# ILLUSTRATED ENCYCLOPEDIA OF BIBLE PLACES

First published in the UK
by Inter-Varsity Press
38 De Montfort Street,
Leicester LE1 7GP

ISBN 0–85110–657–9

First published in the USA
by Baker Books
a division of
Baker Book House Company
Grand Rapids
Michigan 49516
ISBN 0–8010–1093–4

Designed and created by
Three's Company
12 Flitcroft Street
London WC2H 8DJ

Enquiries from publishers to:
Angus Hudson Ltd
Worldwide Co-editions
Concorde House
Grenville Place
London NW7 3SA
United Kingdom
Tel +44 181 959 3668
Fax +44 181 959 3678

Printed in Singapore

ILLUSTRATED ENCYCLOPEDIA OF

# BIBLE PLACES

TOWNS & CITIES•COUNTRIES & STATES
ARCHAEOLOGY & TOPOGRAPHY

CONSULTING EDITOR
**John J. Bimson**

INTER-VARSITY PRESS
Leicester

# ABBREVIATIONS

*AASOR*
*Annual of the American Schools of Oriental Research*

*ABD*
D. N. Freedman, ed., *Anchor Bible Dictionary*, 6 vols., 1992

*ADAJ*
*Annual of the Department of Antiquities of Jordan*

*ad loc.*
(in the relevant passage)

*AfO*
*Archiv für Orientforschung*

*AJA*
*American Journal of Archaeology*

*AJBA*
*Australian Journal of Biblical Archaeology*

*AJSL*
*American Journal of Semitic Languages and Literatures*

*ANEP*
J. B. Pritchard, *The Ancient Near East in Pictures*, 1954; 2nd edition 1965

*ANET*
J. B. Pritchard, *Ancient Near Eastern Texts*, 1950; 2nd edition 1965; 3rd edition 1969

*ANRW*
*Aufstieg und Niedergang der römischen Welt*

*AOLOB*
A. Mazar, *Archeology of the Land of the Bible, 10,000–586 B.C.E.*, 1990

*AOTS*
D. W. Thomas, ed., *Archaeology and Old Testament Study*, 1967

*AS*
*Anatolian Studies*

ASV
*American Standard Version*, 1901 (American version of RV)

AV
*Authorized Version (King James')*, 1611

*BA*
*Biblical Archaeologist*

*BARev*
*Biblical Archaeology Review*

*BASOR*
*Bulletin of the American Schools of Oriental Research*

*BC*
F. J. Foakes-Jackson and K. Lake, *The Beginnings of Christianity*, 5 vols., 1920–33

*BDB*
F. Brown, S. R. Driver and C. A. Briggs, *Hebrew and English Lexicon of the Old Testament*, 1906

*Bib*
*Biblica*

*BJRL*
*Bulletin of the John Rylands Library*

*BS*
*Bibliotheca Sacra*

*BSOAS*
*Bulletin of the School of Oriental and African Studies*

*CAH*
*Cambridge Ancient History*, 12 vols., 1923–39; revised edition 1970–

*CBQ*
*Catholic Biblical Quarterly*

*CIG*
*Corpus Inscriptionum Graecarum*

*CIL*
*Corpus Inscriptionum Latinarum*

*DBS*
*Dictionnaire de la Bible*, Supplément, 1928–

*DOTT*
D. W. Thomas, ed., *Documents of Old Testament Times*, 1958

*EBr*
*Encyclopaedia Britannica*

E. T.
English translation

*EQ*
*Evangelical Quarterly*

*ExpT*
*Expository Times*

f., ff.
and the following page, and the following pages

GTT
J. Simons, *Geographical and Topographical Texts of the Old Testament*, 1959

*HAT*
*Handbuch zum Alten Testament*

*HDAC*
J. Hastings, *Dictionary of the Apostolic Church*, 1915

*HDB*
J. Hastings, ed., *Dictionary of the Bible*, 5 vols., 1898–1904

*HJP*
*E. Schürer, A History of the Jewish People in the Time of Christ*, 2 vols., E. T. 1885–1901; revised edition, M. Black, G. Vermes and F. Millar, eds., 3 vols., 1973–

*HSS*
*Harvard Semitic Series*

*HTR*
*Harvard Theological Review*

*HUCA*
*Hebrew Union College Annual*

*IB*
G. A. Buttrick and others, eds., *Interpreter's Bible*, 12 vols., 1952–57

*IBA*
D. J. Wiseman, *Illustrations from Biblical Archaeology*, 1958

*ibid.*
*ibidem* (the same)

*ICC*
*International Critical Commentary*

*IDB*
G. A. Buttrick and others, eds., *The Interpreter's Dictionary of the Bible*, 4 vols., 1962

*IDBS*
*IDB*, Supplement vol., 1976

*IEJ*
*Israel Exploration Journal*

*IG*
*Inscriptiones Graecae*

*JAOS*
*Journal of the American Oriental Society*

JB
*Jerusalem Bible*, 1966

*JBL*
*Journal of Biblical Literature*

*JCS*
*Journal of Cuneiform Studies*

*JEA*
*Journal of Egyptian Archaeology*

*JNES*
*Journal of Near Eastern Studies*

*JPOS*
*Journal of the Palestine Oriental Society*

*JSOT*
*Journal for the Study of the Old Testament*

*JSS*
*Journal of Semitic Studies*

*JTS*
*Journal of Theological Studies*

*JTVI*
*Journal of the Transactions of the Victoria Institute*

*KB*
L. Köhler and W. Baumgartner, *Hebräisches und aramäisches Lexicon zum Alten Testament*, 3rd edition, 1967

*LA*
*Liber Annus* (Jerusalem)

*LOB*
Y. Aharoni, *The Land of the Bible*, 2nd edition, 1979

LXX (B)
Codex Vaticanus (4th century AD)

NASB
*New American Standard Bible*, 1963

*NBC*
F. Davidson, ed., *The New Bible Commentary*, 1953

*NCB*
*New Century Bible*

*NEAEHL*
Ephraim Stern, ed., *The New Encyclopedia of Archaeological Excavations in the Holy Land*, 4 vols., 1993

NEB
*New English Bible*: NT, 1961; OT, Apocrypha, 1970

*NIDNTT*
C. Brown, ed., *The New International Dictionary of New Testament Theology*, 3 vols., 1975–8

NIV
*New International Version*: NT, 1974; complete Bible, 1978

*NovT*
*Novum Testamentum*

NRSV
*New Revised Standard Version*, 1989

*NTS*
*New Testament Studies*

*op. cit.*
*opere citato* (in the work cited)

*PEQ*
*Palestine Exploration Quarterly*

*PJB*
*Palästina-Jahrbuch*

pl., pls.
plate, plates

POTT
D. J. Wiseman, ed., *Peoples of Old Testament Times*, 1973

*RB*
*Revue Biblique*

*RE*
A. F. Pauly, G. Wissowa and others, eds., *Real-Encyclopädie der klassischen Altertumwissenschaft*, 1893–

*RGTC*
*Répertoire géographique des textes cunéiformes* [Beihefte zum Tübinger Atlas des Vorderen Orients] (Wiesbaden)

RSV
*Revised Standard Version*: NT, 1946; OT, 1952; *Common Bible*, 1973

RV
*Revised Version*: NT, 1881; OT, 1885

*SPT*
W. M. Ramsay, *St Paul the Traveller and Roman Citizen*, 4th edition, 1920

*TA*
Tel Aviv

*TDNT*
G. Kittel and G. Friedrich, eds., *Theologisches Wörterbuch zum Neuen Testament*, 1932–74; E. T. *Theological Dictionary of the New Testament*, ed. G. W. Bromiley, 10 vols., 1964–76

TEV
*Today's English Version*, 4th edition, 1976 (*Good News Bible*)

*TOTC*
*Tyndale Old Testament Commentary*

*TynB*
*Tyndale Bulletin*

*UF*
*Ugarit-Forschungen: Internationales Jahrbuch für die Altertumskunde Syrien-Palästinas*

*VT*
*Vetus Testamentum*

*VT Supp.*
*Vetus Testamentum*, Supplementary vol.

WH
B. F. Westcott and F. J. A. Hort, *The New Testament in the Original Greek*, 2 vols., 1881–82

*WTJ*
*Westminster Theological Journal*

*ZA*
*Zeitschrift für Assyriologie*

*ZAW*
*Zeitschrift für die alttestamentliche Wissenschaft*

*ZDMG*
*Zeitschrift der deutschen morgenländischen Gesellschaft*

*ZDPV*
*Zeitschrift des deutschen Palästina-Vereins*

*ZPEB*
M. C. Tenney, ed., *The Zondervan Pictorial Encyclopaedia of the Bible*, 5 vols., 1975

# LIST OF CONTRIBUTORS

*The information given below was correct at the time of the initial publication of this book.*

The late B. F. C. Atkinson, M.A., Ph.D., formerly Under-Librarian, University of Cambridge.

D. W. Baker, A.B., M.C.S., M.Phil., Ph.D., Professor of Old Testament and Semitic Languages, Ashland Theological Seminary, Ohio.

Mrs M. Beeching, B.A., B.D., M.Ed., formerly Principal Lecturer and Head of Department of Divinity, Cheshire College of Education, Alsager.

J. J. Bimson,B.A., Ph.D., Librarian and Lecturer in Old Testament and Hebrew, Trinity College, Bristol.

J. N. Birdsall, M.A., Ph.D., F.R.A.S., Emeritus Professor of New Testament and Textual Criticism, University of Birmingham.

The late E. M. Blaiklock, O.B.E., M.A., Litt.D., formerly Professor of Classics, University of Auckland.

The late F. F. Bruce, M.A., D.D., F.B.A., formerly Emeritus Rylands Professor of Biblical Criticism and Exegesis, University of Manchester.

J. W. Charley, M.A., Priest in Charge of Great Malvern Priory, Herefordshire and Worcestershire.

D. J. A. Clines, M.A., Professor of Biblical Studies, University of Sheffield.

A. K. Cragg, M.A., D.Phil., D.D., Assistant Bishop in the diocese of Oxford and formerly Vicar of Helme, Huddersfield.

A. E. Cundall, B.A., B.D., formerly Principal, Bible College of Victoria, Australia.

C. J. Davey, B.Sc., M.A., Inspector of Mines, Victoria, Australia.

G. I. Davies, M.A., Ph.D., Lecturer in Old Testament and Intertestamental Studies, University of Cambridge.

C. de Wit, Docteur en philologie et histoire orientales; Conservateur honoraire Musées Royaux d'Art et Histoire, Brussels; Emeritus Professor of the University of Louvain.

J. D. Douglas, M.A., B.D., S.T.M., Ph.D., Lecturer, Singapore Bible College.

The late F. C. Fensham, M.A., Ph.D., D.D., formerly Professor in Semitic Languages, University of Stellenbosch.

G. G. Garner, B.A., B.D., formerly Director, Australian Institute of Archaeology, Melbourne.

R. P. Gordon, M.A., Ph.D., Lecturer in Old Testament, University of Cambridge.

E. M. B. Green, M.A., B.D., Archbishops' Advisor in Evangelism.

G. W. Grogan, B.D., M.Th., formerly Principal, Glasgow Bible College.

R. A. H. Gunner, B.A., M.Th., formerly Lecturer in French, Brooklands Technical College, Weybridge, Surrey.

D. R. Hall, M.A., M.Th., Superintendent Minister of the Rhyl and Prestatyn Circuit of the Methodist Church.

B. F. Harris, B.A., M.A., B.D., Ph.D., formerly Associate Professor of History, Macquarie University, New South Wales.

R. K. Harrison, M.Th., Ph.D., D.D., Professor of Old Testament, Wycliffe College, University of Toronto.

The late J. H. Harrop, M.A., formerly Lecturer in Classics, Fourah Bay College, University of Sierra Leone.

The late C. J. Hemer, M.A., Ph.D., formerly Librarian and Research Fellow, Tyndale House, Cambridge.

N. Hillyer, B.D., S.Th., A.L.C.D., formerly Librarian, Tyndale House, Cambridge.

J. M. Houston, M.A., B.Sc., D.Phil., Chancellor, formerly Principal, Regent College, Vancouver, BC.

D. A. Hubbard, B.A., B.D., Th.M., Ph.D., D.D., L.H.D., formerly President, Fuller Theological Seminary, Pasadena, California.

J. B. Job, M.A., B.D., Minister in the South Bedford and Ampthill Circuit of the Methodist Church; formerly Vice-Principal of Emmanuel College, Ibadan and Tutor in Old Testament, Cliff College, Calver, Derbyshire.

E. A. Judge, M.A., Professor of History, Macquarie University, New South Wales.

J. P. Kane, Ph.D., Dip.Ed., Lecturer in Hellenistic Greek, University of Manchester.

K. A. Kitchen, B.A., Ph.D., Professor of Oriental Studies, University of Liverpool.

J. P. U. Lilley, M.A., F.C.A., Magdalen College, Oxford.

K. L. McKay, B.A., M.A., formerly Reader in Classics, The Australian National University, Canberra.

M. A. MacLeod, M.A., formerly Director, Christian Witness to Israel.

The late G. T. Manley, M.A., sometime Fellow, Christ's College, Cambridge.

I. H. Marshall, B.A., M.A., B.D., Ph.D., Professor of New Testament Exegesis, University of Aberdeen.

R. P. Martin, M.A., Ph.D., Professor of Biblical Studies, University of Sheffield.

The late W. J. Martin, M.A., Th.B., Ph.D., formerly Head of the Department of Hebrew and Ancient Semitic Languages, University of Liverpool.

The late J. W. Meiklejohn, M.B.E., M.A., formerly Secretary of the Inter-School Christian Fellowship in Scotland.

A. R. Millard, M.A., M.Phil., F.S.A., Rankin Professor in Hebrew and Ancient Semitic Languages, University of Liverpool.

T. C. Mitchell, M.A., formerly Keeper of Western Asiatic Antiquities, British Museum.

L. L. Morris, M.Sc., M.Th., Ph.D., formerly Principal, Ridley College, Melbourne; Canon of St Paul's Cathedral, Melbourne.

J. A. Motyer, M.A., B.D., formerly Minister of Christ Church, Westbourne, Dorset, and Principal, Trinity College, Bristol.

The late J. G. G. Norman, B.D., M.Th., formerly Pastor of Rosyth Baptist Church, Fife.

W. Osborne, M.A., M.Phil., Head of Department, Hebrew and Old Testament, The Bible College of New Zealand.

J. H. Paterson, M.A., Emeritus Professor of Geography, University of Leicester.

D. F. Payne, B.A., M.A., Academic Dean, London Bible College.

The late N. H. Ridderbos, D.D., formerly Emeritus Professor of Old Testament, The Free University, Amsterdam.

M. J. S. Rudwick, M.A., Ph.D., Sc.D., formerly Professor of History of Science, The Free University, Amsterdam.

M. J. Selman, B.A., M.A., Ph.D., Lecturer in Old Testament, Spurgeon's College, London.

R. J. A. Sheriffs, B.A., B.D., Ph.D., formerly Lecturer in Old Testament, Rhodes University, Grahamstown, Cape Province.

S. S. Smalley, M.A., B.D., Ph.D., Dean of Chester Cathedral.

F. R. Steele, A.B., M.A., Ph.D., formerly Assistant Professor of Assyriology, University of Pennsylvania.

The late R. A. Stewart, M.A., B.D., M.Litt., formerly Church of Scotland Minister.

J. B. Taylor, M.A., Bishop of St Albans.

J. Thompson, B.A., M.Div., Th.M., Ph.D., Research Consultant, American Bible Society.

J. A. Thompson, M.A., M.Sc., B.D., B.Ed., Ph.D., formerly Reader in Department of Middle Eastern Studies, University of Melbourne.

The late D.H. Tongue, M.A., formerly Lecturer in New Testament, Trinity College, Bristol.

J. C. J. Waite, B.D., Minister of Wycliffe Independent Chapel, Sheffield; formerly Principal, South Wales Bible College.

A. F. Walls, O.B.E., M.A., B.Litt., D.D., D.S.A.Scot., Director of the Centre for the Study of Christianity in the Non-Western World, and Honorary Professor in the University of Edinburgh.

R. J. Way, M.A., formerly Minister of St Columba's United Reformed Church, Leeds.

W. W. Wessel, M.A., Ph.D., Professor of New Testament, Bethel College, St Paul, Minnesota.

D. H. Wheaton, M.A., B.D., Vicar of Christ Church, Ware; formerly Principal, Oak Hill College, London; Canon of St Alban's Cathedral.

The late J. T. Whitney, M.A., L.C.P., Ph.D., formerly Head of Religious Studies, South East Essex Sixth Form College.

B. Winter, B.A., Ph.D., Warden, Tyndale House, Cambridge.

D. J. Wiseman, O.B.E., M.A., D.Lit., F.B.A., F.K.C., F.S.A., Emeritus Professor of Assyriology, University of London.

The late J. S. Wright, M.A., formerly Principal, Tyndale Hall, Bristol; Canon of Bristol Cathedral.

The late E. J. Young, B.A., Th.M., Ph.D., formerly Professor of Old Testament, Westminster Theological Seminary, Philadelphia.

# LIST OF BIBLE PLACES

*Note: Names in CAPITAL LETTERS in this list are the headings of articles or cross-references in the main work. In some cases more than one place may have the same name, as is made clear in the article under that heading.*

*Names in lower case are placenames occurring in the Bible but not treated in articles of their own. They are given in the spellings used by the NIV, with cross-references from alternative spellings, and the Bible references are given.*

ABANA
ABARIM
ABDON
ABEL
Abel-maim, Abel-mayim (2 Chronicles 16:4) *probably another name for Abel of Beth-maachah*
ABEL-MEHOLAH
Abel-mizraim (Genesis 50:11)
ABEL OF BETH-MAACHAH
ABEL-SHITTIM. See *Shittim.
Abez. See *Ebez.
ABILENE
Abronah (Numbers 33:34–35)
ACCAD, AKKAD
ACCO, ACCHO. See *Ptolemais.
ACELDAMA. See *Akeldama.
ACHAIA
ACHMETHA. See *Ecbatana.
ACHOR
ACHSHAPH
ACHZIB
ACRE. See *Ptolemais.
Adadah (Joshua 15:22)
ADAM
ADAMAH
ADAMI-NEKEB
Addar, Adar (Joshua 15:3)
Addon, Addan (Ezra 2:59; Nehemiah 7:61)
Adithaim (Joshua 15:36)
ADMAH
ADONI-BEZEK
ADORAIM
ADRAMYTTIUM
ADRIA
ADULLAM
ADUMMIM
AENON
AFRICA
AHAVA
AHLAB
AI
AIATH. See *Ai.
AIJALON
Ain **1** (Joshua 15:32; 19:7; 21:16; 1 Chronicles 4:32); **2** (Numbers 34:11)
AKELDAMA
AKKAD. See *Accad.
AKRABBIM
ALALAH or ALALAKH
Alammelech. See *Allammelech.
ALEXANDRIA
Alemeth (1 Chronicles 6:60) *also called Almon (Joshua 21:18)*
Allammelech (Joshua 19:26)
Almon (Joshua 21:18) *also called Alemeth (1 Crhonicles 6:60)*
Almon Diblathaim (Numbers 33:46)
Aloth (1 Kings 4:16)
Alush (Numbers 33:14)
Amad (Joshua 19:26)
Amam (Joshua 15:26)
Amana (Song of Songs 4:8)
AMARNA
Ammah (2 Samuel 2:24)
AMMAN. See *Rabbah.
AMMON, AMMONITES
AMPHIPOLIS
Anab (Joshua 11:21; 11:50)
Anaharath (Joshua 19:19)
ANATHOTH
Anem. See *En-Gannim.
Aner (1 Chronicles 6:70)
Anim (Joshua 15:50)
ANTIOCH (PISIDIAN)
ANTIOCH (SYRIAN)
ANTIPATRIS
APHEK, APHEKAH
APOLLONIA
APPII FORUM. See *Forum of Appius.
AR
Arab (Joshua 15:52)
ARABAH
ARABIA
ARAD
Arah, Mearah (Joshua 13:4)
ARAM, ARAMAEANS
ARARAT
ARAVAH. See *Arabah.
AREOPAGUS
ARGOB
ARIEL
ARIMATHEA
ARMAGEDDON
ARMENIA. See *Ararat.
ARNON
AROER
ARPAD
ARPHAD. See *Arpad.
Arubboth, Aruboth (1 Kings 4:10)
ARUMAH. See *Rumah.
ARVAD
ARZOB. See *Bashan.
Ashan (Joshua 15:42; 19:7; 1 Chronicles 4:32))
Ashbea. See *Beth Ashbea.
ASHDOD
ASHDOTH-PISGAH. See *Pisgah.
ASHER
ASHKELON
Ashnah **1** (Joshua 15:33); **2** (Joshua 15:43)
ASHTEROTH-KARNAIM
ASHURITES
ASIA
ASSOS
ASSYRIA
ASWAN. See *Syene.
Atad (Genesis 50:11)
ATAROTH
Ataroth Addar (Joshua 16:5; 18:13)
Athach (1 Samuel 30:30)
ATHENS
Atroth Shophan (Numbers 32:35)
ATTALIA
AVA. See *Ivah.
AVEN
Avith (Genesis 36:35; 1 Chronicles 1:46)
Avva (2 Kings 17:24)
AZEKAH
Azem. See *Ezem.
Azmaveth (Ezra 2:24; Nehemiah 12:29) *also called Beth Azmaveth (Nehemiah 7:28)*
AZOTUS. See *Ashdod.
Azzah. See *Gaza.

Baal. See *Baalath **1**.
Baalah **1** (Joshua 15:29) *also called Balah (Joshua 19:3) or Bilhah (1 Chronicles 4:29)*; **2** (Joshua 15:11); **3** See *Kiriath-jearim.
Baalath **1** (1 Chronicles 4:33) *also called Baalath Beer (Joshua 19:8)*; **2** (Joshua 19:44; 1 Kings 9:18; 2 Chronicles 8:6)
Baalath Beer (Joshua 19:8) *also called Baalath (1 Chronicles 4:33)*
BAAL-GAD
Baal Hamon (Song of Songs 8:11)
BAAL-HAZOR
Baal Hermon (Judges 3:3; 1 Chronicles 5:23)
BAAL-MEON
BAAL OF JUDAH. See *Kiriath-jearim.
BAAL-PEOR. See *Peor.
Baal Perazim (2 Samuel 5:20) *also called Perazim (Isaiah 28:21)*
Baal Shalishah (2 Kings 4:42)
Baal Tamar (Judges 20:33)

**The Theseum, Athens.**

A back street in Bethlehem.

BAAL ZEPHON
BAALE JUDAH. See *KIRIATH-JEARIM.
BABEL
BABYLON
BABYLONIA
BACA, VALLEY OF
BAHURIM
Balah (Joshua 19:3) *also called Baalah (Joshua 15:29)*
BAMAH. See *BAMOTH.
BAMOTH, BAMOTH-BAAL
BASHAN
Bealoth (Joshua 15:24)
BEER
Beer Elim (Isaiah 15:8)
BEER-LAHAI-ROI
Beeroth (Joshua 9:17; 18:25)
Beeroth Bene-jaakan (Deuteronomy 10:16)
BEERSHEBA
BEESHTERAH. See *ASHTAROTH.
BELA. See *PLAIN, CITIES OF THE.
BENE-BERAK
BENE-JAAKAN
BEON. See *BAAL-MEON.
BERACAH
Bered (Genesis 16:14)
BEROEA, BEREA
Berothah (Ezekiel 47:16) *also called Berothai (2 Samuel 8:8) and Cun (or Chun) (1 Chronicles 18:8)*
Berothai (2 Samuel 8:8) *also called Cun (or Chun) (1 Chronicles 18:8) and Berothah (Ezekiel 47:16)*
BETAH. See *TIBHATH.
BETEN
BETHABARA
BETH-ANATH
BETH-ANOTH
BETHANY
Beth Arabah (Joshua 15:6, 61; 18:22)
BETH-ARAM. See *BETH-HARAN.
BETH-ARBEL
Beth Ashbea (1 Chronicles 4:21)
BETH-AVEN
Beth Azmaveth (Nehemiah 7:28) *also called Azmaveth (Ezra 2:24; Nehemiah 12:29)*
Beth Biri, Beth Birei (1 Chronicles 4:31)
Beth Car (1 Samuel 7:11)
BETH-DAGON
BETHEL
Beth Emek (Joshua 19:27)
BETHESDA, BETHZATHA
Beth Ezel (Micah 1:11)
Beth Gader (1 Chronicles 2:51)
Beth Gamul (Jeremiah 48:23)
BETH-GILGAL. See *GILGAL.
Beth Hakkerem (Nehemiah 3:14; Jeremiah 6:1)
BETH HARAM. See *BETH-HARAN.
BETH-HARAN
Beth Hoglah (Joshua 15:6; 18:19)
BETH-HORON
BETH-JESHIMOTH
Beth Lebaoth (Joshua 19:6)
BETHLEHEM
BETH-MARCABOTH
BETH-NIMRAH
Beth Pelet, Beth-palet, Beth-phelet (Joshua 15:27; Nehemiah 11:26)
Beth Pazzez (Joshua 19:21)
BETH-PEOR
BETHPHAGE
BETH-REHAB
BETH-SAIDA
BETHSHEAN, BETHSHAN
BETH-SHEMESH
BETH-SHITTAH
Beth Tappuah (Joshua 15:53)
Beth Togarmah (Ezekiel 27:14; 38:6)
Bethuel (1 Chronicles 4:30) *also called Bethul (Joshua 19:4)*
Bethul (Joshua 19:4) *also called Bethuel (1 Chronicles 4:30)*
BETHZATHA. See *BETHESDA.
BETH-ZUR
Betonim (Joshua 13:26)
Beulah (Isaiah 62:4)
Bezek (1 Samuel 11:8)
BEZER. See *BOZRAH.
BILEAM. See *IBLEAM.
Bilhah (1 Chronicles 4:29) *also called Baalah (Joshua 15:29) or Balah (Joshua 19:3)*
Bithron (2 Samuel 2:19)
BITHYNIA
Biziothiah, Bizjothjah (Joshua 15:28)
BLOOD, FIELD OF. See *AKELDAMA.
Bor Ashan, Chor-ashan (1 Samuel 30:30)
Bokim, Bochim (Judges 2:1–5)
BOZEZ. See *SENEH.
Bozkath, Boscath (Judges 15:39; 2 Kings 22:1)
BOZRAH

Cabbon (Joshua 15:40)
CABUL
CAESAREA
CAESAREA PHILIPPI
CALAH
CALNEH, CALNO
CALVARY
CANA
CANAAN, CANAANITES
CANNEH
CAPERNAUM
CAPHTOR
CAPPADOCIA
CARCHEMISH
CARMEL
CAUDA
CEDRON. See *KIDRON.
CENCHREAE
CHALDEA, CHALDEANS
Charashim. See *Ge Harashim.
Charran. See *Valley of the Craftsmen.
CHEBAR
Chephar-haammonai, Kephar Ammoni (Joshua 18:24)
CHEPHIRAH
CHERITH
Chesalon. See *Kesalon
Chesil. See *Kesil.
CHESULLOTH
CHEZIB. See *ACHZIB.
Chidon. See *Kidon.
Chilmad. See *Kilmad.
CHINNERETH
CHIOS
Chisloth-tabor. See *Kisloth Tabor.
Chor-ashan. See *Bor Ashan.
CHORAZIN
Chozeba. See *Cozeba.
Chun. See *Cun.
CILICIA
CIRCLE OF JORDAN. See *PLAIN, CITIES OF THE.
CITIES OF REFUGE
CITY OF SALT. See *SALT, CITY OF.
CLAUDA. See *CAUDA.
CNIDUS
COELESYRIA
COLOSSAE
CORINTH
COS
Cozeba, Chozeba (1 Chronicles 4:22)
CRETE
Cun (1 Chronicles 18:8) *also called Berothah (Ezekiel 47:16) or Berothai (2 Samuel 8:8)*
CUSH
CUTH, CUTHAH
CYPRUS
CYRENE

Dabbesheth (Joshua 19:11)
DABERATH
DALMANUTHA
DALMATIA
DAMASCUS
DAN
DAN-JAAN
Dannah (Joshua 15:49)
DAUGHTER OF SIDON. See *TYRE.
DAVID, CITY OF. See *JERUSALEM.
DAVID, SEPULCHRE OF. See *SEPULCHRE OF KINGS.
DEAD SEA
DEBIR
DECAPOLIS
DECISION, VALLEY OF
DEDAN
DERBE
DIBLATH, DIBLAH
DIBON
Dibon Gad (Numbers 33:45–46)
Dilean (Joshua 15:38)
Dimnah (Joshua 21:35)
DIMON. See *DIBON.
DIMONAH. See *DIBON.

Dinhabah (Genesis 36:32)
DIZAHAB
Dophkah (Numbers 33:12–13)
DOR
DOTHAN
DUMAH
DURA

EASTERN SEA. See *Dead Sea.
EBAL, MOUNT
EBENEZER
Ebez (see Joshua 19:20)
EBLA
EBRON. See *Abdon.
Ebronah. See *Abronah.
ECBATANA
EDEN
EDEN, GARDEN OF
EDEN, HOUSE OF
EDER, EDAR
EDOM, EDOMITES
EDREI
Eglaim (Isaiah 15:8)
EGLON
EGYPT
EGYPT, RIVER OF
EKRON
ELAH
ELAM, ELAMITES
EL-AMARNA. See *Amarna.
ELATH (ELOTH)
ELEALEH
Eleph, Haeleph (Jopshua 18:28)
ELIAM. See *Helam.
ELIM
ELISHAH
ELLASAR
ELON
Elon Bethhaanon (1 Kings 4:9)
ELOTH. See *Elath.
EL-PARAN. See *Paran.
ELTEKEH
Eltekon (Joshua 15:59)
Eltolad (Joshua 19:4) *also called Tolad (1 Chronicles 4:29)*
EMMAUS
Enam (Joshua 15:34)
ENCAMPMENT BY THE SEA
ENDOR
EN-EGLAIM
EN-GANNIM
EN-GEDI
EN-HADDAH
EN-HAKKORE
EN-HAZOR
EN-RIMMON
EN-ROGEL
EN-SHEMESH
Ephes Dammim (1 Samuel 17:1) *also called Pas Dammim (1 Chronicles 11:13)*
EPHESUS
EPHRAIM
EPHRATH, EPHRATHAH
EPHRON
ERECH
ESDRAELON
Esek (Genesis 26:20)
Eshan (Joshua 15:52)
ESHCOL
ESHTAOL
Eshtemoh (Joshua 15:50)
ETAM
ETHAM
Ether **1** (Joshua 15:42); **2** (Joshua 19:7) *also called Token (1 Chronicles 4:42)*
ETHIOPIA
Eth Kazin (Joshua 19:13)
EUPHRATES
EZEL
Ezem, Azem (Joshua 15:29)
EZION-GEBER

FAIR HAVENS
FORUM OF APPIUS

Gaash (Joshua 24:30)
GABA. See *Geba.
GABBATHA
GAD
GAD, VALLEY OF
GADARENES, GADARA
GAI. See *Gath.
GALATIA
GALEED
GALILEE
GALILEE, SEA OF
Gallim **1** (1 Samuel 25:44); **2** (Isaiah 10:30)
GARDEN OF EDEN. See *Eden, Garden of.
GARDEN TOMB. See *Calvary.
GATH
GATH-HEPHER
Gath Rimmon **1** (Joshua 19:45; 1 Chronicles 6:69); **2** (Joshua 21:25)
GAZA
GAZARA. See *Gezer.
GEBA
GEBAL
Gebim (Isaiah 10:31)
GEDER
GEDERAH
GEDEROTH
GEDEROTHAIM
GEDOR
Ge Harashim (1 Chronicles 4:14); *also called Charran or the Valley of the Craftsmen (Nehemiah 11:35)*
GELILOTH
Gennesaret **1** (Matthew 14:34); **2** See *Galilee, Sea of.
GERAR
GERASENES, GERASA. See *Gadarenes.
GERGESENES, GERGESA. See *Gadarenes.
GERIZIM
GESHUR, GESHURITES
GETHSEMANE
GEZER
Giah (2 Samuel 2:24)
GIBBETHON
GIBEAH
GIBEON
Gidom (Judges 20:45)
GIHON
GILBOA
GILEAD
GILGAL
Giloh (Joshua 15:51)
Gimzo (2 Chronicles 28:18)
GITTAH-HEPHER. See *Gath-hepher.
Gittaim (Nehemiah 11:33).
GITTITE. See *Gath.
Goah, Goath (Jeremiah 31:39)
Gob (2 Samuel 21:18)
GOLAN
GOLGOTHA. See *Calvary.
GOMORRAH. See *Plain, Cities of the.
GOSHEN
GOZAN
GREECE
GUDGODAH
Gur (2 Kings 9:27)
Gur Baal (2 Chronicles 26:7)

HABITATION. See *Naioth.
HABOR
HACHILAH
Hadashah (Joshua 15:37)
Hadid (Ezra 2:33; Nehemiah 11:34)
HADRACH
HADRAMAUT. See *Arabia.
Haeleph (Joshua 18:28)
HALAH
HALAK
Halhul (Joshua 15:58)
Hali (Joshua 19:25)
HAM
HAMATH
Hammath, Hamath (Joshua 19:35; 1 Chronicles 2:55)
Hammon *1* (Joshua 19:28); *2* (1 Chronicles 6:76)
Hamonah (Ezekiel 39:15)
Hamon Gog (Ezekiel 11:15)
HANANEL
HANES
Hannathon (Joshua 19:14)
HARA
Haradah (Numbers 33:24)
HARAN
HAR-MAGEDON. See *Armageddon.
HARMEL. See *Harmon.
HARMON
HAROD
HAROSHETH
HARRAN. See *Haran.
Hasmonah (Numbers 33:29–30)
Hauran (Ezekiel 47:16, 18)

**The Sphinx, Cairo, Egypt.**

HAVILAH
HAVVOTH-JAIR
Hazar Addar, Adda (Joshua 15:3)
Hazar Enan (Numbers 34:9; Ezekiel 48:1)
Hazar Gaddah (Joshua 15:27)
HAZARMAVETH. See *ARABIA.
Hazar Shual (Joshua 15:28; 19:3)
Hazar Susah (Joshua 19:5) *also called Hazar Susim (1 Chronicles 4:31)*
Hazazon Tamar (2 Chronicles 20:2); *also called Hazezon Tamar (Genesis 14:7)*
Hazer Hatticon (Ezekiel 47:16)
HAZEROTH
Hazezon Tamar (Genesis 14:7) *also called Hazazon Tamar (2 Chronicles 20:2)*
HAZOR
HEBRON
HELAM
HELBON
Heleph (Joshua 19:33)
HELKATH
HELKATH-HAZZURIM
Hemath. See *Hammath
HENA
Hepher (Joshua 12:17)
HERMON
HESHBON
Heshmon (Joshua 15:27)
HETHLON
HIDDEKEL
HIERAPOLIS
Hilen (1 Chronicles 6:58) *also called Holon (Joshua 15:51)*
HILL, HILL-COUNTRY
HINNOM, VALLEY OF
HITTITES
HOBAH
Holon **1** (Jeremiah 48:21); **2** (Joshua 15:51) *also called Hilen (1 Chronicles 6:58)*
HOLY LAND. See *PALESTINE.
HOR
HOREB. See *SINAI.
Horem (Joshua 19:38)
HORESH
HOR-HAGGIDGAD. See *GUDGODAH.
HORMAH
HORONAIM
Hosah (Joshua 19:29)
HOUSE OF EDEN. See *EDEN, HOUSE OF.
HUKKOK
HUKOK. See *HELKATH.
Humtah (Joshua 15:54)
HUNDRED, TOWER OF THE

IBLEAM
ICONIUM
Idalah (Joshua 19:15)
IDUMAEA
IIM. See *IYE-ABARIM.
IJON
ILIUM. See *TROAS.
ILLYRICUM
Immer (Ezra 2:59; Nehemiah 7:61)
INDIA
IONIA. See *JAVAN.
Iphtah, Jiphtah (Joshua 15:43)
Iphtah El, Jiphtah-el (Joshua 19:14, 27)
Ir Nahash (1 Chronicles 4:12)
Iron (Joshua 19:38)
Irpeel (Joshua 18:27)
Ir Shemesh (Joshua 19:41)
ISH-TOB. See *TOB.
ISSACHAR
ITALY
Ithnan (Joshua 15:23)
Ittah-kazin. See *Eth Kazin.
ITURAEA
IVAH
IYE-ABARIM

JAAZER. See *JAZER.
JAAR
JABBOK
JABESH-GILEAD
JABEZ
JABNEEL
JACOB'S WELL. See *SYCHAR.
JAFFA. See *JOPPA.
Jagur (Joshua 15:21)
JAHAZ
JANOAH
Janim, Janum (Joshua 15:33)
Japhia (Joshua 19:12)
JAPHO. See *JOPPA.
JARMUTH
JATTIR
JAVAN
JAZER
Jearim, Mount (Joshua 15:10)
JEBUS, JEBUSITE
JEGAR-SAHADUTHA. See *GALEED.
JEHOSHAPHAT, VALLEY OF
Jehud (Joshua 19:45)
Jekabzeel (Nehemiah 11:25)
JERICHO
JERUEL
JERUSALEM
Jeshanah (2 Chronicles 13:19)
JESHIMON
Jeshua (Nehemiah 11:26)
JEZREEL
Jiphtah. See *Iphtah.
Jiphtah-el. See *Iphtah El.
JOGBEHAH
Jokdeam (Joshua 15:56)
JOKMEAM
JOKNEAM
JOKTHEEL. See *SELA.
JOPPA
JORDAN, VALLEY AND RIVER
Jorkeam, Jorkoam (1 Chronicles 2:44)
JOTBAH
JOTBATHAH
JUDAEA
JUDAH
JUDEA. See *JUDAEA.
JUTTAH

KABZEEL
KADESH
KADESH-BARNEA. See *KADESH.
KAIN
KANAH
Karka (Joshua 15:3)
Karkor (Judges 8:10)
KARNAIM. See *ASHTEROTH-KARNAIM.
KARNAK. See *THEBES.
Kartah (Joshua 21:34)
KARTAN. See *KIRIATHAIM.
Kattath (Joshua 19:15)
KEDAR
KEDEMOTH
KEDESH
Kehelathah (Numbers 33:22–23)
KEILAH
KENATH
Kephar Ammoni, Chephar-haammomai (Joshua 18:24)
KERIOTH
Kesalon, Chesalon (Joshua 15:10)
Kesil, Chesil (Joshua 15:30)
Keziz (Joshua 18:21)
KIBROTH-HATTAAVAH
Kibzaim (Joshua 21:22)
Kidon, Chidon (1 Chronicles 13:9) *also called Nacon, Nachon (2 Samuel 6:6)*
KIDRON
Kilmad, Chilmad (Ezekiel 27:23)
Kinah (Joshua 15:22)
KING'S GARDEN
KING'S HIGHWAY
KING'S VALLEY. See *SHAVEH.
KIR
Kiriath (Joshua 18:28)
KIRIATHAIM
KIRIATH-ARBA
KIRIATH-BAAL. See *KIRIATH-JEARIM.
Kiriath Huzoth (Numbers 22:39)
KIRIATH-JEARIM
KIRIATH-SANNA. See *DEBIR.
KIRIATH-SEPHER
KIR OF MOAB, KIR-HARESETH
KISH
KISHON
Kisloth Tabor, Chisloth-tabor (Joshua 19:12)
Kitlish (Joshua 15:40)
Kitron (Judges 1:30)
KITTIM

Laban (Deuteronomy 1:1)
LABO. See *HAMATH.
LACHISH
Lahmas, Lahmam (Joshua 15:40)
LAISH. See *DAN.
Lakkum (Joshua 19:33)
LAODICEA
LASEA
LASHA
LASHARON
LEBANON
Lebaoth (Joshua 15:32)
Lebonah (Judges 21:19)
LEHI
LESHEM. See *DAN.
LIBNAH
LIBYA
LOD. See *LYDDA.
LO-DEBAR
LUHITH, ASCENT OF
LUXOR. See *THEBES.

LUZ
LYCAONIA
LYCIA
LYDDA
LYDIA
LYSTRA

MAACAH, MAACHAH
MAALEH-ACRABBIM. See *Akrabbim.
Maarath (Joshua 15:59)
MAAREH-GEBA
MACEDONIA
MACHAERUS
MACHBENA. See *Meconah.
MACHPELAH
MADMANNAH
MADMEN
MADMENAH
MADON
MAGBISH
MAGDALA, MAGDALENE
Magog (Ezekiel 38:2; 39:6)
MAHANAIM
MAHANEH-DAN
Makaz (1 Kings 4:9)
Makheloth (Numbers 33:25)
MAKKEDAH
MAKTESH
MALTA
MAMRE
MANAHATH
MANASSEH
MAON
MARAH
Maralah (Joshua 19:11)
MARESHAH
MARI
Maroth (Micah 1:12)
MARS HILL. See *Athens.
Mashal (1 Chronicles 6:74)
Masrekah (Genesis 36:36; 1 Chronicles 1:47)
MASSAH
Mattanah (Numbers 21:19)
Mearah. See *Arah.
MECONAH
MEDEBA
MEDIA, MEDES
MEGIDDO
Me Jarkon (Joshua 19:46)
MEKONAH. See *Meconah.
MELITA. See *Malta.
MEMPHIS
MEONENIM, OAK OF
Mephaath (Joshua 13:18)
Merathaim (Jeremiah 50:21)
MEREMOTH. See *Arad.
Meribah **1** (Exodus 17:1); **2** (Numbers 20:13) *also called Meribah Kadesh (Deuteronomy 32:51)*
MEROM, WATERS OF
MERONOTH, MERONOTHITE
MEROZ
MESHA
MESOPOTAMIA
METHEG-AMMAH
MICHMASH, MICHMAS
Micmethath (Joshua 17:7)
Middin (Joshua 15:61)
MIDIANITES
Migdal El (Joshua 19:38)
Migdal Gad (Joshua 15:37)
MIGDOL
MIGRON
MILETUS
MILLO
MINAEANS
MINNI
MINNITH
Misgab (Jeremiah 48:1)
Mishal (Joshua 19:26; 21:30)
MISREPHOTH-MAIM
Mithcah (Numbers 33:28)
MITYLENE
MIZAR
MIZPAH, MIZPEH
MIZRAIM
MOAB, MOABITES
MOLADAH
MOREH
MORESHETH-GATH
MORIAH
MOSERAH, MOSEROTH
MOUNTAIN OF THREE LIGHTS. See *Olives, Mount of.
MOUNT OF OFFENCE. See *Olives, Mount of.
Mozah (Joshua 18:26)
MYRA
MYSIA

NAAMAH
Naaran, Naarath (1 Chronicles 7:28)
NABATAEANS
Nacon, Nachon (2 Samuel 6:6) *also called Kidon, Chidon (1 Chronicles 13:9)*
NAHALAL, NAHALOL
NAHALIEL
NAIN
NAIOTH
NAPHTALI
NAPTHUHIM
NAZARETH
Neah (Joshua 19:13)
NEAPOLIS
Neballat (Nehemiah 11:34)
NEBO
NEGEB
Neiel (Joshua 19:27)
NEKE. See *Adami-nekeb.
NEPHTALIM. See *Naphtali.
NEPHTOAH
NETOPHAH
Nezib (Joshua 15:43)
Nibshan (Joshua 15:62)
NICOPOLIS
NILE
NIMRAH. See *Beth-nimrah.
NIMRIM, WATERS OF
NINEVEH
NIPPUR. See *Calneh.
NO. See *Thebes.
NOB
NOBAH
NOD
NOHAH. See *Manahath.
NOPH. See *Memphis.

The Sea of Galilee from the Mount of Beatitudes.

Nophah (Numbers 21:30)
NUZI

Oboth (Numbers 21:10; 33:43)
OLIVES, MOUNT OF
OLIVET. See *Olives, Mount of.
ON
ONO
Ophel (2 Chronicles 27:3; Nehemiah 3:26; 11:21)
OPHIR
Ophni (Joshua 18:24)
OPHRAH
OREB

PADDAN, PADDAN-ARAM
Pai. See *Pau.
PALESTINE
PALMYRA. See *Tadmor.
PAMPHYLIA
PAPHOS
Parah (Joshua 18:23)
PARAN
PARTHIA
PARVAIM
Pas Dammim (1 Chronicles 11:18) *also called Ephes Dammim (1 Samuel 17:1)*
PATARA
PATHROS, PATHRUSIM
PATMOS
Pau, Pai (Genesis 36:29; 1 Chronicles 1:50)
PEKOD
PENUEL
PEOR
PERAEA
Perazim (Isaiah 28:21) *also called Baal Perazim (2 Samuel 5:20)*
PERGA
PERGAMUM
PERSIA, PERSIANS
PETHOR
PHARATHON. See *Pirathon.
PHARPAR
PHENICE. See *Phoenix.
PHENICIA, PHENICE. See *Phoenicia.

The Forum, Rome.

PHILADELPHIA
PHILIPPI
PHILISTIA, PHILISTINES.
PHOENICIA, PHOENICIANS
PHOENIX
PHRYGIA
PHUT. See *PUT.
PI-BESETH
PIHAHIROTH
PIRATHON
PISGAH, ASHDOTH-PISGAH
PISHON. See *EDEN.
PISIDIA
PITHOM
PLAIN, CITIES OF THE
PLAIN OF MEONENIM. See *MEONENIM, OAK OF.
PLAIN OF ONO. See *ONO.
PONTUS
POOL OF SILOAM. See *SILOAM.
POTTERS FIELD. See *AKELDAMA.
PRAETORIUM
PTOLEMAIS
Pul (Isaiah 66:19, AV)
PUT, PHUT
PUTEOLI

QUMRAN

RAAMAH
RA'AMSES, RAMESES
RABBAH
Rabbith (Joshua 19:20)
Racal (1 Samuel 30:29)
Rakkath (Joshua 19:35)
Rakkon (Joshua 19:46)
RAMAH
RAMATHAIM. See *RAMAH.
RAMATH-LEHI. See *LEHI.
Ramath Mizpah (Joshua 13:26)
RAMESES. See *RA'AMSES.
RAMOTH. See *JARMUTH.
RAMOTH-GILEAD
Recah (1 Chronicles 4:12)
RED SEA
REFUGE, CITIES OF. See *CITIES OF REFUGE.
REHOB
REHOBOTH
REHOBOTH-IR
Rekem (Joshua 18:27)
REMETH. See *JARMUTH.
REMMON. See *RIMMON.
Rephaim (2 Samuel 5:18; Isaiah 17:5)
REPHIDIM
RESEN
REUBEN
REZEPH
RHEGIUM
RHODES
RIBLAH, RIBLATH
RIMMON
Rimmon Perez (Numbers 33:19)
Rissah (Numbers 33:21–22)
Rithmah (Numbers 33:18–19)
ROMAN EMPIRE
ROME
ROSH
RUMAH

SALAMIS
SALECAH, SALCAH
SALEM
SALIM
SALMONE
SALT, CITY OF
SALT, VALLEY OF
SAMARIA
SAMOS
SAMOTHRACE
Sansannah (Joshua 15:31)
SAPHIR. See *SHAPHIR.
SARDIS
SAREPTA. See *ZAREPHATH.
SARID
SCYTHAPOLIS. See *SALIM.
SCYTHIANS
SEA OF ARABAH. See *DEAD SEA.
SEA OF GALILEE. See *CHINNERETH.
SEA OF REEDS. See *RED SEA.
SEBA
SEBAM. See *SIBMAH.
SECACAH
SECU, SECHU
SEIR
Seirah (Judges 3:26)
SELA
Sela Hammahlekoth (1 Samuel 23:28)
SELEUCIA
SENAAH
SENEH
SENIR
SEPHAR
SEPHARAD
SEPHARVAIM
SEPULCHRE OF THE KINGS, SEPULCHRE OF DAVID
SERPENT'S STONE
SEVENEH. See *SYENE.
Shaalim (1 Samuel 9:4)
SHAALBIM, SHAALABBIN
SHAARAIM
Shahazumah (Joshua 19:22)
SHALEM
SHALISHAH
SHAMIR. See *SHAPHIR.
SHAPHIR, SAPHIR
SHARON
SHARUHEN
SHAVEH, VALLEY OF
SHAVEH-KIRIATHAIM. See *KIRIATHAIM.
SHEBA
SHEBAH. See *SHIBAH.
SHEBAM. See *SIBMAH.
Shebarim (Joshua 7:5)
SHECHEM
SHEEP-POOL. See *BETHESDA.
SHELAH. See *SILOAM.
Shen (1 Samuel 7:12)
SHENIR. See *SENIR.
Shepham (Numbers 34:10)
SHEPHELAH
SHIBAH
Shicron. See *Shikkeron
Shihon. See *Shion
SHIHOR. See *EGYPT, RIVER OF.
SHIHOR-LIBNATH
Shikkeron, Shicron (Joshua 15:11)
Shilhim (Joshua 15:32)
SHILOAH. See *SILOAM.
SHILOH
SHIMRON. See *SHIMRON-MERON.
SHIMRON-MERON
SHINAR
Shion, Shihon (Joshua 19:19)
SHITTIM
Shoa (Ezekiel 23:23)
SHOCHO. See *SOCOH.
Shophan. See *Atroth Shophan.
SHUAL, LAND OF
SHULAMMITE
SHUNEM, SHUNAMMITE
SHUR
SHUSHAN. See *SUSA.
SIBMAH
SIBRAIM. See *SEPHARVAIM.
SICHEM. See *SHECHEM.
SIDDIM, VALLEY OF
SIDON
Silla (2 Kings 12:20)
SILOAM
SIN, WILDERNESS OF
SINAI, MOUNT
SINIM. See *SYENE.
SINITES. See *SYENE.
SION
Siphmoth (1 Samuel 30:28)
SIRAH, CISTERN OF
SIRION
SITNAH
SMYRNA
SOCOH
SODOM. See *PLAIN, CITIES OF THE.
SOREK, VALLEY OF
SPAIN
STRAIGHT STREET. See *DAMASCUS.
SUCCOTH
SUMER, SUMERIANS
SUPH
SUSA
SYCHAR
SYCHEM. See *SHECHEM.
SYENE
SYRACUSE
SYRIA, SYRIANS
SYROPHOENICIA

TAANACH
Taanath Shiloh (Joshua 16:6)

Tabbath (Judges 7:22)
Taberah (Numbers 11:3; Deuteronomy 9:22)
TABOR
TADMOR
Tahath (Numbers 33:26–27)
TAHPANHES
TAHTIM-HODSHI
TANACH. See *TAANACH.
TAPPUAH
Tarah. See *Terah.
Taralah (Joshua 18:27)
TARSHISH
TARSUS
TAVERNS, THREE. See *THREE TAVERNS.
TEBAH. See *TIBHATH.
TEHAPHNEHES. See *TAHPANHES.
TEKOA
Tel Abib (Ezekiel 3:15)
TELAIM
TELASSAR
Telem (Joshua 15:24)
Tel Harsha (Ezra 2:59; Nehemiah 7:61)
TEMA
Terah (Numbers 33:27)
THARSHISH. See *TARSHISH.
THEBES
THEBEZ
THESSALONICA
THIMNATHAH. See *TIMNAH.
THREE TAVERNS
THYATIRA
TIBERIAS
TIBHATH
TIGRIS
TIMNAH
TIMNATH-HERES, TIMNATH-SERAH
Tiphsah **1** (1 Kings 4:24); **2** (2 Kings 15:16)
TIRZAH
TISHBITE, THE
TOB
Togarmah. See *Beth Togarmah.
Token (1 Chronicles 4:32) *also called Ether (Joshua 19:7)*
Tolad (1 Chronicles 4:29) *also called Eltolad (Joshua 19:4)*
TOMBS, ROYAL. See *SEPULCHRE OF THE KINGS.
TOPHEL
TOPHETH
TOWER OF BABEL. See *BABEL, TOWER OF.
TOWER OF SILOAM. See *SILOAM.
TRACHONITIS
TRANSJORDAN. See *GILEAD.
TROAS
TROGYLLIUM
TROY. See *TROAS.
TYRE, TYRUS

UGARIT, RAS SHAMRA
ULAI
UMMAH. See *PTOLEMAIS.
UPHAZ
UPPER EGYPT. See *PATHROS.
UR OF THE CHALDEES
UZ
UZAL

VALLEY OF DECISION. See *DECISION, VALLEY OF.
VALLEY OF JEHOSHAPHAT. See *JEHOSHAPHAT, VALLEY OF.
VALLEY OF SALT. See *SALT, VALLEY OF.
VALLEY OF SHAVEH. See *SHAVEH, VALLEY OF.
VALLEY OF SOREK. See *SOREK, VALLEY OF.
Valley of the Craftsmen, Charran (Nehemiah 11:35) *also called Ge Harashim (1 Chronicles 4:14)*
VEDAN. See *UZAL.

WILDERNESS
WILDERNESS OF WANDERING

ZAANAN
ZAANANNIM
ZAIR
ZALMON
Zalmonah (Numbers 33:41–42)
ZANOAH
ZAPHON
ZAREAH. See *ZORAH.
ZARED. See *ZERED.
ZAREPHATH
ZARETAN. See *ZARETHAN.
ZARETHAN
Zareth-shahar. See *Zereth Shahar.
ZARTANA. See *ZARETHAN.
ZARTHAN. See *ZARETHAN.
ZEBOIIM
ZEBOIM
ZEBOYIM. See *ZEBOIIM.
ZEBULUN
ZEDAD
Zela (2 Samuel 21:14)
ZELZAH
ZEMARAIM
ZENAN. See *ZOANAN.
Zephath (Judges 1:17)
ZEPHATHAH
ZER
ZERAD. See *ZEDAD.
ZERED
ZEREDAH. See *ZARETHAN.
ZEREDATHAH. See *ZARETHAN.
Zereth Shahar (Joshua 13:19)
Ziddim (Joshua 19:35)
ZIDON. See *SIDON.
ZIKLAG
ZIN
ZIOR
ZIPH
Ziphron (Numbers 34:9)
ZIZ
ZOAN
ZOAH. See *PLAIN, CITIES OF THE.
ZOBAH
ZOHELETH, STONE OF. See *SERPENT'S STONE.
ZOPHIM
ZORAH
Zuph (1 Samuel 9:5)

A river scene near ancient Ur.

# THE IDENTIFICATION OF BIBLICAL SITES
## Sources and Uncertainties

Many of the entries in this Encyclopedia refer to the problems of site identification. To some readers it may come as a surprise that the locations of so many biblical places are unknown or uncertain, while others may wonder how those which are known were arrived at. Here we introduce briefly some of the sources of information which biblical scholars and archaeologists have at their disposal, and explain the uncertainties which surround the enterprise of site identification.

Very few sites have been more or less continuously occupied since biblical times, thus preserving their identity beyond reasonable doubt (Jerusalem and Damascus are two important places which have), so most identifications depend on various types of evidence which have to be sifted carefully.

The Bible itself sometimes provides useful details. For example, we can deduce from Genesis 12:8 that Bethel and Ai lay close together and south of Shechem, and that Ai lay to the east of Bethel, separated from it by a region of higher ground. In Judges 21:19 the location of Shiloh is given with unusual precision: '. . . north of Bethel, on the east of the highway that goes up from Bethel to Shechem, and south of Lebonah'. Tribal boundary lists, such as we find in Joshua 13–19, are rich sources of information, giving the general locations of many towns in relation to each other, and sometimes in relation to streams, valleys, mountains and the coast. References to military campaigns often list towns which lay close together or on a particular line of march (*e.g.* 2 Kings 15:29; Isaiah 10:28–32).

### Egyptian sources

Egyptian sources provide a valuable complement to the biblical information. The great topographical list of Tuthmosis III (1479–1425 BC) contains the names of some 119 places in Syria-Palestine which came under Egypt's dominion in 1457 BC, following the pharaoh's victory over a Canaanite coalition at Megiddo. Records from the campaigns of Amenophis II (1427–1400 BC), Sethos I (1294–1279 BC) and Ramesses II (1279–1213 BC) also provide useful data, and the campaign list of Sheshonq I (945–924 BC), the biblical Shishak (1 Kings 14:25–28), contains about 140 names, consisting of towns in central Palestine, the Negeb and the southern coastal plain. The Amarna letters (correspondence from Canaanite city-states to the Egyptian court, written around 1350 BC) and Papyrus Anastasi I (a scribe's satirical letter concerning military intelligence, written about 1200 BC) also show us which towns and cities were important in their respective periods, and reveal something of their political and economic relations. By no means all the names in these Egyptian lists can be identified with biblical places, and in many cases identifications are hypothetical.

Later writings are also frequently useful. The books of 1 and 2 Maccabees (in the Apocrypha), both written in the early 1st century BC, indicate the importance of certain towns (*e.g.* Gezer, here called Gadara or Gazara) during the period between the Old and New Testaments. The Jewish historian Josephus (*c.* AD 37–100) produced (among other things) two lengthy works which provide a wealth of information. His *Jewish Wars* (commonly abbreviated *BJ*, from its Latin title *Bellum Judaicarum*) details the course of the Jewish war with Rome, AD 66–74, preceded by a summary of Jewish history from 168 BC to AD 66; it was completed around AD 80. His *Antiquities of the Jews* (*Antiquitates Judaicae*) covers the whole of Jewish history from Creation to his own time, and was completed in AD 93. Although Josephus was not an unbiased recorder of events, these works are a valuable source of information, particularly on the political history and geography of Roman Palestine.

### Early Christian writings

Early Christian pilgrims and church fathers have also left useful records. Of particular importance is a work by Eusebius (*c.* 260–339), who was bishop of Caesarea, the administrative capital of Roman Palestine, from 312 until his death. His *Onomasticon* contains over six hundred entries (biblical places, districts and geographical features) located in relation to Roman towns, roads and milestones. A Latin edition of the *Onomasticon* (originally written in Greek) was produced by Jerome (*c.* 400) who updated and amplified it. The work is not to be treated uncritically; by Eusebius's day, the true locations of many biblical places had already been forgotten and the facts replaced by unreliable traditions. Nevertheless, much of his information has proved to be of value. For example, he tells us that the site of Bethel lay at the twelfth Roman milestone from Jerusalem, on the east side of the road which ran northwards from Jerusalem to Neapolis, the Roman town on the site of biblical Shechem (*Onomasticon* 40.20); and he informs us that in his day Lachish was a village located along the seventh Roman mile from Eleutheropolis as one travelled towards the Negeb (120.20). Both pieces of information have been used by modern scholars and archaeologists seeking to locate these biblical towns.

### Present-day names

The present-day names of ancient sites can provide important clues to their identity. The Arabic name of a ruin or of an existing village will sometimes preserve a form of the biblical name. Thus the name of el-Jib, the site of Gibeon, echoes the Hebrew original; the Arab village of Mukhmâs preserves the name of biblical Michmash; Tell ed-Damiyeh is the site of biblical Adam. Sometimes, however, a name is found to have shifted some way from the true site of the biblical town. This is because, at some time in the post-biblical period, the settlement relocated and took the name with it. In such cases the original site acquires a new name which usually bears no relation to the biblical one. Thus the site of Beth-shan is now known as Tell el-Ḥusn, while the nearby village of Beisân preserves the original name; Old Testament Jericho is represented by the mound of Tell es-Sultan, while the name survives at the village of er-Riḥa, 2 kilometres to the south-east. (New Testament Jericho occupied yet a third site, to the west of the modern village.)

Occasionally a site bears its biblical name in translation. For example the site of Dan is called Tell el-Qadi, which means 'the mound of the judge'; it therefore contains an Arabic translation of the name Dan ('judge'). In many instances, however, a modern name has no onnection whatever with its iblical original. Sometimes a purely ccidental resemblance can be nisleading. Cana of Galilee (John :1; 4:46) has been identified with wo sites north of Nazareth, Kafr anna and Khirbet Qānā, which lie bout 6 kilometres apart. Kafr Kanna ecame the popular site for pilgrims luring the Middle Ages, but either site could fit the information found in ohn's Gospel. In fact the name Cana neans 'reed', while Kafr Kanna ppears to mean 'village of the roof'; here is no possible connection etween the two names. Khirbet Qānā, on the other hand, is situated n the side of the Beth Netofa valley, where reeds still grow in the rainy season, so this is much more likely to e the New Testament town. Most Arabic names for ancient sites are refixed with either 'Khirbet' (which neans a ruin) or 'Tell' (which means ruin-mound, a hill of accumulated lebris). 'Tel' is the Hebrew equivalent of the latter, and occurs in he Old Testament as well as in nodern site-names (*e.g.* Joshua 3:28; 11:13). (The modern city of Tel Aviv was named after the Tel-abib nentioned in Ezekiel 3:15, but has no other connection with it; Ezekiel's settlement was in Babylonia, not on the Mediterranean coast!) 'Khirbet' also has a Hebrew counterpart, 'Ḥorvat'.

**Two names**

Many biblical sites within the borders of modern Israel now have two names, a traditional Arabic name and a recently-created Hebrew one. Sometimes the latter is simply the name of the biblical town with which it has been identified. For example, most scholars are so certain that Tell ed-Duweir is ancient Lachish that the Israel Government Names Committee has renamed it Tel Lachish, and Tell el-Qadi has been renamed Tel Dan. But certainty is rarely available and some changes have turned out to be too hasty. In 1957 the Names Committee decided that the site called Khirbet el-Muqanna' in Arabic should be renamed Tel Eltekeh, in the belief that it was the site of the biblical Eltekeh. But in 1964, when this identification had been rejected in favour of Ekron, the Committee changed the name to Tel Miqne, by simply transcribing the Arabic consonants into Hebrew.

The study of Arabic toponyms to locate biblical sites in Palestine was first undertaken by Edward Robinson, during trips to the Holy Land in 1838 and 1852. Robinson realized that the traditions to be found among the local Christian communities were often unreliable, and so confined his researches to the Arab population, from whom he learnt the Arabic place-names. Many of the identifications which he made have stood the test of time. The data which he collected were greatly added to by the British survey of Palestine (1871–77).

**Archaeological evidence**

Today archaeology provides important evidence for the work of site identification. It is rare, however, for an archaeological find to establish an identification beyond any doubt. Tell el-Qadi was confirmed as the site of Dan by an inscription in Greek and Aramaic from the 2nd century BC, and Gezer's location at Tell el-Jazari is confirmed by eight boundary inscriptions from the Roman period; but these are exceptions. In the vast majority of cases the evidence is never more than circumstantial.

Archaeology can establish whether a site was occupied at the right periods and was the right size to qualify for a proposed identification. For example, an important town such as Lachish could not reasonably be identified with a very small site, and the insubstantial remains at the promisingly-named Umm Lakis were ruled out on those grounds by W. Flinders Petrie last century. The criterion of occupational history, however, is not always as decisive as one might expect. A much debated example is provided by Khirbet et-Tell, commonly identified as the site of Ai, the city which Joshua conquered after destroying Jericho. This site has produced no trace of occupation between about 2300 BC and about 1150 BC, the period during which the Israelite conquest of the town must have occurred. But this has not produced widespread rejection of the identification; instead it has resulted in scepticism concerning the historicity of the biblical tradition.

Such tensions do not occur only between archaeology and the biblical text. Dhiban, commonly held to be the site of biblical Dibon (in Moab), has scant remains from before the Iron Age. However, Thutmosis III and Ramesses II both refer to a town *T-p-n* which some Egyptologists argue is none other than Moabite Dibon. If they are correct, Dibon must have flourished during the Late Bronze Age, and Dhiban cannot be the site.

In short, the interplay between archaeological and textual evidence can be complex and inconclusive. Uncertainty still surrounds the locations of Eglon (Tell 'Aitun or Tell el-Hesi?), Debir (Tell Beit Mirsim or Khirbet Rabûd?) and many other sites; Bethel's long-accepted location at Beitīn has recently been challenged and modern Bīreh proposed as an alternative. We must live with the fact that there will always be many biblical sites which cannot be identified with certainty. And because the Bible does not refer to every town which existed in Palestine during the Old and New Testament periods, there will always be a great many sites known from other ancient sources and from archaeology which have no biblical identification. It has been estimated that Palestine and Transjordan alone contain some 6,000 ancient sites, a vastly higher number than the total of biblical place-names for the same regions. And archaeology reveals that some of these sites without mention in the Bible were large and important cities during the biblical period. This illustrates the importance of archaeology and ancient texts for expanding our knowledge of the historical and political geography of the ancient world.

John Bimson

**Archaeologists at work on site.**

# A

**ABANA.** One of two Syrian rivers mentioned by the leprous Naaman in 2 Kings 5:12. Named Chrysorrhoas ('golden river') by the Greeks, it is probably identical with the modern Barada, which rises in the Anti-Lebanon mountains 29 kilometres north-west of Damascus, and then, after flowing through the city, enters a marshy lake, Bahret-el-Kibliyeh, some 29 kilometres to the east. The fertile gardens and orchards which it waters may explain Naaman's boast.
J. D. Douglas

**ABARIM.** A name for the mountains which rise from the eastern shore of the Dead Sea, where the edge of the *Moabite plateau is broken up by a succession of east-west wadis: literally it means 'the regions beyond', that is, beyond the Dead Sea from the point of view of Judah. At the northern end of the range stands Mount *Nebo, from which Moses could look across over the land of Canaan (Numbers 27:12; Deuteronomy 32:49).

According to the itinerary in Numbers 33 the Israelites' last encampment before they reached the Jordan valley was in these mountains (verses 47–48). *Iye-abarim (verses 44–45; compare Numbers 21:11) must have lain near the southern end of the Dead Sea.

In accordance with modern translations, against the AV which translates 'passages' (compare Targum), Abarim should also be read in Jeremiah 22:20, where two other mountains which overlook Canaan are mentioned.
G. I. Davies

*Further reading*
G. Adam Smith, *The Historical Geography of the Holy Land*, 25th edition, 1931, pp. 380–381
*GTT*, pp. 261, 444.

**ABDON** (Hebrew *'aḇdôn*). A levitical town in Asher (Joshua 21:30, spelt *'eḇrōn* in 19:28, where the territory is described); Tel Avdon, Khirbet 'Abdeh, 6 kilometres inland from *Achzib, commanding a way into the hills.
J. P. U. Lilley

**ABEL.** An element of certain place-names, chiefly in Transjordan. The traditional interpretation 'meadow' is not at all certain, and Baumgartner (in *Hebräisches und aramäisches Lexicon zum Alten Testament*, 3rd edition, p. 7) prefers 'brook, watercourse', comparing Hebrew *'ûḇāl, yûḇāl, yāḇāl*. 'Abel' of the Massoretic text of 1 Samuel 6:18 (compare AV) is probably a textual error, and *'eḇen*, meaning 'stone', should be read (compare the Septuagint and modern versions).

In 2 Samuel 20:18 'Abel' stands for 'Abel (of) Beth-maacah' (verses 14–15), and in 2 Chronicles 16:4 (which may be a corrupt text) Abel-maim seems to be the same place (see 1 Kings 15:20).

The exact locations of Abel-mizraim 'beyond (or 'beside', with NEB) the Jordan' (Genesis 50:11) and Abel-keramim (Judges 11:33: somewhere in Ammon) are unknown, but see the commentaries by Skinner and Kidner on Genesis 50:11, and Aharoni in *LOB* pp. 265 and 429 for possible sites.
G. I. Davies

**ABEL-MEHOLAH.** A town named in conjunction with the flight of the Midianites from Gideon (Judges 7:22). It became part of Solomon's fifth district (1 Kings 4:12) and was Elisha's birthplace (1 Kings 19:16). The site is unknown, but is usually placed in the Jordan valley south of Beth-shean.
D. W. Baker

**ABEL OF BETH-MAACHAH.** The town in northern Naphtali in which Joab besieged Sheba, son of Bichri (2 Samuel 20:14); it was captured by the Syrians under Ben-hadad (*c.* 879 BC, 1 Kings 15:20; 2 Chronicles 16:4) where it is called Abel-maim; and captured by the Assyrians under Tiglath-pileser III (*c.* 733 BC, 2 Kings 15:29). It was possibly part of the Syrian state of *Maacah.

**Abel of Beth-maachah, identified with Tell Abil 20 kilometres north of Lake Huleh.**

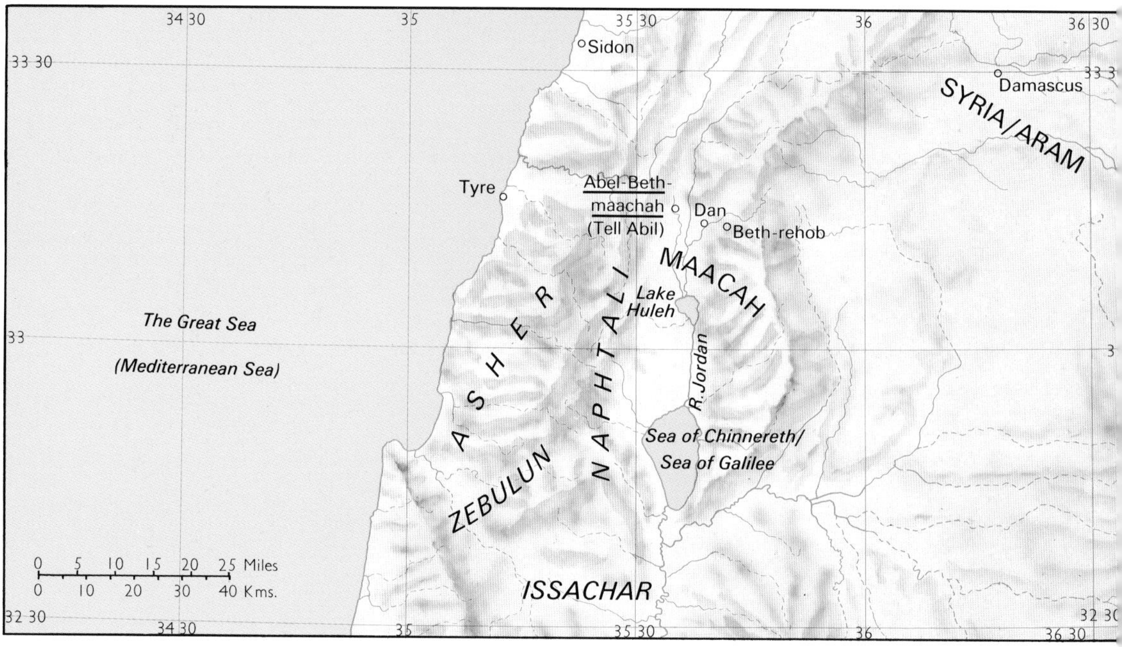

It has been identified with Tell
bil 20 kilometres north of Lake
uleh.
The use of the name Abel alone in
e Egyptian Execration Texts and
2 Samuel 20:18, as well as the use
the explicative conjunction in
Samuel 20:14 ('Abel, *i.e.*
eth-maacah'), shows that these are
vo alternative names rather than
ne consisting of three parts.
W. Baker

**bel-SHITTIM.** See *SHITTIM.

**BILENE.** A region of Anti-Lebanon, ttached to the city of Abila ompare Hebrew *'aḇēl*, 'meadow'), n the bank of the Abana (modern arada), some 29 kilometres north-est of Damascus (its ruins still and round the village of Es-Suk).

Abilene belonged to the Ituraean ingdom of Ptolemy Mennaeus . 85–40 BC) and his son Lysanias I 0–36 BC); it was later detached to rm the tetrarchy of a younger ysanias, mentioned in Luke 3:1. In D 37 it was given by the emperor aius to Herod Agrippa I as part of is kingdom, and in 53 by Claudius Herod Agrippa II. See Josephus, *ewish War*, 2.215, 247; *Antiquities f the Jews,* 18.237; 19.275; 20.138.
F. Bruce

*urther reading*
*JP* 1, 1973, pp. 561–573.

**CCAD, AKKAD.** One of the major ties, with Babylon and Erech, unded by Nimrod (Genesis 10:10). bore the Semitic name of *Akkadu*, umerian *Agade*. Its precise location ear Sippar or Babylon is uncertain, ough some identify it with the ins of Tell Šešubār or even Babylon self.

Inscriptions show that an early emitic dynasty founded by Sargon I . 2350 BC) flourished here. At this me Akkad controlled all Sumer outhern Babylonia), and its armies eached Syria, Elam and southern natolia. With the great trade and rosperity which followed the rule of argon and his successor Naram-Sīn e dynasty became symbolic of a olden age'.

When Babylon later became the apital, the term 'Akkad' continued be used to describe the whole of orthern Babylonia until the late ersian period in the records of the ings of *Assyria and *Babylonia.
. J. Wiseman

**CCO, ACCHO.** See *PTOLEMAIS.

**CELDAMA.** See *AKELDAMA.

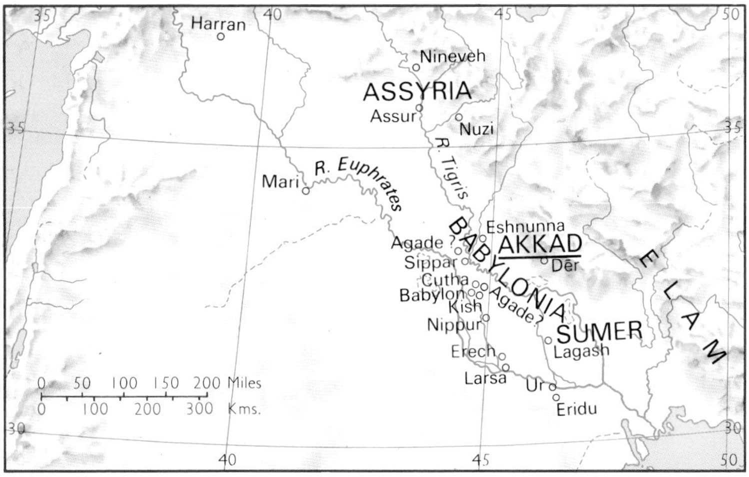


Akkad, the northern part of Babylonia, showing two possible sites for the original city of Agade.

**ACHAIA.** A small region of Greece, on the southern coast of the gulf of Corinth, which twice gave its name to the whole country. In Homer the Greeks are frequently called Achaeans. Again, in the age of the Hellenistic kings, the Achaean confederacy championed the freedom of the republics, and after its defeat by the Romans (146 BC) the name was used by them for Greece in general.

*Under Roman administration*
The area was administered with Macedonia at first, and even after organization as a separate province (27 BC) is linked in common usage with Macedonia (Acts 19:21; Romans 15:26; 1 Thessalonians 1:8).

The province was in the regular senatorial allotment, and was hence governed by a proconsul (*anthypatos*, Acts 18:12), with two exceptions: from AD 15 to 44 it was under the Caesarian legate of Moesia; and from AD 67 Roman supervision was entirely suspended for several years by Nero's benevolence thus giving autonomy in local government and immunity from taxation, and the forty or so republics in the area enjoyed their liberty without even the appearance of permission.

The old confederacy was maintained under the Romans, with its capital at Argos, which until Nero's Principate was the seat of the imperial cult. However, the much larger province was governed from Corinth and the provincial imperial cult was celebrated there from AD 54.

*In the New Testament*
It is always in connection with Corinth that the name Achaia occurs in the New Testament, and it is uncertain whether anything more is meant (see 2 Corinthians 1:1; 9:2; 11:10). We know, however, that there was a church at Cenchreae (Romans 16:1), and there were believers at Athens (Acts 17:34). We may assume, therefore, that in referring to the household of Stephanas as the 'first converts in Achaia' (1 Corinthians 16:15), Paul is applying the term to Corinth as having a primacy due to its position as the Roman capital. He is not thinking of the rest of the province.
E. A. Judge, B. W. Winter

*Further reading*
Pausanias, *Description of Greece*, 8.16.10–17.4
Strabo, *Geography*, 8
*IG*, VIII, 2712
J. Keil in *CAH*, 11, pp. 556–565
A. Spawforth, 'Corinth, Argos and the Imperial Cult: A Reconsideration of Pseudo-Julian *Letters* 198 Bidez', *Hesperia*, 1994.

The view from Acrocorinth, the acropolis of ancient Corinth, looking south-west into the Peloponnese. Achaia was the small region on the southern coast of the gulf of Corinth.

**ACHMETHA.** See *ECBATANA.

**ACHOR** (Hebrew *'āḵôr*). The valley near Jericho where Achan was executed (Joshua 7:26). Jewish and Christian tradition placed it north of Jericho (Eusebius, *Onomasticon,* 18.84), indicating the Wadi Nu'eima. Some authorities think this is meant in Hosea 2:15, relating to the northern kingdom. However the term *'emeq* implies an open valley (see 1 Kings 20:28, and the pastoral picture in Isaiah 65:10), while the mention in Joshua 15:7 suggests that it overlooked Gilgal from the Judah-Benjamin boundary, perhaps not far south of Wadi Qilt; El Buqei'a, the upland vale beyond Nebi Musa, has been proposed but seems too far away.
J. P. U. Lilley

*Further reading*
J. T. Milik, F. M. Cross, *BASOR* 142, 1956, pp. 17–32
*GTT*, 1959, pp. 137, 139, 271
L. E. Stager in *RB* 81, 1974, pp. 94–96.

**ACHSHAPH** (Hebrew *'aḵšāp̄*). An important Canaanite city (Joshua 11:1; 12:20), mentioned in Egyptian lists and *Papyrus Anastasi I* (J. B. Pritchard, *Ancient Near Eastern Texts*, 3rd edition, p. 477) which appears to imply that it lay to the south of Acre (Tel Regev, Khirbet Harbaj [11 kilometres south-east of Haifa], *LOB*, pp. 22, 52, 171; Tel Kison [10 kilometres south-east of Acre], Albright in *BASOR* 83, 1941, p. 33). It was occupied by Asher (Joshua 19:25).

Some authorities favour a site in the hills north east of Acre (Acco); and it is also possible that the city named in Joshua 11 and 12 was in northern Galilee (Noth, in *Josua*).
J. P. U. Lilley

**ACHZIB. 1.** A Canaanite harbour town assigned to Asher (Joshua 19:29) which they never occupied (Judges 1:31). It was taken by Sennacherib in 701 BC (*ANET*, p. 287) and is identified with the modern ez-Zib, 14 kilometres north of Acre (Acco).

**2.** A town of Judah (Joshua 15:44) in the Shephelah. Probably the Chezib of Genesis 38:5, it was conquered by Sennacherib (see Micah 1:14); tentatively identified as the modern Tell el-Beida.
D. W. Baker

**ACRE.** See *PTOLEMAIS.

**ADAM** (Hebrew *'āḏām*). A town 28 kilometres north of Jericho, near *Zarethan, controlling the Jordan fords just below the confluence of the Jabbok; modern Tell ed-Damiyeh. A landslip blocking the Jordan here made it possible for the Israelites to cross at Jericho (Joshua 3:10ff.).

Landslips have occurred at Tell ed-Damiyeh in more recent times with similar effects on the river. In 1267 the Jordan was dammed for 10 hours when part of the bank collapsed, and in 1927 a collapse stopped the river for 2½ hours.
J. P. U. Lilley, J. Bimson

**ADAMAH** (Hebrew *'ᵃḏāmâh*). A town in Naphtali (Joshua 19:36), possibly at Qarn Hattin (*LOB*, pp. 28 *etc.* and *JNES* 19, 1960, pp. 179–181, identify it with Shemesh-adam of Egyptian sources).
J. P. U. Lilley

**ADAMI-NEKEB.** A place mentioned in Joshua 19:33, on the border of Naphtali. It was apparently a pass and has been identified with the modern Khirbet ed-Dâmiyeh or the site of Khirbet et-Tell above it. See *LOB*, pp. 183 and 259.
R. A. H. Gunner

**ADMAH.** One of the Cities of the *Plain (Genesis 14:2, 8; Deuteronomy 29:23), linked specially with *Zeboiim (Hosea 11:8). The association with Gaza (Genesis 10:19) suggests the correctness of the modern locating of the pentapolis as submerged beneath the southern waters of the Dead Sea.

Alternatively, Admah may have been one of a string of Early Bronze Age sites located on the eastern side of the Ghor (the plain at the southern end of the Dead Sea). At least three of these towns were destroyed by fire, but at a date apparently no later than 2200 BC, which is seemingly too early for the time of Abraham. (For the latter suggestion see W. C. van Hattem in *BA* 44/2, 1981, pp. 87–92.)
J. A. Motyer, J. Bimson

**ADONI-BEZEK** (Hebrew *'ᵃḏōnî-ḇezeq*, 'lord of Bezek'). Judah and Simeon, preparatory to conquering their own territory, combined to defeat 10,000 Canaanites at Bezek, probably modern Khirbet Ibziq, 21 kilometres north east of Shechem (Judges 1:4–7). Their king, Adoni-bezek, not to be equated with Adoni-zedek (Joshua 10:1–27), fled, but was recaptured and his thumbs and big toes were cut off.
A. E. Cundall

*Further reading*
*LOB*, p. 197.

**ADORAIM.** City of south west Judah fortified by Rehoboam (2 Chronicles 11:9), identified today with the village of Dura, some 8 kilometres south west of Hebron. It became a major Idumaean city, and as such figured in various historical events in the intertestamental period.
D. F. Payne

**ADRAMYTTIUM**. Seaport in Mysia, in Roman Asia, facing Lesbos: the site is Karatash, but the modern inland town, Edremit, preserves the name. Its commercial importance, once high, was declining by New Testament times.

An Adramyttian coastal ship conveyed Julius and Paul from Caesarea (Acts 27:2). It was doubtless homeward bound, engaging in coastwise traffic with 'the ports along the coast of Asia', where a connection for Rome might be obtained – an expectation soon justified (verses 5f.).
A. F. Walls

*Further reading*
Strabo, *Geography*, 13.1.51, 65–66
Pliny, *Natural History,* 13.1.2 (for a local export)
W. Leaf, *Strabo on the Troad*, 1923, pp. 318ff.

**ADRIA.** The 'sea of Adria' (Acts 27:27), across which the ship of the Alexandrian grain fleet, which was taking Paul to Italy, drifted in a westerly direction for 14 days, was the Central Mediterranean. It refers to the body of water between Crete and Malta with Sicily and the foot of Italy forming its north west boundary (compare Strabo, *Geography,* 2.5.20; Josephus, *Life,* 15; Pausanias, *Description of Greece* 5.25.3; Ptolemy, *Geography,* 3.4.1; 15.1).

It is to be distinguished from the *gulf* of Adria (compare the town of Adria or Hadria north of the Po), which is known to us as the Adriatic Sea.
F. F. Bruce

**ADULLAM.** A Canaanite city in Judah (Joshua 12:15); fortified by Rehoboam (2 Chronicles 11:7); mentioned by Micah (Micah 1:15) and inhabited after the Exile (Nehemiah 11:30). Identified with Tell esh-Sheikh Madhkur (Ḥorvat 'Adullam), midway between Jerusalem and Lachish, the place is usually associated with the cave in which David hid when pursued by

ul (1 Samuel 22:1).
W. Meiklejohn

**DUMMIM.** A steep pass on the
oundary between Judah and
enjamin (Joshua 15:7; 28:17) on
e road from Jericho to Jerusalem.
raditionally the scene of the Good
amaritan story (Luke 10:34), it is
nown today as Tal'at ed-Damm
ascent of blood'), probably from the
d marl of the soil, though Jerome
tributed the name to the murders
nd robberies said to have taken
ace there.
D. Douglas

**ENON** (from Greek *ainōn*,
ountain'). A place west of Jordan
here John baptized (John 3:23),
erhaps to be identified with 'Ainun,
orth east of Nablus, near the
eadwaters of the Wadi Far'ah
ence 'there was much water
ere'). (See also *SALIM.)
An alternative, supported by
usebius and Jerome, is the site of
mm el-Umdan, 13 kilometres south
outh east of Scythopolis (Old
estament Bethshan).
F. Bruce, J. Bimson

## FRICA

### arly knowledge and omenclature

he Greeks designated the
ontinent 'Libya', but of its extent
nd its relation to Asia there was
oubt. Herodotus (5th century BC) is
ready convinced of its being almost
urrounded by sea, and cites (in his
*istory*, 4.42) an alleged circumnavi-
ation by a Phoenician crew in the
ervice of Pharaoh Neco. A
anslation of a Punic document, the
eriplus of the Erythraean Sea,
ccounts a Carthaginian voyage,
vidently as far as Sierra Leone,
efore 480 BC.

The Romans applied 'Africa' to the
hole continent (Pomponius Mela,
.4), but far more regularly to
roconsular Africa, comprising the
rea (roughly modern Tunisia)
nnexed from Carthage in 146 BC,
lus the Numidian and Mauretanian
omains later added. But, though
e Carthaginians may have known
ore about the Trans-Sahara than
e realize, the knowledge of Africa
ossessed by the ancient peoples
ho have left most literary remains
as largely confined to the areas
articipating in, or accessible to, the
lediterranean civilizations, rarely
enetrating the colossal barriers of
e Atlas Mountains, the Sahara and
e perils of the Upper Nile.

### Africa in the Old Testament

*Egypt*
Similarly, Israel's main concerns in Africa were naturally with her powerful neighbour, Egypt. Whether as the granary of the Patriarchs, the oppressor of the bondage or the broken reed of the period of Assyrian advance, the changing roles of Egypt could not be ignored. Despite the cruel past, a tender feeling towards Egypt remained (Deuteronomy 23:7), which prepares us for the prophecies of Egypt's eventually sharing with Israel in the knowledge and worship of the Lord (Isaiah 19 – note the changing tone as the chapter proceeds).

*Cush: south of Egypt*
Other African peoples are mentioned from time to time (see *LIBYA, *PUT), but the most frequent allusions are to Cush (see also *ETHIOPIA), the general designation for the lands beyond Egypt. The characteristic skin and physique of the inhabitants was remarked on (Jeremiah 13:23; Isaiah 45:14 and probably Isaiah 18:2, 7).

At some periods historical circumstances linked Egypt and Ethiopia in Hebrew eyes, and they stand together, sometimes with other African peoples, as representative nations on which God's righteous judgments will be executed (Isaiah 43:3; Ezekiel 30:4ff.; Nahum 3:9), as those who will one day recognize the true status of God's people (Isaiah 45:14), and as those who will ultimately receive Israel's God (Psalm 87:4, and especially Psalm 68:31).

The picture of Ethiopia, symbol of the great African unknown beyond the Egyptian river, stretching out hands to God, was like a trumpet-call in the missionary revival of the 18th and 19th centuries. Even within the biblical period it had a measure of fulfilment; not only were there Jewish settlements in Africa (compare Zephaniah 3:10) but an Ethiopian in Jewish service did more for God's prophet than true-born Israelites (Jeremiah 38), and the high-ranking Ethiopian of Acts 8 was evidently a devout proselyte.

Despite a long tradition of perverted exegesis in some quarters, there is nothing to connect the curse of Ham (Genesis 9:25) with a permanent divinely instituted malediction on the negroid peoples; it is explicitly applied to the Canaanites.

### Africa in the New Testament

Jesus himself received hospitality on African soil (Matthew 2:13ff.). The Jewish settlements in Egypt and Cyrene, prefigured, perhaps, in Isaiah 19:18f. and others, were evidently a fruitful field for the early church. Simon who bore the cross was a Cyrenian, and that his relationship with Christ did not stop there may be inferred from the fact that his children were apparently well known in the primitive Christian community (Mark 15:21).

Egyptian and Cyrenian Jews were present at Pentecost (Acts 2:10); the mighty Apollos was an Alexandrian Jew (Acts 18:24); Cyrenian converts, probably including the prophet Lucius, shared in the epoch-making step of preaching to pagans at Antioch (Acts 11:20f.).

*Origin of the church in Africa*
But we know nothing certain about the foundation of the Egyptian and North African churches, some of the most prominent in the world by the late 2nd century. The tradition, which cannot be traced very early, that Mark was the pioneer evangelist of Alexandria (Eusebius, *Ecclesiastical History*, 2.16) is itself, when applied to 1 Peter 5:13, the only support for the theory of Peter's residence there (but compare G. T. Manley, in *EQ* 16, 1944, pp. 138ff.).

Luke's vivid picture in Acts of the march of the gospel through the northern lands of the Mediterranean may obscure for us the fact that the march through the southern lands must have been quite as effective and probably almost as early. There were Christians in Africa about as soon as there were in Europe.

But Luke does not forget Africa. He shows how, by means the apostolic church never anticipated, and before the real Gentile mission began, the gospel went to the kingdom of Meroë (Acts 8:26ff.), as if in earnest of the fulfilment of the purpose of God for Africa declared in the Old Testament.
A. F. Walls

*Further reading*
M. Cary and E. H. Warmington, *The Ancient Explorers*, 1929
B. H. Warmington, *The North African Provinces*, 1954
——, *Carthage*, 1960
C. K. Meek, *Journal of African History* 1, 1960, pp. 1ff.
C. P. Groves, *The Planting of Christianity in Africa*, 1, 1948, pp. 31ff.

**AHAVA.** A Babylonian town and also, probably, a canal named after the town, where Ezra assembled returning exiles (Ezra 8:15–31). The site may well be the classical Scenae (Strabo, *Geography*, 16.1.27), an important caravan junction not far from Babylon.
D. J. A. Clines

**AHLAB.** Situated in the territory of Asher (Judges 1:31), it is possibly the Mehebel of Joshua 19:29. Probably to be identified with Khirbet el-Maḥālib, 8 kilometres north east of Tyre, the Mahalib captured by Tiglath-Pileser III in 734 BC and later by Sennacherib. See D. J. Wiseman in *Iraq* 18, 1956, p. 129.
D. J. Wiseman

**AI.** The name is always written with the definite article in Hebrew, *hā'ay*, the heap, ruin. The city lay east of Bethel and the altar which Abram built (Genesis 12:8) adjacent to Beth-aven (Joshua 7:2) and north of Michmash (Isaiah 10:28).

The Israelite attack upon it, immediately following the sack of Jericho, was at first repulsed, but after Achan's sin had been punished a successful stratagem was employed. The people of Ai were killed, their king executed, and their city burned and made into 'a heap' (Hebrew *tēl*; Joshua 7:1–8:29).

It became an Ephraimite town (1 Chronicles 7:28, 'Ayyah'), but was inhabited by the Benjaminites after the Exile (Nehemiah 11:31). Isaiah pictured the Assyrian armies advancing on Jerusalem by way of Ai (Isaiah 10:28, 'Aiath').

*The problem of identification: Et-Tell*

Modern Et-Tell (Arabic *tell*, heap, mound) about 3 kilometres south east of Bethel (Tell Beitīn) is usually identified with Ai on topographical grounds and on the correspondence in the meanings of the ancient and modern names.

Excavations in 1933–35 by Mme J. Marquet-Krause and in 1964–72 by J. A. Callaway revealed a city which prospered in the 3rd millennium BC. There was a strong city-wall and a temple containing stone bowls and ivories imported from Egypt. It was destroyed *c.* 2400 BC, perhaps by Amorite invaders. No traces of later occupation were found except for a small settlement which made use of the earlier ruins about 1150–1050 BC.

Those who believe in this identification have made various attempts to explain the discrepancy between the biblical account of Joshua's conquest and the archaeological evidence. It has been suggested that the story originally referred to Bethel but was later adapted to suit Ai or even invented to explain the impressive ruin as the result of an attack by the hero Joshua. There is no evidence to support these hypotheses; indeed, it would be strange to credit a hero with failure at first.

More plausible is the explanation that Ai, with its massive old walls, was used as a temporary stronghold by the surrounding population; but the account points rather to an inhabited town with its own king. While it is possible that Ai is to be located elsewhere, no completely satisfactory solution has yet been proposed.

*The problem of identification: Khirbet Nisya*

The most plausible alternative so far is that of Khirbet Nisya, south east of modern Bireh, proposed by D. Livingston. Excavations here since 1979 have produced pottery from the Middle Bronze and Late Bronze I periods, as well as from the Iron Age, the Persian period and later. On this basis it would appear that Khirbet Nisya's occupational history corresponds more closely than that of Et-Tell to the history of biblical Ai. So far, however, no building remains have been found which can be dated to the time of Joshua's conquest.

(For the question of identification see D. Livingston, in *WTJ* 33, 1970, pp. 20–44; A. F. Rainey, in *WTJ* 33, pp. 175–188; D. Livingston, in *WTJ* 34, 1971, pp. 39–50; J. Bimson and D. Livingston, in *BARev* 13/5, 1987, pp. 40–53.)

The later town (Ezra 2:28; Nehemiah 7:32) may be identified with some other site in the vicinity.

For references to the excavation results at Et-Tell and proposed solutions of the problem they raise, see J. A. Callaway, in *NEAEHL* I, pp. 39–45 and *The Early Bronze Age Citadel and Lower City at Ai (et-Tell)*, 1980; J. M. Grintz, in *Bib* 42, 1961, pp. 201–216.

Ai is also the name of a city in Moab (Jeremiah 49:3) of unknown location.
A. R. Millard, J. J. Bimson

**AIATH.** See *AI.

**AIJALON** (Hebrew *'ayyālôn*). **1.** A town on the hill-side commanding from the south the entrance to the Vale of Aijalon. It is identified with Tell el-Qoq'a, near Yalo (10 kilometres east-south-east of Gezer), first occupied *c.* 2000 BC.

In successive phases of Israel's history it was occupied by Danites (who could not expel the Amorites), Ephraimites and Benjaminites (Joshua 19:42; Judges 1:35; 1 Chronicles 6:69; 8:13). A levitical town, fortified by Rehoboam to guard the north west approach to Jerusalem, it was occupied by Philistines in the reign of Ahaz (2 Chronicles 11:10; 28:18).

See D. Baly, *Geographical Companion*, 1963, pp. 92f.; *LOB*, pp. 26 *etc.*

**2.** A town in Zebulun (Judges 12:12) where the judge Elon was buried; it appears as Ailom in the Septuagint. A possible identification is Khirbet el-Lon at the western end of the Sahl el-Battuf (Abel, *Géographie* II, 1937, p. 241).
J. P. U. Lilley

**AKELDAMA.** Acts 1:19 gives the meaning of the word (in AV Acel-dama) as 'field of blood' – the Aramaic phrase being *ḥ$^a$qēl d$^e$mâ*. The ground was previously known as the Potter's Field, and this has been equated with the Potter's House (Jeremiah 18:2) in the Hinnom Valley.

Jerome placed it on the southern side of this valley; and the site accepted today is there. Eusebius, however, said this ground was north of Jerusalem. The traditional site certainly can provide potter's clay; and it has long been used for burials.

See J. A. Motyer in *NIDNTT* 1, pp. 93–94, for a bibliography and a brief discussion of the problems.
D. F. Payne

**AKKAD.** See *ACCAD.

**AKKADIANS.** See *BABYLON.

**AKRABBIM** (Hebrew *'aqrabbîm*, 'scorpions'). A mountain pass at the southern end of the Dead Sea (Numbers 34:4; Joshua 15:3 ['Maaleh-acrabbim', AV]; Judges 1:36) between the Arabah and the hill-country of Judah, identified with the modern Naqb eṣ-ṣāfā.
J. D. Douglas

**ALALAH** or **ALALAKH** (which is perhaps a more frequent spelling) (Akkadian, Hurrian *a-la-la-aḫ*; Egyptian *'irrḫ*). Capital of a city-state on the river Orontes in the Amq plain of northern Syria from which 468 texts from Level VII (*c.* 1900–1750 BC) and Level IV (*c.* 1500–1470 BC) provide details which may be compared with the patriarchal period of Genesis (see also the

Part of the excavated site at Et-Tell, the possible site of ancient Ai.

entries on *EBLA, *MARI and *UGARIT).

The site of Tell Aṭšānâ (Turkish Açana) was excavated by Sir Leonard Woolley, who in 1937–39 and 1946–49 uncovered sixteen levels of occupation since *c.* 3100 BC (Level XVI) to *c.* 1200 (Level I) with early affinities with both Palestine and Mesopotamia.

*History*
The 172 texts from Yarimlim's palace (Level VII) were primarily contracts and ration lists. The city was controlled by a western Semitic family ruling Aleppo (Halab) whose governor Abba'el (or Abban) suppressed a revolt at Irrid near Carchemish and, *c.* 1720, gave Alalakh to his brother Yarimlim (Alalakh Tablet 1). This early covenant-treaty text, and associated agreements, describes the historical situation, stipulations, divine witnesses and curses, as is common in the later covenant formulae. A separate document by the same scribe lists the religious obligations (Alalakh Tablet 126).

Yarimlim left the city to his son in his will (Alalakh Tablet 6), attested by state officials, perhaps to avoid rivalry on his death (see 1 Kings 1:17–36). However, another son, Irkabtum, succeeded and made peace with the semi-nomadic Hapiru. The city fell to the Hittite Mursilis I when he captured Aleppo (*c.* 1600 BC).

After a gap (Level V), Idrimi, the youngest son of a king of Aleppo, was driven into exile, as he tells in his autobiography, inscribed as a speech on his statue. After living among the Hapiru in Canaan for 7 years he received divine assurance to mount an amphibious operation to recapture Mukish. He re-entered his capital Alalakh to popular acclaim, was made king and built a palace and temple with spoil taken in war (*c.* 1470 BC).

This narrative has been compared with the experiences of David (1 Samuel 22:3ff.). Idrimi made treaties with neighbouring states regulating the extradition of runaway slaves (Alalakh Tablet 3, in *ANET*, 3rd edition, p. 532). Similarly, Shimei entered Philistine territory to search for his two slaves and Achish of Gath returned them on demand (1 Kings 2:39–40). This would imply a similar type of treaty, perhaps between Solomon and Gath, following David's experience there (1 Samuel 27:5ff.). It would also throw light on the provision prohibiting the extradition of Hebrew fugitives in Deuteronomy 23:15–16 (*IEJ* 5, 1955, pp. 65–72).

Another treaty makes city elders responsible for returning fugitives (Alalakh Tablet 2, in *ANET*, 3rd edition, pp. 531f.; Deuteronomy 23:15–16).

Alalakh later came under Hittite control (Level III), as it had earlier been governed by northerners in the 20th–19th centuries BC. It was finally destroyed by 'Sea Peoples', perhaps those allied to the Philistines.

*Significance of the Alalakh texts*
The main interest in the Alalakh texts for the Old Testament lies in the comparison of customs and language with the Genesis narratives.

In marriage contracts (Alalakh Tablets 91–94), the future father-in-law was 'asked' for the bride (compare Genesis 29:18), to whom betrothal gifts were made (Alalakh Tablet 17). Some contracts state that failing a son within 7 years, the husband could marry a concubine (compare Genesis 29:18–21); however, if the first wife later bore a son he would be the first-born (Alalakh Tablet 92; compare Genesis 21:10).

The king held a firm control legally and economically over citizens of all classes including the élite *maryanu*-warriors (who also had religious obligations, Alalakh Tablet 15), the freedmen and the semi-free rural retainers, among whom were listed the *hupšu* (*hop̄šî*, Deuteronomy 15:12–18).

Some individuals were made to work off their debt by going to the palace to 'dwell in the house of the king' (Alalakh Tablets 18–27 and 32; compare Psalm 23:6). Slaves were not numerous and could be received as prisoners of war or as gifts (Alalakh Tablet 224). They were valued at about 25 silver shekels and some contracts included clauses against release at a royal amnesty (Alalakh Tablet 65). The *corvée* (*mas*) was enforced at Alalakh as in later Israel (Alalakh Tablet 246; Joshua 17:13). All this would be in the mind of Samuel at least when the Israelites asked for a similar type of kingship (1 Samuel 8).

Other customs which may illustrate biblical practices are the exchange of villages to preserve inter-state boundaries along natural and defensible features. This may be reflected in Solomon's 'gift' of 20 villages to Hiram of Tyre in return for wood and gold (1 Kings 9:10–14; *JBL* 79, 1960, pp. 59–60).

Treaty ceremonies involved the slaughter of sheep over which the participants declared: 'If ever I take back what I have given . . .', implying 'may the gods cut off my life', a similar idea to that in Old Testament oaths (*e.g.* 1 Samuel 3:17).

In some contracts clothes were given as additional payment, as also in Syria later according to 2 Kings 5:5–27.

Ahab may have attempted to justify his action in confiscating Naboth's property (1 Kings 21:15) on the basis of the practice whereby a rebel against the king had his property taken by the palace after the execution of an evildoer (Alalakh Tablet 17, in *ANET*, 3rd edition, p. 546, no. 15).

The use of *mištannu*, 'equivalent' (Alalakh Tablet 3, in *ANET*, 3rd edition, p. 532), in the manumission of slaves (compare *mišneh*, Deuteronomy 15:18) argues against Jeremiah 16:18 as 'stigmatizing God as unreasonable and unjust' (*HUCA* 29, 1958, pp. 125f.).

The mixed Semitic and Hurrian population of the area from early times (Level VII) gives significant Hurrian parallels to such names as Anah, Aholibamah, Alian, Ajah, Dishon, Ezer (Genesis 36), Anah and Shamgar (Judges 3:31), To'i (2 Samuel 8:9), Agee (2 Samuel 23:11), Eli-hepa (2 Samuel 23:32) (*JTVI* 82, 1950, p.6).

D. J. Wiseman

*Further reading*

C. L. Woolley, *A Forgotten Kingdom*, 1953

*Alalakh*, 1955

D. J. Wiseman, *The Alalakh Tablets*, 1953

*AOTS*, pp. 119–135

*IDBS*, pp. 16–17

Sidney Smith, *The Statue of Idrimi*, 1949; compare *ANET*, 3rd edition, pp. 557–558.

## ALEXANDRIA

### The city

*Location*

Alexandria, a great seaport on the north west coast of the Egyptian Delta, on the narrow isthmus between the sea and Lake Mareotis, was founded in 332 BC by Alexander (the Great) of Macedon and named after himself. A small Egyptian settlement, Rakotis, was its only predecessor on the site and was absorbed into the western side of the new city; in native Egyptian parlance (exemplified by Coptic, centuries later), the name Rakotis was extended to Alexandria.

The city was apparently laid out on a 'grid' plan of cross-streets and *insulae*; but as the remains of the ancient city are inextricably buried underneath its modern successor, any reconstruction of its lay-out and location of its great buildings must draw heavily on the none-too-precise literary references virtually by themselves, and hence cannot be exact. Not until the time of Ptolemy II (*c.* 285–246 BC) did Alexandria first attain to the architectural splendours so famed in later writers' accounts.

Between the shore and the Pharos island stretched a connecting causeway, the 'Heptastadion' ('seven stadia', 1,300 metres long); this divided the anchorage into a Western harbour and an Eastern or Great harbour, whose entrance was dominated by the Pharos lighthouse-tower. It contained also the royal harbour, and was flanked on the east by the royal palace. South of the shore-line, extending all along behind it and as far as Lake Mareotis, stretched the city.

*Population*

Right from the start, Alexandria was a thoroughly cosmopolitan city. Besides its Greek citizens and numerous poor Greek immigrants, there was a considerable Jewish community (compare later, Acts 6:9; 18:24) under their own ethnarch and having their own quarter (though not restricted to it until AD 38), and quite a large native Egyptian populace, especially in the Rakotis district in the west.

In Rakotis was localized the Serapeum, temple of the Egypto-Hellenistic deity Sarapis, whose cult was specially promoted by Ptolemy I, just possibly to serve as a common bond for both Greeks and Egyptians (Sir H. I. Bell).

*The city's role*

Politically, Alexandria became capital of Egypt under the Ptolemies Graeco-Macedonian kings of Egypt *c.* 323 to 30 BC. Under the first and energetic kings of this line it became the greatest Hellenistic city of the day. Alexandria continued as Egypt's administrative capital into the Roman imperial and Byzantine epochs.

Alexandria was the banking-centre of all Egypt, an active manufacturing city (cloths, glass, papyrus, *etc.*) and a thriving port. Thence were transshipped the exotic products of Arabia, India and the East, and thence in Roman time sailed the great grain-ships of Alexandria (see Acts 27:6; 28:11) to bring cheap corn for the Roman plebeians.

Finally, Alexandria quickly became and long remained a brilliant seat of learning. To the reign of either Ptolemy I (323–285 BC) or Ptolemy II (285–246 BC) belongs the founding of the 'Museum', where scholars researched and taught in arts and sciences, and of the Library which eventually contained thousands of works upon many tens of thousands of papyrus scrolls.

### Judaism and Christianity

Alexandria's very large Jewish community was concentrated in the eastern sector, but with places of worship all over the city (Philo, *Legatio ad Gaium* 132). One famous synagogue, magnificently fitted, was so vast that flags had to be used to signal the Amen (Babylonian Talmud *Sukkah* 51b, cited in *BC* 1, pp. 152f.).

*A centre of learning*

But beyond this, Alexandria was the intellectual and literary centre of the Dispersion. It was there that the Greek Old Testament, the Septuagint, was produced, and from there came such works as the Book of Wisdom with its Platonic modifications of Old Testament categories and its Greek interest in cosmology and immortality. It was the home of the voluminous Philo, perhaps the first considerable scholar to use the biblical material as philosophic data – though 'his object is not to investigate but to harmonize' (Bigg, p. 32) – and the first major exponent of the allegorical exegesis of Scripture.

Whatever the demerits of the attempted synthesis of Athens and Jerusalem by Alexandrian Jews (and some of them amount to enormities) the literary remains testify to

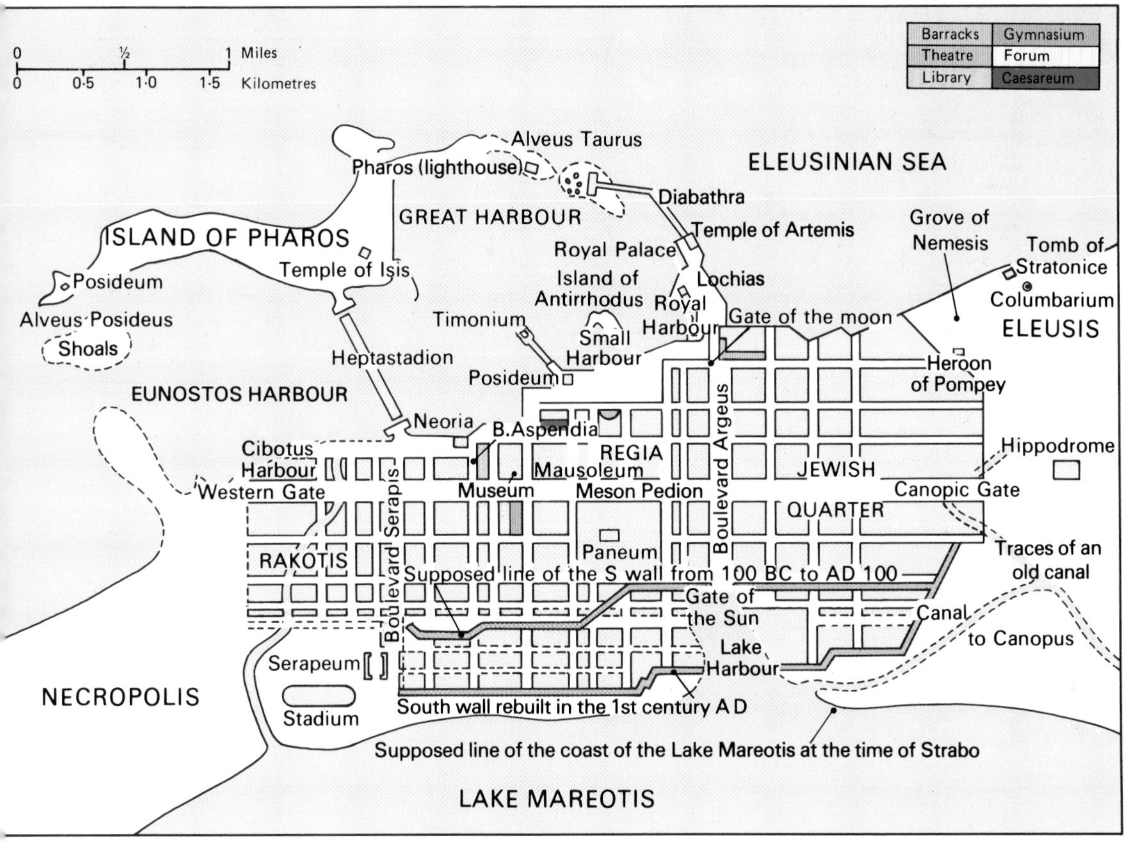


**Plan of Alexandria, 100 BC – AD 100, derived mainly from literary sources, since the old city has never been excavated.**

intellectual energy, missionary concern and, despite audacious departures from traditional formulation, a profound seriousness about the Scriptures.

*Apollos*
These features had considerable indirect influence on early Greek Christianity. It is significant that the eloquent travelling preacher Apollos, who became an important figure in the apostolic church, was an Alexandrian Jew, and 'well versed in the Scriptures' (Acts 18:24). The Epistle to the Hebrews, because of its use of terminology beloved at Alexandria, and its characteristic use of the Old Testament, has been associated, if not necessarily with him, at least with an Alexandrian background; and so, with less reason, have other New Testament books (see J. N. Sanders, *The Fourth Gospel in the Early Church*, 1943; S. G. F. Brandon, *The Fall of Jerusalem and the Christian Church*, 1951).

Apart, however, from unreliable traditions about the agency of the evangelist Mark (which may relate originally to the reception of his Gospel in Alexandria), the origin and early history of the Alexandrian church are completely hidden (see also *AFRICA).

*Alexandrian Christianity*
It has been suggested that Alexandrian Judaism had so philosophized away the Messianic hope that the earliest Christian preaching made slow headway there. There is not sufficient evidence to test this hypothesis. It is unmistakable, however, that when Alexandrian Christianity comes into full view it is patently the heir of Alexandrian Judaism. The missionary zeal, the philosophic apologetic, the allegorical exegesis, the application to biblical commentary and the passion for intellectual synthesis which sometimes leads doctrine to disaster, are common to both.

Some thoroughfare, at present unlit, links Philo and Clement of Alexandria; but it is hardly too bold a conjecture that the road lies through the conversion to Christ of a substantial number of Jews or their adherents in Alexandria during the apostolic or sub-apostolic period.

A. F. Walls

*Further reading*
For a standard historical and cultural background for Alexandria, Ptolemaic and Byzantine, see respectively:
*CAH*, 7, 1928, ch. IV, sect. vii, pp. 142–148, and chs. VIII–IX, pp. 249–311, and *ibid.*, 12, 1939, ch. XIV, sect. i, pp. 476–492.
Useful and compact, with reference to actual remains, is:
E. Breccia, *Alexandrea and Aegyptum, A Guide . . .*, 1922
A popular, readable account of the history and manner of life in ancient Alexandria is:
H. T. Davis, *Alexandria, the Golden City*, 2 vols., 1957
An excellent study of paganism, Judaism and the advent and triumph of Christianity in Egypt generally, and Alexandria also, is provided by:
H. I. Bell, *Cults and Creeds in Graeco-Roman Egypt*, 1953
On Alexandria and Christianity, see also:
J. M. Creed in S. R. K. Glanville (ed.), *The Legacy of Egypt*, 1942, pp. 300–316
A. F. Shore in J. R. Harris (ed.), *The Legacy of Egypt*, 2nd edition, 1971, pp. 390–398
C. Bigg, *The Christian Platonists of Alexandria*, 2nd edition, 1913
J. E. L. Oulton and H. Chadwick, *Alexandrian Christianity*, 1954
L. W. Barnard, 'St Mark and Alexandria', *HTR* 57, 1964, pp. 145–150.

**AMARNA.** (Tell) el-Amarna is the modern name of Akhetaten, capital of Egypt under Amenophis IV

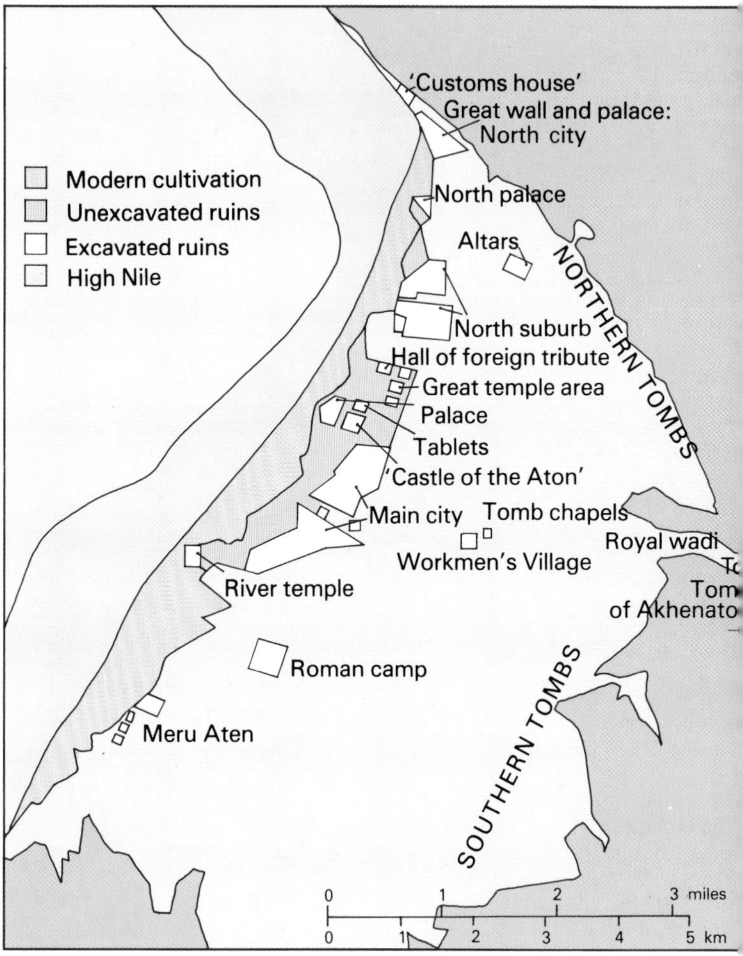


Sketch-map of the site of Amarna, showing areas of excavations.

(Akhenaten) and his immediate successors, *c.* 1375–1360 BC. The ruins lie some 320 kilometres south of Cairo on the east bank of the river Nile. The site extends about 8 by 1 kilometres and has been partially excavated. The impressive remains include temples, administrative buildings, tombs with wall paintings as well as the buildings of many prosperous estates with houses often of uniform plan.

**The Amarna Letters**

The importance of Amarna for biblical studies lies in the series of letters written in cuneiform on clay tablets found by chance in 1887. With subsequent discoveries, the number of documents recovered now totals about 380. The majority are letters from various Asiatic rulers to the pharaohs Amenophis III and IV in the period *c.* 1385–1360 BC; nearly half come from Palestine and Syria. They supply important information concerning the history of the area, providing a vivid picture of the intrigues and inter-city strife which followed the weakening of Egyptian control shortly before the Israelites entered the land.

*Political turmoil*

In southern Syria, Abdi-ashirta and his son Aziru, though protesting their loyalty to their Egyptian overlords, were in reality increasing their own domains with the connivance of the Hittites of northern Syria, and thus preparing the way for the eventual conquest of all Syria by the Hittite Suppiluliuma. Rib-ḫaddi of Byblos, a loyalist who wrote 53 letters to the Egyptian court, describes the uncertainty and chaos which followed his unanswered pleas for military assistance. He reports the capture by Aziru of an adjacent town, where the Egyptian resident had been slain, and the attack on Byblos from which he was forced to flee.

Similarly Lab'ayu of Shechem, despite his protests of innocence (EA 254, see Further reading below), was increasing his hold in the central hills in league with the semi-nomadic 'Apiru, who are frequently named in the texts, mainly as small armed bands. The activities of these 'Apiru are reported by many cities. When Lab'ayu threatened Megiddo, its ruler, Biridiya, begged Egypt for help.

Abdi-ḫeba of Jerusalem makes frequent reports, complaining that Milkilu of Gezer and others are engaged in raids. He cannot, therefore, understand why the pharaoh should allow Gezer, Lachish and Ashkelon to escape from the duty of providing the Egyptian garrison with food when they have plenty. He himself has been robbed by Egyptian troops and warns the pharaoh that his tribute and slaves being sent to Egypt will probably not arrive, as Lab'ayu and Milkilu have planned an ambush (EA 287). The latter might be a ruse to avoid sending any gifts, for in another letter Shuwardata of Hebron warns the pharaoh that Abdi-ḫeba of Jerusalem is a rogue.

*Rulers and officials*

Our knowledge of the political geography of Palestine at this time is helped by references to various local rulers, such as Ammunira of Beirut, Abimilki of Tyre, Akizzi of Qatna and Abdi-tirši of Hazor. Some of these names can be correlated with contemporary texts from *Ugarit (Ras Shamra).

In addition to the local historical evidence, these letters are important for the wider implications of alliances between Egypt and the rulers of Mitanni and Babylon, often concluded, or supported, by marriages between the ruling families.

References to an Egyptian official named Yanḫamu, who attained high office, remind one of the position of Joseph, though the two cannot be identified. Yanḫamu's name is a Semitic form, and one of his functions was the supervision of the grain supply during a time of scarcity for the pharaoh's Syrian subjects.

*Linguistic value*

The tablets are also of great linguistic importance. All but two are written in Akkadian, the *lingua franca* of the whole ancient Near East in this period. The presence at Amarna of Mesopotamian literature (myths of Nergal and Adapa, a story of Sargon of Akkad) and lexical texts including a list of Egyptian and Akkadian words indicates the influence of Akkadian, and this is supported by the discovery in 1946 of a fragment of the Gilgamesh Epic (*c.* 1400 BC) at Megiddo.

The letters from Palestine and Syria are written mainly in local western Semitic dialects of Akkadian, and they provide valuable information about the Canaanite language in its various local forms before the arrival of the Israelites. Letters from King Tushratta of Mitanni have also added considerably to our knowledge of the non-Semitic Hurrian language.

*The 'Apiru and Joshua's Hebrews*
Since some have argued that the 'Apiru of these texts are to be identified with the Hebrews under Joshua, instead of being evidence of the state of the land prior to the Conquest, the following aspects of the Amarna evidence should perhaps be stressed.

The *ḫab/piru* (SA.GAZ) (that is, 'Apiru) here, as indicated also by the Ras Shamra and *Alalakh texts, were occupying the areas not strictly controlled by the larger towns; they operated usually in small numbers throughout Palestine and Syria, and do not appear as besiegers of cities.

Moreover, these texts show a situation different from that under Joshua: Lachish and Gezer, far from being destroyed (Joshua 10), are in active support of the 'Apiru.

The names of the rulers also differ, the king of Jerusalem at this time being Abdi-ḫeba, and whereas the 'Apiru were very active in the Jerusalem area, the city did not become Israelite until the time of David.

Finally, the 'Apiru made use of chariots, but the Israelites knew nothing of this method of warfare until David's reign.

M. J. Selman

*Further reading*

J. A. Knudtzon, *Die El-Amarna-Tafeln*, 2 vols., 1907, 1915 (= EA)
A. F. Rainey, *El Amarna tablets 359–379*, 2nd edition, 1978
W. F. Albright in *ANET*, pp. 483–490
C. J. M. Weir in *DOTT*, pp. 38–45
W. F. Albright, *The Amarna letters from Palestine, CAH*, 2/2, 1975, pp. 98–116
F. F. Bruce in *AOTS*, pp.1–20
K. A. Kitchen, *Suppiluliuma and the Amarna Pharaohs*, 1962
W. F. Moran, *Les Lettres D'El Amarna*, Paris, 1987.

**AMMAN.** See *RABBAH.

**AMMON, AMMONITES.** Ammon (Hebrew *'ammôn*) was the name of the descendants of Ben-ammi, Lot's younger son by his daughter, born in a cave near Zoar (Genesis 19:38). They were regarded as relatives of the Israelites, who were commanded to treat them kindly (Deuteronomy 2:19).

**History**

*Before the Exodus*
At an early date the Ammonites occupied the territory of the Zamzummim between the Arnon and Jabbok rivers (Deuteronomy 2:20–21, 37; 3:11). Later, part of this territory was taken from them by the Amorites, and they were confined to an area to the east of the Jabbok (Numbers 21:24; Deuteronomy 2:37; Joshua 12:2; 13:10, 25; Judges 11:13, 22). Archaeology shows that the Ammonites, like others, surrounded their territories by small fortresses (Numbers 21:24).

At the time of the Exodus, Israel did not conquer Ammon (Deuteronomy 2:19, 37; Judges 11:15). However, the Ammonites were condemned for joining the Moabites in hiring Balaam, and were forbidden to enter the congregation of Israel to the tenth generation (Deuteronomy 23:3–6).

Their chief town was Rabbath Ammon, modern Amman (see also *RABBAH), where the ironstone sarcophagus ('bedstead of iron') of Og, the king of Bashan, rested (Deuteronomy 3:11).

*Judges to Kings*
In the days of the Judges, the Ammonites assisted Eglon of Moab to subdue Israelite territory (Judges 3:13). Again, at the time of Jephthah they encroached on Israelite lands east of Jordan (Judges 11) and were driven out. Their religion influenced some of the Israelites (Judges 10:6), and this caused the Ammonite oppression in Gilead which led to Jephthah's campaign (Judges 10).

Later Nahash, king of the Ammonites, besieged Jabesh-gilead just before Saul became king. Saul rallied Israel and drove off Nahash (1 Samuel 11:1–11; 12:12; 14:47). A few years later Nahash was a friend of David (2 Samuel 10:1–2), but his son Hanun rejected a kindly visit of David's ambassadors and insulted them. He hired Syrian mercenaries and went to war, but David's generals Joab and Abishai defeated them (2 Samuel 10; 1 Chronicles 19).

A year later the Israelites captured Rabbah, the Ammonite capital (2 Samuel 12:26–31; 1 Chronicles 20:1–3) and put the people to work. Some Ammonites befriended David, however, *e.g.* Shobi son of Nahash, who cared for him when he fled from Absalom (2 Samuel 17:27, 29) and Zelek, who was one of his 30 mighty men (2 Samuel 23:37; 1 Chronicles 11:39).

Solomon included Ammonite women in his harem, and worshipped Milcom (Molech) their god (1 Kings 11:1, 5, 7, 33). An Ammonitess, Naamah, was the mother of Rehoboam (1 Kings 14:21, 31; 2 Chronicles 12:13).

In the days of Jehoshaphat, the Ammonites joined Moabites and Edomites in a raid on Judah (2 Chronicles 20:1–30). About 800 BC, Zabad and Jehozabad, both sons of an Ammonitess, conspired to slay Joash king of Judah (2 Chronicles 24:26). Later in the century, both Uzziah and Jotham of Judah received tribute from the Ammonites (2 Chronicles 26:8; 27:5). Josiah defiled the high place that Solomon erected (2 Kings 23:13). Ammonites joined others in troubling Jehoiakim (2 Kings 24:2), and after the fall of Jerusalem in 586 BC, Baalis their king provoked further trouble (2 Kings 25:25; Jeremiah 40:11–14).

They were bitterly attacked by the prophets as inveterate enemies of Israel (Jeremiah 49:1–6; Ezekiel 21:20; 25:1–7; Amos 1:13–15; Zephaniah 2:8–11).

*After the Exile*
After the return from exile Tobiah, the governor of Ammon, hindered the building of the walls by Nehemiah (Nehemiah 2:10, 19; 4:3, 7). Intermarriage between the Jews and the Ammonites was censured by both Ezra and Nehemiah (Ezra 9:1–2; Nehemiah 13:1, 23–31). The Ammonites survived into the 2nd century BC at least, since Judas Maccabeus fought against them (1 Maccabees 5:6).

**Excavations**

A few Middle Bronze tombs from the 17th to 16th century BC, a shrine near Amman and occupation levels in the city of the Late Bronze Age suggest limited sedentary occupation prior to the Iron Age.

There was a vigorous resurgence of urban life at the start of the Iron Age (around 1200 BC or slightly later) which is evidenced by a string of small circular tower fortresses built of large stones. Other structures from the period were square or rectangular.

Several settlements have been investigated, each consisting of a number of flint-block houses together with one or more towers, *e.g.* Khirbet Morbat Bedran. Clearly Ammonite occupation was vigorous during the Iron II period (840–580 BC).

During the 7th century BC Ammon flourished under Assyrian control, as numerous references in Assyrian documents show. Ammon paid considerable tribute to Assyria. Tombs found in the region of Amman give evidence of a high material culture, to judge from the pottery, anthropoid coffins, seals, statues, figures, *etc.*

A growing volume of written material including seals (7th century BC), an inscribed copper bottle from Siran (*c.* 600 BC) and an eight-line fragmentary inscription from the Amman citadel (9th century BC) display a language similar to Hebrew, but a script influenced by Aramaic. The copper bottle contained seeds of emmer wheat, bread wheat and hulled six-row barley, three domesticated grasses in use by the Ammonites of the 6th century BC. At least eleven Ammonite kings can now be listed from various sources.

Archaeological work suggests that sedentary occupation was interrupted by the Babylonian campaigns of the 6th century BC and did not resume until the 3rd century. Bedouin groups occupied the area until the Tobiads (4th-2nd century BC), the Nabataeans (1st century BC) and the Romans (1st century BC-3rd century AD).

An active programme of archaeological research in recent years has uncovered a number of sites. In the general area of the capital Amman numerous graves and a variety of ancient areas of occupation have enlarged our knowledge of the culture of ancient Ammon from the earliest periods of occupation to the Islamic period.

J. A. Thompson

*Further reading*

W. F. Albright, *Miscellanea Biblica B. Ubach*, 1953, pp. 131ff.
P. Bordreuil, *Syria* 50, 1973, pp. 181–195 (seals)
G. Garbini, *Ann. de l'Inst. Or. Napoli* 20, 1970, pp. 249–257
——, *JSS* 19, 1974, pp. 159–168
N. Glueck, *The Other Side of Jordan*, 1940
——, *AASOR* 18, 19, 25–28
P. C. Hammond, *BASOR* 160, 1960, pp. 38–41
S. H. Horn, *BASOR* 193, 1967, pp. 2–13
G. M. Landes, *BA* 24.3, 1961, pp. 66–86
H. O. Thompson, *AJBA* 2.2, 1973, pp. 23–38
—— and F. Zayadine, *BASOR* 212, 1973, pp. 5–11.

**AMORITE.** See *CANAAN.

**AMPHIPOLIS.** An important strategic and commercial centre at the north of the Aegean, situated on the river Strymon (Struma) about 5 kilometres inland from the seaport Eion. Prized by the Athenians and Macedonians as the key both to the gold, silver and timber of Mount Pangaeus and also to the control of the Dardanelles, it became under the Romans a free town and the capital of the first district of Macedonia.

Amphipolis is about 50 kilometres west south west of Philippi on the Via Egnatia, a great Roman highway, and Paul passed through it possibly staying overnight on a three-stage journey of 150 kilometres to Thessalonica (Acts 17:1).

K. L. McKay

**ANATHOTH.** A town in the territory of Benjamin assigned to Levites (Joshua 21:18). The home of Abiathar (1 Kings 2:26) and Jeremiah (Jeremiah 1:1; 11:21), Abiezer (2 Samuel 23:27; 1 Chronicles 11:28; 27:12) and Jehu (1 Chronicles 12:3). It was conquered by Sennacherib (Isaiah 10:30) and repopulated after the Exile (Nehemiah 11:32).

The modern site, Ras el-Ḥarrūbeh, *c.* 5 kilometres north of Jerusalem, lies near the village of 'Anāta (Photo. Grollenberg, *Atlas*, plate 250). However, no Israelite occupation has been traced there and Biran proposes Deir-es-Said as the original location because of the 7th- to 6th-century BC pottery found there (B. Biran, 'On the identification of Anathoth', *Eretz-Israel* 18, 1985, pp. 209–214).

D. J. Wiseman

**ANTIOCH (PISIDIAN).** This Asia Minor city located in Phrygia towards Pisidia, according to Strabo, was one of a number of Antiochs founded in honour of his father by the Macedonian general Seleucus I Nicator (312–280 BC), probably on the site of a Phrygian temple-village. Situated astride a main trading route between Ephesus and Cilicia, it became a prominent centre of Hellenism in the pre-Christian period.

The Seleucids (*i.e.* the rulers of the Seleucid empire, which consisted of Asia Minor, Syria, Palestine and Mesopotamia) brought Jewish colonists into Phrygia for political and commercial reasons, and the more tolerant descendants of these settlers received Paul kindly on his first missionary journey (Acts 13:14). The Romans included Pisidian Antioch in the province of Galatia, and Augustus made it one of a series of Roman colonies in Pisidia.

In Phrygia, women enjoyed considerable prestige and sometimes occupied civic offices. Paul's enemies employed some of these to obtain his expulsion from Antioch (Acts 13:50).

The ruined site is near Yalvaç in modern Turkey, and from that locality have come inscriptions, damaged stelae and other artefacts relating to the cult of the god Mên, which was prominent in Pisidian Antioch in the 1st century AD.

R. K. Harrison

*Further reading*

B. Levick, *JHS* 91, 1971, pp. 80–84.

**ANTIOCH (SYRIAN).** Antioch on the Orontes, now Antakya in south eastern Turkey, some 500 kilometres north of Jerusalem, was founded *c.* 300 BC by Seleucus I Nicator after his victory over Antigonus at Issus (310 BC). It was the most famous of 16 Antiochs established by Seleucus in honour of his father. Built at the foot of Mount Silpius, it overlooked the navigable river Orontes and boasted a fine seaport, Seleucia Pieria. While the populace of Antioch was always mixed, Josephus records that the Seleucids (descendants of Seleucus and rulers of the Seleucid empire) encouraged Jews to emigrate there in large numbers, and gave them full citizenship rights (*Antiquities* 12.119).

Antioch fell to Pompey in 64 BC, and he made it a free city. It became the capital of the Roman province of Syria, and was the third largest city of the empire. The Seleucids and Romans erected magnificent temples and other buildings.

Even under the Seleucids the inhabitants had gained a reputation for energy, insolence and instability which manifested itself in a series of revolts against Roman rule. Nevertheless, Antioch was renowned for its culture, being commended in this respect by no less a person than Cicero (*Pro Archia* 4).

Close by the city were the renowned groves of Daphne, and a sanctuary dedicated to Apollo, where orgiastic rites were celebrated in the name of religion. Despite the bad moral tone, life in Antioch at the beginning of the Christian era was rich and varied.

*The church in Antioch*

Apart from Jerusalem itself, no other

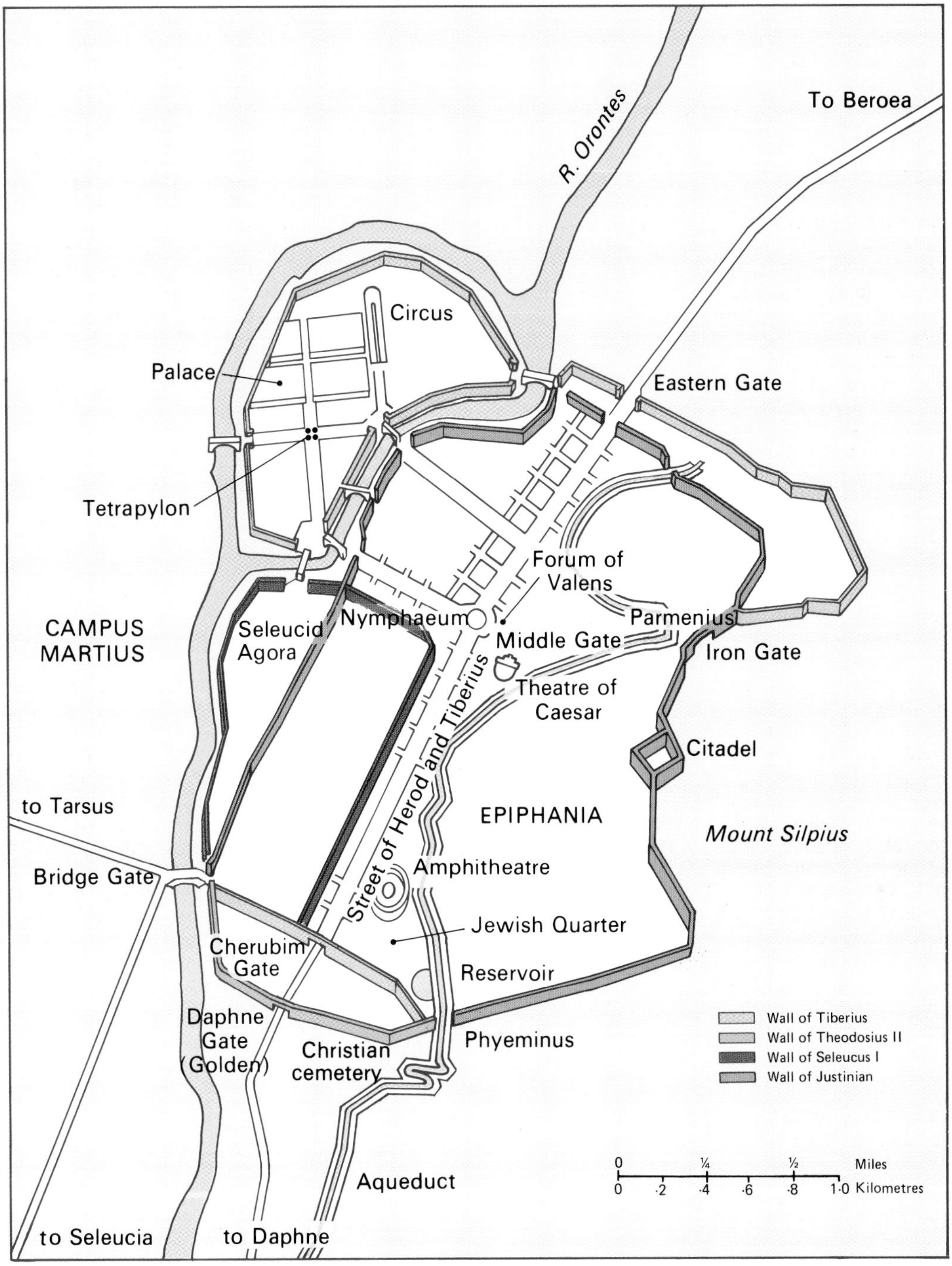


**Plan of the city of Antioch in the first century AD.**

city was so intimately connected with the beginnings of Christianity. Nicolas, one of the seven 'deacons' of Acts 6:5, was of Antioch, and had been a Gentile convert to Judaism. During the persecution which followed the death of Stephen, some of the disciples went as far north as Antioch (Acts 11:19), and preached to the Jews. Later arrivals also took Christianity to the Greek populace, and when numerous conversions occurred the Jerusalem church sent Barnabas to Antioch. When he had assessed the situation he went to Tarsus and brought Saul back with him, and both of them taught in Antioch for a whole year. The disciples were first called 'Christians' there (Acts 11:26).

The energetic nature of the Christians in Antioch was displayed in the way in which alms were sent to the mother church in Jerusalem when famine struck (Acts 11:27–30). It was fitting that the city in which the first Gentile church was founded, and where the Christians were given, perhaps sarcastically, their characteristic name, should be the birthplace of Christian foreign missions (Acts 13:1–3).

Paul and Barnabas set out from the seaport of Antioch and sailed for Cyprus. This first journey into Asia Minor concluded when Paul and Barnabas returned to Antioch and reported to the assembled church.

*The Gentile problem*
Some of the refugees from the persecution over Stephen had taken the lead in preaching at Antioch to Gentiles equally with Jews (Acts 11:20). The Gentile problem came to a head when some Jews visited Antioch and proclaimed the necessity of circumcision for Gentiles as a prerequisite to becoming Christians. Resisting this principle, the church at Antioch sent a deputation headed by Paul and Barnabas to Jerusalem to debate the matter (Acts 15:1–2).

With James presiding, the question of whether or not circumcision was to be obligatory for Gentile Christians was thoroughly discussed. Peter had already encountered the difficulties involved in the relationships between Jews and Gentiles at other than commercial levels (Acts 10:28). Although appearing favourable to such contacts, he had been censured by the Jerusalem church for eating in uncircumcised company (Acts 11:3; compare Galatians 2:12). He now acknowledged that God had not differentiated between Jew and Gentile after Pentecost.

After Paul had related the blessings which the Gentiles had received, James gave his opinion that abstinence from blood, things strangled, idolatry and immorality should alone be required of Gentile converts. These provisions were written into the apostolic letter to the churches of Antioch and its province. Paul returned to Antioch as the recognized apostle to the uncircumcision (Acts 15:22–26).

There is good reason for the view that Galatians was written on the eve of this Jerusalem Council, possibly from Antioch. It appears that the Council settled in principle the contentions for which Paul had to battle in Galatians.

*Missionary journeys*
Paul began and ended his second missionary journey at Antioch. This notable city saw also the start of his third missionary visitation. Its evangelistic zeal afforded Antioch great status in the subsequent history of the church. Archaeological excavations at the site have unearthed over twenty ruined churches dating from the 4th century AD.
R. K. Harrison, C. J. Hemer

*Further reading*
G. Downey, *Ancient Antioch*, 1963.

**ANTIPATRIS.** Formerly Kaphar-Saba, the modern Ras el-Ain, this city has been identified with the Aphek of 1 Samuel 4:1 where the Philistines encamped before their battle with Israel which led to their capture of the Ark of the Covenant (the Covenant Box).

It lies about 42 kilometres south of Caesarea on the road to Lydda, and was rebuilt by Herod the Great in memory of his father Antipater (Josephus, *Antiquities* 16.143; *Jewish War* 1.417).

Paul was taken there on his way from Jerusalem to Caesarea (Acts 23:31). Vespasian occupied it in AD 68 (*Jewish War* 4.443). Codex Sinaiticus reads *Antipatris* instead of *patris* (home-country) in Matthew 13:54, with *anti-* subsequently crossed out. (See also *APHEK.)
D. H. Wheaton

**APHEK, APHEKAH** (Hebrew *'ᵃpēq[â]*, 'fortress'). The name of several places in Palestine.

**1.** Joshua 13:4. Defining the land remaining to be occupied to the north. It was probably Afqa, north east of Beirut at the source of Nahr Ibrahim (*BDB*; Abel, *Géographie de la Palestine*, p. 247; *LOB*, p. 238). A different view places it at *Ras el-'Ain (compare *GTT*, p. 110).

**2.** Joshua 12:18, 1 Samuel 4:1 and 29:1. Later *Antipatris, now Ras el-Ain, Hebrew Tel Afeq, at the source of Nahr el-Auga (Jarkon, Joshua 19:46) on the trunk road to Egypt. It is listed by Tuthmosis III, Amenophis II, Ramesses II and III, and probably by the Execration Texts. Esarhaddon mentions '*Apku* in the territory of Samaria', and it occurs in the Aramaic letter of Adon, *c.* 600 BC (see *ANET*, 242, 246, 292, 329).

Excavations by Tel Aviv University since 1972 have found important Late Bronze Age and Philistine remains. The important Late Bronze Age remains include the palace of a local governor in which were fragments of cuneiform tablets written in a scribal school, one listing words in Babylonian with their Canaanite equivalents, and a letter in Babylonian sent from Ugarit to an Egyptian official. Reports on the excavations are published in the journal *Tel Aviv*. See also P. Beck and M. Kochavi in *NEAEHL* I, pp. 62–72.

**3.** Joshua 19:30 and Judges 1:31 (Aphik). In Asher, modern Tell Kurdaneh, Hebrew Tel Afeq, at the source of Nahr Na'amein which flows into the Bay of Haifa.

**4.** 1 Kings 20:26, 30 and 2 Kings 13:17. Fīq or Afīq at the head of Wadi Fīq, east of the sea of Galilee may preserve the name, the place being 'En-Gev, a tell on the shore (*LOB*, p. 381, note 45).

**5.** Joshua 15:53 (Aphekah). South west of Hebron, it is either Khirbet eḍ-ḍarrame (A. Alt, *Palästina-jahrbuch* 28, pp. 16f.) or Khirbet Kana'an (Abel, *op. cit.*, p. 247).
A. R. Millard

**APOLLONIA.** A town on the Via Egnatia some 43 kilometres west south west of Amphipolis. It lay between the rivers Strymon and Axius (Vardar), but its site is not known for certain. Paul and Silas possibly stayed overnight on their 150-kilometre journey from Philippi to Thessalonica (Acts 17:1).

There were several other towns named Apollonia in the Mediterranean area.
K. L. McKay

**AR.** The chief city of Moab, east of the Dead Sea near the Arnon river.

Something of the early history of the city was known to the Hebrews from records in the Book of the Wars of the Lord (Numbers 21:15), and popular proverbs (Numbers 21:28). Isaiah appears to have had access to similar sources (Isaiah 15:1).

In the later stages of the wilderness wanderings the Hebrews were forbidden to dispossess the Moabite inhabitants of the city and settle there themselves, for this was not the land which the Lord their God had given them (Deuteronomy 2:9, 18, 29; Septuagint 'Seir').

The site is unknown, but el-Misna, 24 kilometres east of the Dead Sea, has been suggested.
R. J. Way

**ARABAH** (Hebrew *'ᵃrāḇâ*). In the AV the word is used only once in its original form (Joshua 18:18), although it is of frequent occurrence in the Hebrew text.

**1.** The root *rb*, meaning 'dry', 'burnt up' and therefore 'waste land', is used to describe the desert steppe (Job 24:5; 39:6; Isaiah 33:9; 35:1, 6; Jeremiah 51:43; RSV usually translates it as 'wilderness' or 'desert').

**2.** Used with the article (*hā-'ᵃrāḇâ*), the name is applied generally to the rift valley which runs from the Sea of Tiberias to the Gulf of Aqabah.

Although the topographical significance of this word was ignored by the earlier commentators, it has a precise connotation in many Old Testament references. Its location is connected with the lake of iberias (Deuteronomy 3:17; Joshua 1:2; 12:3) and as far south as the ed Sea and Elath (Deuteronomy :1; 2:8).

The Dead Sea is called the Sea of rabah (Joshua 3:16; 12:3; euteronomy 4:49; 2 Kings 14:25). oday, the valley of the Jordan ownstream to the Dead Sea is alled the Ghôr, the 'depression', nd the Arabah more properly egins south of the Scorpion cliffs nd terminates in the Gulf of qabah.

For its physical features see JORDAN.

**3.** The plural of the same word, raboth, without the article, is used its primary meaning to describe ertain waste areas within the rabah, especially around Jericho oshua 5:10, RSV 'plains'; 2 Kings 5:5; Jeremiah 39:5, RSV 'plains'), nd the wilderness of Moab.

The Araboth Moab ('plains of Ioab', RSV) is plainly distinguished om the pastoral and cultivated nds of the plateaux above the Rift alley, the Sede-Moab (see Numbers 2:1; 26:3, 63; 31:12; 33:48–50; euteronomy 34:1, 8; Joshua 4:13; :10, *etc.*).

**4.** Beth-arabah (the house of rabah) refers to a settlement tuated near Ain el-Gharba (Joshua 5:6, 61; 18:22).

M. Houston

*urther reading*

. Baly, *Geography of the Bible*, 2nd dition, 1974, pp. 191–209.

## RABIA

### the Old Testament

*eography*

he Arabian peninsula consists of a nge of mountains on the west, sing above 3,000 metres in places, ith a series of strata of younger rmation uptilted against its astern side. In the western ountains, and particularly in the outh western corner of the eninsula, where the annual rainfall xceeds 500 millimetres in parts, ettled life based on irrigation is ossible, and it was in this area, the odern Yemen, that the ancient ngdoms of southern Arabia chiefly ourished.

An area of rainfall of 100–250 illimetres extends north along the estern mountains and east along e coast, and here settled life is also ossible. In the whole of the rest of e peninsula the annual rainfall is egligible and life depends upon ases and wells.

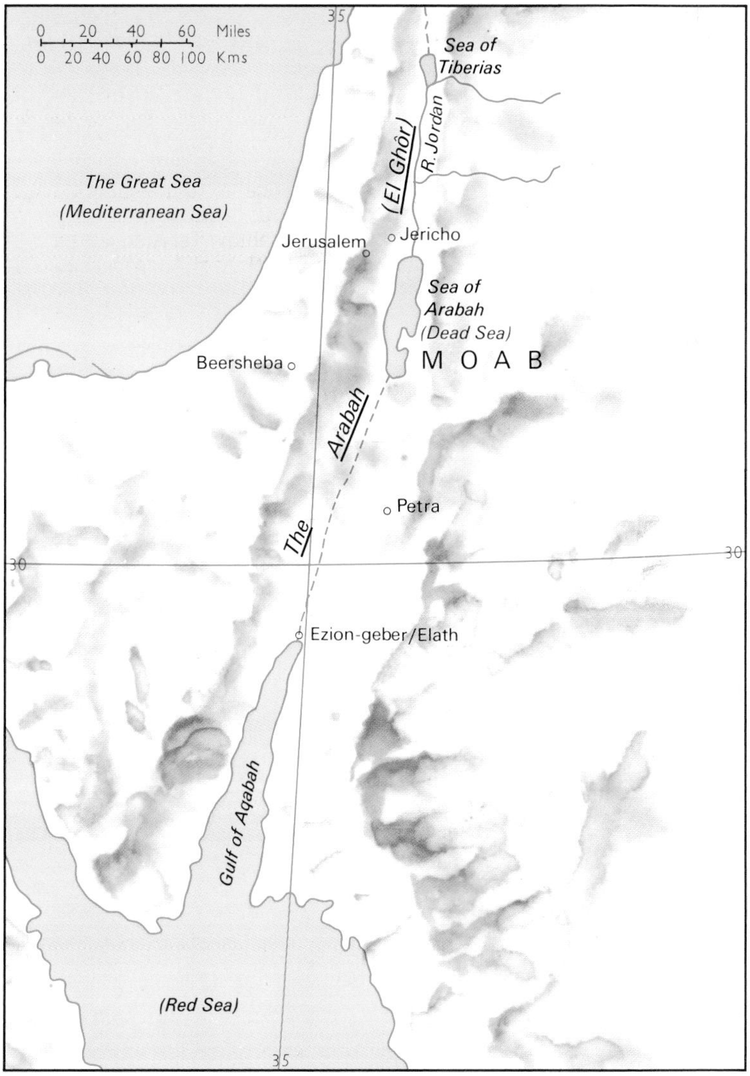


***Above:*** **A dry wadi (river-bed) in the Arabah.**

***Left:*** **The Arabah; the rift valley running from the Sea of Tiberias to the Gulf of Aqabah.**

Between the escarpments formed by the uptilted strata and the eastern coast the scarp slope of the uppermost provides level areas ranging from steppe to sandy desert. The zones of desert widen out in the south into the barren sand desert of al-Rub' al-Ḫāli ('the empty quarter'), and in the north to the smaller desert of al-Nafud.

Along the foot of the escarpments occasional springs provide oases, and consequent trade routes.

Apart from the areas of sandy and rocky desert, the terrain is largely steppe, yielding grass under the sporadic annual rains, and supporting a poor nomadic population. It was where this zone graded into the settled areas of Syria that such metropolises as Petra, Palmyra and Damascus flourished.

*Exploration*

The Danish orientalist, Carsten Niebuhr, visited the Yemen in 1763. In the north, J. L. Burckhardt rediscovered Petra in 1812, but interest was focused on the south when J. R. Wellsted published in 1837 the first southern Arabian inscriptions to be seen in Europe.

Thousands of these inscriptions (known as 'Ḥimyaritic', though stemming from earlier kingdoms) are known, many as a result of explorations in the second half of the last century, but also from more recent expeditions and from numerous individual explorers. A considerable amount of survey work has been undertaken with some archaeological soundings, and there have been a limited number of full scale excavations in the Yemen and Oman.

Many explorations have been made in other parts of Arabia, notable among which are those of the Czech orientalist, A. Musil, in central and northern Arabia (1909–14), N. Glueck in Transjordan and Sinai (1932–71), and G. Ryckmans and H. St J. Philby, who collected some thousands of Arabic inscriptions from Sa'udi Arabia in 1951–52.

Important among inscriptions from the north are the Taima' Stone, which bears an Aramaic inscription of about the 5th century BC, obtained by Huber in 1883 (see also *TEMA), and a second Aramaic inscription of the 4th century BC, found at Taima' in 1982.

*History and civilization*

Apart from the nomads of the steppe lands of Arabia, whose life has continued with little change for millennia, the main areas of historical civilization were in the south western corner of the peninsula, and in the zone to the north where the steppe merges into the settled regions of Syria.

In the 2nd millennium BC various Semitic-speaking tribes arrived from the north in the area of modern Yemen, and formed the settlements which were later to emerge as the kingdoms of Saba' (see also *SHEBA, **2**), Ma'īn (see also *MINAEANS), Qatabān and Ḥaḍramaut (Hazarmaveth, Genesis 10:26). The main cause of their prosperity was their intermediate position on the trade routes from the frankincense lands of the south coast and Ethiopia, to the civilizations in the north.

The first of these kingdoms to emerge was Saba', as revealed by the appearance in about the 8th century of native inscriptions which indicate a well-organized polity under a ruler who evidently combined certain priestly functions in his office. Religion was involved in most aspects of life, and there were annual festivals at the shrines of national deities. Its prosperity is indicated by the fact that it paid tribute to Sargon and Sennacherib, possibly from a northern trading colony.

In *c.* 400 BC the neighbouring kingdom of Ma'īn came into prominence and infringed on much of Sabaean authority. In the 4th century the monarchy was founded in Qatabān, and in the last quarter of the 1st millennium the dominion of Saba', Ma'īn, Qatabān and Ḥaḍramaut fluctuated with turns of fortune, until the area came under the control of the Ḥimyarites.

At their height, the southern Arabian kingdoms had colonies as far afield as northern Arabia, and inscriptions in their characters have been found on the Persian Gulf and in Mesopotamia (Ur, Uruk). The alphabets of the Thamūdic, Liḥyānite and Ṣafāitic inscriptions also show their influence in the north, and the Ethiopic language and script offer similar evidence from Africa.

In the north the history is one of the contacts made by nomads with the settled civilizations of Mespotamia and Syria. In Transjordan the process of infiltration and settlement is evident, though there were periods when this was very sparse. In the early part of the Middle Bronze Age the whole of Transjordan was dotted with settlements, but this was followed by a reduction (though not a total absence, as older books state) of sedentary occupation, *c.* 1900–1200 BC, until settlement was increased again in the Iron Age.

The name 'Arab' first appears in the contemporary inscriptions in the annals of Shalmaneser III, when one Gindibu from 'Arabia' (Kurkh Stele 2.94) fought against him at Qarqar (853 BC), and thereafter they frequently appear in the Assyrian inscriptions as camel-borne raiding nomads, and they are so depicted in the bas-reliefs of Ashurbanipal at Nineveh. One of the unusual episodes in Mesopotamian history was the sojourn of Nabonidus, king of Babylon (556–539 BC) at Taima' (see also *TEMA) in the north. He stayed there for 10 years while his son Bel-šar-uṣur (Belshazzar) ruled for him in Babylon.

In the latter part of the 4th century BC the Aramaic-speaking Arab kingdom of the *Nabataeans, with its capital at Petra, began to emerge and it flourished as a trading state from the 2nd century until well into the Roman period.

Farther south in the same period the Liḥyānite kingdom of *Dedan was formed by Arabs settling at an ancient Minaean colony. In the 1st century BC another Arab state, which adopted Aramaic as its official language, began to come to prominence at Palmyra (see also *TADMOR), and in the Christian era it largely eclipsed Petra as a trading state, and became a serious rival to Rome.

*Biblical references*

Arabia is not often referred to by this name in the Bible, since its inhabitants were generally known by the political or tribal names of the smaller groups to which they belonged. The Table of the Nations in Genesis 10 lists a number of southern Arabian peoples as the descendants of Joktan and of Cush. A number of mainly northern Arabian tribes are listed as being descendants of Abraham through Keturah and Hagar (Genesis 25). Again among the descendants of Esau (Genesis 36) a number of Arabian peoples are mentioned. In the time of Jacob two groups of Abraham's descendants, the Ishmaelites and the Midianites, are found as caravan merchants (Genesis 37:25–36).

It is, however, in the time of Solomon that contacts with Arabia become prominent in the Old Testament narrative, mainly as a result of his extensive trade

Arabs mounted on camels flee from pursuing Assyrians. Part of a relief illustrating the desert campaign of Ashurbanipal, from the king's palace at Nineveh c. 640 BC.

ɿlations, particularly from his port of zion-geber on the Red Sea. This is mphasized by the famous visit of e Queen of *Sheba (1 Kings :26–28; 10), probably a north or entral Arabian group of that name.

The name ʿarāḇ, ʿarāḇî seems to ave originally meant 'desert' or teppe' and by extension 'steppe weller', and therefore in the biblical ontext it referred chiefly to those eople who occupied the emi-desert areas to the east and outh of Palestine. It is not possible, owever, to say whether the word is ways to be taken as a proper name Arab', or as a collective noun teppe dweller'.

In the 9th century, Jehoshaphat of udah received tribute from the rāḇî (2 Chronicles 7:11), but his uccessor Jehoram suffered a raid in hich the ʿarāḇî carried off his wives nd sons (2 Chronicles 21:16–17), nd only Ahaziah, the youngest, was ft (2 Chronicles 22:1). In the 8th entury Uzziah reversed the tuation and restored *Elath to his ominion (2 Kings 14:22).

Though the southern Arabian ingdoms were known (*e.g.* Joel :8), most of the contacts of Israel ith Arabia were with the nomadic ibes of the north. In the time of ezekiah these people were very miliar (Isaiah 13:20; 21:13). In the me of Josiah (Jeremiah 3:2), and in e closing days of the kingdom of udah, the Arabians were coming to ominence as traders (Jeremiah 5:23–24; Ezekiel 27; see also KEDAR).

The growing tendency of the rabs to settle and build trading entres is illustrated by Geshem, the rab who tried to hinder Nehemiah ebuilding Jerusalem (Nehemiah :19; 6:1), presumably because he ared trade rivals. The kingdom of e Nabataeans was to follow, and in e Apocrypha the term 'Arab' sually refers to these people Maccabees 5:39; 2 Maccabees :8).

. C. Mitchell

*urther reading*

. Bright, *A History of Israel*, 2nd dition, 1972

Eph'al, *The Ancient Arabs*, 1982

V. C. Brice, *South-West Asia*, 1966, p. 246–276

J. B. Fisher, *The Middle East. A . . . eography*, 6th edition, 1971, p. 441–478

. Field, *Ancient and Modern Man in outh-western Asia*, 1956, p. 97–124, and folding pocket map

. K. Hitti, *History of the Arabs*, 6th dition, 1956, pp. 1–86

G. W. van Beek in G. E. Wright (ed.), *The Bible and the Ancient Near East*, 1961, pp. 229–248

A. K. Irvine in *POTT*, pp. 287–311

*Proceedings of the Seminar for Arabian Studies* 1– (1970– )

*Atlal* 1– (1977– )

*Raydan* 1– (1978– )

D. T. Potts (ed.), *Araby the Blest: Studies in Arabian Archaeology*, 1988

*Arabian Archaeology and Epigraphy* 1– (1990– ).

## In the New Testament

Arabia did not, as it does today, denote the whole of the great peninsula between the Red Sea and the Persian Gulf, but only the area to the immediate east and south of Palestine. This territory was occupied by an Arab tribe or tribes called the *Nabataeans, who had settled in the area during the 3rd century BC. By the 1st century they had established their control over an area which stretched from Damascus on the north to Gaza to the south and far into the desert to the east. Their capital was the red-rock city of Petra.

Arabia is mentioned only twice in the New Testament. Paul relates how, after his conversion, he went away into Arabia (Galatians 1:17). No other account of this incident occurs in the New Testament. The exact location of this event is very uncertain. Since Arabia to the Graeco-Roman mind meant the Nabataean kingdom, it is likely that he went there, possibly to Petra, the capital city. Why he went is not revealed. Perhaps his purpose was to be alone to commune with God. K. Lake suggests that Paul conducted a preaching mission there, because in the letter to the Galatians, where he mentions this incident, the antithesis is not between conferring with the Christians at Jerusalem and conferring with God in the desert, but between obeying immediately his commission to preach to the Gentiles and going to Jerusalem to obtain the authority to do this (*The Earlier Epistles of St Paul*, 1914, pp. 320f.).

In the only other occurrence of the word Arabia in the New Testament (Galatians 4:25) it is used in the narrower sense to denote the Sinai Peninsula, or the territory immediately to the east, across the Gulf of Aqabah.

W. W. Wessel

*Further reading*

G. A. Smith, *The Historical Geography of the Holy Land*, 1931, pp. 547f., 649

*HDAC*

*IDB*

J. A. Montgomery, *Arabia and the Bible*, 1934.

**ARAD.** A Canaanite town in the wilderness of Judah whose king vainly attacked Israel during the Wandering. Arad was destroyed,

Plan of Arad, showing the Iron Age citadel (late 8th century BC) and the Early Bronze Age II lower city.

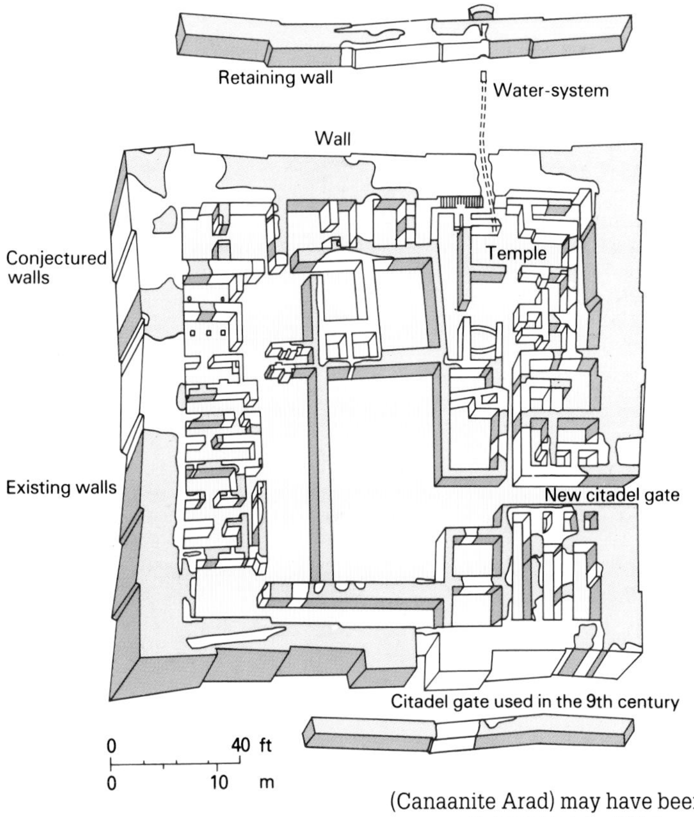


and renamed *Hormah (Numbers 21:1–3; 33:40). Joshua 12:14 lists a king of Arad and a king of Hormah amongst the conquered, while Judges 1:16–17 tells of Kenites settling in the area, and of Judah and Simeon destroying Zephath, renamed Hormah. It is now Tell Arad 30 kilometres north east of Beersheba, excavated from 1962 to 1974 by Y. Aharoni and R. B. K. Amiran.

A large fortified city existed in the Early Bronze Age (Lower City), then the site was deserted until Iron Age I, when a mound at one side was occupied. Here a fortress was built in the 10th century BC that was used until the 6th century.

During several phases of remodelling a shrine with stone altars and pillars existed in one corner. Potsherds inscribed in Hebrew found there include the names of the priestly families Pashhur and Meremoth. More texts were recovered from other parts of the fort, dealing with military affairs and supplies in the troubled years about 600 BC. One mentions 'the house of YHWH'.

Arad of the Late Bronze Age (Canaanite Arad) may have been th present Tell Malḥatah, 12 kilometre to the south west. Two Arads, Arad Rabbat and Arad of Yehuram, were listed by Shishak after his invasion.

A. R. Millard

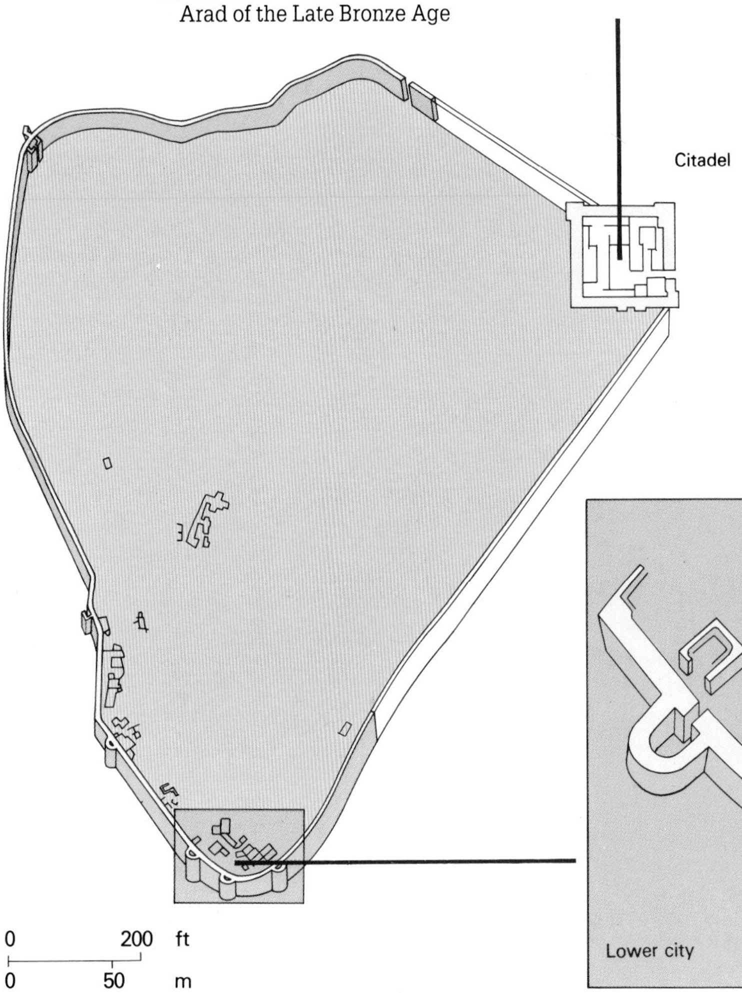


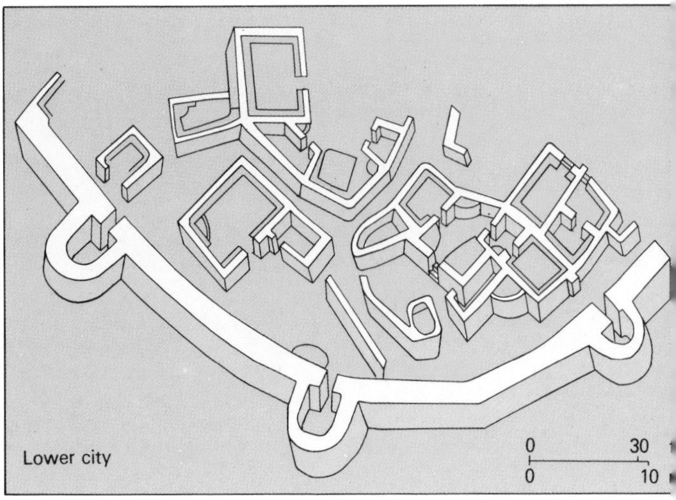


*Further reading*

Y. Aharoni, R. Amiran and others in *NEAEHL* I, pp. 75–87
Y. Aharoni, *Arad Inscriptions*, 1981
Y. Herzog and others, 'The Israelite Fortress at Arad' in *BASOR* 254, 1984, pp. 1–34.

## ARAM, ARAMAEANS

### Origins

Aram and Aramaeans are usually called 'Syria(ns)' in the English Old estament – a misleading ppellation when applied to the eriod before *c.* 1000 BC. From the 3rd illennium BC, western Semitic-peaking semi-nomadic peoples are nown from cuneiform sources to ave been constantly infiltrating into yria and Mesopotamia from almost e whole of the Arabian esert-fringe.

In Mesopotamia under the kings of kkad and of the 3rd Dynasty of Ur . 2400–2000 BC) these 'Westerners' *MAR.TU* in Sumerian, *Amurru* in abylonian) eventually penetrated ght across the Tigris to the eppelands farther east, reaching e Iranian mountains. Evidence iows that they became well stablished there. (For a good scussion of this see J.-R. Kupper, *es Nomades en Mésopotamie au emps des Rois de Mari*, 1957, p. 147f., 166, 177f., 196.)

But these north eastern regions ere no empty land. In the steppes nd hills beyond, the Hurrians were home, and the two populations oubtless mingled. These facts rovide an illuminating background r the origins of the Aramaeans of blical and external sources.

At this period mention is made of a ettlement called Aram(e·i) in the astern Tigris region north of Elam nd east north east of Assyria. If this ct is linked with the presence of estern Semitic-speaking settlers ere, these may justifiably be onsidered as proto-Aramaeans. upper rejects this interpretation, ut has apparently overlooked the nportance of some Old Testament assages here.

This association of the earliest ramaeans' with the east and north ast is evident in Genesis 10:22–23, here Aram, Elam and Assyria occur gether – a mark of very early date. mos 9:7 carries on this tradition in ter times: God brought Israel from gypt (south), the Philistines from aphtor (west) and the Aramaeans om Qir (north east).

Qir occurs only once more (Isaiah 2:6) – standing for Assyria – along ith Elam, so Amos is in line with enesis 10 and with the ascertaina-e north eastern occurrences of oto-Aramaeans.

On the cuneiform evidence (but ot using the biblical passages lduced here), these earliest ramaeans were accepted by A. upont-Sommer (in *VT Supp.* I, 1953, p. 40–49); by S. Moscati (in *The emites in Ancient History*, 1959, p. 66–67, and in earlier works); and y M. McNamara (in *Verbum Domini* 5, 1957, pp. 129–142); but rejected, for example, by I. J. Gelb (*JCS* 15, 1961, p. 28, note 5); D. O. Edzard (in *Die zweite Zwischenzeit Babyloniens*, 1957, p. 43, note 188).

*The name*

Aramu is attested as a personal name in the 3rd Dynasty of Ur (*c.* 2000 BC) and at Mari (18th century BC); at Alalakh in northern Syria about this time occurs the form Arammú – for the doubled 'm' compare the Hebrew *'ᵃrammî*, 'Aramaean'. This corresponds with Aram as an Old Testament personal name about that time.

The name Aram may even be Hurrian; at Alalakh and at Nuzi appear a series of Hurrian-type names compounded with initial Aram- or Arim- (Kupper, *Nomades*, p. 113). 'Aram- may have been the name of a tribal group that first crossed the Tigris into the Hurrian regions, and its name has been applied by the Hurrians to all such western Semitic-speaking infiltrators and settlers (compare the Sumerian and Babylonian use of terms *MAR.TU* and *Amurru*, above) – hence its occurrence in place-names, or it might even have been a Hurrian epithet, which would better explain its occurrence in personal names. As the Hurrians spread right across upper Mesopotamia and into Syria by the beginning of the 2nd millennium, they would then perhaps use this term of the many western Semitic settlers in these regions – known from non-Hurrian cuneiform sources (*e.g.* Mari), Haneans, Suteans and others; but this remains wholly uncertain.

## Early history, 19th–12th centuries BC

*The Patriarchs*

The Hebrew Patriarchs, after leaving Ur, first settled in this upper Mesopotamian area, at Harran (Genesis 11:28–32), in 'Aram-naharaim' (see below). One part of the family stayed on here (Nahor, Bethuel, Laban) as 'Aramaeans' (*i.e.*, named after the place where they lived), while the other (Abraham) went on to Canaan. But the wives of both Isaac and Jacob came from the Aramaean branch of the family (Genesis 24:28ff.), thoroughly justifying the later Israelite confession of descent from 'a wandering Aramaean' (Jacob) in Deuteronomy 26:5.

The speech of Jacob's and Laban's families already showed dialectal differences ('Canaanite' and 'Aramaic'), see Genesis 31:47; note the early form of this Aramaic phrase, using direct (construct) genitive and not circumlocution with *dî*.

*16th–13th centuries*

Aram-naharaim ('Aram of the two rivers') or Paddan-aram was basically the area within the great bend of the river Euphrates past Carchemish bounding it on the west, with the river Habur as limit in the east. In this area arose the Hurrian kingdom of Mitanni (16th-14th centuries BC).

In the Amarna Letters (*c.* 1360 BC) it is called *Naḫrima* with the Canaanite dual in 'm' (like the Hebrew), while in Egyptian texts of *c.* 1520–1170 BC appears the form *Nhrn*, clearly exhibiting an Aramaic-type dual in 'n', not assimilated to the Canaanite as in the Amarna Letters. The form in Egyptian is clear evidence – deriving directly from Egyptian military contact with Aram-naharaim – for Aramaic dialect-forms there from the 16th century BC.

From Ugarit (14th–13th centuries BC) come personal names Armeya and B(e)n-Arm(e)y(a), and a plot of land called 'fields of Aramaeans' (Kupper, *Nomades*, p. 114), which continue the story. An Egyptian mention of Aram occurs under Amenophis III (*c.* 1370 BC), compare E. Edel, in *Die Ortsnamenlisten aus dem Totentempel Amenophis III*, 1966, pp. 28f. Thus the place-name 'the Aram' or 'Pa-Aram' in the Egyptian Papyrus Anastasi III (13th century BC) probably stands for Aram, not Amurru.

It was in the 13th century BC that Balaam was hired from *Pethor (in 'Amaw?) by the Euphrates in Aram (-naharaim) and the 'mountains of the east', in order to curse Israel (Numbers 22:5, RSV; 23:7; Deuteronomy 23:4).

*The Judges' period*

In the chaos that befell the western part of the ancient east just after *c.* 1200 BC when the 'Sea Peoples' destroyed the Hittite empire and disrupted Syria-Palestine (see also *CANAAN; *EGYPT, History), one of Israel's oppressors was the opportunist Cushan-rishathaim, king of Aram-naharaim, whose far-flung but fragile dominion lasted only 8 years (Judges 3:7–11).

Still later in the Judges' period, the gods of Syria proper could already be called 'the gods of Aram' (*c.* 1100 BC?) in Judges 10:6 (Hebrew); this ties up with the accelerating inflow of

Aramaeans and settling in the later 12th and 11th centuries BC in Syria and Mesopotamia, culminating in the founding of Aramaean states.

Just at this time, Tiglath-pileser I of Assyria (1100 BC) was trying unavailingly to stem the advance of 'Akhlamu, Aramaeans' across the length of the middle Euphrates (*ANET*, p. 275). The Akhlamu occur in the 13th, 14th and (as a personal name) 18th centuries BC as Aramaean-type people, thus further witnessing to an Aramaean continuity from earlier to later times.

On this section see also:
Kupper, *Nomades*
R. T. O'Callaghan, *Aram Naharaim*, 1948
A. Malamat, *The Aramaeans in Aram Naharaim and the Rise of Their States*, 1952 (Hebrew)
M. F. Unger, *Israel and the Aramaeans of Damascus*, 1957
*ANET*, p. 259 and note 11.

**Israel and the Aramaean States *c.* 1000–700 BC**

*Saul (*c. *1050–1010 BC)*
During his reign, Saul had to fight many foes for Israel: Moab, Ammon and Edom in the east, the Philistines in the south west and the 'kings of Zobah' in the north (1 Samuel 14:47; or 'king', if the Septuagint be followed). This was probably at the height of his power (*c.* 1025 BC?), before the final disasters of his reign.

*David (*c. *1010–970 BC)*
David's first known Aramaean contact is with Talmai son of Ammihur, king of Geshur, whose daughter he married (Absalom being her son by him) within his first 7 years' reign at Hebron (1010–1003 BC), 2 Samuel 3:3, 5. Talmai still ruled Geshur late in David's reign when Absalom fled there for 3 years (2 Samuel 13:37–39).

In the second half of his reign, David clashed with Hadadezer son of Rehob, king of Aram-zobah (north of Damascus). This king had already extended his rule as far as the Euphrates (subduing the hostile Toi, king of Hamath, 2 Samuel 8:10), but his northern subjects must have revolted, for when David attacked him Hadadezer was then going to 'restore' his conquests there (2 Samuel 8:3).

Perhaps David and Toi found Hadadezer too dangerous; at any rate, David annexed Damascus and Toi of Hamath became his (subject-) ally (2 Samuel 8:5–12). The revolt against Hadadezer probably followed the two heavy defeats that David inflicted on him as ally of Ammon (2 Samuel 10; 1 Chronicles 19) with other Aramaean states (see Unger, pp. 42–46).

No direct time-relation between 2 Samuel 8:3–12 and 2 Samuel 9–12 is stated – but the Ammonite war probably preceded that of 2 Samuel 8. Henceforth, David was doubtless overlord of Hadadezer and all Syria.

The earlier wide but ephemeral power of Hadadezer may be reflected in later Assyrian texts which report how, under Ashur-rabi II (*c.* 1012–972 BC), 'the king of Aram' gained control of Pethor (Pitru) and Mutkinu on either side of the Euphrates; this may mark the foundation there of the Aramaean kingdom of Bit-Adini – perhaps the source of Hadadezer's troops from beyond the Euphrates.

For further discussion, see Landsberger, *Sam'al I*, 1948, p. 35, note 74; and Malamat, *BA* 21, 1958, pp. 101–102.

*Solomon (*c. *970–930 BC)*
Probably it was in the first half of his reign that Solomon overcame 'Hamath-zobah', that is, presumably crushed a revolt in the southern part of the country of Hamath that adjoined Zobah – perhaps a rising against Hamath's subject-ally status? At any rate, Solomon's overlordship was effective enough for him to have store-cities built there (2 Chronicles 8:3–4). But in the last part of David's reign, after the discomfiture of Hadadezer of Zobah, a mere youth, Rezon, went off and gathered a marauding band around himself.

For some time, into Solomon's earlier years, he was probably little more than a petty, roving insurgent. But for the latter half of Solomon's reign he gained control of Damascus and became king there, briefly surviving Solomon, whom he had always opposed (1 Kings 11:23–25); Rezon, it seems, played bandit till *c.* 955 BC, reigning in Damascus perhaps *c.* 955–925 BC, till at last – full of years – he passed away, and a new 'strong man', Hezion, seized the Damascus throne.

*The dynasty of Hezion*
The new opportunist founded a dynasty that lasted a century. Hezion (*c.* 925–915?), his son Tabrimmon (*c.* 915–900?) and grandson Ben-hadad I (*c.* 900–860?) are attested in this order and relationship, from 1 Kings 15:18. (The Melqart Stele, commonly held to show the same line [*DOTT*, pp. 239–241; *ANET*, p. 501], is in fact impossible to read with confidence. These kings speedily made of Damascus the paramount kingdom in Syria proper, rivalled only by Hamath. When attacked by Baasha of Israel, Asa of Judah sought aid from Ben-hadad I (1 Kings 15:18ff.).

The Ben-hadad who clashed with Ahab (1 Kings 20) and was murdered by Hazael in Joram's time, *c.* 843 BC (2 Kings 6:24ff.; 8:7–15) is probably a different king, a Ben-hadad II (*c.* ?860–843), but it is possible to argue with Albright, that this is still Ben-hadad I (then, *c.* 900–843 BC – a long reign but not unparalleled).

This Ben-hadad II/I is almost certainly the Adad-idri ('Hadad-ezer') of Damascus whom Shalmaneser III attacked in 853, 849, 848 and 845 BC, and whose murder and replacement by Hazael are also alluded to by the Assyrian. Double names are common among ancient Near Eastern rulers; Ben-hadad/ Adad-idri is but one more example.

It was Ben-hadad of Damascus and Urhi-leni of Hamath who led the opposition to Assyria and contributed the largest armed contingents, though their efforts were handsomely matched in this respect by Ahab of Israel in 853 BC at Qarqar (*ANET*, pp. 278–281; Wiseman in *DOTT*, p. 47).

*Hazael to Rezin*
The usurper Hazael (*c.* 843–796 BC) almost immediately clashed with Joram of Israel (842/841 BC), see 2 Kings 8:28–29 and 9:15. Jehu gained the Israelite throne at this time, but he and others paid tribute to Assyria (*ANET*, p. 280; *DOTT*, p. 48; *IBA*, p. 57, figure 51), leaving Hazael of Damascus to oppose Assyria alone in 841 and 837 BC (Unger, *op. cit.*, pp. 76–78).

Thereafter, Hazael savagely attacked Israel under Jehu, seizing Transjordan (2 Kings 10:32–33), and throughout the reign of Jehoahaz, *c.* 814/813–798 BC (2 Kings 13:22). But temporary relief did occur; the 'deliverer' sent by God then (2 Kings 13:5) may have been Adad-nirari III of Assyria who intervened against Hazael (called 'Mari') about 805–802 BC.

In the Israelite Joash's early years the pressure was at first maintained by Hazael's son Ben-hadad III (2 Kings 13:3). But as promised by God through Elisha, Joash (*c.* 798–782/781 BC) was able to recover from Ben-hadad the lands previously lost to Hazael (2 Kings 13:14–19, 22–25).

Ben-hadad acceded *c.* 796 BC, and reigned till roughly 770 BC on the evidence of Zakur's stele (see Unger ɒ. *cit.*, pp. 85–89; *DOTT*, p. 242–250). Ben-hadad headed a owerful coalition against Zakur of .amath, a usurper from Lu'ash who ad seized control of the whole ingdom Hamath-Lu'ash. But Zakur nd his allies defeated Ben-hadad's oalition and so spelt the end of the ominance in Syria of the Aramaean ingdom of Damascus.

Shortly after this, discredited amascus came under the verlordship of Jeroboam II of Israel Kings 14:28). Still later, perhaps fter Jeroboam II's death in 753 BC, a ing Rezin (Assyrian *Raḫianu*) ppeared in Damascus and menaced udah as Israel's ally, even (like azael) conquering Transjordan gain; but Ahaz of Judah appealed Tiglath-pileser III of Assyria, who hen in 732 BC defeated and slew ezin (2 Kings 16:5–9; *ANET*, . 283), deporting the unhappy ramaeans to Qir, ironically their ncient homeland, as prophesied by mos (1:4–5).

*ther Aramaean kingdoms*

hese are rarely mentioned in cripture. Sennacherib in 701 BC nocked Hezekiah over the npotence of the kings and gods of Arpad, *Hamath, *Gozan, *Harran, Rezeph (Assyrian *Raṣappa*) and the hildren of Eden in Telassar' (2 ings 18:34; 19:12–13). The ast-named are the people of the ramaean province (former ingdom) of Bit-Adini, the 'House of den' or Beth-eden of Amos 1:5.

*urther reading*

I. F. Unger, R. T. O'Callaghan,
. Malamat (works cited at the end f the section on early history, bove)
. Dupont-Sommer, *Les Araméens*, 949
. R. Millard, *TynB* 41/2, 1990, p. 261–275
pecific studies include:
. de Vaux, *RB* 43, 1934, pp. 512–518
. Jepsen, *AfO* 14, 1941–44, p. 153–172; 16, 1952–53, p. 315–317
. Mazar, *BA* 25, 1962, pp. 98–120 or Aram-Damascus and Israel)
. O. Forrer, in Ebeling and leissner, *Reallexikon der ssyriologie* 1, 1932, pp. 131–139 *Aramu*)
. Landsberger, *Sam'al I*, 1948
/. F. Albright in *AS* 6, 1956, p. 75–85, on Assyrian penetration f Aramaean politics and art
. Malamat, in *POTT*, pp. 134–155
or inscriptions, see:
. C. L. Gibson, *Textbook of Syrian emitic Inscriptions* 2, 1975
W. T. Pitard, *Ancient Damascus*, 1987
H. S. Sader, *Les États Araméens de Syrie*, 1987.

*Language*

It should be recognized that the occurrence of Aramaisms in Old Testament Hebrew often indicates an *early*, not a late, date. Note the 2nd-millennium traces of Aramaic forms (in the section on early history above). Aramaean states in Syria which existed from at least Saul's reign, and marriages in the time of David (Talmai), imply Aramaic linguistic influence in Palestine then.

Finally, some 'Aramaisms' are actually Hebraisms (or Canaanisms) in Aramaic (compare K. A. Kitchen, *Ancient Orient and Old Testament*, 1966, pp. 143–146; A. Hurwitz, *IEJ* 18, 1968, pp. 234–240); for the oldest long Aramaic inscription, bilingual, 9th century BC (kingdom of Guzan), see A. Abon-Assaf, P. Bordreuil, A. R. Millard, *La Statue de Tell Fescherye*, 1982; in English, A. R. Millard, P. Bordreuil, *BA* 45, 1982, pp. 135–141.

*Aramaean culture*

The Aramaeans' one major contribution to ancient Oriental culture was their language: at first, in commerce and diplomacy, then for communication over wide areas (see above), but also as a literary medium (see R. A. Bowman, 'Aramaic, Aramaeans and the Bible', *JNES* 7, 1948, pp. 65–99).

The story and proverbs of Ahiqar are set in the Assyria of Sennacherib and certainly go back in origin to almost that time; from the 5th century BC come the religious texts in demotic (Egyptian) script (Bowman, *JNES* 3, 1944, pp. 219–231) and the Papyri Blacassiani (G. A. Cooke, *A Textbook of North-Semitic Inscriptions*, 1903, pp. 206–210, no. 76).

Still later come magical texts, including one in cuneiform script of the Seleucid era (C. H. Gordon, *AfO* 12, 1937–39, pp. 105–117). Syriac in the Christian epoch was a great province of Christian literature.

The chief gods of the Aramaeans were Baal-shamain and other forms of Baal, Hadad the storm-god, Canaanite deities such as Ashtar, and Mesopotamian ones, including Marduk, Nebo, Shamash, *etc.* (J. A. Fitzmyer, *The Aramaic Inscriptions of Sefîre*, 1967, pp. 33ff.). See Dupont-Sommer, *Les Araméens*, pp. 106–119; Dhorme and Dussaud, *Religions, Babylonie, etc.*, 1949, pp. 389ff.

K. A. Kitchen

## ARARAT

### Biblical evidence

The name Ararat occurs four times in the Bible. It was the mountainous or hilly area (*hārê 'ărāṭ*, 'mountains of Ararat') where Noah's ark came to rest (Genesis 8:4). Traces of wood reported on modern Mount Ararat are possibly remains of shrines erected in the early Christian centuries. There is no evidence that the name 'Ararat' was applied to this mountain before the Christian period. The Hebrew plural 'mountains' shows that the reference is to an area and not a single mountain.

It was the land (*'ereṣ*) to which Adrammelech and Sharezer, the parricides of Sennacherib, fled for asylum (2 Kings 19:37; Isaiah 37:38); and a kingdom (*mamlāḵâ*) grouped by Jeremiah with Minni and Ashkenaz in a prophetic summons to destroy Babylon (Jeremiah 51:27). The AV reads 'Armenia' in both Kings and Isaiah, following *Armenian* in the Septuagint.

### Extra-biblical evidence

There is little doubt that biblical *'ărāṭ* was the *Urarṭu* of the Assyrian inscriptions, a kingdom which flourished in the time of the Assyrian empire in the neighbourhood of Lake Van in Armenia. While it is frequently mentioned by the Assyrian kings as a troublesome northern neighbour, it was much influenced by the Mesopotamian civilization, and in the 9th century the cuneiform script was adopted and modified for writing Urarṭian (also called 'Vannic' or 'Chaldian', not to be confused with 'Chaldean'), a language unrelated to Akkadian. Some 200 Urartian inscriptions are known, and in these the land is referred to as *Biainae* and the people as 'children of Ḫaldi', the national god.

Excavations, notably at Toprak Kale, part of the ancient capital, Ṭušpa, near the shore of Lake Van, at Karmir Blur (ancient Teishebāini), a town site near Erevan (also transliterated Yerevan) in Armenia, and at Altin Tepe, near Erzincan, as well as at Arin-berd, Adilcevaz, Armavir, Haftavan, Bastam and other sites, have revealed examples of art and architecture.

### Urarṭu

In the 13th century, when Urarṭu is first mentioned in the inscriptions of Shalmaneser I, it appears as a small principality between the lakes of Van and Urmia, but it seems to have grown in power in the following centuries when Assyria was suffering a period of decline.

In the 9th century reports of Assyrian campaigns against Urarṭu, whose territory now extended well to the north and west, become more frequent, and about 830 BC a new dynasty was founded by Sardur I, who established his capital at Ṭušpa. His immediate successors held the frontiers, but the kingdom was badly shaken at the end of the 8th century by the Cimmerian invasions, and was only briefly revived in the mid-7th century by Rusa II, who may have been the king who gave asylum to Sennacherib's assassins.

The end of Urarṭu is obscure, but the Indo-European-speaking Armenians must have been established there by the late 6th century BC, as is shown by the Behistun inscription which gives *arminiya* in the Old Persian version where the Babylonian version reads *urašṭu*, and the Aramaic version from Elephantine gives *'rrṭ*. Urarṭu probably disappeared as a state in the early 6th century, at about the time of Jeremiah's prophetic summons.

T. C. Mitchell

*Further reading*

R. D. Barnett, 'Urartu', in *CAH*, III, 1, ch. 8

M. Roaf, *Cultural Atlas of Mesopotamia*, 1990, pp. 172–173 with map

A. Goetze, *Kleinasien*, 2nd edition, 1957, pp. 187–200, 215–216

F. W. König, *Handbuch der chaldischen Inschriften* (*AfO*, Beiheft 8), I, 1955, II, 1957

M. N. van Loon, *Urartian Art*, 1966.

**AREOPAGUS.** See *ATHENS.

**ARGOB.** A district of Transjordan which was ruled over by Og, king of Bashan, before the Israelite conquest under Moses (Deuteronomy 3:3–5). It contained sixty strongly fortified, walled cities and many unwalled towns.

The exact location of the areas has been a matter of dispute. One view which had the support of Jewish tradition and derived additional weight from an unlikely etymology of Argob identified the region with the volcanic tract of land known as el-Leja (see also *TRACHONITIS). This view is no longer favoured.

The name probably indicates a fertile area of arable land (*'argōḇ* probably from *reḡeḇ*, 'a clod'. Compare Job 21:33; 38:38). Its western extent is given as the border of the petty kingdoms of Geshur and Maacah (Deuteronomy 3:14), that is, the Golan Heights.

Some difficulty arises over the reference to the renaming of the cities of Argob, *Havvoth-jair, by Jair the Manassite. In 1 Kings 4:13 the towns of Jair are located in Gilead (see Judges 10:3–4).

J. C. J. Waite

**ARIEL** (Hebrew *'$^{a}$rî'ēl*, 'hearth of El [God]').

**1.** A name for the altar of burnt-offering described by Ezekiel (43:15–16). Several interpretations of this name have been given: 'altar-hearth' (RV); 'mount of God' (compare Ezekiel 43:15–16) or, less likely, 'Lion of God'. In this sense *'r'l* occurs as a personal name on the Moabite Stone (*c.* 830 BC).

**2.** A cryptic name applied to Jerusalem (Isaiah 29:1–2, 7) as the principal stronghold and centre of the worship of God (see **1** above).

D. J. Wiseman

**ARIMATHEA.** 'A city of the Jews', and home of Joseph, in whose sepulchre the body of Jesus was laid (Matthew 27:57; Mark 15:43; Luke 23:51; John 19:38). Identified by Eusebius and Jerome with *Ramah and Ramathaim-zophim, the birthplace of Samuel (1 Samuel 1:19), it is probably identical with the Samaritan toparchy called Rathamein (1 Maccabees 11:34) or Ramathain (Josephus, *Antiquities* 13.127), which Demetrius II added to Jonathan's territory. Possibly it is the modern Rentis, *c.* 15 kilometres north east of Lydda.

J. W. Meiklejohn, F. F. Bruce

*Further reading*

K. W. Clark, 'Arimathaea', in *IDB*.

**ARMAGEDDON** (*WH*, RV, *Har Magedon*; Received Text *Armageddon*; Latin *Hermagedon*; Syriac $^{Gwy.}$ *Magedon*).

The assembly point in the apocalyptic scene of the great Day of God Almighty (Revelation 16:16; unknown elsewhere). If it is symbolic, geographical exactness is unimportant.

The earliest known interpretation, extant only in Arabic, is 'the trodden, *level* place (Arabic *'lmwḏ' 'lwṭv*, possibly meaning the Plain)' (Hippolytus, edited by Bonwetsch).

Of four modern interpretations, namely, 'mountain of Megiddo', 'city of Megiddo', 'mount of assembly' (C. C. Torrey) and 'his fruitful hill', most scholars prefer the first. The fact that the tell of Megiddo was about 21 metres high in John's day, and was in the vicinity of the Carmel range, justifies the use of the Hebrew *har*, used loosely in the Old Testament for 'hill' and 'hill country' (*BDB*, p. 249; compare Joshua 10:40; 11:16).

The 'waters of Megiddo' (Judges 5:19) and the 'valley-plain of Megiddo' (2 Chronicles 35:22) have witnessed important battles, from one fought by Tuthmosis III in 1468 BC to that of Lord Allenby of Megiddo in 1917. The 'mountains of Israel' witness Gog's defeat in Ezekiel 39:1–4. This may be in the writer's mind.

R. J. A. Sheriffs

**ARNON.** A deep wadi (Wadi Môjib) running into the eastern side of the Dead Sea opposite En-gedi. This formed the southern border of Reubenite territory at the time of the settlement (Deuteronomy 3:12, 16), and previously marked the boundary between Moab to the south and Ammon to the north (Judges 11:18–19).

The invading Hebrews crossed the Arnon from south to north, and this proved a turning-point in their career, for they took their first territorial possessions on the northern side (Deuteronomy 2:24). However, the Moabite Stone (line 10) mentions Moabites living in Ataroth, which is to the north of the wadi, suggesting either incomplete conquest on the part of the settlers or later Moabite infiltration.

The importance of the river is confirmed by the number of forts and fords which are found there, the latter being mentioned by Isaiah (Isaiah 16:2).

R. J. Way

**AROER. 1.** In Transjordan, it was on the northern bank of the river Arnon (Wadi Môjib) overlooking its deep gorge (D. Baly, *The Geography of the Bible*, 1957, figure 72 on p. 237), at modern 'Ara'ir (N. Glueck, *Explorations in Eastern Palestine* I [*AASOR* 14, 1934], pp. 3, 49–51 with figure 21a and plate 11), *c.* 22 kilometres east of the Dead Sea (Deuteronomy 2:36; 3:12; 4:48; Joshua 12:2).

It symbolized the southern limit, first, of the Amorite kingdom of Sihon, second, of the tribal territory of Reuben (Joshua 13:9, 16; Judges 11:26 and probably 33) being the seat of a Reubenite family (1 Chronicles 5:8), and third, of the Transjordanian conquests of Hazael of Damascus in Jehu's time (2 Kings 10:33).

About this time, Mesha, king of
/loab, 'built Aroer and made the
oad by the Arnon' (Moabite Stone,
ne 26); Aroer remained Moabite
lown to Jeremiah's time (Jeremiah
8:18–20).
In Numbers 32:34 Gad apparently
elped to repair newly conquered
ities, including Aroer, before the
ormal allotment of Reubenite and
adite territories by Moses.
In 2 Samuel 24:5 probably read
vith RSV that Joab's census for David
tarted from Aroer and the city in the
alley *towards* Gad and on to Jazer.
Isaiah (17:1–3) prophesied
gainst (Moabite-held) Aroer,
longside Damascus and Ephraim.
'he 'city that is in the valley'
Deuteronomy 2:36; Joshua 13:9, 16,
ll RV [but not 12:2, see AV, RSV]; 2
amuel 24:5, RV) may be present
hirbet el-Medeiyineh *c.* 11
ilometres south east of Aroer (*GTT*,
ection 298, pp. 116–117).
For a description, see Glueck, *op.
it.*, p. 36, No. 93.
For excavations, see references, D.
Iomes-Fredericq, J. B. Hennessy,
*rchaeology of Jordan*, I, 1986,
p. 128–129 (under Olavavri), and E.
)lavarri-Goicoechea in *NEAEHL* I,
p. 92–93.
**2.** In Transjordan, 'before Rabbah'
Joshua 13:25, AV, RV, against RSV);
ould be modern es-Ṣweiwinā, *c.* 3.5
ilometres south west of Rabbah
Glueck, *Explorations in Eastern
'alestine* III [*AASOR* 18, 19], 1939,
p. 247, 249. For a description, see
*bid.*, pp. 168–170 and figure 55). But
he existence of this Aroer separate
rom **1** above is doubtful, as Joshua
3:25 might perhaps be rendered
. . . half the land of the Ammonites
nto Aroer, which (land is/extends)
owards/as far as Rabbah' (Glueck,
*p. cit.*, p. 249).
**3.** In Negeb (southland) of Judah,
9 kilometres south east of
eersheba, present Khirbet Ar'areh
N. Glueck, *Rivers in the Desert*,
959, pp. 131–132, 184–185). Among
he Judaeans receiving presents
rom David at Ziklag (1 Samuel
0:26–28) were 'them which were in
roer'; among his mighty men were
wo sons of 'Hotham the Aroerite' (1
hronicles 11:44). For excavations
ee A. Biran in *NEAEHL* I, pp. 89–92.
. A. Kitchen

**RPAD.** Name of a city and
ramaean province in northern
yria, now Tell Rif'at, *c.* 30
ilometres north west of Aleppo,
xcavated in 1956–64. From *c.* 1000
c Arpad (Akkadian *Arpaddu*, Old
ramaic *'rpd*), capital of an
Aramaean tribal territory known as

The mound of Arpad (modern Tell Rif'at).

Bit Agush, opposed Assyria as an ally of Hamath, Damascus, and in 743 BC Urarṭu. (See also *ARARAT.)

Annexed by Tiglath-pileser III after a two-year siege in 740 BC, it rebelled with Hamath, Damascus and Samaria in 720, and was reconquered by Sargon II. This lies behind the boast of Rabshakeh to Jerusalem (2 Kings 18:34; Isaiah 36:19; 37:13, AV 'Arphad'). Its destruction symbolized the overwhelming might of Assyria (Isaiah 10:9; Jeremiah 49:23).

The last ruler of Arpad, Mati'el, signed a vassal treaty under Ashur-nirari V of Assyria in 754 BC, which survives in Assyrian, and another with an unidentified king, 'Bar-Ga'yah of KTK', which was inscribed on stone stelae found at Sefire (see Joshua 8:32).

D. J. Wiseman

*Further reading*
*Excavations:*
V. M. S. Williams, *Iraq* 23, 1961, pp. 68–87
——, *AASOR* 17, 1967, pp. 69–84
*Iraq* 29, 1967, pp.16–33
*Treaty:*
*ANET*, pp. 532f., 659–661
J. A. Fitzmyer, *The Aramaic Inscriptions of Sefire*, 1967.

**ARPHAD.** See *ARPAD.

**ARUMAH.** See *RUMAH.

**ARVAD.** Ezekiel 27:8, 11; 1 Maccabees 15:23 (Aradus) and its inhabitants, the Arvadites, Genesis 10:18; and 1 Chronicles 1:16, it is modern Ruād, a small island 3 kilometres off the coast of Syria (anciently Phoenicia) and about 80 kilometres north of Byblos.

The most northerly of the four great Phoenician cities, Arvad paid tribute to some Assyrian kings, who noted its seafaring skills. A period of independence from *c.* 627 BC was ended by Nebuchadrezzar (*ANET*, p. 308). During these eras it was secondary to Tyre and Sidon. Its commercial fortunes revived under the Persians and Seleucids, but it was displaced by Antaradus (modern Tartûs) in Roman times.

G. G. Garner

**ASHDOD.** Tel Ashdod, 6 kilometres south east of the modern village, was a major Philistinian city, first mentioned in Late Bronze Age texts (Joshua 11:22) dealing with Ugarit. It may have withstood attempts by Judah to conquer it and settle there (Joshua 13:3; 15:46–47). It had a principal port (Ashdod-Yam; in Akkadian sources *Asdudimmu*; compare *ANET*, p. 286) and a temple of Dagon to which the ark was taken (1 Samuel 5:1ff.).

It was attacked by Uzziah of Judah (2 Chronicles 26:6). When it rebelled against Assyria, who replaced King Azuri by his brother, *Asdudu* was sacked, according to Assyrian inscriptions, by Sargon II in 711 BC. These calamities were noted by Amos (1:8) and Isaiah (20:1).

Later besieged by Psamtik I of Egypt for 29 years (Herodotus 2.157), it became a Babylonian province and was weak (Jeremiah 25:20) and derelict (Zephaniah 2:4; Zechariah 9:6). It was partially repopulated after the Exile (Nehemiah 13:23–24).

As Azotus, its idolatry provoked attacks by the Maccabeans (John the Hasmonean and John Hyrcanus, 1 Maccabees 5:68; 10:84). Separated from Judaea by Pompey (Josephus, *Jewish War* 1.156), reconstructed by Gabinius, and given to Salome, Herod's sister, by Augustus, it flourished (Acts 8:40) until it surrendered to Titus.

Excavations (1962–72) confirm

***Opposite:*** **The site of ancient Ashkelon today.**

this history and show Canaanite, Philistinian (temple) and possibly Solomonic occupation (gateway).
D. J. Wiseman

*Further reading*

M. Dothan in *NEAEHL* I, pp. 93–102
F. M. Cross, Jr. and D. N. Freedman, *BASOR* 175, 1964, pp. 48f. (on name).

**ASHDOTH-PISGAH.** See *Pisgah.

**ASHER** (Hebrew *'āšēr*, 'happy, blessed'). **1.** An Israelite tribe (descended from Jacob's eighth son) and its territory. Consisting of five main families or clans (Numbers 26:44–47), Asher shared the organization and fortunes of the tribes in the wilderness journeyings (Numbers 1:13; 2:27; 7:72; 13:13, *etc.*), and shared in Moses' blessing (Deuteronomy 33:24).

Asher's territory as assigned by Joshua was principally the Plain of Acre, the western slopes of the Galilean hills behind it and the coast from the tip of Carmel north to Tyre and Sidon (Joshua 19:24–31, 34). On the south, Asher bordered on Manasseh, *ex*cluding certain border cities (Joshua 17:10–11; translate verse 11, 'Manasseh had *beside* Issachar and *beside* Asher . . . (various towns) . . .'). See Y. Kaufmann, *The Biblical Account of the Conquest of Palestine*, 1953, p. 38. (See also *Helkath and *Ibleam.)

In Asher the Gershonite Levites had four cities (1 Chronicles 6:62, 74–75). However, the Asherites failed to expel the Canaanites, and merely occupied parts of their portion among them (Judges 1:31–32). On topography and resources of Asher's portion, see D. Baly, *The Geography of the Bible*, 1974, pp. 121–127.

In the Judges' period Asher failed to help Deborah but rallied to Gideon's side (Judges 5:17; 6:35; 7:23). Asher provided warriors for David (1 Chronicles 12:36) and formed part of an administrative district of Solomon (1 Kings 4:16).

After the fall of the northern kingdom some Asherites responded to Hezekiah's call to revive the Passover at Jerusalem (2 Chronicles 30:11).

In much later times the aged prophetess Anna, who rejoiced to see the infant Jesus, was of the tribe of Asher (Luke 2:36).

**2.** Possibly a town on the border of Manasseh and Ephraim, location uncertain (Joshua 17:7).
K. A. Kitchen

**ASHKELON.** Modern Asqalōn lies on the southern Palestinian coast between Jaffa and Gaza. The site shows occupation from Neolithic times to the 13th century AD (*IEJ* 5, 1955, p. 271). It is named in Egyptian texts (19th–15th centuries BC) and in the *Amarna letters (14th century BC) when its ruler Widiya helped the Habiru. A pre-Philistinian occupation may be referred to in Deuteronomy 2:23. It was sacked by Merenptah (compare Merenptah stele, *ANET*, p. 378).

It was captured by Judah (Judges 1:18), but regained independence as one of five major Philistine cities (Joshua 13:3); it is associated with *Gaza, *Ashdod and *Ekron (Amos 1:1–7) and sometimes with Gath (2 Samuel 1:20).

Tiglath-pileser III made *Asqaluna* a vassal of Assyria in 733 BC until it was captured by Sennacherib of Assyria, who suppressed the revolt of Sidqa and set Sharruludar on the throne (701 BC).

Ashkelon came under Egyptian domination again, *c.* 630 BC, but was attacked for resisting Nebuchadrezzar in 604 BC (Babylonian Chronicle). Its king, Aga', was killed and prisoners were taken to Babylon in 598 BC (*Mélanges Dussaud* 2, 1939, p. 298). This event, predicted by Jeremiah (47:5–7) and Zephaniah (2:4–7), had a profound effect on Jerusalem, which was to suffer a similar fate a few years later (Jeremiah 52:4–11).

Subordinated to Tyre in Persian times, Ashkelon became a free Hellenistic city in 104 BC. It was captured by Jonathan (1 Maccabees 10:86). Herod the Great embellished the city, which was his birthplace.

Excavations (1921–76) have uncovered successive Canaanite, Philistine, Persian, Hellenistic and predominantly Roman remains.
D. J. Wiseman

*Further reading*

L. Stager in *NEAEHL* I, pp. 103–112.

**ASHTAROTH** (Hebrew *'aštārôṯ*). A city, presumably a centre of the worship of the goddess Ashtaroth, which is probably to be identified with Tell Ashtarah some 30 kilometres east of the Sea of Galilee.

The city, probably *Ashteroth-karnaim of Abraham's day, was the capital of Og, king of Bashan (Deuteronomy 1:4). It was in the territory allotted to Manasseh by Moses (Joshua 13:31), but, though Joshua conquered Og (Joshua 9:10) and took Ashtaroth (Joshua 12:4), it was evidently not held, for it remained among the territories yet to be possessed when Joshua was an old man (Joshua 13:12).

Ashtaroth later became a levitical city (1 Chronicles 6:71; Joshua 21:27, *$b^{e}$ešt$^{a}$râ*, possibly a contraction of *bêṯ 'aštārâ,* which appears in English versions as Beeshterah), and is only subsequently mentioned in the Bible as the home of Uzzia, one of David's mighty men (1 Chronicles 11:44).

The city is perhaps to be identified with the *'s[t']rtm* ('As[ta]rtum?) in the Egyptian Execration Texts of about the 18th century, and with more certainty with the *strt* of the records of Tuthmosis III, the *aš-tar-tu* of the Amarna Letters and the *as-tar-tu* of the Assyrian inscriptions.

A stylized representation of a city with crenellated towers and battlements standing on a mound below the name *as-tar-tu* is given on a bas-relief of Tiglath-pileser III which was discovered at Nimrud (British Museum BM 118908; see *ANEP*, no. 306).

G. Pertinato (*BA* 39, 1976, p. 46 and n. 7) reports that the 3rd-millennium *Ebla texts repeatedly refer to the place Ashtaroth.
T. C. Mitchell

*Further reading*

N. Glueck, *AASOR* 18–19, 1937–39, p. 265
F. M. Abel, *Géographie de la Palestine* 2, 1938, p. 255
W. F. Albright, *BASOR* 83, 1941, p. 33
J. A. Knudzton, *Die el-Amarna Tafeln* 1, 1907, pp. 726, 816; 2, 1915, p. 129
Honigman, *Reallexikon der Assyriologie* 1, 1932, p. 304
W. Helck, *Die Beziehungen ägyptens zu Vorderasien,* 1962, p. 57
R. D. Barnett and N. Falkner, *The Sculptures of Tiglath-Pileser III (745–727 BC),* 1962, pl. LXIX, p. 30.

**ASHTEROTH-KARNAIM.** A city inhabited by the Rephaim, and sacked by Chedorlaomer in the time of Abraham (Genesis 14:5). Some scholars interpret the name as 'Astarte of the Two Horns' and identify this goddess with representations in art of a female with two horns of which Palestinian examples have been found at Gezer and Beth-shan. It is more probable, however, that the name is to be taken as 'Ashteroth near Karnaim' and identified with the city of *Ashtaroth, which lies in the vicinity of Karnaim (mentioned in 1 Maccabees 5:43–44).
T. C. Mitchell

*Further reading*

F. M. Abel, *Géographie*

The Roman province of proconsular Asia (after 133 BC).

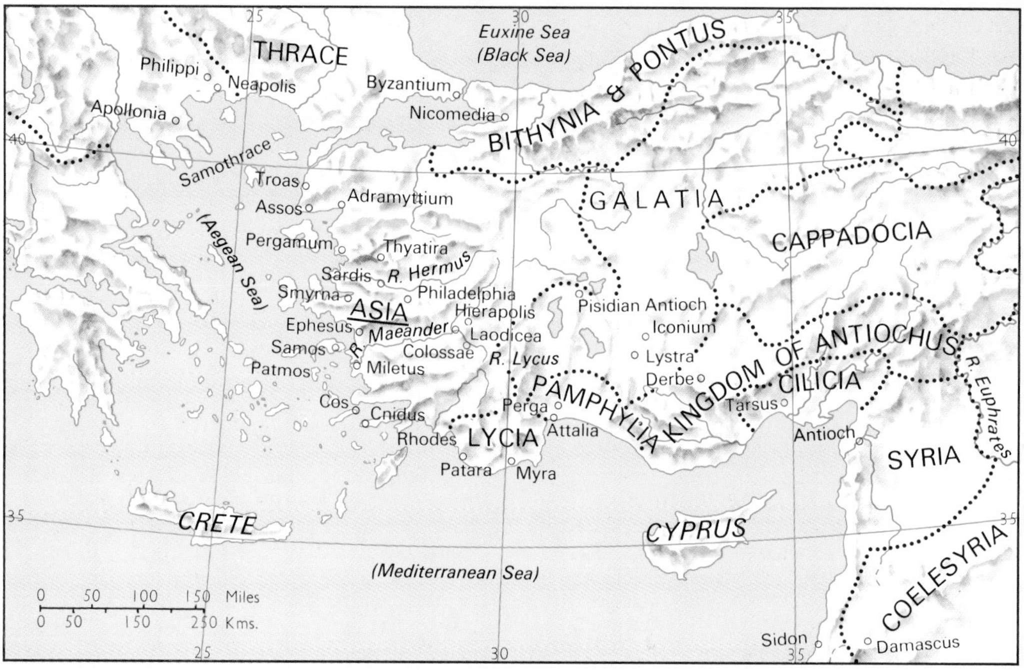


Palestine 2, 1938, p. 255
D. Baly, *The Geography of the Bible*, 1974, pp. 97, 216
H. Tadmor, *IEJ* 12, 1962, p. 121 and n. 30
W. C. Graham and H. G. May, *Material Remains of the Megiddo Cult*, 1935, p. 12.

## ASHURITES

*The name of a people?*

The translation of *Ashuri* (2 Samuel 2:9) by Ashurites, taking it as a gentilic collective, has raised problems. It seems clear that there is no connection with the Ashurites of Genesis 25:3. Some would read Asherites and connect it with Judges 1:32, since the Targum of Jonathan reads Beth-Asher. Some scholars would emend to Geshurites, finding support (see *POTT*, p. 26, note 45) in the Syriac and Vulgate.

The objection to this reading is that Geshur had its own king Talmai (see 2 Samuel 13:37), whose daughter David had married (1 Chronicles 3:2). The Septuagint has *thaseiri*, possibly due to the misreading of the definite article *h* as a *t*.

*The name of a place?*

The use, however, of the preposition *'el* in 2 Samuel 2:9 with the names Gilead, Ashuri and Jezreel rather indicates place-names, as this preposition can have the sense of 'at'. The meaning would then be that these are the names of three administrative centres.

In the choice of such centres consideration would be given to geographical accessibility. In the case of Ashuri, otherwise unknown, this could have been the decisive factor. With the following three names the prepositional *'al* is used, as commonly with 'people' in the phrase 'to reign over', thus: 'and over Ephraim, and over Benjamin, even over all Israel'. The use of the definite article with Ashuri is not unusual with proper names (compare Gilead), and there are other examples of place-names with the ending *i* (*e.g.* Edrei, Ophni).

If the three towns formed a triangle, then Ashuri would be the southern point, with Jezreel on the north and Gilead on the east. Thus geographically an identification with Asher (Joshua 17:7) might be possible.

W. J. Martin

**ASIA.** To Greeks the name either of the continent or more commonly of the region in Asia Minor based on Ephesus. The latter embraced a number of Greek states which in the 3rd century BC fell under the control of the kings of Pergamum.

*Under Roman rule*

In 133 BC the royal possessions were bequeathed to the Romans, and the area was subsequently organized as a province including the whole western coast of Asia Minor together with adjacent islands, and stretching inland as far as the Anatolian plateau. There was a galaxy of wealthy Greek states which suffered at first from Roman exploitation, but recovered in the New Testament period to become the most brilliant centres of Hellenism in the world.

The Roman jurisdiction was exercised through nine or more assizes (*agoraioi*, Acts 19:38) presided over by the senatorial proconsul or his legates (*anthypatoi*, *ibid.*). The imperial cult was well established at the civic level throughout the province.

The Greek republics formed a confederation whose chief expression was the cult of Rome and Augustus, established initially at Pergamum. The 'Asiarchs' (Acts 19:31) were civic and not provincial officials and the term is not synonymous with the *archiereus* of Asia nor the high-priest of the provincial imperial cult. There is extra-biblical evidence for their existence in Paul's day.

*The church in Asia*

Churches were established only in the administrative heart of the province at first. All three metropolitan centres, Pergamum, Smyrna and Ephesus, had churches. Beyond that we know for certain of churches in only two of the nearer assize centres, Sardis in the Hermus valley (Thyatira and Philadelphia being important cities in the same region) and Laodicea (on the Lycus)

t the head of the Maeander valley with the smaller towns of Colossae nd Hierapolis near by).
. A. Judge, B. W. Winter

*urther reading*
liny, *Natural History* 5.28–41
trabo, *Geography* 12–14
. Keil, *CAH*, 11, pp. 580–589
. H. M. Jones, *Cities of the Eastern Roman Provinces*, 2nd edition, 1971, pp. 28–94
. Magie, *Roman Rule in Asia Minor*, vols., 1950
. R. F. Price, *Rituals and Power: The Roman Imperial Cult in Asia Minor*, 1984
. D. Macro, 'The Cities of Asia Minor under the Roman Imperium', *ANRW* II.7.2, 1980, pp. 658–697
. Kearsley, 'Asiarchs', in A. R. Millard and B. W. Winter (eds.), *Documents of New Testament Times*, 1993.

**ASSOS.** A seaport of north west Asia Minor, at the modern Behram Köy on he southern coast of the Troad, lirectly opposite the island of Lesbos. The city was built on a commanding cone of rock over 230 metres high and impressive remains survive of its superb 4th-century-BC fortifications. The shore below is sheltered from the prevalent northerlies, but the harbour was artificial, protected by a mole Strabo, *Geography* 13.1.57).

Acts 20:13–14 records that Paul's companions sailed ahead of him from *Troas to Assos, where he rejoined them after making the swifter 30-kilometre land journey, perhaps wishing to spend as long as possible at Troas without deferring his voyage to Jerusalem.

A harbour village with dwindling trade persisted at Assos into modern times.
C. J. Hemer

**ASSYRIA.** The name of the ancient country whose inhabitants were called Assyrians, it lay in the upper Mesopotamian plain, bounded on the west by the Syrian desert, on the south by the Jebel Hamrin and Babylonia, and on the north and east by the Urarṭian (Armenian) and Persian hills. The most fertile and densely populated part of Assyria lay east of the central river Tigris ('Hiddekel', Genesis 2:14, AV).

The Hebrew *'aššûr* (Assyrian *aššur*) is used both of this land and of its people. The term Assyria was sometimes applied to those territories which were subject to the control of its kings dwelling at Nineveh, Assur and Calah, the principal cities. At the height of its power in the 8th to 7th centuries BC, these territories included Media and southern Anatolia, Cilicia, Syria, Palestine, Arabia, Egypt, Elam and Babylonia.

In the Old Testament Asshur was considered the second son of Shem (Genesis 10:22) and was distinct from Ashuram ('Asshurim'), an Arab tribe descended from Abraham and Keturah (Genesis 25:3), and from the *Ashurites of 2 Samuel 2:9 (where 'Asherites' or 'Geshur' is perhaps to be read; see Judges 1:31–32, see the entry on Ashurites for an alternative view).

Assyria, which is always carefully distinguished from Babylonia, stands for the world power whose invasions of Israel and Judah were divinely permitted, though later it too suffered destruction for its godlessness. There are frequent references to the land (Isaiah 7:18; Hosea 11:5) and to the kings of Assyria (Isaiah 8:4; 2 Kings 15–19).

## History

*Early history down to 900 BC*
Assyria was inhabited from prehistoric times (*e.g.* Jarmo, *c.* 5000 BC) and pottery from the periods known as Hassuna, Samarra, Halaf and 'Ubaid (*c.* 5000–3000 BC) has been found at a number of sites, including Assur, Nineveh and Calah, which, according to Genesis 10:11–12, were founded by immigrants from Babylonia. Although the origins of the Assyrians are still disputed, the Sumerians were present at Assur by 2900 BC and Assyrian language and culture owes much to the southerners. According to the Assyrian king list, the first seventeen kings of Ashur 'lived in tents'.

The kings of Babylonia, including Sargon of Agade (see also *ACCAD), *c.* 2350 BC built in Assyria at Nineveh, and a building inscription of Amar-Su'en of Ur (*c.* 2040 BC) has been found at Assur. After the fall of Ur to Amorite invaders Assur, according to the Assyrian king list, was ruled by independent princes. These established trade connections with Cappadocia (*c.* 1920–1870 BC). Šamši-Adad I (1813–1781 BC) gradually increased his lands, his sons Yasmaḫ-Adad and Zimrilim ruling at *Mari until that city was captured by Hammurapi of Babylon. With the advent of the Mitanni and Hurrian groups in the Upper Euphrates the influence of Assyria declined, though it remained a prosperous agricultural community whose typical life and customs can be seen in the tablets recovered from *Nuzi.

Under Ashur-uballiṭ I (1365–1330 BC) Assyria began to recover something of its former greatness. He entered into correspondence with Amenophis IV of Egypt whereupon Burnaburias II of Babylon objected, declaring him to be his vassal (in the Amarna letters). However, the decline of the Mitanni allowed the trade routes to the north to be reopened and in the reigns of Arik-den-ili (1319–1308 BC) and Adad-nirari I (1307–1275 BC) territories as far west as Carchemish, lost since the days of Šamši-Adad, were recovered.

*Shalmaneser I (1274–1245 BC)* made constant expeditions against the tribes in the eastern hills and against new enemies in Urarṭu. He also sought to contain the Hurrian forces by campaigns in Hanigalbat to the north west. He rebuilt *Calah as a new capital.

His son *Tukulti-Ninurta I (1244–1208 BC)* had to devote much of his attention to Babylonia, of which he was also king for 7 years until murdered by his son Aššurnadinapli.

**The agora (market-place) of Assos from the south.**

Soon afterwards Babylonia became independent again and there was a revival of fortune for a while under *Tiglath-pileser I (1115–1077 BC).*

He vigorously campaigned against the Muški (see also *MESHECH) and Subarian tribes, thrusting also as far as Lake Van in the north and to the Mediterranean, where he received tribute from Byblos, Sidon and Arvad, and making expeditions as far as Tadmor (Palmyra) in his efforts to control the Aramaean (Aḫlame) tribes of the desert. It was the activities of these latter tribes which contained Assyria from *c.* 1100 to 940 BC and left David and Solomon free to strike into Syria (Aram).

*The Neo-Assyrian period (900–612 BC)*

The Assyrians under Tukulti-Ninurta II (890–884 BC) began to take more vigorous military action against the tribes oppressing Assyria.

*Ashurnasirpal II (883–859 BC),* Tukulti-Ninurta's son, in a series of brilliant campaigns subdued the tribes on the Middle Euphrates, and reached the Lebanon and Philistia, where the coastal cities paid him tribute. He also sent expeditions into northern Babylonia and the eastern hills. His reign marked the commencement of a sustained pressure by Assyria against the west which was to bring her into conflict with Israel.

More than 50,000 prisoners were employed on the enlargement of Calah, where Ashurnasirpal built a new citadel, palace and temples, and commenced work on the ziggurat. He employed artists to engrave sculptures in his audience chambers and skilled men to maintain botanical and zoological gardens and a park.

*Shalmaneser III (858–824 BC),* Ashurnasirpal's son, continued his father's policy and greatly extended Assyria's frontiers, making himself the master from Urarṭu to the Persian Gulf and from Media to the Syrian coast and Cilicia (Tarsus). In 857 BC he captured Carchemish and his attack on Bit-Adini (see also *EDEN, HOUSE OF) alerted the major city-states to the south west. Irhuleni of Hamath and Hadadezer of Damascus formed an anti-Assyrian coalition of 10 kings who faced the Assyrian army in the indecisive battle of Qarqar in 853 BC. According to the Assyrian annals, 'Ahab the Israelite (*sir'alaia*)' supplied 2,000 chariots and 10,000 men on this occasion.

After 3 years Shalmaneser undertook a further series of operations directed mainly against Hadadezer (probably Ben-Hadad I). By 841 BC, Shalmaneser's eighteenth year, the coalition had split up, so that the full force of the Assyrian army could be directed against Hazael of Damascus who fought a rearguard action in the Anti-Lebanon mountains and withdrew into Damascus.

When the siege of this city failed, Shalmaneser moved through the Hauran to the Nahr el-Kelb in the Lebanon and there received tribute from the rulers of Tyre, Sidon and 'Jehu (*Ya-ú-a*), son of Omri', an act, in the reign of Jehu, rather than Jehoram, not mentioned in the Old Testament but depicted on Shalmaneser's 'Black Obelisk' at Nimrud (Calah). He had scenes from the other campaigns engraved on the bronze plating of the gates of the temple at Imgur-Bel (Balawat). (These are now in the British Museum.)

*Šamši-Adad V (823–811 BC)* was obliged to initiate reprisal raids in Nairi to counteract the plots of the rebel Ispuini of Urarṭu, and also launched 3 campaigns against Babylonia and the fortress Der on the Elamite frontier.

Šamši-Adad died young, and his influential widow Sammuramat (Semiramis) acted as regent until 805 BC, when their son Adad-nirari III was old enough to assume authority. Meanwhile, the army undertook expeditions in the north and west, and Guzana (see also *GOZAN) was incorporated as an Assyrian province.

Adad-nirari set out to support Hamath in 804 by attacking Damascus, where Hazael, son of Ben-hadad II – whom he called by his Aramaic title *Mari'* – was ruling. This gave Israel a respite from the attacks from Aram (2 Kings 12:17; 2 Chronicles 24:23f.), and many rulers brought the Assyrian gifts in recognition of his aid. He claims that among those bringing tribute were 'Hatti (northern Syria), Amurru (eastern Syria), Tyre, Sidon, Omri-land (Israel), Edom and Philistia as far as the Mediterranean'. A stela from Rimah (Assyria) names 'Joash of Samaria' (*Ya'usu samerinaia*) among these, *c.* 796 BC.

The Assyrian action seems to have enabled Joash to recover towns on his northern border which had previously been lost to Hazael (2 Kings 13:25). Affairs at home appear to have been peaceful, for the Assyrian king built a new palace outside the citadel walls at Calah.

*Shalmaneser IV (782–773 BC),* though harassed by the Urarṭian Argistis I on his northern border, kept up the pressure against Damascus, and this doubtless helped Jeroboam II to extend the boundaries of Israel to the Beqa' ('entrance of Hamath', 2 Kings 14:25–28). But Assyria was now being weakened by internal dissension, for the succession was uncertain, since Shalmaneser had died when young and childless.

A notable defeat in the north was marked by that 'sign of ill omen', an eclipse of the sun, in 763 BC, a date of importance in Assyrian chronology. Once again the west was free to re-group to withstand further attacks, as indicated by the Aramaic treaty of Mati'el of Bit-Agusi (Arpad) with Barga'ayah.

*Tiglath-pileser III (744–727 BC).* The records of Tiglath-pileser III are fragmentary, and the order of events in his reign uncertain. He was, however, a strong ruler who set out to regain, and even extend, the territories which owed allegiance to the national god Ashur. Early in his reign he was proclaimed king of Babylon under his native name Pul(u) (2 Kings 15:19; 1 Chronicles 5:26). In the north he fought Sardur II of Urarṭu, who was intriguing with the Syrian states. By relentless campaigning Tiglath-pileser defeated the rebels in towns along the Anti-Taurus (Kashiari) mountains as far as Kummuḫ, organizing the subdued country in a series of provinces owing allegiance to the king. *Arpad was besieged for 2 years (742–740 BC), and during this time Rezin of Damascus and other neighbouring rulers brought in their tribute.

While Tiglath-pileser was absent in the northern hills in 738 a revolt was stimulated by 'Azriau of Yaudi' in league with Hamath. Yaudi was a small city-state in northern Syria, though there is a possibility that the reference is to Azariah of Judah.

At this time Tiglath-pileser claims to have received tribute from Menahem (*Meni ḫimmu*) of Samaria and Hiram of Tyre. This event is not mentioned in the Old Testament, which records a later payment. Then the amount of 50 shekels of silver extorted from the leading Israelites to meet this demand is shown by contemporary Assyrian contracts to be the price of a slave. It was evidently a ransom to avoid deportation (2 Kings 15:20).

A series of campaigns 2 years later ended with the capture of Damascus n 732 BC. Tiglath-pileser, according o his annals, replaced Pekah, the nurderer of Pekahiah, son of Menahem, by 'Ausi (Hoshea) (see 2 Kings 15:30). This was probably in '34 BC, when the Assyrians marched lown the Phoenician coast and hrough 'the border of Israel' as far as Gaza, whose king, Hanunu, fled across the 'River of *Egypt'.

This action in Palestine was at east in part a response to the appeal of *Iauḫazi* ([Jeho]-Ahaz) of Judah, whose tribute is listed with that of Ammon, Moab, Ashkelon and Edom, or help against Rezin of Damascus and Pekah of Israel (2 Kings 16:5–9). srael (*Bit-Humria*) was attacked, Hazor in Galilee destroyed (2 Kings 15:29), and many prisoners taken nto exile. Ahaz, too, paid dearly for his bid and had to accept religious obligations (2 Kings 16:10ff.), the mported altar being but one symbol of vassalage, another being an mage of the king such as Tiglath-pileser set up in conquered Gaza.

*Shalmaneser V (726–722 BC)*, son of Tiglath-pileser III, also warred in he west. When the Assyrian vassal Hoshea failed to pay his annual ribute after listening to overtures of help promised by Egypt (2 Kings 17:4), Shalmaneser laid siege to Samaria (verse 5). After 3 years, according to the Babylonian Chronicle, 'he broke the resistance of he city of *Šamara'in*' (Samaria?) so the king of Assyria (who) took Samaria' (verse 6) and carried off the sraelites to exile in the Upper Euphrates and Media may be this same Assyrian king. However, since his successor Sargon II later claims he capture of Samaria as his own act, it may be that the unnamed king of verse 6 was Sargon, who could have been associated with Shalmaneser in the siege and have completed the operation on the atter's death.

*Sargon II (721–705 BC)* was a vigorous leader like Tiglath-pileser III. He records that, when the citizens of Samaria were led by Iau-bi'di of Hamath to withhold their taxes, he removed 27,270 (or 27,290) people from the area of Samaria, 'with the gods in which they trusted'.

The exact date of this exile, which broke Israel as an independent nation, cannot be determined as yet from Assyrian records. Hanunu of Gaza had returned from Egypt with military support so Sargon marched to Raphia, where, in the first clash between the armies of the two great nations, he defeated the Egyptians. Despite this, the Palestinian rulers

The tribute of Jehu, depicted on the 'Black Obelisk' of Shalmaneser III at Nimrud.

and peoples still leaned on Egypt for support, and the history of this period is an essential background for the prophecies of Isaiah.

In 715 Sargon intervened once more, sacking Ashdod and Gath and claiming to have 'subjugated Judah'; but there is no evidence in the Old Testament that he entered the land at this time.

Sargon defeated Pisiris of Carchemish in 717 and campaigned in Cilicia. He continued Assyrian raids on the Mannai and tribes in the Lake Van area (714 BC) who were restless under Cimmerian pressure. In the south he invaded Elam, sacked Susa and drove Marduk-apla-iddina II back into the marshland at the head of the Persian Gulf. Sargon died before his new palace at Dur-Šarrukin (Khorsabad) could be completed.

*Sennacherib (704–681 BC)* spent his first years in suppressing revolts which broke out on his father's death. While crown-prince he had been responsible for safeguarding the northern frontier, and this knowledge proved invaluable in his dealings with Urarṭu and Media, and in his military expeditions, which reached as far west as Cilicia, where Tarsus was captured in 698 BC.

Marduk-apla-iddina seized the throne of Babylon (703–701 BC), and it required a concentrated military expedition to dislodge him. It was probably during these years that the Chaldean asked Hezekiah for help (2 Kings 20:12–19). Isaiah's disapproval of this alliance was justified, for by 689 BC the Assyrians had driven Merodach-baladan out of the country and sacked Babylon.

A naval operation which was planned to cross the Gulf in pursuit of the rebel was called off on receipt of the news of his death in Elam. Moreover, in 701 BC Sennacherib had marched to Syria, besieged Sidon and moved south to attack rebellious Ashkelon. It was probably at this time that the Assyrians successfully besieged Lachish (2 Kings 18:13–14), a victory depicted on the bas-reliefs in Sennacherib's palace at Nineveh.

The army next moved to meet the Egyptians at Eltekeh. During these moves in Judah, Hezekiah paid tribute (2 Kings 18:14–16), an act which is recorded in the Assyrian annals. The majority opinion is that it was later in this same campaign and year that Sennacherib 'shut up Hezekiah the Judaean in Jerusalem as a bird in a cage', and demanded his surrender (2 Kings 18:17–19:9). On any interpretation, the Assyrians raised the siege suddenly and withdrew (2 Kings 19:35–36, see Herodotus, 2.141). Another view connects the siege of Jerusalem with a later campaign, perhaps that against the Arabs in 686 BC.

Sennacherib was assassinated by his sons in the month Tebet 681 BC (Isaiah 37:38; 2 Kings 19:37).The Babylonian Chronicle states that Sennacherib was murdered by 'his son', and Esarhaddon, his younger son and successor, claimed to have pursued his rebel brothers, presumably the murderers, into southern Armenia (for a fuller discussion of the seeming discrepancy between the Old Testament and Assyrian texts on the place and number of the assassins, see *DOTT*, pp. 70–73).

Sennacherib, with his western Semitic wife Naqi'a-Zakutu, extensively rebuilt Nineveh, its palaces, gateways and temples, and to ensure water-supplies aqueducts (Jerwan) and dams were built. These were also used to irrigate large parks around the city. Prisoners from his campaigns, including Jews, were used on these projects and are depicted on the palace reliefs.

*Esarhaddon (680–669 BC)* had been designated crown-prince by his father 2 years before he came to the throne, and had served as viceroy in Babylon. When the southern Babylonians rebelled, a single campaign sufficed to subdue them, and Na'id-Marduk was appointed as their new chief in 678. But a series of campaigns was needed to counteract the machinations of their neighbours, the Elamites.

In the hills farther north also periodic raids kept the tribesmen of Zamua and the Median plain subject to Assyrian overlordship. The northern tribes were more restless, due to the plotting of Teušpa and the Cimmerians. Esarhaddon also came into conflict with Scythian tribes (*Išguzai*).

In the west Esarhaddon continued his father's policy of exacting tribute from the city-states, including those in Cilicia and Syria. Baal of Tyre refused payment and was attacked, and Abdi-Milki was besieged in Sidon for 3 years from 676. This opposition to Assyrian domination was incited by Tirhakah of Egypt and provoked a quick reaction. Esarhaddon increased the amount payable, collecting in addition wood, stone and other supplies for his new palace at *Calah and for his reconstruction of Babylon. It may have been in connection with the latter that Manasseh was taken there (2 Chronicles 33:11).

'Manasseh (*Menasi*) of Judah' is named among those from whom Esarhaddon claimed tribute at this time. These included 'Baal of Tyre, Qauš-(Chemosh)-gabri of Edom, Muṣuri of Moab, Ṣili-Bel of Gaza, Metinti of Ashkelon, Ikausu of Ekron, Milki-ašapa of Gebel, . . . Aḫi-Milki of Ashdod as well as 10 kings of Cyprus (*Iadnana*)'.

With these states owing at least a nominal allegiance, the way was open to the fulfilment of Assyria's ambition to control the Egyptian Delta from which so much opposition was mounted. This was accomplished by a major expedition in 672 BC, which resulted in Assyrian governors being installed in Thebes and Memphis. In this same year Esarhaddon summoned his vassals to hear his declaration of Ashurbanipal as crown-prince of Assyria and Šamaš-šum-ukin as crown-prince of Babylonia. In this way he hoped to avoid disturbances similar to those which marked his own succession to the throne.

Copies of the terms and oaths imposed at this ceremony are of interest as indicative of the 'covenant' form of relationship between a suzerain and his vassals. Many parallels can be drawn between this and Old Testament terminology (D. J. Wiseman, *Vassal-Treaties of Esarhaddon*, 1958). It shows that Manasseh, as all the other rulers, would have had to swear eternal allegiance to Ashur, the national god of his overlord (2 Kings 21:2–7, 9).

The end of Esarhaddon's reign saw the beginning of the very revolts these 'covenants' were designed to forestall. Pharaoh Tirhakah incited the native chiefs of Lower Egypt to break away. It was at Harran, while on his way to crush this insurrection, that Esarhaddon died and was succeeded by his sons as planned.

*Ashurbanipal (668–*c. *627 BC)* immediately took up his father's unfinished task and marched against Tirhakah (*Tarqu*); but it required three hard campaigns and the sack of Thebes in 663 (Nahum 3:8, 'No' in AV) to regain control of Egypt.

In Ashurbanipal's reign Assyria reached its greatest territorial extent. Punitive raids on the rebels in Tyre, Arvad and Cilicia brought Assyria into contact with another rising power – Lydia, whose king Gyges sent emissaries to Nineveh seeking an alliance against the Cimmerians. The raids on the Arab tribes and the restoration of Manasseh of Judah, called *Minse* by Ashurbanipal, probably had the one aim of keeping the route open to Egypt.

Nevertheless, Assyria was doomed to fall swiftly. The Medes were increasing their hold over neighbouring tribes and threatening the Assyrian homeland. By 652 BC Šamaš-šum-ukin had revolted and the resultant struggle with Babylonia, which restrained the army from needed operations farther afield, ended in the sack of the southern capital in 648 BC.

This rebellion had been supported by Elam, so Ashurbanipal marched in to sack *Susa in 645 and henceforth made it an Assyrian province. Free from the frequent incursions of the Assyrian army in support of its local officials and tax-collectors, the western city-states gradually loosed from Assyria, and in Judah this new-found freedom was to be reflected in the reforms initiated by Josiah. Once again Egypt was independent and intriguing in Palestine.

The date of Ashurbanipal's death is uncertain (*c.* 631–627 BC), and very few historical texts for this period have yet been found. The hordes of the Scythians (Umman-manda) began to dominate the Middle Euphrates area and Kyaxares the Mede besieged Nineveh. Ashurbanipal may have delegated power to his sons Aššur-eṭel-ilāni (632–628 BC) and Šin-šar-iškun (628–612 BC). Ashurbanipal himself was interested in the arts. He built extensively in *Nineveh, where in his palace and in the Nabu temple he collected libraries of tablets (see the section on literature, below).

*The fall of Assyria.* With the rise of Nabopolassar, the *Chaldeans drove the Assyrians out of Babylonia in 625 BC. The Babylonians joined the Medes to capture Assur (614 BC) and in July/August 612 BC, as foretold by Nahum and Zephaniah, Nineveh fell to their attack. These campaigns are fully told in the Babylonian Chronicle. The walls were breached by floods (Nahum 1:8; Xenophon, *Anabasis* 3.4) and Šin-šar-iškun (Sardanapalus) perished in the flames.

For 2 years the government under Ashur-uballiṭ held out at Harran, but no help came from Egypt, Neco marching too late to prevent the city falling to the Babylonians and Scythians in 609 BC. Assyria ceased to exist and her territory was taken over by the Babylonians.

In later years 'Assyria' formed part of the Persian, Hellenistic (Seleucid) and Parthian empires, and during this time 'Assyria' (Persian *Athura*) continued to be used as a general geographical designation for her former homelands (Ezekiel 16:28; 23:5–23).

### Religion

The Assyrian king acted as regent on earth for the national god Ashur, to whom he reported his activities regularly. Thus Assyrian campaigns were conceived, at least in part, as a holy war against those who failed to avow his sovereignty or breached the borders of his land, and were ruthlessly pursued in the event of rebellion.

Ashur's primary temple was at the capital Assur, and various deities were thought to guard the interests of the other cities. Anu and Adad resided at Assur, having temples and associated ziggurats there, while Ishtar, goddess of war and love, was worshipped at Nineveh,

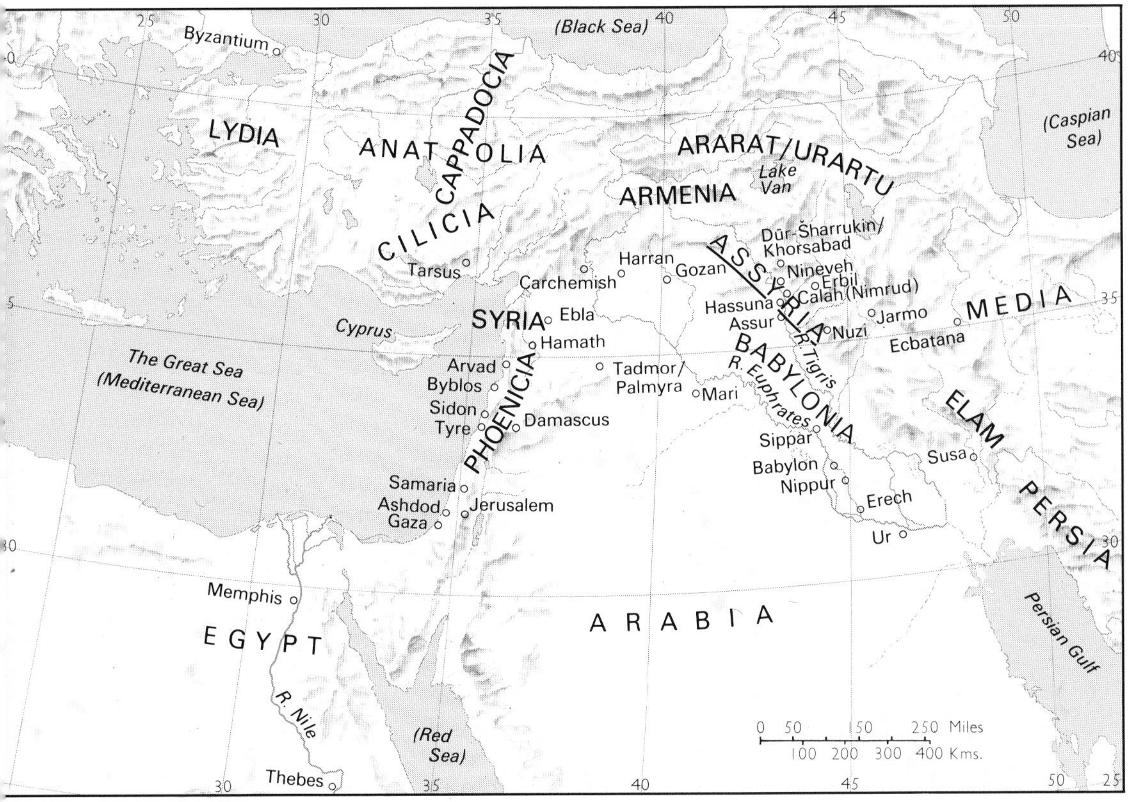


Assyria and surrounding regions.

hough as 'Ishtar of Arbela' she also .eld sway at Erbil. Nabu, god of visdom and patron of the sciences, ad temples at both Nineveh and :alah (Nimrud), where there were braries collected by royal officials nd housed in part in the Nabu (see lso *NEBO) temple.

Sin, the moon-god, and his priests nd priestesses had a temple and loisters at Ehulhul in Harran and were in close association with their ounterpart in Ur. In general, divine onsorts and less prominent deities ad shrines within the major emples; thus at Calah, where the emples of Ninurta, god of war and unting, Ishtar and Nabu have been iscovered, there were places for uch deities as Shala, Gula, Ea and )amkina. In most respects Assyrian eligion differed little from that of Babylonia, whence it had been erived. For the part played by eligion in daily life, see the next ection.

**iterature**

he daily life and thought of the ssyrians is to be seen in the many undreds of letters, economic and dministrative documents, and terary texts found during xcavations. Thus the early 2nd millennium BC is illuminated by the etters from Mari and Shemshara and . 1500, during the period of Hurrian nfluence, from *Nuzi.

The best-known period is, however, that of the Neo-Assyrian empire, when many texts, including some copied from the Middle Assyrian period, enable a detailed reconstruction to be made of the administration and civil service.

Thus the historical annals, recorded on clay prisms, cylinders and tablets, though originally intended as introductions to inscriptions describing the king's building operations, can be supplemented by texts which record the royal requests to a deity (often Shamash) for oracles to guide in decisions concerning political and military affairs. A number of the letters and legal texts, as well as the annals, make reference to Israel, Judah and the western city-states (*DOTT*, pp. 46–75; *Iraq* 17, 1955, pp. 126–154).

*Ashurbanipal's library*

Ashurbanipal, an educated man, created a library by importing or copying texts both from the existing archives at Nineveh, Assur and Calah and from Babylonian religious centres. Thus, in 1852/53 in his palace at Nineveh and in the Nabu temple there, Layard and Rassam discovered 26,000 fragmentary tablets, representing about 10,000 different texts.

This find and its subsequent publication laid the foundation for the study of the Semitic Assyrian language and of Babylonian, from which it differs mainly dialectally. The cuneiform script, employing 600 or more signs as ideographs, syllables or determinatives, was taken over from the earlier Sumerians. Assyro-Babylonian (Akkadian) now provides the major bulk of ancient Semitic inscriptions. Since some texts had interlinear Sumerian translations, this find has been of importance in the study of that non-Semitic tongue which survived, as did Latin in England, for religious purposes.

*The Epic of Gilgamesh*

The discovery among the Nineveh (Kuyunjik) collection, now housed in the British Museum, of a Babylonian account of the flood (Gilgamesh XI), later published by George Smith in December 1872, proved a stimulus to further excavations, and much has been written with special reference to the bearing of these finds on the Old Testament.

The library texts represent scholarly handbooks, vocabularies, sign and word lists, and dictionaries. The mythological texts written in poetic form include the series of twelve tablets now called the 'Epic of Gilgamesh' which describes his quest for eternal life and the story he was told by Uta-napishtim of his own survival of the Flood in a specially

Reconstruction of the façade of the Assyrian temple of the moon-god Sin at Khorsabad (Dūr-Sharrukīn), 8th century BC.

constructed ship.

*Legends and epics*
The Epic of Creation, called *Enuma eliš* after the opening phrase, is principally concerned with the exaltation of Marduk as head of the Babylonian pantheon.

An old Babylonian epic (*Atra-hasīs*) describes the creation of man following a strike against the gods and also the Flood. This provides closer parallels with the Old Testament than either *Enuma eliš* or the Gilgamesh epics.

Other epics include the Descent of Ishtar into the underworld in search of her husband Tammuz. Contrary to many recent theories, no text describing the resurrection of Tammuz has yet been found.

Legends, including that of Sargon of Agade, who was saved at birth by being placed in a reed basket on the river Euphrates until rescued by a gardener, who brought him up to be king, have been compared with Old Testament incidents.

These Akkadian literary texts also contain the legend of Etana, who flew to heaven on an eagle, and that of the plague god Era, who fought against Babylon.

*Wisdom literature*
Wisdom literature includes the poem of the righteous sufferer (*Ludlul bēl nēmeqi*) or the so-called 'Babylonian Job', the Babylonian theodicy, precepts and admonition, among which are counsels of wisdom, sayings and dialogues of a pessimist, and advice to a prince of the same *genre*, but not spirit, as Wisdom literature.

There are also collections of hymns, fables, popular sayings, parables, proverbs and tales ('The poor man of Nippur') which are precursors of later literary forms.

*Religious and scientific literature*
Religious literature is also well represented by tablets grouped in series of up to ninety with their number and title stated in a colophon. The majority are omens derived from the inspection of the liver or entrails of sacrificial animals, or the movements and features of men, animals, birds, objects and planets. Many tablets give instructions for rituals to ensure the king's welfare and that of his country.

Closely allied to these texts are the carefully recorded observations which formed the basis of Akkadian science, especially medicine (prognosis and diagnosis), botany, geology, chemistry, mathematics and law.

For chronological purposes lists covering many of the years from *c.* 1100 to 612 BC gave the name of the eponym or *limmu*-official by whom each year was designated. These, together with the recorded king lists and astronomical data, provide a system of dating which is accurate to within a few years.

**Administration**
The government derived from the person of the king who was also the religious leader and commander-in-chief. He exercised direct authority, although he also delegated local jurisdiction to provincial governors (*e.g.* Rab-shakeh, Rab-saris) and district-governors who collected and forwarded tribute and taxes, usually paid in kind. They were supported by the expeditions of the Assyrian army, the nucleus of which was a highly-trained and well-equipped regular force of chariots, siege-engineers, bowmen, spearmen and slingers.

Conquered territories were made vassal-subjects of the god Ashur on oath and forced to render both political and religious allegiance to Assyria. Offenders were punished by reprisals and invasion, which resulted in the loot and destruction of their cities, death to the rebel leaders, and slavery and exile for the skilled citizens. The remainder were subjected to the surveillance of pro-Assyrian deputies. This helps to explain both the attitude of the Hebrew prophets to Assyria and the fear of 'this cauldron boiling over from the north' (see Jeremiah 1:13) by the small states of Israel and Judah.

**Art**
Many examples of Assyrian art, wall-paintings, painted glazed panels, sculptured bas-reliefs, statues, ornaments, cylinder seals, ivory carvings, as well as bronze and metal work, have been preserved following excavation. Some of the reliefs are of particular interest in that the stele and obelisk of Shalmaneser III from Nimrud mention Israel and may portray Jehu

Sennacherib, on his palace sculptures at Nineveh, depicts the siege of Lachish and the use of Judaean captives to work on his building projects; while the bronze gates at Balawat show the Assyrian army engaged in Syria and Phoenicia.

Other reliefs of Ashurnasirpal II at Nimrud and Ashurbanipal in the 'Lion Hunt' from Nineveh are a pictorial source for the costume, customs, and military and civilian operations of the Assyrians from the 9th to the 7th centuries BC.

**Excavations**
Early explorers searched for biblical *Nineveh (Kuyunjik and Nebi Yunus) opposite Mosul, which was surveyed by C. J. Rich in 1820 and excavated in 1842–43 by Botta, in 1846–47, 1849–51 and 1853–44 by Layard and Rassam, by the British Museum in 1903–05, 1927–32 and subsequently by Iraqi archaeologists.

Other major cities excavated include Assur (Qala'at Shergat) by German expeditions (1903–14); *Calah (Nimrud) by the British – Layard (1842–52), Loftus (1854–55), Mallowan and Oates (1949–63) – and by Iraqis and Poles (1969–76); and Dūr-Sharrukīn (Khorsabad) by the French (1843–45) and Americans

929–35).

Outlying prehistoric sites include ırmo, Hassuna, Thalathat, Umm abaghiyah, Arpachiyah and Tepe ·awra. The principal Middle .ssyrian occupations uncovered in ddition to Assur are Tell Rimah and ılla (Shibaniba). Later Assyrian ıtes of note include Balawat mgur-Bēl).

For sites explored 1842–1939, see . A. Pallis, *The Antiquity of Iraq*, 956; for 1932–56 see M. E. L. Iallowan, *Twenty-Five Years of Iesopotamian Discovery*, 1956; and ubsequently, reports in the journals *'aq*, *Sumer*.

. J. Wiseman

*'urther reading*
*Iistory:*
*'AH* 1, 1971, pp. 729–770
, 1975, pp. 21–48, 274–306, 43–481; 3, 1978
*nscriptions:*
ı. K. Grayson, *Assyrian Royal nscriptions*, 1975–76
V. W. Hallo and W. K. Simpson, *The ıncient Near East; A History*, 1971, h. 5
ı. L. Oppenheim, *Letters from Iesopotamia*, 1967
*Ancient Mesopotamia*, 1964
*Relation to Old Testament:*
*ANET*
*)OTT*
*General:*
*Reallexikon der Assyriologie*, 932–78
I. W. F. Saggs, *The Might that was Assyria*, 1984
*Art:*
R. D. Barnett, *The Assyrian Palace Reliefs*, 1976
*The Sculptures of Ashurbanipal*, 976
M. E. L. Mallowan, *Nimrud and its Remains*, 1966
*Various:*
G. van Driel, *The Cult of Aššur*, 1976
J. N. Postgate, *Taxation and Conscription in the Assyrian Empire*, 974.

**ASWAN.** See *SEVENEH.

**ATAROTH** (Hebrew *'aṭārôṯ*, literally crowns'). **1.** A city on the east of Jordan in Reubenite territory Numbers 32:3, 34), also mentioned on the Moabite Stone; modern Khirbet 'Attarus, 15 kilometres north west of Dibon; see also *ARNON.

A city called Atroth occurs in Numbers 32:35, but this may be an accidental repetition from the previous verse, or else should be taken with the following word, giving the otherwise unknown place-name Atroth-Shophan.

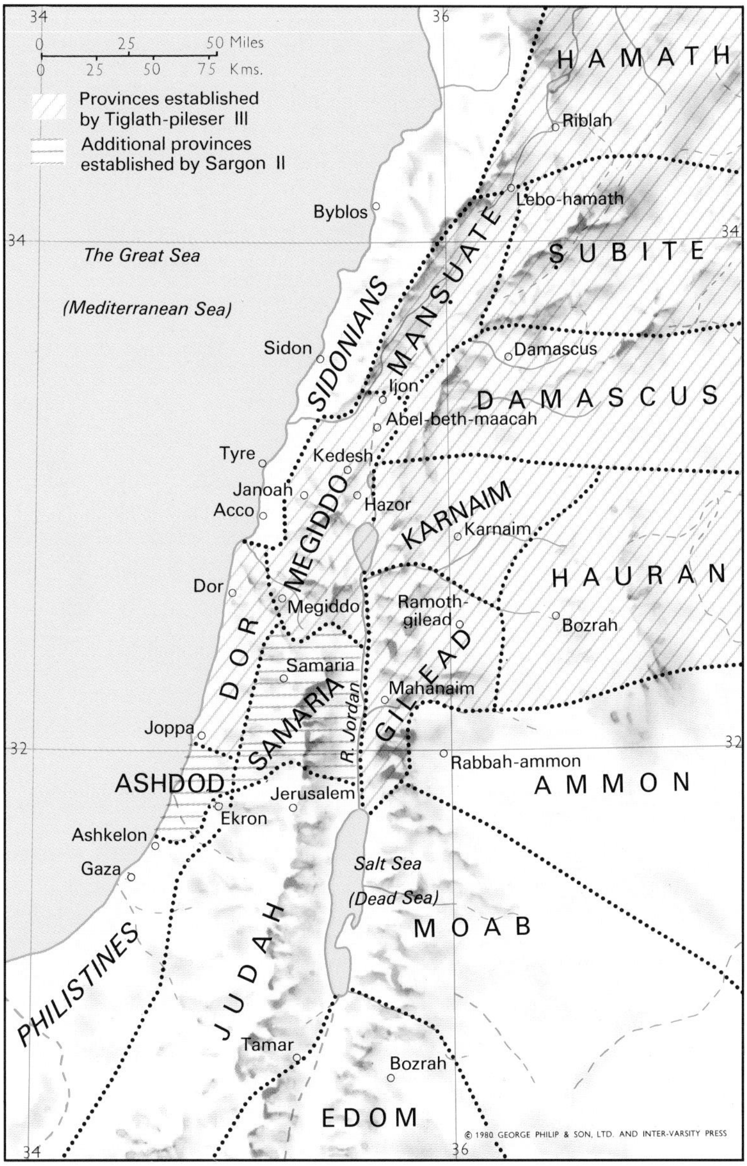


**Provinces established by Tiglath-Pileser II, king of Assyria, 745–727 BC.**

**2.** A city in Ephraim (Joshua 16:2, 7), perhaps the same as Ataroth-Addar (Joshua 16:5; 18:13) which some identify with the site of Khirbet Raddana, 16 kilometres north north west of Jerusalem.

**3.** 'Ataroth, the house of Joab' is mentioned in a Judaean genealogy (1 Chronicles 2:54). This may be understood as 'the crowns (scions, chiefs) of the house of Joab', a description of Bethlehem and Netophathi, whose names immediately precede. See *LOB*.

R. J. Way

**ATHENS.** See p. 48.

**ATTALIA,** modern Antalya, near the mouth of the river Cataractes (modern Aksu), was the chief port of Pamphylia. Founded by Attalus II of Pergamum (159–138 BC), it was bequeathed by Attalus III to Rome.

Paul and Barnabas returned from their missionary journey through Attalia (Acts 14:25).

There was another Attalia in northern Lydia.

K. L. McKay

**AVA.** See *IVAH.

**AVEN. 1.** Abbreviated (Hosea 10:8) for *Beth-aven (Hosea 4:15, *etc.*).

**2.** In Amos 1:5, probably the Beqa' valley between Lebanon and Anti-Lebanon in the Aramaean kingdom of Damascus.

**3.** For Ezekiel 30:17, see *On.

K. A. Kitchen

**AZEKAH.** A Judaean conurbation (Joshua 15:35), lying in the low agricultural plains along the western

**Continued on p. 52**

# ATHENS

**ATHENS.** Athens, the capital of modern Greece, stands in a narrow plain with Mount Parnes to the north, Mount Pentelicus to the east and Mount Hymettus to the south east. Its name is probably derived from that of its patron goddess Athena.

## History

*Council of the Areopagus*
The ancient city-state of Athens rose to prominence as the capital of a unified Attica in the early 7th century BC. By that time Athens had also undergone the transition from monarchy to government by an aristocratic council, known as the Council of the Areopagus after the hill on which it originally met.

This hill, a prominent feature of ancient Athens, was probably so called because of an association with Ares, the Greek god of war (hence the name 'Mars' Hill' in the AV, Acts 17:19, 22, substituting the Roman name of the god).

From the 6th century the reforms of Solon (*c.* 594 BC) and especially Cleisthenes (*c.* 500 BC) moved the government of Athens towards democracy and the Council of the Areopagus lost much of its earlier power and prestige, though it remained a revered institution.

The full flowering of democracy came in the 5th century BC with the rule of Pericles (443–429 BC).

*'The birthplace of western civilization'*
In the 5th and 4th centuries BC Athens was famous for its dramatists (including Aeschylus, Sophocles and Euripides, whose careers spanned the 5th century) and philosophers, including Socrates (470–399 BC), Plato (427–348 BC) and Aristotle (384–322 BC).

The Academy founded in Athens by Plato was the forerunner of the modern university. It continued to exist until AD 529 and helped sustain Athens' reputation as a great cultural and intellectual centre, but the city's most creative period was over by the early 3rd century BC.

*Foreign domination*
Athens successfully led the Greek struggle against Persian domination in the early 5th century BC, but the

**Ancient Athens incoporating the Acropolis.**

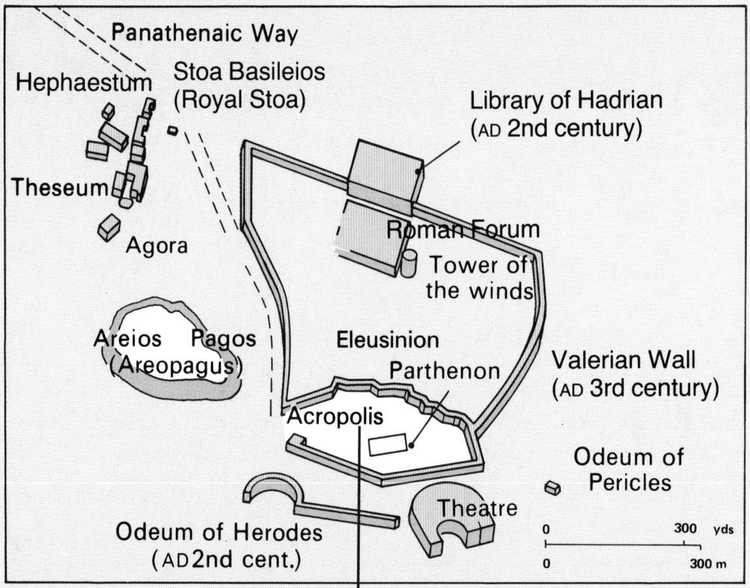


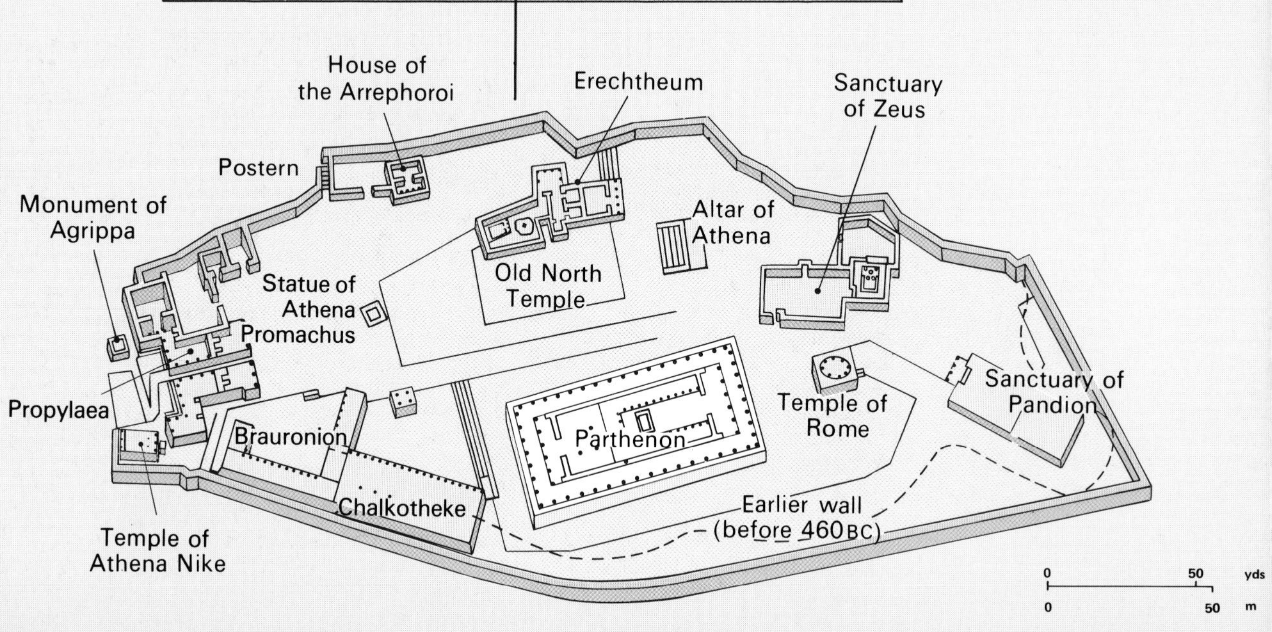

eloponnesian War (431–404 BC)
ıded with its defeat by Sparta. In
38 BC Athens was conquered by
ıilip of Macedon, father of
lexander the Great. However,
ıilip treated the city leniently
ecause of its cultural and
tellectual status.
In later wars with Macedon
00–197 BC and 171–168 BC), Athens
as allied to Rome, and in 168 BC
ome deposed Macedon's last king
ıd reorganized its territories as four
publics. In 88 BC a nationalist
ction in Athens sought independ-
ıce from Rome by overthrowing the
ty's pro-Roman government. In
sponse the Roman general Sulla
ok Athens by storm in 86 BC, but it
covered from this crushing blow
ıd during the period of the Roman
npire it flourished once again as a
ntre of culture and learning.
Athens was well-treated because
its illustrious history and enjoyed
e privileged position of a *civitas
ederata* (a city linked to Rome by
eaty); although it lay in the Roman
ovince of Achaia, it was never
ought into the provincial system, it
ıid no taxes to Rome and had
ternal judicial autonomy.

**ı the New Testament**

*ıul in Athens*
thens was visited by Paul on his
urney from Beroea to Corinth (Acts
7:15–18:1). The account does not
ıy whether Paul reached Athens by
nd or sea, but if he arrived by sea
e would have disembarked at
raeus, the port of Athens on the
egean, some 8 kilometres from the
ty itself.
Assuming that he approached
thens from the west, Paul would
ıve entered through the Dipylon
ate, from which a road led to the
gora. This is often translated
ıarket-place', but in fact the agora
an ancient city was more than
ıis; it was a public square which
ınctioned as the city's social,
olitical and commercial centre. This
ıb of Athens' life provided Paul
ith an ideal place to proclaim the
ospel (Acts 17:17).

*he city*
he Athens of Paul's day was an
nposing city which visibly
splayed its heritage in impressive
culpture and architecture. On the
est side of the agora stood various
vic and religious buildings, and
oove these, on a small hill called the
olonos Agoraios, was the
ephaesteum (a temple to
ephaestus and Athena). Near the

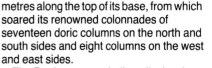

## The Parthenon

The Acropolis, a fortified hill, dominated Athens. It was crowned with temples of exquisite architectural beauty and harmony. The giant statue of the goddess Athena Promachos stood on the Acropolis, and, dwarfing all other buildings in size and magnificence, the Parthenon, the chief temple of the goddess Athena Parthenos. The Parthenon was Greece's largest building and was one of the greatest buildings in the ancient world. It was made entirely of marble. Even the tiles on the roof were marble. It measured 49 metres by 69 metres along the top of its base, from which soared its renowned colonnades of seventeen doric columns on the north and south sides and eight columns on the west and east sides.

The Parthenon was built to display the glory that was Athens. The Athenian statesman Pericles commissioned the architects Ictinus and Caloicrates to build the temple and they worked under the brilliant direction of the sculptor Phidias. The Parthenon was finished in 438 BC, a perfect setting for Phidias's magnificent ivory and gold statue of Athena. In Paul's day visitors came from all over the world to see the Parthenon, not only for the beauty of the building but to admire the intricate craftsmanship and genius of the friezes and sculptures.

**Columns of the Parthenon.**

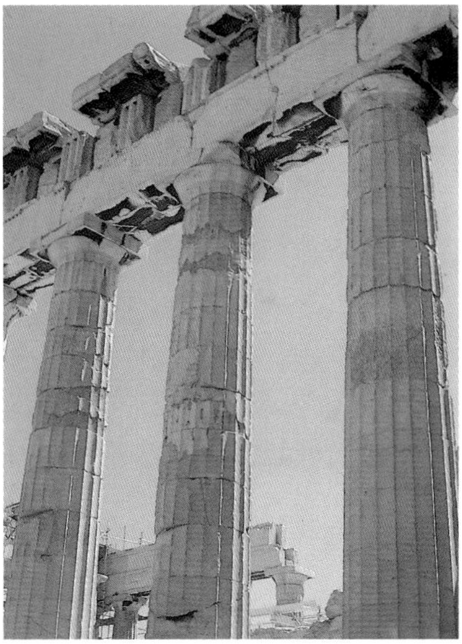

**Caryatids on the Erechtheum.**

**The Parthenon dominates the Acropolis of Athens.**

north-west corner stood the Stoa Basileios or Royal Stoa. (A stoa was a roofed colonnade where public meetings, lectures and discussions took place.) The two-tiered Stoa of Attalus (restored in the 1950s) ran all along the eastern side, and two long, parallel stoas stood on the south.

South of the agora rose the hill of the Areopagus (125 metres high), and to the east of this stood the rocky mass of the Acropolis (156 metres high), still adorned with buildings constructed in the 5th century BC. The enclosed hilltop was entered through an ornamental gateway called the Propylaea, outside and to the south of which stood the temple of Wingless Victory.

The Erectheum (a temple to Erectheus, the reputed first king of Athens, and to Poseidon) stood on the north side, but the hilltop was dominated by the Parthenon, the temple of the goddess Athena.

At the foot of the Acropolis on its south eastern side stood the theatre of Dionysus, partially cut into the steeply-sloping rock. Residential quarters spread out to the south and east of the Acropolis and north of the agora.

Perhaps the most impressive monument of 1st-century Athens was an unfinished temple to Olympian Zeus, which stood near the south eastern edge of the city. Begun in the 6th century BC and left half-built in the 2nd century BC, it was completed by the emperor Hadrian in the 2nd century AD.

No altar with an inscription 'To an unknown god' (Acts 17:23) has been found by excavators of ancient Athens, but the Greek geographer Pausanias (2nd century AD) recorded the existence of 'altars to gods unknown' along the road between the harbour and the city, and Diogenes Laertius wrote of the Athenians erecting such altars to avert a plague.

No trace of the synagogue (Acts 17:17) has been discovered, but a Jewish population is evidenced by Jewish burials in the Kerameikos cemetery on the north western side of the city.

*The Areopagus*

Two views are possible of the references to the Areopagus in Acts 17:19 and 22.

One view takes them as references to the hill of that name, and assumes that Paul was taken to the hill to explain his beliefs at greater length to a more restricted audience. This audience is unlikely to have been the Council of the Areopagus, as this had transferred its meetings to the Royal Stoa during the 4th century BC (though it continued to meet on the Areopagus to try cases of homicide).

The second and more likely view is that 'Areopagus' in these verses is shorthand for the Council of the Areopagus (a usage found in some classical writers), and that Paul was taken to their regular meeting-place in the Royal Stoa in order for the Council to hear and examine his teachings. If this view is correct, then 'Mars' Hill' in the AV (and NEB margin) is a misleading translation.

J. Bimson

*Further reading*

C. J. Hemer, 'Paul at Athens: A Topographical Note', *NTS* 20/3, 1974, pp. 341–350.

**The ancient agora and modern Greek capital viewed from the Acropolis.**

e Theseum, Athens, viewed from the Acropolis.

The reconstructed Stoa, Athens, viewed from the Acropolis.

**Continued from p. 47**
coast, perhaps modern Tell ez-Zahariyeh (also known as Tel Azeqa on the basis of the assumed identity), a large mound at the north eastern end of the Valley of Elah.

Joshua pursued the Amorites as far as Azekah on the day they attacked the newly settled Gibeonite group (Joshua 10:10–11). In the days of Rehoboam it was a fortified border city (2 Chronicles 11:5ff.), and in later times was one of the few strong points to resist the Babylonian incursion under Nebuchadrezzar (Jeremiah 34:7).

Azekah is mentioned, and its capture by Nebuchadrezzar probably implied, in one of the Lachish Letters (*DOTT*, pp. 216f.).

Excavations (1898–99) imply occupation for most of the biblical period (E. Stern, *NEAEHL* I, pp. 123–124).

R. J. Way

# B

**BAAL-GAD.** The northern limit of Israelite conquest, lying at the foot of, and to the west of, Mount Hermon (Joshua 11:17; 13:5; 21:7), replaced simply by Mount Hermon in Judges 3:3.

Identification is uncertain; it may be Hasbeiyah (so F. M. Abel, *Géographie de la Palestine* 2, 1938, p. 258) or Tell Hauš (so *GTT*, 509), and other possibilities are noted by Z. Kallai, *Historical Geography of the Bible*, 1986, p. 226f. There is no clear archaeological evidence.

A. R. Millard

**BAAL-HAZOR.** A mountain 1,016 metres high, 9 kilometres north-north-east of Bethel, modern Jebel el-ʿAṣûr. Absalom gathered his half-brothers to this mountain, perhaps to a settlement of the same name at its foot, at sheep-shearing time and killed Amnon (2 Samuel 13:23). (See also OPHRAH.)

A. R. Millard

**BAAL-MEON.** Known also as Beth-baal-meon (Joshua 13:17), Beth-meon (Jeremiah 48:23) and Beon (Numbers 32:3), this was one of several towns built by the Reubenites in the territory of Sihon the Amorite (Numbers 32:38). It was later captured by the Moabites and was still in their hands in the 6th century BC (Jeremiah 48:23; Ezekiel 25:9). Today the site is known as Maʿîn.

J. A. Thompson

**BAAL-PEOR.** See *PEOR.

**BAAL-ZEPHON** ('Baal [lord] of the north'). The name of a place in the Egyptian eastern Delta near which the Israelites camped during their Exodus (Exodus 14:2, 9; Numbers 33:7), deriving from the name of the Canaanite god Baal-Zephon.

The 'waters of Baal' were in the general area of the Delta residence Pi-Rʿmessē (Qantir) in the 13th century BC; a Phoenician letter of the 6th century BC alludes to 'Baal-Zephon and all the gods of Tahpanhes'. This has led to the suggestion that Tahpanhes, modern Tell Defneh some 43 kilometres south-south-west of Port Said, was earlier the Baal-Zephon of the 'waters of Baal' near Raʿamses and of the Israelite Exodus.

Eissfeldt and Cazelles identify Baal-Zephon and Baal-Hasi (in Ugaritic; later Zeus Casios) and place the Egyptian Zephon/Casios at Ras Qasrun on the Mediterranean shore some 70 kilometres due east of Port Said, backed by Lake Serbonis. However, the deity Baal-Zephon/Casios was worshipped at various places in Lower Egypt, as far south as Memphis, which leaves several possibilities open.

C. de Wit

*Further reading*

R. A. Caminos, *Late-Egyptian Miscellanies*, 1954
N. Aimé-Giron, *Annales du Service des Antiquités de l'Égypte* 40, 1940/41, pp. 433–460
W. F. Albright in *BASOR* 109, 1948, pp. 15–16, and in *Festschrift Alfred Bertholet*, 1950, pp. 1–14
*RB* 62, 1955, pp. 332ff.

**BABEL** (Hebrew *Bāḇel*, 'gate of god'; see also *BABYLON). The name of one of the chief cities founded by Nimrod in the land of Shinar (Sumer), ancient Babylonia. It is named with Erech and Accad (Genesis 10:10) and according to Babylonian tradition was founded by the god Marduk and destroyed by Sargon *c.* 2350 BC when he carried earth from it to found his new capital Agade (see also *ACCAD).

*The city*

The history of the building of the city and its lofty tower is given in Genesis 11:1–11, where the name Babel is explained by popular etymology based on a similar Hebrew root *bālal*, as 'confusion' or 'mixing'. Babel thus became a synonym for the confusion caused by language differences which was part of the divine punishment for the human pride displayed in the building.

There is as yet no archaeological evidence to confirm the existence of a city at Babylon prior to the 1st Dynasty (*c.* 1800 BC) but Babylonian tradition and a text of Sharkalisharri king of Agade *c.* 2250 BC, mentioning his restoration of the temple-tower (*ziggurat*) at Babylon, implies the existence of an earlier sacred city c

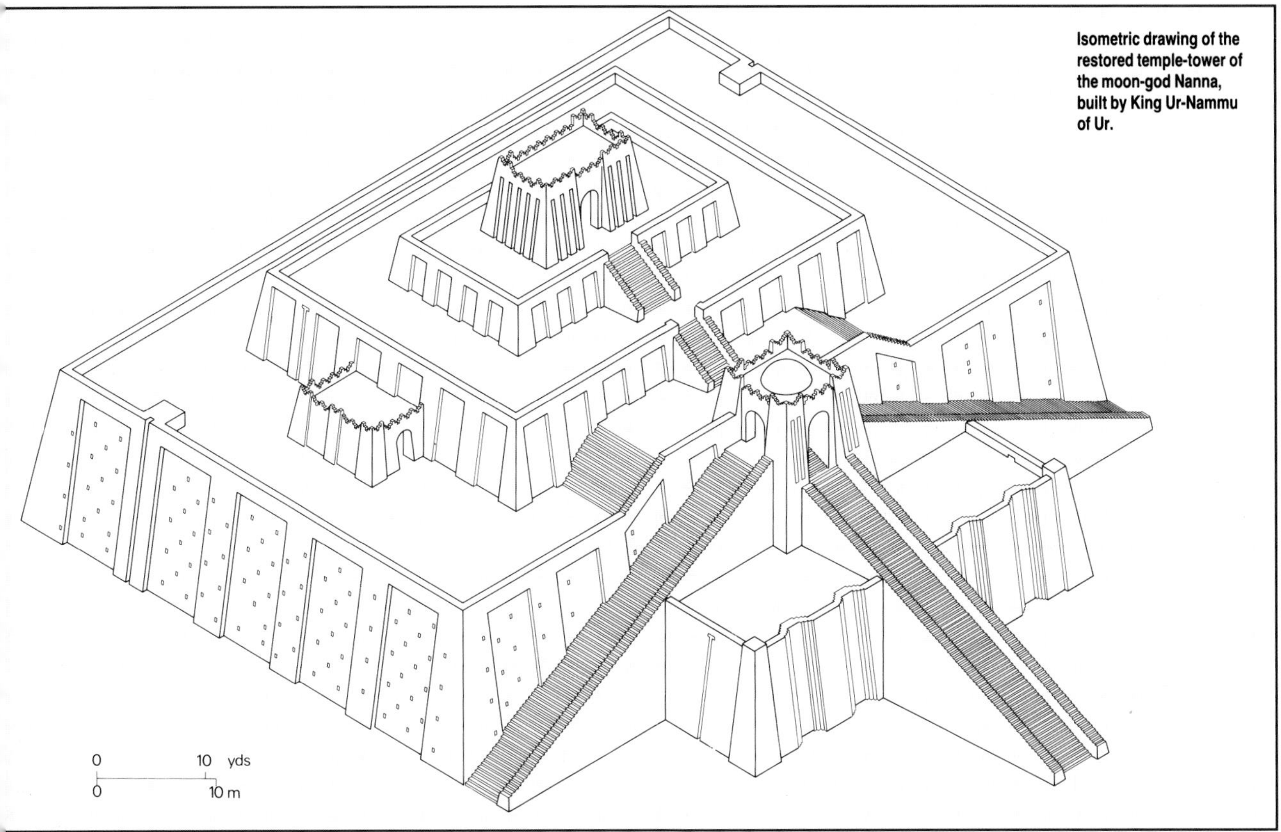


Isometric drawing of the restored temple-tower of the moon-god Nanna, built by King Ur-Nammu of Ur.

Remains of the ziggurat (temple-tower) of Nanna at Ur.

the site. Sargon's action would confirm this.

The use of burnt clay for bricks and of bitumen (AV 'slime') for mortar (Genesis 11:3) is attested from early times. The latter was probably floated down the Euphrates from Hit.

*The tower*

The 'Tower of Babel', an expression not found in the Old Testament, is commonly used to describe the tower (*miḡdōl*) intended to be a very high landmark associated with the city and its worshippers. It is generally assumed that, like the city, the tower was incomplete (verse 8), and that it was a staged temple tower or multi-storeyed *ziggurat* first developed in Babylonia in the early 3rd millennium BC from the low temenos or platform supporting a shrine set up near the main city temples (as at Erech and 'Uqair).

After Sharkalisharri the earliest reference to the *ziggurat* at Babylon is to its restoration by Esarhaddon in 681–665 BC. This was named in Sumerian 'Etemenanki' – 'the Building of the Foundation-platform of Heaven and Earth' – whose 'top reaches to heaven' and associated with the temple of Marduk Esagila, 'the Building whose top is (in) heaven'. It is very probable that such a sacred edifice followed an earlier plan. The tower was severely damaged in the war of 652–648 BC but restored again by Nebuchadrezzar II (605–562 BC). It was this building, part of which was recovered by Koldewey in 1899, which was described by Herodotus on his visit *c.* 460 BC and is discussed in a cuneiform tablet dated 229 BC (Louvre, AO 6555). These enable an approximate picture of the later tower to be given.

The base stage measured 90 by 90 metres and was 33 metres high. Above this were built five platforms, each 6–18 metres high but of diminishing area. The whole was crowned by a temple where the god was thought to descend for intercourse with mankind. Access was by ramps or stairways. A late Babylonian plan of a seven-staged *ziggurat* shows that the architectural form was a height equal to the width at the base with a cubic temple on the summit. Among others, *ziggurats* were found in *Ur, *Erech, *Nineveh and elsewhere in *Assyria and *Babylonia.

The *ziggurat* at Babylon was demolished by Xerxes in 472 BC, and though Alexander cleared the rubble prior to its restoration this was thwarted by his death. The bricks were subsequently removed by the local inhabitants, and today the site of Etemenanki is a pit (*Es-Saḥn*) as deep as the original construction was high.

Travellers of all ages have sought to locate the ruined tower of Babel. Some identify it with the site described above and others with the vitrified remains of a *ziggurat* still visible at Borsippa (modern Birs Nimrūd) 11 kilometres south-south-west of Babylon, which is probably of Neo-Babylonian date. Yet others place this biblical tower at Dūr-Kurigalzu (Aqar Quf), west of Baghdad, a city which was, however, built *c.* 1400 BC. All that can certainly be said is that the Genesis 11 account bears all the marks of a reliable historical account of buildings which can no longer be traced.

Some scholars associate Jacob's vision of a ladder and a 'gate of heaven' (Genesis 28:11–18) with a *ziggurat* of the kind once built at Babel.

*A babble of languages*

According to Genesis 11:9, the intervention of Yahweh at the building of Babel led to the confusion of tongues and the subsequent dispersion of mankind, possibly in the days of Peleg (Genesis 10:25).

Babel, as *Babylon throughout its history, became a symbol of the pride of man and his inevitable fall. Babel was also theologically linked with the confusion and broken fellowship between men and nations when separated from God. Its effects are to be reversed in God's final kingdom, but there is no certainty that the tongues or glossolalia of Acts 2:4 (compare the interpretation of Joel in verses 16–21), which were confined to Jews and proselytes and largely Aramaic- and Greek-speaking peoples, were other than known 'foreign languages' (*JTS* n.s. 17, 1966, pp. 299–307).

D. J. Wiseman

*Further reading*

A. Parrot, *The Tower of Babel*, 1955
D. J. Wiseman, *AS* 22, 1972, pp. 141ff.

**BABYLON.** See p. 55.

**BABYLONIA.** The territory in south-western Asia, now southern Iraq, which derived its name from the capital city of *Babylon. It was also called *Shinar (Genesis 10:10; 11:2; Isaiah 11:11; Joshua 7:21, AV 'Babylonish') and, later, 'the land of the Chaldeans' (Jeremiah 24:5; Ezekiel 12:13).

In earlier antiquity it bore the name of Akkad (Genesis 10:10, AV *ACCAD) for the northern reaches and Sumer for the southern alluvium and the marshes bordering the Persian Gulf; a territory which was later strictly called 'Chaldaea', a term for the whole country after the rise of the 'Chaldaean' dynasty (see the Neo-Babylonian period, below). Thus the Babylonians (*b^enê bābel*, 'sons of Babylon') are also qualified as Chaldaeans (Ezekiel 23:15, 17, 23).

Babylonia, watered by the Tigris and Euphrates rivers, was the probable site of Eden (Genesis 2:14) and of the tower of *Babel, and the country to which the Jews were exiled.

This small flat country of about 20,000 square kilometres was bounded on the north by *Assyria (Samarra-Jebel Hamrîn as the border), on the east by the hills bordering *Elam, on the west by the Arabian desert and on the south by the shores of the Persian Gulf. There is debate whether the latter coastline has changed appreciably since ancient times (*Geographical Journal* 118, 1952, pp. 24–39; compare *JAOS* 95, 1975, pp. 43–57).

The principal cities, of which Babylon, Warka (Erech) and Agade are the first mentioned in the Old Testament (Genesis 10:10), with Nippur, Ur, Eridu and Lagash, were all located on or near the Euphrates.

## History

*Pre-history*

The earliest types of pottery from the lowest level at Eridu in the south imply very early settlement. The pre-'Ubaid culture is to be dated *c.* 4000 BC. The 'Ubaid culture, which is also found in the north, appears to have been introduced by new immigrants.

There is as yet no sure means of identifying the inhabitants of Sumer (possibly biblical *SHINAR), though in the succeeding 'Proto-literate period' (*c.* 3100–2800 BC) pictographic writing is found on clay tablets. Since the language appears to be an early non-Semitic agglutinative Sumerian, employing names for older cities and technical terms in a different language, perhaps Semitic, it is likely that Semites and Sumerians were the earliest, or among the early, settlers. The highly developed art, in pottery, seals and architecture, is generally attributed to the influx of the Sumerians.

*The Early Dynastic period (c. 2800–2400 BC)*

This period saw the advent of kingship and the foundation of great cities. According to the Sumerian king list, 8 or 10 kings ruled before the Flood at the cities of Eridu, Badtibirra, Larak, Sippar and Shuruppak. The governor of the latter was the hero of the Sumerian flood story. The 'flood' deposit found by Woolley at Ur is dated in the 'Ubaid period, and therefore does not correspond with similar levels found at Kish and Shuruppak (Proto-literate – Early Dynastic I; compare *Iraq* 26, 1964, pp. 62–82). There was, however, a strong literary tradition of a flood in Babylonia from *c.* 2000 BC.

After the Flood 'kingship came down again from heaven' and the rulers at Kish and Uruk (Erech) include Gilgamesh and Agga, the heroes of a series of legends, who may well be historical characters.

City-states flourished with centres at Uruk, Kish, Ur (Royal Graves), Lagash, Shuruppak, Abu Ṣalabīkh and as far north as Mari. Often more than one powerful ruler sought to dominate Babylonia at the same time, and clashes were frequent.

Urukagina (*c.* 2351 BC), a social reformer, established the first or 'proto-' imperial domination of Sumer as far as the Mediterranean.

*The Akkadians (c. 2400–2200 BC)*

A strong Semitic family founded a new city at Agade and about this time may have restored Babylon. This 'Akkadian' or Sargonid dynasty (2371–2191 BC), so called after the name of its founder Sargon, developed a new technique of war with the bow and arrow and soon gained the whole of Sumer. This king carried his arms to the Mediterranean and Anatolia.

The Gutians from the eastern hills overran northern Babylonia (2230–2120 BC) and kept their hold over the economy until defeated by a coalition led by Utuḫegal of Uruk. Their rule was, however, somewhat local. Lagash under its ruler Gudea (*c.* 2150 BC) remained independent, dominating Ur and the southern cities. Gudea gradually extended his territory and expeditions as far as Syria (see also *EBLA) to win wood, precious stones and metals, and so

**Continued on p. 59**

# BABYLON

**n the Old Testament**
'he city on the river Euphrates (80 ilometres south of modern 3aghdad, Iraq) which became the olitical and religious capital of 3abylonia and of the empire and ivilization based upon it.

*Jame*
'he Hebrew *Bābel* is translated by he English versions as Babylon except in Genesis 10:10 and 11:9, ee also *BABEL) based on the Greek *3abylōn*. These are renderings of the 3abylonian *bâb-ili*; plural *bâb-ilāni*, vhich in its turn translates the arlier Sumerian name *kà-dingir-ra*, gate of god'. The Egyptians wrote he name *b-bī-r'* (= *bbr* or *bbl*) and he Achaemenids Old Persian *babiruš*.

Other common names for the city n the Babylonian texts are *tin-tir ki*), 'life of the trees', explained by hem as 'seat of life' and *e-ki*, 'place of canals'.

*Sešak* of Jeremiah 25:26 and 51:41 s generally taken to be an *'atbash'* cypher rendering of Babel, but may be a rare occurrence of an old name *šeš-ki*.

*'oundation*
According to Genesis 10:10, Nimrod ounded the city as his capital, while Babylonian religious tradition gives he credit to the god Marduk otherwise apart from the reference o the building of the Tower of *Babel [the *ziggurat*] there are no records of its foundation).

*History*
Sargon I of Agade (*c*. 2400 BC) and his successor Sharkalisharri built temples for the gods Anunitum and Amal and restored the temple-tower according to tradition. It is possible that their city of Agade was built on part of the ruins of the earlier city of Babylon.

In the time of Shulgi of Ur (*c*. 2000 BC) Babylon was attacked and then ruled by governors (*patensi*) appointed from Ur. With the advent of the Amorite 1st Dynasty of Babylon under Sumu-abum the city walls were restored and Hammurapi and his successors enlarged the town, which flourished as capital of their realm until its overthrow by the Hittites *c*. 1595 BC.

After a period under Kassite domination the city revolted and was attacked on several occasions, notably by Tiglath-pileser I of Assyria *c*. 1100 BC. Babylon repeatedly strove for its independence, and once a Chaldaean ruler, Marduk-apla-iddina II (722–710, 703–702 BC), sent embassies to enlist the help of Judah (2 Kings 20:12–18). Isaiah's account of the fate of the city (Isaiah 13) is very similarly worded to the account by Sargon II of Assyria of his sack of the place. In an attempt to remove the chief rebels, some of the leading citizens were deported to Samaria, where they introduced the worship of local Babylonian deities (2 Kings 17:24–30).

Sennacherib made his son king of Babylon but he was killed by pro-Babylonian Elamites in 694 BC. In an attempt to end this upsurge of Babylonian nationalism Sennacherib sacked the city in 689 BC and removed the sacred statues. His son,

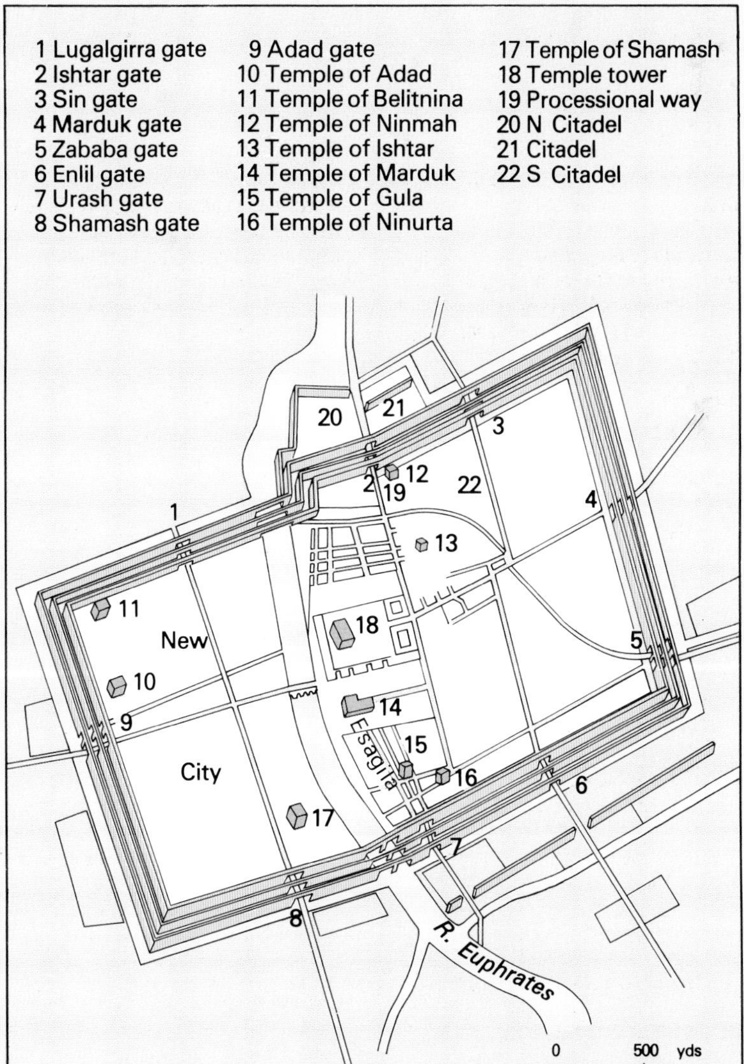


**Plan of Babylon at the time of Nebuchadrezzar II, 605–562 BC.**

## Hanging Gardens

Nebuchadrezzar II, who reigned from 605 to 562 BC, erected many lavish buildings in Babylon, but his most spectacular construction was not a building at all. It was a garden. His awe-inspiring 'Hanging Gardens of Babylon' aroused such admiration in the ancient world that in the 3rd century BC they were included in a list of the seven wonders of the world which all travellers ought to see.

**A jungle in the air**

Nebuchadrezzar had the gardens built inside the walls of his palace in order to please his wife, Amytis, a princess from Media, whom Nebuchadrezzar had married in order to seal a friendship treaty between their two countries. Media was a wild, mountainous country to the north-east of Babylonia, and tradition has it that as Amytis looked out from her palace windows over the flat plains around Babylon she pined for the hills and trees of her homeland. The Hanging Gardens were an attempt to ease her homesickness.

These gardens did not literally 'hang' but were called 'hanging' because they were built high overhead on a series of giant steps. Most of the trees, shrubs and flowers grew straight up so that from the ground it must have looked as if a jungle was hanging in the air.

**Building the gardens**

Nebuchadrezzar's builders began by constructing a row of brick archways, probably 24 metres high. The rounded tops of the archways were filled in to make a strong flat surface on which another row of arches was built, about 3 metres high. This second row was shorter than the first, creating a terrace at one end. Further rows of arches were built, one row on top of another, possibly six in all, each decreasing in length to make an enormous staircase, the top of which was about 40 metres from the ground. Each step was given a waterproof lining of lead, bitumen and reeds, and then filled with the rich earth from the surrounding fields. The result was about six tennis-court-sized flowerbeds in which were planted every kind of flowering shrub and tree from Babylonia.

**Irrigation**

An elaborate irrigation system ensured that the gardens stayed fresh and green in spite of the hot, dry climate. Water from the River Euphrates ran down a series of stone-lined pipes to an underground cistern. Next to the cistern, a tall narrow tower, the height of the top terrace, housed an endless chain of water buckets which were kept moving night and day by slaves working a treadmill. At the top, the water cascaded out from the buckets and splashed down in constantly flowing streams.

The Hanging Gardens were still in existence over 200 years after the death of Nebuchadrezzar, when Alexander the Great conquered Babylon, and it is not known when they finally disappeared. Babylon fell into ruins in the time of Rome, never to be rebuilt, and it is hardly surprising that no firm evidence of the Hanging Gardens has survived. However, Robert Koldewe, a German archaeologist, did unearth an unusual well in the ruins of one of the vaults in Babylon and this could have been used in conjunction with an irrigation system.

Esarhaddon, sought to restore the holy city to which he transported Manasseh as prisoner (2 Chronicles 33:11). He made Babylon a vassal-city under a son, Šamaš-šum-ukin, who, however, quarrelled with his brother Ashurbanipal of Assyria. In the subsequent war of 652–648 BC Babylon was severely damaged by fire, and once again the Assyrians tried appointing a local chief, Kandalanu, as governor.

The decline of the Assyrian empire enabled Nabopolassar, a Chaldaean, to recover the city and found a new dynasty in 626 BC. His work of restoring the city was ably continued by his successors, especially his son, Nebuchadrezzar II, king of Babylonia (2 Kings 24:1), whose boast was of the great city he had rebuilt (Daniel 4:30).

It was to Babylon that the victorious Babylonian army brought the Jewish captives after the wars against Judah. Among these was Jehoiachin, whose captivity there is confirmed by inscriptions found in the ruins of Babylon itself. The plunder from the Temple at Jerusalem, brought with the blinded king Zedekiah (2 Kings 25:7–13), was stored in the main temple of the city, probably that of the god Marduk (2 Chronicles 36:7).

The city was later ruled by Amēl-Marduk and was the place where Daniel served the last Chaldaean ruler Belshazzar, co-regent of Nabonidus.

*Downfall*

As predicted by Isaiah (14:1–23; 21:1–10; 46:1–2; 47:1–5) and Jeremiah (50–51), Babylon was to fall in its turn and be left a heap of ruins (see section on Exploration below). In October 539 the Persians under Cyrus entered the city and Belshazzar was slain (Daniel 5:30). The principal buildings were spared and the temples and their statues restored by royal decree.

There is no extra-biblical record of the government of the city, which now became a subsidiary Persian capital with an Achaemenid palace there. The temple vessels were delivered to Sheshbazzar for restoration to Jerusalem, and the discovery of the record of this, probably in the record office at Babylon, in the reign of Darius I (Ezra 5:16ff.) was the cause of a further return of exiles rallied at Babylon by Ezra (8:1).

Babylon, as of old, was the centre of a number of rebellions, by Nidintu-Bēl in 522 BC, and Araka (521 BC), and by Bel-shimanni and Shamash-eriba in 482 BC. In suppressing the latter, Xerxes destroyed the city (478 BC); although Alexander planned to restore it, he met his death there before work had progressed far, and with the founding of Seleucia on the river Tigris as the capital of the Seleucid rulers after the capture of Babylon in 312 BC, the city once again fell into disrepair and ruins, although, according to cuneiform texts, the temple of Bel continued in existence at least until AD 75.

*Exploration*

Many travellers since Herodotus of Halicarnassus *c.* 460 BC (*History* 1.178–188) have left accounts of their visits to Babylon. Benjamin of Tudela (12th century), Rauwolf (1574), Niebuhr (1764), C. J. Rich (1811–21) and Ker Porter (1818) were among those who were followed by the more scientific explorers who made soundings and plans of the ruins. The preliminary work by Layard (1850) and Fresnel (1852) was succeeded by systematic excavation of the inner city by the Deutsche Orient-Gesellschaft under Koldewey (1899–1917) and more recently by Lenzen in 1956–58 and since 1962 by the Iraqis (including the preservation and restoration of the Ninmah temple).

This work, combined with evidence of more than 10,000 inscribed tablets, recovered from the site by natives digging for bricks, enables a fair picture of the city of Nebuchadrezzar's day to be reconstructed. The deep overlay of debris, the frequent destruction and rebuilding, together with the change in the course of the river Euphrates

**Restored interior of the temple of the goddess Ninmah (Ishtar) at Babylon.**

ınd a rise in the water-table, means hat only a few parts of the city of the earlier period have been uncovered.

The site is now covered by a ıumber of widely scattered mounds. The largest, Qasr, covers the citadel, Merkes a city quarter; to the north, Bāwil, the northern or summer palace of Nebuchadrezzar; Amran bn 'Ali, the temple of Marduk; and Şaḥn, the site of the *ziggurat* or temple-tower.

*Architecture*

The city was surrounded by an ntricate system of double walls, the outer range covering 27 kilometres, strong and large enough for chariots to pass along the top, buttressed by defence towers and pierced by 8 gates.

On the northern side the massive Ishtar gates marked the procession way leading south to the citadel of Esagila, the temple of Marduk and the adjacent *ziggurat* Etemenanki. This paved roadway was *c.* 920 metres long, its walls decorated with enamelled bricks showing 120 lions (symbol of Ishtar) and 575 *mušruššu* – dragons (Marduk) and bulls (Bel) ranged in alternate rows.

From this road another ran west to cross the river Euphrates by a bridge which linked the New Town on the west bank with the ancient capital.

The main palaces on which successive kings lavished attention are now represented by the complex of buildings in the citadel, among which the throne-room (52 by 17 metres) may have been in use in the time of Daniel. At the north-eastern angle of the palace are the remains of vaults thought by Koldewey to be supports for the terraced 'hanging gardens' built by Nebuchadrezzar for Amytis, his Median wife, as a reminder of her homeland.

The temple-tower of Babylon became famous as the Tower of *Babel.

Many details of the city quarters and their temples, of which fifty-three are now known, have been recovered. The names of these quarters were used on occasions to designate the city as a whole (Šu'ana [*JCS* 23, 1970, p. 63], Shushan, Tuba, Tintir, Kullab). The frequent destructions of the city left few of the contents of the temples *in situ*. The possession of the statue of Marduk, housed in Esagila, was a mark of victory, and it was carried off to the conqueror's capital. The religion and civilization were largely synonymous with those of *Assyria and *Babylonia.

D. J. Wiseman

**Bull, possibly representing the god Marduk, one of over 200 decorating the Ishtar gate at Babylon, 7th–6th century BC.**

The ruins of Babylon.

*Further reading*
R. Koldewey, *The Excavations at Babylon*, 1914
E. Unger, *Babylon, Die Heilige Stadt*, 1931
'Babylon', *Reallexikon der Assyriologie*, 1932, pp. 330–369
A. Parrot, *Babylon and the Old Testament*, 1958
O. E. Ravn, *Herodotus' Description of Babylon*, 1932
I. J. Gelb, *Journal of Inst. of Asian Studies* 1, 1955, on the name of Babylon
D. J. Wiseman, *Nebuchadrezzar and Babylon*, 1985

## In the New Testament

**1.** Babylon on the Euphrates, with special reference to the Babylonian Exile (Matthew 1:11–12, 17(2); Acts 7:43).

**2.** In Revelation 14:8 and 18:2, 'Fallen, fallen is Babylon the great' is an echo of Isaiah 21:9 (compare Jeremiah 51:8), but refers no longer to the city on the Euphrates but to Rome, as is made plain by the mention of seven hills in Revelation 17:9 (see also Revelation 16:19; 17:5; 18:10, 21).

The scarlet woman of Revelation 17, enthroned upon the seven-headed beast and bearing the name of mystery, 'Babylon the great', is the city of Rome, maintained by the Roman empire.

The seven heads of the imperial beast are interpreted not only of the seven hills of Rome but also of seven Roman emperors – of whom the five already fallen are probably Augustus, Tiberius, Gaius, Claudius and Nero, and the one currently reigning is Vespasian (Revelation 17:10).

**3.** In 1 Peter 5:13, 'she who is at Babylon, who is likewise chosen', who sends her greetings to the Christians addressed in the epistle, is most probably a Christian church. 'Babylon' here has been identified with the city on the Euphrates, and also with a Roman military station on the Nile (on the site of Cairo); but it is best to accept the identification with Rome.

F. F. Bruce

*Further reading*
E.G. Selwyn, *The First Epistle of St Peter*, 1946, pp. 243, 303ff.
O. Cullmann, *Peter: Disciple, Apostle, Martyr*, 1953, pp. 70ff. and *passim*
R.E. Brown, K. P. Donfried, J. Reumann, *Peter in the New Testament*, 1973
I.T. Beckwith, *The Apocalypse of John*, 1919, pp. 284ff., 690ff.
G.B. Caird, *The Revelation of St John the Divine*, 1966, pp. 211ff.

**:ontinued from p. 54**
ıcreased the prosperity of his city.
 The Sumerian renaissance or 'Golden Age' which followed was ne of economic and artistic wealth.

*rd Dynasty of Ur (2113–2006 BC)*
'ollowing the reigns of Utuḫegal of 'ruk and Namaḫani, the son-in-law f Gudea, in Lagash, Ur once more ecame the centre of power. 'r-Nammu (2113–2096 BC) rebuilt ıe citadel with its *ziggurat* and emples at *Ur and set up statues of imself in Uruk, Isin and Nippur. Gradually Ur extended its influence s far as Assur and Byblos, and for a vhile his successors were accorded ivine honours, depicted on their ıonuments and seals by the horned ıeadgear of divinity (C. J. Gadd, *deas of Divine Rule in the Ancient Near East*, 1944). Similar honours ppear to have been granted to Naram-Sin earlier. Many thousands f documents reveal the administra-ion and religion of this period when Jr traded with places as far distant s India.
 The end came after severe amines, and the Sumerian rulers vere displaced by invaders from Elam and Semitic semi-nomads from he western deserts. It is possible hat the migration of Terah and Abraham (Genesis 11:31) took place t this time of change in Ur's fortune.

*The Amorites (2000–1595 BC)*
The territories formerly controlled by Jr were divided among the local hiefs at Assur, Mari on the Upper Euphrates and Eshnunna. ndependent rule was established y Ishbi-Irra in Isin and Naplanum in Larsa, thus dividing the loyalties of he previously united Sumerians. In Babylon, whose power was growing luring this period, a series of 'igorous rulers in the 1st (Amorite) Dynasty of Babylon (1894–1595 BC) ıeld sway. The sixth of the line, Hammurapi (1792–1750 BC according to the most accepted hronology) eventually defeated Rim-Sin, ruler of Larsa and onqueror of Isin. For the last decade of his reign Hammurapi ruled from he Persian Gulf to *Mari, where he lefeated Zimrilim, a Semite.
 Despite this victory, Hammurapi vas not as powerful as his namesake n Aleppo, and the Mari letters, which afford a remarkable insight nto the diplomacy, trade, history nd religion of those days, show that ıe did not subdue Assyria, Eshnunna or other cities in Babylonia.
 The relations between Babylon, Elam and the west at this time made possible a coalition such as that described in Genesis 14. With the decline of Sumerian influence the increasing power of the Semites was emphasized by the place given to Marduk as the national god, and this encouraged Hammurapi to revise the laws of Babylon to accommodate both traditions. The text bearing this 'code' of 282 laws is based on the earlier reforms of Urukagina, Ur-Nammu and Lipit-Ishtar.

*The Kassites (1595–1174 BC)*
Babylon, as often in its history, was to fall by sudden assault from the north. About 1595 BC the Hittite Mursili I raided the city and the Kassites from the eastern hills gradually took over the country, later ruling from a new capital (Dur-Kurigalzu) built by Kurigalzu I (*c.* 1450 BC).
 In the centuries which followed Babylonia was weak, though independent except for brief periods when under direct Assyrian control (*e.g.* Tukulti-Ninurta I, 1244–1208 BC). Aramaean incursions were frequent, and these raids may well have left the Israelites free to settle in southern Palestine and later to expand their borders under Solomon with little opposition from these desert peoples (see also *ASSYRIA).
 Periodically national heroes were able to maintain local control and trade, as when Nebuchadrezzar I (1124–1103 BC) defeated Elam, but soon Tiglath-pileser I re-established Assyrian overlordship.

*Assyrian domination (745–626 BC)*
About the time of Nabû-naṣir (Nabonassar), whose reign (747–735 BC) marked the beginning of a new era, there began a prolonged struggle for independence from *Assyria. Tiglath-pileser III of Assyria proclaimed himself 'King of Sumer and Akkad', took the hands of Bel (Marduk) and thus claimed the throne in Babylon in 745 BC, using his other name Pul(u) (1 Chronicles 5:26).
 Fifteen years later he had to bring the Assyrian army to fight the rebel Ukin-zēr of Bît-Amuk-kani. He defeated him in Sapia and deported many prisoners. A rival sheikh, Marduk-apla-iddina II, of the southern district of Bît-Yakin, paid Tiglath-pileser tribute at this time (*Iraq* 17, 1953, pp. 44–50). However, the preoccupation with the siege of *Samaria by Shalmaneser V and Sargon II in 726–722 gave Marduk-apla-iddina his opportunity for intrigue. For 10 years (721–710 BC) he held the throne in Babylon until the Assyrian army attacked Der, defeated Ḫumbanigaš of Elam and occupied Babylon. The Assyrian army moved south, but Merodach-baladan was retained as local ruler. It says much for Sargon's diplomacy that he kept him a loyal subject for the rest of his reign.
 On Sargon's death in 705 BC, however, Merodach-baladan again plotted against his masters, and it is likely that it was he, rather than Hezekiah, who initiated the overtures for an alliance against Assyria (2 Kings 20:12–19; Isaiah 39). Isaiah's opposition was well founded, for the Babylonians themselves set their own citizen Marduk-zakir-šum on the throne in 703 BC. This freed Merodach-baladan's hand and he had himself proclaimed king of Babylon, though he lived in the more friendly city of Borsippa.
 Sennacherib marched against him, defeated the rebels and their Elamite supporters in battles at Kutha and Kish, and entered Babylon, where he set a pro-Assyrian, Bel-ibni, on the throne. Bît-Yakin was ravaged, but Merodach-baladan had already fled to Elam, where he died before Sennacherib was able to assemble a punitive naval force in 694 BC.
 For a while Sennacherib's son Esarhaddon had special responsbilities as viceroy at Babylon, and when he came to the throne in 681 did much to repair the city's temples and to restore its fortunes. It may be in conjunction with this that he temporarily deported Manasseh there (2 Chronicles 33:11). Since the Elamites continued to stir up the Babylonian tribes, Esarhaddon led a campaign into the 'sea-lands' in 678 BC and installed Na'id-Marduk as chief.
 In May 672 Esarhaddon made all his vassals swear to support his son Ashurbanipal as crown-prince of Assyria, and his son Šamaš-šum-ukin as crown-prince of Babylonia (*Iraq* 20, 1958). On his death in 669 this arrangement came into force and worked well under the influence of the queen-mother. Nevertheless, by 652 BC the twin brother in Babylon was in open revolt against the central government, and his death followed the sack of Babylon in 648. Ashurbanipal struck at Elam also and captured Susa, from which prisoners were taken with Babylonian rebels to be settled in Samaria (Ezra 4:2). Kandalanu was made viceroy of Babylonia (648–627 BC), while Ashurbanipal kept direct

control of the religious centre of Nippur.

These preoccupations in the south diverted Assyrian attention from the west, and the city-states in Palestine were able to take steps towards independence under Josiah. The end of Ashurbanipal's reign is obscure, but may have followed soon after the death of Kandalanu. In the interregnum which followed, the local tribes rallied to support the Chaldaean Nabopolassar against the Assyrian Sin-šar-iškun.

*The Neo-Babylonian (Chaldaean) period (626–539 BC)*
Nabopolassar, a governor of the 'sea-lands' near the Persian Gulf, was a Chaldaean (*kaldu* hence *CHALDAEA), occupied the throne in Babylon on 22 November 626, and at once made peace with Elam. In the following year he defeated the Assyrians at Sallat, and by 623 Der had broken from their yoke. The Babylonian Chronicle, the principal and reliable source for this period, is silent on the years 623–616 BC, by which time Nabopolassar had driven the Assyrians back along the rivers Euphrates and Tigris.

In 614 the Medes joined the Babylonians to attack Assur, and the same allies, perhaps with Scythian support, captured Nineveh in the summer of 612 BC, the Babylonians pursuing the refugees westwards. Babylonian campaigns in Syria were followed by the assault on Harran in 609 and raids on the northern hill-tribes in 609–606 BC. Nabopolassar, now aged, entrusted the Babylonian army to his crown-prince Nebuchadrezzar, who fought the Egyptians at Kumuḫi and Quramati (Upper Euphrates).

In May-June 605 BC Nebuchadrezzar made a surprise attack on Carchemish, sacked the city and annihilated the Egyptian army at Hamath. Thus the Babylonians now overran all Syria as far as the Egyptian border but do not appear to have entered the hill-country of Judah itself (2 Kings 24:7; Josephus, *Antiquities* 10.6; compare Daniel 1:1). Jehoiakim, a vassal of Neco II, submitted to Nebuchadrezzar, who carried off hostages, including Daniel, to Babylon. While in Palestine, Nebuchadrezzar heard of the death of his father (15 August 605 BC) and at once rode across the desert to 'take the hands of Bel', thus claiming the throne, on 6 September 605 BC.

In 604 BC Nebuchadrezzar received the tribute of 'all the kings of Hatti-land (Syro-Palestine)', among whom must have been Jehoiakim. Ashkelon, however, refused and was sacked, an event which had a profound effect on Judah (Jeremiah 47:5–7). An Aramaic letter appealing for help from the pharaoh against the advancing Babylonian army may be assigned to this time (compare *DOTT*, pp. 251–255).

In 601 the Babylonians fought the Egyptians, both sides sustaining heavy losses; the Babylonians remained at home to re-equip the army during the next year. It was probably as a result of this that Jehoiakim, contrary to the word of Jeremiah (Jeremiah 27:9–11), transferred his allegiance to Neco II after submitting to Babylon for 3 years (2 Kings 24:1).

In preparation for further campaigns the Babylonian army raided the Arab tribes in 599/98 (Jeremiah 49:28–33). In the month Kislev in his 7th year (December 598) Nebuchadrezzar called out his army once more and, according to the Babylonian Chronicle, 'besieged the city of Judah, capturing it on the second day of Adar. He captured its king, appointed a ruler of his own choice and, having taken much spoil from the city, sent it back to Babylon' (BM 21946). The fall of Jerusalem on 16 March 597, the capture of Jehoiachin, the appointment of Mattaniah-Zedekiah and the commencement of the Jewish Exile are thus recorded as in the Old Testament (2 Kings 24:10–17; 2 Chronicles 36:8–10).

In the following year Nebuchadrezzar appears to have marched against Elam (compare Jeremiah 49:34–38). The Babylonian Chronicle is missing from 595 BC, but further Babylonian operations against Judah when Zedekiah rebelled are recorded by Jeremiah (52:3ff.; 2 Kings 25:7). Jerusalem was destroyed in 587 BC and a further deportation effected in 581 (2 Kings 25:8–21), leaving Judah a dependent province under Gedaliah (verses 22–26). A Babylonian text gives a glimpse of an invasion of Egypt in 568/67 BC (Jeremiah 46).

The exiled Jehoiachin, who is named in ration-tablets from Babylon (dated 595–570 BC), was favourably treated by Nebuchadrezzar's successor Amēl-Marduk (Evil-Merodach, 562–560 BC; 2 Kings 25:27). This king was assassinated by Nebuchadrezzar's son-in-law Neriglissar (Nergal-Sharezer, 560–556 BC), who campaigned in Cilicia in an effort to stem the rising power of Lydia. His son, Labaši-Marduk, reigned only 9 months before Nabonidus took the throne and immediately marched to Cilicia, where, according to Herodotus, he mediated between the Lydians and Medes.

The Medes now threatened Babylonia, from which Nabonidus was driven by the people's unwillingness to accept his reforms. He campaigned in Syria and northern Arabia, where he lived at Tema for 10 years while his son Belshazzar acted as co-regent in Babylon. About 544 his people and the kings of Arabia, Egypt and the Medes being favourably disposed, Nabonidus returned to his capital (*AS* 8, 1958), but by this time the country was weak and divided.

*The Achaemenids (539–332 BC)*
Cyrus, who had taken over Media, Persia and Lydia, entered Babylon on 16 October 539 BC, following its capture by his general Gobryas. The course of the river Euphrates had been diverted at Opis to enable the invaders to penetrate the defences along the dried-up river-bed. Belshazzar was killed (Daniel 5:30) and Nabonidus was exiled to Carmania. The identity of Darius the Mede with Cyrus (as Daniel 6:28) or with Gubaru has been proposed.

The rule of Cyrus in Babylon (539–530 BC) was just and favourable to the Jews, whose return from exile he encouraged (Ezra 1:1–11; compare Isaiah 44:24–28; 45:13; Micah 5). For a brief time his son Cambyses acted as co-regent until his father died fighting in the north-eastern hills. He invaded Egypt but his death (522 BC) brought insurgence, and pretenders seized the throne (*AJSL* 58, 1941, pp. 341ff.), until in December 522 Darius I restored law and order. During his reign (522–486 BC) he allowed the Jews to rebuild the temple at Jerusalem under Zerubbabel (Ezra 4:5; Haggai 1:1; Zechariah 1:1).

Henceforth Babylonia was ruled by kings of *Persia; Xerxes (Ahasuerus, 486–470 BC), Artaxerxes I (464–423 BC) and Darius II (423–408 BC), who may be the 'Darius the Persian' so named in Nehemiah 12:22 to distinguish him from 'Darius the Mede'.

Following the capture of Babylon, which he planned to rebuild, Alexander III (the Great) ruled the city (331–323 BC) and was followed by a Hellenistic line; Philip Arrhidaeus (323–316 BC) and Alexander IV (316–312 BC). The country then passed in turn into the hands of the Seleucids (312–64 BC) and then of the Parthians (Arsacids) nd Sassanians until its conquest by ne Arabs in AD 641.

From the Neo-Babylonian period nwards there were a number of ewish settlements in Babylonia naintaining links with Judaea (Acts :9), and after the fall of Jerusalem in D 70 these became influential in the *iaspora*.

## eligion

'rom the 3rd millennium BC onwards sts of the names of deities with heir titles, epithets and temples vere compiled. Although in the final brary version at Nineveh in the 7th entury BC these numbered more han 2,500, many can be identified as arlier Sumerian deities assimilated y the Semites after the time of the st Dynasty of Babylon (*c.* 1800 BC), o that the actual number of deities vorshipped in any one period was onsiderably less.

### *he Pantheon*

he chief gods were Anu (Sumerian *n*) the heaven-god, with his rincipal temple É.anna at Uruk (see lso *ERECH). He was the Semitic 'El, nd his wife Innana, or Innin, was ater confused with Ishtar. Similar yncretistic tendencies can be raced over Enlil, the air-god, whose ttributes were later taken over by Bel (Baal) or Marduk (Merodach). His wife, called Ninlil or Ninhursag, was ater identified also with Ishtar.

The third deity of the supreme riad was Ea (Sumerian *Enki*), 'lord of he deep waters', god of wisdom and hus especially favourable to nankind, to whom he revealed the neans of learning the mind of the gods through divination, and for whom he interceded. His temple É.abzu was at Eridu, and his wife bore the names of Dam-gal, Nin-mah or Damkina, the great wife of earth and heaven.

Among the other principal deities was the Semitic Ishtar, at first perhaps a male deity (compare Arabic *'Athtar*). But later, by the assumption of the powers of Innana through the same process of syncretism, Ishtar became supremely the goddess of love and the heroine of war and was considered to be the daughter of Sin. Sin, the Babylonian moon-god (Sumerian *su'en*), was worshipped with his wife Ningal in temples at Ur and Harran. He was said to be the son of Anu or of Enlil.

Shamash, whose wife Aya was also later considered to be a form of Ishtar, was the sun in his strength (Sumerian *utu*), the son of Sin, the god of power, justice and of war. His main temples (É.babbar, 'the House of the Sun') were at Sippar and Larsa, though like that of all the principal deities his worship was perpetuated in shrines in other cities.

Adad, of western Semitic origin, was the god of storms, the Canaanite Aramaean Addu or Hadad. Nergal and his wife Ereshkigal ruled the underworld, and thus he was the lord of plagues (Irra), fevers and maladies. With the rise of the Amorites the worship of Marduk (Sumerian *amar.utu*, perhaps meaning 'the young bull of the sun'), the eldest son of Enki, became paramount in Babylon.

The Epic of Creation (*enuma eliš*) is a poem concerning the creation of the universe and of order restored by Marduk, whose 50 titles are given. Nabu (Nebo), god of science and writing, had his temple (É.zida) in many cities, including *Nineveh, *Calah and Borsippa.

Many deities were of importance in certain localities. Thus Ashur (*an.šar*) became the national god of Assyria. Amurru (*mar.tu*, 'the west'), who is identified with Anu, Sin and Adad, was a western Semitic deity as was Dagon (Tammuz). Dummuzi was a god of vegetation whose death, but not resurrection, forms the subject of an Ishtar myth. Ninurta was the Babylonian and Assyrian god of war and hunting (perhaps reflected in the biblical Nimrod).

The upper world was peopled with Igigu-gods and the lower by Annunaku. The whole spiritual and material realm was regulated by divine laws (*me*), over a hundred of which are known, ranging from 'godship' to 'victory' and 'a musical instrument', *i.e.* cultural traits and complexes. The gods were immortal yet of limited power. The myths, in which but few of the principal deities figure, illustrate their anthropomorphic character and the conception of any object (*e.g.* a stone) being imbued with 'life'. Spirits and demons abound.

The Sumerians sought by various theological devices to resolve the problems inherent in their polytheistic system. Thus the myths are primarily concerned with such questions as the origin of the universe, the foundation and government of the world and the creation of man and the search for immortality, as in the Epic of the Flood, and man's relationship to the spiritual world.

### *Priesthood*

There were many classes of temple servants, with the king or ruler as the supreme pontiff at certain solemn festivals. In early Sumerian times the whole economy was centred on the temple, where the chief official (*ênû*) was 'the lord of the manor'. In the worship of Sin, the high-priestess (*entu*) was usually a royal princess. The chief priests (*maḫḫu*) had many priests (*šangu*), males of sound body and often married, to assist them. The chief liturgist (*urigallu*) was supported by a host of minor officials who had access to the temple (*ēreb bīti*). In the ceremonial, chanters, psalmists, dirge-singers and musicians played a great part.

In man's approach to the god many specialists might play a role. The exorcist (*ašipu*) could remove the

**Boundary stone of Marduk (Merodach), Babylonia.**

evil spirit or spell with the incantations or ritual prescribed in the texts (*šurpu; maqlu*) involving symbolic substitutions (*kuppuru*), purification by *mašmašu*-priests or by those who cleansed by water (*ramku*). There are many documents describing the action to be taken against evil spirits (*utukki limnūti*), demons of fate (*namtaru*) demons plaguing women (*lamaštu*) or taboos.

The extensive medical literature of the early period was closely allied to religion, as was the astronomy or astrology of the later 'Chaldaean' dynasty. The latter was based on the equation of deities with planets or stars (*e.g.* Nabu equals Mercury), or with parts of the heavens ('The Way of Anu' equals fixed stars).

Others were engaged in ascertaining the will of the gods by omens from livers (the *barû*-priest or 'seer'), or by inquiry by oracle (*ša'ilu*), or by offering prayers. Many women, including sanctuary prostitutes, were attached to the temples (H. A. Hoffner, *Orient and Occident*, 1973, pp. 213–222) and local shrines where travellers prayed have been found at Ur (*Iraq* 22, 1960).

The regular service (*dullu*) included giving the gods something to eat and drink. Statues were dressed and ornamented and votive figures of worshippers set near by. Sacrifices placed on altars were subsequently allocated, wholly or in part, to the priests. The gods had their own chairs, chariots and boats for use in processions.

*Festivals*

Most cities and temples had their own distinctive festivals and sacred days. At Babylon, Erech and Ur, as at Assur, Nineveh and Calah, the New Year Festival (*akitu*) was the most outstanding, held in the spring, but not exclusively, and with varying practices at different centres and periods. At Babylon the ceremonies lasted 2 weeks with numerous rites including a procession of gods to Marduk's temple, the humiliation and restoration of the king who later 'took the hand of Bēl' to lead him in procession to the *akitu*-house outside the city where a re-enactment of the assembly of the gods, the creation debate and struggle (in ritual combat?) and the fixing of the fates for the ensuing year took place. This was sometimes followed by a 'sacred marriage' (king and priestess representing the god) and days of general rejoicing. The Epic of Creation was recited during this time and also at other times later in the year.

Royal festivals included the coronation of the king (texts of Ur-Nammu, Nabopolassar, *etc.*, survive), celebration of victories and the inauguration of a city or temple. Personal festivals include the celebration of birth and of marriage, and the installation of girls as priestesses.

*Literature*

Babylonian literature is already well developed in the Abū Ṣalabīkh tablets (*c.* 2800–2500 BC) with evidence of Semitic scribes copying earlier Sumerian texts and using literary techniques (colophons *etc.*) commonly taught in schools. Throughout its long history (to AD 100) this literature was influential throughout the ancient Near East, copies being found in Anatolia (see also *HITTITE), Syria (see also *EBLA, *UGARIT), Palestine (Megiddo, Hazor, *etc.*), Egypt (see also *AMARNA) and later even Greece. Originals or copies were taken to, or made for, the royal libraries of *Assyria at Assur, Nineveh and Calah.

The range covered some 50 epics about ancient heroes and myths in Akkadian (some translated from Sumerian, and relating to creation, the flood and the establishment of civilization). 'Wisdom literature' includes compositions about 'man and his god', the Babylonian 'Job' (*ludlul bēl nēmeqi*), theodices, disputations, dialogues, practical instructions, proverbs, parables, fables and folk-tales, miniature essays and love-songs. These are also found as part of the school curriculum besides the series of handbooks necessary to a skilled scribe (sign-lists, syllabaries, grammatical paradigms, phrase books, dictionaries and numerous lists, *e.g.* personal and place-names).

'Religious' literature includes psalms, hymns and prayers (to gods and some kings), rituals, incantations, as well as catalogues of such literature, much of which is still lost.

'Scientific' literature covers medicine (prognosis, diagnosis, prescriptions, *vade mecum*, surgery and veterinary texts), chemistry (mainly perfume and glass-making), geology (lists of stones with colour and hardness), alchemy, botany (drug and plant lists) and zoology (lists of fauna).

Mathematics (including geometry and algebra) is represented by both problem and practical texts and is closely related also to astronomy with its tables, procedure, ephemerides and goal-year texts, almanacs and diaries. Texts include predictions for intercalated months to maintain the calendar.

In Babylonia the historical Chronicle was highly developed; extracts from it were included in a whole range of literature (epics, 'dynastic prophecies' and astronomical diaries). Collections of laws (but not law codes) from the 2nd millennium BC (*e.g.* Eshnunna, Hammurapi) are well known and can be compared with practice in more than a quarter of a million texts – letters, legal, economic and administrative from *c.* 3000 to 300 BC. From the 4th century BC developments include horoscopes, the zodiac, and texts written in Greek letters on clay tablets, among other writing materials.

D. J. Wiseman


*Further reading*

*General and History:*

S. N. Kramer, *History Begins at Sumer*, 1958

H. W. F. Saggs, *The Greatness that was Babylon*, 1961

D. J. Wiseman, *Chronicles of Chaldaean Kings*, 1956

——, *Nebuchadrezzar and Babylon*, 1985

A. L. Oppenheim, *Ancient Mesopotamia*, 1964

J. A. Brinkman, *A Political History of Post-Kassite Babylonia*, 1968

W. W. Hallo and W. K. Simpson, *The Ancient Near East*, 1971

*CAH* I.2, 1971; II.2, 1975; III (forthcoming)

*Texts:*

A. K. Grayson, *Assyrian and Babylonian Chronicles,* 1975

*Babylonian Historical-Literary Texts*, 1975

*ANET* for translations of historical, religious, law and other texts

*Religion:*

J. Bottéro, *La religion babylonienne*, 1952

T. Jacobsen, *Treasures of Darkness*, 1976

H. Ringgren, *Religions of the Ancient Near East*, 1967

*Art:*

*ANEP*

H. Frankfort, *The Art and Architecture of the Ancient Orient*, 1954

Seton Lloyd, *The Archaeology of Mesopotamia*, 1978

*Exploration and excavation:*

Reports and texts are published regularly in the journals *Archiv für Orientforschung, Orientalia, Iraq, Sumer, Journal of Cuneiform Studies*

*Other:*

R. S. Ellis, *A Bibliography of Mesopotamian Sites*, 1972

**ACA, VALLEY OF** (Hebrew *'ēmeq abbāḵā'*). A place near Jerusalem ıentioned in Psalm 84:6, so ranslated in the AV and RSV. The raditional rendering 'valley of Veeping' (RV; see 'Valley of the Veeper', JB), as though from *beḵeh* see Ezra 10:1), goes back through erome's Gallican Psalter to the eptuagint; it is accepted by G. R. )river, who suggests the valley may ave been so called because it was ned with tombs.

Other renderings are 'valley of ıulberry (balsam) trees' (AV margin, v margin), as though from *b^ekā'îm* (2 amuel 5:23f.); these are supposed o grow in arid districts, whence erhaps the paraphrase 'thirsty alley' (NEB).

If 'valley of balsam trees' is the orrect rendering, this valley could e the same as the valley of Rephaim 2 Samuel 5:22–23).

. F. Bruce

*urther reading*

. R. Driver, 'Water in the Iountains!', *PEQ* 102, 1970, pp. 87ff.

**AHURIM.** Modern Ras eṭ-Ṭmim, to he east of Mount Scopus, erusalem. Phaltiel, the husband of Iichal, accompanied his wife as far s Bahurim when she went to David o become his wife (2 Samuel :14–16). Shimei, a man of Bahurim, net and cursed David as he reached his locality in his flight from erusalem before Absalom (2 Samuel 6:5), and David's soldiers hid in a vell in Bahurim when pursued by Absalom's men (2 Samuel 17:17–21).

. J. Way

**AMAH.** See *BAMOTH.

**AMOTH, BAMOTH-BAAL.** Bamoth literally, 'heights') is mentioned as a tage in Israel's journey (Numbers 1:19–20). The important shrine on he height was known as Bamoth-baal (Numbers 22:41) and he settlement is later given among he cities of Reuben (Joshua 13:17).

The exact location is unknown but he site was near the river Arnon and n a commanding position for, from t, Balaam could 'see the full extent of he Israelite host'. Baal is probably ısed here in the general sense of lord' relating to the Moabite god Chemosh. Balaam built his own ltars on which to invoke God.

The Moabite Stone refers to nother Moabite 'high place' 'bamah').

. T. Whitney

**BASHAN.** A region east of Jordan lying to the north of Gilead, from which it was divided by the river Yarmuk. Its fertility was famous; see Psalm 22:12; Ezekiel 39:18; Amos 4:1; and Isaiah 2:13; Jeremiah 50:19; Ezekiel 27:5–6. The name, nearly always written with the article (*habbāšān*), had varying connotations. In the wide sense it was counted as extending north to Mount Hermon and east to *Salecah; and in the narrower sense it comprised roughly the area called today en-Nuqra. It included the cities of *Ashtaroth, *Golan and *Edrei, and the regions of *Argob and *Havvoth-jair.

At the time of the conquest Bashan was under the rule of Og, who had his capital at Ashtaroth. He was defeated by the Israelites at Edrei (Deuteronomy 1:4; 3:1–3) and the territory was allotted to the tribe of Manasseh. It formed part of the dominions of David and Solomon, falling within the sixth administrative district of the latter (1 Kings 4:13). It was lost during the Syrian wars, but was regained by Jeroboam II (2 Kings 14:25), only to be taken by Tiglath-pileser III (2 Kings 15:29), after which it formed part of the successive Assyrian, Babylonian and Persian empires. Under the Persians it roughly coincided with the district of Qarnaim, and in the Greek period with that of Batanaea.

T. C. Mitchell

*Further reading*

G. A. Smith, *The Historical Geography of the Holy Land*, 25th edition, 1931, pp. 354–356, 386–397, 445

F. M. Abel, *Géographie de la Palestine* 1, 1933, pp. 274f.

**BEER** (*b^e'ēr*, literally 'a well', 'cistern', usually man-made). **1.** Numbers 21:16. A point on the itinerary of the wandering Hebrews, reached soon after leaving Arnon. This verse records an otherwise unknown story of the provision of water; an important event, for verse 18b suggests that Beer was in a desert place. The site is unknown but the Wadi eth-Themed has been suggested.

**2.** Judges 9:21. The place to which Jotham fled after having denounced the *coup d'état* of his brother Abimelech. The site is unknown but may be el-Bîreh, 11 kilometres north of Bethshean.

R. J. Way

**BEER-LAHAI-ROI.** The name itself and certain elements of Genesis 16:13–14, where it first appears, defy certain translation. As it stands, the name may mean 'The well of the living one who sees me' or 'The well of "He who sees me lives"'. However, the original place-name may have suffered a degree of distortion in transmission, putting the original beyond our discovery. This is not the only proper name in the Old Testament to have suffered in this way.

The exact site is not known, but Genesis 16:7 and 14 places it towards the Egyptian border, whither Hagar, the Egyptian maid, was fleeing from the wrath of Sarai her mistress. God appeared to Hagar here and announced the birth of Ishmael.

Isaac passed through Beer-lahai-roi when waiting for Eliezer to bring him a wife from Mesopotamia (Genesis 24:62), and settled there after the death of Abraham.

R. J. Way

**BEERSHEBA.** The name given to an important well, and also to the local town and district (Genesis 21:14; Joshua 19:2). The present town lies 77 kilometres south-west of Jerusalem and approximately midway between the Mediterranean and the southern part of the Dead Sea.

There are several wells in the vicinity, the largest 3·75 metres in diameter. The digging of this well involved cutting through 5 metres of solid rock. On one stone of the masonry lining the shaft Conder found a date indicating that repairs had been carried out in the 12th century AD. At the time of his visit in 1874, it was 11 metres to the surface of the water.

*Excavations*

Excavations at Tell es-Seba' (Tel Beersheba), 5 kilometres west of the town, have revealed a planned and fortified town of the Judaean monarchy. A well outside the gateway is dated to the 12th century BC by the excavator, and associated with Abraham, setting the stories of the Patriarchs after the Israelite conquest. There is no evidence to support this speculation. No pottery of Bronze Age date has been found at the site, nor anything to prove the place's ancient name.

Iron Age pottery has been found in the modern town (Bir es-Seba'), which was called Berosaba in Roman times, and may yet prove to be the patriarchal site (but modern occupation prohibits extensive excavation).

Plan of the excavated sections of the city of Beersheba (Tel es-Seba').

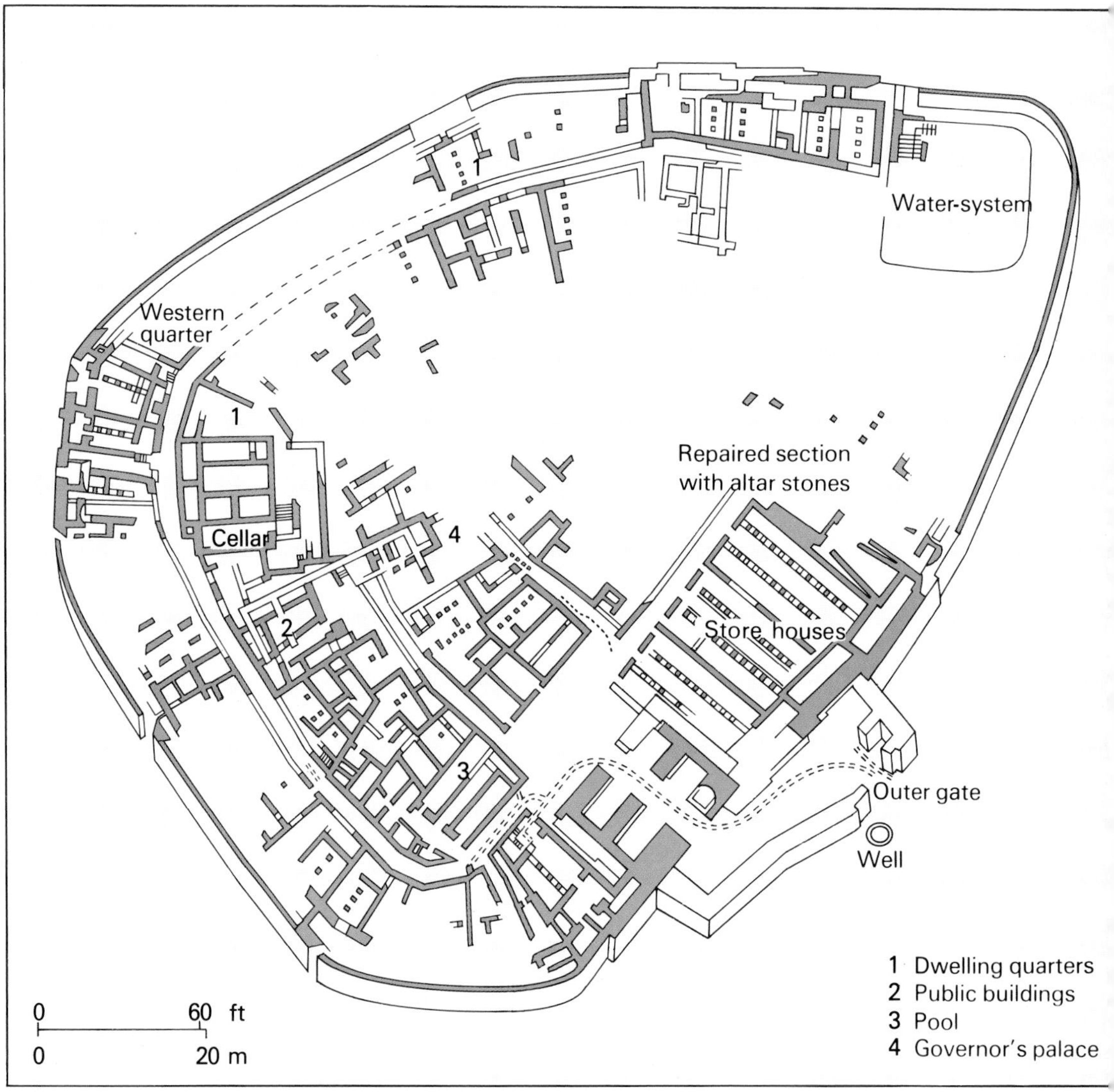


*The name*
The meaning of the name is given in Genesis 21:31, 'The well of seven' (*i.e.* lambs). The alternative interpretation, 'The well of the oath', arises through a misunderstanding of the use of the Hebrew word for 'therefore', which can refer only to an antecedent statement (Genesis 11:9 is not really an exception), and a mistranslation of the Hebrew particle *kî* by 'because', whereas it here introduces an independent temporal clause and should be rendered 'when', or even 'then'. The antecedent statement tells *why* it was done; this clause, *when* it was done. (For a similar use of *kî*, see Genesis 24:41; compare König, *Hebrew Syntax*, 387h.)

The explanation of the alleged second account of the naming of the well by Isaac (Genesis 26:33) is given in verse 18: 'And Isaac dug again the wells of water which had been dug in the days of Abraham his father; for the Philistines had stopped them after the death of Abraham; and he gave them the names which his father had given them.' Since the digging of a well was often a major achievement, filial respect alone would insist that the work of a great father would be thus remembered. In verse 33 the actual wording is: 'He called it Shibah.' The use here of the feminine of the numeral may merely express the numerical group, roughly equivalent to 'It, of the seven'.

*History*
Beersheba has many patriarchal associations. Abraham spent much time there (Genesis 22:19). It was probably a part of Palestine without an urban population, since the seasonal nature of the pasturage would not have been conducive to settled conditions. From here he set out to offer up Isaac. Isaac was dwelling here when Jacob set out for Harran (Genesis 28:10). On his way through to Joseph in Egypt, Jacob stopped here to offer sacrifices (Genesis 46:1). In the division of the land it went to the tribe of Simeon (Joshua 19:2).

In the familiar phrase 'from Dan to Beersheba' (Judges 20:1, *etc.*) it denoted the southernmost place of the land. The town owed its importance to its position on the trade-route to Egypt.

The reference to it in Amos (5:5 and 8:14) indicates that it had become a centre for undesirable religious activities.

Beersheba and its villages (Hebrew 'daughters') were resettled after the captivity (Nehemiah 11:27).

The place referred to by Josephus (*Jewish War* 2.573 and 3.39), which Winckler wanted to identify with the Beersheba of the Old Testament, was a village in lower Galilee (Josephus *Life* 5.188).

W. J. Martin, A. R. Millard

The excavated site of Tell es-Seba' (Tell Beersheba).

*urther reading*
J. Zimmerli, *Geschichte und radition von Beersheba im A. T.*, 932
. Aharoni, *Beer-sheba* 1, 1973
*el-Aviv*, 1, 1974, pp. 34–42; 2, 1975, p. 146–168
. Herzog and others, *Beer-Sheba II. he Early Iron Age Settlements*, 1984
. Herzog in *NEAEHL* I, pp. 167–173.

**EESHTERAH.** See *ASHTAROTH.

**ELA.** See *PLAIN, CITIES OF THE.

**ENE-BERAK.** A town in the rritory of Dan (Joshua 19:45), lentified with modern el-Kheirîyeh ormerly Ibn Ibrâq), about 6 ilometres east of Jaffa. According to ennacherib it was one of the cities elonging to Ashkelon besieged and aken by him (*DOTT*, p. 66; *ANET*, . 237).
D. Douglas

**ENE-JAAKAN.** A camping-ground f the Israelites (Numbers 33:31–32; euteronomy 10:6). Formally it is a ibal name and refers to one of the ans of Seir (1 Chronicles 1:42), which is a name for the mountainous egion west of Wadi Arabah. No iore exact location is possible, as ie section of the itinerary in umbers 33 in which it occurs could efer to one of a number of routes.
. I. Davies

*urther reading*
. R. Bartlett, *JTS* n.s. 20, 1969, p. 1–12

**ENJAMIN.** The tribe descended om Benjamin. The tribe occupied a trip of land in the passes between Iount Ephraim and the hills of udah. The boundary with Judah is early defined (Joshua 18:15ff.; compare 15:5ff.) and passed south of Jerusalem, which however became a Jebusite town until David captured it. Thence it ran to Kiriath-jearim, at one time in Benjamin (Joshua 18:28; RSV 'and' follows the Septuagint, but the text is unclear). Joshua 15:9 supports this, while identifying it with Baalah of Judah; Noth (*Josua*, 2nd edition, comment on 15:9) considers this a gloss, but it is repeated in Joshua 15:60 and 18:14, Judges 18:12 and 1 Chronicles 13:6; see also 1 Chronicles 2:50ff.

The northern border ran from Jericho to the north of *Ophrah, then roughly south-west to the ridges south of *Beth-horon, leaving Luz in Ephraim (but perhaps originally not the sanctuary of *Bethel; see Joshua 18:13).

Under the Divided Monarchy, 'Ephraim' (*i.e.* the northern kingdom) occupied Bethel and part of eastern Benjamin, but the border fluctuated; see 2 Chronicles 13:9. The western border is given as a straight line from Beth-horon to Kiriath-jearim, but there was settlement farther west (1 Chronicles 8:12–13).

With the capital established at Jerusalem, Benjamin was drawn close to Judah (1 Chronicles 8:28), and after the division Rehoboam retained its allegiance (1 Kings 12:21; 2 Chronicles 11; note 1 Kings 11:32, 'for the sake of Jerusalem').

There were two 'Benjamin' gates in the city, one in the Temple (Jeremiah 20:2), the other perhaps the same as the 'sheep gate' in the northern city wall (Jeremiah 37:13; Zechariah 14:10).

Despite the varying fortunes of war, Benjamin remained part of Judah (1 Kings 15:16ff.; 2 Kings 14:11ff.; see also 2 Kings 23:8, 'Geba').
J. P. U. Lilley

*Further reading*
Z. Kallai, *IEJ* 6, 1956, pp. 180–187
*GTT*, pp. 164ff., 170ff.
J. Bright, *History of Israel*, 2nd edition, 1972
J. Grønbaek, *VT* 15, 1965, pp. 421–436
K.-D. Schunk, *ZAW Suppl.* 86, 1963 (reviewed, *JBL* 83, 1964, p. 207)
M. Noth, *History of Israel*, 2nd edition, 1960

**BERACAH** (literally 'blessing'). A valley where Jehoshaphat and his people gave God thanks for the victory which they had gained over the Ammonites, Moabites and Edomites (2 Chronicles 20:26).

It is identified with Wadi Bereikūt between Jerusalem and Hebron, and west of Tekoa. The modern name suggests an earlier form which was pronounced slightly differently from that in the Hebrew text with the meaning 'water pool' (*berēḵâ*).
R. J. Way

**BEROEA, BEREA.** The modern Verria, a city of southern Macedonia probably founded in the 5th century BC. In New Testament times it was evidently a prosperous centre with a Jewish colony.

When Paul and Silas were smuggled out of Thessalonica to avoid Jewish opposition (Acts 17:5–11), they withdrew to Beroea, 80 kilometres away. It was off the major westward route, the Via Egnatia, and a suitable immediate refuge. Here they received a good hearing until the pursuit caught up with them. Beroea was the home of Sopater (Acts 20:4).
J. H. Paterson

**BETEN.** One of the towns of Asher listed in Joshua 19:25. Its location is uncertain. Eusebius's *Onomasticon*, calling it Bethseten, puts it 8 Roman miles east of Ptolemais (Acco). It may be the modern Abtûn, east of Mount Carmel.

The name may be preserved at Khirbet Ibtin, 18 kilometres south-east of Acco, but this site does not have remains from the appropriate periods. Nearby Tell el-Far has been suggested as the original site.

J. D. Douglas

**BETHABARA** (probably from the Hebrew *bêṯ ʿᵃḇārâ*, 'house of [the] ford'). This place is read in many Greek manuscripts at John 1:28 for *'Bethany beyond Jordan': hence it is found in the AV and RV margin. Origen preferred this reading while admitting that the majority of contemporary manuscripts were against him. He gives its etymology as 'house of preparation', which he associated with the Baptist's 'preparation'. In his day, he says, this place was shown as the place of John's baptism. It is probably the present Qasr el-Yehud, on the right bank of the Jordan, east of Jericho, where a monastery of St John stands.

J. N. Birdsall

*Further reading*

F. M. Abel, *Géographie de la Palestine* 2, 1938, pp. 264–265

Raymond F. Brown, *The Gospel according to John* (Anchor Bible), Vol. 1. *I-XII*, 1971, reprinted 1984, pp. 44f., 71f.

**BETH-ANATH** (Hebrew *bêṯ ʿᵃnāṯ*, 'temple of Anat'). Perhaps Safed el-Battikh, north-west of Galilee, and the *bt 'nt* listed by Seti I and Ramesses II. The city was allotted to Naphtali (Joshua 19:38); the original inhabitants were not expelled, but made tributary (Judges 1:33).

A. R. Millard

*Further reading*

*LOB*, pp. 220–221, 235–236

**BETH-ANOTH** (Hebrew *bêṯ ʿᵃnôṯ*, probably 'temple of Anat'). A conurbation (a city with its villages, Joshua 15:59) which was allotted to Judah. It is modern Beit 'Anûn, 6 kilometres north-north-east of Hebron.

J. D. Douglas

**BETHANY. 1.** A village on the farther side of the Mount of Olives, about 3 kilometres from Jerusalem on the road to Jericho. It is first mentioned in the gospels, especially as the home of Jesus' beloved friends, Mary, Martha and Lazarus; hence the modern Arabic name 'el-'Azariyeh. Its most central role in the gospel history is as the place of Jesus' anointing (Mark 14:3–9). Outside the gospels it figures largely in Christian itineraries, traditions and legends.

**2.** The place where John baptized 'beyond the Jordan' (John 1:28). Its identification remains uncertain. Already by the time of Origen (*c.* AD 250) it was unknown (see his *Commentary on John* 6:40, p. 157, ed. Brooke). Origen preferred the reading *Bethabara, since this place was known in his day and, moreover, this choice might in his opinion be corroborated by allegory. 'Bethany', however, should be accepted as the more difficult reading.

A recent suggestion is that this Bethany should be understood as the district of Batanaea (Old Testament Bashan), east of the Sea of Galilee and therefore 'beyond the Jordan'. This allows a coherent reading of John 1:19–2:12 by locating the whole series of events in the north. The suggestion does not conflict with Matthew 3:1ff. because John 1:32–34 merely alludes to Jesus' baptism and does not say it occurred in the same place. See R. Riesner, 'Bethany beyond the Jordan (John 1:28)', *TynB* 38, 1987, 26–63.

The mention of a place so soon unknown is frequently adduced as a token of knowledge of 1st-century Palestine by the Evangelist or his source.

J. N. Birdsall, J. Bimson

**BETH-ARBEL.** A city described (Hosea 10:14) as having been destroyed by Shalman in the 'day of battle'. (This may refer to the Assyrian king Shalmaneser V, 726–722 BC, or to Salamanu, a king of Moab mentioned in the annals of Tiglath-pileser III, 745–727 BC.) The name is known only from this reference, but it may be plausibly identified with modern Irbid, probably the Arbela of Eusebius, some 30 kilometres south-east of the Sea of Galilee.

T. C. Mitchell

*Further reading*

W. F. Albright, *BASOR* 35, 1929, p. 10

G. L. Harding, *The Antiquities of Jordan*, 1959, pp. 54–56

T. C. Mitchell in *CAH* III.1, p. 489

**BETH-AVEN** (Hebrew *bêṯ 'āwen*, 'house of iniquity'). Lying to the west of Michmash (1 Samuel 13:5) and possibly to be distinguished from the Beth-aven said to lie to the east of Bethel (Joshua 7:2). If these two are to be distinguished, it is impossible to be certain which is referred to as a northern boundary mark for Benjamin's allotment (Joshua 18:12). Tell Maryam, 12 kilometres north-east of Jerusalem, has been proposed as the site for at least one Beth-aven.

In Hosea (4:15; 5:8; 10:5) the name may be a derogatory synonym for *Bethel, 'House of the false (god)'.

R. J. Way

**BETH-DAGON** (Hebrew *bêṯ dāḡôn*). **1.** In the lowland of Judah south of *Azekah (Joshua 15:41).

**2.** In Asher, probably north-east of *Helkath (Joshua 19:27).

There were others; Bet Dagan by Tel Aviv, was taken by Sennacherib from Ashkelon (*ANET*, p. 287).

J. P. U. Lilley

*Further reading*

Kallai-Kleinmann, *VT* 8, 1958, pp. 153ff.

B. Mazar, *IEJ* 10, 1960, p. 72

**BETHEL.** Most scholars have identified Bethel with Tell Beitīn on the watershed route 19 kilometres north of Jerusalem.

*In the time of the Patriarchs*

Although traces of earlier occupation have been found, the place was fortified in the Middle Bronze Age. During this period, Abram camped to the east of Bethel where he built an altar to Yahweh (Genesis 12:8). After his visit to Egypt, he returned to this site (Genesis 13:3).

For Jacob, Bethel was the starting-point of his realization of God, who is for him 'God of Bethel' (Genesis 31:13; 35:7). As a result of his vision of Yahweh he named the place 'House of God' (Hebrew *bêṯ 'ēl*) and set up a pillar (Hebrew *maṣṣēḇâ*; Genesis 28:11–22). He was summoned to Bethel on his return from Harran, and both built an altar and set up a pillar, reiterating the name he had given before (Genesis 35:1–15). The site is perhaps Burǵ Beitīn, south-east of Tell Beitīn, the 'shoulder of Luz' (Joshua 18:13).

Excavations at Tell Beitīn yielded some Early Bronze Age traces, with, the excavator claimed, a blood-stained rock high place. This seems to be an improbable interpretation, and the claim that a Middle Bronze Age shrine replaced it is also dubious.

*From before the conquest to the judges*

The prosperous Middle Bronze Age city was destroyed about 1550 BC,

The village of Bethany, with the modern Greek Orthodox Church in the foreground.

The entrance to the traditional site of the tomb of Lazarus, Bethany.

d was followed after an interval by ell-built houses of Late Bronze II. nese in turn were sacked early in e twelfth century BC, and the bsequent Iron Age buildings arked a complete cultural change, hich the excavator related to the raelite conquest (Joshua 12:16; dges 1:22–26).

Bethel was allotted to the Joseph bes who captured it, particularly Ephraim (1 Chronicles 7:28), and rdered the territory of Benjamin oshua 18:13). The Israelites soon settled the town, calling it by the me Jacob had given to the scene of s vision instead of Luz (Judges 23).

When it was necessary for Israel to punish Benjamin, the people sought advice on the conduct of the battle and worshipped at Bethel 'for the ark . . . was there' (Judges 20:18–28; 21:1–4). It was a sanctuary, too, in the time of Samuel, who visited it annually (1 Samuel 7:16; 10:3).

The material remains of this period indicate an unsophisticated and insecure community. The settlement was twice burnt, possibly by the Philistines.

*In the time of kings and prophets*

Under the early monarchy the city prospered, presently becoming the centre of Jeroboam's rival cult, condemned by a man of God from Judah (1 Kings 12:28–13:32). The Judaean Abijah captured it (2 Chronicles 13:19), and his son, Asa, may have destroyed it (2 Chronicles 14:8).

Elisha met a group of the 'sons of the prophets' from Bethel but also the mocking boys (2 Kings 2:3, 23). Amos condemned the rites of the Israelite royal sanctuary (Amos 4:4; 5:5–6; 7:13; compare Hosea 10:15), and Jeremiah showed their futility (Jeremiah 48:13).

The priest sent to instruct the Assyrian settlers in Samaria settled at Bethel (2 Kings 17:28), and worship evidently continued there until Josiah took advantage of Assyrian weakness to invade Israel and destroy its sanctuaries.

No traces of Jeroboam's shrine have been unearthed; it may well have been outside the city proper on the site of the patriarchal altars.

In the 6th century BC the city was destroyed by fire.

*After the Exile*

Returning exiles settled in Bethel (Nehemiah 11:31), but their worship was centred on Jerusalem (Zechariah 7:2–3). The city grew during the Hellenistic period until it was fortified by Bacchides *c.* 160 BC (1 Maccabees 9:50). When Vespasian captured it in AD 69, there was a short break before it was rebuilt as a Roman township. It continued to flourish until the Arab conquest. (See also *BETH-AVEN.)

A. R. Millard

The twin pool north of the Temple area, near St Anne's Church, often identified with Bethesda.

*Further reading*
W. F. Albright and J. L. Kelso, 'The Excavation of Bethel (1934–60)', *AASOR* 39, 1968
D. L. Newlands, 'Sacrificial Blood at Bethel?' *PEQ* 104, 1972, p. 155
J. L. Kelso, *NEAEHL* I, pp. 192–194
For identification with modern Bireh, see D. Livingston, *WTJ* 33, 1970, pp. 20–44; 34, 1971, pp. 39–50; criticized by A. F. Rainey, *WTJ* 33, 1971, pp. 175–188, but see Livingston's reply, *WTJ* 34, 1971, pp. 39–50

**BETHESDA, BETHZATHA.** In the Received Text, the name of a Jerusalem pool (John 5:2), near the Sheep Gate; but there is textual uncertainty about the name itself and about its application. Various names occur in different manuscripts; many scholars take 'Bethzatha' (so RSV, JB, TEV) to be the best reading, though AV, RV, NASB, NEB and NIV accept the Received Text 'Bethesda'. ('Bethsaida', though well attested, is improbable on general grounds.) The name designates either the pool itself (RSV) or a building ('at the Sheep-Pool', NEB).

'Bethesda' may mean 'place (literally, "house") of mercy' (Aramaic *bêṯ ḥesdâ*), or else 'place of outpouring' (Hebrew *bêṯ 'ešdâ*). The latter possibility is enhanced by the occurrence of a dual form of the name in a Qumran document (*bêṯ 'ešdāṯayin*, 3Q15, paragraph 57); the reference is to a (twin) pool near the temple area. This linguistic evidence is the more interesting in view of the fact that Eusebius and the Bordeaux pilgrim speak of twin pools at Bethesda.

A twin pool north of the temple area was discovered in 1856 at St Anne's Church, and many have since identified it with the locale of John 5:2; remains of magnificent porticoes seem to have survived. However, the identification remains uncertain; other pools in the same general area have been proposed; and some scholars have thought the Pool of *Siloam a possibility. If so, the word *probatikē* cannot refer to the 'Sheep [Gate]', which lay north of the temple area; but other renderings are possible (compare, *e.g.*, NEB).
D. F. Payne

*Further reading*
J. Jeremias, *The Rediscovery of Bethesda*, E.T. 1966
A. Duprez, *Jésus et les Dieux Guérisseurs*, 1970
B. M. Metzger, *A Textual Commentary on the Greek New Testament*, 1971
and standard commentaries

**BETH-GILGAL.** See *GILGAL.

**BETH-HARAN** (Numbers 32:36, to be identified with Beth-aram, Joshua 13:27). This site formed part of the allotment of Gad, and so lay on the east of the Jordan. It was probably a border strong-point which the Gadites built (Numbers 32:36) or else an existing settlement which they fortified (Joshua 13:27) to protect themselves and their cattle. The settlement was in good pasture (Numbers 32:1) but in the valley (Joshua 13:27), and so lacked the security of hill fastnesses which those who crossed the river enjoyed.

It is identified with modern Tell Iktanû 12 kilometres north-east of the mouth of the Jordan.
R. J. Way

**BETH-HORON.** A Canaanite place-name meaning 'house of Hauron' (a Canaanite god of the underworld). Upper Beth-horon (Joshua 16:5) is modern Beit 'Ûr al-Fôqâ, 617 metres above sea-leve 16 kilometres north-west of Jerusalem, and Lower Beth-horon (Joshua 16:3) is Beit 'Ûr al-Taḥtâ, 40 metres above the sea and 2 kilometres farther north-west.

These towns were built by Sherah of the tribe of Ephraim (1 Chronicle 7:24). They were within the territo of this tribe, and one of them was assigned to the Levite family of Kohath (Joshua 21:22). They were rebuilt by Solomon (2 Chronicles 8:5 and fortified by the Jews after the Exile (Judith 4:4–5) and by Bacchides the Syrian general (1 Maccabees 9:50).

Upper and Lower Beth-horon controlled the valley of Aijalon, up which went one of the most important ancient routes between the maritime plain and the hill-country. Therefore many armie passed by these towns in biblical times, *e.g.* the Amorites and the pursuing Israelites under Joshua (Joshua 10:10–11), the Philistines (1 Samuel 13:18), and the Egyptian army of Shishak (according to his Karnak inscription), the Syrians under Seron (1 Maccabees 3:16, 24) and under Nicanor (1 Maccabees 7:39), both of whom Judas defeate at Beth-horon, and the Romans under Cestius (Josephus, *Jewish War* 2.516).

Sanballat may have been a nativ of Beth-horon (Nehemiah 2:10). Pseudo-Epiphanius, in *The Lives o the Prophets*, states that Daniel wa born in Upper Beth-horon.
J. Thompson

*Further reading*
E. Robinson, *Biblical Researches in Palestine* 2, 1874, pp. 250–253
G. A. Smith, *Historical Geography c the Holy Land*, 1931, pp. 248–250, 287–292
F. M. Abel, *Géographie de la Palestine* 2, 1938, pp. 274–275

**BETH-JESHIMOTH** (Hebrew *bêṯ hayšimôṯ*, 'house of the deserts', AV 'Jesimoth'). A place near the north-eastern shore of the Dead Se in the plains of Moab (Numbers 33:49; Ezekiel 25:9), allocated by Moses to the tribe of Reuben (Joshu 13:20). Eusebius places it 16 kilometres south-east of Jericho, an Josephus (*Jewish War* 4.438) mentions it by its Greek name *Bēsimōth* (the nearby Khirbet
**Continued on p. 70**

# BETHLEHEM

**ETHLEHEM** (Hebrew *bêṯ leḥem*, ouse of bread', the latter word obably in the wider sense, 'food'). has been suggested that the final ord *leḥem* is Lakhmu, an Assyrian eity; but there is no evidence that is god was ever revered in alestine. There are two towns of e name in the Old Testament, both day given the Arabic name Bayt ahm, the exact equivalent of the ebrew.

**1.** The famed city of David, as it ame to be styled. It lies 9 kilometres outh of Jerusalem. Its earlier name as Ephrath (Genesis 35:19), and it as known as Bethlehem Judah, or ethlehem Ephrathah, to stinguish it from the other city of e same name. Rachel's tomb was ear it; David's ancestors lived there; the Philistines placed a garrison there; and the Messiah was destined to be born there.

Jesus was accordingly born there, and the stories of the shepherds and the Magi centre upon it. Bethlehem's population in the reign of Herod was probably a few hundred (estimates range between 300 and 1,000) and the number of children killed on Herod's orders (Matthew 2:16) cannot have been more than about twenty.

Bethlehem suffered at the hands of Hadrian in the 2nd century AD. All Jews were expelled from it and it seems that the site of the nativity grotto was lost for two centuries; so the Church of the Nativity erected by Helena in the reign of Constantine may or may not mark the true site. It is clear from archaeological finds, however, that the caves beneath the church were part of a complex used for stalls and storage space in the 1st century.

**2.** The second Bethlehem lay in Zebulunite territory (Joshua 19:15); it is 11 kilometres north-west of Nazareth. Most scholars think the judge Ibzan (Judges 12:8) was a resident of it, but ancient tradition favours Bethlehem Judah.

D. F. Payne, J. Bimson

*Further reading*

V. Tzaferis and M. Avi-Yonah in *NEAEHL* I, pp. 204–210

R. T. France, *NovT* 21, 1979, pp. 114–115

**An old entrance in Bethlehem, beside the Church of the Nativity.**

**Modern Bethlehem viewed from the roof of the Church of the Nativity.**

**Continued from p. 68**
Sueimeh), captured by the Roman tribune Placidus during the Jewish revolt. A well and some ruins (Tell el-'Azeimeh) remain.
N. Hillyer

**BETH-MARCABOTH** (Hebrew *bêṯ hammarkāḇôṯ*, 'house of chariots'). A part of the allotment to Simeon (Joshua 19:5; 1 Chronicles 4:31). The site is uncertain but, being connected with Ziklag and Hormah, was probably a strong-point on the Judaean-Philistine border. The partly duplicate list in Joshua 15:31 replaces it with Madmannah, perhaps indicating that the two names refer to the same place.

The name suggests that the settlement may have been a Canaanite arsenal in the days of the conquest. The possession of chariots by the Canaanites prevented the unmounted Hebrew soldiers from entirely occupying the land (Judges 19).
R. J. Way

**BETH-NIMRAH** ('House of pure water' or 'House of leopard'). A city in Gad (Numbers 32:36), probably equalling Nimrah (Numbers 32:3) and Nimrim (Isaiah 15:6; Jeremiah 48:34), it was called Betham-Naram by Eusebius, who located it 8 kilometres north of Livias.

It is possibly either modern Tell Nimrin beside the Wadi Shaîb or nearby Tell Bileibil, some 24 kilometres east of Jericho.
G. W. Grogan

**BETH-PELET.** A town located in the south of Judah, near Beersheba and 'toward the boundary of Edom' (Joshua 15:21, 27). It was reoccupied after the Babylonian exile (Nehemiah 11:26). Its location is unknown. (Petrie's identification of Beth-pelet with the site of Tell el-Fara South is no longer acceptable.)
J. Bimson

**BETH-PEOR** (lit. 'Temple of Peor').

A place in the hill country in the land of Moab (Joshua 13:20) or of the Amorites (Deuteronomy 4:46), to the east of Jordan, which was part of Reubenite territory.

The historical framework of Deuteronomy describes the Hebrews gathering at Mount Pisgah near to Beth-peor to receive their final exhortation before going over into the Promised Land (Deuteronomy 3:29; 4:44–46). Having repeated the law to the immigrants, Moses died, and was buried nearby (Deuteronomy 34:5–6).

Beth-peor may be near, or even the same as, Peor, where Balaam built seven altars (Numbers 23:28). Numbers 25:1–5 mentions the worship of a god Baal Peor (Lord of Peor) by the Moabites. The site is uncertain. Eusebius places it 10 kilometres east of Livias on the road to Esbus (Heshbon); either Khirbet esh-Sheikh Jayel or Khirbet el-Meḥatta would fit this information.
R. J. Way

**BETHPHAGE** (in Aramaic 'place of young figs'). A village on the Mount of Olives, on or near the road from Jericho to Jerusalem and near Bethany (Matthew 21:1; Mark 11:1; Luke 19:29). Its site is unknown but some favour a location 1 kilometre east of the summit of the Mount of Olives, where finds attest occupation between the 2nd century BC and 8th century AD.

See *ZPEB*, p. 112.
J. W. Meiklejohn, J. Bimson

**BETH-REHAB.** See *REHOB.

**BETH-SAIDA.** A town on the northern shores of Galilee, near the Jordan. The name is Aramaic, meaning 'house of fishing' (if *bêṯ ṣaydâ*) or else 'fisherman's house' (if *bêṯ ṣayyāḏâ*). Philip the tetrarch rebuilt it and gave it the name Julias, in honour of Julia the daughter of Augustus.

Pliny and Jerome tell us that Beth-saida was on the east of the Jordan. The site of et-Tell, 3·2 kilometres north of the Sea of Galilee, is most probably the acropolis of Beth-saida-Julius. Excavations have uncovered extensive remains from the New Testament period. An ancient road connected this city with a fishing village at el-Araj, a partly-submerged lakeside settlement which may have been a suburb of the larger town sharing the name Beth-saida. The reference in Mark 8:23 to the *village* of Beth-saida may therefore be to the el-Araj settlement.

A further complication is that in Mark 6:45 the disciples were sent from east of the Jordan to Beth-saida, towards Capernaum (see John 6:17); hence a third Beth-saida has been postulated west of the Jordan – perhaps to be located at 'Ayn al-Tabigha. This is also claimed to be Beth-saida 'of Galilee' (John 12:21), since the political division Galilee did not extend east of the Jordan. But this is unlikely; 'Galilee' is not necessarily used in its political sense here, but i its less formal, geographical sense. suburb of Julias on the west bank may suit Mark 6:45 best; Capernaum was not far away.

Another suggestion is that in Ne Testament times the Jordan followed a different course, so that the el-Araj village stood to the wes of its debouchment.
D. F. Payne, J. Bimson

**BETHSHEAN, BETHSHAN.** A city situated at the important junction o the Valley of *Jezreel with the Jordan valley. The name occurs in the Bible as *bêṯ š$^{e}$'ān* (Joshua 17:11 16; Judges 1:27; 1 Kings 4:12; 1 Chronicles 7:29) and *bêṯ šan* (1 Samuel 31:10, 12; 2 Samuel 21:12), but there is little doubt that both names refer to the same place. The name is preserved in that of the modern village of Beisân, adjacent t which stands Tell el-Ḥosn, the site o the ancient city, which was excavate under the direction of C. S. Fisher (1921–23), A. Rowe (1925–28) and G. M. Fitzgerald (1930–33) and mo recently under Y. Yadin (1983) and A. Mazar (1989–).

*A Canaanite city*
Though a deep sounding was mad revealing settlements of the 4th millennium and an important Canaanite city of the Early Bronze Age, the main excavations were devoted to the nine upper levels which extended from the 14th century BC to Islamic times.

*An Egyptian outpost*
During much of the earlier part of th period, Bethshean was an Egyptian fortified outpost. Already in the 15th century Tuthmosis III mentions it a under his control (scarabs bearing his name were found there), and in the following century one of the Amarna letters speaks of reinforcements sent to garrison *bît-sa-a-ni* o behalf of Egypt.

The earliest main level (IX) probably belongs to this century (th levels have been redated on the basis of pottery sequence, since the original dates of the excavators relied on less certain criteria), and i this an extensive temple dedicated to 'Mekal, the Lord (Ba'al) of Bethshan' was uncovered, in which were found the remains of a sacrificed 3-year-old bull.

Level VIII was comparatively unimportant, dating from about the beginning of the 13th century, but a this time Sethos (Seti) I was seekin to restore Egyptian control in Asia, which had been largely lost under

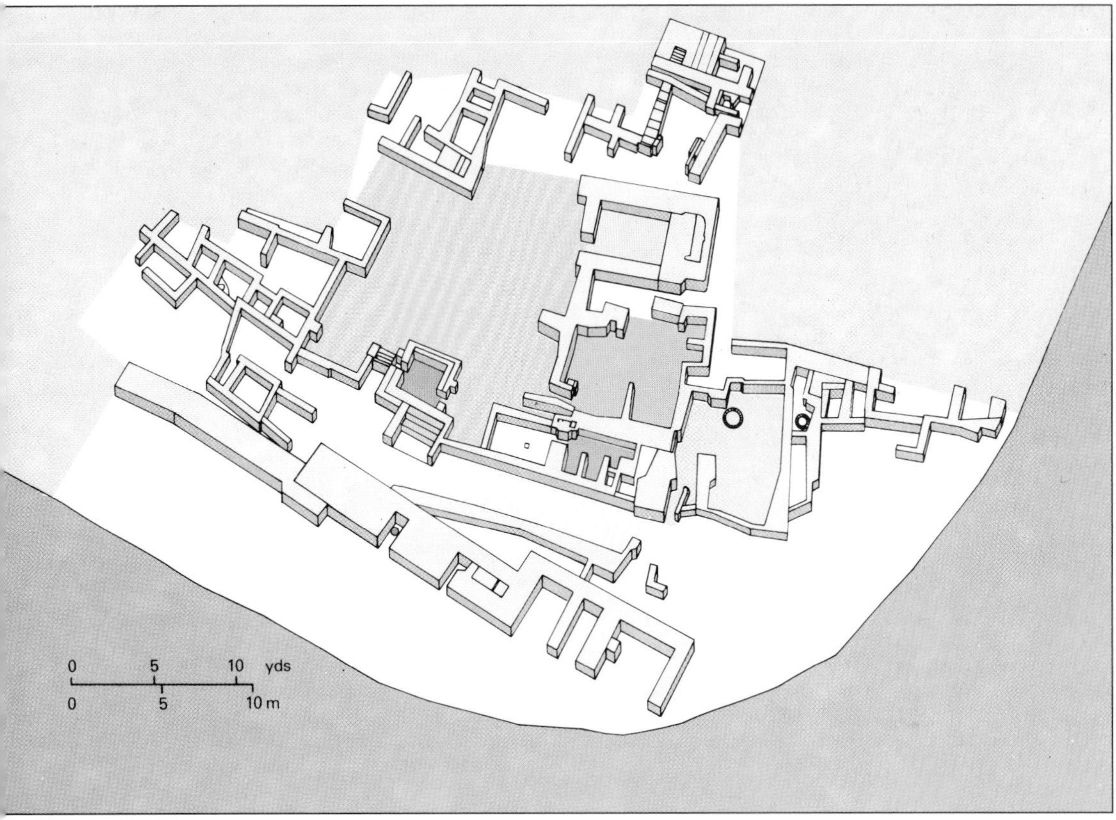


Plan of the temple (level IX) dedicated to 'Mekal, the Lord (Ba'al) of Bethshan'.

| |
|---|
| Altar court |
| Inner court |
| Entrance corridor |
| Inner courts |
| Room with oven and well |
| Room north of the sanctuary |
| Altar (or steps to the roof?) |
| Guard room |
| Water reservoir and well ● |

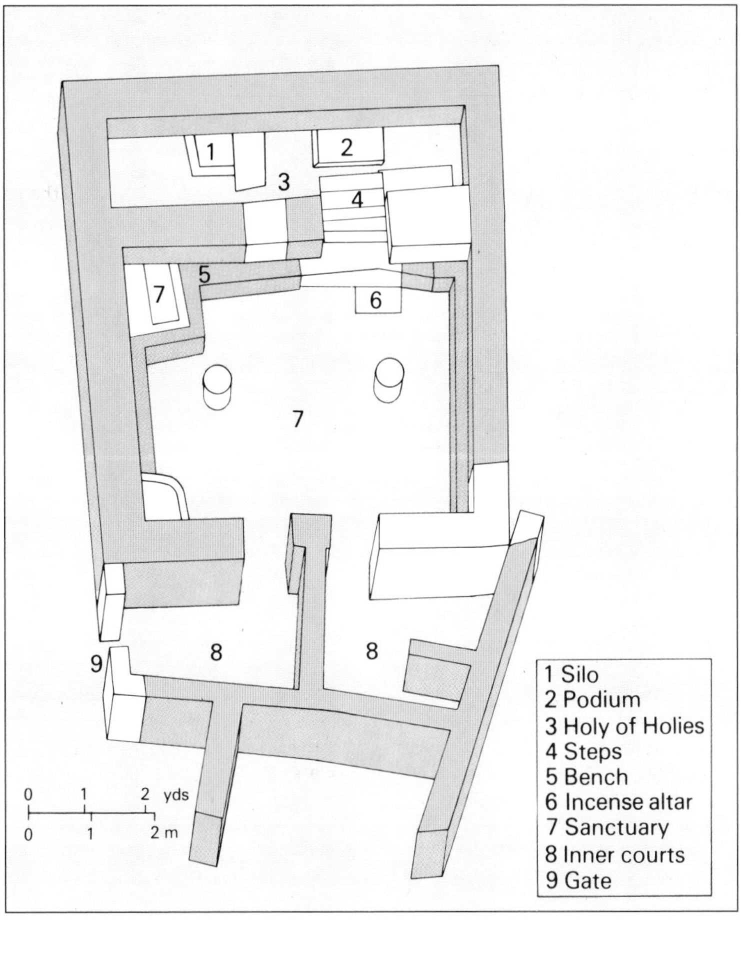


Plan of the temple, level VII, Bethshean.

he later kings of the 18th Dynasty, ınd in his first year he retook 3ethshean. Two of his royal stelae ıave been found there, one of them ecording that he had a clash near by vith the *'pr.w* (Hebrews).

Level VII (*c.* 13th century) contained ı temple in which was found a stela lepicting a goddess with a two-ıorned head-dress (Ashteroth-‹arnaim). In level VI a similar temple vas uncovered. This level probably lates to the 12th century, the time of Ramesses III, of whom a statue was ound there. The discovery in the city emetery of anthropoid clay coffins uggests the presence of an Egyptian garrison, some of the coffins showing ossible feather headdresses, erhaps indicating *Philistine nercenaries among them.

*n Philistine control*

f the 13th-century BC date for the

View of the ruin-mound of Bethshean (Tell el-Ḥosn). Height of mound 80 metres.

Exodus is correct, it was not long before this that the Israelites had arrived in Palestine, and Manasseh, being allotted Bethshean (Joshua 17:11), found it too formidable to take (Joshua 17:16; Judges 1:27), so that it remained in hostile hands until the time of David. Its importance at this time is suggested by the fact that the Bible refers to it as Bethshan 'and her daughters' (*i.e.* dependent villages).

It was still in Philistine hands at the time of Saul, for it was upon its walls that his body and those of his sons were hung, and from which the men of Jabesh-gilead recovered them (1 Samuel 31:10, 12).

In level V (*c.* 10th century) two temples were uncovered, one (the southern temple) dedicated to the god Resheph and the other to the goddess Antit, and Rowe has suggested that these are the temples of Dagon and Ashteroth in which Saul's head and armour were displayed by the Philistines (1 Chronicles 10:10; 1 Samuel 31:10).

*Captured by David*

The city must have fallen finally to the Israelites in the time of David, and the excavations have revealed little material settlement (level IV) from then until the Hellenistic Period (level III). During this time it is mentioned with its environs ('all of Bethshean', *kol-bêṯ š$^e$ān*) as belonging to Solomon's fifth administrative district (1 Kings 4:12), and in the reign of Rehoboam (1 Kings 14:25) Sheshonq (Shishak) claimed it among his conquests.

*A Greek city*

The city was refounded as the Hellenistic centre of Scythopolis, and this later became a part of the *Decapolis.

T. C. Mitchell

*Further reading*

A. Rowe, *Beth-shan* 1, *The Topography and History of Beth-shan*, 1930; 2, i, *The Four Canaanite Temples of Beth-shan*, 1940; with which see G. E. Wright, *AJA* 45, 1941, pp. 483–485
G. M. Fitzgerald, *Beth-shan* 2, ii, 1930; 3, 1931
——, *ANET*, pp. 242, 249, 253
J. Knudtzon, *Die El-Amarna Tafeln* 1, 1907, pp. 874f., no. 289.20; 2, 1915, p. 1343 (*ANET*, p. 489)
W. F. Albright, 'The Smaller Beth-Shan Stele of Sethos I (1309–1290 BC)', *BASOR* 125, 1952, pp. 24–32
G. Posener in J. Bottéro, *Le Problème des Habiru*, 1954, p. 168 (*ANET*, p. 255)
G. E. Wright, *BA* 22, 1959, pp. 53–56, 65
On anthropoid coffins: A. Mazar, *Archeology of the Land of the Bible 10000–586 BCE*, New York, 1990, pp. 283–285, 327
A. Mazar and G. Foerster in *NEAEHL* I, pp. 214–235
Vogel, *HUCA* 42, 1971, pp. 18–19; 52, 1981, p. 18; 58, 1987, p. 11
Y. Yadin and S. Geva, *Investigations at Beth Shean: The Early Iron Age Strata* (*Qedem* 23), Jerusalem, 1986

**BETH-SHEMESH** (Hebrew *bêṯ šemeš*, 'house [temple] of the sun'), a name applied to four places in the Bible. **1.** An important city of Judah (2 Kings 14:11; 2 Chronicles 25:21) on its northern border with Dan (Joshua 15:10), situated in a western-facing valley of the hill-country some 24 kilometres west of Jerusalem and consequently commanding a route from the uplands to the coast plain. The site is probably to be identified with modern Tell er-Rumeileh, situated on the saddle of a hill spur to the west of the later settlement of 'Ain Shems.

*Early history*

Excavations were conducted in 1911–12, 1928–32, and 1971–73. Th site was first settled near the end of the Early Bronze Age, some time before 2000 BC, and flourished as a strongly fortified Canaanite city throughout the Middle and Late Bronze Ages, reaching its zenith in the time of the Egyptian dominatior under the pharaohs of Dynasty 19.

Connections with the north are illuminated by the discovery in the Late Bronze Age levels of a clay tablet inscribed in the cuneiform alphabet of *Ugarit (Ras Shamra).

The close of the Bronze Age is marked by quantities of Philistine pottery, showing that these people, who settled initially along the coast also established themselves well inland, where they became the chie rivals of the newly arrived Israelites

*In the time of the Judges*

The city must have been taken by the Israelites in the period of the Judges, as it was set aside as a levitical city (Joshua 21:16; 1 Chronicles 6:59), and was certainly in their hands by the time of Samuel for thither the captured ark came when the Philistines released it (1 Samuel 6).

*During the monarchy*

It is probable that David strengthened this city in the later phases of his struggle with the Philistines, and it is likely that the casemate walls discovered there date from this period.

There is evidence that the city was destroyed in the 10th century, probably at the hands of the Egyptian king Shishak, who invade Judah in Rehoboam's fifth year (1 Kings 14:25–28).

About a century after this, Beth-shemesh was the scene of the great victory of Joash of Israel over Amaziah of Judah (2 Kings 14:11–13; 2 Chronicles 25:21–23). In the reign of Ahaz, Beth-shemesh was with other cities again taken by the Philistines (2 Chronicles 28:18), but they were driven out by Tiglath-pileser III, to whom Ahaz had appealed and of whom Judah now became a vassal.

Life in the city during the period of the monarchy was illuminated by the discovery of a refinery for olive-oil and installations for copper-working, which last had already existed in the Bronze Age. The city was now in decline, however, and it was finally destroyed by Nebuchadrezzar in the 6th century BC.

It is probable that Ir-Shemesh, 'city [of] the sun' (Joshua 19:41), is to be [e]quated with Beth-shemesh.

*[F]urther reading*
. Mackenzie, 'Excavations at Ain [S]hems', *Annual Report of the [P]alestine Exploration Fund* 1, 1911, [p]p. 41–94; 2, 1912–13, pp. 1–100
. Grant (and G. E. Wright), *Ain [S]hems Excavations* 1–5, 1931–39
. Bunimovitz and Z. Lederman in [N]*EAEHL* I, pp. 249–253
. A. Emerton, *AOTS*, pp. 197–206
[A]lbright, *BASOR* 173, 1964, pp. 51ff. [(t]ablet)
[V]ogel, *HUCA* 42, 1971, p. 21; 52, [1]981, pp. 18–19; 58, 1987, p. 12

**2.** A city on the border of Issachar [(J]oshua 19:22), from which the [C]anaanites were not driven out, but [b]ecame tributary to the Israelites [(J]udges 1:33). It is perhaps to be [id]entified with modern el-ʻAbēdîyeh, [w]hich commands a ford over the [J]ordan some 3 kilometres south of [th]e Sea of Galilee.

*[F]urther reading*
[A]. Saarisalo, *The Boundary between [I]ssachar and Naphtali*, 1927, [p]p. 71–73, 119f.
[A]haroni, *LOB*, p. 432

**3.** A fortified city allotted to [N]aphtali (Joshua 19:38), whose site [i]s unknown, unless it is to be [id]entified with **2.**

**4.** A city in Egypt (Jeremiah 43:13) [p]robably to be identified with [H]eliopolis (which is here given in the [R]SV and NRSV) (See also *On).
. C. Mitchell

**[B]ETH-SHITTAH** (Hebrew *bêṯ šiṭṭâ*, '[h]ouse of [the] acacia'). A town near [A]bel-meholah, to which the [M]idianites fled from Gideon (Judges [7]:22). No definitive identification has [y]et been made but there are two [s]uggestions: Shatta, 8 kilometres [n]orth-west of Bethshan, and Tell [S]leihat, east of the Jordan.
D. Douglas, J. Bimson

**[B]ETH-TOGARMAH.** During the 2nd [m]illennium BC Old Assyrian and [H]ittite texts locate Tegarama near [C]archemish and Harran on a main [tr]ade-route. It was called Til-garimmu [i]n the Annals of Sargon and [S]ennacherib, and was the capital of [K]ammanu on the border of Tabal (see [a]lso *Tubal), until destroyed in 695 BC. [I]t is perhaps to be identified with [c]lassical Gauraena, modern Gürün, [1]20 kilometres west of Malatya.
. J. Wiseman

**BETHZATHA.** See *Bethesda.

**BETH-ZUR** (Hebrew *bêṯ ṣûr*). A city in Judah (Joshua 15:58), not mentioned in the account of the conquest, but settled by the descendants of Caleb the son of Hezron (1 Chronicles 2:45). It was fortified by Rehoboam in the 10th century (2 Chronicles 11:7), was of some importance in the time of Nehemiah (3:16), and was a strategic fortified city during the Maccabean wars (1 Maccabees).

*Excavations*
The name is preserved at the site called Burj eṣ-Ṣur, but the ancient city is represented today by the neighbouring mound of Khirbet eṭ-Ṭubeiqah, about 6 kilometres north of Hebron. The site was identified in 1924, and in 1931 an American expedition under the direction of O. R. Sellers and W. F. Albright carried out preliminary excavations, which, due to the troubled times, were not resumed until 1957, when a further season was undertaken under Sellers.

*In the Bronze Age*
There was little settlement on the site until Middle Bronze Age II (*c.* 19th-16th century BC), in the latter part of which the Hyksos are thought to have dominated Palestine, and it is perhaps to them that a system of massive defensive walls on the slope of the mound is to be attributed.

When the Egyptians finally expelled the Hyksos from Egypt, Beth-zur was destroyed and largely abandoned, and it evidently remained so throughout the Late Bronze Age (*c.* 1550–1200) and therefore offered no resistance to the armies of Joshua, as indicated by its absence from the conquest narratives.

*After the conquest*
The Israelites evidently settled in Beth-zur, for in the 12th and 11th centuries the city was flourishing, though the population seems to have declined towards the end of the 10th century. No certain evidence of Rehoboam's fortifications has come to light, so it may be that he reused the Middle Bronze Age walls and stationed only a small garrison there.

The site was occupied throughout the Monarchy, abandoned during the Exile and resettled in the Persian period.

*The Hellenistic period*
Its zenith of importance came during the Hellenistic period. It was then a garrison city commanding the Jerusalem-Hebron road at the boundary between Judaea and Idumaea, and figured prominently in the Maccabean wars.

A large fortress was uncovered on the summit, in which were found a great number of coins, including many of Antiochus IV Epiphanes, and several stamped Rhodian jar handles, indicating that it had been garrisoned by Greek troops.

The fort had seen three main phases, the second probably due to Judas Maccabaeus, who fortified it after having defeated Antiochus' deputy Lysias there (1 Maccabees 4:26–34, 61), and the third probably to be ascribed to the Macedonian general Bacchides, who fortified it around 161 BC (1 Maccabees 9:52).
T. C. Mitchell

*Further reading*
O. R. Sellers, *The Citadel of Beth-zur*, 1933
*The 1957 Excavations at Beth-zur*, 1968
W. F. Albright, *The Archaeology of Palestine*, revised edition, 1960, *passim*, especially pp. 150–152
F. M. Abel, *Géographie de la Palestine* 2, 1938, p. 283
R. W. Funk in *NEAEHL* I, pp. 259–261
Vogel, *HUCA* 42, 1971, p. 22; 52, 1981, p. 19; 58, 1987, p. 12

**BEZER.** See *Bozrah.

**BILEAM.** See *Ibleam.

**BITHYNIA.** A territory on the Asiatic side of the Bosporus, bequeathed by its last king to the Romans in 74 BC and subsequently administered with Pontus as a single province. The area was partitioned between a number of flourishing Greek republics.

Bithynia early attracted the attention of Paul (Acts 16:7), though he apparently never fulfilled his ambition of preaching there. Others did so, however (1 Peter 1:1), and by AD 111 there was a thoroughly well-established church, even extending to rural areas, which had excited a good deal of local opposition (Pliny, *Letters* 10.96).
E. A. Judge

*Further reading*
B. F. Harris, 'Bithynia: Roman Sovereignty and the Survival of Hellenism', *ANRW* II.7.1, 1980, pp. 857–901

**BLOOD, FIELD OF.** See *Akeldama.

**BOZEZ.** See *Seneh.

***Opposite:*** **Part of the ancient theatre, Caesarea.**

**BOZRAH. 1.** A city of Edom whose early king was Jobab (Genesis 36:33; 1 Chronicles 1:44). Its later overthrow was predicted by Amos (1:12) and taken as symbolic of the defeat of powerful Edom and of God's avenging all his enemies (Isaiah 34:6; 63:1).

Bozrah is usually identified with modern Buseirah, a fortified city of 7·6 hectares atop a crag at the head of the Wadi Hamayideh, *c.* 60 kilometres north of Petra and *c.* 40 kilometres south-south-east of the Dead Sea, controlling the *King's Highway from Elath and thus able to deny passage to the Israelites (Numbers 20:17).

Excavations at Buseirah 1971–76 have uncovered three principal levels of occupation in the 8th century BC and later, though not as yet earlier (C. Bennett, *Levant* 5, 1973, pp. 1–11; 6, 1974, pp. 1–24; R. Reich in *NEAEHL* I, pp. 264–266).

**2.** A city of Moab (Jeremiah 48:24; Septuagint 'Bosor'), perhaps to be identified with Bezer, a town rebuilt by king Mesha *c.* 830 BC, possibly Umm al-'Amad, north-east of Medeba, used as a levitical city of refuge.

**3.** A town of south-east Hauran, *c.* 120 kilometres south of Damascus at the head of the King's Highway, captured by Judas Maccabaeus (165–160 BC; 1 Maccabees 5:26–28; Josephus, *Antiquities* 12.336). Bozrah (modern Busra eski-Sham, and probably the Busruna [Bozrah] of the 14th century BC *Amarna texts) became the most northerly provincial capital of Roman Arabia in New Testament times.

D. J. Wiseman

# C

**CABUL.** The name of a border city in the tribal allocation of Asher (Joshua 19:27), situated 16 kilometres north-east of Carmel. The ironic use in 1 Kings 9:13 probably rests on a popular etymology signifying 'as nothing' (Hebrew $k^{e}$*ḇal*), but possibly Cabul was the chief town of the area, or the border post between Tyrian and Israelite territory.

Modern Kabul preserves the name, but the biblical town probably lay 1·5 kilometres to the north-east at Khirbet Ras ez-Zeitun, where excavations have revealed an early Iron Age town of some 2 hectares.

J. A. Motyer, J. Bimson

*Further reading*
G. W. van Beek, 'Cabul' in *IDB*
*LOB*, pp. 275, 277 n. 51
Z. Gal, *ZDPV* 101, 1985, pp.114–127

**CAESAREA.** This magnificent city, built by Herod the Great on the site of Strato's Tower, stood on the Mediterranean shore 37 kilometres south of Mount Carmel and about 100 kilometres north-west of Jerusalem. Named in honour of the Roman emperor Caesar Augustus, it was the Roman metropolis of Judaea and the official residence both of the Herodian kings and the Roman procurators.

*The city*
Caesarea stood on the great caravan route between Tyre and Egypt, and was thus a busy commercial centre for inland trade. But the city was also a celebrated maritime trading-centre, due largely to the construction of elaborate stone breakwaters north and south of the harbour. A vault discovered in the Caesarea harbour complex has yielded late 3rd century AD Mithraic material. An aqueduct section uncovered in 1974 revealed another legionary inscription, adding to two others previously known. The Caesarea Porphyry statue is thought to represent Hadrian.

The city was lavishly adorned with palaces, public buildings and an enormous amphitheatre. One outstanding architectural feature was a huge temple dedicated to Caesar and Rome, and containing vast statues of the emperor. Traces of this ruin can still be seen south of the site of Kaisarieh on the Plain of Sharon.

Like other New Testament Mediterranean communities, Caesarea had a mixed population, making for inevitable clashes between Jews and Gentiles. When Pilate was procurator of Judaea he occupied the governor's residence in Caesarea. An inscription mentioning Pontius Pilate and the emperor Tiberius was uncovered in 1959 by Italian excavators.

*In the New Testament*
Philip, the evangelist and deacon, brought Christianity to his home city, and subsequently entertained Paul and his companions (Acts 21:8)

**The reconstructed Roman theatre, Caesarea, with the Mediterranean Sea in the background.**

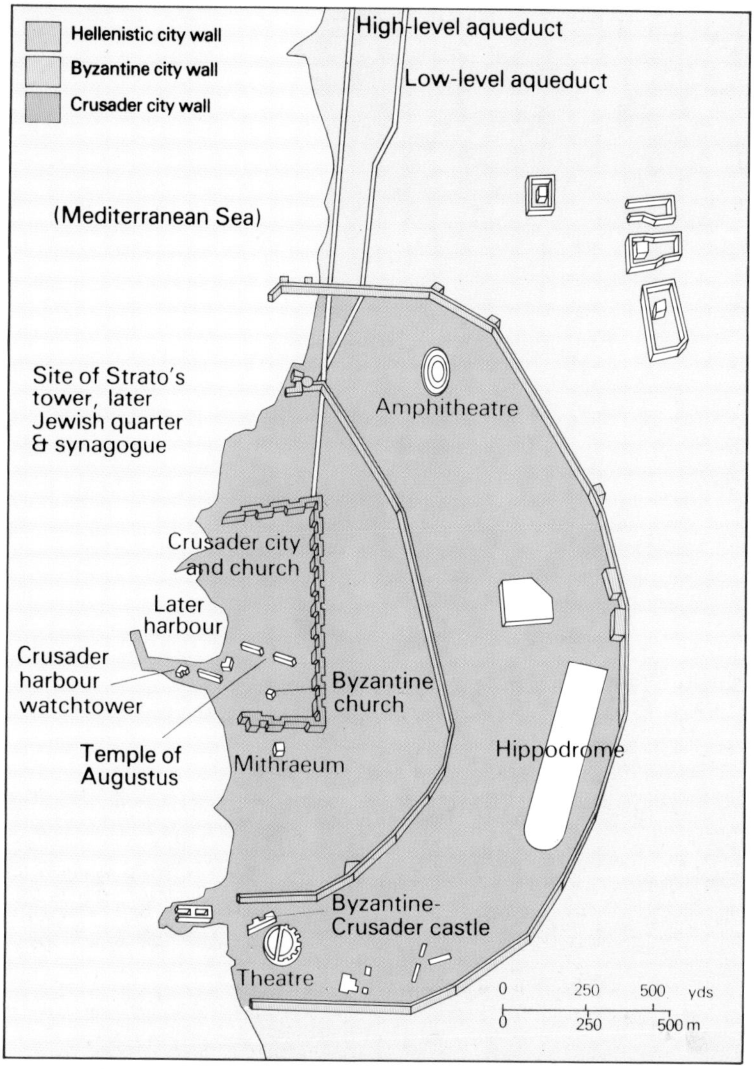


Caesarea: plan of the ancient city.

Paul departed from Caesarea on his way to Tarsus, having escaped his Jewish enemies in Damascus (Acts 9:30). Caesarea was the abode of the centurion Cornelius and the locale of his conversion (Acts 10:1, 24; 11:11). At Caesarea Peter gained greater insight into the nature of the divine kingdom by realizing that God had disrupted the barriers between Gentile and Jewish believers (Acts 10:35), and had dispensed with such classifications as 'clean' and 'unclean'.

Paul landed at Caesarea when returning from his second and third missionary journeys (Acts 18:22; 21:8). Paul's fateful decision to visit Jerusalem was made here also (Acts 21:13), and it was to Caesarea that he was sent for trial by Felix (Acts 23:23–33) before being imprisoned for 2 years. Paul made his defence before Festus and Agrippa in Caesarea, and sailed from there in chains when sent by Festus to Rome on his own appeal (Acts 25:11).

R. K. Harrison

*Further reading*

A. Negev, *IEJ* 22, 1972, pp. 52f., pl. 8
A. Negev and others in *NEAEHL* I, pp. 220–291
L. I. Levine, *Caesarea under Roman Rule*, 1975
——, *Roman Caesarea: An Archaeological-Topographical Study*, 1975
C. T. Fritsch (ed.), *Studies in the History of Caesarea Maritima* 1, 1975
A. Raban, *IEJ* 34, 1984, pp. 274–276
R. L. Vann, *BARev* IX/3, 1983, pp. 10–14

Section of the high-level aqueduct at Caesarea Maritima, built by King Herod.

**AESAREA PHILIPPI.** Caesarea
nilippi has a beautiful locality at the
ɔot of Mount Hermon, on the main
ɔurce of the river Jordan. It is famed
s the place of Peter's confession
Matthew 16:13ff.).

It may be the Old Testament
aal-gad. Baal was the deity
vorshipped there in Old Testament
mes; the Greeks later substituted
neir god Pan, and the town took the
ame Paneas, the shrine itself being
alled Panion. When the Seleucid
uler Antiochus III wrested Palestine
together with the whole of
'oelesyria) from the Ptolemies,
'aneas was the scene of one of the
ecisive battles (200 BC).

Herod the Great built a marble
emple to Augustus Caesar, who had
iven him the town; and Philip the
etrarch later in the same emperor's
eign further adorned the town,
enaming it Caesarea in the
mperor's honour. The addition
Philippi' – *i.e.* of Philip – was to
istinguish it from the coastal
Caesarea (see Acts 8:40). Agrippa II
hen rebuilt the town in Nero's reign,
nd gave it another name, Neronias;
ut this name was soon forgotten.

The town had a considerable
istory in Crusader times. Its ancient
ame persists as Banias today.
'here is a shrine there to the Muslim
l-Khidr, equated with St George.

). F. Payne

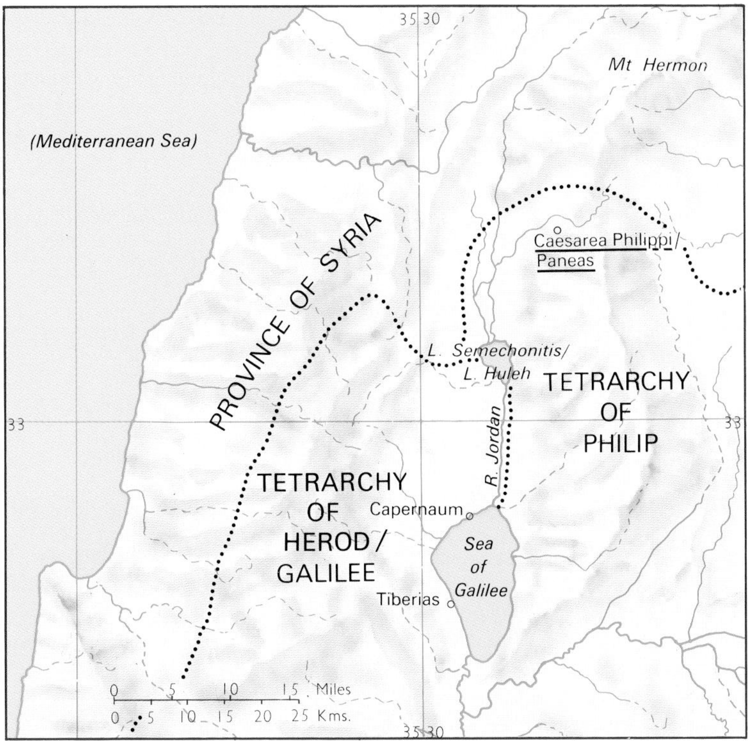


Caesarea Philippi, on the main source of the river Jordan. The town was named after Augustus Caesar and Philip the Tetrarch.

**ALAH.** A city founded by Asshur, a
ollower of Nimrod, moving from
Shinar (Genesis 10:11). The
Assyrian *Kalḫu* (modern Nimrud)
ies 40 kilometres south of Nineveh
n the eastern bank of the river
Tigris. The principal excavations
here by Sir Henry Layard in
845–48, the British School of
Archaeology in Iraq 1949–63 and the
raqi government and Polish
xpeditions 1970–76 have traced the
ity's history from prehistoric to
Hellenistic times.

Soundings show early influences
rom the south before the main
itadel (550 by 370 metres) was
ebuilt by Shalmaneser I (*c.* 1250 BC)
nd again by Ashurnasirpal II in 879
C. The city then covered an area of
40 square kilometres and had a
opulation of about 60,000.

It was from Calah that Shalmaneser III attacked Syria, and his
Black Obelisk recording the
ubmission of Jehu and stelae
nentioning Ahab were originally set
up in the main square. Inscriptions of
Tiglath-pileser III and Sargon II
nention their attacks on Israel and
Judah launched from this Assyrian
nilitary capital. A list of personal

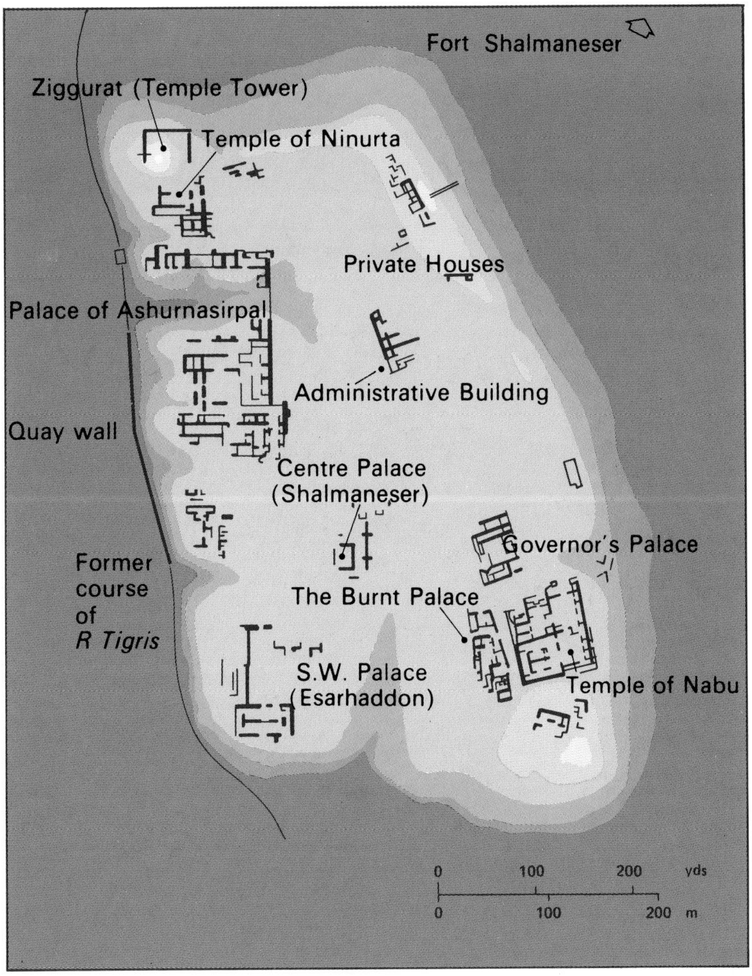


Plan of the citadel at Calah.

*Left:* This rock-formation near the 'Garden Tomb' resembles a skull, which has led to its popular identification as Golgotha (Calvary), the 'Place of a skull' (John 19:17).

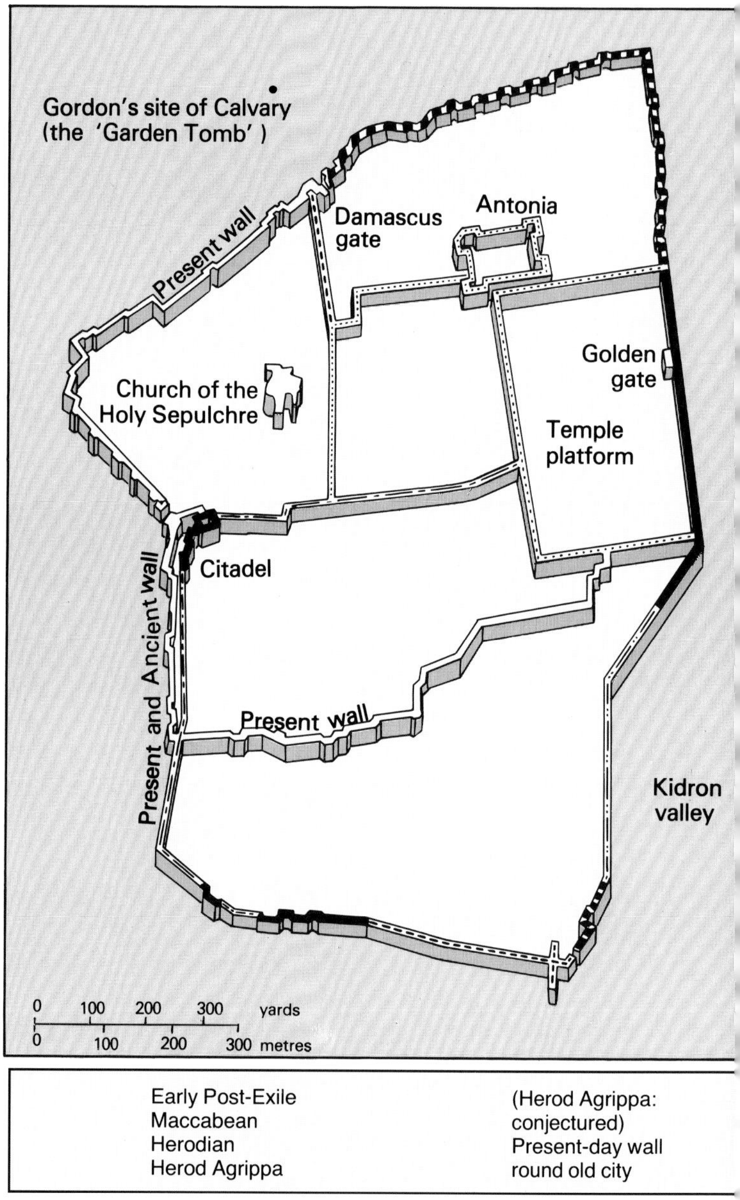


*Right:* Jerusalem: Plan locating the Garden Tomb and the Holy Sepulchre (traditional Calvary) together with the 1st and 2nd north walls of Kenyon.

names written in Aramaic may attest the presence of captives settled here.

Sargon II, conqueror of Samaria, stored his booty here. Esarhaddon subsequently built himself a palace here and recorded his treaties with conquered peoples on tablets set up in the Temple of Nabu.

Many of the discoveries of sculptures, ivories, metal objects and weapons, found in the citadel and barracks of 'Fort Shalmaneser' in the outer town, illustrate the splendour of the booty taken from Syria and Palestine and the might of the Assyrian army.

Calah fell to the Medes and Babylonians in 612 B.C.

D. J. Wiseman

*Further reading*

M. E. L. Mallowan, *Nimrud and its Remains*, 1965

*Iraq* 13–27, 1952–65; 36–38, 1974–77

**CALNEH, CALNO. 1.** Calneh was the name of a city founded by Nimrod in the land of *Shinar (Genesis 10:10, AV). Since no city of this name is known in Babylonia, some scholars propose to point the Hebrew *kullānâ*, 'all of them', as in Genesis 42:36 and 1 Kings 7:37. This would then be a comprehensive clause to cover such ancient cities as Ur and Nippur (identified with Calneh in the Babylonian Talmud). Those who locate Shinar in northern Mesopotamia equate this city with Calno (**2** below) and also with *Canneh.

**2.** Calno (Kalno), Isaiah 10:9; Kalneh, Amos 6:2 (Septuagint *pantes*, 'all', see Calneh above), a town Kullania mentioned in Assyrian tribute lists. It is associated with Arpad, and is modern Kullan Köy 16 kilometres south-east of Arpad (*AJSL* 51, 1935, pp. 189–191).

D. J. Wiseman

*Further reading*

*JNES* 3, 1944, p. 254

**CALVARY**

*The name*

The name occurs once only in the AV, in Luke 23:33, and not at all in most English versions. The word comes from the Vulgate, where the Latin *calvaria* translates the Greek *kranion*; both words translate the Aramaic *gulgoltâ*, the 'Golgotha' of Matthew 27:33, meaning 'skull'. Three possible reasons for such a name have been propounded: because skulls were found there; because it was a place of execution, or because the site in some way resembled a skull.

*The site*

All we know of the site from Scripture is that it was outside Jerusalem, fairly conspicuous, probably not far from a city gate and a highway, and that a garden containing a tomb lay near by.

Two Jerusalem localities are today pointed out as the site of the Lord's cross and tomb; the one is the Church of the Holy Sepulchre, the other Gordon's Calvary, commonly known as the Garden Tomb. Unfortunately it has always proved difficult to debate the question objectively; in some quarters the

**The Church of the Holy Sepulchre, Jerusalem, by tradition built over the site of the hill of Calvary.**

entification one accepts is almost .e touchstone of one's orthodoxy.

*ıe Church of the Holy Sepulchre*
ıis marks the site of a temple to ənus which the emperor onstantine removed, understand- g that it stood over the sacred site. ıe tradition thus goes back at least the 4th century.

Excavations beneath the church self and in the surrounding area ıve provided the following picture. ıe area was certainly outside the ty walls until the reign of Herod grippa, AD 41–43. During the h-1st centuries BC extensive ıarrying was carried out there, eating a large depression. When ıarrying stopped in the 1st century arable soil was tipped into the ıllow, returning the area to ıltivation. Carobs, figs, olives and ıme cereals were grown in gardens ıunded (especially on the west and uth) by a vertical rock-face. At ast two tombs were cut into the rock on the western side, one of which is still partially preserved beneath the Syrian Chapel at the western end of the Church of the Holy Sepulchre. It is of a type datable to the 1st century BC and 1st century AD, but must have been cut before AD 41–43 when a new wall built by Herod Agrippa enclosed this area within the city.

The other tomb, 18 metres to the east, is the one identified in AD 325 as the burial-place of Jesus. Since then it has undergone so many changes that its original form can no longer be ascertained. Forty metres east of this stood a spur of rock, left unquarried because of its poor quality. Since it was uncovered in the 4th century this has been identified as the hill of Golgotha/Calvary and is now incorporated (though probably not in its original size and shape) within the Church of the Holy Sepulchre.

Whether the specific identifications of the tomb and of Calvary are correct or not, there can be no doubt that the area beneath the church consisted of gardens and a cemetery during the 1st century BC to the 1st century AD, agreeing with the details in John 19:41.

*The Garden Tomb*
The Garden Tomb was first pointed out in 1849; a rock formation there resembles a skull; and admittedly the site accords with the biblical data. But there is no tradition nor anything else to support its claim, and the tomb has been confidently dated to the Iron Age; it cannot, therefore, be the 'new tomb' of John 19:41.

The traditional site is much more likely; but any identification must remain conjectural.

*On the Mount of Olives*
A third site for Calvary has recently been proposed by E. L. Martin, who argues for a location on the Mount of Olives (*Secrets of Golgotha*, Alhambra California, 1988). However, the case relies heavily on forced interpretations of verses in the gospels. First, Martin takes Matthew 27:54, Mark 15:39 and Luke 23:47 to mean that the centurion who was present at the crucifixion observed the rending of the temple curtain (referred to in Matthew 27:51; Mark 15:38; Luke 23:45), a phenomenon which he could only have seen from the Mount of Olives.

Secondly, Martin sees in John 19:20 a reference to the site of the crucifixion as 'the place of the city'; he argues that this designates a location which, although outside the city, was involved in the rituals of the temple, namely the place on the Mount of Olives where the sacrifice of the red heifer (Numbers 19:1–8) was carried out.

In fact, neither Matthew, Mark nor Luke explicitly says that the centurion saw the temple veil being torn; they merely record that he was struck by the manner of Jesus' death. The crucial phrase in John 19:20 is correctly translated 'the place was near the city'; this does not indicate a precise spot with cultic associations. Without these arguments from the gospels the rest of Martin's case is seriously weakened and there is no need to look for the site of Calvary on the Mount of Olives.

D. F. Payne, J. Bimson

*Further reading*
L. E. Cox Evans, *PEQ* 1968, pp. 112–136
K. M. Kenyon, *Digging up Jerusalem*,

1974
J. Wilkinson, *Jerusalem as Jesus Knew It*, 1978, pp. 144–159, 180–197
V. C. Corbo, 'Golgotha', *ABD* II, pp. 1071–1073
See also further reading under *Jerusalem.

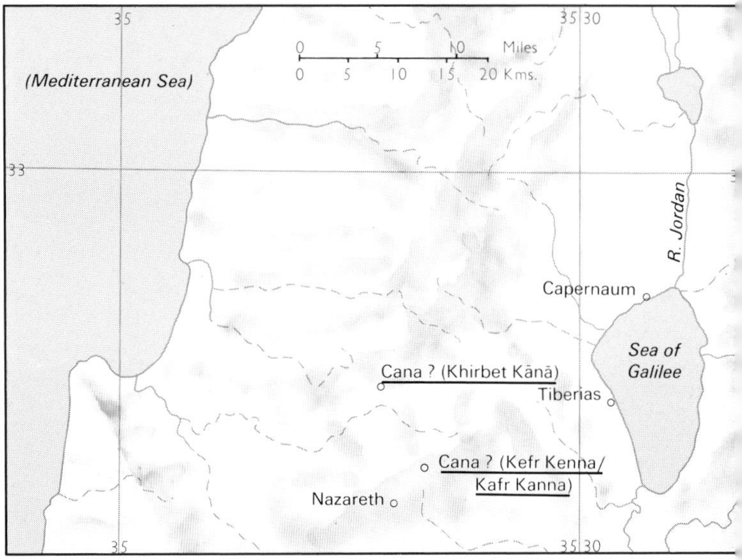


Sites suggested as ancient Cana.

**CANA** (Greek *kana*, probably from the Hebrew *qānâ*, 'place of reeds'). A Galilean village in the uplands west of the lake, mentioned in John's Gospel only. It was the scene of Jesus' first miracle (John 2:1, 11), the place where with a word he healed the nobleman's son who lay sick at Capernaum (4:46, 50), and the home of Nathanael (21:2).

Not definitely located, Cana has been identified by some with Kefr Kenna, about 6 kilometres north-north-east of Nazareth on the road to Tiberias. This site, where excavations have been made, is a likely place for the events of John 2:1–11, having ample water springs, and providing such shady fig trees as that suggested in John 1:48.

Many modern scholars, however, prefer an identification with Khirbet Kānā, a ruined site 14 kilometres north of Nazareth, which local Arabs still call Cana of Galilee. A survey in 1982, and the records of earlier excavations, provide evidence of a well-planned village equipped with many cisterns to ensure an adequate water-supply. The site was occupied from the early Roman to the Byzantine period. (J. F. Strange, Cana of Galilee', *ABD* I, p. 827.)

J. D. Douglas, J. Bimson

**CANAAN, CANAANITES.** A Semitic-speaking people and their territory, principally in Phoenicia. Their racial affinities are at present uncertain.

### The name

The name Canaan (Hebrew *k^ena'an*) of people and land derives from that of their forebear Canaan or Kna' according to both Genesis 10:15–18 and native Canaanite-Phoenician tradition as transmitted by Sanchuniathon and preserved by Philo of Byblos. *Kna'(an)* is the native name of the Canaanites-Phoenicians applied to them both in Greek sources and by the Phoenicians themselves (*e.g.* on coins; see W. F. Albright, p. 1, note 1, in his paper, 'The Role of the Canaanites in the History of Civilization', in *The Bible and the Ancient Near East, Essays for W. F. Albright*, 1961, pp. 328–362; cited hereafter as *BANE* Vol.).

The meaning of *Kn'(n)* is unknown. Outside the Bible, the name occurs both with and without the final *n*. This *n* could be either a final *n* of a common Semitic type, or else a Hurrian suffix (Albright, *op. cit.*, p. 25, note 50). Formerly, some linked *kn'(n)* with words for 'purple dye', especially in Hurrian (with Speiser, *Language* 12, 1936, p. 124), but this was disproved by Landsberger (*JCS* 21, 1967, p. 106f.).

### Extent of Canaan

'Canaan' in both Scripture and external sources has a threefold reference.

**1.** Fundamentally it indicates the land and inhabitants of the Syro-Palestinian coastland, especially Phoenicia proper. This is indicated within Genesis 10:15–19 by its detailed enumeration of Sidon 'the first-born', the Arkite, the Sinite, the Zemarite and Hamath in the Orontes valley. More specifically Numbers 13:29, Joshua 5:1 and 11:3 and Judges 1:27ff. put the Canaanites on the coastlands, in the valleys and plains, and the Jordan valley, with Amorites and others in the hills. Notably the inscription of Idrimi, king of Alalakh in the 15th century BC, mentions his flight to Ammia in coastal Canaan (S. Smith, *The Statue of Idrimi*, 1949, pp. 72–73; *ANET*, 3rd edition, pp. 557–558); N. P. Lemche, *The Canaanites and their Land*, 1991.

**2.** 'Canaan(ite)' can also cover, by extension, the hinterland and so Syria-Palestine in general. Thus, Genesis 10:15–19 includes also the Hittite, Jebusite, Amorite, Hivite and Girgashite, explaining that 'the families of the Canaanite spread abroad' (verse 18); this wider area is defined as extending coastally from Sidon to Gaza, inland to the Dead Sea cities Sodom and Gomorrah and apparently back up north to *Lasha (location uncertain). See also Genesis 12:5 and 13:12; or Numbe 13:17–21 and 34:1–2, with the following delimitation of western Palestinian boundaries; Judges 4:2 and 23–24 calls Jabin (II) of Hazor titular 'king of Canaan'.

This wider use is also encountere in early external sources. In their Amarna letters (14th century BC) kings of Babylon and elsewhere sometimes use 'Canaan' for Egypt's Syro-Palestinian territories generally. And the Egyptian Papyru Anastasi IIIA (lines 5–6) and IV (16 line 4) of 13th century BC mention 'Canaanite slaves from Huru' (that is, Syria-Palestine generally) (see R. A. Caminos, *Late-Egyptian Miscellanies*, 1954, pp. 117, 200).

**3.** The term 'Canaanite' can also bear the more restricted meaning o 'merchant, trafficker', trading being a most charcteristic occupation (Job 41:6; Isaiah 23:8; Ezekiel 17:4; Zephaniah 1:11).

### Canaanites and Amorites

*In the Bible*

Alongside the specific and wider uses of 'Canaan(ite)' noted above, 'Amorite(s)' also has both a specific and a wider reference. Specifically, the Amorites in Scripture are part o the hill-country population of Palestine (Numbers 13:29; Joshua 5:1; 11:3). But in its wider use 'Amorite' tends to overlap directly the term 'Canaanite'. 'Amorite' comes in under 'Canaan' in Genesis 10:15–16 for a start. Then, Israel is to conquer Canaan (that is, Palestine) in Numbers 13:17–21, *etc.*, and duly comes to dwell in the land of the morites, overcoming 'all the eople' there, namely Amorites oshua 24:15, 18). Abraham eaches, and is promised, Canaan ienesis 12:5, 7; 15:7, 18), but ccupation is delayed as 'the iquity of the Amorites is not yet omplete' (Genesis 15:16). Shechem a Canaanite principality under a ivite ruler (Genesis 12:5–6; 34:2, )), but can be called 'Amorite' ienesis 48:22).

The documentary theory of literary iticism has frequently assayed to se these overlapping or double esignations, Canaanites and morites (and other 'pairs'), as arks of different authorship (see, *g.*, S. R. Driver, *Introduction to the iterature of the Old Testament*, 9th dition, 1913, p. 119, or O. Eissfeldt, *he Old Testament, an Introduction*, 965, p. 183). But any such use of ese terms does not accord with the xternal records which have no nderlying 'hands', and it must erefore be questioned.

*non-biblical records*

the 18th century BC Amurru is part Syria in the Alalakh tablets, while morite princes are mentioned in a ari document in relation to Hazor in alestine itself (see J.-R. Kupper, *Les omades en Mésopotamie au temps es Rois de Mari*, 1957, pp. 179–180). s Hazor is the Canaanite city *par xcellence* of northern Palestine, the ingling of people and terms is ready attested in Abraham's day.

In the 14th and 13th centuries BC e specific kingdom of Amurru of bdi-aširta, Aziru, and their uccessors in the Lebanon mountain egion secured a firm hold on a ection of the Phoenician coast and s Canaanite seaports by conquest nd alliance 'from Byblos to Ugarit' Amarna Letter No. 98). This morite control in coastal Canaan is rther attested by the Battle of adesh inscriptions of Ramesses II 3th century BC) mentioning the mely arrival inland of a battle force om a 'port in the land of Amurru' see Gardiner, *Ancient Egyptian nomastica* I, 1947, pp. 188*–189*, nd Gardiner, *The Kadesh scriptions of Ramesses II*, 1960, on is incident). This is independent vidence for a contiguous use of mor(ites) and Canaan(ites) in loses' time.

The use of these terms as the istinguishing marks of different terary hands is thus erroneous. In ny case the situation reflected in e Pentateuch and Joshua by this sage was radically changed by the npact of the 'Sea Peoples' at the beginning of the 12th century BC, after which date the emergence of that usage would be inexplicable.

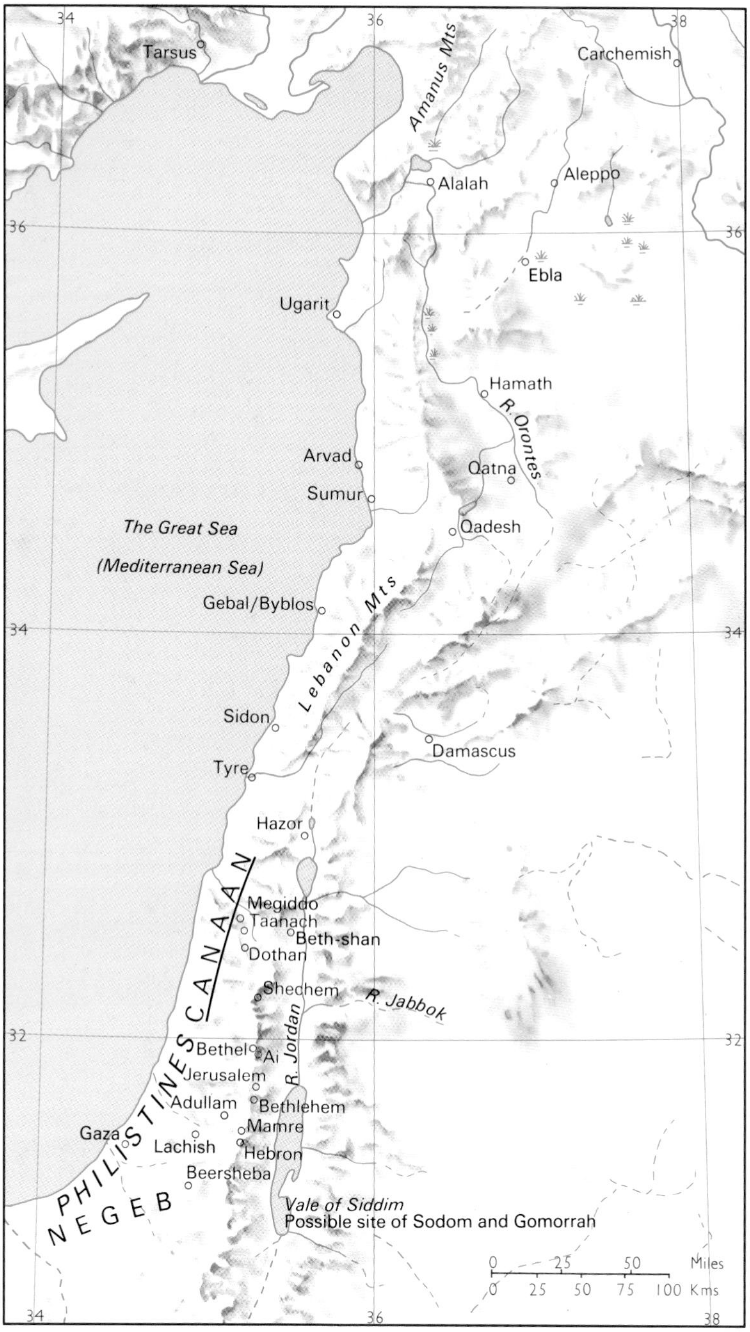


**Canaan and its ancient neighbours.**

## The language

The definition of what is or is not 'Canaanite' is much disputed. Within the general group of the north-west Semitic languages and dialects, biblical Hebrew (see Isaiah 19:18) and the western Semitic glosses and terms in the Amarna tablets can correctly be termed 'southern Canaanite' along with Moabite and Phoenician.

Separate but related are Aramaic and Ya'udic. Between these two groups comes Ugaritic. Some hold this latter to be a separate north-western Semitic language, others that it is Canaanite to be classed with Hebrew, *etc.* Ugaritic itself betrays historical development linguistically, and thus the Ugaritic of the 14th and 13th centuries BC is closer to Hebrew than is the archaic language of the great epics (Albright, *BASOR* 150, 1958, pp. 36–38). Hence it is provisionally possible to view north-western Semitic as including southern Canaanite (Hebrew, *etc.*), northern Canaanite (Ugaritic) and Aramaic. Compare S. Moscati (*The Semites in*

*Ancient History*, 1959, pp. 97–100), who (rather radically) would abolish 'Canaanite'; and J. Friedrich (*Scientia* 84, 1949, pp. 220–223), on this question. The distinction between 'Canaanite' and 'Amorite' is almost illusory, and little more than dialectal.

On north-western Semitic *ā* versus Canaanite *ō*, see *JCS* 15, 1961, pp. 42f. They differ in little more than the sibilants. Texts from the north Syrian city of *Ebla are written in a dialect that appears to be western Semitic and to show affinities with southern Canaanite, according to the decipherer, G. Pettinato, who calls it 'Palaeo-Canaanite' (*Orientalia* n.s. 44, 1975, pp. 361–374, especially 376ff.).

## Canaanite history

*Origins*

The presence of Semitic-speaking people in Palestine in the 3rd millennium BC is so far explicitly attested only by two Semitic place-names in a text of that age: *Ndi'* which contains the element *'il(u)*, 'god', and *n..k..* which begins with *ain*, 'spring, well', both these names occurring in an Egyptian tomb-scene of the 5th/6th Dynasty, *c.* 2400 BC.

However, the question as to whether these indicate the presence of Canaanites, and just when Canaanites appeared in Palestine, is a matter of dispute. It is certain that Canaanites and Amorites were well established in Syria-Palestine by 2000 BC, and a north-western Semitic-speaking element at Ebla in northern Syria by *c.* 2300 BC.

Throughout the 2nd millennium BC, Syria-Palestine was divided among a varying number of Canaanite/Amorite city-states. For the 19th/18th century BC, many names of places and rulers are recorded in the Egyptian Execration Texts. On the organization of some of the separate states in Palestine in this, the patriarchal period, see also A. van Selms, *Oudtestamentische Studiën* 12, 1958 (*Studies on the Book of Genesis*), pp. 192–197.

*16th to 13th centuries BC*

During the period roughly 1500–1380 BC, these petty states were part of Egypt's Asiatic empire; in the 14th century BC the northern ones passed under Hittite suzerainty, while the southern ones remained nominally Egyptian.

Early in the 13th century BC Egypt regained effectual control in Palestine and coastal Syria (the Hittites retaining northern and inner Syria), but this control evaporated as time passed (see H. Klengel in *Geschichte Syriens* 1–3, 1965–70). Thus Israel in the late 13th century met Canaanite/Amorite, but not specifically Egyptian, opposition (except for Merenptah's abortive raid). The 'conquest' by Ramesses III, *c.* 1180 BC, was a sweeping raid, mainly *via* the coast and principal routes, and was superficial.

*The Israelite conquest*

At the end of the 13th century BC the sway of the Canaanite/Amorite city-states, now decadent, was shattered by political upheavals. The Israelites, under Joshua, entered western Palestine from across the Jordan, gaining control of the hill-country first and defeating a series of Canaanite kings.

For the Hebrews, the conquest of Canaan was the fulfilment of an ancient promise to their forefathers (Genesis 17:8; 28:4, 13–14; Exodus 6:2–8). They were to dispossess the peoples of the land as expelled by God, and to destroy those who remained (see Deuteronomy 7:1, 2ff.); this was in consequence of divine judgment on long centuries of persistent wickedness by these peoples (Deuteronomy 9:5, compare Genesis 15:16), and not from any merit on Israel's part.

*The 'Sea Peoples'*

Meantime, the 'Sea Peoples' of the Egyptian records (including Philistines) had destroyed the Hittite empire and swept through Syria and Palestine to be halted on the Egyptian border by Ramesses III; some, especially the *Philistines, establishing themselves on the Palestinian coast.

Finally, Aramaean penetration of inland Syria swiftly increased in the century or so following. The result was that the Canaanites now ruled only in Phoenicia proper with its ports and in isolated principalities elsewhere.

From the 12th century BC onwards, the former Bronze Age Canaanites in their new, restricted circumstances emerged as the more-than-ever maritime *Phoenicians of the 1st millennium BC, centred on the famous kingdom of *Tyre and *Sidon. On the history of the Canaanites, especially as continuing as Phoenicians, see Albright in *BANE* volume, pp. 328–362.

## Canaanite culture

Our knowledge of this is derived from two main sources: first, literary, from the northern Canaanite and Babylonian texts discovered at *Ugarit (Ras Shamra, on the Syrian coast) with odd fragments elsewhere; and second, archaeolog cal, in the sense of being derived from the excavated objects and remains from and of towns and cemeteries in Syria and Palestine.

*Canaanite society*

Most of the Canaanite city-states were monarchies. The king had extensive powers of military appointment and conscription, of requisitioning lands and leasing them in return for services, of taxation, including tithes, customs-dues, real-estate tax, *etc.*, and of corvée to requisition the labour of his subjects for state purposes. This is directly reflected i Samuel's denunciation of a kingshi like that of the nations round about (1 Samuel 8, *c.* 1050 BC), and clearly evident in the tablets from Alalakh (18th-15th centuries BC) and Ugarit (14th-13th centuries BC) (see I. Mendelsohn, *BASOR* 143, 1956, pp. 17–22).

Military, religious and economic matters were under the king's dire oversight; the queen was an important personage sometimes appealed to by high officials; the court was elaborately organized in larger states like Ugarit (for the latter, compare A. F. Rainey, *The Social Stratification of Ugarit*, 1962).

The basic unit of society was the family. For the period of the 19th-15th centuries BC, the great northern Canaanite epics from Ugarit (see *Literature*, below) betra the main features of family life (see A. van Selms, *Marriage and Family Life in Ugaritic Literature*, 1954).

Further information is afforded b legal documents for the 14th/13th centuries BC. Among larger social units, besides the obvious ones of towns with their associated village (in the Ugarit state, see Virolleaud, *Syria* 21, 1940, pp. 123–151, and see briefly, C. H. Gordon, *Ugaritic Literature*, p. 124), for which compare the assignment of towns with their villages ('suburbs') in Joshua 13ff., one may note the widespread organization of guilds. These include primary producers (herdsmen, fowlers, butchers and bakers), artisans (smiths, working i copper [or bronze] and silver, potters, sculptors, and house-, boat and chariot-builders), and traders, both local and long-distance. Priest and other cult-personnel (see below), and also musicians, had guilds or groups; and there were veral special classes of warriors. veral inscribed javelin- or ear-heads found in Palestine rhaps belonged to late-Canaanite ercenary troops of the 12th/11th nturies BC, the sort of people mmanded by a Sisera or Jabin ıdges 4, *etc.*); these also illustrate e free use of early western Semitic phabetic script in the Palestine of e Judges.

It has been suggested that in naanite society in 13th-century BC lestine there was a sharp class stinction between upper-class tricians and lower-class, half-free rfs, the contrast with the relatively mble and homogeneous Israelites ssibly being reflected in the cavated archaeological sites.

*terature*

ıis is principally represented by rthern Canaanite texts from garit. These include long, but sordered and fragmentary, ctions of the Baal Epic (deeds and rtunes of Baal or Hadad), which es back linguistically to perhaps *c.* 00 BC; the legend of Aqhat icissitudes of the only son of good ng Dan'el) perhaps from *c.* 1800 BC; e story of King Keret (bereft of mily, he gains a new wife virtually conquest, and also incurs the rath of the gods) perhaps about the th century BC; and other agments. All extant copies date om the 14th/13th centuries BC.

The high-flown poetry of the early ics has clearly demonstrated the chaic flavour of much Hebrew Old stament poetry in its vocabulary d turns of speech. For full anslations of the epics, so portant for early Canaanite ligions, see C. H. Gordon, *Ugaritic terature*, 1949; G. R. Driver, *naanite Myths and Legends*, 56; A. Caquot, M. Sznycer, A. rdner, *Textes Ougaritiques* I, 74. Selections are given in *ANET*, . 129–155, and in *DOTT*.

*ligion*

e Canaanites had an extensive ntheon, headed by El. More ominent in practice were Baal ord'), *i.e.* Hadad the storm-god, d Dagon, with temples in Ugarit d elsewhere. The goddesses herah, Astarte (Ashtaroth) and ıath – like Baal – had multi-loured personalities and violent aracters; they were goddesses of x and war. Kotharand-Hasis was tificer-god (compare Vulcan), and ıer and lesser deities abounded.

Actual temples in Palestine clude remains at Beth-shan, Megiddo, Lachish, Shechem and especially Hazor (which had at least three), besides those in Syria at Qatna, Alalakh or Ugarit. The Ugaritic texts mention a variety of animals sacrificed to the gods: cattle, sheep (rams and lambs) and birds (including doves) – plus, of course, libations. Animal bones excavated in several Palestinian sites support this picture.

The title of high priest (*rb khnm*) is attested for Canaanite religion at Ugarit. That the *qdšm* of the Ugaritic texts were cult prostitutes is very possible; at any rate, the *qdšm* were as much an integral part of Canaanite religion there as they were forbidden to Israel (Deuteronomy 23:17–18. *etc.*).

Human sacrifice in 2nd-millennium Canaanite religion has not yet been isolated archaeologically with any certainty, but there are indications that it was customary. That Canaanite religion appealed to the bestial and material in human nature is clearly evidenced by the Ugaritic texts and in Egyptian texts of Semitic origin or inspiration; compare Albright, *Archaeology and Religion of Israel*, 3rd edition, 1953, pp. 75–77, 158–159, 197, note 39. When the full import of this is realized it will be the more evident that physically and spiritually the sophisticated crudities of decaying Canaanite culture and emergent Israel with a unique mission could not coexist.

K. A. Kitchen

*Further reading*

A. R. Millard, 'The Canaanites', in *POTT*, pp. 29–52

For discoveries at Ugarit, see Schaeffer's reports in *Syria* since 1929, and the fully documented series of volumes, *Mission de Ras Shamra* by Schaeffer, Virolleaud and Nougayrol.

**CANNEH.** The name of a settlement or town mentioned, with *Haran and *Eden, as trading with Tyre (Ezekiel 27:23). The site is unknown, but the above association suggests the area of the middle Euphrates. It is distinct from Assyrian *Kannu'* (the Hebrew ending *-eh* indicating a final vowel, as against cuneiform *-u'* which indicates a final consonant), which was probably east of the Tigris.

T. C. Mitchell

*Further reading*

E. Lipinski in *Orientalia* 45, 1976, pp. 59–61

## CAPERNAUM

### Name

New Testament manuscripts mostly read *Kapharnaoum*, though *Kapernaoum* appears in minuscules dependent on Codex Alexandrinus. Clearly Kapharnaoum is the original form, directly transcribing Semitic *kᵉp̄ar naḥûm*, 'village of Nahum'. This Semitic form is found at *Qohelet Rabbah* 1.8 and 7.26.

Josephus (*Jewish War* 3.517) refers to the spring *Kapharnaoum*, equivalent to Semitic *'en-kᵉp̄ar-naḥûm*. His *Life* 403 should probably be read *Kepharnakōn* (original of the PRA manuscripts, favoured by Thackeray). This is the same word with *nûn*-ized ending and *k* for *ḥ*.

### Location

Evidence from the New Testament, Josephus, Christian pilgrim-texts, mediaeval Jewish itineraries, extant monumental remains and current excavations indicates that Capernaum was undoubtedly located at *Tell Hum*, and was inhabited continuously from the 1st century BC to the 7th century AD.

The Gospels are almost sufficient

**The Sea of Galilee; the site of Capernaum can be seen among the trees in the middle distance.**

The reconstructed synagogue at Tell Hum (Capernaum), now re-dated to the late 4th/early 5th century AD. The best preserved of all the Galilean synagogues, only the lowest three to four courses of the walls, the column bases and the floor-paving remained *in situ* before the Franciscan reconstructions.

in themselves to fix the site, indicating that Capernaum was (*a*) by the lake-side (Matthew 4:13); (*b*) near a political border, so that a customs-post (Mark 2:14) and military detachment were necessary (Matthew 8:5–13; Luke 7:1–10); (*c*) near Gennesaret (Mark 6:53; John 6:22, 59), which is an area of highly productive land at the north-west of the Lake.

In short, Capernaum was the nearest village to the river Jordan on the north-western shores of the Sea of Galilee, a position occupied in fact by the ruins of *Tell Hum*. This is confirmed by Josephus' *Life* 403, which indicates a village close to Julias (*et-Tell*) in the direction of Magdala/Tarichaeae (*Mejdel*).

Capernaum was also near a most copious spring which watered Gennesaret (*Jewish War* 3.519) and can only be the site *et-Tabgha*. But the Arabic *et-Tabgha* is also undoubtedly a corruption of the Greek *Heptapēgōn* (place of seven springs). This 'Seven Springs' is mentioned by Egeria *c.* AD 383 (Latin *septem fontes*), and by Theodosius (AD 530).

Theodosius provides us with our only detailed early itinerary round the north-western shores of the Sea of Galilee, moving north from Tiberias in Roman miles: 2 miles Magdala, 2 miles Heptapēgōn, 2 miles Capernaum, 6 miles Bethsaida. Thus Capernaum was 2 miles (3·5 kilometres) north of Tabgha, which exactly locates *Tell Hum*.

Monuments are also important in confirming the site of Capernaum. Egeria saw a synagogue there of fine ashlars, approached 'by many steps'. It is in fact an unusual feature of the synagogue remains at *Tell Hum* that they are set up on a high platform, and have a balcony at the front which is reached by high flights of steps from the sides.

Egeria was also shown a church (*ecclesia*) when she came to Capernaum (*c.* AD 383). She says that it had been made from the house of the apostle Peter, and the walls of this house were incorporated into it, still standing in their original form (*ita stant sicut fuerunt*). The pilgrim from Piacenza (AD 570) tells us that he entered Peter's house in Capernaum, but it had been replaced by a basilica.

## History

Until the conversion of Constantine the Great (AD 306–337) Jewish communities flourished in Galilee under their rabbis and Patriarchs. About AD 335 Constantine was informed by a Jew of Tiberias, the Christian convert Joseph, that Tiberias, Sepphoris, Nazareth and Capernaum were entirely inhabited by those of Jewish race, who rigorously excluded Gentiles from their settlements. Joseph secured ready permission from the emperor to build 'churches for Christ' (*ekklēsiai*) in these places (Epiphanius, *Haer.* 30.4.1, in Migne's *Patrologia Graeca* 41.425), and managed to convert a derelict temple of Hadrian at Tiberias and erect a small church at Sepphoris.

Yet it was not perhaps until the 5 century AD that Gentile Christians fully established themselves in thi Jewish 'ghetto'. How far through a this time the 'Judaeo-Christian' se was established at Capernaum an elsewhere in Galilee is difficult to say. From stories in the rabbis one learns of *minîm* (heretics) at Tiberias, Sepphoris and Capernau (2nd/3rd centuries AD). Only one ta is told about Capernaum, that R. Hananya was persuaded by *minîm* to break the sabbath-rule by riding donkey (*c.* AD 110). These Jewish Christians held to the Law, attend synagogue and avoided contact wi Gentiles; but they healed and spo in the name of Jesus. Jerome says that the Pharisees called them 'Nazaraeans'; that they still flourished in his day (late 4th and early 5th centuries AD) 'in the synagogues of the East'; and that they were neither faithful Jews no genuine Christians.

Capernaum was abandoned at t Islamic invasion of Palestine in AD 638.

## Excavations

*The synagogue*

Excavations by the Franciscan *Custodia di Terra Santa*, directed b V. Corbo, began at Capernaum (*Te Hum*) in 1968 and 18 campaigns ha been conducted by 1985. The synagogue had long before (1905) been cleared by Kohl and Watzing

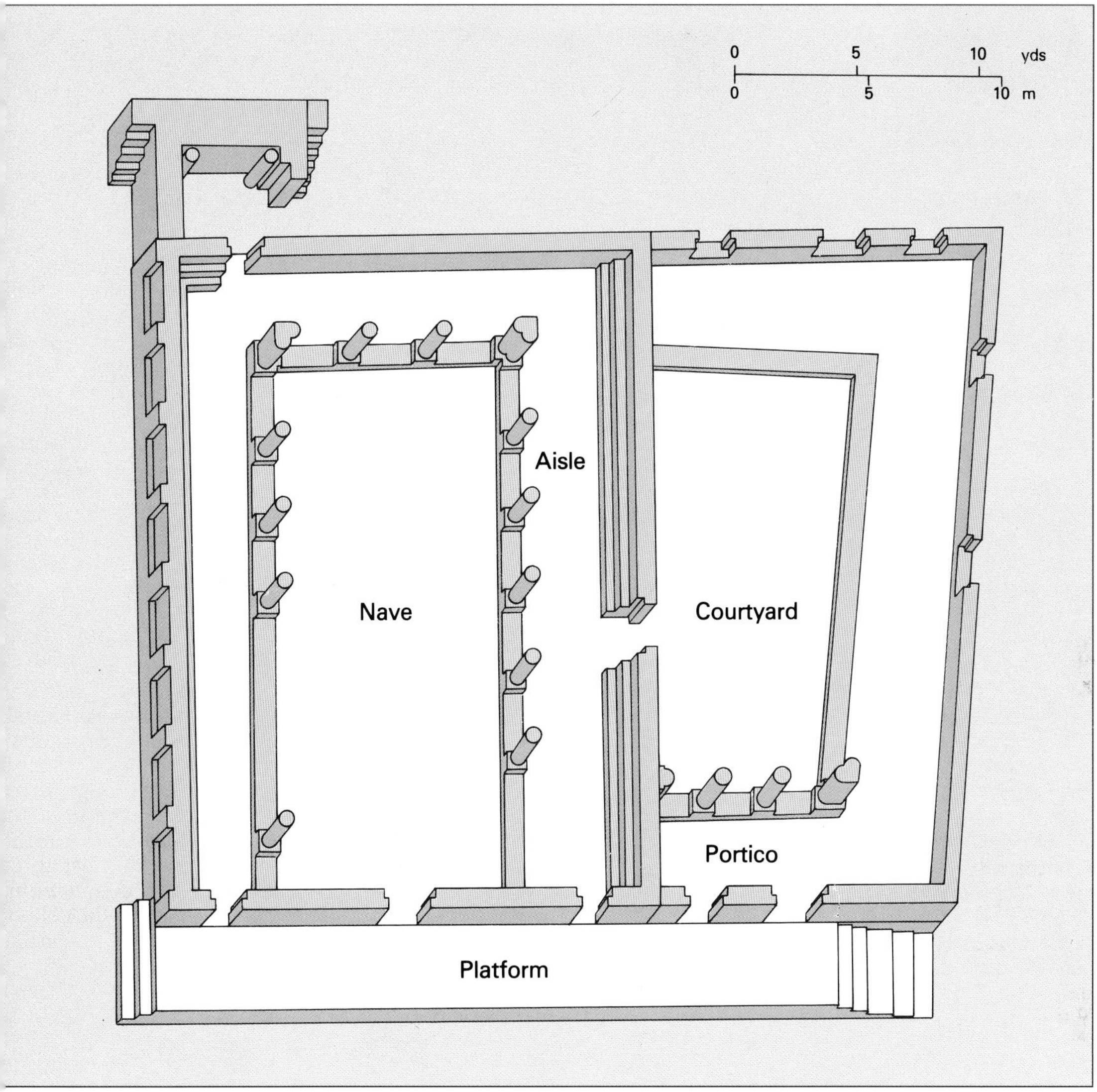


**Ground plan of the Capernaum synagogue. Alongside the roofed prayer-hall was a colonnaded courtyard or annexe, both being raised on a high podium mounted by steps.**

its flagstone pavement, and dated comparison with Severan onuments in Syria to the late 2nd or rly 3rd centuries AD.

The plan which the Germans posed was of a long, colonnaded sembly-hall divided into a central ve and side-aisles; this hall faced ith and was connected on its stern side to an impressive nexe, a colonnaded courtyard. th the hall and annexe were raised on a high platform (*podium*), and d a balcony in front of them iched by imposing flights of steps either side. One would certainly ppose that this was the nagogue seen by Egeria (*c.* AD 383) Capernaum, reached by an ascent 'many steps'.

But if the dates argued for Egeria's grimage by Devos and accepted Wilkinson (AD 381–384) are rrect, she must have seen the nagogue while it was being nstructed. Eighteen trenches in and around the synagogue have yielded pottery (carefully studied by S. Loffreda) and coins establishing that work was begun *c.* AD 350 and completed *c.* AD 450. The rubble fill (stratum B) of the *podium* rests on destroyed houses (stratum A); it is sealed from above by a thick and unbroken mortar (stratum C) in which the flagstones of the hall and annexe were set.

The earliest possible date for the pavement of the hall and its eastern colonnade is AD 383, since the latest coins from the sealed fill beneath the mortar are AD 352–360 (*Cafarnao* 1, pp. 121, 163) and AD 383–408 (*Studia Hierosolymitana*, p. 164, under the stylobate for the eastern colonnade). The latest coin embedded within the thick mortar before it had set (trench 2, stratum C) is also from AD 383 (*LA* 22, 1972, pp. 15–16). These late dates for the synagogue were totally unexpected and have aroused great controversy (*IEJ* 21, 1971, pp. 207–211; 23, 1973, pp. 37–45, 184; *Ariel* 32, 1973, pp. 29–43).

Detailed exploration of the area beneath this 4th-5th century synagogue has revealed traces of an earlier one. This was built on almost the same plan and has roughly the same external measurements as the later building, but was smaller inside because it had thicker walls of black basalt. This earlier synagogue has been identified as the one built by the Roman centurion (Luke 7:5) and in which Jesus taught and healed (Luke 4:31–37).

*The traditional site of Peter's house*
Two successive shrines, totally different from each other, were excavated on the same site only one block of houses distant from the synagogue. The later shrine is the *basilica* seen by the Piacenza pilgrim: a small memorial completed by *c.* AD 450 in the unusual form of a double octagon. Its central ring is

sited exactly over the main room of a house built in the 1st century BC.

The basilica replaced a shrine of the early 4th century AD, possibly built by Joseph of Tiberias, which encapsulated the same early house, leaving its original walls standing, as Egeria was shown. The main room of this house had once again been marked out. In particular its walls were plastered and enlivened by painted designs in bold colours. On fallen pieces of plaster *graffiti* in Greek (a few Semitic) were found, including the words *amen*, *Lord* and *Jesus*. Clearly this was the traditional house of Peter, visited by pilgrims.

*The town*

Excavations of these monuments and of five blocks (*insulae*) of houses indicates that Capernaum was inhabited continuously between the early 1st century BC and the 7th century AD. The houses are part of a village which was *c.* 800 by 250 metres in extent, as sherds and remains indicate.

Of the excavated area, *insulae* 1–3 are the older ones, begun in the 1st century BC; *insulae* 4–5 developed from the 4th century AD. The traditional house of Peter (*insula* 1) and the block between this and the synagogue (*insula* 2) are most fully studied by the excavators, and are reproduced as isometric drawings (*Cafarnao* 1, plates X and XV). Corbo estimates that *insula* 2 could have housed 15 families, about 130 to 150 people. It has only a few entries into the roads outside, and consists of small rooms opening on to a number of internal courtyards. Steps survive, and must have led up to terrace-roofs of earth and straw (as Mark 2:4: healing of the paralytic), since the walls of basalt fieldstones and earth-mortar could not have supported an upper storey. The floors are of basalt cobbles covered by earth.

*Insula* 2 was occupied from the beginning of the 1st century AD to the 7th century without a break; its original walls remained in use unchanged. A succession of floors provides sherds and coins for dating.
J. P. Kane

*Further reading*

E. W. G. Masterman, *PEQ* 1907, pp. 220–229
——, *Studies in Galilee,* 1909
F.-M. Abel, *Capharnaum*, in *DBS* 1, 1928
V. Corbo, *The House of St Peter at Capharnaum,* 1969
——, *Cafarnao 1: Gli edifici della città,* 1975
——, *Studia Hierosolymitana in honore di P. Bellarmino Bagatti* 1, 1976, pp. 159–176
——, 'Capernaum', *ABD* I, pp. 866–869
S. Loffreda, *Cafarnao 2: La Ceramica*, 1974
A. Spijkerman, *Cafarnao 3: Catalogo delle monete della città,* 1975
E. Testa, *Cafarnao 4: I graffiti della case di S. Pietro*, 1972
R. North, *Bib* 58, 1977, pp. 424–431
S. Loffreda and V. Tzaferis in *NEAEHL* I, pp. 291–296
J. Strange, *BARev* IX/6, 1983, pp. 24–31

**CAPHTOR** (*kap̄tôr*). The home of the *kap̄tōrîm* (Deuteronomy 2:23), one of the peoples listed in the Table of Nations as descended, with Casluhim (whence went forth the *Philistines), from Mizraim (Genesis 10:14; 1 Chronicles 1:12). Caphtor was the land from which the Philistines came (Jeremiah 47:4; Amos 9:7), and it is presumably the Philistines, as erstwhile sojourners in Caphtor, who are referred to as Caphtorim in Deuteronomy 2:23.

It is probable that the biblical name is to be identified with Ugaritic *kptr*, and *kap-ta-ra* in a school text from Assur which may well be a copy of one of 2nd-millennium date. It is likewise held by many scholars that the Egyptian *kftyw* is also to be connected with this group, all of which refer in all probability to *Crete.

An alternative view, put forward by J. Strange, identifies Caphtor/ Kaptara/Keftiu with *Cyprus, or at least the south-eastern parts of the island. However, a majority of scholars continue to favour Crete.

At its height in the 2nd millennium, Minoan Crete controlled much of the Aegean area, particularly the adjacent coastlands, and this would accord with the biblical description of Caphtor as an *'î*, a term which can mean both 'island' and 'coastland'.

Western Asia was influenced in art and other ways by the Aegean, and this may explain the occurrence in the Bible of the term *kap̄tôr* as applying to an architectural feature, evidently a column capital, rendered in the AV by 'knop' (Exodus 25:31–36; 37:17–22) and 'lintel' (Amos 9:1; Zephaniah 2:14).
T. C. Mitchell

*Further reading*

A. H. Gardiner, *Ancient Egyptian Onomastica*, Text, I, 1947, pp. 201*–203*
R. W. Hutchinson, *Prehistoric Crete*, 1962, pp. 106–112
A. Malamat, *Mari and Early Israelite Experience* [Schweich lectures 1984], 1989, pp. 57–59
T. C. Mitchell in *AOTS*, pp. 408, 413
K. A. Kitchen in *POTT*, p. 54
J. Strange, *Caphtor/Keftiu: A New Investigation*, 1980

**CAPPADOCIA.** A highland province, much of it around 900 metres, in the east of Asia Minor, bounded on the south by the chain of Mount Taurus, on the east by the Euphrates and on the north by Pontus, but its actual limits are vague.

Cappadocia was constituted a Roman province by Tiberius, AD 17, on the death of Archelaus. In AD 70 Vespasian united it with Armenia Minor as one of the great frontier bulwarks of the empire. Under later emperors, especially Trajan, the size and importance of the province greatly increased. It produced large numbers of sheep and horses. The trade route between Central Asia and the Black Sea ports passed through it, and it was easily accessible from Tarsus through the Cilician Gates.

Jews from Cappadocia were present at Jerusalem on the day of Pentecost (Acts 2:9). Some of the Dispersion to whom Peter wrote lived in Cappadocia (1 Peter 1:1).
J. W. Meiklejohn

**CARCHEMISH.** A city (modern Jerablus) which guarded the main ford across the river Euphrates *c.* 10 kilometres north-east of Aleppo.

Carchemish is first mentioned in text of the 18th century BC as an independent trade-centre (Mari, Alalakh). As a Syrian city-state it had treaties with Ugarit and other states (Mitanni) during the 2nd millennium BC and continued as a neo-Hittite state after Inī-Teṣub (*c.* 1100) until Pisiris was defeated by Sargon II in 717 BC. Thereafter Carchemish was incorporated as an Assyrian province. The event is noted in Isaiah 10:9.

In 609 BC Neco II of Egypt moved *via* Megiddo to recapture the city (2 Chronicles 35:20), which was made a base from which his army harassed the Babylonians. However, in May-June 605 BC Nebuchadrezzar II led the Babylonian forces who entered the city by surprise. The Egyptians were utterly defeated in hand-to-hand fighting in and around the city (Jeremiah 46:2) and pursued to Hamath. Details of this battle, which resulted in the Babylonian ɔntrol of the west, are given in the abylonian Chronicle.

Excavations in 1912 and 1914 ncovered Hittite sculptures, a ɪwer palace area with an open alace (*bît-ḫilani*), and evidence of ɪe battle and later Babylonian ccupation.

. J. Wiseman

*urther reading*

'. L. Woolley, *Carchemish* 1–3, 1914–1952

D. J. Wiseman, *Chronicles of Chaldaean Kings*, 1956, pp. 20–27, 68–69

J. D. Hawkins, *Iraq* 36, 1974, pp. 67–73

W. W. Hallo in C. F. Pfeiffer, *The Biblical World*, 1966, pp. 65–69

**CARMEL** (Hebrew *karmel*, 'garden-land', 'fruitful land'). The word is used as a common noun in Hebrew with this meaning; examples are Isaiah 16:10, Jeremiah 4:26, 2 Kings 19:23 and 2 Chronicles 26:10. It can even be used of fresh ears of grain, as in Leviticus 2:14 and 23:14. Thus, the limestone Carmel hills probably got their name from the luxuriant scrub and woodland that covered them. In the Old Testament two places bear this name.

**1.** A range of hills, *c.* 50 kilometres long, extending from north-west to

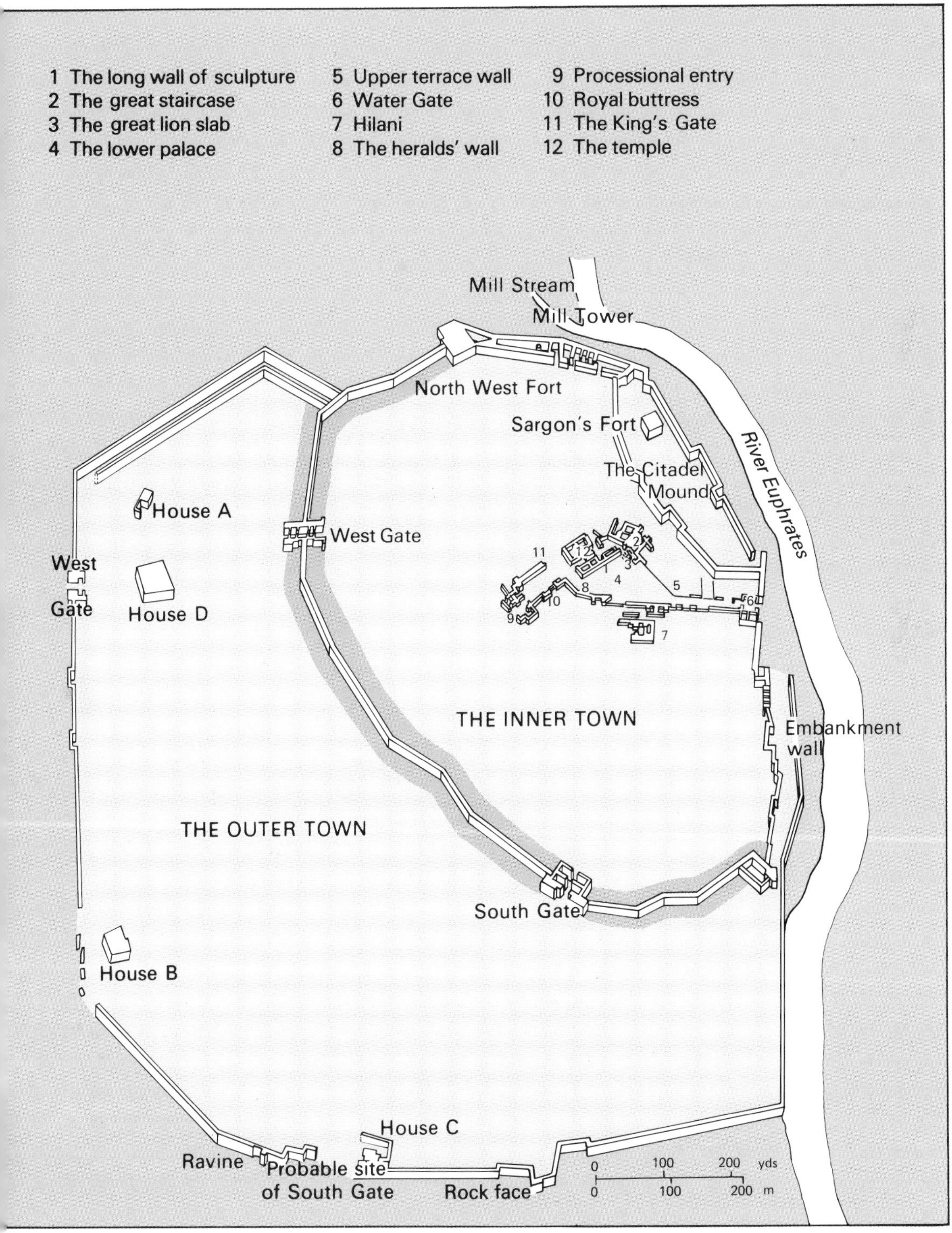


Plan of the site of Carchemish, showing areas of excavations.

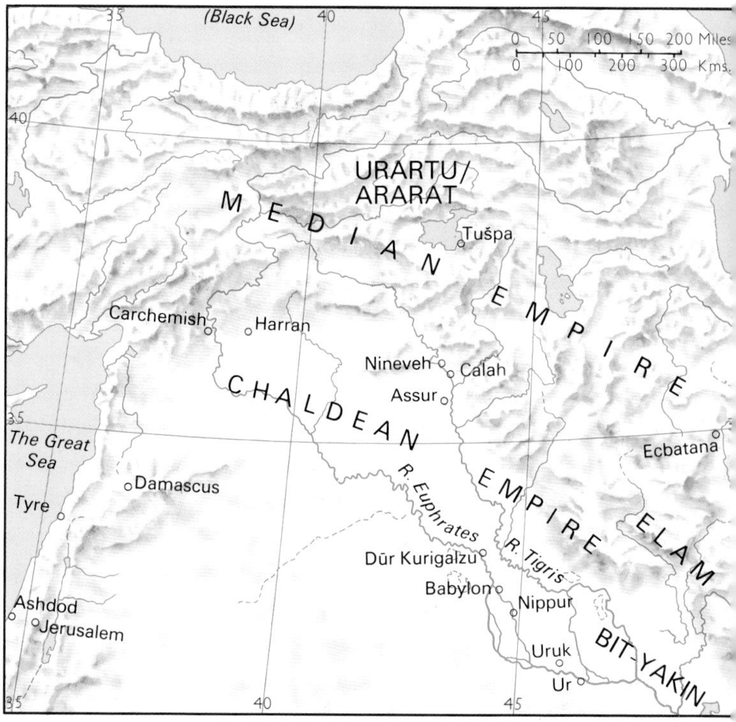

Chaldaea, a name for part of Babylonia taken over for the whole land in the 8th and 7th centuries BC.

south-east, from the Mediterranean (the southern shore of the Bay of Acre) to the plain of Dothan. Strictly, Mount Carmel is the main ridge (maximum height *c.* 530 metres) at the north-western end, running *c.* 19 kilometres inland from the sea, forming a border of Asher (Joshua 19:26).

This densely vegetated and little-inhabited region was a barrier pierced by two main passes, emerging at Jokneam and Megiddo, and a lesser one emerging at Taanach; between the first two, the hills are lower and more barren but have steep scarps. The main north-south road, however, passes by Carmel's hills through the plain of Dothan on the east.

Carmel's luxuriant growth is reflected in Amos 1:2 and 9:3, Micah 7:14 and Nahum 1:4; also in Song of Songs 7:5 in an apt simile for thick, bushy hair. The forbidding figure of Nebuchadrezzar of Babylon marching against Egypt is once compared with the rocky eminences of Carmel and Tabor (Jeremiah 46:18).

Joshua's vanquished foes included 'the king of Jokneam in Carmel' (Joshua 12:22). It was here that Elijah in the name of his God challenged the prophets of Baal and Asherah, the deities promoted by Jezebel, and won a notable victory against them (1 Kings 18; 19:1–2). The text makes it obvious that it was Jezebel's gods that were thus discredited; as she came from Tyre, the Baal was almost certainly Baal-melqart the chief god there.

Baal was still worshipped on Carmel as 'Zeus Heliopolitēs Carmel' in AD 200 (Ap-Thomas, *PEQ* 92, 1960, p. 146). Alt considered this Baal as purely local, a view refuted by the biblical text, and Eissfeldt preferred Baal-shamêm who is less appropriate than Baal-melqart (the latter also advocated by de Vaux).

**2.** A town in Judah (Joshua 15:55), at present-day Khirbet el-Karmil (otherwise known as Kermel or Kurmul), some 12 kilometres south-south-east of Hebron, in a rolling, pastoral region (Baly, p. 164) ideal for the flocks that Nabal grazed there in David's time (1 Samuel 25). His wife Abigail was a Carmelitess, and Hezro, one of David's warriors (2 Samuel 23:35; 1 Chronicles 11:37) probably came from there. Saul passed that way on his return from the slaughter of the Amalekites (1 Samuel 15:12).

*Further reading*
D. Baly, *Geography of the Bible*, 1974, pp. 149 (map 51), 172f.
K. A. Kitchen

**CAUDA,** modern Gavdho (Gozzo), is an island off the south of Crete. Some ancient authorities call it Clauda (as in the AV). Paul's ship was in the vicinity of Cape Matala when the wind changed from southerly to a strong east-north-easterly, and drove it some 40 kilometres before it came under the lee of Cauda, where the crew were at last able to make preparations to face the storm (Acts 27:16).
K. L. McKay

**CENCHREAE,** near the modern resort of Kalamaki on the Sardonic Gulf, served as one of the two ports of Corinth, the other being Lechaion on the Gulf of Corinth. This artificially constructed port was some 14 kilometres from Corinth and had substantial shipping facilities. Pausanias' description of its temples to Isis, Asclepius and Aphrodite and its sanctuary and bronze image to Poseidon on the harbour mole indicates that it was a 'satellite' town. This is confirmed by the archaeological remains uncovered to date.

Early in the arrival of Christianity in Corinth a church was established at this port and Phoebe, a Gentile convert and 'our sister' who served as a deacon in that church, was to be the bearer of Paul's letter to the Romans (Romans 16:1–2).

A large early Christian basilica some 179 metres long has been excavated on the sea-front.
B. W. Winter

*Further reading*
Pausanias, *Description of Greece*, 2.
*Kenchriai, Eastern Port of Corinth*, 3 vols, 1976–78
D. Engels, *Roman Corinth: An Alternative Model for a Classical City*, 1990

**CHALDAEA, CHALDAEANS.** The name of a land, and its inhabitants, in southern Babylonia, later used to denote Babylonia as a whole, especially during the last dynasty of Babylonia (626–539 BC). The Chaldaeans were a semi-nomadic tribe occupying the deserts between northern Arabia and the Persian Gulf (see Job 1:17) who early settled in this area occupying Ur 'of the Chaldees' (Genesis 11:28; Acts 7:4) and were distinct from the Aramaeans.

The proposed derivation from Chesed (Genesis 22:22) is unsubstantiated but the Hebrew *Kaśdîm* may reflect an earlier form of the name than the Assyrian.

From at least the 10th century BC the land of *Kaldu* is named in the Assyrian annals to designate the 'Sea-land' of the earlier inscriptions. Ashurnasirpal II (883–859 BC) distinguished its peoples from the more northerly Babylonians, and Adad-nirari III (*c.* 810 BC) names several chiefs of the Chaldeans among his vassals.

Remains of the synagogue at Chorazin. Date uncertain.

When Marduk-apla-iddina II, the
ief of the Chaldaean district of
t-Yakin, seized the throne of
bylon in 721–710 and 703–702 BC
sought help from the west against
ssyria (Isaiah 39). The prophet
aiah warned of the danger to
dah of supporting the Chaldaean
bels (Isaiah 23:13) and foresaw
eir defeat (43:14), perhaps after
e initial invasion by Sargon in 710
. Since Babylon was at this time
der a Chaldaean king, 'Chaldaean'
used as a synonym for Babylonian
saiah 13:19; 47:1, 5; 48:14, 20), a
e later extended by Ezekiel to
ver all the Babylonian dominions
3:23).
When Nabopolassar, a native
haldaean governor, came to the
bylonian throne in 626 BC, he
augurated a dynasty which made
e name of Chaldaea famous.
mong his successors were
ebuchadrezzar, Amēl-Marduk
vil-merodach), Nabonidus and
lshazzar, 'king of the Chaldaeans'
aniel 5:30). The sturdy
utherners provided strong
ntingents for the Babylonian army
tacking Judah (2 Kings 24–25).
In the time of Daniel the name was
ain used of Babylonia as a whole
aniel 3:8), and Darius the Mede
led the kingdom of the 'Chal-
eans' (Daniel 9:1). The 'tongue of
e Chaldaeans' (Daniel 1:4) was,
rhaps, a semitic Babylonian
alect, the name 'Chaldee' being,
rely in modern times, wrongly
plied to Aramaic.
The prominence of the classes of
iests who, at Babylon and other
ntres, maintained the ancient
aditions of astrology and
ilosophy in the classical
bylonian languages led to the
signation 'Chaldaean' being
applied alike to priests (Daniel 3:8), astrologers and educated persons (Daniel 2:10; 4:7; 5:7, 11).

D. J. Wiseman

*Further reading*

D. J. Wiseman, *Chronicles of Chaldaean Kings,* 1956

A. R. Millard, *EQ* 49, 1977, pp. 69–71, on the use of the name and its origin

**CHEBAR.** The name of a river in Babylonia, by which Jewish exiles were settled; the site of Ezekiel's visions (1:1, 3; 3:15, 23; 10:15, 20, 22; 43:3).

The location is unknown, though Hilprecht proposed an identification with the *nāri kabari* ('great canal'), a name used in a Babylonian text from Nippur for the Shaṭṭ-en-Nil canal running east of that city.

D. J. Wiseman

*Further reading*

E. Vogt, *Biblica* 39, 1958, pp. 211–216

**CHEPHIRAH** (Hebrew *k^e^pîrâh*, possibly meaning 'lion rock'). A Hivite fortress (Joshua 9:17); Khirbet Kefireh, on a spur 8 kilometres west of Gibeon, dominates the Wadi Qatneh, which leads down to *Aijalon. It became Benjaminite territory (Joshua 18:26). The Gola-list (Ezra 2:25; Nehemiah 7:29) associates it with *Kiriath-jearim. For a description see K. Vriezen, *RB* 84, 1977, pp. 412–416.

J. P. U. Lilley

**CHERITH.** A tributary of the river Jordan beside which Elijah was fed when he hid from Ahab at God's command (1 Kings 17:3, 5). Locations south of Gilgal or east of the Jordan have been proposed.

D. W. Baker

**CHESULLOTH** (Hebrew *k^e^sullôṯ*), Joshua 19:18, also Chisloth-tabor, Joshua 19:12. A town in Issachar west of Mount Tabor and near modern Iksal (5 kilometres west of Mount Tabor); Zebulun occupied the hills to the north-west.

J. P. U. Lilley

**CHINNERETH.** A fortified city, Joshua 19:35 (probably modern Khirbet el-Oreimah), also spelt Chinneroth (Joshua 11:2), which gave its name to the sea of Chinnereth (Numbers 34:11), known in the New Testament as the lake of Gennesaret (Luke 5:1), the Sea of Galilee or the Sea of Tiberias. Josephus uses the term Gennesar (*Jewish War* 2.573). The name could be derived from *kinnôr*, harp, from the shape of the lake.

N. Hillyer

**CHIOS.** One of the larger Aegean islands off the west coast of Asia Minor, this was a free city-state under the Roman empire until Vespasian's day.

Paul's ship on the way from Troas to Patara anchored for a night near the island (Acts 20:15).

J. D. Douglas

**CHORAZIN.** A town on the Sea of Galilee associated with the Lord's preaching and miracles, but which he denounced because it did not repent (Matthew 11:21; Luke 10:13).

Now identified with Kerazeh, 4 kilometres north of *Capernaum, the black basalt ruins of its synagogue and various other public and domestic buildings have recently been excavated and partially restored. The synagogue dates from the 3rd-4th centuries AD. No remains of the 1st-century town have yet been identified with certainty.

J. W. Meiklejohn, J. Bimson

*Further reading*

Z. Yeivin, *BARev* XIII/5, 1987, pp. 22–36

Z. Yeivin in *NEAEHL* I, pp. 301–304

**CILICIA.** A region in south-east Asia Minor. The western part, known as Tracheia, was a wild plateau of the Taurus range, the home of pirates and robbers from prehistoric to Roman times. The eastern part, known as Cilicia Pedias, was a fertile plain between Mount Amanus in the south, Mount Taurus in the north and the sea; and the vital trade route between Syria and Asia Minor lay through its twin majestic passes, the Syrian Gates and the Cilician Gates.

Cilicia was officially made a

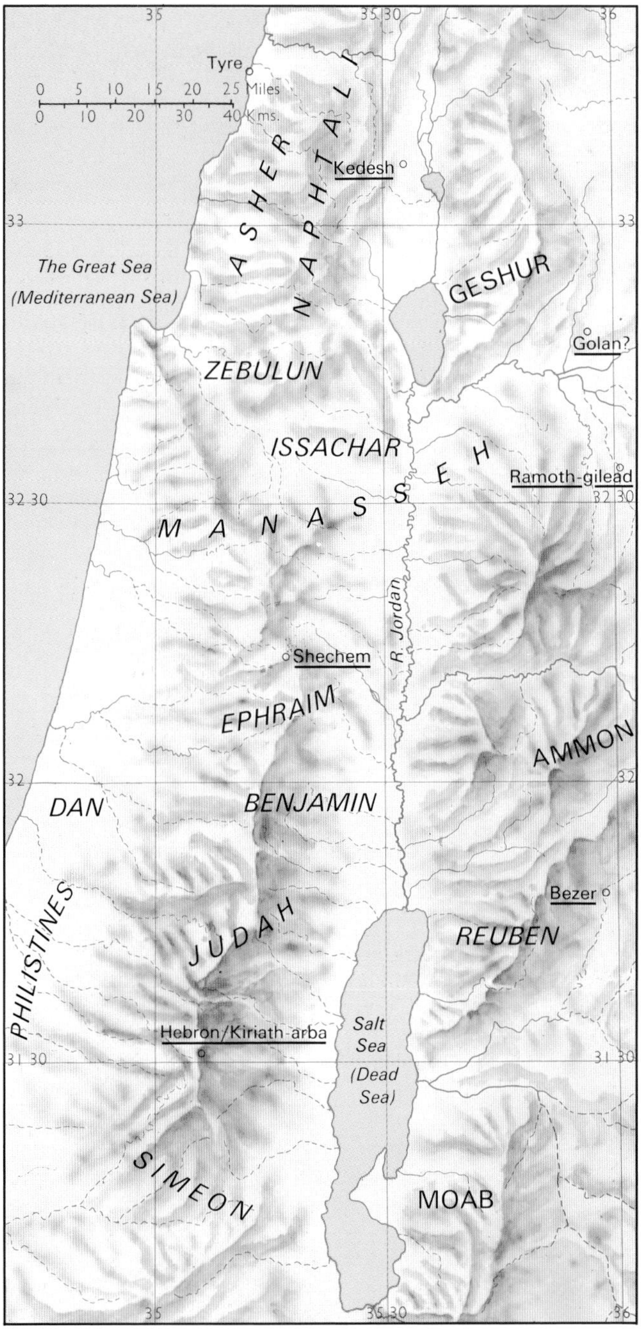


**The cities of refuge (Joshua 20).**

province before 100 BC, but effective rule began only after Pompey's pirate drive in 67 BC. Cicero was governor here in 51 BC. The province apparently disappeared under the Early Empire, Augustus ceding Tracheia partly to the native dynasty and partly to the adjacent client kingdoms of Galatia and Cappadocia.

Pedias, which consists of 16 semi-autonomous cities, of which Tarsus was the most outstanding, was administered by Syria until after Tracheia was taken from Antiochus IV of Commagene in AD 72. Then Vespasian re-combined both regions into the single province of Cilicia (Suetonius, *Vespasian* 8). Thus Paul, its most distinguished citizen, and Luke, both writing accurately of the earlier period, are strictly correct in combining Cilicia (*i.e.* Pedias) in one unit with Syria (Galatians 1:21 variant; Acts 15:23, 41; see E. M. B. Green, 'Syria and Cilicia', *ExpT* 71, 1959–60, pp. 50–53, and authorities quoted there).

E. M. B. Green, C. J. Hemer

**CIRCLE OF JORDAN.** See *PLAIN, CITIES OF THE.

**CITIES OF REFUGE.** These were places of asylum mentioned principally in Numbers 35:9–34 and Joshua 20:1–9 (where they are named). They are also mentioned in Numbers 35:6; Joshua 21:13, 21, 27, 32, 38; and 1 Chronicles 6:57, 67. From these it appears that they were among the cities of the Levites. Deuteronomy 4:41–43 and 19:1–13 deal with the institution indicated by this name (see Exodus 21:12–14).

*Law of retribution*

In Israel's public life the law of retribution was to be applied, and i moreover, specified in the *lex talionis* (see Exodus 21:23–25, *etc.*) which particularly applied in cases of bloodshed (see Genesis 9:5f.; Exodus 21:12; Leviticus 24:17, *etc.* compare also Deuteronomy 21:1–9).

In ancient Israel at least, the duty of punishing the slayer rested upon the *gō'ēl*, the nearest male relative (variously translated as 'next of kin 'nearest relative' and 'kinsman-redeemer' in modern English versions). A distinction was made between slaying a man purposely o unawares. The wilful murderer was to be killed, while the unintentional murderer could find asylum in one of the cities of refuge. It may be said that the institution of the cities of refuge mainly served to prevent excesses which might develop from the execution of what is usually called the 'blood-feud'.

*The altar as an asylum*

In 'the book of the covenant', Israel oldest collection of laws, there is already a stipulation concerning thi matter (Exodus 21:12–14). Perhaps the tendency of this regulation can be described as follows. Israel knew the ancient practice, which also prevailed among other nations, of regarding the altar or the sanctuary as an asylum. Here it is stipulated that the wilful slayer shall not find a refuge near the altar, though the unintentional slayer may do so.

But the altar may be at a great distance, and, moreover, he cannot stay permanently near the altar, in the sanctuary. So the Lord announces that he will make furthe provisions for this matter. The curious expression 'God let him fall into his hand' has been interpreted in the sense that the unintentional murderer is an instrument of God, and accordingly it is only natural tha God should look after his protection

Examples of the altar as an asylum

Israel occur in 1 Kings 1:50–53 and :28–34, while expressions such as ıose used in Psalms 27:4–6 and 1:4, and Obadiah 17 show that this ractice was well known in Israel.

*egulations*

here are characteristic differences etween the two principal groups of gulations concerning the cities of fuge, Numbers 35:9ff. and euteronomy 19:1ff. (compare euteronomy 4:41–43). As to the gulations of Numbers 35, which ere also given in the plains of Moab erse 1), we should note the llowing. The term 'cities of refuge, ties where a person is received (?)' used. In due course Israel is to opoint three cities on the eastern de of Jordan, and three cities on the estern side (verses 13ff.), which ties are to be among the cities of e Levites (verse 6). The ongregation' is to pronounce the nal judgment (verses 12, 24). )uring the wanderings through the esert this body made decisions in ıch cases. Here no further ipulation is made as to what body to act in a similar capacity once rael had settled in Canaan.)

In verses 16–23 criteria are given define accurately whether one has do with intentional or uninten- onal murder. The unintentional ayer is to remain in the city until e death of the high priest (verses 5, 28, 32). In this connection the ay receives the character of an kile, of penance (verses 28, 32). ote also the stipulations of verses )–32, with the important otivation, given in verses 33f.

Deuteronomy 4:41–43 narrates ow 'Moses set apart three cities in ıe east beyond the Jordan'. euteronomy 19:1ff. stipulates that, ter the conquest of Canaan, three ties of refuge shall be appointed on e western side of Jordan, and ıother three in case of a further ktension of Israel's territory (the st regulation was apparently never ırried out).

It is emphasized that the Israelites ıould take care that a slayer who lled ignorantly was within easy ach of a city of refuge (verses 3, f.). To indicate the difference etween a wilful and unintentional urder, an example is given in verse The elders of the slayer's welling-place are to make the final ecision (verse 12).

*he cities*

ccording to Joshua 20, the llowing cities of refuge were opointed during Joshua's lifetime: Kedesh, Shechem, Kiriath-arba (that is, Hebron), Bezer, Ramoth and Golan. Joshua 20 assumes as known both the regulations of Numbers 35 and of Deuteronomy 19. A new feature here is that the elders of the cities of refuge also have a responsibility (verses 4–5).

Nothing is known about the putting into practice of the right of asylum. Except for 1 Kings 1:50–53 and 2:28–34, it is not mentioned, which *per se* need not surprise us. It is possible that, as the central authority established itself more firmly, the right of asylum decreased in significance.

N. H. Ridderbos

*Further reading*

C. L. Feinberg, 'The Cities of Refuge', *BS* 103, 1946, pp. 411–416; 104, 1947, pp. 35–48
W. F. Albright, *Archaeology and the Religion of Israel*, 1956, pp. 120–125
R. de Vaux, *Ancient Israel*, 1961, pp. 160–163
M. Greenberg, 'The Biblical Conception of Asylum', *JBL* 78, 1959, pp. 125–132

**CLAUDA.** See *CAUDA.

**CNIDUS.** A city of Caria in south-west Asia Minor, where Paul's ship changed course on its way to Rome (Acts 27:7). Cnidus had Jewish inhabitants as early as the 2nd century BC (1 Maccabees 15:23), and had the status of free city.

J. D. Douglas

**COELESYRIA** (Greek *koilē syria*, 'hollow Syria'). 1 Esdras 2:17, *etc.*; 2 Maccabees 3:5, *etc.*, the valley lying between the Lebanon and Anti-Lebanon ranges, modern El-Biqa' (compare *biq'aṯ 'āwen*, 'the Valley of Aven', Amos 1:5). As a political region under the Ptomelaic and Seleucid empires it frequently embraces a wider area, sometimes stretching to Damascus in the north and including Phoenicia to the west or Judaea to the south. From 312 to 198 BC it formed part of the Ptolemaic empire, but fell to the Seleucids in consequence of the battle of Panion in the latter year.

Coelesyria was an administrative division of the province of Syria after the Roman occupation (64 BC). Herod was appointed military prefect of Coelesyria by Sextus Caesar in 47 BC and again by Cassius in 43 BC.

F. F. Bruce

**COLOSSAE.** A city in the Roman province of Asia, in the west of what is now Asiatic Turkey. It was situated about 15 kilometres up the Lycus valley from *Laodicea, on the main road to the east. It was originally the point at which the great routes from Sardis and Ephesus joined, and at a defensible place with an abundant water-supply.

Colossae was an important city in the Lydian and Persian periods, but later it declined when the road

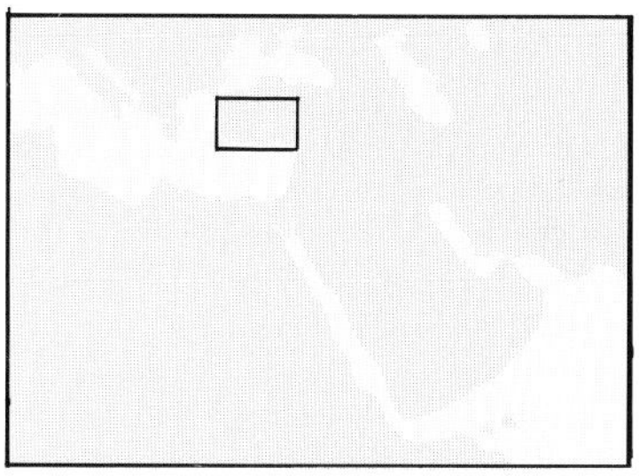

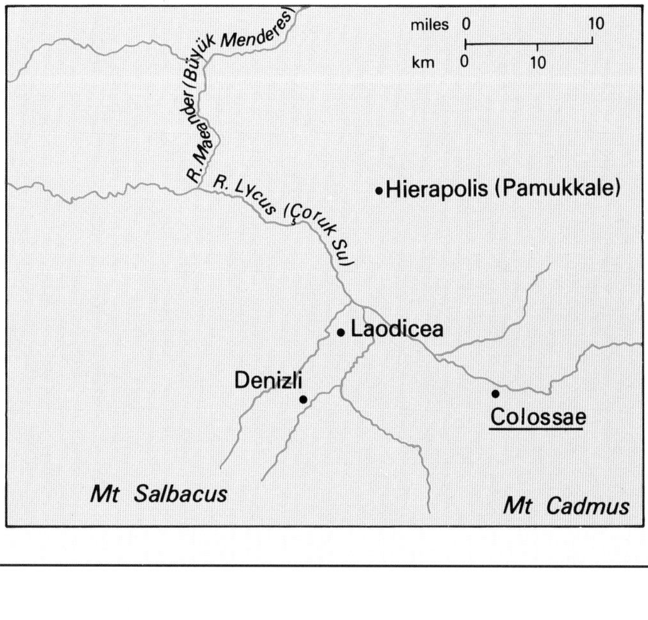


**Colossae, in the Roman province of Asia.**

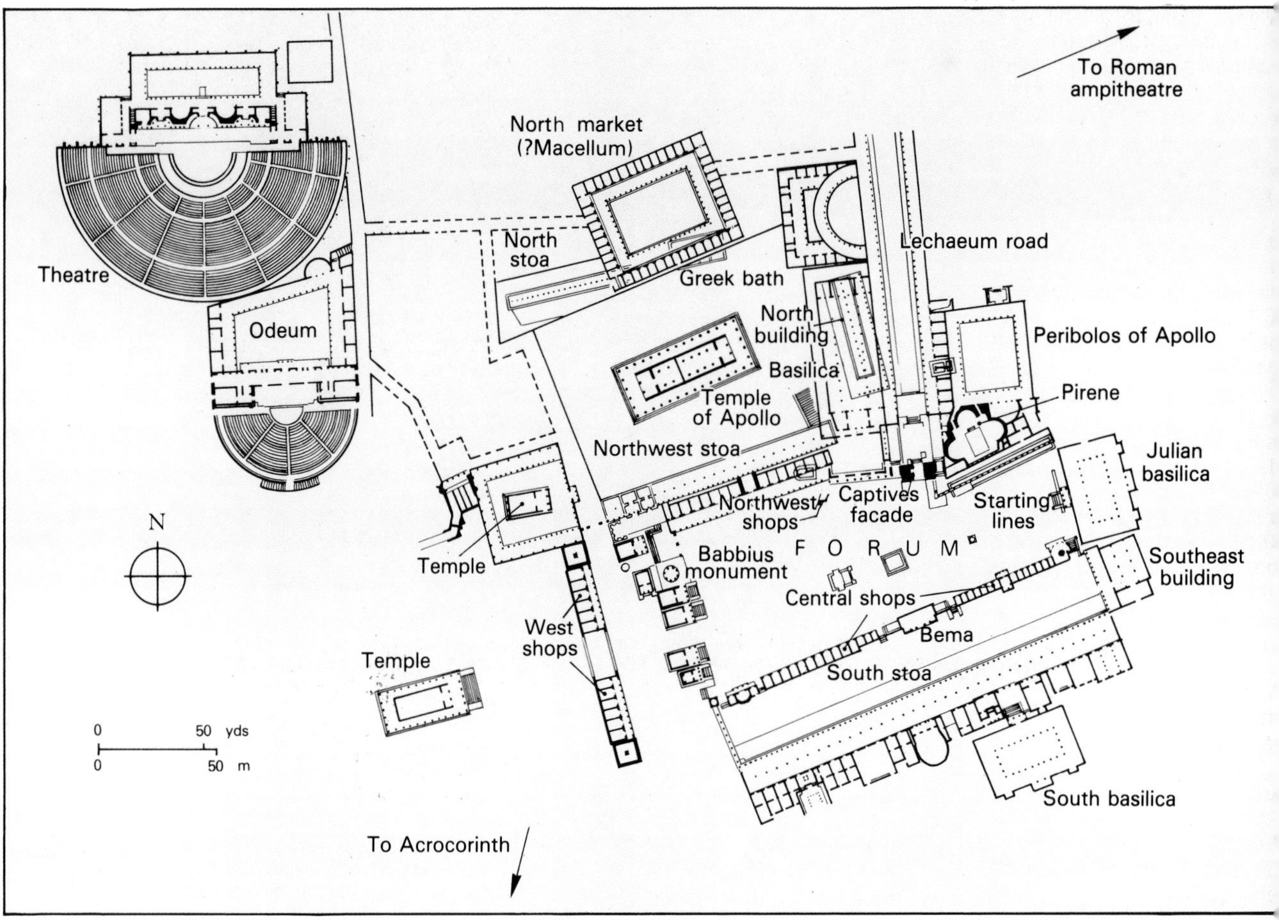


**Plan of the centre of Corinth, refounded as a Roman colony in 44 BC, incorporating the remains of the Greek city dating from *c.* 540 BC.**

through Sardis to Pergamum was resited farther west at the prosperous new foundation of Laodicea.

The site is now uninhabited; it lies near Honaz, 16 kilometres east of the town of Denizli. It has not been excavated.

*The church in Colossae*

The gospel probably reached the district while Paul was living at Ephesus (Acts 19:10), perhaps through Epaphras, who was a Colossian (Colossians 1:7; 4:12–13). Paul had apparently not visited Colossae when he wrote his letter (Colossians 2:1), though his desire to do so (Philemon 22) may have been met at a later date.

Philemon (Philemon 1) and his slave Onesimus (Colossians 4:9; Philemon 10) were members of the early Colossian church. The mixture of Jewish, Greek and Phrygian elements in the population of the city was probably found also in the church: it would have been fertile ground for the type of speculative heresy which Paul's letter was designed to counter.

The neighbourhood was devastated by an earthquake, dated by Tacitus (*Annals* 14.27) to AD 60. There is no hint of this in the Epistle, which we must suppose was written before news of the disaster had reached Rome.

E. M. B. Green, C. J. Hemer

**CORINTH.** A city of Greece at the western end of the isthmus between central Greece and the Peloponnesus, in control of trade routes between northern Greece and the Peloponnese and across the isthmus. The latter was particularly important because much trade was taken across the isthmus rather than round the stormy southern promontories of the Peloponnese.

**The city**

There were two harbours, Lechaeum 2·5 kilometres west on the Corinthian Gulf, connected with the city by long walls; and Cenchreae 14 kilometres east on the Saronic Gulf. Corinth thus became a flourishing centre of trade, as well as of industry, particularly ceramics.

The town is dominated by the Acrocorinth (566 metres), a steep, flat-topped rock surmounted by the acropolis, which in ancient times contained, *inter alia*, a temple of Aphrodite, goddess of love, whose service gave rise to the ancient city's proverbial immorality, notorious already by the time of Aristophanes (Strabo, *Geography*, 378; Athenaeus, *Gastronomers*, 573). However, by Roman times Aphrodite had become the progenitress of the Imperial Family and her connection with her licentious past had been severed.

*History*

From the late 4th century until 196 BC Corinth was held mainly by the Macedonians; but in that year it was liberated, with the rest of Greece, by T. Quinctius Flamininus, and joined the Achaean League. After a period of opposition to Rome, and social revolution under the dictator Critolaus, the city was, in 146 BC, razed to the ground by the consul L. Mummius, and its inhabitants sold into slavery.

In 46 BC Corinth was established as a Roman colony by Julius Caesar. It was relaid in accordance with Roman town planning and the town plan of the colony of Carthage. Augustus made it the capital of the new province of Achaea, now detached from Macedonia and ruled y a separate proconsular governor. s prestige and prosperity attracted eading families from Achaea and by aul's time had approximately 00,000 inhabitants. The Isthmian ames were resumed. The Imperial ult thrived and was established on provincial basis in AD 54.

**aul in Corinth**

aul's 18-months' stay in Corinth in is second missionary journey (Acts 8:1–18) has been dated by an ıscription from Delphi which shows hat Gallio came to Corinth as roconsul in AD 51 or 52 (Acts 8:12–17). His *bēma*, or judgment eat (Acts 18:12), has also been lentified either in the Forum or the ulian Basilica, as has the *macellum* r meat-market (1 Corinthians 0:25). An inscription near the heatre mentions an aedile Erastus, vho possibly is the treasurer of omans 16:23.

. H. Harrop, B. W. Winter

*'urther reading*
'trabo, *Geography*, 378–382
'ausanias, *Description of Greece*, .1–4
\thenaeus, 573
*;orinth I-VIII* (Princeton University 'ress), 1951 onwards
*;Br*, under 'Corinth' (with older ibliography)
;xcavation reports annually from 896 to *AJA, JHS, Hesperia*
I. G. Payne, *Necrocorinthia*, 1931
). Broneer, *BA* 14, 1951, pp. 78ff.
'. Wiseman, 'Corinth and Rome I', *NRW* II.7.1, 1979, pp. 435–548
/. P. Furnish, *BARev* XIV/3, 1988, p. 14–27
). W. J. Gill, 'Erastus the Aedile', *'ynB* 40.2, 1989, pp. 293–301
). Engels, *Roman Corinth: An Alternative Model for a Classical ;ity*, 1990 (but with substantial eservations: see D. W. J. Gill, Corinth: A Roman Colony in \chaea', *BZ* 37, 1993, especially note )
3. W. Winter, 'Theological and ;thical Responses to Religious 'luralism (1 Corinthians 8–10)', *'ynB* 41.2, 1990, pp. 209–226
). W. J. Gill, 'The Meat-Market at ;orinth (1 Corinthians 10:25)', *TynB* 3.2, 1992, pp. 293–301
). G. Romano, 'The Planning of Roman Corinth', *AJA* 96, 1992, p. 337
\. Spawforth, 'Corinth, Argos and he Imperial Cult: A Reconsideration f Pseudo-Julian *Letters* 198 Bidez', *Iesperia*, 1994

**:OS.** Paul's ship after leaving Miletus headed for Cos (Acts 21:1). It vas a massive and mountainous island, one of the Sporades group, off the south-west coast of Asia Minor, near Halicarnassus. Cos was colonized at an early period by Dorian Greeks, and achieved fame as the site of the medical school founded in the 5th century BC by Hippocrates, and again as a literary centre, the home of Philetas and Theocritus, in the 3rd century BC. It was also noted for fine weaving.

The Romans made Cos a free state in the province of Asia, and the emperor Claudius, influenced by his Coan physician, conferred on it immunity from taxes. Herod the Great was a benefactor of the people of Cos.

K. L. McKay

Ruins of Corinth. The acropolis dominates the city in the plain below. View along Lechaeum road towards the city centre.

**CRETE.** A mainly mountainous island in the Mediterranean lying across the southern end of the Aegean. It is about 250 kilometres long, and its breadth varies from 56 kilometres to 11 kilometres. It is not mentioned by name in the Old Testament, but it is probable that the Cherethites, who formed part of David's bodyguard, came from Crete, and the place-name *Caphtor probably referred to the island and the adjacent coastlands which fell within its dominion during the 2nd millennium BC.

*In the New Testament*

Cretans (*Krētes*) are mentioned among those present at Pentecost (Acts 2:11), and later the island (*Krētē*) is named in the account of Paul's journey to Rome (Acts 27:7–13, 21). His ship sailed past Salmone at the eastern end and put into a port called *Fair Havens near Lasea in the centre of the south coast, and Paul advised wintering there. He was overruled, however. The ship set out to coast round to a better wintering-berth at Phoenix in the south-west, but a strong wind drove them out to sea, and finally to Malta.

After his imprisonment at Rome, Paul evidently revisited Crete, for he left Titus there to carry on the work. The unflattering description of the Cretans in Titus 1:12 is a quotation from Epimenides of Crete (quoted also in Acts 17:28a).

*Early history*

Our knowledge of the island's history is derived chiefly from archaeology. There were neolithic settlements on it in the 4th and 3rd millennia BC, but it was in the Bronze Age that a powerful civilization was achieved. This was centred upon Knossos, a site excavated over many years by Sir Arthur Evans.

The Early Bronze Age (Early Minoan I-III, *c.* 2600–1900 BC) was a period of gradual commercial expansion, which was continued during the Middle Bronze Age (Middle Minoan I-III, *c.* 1900–1600 BC). In this latter period writing (on

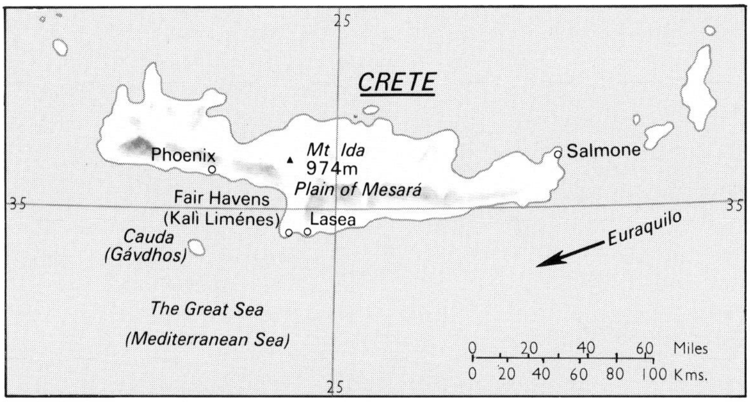


The island of Crete in New Testament times, showing the direction of the wind Euraquilo.

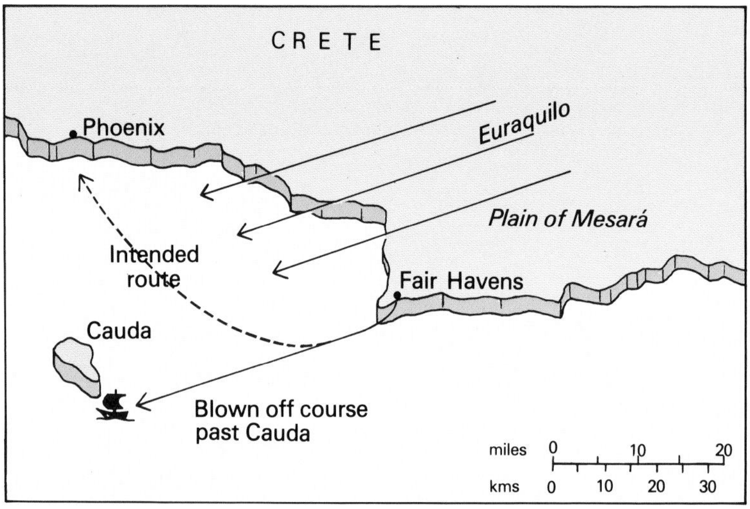


A diagrammatic representation of how far Paul, sailing from Fair Havens, was blown off course past Cauda.

clay and copper tablets) was in use, first of all in the form of a pictographic script (*c.* 2000–1650 BC) and then in a simplified form, known as Linear A (*c.* 1750–1450 BC). Neither of these scripts has been positively deciphered (possible Linear A *ku-ro* is shown by the context to mean 'total' which might point to Semitic *kl* 'all', but the evidence is insufficient to press this).

The peak of Cretan civilization was reached in the early part of the Late Bronze Age (Late Minoan I[-II], *c.* 1600–1400 BC). The Linear A script continued in use during part of this period, but a third script, Linear B, appeared at Knossos (Late Minoan II, known only from Knossos). This was deciphered in 1953 by M. Ventris, and found to be an archaic form of Greek (Mycenaean), suggesting that the Late Minoan II period at Knossos was due to an enclave of Greek-speaking invaders.

Similar tablets have also been found at Mycenae, Pylos, Thebes and Tiryus on the mainland of Greece, where the script continued to be used after the decline of Minoan civilization, a decline which was accelerated by the violent destruction, perhaps by pirates, of most of the towns in Crete, around 1400 BC.

This decline continued through the last phases of the Bronze Age (Late Minoan III, *c.* 1400–1125 BC). Towards the end of this period Dorian Greeks came to the island and ushered in the Iron Age.

Discoveries in Egypt, and at such sites as Ras Shamra (compare the name of King *krt* in the cuneiform tablets), Byblos and Atchana (Alalakh) in Syria, show that Cretan commerce had extended to western Asia by the Middle Minoan II period (1st quarter of the 2nd millennium), and from this time on the folk-movements, in which the Philistines played a part and which culminated in the invasions of the 'Sea Peoples' in the 12th century, were taking place.

Throughout the Iron Age the island was divided among a number of feuding city-states, until it was subdued by Rome in 67 BC.

T. C. Mitchell

*Further reading*

J. D. S. Pendlebury, *The Archaeology of Crete*, 1939
R. W. Hutchinson, *Prehistoric Crete*, 1962
H. J. Kantor, *The Aegean and the Orient in the Second Millennium* BC, 1947
J. Chadwick, *The Decipherment of Linear B*, 1958
*Linear B and related scripts*, 1987
C. H. Gordon, *HUCA* 26, 1955, pp. 43–108
*JNES* 17, 1958, pp. 245–255
F. F. Bruce, *Acts* (Greek Text), pp. 338–339 (on Acts 17:28)

**CUSH. 1.** A region encompassed by the river Gihon (Genesis 2:13); probably in western Asia and unrelated to **2** below; see E. A. Speiser in *Festschrift Johannes Friedrich*, 1959, pp. 473–485.

**2.** The region south of Egypt, *i.e.* Nubia or northern Sudan, the 'Ethiopia' of classical writers (not modern Abyssinia). The name Cush in both Hebrew and Assyrian derives from Egyptian *Kš* (earlier *K's* *K'š*), 'Kush'. Originally the name of a district somewhere between the second and third cataracts of the Nile *c.* 2000 BC, 'Kush' became also a general term for Nubia among the Egyptians, which wider use Hebrews, Assyrians and others took over (G. Posener, in *Kush* 6, 1958, pp. 39–68).

In 2 Chronicles 21:16 Arabians are 'near' the Ethiopians – *i.e.* just across the Red Sea from them; *Syene or Seveneh (modern Aswan) was the frontier of Egypt and Ethiopia in the 1st millennium BC (Ezekiel 29:10).

Invaded in prehistoric times by Hamites from Arabia and Asia, Ethiopia was dominated by Egypt for nearly 500 years beginning with Dynasty 18 (*c.* 1500 BC) and was governed by a viceroy ('King's Son of Kush') who ruled the African empire controlled the army in Africa and managed the Nubian gold mines.

During the 9th century the Ethiopians, whose capital was Napata near the fourth cataract, engaged in at least one foray into Palestine, only to suffer defeat at Asa's hand (2 Chronicles 14:9–15).

Ethiopia's heyday began about 720 BC when Pi-ankhi took advantage of Egypt's internal strife and became the first conqueror of that land in a millennium. For about 60 years Ethiopian rulers (Dynasty 25) controlled the Nile Valley. One of them, Tirhakah, seems to have been Hezekiah's ally and attempted to forestall Sennacherib's invasion (2 Kings 19:9; Isaiah 37:9; J. Bright, *History of Israel*, 2nd edition, 1972, pp. 296ff., discusses the chronological problems in this narrative). Nahum 3:9 alludes to the glory of this period: 'Ethiopia was her (Egypt's)

:ength.'

Invasions by Esarhaddon and shurbanipal reduced the hiopian-Egyptian kingdom to butary status; the destruction of nebes (*c.* 663 BC; Nahum 3:8–10) ought a total eclipse, fulfilling aiah's prophetic symbolism 0:2–6).

Ethiopian troops fought vainly in haraoh Neco's army at Carchemish 05 BC; Jeremiah 46:2, 9). ambyses' conquest of Egypt ought Ethiopia under Persian vay; Esther 1:1 and 8:9 name hiopia as the most remote Persian ovince to the south-west, while blical writers sometimes use her to mbolize the unlimited extent of od's sovereignty (Psalm 87:4; zekiel 30:4ff.; Amos 9:7; phaniah 2:12).

'Beyond the rivers of Ethiopia' saiah 18:1; Zephaniah 3:10) may fer to northern Abyssinia, where wish colonists had apparently ttled along with other Semites om southern Arabia. The ronicler is cognizant of this close lationship between Ethiopia and uthern Arabia (2 Chronicles 21:16).

The 'topaz' came from this land ob 28:19) of unchangeably dark ins (Jeremiah 13:23), as did bed-melech at the Judaean court eremiah 38:7ff.; 39:15ff.), and ueen Candace's minister (Acts 27). The runner who bore news of bsalom's death to David was a ushite' (2 Samuel 18:21, 23, 31–32).

Ethiopia recurs in the prophecies Ezekiel 38:5 and Daniel 11:43. The ushite woman' whom Moses arried (Numbers 12:1) was either a ubian who left Egypt along with e Israelites or, if 'Cushite' here is erived from Cushan (a region linked ith Midian in Habakkuk 3:7), a oman of allied stock to his first wife pporah (if this is not in fact a ference to Zipporah herself).

Modern Ethiopians (Abyssinians) ave appropriated biblical ferences to Ethiopia and consider e Ethiopian eunuch's conversion be a fulfilment of Psalm 68:31.

A. Hubbard, K. A. Kitchen

*urther reading*

A. W. Budge, *History of Ethiopia*, 928
A. Kitchen, *Third Intermediate eriod in Egypt (1100–650 BC)*, 2nd lition, 1986
Ullendorff, *The Ethiopians*, 1960
—, *Ethiopia and the Bible*, 1968
Wilson, *The Burden of Egypt*, 1951

**UTH, CUTHAH.** An ancient city in abylonia (Akkadian *kûtu* from the Sumerian *gu-du-a*), the seat of the god Nergal, whose inhabitants were deported by Sargon to repopulate Samaria (2 Kings 17:24, 30). The site, represented today by the mound called Tell Ibrahīm, was briefly excavated in 1881–82 by Hormuzd Rassam, who noted that it had at one time been a very extensive city.

T. C. Mitchell

*Further reading*

H. Rassam, *Asshur and the Land of Nimrod*, 1897, pp. 396, 409–411

**CYPRUS.** The island of Cyprus, some 225 kilometres long, and 100 kilometres wide at its broadest, lies in the eastern Mediterranean some 100 kilometres west of the coast of Syria and about the same distance from the Turkish coast.

*In the Old Testament*

Cyprus is not mentioned by that name in the Old Testament, where it is probably referred to as *Elishah; the people called Kittim in Genesis 10 were probably the Phoenician settlers at Kition (modern Larnaca). It has been argued that biblical *Caphtor should be identified with at least a part of Cyprus, but most scholars prefer to identify Caphtor with *Crete.

*In the New Testament*

The island is named *Kypros* in Acts. Barnabas was a native of it (4:36), as were some of the other early disciples, and the church in the island was further augmented by refugees from the first persecution (Acts 11:19–20; 21:16). Paul and Barnabas travelled across the island from Salamis to Paphos at the beginning of their first missionary journey (Acts 13:4–13). It was at Paphos that they encountered Bar-jesus, the sorcerer, and the proconsul (*anthypatos*) Sergius Paulus.

Paul did not visit the island on his second missionary journey, but Barnabas went there separately with Mark (Acts 15:39). When returning from his third journey, Paul's ship passed it to the south-west (Acts 21:3), and on the voyage to Rome contrary winds prevented him from landing (Acts 27:4).There is no other mention of the island in the Bible, but the church there continued to flourish, sending three bishops to the Council of Nicaea in AD 325.

*Excavations*

There are traces of neolithic settlement on the island, and its Bronze Age culture shows evidence of contacts with Asia Minor and Syria. In the 15th century BC the Minoan civilization of *Crete extended to Cyprus, and in the following century there is evidence of colonization by the Mycenaeans, who were succeeding to the Cretan power on the Greek mainland. It was probably in this century that the copper mines, which in Roman times became famous enough for the metal to be named after the island (Latin *cyprium*), first came into extensive use, and as a result of this Cyprus appears frequently in the records of the surrounding nations (see also *ELISHAH) at this period.

In spite of outside influence, the basic Minoan-Mycenaean culture remained dominant, being evidenced particularly by the so-called Cypro-Minoan inscriptions (two early collections 15th and 12th centuries BC), which show close affinities with the Cretan Linear scripts. This script was still found in use in the late 1st millennium, together with the dialect of Greek most closely related to that in the Minoan Linear B Tablets, Arcadian, which had presumably been superseded in southern Greece and Crete by Doric.

Cyprus lay in the path of the 'Sea Peoples', and excavations at Enkomi and Sinda have revealed a late type of Mycenaean pottery from which the so-called *'Philistine' pottery of Palestine was clearly a development. In the 9th or 8th century BC Phoenicians settled on the island and later a number of bilingual inscriptions occur (*c.* 600–200 BC), of Phoenician and Greek each with the Cypro-Minoan, now called classical Cypriot, script which was still in use at this time. That the Phoenicians did not gain much power is shown by an account of tribute to Esarhaddon in 672 BC, when only one Phoenician, as opposed to nine Greek kings, is mentioned (tribute had also been paid to Sargon in 709).

In the 6th century Egypt dominated the island until it became part of the Persian empire under Cambyses in 525. In 333 BC it submitted to Alexander, and after a brief period under Antigonus it passed to the Ptolemies. It was made a Roman province in 58 BC, and after various changes it became a Senatorial province in 27 BC, from which time it was governed by a proconsul (Greek *anthypatos*; compare Acts 13:7).

T. C. Mitchell

*Further reading*
G. F. Hill, *A History of Cyprus*, 1940
E. Gjerstad, *The Swedish Cyprus Expedition* 4, 2, 1948 (Geometric, Archaic and Classical periods); 4, 3, 1956 (Hellenistic and Roman periods)
V. Karageorghis, *The Ancient Civilization of Cyprus*, 1969
——, *Cyprus: From the Stone Age to the Romans*, 1982
J. Chadwick, *Linear B and Related Scripts*, 1987, pp. 50–56
T. C. Mitchell, *CAH*, 2nd edition, III.2, p. 399 (Kittim)

**CYRENE.** A port in North Africa, of Dorian foundation, rich in corn, silphium, wool and dates. It became part of the Ptolemaic empire in the 3rd century BC, and was bequeathed to Rome in 96 BC, becoming a province in 74 BC.

Josephus quotes Strabo as stating that Cyrene encouraged Jewish settlement, and that Jews formed one of the four recognized classes of the state (*Antiquities*, 14.114). Josephus mentions also a Jewish rising there in Sulla's time, and Dio Cassius (68) another in Trajan's.

To this Jewish community belonged Simon the cross-bearer (Mark 15:21 and parallels), some of the missionaries to Antioch (Acts 11:20) and the Antiochene teacher Lucius. It was also represented in the Pentecost crowd (Acts 2:10) and evidently had its own (or a shared) synagogue in Jerusalem (Acts 6:9).
J. H. Harrop

*Further reading*
P. Romanelli, *La Cirenaica Romana*, 1943
A. Rowe, D. Buttle and J. Gray, *Cyrenaican Expeditions of the University of Manchester*, 1956
J. Reynolds, *JTS* n.s. 11, 1960, pp. 284ff.

# D

**DABERATH.** A levitical city of Issachar (1 Chronicles 6:72; Joshua 21:28, where the AV has 'Dabareh'), probably on the border of Zebulun (Joshua 19:12). It is usually identified with the ruins near the modern village of Debûriyeh, at the western foot of Mount Tabor.
J. D. Douglas

**DALMANUTHA.** In Mark 8:10 a district on the coast of the Lake of Galilee, to which Jesus and his disciples crossed after the feeding of the four thousand. It has never been satisfactorily identified. (Magadan in the parallel passage, Matthew 15:39, is equally unknown though some manuscripts read Magdala here, a town on the western shore of the lake.) Various emendations have been proposed (including F. C. Burkitt's suggestion that it represents a corruption of Tiberias combined with its earlier name Amathus), but it is best to keep the attested reading and await further light.

An interesting recent suggestion is that the name reflects an Aramaic word for 'enclosure/anchorage', and refers to an anchorage somewhere near Magdala. Exceptionally low water levels in 1970 revealed a number of previously unknown ancient anchorages around the lake including one near Magdala and another between Magdala and Capernaum. One of these could have provided the name for the stretch of coast in Mark 8:10.
F. F. Bruce, J. J. Bimson

*Further reading*
J. F. Strange, 'Dalmanutha', *ABD* II, p. 4

**DALMATIA.** A Roman province in the mountainous region on the east of the Adriatic, formed by the emperor Tiberius. Its name was derived from an Illyrian tribe that inhabited it. It was bounded on the east by Moesia and the north by Pannonia. It is mentioned in 2 Timothy 4:10, and is identical with *Illyricum (Romans 15:19).
B. F. C. Atkinson

**DAMASCUS**

*Location*
The capital city of Syria (Isaiah 7:8), situated east of the Anti-Lebanon Mountains and overshadowed in the south-west by Mount Hermon (Song of Songs 7:4). It lies in the north-west of the Ghuta plain 700 metres above sea-level and west of the Syrian-Arabian desert. The district is famous for its orchards and gardens, being irrigated by the clear Abana (modern Barada) and adjacent Pharpar rivers, which compared favourably with the slower, muddy Jordan (2 Kings 5:12) and Euphrates rivers (Isaiah 8:5–8).

Damascus is a natural communications centre, linking the caravan route to the Mediterranean coast

A typical house-construction on the ancient wall of Damascus. From such a place Paul would have escaped from the city.

100 kilometres to the west)
rough Tyre (Ezekiel 27:18) to
ypt with the tracks east across the
sert to Assyria and Babylonia,
uth to Arabia, and north to Aleppo.
e city was of special importance
head of an *Aramaean state in the
th-8th centuries BC.
The centre of the modern city lies
side the Barada river, part of it
cupying the area of the old walled
y. Some streets follow the lines of
man times, including Straight
eet (*Darb al-mustaqim*) or Long
eet (*Sūq al-Tawilēh*) as in Acts
11. The great mosque built in the
century AD is said to cover the site
the temple of Rimmon (2 Kings
18).

*me*

e meaning of Damascus (Greek
*maskos*; Hebrew *Dammeseq*;
amaic *Darmeseq*; 1 Chronicles
:5; 2 Chronicles 28:5) is unknown.
e *'ᵃram darmeseq* of 1 Chronicles
:6 corresponds to the modern
*imašk-)eš-šām* as 'Damascus of
e North (Syria)'. The name is found
Egyptian *Tjmšqw* (Tuthmosis III)
d Amarna Letters (14th century)
d cuneiform inscriptions as
*mašqi*. Other names in the latter
xts are *ša imerišu* (perhaps 'caravan
y') and *Bīt-Haza'-ili* ('House of
zael') in the 8th century BC (*DOTT*,
57). See *ANET*, p. 278, note 8.

*story*

mascus appears to have been
cupied from prehistoric times. In
e 2nd millennium BC it was a
ell-known city near which
raham defeated a coalition of
ngs (Genesis 14:15). It is possible
at his servant Eliezer was from this
y (Genesis 15:2; Syriac and
rsions).
David captured and garrisoned
mascus after his defeat of the
ops it had contributed in support
Hadadezer of Zobah (2 Samuel
5f.; 1 Chronicles 18:5). Rezon of
bah, who escaped from this battle,
er entered the city which was
ade the capital of a newly formed
amaean city-state of *Aram (Syria;
Kings 11:24). The city increased its
fluence under Rezon's successors
zion and his son Tabrimmon.
By the time of the accession of
brimmon's son Ben-hadad I (*c.*
0–860 BC) Damascus was the
minant partner in the treaty made
Asa of Judah to offset the
essure brought against him by
asha of Israel (2 Chronicles 16:2).
e same king (if not Ben-hadad II)
ade the provision of merchants'
arters in Damascus a term of a
treaty made with Ahab (1 Kings 20:34). The aim of this treaty was to gain the support of Israel for the coalition of city-states to oppose the Assyrians. Ben-hadad (Assyrian Adad-idri) of Damascus provided the largest contingent of 20,000 men at the indecisive battle of Qarqar in 853 BC. Ben-hadad may be the unnamed 'king of Aram', in fighting whom Ahab met his death (see 1 Kings 22:29–36).

In the plain near Damascus the prophet Elijah anointed Hazael, a Damascene noble, as the future king of Syria (1 Kings 19:15), and Elisha, who had healed the general Naaman of Damascus, was invited there by Hazael to advise on Ben-hadad's health (2 Kings 8:7). In 841 BC Hazael had to face renewed attacks by the Assyrians under Shalmaneser III. For a time he held the pass leading through the Lebanon Mountains, but having lost 16,000 men, 1,121 chariots and 470 cavalry was forced to retreat within Damascus, where he successfully withstood a siege. The Assyrians fired orchards and plantations round the city before they withdrew (*DOTT*, p. 48; *ANET*, p. 280). In 805–803 BC Adad-nirari III led fresh Assyrian attacks on Hazael and Damascus. A further campaign in 797 BC by Adad-nirari so weakened Damascus that J(eh)oash of Israel was able to recover towns on his northern border previously lost to Hazael (2 Kings 13:25).

Under Rezin (Assyrian *Raḫianu*) Aram again oppressed Judah (2 Kings 16:6), and in 738 was, with Menahem of Israel, a vassal of Tiglath-pileser III of Assyria. Soon thereafter Rezin revolted, captured Elath and took many Judaeans captive to Damascus (2 Chronicles 28:5). Ahaz of Judah thereupon appealed for help to Assyria who responded by launching a series of punitive raids in 734–732 BC, which culminated in the capture of Damascus, as prophesied by Isaiah (17:1) and Amos (1:4–5), and the death of Rezin.

The spoiling of the city (Isaiah 8:4), the deportation of its inhabitants to Kir (2 Kings 16:9), and its destruction were cited as an object-lesson to Judah (Isaiah 10:9f.). In return for this assistance Ahaz was summoned to pay tribute to the Assyrian king at Damascus, where he saw and copied the altar (2 Kings 16:10–12) which led to the worship of Syrian deities within the Temple at Jerusalem (2 Chronicles 28:23).

Damascus was reduced to a subsidiary city within the Assyrian province of Hamath and henceforth lost its political, but not completely its economic, influence (see Ezekiel 27:18). Judaean merchants continued to reside in the city, and the border of Damascus was considered the boundary of the ideal Jewish state (Ezekiel 47:16–18; 48:1; Zechariah 9:1).

In the Seleucid period Damascus lost its position as capital, and thus much trade, to Antioch, though it was restored as capital of Coelesyria under Antiochus IX in 111 BC. The Nabataean Aretas won the city in 85 BC, but lost control to Tigranes of Armenia. Damascus was a Roman city from 64 BC to AD 33.

*In the New Testament*

By the time of Paul's conversion Aretas IV (9 BC-AD 40), who had defeated his son-in-law Herod Antipas, had an ethnarch in the city (2 Corinthians 11:32–33). The city had many synagogues (Acts 9:2; Josephus, *Jewish War* 2.20) and in these, after being led to the house of Judas in Straight Street (9:10–12) where he was visited by Ananias, Paul first preached. Opposition forced Paul to escape over the city wall (9:19–27) but he returned to the city after a period spent in nearby Arabia (Galatians 1:17). Damascus continued to be subsidiary to Antioch, both politically and economically, until its supremacy was restored by the Arab conquest of AD 634.

D. J. Wiseman

*Further reading*

M. F. Unger, *Israel and the Aramaeans of Damascus,* 1957
A. Jepsen, *AfO* 14, 1942, pp. 153–172
W. T. Pitard, *Ancient Damascus*, Winona Lake, 1987

**DAN** (Hebrew *dān*, commonly treated as the active participle of *dîn*, 'to judge'). **1.** One of the 12 tribes of Israel. Its first settlement lay between the territories of Ephraim, Benjamin and Judah (Joshua 19:40ff.). Pressed back into the hill-country by the Amorites, who themselves were being pressed from the west by the Philistines and other sea peoples who had occupied the Mediterranean seaboard, the majority of the Danites migrated north to find a new home near the source of the Jordan (Joshua 19:47; Judges 1:34; 18:1ff.).

Some members of the tribe, however, remained in their earlier settlement, with the Philistines as their western neighbours; it is in this region that the stories of Samson, a

The Dead Sea.

Danite hero, have their setting (Judges 13:1ff.). It is possibly the remnant of the tribe that stayed in its first home that is described in Deborah's song (Judges 5:17) as remaining 'with the ships' – however we are to understand the 'ships' (various uncertain emendations have been proposed). M. Noth, on the other hand, suggests that Dan had to 'buy its settlement' in the north 'by accepting a certain amount of compulsory labour service in southern Phoenician seaports' (*The History of Israel*, p. 80). The southern remnant appears to have been absorbed ultimately in Judah; the northern Danites were deported by Tiglath-pileser III in 732 BC (2 Kings 15:29). The aggressive qualities of the Danites are celebrated in the benedictions of Genesis 49:16f. and Deuteronomy 33:22.

Dan is missing from the list of tribes in Revelation 7:5–8, either intentionally or by a primitive corruption. Irenaeus (*Against Heresies* 5.30.2) explains the omission by saying that antichrist is to come from the tribe of Dan – a belief which he bases on the Septuagint of Jeremiah 8:16 ('from Dan shall we hear the noise of his swift horses').

**2.** A city in the northern Danite territory, modern Tell el-Qadi or Tell Dan, near one of the sources of Jordan. Its earlier name was Laish (Judges 18:29; called Leshem in Joshua 19:47), appearing as Lus(i) in Egyptian texts of *c.* 1850–1825 BC. It was the most northerly Israelite city, hence the phrase 'from Dan to Beersheba' (*e.g.* Judges 20:1).

The shrine established here under the priesthood of Moses' grandson Jonathan and his descendants (Judges 18:30) was elevated (along with Bethel) to the status of a national sanctuary by Jeroboam I (1 Kings 12:29f.), and so remained until 'the captivity of the land' under Tiglath-pileser III.

Excavations begun in 1966 have revealed a series of prosperous cities from the Early, Middle and Late Bronze Ages. The excavator, A. Biran, associates the arrival of the Danites with an apparent change of occupants at the beginning of the Iron Age (early 12th century BC). However, there is no evidence of the city's destruction by fire, referred to in Judges 18:27. An Iron Age city flourished until the Babylonian conquest.

A cultic building on the northern edge of the site is interpreted by Biran as the sanctuary founded at Dan by Jeroboam I (1 Kings 12:26–30).

Dan flourished again in the Hellenistic and Roman periods.

F. F. Bruce

*Further reading*

H. H. Rowley, 'The Danite Migration to Laish', *ExpT* 51, 1939–40, pp. 466–471
M. Noth, *The History of Israel*, 1960, pp. 67ff. *et passim*
J. Gray, *Joshua, Judges and Ruth*, *NCB*, 1967, pp. 287f.
Y. Yadin, *AJBA* 1, 1965, pp. 9–23
A. Biran, *BA* 43, 1980, pp. 168–182
*BA* 44, 1981, pp. 139–144
*IEJ* 34, 1984, pp. 1–19

**DAN-JAAN.** Joab and his companions came to Dan-jaan in compiling the census ordered by David (2 Samuel 24:6–9). Starting from *Aroer, east of the Dead Sea, they camped south of the city in the valley of the Gadites (the Arnon basin), then went north to Jazer, through Gilead and other territory to Dan-jaan and its environs, and to Sidon (probably the territorial boundary is meant). Thence they moved south, past a Tyrian outpost, ending in Beersheba.

As Beersheba is also mentioned in David's instructions along with Dan (verse 2), some scholars identify Dan-jaan with the well-known Dan. More probably it was a northern town in the district of Dan, perhaps *Ijon of 1 Kings 15:20 (*LOB*, p. 264). Among readings given by the Septuagint is Dan-jaar, perhaps 'Dan of the Woods'. Another Septuagint reading, 'and from Dan they turned round to Sidon', seems indefensible. Jaan might be a personal name (see 1 Chronicles 5:12 for a possible cognate); a place name *y'ny* is known in Ugaritic.

W. J. Martin, A. R. Millard

**DAUGHTER OF SIDON.** See *TYRE.

**DAVID, CITY OF.** See *JERUSALEM.

**DAVID, SEPULCHRE OF.** See *SEPULCHRE OF KINGS.

**DEAD SEA.** Old Testament: 'Salt Sea' (Genesis 14:3), 'Eastern Sea' (Ezekiel 47:18), 'Sea of the Arabah' (Deuteronomy 4:49); classical: *Asphaltites*, later 'Dead Sea'; Arabic: 'Sea of Lot'.

*The Sea and its rivers*

The great rift valley reaches its deepest point at the Dead Sea basin. The surface of the water is on average 427 metres below sea-level and the deepest point of the bed some 433 metres lower still. The Sea is about 77 kilometres long and stretches from the sheer cliffs of Moab some 10 or 14 kilometres across to the hills of Judah. On this western side is a narrow shore bounded by many terraces, the remains of earlier beaches. Except for a few springs (*e.g.* 'Ain Feshkha and Engedi, compare Song of Songs 1:14), the Judaean coast is arid and bare.

Four main streams feed the Sea from the east: the Mojin (Arnon), Zerqa Ma'in, Kerak and the Zered. The rate of evaporation is so great (the temperature reaches 43°C in summer) that the inflow of these waters and the Jordan serves only to keep the sea-level constant. The annual rainfall is about 5 centimetres.

Luxuriant vegetation is to be found where the rivers flow in or where there are fresh-water springs

ıe oases around the Kerak and the ›red delta show how fertile this ısin could be (compare Genesis :10), as Ezekiel saw in his vision of river of pure water flowing from rusalem to sweeten the Salt Sea zekiel 47:8–12).

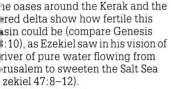

Until the mid-19th century it was ssible to ford the sea from Lisan ongue'), a peninsula which ojects from beside the Kerak to ithin 3 kilometres of the opposite ore. Traces of a Roman road remain. asada, an almost impregnable rtress built by the Maccabees and Herod, guarded this road on the lge of Judaea. South of the Lisan, e sea is very shallow, gradually sappearing into the salty marsh ephaniah 2:9) called the Sebkha.

*re, brimstone and salt*

ıe concentrated chemical deposits alt, potash, magnesium, and lcium chlorides and bromide, 25% the water), which give the Dead a its buoyancy and its fatal effects fish, may well have been ignited ring an earthquake and caused e rain of brimstone and fire estroying Sodom and Gomorrah. ot's wife, stopping to look back, as overwhelmed by the falling salt, hile her family, hastening on, caped (Genesis 19:15–28).

Archaeological evidence suggests break of several centuries in the dentary occupation from early in e 2nd millennium BC. A hill of salt *ebel Usdum*, Mount Sodom) at the uth-western corner is eroded into range forms, including pillars hich are known as 'Lot's Wife' by cal Arabs (compare Wisdom 10:7).

Salt was obtained from the shore zekiel 47:11), and the Nabataeans aded in the bitumen which floats the surface (see P. C. Hammond, 4 22, 1959, pp. 40–48).

Throughout the Old Testament riod the sea acted as a barrier etween Judah and Moab and Edom ee 2 Chronicles 20:1–30), although may have been used by small ading boats, as it was in Roman nes. (See also *PLAIN, CITIES OF THE; ORDAN; *ARABAH.)

R. Millard

*urther reading*

A. Smith, *Historical Geography of e Holy Land*, 1931, pp. 499–516

Baly, *The Geography of the Bible*, 74

Biran in *NEAEHL* I, pp. 323–332

**EBIR** (Hebrew *d^e^bîr*). **1.** A city on e southern side of the Judaean lls, held by the Anakim before the raelite invasion, then by Kenizzites (Joshua 10:38; 11:21; 15:15 and Judges 1:11). It was previously known as *Kiriath-sepher (Joshua 15:15, and verse 49 Kiriath-sanna). It was a levitical city (Joshua 21:15).

Khirbet Rabud, on the south-eastern side of the Nahal Hevron 13 kilometres south-west of Hebron, is in a very strong position with Late Bronze and Israelite occupation and walls enclosing about 6 hectares. It matches the biblical data better than Tell Beit Mirsim, proposed by Albright (*BASOR* 15, 1924; 47, 1932), which for a time was widely but not universally accepted.

The springs mentioned in Joshua 15:19 may be located 3 kilometres to the north, up a side valley. For a full account and discussion see M. Kochavi, *Tel Aviv* 1, 1974, pp. 2–33.

**2.** On the northern border of Judah (Joshua 15:7; 'facing northwards towards Gilgal' rather than 'turning', compare verse 2); probably above the Wadi Debr, the lower part of the Wadi Mukallik, or near Tugret ed-Debr, south of the Ascent of *Adummim. See J. Simons in *GTT*, p. 137.

**3.** In the north of Gad (Joshua 13:26; Massoretic Text *lid^e^bir*, which may indicate *Lo-debar); probably

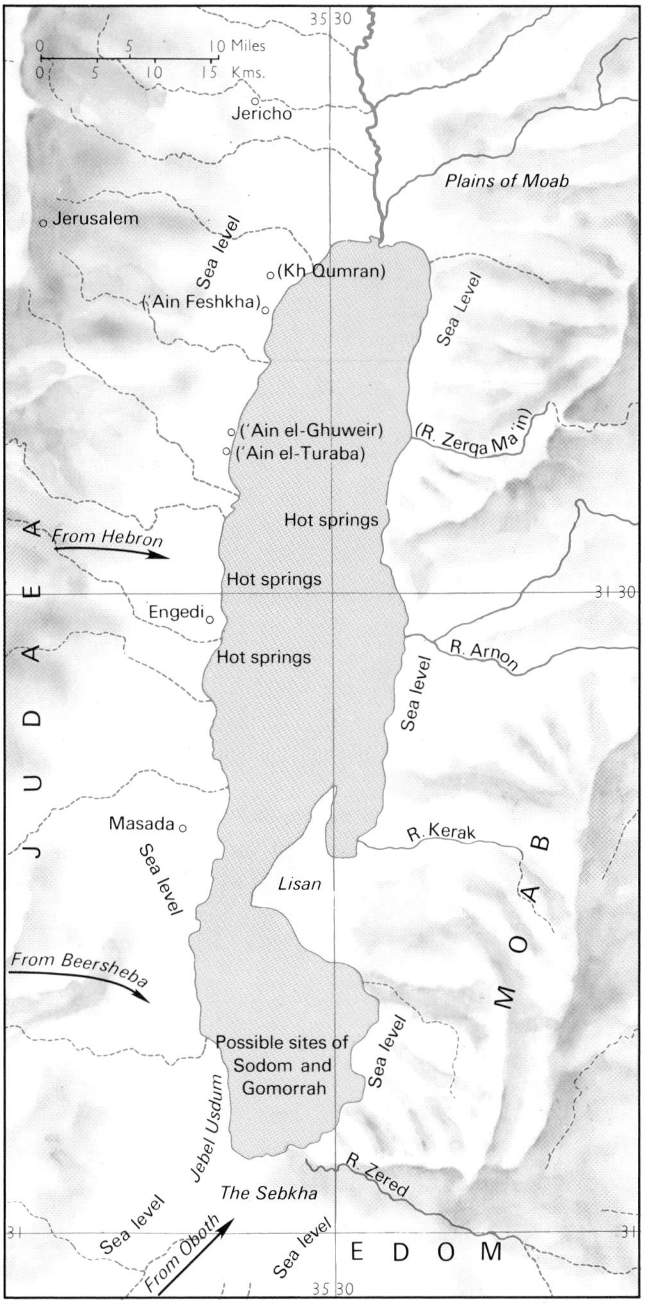

The Dead Sea, also called the Salt Sea or Sea of the Arabah.

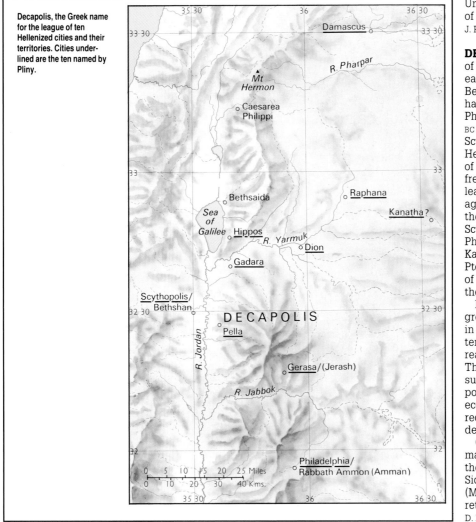

Decapolis, the Greek name for the league of ten Hellenized cities and their territories. Cities underlined are the ten named by Pliny.

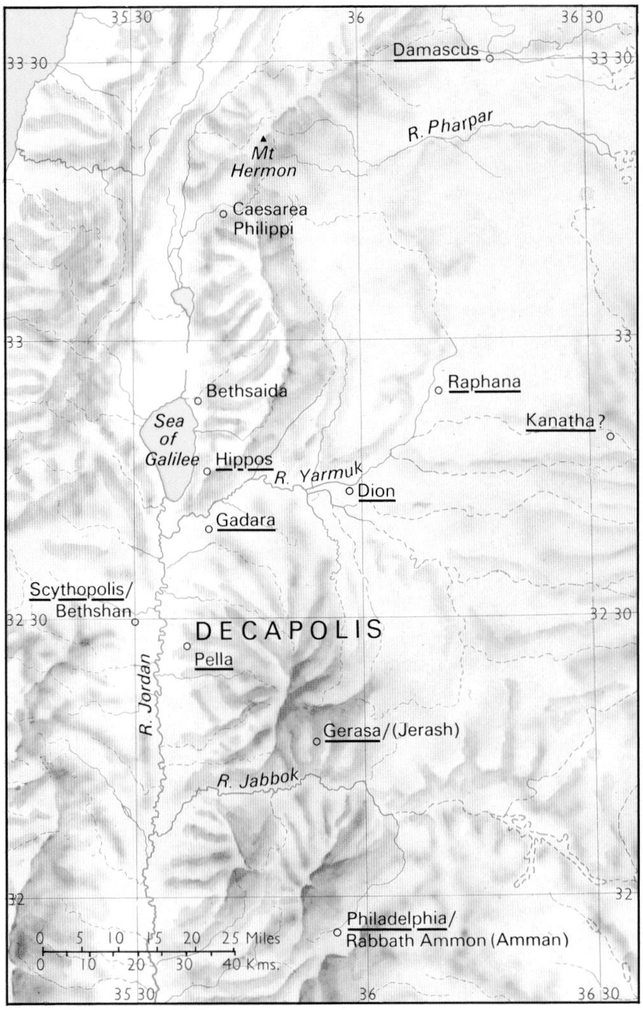


Umm ed-Debar, 16 kilometres south of Lake Galilee.

J. P. U. Lilley

**DECAPOLIS.** A large territory south of the Sea of Galilee, mainly to the east of Jordan, but including Beth-shean to the west. The Greeks had occupied towns like Gadara and Philadelphia as early as 200 BC. In 63 BC Pompey liberated Hippos, Scythopolis and Pella from the Jews. He annexed the cities to the province of Syria, but gave them municipal freedom. About AD 1 they formed a league for trade and mutual defence against Semitic tribes. Pliny named the ten original members as Scythopolis, Pella, Dion, Gerasa, Philadelphia, Gadara, Raphana, Kanatha, Hippos and Damascus. Ptolemy included other towns south of Damascus in a list of 18 cities in the 2nd century AD.

Inhabitants of Decapolis joined the great crowds which followed Christ in Matthew 4:25. He landed in the territory at Gerasa (Mark 5:1; Origen reads Gergesa, a site on the cliff). The presence of so many swine suggests a predominantly Gentile population who, on suffering economic loss through the miracle, requested Christ's departure, despite the demoniac's testimony.

Christ revisited Decapolis when making an unusual detour through the Hippos area on a journey from Sidon to the eastern shore of Galilee (Mark 7:31). The Jewish church retired to Pella before the war of AD 70.

D. H. Tongue

Hippos, one of the ten cities (Decapolis) around the Sea of Galilee.

*urther reading*
*CG*
. A. Smith, *Historical Geography of ıe Holy Land,* 1931, pp. 595–608
. Bietenhard, 'Die Dekapolis von ɔmpeius bis Traian', *ZDPV* 79, 963, pp. 24–58
liny, *Natural History* 5.18.74

**ECISION, VALLEY OF.** Mentioned ı Joel 3:14 as the place of God's ıdgment on the nations, the 'valley ⁝ decision' is also called (verses 2, 2) 'the valley of Jehoshaphat'. erse 16 suggests proximity to Zion, ut, as Amos 1:2 shows, this ording may be a prophetic formula ıther than an indication of location. ehoshaphat', meaning 'Yahweh ıdges', may be symbolic rather than ɔpographic.

2 Chronicles 20 would explain the ymbolism: in the valley of Beracah, 4 kilometres south of Jerusalem, ing Jehoshaphat observed ahweh's victory over heathen ations, a microcosm of the Day of ahweh.

However, from the 4th century AD nwards the name 'valley of ehoshaphat' has been given to the alley between the Temple Hill and ıe Mount of Olives.
A. Motyer

**EDAN.** A city and people of orth-western *Arabia, famous for s role in the caravan trade (Isaiah 1:13; Ezekiel 27:20 – the reference ı the Massoretic Text of verse 20 is robably due to a textual error – ompare RSV), since it lay on the vell-known 'incense route' from outhern Arabia to Syria and the lediterranean.

Dedan is mentioned in close ssociation with Sheba in the Table f *Nations (Genesis 10:7 – compare Chronicles 1:9) and elsewhere Genesis 25:3; 1 Chronicles 1:32; zekiel 38:13), and probably played part in the trading relations stablished by Solomon with the ueen of Sheba (1 Kings 10). But it nly comes into prominence in Old estament texts in the 7th century BC Jeremiah 25:23; 49:8; Ezekiel 5:13; 27:20), when it may have een a Sabaean trading colony (see on Wissman); this would help to xplain why, in the biblical enealogies, it is associated with oth northern and southern Arabian eoples.

It is mentioned by Nabonidus in ne of his inscriptions (*ANET*, . 562), and seems to have been at east temporarily conquered by him mid-6th century BC): some Arabian ıscriptions found near Taima', which mention Dedan, may refer to his wars (*POTT*, p. 293).

The site of the city of Dedan is that now known as al-'Ula, some 110 kilometres south-west of Taima'. A number of Dedanite inscriptions are known, and give the names of one king and several gods of the Dedanites (*POTT*, p. 294).

Subsequently the kingdom seems to have fallen into Persian hands, and later still (3rd-2nd centuries BC?) came under Lihyanite rule. With the arrival of the Nabataeans Dedan gave place to the neighbouring city of Hegra (Medain Salih) as the main centre in the area.
G. I. Davies

*Further reading*
*POTT*, pp. 287–311, especially 293–296, with bibliography, to which add:
W. F. Albright, *Geschichte und Altes Testament* (*Festschrift* A. Alt), 1953, pp. 1–12
H. von Wissmann, *RE* Supp. Bd. 12, cols. 947–969
M. C. Astour, *IDBS*, p. 222

**DERBE** (Lycaonian *delbeia*, 'juniper'). In Acts 14:6ff. a city of Lycaonia, the most easterly place visited by Paul and Barnabas when they founded the churches of southern Galatia. Paul and Silas visited it on their westward journey through Asia Minor (Acts 16:1). Paul's fellow-traveller Gaius came from Derbe (Acts 20:4; the Western Text brings him from Doberus in Macedonia).

The site of Derbe was identified in 1956 by M. Ballance at Kerti Hüyük, 21 kilometres north-north-east of Karaman (Laranda), some 100 kilometres from Lystra (whence Acts 14:20b must evidently be translated: 'and on the morrow he set out with Barnabas for Derbe'). In 1964 M. Ballance attempted to identify the site even more precisely at Devri Şehri, 4 kilometres south-south-east of Kerti Hüyük. It may have lain beyond the eastern frontier of Roman Galatia, in the client kingdom of Commagene.
F. F. Bruce

*Further reading*
M. Ballance, 'The Site of Derbe: A New Inscription', *AS* 7, 1957, pp. 147ff.
——, 'Derbe and Faustinopolis', *AS* 14, 1964, pp. 139ff.
A. G. Ogg, 'Derbe', *NTS* 9, 1962–63, pp. 367–370
B. Van Elderen, 'Some Archaeological Observations on Paul's First Missionary Journey', in W. W. Gasque and R. P. Martin (eds.), *Apostolic History and the Gospel*, 1970, pp. 156ff.

**DIBLATH, DIBLAH.** Occurring only in Ezekiel 6:14, no place of this name has been identified, and it is probably an ancient scribal error for *Riblah as the RSV text; the Septuagint already read 'Diblah'.
J. D. Douglas

**DIBON. 1.** A town in Judah, occupied after the Exile (Nehemiah 11:25) but not identifiable today.

**2.** Dibon (Hebrew *dîḇôn*) of Moab, marked by the modern village of Dhiban, to the east of the Dead Sea and 6 kilometres north of the river Arnon. The city is mentioned by Ramesses II, who claimed its capture (K. A. Kitchen, *JEA* 50, 1964, pp. 63–70).

Originally Dibon belonged to Moab, but it was captured by Sihon, king of the Amorites, in pre-Israelite times (Numbers 21:26). The Israelites took it at the time of the Exodus (Numbers 21:30), and it was given to the tribes of Reuben and Gad (Numbers 32:2–3). Gad built Dibon, however (Numbers 32:34), and hence it is called Dibon-gad (Numbers 33:45), although in Joshua 13:15ff. it is reckoned to Reuben. It is probably one of the halting-places on the Exodus journey and is referred to in Numbers 33:45–46. Israel lost it later; it was regained by Omri and lost again to Mesha, king of Moab, who speaks of it on the Moabite Stone, lines 21 and 28. Isaiah and Jeremiah knew it as a Moabite town (Isaiah 15:2; Jeremiah 48:18, 22).

Archaeological excavations were carried out by the American Schools of Oriental Research in 1950–56 in the south-east, north-west and north-east corners of the mound, with a further season in 1965. There is some evidence for Early Bronze Age occupation, some levels at bedrock, a wall and pottery from Early Bronze III.

Nothing at all was found from the Middle or Late Bronze Ages, which is surprising in view of biblical and Egyptian references which attest its existence at least during the latter period. Either the relevant remains escaped detection or the town flourished at another site during the Late Bronze (and perhaps also Middle Bronze) Age. The Moabite occupation proper dates from Iron I and is represented by several large buildings. In the south-eastern corner the remains are from Iron II extending from the mid-9th century to the destruction by Nebuchadrezzar in 582 BC. Here lay a royal quarter, possibly built by Mesha.

During archaeological work in 1950 a small fragment of a Moabite stele was found on the surface of the mound which is thought to antedate the Moabite Stone by a few decades. It contains only two complete letters, not sufficient to permit any translation. Later remains come from the Nabataean, Byzantine and Arab periods.

J. A. Thompson

*Further reading*

F. M. Abel, *Géographie de la Palestine* 2, 1937, pp. 304–305
N. Glueck, *Explorations in Eastern Palestine* 3
*AASOR* 18–19, 1937–38, pp. 115, 224ff.
W. H. Morton, *BASOR* 140, 1955, pp. 5ff.
R. E. Murphy, *BASOR* 125, 1952, pp. 20–23
W. L. Reid, *BASOR* 146, 1957, pp. 6–10
A. D. Tushingham, *BASOR* 133, 1954, pp. 6–26; 138, 1955, pp. 29–34
*AASOR* 40, 1972
F. V. Winnett, *BASOR* 125, 1952
—— and W. L. Reid, *AASOR* 36–37, 1961
A. D. Tushingham in *NEAEHL* I, pp. 350–352

**DIZAHAB.** One of the places named in Deuteronomy 1:1 to define the site of the speeches which follow. It has often been identified with Ḏahab on the eastern coast of the Sinai peninsula (*e.g.* Rothenberg and Aharoni), but this is not easily reconciled with the other data given (compare verse 5). A location in northern Moab is required, and eḏ-Ḏheibe (30 kilometres east of Ḥesbân/Heshbon) seems the most probable suggestion so far.

G. I. Davies

*Further reading*

F. M. Abel, *Géographie de la Palestine* 2, 1937, p. 307 and map 4
B. Rothenberg and Y. Aharoni, *God's Wilderness*, 1961, pp. 144, 161

**DOR.** A city on the Mediterranean coast of Palestine, just south of Carmel. Its king joined with Jabin, king of Hazor, in his fight against Israel and shared in his defeat (Joshua 11:1–2; 12:23). Though on the borders of Asher, it was given to Manasseh, who failed to drive out the Canaanite inhabitants (Judges 1:27). See also 1 Kings 4:11 and 1 Chronicles 7:29.

It is associated with, but distinguished from, En-dor (Joshua 17:11). It is mentioned as 'a town of the Tjeker' in the Wen-Amon story, 11th century BC (*ANET*, p. 26). In Graeco-Roman times it was called Dora (neuter plural) (compare Josephus, *Antiquities* 5.87; 8.35; *Against Apion* 2.114, 116; *Life* 31).

Dor is identified with the mound of Khirbet el-Burj, which has been excavated a number of times since the 1920s. The most recent excavations, begun in 1980, have uncovered extensive remains from the Hellenistic and Roman periods, but occupation clearly goes back at least to the start of the Late Bronze Age.

G. T. Manley, J. Bimson

*Further reading*

E. Stern in *NEAEHL* I, pp. 357–368
E. Stern, *ABD* II, pp. 223–225

**DOTHAN.** The fertile plain of Dothan separates the hills of Samaria from the Carmel range. It provides an easy pass for travellers from Bethshan and Gilead on their way to Egypt. This was the route of the Ishmaelites who carried Joseph into Egypt. The good pasturage had attracted Jacob's sons from Shechem, 32 kilometres to the south. Near the town (now *tell dōṯā*) are rectangular cisterns about 3 metres deep similar to the pit into which Joseph was put (Genesis 37:17ff.).

Elisha led the Syrian force, which had been sent to capture him, along the hill road to Samaria, 16 kilometres to the south. His servant was encouraged by a vision of heavenly forces arrayed on the hill to the east of the town (2 Kings 6:13–23).

Excavations (1953–60) revealed a walled city of the Early and Middle Bronze Ages, and a Late Bronze Age settlement apparently using the older city wall. Thothmes III lists Dothan among his conquests (*c.* 1459 BC). It was probably one of the towns which was absorbed by the Israelites, but not actually conquered (see Judges 1:27).

Areas of the Iron Age town which have been cleared show the narrow streets and small houses with storage-pits and bread-ovens of Elisha's day. A large tomb used in the Late Bronze and Early Iron Ages contained over 1,000 pots and other objects. Another find was 15 pieces of silver. There was also settlement in the Assyrian and Hellenistic periods (compare Judith 4:6; 7:3).

A. R. Millard

*Further reading*

Excavation reports by J. P. Free, *BA* 19, 1956, pp. 43–48, 1953–55 season; *BASOR* 131, 1953, pp. 16–29; 135, 1954, pp. 14–20; 139, 1955, pp. 3–9; 143, 1956, pp. 11–17; 147, 1957, pp. 36–37; 152, 1958, pp. 10–18; 15[illegible] 1959, pp. 22–29; 160, 1960, pp. 6–1[illegible]
D. Ussishkin in *NEAEHL* I, pp. 372–373

**DUMAH. 1.** Son of Ishmael and founder of an Arab community (Genesis 25:14; 1 Chronicles 1:30). These descendants gave their name to Dumah, capital of a district known as the Jawf, about halfway across northern Arabia between Palestine and southern Babylonia.

Dumah is modern Arabic Dûmat-al-Jandal, and the Adummatu of Assyrian and Babylonian royal inscriptions in the 7th-6th centuries BC (references in Ebeling and Meissner, *Reallexikon der Assyriologie* 1, 1932, pp. 39–40).

**2.** The name is apparently used figuratively of that nearer semi-desert land, Edom (Seir), in a brief oracle of Isaiah (21:11–12).

**3.** A township in Judah (Joshua 15:52), usually identified with the present ed-Dômeh or ed-Dûmah, *c.* 18 kilometres south-west of Hebron. The name Rumah in 2 Kings 23:36 might conceivably be for Dumah in Judah; see *GTT*, section 963, p. 368

K. A. Kitchen

**DURA** (Aramaic *Dûrā'*; Septuagint *Deeira*). The place in the administrative district of Babylon where King Nebuchadrezzar set up an image for all to worship (Daniel 3:1). It is possibly to be identified with Tell Dēr (27 kilometres south-west of Baghdad), though there are several Babylonian places named Dūru. Oppert reported structures south-south-east of Babylon at 'Doura' (*Expédition scientifique en Mésopotamie* 1, 1862, pp. 238–240). Pinches (in *ISBE*) proposed the general interpretation of the plain of the 'Wall' (Babylonian *dūru*), part of the outer defences of the city.

For the name Dura, compare Dura (Europos); Old Babylonian *Da-mara* (*Orientalia* 21, 1952, p. 275, note 1).

Other identifications proposed include Tell al-Lahm near Ur (*ZA* 65 1970, p. 219) or a military centre near Uruk (Erech) in the Ur III period (*Mesopotamia* 12, 1977, pp. 83, 96).

D. J. Wiseman

# E

**ASTERN SEA.** See *Dead Sea.

**BAL, MOUNT.** The northern, and gher, of two mountains which ershadowed Shechem, the odern Nablus. It lies north of the ale of Shechem, 427 metres above e valley and 938 metres above a-level.

The space between Ebal and its ighbour Gerizim, south of the ale, provides a natural nphitheatre with wonderful oustic properties.

At the close of his discourse in euteronomy 5–11 Moses points to e two mountains on the western orizon beyond Gilgal and Moreh hechem) and announces that hen they have entered the land a lessing shall be set on Gerizim and curse on Ebal.

After the laws of Deuteronomy 2–26 the narrative is resumed, and loses gives detailed instructions. irst, great stones were to be set up n Mount Ebal, covered with ement, and the law inscribed on iem. The practice of writing on laster laid on stones, previously nown from Egypt, is now attested Palestine itself, in the 8th century wall-inscriptions from Tell Deir lla (J. Hoftijzer, *BA* 39, 1976, p. 11; r the date, see p. 87). After this an tar of unhewn stones was to be ected and sacrifices offered Deuteronomy 27:1–8).

The Samaritan Pentateuch reads Gerizim' for 'Ebal' in verse 4; the xtual variation seems to be onnected in some way with the xistence of a Samaritan temple on Iount Gerizim, but it is not certain hich reading is the more original. nother possibility is that the amaritan reading is due to the neasiness felt in a late period at acrifice (verses 6–7) being offered n 'the mountain of the curse' ompare 11:29).

In a further address (Deuteronomy 7:9–28:68), Moses ordered that six tribes should stand on Gerizim to pronounce blessing on obedience and six should stand on Ebal to lay curses on disobedience (27:9–13). Following upon this, the Levites shall call down curses on the tribes for sins against God or man, many of which could be done in secret (27:15–26). By their response of 'Amen' the people are to condemn such practices openly. After victories in the centre of Palestine, Joshua gathered the people at Shechem, where these ceremonies were duly performed (Joshua 8:30–35).

The rituals described have been seen as evidence for regarding Deuteronomy as a document in treaty-form (M. G. Kline, *The Treaty of the Great King*, 1963, ch. 2, especially pp. 33–34) and for supposing that in early times there was a recurring festival for the renewal of the covenant at Shechem (G. von Rad, *The Problem of the Hexateuch and Other Essays*, English translation 1966, pp. 37–38). Whatever the merits of these particular theories, Deuteronomy 27 certainly contains early material of great importance for the early history of Israelite religion.

A stone structure was discovered on the north-east slopes of Mount Ebal in 1980 and after excavation (1982–84) it was identified as an altar dating from the late 13th and early 12th centuries BC. It could therefore be the remains of the altar mentioned in Joshua 8:30–32, though not all archaeologists are convinced by this interpretation. Further excavations in 1986 and 1987 have exposed the remains of two other buildings in the vicinity of the central structure.

G. T. Manley, G. I. Davies

*Further reading*

G. Adam Smith, *The Historical Geography of the Holy Land*, 25th edition, 1931, ch. 6 ('The View from Mt Ebal')

R. J. Coggins, *Samaritans and Jews*, 1975, pp. 73, 155

A. Zertal, 'Has Joshua's Altar been found on Mount Ebal?', *BARev* 1985, pp. 26–43

*Excavations and Surveys in Israel* 5, 1986, pp. 77–78; 6, 1987/88, pp. 82–84

I. Finkelstein, *The Archaeology of the Israelite Settlement*, 1988, pp. 82–85

A. Zertal in *NEAEHL* I, pp.375–377

**EBENEZER** (Hebrew *'eḇen 'ēzer*, 'stone of help').

**1.** The site of the dual defeat of Israel at the hands of the Philistines near Aphek in the north of Sharon. The sons of Eli were slain, the ark taken (1 Samuel 4:1–22), and a period of Philistine overlordship begun which continued until the days of national reinvigoration under the Monarchy.

The site may be 'Izbet Sartah, 3 kilometres east of Aphek. This small settlement dates from the 12th to 10th centuries BC.

**2.** The name of the stone which Samuel erected between Mizpah and Shen some years after this battle, to commemorate his victory over the Philistines (1 Samuel 7:12). The stone was probably given the same name as the site of Israel's earlier defeat in order to encourage the impression that that defeat had now been reversed. The exact site of the stone is unknown.

R. J. Way

**EBLA.** Capital of a city-state, 70 kilometres south of Aleppo, Ebla is the modern Tell Mardiḥ. It has been excavated by the Italian archaeological mission to Syria since 1964. The discovery of an archive of more than 18,000 texts dated *c.* 2300 BC is of importance for the history of the region and background to the Genesis narratives.

The city was occupied during the Proto-Syrian I (*c.* 3000–2400 BC) and II (*c.* 2400–2000 BC) periods; from the latter period texts have been found both in the royal palace and on the acropolis. The city was destroyed either by Sargon or by Naram-Sin of Akkad. As a commercial centre it was ruled by kings including Igris-Halam, Irkab-Damu and Ibbi-zikir; the name of one of its high officials was Eb(e)rum, variously compared with *Eber (Genesis 10:24) or *'iḇrî* ('Hebrew-Hapiru').

Ebla is later named in texts from *Ur, *Alalakh, Kanish in Anatolia and *Egypt, and thrived till *c.* 1450 BC.

*The texts*

The texts are written in Sumerian and an early north-west Semitic dialect (called initially 'Palaeo-Canaanite' or 'Eblaic/Eblaite'). These show the Semitic influence in the area from an early period.

The literary types follow the contemporary Mesopotamian styles (Fara, Abū Salabikh) and the school tradition which survived into the Akkadian texts of *Ugarit. They include accounts of creation and a flood, mythologies, incantations, hymns and proverbs. Historical and legal texts, royal edicts, letters and possibly some laws show the great potential of this site.

Lexical texts include thirty-two bilinguals (Sumerian-Eblaite) and many duplicates. These, with many administrative and economic texts, show the activity of a commercial centre with a quarter of a million inhabitants trading with Cyprus, Palestine and the major capitals in grain, textiles, wood and wine. The royal family held much power but employed 'elders' (*abū*) and 'governors' (*šāpiṭum*) whose role was similar to the later biblical judges.

Lexical texts cover the usual school lists of animals, fish, birds, professions and objects (for these with proverbs, see 1 Kings 4:32–33). More than 500 place-names listed are said to include Hazor, Lachish, Gezer, Dor, Megiddo, Ashtaroth, Jerusalem, Joppa and Sinai (though some of these readings are debated).

Personal names so far cited include Išra'el, Isma'el, Abarama, Mika'el, Mikaya, but there is as yet no evidence that these are to be identified with similar biblical names or that the names ending hypocoristic *-ya* refer to an early use of the divine name Yah(weh).

It is anticipated that these texts, like the later ones from Syria (see also *MARI, *ALALAKH) will be of importance for our understanding of the patriarchal age and provide new details of the language, life and literature of early Semitic peoples. They are generally too early to have direct bearing on the Old Testament other than the tradition of early writing and literature. Decisive comment must await full publication.

D. J. Wiseman

*Further reading*

*BA* 39, 1976, pp. 44–52

Articles by P. Mattiae and G. Pettinato in journals (*Orientalia* 44, 1975, pp. 367f., *etc.*)

L. Cagni, ed., *Ebla 1975–1985*, Naples, 1987

**EBRON.** See *ABDON.

**ECBATANA (AV ACHMETHA),** modern Hamadan. The former capital of the Median empire, it became the summer residence of the Persian kings after Cyrus had founded the *Persian empire (*c.* 540 BC). Herodotus (1.98) and Judith 1:1–4 describe the magnificence of the city.

The decree of Cyrus (Ezra 6:3–5), authorizing the rebuilding of the Temple under Zerubbabel (Ezra 1:2; 3:8–13), was filed here in the royal archives, and re-issued with additions by Darius (Ezra 6:6–12).

D. J. A. Clines

**EDEN.** A place that traded with Tyre, associated with Harran and Canneh (Ezekiel 27:23). This Eden and its people are identical with the Beth-eden (House of Eden) of Amos 1:5 and the 'children' of Eden of 2 Kings 19:12 and Isaiah 37:12 – and these comprise the Assyrian province (and former kingdom) of Bit-Adini between Harran and the Euphrates at Carchemish. See also the articles on *TELASSAR and *EDEN, HOUSE OF, and the literature cited there.

K. A. Kitchen

**EDEN, GARDEN OF.** The place which God made for Adam to live in, and from which Adam and Eve were driven after the Fall.

### The name

The Massoretic Text states that God planted a garden in Eden (*gan-b*$^{e}$*'ēḏen*; Genesis 2:8), which indicates that the garden was not co-extensive with Eden, but must have been an enclosed area within it.

Of possible origins of the name: *a* direct from the Sumerian *edin*, 'plain, steppe'; *b* from the Sumerian *edin* via Akkadian *edinu*; or *c* from the Common West Semitic *'ḏn*, 'pleasure, luxury', the last, already long noted by commentators as a 'homophonous' root, seems most plausible, with a possible derived meaning of 'place with abundance of water' or the like. The question must remain open, however, since the name might go back to some quite unknown earlier language.

From its situation in Eden the garden came to be called the 'garden of Eden' (*gan-'ēḏen*; Genesis 2:15; 3:23–24; Ezekiel 36:35; Joel 2:3), but it was also referred to as the 'garden of God' (*gan-*$^{e}$*lōhîm*; Ezekiel 28:13; 31:9) and the 'garden of the Lord' (*gan-YHWH*; Isaiah 51:3).

In Genesis 2:8ff. the word *gan*, 'garden', and in Isaiah 51:3 *'ēḏen* itself, is rendered *paradeisos* by the Septuagint, this being a loan-word from Old Iranian (Avestan) *pairidaēza*, 'enclosure', which came to mean 'park, pleasure ground', and from this usage came the English 'paradise' for the garden of Eden.

### The rivers

A river came from Eden, or the plain, and watered the garden, and from thence it was parted and became four heads (*rā'šîm*, Genesis 2:10). The word *rō'š*, 'head, top, beginning', is interpreted variously by scholars to mean either the beginning of a branch, as in a delt going downstream, or the beginni or junction of a tributary, going upstream. Either interpretation is possible, though the latter is perhaps the more probable.

The names of the four tributarie or mouths, which were evidently outside the garden, are given as *pîšôn* (Genesis 2:11), *gîḥôn* (2:13), *ḥiddeqel* (2:14) and *p*$^{e}$*rāṯ* (2:14). Th last two are identified, without dissent, with the *Tigris and *Euphrates respectively, but the identifications for the Pishon and Gihon are almost as diverse as the are numerous, ranging from the Ni and Indus to tributaries of the Tigr in Mesopotamia. Sufficient data ar not available to identify either of these two rivers with certainty.

Genesis 2:6 states that 'an *'ēḏ* went up from the earth, and watere the whole face of the ground'. The etymology of *'ēḏ* has been much debated, the main suggestions being: *a* from the Sumerian *id*, 'river'; *b* from the Sumerian *id* via Akkadian *id* (though the more usua Akkadian reading of the ideogram *naru*); *c* from the Sumerian *e 4 -de*, 'high water'; and *d* from the Sumerian *e 4 de(-a)* via Akkadian *edû*, 'flood'.

Of these the third, from the Sumerian *e 4 d-de* possibly via another language such as Hurrian, i perhaps the most plausible, but th possibility of an origin in an unknown earlier language must leave the question open. The sense seems to be of some form of natura irrigation. It seems reasonable to understand this as relating to the inside of the garden.

### The contents of the garden

If the statement in Genesis 2:5–6 may be taken to indicate what did subsequently take place within the garden, an area of arable land (*śāḏeh*, AV 'field') to be tilled by Adam may be postulated. On this were to grow plants (*śîªḥ*) and herb (*'ēśeḇ*), perhaps to be understood a shrubs and cereals respectively.

There were also trees of every kind, both beautiful and fruit-bearin (Genesis 2:9), and two in particular in the middle of the garden, the tre of life, to eat from which would mak a man live for ever (Genesis 3:22), and the tree of knowledge of good and evil, from which man was specifically forbidden to eat (Genesi 2:17; 3:3).

Many views of the meaning of 'th knowledge of good and evil' in this context have been put forward. On

the most common would see it as
e knowledge of right and wrong,
t it is difficult to suppose that
lam did not already possess this,
d that, if he did not, he was
bidden to acquire it.
Others would connect it with the
orldly knowledge that comes to
an with maturity, and which can
put to either a good or bad use.
Another view would take the
pression 'good and evil' as an
ample of a figure of speech
hereby an autonymic pair signifies
tality, meaning therefore
verything' and in the context
iversal knowledge. Against this is
e fact that Adam, having eaten of
e tree, did not gain universal
owledge.
Yet another view would see this as
quite ordinary tree, which was
lected by God to provide an ethical
st for the man, who 'would acquire
experiential knowledge of good or
il according as he was stedfast in
edience or fell away into
sobedience' (*NBC*, pp.78f.).
There were also animals in the
rden (*b*$^{e}$*hēmâ*, beast), and beasts
the field (Genesis 2:19–20), by
hich may perhaps be understood
ose animals which were suitable
r domestication. There were also
rds.

**e neighbouring territories**
ree territories are named in
nnection with the rivers. The
gris is said to have gone 'east of
ssyria' (*qiḏmaṯ 'aššûr*, literally 'in
ont of *'aššûr*'; Genesis 2:14), an
pression which could also mean
etween *'aššûr* and the spectator'.
e name *'aššûr* could refer either to
e state of Assyria, which first
egan to emerge in the early 2nd
illennium BC, or the city of Assur,
odern Qal'at Sharqât on the west
nk of the Tigris, the earliest capital
Assyria, which was flourishing, as
cavations have shown, in the early
d millennium BC. Since even at its
nallest extent Assyria probably lay
both sides of the Tigris, it is
obable that the city is meant and
at the phrase correctly states that
e Tigris ran to the east of Assur.
Secondly, the river Gihon is
escribed as winding through
*āḇaḇ*) 'the whole land of Cush'
*ûš*, Genesis 2:13). *Cush in the
ble usually signifies Nubia, and
as commonly been taken in this
assage (*e.g.* AV) to have that
eaning; but there was also a region
the east of the Tigris, from which
e Kassites descended in the 2nd
illennium, which had this name,
d this may be the meaning in this
passage.

Thirdly, the Pishon is described as winding through the whole land of *Havilah (Genesis 2:11). Various products of this place are named: gold, bdellium and *šōham*-stone (Genesis 2:11–12), the latter being translated 'onyx' in the English versions, but being of uncertain meaning. Since bdellium is usually taken to indicate an aromatic gum, a characteristic product of southern Arabia, and the two other biblical usages of the name Havilah also refer to parts of Arabia, it is most often taken in this context to refer to some part of that peninsula.

This is the evidence which can be derived from the sources at present known, but other rivers with these names may have been known elsewhere.

**The location of the garden of Eden**
Theories as to the location of the garden of Eden are numerous. That most commonly held, by Calvin, for instance, and in more recent times by F. Delitzsch and others, is that the garden lay somewhere in southern Mesopotamia, the Pishon and Gihon being either canals connecting the Tigris and Euphrates, tributaries joining these, or in one theory the Pishon being the body of water from the Persian Gulf to the Red Sea, compassing the Arabian peninsula.

These theories assume that the four 'heads' (AV) of Genesis 2:10 are tributaries which unite in one main stream, which then joins the Persian Gulf; but another group of theories takes 'heads' to refer to branches spreading out from a supposed original common source, and seeks to locate the garden in the region of Armenia, where both the Tigris and Euphrates take their rise. The Pishon and Gihon are then identified with various smaller rivers of Armenia and Trans-Caucasia, and in some theories by extension, assuming an ignorance of true geography in the author, with such other rivers as the Indus and even Ganges.

The expression 'in Eden, in the east' (Genesis 2:8), literally 'in Eden from in front', could mean either that the garden was in the eastern part of Eden or that Eden was in the east from the narrator's point of view, and some commentators have taken it as 'in Eden in old times', but in either case, in the absence of certainty as to the meaning of the other indications of locality, this information cannot narrow it down further.

In view of the possibility that, if the Deluge was universal, the geographical features which would assist in an identification of the site of Eden would have been altered, the site of Eden remains unknown.

**Dilmun**
Among the Sumerian literary texts discovered early this century at Nippur in southern Babylonia, one was discovered which described a place called Dilmun, a pleasant place, in which neither sickness nor death were known. At first it had no fresh water, but Enki the water-god ordered the sun-god to remedy this, and, this being done, various other events took place, in the course of which the goddess Ninti (Eve) is mentioned.

In later times the Babylonians adopted the name and idea of Dilmun and called it the 'land of the living', the home of their immortals.

Certain similarities between this Sumerian notion of an earthly paradise and the biblical Eden emerge, and some scholars therefore conclude that the Genesis account is dependent upon the Sumerian. But an equally possible explanation is that both accounts refer to a real place, the Sumerian version having collected mythological accretions in the course of transmission.

T. C. Mitchell

*Further reading*
C. Westermann, *Genesis 1–11*, 1984, pp. 208–219
W. F. Albright, 'The Location of the Garden of Eden', *AJSL* 39, 1922, pp. 15–31
E. A. Speiser, 'The Rivers of Paradise', *Festschrift Johannes Friedrich*, 1959, pp. 473–485
M. G. Kline, 'Because It Had Not Rained', *WTJ* 20, 1957–58, pp. 146ff.
D. T. Tsamura, *The Earth and the Waters in Genesis 1 and 2*, 1989
On Dilmun:
S. N. Kramer, *History Begins at Sumer*, 3rd edition, 1981, pp. 141–147
N. M. Sarna, *Understanding Genesis*, 1966, pp. 23–28

**EDEN, HOUSE OF** (Hebrew *bêṯ 'eḏen*, Amos 1:5; sometimes written *b*$^{e}$*nê 'eḏen*, 2 Kings 19:12 and Isaiah 37:12, which may be a contraction of *b*$^{e}$*nê bêṯ 'eḏen*, 'children of the house of Eden'), and its association with Gozan and Harran suggests a location in northern Syria.

The Eden referred to in Ezekiel 27:23 (without *bêṯ*, 'house of'), among the far flung places trading with Tyre, has been connected plausibly with cuneiform Hindanu, original 'Iddan/Giddan on the middle Euphrates.

It is very probably to be identified

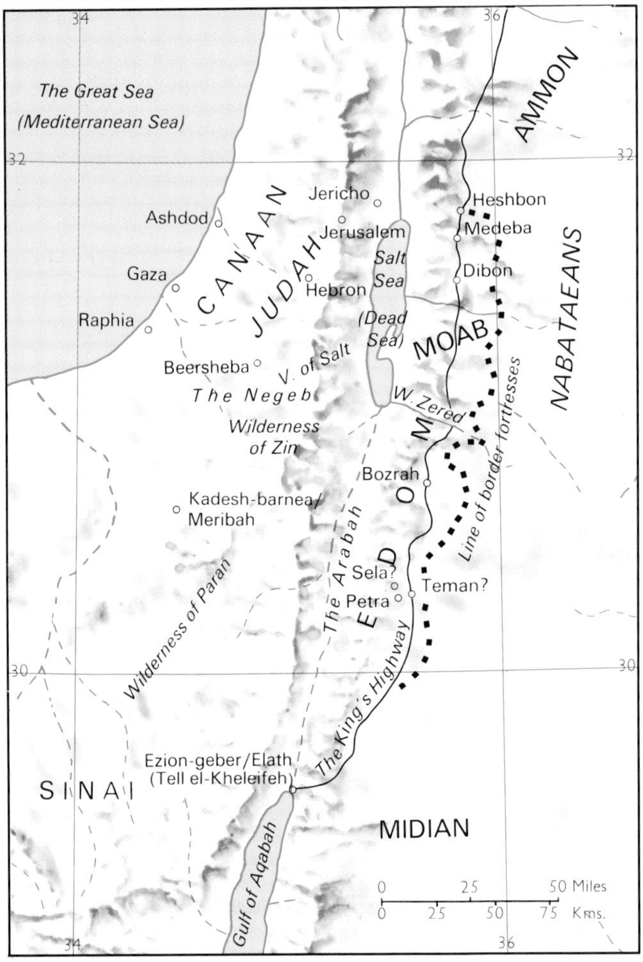

The land of the Edomites between the Dead Sea and the Gulf of Aqabah.

with the Aramaean state of Bît-Adini which lay between the river Baliḫ and the Euphrates, and blocked the path of the Assyrian expansion to northern Syria. Under these circumstances it could not last long, and its main city Til Barsip, modern Tell Aḥmar, on the east bank of the Euphrates, was taken by Shalmaneser III, and in 855 BC the state became an Assyrian province. It is presumably to this conquest that both Amos and Rabshakeh referred over a century later (*BASOR* 129, 1953, p. 25).
T. C. Mitchell

*Further reading*
Honigmann, *Reallexikon der Assyriologie* 2, 1933–38, pp. 33–34
E. Forrer, *Die Provinzeinteilung des assyrischen Reiches*, 1920, pp. 12f., 25f.
F. Thureau Dangin and M. Dunand, *Til Barsib*, 1936
W. W. Hallo, *BA* 23, 1960, pp. 38–39
S. Parpola, *Neo-Assyrian Toponyms*, 1970, pp. 75–76
E. Lipinski, *Orientalia* 45, 1976, pp. 60–61

**EDER, EDAR** (Hebrew *'ēḏer*, 'flock'). **1.** The place of Israel's encampment between Bethlehem and Hebron (Genesis 35:21). In Micah 4:8 'tower of the flock' (RV margin 'of Eder') was probably the site of a watch-tower erected against sheep thieves.

**2.** A town to the south of Judah near to the Edomite border; perhaps modern Khirbet el-'Adar 8 kilometres south of Gaza (Joshua 15:21). Y. Aharoni proposed to emend this name to *Arad, following a reading in the Septuagint (*LOB*, pp. 117, 353).
R. J. Way

## EDOM, EDOMITES

### Biblical

The term Edom (*'$^{e}$ḏôm*) denotes either the name of Esau, given in memory of the red pottage for which he exchanged his birthright (Genesis 25:30; 36:1, 8, 19), or the Edomites collectively (Numbers 20:18, 20–21; Amos 1:6, 11; 9:12; Malachi 1:4), or the land occupied by Esau's descendants, formerly the land of Seir (Genesis 32:3; 36:20–21, 30; Numbers 24:18).

*The land*
Edom stretched from the Wadi Zered to the Gulf of Aqabah for *c.* 160 kilometres, and extended to both sides of the Arabah or wilderness of Edom (2 Kings 3:8, 20), the great depression connecting the Dead Sea to the Red Sea (Genesis 14:6; Deuteronomy 2:1, 12; Joshua 15:1; Judges 11:17–18; 1 Kings 9:26, *etc.*

It is a rugged, mountainous area, with peaks rising to 1,067 metres. While not a fertile land, there are good cultivable areas (Numbers 20:17, 19). In Bible times the king's highway passed along the eastern plateau (Numbers 20:14–18). The capital, *Sela, lay on a small plateau behind Petra. Other important towns were Bozrah and Teman.

*The people*
The Edomites (*'$^{e}$ḏôm, '$^{a}$ḏômîm*) were descendants of Edom (Esau, Genesis 36:1–17). Modern archaeology has shown that the land was occupied before Esau's time. We conclude that Esau's descendants migrated to that land and in time became the dominant group incorporating the original Horites (Genesis 14:6) and others into their number. After *c.* 1850 BC there was a break in the culture of Edom till just before *c.* 1200 BC and the land was occupied by nomads.

*History*
Esau had already occupied Edom when Jacob returned from Harran (Genesis 32:3; 36:6–8; Deuteronomy 2:4–5; Joshua 24:4). Tribal chiefs (AV 'dukes') emerged here quite early (Genesis 36:15–19, 40–43; 1 Chronicles 1:51–54), and the Edomites had kings 'before any king reigned over the Israelites' (Genesis 36:31–39; 1 Chronicles 1:43–51).

At the time of the Exodus, Israel sought permission to travel by the king's highway, but the request was refused (Numbers 20:14–21; 21:4; Judges 11:17–18). Notwithstanding this discourtesy, Israel was forbidden to abhor his Edomite brother (Deuteronomy 23:7–8). In those days Balaam predicted the conquest of Edom (Numbers 24:18).

Joshua allotted the territory of Judah up to the borders of Edom (Joshua 15:1, 21), but did not encroach on their lands. Two centuries later King Saul was fighting the Edomites (1 Samuel 14:47) although some of them were in his service (1 Samuel 21:7; 22:9, 18).

David conquered Edom and put garrisons throughout the land (2 Samuel 8:13–14; emend *'$^{a}$rām* in rse 13 to *'ᵉḏôm* because of a scribal nfusion of *resh* 'r' and *daleth* 'd'; mpare 1 Chronicles 18:13). There as considerable slaughter of the lomites at this time (2 Samuel 13), and 1 Kings 11:15–16 speaks Joab, David's commander, maining in Edom for six months ntil he had cut off every male in lom'. Some must have escaped, for adad, a royal prince, fled to Egypt d later became a trouble to lomon (1 Kings 11:14–22).

This conquest of Edom enabled lomon to build a port at ion-geber on the Gulf of Aqabah Kings 9:26), and possibly to ploit the copper-mines in the gion, though the archaeological idence relates only to earlier yptian workings.

In Jehoshaphat's time the lomites joined the Ammonites and oabites in a raid on Judah (2 ronicles 20:1), but the allies fell to hting one another (verses 22–23). hoshaphat endeavoured to use the rt at Ezion-geber, but his ships ere wrecked (1 Kings 22:48). At is time Edom was ruled by a puty, who acted as king (1 Kings :47). This 'king' acknowledged the premacy of Judah and joined the dah-Israel coalition in an attack on esha, king of Moab (2 Kings 4–27).

Under Joram (Jehoram), Edom belled, but, although Joram feated them in battle, he could not duce them to subjection (2 Kings 20–22; 2 Chronicles 21:8–10), and lom had a respite of some 40 years. Amaziah later invaded Edom, slew ,000 Edomites in the Valley of Salt, ptured Sela their capital and sent ,000 more to their death by casting em from the top of Sela (2 Kings :7; 2 Chronicles 25:11–12).

Uzziah, his successor, restored the rt at Elath (2 Kings 14:22), but der Ahaz, when Judah was being tacked by Pekah and Rezin, the lomites invaded Judah and carried captives (2 Chronicles 28:17). The rt of Elath was lost once again. ead 'Edom' for 'Aram' in 2 Kings :6, as RSV). Judah never again covered Edom. Assyrian scriptions show that Edom came a vassal-state of Assyria ter *c.* 736 BC.

After the fall of Judah, Edom joiced (Psalm 137:7). The prophets retold judgment on Edom for her tter hatred (Jeremiah 49:7–22; mentations 4:21–22; Ezekiel :12–14; 35:15; Joel 3:19; Amos 12; Obadiah 10ff.). Some Edomites essed into southern Judah and ttled to the south of Hebron (see also *IDUMAEA).

Edom proper fell into Arab hands during the 5th century BC, and in the 3rd century BC was overrun by the Nabataeans. Through these centuries yet other Edomites fled to Judah. Judas Maccabaeus later subdued them (1 Maccabees 5:65), and John Hyrcanus compelled them to be circumcised and incorporated into the Jewish people. The Herods were of general Edomite stock.

**Archaeological**

If we date the emergence of the Edomites proper from the end of the Late Bronze Age and the beginning of the Iron Age, there is a limited range of archaeological evidence throughout the centuries until Roman times.

A few important sites have been excavated – Tawilân was occupied from the 8th to the 6th centuries BC. Finds from Tell el-Kheleifeh on the Gulf of Aqabah have recently been reassessed and occupation seems to have spanned the 8th to the 5th centuries BC (and not to have begun in the time of Solomon, as once believed). The earliest settlement found at Bozrah also dates from the 8th century BC. Umm el-Biyāra (behind Petra) has been investigated.

A variety of small Iron Age fortresses on the borders of Edom is known.

Important data are preserved on Assyrian records from about 733 BC to the end of the Assyrian empire in 612 BC. Some aspects of the general culture are beginning to emerge, *e.g.* several important seals and ostraca reveal names and deities and throw light on commercial transactions. The name of the deity *Qaus* appears in personal names. But, in general, the archaeological information is comparatively sparse at present. However excavations continue on a much larger scale at a large site like Petra and at several separate, but smaller, sites.

J. A. Thompson

*Further reading*

F. M. Abel, *Géographie de la Palestine* 2, 1937, pp. 281–285
D. Baly, *The Geography of the Bible*, 1974
C. M. Bennett, *RB* 73, 1966, pp. 372ff.; 76, 1969, pp. 386ff.
Nelson Glueck, *The Other Side of Jordan*, 1940
*AASOR* 15, 18–19
Various articles in *BASOR* 71–72, 75–76, 79–80, 82, 84–85
*BA* 28, 1965, pp. 70ff.
J. Lindsay, *Tyndale Paper* 21, 3, 1976, Melbourne
B. Rothenberg, *PEQ* 94, 1962, pp. 5ff.
J. R. Bartlett in *POTT*, pp. 229–258
Aharoni, *LOB*, pp. 40–42, 61–62
Various articles in A. Hadidi (ed.), *Studies in the Archaeology and History of Jordan* I, 1982; II, 1985; III, 1987, Amman
J. R. Bartlett, *Edom and the Edomites*, JSOT Supp. 77, 1989
P. Bienkowski (ed.), *Early Edom and Moab*, 1992

**EDREI** (Hebrew *'eḏre'î*). **1.** A chief city of the Amorite kingdom of Og, where Israel defeated the Amorites in a pitched battle (Numbers 21:33; Deuteronomy 1:4; 3:1; Joshua 12:4; 13:12, 31). Usually identified (following Eusebius) with Der'a (95 kilometres south of Damascus), a key point for communications in the Bashan area, with remains dating from the Early Bronze Age; but R. Hill (in *VT* 16, 1966, pp. 412–419) points out that it lacks natural defence, and prefers Zorah/Ezra 30 kilometres north-north-east (not incompatible with Eusebius' 25 miles from Bozrah).

**2.** A town in Naphtali (Joshua 19:37); named next to Abel-beth-maacah in the list of Tuthmosis III (*LOB*, p. 162).

J. P. U. Lilley

**EGLON** (Hebrew *'eglôn*). Not far from Lachish, but an independent state in the southern confederacy against Joshua; eventually occupied by Judah (Joshua 10:3; 15:39).

Albright's identification with Tell el-Hesi (*BASOR* 15, 1924 and 17, 1925) has been widely accepted (J. Simons, *GTT*, p. 147; *LOB*, pp. 124, 218f.) and is not inconsistent with the sequence in Joshua 10:34; Khirbet Ajlan, may preserve the name. The westerly position and small Iron Age fortification count against it, however, and Noth's suggestion of Tel Eton (Tell Eitun) may be right. Tell en-Najileh is now ruled out by the lack of Late Bronze remains.

J. P. U. Lilley

*Further reading*

G. E. Wright, *BA* 34, 1971, pp. 76–86
V. Fargo, K. O'Connell, *BA* 41, 1978, pp. 165–182
D. Dorsey, *Tel Aviv* 7, 1980, p. 187
L. Toombs, *IEJ* 32, 1982, pp. 67ff.

**EGYPT.** See p. 108.

**EGYPT, RIVER OF.** The correct identification of 'River of Egypt' is still uncertain; several distinct

**Continued on p. 122**

The pyramids, near Cairo.

# EGYPT

**EGYPT.** The ancient kingdom and modern republic in the north-eastern corner of Africa and linked with western Asia by the Sinai isthmus.

## Name

*Egypt*

The word 'Egypt' derives from the Greek *Aigyptos*, Latin *Aegyptus*. This term itself is probably a transcript of the Egyptian *Ḫ(wt)-k'-Pt(ḥ)*, pronounced roughly H̆a-ku-ptah, as is shown by the cuneiform transcript *Ḫikuptaḫ* in the Amarna letters, *c.* 1360 BC. 'Hakuptah' is one of the names of Memphis, the old Egyptian capital on the western bank of the Nile just above Cairo (which eventually replaced it).

If this explanation is correct, then the name of the city must have been used *pars pro toto* for Egypt generally besides Memphis by the Greeks, rather as today Cairo and Egypt are both *Miṣr* in Arabic.

*Mizraim*

The regular Hebrew (and common Semitic) word for Egypt is *miṣrayim*. The word first occurs in external sources in the 14th century BC: as *mṣrm* in the Ugaritic (northern Canaanite) texts and as *miṣri* in the Amarna letters. In the 1st millennium BC, the Assyrian-Babylo nian texts refer to *Muṣur* or *Muṣri*; unfortunately they use this term ambiguously: for Egypt on the one hand, for a region in northern Syria/southern Asia Minor on the other, and (very doubtfully) for par of northern Arabia (see literature cited by Oppenheim in *ANET*, p. 27 note 9).

For the doubtful possibility of the northern Syrian *Muṣri* being intended in 1 Kings 10:28, see *MIZRAIM.

The term *Muṣri* is thought to mea 'march(es)', borderlands, and so to be applicable to any fringe-land (Egyptian, Syrian or Arabian; compare Oppenheim, *loc. cit.*). However true from an Assyrian military point of view, this explanation is hardly adequate to account for the Hebrew/Canaanite form *miṣrayim/mṣrm* of the 2nd millennium, or for its use.

That *miṣrayim* is a dual form reflecting the duality of Egypt (see the section on geography, below) i possible but quite uncertain.

Spiegelberg, in *Recueil de Travau* 21, 1899, pp. 39–41, sought to deriv

sr from the Egyptian (*i*)*mḏr*, ortification)-walls', referring to the ard-forts on Egypt's Asiatic ntier from *c.* 2000 BC onwards, the st feature of the country to be countered by visiting Semites m that time. The fact that the term ght be assimilated to Semitic *āṣôr*, 'fortress', adds weight to this. owever, a final and complete planation of *miṣrayim* cannot be fered at present.

### atural features and geography

*eneral*

e present political unit 'Egypt' is ughly a square, extending from the editerranean coast of Africa in the rth to the line of 22° N latitude 100 kilometres from north to uth), and from the Red Sea in the st across to the line of 25° E ngitude in the west, with a total rface-area of roughly 1,000,250 uare kilometres. However, of this hole area, 96% is desert and only % usable land; and 99% of Egypt's pulation live in that 4% of viable nd.

The real Egypt is the land reached by the Nile, being Herodotus' oft-quoted 'gift of the Nile'. Egypt is in a 'temperate zone' desert-belt having a warm, rainless climate: in a year Alexandria has barely 19 centimetres of rain, Cairo 3 centimetres and Aswan virtually nil. For life-giving water, Egypt depends wholly on the Nile.

*The two Egypts*

Historically ancient Egypt consists of the long, narrow Nile valley from the first cataract at Aswan (not from the second, as today) to the Memphis/Cairo district, plus the broad, flat triangle (hence its name) of the Delta from Cairo to the sea. The contrast of valley and delta enforce a dual nature upon Egypt.

*a. Upper Egypt.* Bounded on either side by cliffs (limestone to the north and sandstone to the south of Esna some 530 kilometres south of Cairo), the valley is never more than *c.* 19 kilometres wide and sometimes narrows to a few hundred metres (as at Gebel Silsileh). At its annual inundation the *Nile deposited fresh silt upon the land beyond its banks each year until the Aswan barrages halted deposition in modern times. As far as the waters reach, green plants can grow; immediately beyond, all is desert up to the cliffs.

*b. Lower Egypt.* Some 20 kilometres north of Cairo, the Nile divides into two main branches. The northern branch reaches the sea at Rosetta, and the eastern at Damietta about 145 kilometres away; from Cairo to the sea is roughly 160 kilometres.

Between the two great arms of the Nile, and over a considerable area beyond them to the east and west, stretches the flat, swampy Delta-land, entirely composed of river-borne alluvium and intersected by canals and drainage-channels. Lower Egypt has, from antiquity, always included the northernmost part of the Nile valley from just south of Memphis/Cairo, in addition to the Delta proper.

In ancient times tradition held that the Nile had seven mouths on the Delta coast (Herodotus), but only three are recognized as important in ancient Egyptian sources.

# Pyramids at Giza

On a high rocky plateau on the west bank of the Nile, at Giza, 24 kilometres north of the ancient capital of Memphis, and now in the suburbs of Cairo, you can still see the Great Pyramid of Giza, perhaps the largest building ever to be constructed. Close by are two other pyramids, and the three pyramids together were classed as one of the seven wonders of the ancient world. At their feet lie the remains of a town of temples, smaller pyramids and scores of flat-topped mastabas, all linked by ceremonial roadways. The three large pyramids are gigantic tombs, built for three great kings of Egypt; the smaller pyramids are thought to be the tombs of the kings' queens and the mastabas were for the kings' dead families and courtiers. Nearby is the Sphinx, an enormous stone lion with a bearded human face, crouching by the town of dead people as if guarding it.

**The structure**

The great pyramid was built for King Khufu (sometimes known today by the Greek form of his name, Kheops), the second king of the Fourth Dynasty. Built between 2600 and 2500 BC, before the Egyptians knew the pulley or had wheeled vehicles, the pyramid was ancient when Abraham visited Egypt. It is immense. Its north side was originally 230·3 metres, its west side 230·4 metres, its south side 230·5 metres and its east side 230·4 metres. It was orientated very closely to the points of the compass, with each side at an exact elevation of 51° 52′. These figures reveal the mathematical precision and engineering brilliance of the construction. Its square base covered an area of 5·3 hectares, an area large enough for ten jumbo jets to park. Its height was 145·7 metres, and its peak was only 10 centimetres wide.

**The interior**

There was one door, in the north-facing wall. Descending passageways led to the Queen's Chamber; a Grand Gallery, 46 metres long; an unfinished underground chamber; and, above all, the King's Chamber, the size of a small house, lined with polished pink granite. Here the King's mummified body was put to rest within a sarcophagus that had been exquisitely carved from a single stone. Originally the room would have been filled with the belongings that his spirit needed in the after-life, but ancient Egyptian robbers, with no respect for the dead, and defying the curse laid on anyone who opened the door, were in the habit of robbing all tombs, including the pyramids. After the king was buried, all the passageways were filled with rubble, and the door itself was hidden.

**The building**

To build the pyramid, Egyptian labourers used 2,300,000 colossal blocks of granite and limestone, each weighing an average of 2,300 kilos. The outer surface was faced with finer light-coloured limestone, which was smoothed down until the sides were sheer (over the centuries plunderers have taken away this outer surface for other buildings).

Most of this rock was quarried from cliffs lower down the Nile, and brought up the river on great rafts. From the river the rocks were hauled along a specially constructed causeway, probably on sledges balanced on top of rollers. At the building site the blocks of stone were most likely pulled and pushed up sloping embankments, using sledges, rollers and levers.

The planner and director of this vast enterprise was known as the master builder and was a trusted adviser to the pharaoh. He supervised scores of foremen and superintendents, all of whom had their own subordinates. According to the Greek historian Herodotus, the Great Pyramid took 100,000 men 20 years to construct. Peasants, not slaves, formed the major part of the work force, generally labouring on the pyramids when the Nile flooded their fields and agricultural work had to stop. Their overseers took great care of the health and welfare of their workers. From manpower to materials, everything had to be the very best for this great testimony to the greatness of Egypt.

**The Sphinx, a huge stone lion with a bearded human face.**

*The Egypt of antiquity*

To the west of the Nile valley stretches the Sahara, a flat, rocky desert of drifted sand, and parallel with the valley a series of oases – great natural depressions, where cultivation and habitation are made possible by a supply of artesian water. Between the Nile valley and Red Sea on the east is the Arabian desert, a mountainous terrain with some mineral wealth: gold, ornamental stone, including alabaster, breccia and diorite. Across the Gulf of Suez is the rocky peninsula of Sinai.

Egypt was thus sufficiently isolated between her deserts to develop her own individual culture, but, at the same time, access from the east by either the Sinai isthmus or Red Sea and Wadi Hammamat, and from the north and south by way of the Nile was direct enough for her to receive (and give) external stimulus.

The ancient geography of pharaonic Egypt is a subject of considerable complexity. The historic nomes or provinces first clearly emerge in the Old Kingdom (4th Dynasty) in the 3rd millennium BC, but some probably originated earlier as territories of what were originally separate little communities in prehistory. There were reckoned 22 of these nomes for Upper Egypt and 20 for Lower Egypt in the enumeration that was traditional by Graeco-Roman times, when geographical records are fullest.

## People and language

*People*

The earliest evidences of human activity in Egypt are flint tools of the Palaeolithic age from the Nile terraces. But the first real Egyptians who settled as agriculturists in the Nile valley (and of whom physical remains survive) are those labelled as Taso-Badarians, the first predynastic (prehistoric) culture. They appear to be of African origin, together with the two successive prehistoric culture-phases, best called Naqada I and II, ending about 3000 BC or shortly thereafter. Modern Egyptians are in direct descent from the people of ancient Egypt.

*Language*

The ancient Egyptian language is of mixed origin and has had a very long history. It is usually called 'Hamito-Semitic', and was basically a Hamitic tongue (*i.e.* related to the Libyco-Berber languages of North

**The colossal (*c.* 20 metres high) statue of King Ramesses II at his temple at Abu Simbel, lower Egypt, 1301–1234 BC.**

'rica) swamped at an early epoch
ı prehistory) by a Semitic
nguage. Much Egyptian
ocabulary is directly cognate with
emitic, and there are analogies in
ntax. Lack of early written matter
nders proper comparison with
mitic.

On the affinities of the Egyptian
nguage, see A. H. Gardiner,
*yptian Grammar*, section 3, and
ı more detail) G. Lefebvre,
*ıronique d'Égypte*, 11, No. 22,
·36, pp. 266–292.

In the history of the Egyptian
nguage, five main stages may
nveniently be distinguished in the
ritten documents.

*Old Egyptian* was an archaic and
rse form, used in the 3rd
illennium BC.

*Middle Egyptian* was perhaps the
rnacular of Dynasties 9–11
200–2000 BC) and was used
iversally for written records
ıring the Middle Kingdom and
rly New Kingdom (to *c.* 1300 BC),
ıd continued in use in official texts,
a slightly modified form, as late as
'aeco-Roman days.

*Late Egyptian* was the popular speech of the New Kingdom and after (16th–8th centuries BC), but was already coming into popular use two centuries before this time (1800–1600). It is also the language of documents and New Kingdom literature and official texts from Dynasty 19 onwards. Old, Middle and Late Egyptian were written in hieroglyphic and hieratic scripts.

*Demotic* is really the name of a script, applied to the still more evolved form of Egyptian current in documents dating from the 8th century BC to Roman times.

*Coptic*, the last stage of Egyptian, and the native language of Roman-Byzantine Egypt, has several dialect forms and was turned into a literary medium by Egyptian Christians or Copts. It was written, not in Egyptian script, but in the Coptic alphabet, which is composed of the Greek alphabet plus seven extra characters taken over from the old Demotic script. Coptic has survived as the purely liturgical language of the Coptic (Egyptian) Church down to modern times, its use being equivalent to that of Latin in the Roman Catholic Church.

### History

Of Egypt's long history only the salient features and those periods of direct relevance to biblical studies are discussed below. For further detail, see the classified *Further Reading* at the end of the article.

*Egypt before 2000 BC*

*a. Predynastic Egypt.* During the three successive phases of predynastic settlement the foundations for historic Egypt were laid. Communities grew up having villages, local shrines and belief in an after-life (evidenced by burial-customs).

Late in the final prehistoric phase (Naqada II) definite contact with Sumerian Mesopotamia existed and Mesopotamian influences and ideas were so strong as to leave their mark on formative Egyptian culture (compare H. Frankfort, *Birth of Civilisation in the Near East*, 1951, pp. 100–111). It is at this point that hieroglyphic writing appears, Egyptian art assumes its characteristic forms and monumental architecture begins.

*b. Archaic Egypt.* The first pharaoh of all Egypt was apparently Narmer of Upper Egypt, who conquered the rival Delta kingdom; he was perhaps the Menes of later tradition, and certainly the founder of Dynasty 1. Egyptian culture advanced and matured rapidly during the first two Dynasties.

*c. Old Kingdom.* In Dynasties 3–6, Egypt reached a peak of prosperity, splendour and cultural achievement. King Djoser's step-pyramid and its attendant buildings is the first major structure of cut stone in history (*c.* 2650 BC).

In Dynasty 4 the pharaoh was absolute master, not in theory only (as was always the case) but also in fact, as never occurred before or after. Next in authority to the divine king stood the vizier, and beneath him the heads of the various branches of administration. At first members of the royal family held such offices.

During this period material culture reached high levels in architecture (culminating in the Great Pyramid of Kheops, Dynasty 4), sculpture and painted relief, as well as in furnishings and jewellery.

In Dynasty 5 the power of the kings weakened economically, and the priesthood of the sun-god Rē' stood behind the throne.

In Dynasty 6 the Egyptians were

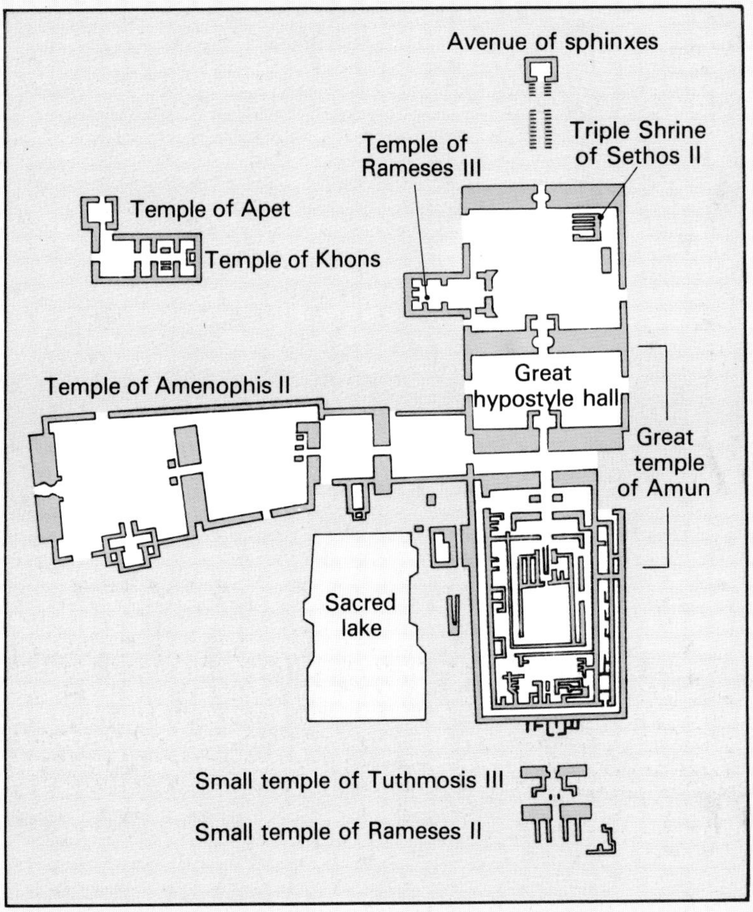


**Plan of the temple at Karnak, including the Great Hypostyle Hall built by Sethos I and Ramesses II, *c.* 1300–1220 BC.**

actively exploring and trading in Nubia (later Cush). Meanwhile the decline in the king's power continued. This situation reached its climax late in the 94 years' reign of Pepi II. The literature of the time included several wisdom-books: those of Imhotep, Hardidief, (?Kairos) to Kagemni, and, of especial note, that of Ptah-hotep.

*d. First Intermediate Period.* In the Delta, where the established order was overthrown, this was a time of social upheaval (revolution) and of Asiatic infiltration. New kings in Middle-Egypt (Dynasties 9 and 10) then took over and sought to restore order in the Delta. But eventually they quarrelled with the princes of Thebes in Upper Egypt, and these then declared their independence (Dynasty 11) and eventually vanquished their northern rivals, reuniting Egypt under one strong sceptre (that of the Intef and Mentuhotep kings).

The disturbances of this troubled epoch shattered the bland self-confidence of Old Kingdom Egypt and called forth a series of pessimistic warnings that are among the finest and the most remarkable in Egyptian literature.

*The Middle Kingdom and Second Intermediate Period*

*a. Middle Kingdom.* Eventually the 11th Dynasty was followed by Amenemhat I, founder of Dynasty 12, the strong man of his time. He and his Dynasty (*c.* 1991 BC) were alike remarkable.

Elected to an unstable throne by fellow-nobles jealous for their local autonomy, Amenemhat I sought to rehabilitate the kingship by a programme of material reform announced and justified in literary works produced as royal propaganda (see G. Posener, *Littérature et Politique dans l'Égypte de la XII$^e$ Dynastie*, 1956). He therein proclaimed himself the (political) saviour of Egypt. He accordingly rebuilt the administration, promoted agricultural prosperity and secured the frontiers, placing a series of forts on the Asiatic border.

The administration was no longer at 11th-Dynasty Thebes, which was too far south, but moved back to the strategically far superior area of Memphis, to Ithet-Tawy, a centre specifically built for the purpose. Sesostris III raided into Palestine, as far as Shechem ('Sekmem').

The extent of Egyptian influence in Palestine, Phoenicia and southern Syria in Dynasty 12 is indicated by the execration texts (19th century BC) which record the names for magical cursing of possibly-hostile Semitic princes and their districts, besides Nubians and Egyptians. (See W. F. Albright, *JPOS* 8, 1928, pp. 223–256; *BASOR* 83, 1941, pp. 30–36.)

This was the golden age of Egypt's classical literature, especially short stories. This well-organized 12th-Dynasty Egypt, careful of its Asiatic frontier, was in all probability the Egypt of Abraham. The charge which pharaoh gave to his men concerning Abraham (Genesis 12:20) when he left Egypt is exactly paralleled (in reverse) by that given with regard to the returning Egyptian exile Sinuhe (*ANET*, p. 21, lines 240–250) and, pictorially, by the group of 37 Asiatics visiting Egypt, shown in a famous tomb-scene at Beni-hasan (see, *e.g.* *IBA*, figure 25, pp. 28–29). Amūn of Thebes, fused with the sun-god as Amen-Rē', had become chief national god; but in Osiris resided most of the Egyptians' hopes of the after-life.

*b. Second Intermediate Period and Hyksos.* For barely a century after 1786 BC, a new line of kings, the 13th Dynasty, held sway over most of Egypt, still ruling from Ithet-Tawy. Their reigns were mostly brief so that a vizier might thus serve several kings. Deprived of settled, firm, personal royal control, the machinery of state inevitably began to run down.

At this time many Semitic slaves were to be found in Egypt, even as far as Thebes, and eventually Semitic chiefs (Egyptian 'chiefs of foreign lands' *ḥḳ'w-ḫ'swt*, that is, Hyksos) gained prominence in Lower Egypt and then (perhaps by swift *coup d'état*) took over the kingship of Egypt at Ithet-Tawy itself (forming the 15th to 16th 'Hyksos' Dynasties), where they ruled for about 100 years. They established also an eastern Delta capital, Avaris (on the south of modern Qantir). These Semitic pharaohs assumed the full rank and style of traditional royalty.

The Hyksos at first took over the Egyptian state administration as a going concern, but as time passed, Semitic officials were appointed to high office; of these the chancellor Ḥūr is the best-known.

Into this background, Joseph (Genesis 37–50) fits perfectly. Like so many others, he was a Semitic servant in the household of an

**Continued on p. 114**

# Tutankhamun's treasure

### The discovery

When Howard Carter, the English Egyptologist, broke through a sealed door on 5th November, 1922, as he excavated in the Valley of the Kings, he discovered the entrance to the only tomb of a pharaoh ever found that has not been ransacked by grave-robbers. It was Tutankhamun's tomb, a tomb Carter had been convinced must exist somewhere in the Valley and which he had spent 10 years searching for. When he had come across the steps leading to this sealed door, hidden below huts used by ancient Egyptian decorators, he had almost given up hope.

This door was removed on 25th November, revealing a tunnel, almost entirely filled with rubble. All that day and until mid-afternoon the following day was spent clearing out the rubble, but at last Carter found himself at the end of the nine-metre-long passageway and in front of a second sealed door. Behind him in the flickering candle-light were Lord Carnarvon, who had provided the money for the patient excavations, and Lord Carnarvon's daughter. Carter made a hole in the top of the door, pushed his candle through and peered in. He later wrote, '. . . as my eyes grew accustomed to the light, details of the room within emerged slowly from the mist; strange animals, statues and gold – everywhere the glint of gold. For the moment I was struck dumb with amazement, and when Lord Carnarvon, unable to stand the suspense any longer, inquired anxiously, "Can you see anything?" it was all I could do to get out the words, "Yes, wonderful things!"'

Carter's discovery was to be the most spectacular archaeological discovery yet made.

### The tomb

The inner door opened into the largest of four rooms. Three of the rooms were crammed with objects – furniture, including three wooden beds with carved animal heads, chairs, a beautiful gold-covered ornamental throne, and stools; also gaming boards inlaid with gold and ivory; walking sticks; two life-sized statues; weapons; four dismantled chariots; twenty-nine bows, some of which were gold-plated; flowers; two gold trumpets; and clothes – everything that Tutankhamun might need in the after-life.

A magnificent wooden chest is decorated with scenes from the king's life. This box has four carrying poles, which slide through rings on the base, a method of carrying also used for the Israelite ark of the covenant which held the Ten Commandments.

One room, later called the treasury, was guarded by the life-sized statue of a dog, Anubis, the Egyptian god of mummification and rebirth. This room contained the most valuable of the jewels and ornaments: necklaces, earrings, diadems, rings, pectorals, pendants and amulets. The craftsmanship has hardly been surpassed in the history of jewellery.

### Burial chamber

The second largest room was filled almost entirely by a wooden shrine covered with hammered gold. Inside this was a second shrine, and then a third and a fourth, all covered with gold, and engraved with spells to ensure the safe passage of pharaoh's spirit. Gold jewellery, amulets and other precious objects lay between the walls of the shrines. These shrines had been brought into the tomb in pieces and assembled in the burial chamber. The sides were held together by rods inserted through silver rings. The tabernacle which the Israelites made and carried through the wilderness was constructed in this way, while the ark of the covenant was similarly overlaid with gold.

It took Carter a year to separate the pieces of the shrine. Inside the fourth shrine was a yellow quartzite sarcophagus. When the lid was lifted and the layers of linen removed, Carter and those with him were astonished to see a golden coffin of exquisite workmanship in the shape of a mummy. Fitted tightly inside was a second coffin made, like the first, of wood covered with gold. Within this was a third mummy-shaped coffin, this time made entirely of gold. Then at last Carter saw the mummy. The face was concealed by an amazing mask in the likeness of the king, made of gold inlaid with precious stones and lapis lazuli. More precious stones, amulets and jewellery had been carefully inserted between the bandages covering the body.

### Tutankhamun

A post-mortem revealed that Tutankhamun was between 18 and 20 years old when he died. The death of the boy king may have taken the tomb makers by surprise. The tomb shows signs of being hastily cut, and the burial chamber, with its decorated walls, is the only room that was finished.

Tutankhamun lived 3,300 years ago and ruled for only 9 years, from about 1336 to 1327 BC. He was an unimportant puppet king, the son-in-law of the great King Akhenaten, and his was the smallest royal tomb in the Valley of the Kings. The amazing riches and intricate works of craftsmanship must have been only a small reflection of the magnificence of the Egyptian court. Since Tutankhamun lived only about a hundred years before Moses, we have here a glimpse of the life-style which Moses knew and which he abandoned in order to be identified with the people of God.

The tomb took 10 years to clear and work on its contents has not yet finished. The treasure is kept in the Egyptian Museum, and remains the largest collection of gold and jewellery in the world.

The gold mask of Tutankhamun.

**Continued from p. 112**
important Egyptian. The royal court is punctiliously Egyptian in etiquette (Genesis 41:14; 43:32), yet the Semite Joseph is readily appointed to high office (as in the case of Ḥūr, perhaps, a little later). The peculiar and ready blend of Egyptian and Semitic elements mirrored in the Joseph-narrative (independent of its being a Hebrew story set in Egypt) fits the Hyksos period perfectly. Furthermore, the eastern Delta is prominent under the Hyksos (Avaris), but not again in Egyptian history until Moses' day (*i.e.* the 19th Dynasty, or, at the earliest, the very end of the 18th).

Eventually princes at Thebes clashed with the Hyksos in the north; King Kamose took all Egypt from Apopi III ('Awoserrē) except for Avaris in the north-eastern Delta, according to his historical stele (see L. Habachi, *The Second Stela of Kamose*, 1972). Finally, Kamose's successor Ahmose I (founder of the 18th Dynasty and the New Kingdom) expelled the Hyksos regime and its immediate adherents (Egyptian as well as Asiatic) from Egypt and worsted them in Palestine. An outline of this period's culture (illustrated) is in W. C. Hayes, *Scepter of Egypt* 2, 1959, pp. 3–41.

*New Kingdom – the Empire*

The next five centuries, from *c.* 1552 to *c.* 1069 BC, witnessed the pinnacle of Egypt's political power and influence and the age of her greatest outward grandeur and luxury, but also, by their end, the breakdown of the old Egyptian spirit and eventual dissolution of Egyptian life and civilization which came about during the Late Period.

*a. Dynasty 18.* The first kings of this line (except Tuthmosis I) were apparently content to expel the Hyksos and to rule Egypt and Nubia in the old 12th-Dynasty tradition. But the energetic Tuthmosis III took up the embryo policy of his grandfather Tuthmosis I, aiming to conquer Palestine–Syria and set the national boundary as far from Egypt proper as possible, in order to avoid any repetition of the Hyksos dominion. The princes of the Canaanite/Amorite city-states were reduced to tribute-paying vassals.

This structure lasted almost a century till late into the reign of Amenophis III (*c.* 1360 BC); for this brief spell, Egypt was the paramount power in the ancient Near East.

Thebes was not sole capital at this time: Memphis in the north was more convenient administratively (especially for Asia).

Amenophis III showed particular predilection for Aten, the sun-god manifest in the solar disc, while seeking to curb priestly ambition and still officially honouring Amūn. But his son Amenophis IV broke completely with Amūn and then with almost all the old gods, proscribing their worship and excising their very names from the monuments. Amenophis IV proclaimed the sole worship of Aten, changed his own name to Akhenaten and moved to his own newly-created capital-city in Middle Egypt (Akhet-Aten, the modern Tell el-Amarna). Only he and the royal family worshipped Aten directly; ordinary men and women worshipped Aten in the person of the divine pharaoh Akhenaten himself.

Meantime, Egypt's hold on Syria–Palestine slackened somewhat. The petty princes there were free to fight each other in pursuit of personal ambition, denouncing each other to the pharaoh and seeking military aid from him to further their own designs. This information comes from the famous Amarna Letters. At home, Akhenaten eventually had to compromise with the opposing forces, and within two or three years of his death Amūn's worship, wealth and renown were fully restored.

General Haremhab now assumed control and began to set the affairs of Egypt to rights again. At his death the throne passed to his colleague Paramessu, who, as Ramesses I, founded Dynasty 19 and reigned for one year.

*b. Dynasty 19* (roughly 1300–1200 BC). Following Haremhab's internal restoration of Egypt, Sethos I (son of Ramesses I) felt able to reassert Egyptian authority in Syria. His clash with the Hittites was not unsuccessful and the two powers made a treaty.

Sethos began a large building programme in the north-eastern Delta (the first since Hyksos times) and had a residence there. He may have founded the Delta capital so largely built by his son Ramesses II, who named it after himself, 'Pi-Ramessē', 'House of Ramesses' (the Raamses of Exodus 1:11). Ramesses II posed as the imperial pharaoh *par excellence*, dazzling later generations to such an extent that nine later kings took his name (Ramesses III-XI).

Besides the Delta residence, this king undertook extensive building throughout all Egypt and Nubia during his long reign of 66 years.

In Syria he campaigned (usually against the Hittites) for 20 years (including the battle of Qadesh) until, wearied of the struggle, and with other foes to face, he and his Hittite contemporary Hattusil III finally signed a treaty of lasting peace between them. His successc Merenptah made one brief raid intc Palestine (his capture of Gezer is attested by an inscription at Amad independent of the famous Israel Stele), apparently brushing with a few Israelites among others, and ha to beat off a dangerous invasion (th of the 'Sea Peoples') from Libya; hi successors were ineffective.

The first half of Dynasty 19 apparently witnessed the Israelite oppression and Exodus. The restoration of firm order under Haremhab and the great impetus given to building activity in the eastern Delta by both Sethos I and Ramesses II, with the consequent need of a large and economic labour-force, set the background fc the Hebrew oppression which culminated in the work on Pithom and Ra'amses described in Exodus 1:8–11. Ra'amses was the great Delta-residence of the pharaoh, an *Pithom a township in the Wadi Tumilat. Exodus 1:12–22 gives som details of the conditions of this slavery.

As for the early life of Moses, ther is nothing either exceptional or incredible in a western Semite's being brought up in Egyptian cour circles, perhaps in a *harim* in a Delt pleasure-residence, the pharaohs having several such scattered *harims* (compare J. Yoyotte in G. Posener, *Dictionary of Egyptian Civilization*, 1962). At least from th reign of Ramesses II onwards, Asiatics were brought up in royal *harims*, with the purpose of holdin office (see S. Sauneron and J. Yoyotte, *Revue d'Égyptologie* 7, 1950, pp. 67–70). The thoroughly Semitic Ben-'Ozen from Ṣûr-Bāšān ('Rock of Bashan') was royal cupbearer (*wb'-nsw*) to Merenptah (J. M. A. Janssen, *Chronique d'Égypte* 26, No. 51, 1951, pp. 54–5 and figure 11), and another Semitic cupbearer of his was called Pen-Ḥaṣu[ri], ('he of Hazor')(compa Sauneron and Yoyotte, *op. cit.*, p. 6 note 6). On a lower level, an Egyptia of *c.* 1170 BC scolds his son for joinin in blood-brotherhood with Asiatics in the Delta (J. Černý, *JNES* 14, 1955 pp. 161ff.).

Hence the Egyptian training and upbringing of Moses in Exodus 2 is entirely credible; the onus of proof

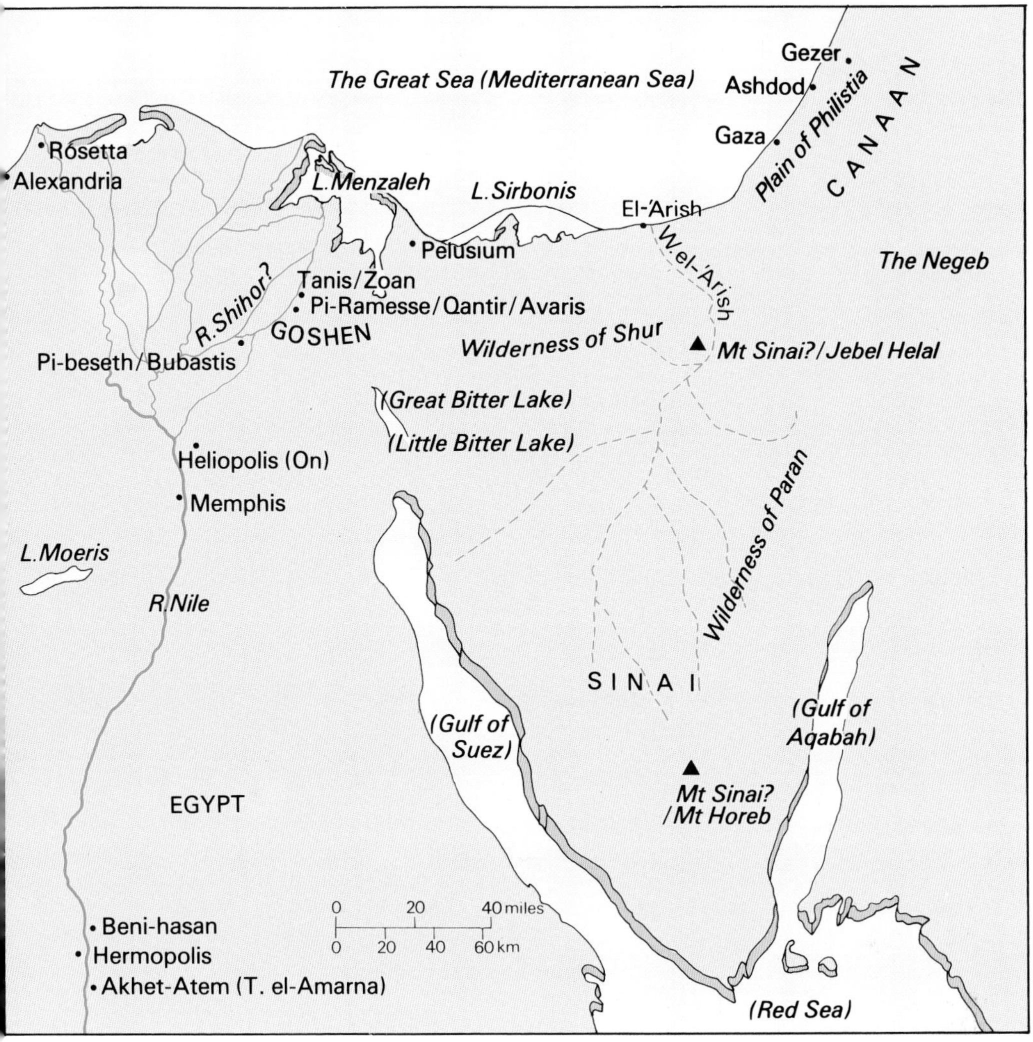


Egypt, showing the Wadi el-'Arish and the river Shinor, both possible identifications with the 'River of Egypt'.

›s upon any who would discredit e account. A further implication is at Moses would have an Egyptian ucation, one of the best available his day.

For the flight of fugitives omparable to that of Moses in codus 2:15), compare the flight of o runaway slaves in Papyrus nastasi V (*ANET*, p. 259) and uses on the extradition of gitives in the treaty between ımesses II and the Hittites (*ANET*, ). 200–203).

For the number of Israelites at the codus, see the article *WILDERNESS OF ANDERING. Between Egypt and naan at this period there was nstant coming and going ompare the frontier-reports in VET, pp. 258–259).

The age of the 19th Dynasty was e most cosmopolitan in Egyptian story. More than in Dynasty 18, ebrew-Canaanite loan-words netrated Egyptian language and literature by the score, and Egyptian officials proudly showed off their knowledge of the Canaanite tongue (Papyrus Anastasi I, see *ANET*, p. 477b). Semitic deities (Baal, Anath, Resheph, Astarte or Ashtaroth) were accepted in Egypt and even had temples there. Thus the Hebrews could hardly fail to hear something of the land of Canaan, and Canaanites with their customs were before their eyes, before they had even stirred from Egypt; the knowledge of such matters displayed in the Pentateuch does not imply a date of writing after the Israelite invasion of Canaan, as is so often erroneously surmised.

*c. Dynasty 20.* In due course, a prince Setnakht restored order. His son Ramesses III was Egypt's last great imperial pharaoh. In the first decade of his reign (*c.* 1190–1180 BC) great folk-movements in the eastern Mediterranean basin swept away the Hittite empire in Asia Minor, entirely disrupted the traditional Canaanite–Amorite city-states of Syria–Palestine and threatened Egypt with invasion from both Libya and Palestine. These attacks Ramesses III beat off in three desperate campaigns, and he even briefly carried Egyptian arms into Palestine.

Since his successors Ramesses IV–XI were for the most part ineffective personally, the machinery of state became increasingly inefficient and corrupt, and chronic inflation upset the economy, causing great hardship for the common people. The famous robberies of the royal tombs at Thebes reached their peak at this time.

*Late-Period Egypt and Israelite History*

From now on, Egypt's story is one of a decline, halted at intervals, but then only briefly, by occasional kings of outstanding character. But the memory of Egypt's past greatness lingered on far beyond her own borders, and served Israel and Judah ill when they were foolish enough to depend on the 'bruised reed'.

*a. Dynasty 21 and the united monarchy.* Late in the reign of Ramesses XI the general Herihor (now also high priest of Amūn) ruled Upper Egypt and the prince Nesubanebded I (Smendes) ruled Lower Egypt; this was styled, politically, as a 'renaissance' (*wḥm-mswt*). At the death of Ramesses XI (*c.* 1069 BC), Smendes at Tanis became pharaoh, the succession being secured for his descendants (Dynasty 21), while, in return, Herihor's successors at Thebes were confirmed in the hereditary high-priesthood of Amūn, and in the rule of Upper Egypt under the Tanite pharaohs. So in Dynasty 21, one half of Egypt ruled the whole only by gracious permission of the other half!

These peculiar circumstances help to explain the modest foreign policy of this Dynasty in Asia: a policy of friendship and alliance with neighbouring Palestinian states, military action being restricted to 'police' action to safeguard the frontier in the south-western corner of Palestine nearest the Egyptian border. Commercial motives would also be strong, as Tanis was a great port. All this links up with contemporary Old Testament references.

When King David conquered Edom, Hadad the infant Edomite heir was taken to Egypt for safety. There he found a welcome so favourable that, when he was grown up, he gained a royal wife (1 Kings 11:18–22).

A clear example of 21st Dynasty foreign policy occurs early in Solomon's reign. A pharaoh 'smote Gezer' and gave it as dowry with his daughter's hand in marriage-alliance with Solomon (1 Kings 9:16; compare 3:1; 7:8; 9:24; 11:1). The combination of 'police' action in south-western Palestine (Gezer) and alliance with the powerful Israelite state gave Egypt security on her Asiatic frontier and doubtless brought economic gain to both states. At Tanis was found a damaged triumphal relief-scene of the pharaoh Siamūn smiting a foreigner – apparently a Philistine, to judge by the Aegean-type axe in his hand. This very specific detail strongly suggests that it was Siamūn who conducted a 'police' action in Philistia (reaching Canaanite Gezer) and became Solomon's ally. (For this scene, see P. Montet, *L'Égypte et la Bible*, 1959, p. 40, figure 5.)

*b. The Libyan Dynasties and the divided monarchy.* (i) Shishak. When the last Tanite king died in 945 BC a powerful Libyan tribal chief (? of Bubastis/Pi-beseth) acceded to the throne peacefully as Sheshonq I (biblical Shishak), thereby founding Dynasty 22. While consolidating Egypt internally under his rule, Sheshonq I began a new and aggressive Asiatic foreign policy. He viewed Solomon's Israel not as an ally but as a political and commercial rival on his north-eastern frontier, and therefore worked for the break-up of the Hebrew kingdom.

While Solomon lived, Sheshonq shrewdly took no action apart from harbouring political refugees, notably Jeroboam son of Nebat (1 Kings 11:29–40). At Solomon's death Jeroboam's return to Palestine precipitated the division of the kingdom into the two lesser realms of Rehoboam and Jeroboam. Soon after, in Rehoboam's 'fifth year', 925 BC (1 Kings 14:25–26; 2 Chronicles 12:2–12), and apparently on pretext of a Bedouin border incident (stele-fragment, Grdseloff, *Revue de l'Histoire Juive en Égypte* 1, 1947, pp. 95–97), Shishak invaded Palestine, subduing Israel as well as Judah, as is shown by the discovery of a stele of his at Megiddo (C. S. Fisher, *The Excavation of Armageddon*, 1929, p. 13 and the figure).

Many biblical place-names occur in the list attached to the triumphal relief subsequently sculptured by Shishak on the temple of Amūn (Karnak) in Thebes (see *ANEP*, p. 118 and figure 349). Sheshonq's purpose was limited and definite: to gain political and commercial security by subduing his immediate neighbour. He made no attempt to revive the empire of Tuthmosis or Ramesses.

(ii) Zerah. It would appear from 2 Chronicles 14:9–15 and 16:8 that Sheshonq's successor Osorkon I sought to emulate his father's Palestinian success but was too lazy to go himself. Instead, he apparently sent as general Zerah the Ethiopian, who was soundly defeated by Asa of Judah *c.* 897 BC. This defeat spelt the end of Egypt's aggressive policy in Asia. However, again like Sheshonq I, Osorkon I maintained relations with Byblos in Phoenicia, where statues of both pharaohs were found (*Syria* 5, 1924, pp. 145–147 and plate 42; *Syria* 6, 1925, pp. 101–117 and plate 25).

(iii) Egypt and Ahab's dynasty. Osorkon I's successor, Takeloth I, was apparently a nonentity who allowed the royal power to slip through his incompetent fingers. Thus the next king, Osorkon II, inherited an Egypt whose unity w already menaced: the local Libya provincial governors were becom increasingly independent, and separatist tendencies appeared i Thebes. Hence, he apparently returned to the old 'modest' foreig policy of (similarly-weak) Dynasty 21, that of alliance with his Palestinian neighbours.

This is hinted at by the discove in Omri and Ahab's palace at Samaria, of an alabaster vase of Osorkon II, such as the pharaohs included in their diplomatic prese to fellow-rulers (illustrated in Reisner, *etc.*, *Harvard Excavations Samaria* 1, 1924, figure on p. 247). This suggests that Omri or Ahab h links with Egypt as well as Tyre (compare Ahab's marriage with Jezebel). Osorkon II also presente statue at Byblos (M. Dunand, *Fouilles de Byblos* 1, pp. 115–116 and plate 43).

(iv) Hoshea and 'So king of Egyp The 'modest' policy revived by Osorkon II was doubtless continu by his ever-weaker successors, under whom Egypt progressively f apart into its constituent local provinces with kings reigning elsewhere (Dynasty 23) alongside the main, parent 22nd Dynasty at Tanis/Zoan. Prior to a dual rule (perhaps mutually agreed), the Egyptian state was rocked by bitt civil wars centred on Thebes (compare R. A. Caminos, *The Chronicle of Prince Osorkon*, 1958) and could hardly have supported a different external policy.

All this indicates why Israel's la king, Hoshea, turned so readily fo help against Assyria to 'So king of Egypt' in 725/24 BC (2 Kings 17:4), and how very misplaced was his trust in an Egypt so weak and divided. No help came to save Samaria from its fall. The identity 'So' has long been obscure. He is probably Osorkon IV, last pharaoh Dynasty 22, *c.* 730–715 BC. The rea power in Lower Egypt was wielde by Tafnekht and his successor Bekenrenef (Dynasty 24) from Sais the western Delta; so powerless w Osorkon IV that in 716 BC he boug off Sargon of Assyria at the border of Egypt with a gift of twelve hors (H. Tadmor, *JCS* 12, 1958, pp. 77–7

*c. Ethiopia – the 'bruised reed'.* Nubia (Cush) there had meantime arisen a kingdom ruled by princes who were thoroughly Egyptian in

Fertile land beside the river Nile, Egypt.

ture. Of these, Kashta and nkhy laid claim to a protectorate er Upper Egypt, being worship- rs of Amūn of Thebes. In one mpaign, Piankhy subdued nekht of Lower Egypt to keep ebes safe, but promptly returned Nubia.

However, his successor Shabaka 716–702 BC) promptly re- nquered Egypt, eliminating kenrenef by 715 BC. Shabaka was a endly neutral towards Assyria; in 2 he extradited a fugitive at rgon II's request, and sealings of abaka (possibly from diplomatic cuments) were found at Nineveh. Doubtless, Shabaka had enough to inside Egypt without meddling road; but unfortunately his ccessors in this Dynasty (the 25th) ere less wise. When Sennacherib Assyria attacked Hezekiah of dah in 701 BC the rash new hiopian pharaoh Shebitku sent his ually young and inexperienced other Tirhakah to oppose Assyria Kings 19:9; Isaiah 37:9), resulting dire defeat for Egypt. The hiopian pharaohs had no preciation of Assyria's superior ength – after this setback, hakah was defeated twice more Assyria (*c.* 671 and 666/65, as ng) and Tanutamen once – and eir incompetent interference in lestinian affairs was disastrous for ypt and Palestine alike. They ere most certainly the 'bruised ed' of the Assyrian king's jibe Kings 18:21; Isaiah 36:6).

Exasperated by this stubborn meddling, Ashurbanipal in 664/63 BC finally sacked the ancient holy city of Thebes, pillaging fourteen centuries of temple treasures. No more vivid comparison than the downfall of this city could the prophet Nahum find (3:8–10) when proclaiming the on-coming ruin of Nineveh in its turn. However, Assyria could not occupy Egypt, and left only key garrisons.

*d. Egypt, Judah and Babylon.* In a now disorganized Egypt, the astute local prince of Sais (western Delta) managed with great skill to unite all Egypt under his sceptre. This was Psammetichus I, who thereby established the 26th (or Saite) Dynasty. He and his successors restored Egypt's internal unity and prosperity. They built up an effective army round a hard core of Greek mercenaries, greatly enhanced trade by encouraging Greek merchants and founded strong fleets on the Mediterranean and Red Seas. But, as if in compensation for the lack of real, inner vitality, inspiration was sought in Egypt's past glories; ancient art was copied and archaic titles were artificially brought back into fashion.

Externally, this dynasty (except for the headstrong Hophra) practised as far as possible a policy of the balance of powers in western Asia. Thus, Psammetichus I did not attack Assyria but remained her ally against the reviving power of Babylon. So, too, Neco II (610–595 BC) was marching to help a reduced Assyria (2 Kings 23:29) against Babylon, when Josiah of Judah sealed Assyria's fate by delaying Neco at Megiddo at the cost of his own life.

Egypt considered herself heir to Assyria's Palestinian possessions, but her forces were signally defeated at Carchemish in 605 BC so that all Syria–Palestine fell to Babylon (Jeremiah 46:2). Jehoiakim of Judah thus exchanged Egyptian for Babylonian vassalage for 3 years. But as the Babylonian chronicle-tablets reveal, Egypt and Babylon clashed in open conflict in 601 BC with heavy losses on both sides; Nebuchadrezzar then remained 18 months in Babylonia to refit his army.

At this point Jehoiakim of Judah rebelled (2 Kings 24:1f.), doubtless hoping for Egyptian aid. None came; Neco now wisely kept neutral. So Nebuchadrezzar was not molested in his capture of Jerusalem in 597 BC.

Psammetichus II maintained the peace; his state visit to Byblos was linked rather with Egypt's acknowledged commercial than other interests in Phoenicia. He fought only in Nubia. But Hophra (589–570 BC; the Apries of the Greeks) foolishly cast dynastic restraint aside, and marched to support Zedekiah in his revolt against Babylon (Ezekiel 17:11–21; Jeremiah 37:5), but returned in haste to Egypt when Nebuchadrez-zar temporarily raised his (second) siege of Jerusalem to repulse him – leaving Jerusalem to perish at the

Babylonian's hand in 587 BC. After other disasters, Hophra was finally supplanted in 570 BC by Ahmose II (Amasis, 570–526 BC).

As earlier prophesied by Jeremiah (46:13ff.), Nebuchadrezzar now marched against Egypt (as referred to in a damaged Babylonian tablet), doubtless to prevent any recurrence of interference from that direction. He and Ahmose must have reached some understanding, for henceforth, till both were swallowed up by Medo-Persia, Egypt and Babylon were allies against the growing menace of Media. But in 525 BC Egypt followed her allies into Persian dominion, under Cambyses. On this period, see further, *BABYLONIA and *PERSIA.

*e. The base kingdom.* At first Persian rule in Egypt (Darius I) was fair and firm; but repeated Egyptian rebellions brought about a harshening of Persian policy. The Egyptians manufactured anti-Persian propaganda that went down well in Greece (compare Herodotus); they shared a common foe.

Briefly, during *c.* 400–431 BC, Egypt's last native pharaohs (Dynasties 28–30) regained a precarious independence until they were overwhelmed by Persia to whom they remained subject for just 9 years, until Alexander entered Egypt as 'liberator' in 332 BC. (See F. K. Kienitz, in the list of books for further reading below, and G. Posener, *La Première Domination Perse en Égypte*, 1936).

Thereafter, Egypt was first a Hellenistic monarchy under the Ptolemies and then fell under the heel of Rome and Byzantium. From the 3rd century AD, Egypt was a predominantly Christian land with its own, eventually schismatic (Coptic) church. In AD 641/42 the Islamic conquest heralded the mediaeval and modern epochs.

## Literature

*Scope of Egyptian literature*

*a. 3rd millennium BC.* Religious and wisdom-literature are the best-known products of the Old Kingdom and 1st Intermediate Period. The great sages Imhotep, Hardidief [?Kairos] to Kagemni, and Ptahhotep produced 'Instructions' or 'Teachings' (Egyptian *sb'yt*), written collections of shrewd maxims for the wise conduct of everyday life, especially for young men hopeful of high office, so beginning a very long tradition in Egypt. The best-preserved is that of Ptahhotep; see Z. Žába, *Les Maximes de Ptahhotep*, 1956. For the Pyramid Texts and Memphite Theology, see the section on religion, below.

In the 1st Intermediate Period, the collapse of Egyptian society and the old order may be pictured in the *Admonitions of Ipuwer*, while the *Dispute of a Man Tired of Life with his Soul* reflects the agony of this period in terms of a personal conflict which brings man to the brink of suicide. The *Instruction for King Merikarē* shows remarkable regard for right dealing in matters of state, while the *Eloquent Peasant*'s nine rhetorical speeches within a narrative prose prologue and epilogue (compare Job) call for social justice.

*b. Early 2nd millennium BC.* In the Middle Kingdom, stories and propaganda-works are outstanding. Finest of the narratives is the *Biography of Sinuhē*, an Egyptian who spent long years of exile in Palestine. The *Shipwrecked Sailor* is a nautical fantasy.

Among the propaganda, the *Prophecy of Neferty* ('*Neferrohu*' of older books) is a pseudo-prophecy to announce Amenemhat I as saviour of Egypt. On prediction in Egypt, see Kitchen, *Tyndale House Bulletin* 5/6, 1960, pp. 6–7 and references.

Two loyalist 'Instructions', *Sehetepibrē* and *A Man to his Son*, were intended to identify the good life with loyalty to the throne in the minds of the ruling and labouring classes respectively. The poetry of the *Hymns to Sesostris III* apparently also expresses that loyalty. For administrators in training, the *Instruction of Khety son of Duauf* or *Satire of the Trades* points out the advantages of the scribal profession over all other (manual) occupations by painting these in dark colours.

*c. Late 2nd millennium BC.* During this period the Empire produced further stories, including delightful fairy-tales (*e.g. The Foredoomed Prince; Tale of the Two Brothers*), historical adventure (*The Capture of Joppa*, a precursor of *Alibaba and the Forty Thieves*) and biographical reports such as the *Misadventures of Wenamūn*, who was sent to Lebanon for cedarwood in the ill-starred days of Ramesses XI.

Poetry excelled in three forms: lyric, royal and religious. Under the first head come some charming love-poems, in general style heralding the tender cadences of the Song of Songs. The Empire pharaohs commemorated their victories with triumph-hymns, the finest being those of Tuthmosis III, Amenophis III, Ramesses II and Merenptah (Israel Stele). Though less prominent, wisdom is still well represented; beside the 'Instructions' of Ani and Amennakhte, the is a remarkable ode on the immortality of writing. For Amenemope's wisdom see the section on Egyptian literature and the Old Testament, below.

*d. 1st millennium BC.* Less new literature is known from this epoc so far. In Demotic the 'Instruction' 'Onchsheshonqy dates to the last centuries BC, and the *Stories of the High Priests of Memphis* (magiciar to the 1st centuries AD. Most Copti (Christian) literature is translated from Greek church literature, Shenoute being the only outstandi native Christian writer.

*Egyptian literature and the Old Testament*

The very incomplete survey given above will serve to emphasize the quantity, richness and variety of early Egyptian literature; besides the additional matter under Religi below, there is a whole body of historical, business and formal tex Egypt is but one of the Bible lands the neighbouring countries, too, offer a wealth of writings (see *ASSYRIA; *CANAAN; *HITTITES).

The relevance of such literatures twofold: firstly, with regard to questions of direct contact with th Hebrew writings; and secondly, i so far as they provide dated, first-hand comparative and contemporary material for objecti control of Old Testament literary forms and types of literary criticis

*a. Questions of direct contact.* (i) Genesis 39 and Psalm 104. In times past the incident of Potiphar unfaithful wife in Genesis 39 has occasionally been stated to be bas on a similar incident in the mythic *Tale of Two Brothers*. But an unfaithful wife is the only commor point; the *Tale* is designedly a wo of pure fantasy (the hero is change into a bull, a persea-tree, *etc.*), whereas the Joseph-narrative is biography, touching actuality at every point. Unfortunately, unfaithful wives are not mere myt either in Egypt or elsewhere (see a incidental Egyptian instance in *JNES* 14, 1955, p.163).

Egyptologists today do not usua consider that Akhenaten's 'Hymn Aten' inspired parts of Psalm 104 a Breasted once thought (compare J. H. Breasted, *Dawn of Conscienc* 1933, pp. 366–370). The same universalism and adoration of the deity as creator and sustainer occ hymns to Amūn both before and ter the Aten hymn in date, which uld carry these concepts down to e age of Hebrew psalmody (so, g., J. A. Wilson, *Burden of ypt/Culture of Ancient Egypt*, ). 224–229). But even this tenuous ık-up can carry no weight, for the me universalism occurs just as rly in western Asia (compare the amples given in W. F. Albright, *om Stone Age to Christianity*, 1957 lition, pp. 12–13, 213–223) and is erefore too generally diffused to low of its being made a criterion to ove direct relationship.

The same point might be made ith regard to the so-called nitential psalms of the Theban cropolis-workers of Dynasty 19. A nse of shortcoming or sin is not culiar to Egypt (and is even, in ct, quite atypical there); and the yptian psalms should be mpared with the confession of an's sinfulness made by the Hittite ng, Mursil II (*ANET*, p. 395b) and ith the Babylonian penitential les. The latter again show the wide ffusion of a general concept lthough it may have different local nphases); and they cannot be used establish direct relationship ompare G. R. Driver, *The Psalmists*, l. D. C. Simpson, 1926, pp. 109–175, pecially 171–175).

(ii) The Wisdom of Amenemope d Proverbs. Impressed by the ose verbal resemblances between rious passages in the Egyptian nstruction' of Amenemope (*c.* 1100 , see below) and the 'words of the ise' (Proverbs 22:17–24:22) quoted y Solomon (equating the 'my nowledge' of 22:17 with that of olomon from 10:1), many have sumed, following Erman, that roverbs was debtor to Amenemope; ly Kevin and McGlinchey ventured take the opposite view. Others, ith W. O. E. Oesterley, *Wisdom of gypt and the Old Testament*, 1927, oubted the justice of a view at ther extreme, considering that erhaps both Amenemope and roverbs had drawn upon a common nd of Ancient Oriental proverbial re, and specifically upon an older ebrew work.

The alleged dependence of roverbs upon Amenemope is still e common view (*e.g.* P. Montet, *'Égypte et la Bible*, 1959, pp. 113, 72), but is undoubtedly too simple. y a thoroughgoing examination of oth Amenemope and Proverbs gainst the entire realm of ancient ear Eastern Wisdom, recent search has shown that in fact there *no* adequate basis for assuming a

A bronze statue of the sacred bull Apis, found at Memphis.

special relationship either way between Amenemope and Proverbs.

Two other points require note. First, with regard to date, Plumley (*DOTT*, p. 173) mentions a Cairo ostracon of Amenemope that 'can be dated with some certainty to the latter half of the Twenty-first Dynasty'. Therefore the Egyptian Amenemope cannot be any later than 945 BC (the end of Dynasty 21), and Egyptologists now tend to favour a date in Dynasties 18–20. In any case, there is no objective reason why the Hebrew Words of the Wise should not be as old as Solomon's reign, *i.e.* the 10th century BC.

The second point concerns the word *šilšôm*, found in Proverbs 22:20, which Erman and others render as 'thirty', making Proverbs imitate the 'thirty chapters' of Amenemope. But Proverbs 22:17–24:22 contains not 30 but 33 admonitions, and the simplest interpretation of *šlšwm* is to take it as elliptical for *'eṯmôl šilšôm*, 'formerly', 'already', and to render the clause simply as, 'Have I not written for thee, already, in/with counsels of knowledge?'

*b. Literary usage and Old Testament criticism.* It is singularly unfortunate that the conventional methods of Old Testament literary criticism have been formulated and developed, over the last century in particular, without any but the most superficial reference to the actual characteristics of the contemporary literature of the Bible world, alongside which the Hebrew writings came into existence and with the literary phenomena of which they present very considerable external, formal similarities. The application of such external and tangibly objective controls cannot fail to have drastic consequences for these methods of literary criticism. While Egyptian texts are a specially fruitful source of such external control-data, Mesopotamian, northern Canaanite (Ugaritic), Hittite and other literatures provide valuable confirmation. See for preliminary survey, K. A. Kitchen, *Ancient Orient and Old Testament*, 1966, chapters 6–7.

## Religion

*The gods and theology*

Egyptian religion was never a unitary whole. There were always local gods up and down the land, among whom were Ptah, artificer-god of Memphis; Thoth, god of learning and the moon at Hermopolis; Amūn 'the hidden', god of Thebes, who overshadowed the war-god Mentu there and became state god of 2nd-millennium Egypt; Hathor, goddess of joy at Dendera; and many more.

Then there were the cosmic gods:

**A silver statuette of the Egyptian god Amen-Rē, partly overlaid with gold foil. Late period *c.* 900.**

first and foremost Rē' or Atum the sun-god, whose daughter Ma'et personified Truth, Justice, Right and the cosmic order; then Nūt the sky-goddess and Shu, Geb and Nu, the gods of air, earth and the primordial waters respectively.

The nearest thing to a truly national religion was the cult of Osiris and his cycle (with his wife, Isis, and son, Horus). The story of Osiris had great human appeal: the good king, murdered by his wicked brother Seth, becoming ruler of the realm of the dead and triumphing in the person of his posthumous son and avenger Horus, who, with the support of his mother Isis, gained his father's kingship on earth. The Egyptian could identify himself with Osiris the revivified in his kingdom of the hereafter; Osiris's other aspect, as a god of vegetation, linking with the annual rise of the Nile and consequent rebirth of life, combined powerfully with his funerary aspect in Egyptian aspirations.

*Egyptian worship*

Egyptian worship was a complete contrast to Hebrew worship in particular, and to Semitic in general. The temple was isolated within its own high-walled estate. Only the officiating priesthood worshipped in such temples; and it was only when the god went forth in glittering procession on great festivals that the populace actively shared in honouring the great gods. Apart from this, they sought their solace in household and lesser gods.

The cult of the great gods followed one general pattern, the god being treated just like an earthly king. He was awakened from sleep each morning with a hymn, his image was washed and dressed, he breakfasted (morning offering), did a morning's business, and had midday and evening meals (corresponding offerings) before retiring for the night.

The contrast could hardly be greater between the ever-vigilant, self-sufficient God of Israel with his didactic sacrificial system, symbolizing the need and means of atonement to deal with human sin, and of peace-offerings in fellowship at tabernacle or Temple, and those earthly Egyptian deities of nature.

For Egyptian temple-worship, see H. W. Fairman, *BJRL* 37, 1954, pp. 165–203.

*Religious literature*

To the 3rd millennium BC belong the Pyramid Texts (so-called from their being inscribed in 6th-Dynasty pyramids), a large body of 'spells', apparently forming incredibly intricate royal funerary rituals, and also the Memphite Theology, which glorifies the god Ptah as first cause, conceiving in the mind ('heart') and creating by the word of power ('tongue') (a distant herald of the *logos*-concept of John's Gospel [1:1ff.] transformed through Christ). At all times there are hymns and prayers to the gods, usually full of mythological allusions. In the Empire certain hymns to Amūn, and Akhenaten's famous Aten-hymn, remarkably illustrate the universalism of the day; see the section on Literature, above.

Epics of the gods which at present remain to us exist only in excerpts. A ribald part of the Osiris-cycle survives in the *Contendings of Horus and Seth.* The Coffin Texts of the Middle Kingdom (usually painted inside coffins at that time) and the 'Book of the Dead' of the Empire and Late Period are nothing more than collections of magical spells to protect and benefit the deceased in the after-life; special guide-books to 'infernal' geography were inscribed on the tomb-walls of Empire pharaohs. See *ANET* for translations from religious texts.

*Funerary beliefs*

The Egyptians' elaborate beliefs about the after-life found expression in the concrete, material terms of a more-glorious, other-worldly Egypt ruled by Osiris. Alternative hereafters included accompanying the sun-god Rē' on his daily voyage across the sky and through the underworld, or dwelling with the stars.

The body was a material attachment for the soul; mummification was simply a means of preserving the body to this end, when tombs early became too elaborate for the sun's rays to desiccate the body naturally, as it did in prehistory's shallow graves.

Objects in tombs left for the use of the dead usually attracted robbers. Egyptian concern over death was not morbid; this cheerful, pragmatic materialistic people simply sought to take the good things of this world with them, using magical means to do so. The tomb was the deceased's eternal physical dwelling. The pyramids were simply royal tombs whose shape was modelled on that of the sacred stone of the sun-god Rē' at Heliopolis (see I. E. S. Edwards, *The Pyramids of Egypt*, 1961). The Empire pharaohs' secret rock-hewn tombs in the Valley of Kings at Thebes were planned to foil the robbers, but failed, like the pyramids they replaced.

K. A. Kitchen

*ırther reading*
*eneral*
ɔpular introductions to ancient
ɜypt are:
Cottrell, *The Lost Pharaohs*, 1950
—, *Life under the Pharaohs*, 1955
Montet, *Everyday Life in Egypt in*
*e Days of Ramesses the Great*, 1958
ery useful is:
R. K. Glanville (ed.), *The Legacy of*
*gypt*, 1942 (new edition, 1965)
ell illustrated are:
. C. Hayes, *Sceptre of Egypt* 1,
53; 2, 1959
. Posener, S. Sauneron and J.
ɔyotte, *Dictionary of Egyptian*
*ivilization*, 1962
n Egypt and Asia:
. Helck, *Die Beziehungen*
*gyptens zum Vorderasien im 3. und*
*Jahrtausend v. Chr.*, 1962
standard work is:
. Kees, *Ägypten*, 1933, being part 1
the *Kulturgeschichte des Alten*
*rients* in the *Handbuch der*
*ltertumswissenschaft* series
—, *Ancient Egypt, a Cultural*
*ɔpography*, 1961 (useful and
liable)
ıll bibliography is obtainable from:
A. Pratt, *Ancient Egypt*, 1925
—, *Ancient Egypt (1925–41)*, 1942,
r nearly everything pre-war
. Federn, 8 lists in *Orientalia* 17,
948; 18, 1949; and 19, 1950, for the
ears 1939–47
M. A. Janssen, *Annual*
*gyptological Bibliography*, 1948ff.
ɔr 1947 onwards)
J. Kemp, *Egyptology Titles*,
nnually.
ɔrter-Moss, *Topographical*
*ibliography*, 7 vols.
Baines, J. Malek, *Atlas of Ancient*
*gypt*, 1980
. Hobson, *Exploring the World of*
*e Pharaohs*, 1987.

*rigin of name*
rugsch, *Geographische Inschriften*
1857, p. 83
. H. Gardiner, *Ancient Egyptian*
*nomastica* 2, 1947, pp. 124*, 211*

*eography*
ery valuable for the physical
ructure and geography of Egypt is:
Ball, *Contributions to the*
*eography of Egypt*, 1939
ɔr modern statistics, see survey in
*he Middle East, 1958*
uch information is contained in
*aedeker's Egypt*, 1929
he deserts find some description in:
. E. P. Weigall, *Travels in the Upper*
*gyptian Deserts*, 1909
n the early state and settlement of
e Nile valley:
. C. Hayes, 'Most Ancient Egypt' =
*VES* 22, 1964

For ancient Egyptian geography, a mine of information is:
Alan Gardiner, *Ancient Egyptian Onomastica*, 3 vols., 1947 (with good discussions and references to literature)
See also *EGYPT, RIVER OF, *HANES, *MEMPHIS, *NAPHTUHIM, *NILE, *ON, *PATHROS, *PI-BESETH, *THEBES, *ZOAN, *etc.*

*Language*
For details of, and bibliography on, the Egyptian language:
A. H. Gardiner, *Egyptian Grammar*, 3rd edition, 1957
For Coptic:
W. C. Till, *Koptische Grammatik*, 1955
A. Mallon, *Grammaire Copte*, 1956, for full bibliography
C.C. Walters, *An Elementary Coptic Grammar*, 1972

*History*
The standard work is:
É. Drioton and J. Vandier, *L'Égypte* (Collection '*Clio*'), 4th edition, 1962 (with full discussions and bibliography)
Valuable is:
J. A. Wilson, *The Burden of Egypt*, 1951, reprinted as a paperback, *The Culture of Ancient Egypt*, 1956
J. H. Breasted's *History of Egypt*, various dates, is now out of date, as is H. R. Hall's *Ancient History of the Near East*
See also:
A. H. Gardiner, *Egypt of the Pharaohs*, 1961
and especially:
*CAH*, 3rd edition, 1 and 2, 1970ff.
B. G. Trigger, B. J. Kemp, D. O'Connor, A. B. Lloyd, *Ancient Egypt, a Social History*, 1983
On Egyptian historical writings:
L. Bull in R. C. Dentan (ed.), *The Idea of History in the Ancient Near East*, 1955, pp. 3–34
C. de Wit, *EQ* 28, 1956, pp. 158–169
D. B. Redford, *Pharaonic King-Lists, Annals and Daybooks*, 1986
On rival Egyptian priesthoods:
H. Kees, *Das Priestertum im Ägyptischen Staat*, 1953, pp. 78–88 and 62–69
*Nachträge*, 1958
J. A. Wilson, *Burden of Egypt/ Culture of Ancient Egypt*, ch. ix.
Late Period:
K. A. Kitchen, *The Third Intermediate Period in Egypt (1100–650 BC)*, 2nd edition, 1986, especially Part IV
On Egypt under Persian dominion:
F. K. Kienitz, *Die Politische Geschichte Ägyptens, vom 7. bis zum 4. Jahrhundert vor der Zeitwende*, 1953

For the Babylonian chronicle-tablets:
D. J. Wiseman, *Chronicles of Chaldaean Kings*, 1956
For a small but very important correction of Egyptian 26th Dynasty dates:
R. A. Parker, *Mitteilungen des Deutschen Archäologischen Instituts, Kairo Abteilung* 15, 1957, pp. 208–212
For Graeco-Roman Egypt:
*CAH*, later volumes
H. I. Bell, *Egypt from Alexander the Great to the Arab Conquest*, 1948
——, *Cults and Creeds in Graeco-Roman Egypt*, 1953 and later editions
W. H. Worrell, *A Short Account of the Copts*, 1945

*Literature*
For literary works:
W. K. Simpson (ed.), *The Literature of Ancient Egypt*, 1972
M. Lichtheim, *Ancient Egyptian Literature* 1–2, 1973–76
Many historical texts in:
J. H. Breasted, *Ancient Records of Egypt*, 5 vols., 1906/07
Considerable but abbreviated selections appear in *ANET*
Brilliant work in listing, identifying and restoring Egyptian literature:
G. Posener, *Recherches Littéraires* 1–7, in the *Revue d'Égyptologie* 6–12, 1949–60
Still valuable in its field is:
T. E. Peet, *A Comparative Study of the Literatures of Egypt, Palestine and Mesopotamia*, 1931
On wisdom literature and the Old Testament:
J. Ruffle, *TynB* 28, 1979, 29–68

*Religion*
For Egyptian religion, a convenient outline in English is:
J. Černý, *Ancient Egyptian Religion*, 1952
Fuller detail and bibliography in:
J. Vandier, *La Religion Égyptienne*, 1949
H. Kees, *Der Götterglaube im alten Ägypten*, 1956
S. Morenz, *Egyptian Religion*, 1973

**Continued from p. 107**
Hebrew terms must be carefully distinguished. *y*$^{e}$*'ôr miṣrayim*, 'river (*i.e*, the *Nile) of Egypt', refers exclusively to the Nile proper: its seasonal rise and fall being mentioned in Amos 8:8, and its upper Egyptian reaches in Isaiah 7:18 (plural). The term *n*$^{e}$*har miṣrayim*, '(flowing) river of Egypt', occurs once only (Genesis 15:18), where by general definition the promised land lies between the two great rivers, Nile and Euphrates.

These two terms (*y*$^{e}$*'ôr/n*$^{e}$*har miṣrayim*) are wholly separate from, and irrelevant to, the so-called 'river of Egypt' proper, the *naḥal miṣrayim* or 'torrent-wadi of Egypt'. The identification of this term, however, is bound up with that of Shihor, as will be evident from what now follows.

*Shihor*

In the Old Testament it is clearly seen that Shihor is a part of the Nile; see the parallelism of Shihor and *y*$^{e}$*'ôr* (Nile) in Isaiah 23:3, and Shihor as Egypt's Nile corresponding to Assyria's great river (Euphrates) in Jeremiah 2:18. Shihor is the extreme south-western limit of territory yet to be occupied in Joshua 13:3 and from which Israelites could come to welcome the ark into Jerusalem in 1 Chronicles 13:5, and Joshua 13:3 specifies it as east of Egypt. Hence Shihor is the lowest reaches of the easternmost of the Nile's ancient branches (the Pelusiac), flowing into the Mediterranean just west of Pelusium (Tell Farameh).

This term Shihor is by origin the Egyptian *š-ḥr*, 'waters of Horus'; the Egyptian references agree with the biblical location in so far as they mention Shihor's producing salt and rushes for the not-distant Delta-capital Pi-Ramessē (Tanis or Qantir) and as the 'river' of the 14th Lower-Egyptian nome (province); see R. A. Caminos, *Late-Egyptian Miscellanies*, 1954, pp. 74 and 78 (his Menzalah-identification is erroneous), and especially A. H. Gardiner, *JEA* 5, 1918, pp. 251–252.

*The Shihor and the River of Egypt*

The real question is whether or not the *naḥal miṣrayim*, 'river (torrent-wadi) of Egypt', is the same as the Shihor, easternmost branch of the Nile.

Against the identification stands the fact that elsewhere in Scripture the Nile is never referred to as a *naḥal*. The river of Isaiah 11:15 is often taken to be the Euphrates (note the Assyro-Egyptian context here, especially verse 16), and the threat to smite it into seven *n*$^{e}$*ḥālîm*, wadis traversable on foot, represents a transformation of (not the normal description for) the river concerned, whether Nile or Euphrates.

*The Wadi el-'Arish*

If the 'wadi of Egypt' is not the Nile, the best alternative is the Wadi el-'Arish, which runs northwards out of Sinai to the Mediterranean 145 kilometres east of Egypt proper (Suez Canal) and 80 kilometres west of Gaza in Palestine.

In defence of this identification can be argued a perceptible change of terrain west and east from el-'Arish. Westward to Egypt there is only barren desert and slight scrub; eastward there are meadows and arable land (A. H. Gardiner, *JEA* 6, 1920, p. 115). Hence Wadi el-'Arish would be a practical boundary, including the usable land and excluding mere desert, in the specific delimitations of Numbers 34:5 and Joshua 15:4 and 47 (compare also Ezekiel 47:19; 48:28). This is then simply echoed in 1 Kings 8:65 (2 Chronicles 7:8), 2 Kings 24:7 and Isaiah 27:12. Joshua 13:3 and 1 Chronicles 13:5 would then indicate the uttermost south-western limit (Shihor) of Israelite activity (see above).

*Assyrian evidence*

Sargon II and Esarhaddon of Assyria also mention the Wadi or Brook of Egypt in their texts. In 716 BC Sargon reached the 'Brook (or Wadi) of Egypt' (*naḥal muṣur*), 'opened the sealed harbour of Egypt' mingling Assyrians and Egyptians for trade purposes, and mentioning 'the border of the City of the Brook of Egypt', where he appointed a governor. Alarmed by the Assyrian activity, the shadow-pharaoh Osorkon IV sent a diplomatic present of '12 big horses' to Sargon (H. Tadmor, *JCS* 12, 1958, pp. 34, 78).

All this fits well with *naḥal muṣur* being Wadi el-'Arish and the 'City' there being the settlement El-'Arish, Assyrian *Arzâ* (Tadmor, article cited, p. 78, note 194, with the further bibliography on 'River of Egypt').

*Debatable evidence*

One or two points apparently favouring the alternative view, namely that the 'Wadi of Egypt' is the Shihor/Pelusiac Nile-arm, must, however, not be overlooked. Many are inclined to equate precisely the terms of Joshua 13:3, Shihor, and Numbers 34:5 and Joshua 15:4, 47 (likewise 1 Kings 8:65 and 1 Chronicles 13:5), *naḥal miṣrayim*, making Wadi of Egypt another nam of the Shihor-Nile. But this would make no allowance for different nuances in the Scripture texts concerned as outlined above.

Further, it is true that Sargon II could well have reached the Pelusia (easternmost) arm of the Nile; his 'City' there would then be Pelusiun – which would most decidedly alar Osorkon IV. But the 'City' is certainl the 'Arza(ni) of Esarhaddon's inscriptions (*ANET*, pp. 290–292) which corresponds well to 'Arish bu not Pelusium (Egyptian *sinw*, *swn*)

Finally, Egyptians and the 19th Dynasty evidently regarded the Pelusiac area as *de facto* the edge c Egypt proper: in Papyrus Anastasi III, 1:10, Ḫuru (Palestine generally) extends 'from Silē to 'Upa (that is, Damascus)'; Silē ('Thel') is modern Qantara a few kilometres south and east of the former Pelusiac Nile-arm (R. A. Caminos, *Late-Egyptian Miscellanies*, pp. 69 and 73 and references).

But this proves nothing about Israel's boundaries; as already mentioned, from Qantara to 'Arish a desolate no-man's-land. In any case, 19th-Dynasty Egypt did asser authority and maintain wells across the entire coast-strip, Qantara–'Arish–Gaza (see A. H. Gardiner, *JEA* 6, 1920, pp. 99–116, on the military road there).

The Shihor/Nile identification of the Wadi of Egypt has been advocated by H. Bar-Deroma, *PEQ* 92, 1960, pp. 37–56, but he takes nc account of the contemporary Egyptian and Assyrian sources, the post-biblical matter cited being imprecise and of too late a date.

The subject is not closed, but Wac el-'Arish is more likely to be the 'River (Wadi) of Egypt' than is the eastern Nile on present evidence.

K. A. Kitchen

**EKRON.** One of the five principal Philistine cities, and a place of importance, having villages dependent upon it (Joshua 15:45–46). It is now generally identified with Khirbet al-Muqanna (Tel Miqne), 35 kilometres west of Jerusalem. A long term project to excavate the site began in 1981. Pottery attests occupation in the Chalcolithic, Early Bronze and Middle Bronze Ages, and a Late Bronze Age city extended over mos of the large site.

The arrival of the Philistines is marked by new pottery styles beginning in Stratum VII, which thu dates from *c.* 1177 BC (*i.e.* the 8th yea

The view east over the valley of Elah, from near Socoh.

of Ramesses III, when the Philistines and other 'Sea Peoples' advanced on Egypt and the southern coastal plain). Iron Age occupation continued until the 6th century BC.

In the allotment of territories Ekron was placed on the border between Judah and Dan (Joshua 15:11, 45–46; 19:43), but at the death of Joshua it remained to be possessed. It was finally taken by Judah (Judges 1:18), but must have been recaptured by the Philistines, for they took the ark there when it was removed from Gath (1 Samuel 5:10), and it was from there that it was despatched to Beth-shemesh on the cow-drawn cart (1 Samuel 6).

It appears that Ekron was again temporarily in Israelite hands in the time of Samuel (1 Samuel 7:14), but the Philistines had retaken it by Saul's time (1 Samuel 17:52), and it was still held by them in the time of Amos (1:8). In 701 BC Padi the ruler of Ekron, a vassal of the Assyrians, was expelled by certain Ekronites and held captive by Hezekiah in Jerusalem, but Sennacherib, in his campaign of that year, retook Ekron (*am-qar-ru-na*) and restored Padi (*ANET*, pp. 287–288; *DOTT*, pp. 66–67).

The city is mentioned in the Annals of Esarhaddon as tributary (*ANET*, p. 291; *DOTT*, p. 74), but was still at that time regarded as a Philistine city from the ethnic point of view (Jeremiah 25:20; Zephaniah 2:4; Zechariah 9:5, 7).

The Bible is not concerned with the subsequent history of the city, though the name of the city god, Baal-zebub (2 Kings 1:2–3), is familiar from the New Testament.

T. C. Mitchell, J. Bimson

*Further reading*

S. Gitin and T. Dothan, *BA* 50, 1987, pp. 197–222
Vogel, *HUCA* 58, 1987, p. 17
Honigmann, *Reallexikon der Assyriologie* 1, 1932, p. 99
T. Dothan and S. Gitin, 'Tel Miqne', *NEAEHL* III, pp. 1051–1059

**ELAH** (Hebrew *'ēlâ*, 'terebinth'). A valley used by the Philistines to gain access to Central Palestine. It was the scene of David's victory over Goliath (1 Samuel 17:2; 21:9), and is generally identified with the modern Wadi es-Sant, 18 kilometres south-west of Jerusalem.

J. D. Douglas

**ELAM, ELAMITES.** The ancient name for the plain of Khuzistan, watered by the Kerkh river, which joins the Tigris just north of the Persian Gulf.

*Earliest history*

Civilization in this area is as old as, and closely connected with, the cultures of lower Mesopotamia. A local pictographic script appeared very soon after the invention of writing in Babylonia.

The Elamites cannot be certainly linked with any other known race, although their language may be related to the Dravidian family. The reference to Elam as a son of Shem (Genesis 10:22) may well reflect the presence of early Semites in this area, and there is archaeological evidence in the time of Sargon I (*c.* 2350 BC) and his successors of their influence on local culture. Rock sculptures depict typical Akkadian figures and bear Akkadian inscriptions, although carved for Elamite rulers.

The mountainous region to the north and east was known as Anshan and, from an early period, formed a part of Elam. Sumerian and Semitic plainsmen looked upon these ranges as the abode of evil spirits, and early epics describe the terrors they held for those who crossed them in search of the mineral wealth of states beyond (see S. N. Kramer, *History Begins at Sumer*, 1958, pp. 57ff., 230ff.).

*2000–1000 BC*

Its control of the trade routes to the Iranian plateau, and to the south-east, made Elam the object of constant attacks from the plains of Mesopotamia. These in turn offered great wealth to any conqueror. A strong Elamite dynasty, a king being succeeded by his brother, then his son, arose about 2000 BC and gained control of several cities in Babylonia, destroying the power of the Sumerian rulers of Ur and sacking it (see *ANET*, pp. 455ff., 480f.).

To this period of Elamite supremacy should Chedorlaomer probably be assigned (Genesis 14:1).

Hammurapi of Babylon drove the Elamites out *c.* 1760 BC, but the 'Amorite' dynasty, to which he belonged, fell before Hittite and Elamite attacks *c.* 1595 BC. Invasions of Kassites coming from the central Zagros mountains (see also *Babylonia) drove the Elamites back to Susa, until a resurgence of power enabled them to conquer and rule Babylon for several centuries (*c.* 1300–1120 BC). Among trophies taken to Susa at this time was the famous Law stele of Hammurapi.

*Kings and prophets*
Elamite history is obscure from *c.* 1000 BC until the campaigns of Sargon of Assyria (*c.* 721–705 BC). Sennacherib and Ashurbanipal subjected the Elamites and deported some of them to Samaria, taking Israelites to Elam (Ezra 4:9; Isaiah 11:11).

After the collapse of *Assyria, Elam was annexed by the Indo-Europeans, who had gradually gained power in Iran following their invasions *c.* 1000 BC. Teispes (*c.* 675–640 BC), ancestor of Cyrus, bore the title 'king of Anshan' and Susa eventually became one of the three chief cities of the Medo-Persian empire.

Elam is called upon by Isaiah to crush Babylon (Isaiah 21:2) and this was carried out (see Daniel 8:2). Yet Elam will be crushed in turn, even the famous archers defeated (Jeremiah 25:25; 49:34–39; compare Isaiah 22:6; Ezekiel 32:24).

*New Testament times*
The crowd at Pentecost (Acts 2:9) contained men from as far away as Elam, presumably members of Jewish communities who had remained in exile in the semi-autonomous state of Elymais, though using Aramaic, the last flicker of Elamite independence. (See also *Media; *Persia; *Susa.)
A. R. Millard

*Further reading*
W. Hinz, *The Lost World of Elam*, 1972
E. Porada, *Ancient Iran*, 1965

**EL-AMARNA.** See *Amarna.

**ELATH (ELOTH).** Whether or not it took its name from such as the early Edomite chief Elah (Genesis 36:41), Elath is mentioned as separate from *Ezion-geber (Deuteronomy 2:8), as is also implied in 1 Kings 9:26 (Solomon's ships were built 'at Ezion-geber, which is near Eloth on the shore of the Red Sea . . .'). Around 780 BC Azariah (Uzziah) of Judah 'rebuilt Elath and restored it to Judah' (2 Kings 14:22) – perhaps after an Edomite occupation. But within 20 years or so, under Aramaean pressure, his grandson Ahaz lost Elath to the Edomites, permanently (2 Kings 16:5–6).

Clearly, Elath was at the head of the Gulf of Aqabah, by its association with nearby Ezion-geber, base for Solomon's fleet. The name probably reappears in classical Aelana or Aila, at or near modern Aqabah. Barely 5 kilometres west of Aqabah is the ancient site of Tell el-Kheleifeh, dug by Nelson Glueck who believed it to be both Ezion-geber and Elath (as one site). It cannot be Ezion-geber, but it may have served as an adjunct fort for Elath if it is not Elath itself.

A drastically revised interpretation of the archaeological remains indicates a rectangular fort with 'casemate' walls and a central building within, replaced (in the 8th century BC) by a larger solid-wall fortress of the 8th–6th centuries BC; see G. Pratico, *BASOR* 259, 1985, pp. 1–32, and his summaries in *BA* 45, 1982, pp. 120–121, and *BARev* 12/5, 1986, pp. 24–35.

It is at least possible that the original 'casemate' for it was the work of Uzziah, though this can only be speculation at present. The larger settlement of *c.* 700–580 BC would then represent the Edomite reoccupation. Its pottery bears the seal-impression of 'Qos'anal, servant of the king' (*i.e.*, of Edom), of 7th/6th century date – perhaps the stamp of the Edomite governor of Elath and district.

Tell el-Kheleifeh was also occupied in the Persian period. The seal of one Jotham (Level III) of the 7th/6th centuries BC would have belonged to an Edomite official, not to the son of Uzziah as at first thought (*e.g.* by N. Avigad, *BASOR* 163, 1961, pp. 18–22). See also J. R. Bartlett, *Edom and the Edomites*, 1990, pp. 46–47, section 4. For full publication see G. Pratico, *Nelson Glueck's 1938–1940 Excavations at Tell el-Kheleifeh: A Reappraisal*, ASOR, Atlanta, 1993.
K. A. Kitchen

**ELEALEH** (Hebrew *'el'ālēh*, 'God is exalted'). A town east of Jordan always mentioned in conjunction with Heshbon. Conquered by Gad and Reuben (Numbers 32:3), rebuilt by the latter tribe (32:37), and later Moabite, it was the subject of prophetic warnings (Isaiah 15:4; 16:9; Jeremiah 48:34).

It is identified with the modern el-'Al, 4 kilometres north-east of Heshbon.
J. D. Douglas

**ELIAM.** See *Helam.

**ELIM** (Hebrew 'terebinths' or 'oaks'). Second stopping-place of th[e] Israelites after their crossing of the Re(e)d Sea from Egypt. Beyond the wilderness of *Shur, east of the modern Suez canal, they first encamped at Marah in the wilderness of Etham not far away (because named after Etham in the eastern Delta), and thence reached Elim with its twelve springs and seventy palm-trees. After this the Israelites went on 'and pitched by the Red Sea', before eventually reaching the wilderness of *Sin (Exodus 15:27; 16:1; Numbers 33:9–10).

By putting the stop at Elim shortl[y] after the escape from Egypt and passage of its desert edge (Shur), and before a stop by the Red Sea prior to reaching the wilderness of Sin, the biblical references suggest that Elim is situated on the western side of the Sinai peninsula, facing o[n] to the Gulf of Suez. Any closer location is still not certain, but a plausible suggestion of long standing is Wadi Gharandel (or, Ghurundel), a well-known watering-place with tamarisks and palms, *c.* 60 kilometres south-south-east of Suez along the western side of *Sinai. (See also *Wilderness of Wandering.
K. A. Kitchen

*Further reading*
E. Robinson, *Biblical Researches in Palestine* 1, 1841, pp. 99–100, 105–106, and map at end
A. P. Stanley, *Sinai and Palestine*, 1887, pp. 37–38
Wright and Filson, *Westminster Historical Atlas to the Bible*, 1956, pp. 38–39 and plate V
W. M. F. Petrie, *Researches in Sinai*, 1906, pp. 205, 207

**ELISHAH.** The eldest son of Javan (Genesis 10:4; 1 Chronicles 1:7), whose name was later applied to the geographical area in which his descendants settled (*'iyyê*, 'isles' or 'coastlands') which traded purple to Tyre (Ezekiel 27:7). It is very probable that the biblical name *'elîšā* (Septuagint *Elisa*) is to be equated with Alašia of the extra-biblical sources. This name occurs in the Egyptian and cuneiform (Boghaz-Koi, Alalakh, Ugarit) inscriptions, and it was the source of eight of the Amarna letters, in which it usually occurs in the form *a-la-ši-ia*.

These texts indicate that Alašia was an exporter of copper, and it is possible, though not universally

:cepted, that it is to be identified
'ith the site of Enkomi on the
astern coast of Cyprus, where
xcavations under C. F. A. Schaeffer
ave revealed an important
ading-centre of the Late Bronze
ge.
The name Alašia would also apply
the area under the political
omination of the city, and may at
mes have included outposts on the
hoenician coast.
C. Mitchell

*urther reading*
. Dussaud in C. F. A. Schaeffer,
*nkomi-Alasia*, 1952, pp. 1–10
*S* 6, 1956, pp. 63–65
*B*, 3rd edition, p. 55

**LASAR.** The city or kingdom ruled
y Arioch, an ally of Chedorlaomer
ng of Elam, who attacked Sodom
nd captured Lot, Abraham's
ephew (Genesis 14:1, 9).
Identifications suggested depend
n those proposed for the kings
volved. These include: *a āl Aššur* –
shur/Assyria (so Dhorme, Böhl,
ossin); *b* Ilânsura – in the Mari
xts, between Harran and
archemish (Yeivin); *c* Telassar – (2
ings 19:12; Isaiah 37:12) in
orthern Mesopotamia as a parallel
*Shinar (Singara), but the name is
be read Til-Bašeri; *d* Larsa – in
outhern Babylonia. This depends
n the outmoded equation Amraphel
hat is, Hammurapi of Babylon).
J. Wiseman

*urther reading*
I. C. Astour in *Biblical Motifs*, ed. A.
ltmann, 1966, pp. 77–78

**LON** (Hebrew *'ēlôn*). A southern
anite town (Joshua 19:43);
ossibly Khirbet Wadi Alin, 2
ilometres east of Beth-shemesh
*TT*, p. 349).
Elon-beth-hanan (1 Kings 4:9) may
e the same (Mazar, *IEJ* 10, 1960,
. 67), or *Aijalon **1** (*LOB*, p. 311). The
ame, like *Elah, means 'terebinth'
SV 'oak' in *Zaanannim, Joshua
9:33).
P. U. Lilley

**LOTH.** See *ELATH.

**L-PARAN.** See *PARAN.

**LTEKEH.** A city in Palestine
llotted to the tribe of Dan (Joshua
9:44) and later made a levitical city
Elteke, Joshua 21:23). Sennacherib
entions it (Altakū) together with
imnā among his conquests in his
nnals for 701/700 BC (Chicago
ylinder 3.6; Taylor Cylinder
2.82–83).

It was once identified with Khirbet el-Muqanna' (Tel Miqne), 35 kilometres west of Jerusalem, but this is now generally held to be *Ekron; Tell-esh-Shalaf, 16 kilometres north-north-east of Ashdod, is an alternative (Mazar), but some regard this as too far to the south. Khirbet el-Muqanna' therefore still has a few supporters, but if this is Eltekeh an alternative is required for Ekron.
T. C. Mitchell

*Further reading*
D. D. Luckenbill, *The Annals of Sennacherib*, 1924, p. 32
W. F. Albright, *BASOR* 15, 1924, p. 8
B. Mazar, *IEJ* 10, 1960, pp. 72–77
R. Boling, 'Levitical Cities: Archaeology and Texts', in *Biblical and Related Studies Presented to Samuel Iwry*, ed. A. Kort and S. Morschauser, 1985, pp. 23–32

**EMMAUS.** A village, said to be 60 furlongs (11 kilometres) from Jerusalem, to which Cleopas and another disciple were journeying when Jesus appeared to them after his resurrection (Luke 24:13). The site cannot be certainly identified.

One possibility is the town still known as 'Amwas, 32 kilometres west-north-west of Jerusalem, where Judas Maccabaeus defeated Gorgias in 166 BC (1 Maccabees 3:40, 57; 4:3). But this is at the wrong distance from Jerusalem, as given by Luke (unless the variant reading of 160 furlongs found in Codex Sinaiticus and other manuscripts preserves the original text); it also demands a long, though by no means impossible, walk by the travellers.

Of places within about 11 kilometres from Jerusalem two have been suggested. There was a village at El-qubeibeh in the 1st century, and Crusaders found a fort here named Castellum Emmaus; unfortunately the name cannot be traced back to the 1st century.

Josephus (*Jewish War* 7.217) refers to a military colony of Vespasian at Ammaous, some 6 kilometres west of Jerusalem. This has been identified with Kaloniye (Latin *colonia*) or with Khirbet Beit Mizza (ancient Mozah); here again the distance is wrong, unless we suppose that Luke's 60 furlongs was meant as the total length of the outward and return journeys.
I. H. Marshall

*Further reading*
J. Finegan, *The Archaeology of the New Testament*, 1969, pp. 177–180
I. H. Marshall, *The Gospel of Luke*, 1978, pp. 892f.

**ENCAMPMENT BY THE SEA.** The place where the Israelites camped by the sea and made the crossing (Exodus 13:18; 14:2) has been the subject of much controversy during the last 100 years. The question is inseparable from that of the location of such places as Baal-zephon, Etham, Migdol, Pihahiroth, Sea of Reeds and Succoth.

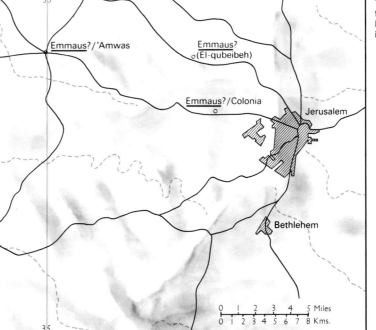

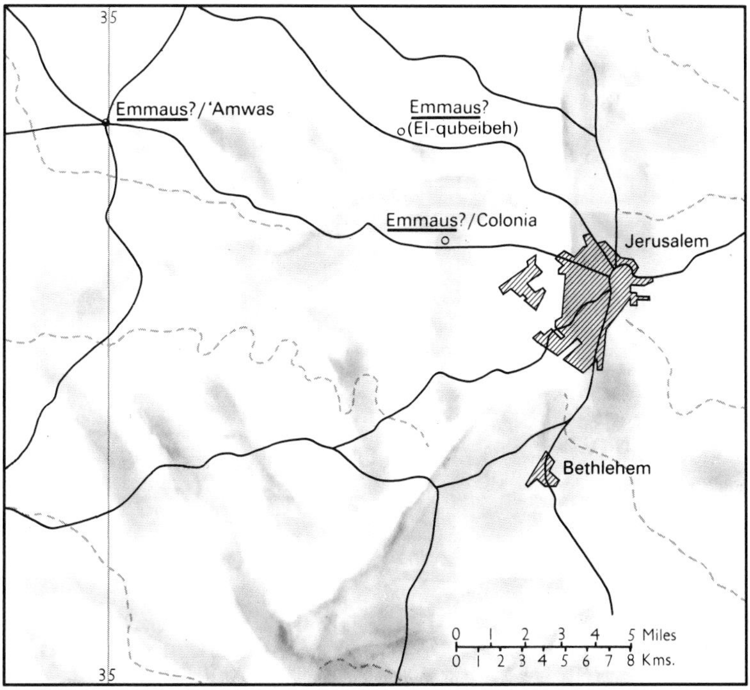


Three possible sites for the village of Emmaus, mentioned in Luke 24:13.

Two main traditions have grown up around the route of the Exodus out of Egypt: the 'Southern' theory favouring a route from the Wadi Tumilat region south-east to the Suez area, and the 'Northern' theory advocating a crossing near Lake Menzaleh to the south of Port Said.

*Southern theory*
The Southern theory was foreshadowed by Josephus (*Antiquities* 2.315), who considered the Israelites to have started from Latopolis (Egyptian Babylon, Old Cairo) to a Baal-zephon on the Red Sea; Pierre Diacre and Antonin de Plaisance had a tradition of the Hebrews passing Clysma near the present-day Suez. Among moderns, Lepsius, Mallon, Bourdon (with a crossing at Clysma), Cazelles and Montet favoured this view.

*Northern theory*
The northern route was championed by Brugsch, identifying the Sea of Reeds, *yam-sûp̄*, with the Egyptian *p'-ṯwf* and placing it in Lake Serbonis on the Mediterranean shore with Baal-zephon at Ras Qasrun there. But this hardly agrees with the biblical account, in which God forbade Israel to go by 'the way of the land of the Philistines' (Exodus 13:17–18).

Gardiner was the next to espouse the northern route (*JEA* 5, 1918, pp. 261–269; *Recueil Champollion*, 1922, pp. 203–215), likewise O. Eissfeldt and N. Aimé-Giron, the former identifying Casios and Baal-zephon on the Mediterranean shore and the latter equating Baal-zephon with Tahpanhes (Phoenician papyrus). For Albright, see below.

*Summary*
H. Cazelles summed up the whole problem. He considers that later tradition from the Septuagint onward (note the Septuagint's *thalassa erythra*, 'Red Sea') speaks for a southern route, but that study of the names in the Hebrew text suggests that this latter indicates a northern route by the Mediterranean; according to Cazelles, these northern locations were due to an editor of J and E documents who (like Manetho and Josephus) associated the Hebrew Exodus with the expulsion of the Hyksos from Egypt. However, this is speculative.

*A third view*
Finally, there is an entirely different suggestion by W. F. Albright (*BASOR* 109, 1948, pp. 15–16). He placed Ra'amses at Tanis in the north, brought the Israelites south-east past the places in the Wadi Tumilat (Pithom at Retabeh, Succoth at Tell el-Maskhutah) and then sharply back up north again (compare 'that they turn back', Exodus 14:2) by the Bitter Lakes to the region of a Baal-zephon located at later Tahpanhes (Defneh); Migdol is then Tell el-Her just south of Pelusium, with the Sea of Reeds (*yam-sûp̄*) in this general area. Having thus left Egypt proper, the Israelites would then flee to the south-east into the Sinai peninsula, so that Albright's route in its end-result becomes a 'southern' one (*i.e.* he does not take Israel by the forbidden way of the Philistines).

Noth's reserves (*Festschrift Otto Eissfeldt*, 1947, pp. 181–190) are largely based on literary-critical considerations of doubtful relevance.

As will be evident, the route of the Exodus is still a very live issue.

C. de Wit

*Further reading*
N. Aimé-Giron, *Annales du Service des Antiquités de l'Égypte* 40, 1940–41, pp. 433–460
Bourdon, *RB* 41, 1932, pp. 370–382, 538–549
H. Cazelles, *RB* 62, 1955, pp. 321–364
O. Eissfeldt, *Baal-Zaphon, Zeus Casios und der Durchzug der Israeliten durch das Meer*, 1932
Lepsius, *Zeitschrift für Ägyptische Sprache* 21, 1883, pp. 41–53
Mallon, 'Les Hébreux en Égypte', *Orientalia* 3, 1921
Montet, *Géographie de l'Égypte Ancienne* 1, 1957, pp. 218–219
——, *L'Égypte et la Bible*, 1959, pp. 59–63
E. Uphill, *Pithom and Raamses JNES* 27, 1968, pp. 291–316, and 28, 1969, pp. 15–39.
For much older bibliography, see also:
H. H. Rowley, *From Joseph to Joshua*, 1950
C. de Wit, *The Date and Route of the Exodus*, 1960 (for more specifically Egyptian aspects)
Invaluable for eastern Delta topography and conditions:
M. Bietak, *Tell El-Dab'a II*, Vienna, 1975

**ENDOR.** A town in the vicinity of the Esdraelon plain. Modern 'En-dûr, 6 kilometres south of Mount Tabor, must now be ruled out because archaeological surveys have revealed no trace of occupation in the Old Testament period.

Other candidates are: Khirbet Safsafeh, a few kilometres away from the modern Arab town; Tell el-'Ajjul; Khirbet Jadurah and Tell Abu Qudeis. The biblical references imply a location on the southern side of the plain, which would favour one of the latter two sites, the others being on the northern side.

The town was assigned to Manasseh, but was never wrested from Canaanite possession (Joshua 17:11–12).

The medium of Endor, of whom Saul inquired before his last battle (1 Samuel 28:7), was probably from this Canaanite stock, for an attempt had been made to do away with such practices among the Hebrews (1 Samuel 28:3).

R. J. Way

*Further reading*
N. Zori, *PEQ* 84, 1952, pp. 114–117
O. Margalith, *ZAW* 97, 1985, pp. 109–111

**EN-EGLAIM** (Hebrew *'ên-'eg̱layim*, 'spring of the two calves'). A place mentioned once only (Ezekiel 47:10) as lying on the shore of the Dead Sea. Though the site is unknown, the reference to *En-gedi suggests a location somewhere in the north-western sector.

This site is probably distinct from Eglaim (*'eg̱layim*, Isaiah 15:8), a town in Moab, though their identity has been argued by G. A. Herion, *ABD* II, p. 501.

T. C. Mitchell

*Further reading*
*GTT*, pp. 459–460
W. R. Farmer, *BA* 19, 1956, pp. 9–21

**EN-GANNIM** (Hebrew *'ên-gannîm*, 'spring of gardens'). **1.** A town in Judah's inheritance in the Shephelah (Joshua 15:34); perhaps modern Beit Jamal, 3 kilometres south of Beth-shemesh.

**2.** A levitical city in Issachar's territory (Joshua 19:21; 21:29; called Anem, 1 Chronicles 6:73). It is variously identified with Jenin, Olam and Khirbet Beit Jann, south-west of Tiberias.

G. G. Garner

**EN-GEDI** (Hebrew *'ên-geḏî*, 'spring of the kid'). Important oasis and fresh water spring west of the Dead Sea, allotted to Judah at the conquest (Joshua 15:62). David hid there (1 Samuel 23:29; 24:1ff.), its rugged terrain and fertility making it an ideal refuge. It was famous for aromatic plants and perfume (Song of Songs 1:14).

Excavations in 1949 and 1961–65 revealed several fortresses and a late

nagogue. In 1971–72 excavations covered four separate Ghassulian )00–3150 BC) structures linked gether by a stone wall. Included ıs a broadroom sanctuary. The site ıs abandoned and left to decay at e end of the Ghassulian era. ızazon-tamar is identified with -gedi (Genesis 14:7; 2 Chronicles :2).
G. Garner, J. Bimson

*rther reading*
Mazar and D. Barag in *NEAEHL* II, . 399–401
1 7:1, 1980, pp. 1–44

**I-HADDAH.** 'Sharp spring', the me of a place which was allotted the tribe of Issachar (Joshua :21). Suggested identifications ve been made (see *GTT*, p. 185), t the site has not been definitely entified.
C. Mitchell

**I-HAKKORE** (Hebrew *'ên-qqôrē'*). The spring in Lehi from nich Samson refreshed himself er slaughtering the Philistines th the jawbone of an ass (Judges :19). None of the places entioned in the story has been entified.
En-hakkore could mean 'the ring of the partridge' (compare -gedi, 'the spring of the goat'), but dges 15 gives a coherent account the origin of the name, indicating at it means 'the spring of him who lled'.
A. Motyer

**I-HAZOR.** The name of a place hich was allotted to the tribe of ıphtali (Joshua 19:37). The site is known, though suggestions have en made (see *GTT*, p. 198). ıaroni tentatively suggests an entification with *'ny* in the great nquest list of Tuthmosis III on lons 6 and 7 at Karnak, but this can ly be a speculation. It is distinct om *Hazor.
C. Mitchell

*rther reading*
*)B*, p. 162 no. 86

**I-RIMMON** (Hebrew *'ên-rimmôn*, ring of the pomegranate'). A lage in Judah reoccupied after the ile (Nehemiah 11:29). Either it as formed by the coalescing of two parate villages Ain and Rimmon, more probably, reading Joshua :32, 19:7 and 1 Chronicles 4:32 all En-rimmon, it was always a single wn, originally in Judah's heritance (Joshua 15:32), but soon transferred to Simeon (Joshua 19:7).

It has been identified with Umm er-Ramāmîn, 15 kilometres north of Beersheba.
M. A. MacLeod

**EN-ROGEL** (Hebrew *'ên-rōgēl*, 'well of the fuller'). A water source just outside Jerusalem, some 200 metres south of the confluence of the Valley of Hinnom and the Kidron Valley. It is almost certainly the source known today as Job's Well (Bir Eyyub), rather than the Virgin's Fountain. The well marked a point on the northern boundary of Judah (Joshua 15:7) before David captured Jerusalem (2 Samuel 5:6ff.).

The narrative of Adonijah's abortive attempt to gain the throne in David's old age suggests the site had cultic associations (1 Kings 1:9ff.).
R. J. Way

**EN-SHEMESH** (Hebrew *'ên-šemeš*, 'spring of the sun'). A point on the Judah-Benjamin border 4 kilometres east of Jerusalem (Joshua 15:7; 18:17), below Olivet, and just south of the Jericho road, and now sometimes called the 'Spring of the Apostles'; modern 'Ain Hod.
J. D. Douglas

**EPHESUS.** See p. 128.

**EPHRAIM.** The second son of Joseph, born to him by Asenath, the daughter of Potipherah, before the years of famine came (Genesis 41:50–52). The sick Jacob acknowledged the two sons of Joseph (Genesis 48:5), blessing Ephraim with his right hand and Manasseh with his left (verses 13–14), thus signifying that Ephraim would become the greater people (verse 19).

From the beginning the tribe of Ephraim occupied a position of prestige and significance. It complained to Gideon that he had not called it to fight against the Midianites. His reply reveals the superior position of Ephraim. 'Is not the gleaning of the grapes of Ephraim better than the vintage of Abi-ezer?' (Judges 8:2). The men of Ephraim complained again in similar terms to Jephthah, and this led to war between the Ephraimites and the Gileadites.

The boundaries of Ephraim are recorded in Joshua 16, and with Manasseh in Joshua 17. Only some of the main topographical features of these boundaries have so far been determined beyond dispute; most of the places mentioned cannot be precisely located at present.

*Southern boundary*
The southern boundary of Ephraim is most clearly expressed in Joshua 16:1–3, where, however, it is given as the (southern) boundary of 'the children of Joseph', that is, Ephraim-Manasseh. But as Manasseh was situated wholly to the north and north-east of Ephraim, this boundary is, in practice, that of Ephraim. It ran (east to west) up from the Jordan and Jericho inland to Bethel (Beitin, *c.* 16 kilometres north of Jerusalem), Luz (perhaps near by) and Ataroth (site uncertain), then *via* the border of Lower Beth-horon to Gezer – a well-known site – and the Mediterranean sea-coast (Joshua 16:1–3). Verse 5 is difficult, but may perhaps further define part of this southern boundary.

*Northern boundary*
The northern boundary from a point Michmetha(t)h (16:6) 'before Shechem' (17:7) turned west; its course in that direction ran from Tappuah (location still disputed) to and along the brook of Qanah (perhaps the present Wadi Qānah, which joins Wadi Aujah, and reaches the Mediterranean *c.* 6·5 kilometres north of Joppa) to the sea (16:8).

East from Michmetha(t)h, the border turned by Taanath-shiloh (south) along the east of Janoah to (another) Ataroth, Naarah, and back to Jericho and the Jordan (16:6–7).

On the north, Shechem apparently was within Ephraim's share, to judge from the levitical city-lists (Joshua 21:20–21; 1 Chronicles 6:67).

*Geography*
The region in central western Palestine that fell to Ephraim is mainly relatively high hill-country with better rainfall than Judaea and some good soils; hence some biblical references to the fruitfulness of the Ephraim district. The Ephraimites had direct but not over-easy access to the great north–south trunk road through the western plain.
K. A. Kitchen

*Further reading*
D. Baly, *The Geography of the Bible*, 2nd edition, 1974, pp. 164–176
*GTT*, pp. 158–169
Y. Kaufmann, *The Biblical Account of the Conquest of Palestine*, 1953, pp. 28–36
E. Jenni, *ZDPV* 74, 1958, pp. 35–40, with some detailed bibliography
F. M. Abel, *Géographie de la*
**Continued on p. 132**

# EPHESUS

**EPHESUS.** The most important city in the Roman province of Asia, on the west coast of what is now Asiatic Turkey. It was situated at the mouth of the Caÿster River between the mountain range of Coressus and the sea. A magnificent road, 11 metres wide and lined with columns, ran down through the city to the fine harbour, which served both as a great export centre at the end of the Asiatic caravan-route and also as a natural landing-point from Rome.

The city, now uninhabited, has been undergoing excavation for many years, and is probably the most extensive and impressive ruined site of Asia Minor.

The sea is now some 10 kilometres away, owing to the silting process which has been at work for centuries. The harbour had to undergo extensive clearing operations at various times from the 2nd century BC; is that, perhaps, wh Paul had to stop at Miletus (Acts 20:15–16)?

The ruins of the Temple of Artemis, Ephesus, ranked as one of the seven wonders of the world.

The main part of the city, with it theatre, baths, library, agora and paved streets, lay between the Coressus ridge and the Caÿster, bu the temple for which it was famed lay over 2 kilometres to the north-east. This site was originally sacred to the worship of the Anatolian fertility goddess, later identified with Greek Artemis and Latin Diana. Justinian built a churc to St John on the hill nearby (hence the later name Ayasoluk – a corruption of *hagios theologos*), which was itself succeeded by a Seljuk mosque. The neighbouring settlement is now called Selçuk.

*History*

The original Anatolian settlement was augmented before the 10th century BC by Ionian colonists, and joint city was set up. The goddess Ephesus took a Greek name, but clearly retained her earlier characteristics, for she was repeatedly represented at later periods as a many-breasted figure.

Ephesus was conquered by Croesus shortly after his accession *c.* 560 BC, and owed some of its artistic glories to his munificence. After his fall in 546 it came under Persian rule. Croesus shifted the sit of the archaic city to focus upon th temple of Artemis: Lysimachus, or of the successors of Alexander, forcibly replanted it around the harbour early in the 3rd century BC

Ephesus later formed part of the kingdom of Pergamum, which Attalus III bequeathed to Rome in 133 BC. It became the greatest commercial city of the Roman province of Asia. It then occupied vast area, and its population may have numbered a third of a million. is estimated that the great theatre built into Mount Pion in the centre the city had a capacity of about 25,000.

*Emperor cult*

Ephesus also maintained its religious importance under Romar rule. It became a centre of the emperor cult, and eventually possessed three official temples, thus qualifying thrice over for the proud title *neōkoros* ('temple-warden') of the emperors, as well being *neōkoros* of Artemis (Acts 19:35). It is remarkable that Paul h friends among the Asiarchs (*Asiarchai*, Acts 19:31), who were officers of the 'commune' of Asia, whose primary function was actua

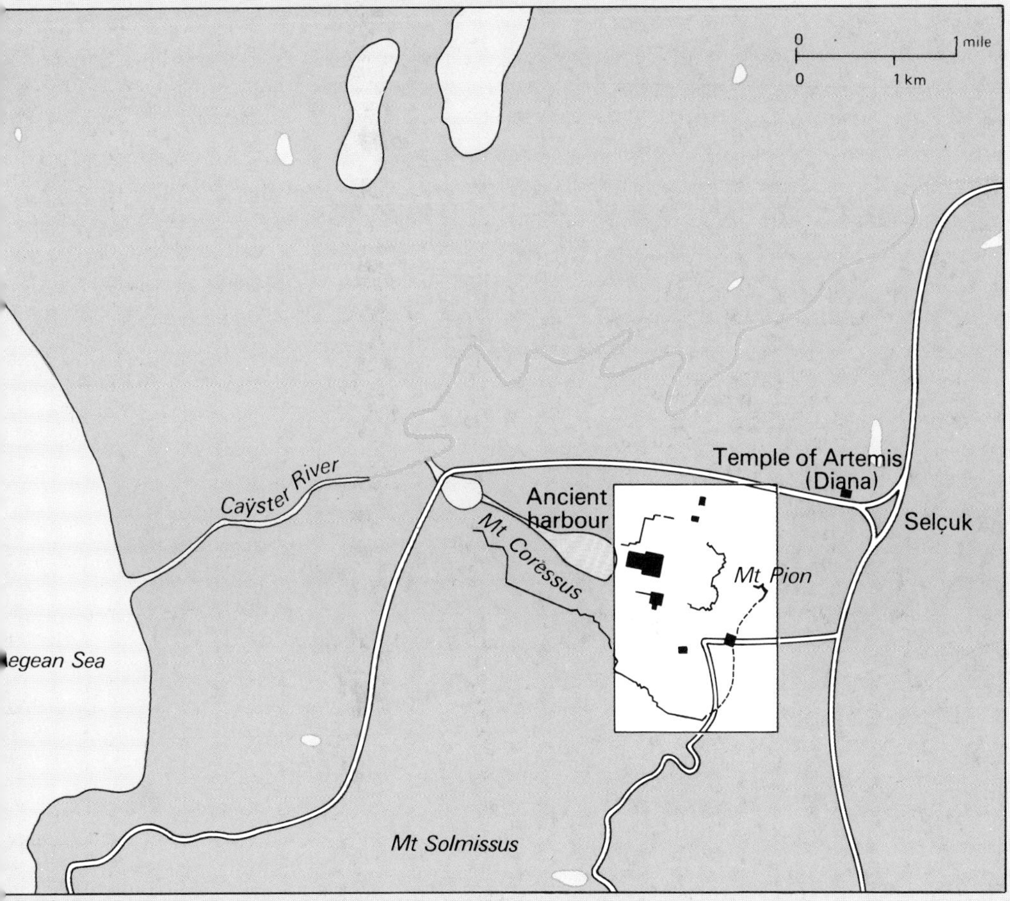


Plan showing the main buildings of Ephesus so far recovered. The city was destroyed by the Goths in AD 263.

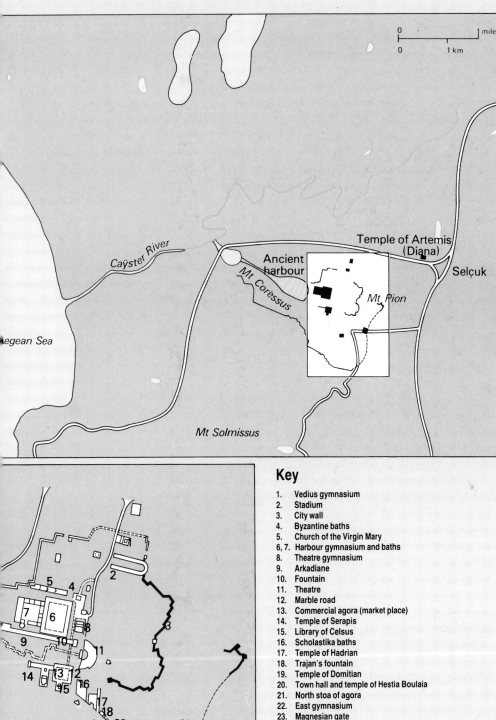

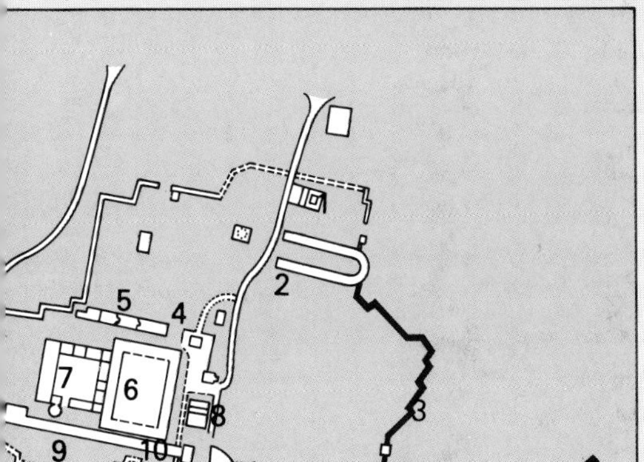


## Key

1. Vedius gymnasium
2. Stadium
3. City wall
4. Byzantine baths
5. Church of the Virgin Mary
6, 7. Harbour gymnasium and baths
8. Theatre gymnasium
9. Arkadiane
10. Fountain
11. Theatre
12. Marble road
13. Commercial agora (market place)
14. Temple of Serapis
15. Library of Celsus
16. Scholastika baths
17. Temple of Hadrian
18. Trajan's fountain
19. Temple of Domitian
20. Town hall and temple of Hestia Boulaia
21. North stoa of agora
22. East gymnasium
23. Magnesian gate
24. City wall

***Opposite:* The theatre at Ephesus, constructed during the Hellenistic period (3rd–2nd century BC) but altered in the reigns of Claudius (AD 41–54), Nero (AD 54–68) and Trajan (AD 98–117). The auditorium seated 24,000.**

to foster the imperial cult.

*Temple of Artemis*

The temple of Artemis itself had been rebuilt after a great fire in 356 BC, and ranked as one of the seven wonders of the world until its destruction by the Goths in AD 263. After years of patient search J. T. Wood in 1870 uncovered its remains in the marsh at the foot of Mount Ayasoluk. It had been the largest building in the Greek world.

It contained an image of the goddess which, it was claimed, had fallen from heaven (compare Acts 19:35). Indeed, it may well have been a meteorite originally. Silver coins from many places show the validity of the claim that the goddess of Ephesus was revered all over the world (Acts 19:27). They bear the inscription *Diana Ephesia* (compare Acts 19:34).

*The coming of Christianity*

There was a large colony of Jews at Ephesus, and they had long enjoyed a privileged position under Roman rule (Josephus, *Antiquities* 14.225ff.; 14.262ff.).

The earliest reference to the coming of Christianity there is in *c.* AD 52, when Paul made a short visit and left Aquila and Priscilla there (Acts 18:18–21).

Paul's third missionary journey had Ephesus as its goal, and he stayed there for over 2 years (Acts 19:8, 10), attracted, no doubt, by its strategic importance as a commercial, political and religious centre. His work was at first based on the synagogue: later he debated in the lecture-hall of Tyrannus, making Ephesus a base for the evangelization of the whole province of Asia.

The spread of Christianity, which refused syncretism, began to incur the hostility of vested religious interests. It affected not only the magic cults which flourished there (Acts 19:13ff. – one kind of magic formula was actually called *Ephesia grammata*) but also the worship of Artemis (Acts 19:27), causing damage to the trade in cult objects which was one source of the prosperity of Ephesus. There followed the celebrated riot described in Acts 19.

Inscriptions show that the *grammateus* ('town clerk') who gained control of the assembly on this occasion was the leading civic official, directly responsible to the Romans for such breaches of the peace as illicit assembly (Acts 19:40). It has been suggested that his assertion 'there are proconsuls' (19:38), if it is not a generalizing plural, may fix the date with some precision. On Nero's accession in AD 54, M. Junius Silvanus, the proconsul of Asia, was poisoned by his subordinates Helius and Celer, who acted as proconsuls until the arrival of a regular successor.

*Paul and Ephesus*

Christianity evidently spread to *Colossae and other cities of the Lycus valley at the period of Paul's stay in Ephesus (see Colossians 1:6–7 and 2:1). It was Paul's headquarters for most of the time of the Corinthian controversy and correspondence (1 Corinthians 16:8), and the experience which he describes as 'fighting with wild beasts' happened there (1 Corinthians 15:32). This seems to be a metaphorical allusion to something already known to the Corinthians, perhaps mob violence or even the provincial imperial cult which was regularly celebrated with wild beast or gladiatorial shows. (There was no amphitheatre at Ephesus, though the stadium was later adapted to accommodate beast-fighting.)

G. S. Duncan in *St Paul's Ephesian Ministry* (1929) has maintained that Paul was imprisoned two or three times at Ephesus, and that all the captivity Epistles were written from there and not from Rome.

E. J. Goodspeed (in *Introduction to the New Testament*, 1937), followed by C. L. Mitton and J. Knox, have located at Ephesus the collection of the Pauline group of letters. There are difficulties in the hypothesis of an Ephesian imprisonment which suits the case, and although B. Reicke and J. A. T. Robinson have revived the idea that some or all of the captivity Epistles were written from Caesarea, it remains preferable to place them in Rome (see C. H. Dodd, *BJRL* 18, 1934, pp. 72–92).

After Paul's departure Timothy was left at Ephesus (1 Timothy 1:3). The Pastoral Letters give a glimpse of the period of consolidation there. It is thought by many that Romans 16 was originally addressed by Paul to Ephesus.

*John and Ephesus*

The city was later the headquarters of the John who had jurisdiction over the seven leading churches of Asia addressed in the Apocalypse. The church in Ephesus is addressed first of the seven (Revelation 2:1–7), as being the most important church in the *de facto* capital, and as being the landing-place for a messenger from Patmos, and standing at the head of a circular road joining the seven cities in order.

This church is flourishing, but is troubled by false teachers, and has lost its 'first love'. The false apostl (2:2) are most probably like the Nicolaitans, who seem to have advocated compromise with the power of paganism for the Christia under pressure. The Ephesians we steadfast, but deficient in love.

Sir William Ramsay characterize Ephesus as the 'city of change'. Its problems were the problems of a successful church coping with changing circumstances: the city t had had a long history of shifting sites (see Revelation 2:5b). The promise of eating of the tree of life here probably set against the background of the sacred date-pal of Artemis, which figures on Ephesian coins.

*Decline*

According to Irenaeus and Eusebiu Ephesus became the home of John the Apostle. A generation after his time Ignatius wrote of the continuing fame and faithfulness c the Ephesian church (*Ephesians* 8–9).

The third General Council of the church took place here in AD 431 to condemn Nestorian Christology, a sat in the double church of St Mary the ruins of which are still to be see

The city declined, and the progressive silting of its gulf finally severed it wholly from the sea.

E. M. B. Green, C. J. Hemer

*Further reading*

W. M. Ramsay, *The Letters to the Seven Churches*, 1904
J. T. Wood, *Modern Discoveries on the Site of Ancient Ephesus*, 1890
D. G. Hogarth, *Excavations at Ephesus: the Archaic Artemisia*, 1908
*RE*, 'Ephesos'
L. Robert, *Les Gladiateurs dans l'Orient Grec*, 1940, ch. 5
G. E. Bean, *Aegean Turkey. An Archaeological Guide*, 1966
E. Akurgal, *The Ancient Ruins and Civilisations of Turkey*, 1973
C. J. Hemer, 'Ephesus', *The Letter. to the Seven Churches of Asia in their Local Setting*, 1986, ch. 3
R. E. Oster, 'Ephesus as a Religiou Center under the Principate, I. Paganism before Constantine', *ANRW* II.18.3, 1990, pp. 1661–1728
G. M. Rogers, *The Sacred Identity* of *Ephesos*, 1991

**Continued from p. 127**
*Palestine* 1–2, 1933–38
For the archaeology of the region:
I. Finkelstein, *The Archaeology of the Israelite Settlement*, 1988, especially pp. 65–80, 119–204

**EPHRATH, EPHRATHAH. 1.** The ancient name of *Bethlehem Judah (see Genesis 35:19 *etc.*, 'Ephrathah, that (is) Bethlehem'), which occurs in all cases but one (Genesis 48:7, *'ep̄rāṯ*) in the form *'ep̄rāṯâ*.

Rachel was buried on the route there from Bethel (Genesis 35:16, 19; 48:7; compare 1 Samuel 10:2); it was the home of Naomi's family (Ruth 4:11), who are described as Ephrathites (*'ep̄rāṯî*, Ruth 1:2), of Ruth's descendant David (1 Samuel 17:12; see Psalm 132:6), and of the Messiah, as foretold in Micah 5:2.

**2.** The gentilic *'ep̄rāṯî* is applied three times to Ephraimites (Judges 12:5; 1 Samuel 1:1; 1 Kings 11:26).
T. C. Mitchell

*Further reading*
G. Adam Smith, *Historical Geography of the Holy Land*, 1931, pp. 214–215, note 3

**EPHRON 1.** A hill area between Nephtoah and *Kiriath-jearim which marked the border of Judah (Joshua 15:9; 18:15, RSV amended text).

**2.** A place near *Bethel taken by Abijah from Jeroboam I (2 Chronicles 13:19). RSV 'Ephron'; Massoretic Text 'Ephrain', AV 'Ephraim'; see 2 Samuel 13:23) to be identified with Ophrah (Joshua 18:23). Perhaps the word means 'province' (*VT* 12, 1962, p. 339). Generally it is identified as et-Taiyibeh *c.* 7 kilometres north-east of Bethel.

**3.** A fort between Ashtoreth-karnaim (Carmion) and Beth-shan (Scythopolis) captured by Judas Maccabaeus (1 Maccabees 5:46–52; 2 Maccabees 12:27–29; Josephus, *Antiquities* 12.346). It is possibly the modern et-Taiybeh south-east of Galilee.
D. J. Wiseman

**ERECH.** An ancient city of Mesopotamia mentioned in the Table of Nations (Genesis 10:10) as one of the possessions of Nimrod in the land of *Shinar. Known to the Sumerians as *Unu(g)* and to the Akkadians as *Uruk*, it was one of the great cities of Sumerian times. It is named in the Sumerian king lists as the seat of the 2nd Dynasty after the Flood, one of whose kings was Gilgamesh, who later became one of the great heroes of Sumerian legend.

Though the city continued in occupation during later periods (Greek *Orchoē* in Seleucid times), it never surpassed its early importance.

Uruk is represented today by the group of mounds known to the Arabs as *Warka*, which lies in southern Babylonia some 64 kilometres north-west of Ur and 6 kilometres east of the present course of the *Euphrates. While the site was investigated over a century ago by W. K. Loftus (*Travels and Researches in Chaldaea and Susiana*, 1857), the principal excavations have been conducted by a series of German expeditions in 1912, 1928–39 and from 1954 onwards. The results are of outstanding importance for the early history of Mesopotamia.

Prehistoric remains of the Ubaid Period (see also *SUMER) were followed by monumental architecture and stone sculpture of the Late Prehistoric Period which richly illustrate the material culture of Mesopotamia at the beginning of history. It was in these levels, dating from the 4th millennium BC, that the earliest inscriptions so far known were found. These are in the form of clay tablets, and, though the signs are only pictographic, it is probable that the language behind them was Sumerian.
T. C. Mitchell

*Further reading*
R. North, 'Status of the Warka Excavations', *Orientalia* n.s. 26, 1957, pp. 185–256
S. A. Pallis, *The Antiquity of Iraq*, 1954, pp. 349–350 (publication series continuing)

**ESDRAELON.** The Greek form of the name *Jezreel. However, the Greek and Hebrew names really apply to two distinct but adjacent lowlands, even though in some modern works the term Jezreel is loosely extended to cover both regions. The vale of Jezreel proper is the valley that slopes down from the town of Jezreel to Beth-shan overlooking the Jordan rift-valley, with Galilee to the north and Mount Gilboa to the south.

Esdraelon is the triangular alluvial plain bounded along its south-western side by the Carmel range from Jokneam to Ibleam and Engannim (modern Jenin), along its northern side by a line from Jokneam to the hills of Nazareth, and on the east by a line thence back down to Ibleam and Engannim.

On the east, Jezreel guards the entry to its own valley, while in the west the south-western spur of hills from Galilee leaves only a small ga by which the river Kishon flows ou into the plain of Acre after crossing the Esdraelon plain.

At the foot of the north-east-facin slopes of Carmel the important towns of *Jokneam, *Megiddo, *Taanach and *Ibleam controlled t main passes and north–south rout through western Palestine, while these and the town of Jezreel also controlled the important route running east–west from the Jorda valley to the Mediterranean coast, the only one unimpeded by ranges hills.

Esdraelon was a marshy region, important mainly for these roads; the vale of Jezreel was agricultural valuable as well as being strategically placed.

For the geographical backgroun see D. Baly, *Geography of the Bible* 1974, pp. 39 and 144–151.
K. A. Kitchen

**ESHCOL.** The valley where the spie sent out by Moses gathered a huge cluster (Hebrew *'eškōl*) of grapes, typical of the fruitfulness of the lan (Numbers 13:23–24; 32:9; Deuteronomy 1:24). Traditionally thought to be located a few kilometres north of Hebron (alread in Jerome, *Letters* 108.11, printed i Migne's *Patrologia Latina* 22.886), where the vineyards are still famou for the quality of their grapes.

Some scholars prefer a location south of Hebron (Gray; Noth), but although the texts are not explicit about the direction, it does seem to be implied that the spies continued north from Hebron to the Valley of Eshcol (Numbers 13:22–23).
G. T. Manley, G. I. Davies

*Further reading*
G. B. Gray, *Numbers* (ICC), 1903, pp. 142–143
P. Thomsen, *Loca Sancta*, 1907, p. 6
*IDB* 2, p. 142

**ESHTAOL** (*'eštā'ōl*, from the verb *šā'al*, 'to ask'). A lowland city, west of Jerusalem, tentatively identified with Khirbet Deir Shubeib, near the modern Eshwa'. It was included in the territory of both Judah (Joshua 15:33) and Dan (Joshua 19:41), an anomaly which is partially explaine by the fluidity of the border, a fact attributable to Amorite (Judges 1:34) and then Philistine pressure. The Eshtaolites are numbered amongst the Calebites, traditionall associated with Judah (1 Chronicle 2:53).

It was at Eshtaol that the Danite Samson was first moved by the Spiri

the Lord (Judges 13:25) and ıere he was finally buried in the ꟷnb of his father (Judges 16:31). om Eshtaol and neighbouring rah originated the Danite quest for settled habitation (Judges 18:2, ).
E. Cundall

**'AM. 1.** A place in the hill-country Judah, rebuilt by Rehoboam (2 ronicles 11:6), probably referred in 1 Chronicles 4:3, and in the ptuagint of Joshua 15:59 (*Aitan*). e site is usually identified with odern Khirbet el-Ḫoḫ, some 10·5 ometres south-south-west of rusalem.
**2.** A village in the territory of meon (1 Chronicles 4:32). The site unknown, though some scholars ould equate the place with **1** above.
**3.** The cave (*s*e*ʿîp sela'*, 'cleft of ck') where Samson took refuge om the Philistines (Judges 15:8, ). The site is unknown, but must in western Judah.
C. Mitchell

*rther reading*
M. Abel, *Géographie de la lestine* 2, 1938, p. 32
*DB*, p. 434

**THAM.** Camp of the Israelites mewhere on the isthmus of Suez xodus 13:20; Numbers 33:6–7), oout whose precise location holars differ. Müller suggested a nnection with the name of the yptian god Atum; Naville oposed Edom; Clédat, Gauthier, urdon, Lagrange, Abel and ontet would connect it with the d Egyptian word for 'fort' (*ḫtm*), a me which was given to several aces; but none of these ggestions seems very likely. The d Egyptian *ḫtm* seems rather to signate the frontier-city of Sile. ee also *Encampment by the Sea.)
de Wit

**THIOPIA.** Settled by the escendants of *Cush (Genesis :6), biblical Ethiopia (Greek *ithiōps*, 'burnt face', see Jeremiah :23) is part of the kingdom of ıbia stretching from Aswan (see so *Seveneh) south to the junction the Nile near modern Khartoum.
In Acts 8:27 Ethiopia refers to the lotic kingdom of Candace, who led at Meroë, where the capital d been moved during the Persian riod.
A. Kitchen

**UPHRATES.** The largest river in estern Asia, and on this account generally referred to as *hannāhār*, 'the river', in the Old Testament (*e.g.* Deuteronomy 11:24). It is sometimes mentioned by name, however, the Hebrew form being *p*e*rāṯ* (*e.g.* Genesis 2:14; 15:18), derived from the Akkadian *purattu*, which represents the Sumerian *buranun*, and the New Testament form *Euphratēs* (Revelation 9:14; 16:12).

The Euphrates takes its source in two main affluents in eastern Turkey, the Murad-Su, which rises near Lake Van, and the Kara-Su, which rises near Erzerum, and runs, joined only by the Ḫâbûr (see also *Habor) for 2,000 kilometres to the Persian Gulf.

From low water in September it rises by degrees throughout the winter to some 3 metres higher by May, and then declines again until September, thus enjoying a milder regime than the *Tigris.

In the alluvial plain of Babylonia (see also *Mesopotamia) its course has shifted to the west since ancient times, when most of the important cities, now some kilometres to the east of it, lay on or near its banks.

This is illustrated by the fact that the Sumerians wrote its name ideographically as 'river of Sippar', a city whose ruins lie today some 6 kilometres to the east (see also *Sepharvaim).

In addition to the many important cities, including Babylon, which lay on its banks in the southern plain, the city of Mari was situated on its middle course, not far from the junction with the Ḫâbûr, and the strategic crossing-place from northern Mesopotamia to northern Syria was commanded by the fortress city of *Carchemish.
T. C. Mitchell

*Further reading*
W. B. Fisher, *The Middle East*, 6th edition, 1971, pp. 345–347
S. A. Pallis, *The Antiquity of Iraq,* 1956, pp. 4–7
D. T. Tsamura, *The Earth and the Waters in Genesis 1 and 2*, 1989, pp. 138–139
R. Zadok, *RGTC* 83, 1985, pp. 396–398

**EZEL.** The agreed rendezvous of David and Jonathan, occurring in 1 Samuel 20:19 (AV, RV, RSV margin). It is sometimes taken to mean 'departure', but the RV margin and the RSV, following the Septuagint, read 'this mound' and 'yonder stone heap' respectively, and assume corruption in the Hebrew text. See also the margin of 1 Samuel 20:41.
G. W. Grogan

**EZION-GEBER.** Ezion-geber first appears along the route of the Hebrews from Mount Sinai to Qadesh (Barnea), in Numbers 33:35–36, being distinguished from *Elath in Deuteronomy 2:8. That distinction is maintained in the accounts of Solomon (*c.* 950 BC) specifying Ezion-geber as 'near Elath', when using it as a base to dispatch his fleet down the Red Sea under Hiram's men to fetch gold from Ophir (1 Kings 9:26–28; 2 Chronicles 8:17–18). Barely a century after (*c.* 850), Jehoshaphat king of Judah failed to match Solomon's enterprise when 'his ships were wrecked at Ezion-geber' (1 Kings 22:48–49; 2 Chronicles 20:35–37).

*Location*
Following a suggestion by F. Frank (*ZDPV* 57, 1934, pp. 234–235), N. Glueck identified Ezion-geber with the mound of Tell el-Kheleifeh (at the southern end of the Arabah valley) where he excavated in 1938–40, finding a fortress within which he identified some remains as a smeltery (for a full bibliography, see E. K. Vogel, *Bibliography of Holy Land Sites* I, 1971, pp. 85–86; II, 1981, pp. 49–50).

However, the smeltery proved to be illusory (see B. Rothenberg, *PEQ* 94, 1962, pp. 44–56), as Glueck himself later conceded (see *BA* 28, 1965, p. 73; *The Other Side of the Jordan*, 2nd edition, 1970, pp. 113–115). Also, the shelving beach just south of Tell el-Kheleifeh was not a suitable site from which to dispatch such fleets as Solomon's.

A more appropriate location for Ezion-geber has been placed at the coast, anchorage and island of Gezirat al-Faraun ('Coral Island'), some 24 kilometres farther west-south-west along the coast from Tell el-Kheleifeh. The island itself has a small inner harbour; occupation of the island began no later than the 13th/12th centuries BC, as shown by finds of 'Midianite' pottery there (B. Rothenberg, J. Glass, in J. F. A. Sawyer, D. J. A. Clines [eds.], *Midian, Moab and Edom*, 1983, pp. 76–77).

Between the island and the shore is a safe anchorage and remains of two quays projecting from the shore. Such an anchorage could have accommodated Solomon's fleet, and the rocks and wilder water beyond the island could have occasioned the wreck of Jehoshaphat's ships.
K. A. Kitchen

*Further reading*
On the Gezirat al-Faroun location, see:
A. Flinder, *International Journal of Nautical Archaeology* 6, 1977, pp. 127–139
——, *BARev*, 15/4, 1989, pp. 30–43
Simple account:
A. Flinder, *Secrets of the Bible Seas*, 1985, pp. 42–82 with plates
See also:
J. R. Bartlett, *Edom and the Edomites*, 1990, pp. 47–48, section 5
B. Rothenberg and others, *God's Wilderness*, 1961, pp. 86–92 and 185–189 (but note that his Iron I pottery is not Solomonic, but the earlier 'Midianite')

# F

**FAIR HAVENS,** modern Kaloi Limenes, a small bay on the southern coast of Crete, a few kilometres east of Cape Matala. Although protected by small islands, it is too open to be an ideal winter harbour (Acts 27:8), but it would be the last place where Paul's ship could stay to avoid the north-westerly wind, as the coast swings northwards beyond Cape Matala.
K. L. McKay

*Further reading*
C. J. Hemer, *The Book of Acts in the Setting of Hellenistic History*, 1989, pp. 136–137

**FORUM OF APPIUS.** A market town and staging-post in Latium, a foundation of Appius Claudius Caecus, the builder of the Via Appia, on which the town stands. It is 45 kilometres from Rome, a place 'packed with bargees and extortionate innkeepers', if the poet Horace is to be believed.

The town was the northern terminus of the canal through the Pontine Marshes. This was one of the places where the Roman Christians met Paul (Acts 28:15); see also *THREE TAVERNS.
E. M. Blaiklock

# G

**GABBATHA.** An Aramaic word meaning 'height', 'eminence'; the local, native word for the area. It must have been on a height.

*Gabbatha* identifies the same location as the other term, 'the Pavement' (*lithostrōton*), but does not describe exactly the same thing. As John 19:13 specifies, it is a 'place' called either the Height or the Pavement. One may suppose that the Pavement was laid by Herod in front of his palace in the Upper City (at the north-western angle of the first north wall). This palace was the official residence of the Roman governors, including Pilate, as is clear from incidents described by Josephus.

*A paved area*
The Greek word *lithostrōton* was adopted by the Romans to describe paved area, either of marquetry (*opus sectile*) or of flagstones. Both types of work are known to have been used by Herod; marquetry at Jericho (inlaid stones, some coloured, set in a pattern) and flags at Jerusalem, notably for the streets and terraces outside the immense walls of the Temple Mount (now excavated by Mazar). The foundations of this palace in the Upper City have been excavated, but the superstructures were missing. Nor has the Pavement been found as yet.

*The traditional site*
The site for 'the Pavement' favoured by Christian pilgrims at the Convent of the Sisters of Zion is to be rejected. Its adherents err in claiming that Jesus was brought to trial at the Antonia fortress on the Temple Mount; as stated above, the palace in the Upper City was Pilate's headquarters. Moreover the location of this pavement is slightly wrong even for the Antonia; it is probably part of the public square at the

stern gate of Hadrian's Aelia pitolina. The pools beneath it ›re filled in and had siege-engines ›cted on them when the Romans der Titus attacked the Antonia ;t Revolt). At the time of Jesus they ›re open pools *outside* the walls of ə Antonia. The pavement set over əm, now shown as the *lithostrōton*, d not been laid.

'. Kane

**AD** ('good fortune'). An Israelite be descended from Gad, and the 'ritory they occupied. The tribe in ɔses' time had seven clans umbers 26:15–18), was mmanded and represented by one .asaph (Numbers 1:14; 2:14; 7:42; :20), and supplied a spy for the ploration of Canaan (Numbers :15).

*ıd's share of the land*

hen Israel reached the plains of ɔab, Reuben, Gad and half-Manas-h sought permission to settle in ansjordan, which they desired as əir share in the promised land, cause *Gilead was so suitable for eir considerable livestock. To this ɔses agreed, on condition that they st help their fellow-Israelites to tablish themselves in western lestine (Numbers 32). The Gadites d Reubenites then hastily paired cities (including Ataroth) d sheepfolds to safeguard their milies and livestock (Numbers :34–38, compare 26–27) while eparing to help their brethren, a omise of help duly kept (Joshua :1–8). Then came the incident of e altar of witness (Joshua :9–34).

As tribal territory, Reuben and ıd received the Amorite kingdom Sihon: Reuben had the land from roer on the Arnon river, north to a ıe running from the Jordan's outh east to the region of Heshbon ɔshua 13:15–23). North of this line, ıd had all southern Gilead, from e Jordan valley east as far as the uth-to-north course of the upper bbok (the border with Ammon), d north generally as far as the .st-to-west course of the lower bbok, but with two extensions ›yond this: first, all the Jordan lley on the eastern side of the rdan river (formerly Sihon's) ›tween the Dead Sea and the Sea of alilee (or Chinneroth), and second, ross the north-eastern angle of the ver Jabbok to include the district of Mahanaim and a fertile tract nking the eastern side of northern lead north over Jebel Kafkafa to rategic Ramoth-Gilead at modern Tell Ramith, 32 kilometres north-east of Jerash (compare Joshua 13:24–28).

Heshbon was assigned as a levitical city out of the territory of Gad (Joshua 21:38–39); hence perhaps read Joshua 13:16–17 as (Reuben's) 'border was from Aroer . . . and all the plain by Medeba, [unto] Heshbon . . .' (emending only by the addition of one letter, locative-*h*). Dibon, *etc.*, are then cities between these limits, and Heshbon would be the southernmost territory of Gad.

*Gad's share of the troubles*

The Gadites doubtless shared the troubles of Transjordanian Israel generally in the judges' period (*e.g.* Judges 10–12). In Saul's day the wooded Gileadite hills of Gad offered a place of refuge (1 Samuel 13:7), and Gadites among others joined the fugitive David and supported his becoming king (1 Chronicles 12:1, 8–15, 37–38).

Gadites likewise shared in, and were subject to, David's administration (2 Samuel 23:36; 24:5; 1 Chronicles 26:32). On his Moabite Stone, roughly 840/830 BC, King Mesha mentions that the Gadites had long dwelt in the land of Ataroth. Just after this, within Jehu of Israel's reign, Hazael of Damascus ravaged all Gilead, Gad included (2 Kings 10:32–33).

In the 8th century BC Gadite settlement apparently extended north-east into Bashan (1 Chronicles 5:11–17), until Tiglath-pileser III carried the Transjordanians into exile (2 Kings 15:29; 1 Chronicles 5:25–26). Then the Ammonites again invaded Gad (Jeremiah 49:1–6). Gad is assigned the southernmost zone in Ezekiel's vision of the tribal portions (48:27–28).

For geographical background, see D. Baly, *Geography of the Bible*, 2nd edition, 1974, pp. 210ff., 221ff., 227–232.

K. A. Kitchen

**GAD, VALLEY OF.** The place where the census ordered by David was begun is given as 'Aroer, on the right side of the city that is in the middle of the valley (Hebrew *naḥal*) of Gad' (2 Samuel 24:5, RV). In Deuteronomy 2:36 Aroer is described as 'on the edge of the valley (*naḥal*) of the Arnon'. Since the census would naturally begin at the southern border of the Transjordan territory, this is probably the place intended. Various manuscripts of the Septuagint indicate corruptions in the text of 2 Samuel 24:5, which should read 'toward Gad and Jazer' (so RSV).

G. T. Manley

**GADARENES, GADARA.** The place where Jesus healed a demon-possessed man, allowing the demons to enter a herd of pigs which then rushed into the Sea of Galilee (Matthew 8:28–34; Mark 5:1–20; Luke 8:26–39), is variously named in the Gospel accounts. The best Greek text reads 'the country of the Gadarenes' in Matthew but '. . . of the Gerasenes' in Mark and Luke (as in RSV, NRSV and NIV); however, all three Gospels have variant readings, with '. . . of the Gergesenes' appearing as a third alternative.

**Remains of the 5th century church built at Kursi, since the 4th century identified as Gergesa.**

*Gadara*
The name 'Gadarenes' would indicate an association with Gadara, a city some 10 kilometres south-east of the southern tip of the Sea of Galilee, near the gorge of the Yarmuk. The ruins of Umm Qeis mark the site. Its history extends back at least to the 3rd century BC and in the 1st century BC it became a city of the Decapolis. This cannot, however, be the site of the miracle, which clearly occurred near the shore of the Sea of Galilee (Matthew 8:32, *etc.*). If 'Gadarenes' is the correct reading it must refer to a lakeside district under Gadara's administration.

*Gerasa*
The same explanation would apply in the case of 'Gerasenes', as this refers to Gerasa, another Decapolis city even further from the Sea of Galilee (60 kilometres to the south-east). Gerasa (modern Jerash) probably became a significant town in the Hellenistic period, and during the 1st century AD it was largely rebuilt on a Roman plan.

The town's most impressive remains date from the 2nd century AD and include a triumphal arch commemorating a visit by the emperor Hadrian in AD 129–130. Colonnades were added to the main streets and it was possibly at this time (if not in the 1st century) that a hippodrome seating 15,000 spectators was built outside the city to the south.

*Gergesa*
Of the three attested variants only Gergesa can be related directly to a site on the eastern shore of the Sea of Galilee. From the 4th century tradition has identified Gergesa with the place now known as El Kursi, just south of the Wadi Samak and 5 kilometres north of En Gev. A church and monastic complex were built there in the 5th century. Excavated by V. Tzaferis in the 1970s, the church has been extensively restored. On the shore to the west of the monastic area lie the remains of a village of the Roman period with an anchorage and breakwater.

*Tel Samra*
However, G. Franz has recently questioned the association of El Kursi with the healing of the demoniac. On the basis of the mosaics in the El Kursi church, he suggests it was actually built to commemorate the feeding of the 4,000 (Matthew 15:32–39) and proposes a site for the healing miracle some 12 kilometres further south.

In 1985 an ancient harbour was discovered just south of Tel Samra on the south-eastern shore of the Sea of Galilee. With a breakwater 250 metres long this is the largest harbour on the eastern side of the sea and may have served the city of Gadara, 1·5 kilometres to the south-east, and thus have been reckoned within 'the country of the Gadarenes'. Roman sarcophagi from Tel Samra provide evidence of a nearby cemetery (compare Mark 5:3) and 10 kilometres to the south-west a cliff drops directly down to the water, fitting the description of 'a steep slope' down which the swine rushed into the sea.

If Gadara is the correct reading of the place-name this last theory has much to commend it. However, confusion over the name means that certainty will never be available.
J. Bimson

*Further reading*
S. Applebaum and A. Segal, 'Gerasa', *NEAEHL* II, pp. 470–479
U. Wagner-Lux, *ADAJ* 24, 1980, pp. 157–161
*ADAJ* 28, 1984, pp. 87–90
V. Tzaferis, *BARev* 15/2, 1989, pp. 44–51
G. Franz, *ABR* [= *Archaeology and Biblical Research*] 4/4, 1991, pp. 111–121

**GALATIA. 1.** The ancient ethnic kingdom of Galatia located in the north of the great inner plateau of Asia Minor, including a large portion of the valley of the Halys river.

A great population explosion in central Europe brought Gauls into this area during the 3rd century BC. Although never in the majority, the Gauls gained the upper hand and ruled over the more numerous tribes of Phrygians and Cappadocians.

Ultimately the Gauls separated into three tribes, each inhabiting a separate area: the Trokmi settled in the east which bordered on Cappadocia and Pontus, with Tavium as their capital; the Tolistobogii inhabited the west bordering on Phrygia and Bithynia, with Pessinus as their chief town; and the Tektosages settled in the central area with Ancyra as their principal city.

**2.** The Roman province of Galatia. In 64 BC Galatia became a client of the Romans and, after the death of Amyntas, its last king, was given full status as a Roman province (25 BC). The new province of Galatia included not only the old ethnic territory but also parts of Pontus, Phrygia, Lycaonia, Pisidia, Paphlagonia and Isauria.

Within the provincial Galatia we the towns which the apostle Paul evangelized on his first missionary journey, namely Antioch, Iconium, Lystra and Derbe (Acts 13–14). Th latter two cities were Roman colonies, and the former two had been Romanized by the emperor Claudius. Large numbers of Roman Greeks and Jews were attracted to these population centres because their strategic geographical locatic

*The meaning of 'Galatia'*
A particularly difficult question arises out of Paul's use of the word 'Galatia' in the Epistle to the Galatians (1:2). Does Paul use the term in its geographical sense, *i.e.*, denote the ancient ethnic kingdom of Galatia, or in its political sense, t denote the Roman province by tha name? New Testament scholars ar almost evenly divided on this question.

It is clear from the account in Ac 13–14 that Paul visited southern Galatia and established churches there. Did he ever conduct a missic in northern Galatia? Two texts especially have been used to suppo such a ministry. The first (Acts 16: reads: 'And they went through the region of Phrygia and Galatia. . . .' Northern Galatian proponents understand 'Phrygia' here to be the territory in which Antioch and Iconium were located, whereas 'Galatia' refers to the geographical or ethnic kingdom by that name. Ramsay, however, takes the phras *tēn Phrygian kai Galatikēn chōran* be a composite term describing a single area – the Phrygian-Galatic region. The word *chōra*, 'territory', was the official word used to describe one of the *regiones* into which Roman provinces were divided. Part of the old kingdom of Phrygia belonged to the Roman province of Galatia and another pa belonged to the province of Asia. Thus Acts 16:6 refers to the parts c Phrygia which had been incorporated into the Roman province of Galatia.

This interpretation is supported by the following statement in the Acts account, 'having been forbidden by the Holy Spirit to spea the word in Asia'. The plan of the missionary party apparently was to strike out directly in a westerly direction from Antioch of Pisidia, which would have taken them into the province of Asia. Instead they

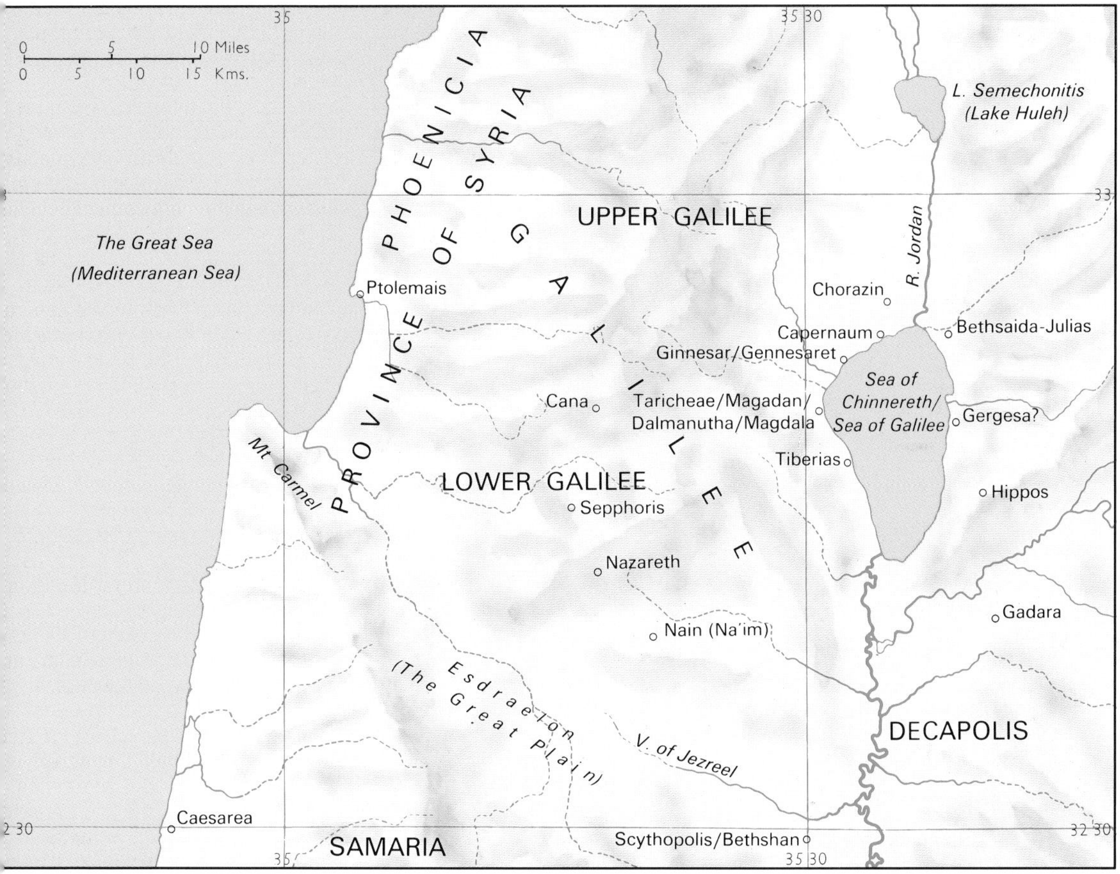


New Testament Galilee, the scene of Christ's childhood and early ministry.

ent north towards Bithynia, ossing only a part of Asia.

The other passage is Acts 18:23. ere the order of the words is versed: '. . . and went from place to ace through the region of Galatia nd Phrygia, strengthening all the isciples'. The 'region of Galatia' ere is probably 'Galatic Lycaonia, ɔ called to distinguish it from astern Lycaonia, which lay, not in e province of Galatia, but in the rritory of King Antiochus' (F. F. ruce, *The Book of the Acts*, 1954, 380). 'Phrygia' then would robably include both Galatic and siatic Phrygia, since on this ccasion there was no prohibition to revent Paul preaching the word in sia.

In neither of these passages in cts does there seem to be any good ason to suppose that Galatia eans northern Galatia. It is oubtful that Paul ever visited the ncient kingdom to the north, much ss that he conducted an extensive ission there.

There are three other occurrences 'Galatia' in the New Testament. 2 imothy 4:10 (which has the variant Gaul') and 1 Peter 1:1 are almost ertain references to the Roman rovince, while a decision on 1 orinthians 16:1, 'the churches of Galatia', will depend on one's view of the passages discussed above.

W. W. Wessel

*Further reading*

W. M. Ramsay, *An Historical Commentary on St. Paul's Epistle to the Galatians*, 1899, *passim*

——, *SPT*, pp. 89–151, 178–193

——, *The Church in the Roman Empire*, 3rd edition, 1894, pp. 74–111

*HDB*

*HDAC*

*IDB*

K. Lake, *BC* 5, 1933, pp. 231ff.

G. H. C. Macgregor, *IB* 9, 1954, pp. 213f., 247, 252

R. T. Stamm, *IB* 10, 1953, pp. 435ff.

S. Mitchell, 'Population and Land in Roman Galatia', *ANRW* II.7.2, 1980, pp. 1053–1081

C. J. Hemer, 'The Galatian Question', *The Book of Acts in the Setting of Hellenistic History*, 1989, ch. 7

**GALEED** (Hebrew *gal'ēḏ*, 'witness pile'). The name given to the cairn erected by Jacob and Laban as a memorial to their covenant made in northern Transjordan (Genesis 31:47–48). By Laban it was given the equivalent Aramaic name *Yegar-sahadutha*.

Documents of the earlier 2nd millennium BC reveal a great mixture of ethnic groups in northern Mesopotamia. It is quite possible that some Aramaeans were included among them and that their dialect had been adopted by other Semitic groups. Specific evidence of Aramaeans in this area at this date is not yet available (see also *ARAM).

A. R. Millard

**GALILEE** (Hebrew *gālîl*, 'ring, circle', hence a 'district, region'). The regional name of part of northern Palestine, which was the scene of Christ's boyhood and early ministry.

The origin of the name as applied here is uncertain. It occurs occasionally in the Old Testament (*e.g.* Joshua 20:7; 1 Kings 9:11), and notably in Isaiah 9:1. The latter reference probably recalls the region's history: it originally formed part of the lands allocated to the twelve tribes, but, owing to the pressure from peoples farther north, its Jewish population found themselves in a kind of northern salient, surrounded on three sides by non-Jewish populations – 'the nations'. Under the Maccabees, the Gentile influence upon the Jews became so strong that the latter were actually withdrawn to the south for half a century. Thus Galilee had to be recolonized, and this fact,

The Sea of Galilee.

together with its diversity of population, contributed to the contempt felt for the Galileans by the southern Jews (John 7:52).

*Physical features*
Exact demarcation of the Galilee region is difficult, except in terms of the provincial boundaries of the Roman empire. The name was evidently applied to the northern marchlands of Israel, the location of which varied from time to time. In the time of Christ, however, the province of Galilee formed a rectangular territory some 70 kilometres from north to south, and 40 kilometres from east to west, bordered on the east by the Jordan and the Sea of *Galilee, and cut off from the Mediterranean by the southern extension of Syro-Phoenicia down the coastal plain.

Thus defined, Galilee consists essentially of an upland area, bordered on all sides save the north by plains – the coastlands, the plain of Esdraelon and the Jordan Rift. It is, in fact, the southern end of the mountains of Lebanon, and the land surface falls, in two steps, from north to south across the area.

The higher 'step' forms Upper Galilee, much of which is at 1,000 metres above sea-level; in New Testament times it was a forested and thinly inhabited hill-country. The lower 'step' forms Lower Galilee, 450–600 metres above sea-level, but falling steeply to more than 180 metres below sea-level at the Sea of Galilee.

It is to this area of Lower Galilee that most of the gospel narrative refers. Well watered by streams flowing from the northern mountains, and possessing considerable stretches of fertile land in the limestone basins among its hills, it was an area of dense and prosperous settlement. It exported olive oil and cereals, and fish from the lake.

*Politics and people*
'Outside the main stream of Israelite life in Old Testament times, Galilee came into its own in the New Testament' (D. Baly, *The Geography of the Bible*, 1957, p. 190). The Roman region was governed successively by Herod the Great (died 4 BC), Herod Antipas and Herod Agrippa. Cut off from Judaea – at least in Jewish eyes – by the territory of Samaria, Galilee nevertheless formed an integral part of 'the land', and the Galileans had, in fact, resisted the Romans even more doggedly than the southern Jews. In the time of Christ the relationship between the two groups is well described as having been that of 'England and Scotland soon after the Union' (G. A. Smith, *Historical Geography of the Holy Land*, 25th edition, 1931, p. 425).

This, then, was the region in which Christ grew up – at Nazareth, in the limestone hills of Lower Galilee. Thanks to its position, it was traversed by several major routeways of the empire, and was therefore far from being a rural backwater. Its agriculture, fisheries and commerce provided him with his cultural background, and are reflected in his parables and teaching. Its people provided him with his first disciples, and its dense scattering of settlements formed their first mission field.

*Galilee today*
Today, Galilee and the plain of Esdraelon form the core area of northern Israel, but its modern inhabitants have the task of rehabilitating an area which has lost much of the prosperity it enjoyed in New Testament days. Its forests have been largely replaced by *maquis*, the characteristic scrub of the Mediterranean, and many of its towns and villages, places which Christ knew and visited, have disappeared from the map, leaving hardly a trace behind them.

J. H. Paterson

*Further reading*

G. A. Smith, *The Historical Geography of the Holy Land*, 25th edition, 1931, pp. 413–436
Z. Gal and M. Aviam in *NEAEHL* II, pp. 450–458
D. Baly, *The Geography of the Bible*, 1957

**GALILEE, SEA OF.** A lake in the region of Galilee, also referred to, in the Old Testament, as the 'sea of *Chinnereth' (Numbers 34:11) or Chinneroth (Joshua 12:3), and in the New Testament as the 'lake of Gennesaret' (Luke 5:1) and the 'Sea of Tiberias' (John 21:1). Its modern Hebrew name is Yam Kinneret.

The lake is some 21 kilometres long and up to 11 kilometres broad, and it lies at 211 metres below sea-level. The river Jordan flows through it from north to south; its waters are therefore sweet – unlike those of the Dead Sea – and its fisheries, so prominent in the New Testament narrative, were famous throughout the Roman empire and produced a flourishing export trade. On the other hand, the position of the lake, in the depths of the Jordan Rift and surrounded by hills, renders it liable to atmospheric downdraughts and sudden storms.

The lake is bordered by a plain of varying width; in general, the slopes on the eastern side are abrupt (Mark 5:13), and are somewhat gentler on the west. To the north and south are the river plains of the Jordan as it enters and leaves the lake.

*Lakeside towns*
The shores of the lake were the site of towns – Capernaum, Bethsaida, *etc.* – where much of Christ's ministry was carried out. In his time they formed a flourishing, and almost continuous, belt of settlement around the lake, and communicated and traded across it with each other. Today, only *Tiberias remains as a town – even

The town of Tiberias viewed from the shore of the Sea of Galilee.

the sites of several other former towns are uncertain – and changed patterns of commerce have robbed the lake of its focal importance in the life of the region.

J. H. Paterson

*Further reading*

G. A. Smith, *The Historical Geography of the Holy Land*, 25th edition, 1931, pp. 437–463

**GARDEN OF EDEN.** See *EDEN, GARDEN OF.

**GARDEN TOMB.** See *CALVARY.

**GATH.** One of the five principal Philistine cities, and formerly occupied by the Anakim (Joshua 11:22). The gentilic from the name *gaṯ* was *gittî* or *gittîm* (Joshua 13:3), and this accounts for the 'Gittite' of the English versions. When the Philistines captured the ark and it brought ill fortune to Ashdod it was moved to Gath, where the people were struck with bubonic plague, so it was moved on to Ekron (1 Samuel 5:6–10; 6:17).

Gath was famous as the home of Goliath (1 Samuel 17), whom David killed. David later feigned madness to avoid retribution at the hands of Achish, king of Gath, when fleeing from Saul (1 Samuel 21:10–15), but subsequently took service under Achish, and lived for more than a year in his territory (1 Samuel 27). When David's fortunes revived, and later during Absalom's rebellion, after he had added Gath to his dominions (1 Chronicles 18:1), he had Gittite friends in his retinue (2 Samuel 6:10–11; 15:19–21; 18:2) and a Gittite contingent among his mercenaries (2 Samuel 15:18).

Another interesting Gittite is mentioned in 2 Samuel 21:20 (1 Chronicles 20:6). He was very tall and had six digits on each extremity. Though Achish is still spoken of as king of Gath (1 Kings 2:39–41), the city was probably subservient to David, and evidently continued subject to Judah in the time of Rehoboam, who fortified it (2 Chronicles 11:8).

It was captured by Hazael of Damascus in the late 9th century (2 Kings 12:17), and may have regained its independence by the time Uzziah broke down its wall when he campaigned in Philistia (2 Chronicles 26:6). Soon afterwards Amos describes it as belonging to the Philistines (6:2), so it may have been a Philistine enclave, in loose vassalage, in the territory of Judah. Gath was besieged and conquered by Sargon of Assyria in the late 8th century.

The site has not been identified beyond doubt. The most likely candidate is the mound of Tell eṣ-Ṣafi in the Shephelah, but certainty must await further investigation.

T. C. Mitchell

*Further reading*

E. K. Vogel, *HUCA* 42, 1971, p. 88; 52, 1981, p.11; 58, 1987, p.17
K. A. Kitchen, *POTT*, pp. 62ff.
E. Stern, 'Tel Zafit', *NEAEHL* IV, pp. 1522–1524
G. E. Wright, *BA* 29, 1966, pp. 78–86
*LOB*, p. 271

**GATH-HEPHER** (Hebrew *gaṯ-haḥēper*, 'winepress of digging'). The rendering Gittah-hepher of Joshua 19:13 in the AV arose through a misunderstanding of the *he locale*. A town on the border of Zebulon and Naphtali (Joshua 19:13), it was the birthplace of the prophet Jonah (2 Kings 14:25). It has been identified with Khirbet ez-Zurra' and nearby el-Meshhed, 5 kilometres north-east of Nazareth. Ancient and continuous tradition indicated this as the birthplace and tomb of the prophet. Jerome in the 4th century AD said that Jonah's tomb was about 3 kilometres from Sepphoris, which would coincide with Gath-hepher.

M. A. MacLeod

**GAZA** (Hebrew *'azzâ*, Septuagint *Gaza*). One of the five principal

**Proposed locations for Gath and Gaza, two of the five principal Philistine cities.**

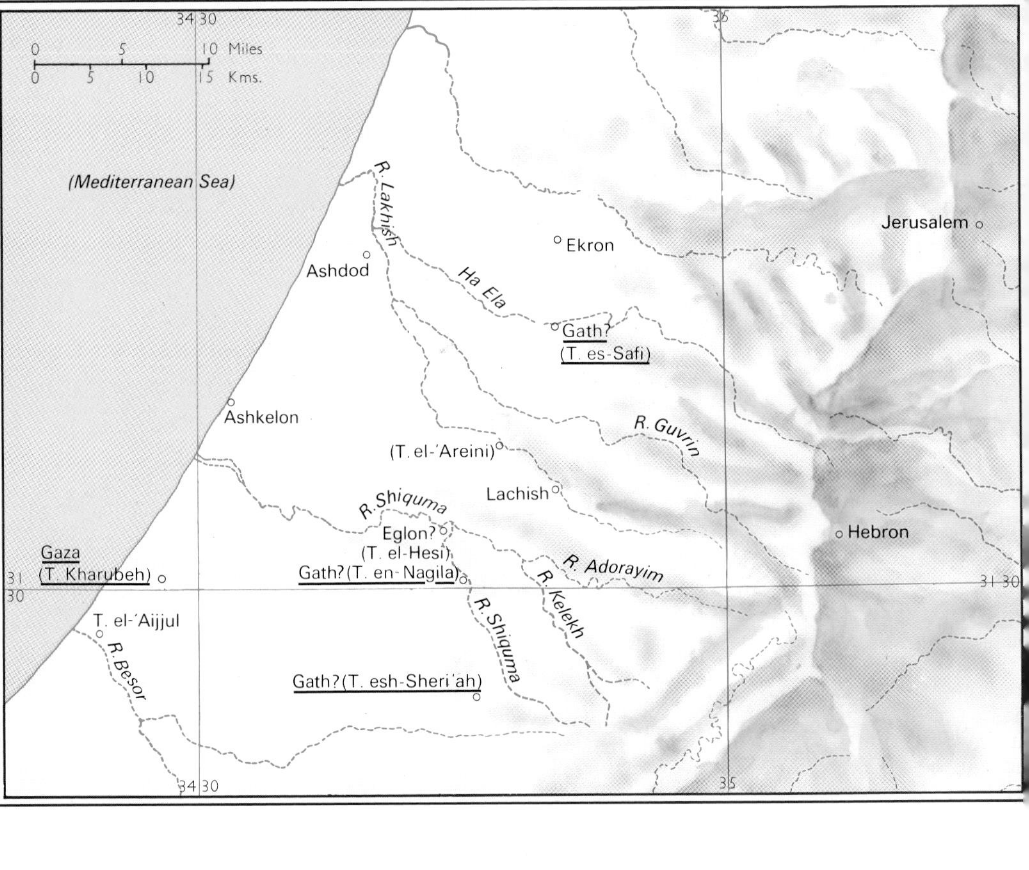

ilistine cities. Originally inhabited the Arvim, driven out by the phtorim (see also *CAPHTO; uteronomy 2:23), it was considered mark the southern limit of Canaan the point on the coast where it s situated (Genesis 10:19).

*story*
shua conquered Gaza (Joshua :41) and found that some Anakim nained there (Joshua 11:21–22); city was lost to Israel during his etime (Joshua 13:3). Judah, to om it was allotted (Joshua 15:47), aptured the town (Judges 1:18; ough some hold that this refers to same campaign as Joshua 10:41). n the period of the Judges Samson nsorted with a harlot of Gaza in nnection with which a description the city gate is given (Judges :1–3). Israel's hold over Gaza must ve been lost again at this period, when the Philistines finally ptured Samson they imprisoned n there, and it was there that he ade sport' for them, and dislodged pillars of the house, killing many them (Judges 16:21–31). It has en pointed out that the description Samson 'making sport' in front of a lared building with spectators on roof is reminiscent of some of the atures of Cretan civilization, and s is to be expected in view of the gins of the *Philistines.

At the time of the Philistine pture of the ark, Gaza with the er cities suffered from bubonic gue and made an offering of an erod and a mouse of gold to avert 1 Samuel 6:17).

The city occupied an important sition on the trade routes from ypt to western Asia, and from the century it is frequently ntioned among Assyrian nquests. Tiglath-pileser III ptured it (*Ḫa-az-zu-tu*) in 734 BC, rhaps at the request of Jehoahaz Judah, the ruler, Hanno, fleeing to ypt, and Tiglath-pileser set up an age of himself in the palace. Sargon had to repeat the action in 2 BC, for Hanno had returned to za in support of a rebellion led by math. Hanno was taken prisoner Assyria. The city remained faithful Assyria, for Sennacherib, when he oceeded against Hezekiah in rusalem, gave some of the territory ken from Judah to Ṣillibel, king of za, and Esarhaddon put a strain this loyalty when he laid heavy bute on him and twenty other ngs of the Hittite country.

In the time of Jeremiah the city s captured by Egypt (Jeremiah :1).

Gaza was taken by Alexander the Great in 332 BC after a 5-month siege, and finally desolated – as prophesied by Amos (1:6–7), Zephaniah (2:4) and Zechariah (9:5) – by Alexander Jannaeus in 96 BC.

*Excavations*
The site of ancient Gaza, Tell Kharubeh (Ḥarube), lies in the modern city. Small excavations showed that it was occupied in the Late Bronze and Iron Ages, and pieces of Philistine pottery were found.

Various remains show the importance of the place in Hellenistic and Roman times. Gabinius, the proconsul, rebuilt it in 57 BC on a new site to the south of the old, nearer the sea. It was presumably to distinguish the old abandoned site from this that the angel, who wanted Philip to go to the old site, qualified the name Gaza with the phrase 'this is a desert road' (*hautē estin erēmos*, Acts 8:26).

At Tell el-'Ajjul, 6 kilometres to the south-west, Flinders Petrie found extensive cemeteries and a town that flourished during the 2nd millennium BC. He mistakenly considered this to be the site of Gaza, but it is probably Old Testament Sharuhen. Numerous pieces of gold jewellery were discovered in tombs and buildings of *c.* 1400 BC. Nearby later burials have been uncovered containing so-called Philistine clay-coffins.

T. C. Mitchell, A. R. Millard

*Further reading*
J. Garstang, *Joshua-Judges*, 1931, pp. 375f.
A. Ovadiah in *NEAEHL* II, pp. 464–467

**GAZARA.** See *GEZER.

**GEBA** (Hebrew *geḇa'*, 'a hill'). A town belonging to Benjamin, 11 kilometres north of Jerusalem and 5 kilometres from Gibeah, from which it is to be distinguished; compare Joshua 18:24, 28 and Isaiah 10:29. It was assigned to the Levites under Joshua (Joshua 21:17; 1 Chronicles 6:60). It was in the descent from here that Jonathan and his armour-bearer revealed themselves to the Philistines during their daring attack (1 Samuel 14:1ff.). In the days of Asa, king of Judah, it was fortified, and then regarded as the northern limit of Judah; it replaced the name of Dan in the saying 'from Dan to Beersheba' (2 Kings 23:8). It remained prominent after the Exile (Nehemiah 11:31; 12:29). The modern town of Jeba stands on the same site.

M. A. MacLeod

**GEBAL. 1.** A Canaanite and Phoenician port whose ruins lie at Jebeil, 40 kilometres north of Beirut. Its name, western Semitic *g$^{e}$ḇal*, Akkadian *gubla*, Egyptian *kpn*, means 'hill, bluff'. The Greek name Byblos may involve a phonetic shift *g-b*, or imply that it was the place where Greeks first saw papyrus (Greek *byblos*) imported from Egypt as writing material.

*Excavations*
Excavations, begun in 1919 by M. Dunand, have revealed a city that flourished from Neolithic times to the Crusades. By the mid-3rd millennium BC it was a centre for exporting cedar wood to Egypt, receiving Egyptian luxury goods in exchange. Strong stone ramparts guarded the city. Inside were temples, houses and tombs.

At the end of the 3rd millennium it was sacked, but soon recovered. One temple was devoted to the city's patron goddess (Baalat Gebal), another was a memorial shrine filled with obelisks commemorating the dead, originally probably plastered and inscribed. Dozens of jars containing bronze weapons, jewellery and figures of gods were buried around the temples as offerings.

Tombs of Byblian kings were furnished with Egyptian and stone vessels of about 1800 BC. From this time scribes at Byblos, trained to write in Egyptian, seem to have invented a simpler script, the Byblos hieroglyphic, a syllabary of about eighty signs known from texts engraved on stone slabs and copper plates.

It may have been here that the alphabet arose. Certainly it was used here fully developed by about 1000 BC, the date of the stone coffin of King Ahiram which bears the longest early alphabetic inscription. Other texts from *c.* 900 BC show continuing links with Egypt.

Byblos declined as the power of Tyre and Sidon grew.

*In the Old Testament*
Joshua 13:5 includes Gebal as part of the Promised Land then unconquered, and in fact Israel never ruled it. Solomon hired masons there (1 Kings 5:18), and its skilled shipbuilders are mentioned in Ezekiel 27:9. The Egyptian story of Wen-amun describes the city about 1100 BC (*ANET*, pp. 25–29).

**2.** A mountain region in Transjordan whose inhabitants allied with Israel's other neighbours against her (Psalm 83:7).
A. R. Millard

*Further reading*
M. Dunand, *Fouilles de Byblos*, 1937–
N. Jidejian, *Byblos through the Ages*, 1968

**GEDER.** A southern Canaanite town (Joshua 12:13). The Septuagint (B) reads *asei*, and other minuscules suggest 's' as the second letter; *Goshen* may be the correct reading. (Joshua 11:16 refers to an area called Goshen in the south of Judah; this is not to be confused with *Goshen in Egypt, Genesis 47:6, *etc.*). Y. Aharoni (in *LOB*, p. 231) suggests Gerar.
J. D. Douglas

**GEDERAH** (Hebrew *g$^{e}$ḏērâh*, 'wall', 'defence'). **1.** In the Shephelah (Joshua 15:36); probably Khirbet Judraya, on the northern side of the Vale of Elah, opposite *Socoh (see F. M. Cross, J. T. Milik, *JBL* 75, 1976, pp. 215, 217). Abel, in his *Géographie* 2, p. 329, points to Khirbet Sheikh Jadir, 6 kilometres north-north-west of Zorah (with Khirbet Hadatha for Adithaim another 8 kilometres north-north-east); but this might stretch the district too far.
**2.** 'The Potteries' of the Monarchy (1 Chronicles 4:23; AV 'hedges'); perhaps Khirbet Judeideh on a ridge between Tel Goded (*Moresheth-Gath?) and *Mareshah (see Albright in *JPOS* 5, 1925, pp. 50ff.).
**3.** In Benjamin (1 Chronicles 12:4); possibly Judeira, north-east of Gibeon, or Khirbet Juderia, 10 kilometres farther west.
J. P. U. Lilley

**GEDEROTH** (Hebrew *g$^{e}$ḏērôṯ*). A town in the Lachish district of Judah (Joshua 15:41; 2 Chronicles 28:18). Abel (following Eusebius) suggested a site near modern Gederah, but this is too far west and out of context (see Noth's commentary on Joshua 15:41, and *GTT*, p. 147).
J. P. U. Lilley

**GEDEROTHAIM** (Hebrew *g$^{e}$ḏērōṯaim*). May be a variant of *Gederah (Joshua 15:36); the count is correct without it. The Septuagint ('its penfolds') read as *giḏrōṯêhâh*.
J. P. U. Lilley

**GEDOR** (Hebrew *g$^{e}$ḏôr*). **1.** A town in the hills of Judah (Joshua 15:58, and perhaps 1 Chronicles 4:4); Khirbet Jedur, on the edge of the central ridge 2 kilometres north-west of Beit Ummar; possibly the Beth-gader of 1 Chronicles 2:51 (*GTT*, p. 155).
**2.** In the Negeb, near *Socoh and *Zanoah **2** (1 Chronicles 4:18). The 'outskirts of Gedor', RSV 'entrance' (1 Chronicles 4:39), may be the outfall of the Nahal Hevron, but the context indicates an area further south-east. The Septuagint has 'Gerar'; see *LOB*, pp. 218 and 388.
**3.** In Benjamin (1 Chronicles 12:7), perhaps *Gederah **3**, as in verse 4.
J. P. U. Lilley

**GELILOTH.** Perhaps means 'circuit, circle' (of stones), see *Gilgal. The name only appears in Joshua 18:17, where it refers to a place on the border between Judah and Benjamin, in terms almost identical with those used of Gilgal (Joshua 15:7). As Geliloth and Gilgal have more or less the same meaning, both derived from Hebrew *gālal*, 'to roll', they may be variant-names for one and the same place. J. Simons thinks of Geliloth as a small region near Jericho (see *GTT*, p.173, section 326). Y. Aharoni sought it near Tal'at ed-Damm, south of the Wadi Qilt (see *LOB*, p. 255).
K. A. Kitchen

**GEOGRAPHY OF PALESTINE.** See *PALESTINE.

**GEOLOGY OF PALESTINE.** See *PALESTINE.

**GERAR** (Hebrew *g$^{e}$rār*, 'circle'). An ancient city south of Gaza (Genesis 10:19) in the foothills of the Judaean mountains.
Both Abraham (Genesis 20–21) and Isaac (Genesis 26) stayed in Gerar, digging wells, and had cordial relations with Abimelech its king, though Isaac quarrelled with him at one stage. The city lay in the 'land of the *Philistines' (*'ereṣ p$^{e}$lištîm*, Genesis 21:32 and 34; see also 26:1 and 8), not necessarily an anachronistic designation. In the early 9th century BC it was the scene of a great victory by Asa of Judah over the invading Ethiopian army of Zerah (2 Chronicles 14:13–14).
The site of Gerar was identified with modern Tell Jemmeh by W. M. Flinders Petrie, but following a survey by D. Alon, the site of Tell Abu Hureira (Tel Haror), a mound about 18 kilometres south-east of Gaza, in the Wadi Eš-Šari'ah has been proposed as more likely. As no pre-Iron-Age remains had been found near it, this site had hitherto been believed to be a natural hill, bu Alon's survey showed that it was first inhabited in Chalcolithic time and continued in occupation throug every period of the Bronze and Iron Ages.
Excavations by E. D. Oren from 1982 onwards have confirmed this picture. During the 18th-16th centuries BC the Middle Bronze Ag city was one of the largest in southern Canaan, covering some 1 hectares.
T. C. Mitchell

*Further reading*
Y. Aharoni, 'The Land of Gerar', *IE* 6, 1956, pp. 26–32
F. M. Cross Jr. and G. E. Wright, *JE* 75, 1956, pp. 212–213
W. F. Albright, *BASOR* 163, 1961, p. 48
E. D. Oren and M. A. Morrison, *BASOR Sup.* 24, 1986, pp. 57–87
*LOB*, p. 435

**GERASENES, GERASA.** See *GADARENES.

**GERGESENES, GERGESA.** See *GADARENES.

**GERIZIM.** The more southerly of t two mountains which overshadow the modern town of Nablus, 4 kilometres north-west of ancient Shechem, called Jebel eṭ-Ṭôr in Arabic. It has been called the mou of blessing, because here the blessings for obedience were pronounced at the solemn assemb of Israel described in Joshua 8:30–35 (see also *EBAL, MOUNT).
A ledge halfway to the top is popularly called 'Jotham's pulpit', from which he once addressed the men of Shechem (Judges 9:7).
On the summit are the bare ruin of a Christian church of the 5th century. Still earlier there stood there a temple of Jupiter, to which staircase of 300 steps led up, as shown on ancient coins found in Nablus.

*The Samaritan tradition*
Gerizim remains the sacred mount the Samaritans; for they have 'worshipped on this mountain' (Joh 4:20) for countless generations, ascending it to keep the feasts of Passover, Pentecost and Tabernacles. According to Samaritan tradition, Gerizim is Mount Moriah (Genesis 22:2) and the place wher God chose to place his name (Deuteronomy 12:5). Accordingly i was here that the Samaritan templ was built with Persian authorizatic in the 4th century BC – the temple

hich was demolished by John yrcanus when he captured 1echem and the surrounding area 128 BC.

A large building complex xcavated at Tell er-Râs, the orthernmost peak of Mount erizim, has been interpreted as the emains of the Samaritan temple. he temple of Jupiter was erected on e ruins of this temple in the 2nd entury AD by the Emperor Hadrian.

T. Manley, F. F. Bruce

*urther reading*

Robertson, *The Old Testament roblem*, 1950, pp. 157–171

. E. Wright, *Shechem*, 1965, p. 170–184

J. Bull, *BASOR* 190, 1968, pp. 4–19

Magen in *NEAEHL* II, pp. 484–492

**ESHUR, GESHURITES. 1.** In the st of David's sons in 2 Samuel 3:3 e third is 'Absalom the son of aacah the daughter of Talmai king Geshur', a city in Syria (2 Samuel 5:8; 1 Chronicles 3:2), north-east of ashan (Joshua 12:5; 13:11, 13).

It was this city to which Absalom ed after the murder of his brother mnon (2 Samuel 13:37) and to hich David sent Joab to bring him ack (14:23). The young man eturned to Jerusalem, but only to ot rebellion against his father (2 amuel 14:32; 15:8).

**2.** Another group called eshurites' is attested in Joshua 3:2 and 1 Samuel 27:8 as resident in e Negeb, near the Egyptian border.

F. Bruce

**ETHSEMANE** (from the Aramaic at šemen, 'an oil press'). A garden *ēpos*, John 18:1), east of Jerusalem eyond the Kidron valley and near e Mount of Olives (Matthew 26:30).

Gethsemane was a favourite retreat frequented by Christ and his disciples, which became the scene of the agony, Judas' betrayal and the arrest (Mark 14:32–52). It should probably be contrasted with Eden, as the garden where the second Adam prevailed over temptation. Christ's action in Gethsemane (Luke 22:41) gave rise to the Christian custom of kneeling for prayer.

*The site of Gethsemane*

The traditional Latin site lies east of the Jericho road-bridge over the Kidron, and contains olive trees said to date back to the 7th century AD. It measures 50 metres square, and was enclosed with a wall by the Franciscans in 1848. It corresponds to the position located by Eusebius and Jerome, but is regarded by Thomson, Robinson and Barclay as too small and too near the road.

The Greeks enclosed an adjacent site to the north. There is a broad area of land north-east of the Church of St Mary where larger, more secluded gardens were put at the disposal of pilgrims, and Thomson locates the genuine site here. The original trees were cut down by Titus (Josephus *Jewish War* 5.523).

D. H. Tongue

*Further reading*

W. M. Thomson, *The Land and the Book*, 1888, p. 634

G. Dalman, *Sacred Sites and Ways*, 1935, pp. 321ff.

J. Wilkinson, *Jerusalem as Jesus Knew It*, 1978, pp. 125–131

**GEZER.** One of the chief cities of pre-Roman Palestine from at least 1800 BC. It is strategically located on the road from Jerusalem to Joppa on the most northerly ridge of the Shephelah, some 12 kilometres from the main highway between Egypt and Mesopotamia.

Strong Canaanite defences were overthrown by Pharaoh Thutmosis III *c.* 1468 BC. Egypt then controlled the city. Ten el-*Amarna letters from Gezer show the city vacillated but finally remained loyal to Egypt in the 14th century. At the time of the Hebrew conquest its Canaanite king, Horam, tried to help Lachish but was defeated (Joshua 10:33; 12:12); Gezer however was not taken by the Israelites (Joshua 16:10; Judges 1:29). Even so, the city was included in Ephraim's territory as a levitical city (Joshua 21:21).

Soon after the Conquest Pharaoh Merenptah claims, on his stele, to have recaptured it. Archaeological evidence indicates that after 1200 BC the Philistines controlled the city, possibly with Egyptian approval, which may explain David's battles in this region (2 Samuel 5:25).

Gezer became an Israelite possession when the Egyptian pharaoh gave it to his daughter on her marriage to Solomon, who rebuilt the city and its defences (1 Kings 9:15–17). Excavations (1964–73) have uncovered a typical Solomonic gate and defences. This area has also yielded great quantities of calcined stone, evidence of Pharaoh Shishak's assault on Judah *c.* 918 BC (1 Kings 14:25ff.). Questions about the interpretation of the site led to a further dig in 1984.

There are also indications of later occupations – Persian, Seleucid and Maccabean. Gezer (Gazara) figures frequently in the Maccabean struggle. Two interesting archaeological finds are the Gezer Calendar (an inscription from the 10th century BC) and a ten monolith 'High Place' (*c.* 1600 BC onwards).

G. G. Garner

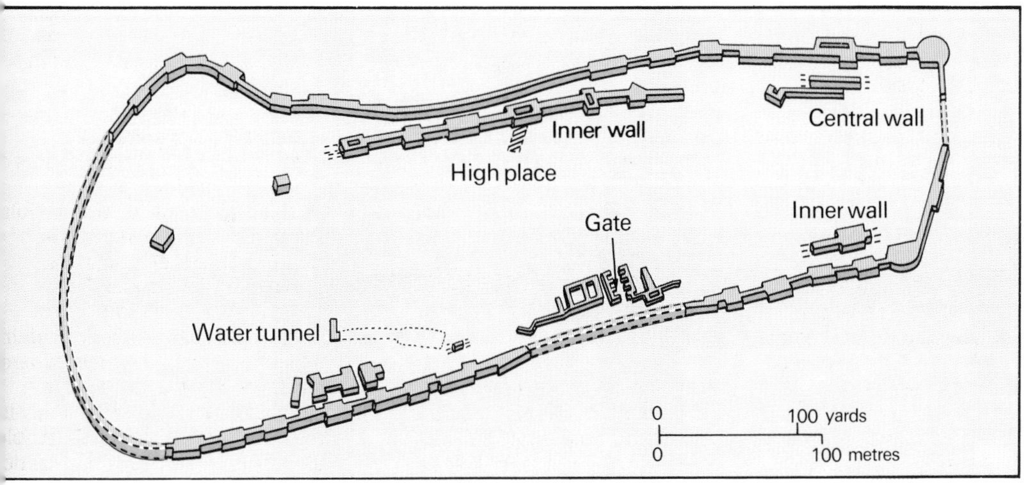


Plan of Gezer.

*Further reading*
R. A. S. Macalister, *The Excavations of Gezer*, 1912
W. G. Dever (ed.) *Gezer* 1, 2 (and following vols.), 1970, 1974
W. G. Dever in *NEAEHL* II, pp. 496–506
*BASOR* 262, 1986, pp. 9–34; 277/278, 1990, pp. 109–130
*BA* 47, 1984, pp. 206–218

**GIBBETHON** (Hebrew *gibb*$^{e}$*ṯôn*, 'mound'). A city in Dan (Joshua 19:44), given to the Kohathite Levites (Joshua 21:23). For some time it was in Philistine hands and was the scene of battles between them and northern Israel. Here Baasha slew Nadab (1 Kings 15:27) and, about 26 years later, Omri was acclaimed king (1 Kings 16:17). Sargon of Assyria depicted the conquest of the city on the walls of his palace, amongst the triumphs of his 712 BC campaign (see P. E. Botta, *Monument de Ninive*, 1849, 2, plate 89).

Probably it is modern Tell el-Melât, west of Gezer; trial probes have revealed evidence of occupation from the Early Bronze Age to the Byzantine period.
G. W. Grogan

**GIBEAH** (Hebrew *giḇ*$^{e}$*'â, giḇ*$^{e}$*aṯ*). A noun meaning 'hill', and often so used in the Bible (*e.g.* 2 Samuel 2:25 and probably in 2 Samuel 6:3 with RV and RSV), but also used as a place-name. Owing to its similarity in form with the place-name *geḇa'* (see also *GEBA), these two are sometimes confused (*e.g.* Judges 20:10).

**1.** A city in the hill country of Judah (Joshua 15:57), possibly to be identified with modern el-Jeba' near Bethlehem.

**2.** A city in Benjamin (Joshua 18:28), evidently north of Jerusalem (Isaiah 10:29). As a result of a crime committed by the inhabitants, the city was destroyed in the period of the Judges (Judges 19–20; see Hosea 9:9; 10:9).

It was famous as the birthplace of Saul (1 Samuel 10:26), *giḇ*$^{e}$*'aṯ šā'ûl*, 'Gibeah of Saul' (1 Samuel 11:4), and it served as his residence while he was king (1 Samuel 13–15), and after David was anointed in his place (1 Samuel 22:6; 23:19; 26:1). When David was king it was necessary to allow the Gibeonites to hang up the bodies of seven of Saul's descendants on the walls of Gibeah to make amends for his slaughter of them (2 Samuel 21:6; Septuagint 'Gibeon').

Biblical Gibeah of Saul is almost certainly to be identified with the mound of Tell el-Ful, about 5 kilometres north of Jerusalem. The site was excavated by W. F. Albright in 1922–23 and 1933, with results that agreed with this identification. Further excavations were made by P. W. Lapp in 1964, bringing some changes to Albright's conclusions.

The situation of the place away from running water meant that it was not permanently occupied until the Iron Age, when rain-water cisterns came into common use in the hill country. The first small settlement belonged to the 12th century BC, perhaps being destroyed in the episode which Judges 19–20 relate. After an interval, a small fortress was erected and manned about 1025–950 BC, the time of Saul. Albright had restored its plan as a rectangle with a tower at each corner, but only one tower has been uncovered, and Lapp's work has shown that the plan is uncertain.

An iron plough-tip from this period was found, indicating the introduction of iron. There are signs that the fortress was pillaged and then abandoned for a few years, presumably at the death of Saul, but the site was soon reoccupied, possibly as an outpost in David's war with Ishbosheth. It must have lost its importance with David's conquest of the whole kingdom, however, and the excavations indicate that it lay deserted for about 2 centuries.

The fortress was rebuilt with a watchtower, possibly by Hezekiah, and destroyed soon after (see Isaiah 10:29), to be refortified in the 7th century BC with a casemate wall. After a destruction attributed to Nebuchadrezzar's forces, there was quite an extensive village on the site until about 500 BC.

A further period of abandonment ensued until the spread of a new village across the site in the Maccabean age. Thereafter there was sporadic occupation until the expulsion of all Jews from Jerusalem, when Gibeah presumably fell under the same ban because of its proximity to the city.

In a recent challenge to Albright's view, P. M. Arnold has revived the case for identifying Gibeah with Geba and locating it at modern Jeba.
T. C. Mitchell, A. R. Millard

*Further reading*
W. F. Albright, *AASOR* 4, 1924
L. A. Sinclair, 'An Archaeological Study of Gibeah', *AASOR* 34, 1960
P. W. Lapp, *BA* 28, 1965, pp.2–10
N. W. Lapp, *BASOR* 223, 1976, pp. 25–42
N. L. Lapp, 'Tell el-Fûl', *NEAEHL* II, pp. 445–448
P. M. Arnold, *Gibeah: The Search* [in] *a Biblical City*, JSOT Supp. 79, 199[0]

**GIBEON.** At the time of the Israelit[e] invasion of Canaan this was an important city inhabited by Hivite[s] (Joshua 9:17; Septuagint 'Horites' perhaps preferable) and apparentl[y] governed by a council of elders (Joshua 9:11; see 10:2).

Following the fall of Jericho and Ai, the Gibeonites tricked Joshua into making a treaty with them as vassals. They were reduced to menial service and cursed when their deceit was discovered. The Amorite kings of the southern hill-country attacked Gibeon for its defection to the Israelites, but Joshua led a force to aid his allies and, by means of a hailstorm and a miraculous extension of the daylight, routed the Amorites (Joshua 9–10; 11:19). The city was allotted to Benjamin and set apart f[or] the Levites (Joshua 18:25; 21:17).

During the struggle between David and the adherents of Ishbosheth the two sides met at Gibeon. Twelve warriors from eith[er] side were chosen for a contest, but each killed his opposite number an[d] only after a general mêlée were David's men victorious (2 Samuel 2:12–17).

At 'the great stone which is in Gibeon' Joab killed the dilatory Amasa (2 Samuel 20:8). This may have been merely a notable landmark, or it may have had some religious significance connected with the high place where the tabernacle and the altar of burnt-offering were, and where Solomon worshipped after his accession (1 Chronicles 16:39; 21:29; 2 Chronicles 1:3, 13; 1 King[s] 3:4–5). The 'Geba' of 2 Samuel 5:2[5] should probably be altered to 'Gibeon' in view of 1 Chronicles 14:16, Isaiah 28:21 and the Septuagint.

The Gibeonites still retained the treaty rights in David's time, so tha[t] the only way of removing the guilt incurred by Saul's slaughter of Gibeonites was to hand over seve[n] of his descendants for execution (2 Samuel 21:1–11). The close connection of Saul's family with Gibeon (1 Chronicles 8:29–30; 9:35–39) may well have made his deed appear all the worse.

Shishak of Egypt numbers Gibe[on] among the cities he captured (*ANE*[T] p. 242; compare 1 Kings 14:25). Th[e] assassins of Gedaliah, the govern[or] of Judah appointed by Nebuchadre[z]zar, were overtaken by the 'great

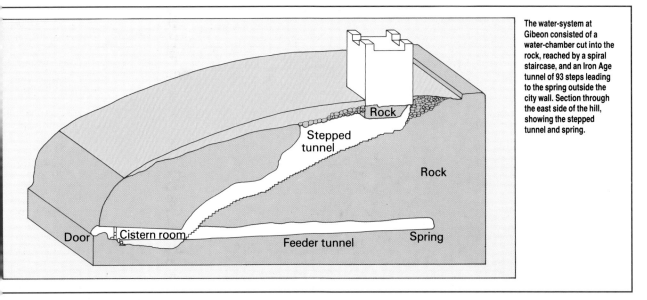

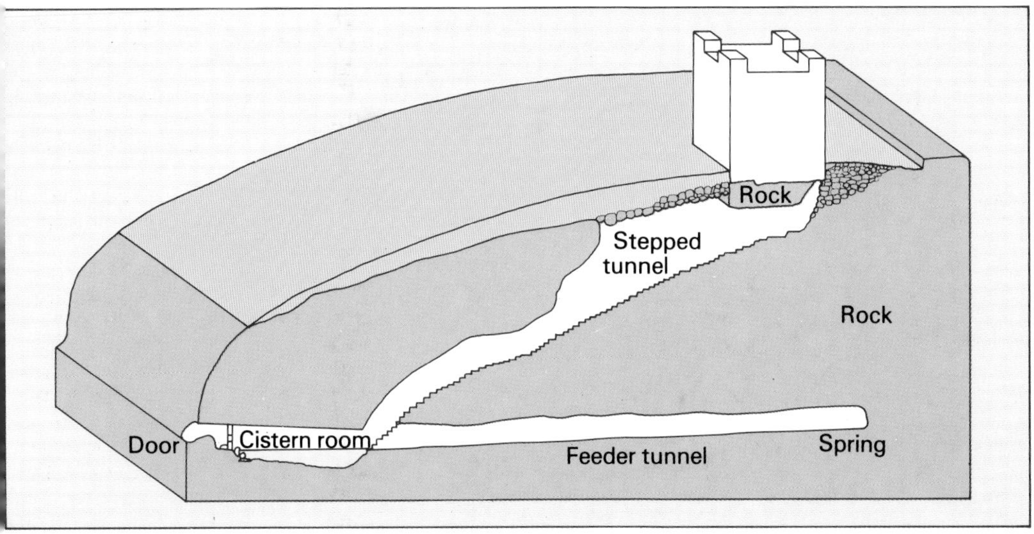


**The water-system at Gibeon consisted of a water-chamber cut into the rock, reached by a spiral staircase, and an Iron Age tunnel of 93 steps leading to the spring outside the city wall. Section through the east side of the hill, showing the stepped tunnel and spring.**

aters' of Gibeon and the prisoners ey had taken set free (Jeremiah :11–14). Gibeonites helped ehemiah to rebuild the walls of rusalem (Nehemiah 3:7).

*cavations*

cavations at el-Jib, some 9 ometres north of Jerusalem, tween 1956 and 1962 have vealed remains of cities of the rly and Middle II Bronze Age, and the Iron Age from its beginning to e Persian period. There was also a rge town during Roman times. No mains of a Late Bronze Age ttlement, which might be nsidered contemporary with shua, have been discovered, but rials of the time showed there had en life there.

Some time in the Early Iron Age a rge pit with a stairway descending ound it was dug to a depth of 11 etres in the rock. Steps led down a nnel a further 12 metres to a ater-chamber, perhaps the 'pool' of Samuel 2 and the 'waters' of remiah 41. It seems that this pit as often almost full of water. Later, nother tunnel was cut leading from e city to a spring outside the walls. he filling of the great pit contained e handles of many storage jars, amped with a royal seal or scribed with the owners' names nd the name Gibeon.

Examination of the area around e pit has shown that it was the site an extensive wine-making dustry in the 7th century BC. Sealed rs of wine were stored in cool ck-cut cellars. The evidence ggests that the inscriptions relate this site and so identify it.

. R. Millard

*Further reading*

J. B. Pritchard, *Hebrew Inscriptions and Stamps from Gibeon*, 1959
——, *The Water System of Gibeon*, 1961
——, *Gibeon where the Sun stood still*, 1962
——, *The Bronze Age Cemetery at Gibeon*, 1964
——, *Winery, Defences and Soundings at Gibeon*, 1964
J. B. Pritchard in *NEAEHL* II, pp. 511–514

**GIHON** (Hebrew *gîḥôn*, 'stream').

**1.** One of the four rivers of the Garden of *Eden, which has been identified variously with the Oxus, Araxes, Ganges, Nile and many other rivers.

The Nile identification arises from the statement that it wound through (*sāḇaḇ*) the land of *Cush (Genesis 2:13), which is identified with Nubia, but it is more probable that the Cush here referred to is the area to the east of Mesopotamia from which the Kassites later descended. If this is so, some river descending to Mesopotamia from the eastern mountains, perhaps the Diyala or the Kerkha, is possible, though the possibility of changed geographical features makes any identification uncertain.

**2.** The name of a spring to the east of Jerusalem, where Solomon was anointed king (1 Kings 1:33, 38, 45). It was from this spring that Hezekiah cut a conduit to take the water to the pool of Siloam (2 Chronicles 32:30) inside the city walls, and it was still outside the outer wall built by Manasseh (2 Chronicles 33:14). It is probably to be identified with modern 'Ain Sitti Maryām.

T. C. Mitchell

*Further reading*

On **1** see E. A. Speiser, 'The Rivers of Paradise', *Festschrift Johannes Friedrich*, 1959, pp. 473–485
On **2** see J. Simons, *Jerusalem in the Old Testament*, 1952, pp. 162–188

**GILBOA** (Hebrew *gilbōa'*, probably 'bubbling fountain', although there is some doubt about this). Sometimes the name appears without the article, while 'Mount Gilboa' also occurs. It was a range of mountains in the territory of Issachar, and so, in 2 Samuel 1:21, David exclaims, 'O mountains of Gilboa'.

It was the scene of Saul's final clash with the Philistines and of his death (1 Samuel 28:4; 31). It may seem surprising to find the Philistines so far north, but the route from Philistia to Esdraelon was an easy one for armies on the march.

The hills are now called Jebel Fuḳû'a, but the ancient name is perpetuated in the village of Jelbôn on the hillside.

G. W. Grogan

**GILEAD.** The name applied to the whole or part of the Transjordanian lands occupied by the tribes of Reuben, Gad and half-Manasseh.

*Extent*

Geographically, Gilead proper was the hilly, wooded country north of a line from Heshbon west to the northern end of the Dead Sea, and extending north towards the present-day river and Wadi Yarmuk but flattening out into plains from *c.* 29 kilometres south of Yarmuk. The northern extension of these plains forms the territory of Bashan. Gilead thus defined is divided into northern and southern halves by the east-west course of the lower Jabbok river.

South of Gilead proper (*i.e.* south of the Heshbon-Dead Sea line) and reaching to the Arnon river, there is a rolling plateau suitable for grain-growing, cattle and flocks. This tract, too, was sometimes included under 'Gilead'.

But the term Gilead could in its widest application be extended to cover all (Israelite) Transjordan (see Deuteronomy 2:36 and especially 34:1; Judges 10–12; 20:1; 2 Kings 15:29). 1 Samuel 13:7 is interesting in that it uses 'Gad' in reference to a particular section, and 'Gilead' of the territory in general. It is also used as a general term in 2 Kings 10:33, where 'all the land of Gilead', *i.e.* (Israelite) Transjordan, includes 'Gilead (*i.e.* Gilead proper, plus the land to the Arnon) and Bashan'.

For Gilead in the narrower sense, as the wooded hill-country stretching to the north and south of the Jabbok, see Deuteronomy 3:10, where it is described as lying between the cities of the plain or tableland south of Heshbon and Bashan in the north, and Joshua 13:11 (in context).

Either half of Gilead proper could be called simply 'Gilead' (referring to the north, see Deuteronomy 3:15; Joshua 17:1, 5–6). Where fuller designations were used, Gilead south of the Jabbok (which fell to Gad) was sometimes called 'half the hill-country of Gilead' (RV, Deuteronomy 3:12, compare 16; Joshua 12:2, 5, compare 13:25), a name also used of Gilead north of the Jabbok (Joshua 13:31). The northern half was also known as 'the rest of Gilead' (Deuteronomy 3:13). In Deuteronomy 3:12 with 16, and 13 with 15, the sequence of full and abbreviated terms is particularly noteworthy.

The simultaneous use of a term or title in both wide and restricted senses, or in both full and abbreviated forms, is a common phenomenon in antiquity and modern times alike. In most Old Testament references to Gilead study of context usually shows the nuance intended.

*In the Old Testament*

The balm of Gilead was proverbial (Jeremiah 8:22; 46:11; compare Genesis 37:25). The rich woodland covering its hills is cited with Lebanon and Carmel as a symbol of luxury (Jeremiah 22:6; 50:19; Zechariah 10:10). It was the grazing-ground of goats (Song of Songs 4:1; 6:5), and also provided refuge for fugitives.

Among those who sought refuge in Gilead were Jacob when he fled before Laban (Genesis 31:21–55), the Israelites who feared the Philistines in Saul's time (1 Samuel 13:7), Ishbosheth (2 Samuel 2:8–9) and David during Absalom's revolt (2 Samuel 17:22ff.).

K. A. Kitchen

*Further reading*

On natural geography:
D. Baly, *The Geography of the Bible*, 1974, pp. 219–225
On archaeology:
N. Glueck, *Explorations in Eastern Palestine*, 3
*AASOR* 18/19, 1939, pp. 151–153, 242–251 (extent and history), and pp. 153–242, 251ff. (archaeology)
In general:
M. Ottoson, *Gilead,* 1969
M. Wüst, *Untersuchungen zu den siedlungsgeographischen Texten des Alten Testaments*
1. *Ostjordanland*, 1975 (speculative)

See also *REUBEN, *GAD, *MANASSEH, *RAMOTH-GILEAD and *MAHANAIM.

**GILGAL.** The name can mean 'circle (of stones)', or 'rolling', from the Hebrew *gālal*, 'to roll'. In its latter meaning the name was used by God through Joshua when the people were circumcised at Gilgal to serve as a reminder to Israel of their deliverance from Egypt: 'This day I have rolled away (*gallôṯî*) the reproach of Egypt from you' (Joshua 5:9).

**1.** Gilgal to the east of Jericho, between it and the Jordan. The exact site of Gilgal within this area is still uncertain. J. Muilenburg very tentatively suggests a site just north of Khirbet el-Mefjir, about 2 kilometres north-east of Old Testament Jericho (Tell es-Sulṭan). In support of this approximate location, Muilenburg adduces the combined testimony of the Old Testament references and of later writers (Josephus, Eusebius, *etc.*), and a trial excavation revealed Early Iron Age remains there.

J. Simons criticized Muilenburg's view on the ground that Khirbet el-Mefjir is more fairly north than east of Jericho; but this is not a very strong objection because Khirbet el-Mefjir is as much east as it is north. Examination of an alternative site, just west of Khirbet el-Mefjir, produced inconclusive results.

*During the Conquest*

Gilgal became Israel's base of operations after the crossing of Jordan (Joshua 4:19), and was the focus of a series of events during the conquest: twelve commemorative stones were set up when Israel pitched camp there (Joshua 4:20); the new generation grown up in the wilderness were circumcised there; the first Passover in Canaan was held there (Joshua 5:9–10) and the manna ceased (Joshua 5:11–12).

From Gilgal, Joshua led Israel against Jericho (Joshua 6:11, 14ff.) and conducted his southern campaign (Joshua 10) after receiving the artful Gibeonite envoys (Joshua 9:6), and there began to allot tribal territories (Joshua 14:6).

Gilgal thus became at once a reminder of God's past deliverance from Egypt, a token of present victory under his guidance, and sa[me] the promise of inheritance yet to be gained.

On the camp at Gilgal in Joshua's strategy, compare Kaufmann (see *Further reading* below), who also incisively refutes Alt's and Noth's erroneous views about Gilgal as an early shrine of Benjaminite traditic[n].

*In the time of the Judges and King[s]*

In later days God's angel went up from Gilgal to Bochim in judgment against forgetful Israel (Judges 2:1); thence Ehud returned to slay a Moabite king for Israel's deliveran[ce] (Judges 3:19). Samuel used to visit Gilgal on circuit (1 Samuel 7:16); there Saul's kingship was confirme[d] after the Ammonite emergency wi[th] joyful sacrifices (1 Samuel 11:14–1[5]; see 10:8). But thereafter, Saul offered precipitate sacrifice (1 Samuel 13:8–14), and it was at Gilg[al] that Samuel and Saul parted for ev[er] after Saul's disobedience in the Amalekite war (1 Samuel 15:12–35).

After Absalom's abortive revolt, the Judaeans welcomed David bac[k] at Gilgal (2 Samuel 19:15, 40). In th[e] days of Ahab and Joram, Elijah an[d] Elisha passed that way just before Elijah's translation to heaven (2 Kings 2:1; although some, quite unnecessarily it would seem, consider this place to be distinct from the historic Gilgal), and there Elisha sweetened the wild gourds [in] the cooking-pot of a group of prophets who feared poison (2 Kin[gs] 4:38).

*Condemned by the prophets*

But during the 8th century BC, at least under the kings Uzziah to Hezekiah, Gilgal became a centre o[f] formal and unspiritual worship which like Bethel drew condemnation from Amos (4:4; 5:5) and Hose[a]

15; 9:15; 12:11). The association Bethel and Gilgal (reflected also in :ings 2:1–2) was strengthened by important road that connected em (see Muilenburg, p. 15). nally, Micah (6:5) reminds his ople of Gilgal's first role in their ritual pilgrimage, witnessing to od's righteousness and saving wer, 'from Shittim to Gilgal', *i.e.* ross Jordan into the promised land.
**2.** In Joshua 15:7, the northern undary of Judah at least came in ew of a Gilgal that was 'opposite e ascent of Adummim'; in the rallel description of this line, as o the southern boundary of njamin (Joshua 18:17), Geliloth is described. But whether *this* lgal/Geliloth is the same as the nous Gilgal east of Jericho mains quite uncertain though just ssible. Otherwise, it must be some ner local 'circle' farther west. An ea of ruins 1·5 kilometres west of an el-Ahmar (the traditional ation of the Inn of the Good maritan) provides one possibility. ggestions about this boundary ll be found in Simons (*GTT*, . 139–140, section 314, and p. 173, ction 326), who, however, makes o free a use of emendation.
**3.** In Deuteronomy 11:30, the rase 'opposite Gilgal' may refer to e Canaanites dwelling in the abah (Jordan rift valley), rather an to the mountains Ebal and rizim. If so, then this is simply the storic Gilgal, see **1** above. ompare *GTT*, p. 35, sections –88.)
**4.** Among Joshua's defeated emies occurs the king of Goyyim longing to Gilgal (Joshua 12:23) tween the kings of Dor and Tirzah. is Gilgal might be the capital of a ng ruling over a mixed population the edge of the maritime plain of aron, if – as is sometimes ggested – it is to be placed at jūliyeh, about 5 kilometres north of hek or about 22 kilometres rth-east of the coast at Joppa.
**5.** The Beth-gilgal from which ngers came to the dedication of the alls of Jerusalem by Nehemiah and ra is either the famous Gilgal (**1** ove) or else remains unidentified ehemiah 12:29).
A. Kitchen

*rther reading*
n **1**:
Muilenburg, *BASOR* 140, 1955, . 11–27, and map on p. 17, fig. I
Simons, *GTT*, pp. 269–270, section 4
M. Bennett, *PEQ* 104, 1972, . 111–122
Y. Kaufmann, *The Biblical Account of the Conquest of Palestine*, 1953, pp. 67–69 and 91–97, especially 92, 95f.

**GITTITE.** See *GATH.

**GOLAN.** The northern city of refuge in Transjordan, in Manasseh's territory of Bashan (Deuteronomy 4:43), and a levitical city (Joshua 21:27). The location is uncertain, but it may be identified with Sahm el-Jolan, 22 kilometres east of Aphek (Hippos). The district of Gaulanitis was later named after it.
N. Hillyer

*Further reading*
*LOB*, p. 435

**GOMORRAH.** See *PLAIN, CITIES OF THE.

**GOSHEN. 1.** The territory assigned to Israel and his descendants during their Egyptian sojourn. Its exact location and extent remain uncertain, but it was certainly in Egypt (Genesis 47:6, 27), and in the eastern Nile Delta: Genesis 47:6 with 11 clearly equate Goshen with 'the land of Rameses', so named from the residence-city Pi-Ramessē, biblical *Ra'amses, in the north-eastern Delta. The Septuagint's topographical interpretations are of uncertain authenticity. The eastern Delta would be suitably 'near' the court (Genesis 45:10) for Joseph serving his (probably Hyksos) pharaoh at *Memphis (near Cairo) or Avaris (north-eastern Delta), compare also Genesis 46:28–29; likewise for Moses interviewing his pharaoh at Pi-Ramessē (Exodus 7–12).

Goshen was a well-favoured region suited to flocks and herds (Genesis 46:34; 47:1, 4, 6, 27; 50:8). It remained the habitat of the Hebrews until the Exodus, being therefore largely shielded from the plagues (Exodus 8:22; 9:26); nevertheless, contact was close with Egyptians living in the same general region (*e.g.* compare Exodus 11:2–3; 12:35–36).

The name *Gsmt* occurring in certain Egyptian texts, once equated with Hebrew Goshen through the Septuagint's 'Gesem', should be read *Šsmt* and is therefore irrelevant.

**2.** A district in the south of Palestine (Joshua 10:41; 11:16), probably named after **3**, a town in the hills of southern Palestine (Joshua 15:51), possibly near Ẓāhiriyeh, *c.* 19 kilometres south-west of Hebron (so Abel) or else somewhat farther east (*GTT*, 1959, sections 285–287, 497). (See also *GEDER.)
K. A. Kitchen

**GOZAN** is identified with ancient Guzana, modern Tell Halaf, on the Upper Habur river. Israelites from Samaria were deported here in 722 BC (2 Kings 17:6; 18:11). Sennacherib, in his letter to Hezekiah (2 Kings 19:12; Isaiah 37:12), refers to the heavy punishment inflicted on this Assyrian provincial capital when it rebelled in 759 BC.

Excavations in 1899, 1911–13 and 1927 (M. von Oppenheim, *Tell Halaf*, 1933) produced tablets of the 8th-7th centuries BC, in which Western Semitic names may attest, or explain, the presence of the Israelite exiles (*AfO* Beiheft 6).
D. J. Wiseman

**GREECE.** Who the Greeks were is a famous crux. Their language is Indo-European and its earliest known location is in the Mycenaean states of the Peloponnesus (as established by the decipherment of the Linear B script) in the 2nd millennium BC. When they emerge into history well into the 1st millennium they belong indifferently to either side of the Aegean.

*The spread of Hellenism*
The first flowering of the two institutions that became the hall-marks of Hellenism, speculative philosophy and republican government, apparently occurred on the Ionian coast of Asia Minor. Ionia is perhaps the Old Testament Javan (Isaiah 66:19). The area of Greek settlement was never static. The republics were early established throughout the Black Sea, Sicily and southern Italy, and as far west as Marseilles and Spain. After Alexander there were Greek states as far east as India.

Under Seleucid and more especially Roman control the wealthy and ancient nations of Asia Minor and the Levant were systematically broken up into many hundreds of Greek republics, leaving only the most backward regions under the indigenous royal or priestly governments.

This political fragmentation was always characteristic of the Greeks, as was the consequent subordination to foreign powers. Greece was never a political entity. 'The king of Greece' (*yāwān*, Daniel 8:21) must be one of the *Macedonian rulers, Alexander or a Seleucid, who controlled the affairs of many but by no means all Greek states. 'Greece'

(*Hellas*) in Acts 20:2 must refer to the Roman province of *Achaia, which, while it contained many Greek states, was now almost a backwater of Hellenism.

On the other hand, the ever-increasing diffusion of Greek institutions brought unification at a different level. The whole of the eastern Mediterranean and much beyond was raised to the common norm of civilization that Hellenism supplied. Both the opulence of the states and the degree of standardization are attested by the splendid ruins that indiscriminately litter these parts today. The ideal of a free and cultivated life in a small autonomous community, once the boast of a few Aegean states, was now almost universally accepted. *Athens was still a home of learning, but Pergamum, Antioch and Alexandria, and many others in the new world, rivalled or eclipsed her.

*The civilized man*

The states provided not only education but brilliant entertainment and a wider range of health and welfare services than most modern communities. It was membership in such a republic and use of the Greek language that marked a man as civilized (Acts 21:37–39). Such a person might be called a Greek, whatever his race (Mark 7:26); all others were 'barbarians' (Romans 1:14). The term 'Hellenists' in Acts 6:1 and 9:29 presumably shows that this distinction applied even within the Jewish ethnic community. The term 'Greek' (*hellēn*, Acts 11:20; 19:17; Romans 1:16, *etc.*) is, however, the regular New Testament usage for non-Jews, being virtually equivalent to 'Gentile'.

Greeks were frequently associated with the synagogues as observers (John 12:20; Acts 14:1; 17:4; 18:4), but the exclusiveness of Israel as a nation was jealously preserved. It was the agonizing delivery of the gospel from this constricting matrix that marked the birth of the Christian religion in its universal form. The translation from Hebrew into Greek opened the gospel to all civilized men. It also produced the New Testament.

E. A. Judge

*Further reading*

A. H. M. Jones, *The Greek City from Alexander to Justinian*, 1940
M. I. Finley, *The Ancient Greeks*, 1963
A. Andrewes, *The Greeks*, 1967
M. Hengel, *Judaism and Hellenism*, 1974

**GUDGODAH.** One of the Israelite encampments in the wilderness according to Deuteronomy 10:7. Hor-haggidgad in Numbers 33:32–33 is probably another form of the same name. Its location is not known, although its proximity to *Bene-jaakan and *Jotbathah suggests that it was somewhere in the mountains west of Wadi Arabah.

The suggestion that the name survives in Wadi Ḫadaḫid, in this area, is unlikely from a linguistic point of view. Baumgartner, comparing an Arabic word, has suggested that it may be an animal name, 'a cricket': the first element of the longer form, Hor, appears to mean 'cave'.

G. I. Davies

*Further reading*

*KB*, pp. 169, 335 (bibliography)

# H

**HABITATION.** See *Naioth.

**HABOR.** A river (the modern Ḫâbû which carries the waters of severa streams draining the Mardin area south-west to the middle Euphrate It ran through the Assyrian provinc of *Gozan (*n$^e$har gôzān*, 'river of Gozan') and was one of the locatio to which the Israelites were deported by the Assyrians (2 Kings 17:6; 18:11; 1 Chronicles 5:26).

T. C. Mitchell

*Further reading*

W. B. Fisher, *The Middle East*, 6th edition, 1971, pp. 353–354
T. C. Mitchell, *CAH* III.2, p. 341

**HACHILAH** (Hebrew *ḥ$^a$ḵîlâ*, 'drought'). A hill in the wilderness Judah where David was hidden when the Ziphites plotted to betray him to Saul (1 Samuel 23:19; 26:1, 3 The site is uncertain, but is generall regarded as being near Dahret el-Kôlâ, between Ziph and *En-ged

J. D. Douglas

**HADRACH.** A place on the norther boundaries of Syria (Zechariah 9:1) Mentioned in the Aramaic inscription of Zakur of Hamath, *c.* 78 BC, it is the Hatarikka of Assyrian inscriptions, once the seat of a district governor, near Qinneṣrin, 2 kilometres south of Aleppo (*HUCA* 18, 1944, p. 449, note 108).

A. R. Millard

**HADRAMAUT.** See *Arabia.

**HALAH.** A place in Assyria to whic Israelites were deported from Samaria (2 Kings 17:6; 18:11; 1 Chronicles 5:26; see Obadiah 20, R 'exiles in Halah' by a small emendation). There is no doubt thi was Assyrian Halahhu, a town and district north-east of Nineveh, givin its name to one of the gates of that city. Other proposed locations are f less likely.

A. R. Millard

**LAK** (Hebrew *ḥālāq*, 'smooth, ld'). A mountain (literally 'the bald ountain') in Judaea which marked e southern limit of Joshua's nquests (Joshua 11:17; 12:7). Its ality is described as 'going up to ir'. It is probably the modern Jebel làq, west of the Ascent of rabbim.
G. Norman

**M** (Hebrew *hām*). The name of a y whose inhabitants, the Zuzim, ere defeated by Chedorlaomer in e time of Abraham (Genesis 14:5). e site, though probably mewhere in Transjordan, is known. It may feature as *Hum* in a pographical list of the pharaoh thmosis III (*c.* 1460 BC), but its ce in the list does not help locate

The modern village of Hām in rthern Jordan may mark the site of e or both of these places, but as e mound has not been excavated it uncertain whether its occupational story suits either the biblical or the yptian reference.

The Septuagint (*hama autois*) erprets the Hebrew *b$^{e}$hām* 'in m' as *bāhem*, 'with them'.
C. Mitchell, J. Bimson

**AMATH** (Hebrew *ḥ$^{a}$maṯ*, 'fortress, adel'). City on the east bank of the ontes, lying on one of the main de-routes to the south from Asia nor. Genesis 10:18 describes it as naanite.

In David's time, under King Toi (or u), it was friendly towards Israel Samuel 8:9–10; 1 Chronicles :9–10). Toi's son is named Joram 2 Samuel 8:10. This is probably not Yahweh name ('Yah is exalted'), t an abbreviation of Hadoram as ven in 1 Chronicles 18:10. The nnection of a Hamathite rebel lled *Ya'u-bidi* by Sargon of Assyria ith Yahweh is also unlikely (see *NET*, p. 285; *DOTT*, p. 59).

Solomon controlled Hamath (2 ronicles 8:4), and it was nquered by Jeroboam II (*c.* 780 BC, Kings 14:28) and Sargon (*c.* 721 BC, e 2 Kings 18:33f.; Isaiah 36:18f.; :13, 18f.), some of its inhabitants ing settled by the Assyrians in amaria worshipping their deity shima there (2 Kings 17:24ff.).

Palace buildings of the 9th and 8th nturies BC were excavated by a anish team, 1931–38 (see E. gmann, *Hama, l'Architecture des ériodes préhellénistiques,* 1958). scriptions in Hittite hieroglyphs, neiforms and Aramaic were found.

According to the Babylonian hronicle, it was at Hamath that Nebuchadrezzar overtook the Egyptians fleeing from Carchemish in 605 BC (see D. J. Wiseman, *Chronicles of Chaldaean Kings*, 1956, p. 69).

The city was known in Greek and Roman times as Epiphaneia; today it is *Ḥamāh*.

*Labo of Hamath*

The ideal northern boundary of Israel reached 'Labo of Hamath', formerly rendered 'the entering in of Hamath', *e.g.* Numbers 34:8, Joshua 13:5 and Amos 6:14, but probably it is modern Lebweh, north-north-east of Baalbek, at the watershed of the Beqa' valley, near one source of the Orontes, so at the head of the road north to Hamath, Assyrian Laba'u in the province of Supite (see also *Zobah). For a discussion see R. North, *Mélanges de l'Université S. Joseph* 46, 1970–71, pp. 71–103.
J. G. G. Norman, A. R. Millard

**HANANEL.** In Nehemiah 3:1 and 12:39, a *Jerusalem tower, lying between the Sheep and Fish Gates, in the northern part of the city. It also receives mention in Jeremiah 31:38 and Zechariah 14:10. It is closely connected with the Tower of the *Hundred, and some scholars would equate the two, or else make them two parts of the same fortress, perhaps the 'castle' mentioned in Nehemiah 7:2. AV spells the name 'Hananeel'; the Hebrew is *ḥ$^{a}$nan'ēl*, 'God is gracious'.

The Targum of Zechariah 14:10 seems to place the tower on the west of the city, by identifying it with the later Hippicus; this cannot be correct.
D. F. Payne

**HANES.** Often identified with the Egyptian *Ḥ(wt-nni-)nsw*, the Greek-Latin 'Heracleopolis magna', modern Ihnâsyeh el-Medîneh or Ahnaâs, about 80 kilometres upstream (*i.e.* south) of Cairo, and an important city in Middle Egypt. However, this does not really suit Isaiah 30:4, in the two parallel clauses: 'His officials are at Zoan, and his envoys reach Hanes.' *Zoan is Tanis in the north-eastern Delta, the seat of the 22nd-23rd Dynasty pharaohs, and Lower Egypt advanced-headquarters of the Ethiopian 25th Dynasty, for Asiatic affairs. Hence the parallelism of the verse seems to demand that Hanes be closely linked with eastern Delta Tanis, not Upper Egypt Heracleopolis, far distant and irrelevant.

Two solutions are possible. W. Spiegelberg, in *Aegyptologische Randglossen zum Alten Testament,* 1904, pp. 36–38, postulated a 'Heracleopolis parva' in the eastern Delta, arguing from Herodotus' mention of a province and city of Anysis there (2.166, 137); this would then be the Egyptian *Ḥ(wt-nni-)nsw* of Lower Egypt, Hebrew *Ḥanes*, and Assyrian *Ḫininsi*. See Caminos in *JEA* 50, 1964, p. 94. Or Hanes may merely be a Hebrew transcription of an Egyptian *ḥ(wt)-nsw*, 'mansion of the king', as the name of the pharaoh's palace in Zoan/Tanis itself.

Either interpretation is plausible; neither is proven. Some refer the 'his' (princes, envoys) of Isaiah 30:4 to the Judaean king; but the natural antecedent is pharaoh in verse 3. Hence, with É. Naville, *Ahnas el Medineh*, 1894, p. 3, these are pharaoh's officials at Zoan and his envoys who come to treat with the Jewish emissaries, either at Hanes as an advance post for Zoan (Naville, Spiegelberg), or summoned to the 'Ha-nesu', the king's palace, in Zoan itself.
K. A. Kitchen

*Further reading*

K. A. Kitchen, *Third Intermediate Period in Egypt (1100–650 BC)*, 2nd edition, 1986, p. 374, note 749

**HARA.** With *Halah, *Habor and *Gozan, a place to which Tiglath-pileser III removed rebellious Israelites in 734–732 BC (1 Chronicles 5:26). An Assyrian site of this name is not known. 2 Kings 17:6 and 18:11, however, interpret *hārā'* as '*cities* of the Medes' and the Septuagint 'mountains' may represent the Hebrew *hārê*, 'hill-country'.
D. J. Wiseman

**HARAN** (Hebrew *ḥar(r)an*; Akkadian *ḫarrānu*, 'cross-roads'; Greek *charrhan*, Acts 7:4). The city *c.* 32 kilometres south-east of Urfa (Edessa), Turkey, on the river Baliḫ, lies on the main route from Nineveh to Aleppo.

Terah lived there with Abram (Genesis 11:31; compare Acts 7:2, 4) before the latter migrated to Canaan (Genesis 12:1). It was the home of Isaac's bride Rebekah. Jacob fled there to escape Esau (Genesis 29:4), married Leah and Rachel, daughters of Laban, and all his children (except Benjamin) were born there (Genesis 29:32–30:24).

Harran is referred to in texts from the Ur III period *c.* 2000 BC as a temple (*é.ḫul.ḫul*) for the worship of Sin the moon-god, and its occupation is confirmed by archaeological evidence.

Its strategic position made it a focus for Amorite tribes according to Mari texts of the 2nd millennium BC, and later an Assyrian centre fortified by Adad-nirari I (*c.* 1310 BC) with a temple embellished by Tiglath-pileser I (*c.* 1115 BC). Harran rebelled and was sacked in 763 BC, an event used by Sennacherib's officials to intimidate Jerusalem (2 Kings 19:12 and Isaiah 37:12). The city was restored by Sargon II, and the temple repaired and refurnished by Esarhaddon (675 BC) and by Ashurbanipal.

After the fall of Nineveh (612 BC) Harran became the last capital of Assyria until its capture by the Babylonians in 609 BC. The Chaldean Dynasty's interest in the Babylonian temples led to the restoration of the Sin temples at Harran and at Ur. At the former the mother of Nabonidus (who lived to 104), and at the latter his daughter, were made the high priestesses. It was a thriving commercial city in contact with Tyre (Ezekiel 27:23).

The site, excavated in 1951–53 and 1959, indicates clearly an occupation before the Assyrian period. The existing ruins are mainly from the Roman city near which the Parthians slew Crassus (53 BC) and from the later occupation by Sabaean and Islamic rulers in Harran, then called Carrhae. In the AV of Acts 7:4 the city is named Charran.

D. J. Wiseman

*Further reading*

S. Lloyd and W. Brice, *AS* 1, 1951, pp. 77–112

D. S. Rice, *AS* 2, 1952, pp. 36–84

C. J. Gadd, *AS* 8, 1958, pp. 35–92

K. Prag, *Levant* 2, 1970, pp. 63–94

**HAR-MAGEDON.** See *ARMAGEDDON.

**HARMEL.** See *HARMON.

**HARMON.** A place (RSV, Amos 4:3) otherwise not mentioned in the Old Testament (AV interprets as 'the palace', from versions). The Septuagint has 'the mountains of Rimmon', possibly the hill of *Rimmon (Judges 20:45, 47).

Various emendations, 'naked' (*'armôṯ*), 'devoted to destruction', have been suggested, but the most plausible is 'Hermon'; as Mount Hermon lay on the northern side of Bashan (referred to in Amos 4:1) this would fit the context well. However, others prefer the suggestion, on the basis of Ugaritic *hrmn*, that this may be Harmel (south of *Kadesh on the Orontes).

D. J. Wiseman

*Further reading*

*BASOR* 198, 1970, p. 41

**HAROD** (Hebrew *ḥ$^{a}$rōḏ*, 'trembling'). A copious and beautiful spring at the foot of Mount Gilboa, east of Jezreel, which flows east into the Beth-shean valley.

Here Gideon, confronting the Midianite hordes, reduced his army in two stages from 32,000 to 300 (Judges 7:1–8). Probably Saul and his army camped here prior to the fatal battle on Mount Gilboa (1 Samuel 29:1; compare 31:1). Two of David's 'mighty men', Shammah and Elika (2 Samuel 23:25; 1 Chronicles 11:27), came from Harod, possibly to be identified with the modern 'Ain Jalud.

A. E. Cundall

**HAROSHETH** (Hebrew *ḥ$^{a}$rōšeṯ*), the home of Sisera the Canaanite general (Judges 4:2, 13, 16), called *ḥ$^{a}$rōšeṯ hagôyīm* ('of the nations') each time; the meaning has been sought in Akkadian *hursanu*, 'mountains', and in a rendering 'forest' in one text in the Septuagint (A); neither suits the context of a chariot concentration.

Reference in an Amarna letter (365.11) to *errisu/ahrisu*, for cultivation in the Jezreel valley, suggests 'estates' as a possible translation. The name does not occur elsewhere, and identifications of particular sites have been unsuccessful; Tell 'Amr, near el-Hartiyeh, north-west of Megiddo, lacks evidence of settlement before the Monarchy, and Khirbet Harbaj, south- east of Haifa, was probably *Achshaph.

J. P. U. Lilley

*Further reading*

B. Mazar, *HUCA* 24, 1952–53, pp. 80–84

*LOB*, pp. 221–223, 279 n. 103

A. F. Rainey, *Tel Aviv* 10, 1983, pp. 46–48

**HARRAN.** See *HARAN.

**HAVILAH** (Hebrew *ḥ$^{a}$wîlâ*, 'circle', 'district'). **1.** A land (*'ereṣ*) in the neighbourhood of *Eden, through which meandered (*sābab*) the river Pishon, and in which was found gold, bdellium and *shoham*-stone (Genesis 2:11–12). The location of the place is unknown.

**2.** An area mentioned in the phrase 'from Havilah to Shur'; inhabited by the Ishmaelites (Genesis 25:18) and Amalekites (1 Samuel 15:7). It probably lay therefore in the area o[f] Sinai and north-western Arabia.

T. C. Mitchell

*Further reading*

J. A. Montgomery, *Arabia and the Bible*, 1934, p. 39

**HAVVOTH-JAIR** (Hebrew *ḥawwō[ṯ] yā'îr*, 'the camps of Jair'). Probably i[n] the hills between Mount Gilead proper and the Yarmuk, which we[re] dotted with settlements called *'$^{a}$yārîm* (Judges 10:4); this could be [a] unique plural of *'îr*, 'town', or a diminutive (so Rashi, *Commentary*) homonymous with 'ass-colts'. The area may have been known earlier a[s] Havvoth-Ham (Numbers 32:41 as emended by Bergman, *JPOS* 16, 1936, pp. 235ff., since *ḥawwōṯêhe[m]* 'their villages', has no plural antecedent); compare Genesis 14:[5].

Havvoth-Jair was associated wit[h] the Argob, north of the Yarmuk, as part of Bashan, of which Og was th[e] last king. Jair was credited (Deuteronomy 3:14; 1 Chronicles 2:23f.) with the conquest of the whole region , including the Argob to which the '60 towns' of Joshua 13:30; 1 Chronicles 2:23; 1 Kings 4:13 refer.

See Aharoni, *LOB*, p. 209, for a possible mention in Assyrian records; and D. Baly, *Geography*, pp. 213–216, for a general description of the area.

J. P. U. Lilley

**HAZARMAVETH.** See *ARABIA.

**HAZEROTH.** A stopping-place on the desert journey of the Israelites (Numbers 11:35; 33:17–18), where Miriam became a leper (Numbers 12:1–16; compare Deuteronomy 1:1). It is generally identified with 'Ayin Khodara, an oasis with a wel[l] on the way from Sinai to Aqabah. (See also *ENCAMPMENT BY THE SEA.)

C. de Wit

**HAZOR** (Hebrew *ḥāṣôr*). A place-name, probably meaning 'settlement' or 'village', and therefore used of several places in the Old Testament, of which the most important was a fortified city i[n] the territory of Naphtali (Joshua 19:36).

### In the Old Testament

This city lay in northern Palestine, and at the conquest it was the roya[l] seat of Jabin (called 'king of Hazor' *meleḵ-ḥāṣôr*, Joshua 11:1), who organized a coalition against Joshua. The Israelites defeated thi[s]

Hazor: the remains of the Israelite citadel. 9th–8th century BC.

owever, Jabin was killed, and azor was destroyed and burnt oshua 11:1–13; 12:19). Hazor was e only city thus burnt, perhaps ecause of its former importance oshua 11:10), but in spite of this estruction a later king of the same ame, who this time was styled 'king Canaan' (*meleḵ-kᵉna'an*, Judges 2, 24) threatened Israel in the time Deborah. Though his general, sera, had 900 chariots at his sposal, the Israelites under Barak ere able to defeat him, and crush bin (Judges 4; 1 Samuel 12:9). Some two centuries later Hazor as fortified, together with rusalem, Megiddo and Gezer, by olomon when he was organizing s kingdom (1 Kings 9:15), but in the h century, in the time of Pekah of rael, Tiglath-pileser III of Assyria ame and destroyed the city and arried off its remaining inhabitants Assyria (2 Kings 15:29).

### xcavation

he site of Hazor was identified in 375 by J. L. Porter with the bandoned mound of Tell el-Qedah ome 8 kilometres south- west of ake Huleh in Galilee. J. Garstang ade some trial soundings in 1928, ut the first major excavations were arried out from 1955 to 1958 and 968 to 1969 by an Israeli expedition nder Yigael Yadin.

The site lies on a north-east facing ope, and consists of the city tell ccupying some 10 hectares at the outhern end, and adjoining this to the north a much larger area of about 69 hectares with an earthen rampart on the western or uphill side. The main tell was founded in the 3rd millennium and the lower city added to it in the early part of the 2nd millennium.

*The lower city*

Though Garstang assumed the lower city to be a camping enclosure for horses and chariots, excavation revealed that the whole of this area had been occupied by a built city, which at its height must, with the tell proper, have accommodated up to 40,000 souls. Hazor was in fact the largest Canaanite city throughout the Middle and Late Bronze Ages.

A further indication of the importance of the city at this time is given by the discovery of a pottery jug with an Akkadian inscription (the earliest known in Palestine) scratched on it. Though crudely done, the inscription has been read as *Iš-me-ilam*, an Akkadian personal name, perhaps that of a Mesopotamian merchant.

The lower city was occupied for only about five centuries, having been destroyed in the 13th century (Level XIII). This destruction is attributed by the excavators to Joshua. Among the remains in this destroyed city were found a Canaanite temple and a small shrine.

*The tell*

While the lower city lay barren, the tell was reoccupied by the Canaanites, and then by the Israelites. A city gate and casemate wall from the time of Solomon, almost exactly matching those found at *Megiddo and *Gezer (compare 1 Kings 9:15), were uncovered. Evidence from the later Israelite period included a pillared public building of the time of Ahab (taken by Garstang to be stables), a huge underground water system and a fortress containing a thick layer of ash, in which was a fragment of a wine jar bearing the name Pekah (*pqḥ*), and other signs of violent destruction, probably due to Tiglath-pileser III, who took the city in 732 BC (2 Kings 15:29).

A new series of excavations began in 1990 under A. Ben-Tor. One aim of these campaigns is to test Yadin's theory that an important archive may exist in the Middle Bronze Age palace which lies beneath the Iron Age buildings on the tell proper. During the 1991 season a fragment of a clay tablet was found, addressed to a king of Hazor with the name Ibni [Addu]. This tablet is of Old Babylonian date (1800–1600 BC) but was found out of context in Israelite levels. The king named on it may be the same Ibni-Adad already known from the Mari archives (see below).

### In extra-biblical texts

Hazor is first mentioned in the Egyptian Execration Texts of the 19th century BC, as a Canaanite city likely to be a danger to the empire. It figures (*ḫa-ṣu-ra*) in the Mari archives of the first quarter of the 2nd millennium, and in a slightly later Babylonian text, as an important political centre on the route from Mesopotamia, perhaps to Egypt. In one tablet the ruler is spoken of as a 'king' (*šarrum*), a title not usually applied to city rulers (compare Joshua 11:1), and his importance is further indicated by the mention of ambassadors from Babylon travelling to see him.

One king's name is given in the Mari archives (18th century BC) as Ibni-Adad, an Akkadian form suggesting Babylonian influence. (The first part of this name is a form of the Old Testament 'Jabin', implying this may have been a dynastic name among kings of Hazor. Compare the tablet discovered at Hazor in 1991, mentioned above.)

There was also contact with the north and west, as manifested in gifts from the king to Ugarit and Crete (*Kaptara*). Hazor is mentioned in the lists of their dominions made by the Egyptian kings Tuthmosis III, Amenhotep II and Seti I in the 15th and 14th centuries BC.

The city is later mentioned in the Amarna letters, of the 14th century, the ruler still being spoken of as a king (*šar ḫa-zu-ra*). Finally, from the next century, the city is mentioned in an Egyptian papyrus (Anastasi I) in a military context. Thus the texts and excavations amply bear out the biblical testimony to the importance of the site.

**Other places of the same name**

**1.** A place in the south of Judah (Joshua 15:23) whose site is unknown.

**2.** (*ḥāṣôr ḥᵃdattâ*) 'New Hazor' (Joshua 15:25), a place in southern Judah whose site is unknown.

**3.** Another name for Kerioth-hezron (Joshua 15:25) in southern Judah, site unknown, perhaps the same as **2.**

**4.** A place in Benjamin (Nehemiah 11:33) probably modern Khirbet Hazzur.

**5.** An area occupied by semi-nomadic Arabs, mentioned by Jeremiah (49:28, 30, 33).

T. C. Mitchell

*Further reading*

Y. Yadin and others, *Hazor I*, 1958, *Hazor II*, 1960, *Hazor III-IV*, 1961
——, *Hazor* (Schweich Lectures, 1970), 1972
Y. Yadin and A. Ben-Tor in *NEAEHL* II, pp. 594–606
A. Malamat, *JBL* 79, 1960, pp. 12–19
E. K. Vogel, *HUCA* 42, 1971, pp. 35–36; 52, 1981, p. 35; 58, 1987, pp. 24–25
P. Bienkowski, *PEQ* 119, 1987, pp. 50–61

**HEBRON** (Hebrew *ḥeḇrôn*, 'confederacy'; compare its alternative and older name Kiriath-arba, 'tetrapolis'), the highest town in Palestine, 927 metres above the level of the Mediterranean, 30 kilometres south-south-west of Jerusalem.

The statement that it 'was built seven years before Zoan in Egypt' (Numbers 13:22) was once thought to place Hebron's founding in the 18th century BC, but it is now clear that Zoan (that is, Tanis) itself was not founded until the 11th century BC. However, excavations at Jebel er-Rumeideh (Old Testament Hebron) show that a town of the Middle Bronze Age (*c.* 1900–1500 BC) was followed by a gap in occupation until the site was resettled late in the Iron Age Ib period (*c.* 1100–1000 BC). Numbers 13:22 may therefore be taken to refer to the building of Israelite Hebron some time in the 11th century BC, and not to the earlier town of Abraham's day.

*The patriarchal period*

Abraham lived in the vicinity of Hebron for considerable periods (see also *MAMRE); in his days the resident population ('the people of the land') were 'sons of Heth' ('Hittites' in modern English versions), from whom Abraham bought the field of Machpelah with its cave to be a family burying-ground (Genesis 23). There he and Sarah, Isaac and Rebekah, Jacob and Leah were buried (Genesis 49:31; 50:13). According to Josephus (*Antiquities* 2.199; 3.305), the sons of Jacob, with the exception of Joseph, were buried there too. The traditional site of the Patriarchs' sepulchre lies within the great *Ḥaram el-Ḫalîl*, the 'Enclosure of the Friend' (*i.e.* Abraham; compare Isaiah 41:8), with its Herodian masonry.

*After the Exodus*

During the Israelites' wilderness wandering the twelve spies sent out to report on the land of Canaan explored the region of Hebron; at that time it was populated by the 'descendants of Anak' (Numbers 13:22, 28, 33).

After Israel's entry into Canaan, Hoham, king of Hebron, joined the anti-Gibeonite coalition led by Adoni-zedek, king of Jerusalem, and was killed by Joshua (Joshua 10:1–27). Hebron itself and the surrounding territory were conquered from the Anakim by Caleb and given to him as a family possession (Joshua 14:12ff.; 15:13f. Judges 1:10, 20).

In Hebron David was anointed king of Judah (2 Samuel 2:4) and 2 years later king of Israel also (2 Samuel 5:3); it remained his capital for 7½ years. It was here too later in his reign, that Absalom raised the standard of rebellion against him (2 Samuel 15:7ff.). It was fortified by Rehoboam (2 Chronicles 11:10).

Hebron is one of the four cities named on royal jar-handle stamps found at *Lachish and other sites, which probably points to its importance as a major Judaean administrative centre in the reign of Hezekiah.

*After the captivity*

After the Babylonian captivity it wa one of the places where returning exiles settled (Nehemiah 11:25; Kiriath-arba was Hebron). Later it was occupied by the Idumaeans, from whom Judas Maccabaeus captured it (1 Maccabees 5:65). During the war of AD 66–70 it was occupied by Simon bar-Giora, but was stormed and burnt by the Romans (Josephus, *Jewish War* 4.529, 554).

Under the name of el-Ḫalîl Hebron is one of the four sacred cities of the Muslims.

F. F. Bruce

*Further reading*

L. H. Vincent and E. J. H. Mackay, *Hébron, le Ḥaram el-Khalil, sépulture des patriarches*, 2 vols., 1923
D. Baly, Geography of the Bible, *2nd edition, 1974*
*P. C. Hammond, RB* 72, 1965, pp. 267–270
*RB* 73, 1966, pp. 566–569
*RB* 75, 1968, pp. 253–258
A. Mazar, *Archaeology of the Land of the Bible*, 1990, pp. 332–334
A. Ofer in *NEAEHL* II, pp. 606–609

**HELAM.** A city in Transjordan, probably the modern 'Alma, the location of the defeat of Hadadezer Syrian forces, reinforced by Syrian troops from beyond the Euphrates, by David (2 Samuel 10:16f.), following the defeat of an Ammonite-Syrian alliance by David's captain Joab.

The mention of the Greek form, Eliam, constituting part of a place-name in the Septuagint of Ezekiel 47:16, has led to a proposed

The city of Hebron today.
Inset: The Haram el-Ḥalîl, 'Enclosure of the Friend' (centre, traditional burial place of Abraham and Sarah, Isaac and Rebekah, Jacob and Leah).

alternative location on the border between Damascus and Hamath. A connection with Alema (1 Maccabees 5:26) has also been suggested.
R. A. H. Gunner

**HELBON** (Hebrew *ḥelbôn*, 'fat', 'fruitful'). A town mentioned in Ezekiel 27:18 as trading wine to Tyre. This has been identified with the village of Khalbun, 25 kilometres north of Damascus.

The author of the Genesis Apocryphon from Qumran wrote Helbon for the place-name *Hobah of Genesis 14:15, described as 'on the left hand of' or 'north of' Damascus, and this gives interesting evidence for thus identifying an otherwise unknown site.
J. D. Douglas

**HELKATH.** In the border-territory of Asher (Joshua 19:25) and a levitical city (Joshua 21:31). 1 Chronicles 6:75 gives Hukok as a variant for Helkath. The exact location in the Kishon valley is disputed: a likely site for it is Tell el-Harbaj nearly 10 kilometres south-east of Haifa (A. Alt, *Palästinajahrbuch* 25, 1929, pp. 38ff.), or perhaps even better, Tell el-Qasis (or Kussis) 8 kilometres south-south-east of Tell el-Harbaj (Y. Aharoni, *IEJ* 9, 1959, pp. 119–120).

Helkath is probably the *ḥrḳt* in topographical lists of the pharaoh Tuthmosis III, *c.* 1460 BC.
K. A. Kitchen

**HELKATH-HAZZURIM** (Hebrew *ḥelqaṯ haṣṣurîm*, 'field of flints' or 'field of (sword)-edges'). This is the name given to the place in Gibeon where there was a tournament between the champions of Joab and Abner, which led on to a battle (2 Samuel 2:16).

Other meanings conjectured include 'field of plotters', based on the Septuagint *meris tōn epiboulōn*, 'field of sides' and 'field of adversaries'. (Compare S. R. Driver, *Notes on the Hebrew Text of the Books of Samuel*, 1913.)
J. G. G. Norman

**HENA.** A city whose god, the Assyrians boasted, could not save it (2 Kings 18:34). It is identified by the Septuagint with Ana on the Euphrates. Hena and Ivvah have been identified as Arabic star names, and consequently taken as the names of deities. This is, however, unlikely, as the latter is almost certainly a place-name identical with Avva (2 Kings 17:24, 31).
M. A. MacLeod

**HERMON** (Hebrew *ḥermôn*, 'sanctuary'). A mountain in the Anti-Lebanon Range, and easily the highest (2,814 metres) in the neighbourhood of Palestine. It is called also Mount Sirion (Hebrew Sion, Deuteronomy 4:48), and known to the Amorites as S(h)enir (Deuteronomy 3:9). Note, however, that Song of Songs 4:8 and 1 Chronicles 5:23 explicitly distinguish between Hermon and *Senir (compare *GTT*, p. 41; *DOTT*, p. 49).

Regarded as a sacred place by the original inhabitants of Canaan (compare 'Baal-hermon', Judges 3:3; 'Baal-gad', Joshua 13:5, *etc.*), it formed the northern boundary of Israel's conquests from the Amorites (Deuteronomy 3:8; Joshua 11:17, *etc.*). Snow usually lies on the top all year round, causing plentiful dews in stark contrast to the parched land of that region (hence probably the Psalmist's allusion in Psalm 133:3), and the melting ice forms a major source of the Jordan.

Hermon is identified with the modern Jebel es-Sheik, 'the Sheik's mountain', 48 kilometres south-west of Damascus (but on this point see *GTT*, p. 83). Its proximity to Caesarea Philippi has made some suggest Hermon as the 'high mountain' (Mark 9:2, *etc.*) of the transfiguration.

A misleading reference to 'the Hermonites' (Psalm 42:6, AV) should probably be amended to RV 'The Hermons', signifying the three summits of Mount Hermon.
J. D. Douglas

**HESHBON** (Hebrew *ḥešbôn*, 'device'). A city of Moab, taken by Sihon king of the Amorites and made his royal city (Numbers 21:26). After his defeat by the Israelites (21:21–24) it was given to Reuben (32:37), but later passed over to Gad, whose land bordered on Reuben, and was assigned by them to the Levites (Joshua 21:39). By the time of Isaiah and Jeremiah, at the height of its prosperity, Moab had retaken it (Isaiah 15:4; Jeremiah 48:2, *etc.*), but by the time of Alexander Jannaeus it is once more in the hands of Israel (Josephus, *Antiquities* 13.397).

Remains of old pools and conduits may be seen in a branch of the present Wadi Hesbān which flows by the city (see Song of Songs 7:4).

Excavations during 1968–75 at Tell Hesbān have found buildings from the Iron Age, *c.* 1200 BC onwards, but no late Bronze Age remains that might be associated with Sihon. There are a few Late Bronze Age sites nearby, however, and one of these may have been th[e] Amorite capital. S. Horn has suggested that Jalul is the site.
M. A. MacLeod, A. R. Millard

*Further reading*

L. T. Geraty, *Ann. Department of Antiquities of Jordan* 20, 1975, pp. 47–56
L. T. Geraty in *NEAEHL* II, pp. 626–630

**HETHLON** (Hebrew *ḥeṯlôn*). A city on the ideal northern boundary of Palestine as seen by Ezekiel, near Hamath and Zedad and referred to only by him (Ezekiel 47:15; 48:1).

It is identified with the modern Heitela, north-east of Tripoli, Syria.
J. D. Douglas

**HIDDEKEL.** The ancient name of th[e] river *Tigris used in the account of the Garden of Eden (Genesis 2:14) and in Daniel's description of his visions (Daniel 10:4) in the third yea[r] of Cyrus. The name comes from the Akkadian *idiqlat*, which is equivalent to the Sumerian *idigna*, *i.e.* 'flowing river'.
T. C. Mitchell

*Further reading*

D. O. Edzard and others, *Répertoire Géographique des Textes Cunéiformes* 1, 1977, pp. 216–217
W. G. Lambert, *Reallexikon der Assyriologie* 5, 1976, pp. 31–32
D. T. Tsamura, *The Earth and the Waters in Genesis 1 and 2*, 1989, pp. 137–138
R. Zadok, *RGTC* 8, 1985, p. 361

**HIERAPOLIS.** A city in the Roman province of Asia, in the west of wh[at] is now Asiatic Turkey. It was situated about 10 kilometres north o[f] *Laodicea, on the opposite side of the broad valley of the Lycus.

The city was built around copiou[s] hot springs, which were famed for their medicinal powers. There was also a subterranean vent of poisonous gases (the Plutonium), which was later filled in by the Christians in about the 4th century AD. When the hot water flows over the edge of the city terrace it forms spectacular pools and cascades encrusted with lime. The resulting white cliffs give the site its modern name Pamukkale ('cotton castle').

These natural features made Hierapolis ('sacred city', for earlier 'Hieropolis', 'city of the sanctuary') an ancient centre of pagan cults, from which its importance and prosperity mainly derived.

The church in Hierapolis was
obably founded while Paul was
ing at Ephesus (Acts 19:10),
rhaps by Epaphras. It is
entioned only in conjunction with
s close neighbours, *Colossae and
aodicea (Colossians 4:13). There
ay be a reminiscence of its
mous hot waters in Revelation
15–16, in contrast with the cold
aters of Colossae and the tepid of
odicea.
According to Polycrates, bishop of
ohesus *c.* AD 190, as quoted by
isebius (*Church History* 3.31), the
ostle Philip was buried at
erapolis, though the authorities
ow confusion between apostle
d evangelist. Papias and the Stoic
ilosopher Epictetus were also
nnected with the city.
J. S. Rudwick, C. J. Hemer

*urther reading*
J. Hemer, *The Letters to the Seven*
*hurches of Asia in their Local*
*etting*, 1986, pp. 178–183

**LL, HILL-COUNTRY.** These terms
anslate the Hebrew words *giḇ'â*
d *har*. The root-meaning of the
rmer is convexity; bare hills, like
i inverted basin, are a common
ature of Palestine, notably the area
Judah. But *giḇ'â* is often a proper
ime (Gibeah) to indicate towns
ilt on such eminences, coupled
ith a distinguishing 'surname' (*e.g.*
f Saul', 1 Samuel 11:4).
The second word, *har*, may
dicate a single eminence or a range
hills; this led to some confusion in
e AV, but recent English versions
ake it clear when a range of hills is
eant. The mountainous backbone
Palestine is so styled sometimes
vided into the northern and
uthern parts of it, respectively
lled the hill-country 'of Ephraim'
id 'of Judah'. It should, however,
e noted that it is not always
ossible to decide whether a single
ll or a hilly region is meant.
F. Payne

**INNOM, VALLEY OF.** A valley to
e south of Jerusalem, also styled
he valley of the son (or sons) of
innom'. It was associated in
eremiah's time with the worship of
olech. Josiah defiled this shrine,
d put an end to the sacrifices
fered there.

*he mouth of hell'*
the New Testament and Jewish
ritings of the intertestamental
eriod the place becomes a
etaphor for hell, the Hebrew
rase *gê* ('valley of') *hinnōm*
becoming *geenna* in Greek, whence Gehenna in Latin and English. This is often said to be because the valley was used for burning corpses and refuse, but this traditional explanation cannot be traced earlier than *c.* AD 1200 and there is no evidence to support it. The valley's association with the fiery worship of Molech (2 Kings 23:10) provides a more likely explanation, as Molech was a god of the underworld and altars to Molech would have been thought of as entry-points into his realm. Thus Jewish tradition at one time held that the mouth of hell was in the valley.

*The problem of identification*
The identification of the valley presents problems. It formed part of the boundary between Judah and Benjamin, and lay between the 'south side of the Jebusite; the same is Jerusalem' and Enrogel (Joshua 15:7f., AV). So clearly the identification of these two localities will affect our identification of the Valley of Hinnom.

If *En-rogel was the Virgin's Fountain, the Valley of Hinnom can be equated with the Kidron valley, which runs from the east to the south-east of Jerusalem. But if it was what is now called Bir Eyyub, two possibilities remain: the valley was either the Tyropoeon valley, running from the centre of Jerusalem to the south-east, or the valley encircling the city on the west and south, now called the Wadi al-Rababi. Each of these three valleys, at its south-eastern extremity, terminates near Siloam.

Muslim tradition supports the Kidron valley identification, but that is the least likely; the great majority of scholars accept the Wadi al-Rababi as the correct identification.
D. F. Payne

*Further reading*
L. R. Bailey, *BA* 49/3, 1986, pp. 187–191

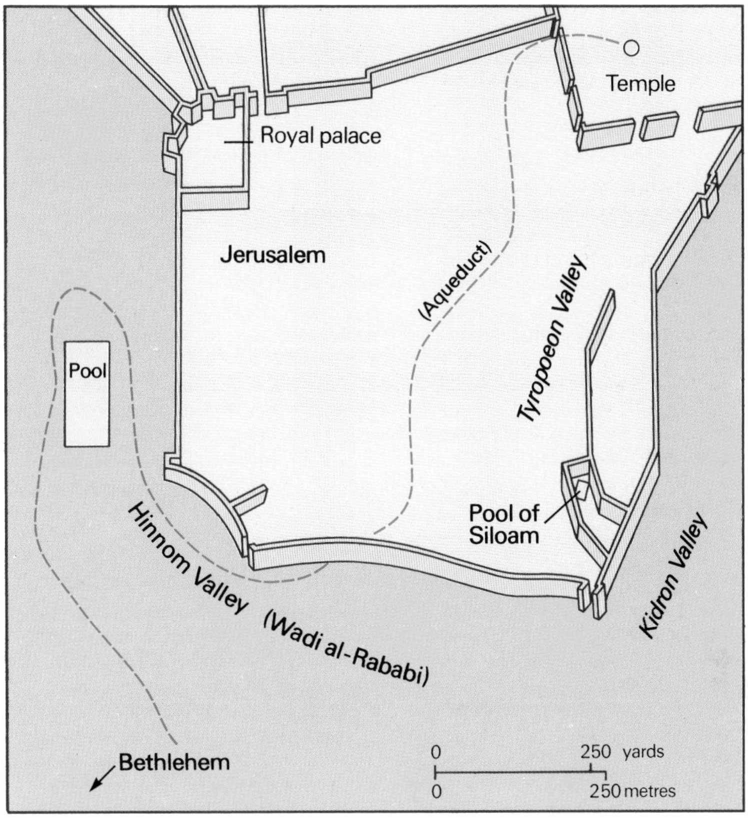

The Hinnom (Gehenna) valley, Jerusalem.

**HITTITES** (Hebrew *ḥittîm, b^enê ḥēṯ*). In the Old Testament the Hittites are, firstly, a great nation which gave its name to the whole region of Syria, 'from the wilderness and this Lebanon as far as the great river, the river Euphrates, all the land of the Hittites to the Great Sea toward the going down of the sun' (Joshua 1:4). Secondly, they are an ethnic group living in Canaan from patriarchal times until after the Israelite settlement (Genesis 15:20; Deuteronomy 7:1; Judges 3:5), called literally 'the children of Heth' (Genesis 23:3, etc.) after their eponymous ancestor Heth, a son of Canaan (Genesis 10:15).

### The Hittite empire

The Hittite empire was founded *c.* 1800 BC by an Indo-European nation which had settled in Asia Minor in city-states some two centuries before. They derived the name 'Hittite' from the Hatti, the earlier inhabitants of the area where they settled, whose legacy is clearly traceable in Hittite art and religion and in divine and royal names and titles. With the spread of the Hittite empire the designation 'Hittites' was extended to the peoples and lands which it incorporated.

*Hittite kings*

An early Hittite king, Tudhaliyas I (*c.* 1720 BC), has been identified (precariously) with 'Tidal king of nations' of Genesis 14:1. About 1600 BC Hattusilis I extended his rule over parts of northern Syria. His successor, Mursilis I, established a new capital at Hattusas (modern Boğaz-köy), east of the Halys; it is largely to the archives uncovered there since 1906 that we owe our knowledge of Hittite history and literature.

Mursilis I captured Aleppo and subsequently (*c.* 1560 BC) raided Babylon – an event which precipitated the fall of the first Babylonian Dynasty.

King Telepinus (*c.* 1480 BC) was the great Hittite legislator. There are some striking affinities between the Hittite law-codes and those of the Pentateuch, although affinities are found in matters of detail and arrangement rather than in general conception. Whereas the Pentateuchal codes resemble the great Semitic law-codes of the ancient Near East in employing the *lex talionis* as a basic principle, the Hittite laws are dominated by the distinctively Indo-European principle of compensation (*Wergild*). Some analogy has also been discerned between Hittite treaty forms and Old Testament covenant terms. Other notable points of contact are found in the levirate marriage and in the procedures for ascertaining the divine will or the unknown future by means of teraphim and *'ōḇôṯ* ('familiar spirits').

*Peak of Hittite power*

The Hittite empire reached the peak of its power under Suppiluliumas I (*c.* 1380–1350 BC). It was in his province of Kizzuwatna, in south-east Asia Minor, that iron was first smelted in the Near East on a scale which justifies one in speaking of the beginning of the Iron Age. He extended his empire over Upper Mesopotamia and over Syria as far south as the Lebanon. The Hittites thus collided with the northern thrust of the Egyptian empire in Asia, and hostilities continued between the two powers until 1284 BC, when a non-aggression pact between Hattusilis III and Rameses II recognized the Orontes as their common frontier.

*Fall of the empire*

The Hittite empire collapsed aroun[d] 1200 BC as the result of blows from western enemies.

### The Hittite kingdoms

With the fall of the Hittite empire, 2[4] city-states of the Tabali ('Tubal' in the Old Testament) became heirs t[o] the Hittite home territory north of th[e] Taurus range. In Syria seven city-states which had belonged to the Hittite empire perpetuated the name 'Hittite' for several centuries[;] their rulers were called 'the kings o[f] the Hittites'. Hamath on the Oronte[s] and Carchemish on the Euphrates were among the most important of the seven. Hamath was allied with David (2 Samuel 8:9ff.), whose kingdom bordered on 'Kadesh in th[e] land of the Hittites' (2 Samuel 24:6[;] see also *TAHTIM-HODSHI).

Solomon traded and intermarried with these 'kings of the Hittites' (1 Kings 10:28f.; 11:1). In the 9th century BC their military reputation could throw the army of Damascus into panic (2 Kings 7:6). But in the following century they were reduce[d] one by one by the Assyrians; Hamath fell in 720 BC and Carchemish in 717 (see 2 Kings 18:34; 19:13; Isaiah 10:9).

The Assyrian and Babylonian records of the period (as late as the

General view of the ruins of the great Hittite temple (Temple I) at Hattusas, perhaps dedicated to the weather god.

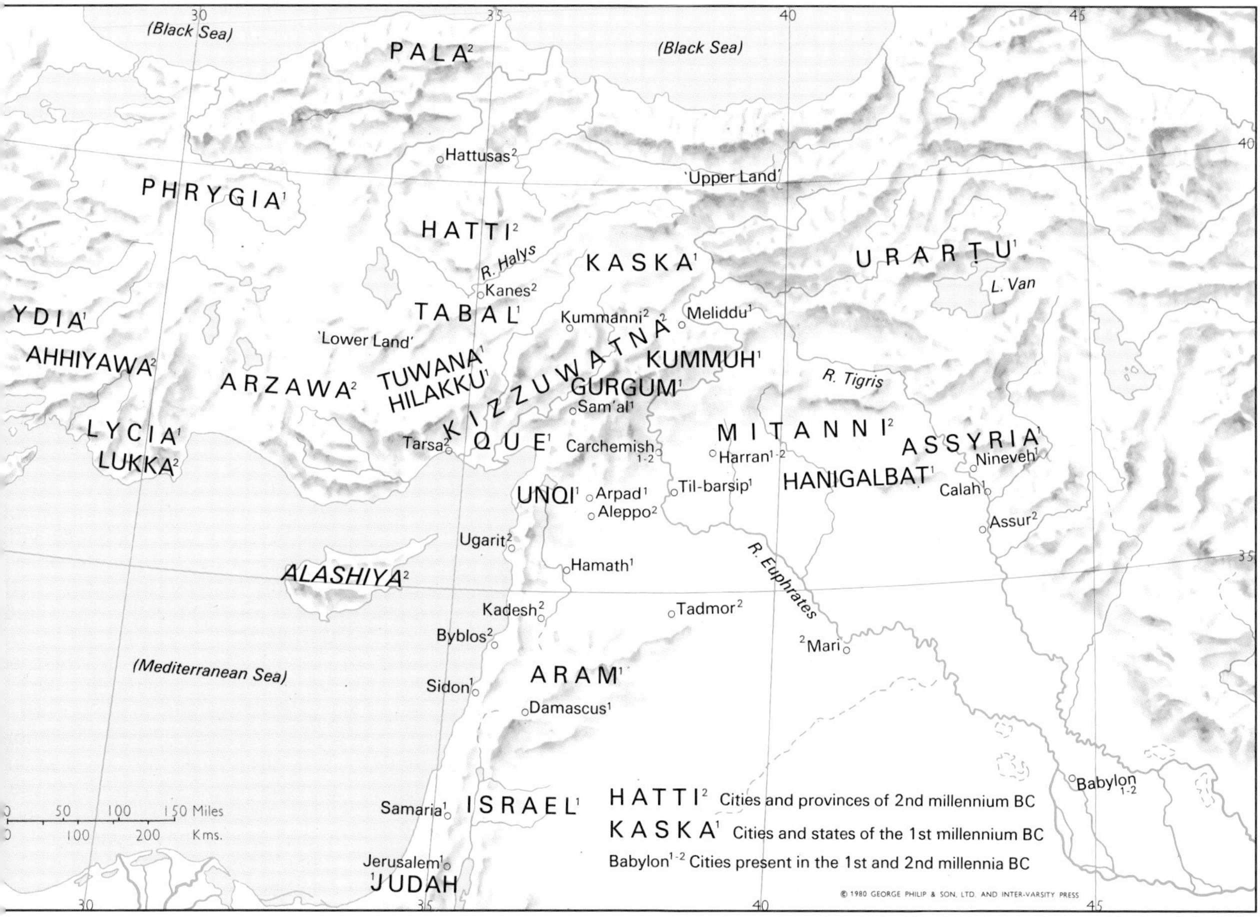


Areas under Hittite influence.

ıaldaean dynasty) regularly refer the whole of Syria (including ılestine) as the 'Hatti-land'; Sargon ın 711 BC can speak of the people of ıhdod as 'the faithless Hatti'.

*ınguage*

ıe language of the seven Hittite ıngdoms is known from hiero-yphic texts which have been ciphered in recent years; bilingual scriptions in hieroglyphic Hittite ıd Phoenician, discovered at ıratepe in Cilicia (1946–47), have ılped considerably in their cipherment. The language of ese texts is not identical with the ficial language of the earlier Hittite ıpire, which was written in ıneiform script and identified as an do-European language in 1917; it sembles rather a neighbouring do-European language called ıvian.

*ıe Hittites of Canaan*

ıe Hittites of Canaan in patriarchal ıes appear as inhabiting the ntral ridge of Judah, especially the ebron district. It has been surmised at they were a branch of the e-Indo-European Hatti, or early igrants from some part of the Hittite empire; the Hittite empire itself never extended so far south.

They may, on the other hand, have had nothing in common with the northern Hittites but their similar (though not identical) name. In Genesis 23 the Hittites are the resident population of Hebron ('the people of the land') among whom Abraham lives as 'a stranger and a sojourner' and from whom he buys the field of Machpelah, with its cave, as a family burying-ground. The record of the purchase is said to be 'permeated with intricate subtleties of Hittite laws and customs, correctly corresponding to the time of Abraham' (M. R. Lehmann, *BASOR* 129, 1953, p. 18; but see for another opinion G. M. Tucker, *JBL* 85, 1966, pp. 77ff.).

Esau grieved his parents by marrying two 'Hittite women . . . women of the land' (Genesis 27:46; see also 26:34f.) – apparently in the Beersheba region.

Jerusalem, according to Ezekiel 16:3, 45, had a mixed Hittite and Amorite foundation. The name of Araunah the Jebusite (2 Samuel 24:16ff.) has been thought to be Hittite, and Uriah the Hittite, evidently a Jerusalemite, was one of David's mighty men (2 Samuel 23:39). Ahimelech, one of David's companions in his days as an outlaw, is called a Hittite (1 Samuel 26:6).

The last reference to the Hittites of Canaan is in Solomon's reign (2 Chronicles 8:7). Thereafter they were merged in the general population of the land.

F. F. Bruce

*Further reading*

O. R. Gurney, *The Hittites*, revised edition, 1981
—, *Some Aspects of Hittite Religion*, 1976
— and J. Garstang, *The Geography of the Hittite Empire*, 1959
S. Lloyd, *Early Anatolia*, 1956
L. Woolley, *A Forgotten Kingdom*, 1953
E. Neufeld, *The Hittite Laws*, 1951
E. Akurgal, *The Art of the Hittites*, 1962
G. Walser (ed.), *Neuere Hethiter-forschung*, 1964
H. A. Hoffner, 'Some Contributions of Hittitology to OT Study', *TynB* 20, 1969, pp. 29ff.
—, 'The Hittites and Hurrians' in *POTT*, pp. 197ff.
J.G. Macqueen, *The Hittites*, 1975
J. Lehmann, *The Hittites*, 1977

**HOBAH.** The name of the place to which Abraham pursued the four kings who had pillaged Sodom and Gomorrah and carried off Lot (Genesis 14:15). It lay 'on the left hand of', that is (to one facing east) to the north of Damascus.

Though modern sites have been suggested, the place is unknown. A district Apu/Upu, which might be the same place, is mentioned in the *Amarna letters and identified by some with Tell el-Salihiye *c.* 20 kilometres east of Damascus.

T. C. Mitchell

*Further reading*

J. Lewy, *Orientalia* 21, 1952, p. 414 note 1

**HOLY LAND.** See *Palestine.

**HOR. 1.** A mountain on the border of Edom where Aaron was buried (Numbers 20:22–29; 33:37–39; Deuteronomy 32:50), possibly Moserah (Deuteronomy 10:6), although Numbers 33:30 and 39 distinguishes them. The place was in the region of Kadesh (Numbers 20:22; 33:37). More accurately it is 'Hor, the mountain', suggesting that it was a prominent feature.

Josephus (*Antiquities* 4.82) thought it was near Petra, and tradition has identified it with Jebel Nebi Harun, a lofty peak 1,460 metres high, to the west of Edom. This, however, is far from Kadesh.

Jebel Madeira, 24 kilometres north-east of Kadesh, on the north-western border of Edom has been suggested, for Israel began the detour round Edom at Mount Hor (Numbers 21:4), and Aaron could well have been buried here 'in the sight of all the congregation' (Numbers 20:22–29).

However, the site should be sought on 'the way of Atharim' from Kadesh-barnea to the vicinity of Arad, because it is always mentioned on the line of this journey (see references above).

**2.** A mountain on the northern border of Israel, mentioned only in Numbers 34:7–8; probably one of the northern summits of the Lebanese range in the vicinity of the coast. From Joshua 13:4 the northern border of 'the land that remains' included the region of Byblos and extended to Aphek on the Amorite border. Mount Hor was thus probably one of the north-western peaks of the Lebanese range north of Byblos, such as Ras Shaqqah.

J. A. Thompson

**HOREB.** See *Sinai.

**HORESH.** A place in the wilderness of Ziph (1 Samuel 23:15–19), possibly to be identified with Khirbet Khoreisa some 9–10 kilometres south of Hebron. The AV and RV 'wood' is grammatically possible but topographically unlikely; trees could scarcely have grown in this region.

R. P. Gordon

**HOR-HAGGIDGAD.** See *Gudgodah.

**HORMAH** (Hebrew *ḥormâh*). A town in the Negeb (Joshua 15:30; 19:4; 1 Chronicles 4:30); David shared the Amalekite spoils with its inhabitants (1 Samuel 30:30).

Formerly Canaanite Zephath, Hormah was destroyed by Judahites and Simeonites (Judges 1:17); its king is listed in Joshua 12:14. The Israelite name 'sacred' recalled the sacrifice of the captured town under the national vow made after a previous defeat (Numbers 21:1–3); there is no clear link with Numbers 14:45 (Deuteronomy 1:44), in which Hormah is named as the limit of pursuit after an abortive attempt to invade the hills.

The mention of *Arad with Hormah in Numbers 21 (and nowhere else, apart from Joshua 12) led many scholars to identify the two, or to suggest that Hormah was the chief city of a region Arad (B. Mazar, *JNES* 24, 1965, pp. 297–303).

Garstang proposed Tel Malhata, Tell el-Milh (20 kilometres east of Beersheba), but no Late Bronze remains were found. Meanwhile Tel Arad, 12 kilometres to the north-east, had been excavated and proved to have been a major fort under the Monarchy; but again, evidence of Late Bronze occupation was lacking.

A solution may have been found through excavations in the area of Tel Masos/Khirbet Meshash (15 kilometres east of Beersheba). Here were unwalled villages towards the end of the 2nd millennium BC, but later the site was abandoned and a fort built at Khirbet el-Gharra, Tel Ira, 150 metres above the river-bed.

J. P. U. Lilley

*Further reading*

Y. Aharoni, *LOB*, pp. 201, 215ff., 353

—— in *BA* 39, 1976, pp. 55–76

V. Fritz, *BASOR* 241, 1981, pp. 61–74

A. Frendo, *PEQ*, 1987, pp. 156f. (reviewing excavation reports by A. Kempinski)

**HORONAIM.** A town of Moab (Isaiah 15:5; Jeremiah 48:3, 5, 34) which lay at the foot of a plateau close to Zoar. The Moabite Stone refers to it in line 32.

Some would identify it with el-'Araq, 500 metres below the plateau, where there are springs, gardens and caves. Other possible sites are Kathrabba, 7 kilometres north of el-'Araq, and Tell el Mise, south-east of Kathrabba. It may, however, be Oronae, taken by Alexander Jannaeus from the Arabs and restored to the Nabataean king by Alexander Jannaeus (Josephus, *Antiquities* 13.397; 14.18).

J. A. Thompson

*Further reading*

S. Mittmann, 'The Ascent of Luhith' in A. Hadidi, ed., *Studies in the Archaeology and History of Jordan* 1, Amman, 1982, pp. 175–180

**HOUSE OF EDEN.** See *Eden, House of.

**HUKKOK.** A town on the southern border of Naphtali, listed with Aznoth-tabor (Joshua 19:34). It is generally identified with Yakuk, 8 kilometres west of the suggested site of Capernaum. 1 Chronicles 6:75 gives it as a Levitical city in Asher, but this may be a mistake for Helkath, as in the parallel passage in Joshua 21:31. Y. Aharoni (*LOB*, p. 436) proposed Khirbet el-Jemeijmeh. For a discussion, see Z. Kallai in *Historical Geography of the Bible*, 1986, pp. 190–192.

J. D. Douglas, A. R. Millard

**HUKOK.** See *Helkath.

**HUNDRED, TOWER OF THE.** In Nehemiah 3:1 and 12:39, a Jerusalem tower which stood between the Sheep and Fish Gates in the northern part of the city. The Hebrew is *ham-mē'â*, meaning 'the hundred'. The AV reads 'Meah', omitting the definite article, while the RSV translates it literally. The name may refer to its height – perhaps 100 cubits; or to the number of its steps; or to the number of the garrison it housed. (See also *Hananel and *Jerusalem.)

D. F. Payne

**LEAM.** A Canaanite town in the
rthern borderland of Manasseh,
iose territory extended to (not
') Issachar (Joshua 17:11; Y.
ufmann, *The Biblical Account of
e Conquest of Palestine*, 1953,
38). During the Israelite
ttlement, its Canaanite
iabitants were subdued, not
pelled (Judges 1:27).
The site of Ibleam is now Khirbet
'ameh, *c.* 16 kilometres south-east
Megiddo on the road from
th-shean (2 Kings 9:27). It is
obably the Bileam of 1 Chronicles
70, a levitical city. Ibleam occurs in
yptian lists as *Ybr'm*.
A. Kitchen

**ONIUM.** A city of Asia Minor
entioned in Acts 13:51, 14:1, *etc.*
d 2 Timothy 3:11 as the scene of
ul's trials, and in Acts 16:2 as a
ice where Timothy was
mmended.
Standing on the edge of the
ateau, Iconium was well watered,
productive and wealthy region. It
is originally Phrygian, its name
wania: its religion remained
rygian into Roman times, the
orship of a mother goddess with
nuch priests. After being for a
ne the chief city of Lycaonia, and
ssing through various political
tunes, it was at length included in
kingdom of Galatia and a little
er in the Roman province of
latia.
conium was the site of a colony
m at least the time of Augustus, as
cently published coins show. This
is not an honorary title, as was
eviously thought. A separate
mmunity of colonists existed with
own coinage and decrees,
ongside a Greek *polis*. The latter
is honoured by Claudius with the
e of Claudiconium. In New
stament times, then, it
intained the polity of a Hellenistic
y, the juridical powers of the
sembly being vested in the two
gistrates annually appointed.

*Paul in Iconium*

The passage in Acts 14, though brief, gives occasion for differing interpretations. The so-called Western Text implies two attacks on Paul, one open, the second more subtle, after which the apostles flee. Two classes of Jewish leaders are mentioned, 'chief men of the synagogue' and 'rulers', a distinction epigraphically defensible.

The Codex Vaticanus and its allies have a more difficult text with only one attack of fairly long duration implied. Here the rulers of verse 5 may plausibly be identified with the magistrates of the city, as Ramsay suggests. Whether the Codex Vaticanus text is a bad abbreviation, or the Western Text an attempt at correction of a text perhaps corrupt, has not yet been finally decided.

Iconium is the scene of the well-known apocryphal story of Paul and Thecla, contained in the longer *Acts of Paul*. Apart from the scarcely doubtful existence of an early martyr of the name, there is no ascertainable historical content to be found in the story.

J. N. Birdsall

*Further reading*

Commentaries on Acts, especially *BC* 3, pp. 129–132; 4, pp. 160–162
W. M. Ramsay, *Cities of St Paul*, 1907, part iv
Albert C. Clark, *The Acts of the Apostles*, 1933, pp. 85–87, 357 ref. xiv.2
M. E. Boismard, A. Lamouille, *Texte Occidental des Actes des Apôtres*, 1984, vol. I, pp. 172f., vol. II, pp. 96f.
G. H. R. Horsley, 'Galatia in recent research' in *New Documents illustrating early Christianity*, vol. 4, 1987, pp. 138f.

**IDUMAEA.** The Greek form (*idoumaia*) of the Hebrew *'ᵉdôm* refers to an area in western Palestine, rather than to Edom proper. At the time of the Exodus, Edom extended to both sides of the Arabah, and the western portion reached close to Kadesh (Numbers 20:16).

David subdued Edom, but there was continual conflict between *Edom and Judah. After the fall of Jerusalem in 587 BC the Edomites took advantage of the calamity to migrate into the heart of southern Judah, south of Hebron. Several prophets inveighed against Edom for this (Jeremiah 49:7–22; Lamentations 4:21–22; Ezekiel 25:12–14; 35:3; Obadiah 10ff.).

Later, as various Arab groups, notably the Nabataeans, pressed into old Edom, more migrants settled in Judah, and the area they occupied became known as Idumaea (1 Maccabees 4:29; 5:65). Judas Maccabaeus had successful campaigns against these people, and John Hyrcanus subdued them *c.* 126 BC, placed them under Antipater as governor and compelled them to be circumcised (Josephus, *Antiquities* 13.258). Antipater was the grandfather of Herod the Great.

The word Idumaea occurs in the New Testament only in Mark 3:8.

J. A. Thompson

**IIM.** See *IYE-ABARIM.

**IJON.** A town in northern Naphtali taken by the Syrians under Ben-hadad along with *Dan and *Abel of Beth-maacah (1 Kings 15:20; 2 Chronicles 16:4). Subsequently the town was captured by Tiglath-pileser III in 733 BC (2 Kings 15:29).

**The Selimiye Kamii mosque, Konya (Turkey), ancient Iconium.**

Possibly it is the Dan-jaan of 2 Samuel 24:6.

Ijon is generally identified with Tell Dibbin, 30 kilometres north of Lake Huleh. The site has not been excavated, but surface surveys have produced pottery from the Bronze Age to the Arabic period.

D. W. Baker, J. J. Bimson

**ILIUM.** See *TROAS.

**ILLYRICUM.** The name of the large mountainous region on the east of the Adriatic, extending to the central Balkans in the east and reaching from north-eastern Italy and the Celtic tribes in the north to Macedonia in the south. Its name was derived from that of one of the first tribes within its boundaries whom the Greeks came across. Its inhabitants spoke dialects which were probably the linguistic ancestors of modern Albanian.

The Romans had first come into conflict with some of the tribes of Illyricum in the 3rd century BC, but it was not finally conquered till the early 1st century AD. In the Flavian period (AD 69–96) it was divided into two provinces, later called Pannonia and Dalmatia.

*Paul's links with Illyricum*

Paul says at the time of writing the Epistle to the Romans (15:19) that Illyricum was the limit of his evangelistic activity. His reference to it appears to be inclusive, but it is not known when, or from what direction, he had entered it (possibly from Macedonia when he revisited that province after his Ephesian ministry, Acts 20:1). It was the first Latin-speaking province which he visited in the course of his apostolic ministry, and could have prepared him for his projected mission in Latin-speaking Spain (Romans 15:24, 28).

B. F. C. Atkinson

**INDIA**

**Early period**

Hebrew *hōddû*, from Old Persian *hindu* (compare Sanskrit *sindhu*), in inscriptions of Darius I and Xerxes I of Persia. The area so designated was that part of the Indus valley and plains east of the Afghan mountains incorporated into the Persian empire by Darius I, who made it his eastern boundary (Herodotus, 3.94; 4.40, 44).

In Esther 1:1 and 8:9 the limits of the dominion of Ahasuerus (Xerxes I) are 'from India unto Ethiopia', *hōddû* and *kûš*; this corresponds with Xerxes I's own Old Persian inscriptions, see the list of countries including 'Sind' or India (*Hiduš*) and Ethiopia (*Kušiya*) in R. G. Kent, *Old Persian: Grammar, Texts, Lexicon*, 1953 edition, p. 151, lines 25 and 29 and section 3.

But long before this, trade between India and Mesopotamia is known as early as *c.* 2100 BC (Ur III period), both in texts and by the presence of Indus Valley seals in Mesopotamia. Some think that *Ophir might be the Indian (S)upāra.

India was the source of the war-elephants used by Alexander and his Seleucid successors in Syria, and in the Graeco-Roman period many exotic products came from India, usually through southern Arabia, either up the Red Sea or overland up the western side of Arabia. On routes and navigation, see van Beek and Hourani in *JAOS* 78, 1958, pp. 146–147; and 80, 1960, pp. 135–139.

Greek principalities maintained themselves for some time in parts of north-western India; see W. W. Tarn, *The Greeks in Bactria and India*, 1938. For Indians in Egypt in the Graeco-Roman period, see Sir H. I. Bell, *Cults and Creeds in Graeco-Roman Egypt*, 1953, p. 48; E. Bevan, *History of Egypt under the Ptolemaic Dynasty*, 1927, p. 155; models from Memphis: Petrie, *Memphis I*, 1909, pp. 16–17, plate 39.

**Later period**

Between the 1st century BC and *c.* AD 200, India and the Mediterranean lands entered into closer commercial and cultural relations, stimulated by the Roman market for Eastern luxuries and facilitated by the discovery of the nature of the monsoons, with the subsequent opening of a regular sea-route to the Tamil towns (modern Cranganore and Kottayam) and even to Madras (*Sopatma*) and beyond.

*Origin of the church in India*

Against this background we must view the stories of the first introduction of Christianity to India. The unanimous tradition of the old South India church traces its foundation to Thomas the apostle. The narrative of the gnosticizing *Acts of* (Judas) *Thomas* also sets Thomas's activities in India. In itself it is the wildest legend, but J. N. Farquhar argued that it reflects accurate knowledge of 1st-century India and postulated that Thomas worked first in the Punjab and later in the south (*BJRL* 11, 1926; 12, 1927). There seems, however, no other early account of Thomas in India clearly independent of these *Acts* (A. Mingana, *BJRL* 11, 1926; 1[illegible] 1927).

The peripatetic Pantaenus is sai[d] to have been a missionary in India some time before AD 180, and to hav[e] found Christians there with Matthew's Gospel in Hebrew left b[y] Bartholomew (Eusebius, *Church History* 5.10); but a loose designation of Aden or some other part of Arabia may be involved.

That the Syriac South India chur[ch] is very ancient is undeniable: the question of apostolic or subaposto[lic] foundation remains open.

K. A. Kitchen

*Further reading*

E. H. Warmington, *Indian Commerce*, 1928

L. W. Browne, *The Indian Christia[ns] of St Thomas*, 1956

**IONIA.** See *JAVAN.

**ISSACHAR.** Issachar's tribal porti[on] fell between Mount Gilboa and the hills of Lower Galilee, at the easte[rn] end of the Valley of Jezreel, but the boundaries cannot be drawn precisely. In some of the lists (*e.g.*, Judges 1:30) Issachar is not mentioned and may have been included with Zebulun (as Simeon was incorporated with Judah). Manasseh also seems to have expanded northwards into the territory of Issachar. Sixteen cities and their associated villages were assigned to Issachar (Joshua 19:17–23; compare 17:10–11).

The close connection between Zebulun and Issachar is shown in their inclusion in a common blessi[ng] (Deuteronomy 33:18–19). The mountain mentioned is undoubted[ly] Tabor, where there was a commo[n] sanctuary.

Issachar was involved in the campaign led by Deborah, who probably came from this tribe (Judges 5:15), although it is not mentioned in the prose account (ch. 4). The battle began in Issachar's territory and completely broke the Canaanite domination o[f] the low-lying areas. The minor judge, Tola, was a man of Issachar (Judges 10:1) as was also the usurper, Baasha (1 Kings 15:27).

Issachar was one of the twelve administrative districts set up by Solomon (1 Kings 4:17).

The blessing of Jacob (Genesis 49:14–15) has been viewed as evidence that part of Issachar was resident in the land in the Amarna period, maintaining its position by

ing a certain amount of npulsory labour to its Canaanite erlords. But the implied reproach y be merely a statement of the t that Issachar's material sperity made it submissive and ete. At the time of David, wever, the tribe had gained a outation for wisdom (1 Chronicles .32), a fact which re-emerges in Talmudic statement that the sest members of the Sanhedrin ne from Issachar.
E. Cundall

*rther reading*
*B*, pp. 200, 212, 223, 232f.
Alt, *PJB* 24, 1928, pp. 47ff.
F. Albright. *JAOS* 74, 1954, pp. 2f.
Yeivin, *Mélanges A. Robert*, 1957, . 100ff.

**ALY** (Greek *Italia*). The name *Italia* s probably a Greek form of *Italic* *elia*, 'calf-land', which was ginally a reference to the southern lf of the 'toe'. It was finally unified der Augustus who divided it into ven administrative districts. By middle of the 1st century the me had come to have substantially modern geographical meaning. en before the time of Christ many ws had resorted to Italy, especially the metropolis.
It was because the emperor audius had evicted the Jews from me that Paul met Aquila and scilla (Acts 18:2). Rome was the ostle's destination when after his peal to Caesar he and other soners embarked at Caesarea cts 27:1, 6).
In Hebrews 13:24 'those who me from Italy' greet the dressees.
). Douglas, B. W. Winter

**URAEA** (Greek *Itouraia*, Luke 3:1). e name, mentioned in conjunction th *Trachonitis, almost certainly mes from the Hebrew *y$^{e}$ṭûr* etur'), a son of Ishmael (Genesis :15–16; 1 Chronicles 1:31), ntioned also as a tribe at war with Israelites east of the Jordan (1 ronicles 5:19). Little or nothing is own of them thereafter until the ne of the Jewish king Aristobulus I 05–104 BC), who is recorded as ving fought against the Ituraeans d taken from them a portion of eir land (Josephus, *Antiquities* .318). Thereafter frequent allusion made to them by classical writers osephus, Strabo, Pliny, Dio ssius, *etc.*). Sometimes they are lled Syrians, sometimes Arabians. At the time of the Roman conquest they were known as a wild robber tribe especially proficient in the use of the bow, but not associated with any precisely defined geographical location. It was part of the territory ruled by Herod the Great, after whose death in 4 BC his kingdom was partitioned, and certain lands including Trachonitis and what was called 'the house of Zeno (or Zenodorus) about Paneas' formed the tetrarchy of Philip. If, as seems likely, this latter section was inhabited by Ituraeans, it may have been known as Ituraea, for migratory tribes frequently gave their name to their new home.

Josephus, in defining the limits of Philip's sovereignty, does not specifically mention Ituraea – some would say because it was indistinguishable from Trachonitis (*Antiquities* 17.189).

Is Luke's reference, then, to be understood as a noun or as an adjectival form? Does he intend the place or the people? No certainty is possible. Place-names of this region and time are notoriously elastic and liable to corruption, and overlapping is frequently found. The most we can safely say is that it was, in W. Manson's words (*Luke* in *MNTC*), 'a hilly country in the Anti-Lebanon range, inhabited by roving Arabs'.

Caligula gave it to Herod Agrippa I. When the latter died it was incorporated into the province of Syria under procurators.
J. D. Douglas

*Further reading*
Discussions by W. M. Ramsay and G. A. Smith in *The Expositor* 4, 9, 1894, pp. 51–55, 143–149, 231–238
E. Schürer, *HJP* 1, 1973, pp. 561–573
A. H. M. Jones, *The Herods of Judaea*, 1938, pp. 9–11, *passim*

**IVAH.** A foreign town conquered by the Assyrians during the time of Isaiah and used as an illustration of the inevitability of the defeat of Samaria (2 Kings 18:34; 19:13; Isaiah 37:13). Probably it is the Ava of 2 Kings 17:24. The location is unknown.
D. W. Baker

**IYE-ABARIM,** a stopping-place on the Exodus journey on the borders of Moab (Numbers 21:11; 33:44–45). Iye-abarim (Hebrew *'iyyê hā'$^{a}$ḇārîm*, ruins of Abarim, or of the regions beyond) is abbreviated in Numbers 33:45 AV to Iim.

Abel identifies Iye-abarim with the ancient site of Maḥaiy to the south-east of Moab, Glueck places it farther west, and du Buit chooses a site near the river Arnon. Its position is still debatable.
J. A. Thompson

# J

**JAAR** (Hebrew *ya'ar*, 'forest') in the Old Testament usually means 'forest', but once only it may be a proper name (Psalm 132:6) as a poetical abbreviation for *Kiriath-jearim (city of forests).

The allusion in Psalm 132 is to the bringing of the ark to Jerusalem from Kiriath-jearim, where it had lain for 20 years or more after it was recovered from the Philistines (1 Samuel 7:1–2; 1 Chronicles 13:5). Some take the word here, as elsewhere, to mean forest and refer 'it' to the oath in the preceding verses.

M. A. MacLeod

**JABBOK.** A river flowing west into the river Jordan, some 32 kilometres north of the Dead Sea. It rises near Amman (see also *RABBAH) in Jordan and in all is over 96 kilometres long. It is today called the Wadi Zerqa. It marked a boundary line between Ammonite and Gadite territory (Deuteronomy 3:16), once the Israelites had defeated the Amorite king Sihon south of the Jabbok (Numbers 21:21ff.).

The Jabbok was also the river forded by Jacob (Genesis 32:22) on the occasion of his wrestling with the angel and subsequent change of name. Several scholars have noted a probable word-play in verses 22–24 involving 'Jacob' (*ya'aqōb*), 'and he wrestled' (*wayyē'ābēq*) and 'Jabbok' (*yabbōq*).

D. F. Payne, J. J. Bimson

*Further reading*
C. Westermann, *Genesis 12–36*, 1985, pp. 512–520
H. A. McKay, *JSOT* 38, 1987, pp. 3–13

The river Jabbok (modern Zerqa) near its source at Amman, Jordan.

**JABESH-GILEAD** (Hebrew *yāḇēš gil'āḏ*). An Israelite town east of the Jordan which kept out of the war against Benjamin and suffered severe reprisals (Judges 21). Here Saul proved his kingship, routing the Ammonites who were besieging it (1 Samuel 11). The citizens rescued Saul's body from the walls of Beth-shan after the battle of Gilboa (1 Samuel 31; 1 Chronicles 10).

Jabesh was obviously in a strong position near the Wadi Yabis, which enters the Jordan 12 kilometres south of Beth-shan. Most authorities identify it with Tell el-Maqlub, which agrees with the indication in Eusebius, *Onomasticon* 110 (6 Roman miles from Pella towards Gerasa). No other site upstream has pre-Roman remains.

Glueck argued that it was an unlikely location for the attack described in 1 Samuel 11:11, and to far from Beth-shan in view of 1 Samuel 31:11f.; he proposed Tell ab Kharaz, on a hill dominating the outfall of the Wadi Yabis. The relationship between these sites ha yet to be clarified; if they were contemporary, Glueck's argument has some force.

J. P. U. Lilley

*Further reading*
N. Glueck in *BASOR* 89 and 91, 194
——, *The River Jordan*, 1946, pp. 159–166
J. Simons, *GTT*, p. 315
Y. Aharoni, *LOB*, p. 127

**JABEZ** (Hebrew *ya'bēṣ*, 'he makes sorrowful' or 'he fashions'). A city, evidently in Judah, inhabited by 'th families of the scribes' (1 Chronicle 2:55). The site, apparently near Bethlehem, has not been identified.

J. D. Douglas

**JABNEEL** (Hebrew *yaḇn*[e]*'ēl*, 'God (El) causes to build'), a name, of which a comparable form *Jabni-ilu* occurs in the Amarna letters. It is used of two places in the Bible.

**1.** A city on the south-western boundary of Judah (Joshua 15:11) and probably to be identified with Jabneh, a Philistine city which was captured by Uzziah (2 Chronicles 26:6). Jabneh was called Jamnia in the Greek and Roman periods, and was at this city that the Sanhedrin was re-formed after the destructio of Jerusalem in AD 70.

Two sites vie for identification with Jabneh/Jamnia: Yibna, on the coastal plain south of Nahal Sorek, and Yavneh-Yam on the coast. Both are largely unexcavated so neither theory can be substantiated.

**2.** A town of Naphtali (Joshua 19:33), possibly to be identified wi modern Khirbet Yamma. However, surface pottery at this site does no suggest occupation in the Late Bronze or Iron Ages, and for this reason Tel Yin'am (1·5 kilometres t the north-east), which does have remains from those periods, is to b preferred.

T. C. Mitchell, J. B. Bimson

*Further reading*
M. Avi-Yonah, *Gazetteer of Roman Palestine* (Qedem, 5), 1976, p. 67
S. Z. Leiman, *The Canonization of Hebrew Scripture*, 1976, pp. 120–1
R. Beckwith, *The Old Testament Canon of the New Testament Church*, 1985, pp. 276–277

**COB'S WELL.** See *SYCHAR.

**FFA.** See *JOPPA.

**HAZ** (Hebrew *yahaṣ*). A site in the ins of Moab where Israel defeated on, the Amorite king (Numbers :23; Deuteronomy 2:32; Judges :20). The name occurs in several ms – Jahzah, Jahaza (Joshua :18), and Jahazah (Joshua 21:36; emiah 48:21). It fell in the portion Reuben, and was assigned to the rarite Levites (Joshua 13:18; :34, 36). The area was later lost to ael, but Omri reconquered the d as far as Jahaz.

The Moabite Stone (lines 18–20) tes that the Israelites dwelt there ile they fought Mesha. Finally, sha drove them out and added naz to his domains.

M. du Buit would place the site just the central highlands road on the ht of the Wadi Wali. Y. Aharoni s proposed Khirbet el-Medeiyineh the fringe of the desert (*LOB*, 339). No fewer than five other sites ve been suggested but deiyineh, the largest Iron Age e in the immediate area, remains e most likely.

The city was still in Moabite hands the days of Isaiah and Jeremiah aiah 15:4; Jeremiah 48:21, 34).

A. Thompson

**NOAH** (Hebrew *yānôaḥ, yānôḥâ*, st'). **1.** A town of Naphtali seized Tiglath-pileser during Pekah's gn (2 Kings 15:29); possibly odern Yanūḥ, north-west of Acco *OB*, p. 379).

**2.** A town of Ephraim, south-east m Shechem, used in defining hraim's border with Manasseh oshua 16:6–70; AV 'Janohah'). It is her Yanun, 11 kilometres uth-east of Nablus (Shechem), or irbet Yānum, 1·5 kilometres rth-east of Yanum.

G. G. Norman

**RMUTH** (Hebrew *yarmûṯ*). **1.** A naanite royal city (Joshua 10:3); er a town in the Socoh district oshua 15:35), re-occupied after the ile (Nehemiah 11:28). Apparently became important in the 15th ntury BC. It is usually taken to be l Yarmut, Khirbet el-Yarmuk, on a ge above a branch of the Wadi rar, 5 kilometres south of th-shemesh; but excavations ve revealed a large Early Bronze y, with scanty Late Bronze and bsequent occupation mainly on e acropolis. The identification ust therefore be treated with serve.

**2.** A levitical town in Issachar, Joshua 21:29, otherwise Remeth (Joshua 19:21; compare the Septuagint (B) Joshua 21:29) or Ramoth (1 Chronicles 6:73); perhaps Kokhav-hayyarden, Belvoir of the Crusaders, overlooking the Jordan Valley between Beth-shan and Lake Galilee. The Egyptians called the district 'Hills of Yarmuta' (stele of Seti I found at Beth-shan, *ANET*, p. 255).

J. P. U. Lilley

*Further reading*

On **1**:

W. F. Albright in *BASOR* 87, 1942, pp. 32–38

Y. Aharoni, *LOB*, pp. 174, 212

A. Ben-Tor in *IEJ* 21, 1971, pp. 173–178

——, *Qedem* 1, 1975

P. de Miroschedji, excavation reports in *IEJ* 31–38, 1981–1988

On **2**:

Y. Aharoni, *LOB*, pp. 28, 179

**JATTIR** (Hebrew *yattir*). Hurvat Yatir, on the south-western escarpment of the Hills of Judah, 21 kilometres from Hebron; assigned to the priests (Joshua 21:14). David shared the spoils of the Amalekites with its inhabitants (1 Samuel 30:27).

J. P. U. Lilley

**JAVAN.** One of the sons of Japheth (Genesis 10:2; 1 Chronicles 1:5) and father of a group of peoples, *Elishah, *Tarshish, *Kittim and Dodanim (Genesis 10:4; 1 Chronicles 1:7), whose associations are with the regions to the north and west of the Middle East.

It is generally accepted that this name (Hebrew *yāwān*) is to be identified with the Greek *Iōnes*, which occurs as *Iaones*, probably for *Iawones*, in Homer (*Iliad* 13.685), and refers to the people who later gave their name to Ionia. The name also occurs in Assyrian and Achaemenian inscriptions (*Iâmanu* and *Yauna* respectively).

Isaiah mentions the descendants of Javan (Septuagint *Hellas*) beside Tubal as one of the nations (*gôyīm*) inhabiting distant islands and coastlands (*'iyyîm*, Isaiah 66:19).

In the time of Ezekiel the descendants of Javan (Septuagint *Hellas*) were known as traders in men, bronze vessels and yarn, with Tyre (Ezekiel 27:13, 19; in verse 19 the RSV prefers to read *mē'ûzāl*, 'from Uzal', for *m$^{e}$ûzzāl*, 'that which is spun, yarn').

The name Javan ('Greece' in English versions) is used in the prophecies of Daniel to refer to the kingdom of Alexander of Macedon (Daniel 8:21; 10:20; 11:2), and in Zechariah 9:13 the term (English verions 'Greece', Septuagint *Hellēnes*) is probably used of the Seleucid Greeks.

T. C. Mitchell

*Further reading*

P. Dhorme, *Syria* 13, 1932, pp. 35–36

W. Brandenstein and M. Mayrhofer, *Handbuch des Altpersischen*, 1964, p. 156

**JAZER.** A town of the Amorite kingdom of Sihon captured by Israel (Numbers 21:32) and part of the pasture-lands allotted to the tribe of Gad. It was later given to the Merarite families of the tribe of Levi.

During David's reign, Jazer furnished 'mighty men of valour' (1 Chronicles 26:31) and was one of the towns on the route of the census-takers (2 Samuel 24:5). The Moabites gained control of it, probably a little before the fall of Samaria (Isaiah 16:8–9; Jeremiah 48:32, where 'sea of' has been considered a scribal error). Judas Maccabaeus captured and sacked the town *c.* 164 BC (1 Maccabees 5:7–8).

The site may be Khirbet Gazzir on the Wadi Ša'īb near es-Salt.

A. R. Millard

*Further reading*

Z. Kallai, *Historical Geography of the Bible*, 1986, pp. 268–270

**JEBUS, JEBUSITE.** Jebusite was the ethnic name of a people dwelling in the hills (Numbers 13:29; Joshua 11:3) round about Jerusalem (Joshua 15:8; 18:16). Descended from the third son of Canaan (Genesis 10:16; 1 Chronicles 1:14), they are, however, listed as a distinct, but minority, group of people living alongside such peoples as Amorites and Heth.

Jebus was a name given to *Jerusalem, the principal city in their territory (Judges 19:10–11; 1 Chronicles 11:45; called Jebusi in Joshua 18:16, 28, RSV), and 'Jebusite' described the inhabitants of the city (Genesis 15:21; Exodus 3:8). Later the term is used of the former inhabitants (Ezekiel 16:3, 45; Zechariah 9:7).

Specifically, Jebus should probably be identified with the eastern hill of Jerusalem, referred to as 'the shoulder of the Jebusites' (Joshua 18:16). However, while Jerusalem is referred to in Egyptian Execration Texts of the 19th-18th centuries BC, and in the 14th century

Jericho seen from Tulul Abe al-'Alayiq, site of the magnificent Hasmonaean and Herodian winter palace complexes.

BC Amarna tablets, these sources do not use the name Jebus. This has led some scholars to suggest that the name was applied to Jerusalem only in a secondary sense because it was controlled by the Jebusites, and that the original Jebus lay elsewhere. Thus J. M. Miller suggests that Jebus should actually be located at present-day Sha'fat, slightly north of Jerusalem (J. M. Miller, *ZDPV* 90, 1974, pp. 115–127).

D. J. Wiseman, J. J. Bimson

**JEHOSHAPHAT, VALLEY OF.** The name which Joel gives to the place of final judgment in Joel 3:2 and 12. In both of these verses 'Jehoshaphat' (meaning 'Yahweh has judged') is associated with statements that God will judge (Hebrew *šāpaṭ*). Therefore it is probable that 'the valley of Jehoshaphat', like 'the valley of decision' in verse 14, is a term symbolic of the judgment, not a current geographical name.

The valley of Jehoshaphat has been variously identified. Some have thought that Joel had no definite place in mind; *e.g.* Targum Jonathan translates this name 'the plain of the decision of judgment', and Theodotion renders 'the place of judgment'.

Since Joel uses the geographical term 'valley', most students have thought that some location was intended. Ibn Ezra suggests the valley of Berachah south of Bethlehem, where Jehoshaphat's forces gathered after the destruction of enemies (2 Chronicles 20:26), but Zechariah 14 locates the judgment near Jerusalem, and according to 1 Enoch 53:1 all people gather for judgment in a deep valley near the valley of *Hinnom. This tradition may be based on the prophecy in Jeremiah 7:32–34 and 19:6–8 that God would turn the valley of Hinnom into a place of slaughter because of the sins of Jerusalem.

Jewish, Christian and Muslim traditions identify the place of final judgment as the Kidron valley, between Jerusalem and the Mount of Olives. Therefore many have been buried there, Muslims especially on the western slope and Jews especially on the eastern slope of the valley. A Graeco-Roman tomb on the eastern slope has been called mistakenly the tomb of King Jehoshaphat. As early as the Bordeaux pilgrim (AD 333) and Eusebius' *Onomasticon* (under *Koilas*), the name Jehoshaphat was associated with this valley. Some object that Joel uses the word *'ēmeq*, 'broad valley', while the Kidron valley is called *naḥal*, 'ravine' (2 Samuel 15:23).

Other identifications are 'the king's dale' (2 Samuel 18:18), which runs into the Kidron valley from the north-west (so C. F. Keil, E. G. Kraeling) and the valley of Hinnom, west and south of Jerusalem (so G. W. Wade).

J. Thompson

*Further reading*

E. Robinson, *Biblical Researches in Palestine* 1, 1856, pp. 268–273

J. A. Bewer in *ICC*, 1912, on Joel 3 (Massoretic Text 4):2

E. G. Kraeling, *Rand McNally Bible Atlas*, 1956, p. 342

## JERICHO

### Name

The original meaning of the name Jericho is open to doubt. It is simplest to take the Hebrew *y<sup></sup>*ᵉ*rîḥ*... as from the same root as *yārēaḥ*, 'moon', and to connect it with the early western Semitic moon-god *Yariḥ* or *Yeraḥ*. See remarks by Albright in *Archaeology and the Religion of Israel*, 1953 edition, pp. 83, 91–92, 197 note 36, and in *AASOR* 6, 1926, pp. 73–74.

Some suggest *rwḥ*, 'fragrant pla[ce]' (*BDB*, p. 437b, after Gesenius), or [a] 'founded by (deity) Ḥô' (*PEQ* 77, 1945, p. 13), but this is improbable.

### Sites

Old Testament Jericho is generally identified with the present mound Tell es-Sultan *c.* 16 kilometres north-west of the present mouth of the Jordan at the Dead Sea, 2 kilometres north-west of er-Riḥa village (modern Jericho), and about 27 kilometres east-north-east of Jerusalem. The imposing, pear-shaped mound is about 400 metres long from north to south an[d] roughly 200 metres wide at the broad northern end, and some 20 metres thick.

Herodian and New Testament Jericho is represented by the mounds of Tulul Abu el-'Alayiq, 2 kilometres west of modern er-Riḥa and so is south of Old Testament Jericho.

The mountains of Judaea rise abruptly from the plains of Jericho [a] little distance to the west.

### History

*Before Joshua*

*(i) Beginnings.* The story of Jericho [is] virtually a précis of the whole archaeological history of Palestine between *c.* 8000 and *c.* 1200 BC. (F[or] the special abbreviations used her[e]

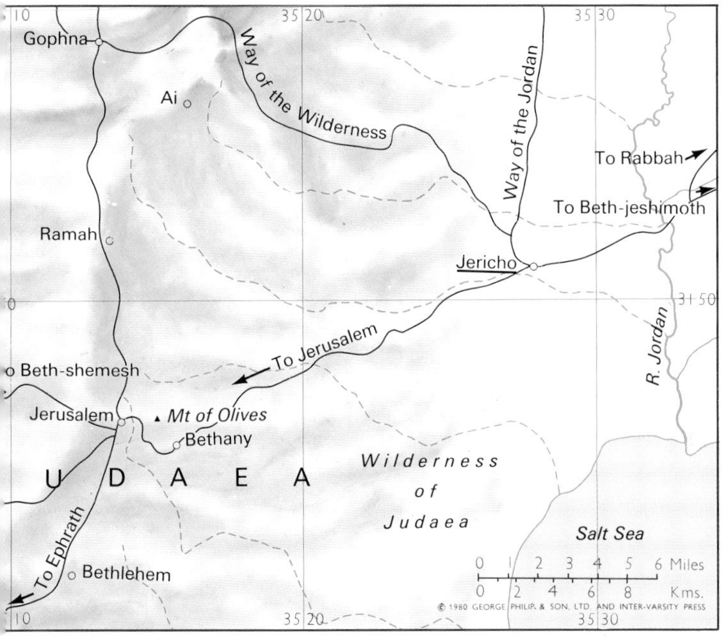


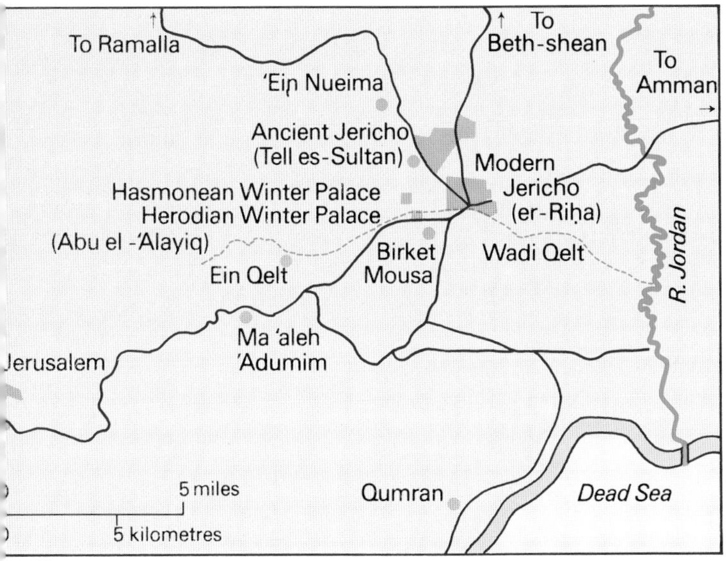


***Top:* The highways running through Jericho.**
***Bottom:* Jericho and adjacent ancient sites.**

e *Further reading* at the end of this ticle.) Every settlement at Jericho s owed its existence to the fine rennial spring there and the isis' which it waters (*DUJ*, plate 1); the Old Testament Jericho is metimes called 'the city of palm ees' (Deuteronomy 34:3).

Already *c.* 9600/7700 BC, od-gathering hunters may have d a shrine there, and Palestine's rliest-known agriculturists built ts by the spring (*AHL*, pp. 24–26; ate 8).

Early in the 8th millennium BC arbon-14 date), the oldest *town* of richo was built with a stone vetment-wall that included at least e tower (with built-in stairway) d round houses. Subsequently, acious rectangular houses became fashionable and skulls of venerated ancestors (?) were embodied in clay-moulded portrait heads of remarkable realism (*DUJ*, pp. 67–73 and plates 25, 29–30, or *AHL*, pp. 26–30 and plates 13–15 for 'prepottery Neolithic, phase A'; *DUJ*, pp. 51–67 and pls. 20–22, or *AHL*, pp. 31–40 and plates 16–25, for 'phase B').

In the 5th and 4th millennia BC later Jericho citizens learnt to make pottery, but eventually abandoned the place ('Pottery Neolithic A and B', 'Jericho IX and VIII' of older books, *DUJ*, pp. 79–94, *AHL*, pp. 43–50).

Ancient Jericho is currently the primary source of information on the earliest settled life of Palestine (see also *W*, chs. 2–4 and *GSJ*, pp. 55–72).

*(ii) Early historical period.* From *c.* 3200 BC Jericho was again inhabited as a walled and towered town of the Early Bronze Age, when towns famous later (*e.g.* Megiddo) were first founded, contemporary with Egypt's Pyramid Age and the Sumerian civilization in Mesopotamia (*DUJ*, pp. 167–185; *AHL*, pp. 84–118; *W*, ch. 5; *GSJ*, pp. 75–88, cities I and II).

But *c.* 2300 BC Jericho perished violently at the hands of uncultured newcomers who eventually resettled the site (Albright's Middle Bronze Age I; K. M. Kenyon's Intermediate Early/Middle Bronze Age, compare *DUJ*, pp. 186–209; *AHL*, pp. 119–147). These coalesced with the Canaanites of the Middle Bronze Age proper (*c.* 1900–1550 BC). Biblically this was the period of Abraham, Isaac and Jacob; the remains from contemporary Jericho throw a vivid light on the daily life of Abraham's Canaanite/Amorite town-dwelling neighbours.

The tombs have preserved more than the badly-denuded town buildings. Splendid pottery, wooden three- and four-legged tables, stools and beds, trinket-boxes of bone inlay, basketry, platters of fruit and joints of meat, metal daggers and circlets – all have been preserved by peculiar atmospheric conditions (*DUJ*, pp. 210–232 [city], 233–255 [tombs]; *AHL*, pp. 148–179; *GSJ*, pp. 91–108). For the restoration of a Jericho house-interior, see *DUJ*, endpapers. For reconstructions of the walled city on its mound, see *Illustrated London News*, 19 May 1956, pp. 554–555; see *AHL*, figure 48 on p. 163 for a section of the defences.

*Jericho and the Old Testament*

*(i) Joshua's invasion.* After *c.* 1550 BC the Middle Bronze Age city at Jericho was violently destroyed, probably by Egypt's 18th Dynasty imperial pharaohs. After this the only (Late Bronze) occupation found at Jericho dates mainly between *c.* 1400 and 1275 BC; from the late 13th century BC, the date of the Israelite conquest, virtually nothing is known (*DUJ*, pp. 259–263; *AHL*, pp. 181–182, 207–208). Garstang's 'Late Bronze Age' walls (*GSJ*, chapter 7) actually date from the Early Bronze Age, over 1,000 years before Joshua, because of the associated Early Bronze remains, and they are overlaid by Middle Bronze material, only subsequently identified in Dame Kathleen Kenyon's excavations (*e.g.* *DUJ*, pp. 170–171, 176–177, and especially 181).

Part of the extensive excavations at Jericho.

It is possible that in Joshua's day (13th century BC) there was a small town on the eastern part of the mound, later wholly eroded away. Such a possibility is not just a 'harmonistic' or heuristic view, but one suggested by the evidence of considerable erosion of the older settlements at Jericho. The tombs conclusively prove the importance of Middle Bronze Age Jericho (patriarchal period), although on the city mound most of the Middle Bronze town – and even much of the Early Bronze one before it – was eroded away between *c.* 1550 and *c.* 1400 BC (see *DUJ*, pp. 170–171, and also 45, 93, 259–260, 262–263).

When so much damage was done by the elements in barely 150 years it is easy to see how much havoc natural erosion must have wrought on the deserted mound in the 400 years that separated Joshua from Jericho's refounding by Hiel the Bethelite (1 Kings 16:34) in Ahab's reign. It seems highly likely that the washed-out remains of the last Late Bronze Age city are now lost under the modern road and cultivated land along the eastern side of the town mound, as the main slope of the mound is from west down to east. It remains highly doubtful whether excavation here (even if allowed) would yield much now.

The narrative of Joshua 3–8 with which the fall of Jericho is recount[ed] is known to reflect faithfully conditions in, and topography of, th[e] area, while Joshua's generalship is recounted in a realistic manner. On terrain, see Garstang, *Joshua-Judges*, 1931, pp. 135–148 (his earth-tremors, providentially sent, remain a valid suggestion, even though his 'Late Bronze' [actually Early Bronze] walls do not now cou[nt] as direct evidence for Joshua's day. On Joshua's generalship, compare Garstang, pp. 149–161, and Y.

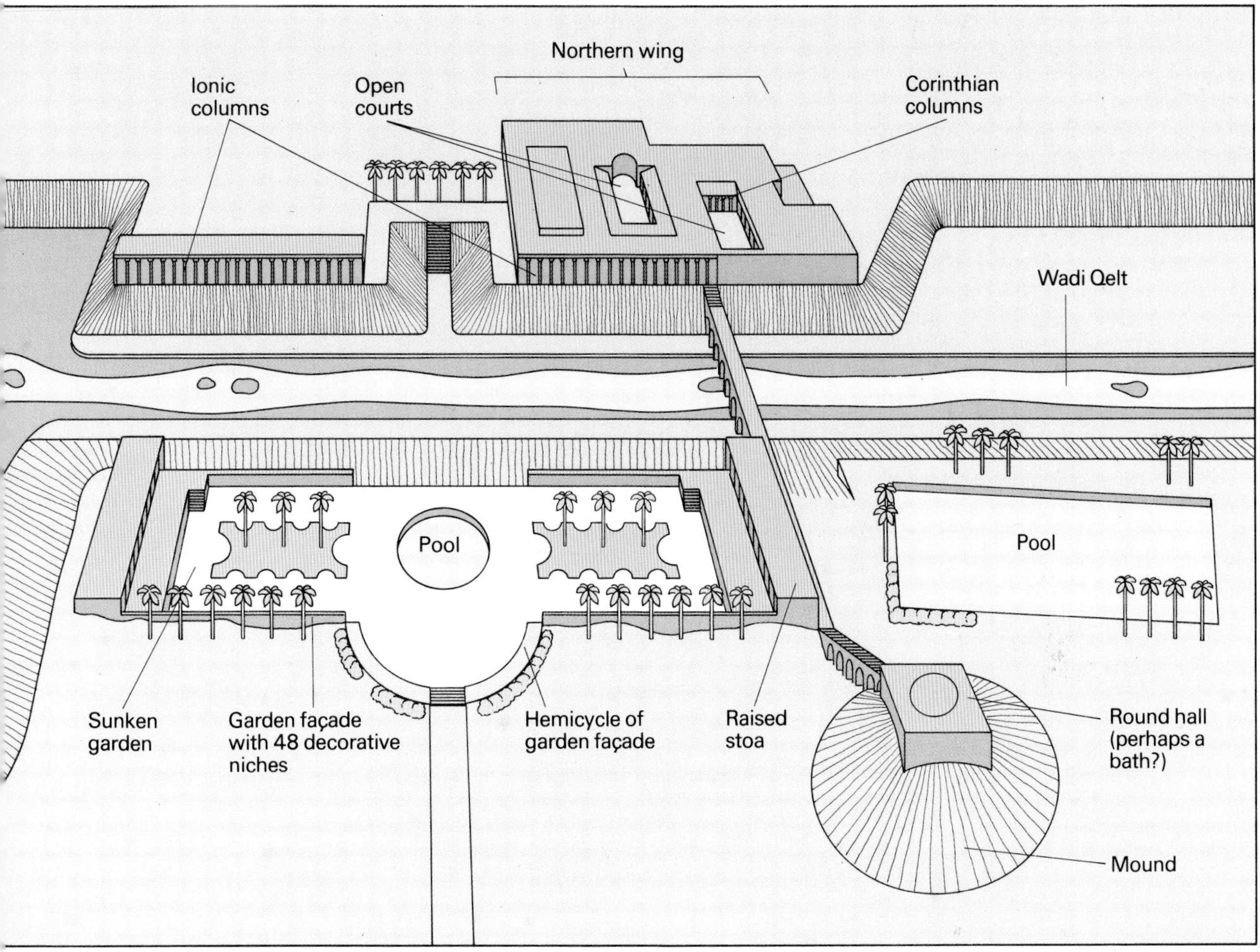


Reconstruction of the royal winter palace built by Herod the Great at Jericho.

aufmann, *The Biblical Account of e Conquest of Palestine*, 1953, p. 91–97.

*(ii) From Joshua to Nehemiah.* For nturies no attempt was made to build the town-mound of Jericho in we of Joshua's curse (Joshua 6:26), it the spring and oasis were still equented, perhaps supporting a amlet there. Pottery from the arliest (German) excavations, 907–09 and 1911, has recently been ssigned to the Iron Age I-II periods . 1200–800 BC).

In the time of the judges, Eglon ng of Moab temporarily occupied e oasis (Judges 3:13) and David's nvoys stayed there after being utraged by Hanun of Ammon (2 amuel 10:5; 1 Chronicles 19:5); the lockhouse' may have been a uard-post in this period (10th entury BC: so Albright and Wright, ted by Tushingham in *BA* 16, 1953, 67).

Then in Ahab's reign (*c.* 74/3–853 BC) Hiel the Bethelite efounded Jericho proper and finally lfilled the ancient curse in the loss f his eldest and youngest sons (1 ings 16:34). This humble Iron Age Jericho was that of Elijah and Elisha (2 Kings 2:4–5, 18–22), and it was in the plains of Jericho that the Babylonians captured Zedekiah, last king of Judah (2 Kings 25:5; 2 Chronicles 28:15; Jeremiah 39:5; 52:8). The remains of this Jericho (9th–6th centuries BC) are very fragmentary (erosion again to blame), but quite definite: buildings, pottery and tombs; Iron Age occupation did not become extensive until the 7th century BC and probably the Babylonians destroyed the place in 587 BC (see *BA* 16, 1953, pp. 66–67; *PEQ* 85, 1953, pp. 91, 95; *DUJ*, pp. 263–264).

After the Exile, a modest Jericho still existed in Persian times. Some 345 Jerichoans returned to Judaea with Zerubbabel (Ezra 2:34; Nehemiah 7:36), and their descendants in Jericho helped with repairing Jerusalem's walls in 445 BC under Nehemiah (Nehemiah 3:2); a pottery jar-stamp (*c.* 4th century BC) 'belonging to Hagar (daughter of) Uriah' is the last memento of Old Testament Jericho (Hammond, *PEQ* 89, 1957, pp. 68–69, with plate 16, corrected in *BASOR* 147, 1957, pp. 37–39; compare also Albright in *BASOR* 148, 1957, pp. 28–30).

*New Testament Jericho*

In New Testament times, the town of Jericho was sited south of the old mound. In that region, Herod the Great (40/37–4 BC) built three palaces, including an elaborate winter palace which covered 2·8 hectares and lay on both sides of the Wadi Qilt (as excavations have revealed). See Kelso and Baramki, 'Excavations at New Testament Jericho' in *AASOR* 29/30, 1955, and *BA* 14, 1951, pp. 33–43; Pritchard, *The Excavation at Herodian Jericho* in *AASOR* 32/33, 1958, and *BASOR* 123, 1951, pp. 8–17; E. Netzer in *BASOR* 228, 1977, pp. 1–13. Herod brought water by aqueduct from the Wadi Qilt (Perowne, *Life and Times of Herod the Great*, 1956, plates opposite pp. 96–97).

The environs of New Testament Jericho witnessed Christ's healing of blind men, including Bartimaeus (Matthew 20:29; Mark 10:46; Luke 18:35). Zacchaeus (Luke 19:1) was not the only wealthy Jew who had

**Continued on p. 178**

# JERUSALEM

## Introduction and general description

Jerusalem is one of the world's famous cities. Under that name, it dates from at least the early 2nd millennium BC; and today is considered sacred by the adherents of the three great monotheistic faiths, Judaism, Christianity and Islam.

*Jerusalem's hills and valleys*
The city is set high in the hills of Judah, about 50 kilometres from the Mediterranean, and over 30 kilometres west of the northern end of the Dead Sea. It rests on a none-too-level plateau, which slopes noticeably towards the south-east. To the east lies the ridge of Olivet.

Access to the city on all sides except the north is hampered by three deep ravines, which join in the Siloam Valley, near the well Bir Eyyub, south-east of the city. The eastern valley is Kidron; the western is now called the Wadi al-Rababi, and is probably to be equated with the Valley of Hinnom; and the third cuts the city in half before it runs south, and slightly east, to meet the other two. This latter ravine is not mentioned or named in Scripture (although Maktesh, Zephaniah 1:11, may well have been the name of part of it), so it is usually referred to as the Tyropoeon Valley, *i.e.*, the Valley of the Cheesemakers, after Josephus.

Eminences rise each side of the Tyropoeon Valley, and the city can at once be divided into western and eastern halves. Ignoring lesser heights, we may subdivide each of these two sections into northern and southern hills. When considering the growth and development of the city (see below) it will be important to visualize these details.

In discussing the respective heights and depths of these hills and valleys, it must be realized that they have changed considerably over the centuries. This is inevitable in any city continuously inhabited for centuries, and particularly when periodic destructions have taken place. Layer after layer of rubble and debris piles up, amounting here and there to more than 30 metres in parts of Jerusalem. In the case of Jerusalem there is also the factor that deliberate attempts have been made at various periods to fill in valleys (especially the Tyropoeon) and diminish hills.

*Water supply*
Jerusalem's water-supply has always presented problems. Apart from Bir Eyyub, the well mentioned above, there is only the Virgin's Spring, which is connected by an aqueduct with the Pool of Siloam. There are, and have been, other reservoirs, of course, such as Bethesda in New Testament times and Mamilla Pool today, but they all depend on the rains or else on aqueducts to fill them.

Bir Eyyub and the Virgin's Spring are in all probability the biblical En-rogel and Gihon respectively. Bir Eyyub lies south-east of the city, at the junction of the three ravines mentioned above. The Virgin's Spring is due north of Bir Eyyub, eas and a little south of the Temple are Thus it is evident that only the south-eastern part of Jerusalem ha a reliable water supply. (See A. Mazar, 'The Aqueducts of Jerusalem', in Yadin, *Jerusalem Revealed*, pp. 79–84.)

## Name

The meaning of the name is not certain. The Hebrew word is usuall written *y*$^{e}$*rûšālaim* in the Old Testament, but this is an anomalou form, since Hebrew cannot have tw consecutive vowels. The anomaly was resolved in later Hebrew by inserting the letter 'y', thus giving *y*$^{e}$*rûšālayim*; this form does in fact occur a few times in the Old Testament, *e.g.*, Jeremiah 26:18. This may well have been understoo to be a dual (for the ending *-ayim* is dual), viewing the city as twofold. (Similarly, the Hebrew name for 'Egypt', *miṣrayim*, appears to be dual.) But there can be little doubt that the original form of the word ir Hebrew was *y*$^{e}$*rušālēm*; this is evidenced by the abbreviation *šālēn* (English 'Salem') in Psalm 76:2, anc by the Aramaic form of the name *y*$^{e}$*rûšlēm*, found in Ezra 5:14, *etc.*

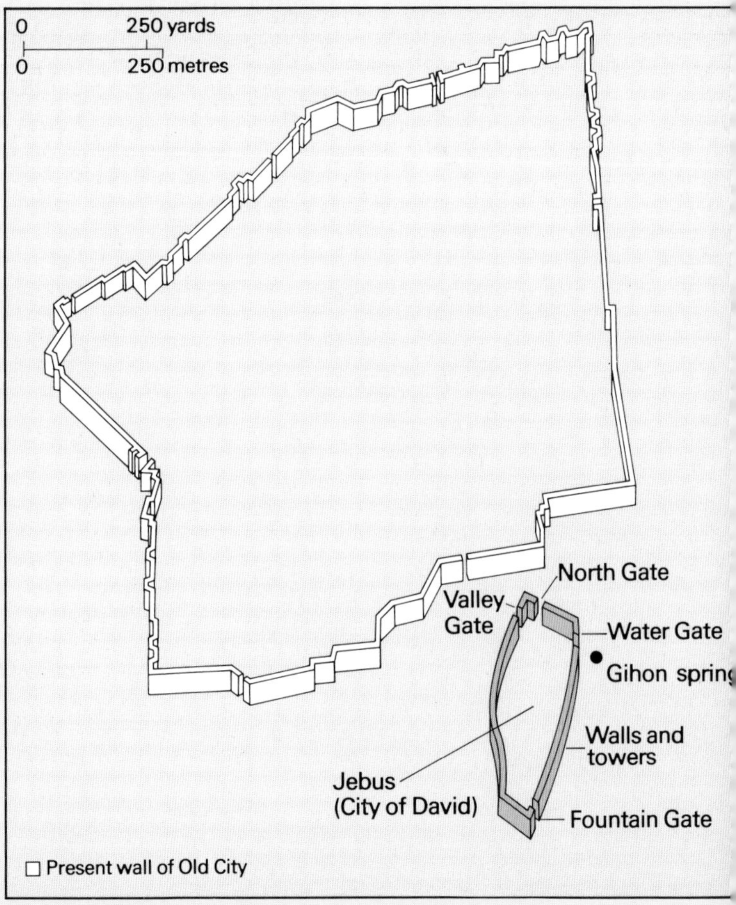


**Jebus, the site of the City of David, Jerusalem, on the south-east hill, Mount Zion.**

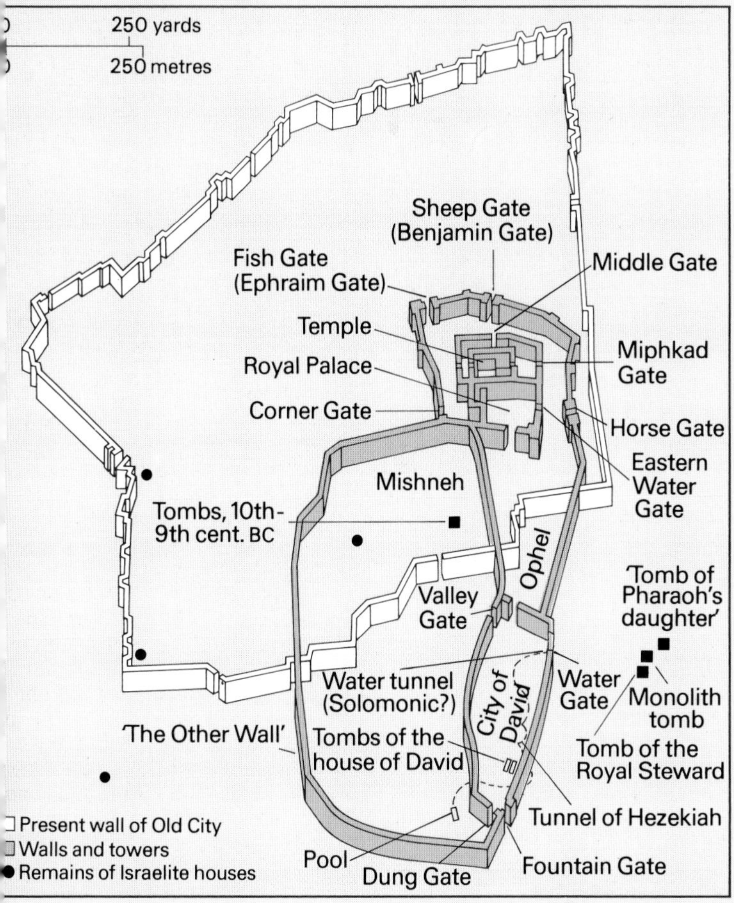

***Left:*** **Jerusalem from Solomon to Hezekiah, showing extensions to the north and west, including to the Temple area.**
***Above:*** **Mount Ophel, Jerusalem, showing part of the excavated Jebusite wall.**

The name is pre-Israelite, appearing in the Egyptian Execration Texts (19th-18th century; the form appears to be Rushalimum) and in later Assyrian documents (as *Urusalim* or *Urisalimmu*). The first part of the name is usually thought to mean 'foundation'; the second element, though cognate with the Hebrew word for 'peace', probably originally referred to a Canaanite deity Shalem. Thus 'foundation of Shalem' is probably the original sense of the name; in course of time, however, the second element will have been associated with 'peace' (Hebrew *šālôm*) in Jewish minds; compare Hebrews 7:2.

In New Testament Greek the

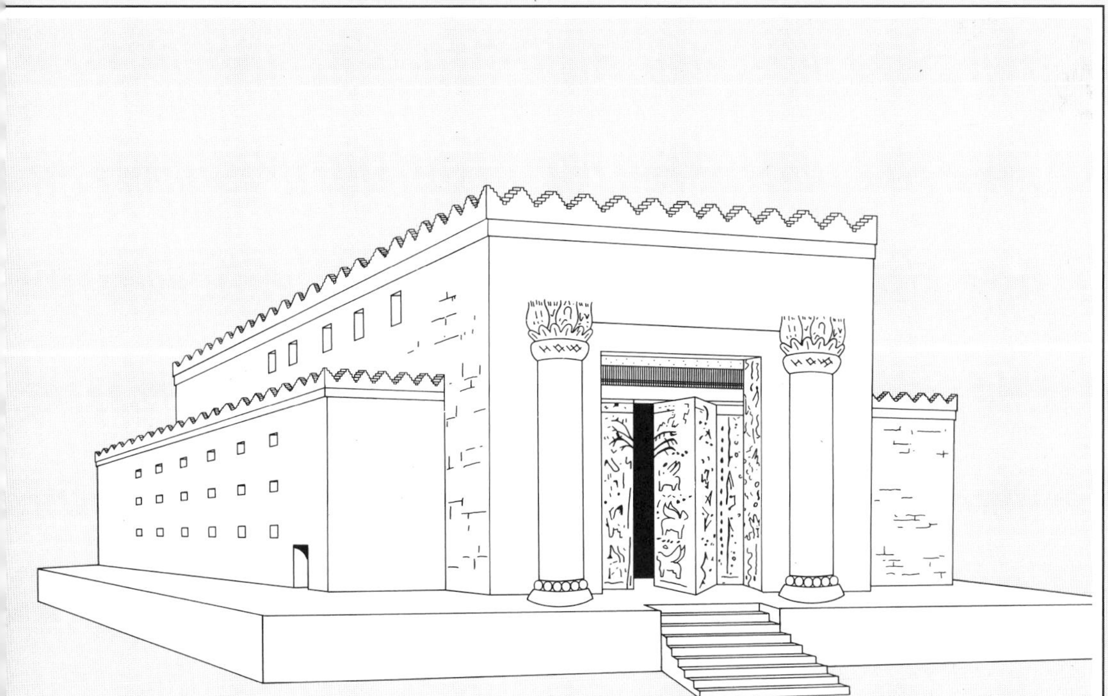

**Steven's reconstruction of Solomon's Temple, showing the twin free-standing pillars (Jachin and Boaz), the vestibule and side storage-chambers.**

name is transliterated in two different ways, *Hierosolyma* (as in Matthew 2:1) and *Hierousalēm* (as in Matthew 23:37). The latter is evidently a close approximation to the Hebrew pronunciation, and incidentally an additional evidence for an *'e'* as the original final vowel in Hebrew. The former is deliberately Hellenized, to make a Greek-sounding word; the first part of the word at once recalls the Greek word *hieros*, 'holy', and probably the whole was understood to mean something like 'sacred Salem'.

The Septuagint has only the form *Hierousalēm*, whereas Greek classical writers use *Hierosolyma* (*e.g.* Polybius; so too Latin, *e.g.* Pliny).

*The holy city*

Jerusalem is described in Isaiah 52:1 as the holy city, and to this day it often receives this title. The Hebrew phrase is *'îr haq-qōḏeš*, literally 'the city of holiness'. Probably the reason for this title was that Jerusalem contained the Temple, the shrine where God deigned to meet his people. Hence, the word *qōḏeš* came to mean 'sanctuary' as well as 'holiness'. To Judaism, then, Jerusalem was the holy city without a rival. It was natural for Paul and

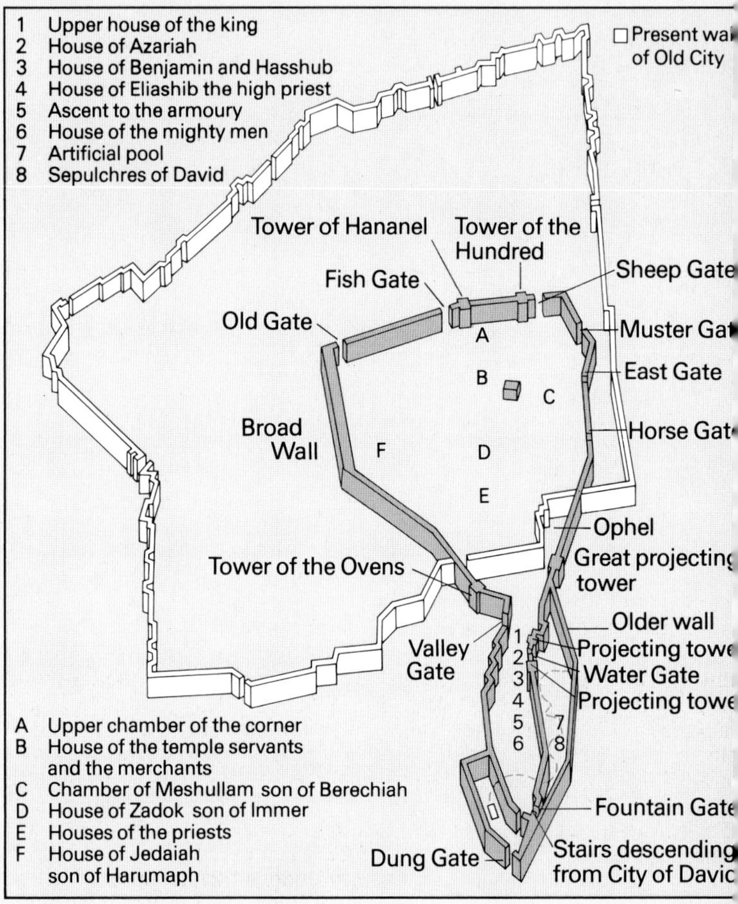


Probable reconstruction of Jerusalem as rebuilt by Nehemiah in the 5th century BC.

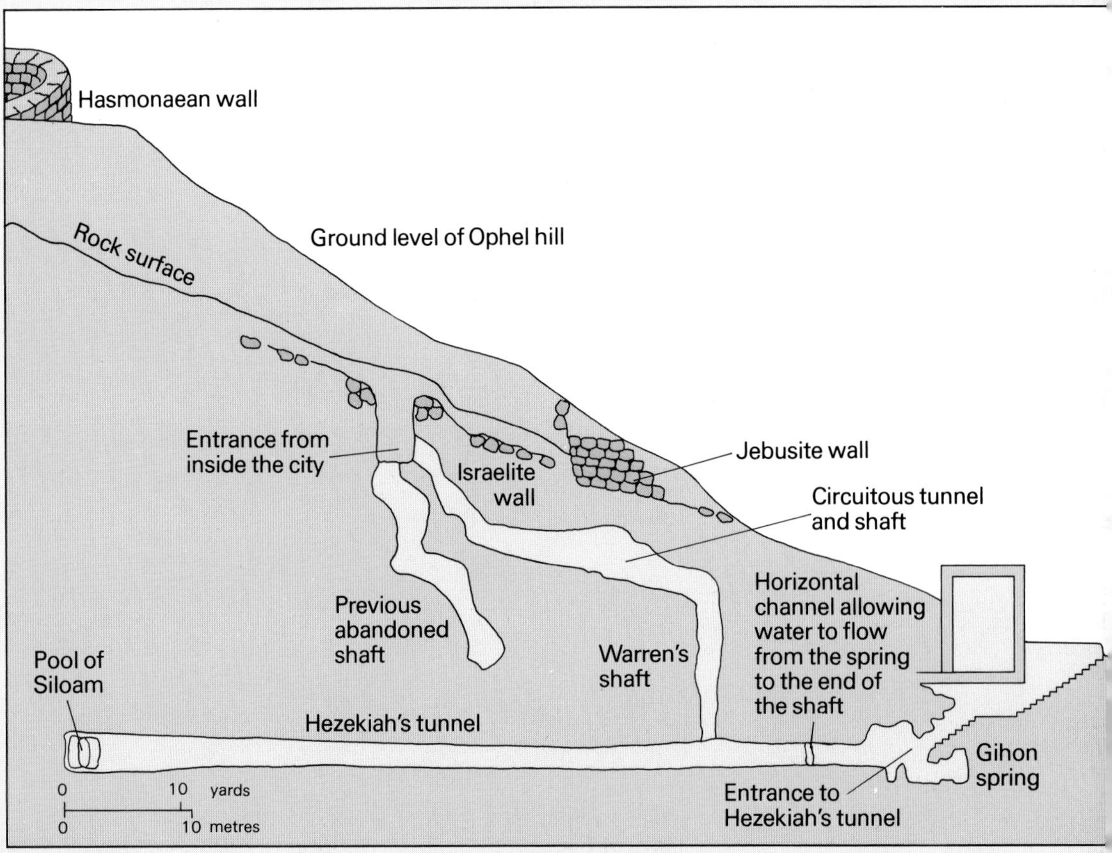


Cross-section of the water-system of ancient Jerusalem, including Hezekiah's tunnel.

A view of the Old City of Jerusalem from the Mount of Olives, showing clearly the Temple Mount area.

hn, seeing that the earthly city as far from perfect, to designate e place where God dwells in true oliness as 'Jerusalem which is ove' (Galatians 4:26) and 'new rusalem' (Revelation 21:2).
For other names the city has rne, see below.

## istory

*efore the Conquest*

aces of prehistoric settlement at rusalem have been found, but its rly history cannot be traced. After oare mention in the Egyptian ecration Texts early in the 2nd illennium BC, it reappears in the th-century el-Amarna letters, led by a king named Abd Khiba. At at time it was under the suzerainty Egypt, and was probably little ore than a mountain fortress.
Possible Pentateuchal references Jerusalem are as Salem (Genesis :18) and the mountain in the 'land Moriah' of Genesis 22:2.
ccording to very ancient tradition, e latter was the place where later e Temple was built, but there is no ossible proof of this. As for Salem, it almost certainly to be identified ith Jerusalem (compare Psalm :2); if so, it was ruled in oraham's day by an earlier king, elchizedek, who was also 'priest of od Most High' (*'ēl 'elyôn*).

*shua and Judges*

hen the Israelites entered Canaan ey found Jerusalem in the hands of indigenous Semitic tribe, the busites, ruled over by a king amed Adoni-zedek. This ruler formed an alliance of kings against Joshua, who soundly defeated them; but Joshua did not take the city, owing, doubtless, to its natural strength of position.

The city remained in Jebusite hands, bearing the name *Jebus. From a comparison of Judges 1:8 with Judges 1:21, it appears that Judah overcame the part of the city outside the fortress walls, and that Benjamin occupied this part, living peaceably alongside the Jebusites in the fortress. This was the situation when David became king.

*A royal city*

David's first capital was Hebron, but he soon saw the value of Jerusalem, and set about its capture. This was not only a tactical move but also a diplomatic one, for his use of a city on the Benjamin-Judah border would help to diminish the jealousy between the two tribes.

The Jebusites felt confident of their safety behind the fortress walls, but David's men used an unexpected mode of entry, and took the citadel by surprise (2 Samuel 5:6ff.). In this passage we meet a third name, 'Zion'. This was probably the name of the hill on which the citadel stood. Vincent, however, thinks the name originally applied rather to the fortress building than to the ground it occupied.

Having taken the city, David improved the fortifications and built himself a palace; he also installed the ark in his new capital.

Solomon carried the work of fortification further, but his great achievement was the construction of the Temple. After his death and the subsequent division of the kingdom, Jerusalem naturally declined somewhat, being now capital only of Judah.

As early as the 5th year of Solomon's successor, Rehoboam, the Temple and royal palace were plundered by Egyptian troops (1 Kings 14:25f.). Philistine and Arab marauders again plundered the palace in Jehoram's reign. In Amaziah's reign a quarrel with the king of the northern kingdom, Jehoash, resulted in part of the city walls being broken down, and fresh looting of Temple and palace. Uzziah repaired this damage to the fortifications, so that in the reign of Ahaz the city was able to withstand the attack of the combined armies of Syria and Israel.

Soon after this the northern kingdom fell to the Assyrians. Hezekiah of Judah had good reason to fear Assyria too, but Jerusalem providentially escaped. In case of siege, he made a conduit to improve the city's water-supply.

*After the Exile*

Nebuchadrezzar of Babylon captured Jerusalem in 597 and in 587 BC destroyed the city and Temple. At the end of that century the Jews, now under Persian rule, were allowed to return to their land and city, and they rebuilt the Temple, but the city walls remained in ruins until Nehemiah restored them in the middle of the 5th century BC.

Alexander the Great ended the power of Persia at the end of the 4th

The Herodian city of Jerusalem.

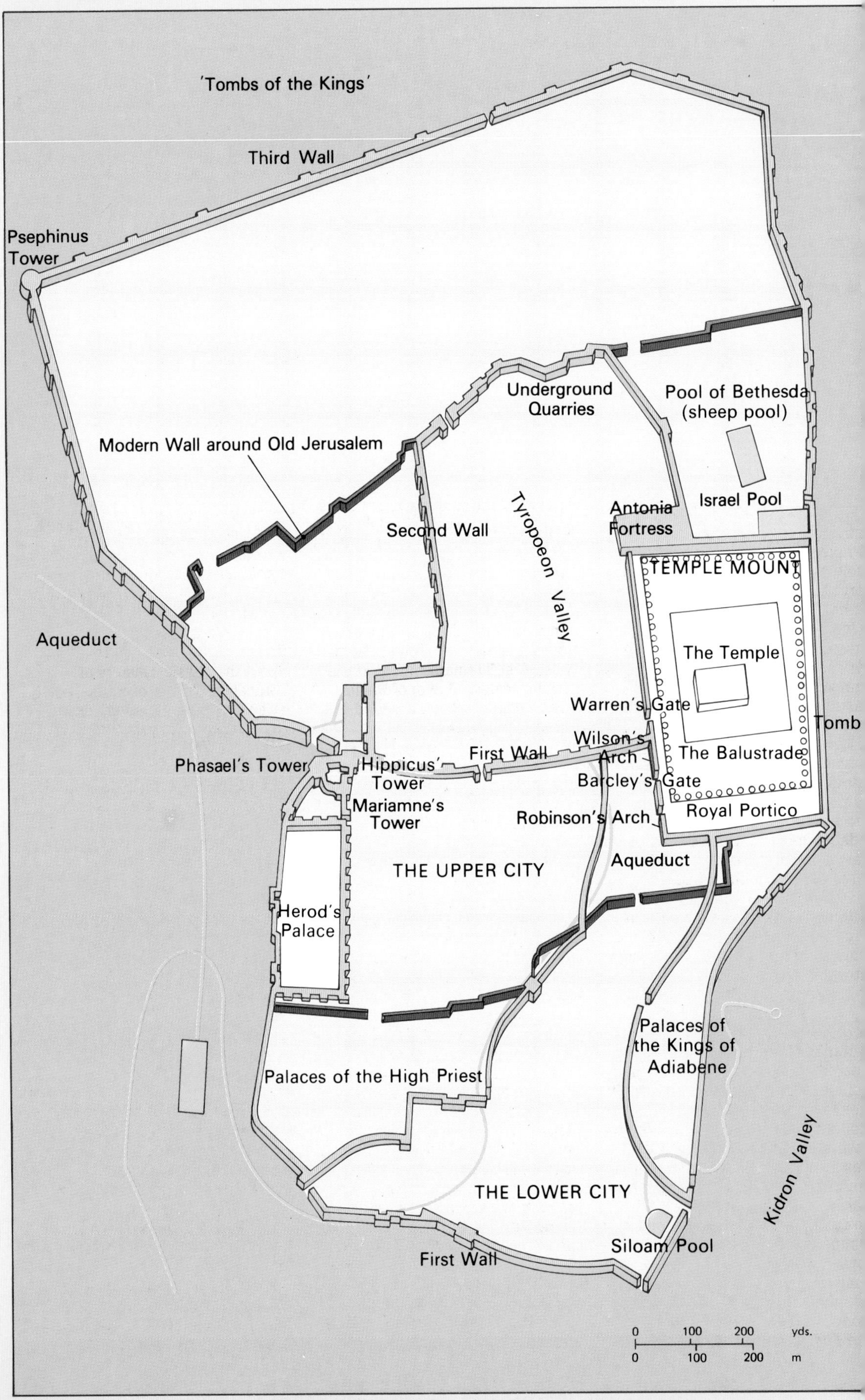
'Tombs of the Kings'
Third Wall
Psephinus Tower
Modern Wall around Old Jerusalem
Underground Quarries
Pool of Bethesda (sheep pool)
Israel Pool
Antonia Fortress
Second Wall
Tyropoeon Valley
TEMPLE MOUNT
The Temple
Aqueduct
Warren's Gate
Tomb
Wilson's Arch
The Balustrade
Phasael's Tower
Hippicus' Tower
First Wall
Barcley's Gate
Mariamne's Tower
Robinson's Arch
Royal Portico
Aqueduct
THE UPPER CITY
Herod's Palace
Palaces of the Kings of Adiabene
Palaces of the High Priest
Kidron Valley
THE LOWER CITY
Siloam Pool
First Wall
0 100 200 yds.
0 100 200 m

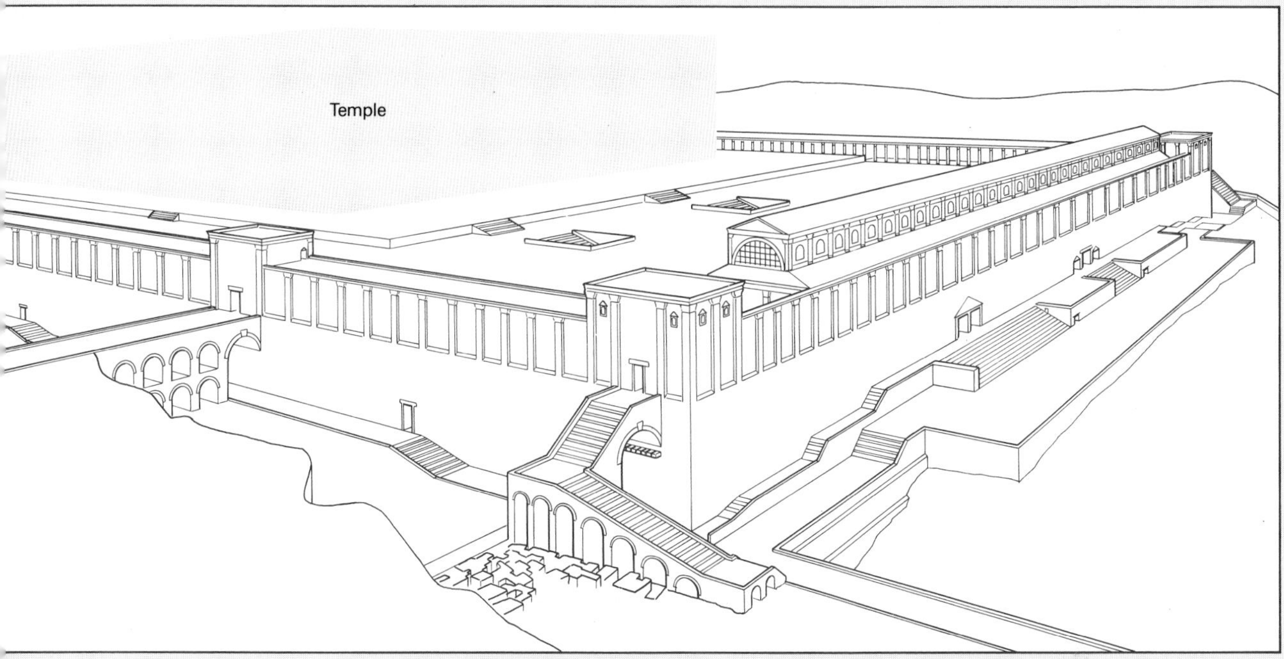


Reconstruction of the south-west approach to Herod's Temple following recent excavations. A monumental stairway leads to the portal of the Royal Stoa at the junction of the west and south walls. To the right are the Huldah Gates.

›ntury, and after his death his ›eneral Ptolemy, founder of the :olemaic dynasty in Egypt, entered ›rusalem and included it in his ›alm.

In 198 BC Palestine fell to ntiochus II, the Seleucid king of ›ria. About 30 years later, ntiochus IV entered Jerusalem, ›estroying its walls and plundering ıd desecrating the Temple; and he ›stalled a Syrian garrison in the city, ı the Akra. Judas the Maccabee led Jewish revolt, and in 165 BC the ›emple was rededicated. He and his ıccessors gradually won ıdependence for Judaea, and the ›asmonaean dynasty ruled a free ›rusalem until the middle of the 1st ›ntury BC, when Rome intervened. Roman generals forced their way ıto the city in 63 and 54; a Parthian ›my plundered it in 40; and 3 years ›ter that Herod the Great had to ›ht his way into it, to take control.

*›erod the Great*

›erod first had to repair the damage ›eated by the Roman and Parthian ›cursions and his own invasion. He ›en launched a big building ›ogramme, erecting some notable ›wers. His most renowned work ›as the rebuilding of the Temple on much grander scale, although this ›as not finished within his lifetime. ›ne of his towers was Antonia, ›mmanding the Temple area (it ›oused the Roman garrison which ›me to Paul's aid, Acts 21:34).

*›om AD 70*

›e Jewish revolt against the Romans in AD 66 could have but one conclusion; in AD 70 the Roman general Titus systematically forced his way into Jerusalem and destroyed the fortifications and the Temple. He left three towers standing; the base of one of them, Phasael, still remains, incorporated in the so-called 'Tower of David'.

But further disaster awaited the Jews: another revolt in AD 132 led to the rebuilding of Jerusalem (on a much smaller scale) as a pagan city, dedicated to Jupiter Capitolinus, from which all Jews were excluded. This was the work of the emperor Hadrian; he called the newly constructed city Aelia Capitolina (the name even found its way into Arabic, as Iliya).

It was not until the reign of Constantine (early 4th century) that the Jews were again permitted to enter the city. From his reign on, the city became Christian instead of pagan, and many churches and monasteries were built, notably the Church of the Holy Sepulchre.

Jerusalem has suffered many vicissitudes since the 2nd century, and has been captured and held at various times by Persian, Arab, Turkish, Crusader, British and Israeli troops and administrations. The most important building developments in the Old City (as opposed to the rapidly growing modern suburbs) were due to the early Muslims, the Crusaders and finally the Turkish sultan Suleiman the Magnificent who in 1542 rebuilt the city walls as they can be seen today. The Israelis give the city its ancient Hebrew name, *y*$^{e}$*rûšālayim*; the Arabs usually call it *al-Quds* (*al-Sharîf*), 'the (noble) Sanctuary'.

**Growth and extent**

It must be stated at the outset that there is a good deal of uncertainty about the physical history of Jerusalem. This is, of course, partly due to the periodic disasters and destructions, and to the layers upon layers of rubble that have piled up over the centuries. These factors have caused difficulty elsewhere, of course, but archaeologists have often been able to surmount them to a large extent. The particular problem with Jerusalem is that it has been continuously inhabited and still is, so that excavations can be made only with difficulty. Archaeologists here have to dig where they can, not where they think it might be profitable.

On the other hand, there is an abundance of traditions, Christian, Jewish, and Muslim; but in many cases it is not easy to evaluate them. So uncertainty and controversy remain; however, much valuable archaeological work has been done during the last century, and it has solved some problems.

Scripture nowhere gives a systematic description of the city. The nearest approach to such a description is the account of the rebuilding of the walls by Nehemiah. But there are a great number of references giving some information. These have to be pieced together, and fitted in with the picture we get from archaeology. Our earliest

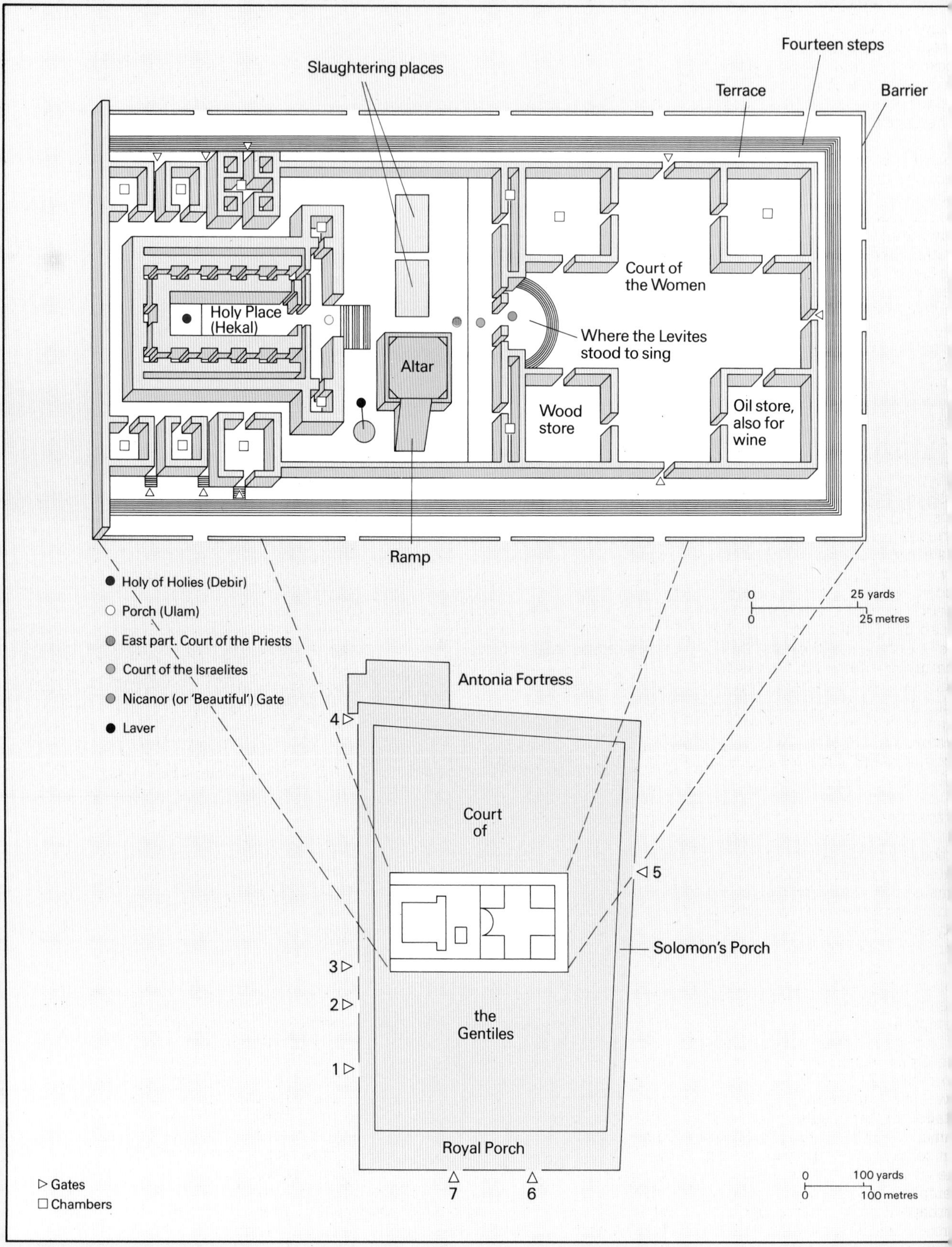

Slaughtering places
Fourteen steps
Terrace
Barrier
Court of the Women
Holy Place (Hekal)
Where the Levites stood to sing
Altar
Wood store
Oil store, also for wine
Ramp
Holy of Holies (Debir)
Porch (Ulam)
East part. Court of the Priests
Court of the Israelites
Nicanor (or 'Beautiful') Gate
Laver
0 25 yards
0 25 metres
Antonia Fortress
Court of the Gentiles
Solomon's Porch
Royal Porch
1
2
3
4
5
6
7
0 100 yards
0 100 metres
Gates
Chambers

scription of the city is that of
sephus (*Jewish War* 5.136–141);
sephus is here laying a
ckground for his account of the
adual capture of the city by Titus
d the Roman armies. This too has
be fitted into the picture.

*e earliest city*
cavations have conclusively
own that the earliest city was on
e south-eastern hill, an area now
holly outside the city walls (the
uthern wall was retracted north in
e 2nd century AD). It must be
early borne in mind that the
iginal Zion lay on the eastern
lge; the name was by the time of
sephus already erroneously
tached to the south-western hill.
Few traces remain from the
e-Jebusite period, but it may be
ferred that a small town grew on
e south-eastern ridge, within easy
ach of the spring Gihon in the
lley to the east. The Jebusites
larged the city to a limited extent,
ost notably by the construction of
rraces to the east, so that their
stern wall lay well down the slope
wards the spring. This terracing
d eastern wall seem to have
eded frequent maintenance and
pair till their final destruction by
e Babylonians in the early 6th
ntury BC, after which the eastern
all was again retracted to the
lge. Present opinion is inclined to
nsider the word *'Millo' (*e.g.* 2
muel 5:9; 1 Kings 9:15), which
rives from a Hebrew root meaning
l', to refer to this terracing.

*the reigns of David and Solomon*
times of peace it was common
actice for houses to be built
itside the walls, which from time to
ne necessitated new walls and
rtifications. David's and Solomon's
ty extended northwards, in
rticular, the Temple being built on
e north-eastern hill; the royal
lace was probably situated in the
ea between the older city and the
emple area.
This intermediate area is probably
e 'Ophel' of such passages as 2
hronicles 27:3 (the name means
welling', and was used of the
tadel of other cities too, *e.g.*
maria, compare 2 Kings 5:24, NEB);
it some scholars apply the term to
e whole eastern ridge south of the
emple. The Jebusite city, or
erhaps more strictly the central
rtress of it, already bore the name
ion' (the meaning of which is
certain, perhaps 'dry area' or
minence') at the time of David's
pture, after which it was also
called 'the city of David' (see 2 Samuel 5:6–10; 1 Kings 8:1). The name 'Zion' became, or remained, synonymous with Jerusalem as a whole.

A massive stepped-stone structure excavated near the crest of the hill, on its eastern side, may have been part of the city's defences during the time of David and/or Solomon. David's Jerusalem covered about 6 hectares, a size which suggests a population of around 2,000.

Nothing remains of Solomon's Temple. Its subsequent destruction and rebuilding have obliterated all traces of the original structure.

*The 8th century*

It was in the prosperous days of the 8th century BC that the city first spread to the western ridge; this new suburb seems to have been called the Second Quarter or Mishneh (2 Kings 22:14). A wall later enclosed it, built either in Hezekiah's reign (compare 2 Chronicles 32:5) or somewhat later. (65 metres of a massive fortification wall 7 metres thick, excavated by N. Avigad in the Jewish Quarter, was associated

## The Antonia Fortress

In the days of Nehemiah, Jerusalem had a 'citadel by the temple', under the command of Hananiah (Nehemiah 2:8; 7:2). Such a citadel formed a last line of defence should the walls of a city be breached. This citadel was rebuilt by the Hasmonaean kings, who named it the Bira.

When Herod became king he strengthened the internal security of Jerusalem by building a fortified palace for himself on the western walls of the city on the site of a second Hasmonaean fortress. He also rebuilt the Temple citadel on palatial lines, renaming it 'Antonia', in honour of his patron, Mark Antony. Very cleverly, he joined it on to his rebuilt Temple platform, so that the soldiers in the fortress could keep a watch on the activities of the Temple.

The fortress was built on a stone platform on top of a steep rock. The Jewish historian Josephus wrote that the rock was 50 cubits high (about 25 metres). He tells us that the fortress itself was 40 cubits (about 20 metres) high, with four towers. Three of the towers were about 25 metres high. The tower at the south-eastern corner, overlooking the Temple, was 35 metres high. From this great height everything that happened in the Temple courtyards could easily be seen.

Walls surrounded a large enclosure, in which were a number of buildings, including a soldiers' barracks. The Romans were responsible for civil order in Jerusalem, and the Roman military tribune therefore doubled up as chief of police. Roman soldiers were permanently garrisoned in the barracks, but extra contingents were drafted down from Caesarea and Samaria during the Festivals. At these times soldiers were on guard, night and day, on the castle walls overlooking the Temple.

At the back of the fortress, two flights of steps led down to the Temple porticoes. Paul probably owed his life to the presence of these steps and the immediate access they gave to the Temple (Acts 21:30–32). After the soldiers had arrested him, thus ensuring his safety, Paul used the steps as a pulpit from which to address the crowd. It has traditionally been held that it was to the Antonia that Jesus was taken for his interrogation by Pilate; but see *PRAETORIUM.

**A model of first-century Jerusalem, showing the Antonia Fortress.**

***Opposite:*** **One proposed plan of Herod's Temple, with indication of its position within the Temple enclosure.**

with pottery of the 8th-7th centuries BC.) It is certain that this extension included the north-western hill, but whether the south-western hill was now occupied is as yet unresolved. Israeli archaeologists conclude that it was, and that the Pool of Siloam was inside the city walls in Hezekiah's reign; but K. M. Kenyon opposed this view.

If M. Broshi's estimates are correct, Jerusalem expanded to cover 50 hectares in Hezekiah's reign, with a population of about 25,000.

*Babylonian destruction*
Jerusalem was sacked by Nebuchadrezzar's troops in 587 BC; most of the buildings were destroyed, and the city walls were demolished. Layers of ash and numerous arrowheads provide archaeological evidence of the Babylonian destruction. In the remains of one burnt house on the eastern hill, Y. Shiloh found over 50 clay seal-impressions, including one bearing the name 'Gemaria ben-Shaphan'; this may be the official mentioned in Jeremiah 36.

*After the Exile*
The Temple was rebuilt at the end of the century, and Jerusalem had a small population once again; but it was not until the mid-5th century that the Persian authorities permitted the rebuilding of the city walls, by Nehemiah.

No doubt Nehemiah rebuilt earlier walls so far as was practicable but it is clear from excavations that the western ridge was abandoned, and also the eastern slopes of the south-east hill. The Jebusite terracing had been too thoroughly demolished for repair, and Nehemiah therefore retracted the eastern wall to the ridge itself. The city shrank to about 12 hectares, with a probable population of 4,500.

Nehemiah's description of contemporary Jerusalem unfortunately presents numerous problems. For one thing, it is not clear which gates were in the city wall and which led into the Temple. For another, there are numerous textual difficulties in the relevant passages of Nehemiah. Again, Nehemiah gives no indication of direction or changes of direction. Add to that the fact that names of gates changed from time to time. Earlier attempts to interpret Nehemiah's data now all require revision in the light of recent excavations. It is fairly clear, however, that the circuit described in Nehemiah 3 is in an anti-clockwise direction, and begins at the north of the city.

*From the 2nd century BC to AD 70*
There is little evidence that the city spread to the western ridge again until the 2nd century BC. After the Maccabean revolt, the city began t grow once more. Herod the Great was responsible for a major buildi programme in the late 1st century B and the city continued to develop until its destruction at the end of t Jewish War (AD 66–70).

During Herod's reign the city covered an area of about 90 hectar and probably had a population of 40,000; by the time of its destructi it had grown to 180 hectares and a population of some 80,000. Our major literary source for this whole period is Josephus; but his information leaves us with a numb of problems as yet unresolved.

The first of these problems is the position of the 'Akra', the Syrian fortress set up in Jerusalem in 169 B Its purpose was plainly to keep the Temple courts under close surveillance, but neither Josephus nor 1 Maccabees makes it clear whether the garrison was located north, west or south of the Temple Opinions remain divided, but rece excavations tend to support the thi of these possibilities. (See *BASOR* 176, 1964, pp. 10f.)

A second problem concerns the course of the 'Second Wall' and the 'Third Wall' mentioned by Joseph who tells us that the Romans penetrated Jerusalem in AD 70 by progressively breaching three

**The Damascus Gate into the Old City of Jerusalem.**

The Church of the Holy Sepulchre, traditional site of the crucifixion and burial of Christ.

rthern walls. Josephus describes ; termini of the three walls, but he es not give information as to the e followed by any of them. cavations have supplemented his ormation here and there, but ıny uncertainties remain.

osephus numbers the three walls he order in which they were built. e 'First Wall' he believed dated m the time of Solomon. In this he ıs mistaken; it was built in the 2nd ntury BC, but it did follow the line of earlier wall built probably in the ıe of Hezekiah and destroyed by ; Babylonians. The First Wall ran st from the northern end of Herod ; Great's palace to the Temple ırts.

The remains of an ancient wall at ; present-day Damascus Gate ve been identified by K. M. Kenyon d J. B. Hennessy as part of the ird Wall, but by Israeli haeologists as part of the Second ıll; and finds considerably further rth have been linked with the ird Wall by the latter, but with a ıll dating to the Jewish War by the tish excavators. (While Kenyon ought this was a wall of cumvallation erected by Titus, W. Hamrick has shown that it is re plausibly a barrier wall erected *ainst* Titus by the Jews.)

The Third Wall was begun by rippa I (AD 41–44), and scarcely ished by the outbreak of the wish War AD 66, so that atigraphical methods would ırcely serve to distinguish Agrippa's Wall from Titus' Wall. The evidence of coins found in foundation deposits seems to favour the British team's interpretation, but certainty is not available.

*The site of the crucifixion*

One special point of interest concerning the Second Wall, which must have been built in the 2nd or 1st century BC (Josephus does not date its construction) is its relationship to the Church of the Holy Sepulchre. If the church has any claim to marking the authentic site of the crucifixion and burial of Christ, its site must have lain outside the city walls; but for many years it was considered doubtful whether the site lay inside or outside the line of the Second Wall (the Third Wall was not then in existence). It has now been established that this area lay to the north of the wall; the site may therefore be authentic. (See also *CALVARY.)

*After AD 70*

The city lay in ruins between AD 70 and the Bar-Kokhba revolt 60 years later. The emperor Hadrian then rebuilt the city, naming it Aelia Capitolina; his city was much smaller than its predecessor, with the permanent retraction of the southern wall. During the Christian era, the size of Jerusalem has been by no means constant. The present-day walled area ('the Old City') was given its definitive shape by Suleiman the Magnificent in the 16th century.

D. F. Payne, J. Bimson

*Further reading*

On history and archaeology, see especially:
K. M. Kenyon, *Digging Up Jerusalem*, 1974, and bibliography listed there
Y. Yadin (ed.), *Jerusalem Revealed*, 1975
B. Mazar, *The Mountain of the Lord*, 1975
—— and others in *NEAEHL* II, pp. 698–804
J. Wilkinson, *Jerusalem as Jesus Knew It*, 1978
M. Broshi, *BARev* 4, 1978, pp. 10–15
N. Avigad, *Discovering Jerusalem*, 1983
Y. Shiloh, *Excavations at the City of David* I, *1978–1982* (*Qedem* 19), 1984
A. D. Tushingham, *Excavations in Jerusalem 1961–1967*, 1985
——, *Levant* XIX, 1987, pp. 137–143
E. W. Hamrick, *Levant* XIII, 1981, pp. 262–266
J. Murphy-O'Connor, *The Holy Land: An Archaeological Guide*, 3rd edition, 1992, pp. 11–149
On economic and social conditions:
J. Jeremias, *Jerusalem in the Time of Jesus*, 1969
On theology:
*TDNT* 7, pp. 292–338
W. D. Davies, *The Gospel and the Land*, 1974

**Continued from p. 167**
his home in this fashionable district. Few private dwellings have been excavated, but a large cemetery provides indirect evidence for an extensive Jewish population during the 1st century BC to 1st century AD.

The immortal story of the good Samaritan is set on the narrow, bandit-infested road from Jerusalem down to Jericho (Luke 10:30–37).
K. A. Kitchen

*Further reading*
Sir Charles Warren sank shafts at Jericho in about 1868 with little result. The first scientific excavation there (1907–09) was by Sellin and Watzinger (*Jericho*, 1913), but they could not date their finds properly. Apart from his errors over 'Joshua's Jericho' (see above), Garstang in 1930–36 put the archaeology of the site on a sound basis. See J. and J. B. E. Garstang, *The Story of Jericho*, 1948 (*GSJ*). Detailed preliminary reports are in *Liverpool Annals of Archaeology and Anthropology* 19, 1932, to 23, 1936, and in *PEQ* for the same years. Dame Kathleen Kenyon reviewed Garstang's results in *PEQ* 83, 1951, pp. 101–138. Further older bibliography is in Barrois, *Manuel d'Archéologie Biblique* 1, 1939, pp. 61, 63.

Detailed preliminary reports of Dame Kathleen Kenyon's excavations from 1952 to 1958 are in *PEQ* 84, 1952, to 92, 1960; *BASOR* 127, 1952, pp. 5–16; *BA* 16, 1953, pp. 45–67, and 17, 1954, pp. 98–104.

For an instructive (and humorous) general account, see *W, i.e.*, M. Wheeler, *The Walls of Jericho*, 1956 (paperback, 1960).

The best detailed over-all account is *DUJ, i.e.*, K. M. Kenyon, *Digging Up Jericho*, 1957 (fully illustrated), supplemented for the earliest periods by *AHL, i.e.*, K. M. Kenyon, *Archaeology in the Holy Land*, 4th edition, 1979.

The definitive publication is now K. M. Kenyon, *Excavations at Jericho*, vol. 1, 1960; vol. 2, 1965; vol. 3, 1981; K. M. Kenyon and T. A. Holland, *Excavations at Jericho*, vol. 4, 1982; vol. 5, 1983. For a summary see J. R. Bartlett, *Jericho*, 1982.

On the Late Bronze Age finds see P. Bienkowski, *Jericho in the Late Bronze Age*, 1986

For a recent re-evaluation of the Middle and Late Bronze Ages at Jericho with reference to the Old Testament, see B. G. Wood, *BARev* 16/2, 1990, pp. 44–58.

On the Iron Age, see H. Weippe and M. Weippert, *ZDPV* 92, 1976, pp. 105–148.

For New Testament Jericho, see above and good background by L. Mowry, *BA* 15, 1952, pp. 25–42. Fo an over-all bibliography, see E. K. Vogel, *Bibliography of Holy Land Sites*, 1974, pp. 42–44; survey, see K. M. Kenyon and E. Netzer in *NEAEHL* II, pp. 674–697.

The land around Jezreel.

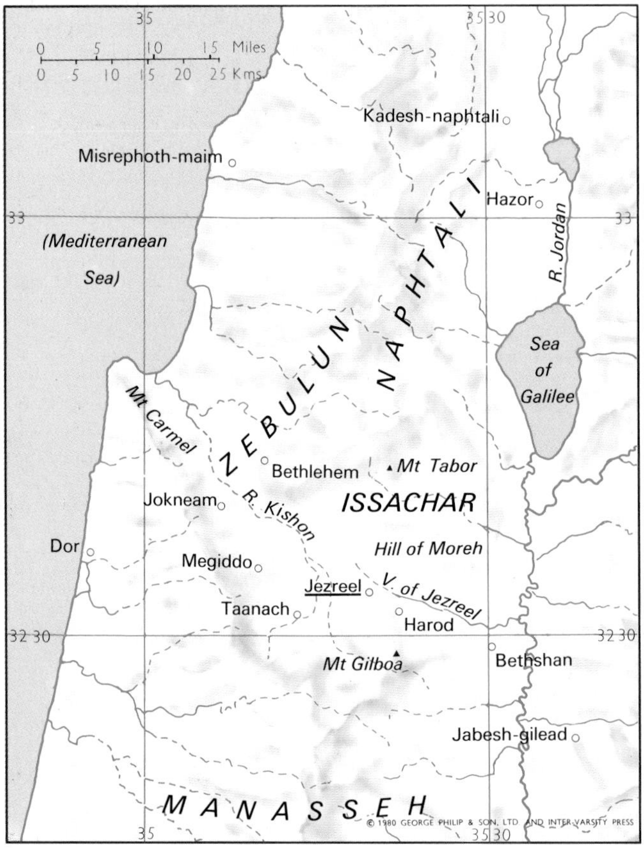


**JERUEL** (Hebrew *yᵉrû'ēl*, 'founde by El'; Septuagint 'Jeriel'). Mentioned by the prophet Jahazie as the wilderness where Jehoshaphat would meet and conquer the Moabites and Ammonites (2 Chronicles 20:16). Possibly it is identical with, or a pa of, the wilderness of *Tekoa, the country extending from the weste shores of the Dead Sea north of En-gedi.
J. D. Douglas

**JERUSALEM.** See p. 168.

**JESHIMON** (Hebrew *yᵉšîmōn*, 'waste', 'desert'). Apparently usec as a proper noun in Numbers 21:2 23:28; 1 Samuel 23:19, 24; and 26 3. G. A. Smith, followed by G. E. Wright and F. V. Filson, identifies t name simply with the Wilderness Judaea, but there is reason to thin that in the Numbers references a location north-east of the Dead Sea indicated. (See *GTT*, pp. 22f.)
R. P. Gordon

**JEZREEL** (Hebrew *yizrᵉ'e'l*, 'God sows'). **1.** The town in the mountai of Judah (Joshua 15:56); the nativ place of Ahinoam, one of David's wives (1 Samuel 25:43).

**2.** A city in Issachar and the plai (see *Esdraelon for location) on which it stood (Joshua 19:18; Hos 1:5). The city and general neighbourhood are associated wit several notable events. By its fountain the Israelites assembled before engaging the Philistines at Gilboa (1 Samuel 29:1). It was a pa of Ish-bosheth's short-lived kingdo (2 Samuel 2:8ff.); an administrativ district of Solomon (1 Kings 4:12); and the scene of the tragedy of Naboth and his vineyard (1 Kings 21:1). Here Joram, who had earlie come to convalesce from war wounds (2 Kings 8:29), was slain Jehu, and his body significantly ca into the vineyard so cruelly appropriated by Ahab and Jezebe (2 Kings 9:24–26). Thereafter at Jehu's instigation Jezebel herself Kings 9:30–37) and the remnant c ab's household (2 Kings 10:1–11) re slain.

ezreel is identified with the dern Zer'in, about 90 kilometres th of Jerusalem. There have been major excavations and its history nains unknown apart from the lical references.

. Douglas

**GBEHAH** (Hebrew *yōgb$^{e}$hâ*, ight'). A town in Gilead assigned Gad (Numbers 32:35), named also Gideon's pursuit of the Midianites dges 8:11). It is the modern beihât, about 10 kilometres th-west of Amman and 1057 tres above sea-level.

. Douglas

**KMEAM** (Hebrew *yoqm$^{e}$'ām*). A itical town in Ephraim (1 ronicles 6:68; Massoretic Text se 53), probably the Kibzaim of hua 21:22. Tell el-Mazar, at the uth of the Wadi Fari'a (in the dan valley, 22 kilometres ith-east of Shechem [modern blus]), has been suggested (B. zar, *VT Supplement* 7, 1960, 98). This may have been the ithern end of Solomon's fifth trict, 1 Kings 4:12, though the text not entirely clear; Gray and Noth e the site to be *Jokneam at the thern end.

. U. Lilley

**KNEAM** (Hebrew *yoqn$^{e}$'ām*). A naanite city (Joshua 12:22), mber 113 in the list of Tuthmosis a levitical city in Zebulun (Joshua :34). Tel Yoqneam, Tell Qeimun kilometres north-west of giddo), guards the most westerly ss from the Vale of Jezreel to the ist south of Carmel. The brook posite Jokneam' (Joshua 19:11) rked the tribal boundary; since city was within Zebulun, the *hal* is likely to have been a butary rather than the Kishon elf, and may refer to the pass. Excavations since 1977 have ealed a site occupied from the rly Bronze Age to the Ottoman riod, *i.e.* spanning some 4,500 ars. No other site in Palestine, cept Jerusalem, matches this time an.

. U. Lilley

*rther reading*

Noth, *Josua*, 2nd edition, 1953, on 11

Simons, *GTT*, pp. 206, 350

Aharoni, *LOB*, pp. 152, 257 *etc.*

Ben-Tor, *IEJ* 33, 1983, pp. 30–54

**KTHEEL.** See *Sela.

The Jordan near to the southern end of the Sea of Galilee.

**JOPPA.** The name in Hebrew is *yāpō*, Greek *Ioppē*, Arabic *Yâfâ* (whence modern English 'Jaffa'). As the only natural harbour between the Bay of Acco (near modern Haifa) and the Egyptian frontier, Joppa has a long history; excavations have shown that it dates back to the 18th century BC or earlier, and it is mentioned in several Egyptian records of the 15th and 14th centuries BC.

After the Israelite occupation of Canaan, it was a border city of Dan (Joshua 19:46), but soon fell into Philistine hands. It was rarely under Israelite control thereafter, though it must have served as the seaport for Jerusalem, about 55 kilometres away. In the 2nd century BC Simon wrested it from the Syrians and annexed it to Judaea (1 Maccabees 13:11). It features in the story of Acts 10. Today it forms the southern part of the municipality of Tel Aviv-Jaffa.

Parts of Joppa have been excavated in several archaeological campaigns since World War II. Of special interest is a pre-Philistine temple (13th century BC), dedicated to a lion cult.

D. F. Payne

*Further reading*

J. Kaplan and H. Ritter-Kaplan, 'Jaffa', *NEAEHL* II, pp. 655–659

**JORDAN, VALLEY AND RIVER.** The Jordan depression is unique among the features of physical geography. Formed as a result of a rift valley, it is the lowest depression on earth. The headwaters of the river Jordan, fed by springs, collect into Lake Huleh, 70 metres above sea-level. Ten kilometres south at Lake Tiberias the river is already nearly 200 metres below the Mediterranean, while at the northern end of the *Dead Sea the floor of the trench has dropped a further 177 metres and the river has plunged to 393 metres below sea-level. Thus the name 'Jordan' (Hebrew *yardēn*) aptly means 'the descender'.

The river is the largest perennial course in Palestine, and its distance of some 120 kilometres from Lake Huleh to the Dead Sea is more than doubled by its meander. No other river has more biblical allusions and significance.

### Archaeological sites

Archaeological sites in the Jordan valley have revealed it to be one of the earliest loci of urban settlement in the world. The Natufian transition from hunting to urban life at Jericho may be as old as 7000 BC.

A pottery-making people arrived about 5000 BC, and with the later pottery (Neolithic B culture) the first evidence occurs of links with other Jordan valley sites and the northern Fertile Crescent. Copper was introduced in the Chalcolithic period (4500–3200 BC), such as at Teleilat Ghassul, just north of the Dead Sea.

At Ghassul, three city levels existed from the 4th millennium onwards, with evidence of irrigation farming. This Ghassulian culture is identified widely in Palestine, but it was especially prevalent in the Jordan valley, at Mefjar, Abu Habil, Jiftlik Beth-shan, En-gedi and Tell esh-Shuneh, south of the Sea of Galilee.

At the end of the 4th millennium at least three groups of peoples entered the Jordan valley from the north, to settle in unwalled villages

**The Jordan valley in Old Testament times.**

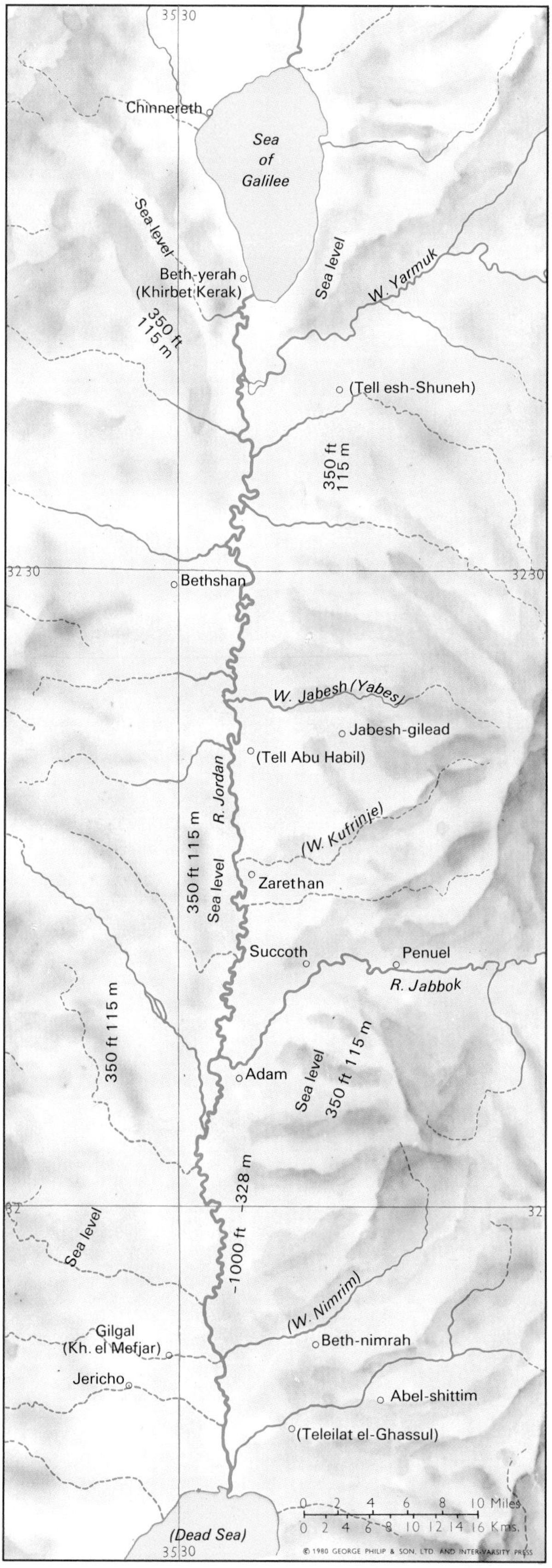


in the plains of Esdraelon, or from t east via Jericho. This period K. M. Kenyon has called proto-urban.

City-states then began to appea in the Jordan valley, such as Jeric in the south, Beth-shan in the cen and Beth-yerah (Khirbet Kerak) in the north, and these traded with Egypt and Mesopotamia.

About 2200 BC many of the urba centres were destroyed. This may have been caused by a vast gener eruption of peoples that went on from 2300 to 1900 BC, that is, to the beginning of the Middle Bronze Ag Abraham may have come into the Jordan valley in association with th period of nomadic unrest.

During the Middle Bronze Age elaborate urban defences in depth were built at such towns as Jerich As Egypt forged its empire from th 15th century BC onwards, the grea fortress towns of the Jordan valley such as Beth-shan and Hazor, wer equipped with Egyptian garrisons Then later in the Bronze Age, at lea by 1220 BC, the Israelites entered Palestine through the Jordan valle There is evidence of the destructi of the cities of Hazor, Debir and Lachish, but the archaeological evidence for Joshua's capture of Jericho is obscure (see *JERICHO).

## Topographical features

*The Huleh basin*

The Jordan valley begins below Mount Hermon (2814 metres), out whose limestone springs issue the headwaters of the Jordan. Banias, later called Caesarea Philippi, may have been the centre of Baal-gad i the valley 'of Lebanon' (Joshua 12:7). It was the territory of Dan, t northern limit of Israel, whose inhabitants controlled the vital tra route into Syria and were likened t nest of vipers (Genesis 49:17).

Moving down the upper valley i the Huleh area, a depression some 5 × 15 kilometres, where ancient lava flows blocked the valley, so t the Jordan plunges 280 metres in kilometres of gorges. On the plate overlooking the Huleh plain stand the site of Hazor, the great Canaanite town.

*The Tiberias district*

Beyond the Huleh gorges, at abou 213 metres below sea-level, the Jordan enters the Sea of Galilee, a harp-shaped lake, 21 kilometres long, and about 13 kilometres acro Fed by numerous thermal springs its fresh waters are well stocked with fish, the maximum depth of 5 metres permitting vertical

ɟrations of the fish with the
ısonal temperatures. It was,
refore, probably in the hot
ımer season when the normal
ıter temperature of 13°C lies 37
tres below the surface of the lake,
.t Jesus advised the fishermen to
st into the deep' (Luke 5:4). The
thods of catching fish referred to
he gospels are still practised: the
gle-hook line (Matthew 17:27);
circular fishing net (Matthew
8; Mark 1:16); the draw-net cast
: by a boat (Matthew 13:47f.);
ep-sea nets (Matthew 4:18f.;
ırk 1:19f.); and deep-sea fishing
dertaken with two boats (Luke
0).

\ dense population clustered
ınd the lake in our Lord's day, and
vas the sophisticated city folk of
orazin, Bethsaida and Capernaum
ıt he condemned (Matthew
·20–24). 'There is no spot in the
ıole of Palestine where memories
ap themselves up to such an
tent as in Capernaum' (G.
lman). Jewish life throbbed in its
ıagogues (Matthew 12:9; Mark
21; 3:1; 5:22; Luke 4:31; 6:6;
11). There lived Jairus, the chief of
synagogue (Mark 5:22), the
nturion who built a synagogue
ıke 7:5) and Levi the customs
icial (Matthew 9:9; Mark 2:14;
ke 5:27).

East of Capernaum was Bethsaida
m which Philip, Andrew and Peter
me (John 1:44), and beyond that
less populous district of the
adarenes, where the heathen
ared their pigs (Luke 8:32). The
ce, plains and steep rocky slopes,
erspersed with boulders and
ıstle-fields, provide the setting for
e parable of the sower (Mark
2–8), while in spring the flowered
rpets of asphodels, anemones and
ses are also telling sermons.

Dominating this lake environment
e the surrounding mountains,
pecially those of the north-west,
ıich played so vital a part in the
ayer-life of our Lord, where he
ught his disciples (Matthew 5:1)
d from which he appeared as the
sen Lord (Matthew 28:16). The
rth-eastern corner of the lake is
pposedly the scene of the miracle
the feeding of the five thousand
uke 9:10–17).

*ıe 'Ghor' or Jordan valley*

ıis runs for over 105 kilometres
tween Lake Tiberias and the Dead
a. The Yarmuk, entering the left
ınk of the Jordan 8 kilometres
ɔwnstream from the lake, doubles
e volume of flow, and the valley is
ogressively deepened to as much

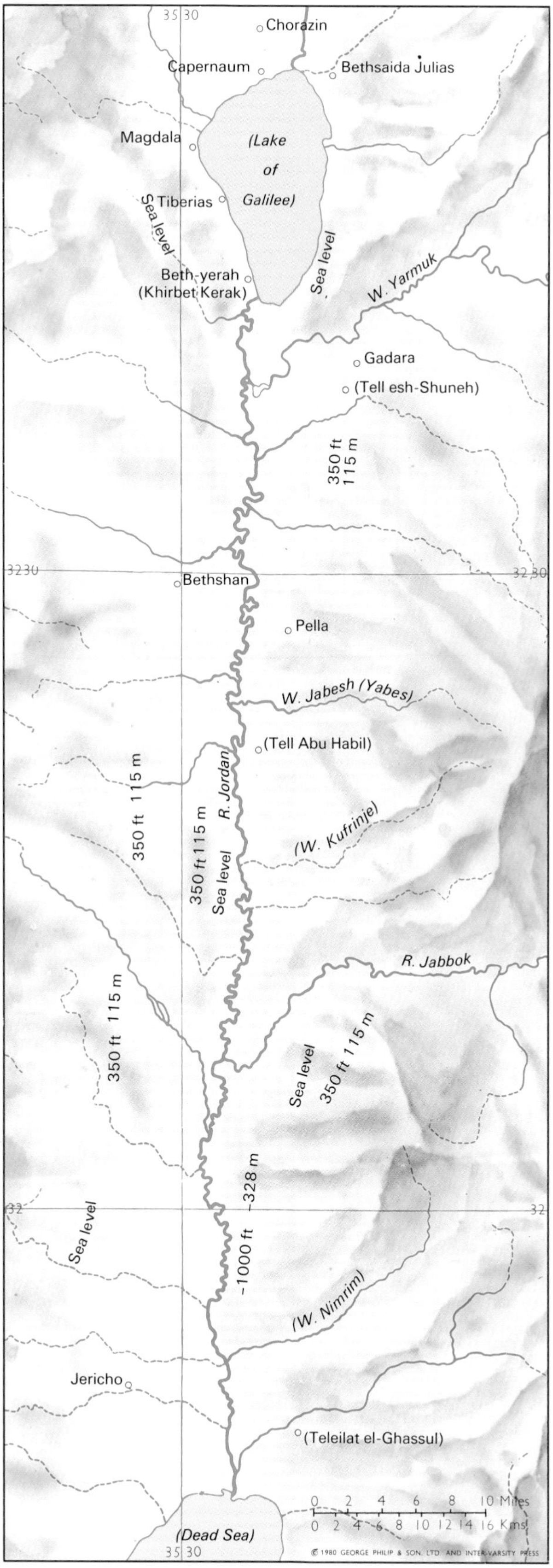


**The Jordan valley in New Testament times.**

as 50 metres below the floor of the trough.

In this sector, three physical zones are distinguishable: the broad upper terrace of the Pliocene trough, the Ghor proper; the lower Quaternary terrace and the flood plain of the river, the Zor; and between them the deeply dissected slopes and badlands of the Qattara. It is the Qattara and the Zor together, rather than the river Jordan, which have created the frontier character of this obstacle (Joshua 22:25).

The northern half of the Ghor is a broad, well-cultivated tract, but the Judaean-Gilead dome, crossing the trough, narrows the valley south of Gilead. Beyond it, the trough becomes increasingly more arid, until at the head of the Dead Sea there is scarcely more than 5 centimetres mean annual rainfall. The Qattara badlands, carved grotesquely in soft marls and clays, create a steep, desolate descent to the valley floor.

The Zor, making its way in vivid green vegetation cover, stands out in sharp contrast below, hence its name *gā'ôn* ('luxuriant growth') of Jordan (Jeremiah 12:5; 49:19; 50:44; Zechariah 11:3; compare Psalms 47:4; 59:12; Proverbs 16:18). The haunt of wild animals (Jeremiah 49:19), it is partly flooded in spring (Joshua 3:15). Thus the question can be understood, 'And if in a safe land you fall down, how will you do in the jungle of the Jordan?' (Jeremiah 12:5).

Between the Yarmuk in the north and the Jabbok are nine other perennial streams entering the left bank of the Jordan, and their water supply explains why all the important settlements were located on the eastern side of the Ghor, towns such as Succoth, Zaphon, Zarethan, Jabesh-gilead and Pella. With the aid of irrigation, this was probably the view Lot saw 'like the garden of the Lord' (Genesis 13:10).

The brook Cherith may well have been a seasonal tributary of the Jabesh farther north, where Elijah, a native of Jabesh-gilead, hid himself from Ahab (1 Kings 17:1–7).

Between Succoth and Zarethan (identified by Glueck as Tell es-Saidiyeh) Solomon had his copper cast in earthen moulds, using local clay and fuel (1 Kings 7:46; 2 Chronicles 4:17). In this section of the valley, there are a number of fords, though the river was not bridged until Roman times. Near the mouth of the Jabbok, both Abraham and Jacob crossed it (Genesis 32:10). Somewhere here, the Midianites crossed pursued by Gideon (Judges 7:24; 8:4–5). Twice David crossed it in the rebellion of Absalom (2 Samuel 17:22–24; 19:15–18).

Between the Jabbok confluence and the Dead Sea, crossings are more difficult, owing to the swift current. The miraculous crossing of the Israelites took place in the vicinity of Jericho while the river was blocked by a landslide at *Adam (modern Tell Dâmiyeh), 26 kilometres north of Jericho (Joshua 3:1–17; 4:1–24; Psalm 114:3, 5).

Between the Jabbok and Beth-nimrah for 26 kilometres (Isaiah 15:6) there are no streams entering the Jordan, and little settlement. Oasis towns occur near springs, such as Jericho west of the Jordan, and in the plains of Moab (Numbers 20:1) to the east was Shittim, from where the spies were sent (Joshua 2:1–7).

J. M. Houston

*Further reading*

D. Baly, *The Geography of the Bible*, 2nd edition, 1974
G. Dalman, *Sacred Sites and Ways*, trans. by P. P. Levertoff, 1935
J. and J. B. E. Garstang, *The Story of Jericho*, 1948
N. Glueck, *The River Jordan*, 1946
K. M. Kenyon, *Jericho I*, 1960
E. B. Smick, *Archaeology of the Jordan Valley*, 1973

**JOTBAH** (Hebrew *yot'bah*). Birthplace of the wife of Manasseh (2 Kings 21:19); earlier, overrun by Tiglath-pileser III in his invasion of Galilee (*ANET*, p. 283).

Probably biblical Jotbah is Khirbet Jefat (Shifat), Hurvat Yodefat (15 kilometres north of Nazareth); Josephus in his *Jewish War* 2.573 refers to it as Jotapata. However, no Iron Age finds have turned up at the site and this has led to the suggestion that while Khirbet Jefat is Jotapata, Old Testament Jotbah should be sought at Kerem el-Ras (10 kilometres south-south-east of Khirbet Jefat) where pottery from the 10th-8th centuries BC has been collected in surveys.

J. P. U. Lilley, J. Bimson

**JOTBATHAH.** A stopping-place in the Israelites' wilderness wanderings (Numbers 33:33–34; Deuteronomy 10:7). Described in Deuteronomy as 'a land of brooks of water', it is identified with either 'Ain Ṭābah in the Arabah north of Elath or perhaps more accurately with Ṭabeh, about 11 kilometres south of Elath on the western shore of the Gulf of Aqabah (*LOB*, pp. 199–200).

W. Osborne

**JUDAEA.** The Greek and Roman designation of the land of *Judah. The word is actually an adjective ('Jewish') with *gē* ('land') or *chōra* ('country') understood. After the Roman conquest (63 BC) it appears both in a wider sense, denoting all Palestine, including Galilee and Samaria, and in the narrower sens which excludes these two regions.

Herod's kingdom of Judaea (37–4 BC) included all Palestine and son districts east of the Jordan. Archelaus' ethnarchy of Judaea (4 – AD 6) embraced Judaea in the narrower sense and Samaria, and the same is true of the Roman province of Judaea from AD 6 to 41. After the death of Herod Agrippa I in AD 44 the Roman province of Judaea included Galilee also.

The 'wilderness of Judaea' (Matthew 3:1), associated with Jo the Baptist, is probably identical with the 'wilderness of Judah' (Judges 1:16, *etc.*), *i.e.*, the desert the west of the Dead Sea.

J. D. Douglas

**JUDAH** (Hebrew *y$^{e}$hûḏâ*). In Genesis 29:35 the name is explain as meaning 'praised', from the roo *ydh*, 'to praise'. The derivation is widely rejected but no other suggested etymology has been generally accepted (for literature, see *KB*).

## The tribe of Judah

*From the Exodus till Saul*

The tribe plays no special role in th story of the Exodus and of the wilderness wanderings, though it to be noted that Judah was the leader of the vanguard (Numbers 2:9). There is no significant chang in the two census figures from this period (Numbers 1:27; 26:22).

Achan, a member of the tribe, w the cause of the defeat of Israel before Ai (Joshua 7). This may be th reason for the special task laid on Judah to lead an independent atta on the Canaanites (Judges 1:1–2). No explanation is given, but it is clear that Judah's portion was allocated not by lot in Shiloh (Josh 18:1–10) but before its conquest (Judges 1:3); compare the similar treatment of Ephraim and half Manasseh (Joshua 16–17).

Judah was bounded on the nort by the portions of Dan and Benjami and ran approximately east and we from the northern end of the Dead Sea, south of Jerusalem and the beonite tetrapolis to the editerranean. Its western and stern frontiers were the editerranean and the Dead Sea, d it extended south as far as ltivation permitted (see Joshua ).

Judah first overran most of the astal plain, soon to be occupied by e Philistines (Judges 1:18), but idently quickly withdrew from the uggle (Judges 1:19; 3:3; Joshua :22; 13:2–3). Since it was the best the land apportioned to him that dah voluntarily abandoned to meon (Joshua 19:1, 9), it is asonable to suppose that he hoped have Simeon as a buffer between m and the unconquered coastal ain.

The story of the conquest of the uth in Judges 1:1–17 has been ry widely interpreted to mean that ıdah (and other tribes) entered the nd from the south *before* the vasion under Joshua (see H. H. owley, *From Joseph to Joshua*, 950, pp. 4f., 101f., 110ff., with erature), but the whole trend of odern archaeological discovery ems to be unfavourable to the eory, which is unacceptable on her, general grounds.

The failure to maintain a hold on erusalem (Judges 1:8, 21), mbined with the existence of the mi-independent Gibeonite trapolis (Joshua 9; 2 Samuel 1:1–2), created a psychological ontier between Judah and the entral tribes. Though there was no arrier to communications (see udges 19:10–13), Judah will creasingly have looked south to ebron rather than to the sanctuary Shiloh.

While Judah provided the first of e judges, Othniel (Judges 3:9–11), nd shared in the early action ainst Benjamin (Judges 20:18), he oes not seem even to have been xpected to join against Jabin and isera (Judges 5). As a result, when udah became tributary to the hilistines (Judges 15:11), he ppears not to have appealed to the ther tribes, nor do they seem to ave been concerned.

The fact of this division seems to ave been generally recognized, for y Saul's time we find the contingent om Judah separately enumerated Samuel 11:8; 15:4; 17:52; 18:16).

*nder David and Solomon*

fter Saul's death this growing split vas perpetuated by David's being rowned as king in Hebron over udah (2 Samuel 2:4). A. Alt is robably correct in maintaining (in 'The Formation of the Israelite State in Palestine', in *Essays on Old Testament History and Religion*, 1966, pp. 216ff.) that the crowning of David as king over 'all Israel' (2 Samuel 5:1–5) made him king of a dual kingdom in which Judah kept its separate identity. Certainly during Absalom's rebellion Judah seems to have maintained its neutrality, while the north followed the rebel.

## The kingdom of Judah

*Its relations with Israel*

If A. Alt's view is correct, Judah and Israel in accepting different kings were acting in accordance with their rights as separate political entities. Apart from Jeroboam himself, the kings of Israel do not seem to have sought the destruction of Judah (see 2 Kings 14:13–14), and the prophets never questioned the right of Israel to exist, though they foresaw the time when it would return to its allegiance to 'David'.

The heritage of Solomon's riches seemed to give Judah the advantage at the disruption, despite its less fertile land and smaller population compared with the north. In spite of claims to the contrary, there is no evidence that Rehoboam later disregarded the command of Shemaiah (1 Kings 12:22–24) and attacked Jeroboam. The suggestion that Shishak's attack on Judah (1 Kings 14:25–26) was in support of his ally Jeroboam lacks positive evidence in its support. The resultant loss of the wealth Solomon had amassed, even though Israel seems to have suffered from Shishak's attack as well, meant that Judah now stood permanently in a position of material inferiority compared with Israel. The evidence suggests that Judah needed a prosperous Israel for its own prosperity.

One effective test of the absolute, rather than relative, prosperity of Judah was its ability to control Edom, or as much of it as was necessary for the safeguarding of the trade-route to the Gulf of Aqabah. Rehoboam made no effort to maintain his father's precarious hold on the area. Jehoshaphat evidently completely subdued the country (1 Kings 22:47), but later he had to install a vassal king (2 Kings 3:9). Edom regained its independence under his son Jehoram (2 Kings 8:20–22). Amaziah, about half a century later, reconquered Edom (2 Kings 14:7). This time the conquest was more effective, and not until the troubles of Ahaz' reign 60 years later was Edom finally able

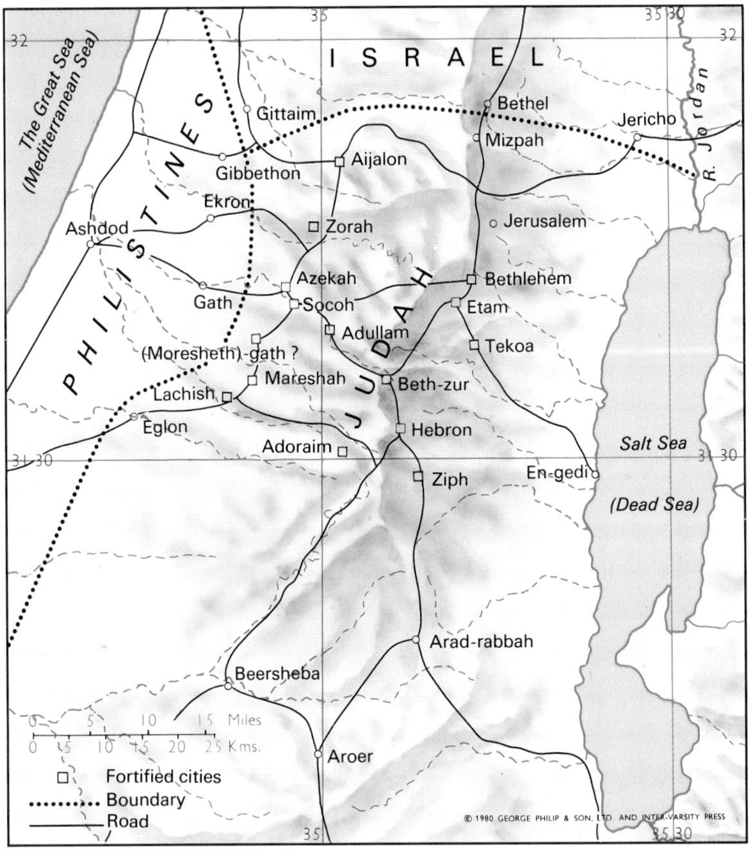


Judah at the time of Rehoboam (*c.* 931–913).

to free itself (2 Kings 16:6). After this Judah does not seem even to have attempted conquest.

It was only a decisive victory by Abijah (or Abijam) that restored a measure of parity between the kingdoms (2 Chronicles 13). Asa, faced with the capable Baasha, could maintain it only by allying himself with Ben-hadad, king of Damascus (1 Kings 15:18–20). The dynasty of Omri, disturbed both by the increasing power of Damascus, and even more by the threat from *Assyria, made peace with Judah, which was later sealed by the marriage of Athaliah, Ahab's daughter, or perhaps sister (2 Kings 8:26), with Jehoram.

It is widely held that at this time Judah was Israel's vassal. So far from this being true, the evidence suggests that Jehoshaphat used Israel as a buffer between him and Assyria. This is the most likely explanation why Judah does not figure on Shalmaneser's list of his enemies at the battle of Qarqar, nor for that matter on the 'Black Obelisk'. Jehoshaphat seems to have looked on, with the sole exception of the battle of Ramoth-gilead (1 Kings 22:1–38), while Israel and Damascus tore at one another's vitals. Hence, by the end of his long reign, he felt himself strong enough to refuse Ahaziah's request for a joint venture to Ophir after the first had failed (1 Kings 22:48–49 compared with 2 Chronicles 20:35–37). The relative equality between the kingdoms at this time is seen in the fact that Jehu, though he had killed Ahaziah of Judah (2 Kings 9:27), did not venture to carry his anti-Baal campaign into Judah, nor, on the other hand, did Athaliah try to avenge her son's death.

In the century between the accession of Jehu and the deaths of Jeroboam II and Uzziah the fortunes of Judah seem to have kept pace with those of Israel both in affliction and prosperity. Probably the latter came more slowly to the south, even as the hollowness of its prosperity was revealed somewhat later than in Israel.

*Earlier foreign enemies*

Until the collapse of Israel the history of Judah is singularly uninfluenced by foreign threats. Shishak's invasion was a last stirring of Egypt's ancient power until the Assyrian advance forced it to measures of self-defence.

The Philistines had been so weakened that we find them as aggressors only when Judah was weakest, namely under Jehoram (2 Chronicles 21:16) and Ahaz (2 Chronicles 28:18).

At the height of Hazael's power, when he had almost destroyed Israel, Jehoash was forced to become tributary to Damascus, but this cannot have lasted long.

In fact, the only two major threats of this period were from those sudden movements that the nomads and semi-nomads of the desert have periodically thrown up. Zerah 'the Cushite' (2 Chronicles 14:9) is more likely to have been an Arabian (compare Genesis 10:7) than an Ethiopian, *i.e.* a Sudanese. The second was from a sudden movement of the inhabitants of the Transjordan steppe-land (2 Chronicles 20:1, 10).

*Judah and Assyria*

As stated above, the earlier advances of Assyria do not seem to have affected Judah. When Damascus and Israel attacked Ahaz (2 Kings 16:5), it was a last desperate attempt to unite the remnants of the West against the advance of Tiglath-pileser III. There are no grounds for thinking that Judah was threatened by the Assyrians, for until they wanted to challenge Egypt they would hardly alarm it by advancing prematurely to its desert frontier.

By accepting the suzerainty of Assyria Ahaz virtually sealed the fate of Judah. On the one hand, it remained a vassal until the approaching doom of Assyria (612 BC) could be foreseen; on the other, it was caught up in the intrigues stirred up by Egypt, for which it duly suffered. Hezekiah's revolt in 705 BC, crushed by Sennacherib 4 years later, reduced Judah to a shadow of its former self, at least two-thirds of the population perishing or being carried away captive, and a large portion of its territory being lost.

For details, see J. Bright, *A History of Israel*, 3rd edition, 1980, pp. 284–288, 298–309, and *DOTT*, pp. 64–70.

*Revival and downfall*

A revival of religious and nationalistic feeling under the young Josiah began just after Ashurbanipal's death (631 BC), when the weakness of Assyria was already becoming manifest. The steps in reform indicated in 2 Chronicles 34:3 and 8 suggest how closely interwoven religion and politics had become, for each step was in itself also a rejection of Assyrian religious and therefore political control.

By the height of the reform in 621 BC Josiah, though probably still nominally tributary to Assyria, was in fact independent. With or without the approval of his nominal overlord he took over the Assyrian provinces of Samaria and eastern Galilee (2 Chronicles 34:6) and doubtless recovered the territory that Hezekiah had lost as a punishment for his rebellion. There is no reliable evidence that the Scythian inroad, which did so much to give Assyria its mortal wound, affected or even reached Judah.

There is no indication that Josiah offered any opposition to Pharaoh Psammetichus' expedition in aid of Assyria in 616 BC, but when Pharaoh Neco repeated the expedition in 60[illegible] BC Josiah evidently felt that in the new international position his only chance of maintaining Judah's independence was to fight, but in the ensuing battle at Megiddo he met his death. There is no evidence for the suggestion that he was acting in alliance with the rising star of *Babylon, though the possibility must not be rejected.

Egypt marked its victory by deposing Josiah's son Jehoahaz and replacing him by his brother Jehoiakim, who had, however, to accept Babylonian overlordship soon after Nebuchadrezzar's victory at Carchemish (605 BC) (Daniel 1:1; 2 Kings 24:1).

In 601 BC Nebuchadrezzar was checked by Neco in a battle near the Egyptian frontier, and on his withdrawal to Babylon Jehoiakim rebelled. Judah was ravaged by Babylonian troops and auxiliary levies (2 Kings 24:2). Jehoiakim died an obscure death in December 598 BC, before he could suffer the full penalty of rebellion, and Jehoiachin his 18-year-old son, surrendered Jerusalem to Nebuchadrezzar on 16 March 597 BC.

His uncle Zedekiah became the last king of Judah, but revolted in 589 BC. By January 588 BC the Babylonian armies were before the walls of Jerusalem. In July 587 BC the walls were breached and Zedekiah was captured to meet a traitor's fate (2 Kings 25:6–7); a month later the city was burnt down and the walls razed.

*Religion under the Monarchy*

Popular religion in Judah was probably as degraded by concepts of nature-religion as in Israel, but its relative isolation and openness to the desert will have made it less influenced by its Canaanite forms. Its lack of major sanctuaries – only ebron and Beersheba are known to ;, with Gibeon in Benjamin – creased the influence of Jerusalem ıd its Solomonic Temple.

It is questionable whether any ng of Israel could even have tempted the centralizing reforms Hezekiah and Josiah. The Davidic ovenant (2 Samuel 7:8–16), far more an the general atmosphere of the ertile Crescent', made the king the ıdisputed leader of the national ligion, even though cultic nctions were denied him Chronicles 26:16–21).

The power of the king might be sed for good, as in the reformations, ıt where national policy seemed to emand an acceptance of aal-worship, as under Jehoram, haziah and Athaliah, or a cognition of the Assyrian astral eities, as under Ahaz and anasseh, there was no effective ower that could resist the royal will. ne royal authority in matters of ligion will also have helped to ake the official cult for many erely an external and official atter.

*xile (597–538 BC)*

part from an unspecified number of dinary captives destined to avery, Nebuchadrezzar deported e cream of the population in 597 BC Kings 24:14; Jeremiah 52:28 – the fference in figures is doubtless due different categories of captives eing envisaged). A few, including e royal family, became 'guests' of ebuchadrezzar in Babylon; others, *g.* Ezekiel, were settled in mmunities in Babylonia, where ey had apparently full freedom oart from the right to change their omicile; the skilled artisans ecame part of a mobile labour force sed by Nebuchadrezzar in his ıilding operations. The destruction Jerusalem added to the general tal of captives (2 Kings 25:11), and eremiah 52:29 shows there was ıother group of designated eportees.

The murder of Gedaliah, whom ebuchadrezzar had made governor Judah, led to a large-scale flight to gypt (2 Kings 25:25–26; Jeremiah :1–43:7). This, in turn, was llowed in 582 BC by another, oviously punitive, deportation to abylonia (Jeremiah 52:30).

Although the population was eatly reduced by the deportations, ıdah was not left empty. The abylonians 'left some of the poorest the land to be vine-dressers and oughmen' (2 Kings 25:12), *i.e.* to ork the land for the benefit of the empire's economy. After the fall of Jerusalem Mizpah functioned as the administrative capital, but when Gedaliah was murdered the town's population moved to Egypt (2 Kings 25:25–26).

The land south of a line between Beth-zur and Hebron seems to have been detached from Judah in 597 BC; into it the Edomites gradually moved. As a result, this area was lost to Judah until its capture by John Hyrcanus after 129 BC and the forcible Judaizing of its population. The remainder was placed under the governor of Samaria.

## Post-exilic Judah

*Restoration*

Babylon fell to Cyrus in 539 BC, and the next year he ordered the rebuilding of the Jerusalem Temple (Ezra 6:3–5); he accompanied this with permission for the deportees and their descendants to return (Ezra 1:2–4). The list of names, involving a total of some 43,000 persons, in Ezra 2 may well cover the period 538–522 BC, but there are no solid grounds for doubting that there was an immediate and considerable response to Cyrus' decree.

Sheshbazzar, a member of the Davidic royal family, was responsible for overseeing the rebuilding of the Temple; he will have returned (or died?) after the laying of the foundations (Ezra 5:14, 16).

In spite of the fact that Sheshbazzar and later Zerubbabel are both styled 'governor' (*pēḥâ*) (Ezra 5:14; Haggai 1:1) it has long been held that they were actually officials of lesser status, Judah being under the control of Samaria until the time of Nehemiah (444 BC). However, recent evidence suggests that this is incorrect and that Judah was indeed under its own governors from the beginning of Persian rule (H. G. M. Williamson in *TynB* 39, 1988, pp. 59–82).

By the time of Ezra in the middle of the 5th century it had become apparent to most that political independence and the restoration of the Davidic monarchy were no more than a hope for the distant future. Ezra transformed the Jews from a national state into a 'church', making the keeping of the Torah the purpose of their existence. The political insignificance of Judaea under the Persians and the relatively peaceful conditions of the country favoured the steady instruction of the mass of the people in the Torah. The only political upheaval of the period may have been a deportation to Babylonia and Hyrcania, though many doubt it (see Josephus, *Against Apion* 1.194).

*The end of Judah*

The campaigns of Alexander the Great will hardly have affected Judaea, but his founding of Alexandria provided a centre for a western, and for the most part voluntary, dispersion, which soon rivalled that of Babylonia and Persia in numbers and surpassed it in wealth and influence. The division of Alexander's empire among his generals meant that Palestine became a debatable land between Syria and Egypt. Till 198 BC it was normally in the hands of the Egyptian Ptolemies, but then it became part of the Syrian Seleucid empire.

The extravagances of the rich Hellenized upper classes of Jerusalem, in large proportion priests, and the unbalanced efforts of Antiochus Epiphanes (175–163 BC) to Hellenize his empire, which led him to forbid circumcision and Sabbath-keeping and to demand the worship of Greek deities, created an alliance between religious zeal and dormant nationalism. The Jews achieved first religious autonomy and then political freedom (140 BC) for the first time since Josiah.

By 76 BC their boundaries extended virtually from the traditional Dan to Beersheba. However, the outbreak of civil war brought the intervention of Rome and in 63 BC Judaea was greatly reduced and became tributary to Rome. From 37 to 4 BC Herod the Great ruled ably in the interests of the emperor and acquired additional territory. On his death his kingdom was divided among three sons, Archelaus governing Judaea and Samaria. His unpopular reign ended with his removal and Judaea was governed by Roman prefects until the outbreak of war with Rome in AD 66 (except for the years 41–44 when it was ruled by Herod Agrippa I).

When the Romans destroyed the last vestiges of political independence in AD 70, and especially after the crushing of Bar Kochba's revolt in AD 135, Judaea ceased to be a Jewish land, but the name of Judah in its form of Jew became the title of all dispersed through the world who clung to the Mosaic law, irrespective of tribal or national origin.

H. L. Ellison

*Further reading*

Archaeological discovery has put all

earlier treatments of the subject to a greater or less degree out of date. John Bright, *A History of Israel*, 3rd edition, 1980, gives a balanced presentation with a mention of the most important literature. See also: A. R. Millard, 'The Meaning of the Name Judah', *ZAW* 86, 1974, pp. 246f.
For the text of Kings:
J. A. Montgomery and H. S. Gehman, *The Books of Kings,* (ICC), 1951
For extra-biblical texts naming Judah:
J. B. Pritchard, *ANET*, 3rd edition, 1969
*DOTT*
For the post-exilic period:
W. O. E. Oesterley, *A History of Israel* 2, 1932
F. F. Bruce, *Israel and the Nations*, 1963

**JUDEA.** See *JUDAEA.

**JUTTAH** (Hebrew *yûṭâh, yuṭṭâh*). A walled town on a hill 8 kilometres south of Hebron, 5 kilometres south-west of Ziph, assigned to the priests (Joshua 15:55; 21:16; compare 1 Chronicles 6:59, where the Septuagint read additionally *Atta*, and this is needed to make the count). It is modern Yatta; no excavations have been carried out.

In Luke 1:39 some commentators would read 'city of Juttah' instead of 'city of Judah'; Abel disagrees emphatically (in *Géographie de la Palestine* 2, 1938, p. 367). See Aharoni, *LOB*, p. 379.
J. P. U. Lilley

# K

**KABZEEL** (Hebrew *qabs''el* 'God gathers'), a town in southern Judah (Joshua 15:21), birthplace of Benaiah, captain of David's bodyguard (2 Samuel 23:20; 1 Chronicles 11:22); resettled after the Exile (Nehemiah 11:25, where it is spelt 'Jekabzeel' [the Hebrew variant may be due to the preposition 'in']).

Usually Kabzeel is identified with Khirbet el-Gharra, Tel Ira, on a high hill fortified during the Monarchy, 17 kilometres east of Beersheba and north-east of Tel Masos (Aharoni, *IEJ* 8, 1958, pp. 36–38); but this might be too close to *Hormah. Abel, in *Géographie* 2, pp. 89 and 353, suggested Khirbet Hora, Hurvat Hor, on the south-western edge of the Judaean hills.
J. P. U. Lilley

**KADESH. 1.** Kadesh-barnea. A location apparently in the north-east of the Sinai peninsula: a well, a settlement, and a wilderness region (Psalm 29:8).

*History*
When Chedorlaomer and his allies marched south through Transjordan they penetrated Mount Seir as far as El Paran, turned back to the north-west, came to En-mishpat (*i.e.* Kadesh) and subdued the Amalekites, before returning to defeat the kings of the Cities of the (Dead Sea) Plain (Genesis 14:5–9).

In the narrative of the fugitive Hagar's experience of God, the well Beer-lahai-roi is 'between Kadesh and Bered', on the way to Shur (Genesis 16:7, 14); Kadesh is also associated with the way to Shur in Genesis 20:1.

Journeying through the Sinai wilderness, the Israelites stayed in the region of Kadesh on the edges of the wilderness of Paran and Zin more than once (Numbers 13:26; 20:1; Deuteronomy 1:19, 46); from here Moses sent his spies into Canaan. From Horeb or Sinai to Kadesh was 11 days' journey *via* Mount Seir (Deuteronomy 1:2). From the traditional Mt Sinai to Dahab on the eastern coast of Sinai and up the coast and across to Kadesh (Qudeirat) is indeed 11 days' travel, as observed by Y. Aharoni (*The Holy Land: Antiquity and Survival* 2, 2/3, pp. 289–290 and 293, figure 7; Dahab).

At Kadesh, after doubting God's ability to give them the promised land, Israel was condemned to wander for 40 years until a new generation should arise (Numbers 14:32–35; compare Deuteronomy 2:14). After some time, Israel returned to Kadesh (Numbers 33:36–37), Miriam being buried there (Numbers 20:1). At this time, too, for failing to glorify God when striking water from the rock (Numbers 20:10–13; 27:14; Deuteronomy 32:51) Moses was denied entry to the promised land; thence, also, he sent messengers in vain to the king of Edom, to grant Israel permission to pass through his territory (Numbers 20:14–21; Judges 11:16–17).

Kadesh-barnea was to be the southern corner of the south-west boundary of Judah, turning west then north-west to reach the Mediterranean along the 'River of Egypt' (Numbers 34:4; Joshua 15:3); it was also included as a boundary-point by Ezekiel (47:19; 48:28). The south-eastern to south-western limits of Joshua's southern Canaanite campaign were marked by Kadesh-barnea and Gaza respectively (Joshua 10:41).

*Site*
Kadesh-barnea is often identified with the spring of 'Ain Qudeis, som[e] 106 kilometres south-west from the southern end of the Dead Sea, or about 80 kilometres south-west of Beersheba. However, the water-supply at 'Ain Qudeis is insignificant; see the unflattering but realistic comments by Woolley and Lawrence ('The Wilderness of Zin', in *Palestine Exploration Fund Annual* 3, 1914–15, pp. 53–57, and plates 10–12, also Baly, *Geography of the Bible,* 1974, p. 250). The name Qudeis may, indeed, have no connection with 'Kadesh' (see Woolley and Lawrence, p. 53 and note *).

'Ain Qudeirat, roughly 8 kilometres north-west of 'Ain Qudeis, has much more water (the spring produces 40 cubic metres pe[r] hour) and vegetation and is a more suitable location for Kadesh-barnea

ɔr this see Aharoni, *op. cit.*, ɔ. 295–296 and figures 1–3 ɔpposite p. 290; and Woolley and ıwrence, pp. 59–62, 69–71 and ates 13–15). Probably the whole oup of springs was used by the raelites, Qudeirat being the main e. The general location of ıdeirat/Qudeis sufficiently suits e topographical requirements of e biblical narratives.

Excavations have revealed three ıperimposed fortresses spanning e 10th-6th centuries BC, followed y some occupation in the Persian eriod. There is no evidence of a ttlement there in the Late Bronze ge, the time of Israel's wanderings the wilderness. Note, however, at the Hebrew presence there for ıany days' does *not* necessarily ıply a whole generation (or ngible settlement) – hence chaeological traces of them may ever be found there.

On the site, see R. Cohen, *BARev* '3, May-June 1981, pp. 2–33; R. ohen in *NEAEHL* III, pp. 843–847; eferences in E. K. Vogel, *ibliography of Holy Land Sites*, 974, p. 6; and especially Y. Aharoni B. Rothenberg, *God's Wilderness*, 961, pp. 121ff. Also T. L. Thompson, *he Settlement of Sinai and the egev in the Bronze Age*, 1975, 101:0900. 11, and references. See ırther, *WILDERNESS OF WANDERING.

**2.** Kedesh in Joshua 15:23, in the outhernmost territory of Judah, is ther another otherwise unknown adesh, or else is probably identical ith Kadesh-barnea (see 15:3).

Finally, the emendation of Tahtim-Hodshi in 2 Samuel 24:6 to he land of the Hittites towards adesh' is not very convincing, articularly as the Kadesh on rontes thus referred to had long assed from history by David's day.

A. Kitchen

**ADESH-BARNEA.** See *KADESH.

**AIN** (Hebrew *qayin*). A town in the istrict of *Ziph (Joshua 15:57); hirbet Yaqin (5 kilometres outh-east of Hebron) has been ıggested, but its antiquity is ncertain. It has been suggested, owever, that Kain should be nderstood as a genitive attached to e preceding name, *i.e.* 'Zanoah of e Kenites'. This may explain its mission from the Septuagint, which ives a count of nine cities instead of n in Joshua 15:57. See also Zanoah **2**.

D. Douglas, J. Bimson

**ANAH** (Hebrew *qānâh*). **1.** A wadi running west from the watershed at the head of the Michmethath valley, 8 kilometres south-west of Shechem; its lower course was the boundary between Ephraim and Manasseh (Joshua 16:8). For a discussion see E. Danelius in *PEQ* 90, 1958, pp. 32–43.

**2.** A town in the Lebanon foothills, assigned to Asher (Joshua 19:28); probably modern Qana (11 kilometres south-east of Tyre), on an important road from Galilee to Tyre (*LOB*, pp. 61, 181, 372; *ANET*, p. 283). It is to be distinguished from the New Testament *Cana of Galilee.

J. P. U. Lilley

**KARNAIM.** See *ASHTEROTH-KARNAIM.

**KARNAK.** See *THEBES.

**KARTAN.** See *KIRIATHAIM.

**KEDAR** (Hebrew *qēḏār*, probably 'black', 'swarthy'). Nomadic tribesfolk of the Syro-Arabian desert from Palestine to Mesopotamia. Their name is sometimes used in the Old Testament to refer to the eastern desert regions in which they lived.

In the 8th century BC, they were known in southern Babylonia (I. Eph'al, *JAOS* 94, 1974, p. 112), Isaiah prophesying their downfall (Isaiah 21:16–17). They developed 'villages' (Isaiah 42:11), possibly simple encampments (H. M. Orlinksy, *JAOS* 59, 1939, pp. 22ff.), living in black tents (Song of Songs 1:5). As keepers of large flocks (Isaiah 60:7), they traded over to Tyre (Ezekiel 27:21). Geographically, Kittim (Cyprus) to the west in the Mediterranean and Kedar east into the desert were like opposite poles (Jeremiah 2:10). Dwelling with the Kedarites was like a barbaric exile to one psalmist (Psalm 120:5).

Alongside Arabian tribes, Nebaioth, *etc.*, Kedarites clashed with Ashurbanipal in the 7th century BC (M. Weippert, *Welt des Orients* 7, 1973–74, p. 67). Likewise they suffered attack by Nebuchadrezzar II of Babylon in 599 BC (see D. J. Wiseman, *Chronicles of Chaldaean Kings*, 1956, p. 32), as announced by Jeremiah (Jeremiah 49:28).

By the Persian period, a regular succession of kings of Kedar controlled a realm astride the vital land-route from Palestine to Egypt, regarded as its guardians by the Persian emperors. Such was Geshem (Gashmu) – opponent of Nehemiah (Nehemiah 6:1–2, 6) – whose son Qaynu is entitled 'King of Kedar' on a silver bowl from a shrine in the Egyptian eastern Delta. On this and these kings, see I. Rabinowitz, *JNES* 15, 1956, pp. 1–9, plate 7; W. J. Dumbrell, *BASOR* 203, 1971, pp. 33–34; A. Lemaire, *RB* 81, 1974, pp. 63–72.

J. D. Douglas, K. A. Kitchen

**KEDEMOTH.** A levitical city (Joshua 21:37; 1 Chronicles 6:79) from the inheritance of Reuben (Joshua 13:18), giving its name to a nearby desert area (Deuteronomy 2:26).

Kedemoth may be one of two sites known today as Qasr ez-Za'feran. These lie about 1 kilometre apart, *c.* 16 kilometres north of the Arnon. However, A. H. van Zyl has argued that Kedemoth should be sought further to the south-east than this, and proposes es-Saliyeh, on the northern side of the Wadi Saliyeh. Pottery from this site attests occupation in the Late Bronze Age and Iron Age I–II.

N. Hillyer, J. Bimson

*Further reading*

F. M. Abel, *Géographie de la Palestine*, 1938, p. 69

A. H. van Zyl, *The Moabites*, 1960

**KEDESH.** Meaning 'holy place' or 'sanctuary', this was the name of at least three Old Testament towns.

**1.** Originally a Canaanite royal city (Joshua 12:22), Kedesh became an Israelite city of refuge (Joshua 20:7) and was assigned to the Levites (21:32). It was distinguished from other towns of the same name by its location in Galilee (Joshua 20:7; 21:32; 1 Chronicles 6:76). It was one of the cities which fell to Tiglath-pileser III of Assyria when he invaded northern Israel in 734–732 BC (2 Kings 15:29). In the 2nd century BC it was the scene of a great victory by Jonathan, brother of Judas Maccabaeus, over the forces of the Seleucid king Demetrius (1 Maccabees 11:63–74).

Today the site is Tell Qades, north-west of the Huleh basin. Surveys and soundings show it to have been occupied during the Early, Middle and Late Bronze Ages, Iron Age I–II, and the Hellenistic, Roman and Arab periods.

**2.** 'Kedesh in Naphtali' was the home of Barak and the place where he gathered his forces for war against Sisera (Judges 4:6–10). Some scholars regard it as the same as **1**, which also lay in the territory of Naphtali (Joshua 20:7), but this lay too far from Mount Tabor (see Judges 4:6). Aharoni suggested identifying Kedesh in Naphtali with the ruins of Khirbet Qedish, high on the slopes above the south-western shore of the Sea of Galilee.

*Opposite:* **The Kidron Valley is a vast cemetery, and contains a number of unusual tombs, such as the 'Tomb of Absalom' and the 'Tomb of Zachariah' (seen here), which belonged in fact to the priestly family of the Bene Hezir (1 Chronicles 24:15).**

**3.** A town of Issachar given to Gershonite Levites (1 Chronicles 6:72). It is called (or is replaced by) Kishion in the list of Joshua 21:28. This Kedesh is identified with modern Tell Abu Qedes, south-south-west of Megiddo, where excavations reveal Iron Age occupation from the 12th–9th centuries BC.

Some scholars suggest that this town, rather than Kedesh in Naphtali, was the place near which Sisera met his death (Judges 4:11–22); in other words, they would distinguish the Kedesh of Judges 4:11 from 'Kedesh in Naphtali' in Judges 4:6–10. The logic of this argument depends on the assumption that Kedesh in Naphtali is the same as **1**, for then it would be too far from the field of battle for Sisera to have fled there on foot (Judges 4:17). However, if we follow Aharoni's proposal concerning Kedesh in Naphtali, this difficulty disappears and the latter could easily be the place to which Sisera fled.

**4.** A town in southern Judah near the border with Edom, possibly to be identified with Kadesh-barnea (see also *KADESH).

J. Bimson

*Further reading*

*LOB*, pp. 223–224, 303

**KEILAH** (Hebrew *q*$^{e}$*'îlâh*). A town in the Shephelah (Joshua 15:44); mentioned in the Amarna letters, where the 'men of Keilah' are accused of encouraging rebellion. In Saul's time, David relieved it from a Philistine attack, but found Saul's influence there too strong for his safety (2 Samuel 23). After Judah's return from Babylonian exile it provided two district chiefs (Nehemiah 3:17f.).

Khirbet Qila, near the head of the valley between the Shephelah and the Hills, commands the ascent to Hebron from Socoh.

J. P. U. Lilley

**KENATH** (Hebrew *q*$^{e}$*nāṯ*, 'possession'). A city in northern Transjordan taken from the Amorites by Nobah, who gave it his name (Numbers 32:42), and later taken by Geshur and Aram (1 Chronicles 2:23). The name appears in several Egyptian texts of the 2nd millennium (see *LOB*, index). It is usually identified with the extensive ruins at Qanawât, some 25 kilometres north-east of Bozrah; but see F.-M. Abel, *Géographie de la Palestine* 2, p. 417, and M. Noth, *Numbers*, p. 241 (compare *PJB* 37, 1941, pp. 80–81), who prefers a location west or north-west of modern Amman, comparing Judges 8:11.

J. D. Douglas, G. I. Davies

**KERIOTH. 1.** A town in the extreme south of Judah, known also as Kerioth-Hezron or Hazor, possibly the modern Khirbet el-Qaryatein (Joshua 15:25).

**2.** A city of Moab (Jeremiah 48:24), formerly fortified (Jeremiah 48:41), and possessing palaces (Amos 2:2). Probably it is El-Qereiyat, south of Ataroth. Some writers identify it with Ar, the ancient capital of Moab, because when Ar is listed among Moabite towns Kerioth is omitted (Isaiah 15–16), and *vice versa* (Jeremiah 48).

From the Moabite Stone we learn that there was a sanctuary at Kerioth for Chemosh, to which Mesha dragged Arel the chief of Ataroth.

J. A. Thompson

**KIBROTH-HATTAAVAH** (Hebrew *qiḇrôṯ hatta'*$^{a}$*wâ*, 'graves of craving'). A camp of the Israelites a day's journey from the wilderness of Sinai. There the people, having craved flesh to eat and been sent quails by the Lord, were overtaken by plague, which caused many fatalities (Numbers 11:31–34; 33:16; Deuteronomy 9:22; compare Psalm 78:27–31).

Some have suggested that the incident at Taberah (Numbers 11:1–3) had the same location as that at Kibroth-hattaavah, but Deuteronomy 9:22 seems to argue against this. Grollenberg makes an identification with Ruweis el-Ebeirig, north-east of Mt Sinai.

J. D. Douglas

**KIDRON.** The brook Kidron, the modern Wadi en-Nar, is a torrent-bed, which begins to the north of Jerusalem, passes the Temple mount and the Mount of Olives *en route* to the Dead Sea, which it reaches by way of the wilderness of Judaea. Its modern name means 'the Fire wadi', and this bears witness to the fact that it is dry and sun-baked for most of the year. Only for short periods during the rainy seasons is it filled with water. It was also called 'the Valley of *Jehoshaphat'.

On the western side of the Kidron there is a spring known as the *Gihon ('Gusher', 1 Kings 1:33, 38, 45), today known as the 'Virgin's Fountain', the flow of which was artificially diverted under Hezekiah's orders to serve the need of Jerusalem and to protect its water-supply from the enemy (2 Chronicles 32:30). This was the latest of several tunnels and shafts connected with the spring.

As its name would suggest, the water does not come through in a steady flow, but accumulates underground in a reservoir and breaks out from time to time. In 188 a Hebrew inscription was discovered in which information wa recorded concerning the making of Hezekiah's tunnel (see also *SILOAM For the archaeology, see K. M. Kenyon, *Digging up Jerusalem*, 1974, pp. 84–89, 151–159.

David passed over the brook Kidron on his way out of Jerusalem during Absalom's revolt (2 Samuel 15:23). The reforming kings, such a Asa, Hezekiah and Josiah, used the valley as a place of destruction where heathen idols, altars, *etc.*, were burned or ground to powder ( Kings 15:13, *etc.*). It seems to be taken as one of the boundaries of Jerusalem in 1 Kings 2:37 and Jeremiah 31:40.

Some suggest a reference to the Kidron in Ezekiel 47, where the prophet sees a stream of water issuing from the threshold of the Temple and pursuing its way towards the Dead Sea, making the land fertile in the process. See especially G. Adam Smith, *The Historical Geography of the Holy Land,* 1931, pp. 510ff.; and W. R. Farmer, 'The Geography of Ezekiel' River of Life', *BA* 19, 1956, pp. 17ff. That Ezekiel was thinking of the filling-up of the dry bed of the Kidror by the healing stream of water seems probable, but cannot be maintained with any degree of certainty.

G. W. Grogan

**KING'S GARDEN.** An area in the Kidron valley at the southern end o the City of David, near 'the gate between the two walls' (2 Kings 25:4; Jeremiah 39:4; 52:7) and clos to the Pool of *Siloam (Nehemiah 3:15). The garden was probably irrigated by the outflow from the pool, which was in turn fed by the Gihon spring (2 Kings 20:20; 2 Chronicles 32:30).

J. D. Douglas

*Further reading*

N. Grollenberg, *Atlas*, Maps 24B, C

W. H. Mare, *The Archaeology of the Jerusalem Area*, 1987, p. 123

**KING'S HIGHWAY.** The name give to the direct road running from the

Gulf of Aqabah to Damascus in Syria, east of the Dead Sea and Jordan valley. The route was in use as early as the 23rd century BC, being marked along its length by Early Bronze Age settlements and fortresses. It was, therefore, likely that Chedorlaomer and his allies approached Sodom and Gomorrah by this way and were pursued up it by Abraham (Genesis 14).

The highway remained important for international commerce throughout antiquity. The Edomites and the Ammonites prevented Moses and the Israelites from using it (Numbers 20:17; 21:22; compare Deuteronomy 2:27). In Solomon's reign the highway played an important part as a trade-link between Ezion-geber, Judah and Syria. Israel and Judah lost control of it when Moab and Edom achieved independence in the 9th century BC (2 Kings 1:1; 8:20), but in the following century both kingdoms regained it (2 Kings 14:7–10, 25).

Roman milestones show that the highway was incorporated into Trajan's road built in the 2nd century AD and was used by the Nabataeans. The modern motorway follows part of the old track, which is still called Tarīq es-Sulṭan.

D. J. Wiseman

*Further reading*

N. Glueck, *The Other Side of the Jordan*, 1945, pp. 10–16

J. A. Thompson, *Archaeology and the Old Testament*, 1957, pp. 57–58

*LOB*, pp. 54–57

**KING'S VALLEY.** See *SHAVEH.

**KIR.** In the Hebrew text the name of the place of exile of the Syrians (2 Kings 16:9; Amos 1:5), and a country, not necessarily the same, from which Yahweh brought them (Amos 9:7). This is perhaps not their original home, but a land occupied at some earlier stage in their history, parallel to Israel in Egypt and the *Philistines in *Caphtor (see also *ARAM). In Isaiah 22:6 Kir is parallel to Elam.

A tablet found at Emar on the mid-Euphrates mentions a ruler of 'the people of the land of *Qi-ri* about 1200 BC, and this place, presumably somewhere in central Syria, could be the land Amos mentioned. However, the word simply means 'city', so need not be specific.

The Septuagint does not use a proper name in any of these passages, but translates 'from a pit' (Amos 9:7, Greek *ek bothrou*), 'called as an ally' (Amos 1:5, Greek *epiklētos*) and 'congregation' (Isaiah 22:6, Greek *synagōgē*), feasible translations of an unpointed Hebrew text.

The Vulgate follows the mistaken identification with Cyrene made by Symmachus. Kir has been altered to read Koa' (by Cheyne), and said to be Gutium in the Kurdish hills (see Ezekiel 23:23; Isaiah 22:5–6). The problem is not yet solved.

A. R. Millard

**KIRIATHAIM.** The dual form of the Hebrew *qiryâ*, 'city, town', and meaning therefore 'double city', a name applied to two cities in the Bible.

**1.** A place in the territory allotted to Reuben (Joshua 13:19) which had already been conquered and rebuilt by the Reubenites (Numbers 32:37). It is possible that Shaveh-Kiriathaim, which is mentioned in the account of the invasion of Chedorlaomer in the time of Abraham (Genesis 14:5), refers to this locality, as the 'plain' of Kiriathaim (RVmargin), though *šāwēh* is a rare word of uncertain meaning.

The city was later in the hands of the Moabites (Jeremiah 48:1, 23; Ezekiel 25:9), and is mentioned in the 9th-century inscription of King Mesha of Moab (*qrytn*, line 10) as having been rebuilt by him, so it cannot have remained under Israelite control for more than about 3 centuries.

The site is possibly near to modern El Quraiyāt about 10 kilometres north-west of Dibon in Jordan, but the place has not yet been located (compare *LOB*, pp. 140, 337, 438; H. Donner and W. Röllig, *Kanaanäische und aramäische Inschriften*, 1962–64, pp. 174–175).

**2** A levitical city in Naphtali (1 Chronicles 6:76), possibly to be identified with Kartan (*qartān*) of Joshua 21:32. The site is unknown, though various suggestions have been made (see *GTT*, sections 298, 337, 357; *LOB*, p. 304).

T. C. Mitchell

**KIRIATH-ARBA** (Hebrew *qiryaṯ 'arba'*, 'city of four', *i.e.* 'tetrapolis'), an earlier name of *Hebron. According to Joshua 14:15, it was 'the metropolis of the Anakim' (so Septuagint; the Massoretic Text makes the numeral *'arba'*, 'four', into a personal name).

The name Kiriath-arba occurs once in the story of Abraham (Genesis 23:2) and a few times in the narrative of the Conquest (Joshua 14:15; 15:54; 20:7; Judges 1:10); thereafter it evidently fell into disuse. Some attempt may have been made to revive it in the post-exilic age (Nehemiah 11:25), but with the Idumaean occupation of the place soon afterwards the old name was completely discontinued.

F. F. Bruce

**KIRIATH-BAAL.** See *KIRIATH-JEARIM.

**KIRIATH-JEARIM** (Hebrew *qiryaṯ-y$^{e}$'ārîm*, 'city of forests'). A chief city of the Gibeonites (Joshua 9:17), on the Judah-Benjamin border (Joshua 18:14–15; compare Judges 18:12), assigned first to Judah (Joshua 15:60), then, assuming an identification with 'Kiriath', to Benjamin (Joshua 18:28). It is called also Kiriath-baal (Joshua 15:60, suggesting that it was an old Canaanite high place), Baalah (Joshua 15:9–10), Baale-judah (2 Samuel 6:2) and Kiriath-arim (Ezra 2:25).

Here the ark was brought from Beth-shemesh and entrusted to the keeping of Eleazar (1 Samuel 7:1), whence after 20 years David took it to Jerusalem (2 Samuel 6:2; 1 Chronicles 13:5; 2 Chronicles 1:4). The home of Uriah the prophet was in Kiriath-jearim (Jeremiah 26:20).

Its precise location has not been determined, but the consensus of opinion favours Tell Deir el-'Azar in Abu Ghosh, a flourishing little village 14 kilometres west of Jerusalem on the Jaffa road. It is a well-wooded district (or has been in the past) and it meets other geographical requirements.

J. D. Douglas

*Further reading*

*LOB*, p. 255

**KIRIATH-SANNA.** See *DEBIR.

**KIRIATH-SEPHER** (Hebrew *qiryaṯ-sēp̄er*, 'city of the book', but the name was Canaanite, so we cannot be certain of the meaning). It is given as the earlier name of *Debir **1** in the story of Othniel and Achsah (Joshua 15:15f.; Judges 1:11f.). Kiriath-sepher appears as 'Kiriath-Sanna' in Joshua 15:49; Noth, in *Josua, ad loc.*, considers 'Debir' an incorrect gloss, but it is more likely that 'Sanna' is a mis-spelling (Orlinsky, *JBL* 58, 1939, p. 255).

J. P. U. Lilley

**KIR OF MOAB, KIR-HARESETH.** A fortified city of southern Moab, attacked but not taken by the kings of Israel, Judah and Edom (2 Kings 3:25). During the siege, Mesha, king of Moab, offered up his eldest son 'for a burnt offering upon the wall'.

'The Hebrew name (*qîr ḥ<sup></sup>ᵃreśeṯ*) eans 'the wall of potsherds'. The ·ptuagint rendering of Isaiah 16:11 esupposes the Hebrew *qîr ḏešeṯ*, 'the new city'. Normally the wn is called Kir of Moab (Isaiah ;:1). Some writers see in Jeremiah ':36–37 a play on words in which r Heres is parallel to 'bald' [ebrew *qorḥâ*).

It is suggested that the original oabite name was QRḤH, probably e town referred to in the Moabite one (lines 22ff.), where Mesha tablished a sanctuary for Chemosh ıd carried out a building project. ıis would place it near Dibon.

Most writers, however, identify it ith Kerak, following the Targum ndering, Kerak of Moab. If that is ı, the place was built on a strategic cky hill 1,027 metres above a-level, surrounded by steep ılleys, some 18 kilometres east of e Dead Sea and 24 kilometres uth of the Arnon River. Today a ediaeval castle crowns the hill.

A. Thompson

*ırther reading*

M. Abel, *Géographie de la ılestine* 2, 1933, pp. 418–419

. Glueck, *AASOR* 14, 1934, p. 65

**ISH** (Hebrew *qîš*, 'bow', 'power'). ame of the capital of a city-state *c.* ) kilometres south-east of Babylon ıodern Tell el-Ukheimer) where, cording to Sumerian tradition ing List), the first dynasty after the ood ruled. It flourished *c.* 200–3000 BC as a rival of *Erech hen it was linked with the gendary Etana and with King Agga ho opposed Gilgamesh. ocuments from the earlier cupation and from the 2nd illennium are extant.

Kish was excavated by the French 914) and by a joint Oxford shmolean Museum) and Chicago 'ield Museum) expedition 922–33). Finds include early alaces, tablets and a major ood-deposit level dated *c.* 3300 BC.

J. Wiseman

*ırther reading*

C. Watelin, S. H. Langdon, *xcavations at Kish*, 1925–34

*aq* 26, 1964, pp. 83–98; 28, 1966, ). 18–51

**ISHON.** The river, modern Nahr -Muqaṭṭa', which, rising in the hills ī northern Samaria, drains the plain f Esdraelon and debouches in the ay of Acre, east of Mount Carmel. hough it winds about, in a general ense it flows in a north-westerly direction parallel with, and to the north-east of, the mountain range which runs from Samaria to Carmel. Taanach, Megiddo and Jokneam lie in the north-eastern passes of this mountain range.

The name Kishon is not often used, the river sometimes being indicated by reference to one of the towns overlooking it. Thus it is probably first mentioned in Joshua 19:11, where the 'brook which is east of Jokneam' is given as part of the boundary of Zebulun, though in this case it is only a small section of the river in the vicinity of Jokneam that is referred to.

The best-known reference to the river is that connected with the victory of the Israelites under Barak over the Syrians under Sisera (Judges 4–5; Psalm 83:9). The forces of Sisera, fully armed with chariots, were deployed in the plain, and the Israelites made their attack from the mountains south-west of the river. The success of the Israelites was in large measure due to the river, which was running high, and must have made the surrounding plain too soft for Sisera's chariots, which became bogged down and useless. The river or one of its feeders is referred to in the Song of Deborah as 'the waters of Megiddo' (Judges 5:19).

The river is next mentioned as the scene of the slaughter by Elijah of the prophets of Baal, after the contest on Mount Carmel (1 Kings 18:40). It is referred to here as a brook (*naḥal*), suggesting that the long drought preceding these events had reduced the river to a low level. The rains which followed must have washed away the traces of the execution.

T. C. Mitchell

*Further reading*

G. A. Smith, *The Historical Geography of the Holy Land*, 25th edition, 1931, pp. 394–397

W. F. Albright, *The Archaeology of*

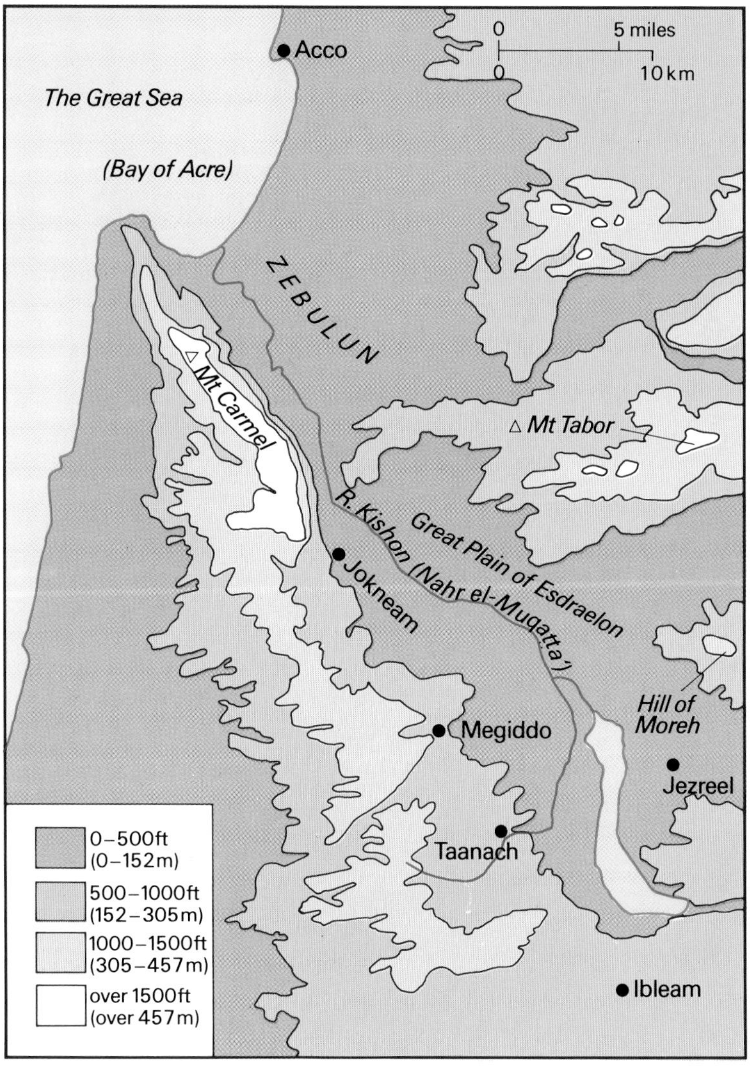


The course of the river Kishon.

*Palestine*, 1960, pp. 117–118
*LOB*, pp. 224–225

**KITTIM.** One of the sons of Javan (Genesis 10:4 and 1 Chronicles 1:7; Hebrew *kittîm*) whose descendants settled on the island of Cyprus where the name (*kt, kty*) is found in Phoenician inscriptions applied to the town of Kition (modern Larnaka), where a significant part of the population were Phoenicians. They engaged in sea trade (Numbers 24:24), and the name seems to have come to apply to the whole island of Cyprus (Isaiah 23:1, 12), and then in a more general way to the coastlands and islands of the eastern Mediterranean (*'iyyê kittiyyîm*: Jeremiah 2:10; Ezekiel 27:6). The ostraca of *c.* 600 BC from Arad refer to *ktym*, probably mercenaries, principally perhaps Greeks, from the islands and coastlands.

In Daniel's fourth vision, which probably deals with the period from Cyrus to Antiochus Epiphanes, the latter's failure to conquer Egypt, due to the intervention of Rome, is probably referred to in 11:30, where 'the ships of Kittim' must be Rome. The author probably saw in Rome's intervention the fulfilment of Numbers 24:24, where the Vulgate translates Kittim by 'Italy' (so also in Daniel 11:30) and the Targum of Onkelos by 'Romans'.

The name occurs in the Dead Sea Scrolls, also probably with reference to Rome, being used, for instance, in the commentary on Habakkuk as an interpretation of the 'Chaldeans' of that prophet (Habakkuk 1:6).
T. C. Mitchell

*Further reading*

A. Lemaire, *Inscriptions hébraïques*, 1, 1977, p. 156
Y. Yadin, *The Scroll of the War of the Sons of Light Against the Sons of Darkness*, 1962, pp. 22–26
T. C. Mitchell, *CAH* III.2, p. 399

# L

**LABO**. See *HAMATH.

**LACHISH** (Hebrew *lāḵîš*, Septuagint *Lachis*). A large fortified city identified with modern Tell ed-Duweir 40 kilometres south-west of Jerusalem. This site was excavated by the Wellcome-Marston Archaeological Expedition 1932–38 and since 1973 by the University of Tel Aviv. Y. Aharoni excavated there on a small scale in 1966 and 1968.

*Beginnings*

While the area is known to have been inhabited by cave-dwellers from at least as early as the 8th millennium BC it was not until *c.* 2500 BC that the hill which is now Tell ed-Duweir was first settled. By *c.* 1750 BC the city was strongly fortified with a wall built on the crest of a steep rampart which sloped down to a ditch or fosse at the base of the tell. Throughout this period the surrounding caves previously used for habitation served as tombs.

*The Canaanite city*

Letters from two rulers of Lachish, Yabni-ilu and Zimrida (numbers 328–329) were found at *Amarna. In another letter (number 288), Abdi-Ḫeba, king of Jerusalem, accuses Zimrida of conspiring with the Ḫapiru, while a letter found at Tell el-Ḥesi says that he has made a treaty with another king, Šipti-Ba'lu.

The religious practices of the Canaanites have been illustrated by a series of temples in use between 1550 and 1200 BC and situated in the fosse north-west of the tell. The altar was constructed of unhewn stones (compare Joshua 8:31) and had a flight of stairs ascending it (compare Exodus 20:24ff.). Offerings had been placed in bowls which were deposited on the benches in the temple and over 100 lamps were found scattered around the building. Bones of young sheep or goats were plentiful and practically all the identified specimens were from the right foreleg which in Hebrew religion formed part of the priests' portion of the peace offering (Leviticus 7:32).

*The conquest*

Japhia, king of Lachish, was a member of the Amorite coalition that fought Joshua at Gibeon (Joshua 10:3, 5) and was executed at Makkedah (Joshua 10:22–27) after Joshua's victory. Lachish subsequently fell to Joshua (Joshua 10:31f.).

The destruction by fire of Level VI was initially dated *c.* 1220 BC and associated with the Israelites' conquest of the city. More recent excavations have redated this destruction to about 1130 BC, which is too late for the time of Joshua. Whether the Israelite conquest of Lachish can be identified with an earlier destruction of the city is still uncertain at this stage in the excavations.

*In the time of the kings*

The end of Level VI was followed by a long period of abandonment. Level V is an Iron Age settlement established around 1000 BC, in the time of the united monarchy. A small room dated to *c.* 925 BC has been excavated on the tell and found to contain a large number of religious objects including an altar, a *maṣṣeb*[ah] and incense burners, which together with figurine fragments found nearby indicate the presence of Canaanite religion in Israel. These practices at Lachish may have been referred to later by the prophet Micah (1:13), who said that the city was 'the beginning of sin to the daughter of Zion'.

Level IV probably represents Rehoboam's rebuilding of the city (2 Chronicles 11:5–10) to a completely new plan as part of a comprehensive system of defence against the Egyptians. The city had large palace-fort with a storehouse and possibly stables.

The palace-fort complex was rebuilt in Level III, which begins in the 8th century BC. The fortifications were also rebuilt. Two walls surrounded the city; the inner one was erected on the crest of the tell and was 6 metres thick, while the second was built 16 metres down the slope. A large three-chambered gate in the inner wall led to an outer gate from which a walled ramp ran down the slope of the tell.

These defences are portrayed in relief sculpture from Sennacherib's palace at Nineveh (now in the British

seum) which relate his siege and
ture of Lachish in 701 BC.
owheads, scale armour,
g-stones and an Assyrian helmet
st were found in the vicinity of the
e, testifying to this battle. A
ssive Assyrian siege ramp was
lt against the south-western
ner of the city, and the defenders
cted a counter-ramp along the
ide of the inner wall in a
sperate attempt to prevent the
's capture. But their efforts were
ain. The city was razed by the
syrians, leaving an ash and
struction layer over the site. By
turing Lachish, Sennacherib
vented any Egyptian assistance
ching Jerusalem where he sent
messengers to demand
zekiah's surrender (2 Kings
17; 19:8; Isaiah 36:2; 37:8).
After this destruction the site was
andoned for a time. The city was
bably rebuilt under Josiah
9–609 BC). This was the Level II
, poorer and less strongly
tified than its predecessor.
Neither the Bible nor the
bylonian Chronicle mentions a
struction of Lachish in
buchadrezzar's early campaigns
Palestine. However, the evidence
Level II shows that it was
stroyed with the remainder of
dah in 588–587 BC when it was the
y fortified outpost from Jerusalem
remiah 34:7) in addition to
zekah.

*ter the Exile*

chish was resettled by returning
aelites (Nehemiah 11:30) and the
haeological evidence suggests it
s rebuilt as a governmental centre
vel I). The wall and gate were
stored and a number of buildings
cluding a governor's Residency
d a temple) were erected on the
mmit. The town was abandoned
the Hellenistic period.

*scriptions*

number of inscribed objects of the
onze Age have been found at
chish. Pictographic signs were
ised on a dagger of *c.* 1700 BC and
oto-Canaanite scripts appear on a
erd of *c.* 1600 BC, an ewer of *c.* 1200
and a bowl of the same date.
Inscriptions from the time of the
daean monarchy are numerous
d are most important for the
story of Hebrew script. The first
e letters of the Hebrew alphabet
ere found carved on one of the
eps of a large building of *c.* 800 BC.
seal impression appears on a bulla
m Lachish which had traces of
pyrus fibres on the reverse,

A reconstruction of the siege of Lachish by Sennacherib's Assyrian army in 701 BC. This painting shows the double walls, city gate, siege-ramp and battering rams as well as the offensive and defensive weapons employed. Judaean refugees are leaving the city.

revealing that it had sealed a rolled papyrus document. The seal bore the name of Gedaliah, the royal steward (Hebrew 'who is over the house'), and may well be the person appointed governor over Judah by Nebuchadrezzar (2 Kings 25:22; Jeremiah 40:11–12). About seventeen other clay bullae and many jar handles bearing seal impressions with Hebrew names have also been found.

*Military correspondence*

A total of twenty-two ostraca (inscribed potsherds) came from Level II, and of these sixteen appear to be military correspondence written during the last few weeks before Nebuchadrezzar's conquest in 588–587 BC. They were found in the ruins of a guardroom just inside the outer gate. Although the language is biblical Hebrew, the cursive script has been almost obliterated on some of the ostraca making reading impossible. The legible examples reveal that the collection is the correspondence of a subordinate, Hoshayahus, who is in charge of an outpost, to his superior, Yaush, who is the commanding officer of a garrison, presumably at Lachish itself.

Hoshayahu commences the letters with the greeting 'May YHWH cause my lord to hear tidings of peace this day' before proceeding with the business which in most of the letters is answering the charge that he has read confidential letters from the king. In letter II, he replies in words reminiscent of those spoken by Mephibosheth to David (2 Samuel 9:8); 'Who is your servant (but) a dog . . . May YHWH afflict those who re[port] an (evil) rumour about which you are not informed.'

It has been suggested that the ostraca were stored in the gate pending a trial, but it is more likely that the military command to which the letters were sent was situated in the gate building.

Letter IV concludes, 'we are watching for the signals of Lachish, according to all the indications which my lord has given, for we cannot see Azekah'. This recalls the situation mentioned by Jeremiah (34:7) when Azekah, Lachish and Jerusalem were the only fortified Judaean cities left. Azekah is 11 kilometres north-east of Lachish and the fact that Hoshayahu could not see its signals may indicate that it had already fallen.

Letters III and XVI refer to 'the prophet'. Attempts to identify him with Jeremiah or with Uriah who fled to Egypt (Jeremiah 26:20–22) during Jehoiakim's reign are purely hypothetical. More important than the man's identity is that the letter testifies to the recognition of prophets in ancient Israel and their participation in affairs of state. Letter III also mentions an expedition to Egypt by the commander of the army which may have been a last desperate attempt by Zedekiah to obtain Egyptian assistance to withstand the inevitable Babylonian attack (see Jeremiah 37:5–10).

C. J. Davey, J. Bimson

Map showing the strategic position of Laodicea in Asia Minor.

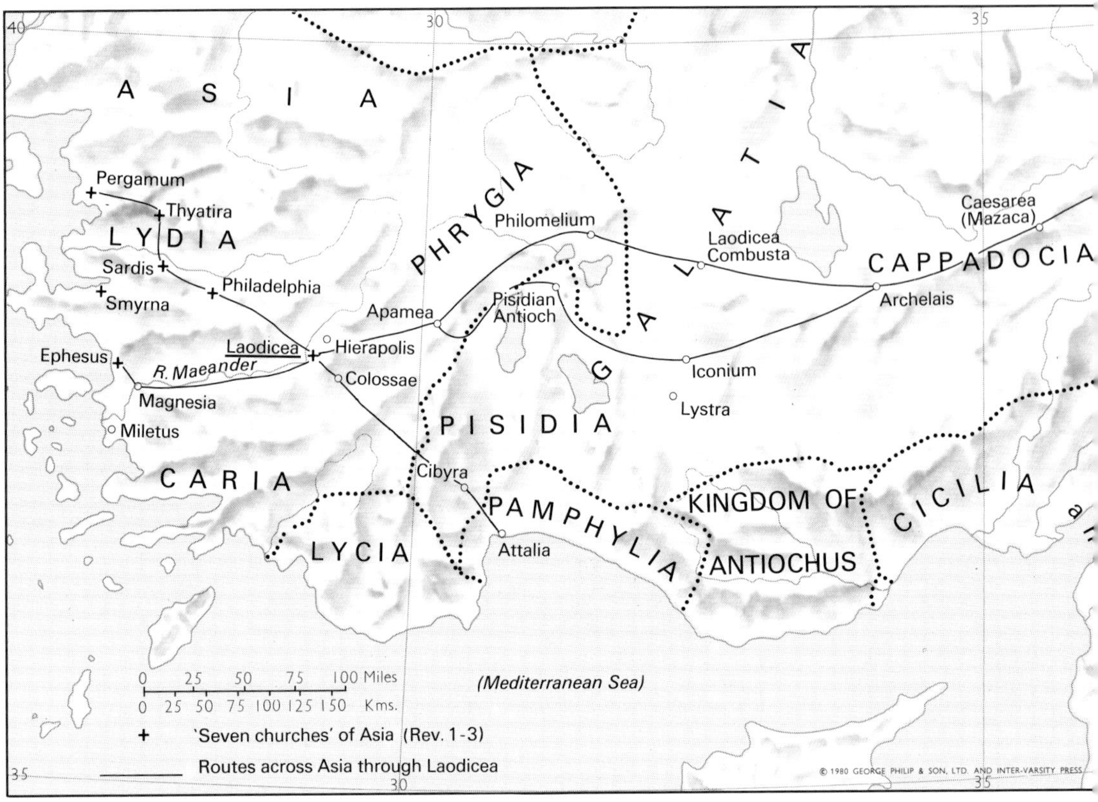


*Further reading*

Excavation Reports:
*Lachish I*, H. Torczyner, *The Lachish Letters*, 1935
*II*, O. Tufnell, *The Fosse Temple*, 1940
*III, The Iron Age*
*IV, The Bronze Age*
Y. Aharoni, *Lachish V*, 1975
D. Ussishkin, preliminary reports of excavations since 1973 in *Tel Aviv* 5, 1978, pp. 1–97; 10, 1983, pp. 97–175
——, *The Conquest of Lachish by Sennacherib*, 1982
'The "Lachish Reliefs" and the City of Lachish,' *IEJ* 30, 1980, pp. 174–195
'Lachish: Key to the Israelite Conquest of Canaan?', *BARev* XIII/1, 1987, pp. 18–39
'Lachish' in *ABD* vol. 4, pp.114–126
R. A. di Vito, 'Lachish Letters', *ABD* vol. 4, pp. 126–128
K. A. D. Smelik, *Writings From Ancient Israel*, 1991, pp. 116–131
D. Ussishkin in *NEAEHL* III, pp. 897–911

**LAODICEA.** A city of south-western Phrygia, in the Roman province of Asia, in the west of what is now Asiatic Turkey. It was founded by the Seleucid Antiochus II in the 3rd century BC, and called after his wife Laodice. It lay in the fertile valley of the Lycus (a tributary of the Maeander), close to *Hierapolis and *Colossae, and was distinguished by the epithet 'on Lycus' from several other cities of the name.

Laodicea was at a very important cross-road: the main road across Asia Minor ran west to the ports of *Miletus and *Ephesus about 160 kilometres away and east by an easy incline on to the central plateau and thence towards Syria; and another road ran north to *Pergamum and south to the coast at *Attalia.

This strategic position made Laodicea an extremely prosperous commercial centre, especially under Roman rule. When destroyed by a disastrous earthquake in AD 60 (Tacitus, *Annals* 14.27) it could afford to dispense with aid from Nero. It was an important centre of banking and exchange (see Cicero, *Letters to his Friends* 3.5.4, *etc.*).

Laodicea's distinctive products included garments of glossy black wool (Strabo, *Geography* 12.8.16 [578]), and it was a medical centre noted for ophthalmology.

The site had one disadvantage: being determined by the road-system, it lacked a sufficient and permanent supply of good water. Water was piped to the city from hot springs some distance to the south, and probably arrived lukewarm. The deposits still encrusting the remains testify to it[s] warmth.

The site of Laodicea was eventually abandoned, and the modern town (Denizli) grew up nea[r] the springs.

*The church in Laodicea*

The gospel must have reached Laodicea at an early date, probably while Paul was living at Ephesus (Acts 19:10), and perhaps through Epaphras (Colossians 4:12–13). Although Paul mentions the church there (Colossians 2:1; 4:13–16), there is no record that he visited it. I[t] is evident that the church maintained close connections with the Christians in Hierapolis and Colossae. The 'letter from Laodicea' (Colossians 4:16) is often thought t[o] have been a copy of our Ephesians which had been received in Laodicea.

*e Letters to the seven churches*
e last of the Letters to 'the seven urches of Asia' (Revelation 14–22) was addressed to odicea. Its imagery owes atively little to the Old Testament, t contains pointed allusions to the aracter and circumstances of the y. For all its wealth, it could oduce neither the healing power of t water, like its neighbour erapolis, nor the refreshing power cold water to be found at Colossae, t merely lukewarm water, useful ly as an emetic.

The church was charged with a nilar uselessness: it was lf-sufficient, rather than lf-hearted. Like the city, it thought had 'need of nothing'. In fact it was iritually poor, naked and blind, d needed 'gold', 'white garments' d 'eye-salve' more effective than bankers, clothiers and doctors uld supply. Like citizens hospitable to a traveller who offers em priceless goods, the odiceans had closed their doors d left their real Provider outside. rist turns in loving appeal to the dividual (verse 20).

J. S. Rudwick, C. J. Hemer

*rther reading*
. M. Ramsay, *The Letters to the ven Churches of Asia,* 1904
J. S. Rudwick and E. M. B. Green, *pT* 69, 1957–58, pp. 176–178
J. Hemer, 'Laodicea,' *The Letters the Seven Churches of Asia in eir Local Setting*, 1986, chapter 9

**SEA,** presumably the same town the Lasos mentioned by Pliny *atural History* 4.59), has been entified with ruins some 8 ometres east of *Fair Havens.

L. McKay

**SHA.** Probably *leša'*, but written *ša'* in the interests of prosody in its le occurrence, which is at the end a verse (Genesis 10:19). It figures the designation of the limits of the rritory of Canaan in a context hich suggests that one travelling m the Mediterranean coast would counter it as the farthest inland of group consisting of Sodom, omorrah, Admah and Zeboim. This ints to a locality somewhere near e south-eastern shore of the Dead a, but no site of this name is own there.

Ancient tradition equated Lasha th the hot springs of *Kallirrhoē*, odern Zarqa Ma'in south-west of adaba near the eastern coast of the ad Sea, and some modern scholars efer to identify it with *layiš* of

The site of the arena of the ancient city of Laodicea.

*Dan, but neither of these can be substantiated.

T. C. Mitchell

*Further reading*
H. Donner, *ZDPV* 79, 1963, pp. 60–61

**LASHARON** (RV 'Lassharon', AV margin 'Sharon'). A Canaanite royal city mentioned with Aphek as taken by Joshua (12:18). The Septuagint (B) reads 'the king of Aphek in Sharon'. However, Eusebius (*Onomasticon*, under 'Sharon') mentions a district called Sarona, between Mount Tabor and the Sea of Tiberias, and this ancient site, 10 kilometres south-west of Tiberias, may be the biblical Lasharon.

J. D. Douglas

**LEBANON.** A mountain range in Syria. The name is also more loosely applied to the adjoining regions (Joshua 13:5), and is also that of a modern republic.

## Name

The Hebrew *l*$^{e}$*ḇānôn* is derived from the root *lbn*, 'white'. The range owes this name to two factors: the white limestone of the high ridge of Lebanon and especially the glittering snows that cap its peaks for 6 months of the year; see Jeremiah 18:14. Lebanon is attested in ancient records from at least the 18th century BC onwards; see on history, below.

The Assyrians called it *Lab'an*, then *Labnanu*; the Hittites, *Niblani*; the Egyptians, *rmnn* or *rbrn*; and the Canaanites themselves, *e.g.* at Ugarit, *Lbnn* just as in Hebrew.

## Topography

The southern end of the Lebanon range is a direct continuation of the hills of northern Galilee, and is divided from them only by the deep east-west gorge of the lower reaches of the Litani river, which enters the sea a few kilometres north of Tyre.

The Lebanon range is a ridge almost 160 kilometres long, following the south-west to north-east trend of the Phoenician coast from behind Sidon north to the east-west valley of the Nahr el-Kebir river (the river Eleutherus of antiquity), which divides Lebanon from the next north-south mountain range extending still farther north (Nuseiri or Ansariya Mountains).

This ridge is marked by a series of peaks. These high mountains and the coastal strip have a good rainfall, but in the 'rain-shadow' area Damascus and the northern half of the Biqā' plain have less than 25 centimetres a year and must depend on stream water.

The western flanks of this range sweep right down to the Mediterranean, leaving only a narrow coastal plain for the Canaanite/Phoenician cities, and sometimes reach the sea, roads having had to be cut by man round such headlands. Typical of these is the headland of the Nahr el-Kelb just north of Beirut.

The eastern flanks of Lebanon descend into the Biqā'. This plain, or broad vale, is highest in the vicinity of Baalbek, and it is the 'valley (*biq'aṯ*) of Lebanon' of Joshua 11:17. It descends north with the Orontes and south with the Litani and headwater streams of the Jordan. It

The Lebanon range of mountains.

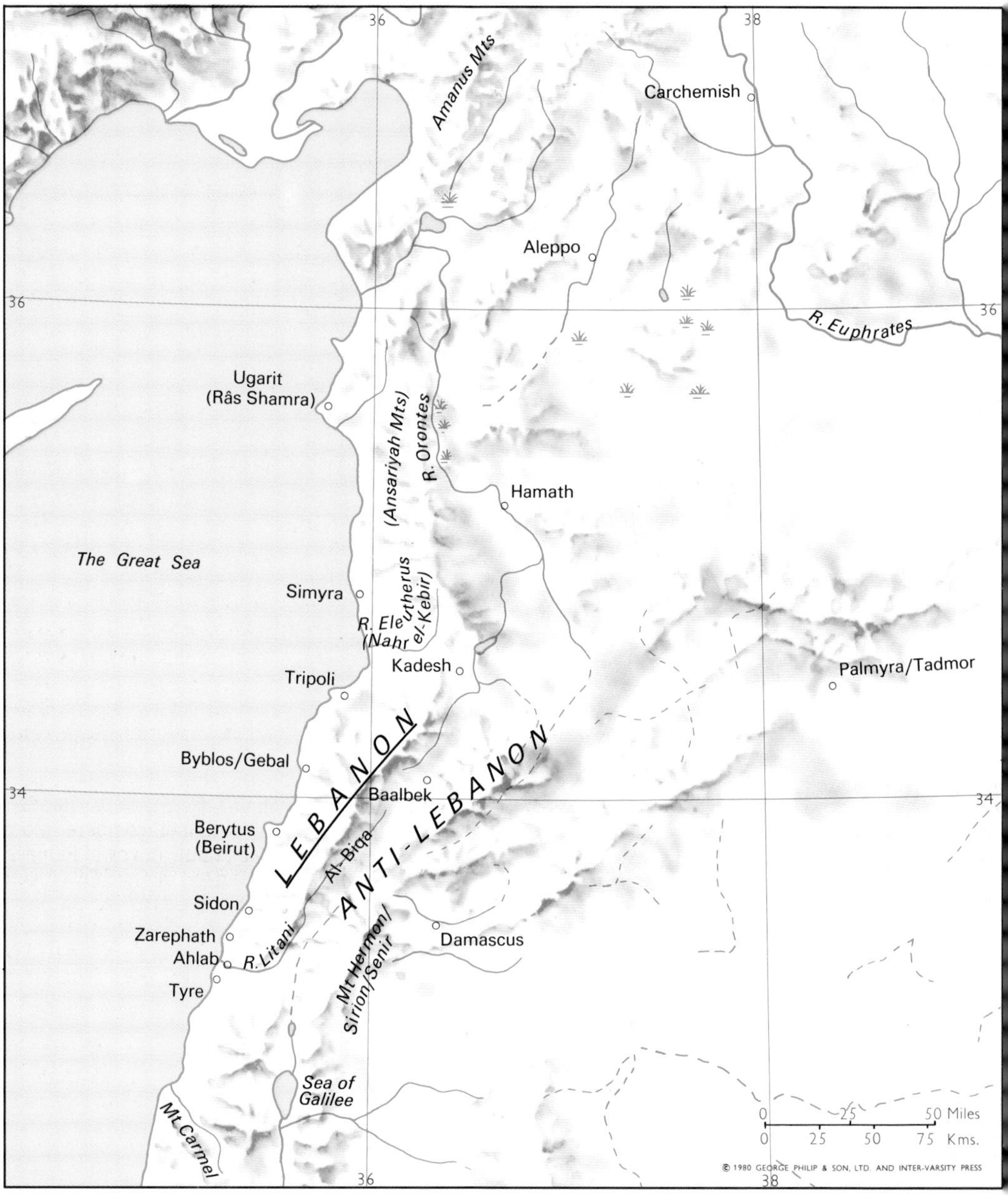


is the classical *Coelesyria ('Hollow Syria') and is bounded along its eastern side by the corresponding mountain range of Anti-Lebanon. This latter range also runs from south-west to north-east and is broken in two by the plateau from which the Barada river descends east to water the incredibly rich oasis of Damascus.

The highest peak is Mount Hermon (over 2,800 metres) in the southern half of the range. The structure of the whole region is clearly expressed in the diagram of D. Baly in *Geography of the Bible*, 1957, p. 11, figure 3. For routes connecting the Biqā', Anti-Lebanon and Damascus, see *ibid.*, pp. 110–111.

Mount Hermon in Anti-Lebanon was called Sirion by the Sidonians (*i.e.* Phoenicians), and Senir by the Amorites (Deuteronomy 3:9). Both names are independently attested in antiquity. Senir is mentioned as Saniru by Shalmaneser III of Assyria in 841 BC (*ANET*, p. 280b; *DOTT*, p. 48). Besides a Hittite mention of Sirion as Sariyana about 1320 BC (*ANET*, p. 205a), the use of the name Sirion for Hermon by the Canaanites/Phoenicians is confirmed by the Ugaritic texts of the 14th/13th centuries BC that picture Lebanon and Sirion as yielding timber for Baal's temple (*ANET*, p. 134a, section vi).

Hermon is often thought to be th[e] 'many-peaked mountain, mountain of Bashan' in Psalm 68:15; but Baly (*op. cit.*, pp. 194, 220, 222) suggests that it could equally well be the impressive peaks of the Gebel Druz[e] (See also *BASHAN, *HERMON, *SENIR, and *SIRION).

The biblical writers sometimes define the promised land in genera[l] terms as extending 'from the wilderness and Lebanon and from the River . . . Euphrates to the western sea' (Deuteronomy 11:24; Joshua 1:4), *i.e.* within these south-north and east-west limits. For the Phoenician coastal cities, th[e] Lebanon mountain range formed a natural barrier to invaders from land. The Assyrian king amshi-Adad I reached Lab'an in e 18th century BC (*ANET*, p. 274b) ıd the Hittite emperor Suppiluliuma ade it his south-western boundary the 14th century BC (Mount blani, *ANET*, p. 318b), without eir disturbing the coastal cities to ıy extent.

**esources**

ebanon was above all famous for its rmer dense forest cover. The nple November and March rainfall ıd limestone ridges gave rise to any springs and streams flowing own to east and west (Song of ongs 4:15; Jeremiah 18:14). The astland, Biqā', and lower ountain-slopes support arden-cultivation, olive-groves, neyards, fruit-orchards nulberries, figs, apples, apricots, alnuts) and small cornfields awlinson, *Phoenicia*, p. 17).

Higher still rises the forest-cover myrtles and conifers, culminating the groves of mighty cedars, of hich, alas, only one or two isolated roves survive (because of excessive eforestation), the main one being at sharreh south-east of Tripoli icture in L. H. Grollenberg, *Shorter tlas of the Bible,* 1959, p. 13).

The fertility and fruitfulness of the ebanon region is reflected in riptures such as Psalm 72:16; Song Songs 4:11; Hosea 14:5–7, as well s in early inscriptions (Tuthmosis I, 5th and 7th campaigns, 15th entury BC, *ANET*, p. 239a and b). Vild beasts also lurked there (*e.g.* Kings 14:9; Song of Songs 4:8).

*edars of Lebanon*

ne mighty cedars were apt symbols f majesty and strength in biblical nagery; see Judges 9:15; 1 Kings :33; 2 Kings 14:9 (2 Chronicles 5:18); Psalms 92:12; 104:16; Song f Songs 5:15; Isaiah 35:2 and 60:13. ney were also symbols of earthly ride subject to divine wrath; see salm 29:5–6; Isaiah 2:13; 10:34; eremiah 22:6; Ezekiel 31:3–14; and echariah 11:1–2.

These forests afforded a refuge eremiah 22:23). But above all, ebanon's cedars and conifers (firs, ypresses, *etc.*) furnished the finest uilding timber in the ancient East, ought by the rulers of Egypt, lesopotamia and Syria-Palestine like. The most celebrated of such eliveries of timber were those sent Solomon by Hiram I of Tyre for the emple at Jerusalem (1 Kings 5:6, 9, 4 (2 Chronicles 2:8, 16); 7:2; 10:17, 1 (2 Chronicles 9:20). The firs of ebanon and Anti-Lebanon (Sirion) provided ships for Tyre (Ezekiel 27:5) and sacred barges for Egypt (*ANET*, pp. 25b, 27a; *c.* 1090 BC), as well as furniture (Song of Songs 3:9). Wood for the second Jerusalem Temple was also cut in Lebanon (Ezra 3:7).

Snow-capped mountain ridges in the Lebanon with cedars at Kadesh.

**History**

The history of Lebanon is essentially that of the Phoenician cities on its littoral and the story of the exploitation of its splendid timber. From south to north, the Canaanite/ Phoenician cities of Tyre, Ahlab, Zarephath, Sidon, Beirut, Byblos (Gebal, modern Jebail) and Simyra (north of Tripoli) all had the wealth of the Lebanon as their hinterland besides their maritime trade. For their detailed histories (except Beirut and Simyra), see the separate articles; see also *CANAAN and *PHOENICIA.

The Lebanon timber-trade goes back to the earliest times. The 4th Dynasty pharaoh Snofru fetched 40 shiploads of cedars as early as *c.* 2600 BC (*ANET*, p. 227a), and various of his successors followed suit in later centuries. Byblos in particular became virtually an Egyptian dependency and its princes thoroughly assimilated to Egyptian culture, even writing their Semitic names in hieroglyphs (see *ANET*, p. 229a). In exchange for timber, they received handsome gold jewellery from the 12th Dynasty pharaohs (*c.* 1900–1800 BC).

When the New Kingdom pharaohs conquered Syria they exacted a regular annual tribute of 'genuine cedar of Lebanon' (*ANET*, p. 240b: Tuthmosis III, *c.* 1460 BC), and a relief of Sethos I (*c.* 1300 BC) actually depicts the Syrian princes hewing down the timbers of Lebanon for the pharaoh (*ANEP*, p. 110, figure 331, or Grollenberg, *Shorter Atlas of the Bible*, p. 14; see *ANET*, p. 254, section c, end).

In later days (20th Dynasty) the pharaohs had to pay handsomely for such timber (compare Solomon), as Wenamun, envoy of Ramesses XI, found to his cost (*ANET*, p. 27a).

From Canaan itself in the 2nd millennium BC, the Ugaritic epics about Baal and Anath and Aqhat allude to 'Lebanon and its trees; Sirion, its choice cedars' providing timber for the house (*i.e.* temple) of Baal (*ANET*, p. 134a, section vi; C. H. Gordon, *Ugaritic Literature*, 1949, p. 34), and furnishing material for a bow (*ANET*, p. 151b, section vi; Gordon, *op. cit.*, p. 90).

The Assyrians, too, exacted a tribute of timber from Lebanon for temple-building – so Tiglath-pileser I, *c.* 1100 BC (*ANET*, p. 275a) and Esarhaddon about 675 BC (*ANET*, p. 291b) – but also often drew upon the Amanus forests farther north (*ANET*, pp. 276b, 278a); compare here, 2 Kings 19:23 and Isaiah 37:24. Nebuchadrezzar followed their example (*ANET*, p. 307; *DOTT*, p. 87). Habakkuk (2:17) refers to Babylonian despoliation of Lebanon, which was also foreseen by Isaiah (14:8).

K. A. Kitchen, A. K. Cragg

*Further reading*

In addition to the works already cited above for particular points, see also:

P. K. Hitti, *Lebanon in History*, 1957

——, *History of Syria with Lebanon and Palestine*, 1951
J. P. Brown, *The Lebanon and Phoenicia* 1, 1969 (on ancient sources)

**LEHI** (Hebrew *l$^e$ḥî*, 'jawbone', Judges 15:9, 14, 19; 'Ramath-lehi' in Judges 15:17). The place in Judah where Samson slew 1,000 men with the jawbone of an ass. The site is unknown, but some scholars suggest Khirbet es-Siyyaj, where Siyyaj may be a loanword from the Greek *siagōn* ('jawbone'), the rendering of Lehi found in some Greek translations of the Old Testament. The site is 7 kilometres east of Tel Batash (biblical Timnah). Others prefer Khirbet Lāqīya, near Beersheba.
J. D. Douglas, J. Bimson

**LIBNAH** (Hebrew *liḇnâh*, 'white'). **1.** An important town in the Shephelah, taken by Joshua (Joshua 10:29f.; 15:42); assigned to the priests (Joshua 21:13); revolted from Jehoram (2 Kings 8:22); besieged by Sennacherib, whose army was decimated by pestilence (2 Kings 19:8, 35); the birthplace of Josiah's wife Hamutal (2 Kings 23:31).

Bliss and Macalister proposed Tel Zafit, Tell es-Safi, which they excavated in 1899; the Crusader Blanchegarde, it is on a limestone outlier 7 kilometres west of *Azekah. This appears doubtful, given that Azekah was in the Socoh district (Joshua 15:35; but see Rainey in *BASOR* 251, 1983, pp. 1–22); and Sennacherib would hardly have passed it to attack Lachish first.

There is now strong support for Tel Zafit as the site of *Gath (*LOB*, p. 271). Noth and Aharoni place Libnah at Tel Burna, Tell Bornat (30 kilometres east of Ashkelon); surveys suggest occupation in the Early Bronze, Late Bronze, Iron I, Iron II, Persian and Arab periods. This is closer to Mareshah than to Lachish, but seems too small for the role of Libnah.

Tell el-Beida, 7 kilometres north-east of Mareshah, has also been proposed, as being a larger site with Late Bronze remains.

Tell ej-Judeideh has also been suggested. This lies 10 kilometres north-east of Lachish; surveys have revealed Early Bronze, Iron I, Iron II, Persian and later occupation. Many scholars, however, prefer to identify this site with *Moresheth-Gath.

**2.** An unidentified camping-place in the desert, Numbers 33:20, perhaps also Deuteronomy 1:1.
J. P. U. Lilley, J. Bimson

*Further reading*
For **1**:
F. M. Cross, J. T. Milik, *JBL* 75, 1956, pp. 217f.
G. E. Wright, *BA* 34, 1971, pp. 76–86
*LOB*, pp. 86, 332
Rainey, *Tel Aviv* 7, 1980, pp. 195, 198

**LIBYA (LUBIM**, AV). First occurs as *Rbw* (that is, Libu) in Egyptian texts of the 13th-12th centuries BC, as a hostile Libyan tribe (Sir A. H. Gardiner, *Ancient Egyptian Onomastica*, 1, 1947, pp. 121*–122*). Libu as *lûḇîm* became a Hebrew term for Libya, Libyans, and as *libys* became the general Greek term 'Libyan' for the land and people west of Egypt. Thus the Hebrew and Greek terms cover other Libyans besides the tribe *Rbw*.

During the 12th–8th centuries BC, Libyans entered Egypt as raiders, settlers or soldiers in Egypt's armies. Hence the prominence of Lubim in the forces of Shishak (2 Chronicles 12:3); of Zerah (2 Chronicles 14:9 with 16:8); and among the troops of the Ethiopian pharaohs that failed to protect No-Amon (Thebes) from Assyrian devastation (Nahum 3:9).

*Lubbîm*, Daniel 11:43, may be the same word. (See also *PUT.)
K. A. Kitchen

*Further reading*
M. A. Leahy (ed.), *Libya and Egypt c.1300–750 BC*, 1990

**LOD.** See *LYDDA.

**LO-DEBAR** (Hebrew *lô d$^e$ḇār*). Where Mephibosheth lived before David recalled him (2 Samuel 9:4); recaptured (Amos 6:13), probably by Joash son of Jehoahaz after having been lost to the Syrians (see 2 Kings 13:25). It was east of the Jordan beyond Mahanaim (2 Samuel 17:27, compare Joshua 13:26, spelt respectively *lō' d$^e$ḇār, lid$^e$ḇir*); possibly Debir **3**. Amos may have been punning on the name, which sounds like 'No Matter'.
J. D. Douglas

**LUHITH, ASCENT OF.** A place in Moab where the people fled from the Babylonians (Isaiah 15:5; Jeremiah 48:5). Eusebius places it between Areopolis and Zoar, but it has not yet been certainly identified.
J. D. Douglas

**LUXOR.** See *THEBES.

**LUZ.** The ancient name of *Bethel, which was so named by Jacob when he had dreamed of the ladder from heaven to earth after spending the night near to the city (Genesis 28:1 35:6; 48:3). It was the site of Jacob sojourn near to the city, rather tha the city itself, that received the nam Bethel (Joshua 16:2), but this site later became so important that the name was applied to the city as w (Joshua 18:13; Judges 1:23).

The city was, however, still know to the Canaanite inhabitants as Lu because when the Israelites took th city at the time of the conquest a Canaanite whom they pressed to show them the entrance to it in return for his life escaped to the 'lan of the Hittites' and founded anoth city of that name (Judges 1:24–26)
T. C. Mitchell

*Further reading*
F. M. Abel, *Géographie de la Palestine* 2, 1938, p. 371

**LYCAONIA,** a territory in southern-central Asia Minor, so called from the *Lykaones* who inhabited it, mentioned by ancient writers from Xenophon (early 4th century BC) onwards. In Pompey's settlement of western Asia Minor ( BC) the western part of Lycaonia w added to Cilicia, the eastern part t Cappadocia, and the northern part *Galatia, which became a Roman province in 25 BC. Eastern Lycaoni later became independent of Cappadocia and from AD 37 onwar formed part of the client kingdom Antiochus, king of Commagene, a was known as Lycaonia Antiochian

In the New Testament 'Lycaonia denotes that part of the territory which constituted a region of the province of Galatia, Lycaonia Galatica. Lystra and Derbe are designated 'cities of Lycaonia' in Acts 14:6, in a context which implie that Iconium lay on the Phrygian si of the frontier separating Lycaonia Galatica from Phrygia Galatica.

W. M. Ramsay has put it on recor that it was this geographical note that led to his 'first change of judgment' with regard to the historical value of Acts. Paul and Barnabas on their first 'missionary journey' (AD 47–48) doubtless recognized that they had crossed a linguistic frontier between Iconiu and Lystra, for in the latter place (near modern Hatunsaray) they heard the indigenous population speak 'in Lycaonian' (Acts 14:11, Greek *lykaonisti*).

Lycaonian personal names have been identified in inscriptions hereabout, *e.g.* in one at Sedasa which records the dedication to Zeu of a statue of Hermes (compare Act 14:12). When, after leaving Lystra, aul and Barnabas came to Derbe nodern Kerti Hüyük) and planted a nurch there, they turned back; had ey gone farther they would have rossed into the kingdom of ntiochus, but it was no part of their lan to evangelize non-Roman erritory.

F. Bruce

*urther reading*

V. M. Ramsay, *Historical 'ommentary on Galatians*, 1899, p. 185f., 215ff.

1. H. Ballance, *AS* 7, 1957, pp. 147ff.; 4, 1964, pp. 139f.

. Van Elderen, 'Some Archaeological Observations on Paul's First lissionary Journey', in *Apostolic istory and the Gospel*, ed. W. W. asque and R. P. Martin, 1970, p. 156–161

**YCIA.** A small district on the outhern coast of Asia Minor ontaining the broad valley of the iver Xanthus, mountains rising to ver 3,000 metres, and the seaports Patara and *Myra (Acts 21:1; 27:5).

Although some sculptures and nscriptions have been preserved, ne origin of the Lycian people is bscure. They alone of the peoples of vestern Asia Minor successfully esisted the Lydian kings, but they uccumbed in 546 BC to the Persians.

Freed by Greeks in the following entury, they were greatly nfluenced by Greek civilization and ventually submitted voluntarily to lexander. They adopted the Greek anguage and script, and were horoughly Hellenized by the time hey came under Roman protection n the 2nd century BC.

Claudius in AD 43 annexed Lycia to he province of Pamphylia, but pparently Nero restored their reedom, for Vespasian again educed them to provincial status Suetonius, *Vespasian* 8). Through hese changes the federation of ycian cities maintained its general olitical framework.

. L. McKay

**YDDA.** A town some 18 kilometres outh-east of the coast at Jaffa, in the hephelah plain, referred to in Acts ):32, 35 and 38. It is almost certainly o be identified with the Old Testament Lod, which is mentioned n the Karnak list of Thothmes III.

In Israelite times it was a Benjaminite town (1 Chronicles ):12); reoccupied after the Babylonian Exile (Ezra 2:33; Nehemiah 11:35). It later fell to the uthority of the governor of Samaria, nd was not reclaimed by the Jews till 145 BC (1 Maccabees 11:34). It was burnt down in Nero's reign.

After the fall of Jerusalem (AD 70) Lydda became a rabbinical centre for a period. It had a bishop in the early Christian centuries. Since then it has borne the names Diospolis, Ludd and Lod again (today).

D. F. Payne

**LYDIA,** a district in the centre of the western slope of Asia Minor, including the Caÿster and Hermus valleys, the most fertile and highly cultivated areas of the peninsula, and between them the mountains of Tmolus, rising to 2,000 metres. Besides its natural wealth, its position on the main routes from the coast to the interior of Asia Minor gave its cities (including *Sardis, *Thyatira and *Philadelphia) great commercial importance. Lydia was bordered by Mysia, Phrygia and Caria. Some of the coastal cities (including Smyrna and Ephesus) were sometimes reckoned as Lydian, sometimes as Greek.

The origins of the Lydian race are obscure, but there may have been Semitic elements (see also *LUD). Croesus, the last king of Lydia, dominated the whole of Asia Minor before he was conquered by Cyrus the Persian in 546 BC. The region was subsequently ruled by Alexander and his successors, and became part of the Attalid kingdom of Pergamum before becoming part of the Roman province of Asia in 133 BC.

Some Lydian inscriptions of the 4th century BC have been discovered, but by the beginning of the Christian era Greek had become the common language and, according to Strabo, Lydian was little used.

Lydia was the first state to use coined money and was the home of some innovations in music.

K. L. McKay

**LYSTRA.** An obscure town on the high plains of Lycaonia (near modern Hatunsaray), singled out by Augustus as the site of one of a number of Roman colonies that were intended to consolidate the new province of Galatia. Its advantages are not known. Its remote position and proximity to the unsettled southern mountains suggest defensive motives, as also does the considerable Latin-speaking settlement implied by surviving inscriptions.

If it was the security of such a place that attracted Paul and Barnabas in their hasty retreat from Iconium (Acts 14:6) they were badly let down. Superstitious veneration, disabused by the apostles themselves, was converted by agitators into drastic hostility, which apparently secured official support for the stoning that was inflicted upon Paul (verse 19). There is no suggestion of Roman order or justice. Nor does the New Testament even disclose that it was a colony. There was plainly a substantial non-hellenic population (verse 11), as well as the usual Greeks and Jews (Acts 16:1). Nevertheless a church was established (Acts 14:20–23) which provided in Timothy (unless, as is just possible, he came from the nearby Derbe, Acts 16:1–2) Paul's most devoted 'son'.

E. A. Judge

*Further reading*

B. Levick, *Roman Colonies in Southern Asia Minor*, 1967

Rock-tombs at Myra, Lycia.

# M

**MAACAH, MAACHAH.** The name for a small state to the south-west of Mount Hermon, on the edge of the territory of the half-tribe of Manasseh (Deuteronomy 3:14; Joshua 13:8–13) and possibly extending across the Jordan to Abel-beth-Maacah. At the time of David, its Aramaean king provided 1,000 soldiers for the Ammonite and Aramaean attempt to crush Israel.

Following the defeat at Helam, Maacah probably became tributary to David (2 Samuel 10), Maacah was later absorbed into the kingdom of Damascus, which had been re-established during Solomon's reign (1 Kings 11:23–25).

A. R. Millard

*Further reading*

B. Mazar, 'Geshur and Maacah', *The Early Biblical Period, Historical Studies*, 1986, pp. 113–125

**MAALEH-ACRABBIM.** See *Akrabbim.

**MAAREH-GEBA** (Judges 20:33, RV; AV 'meadows of Gibeah'). The Hebrew *ma'ᵃrēh* means 'open, bare place', but the Septuagint (A) *dysmōn* and the Vulgate *occidentali urbis parte* suggest the Hebrew *ma'ᵃrāḇ*, 'west', which yields a better sense here. (See also *Geba.)

A. R. Millard

**MACEDONIA.** A splendid tract of land, centred on the plains of the gulf of Thessalonica, and running up the great river valleys into the Balkan mountains. It was famous for timber and precious metal.

*Government*

Anciently ruled by cavalry barons under a hellenized royal house, its kings dominated Greek affairs from the 4th century BC, and after Alexander Macedonian dynasties ruled throughout the eastern Mediterranean until superseded by the Romans.

The home monarchy was the first to go when in 167 BC Macedonia was constituted a series of four federations of republics (to which structure Acts 16:12 may refer), thus completing its hellenization. They were subsequently grouped under Roman provincial control, and, until the consolidation of Moesia and Thrace as provinces in New Testament times, were heavily garrisoned against the intractable northern frontier.

The province embraced the northern part of modern Greece from the Adriatic to the Hebrus river, and was crossed by the Via Egnatia, the main land route from Italy to the east.

After 44 BC the proconsul sat at Thessalonica, while the assembly of the Greek states met at Beroea, the seat of the imperial cult. The province included six Roman colonies, of which Philippi was one. There were also tribally organized communities. In spite of this diversity, the area is normally treated in the New Testament as a unit, following Roman usage.

*Paul in Macedonia*

Paul's vision of 'a man of Macedonia' (Acts 16:9) marks a distinct development in his methods of evangelism. At Philippi (Acts 16:37) for the first time he took advantage of his high civil station. He now enjoyed support in the cultivated circles to which he naturally belonged (Acts 16:15; 17:4, 12) in contrast to their hostility at earlier points on his route (Acts 13:50; 14:5).

Paul looked back upon Macedonia with profound affection (1 Thessalonians 1:3; Philippians 4:1), and was always eager to return (Acts 20:1; 2 Corinthians 1:16). The Macedonians were willing donors to his Jerusalem fund (2 Corinthians 8:1–4), and several of their number were added to his regular retinue of assistants (Acts 19:29; 20:4). It was in Macedonia then, it seems, that Paul finally proved himself as an independent missionary leader.

E. A. Judge

*Further reading*

J. Keil, *CAH* 9, pp. 566–570

J. A. O. Larsen, *Representative Government in Greek and Roman History*, 1955, pp. 103–104, 113–115

——, in T. Frank, *An Economic Survey of Ancient Rome* 5, 1940, pp. 436–496

N. G. L. Hammond, *The Macedonian State*, 1989

**MACHAERUS.** A fortress east of th Dead Sea (modern el-Mekawar), near the southern frontier of the region of Peraea, built by Alexande Jannaeus (103–76 BC), destroyed b the Roman commander Gabinius (5 BC), and rebuilt by Herod (37–4 BC), who appreciated the hot springs at Calirrhoe not far away (Wadi Zerka Ma'in).

Here, according to Josephus (*Antiquities* 18.112, 119), Herod Antipas imprisoned John the Bapti and later had him put to death. Here too, Antipas's first wife, the daughter of the Nabataean king Aretas IV, broke her journey on her way home to her father's capital at Petra when Antipas divorced her fo Herodias.

When Peraea was added to the province of Judaea (AD 44), Machaerus was occupied by a Roman garrison, which evacuated the place on the outbreak of war in A 66. It was then occupied by a force o Jewish insurgents, but surrendere to the governor Lucilius Bassus in AD 71.

F. F. Bruce

*Further reading*

Josephus, *Jewish War* 7.163–209

**MACHBENA.** See *Meconah.

**MACHPELAH.** The name applied t the field, cave and surrounding lan purchased by Abraham as a burial-place for his wife Sarah (Genesis 23). It was purchased from Ephron, a Hittite, for 400 shekels of silver (verses 8–16). It lay east of Mamre (verse 17) in the district of Hebron. Here were later buried Abraham (Genesis 25:9), Isaac and Rebekah (Genesis 49:31) and Jacob (Genesis 50:13).

The Hebrew (*hammaḵpēlâ*) implies that the name is in some wa descriptive and the Greek (*to diploun*, 'the double') is taken to describe the form of the cave in Genesis 23:17 (Septuagint). The reading of Shechem for Hebron in Acts 7:16 may be due to the summary nature of the record of thi speech, which originally referred also to Joseph's burial at Shechem.

The modern site of the burial-cav (60 metres × 34 metres), now incorporated in the southern end of the Ḥaram al-Ḥalîl at Hebron, is much venerated by Jews, Christian and Muslims. It is jealously guarde by massive stone walls of Herodian date. The antiquity of the cave itsel and its furnishings has not been verified by archaeological research. The 'cenotaph of Sarah' is still to be

The burial-cave of Machpelah is now incorporated in the southern end of the Haram al-Halil at Hebron.

en among others in the mosque ɔove the cave (see Vincent, Mackay ıd Abel, *Hébron, le Haram al Khalîl,* 923).

The antiquity of the details of braham's purchase of Machpelah ;enesis 23) has been thought to ıd support in Middle Assyrian and ittite laws prior to 1200 BC (*BASOR* 29, 1953, pp. 15–23), but this claim as now been questioned (*JBL* 85, 966, pp. 77–84).

J. Wiseman

**ADMANNAH** (*maḏmannâh*). A wn in south-western Judah; at one me Calibbite (1 Chronicles 2:49), it ay have passed to Simeon and ecome known as Beth-marcaboth ompare Joshua 15:31 with 19:5; lbright, *JPOS* 4, 1924, pp. 159f.; . M. Cross, J. T. Milik, *JBL* 75, 1956, 214).

Khirbet Tatrit, 27 kilometres ɔuth-west of Hebron, where the ahal Hevron leaves the hills, is now referred to Khirbet Umm-Deimneh, 5 kilometres farther north, which ay preserve the name but lacks raelite remains (A. F. Rainey, *IDB upplement*, 1976, p. 561, after ochavi).

P. U. Lilley

**ADMEN.** A town of Moab against hich Jeremiah prophesied (48:2). Since this place is otherwise nknown, it has been suggested, ther that the Hebrew text read *n-dmm tdmm*, 'also thou (Moab) ıalt be utterly silenced' (Septuant, Syriac, Vulgate), or that it stands for Dimon, a possible (but unlikely) rendering of the capital *Dîḇôn*.

Modern Khirbet Dimneh may be the site. Madmen is unlikely to be the same as *Madmannah, which lay in the Negeb (Joshua 15:31; 1 Chronicles 2:49), or *Madmenah, north of Jerusalem (Isaiah 10:31).

D. J. Wiseman

**MADMENAH.** A place mentioned only in Isaiah's description of the route whereby an invading army approached Jerusalem from the north (Isaiah 10:31). Shu'fat, 2 kilometres north of Mount Scopus, is the supposed site.

A. R. Millard

**MADON** (Hebrew *māḏôn*). A city of northern Canaan (Joshua 11:1; 12:19). Some scholars (*e.g.* Abel, Simons) would locate Madon at Khirbet Madjan, near Qarn Hattin (west of Tiberias), on the basis of the similar name. But this site was more probably *Adamah.

There is no other reference to a town called Madon. However, the Septuagint reads *marrōn* in both Joshua 11:1 and 12:19, and this is also the Septuagint rendering of Merom in 11:7. This probably indicates that *d* in the Hebrew is a transcriptional error for *r*, the original name being Merom. A town of this name, near the Waters of Merom, is known from Egyptian and Assyrian sources. (See *MEROM, WATERS OF.)

J. P. U. Lilley

*Further reading*
*LOB*, pp. 117f., 226, 280 n. 17

**MAGBISH.** Either a town in Judah (*GTT*, p. 380) or the name of a clan. Ezra 2:30 records that 156 of its 'sons' (or 'inhabitants') returned after the Exile. It is inexplicably omitted from the parallel list in Nehemiah 7.

D. J. A. Clines

**MAGDALA, MAGDALENE.** The name 'Magdala' occurs only once in the New Testament (Matthew 15:39, AV), where the best manuscripts (followed by RSV, NEB) read 'Magadan'. Some manuscripts, however, also read 'Magdala' or 'Magadan' for *'Dalmanutha' (otherwise unknown) in Mark 8:10.

The town of Magdala (or Tarichaea) stood on the western shore of the Sea of Galilee, north of Tiberias and Hamath, and south of Capernaum. The name derives from the Hebrew *miḡdāl*, 'tower'. It is probable that the modern Khirbet Mejdel stands on the site today.

Magadan was the *locality* on the western shore of the lake to which Jesus crossed after feeding the crowds, and it probably included the town of Magdala. Evidently Mary called Magdalene came from this town or area.

S. S. Smalley

**MAHANAIM** (Hebrew *maḥ*$^{a}$*nayim*, 'two camps'). A place in Gilead where Jacob saw the angels of God before he reached Penuel and met

Esau (Genesis 32:2).

Appointed to be a levitical (Merarite) city from the territory of Gad (Joshua 21:38; 1 Chronicles 6:80), Mahanaim was on the border of Gad with Gileadite Manasseh (Joshua 13:26, 30). It was briefly the capital of Ishbosheth, Saul's son (2 Samuel 2:8, 12, 29), and later David's refuge from Absalom (2 Samuel 17:24, 27; 19:32; 1 Kings 2:8), and then became the seat of a district-officer of Solomon's (1 Kings 4:14).

The location of Mahanaim is still uncertain; see J. R. Bartlett in *POTT*, p. 252, note 47. It is usually placed in the middle of northern Gilead at Khirbet Mahneh, 20 kilometres north of the Jabbok river, but as the boundary of Gad is linked with the course of the Jabbok, Mahanaim is probably better located somewhere on (or overlooking) the northern bank of the Jabbok. Mahanaim is now often located at Tell edh-Dhahab el-Gharbi; compare *LOB*, p. 34 and D. Homes-Fredericq, J. B. Hennessy, *Archaeology of Jordan* I, 1986, p. 71.

Mahanaim was at some distance from the Jordan, on the evidence of 2 Samuel 2:29, however 'Bithron' be interpreted. If (as is commonly taken) Bithron means 'cleft, ravine', Abner went from Jordan up the vale of the Jabbok east and through its narrow part before reaching Mahanaim. If the RSV reading be adopted, then 'the whole forenoon' was needed in any case for Abner's eastward flight. Hence perhaps Mahanaim was in the Jerash area, or up to 10–15 kilometres south-south-west of Jerash, overlooking the northern bank of the river Jabbok. See K.-D. Schunck, *ZDMG* 113, 1963, pp. 34–40. (See also *GAD, *GILEAD.)

K. A. Kitchen

**MAHANEH-DAN** (Hebrew *maḥ$^{a}$nēh-ḏān*, 'camp of Dan'). Where Samson experienced the stirring of God's Spirit (Judges 13:25), and the first staging-post of the Danites in their quest for an inheritance (Judges 18:12).

The geographical references given, 'between Zorah and Eshtaol' and 'west of Kiriath-jearim', cannot be reconciled, and the name itself suggests a temporary settlement. As the Danites had no secure inheritance (Judges 18:1), probably due to Philistine pressure, there is no problem in two places bearing the same name. It is not surprising that no trace of such temporary encampments has survived.

A. E. Cundall

**MAKKEDAH** (Hebrew *maqqēḏâh*). A town in the Shephelah captured by Joshua (Joshua 10:28; 12:16); Adoni-zedek and his allies hid in a cave nearby after their defeat (10:16ff.).

Makkedah was in the district of *Lachish (15:41); but apparently *Libnah lay between them (10:29–31). Eusebius, in *Onomasticon* p. 126, put Makkedah 8 miles from Beit Guvrin (*Mareshah). This could be Khirbet Beit Maqdum, which does not, however, have pre-Roman remains; but Khirbet el-Qom, on a spur 0·5 kilometres to the south-west, is an Early Iron site near the head of the valley leading to Lachish, still in the Shephelah but close to the hills (D. Dorsay, *Tel Aviv* 7, 1980, pp. 185–193). Late Bronze material however has not been found (Holladay, *IEJ* 31, 1971, pp. 106–108). Simons, in *GTT*, 1959, p. 273, lists earlier suggestions as 'none quite satisfactory'.

J. P. U. Lilley

**MAKTESH.** A site in Jerusalem or nearby (Zephaniah 1:11). The name means 'mortar' (as in RSV, NRSV) or 'trough'. The oldest suggestion is that it was the Kidron Valley; so says the Targum. But most scholars today believe it to have been some part of the Tyropoean Valley, within the walls of the city, where foreign merchants gathered; compare NEB 'Lower Town', NIV 'market district'.

D. F. Payne

**MALTA** (Greek *Melitē*; Acts 28:1, AV 'Melita'). An island in the centre of the Mediterranean, 100 kilometres south of Sicily and in area about 246 square kilometres (not to be confused with the island Mljet or Melitene off the Dalmatian coast; see O. F. A. Meinardus, 'St Paul Shipwrecked in Dalmatia', *BA* 39, 1976, pp. 145–147).

Here Paul's ship was driven from Crete by the east-north-east wind Euraquilo (27:14, RSV 'the northeaster'). After being shipwrecked he spent 3 months on the island before continuing his journey to Rome *via* Syracuse, Rhegium and Puteoli (28:11–13). Paul performed acts of healing, and the party was treated with great respect.

Malta had been occupied from the 7th century BC by Phoenicians. The name itself means 'refuge' in that language (J. R. Harris in *ExpT* 21, 1909–10, p. 18). Later, Sicilian Greeks also came; there are bilingual inscriptions of the 1st century AD on the island.

In 218 BC the island passed from Carthaginian to Roman control (Liv 21.51), later gaining the 'civitas'. It inhabitants were *barbaroi* (28.2, 4) only in the sense of not speaking Greek. Luke may refer to one of the gods in verse 4 as *Dikē* (Justice). Publius, 'the chief man' (verse 7), probably served under the propraetor of Sicily. His title (Greek *prōtos*) is attested by inscriptions (*CIG*, 14.601; *CIL*, 10.7495).

The site of the shipwreck is thought to have been 'St Paul's Ba 13 kilometres north-west of moder Valetta (see W. M. Ramsay, *St Paul the Traveller and Roman Citizen*, 4 edition, pp. 314ff.).

B. F. Harris

*Further reading*

J. Smith, *Voyage and Shipwreck of Paul*, 4th edition, 1880

W. Burridge, *Seeking the Site of St Paul's Shipwreck*, 1952

J. D. Evans, *Malta*, 1959

C. J. Hemer, 'Euraquilo and Melita *JTS* n.s. 26, pp. 100–111

**MAMRE** (Hebrew *mamrē'*). A plac in the Hebron district, west from Machpelah (Genesis 23:17, 19; 49:30; 50:13), associated with Abraham (Genesis 13:18; 14:13; 18:1) and Isaac (Genesis 35:27). Abraham resided for considerable periods under the terebinth of Mamre; there he built an altar, the he learnt of the capture of Lot, the he received Yahweh's promise of a son and pleaded for Sodom, and fro there he saw the smoke of Sodom and its neighbour-cities ascend.

The site has been identified as Râmet el-Khalîl, 4 kilometres north Hebron. Here Constantine built a basilica beside an ancient terebint which was pointed out in his day ( by Josephus 250 years earlier) as th tree beneath which Abraham 'entertained angels unawares' (Genesis 18:4, 8). There was a shrir there under the Monarchy, but it w a sacred place before Abraham's time in the Early Bronze Age.

F. F. Bruce

*Further reading*

E. Mader, *Mambre*, 2 vols., 1957

**MANAHATH.** The name of a city t which certain Benjaminites were carried captive (1 Chronicles 8:6), and which seems to have been somewhere in the vicinity of Bethlehem (so *GTT*, p. 155). Grollenberg suggests an identifica tion with Manocho, a town in the hill-country of Judah listed in Joshu 15:59, Septuagint, and probably to e identified with the modern ɪaliha, south-west of Jerusalem.

Manahath may also be the 'Nohah' f Judges 20:43, for both names ɪean 'resting-place'. Amarna Letter 92 (*ANET*, p. 489) mentions a ɪanhatu in the realm of Gezer which s probably the same place.

D. Douglas

**ɪANASSEH** ('making to forget'). ɪanasseh was the elder son of oseph. The tribe of Manasseh erived from seven families: one om Machir, and the remaining six om Gilead. They occupied land on oth sides of Jordan; the eastern ortion being granted by Moses, the vestern by Joshua (Joshua 22:7). fter the crossing of Jordan and the ettlement in the land, Joshua ermitted the half-tribe of Manasseh, ogether with Reuben and Gad, to eturn to the conquered territory of ihon, king of Heshbon, and Og, king f Bashan (Numbers 32:33).

The eastern allotment of the alf-tribe of Manasseh covered part f Gilead and all of Bashan Deuteronomy 3:13). The western alf of the tribe was granted good ınd north of Ephraim, and south of ebulun and Issachar (Joshua 7:1–12). This western part was ivided into ten portions: five to nose families having male escendants, and five to Manasseh's ixth family, *i.e.* the posterity of epher, all females and daughters of elophehad (Joshua 17:3).

Western Manasseh included a hain of Canaanite fortresses and trong cities, among which were Megiddo, *Taanach, *Ibleam and Bethshan. These they failed to onquer but compelled their ıhabitants eventually to pay tribute.

Though the lot of Manasseh and phraim, the tribe of Joseph, was ırge, they lodged a complaint with oshua for more land. In reply he dvised them to show their worth by learing the unclaimed forest areas Joshua 17:14–18). Golan, a city of ashan, in eastern Manasseh, was ne of the six *'cities of refuge' Joshua 20:8; 21:27; 1 Chronicles :71).

The tribe was renowned for its alour; among its heroes were ideon in the west and Jephthah in ıe east (Judges 11:1). Some of the ibe of Manasseh deserted to David t Ziklag (1 Chronicles 12:19–20), nd also rallied to his support at ebron (verse 31). Manassites were mong those deported to Assyria by iglath-pileser (1 Chronicles :18–26).

J. A. Sheriffs

**MAON.** The town Maon features in Judah in the list in Joshua 15:55. In this area David and his men sheltered from Saul (1 Samuel 23:24–25), and the churlish Nabal lived there (1 Samuel 25:2). The Maonites are mentioned in the official list of those who returned from Exile (Ezra 2:50), AV 'Mehunim', RSV 'Meunim'; Nehemiah 7:52, 'Meunim').

Khirbet-el-Ma'în, 14 kilometres south of Hebron and 65 kilometres west of Gaza, marks the ancient site. Traces of Early Iron Age I pottery and a remarkable late 4th–6th century AD synagogue with mosaics were found there. It is surrounded by pasture-lands, probably the 'wilderness of Maon' where David sought refuge from Saul (1 Samuel 23:24–25) and was saved by a Philistine raid (1 Samuel 23:27f.).

J. A. Thompson

**MARAH** (Hebrew *mārâ*, 'bitter'). This was the first named camp of the Israelites after the Red Sea crossing, called Marah because only bitter water was found there (Exodus 15:23; Numbers 33:8–9), and perhaps also by comparison with the sweet water of the Nile Valley to which they had been accustomed.

On the likely assumption that the route from the crossing led to the mountains in the south of the Sinai peninsula, Marah is often identified with the modern Ain Hawarah, *c.* 75 kilometres south-south-east of Suez. However, H. H. Rowley (*From Joseph to Joshua*, 1950, p. 104) and J. Gray (*VT* 4, 1954, pp. 149f.) identify Marah with *Kadesh, a view refuted by *GTT*, p. 252, n. 218; B. Rothenberg and Y. Aharoni, in *God's Wilderness*, 1961, pp. 11, 93f., 142ff., present both views. (See also *WILDERNESS OF THE WANDERING.)

J. D. Douglas, G. I., Davies

*Further reading*

B. S. Childs, *Exodus*, 1974, pp. 265–270

**MARESHAH** (Hebrew *mārē'šâh*). A town in the Shephelah (Joshua 15:44), covering the road up the Wadi Zeita to Hebron; now Tel Mareshah, Tell Sandahanna, on a spur running just south of Beit Jibrin. The inhabitants claimed descent from Shelah (1 Chronicles 4:21).

Rehoboam fortified it; Asa defeated Zerah the Ethiopian in this area; Eliezer the prophet was born here (2 Chronicles 11:8; 14:10; 20:37). Later it was a Sidonian colony and then an important stronghold of Idumaea (1 Maccabees 5:66; 2 Maccabees 12:35; Josephus, *Antiquities* 12.8.6, 14.4.4). The Parthians destroyed it in 40 BC (*Antiquities* 14.13.9); in its place, but nearer the river, rose Eleutheropolis, which Eusebius used as a main point of reference. The name, probably derived from *rō'š* ('head'), was probably not unique (Rudolph on 1 Chronicles 2:42).

Limited excavations at the site in 1900 uncovered only a Hellenistic city of the 3rd–1st centuries BC and an Iron Age stratum from the 8th–7th centuries BC.

J. P. U. Lilley

**MARI.** Excavations at Mari, modern Tell Ḥarīri, in south-eastern Syria, *c.* 12 kilometres north-north-west of Abu Kemal by the Euphrates, were conducted in 1933–39 and 1951–64 by André Parrot for the Musée de Louvre. While not mentioned in the Old Testament, this strategic site proved to be the capital of a major *Amorite city-state in the 2nd millennium BC. More than 22,000 inscribed clay tablets, a quarter of them state letters, provide important information for the background of the Patriarchal Age.

*History*

Founded in the 3rd millennium BC, Mari was already a powerful centre when it was conquered by Sargon of Agade *c.* 2250 BC. Thereafter it was ruled by governors dependent on *Ur until freed by the Amorite Ishbi-Irra. About 1820 BC a strong ruling house under King Yahdun-Lim, son of Yaggid-Lim, controlled the region as far as the Mediterranean. He held the surrounding semi-nomad tribes in a firm but just hand, among them the Sutu, Amnanum, Ben-Yamini ('Benjaminites') and later Ḫapiru ('Hebrews'), not the same as their later biblical counterparts. His successors Yasmah-Adad and Zimri-Lim (*c.* 1775 BC), though powerful, found themselves hemmed in by the strong city-states of Aleppo (Yamhad), Assyria (Nineveh) and Babylon.

The dynasty fell *c.* 1760 BC to Hammurapi of Babylon, of whom one of Zimri-Lim's agents reported that 'there is no king really powerful in himself. Ten or fifteen kings go with Hammurapi of Babylon, the same number with Rim-Sin of Larsa, with Ibal-pī'el of Eshnunna and with Amut-pī'el of Watānum. Twenty go with Yarimlim of Yamhad.'

*Diplomacy*

Diplomacy was a major subject of international correspondence and

**Axonometric projection of the palace of Zimri-Lim as excavated at Mari, *c.* 1775 BC.**

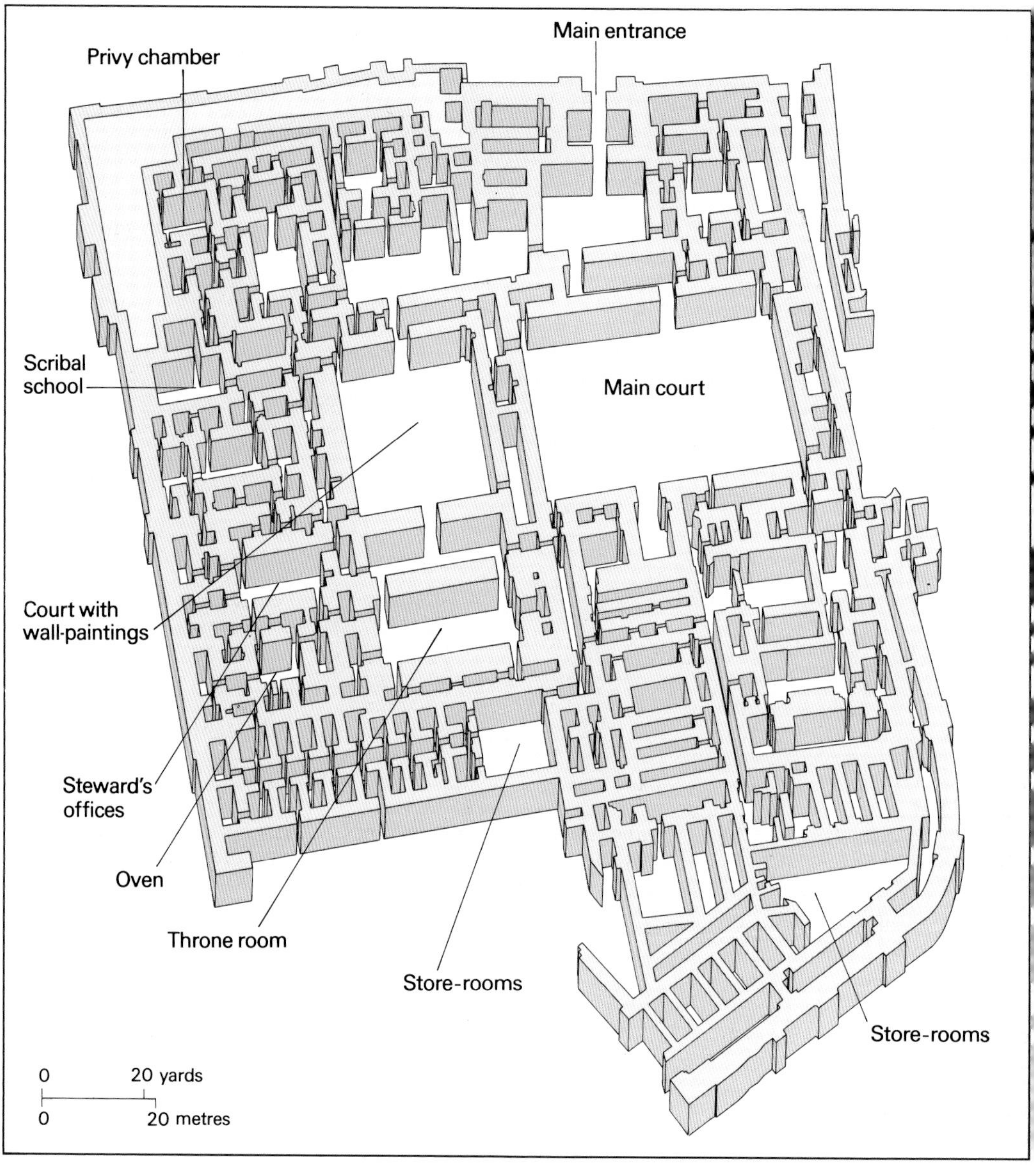


gifts between rulers (*Iraq* 18, 1958, pp. 68–110), equals addressed each other as 'brothers' and vassals referred to their overlords as 'father' or 'lord'. Tribal chiefs were designated 'fathers' and, as at Ebla, local administration was in the hands of sub-governors (*šāpiṭum*; compare Hebrew *šōpēṭ*, often mistranslated 'judge') responsible for law and order, collection of taxes, hospitality to passing dignitaries, *etc.*, much as the role adopted by Abraham (*BS* 134, 1977, pp. 228–237).

Relations with neighbours were regulated by written treaty or covenant. These followed a pattern close to those in use in Syria, Mesopotamia and Palestine in the following centuries. At Mari some covenants were ratified in a ritual requiring the 'killing of an ass' (*hayaram qatālum*) which occurs also in Hebrew and seems to have been preserved by the Shechemite Bene Hamar ('sons of an ass', Joshua 24:13) who entered into covenant with Jacob (Genesis 33:14; 34:1–3).

*Religion*

At Mari prophets, the *āpil(t)u*, 'male (or female) answerer', put questions to a deity, might function in a group, and received government maintenance. Others, *muhhû*, were low-ranking cult officials who were perhaps ecstatics and spoke for the god in the first person. Yet others were called 'speakers' (*qabbātum*) and were each attached to a god o temple. It was also known for lay persons to make divine pronounce ments or report visions. In association with music some temp officials (*e.g. assinnu*) declared 'Thus says the god . . .'.

One report from Itur-Asdu to Kin Zimri-Lim tells of a dream revelatic in the temple of Dagan at Terqa. T message was not good, because th king had failed to report regularly t his god. 'If he had done so I would have delivered the sheiks of the Benjaminites into the hands of Zimri-Lim.' In this way too the king was told of the sacrifices required him. Another prophet appears to have foretold the downfall of a city

This activity relied largely on

inatory and magic techniques, eams, the reading of the entrails of crificial animals and some tronomical observations. This is in irked contrast with the clarity, ige, content and purpose of ophecies in Israel.

At Mari, as in Israel, the census is of particular religious and ritual portance above any immediate litical, military or economic gnificance (compare 2 Samuel 24). hile it involved political reform and estions of land tenure, it was ought to concern the purification the people (Hebrew *kōper*, Mari *ibtum*), their enrolment (*pqd*, lled to account'; compare Exodus :13–14) and status.

*xts*

e many lists show personal names a wide cosmopolitan range, some nilar to, but not to be identified th, Old Testament persons: iukku (compare Arioch of Genesis :1), Abarama, Yaqub-'el, or the e *dawīdum*, 'chief' (compare avid'), now thought to be a word 'defeat' (*JNES* 17, 1958, p. 130). ace-names mentioned in the texts clude a number round Har(r)an, hur (Nahor), Til-Turahi (Terah) d Sarug (Serug; compare Genesis :23–24). The only city of Palestine entioned directly is *Hazor.

The texts provide a detailed sight into daily life, especially in e 300-room (6-hectare) royal lace with its various archives cording not merely inter-state fairs but the detail of imports of ne, honey, oil, wool, ice and other mmodities. Other notes detail the ues from the palace stores both for e royal hospitality and for the ritual asts which were part of the orship of ancestors. The pantheon Mari included the sun (Saps), oon (Sin, Yerah), the storm-god dad) as well as the goddess Ishtar, tar, the god Dagan (Dagon), Ba'al, , Rasap (the underworld god) and any others (including Lim, 'the ousand gods'). All these could ve been known to Terah (Joshua :2).

Such an abundance of sources, cluding that for the position of omen and the family, written in a mitic dialect very similar to early oks of the Pentateuch, will yet row much light on the practices of e patriarchal period.

J. Wiseman

*irther reading*

Parrot, *Mari, Capitale fabuleuse*, 74

Dossin and others, *Archives royales de Mari*, 1–15, 1941–78

J.-R. Kupper, *Les nomades en Mésopotamie au temps des rois de Mari*, 1957

B. F. Batto, *Studies in Women at Mari*, 1974

On the Mari prophecies:

*VT Supp.* 15, 1966, pp. 207–227; 17, 1969, pp. 112–138

*HTR* 63, 1970, pp. 1–28

*VT* 27, 1977, pp. 178–195

E. Noort, *Untersuchungen zum Gottesbescheid in Mari*, 1977

**MASADA.** See p. 206.

**MASSAH.** According to Deuteronomy 6:16 and 9:22, a place in the wilderness where Israel put God to the test: Massah (from *nissâ*, 'to test') means 'testing'.

In Exodus 17:7 the name is coupled with Meribah (which means 'quarrel, complaint', from *rîḇ*, 'strive, complain') in a story from the older Pentateuchal sources which shows the Israelites protesting because of lack of water at *Rephidim, close to Mount Horeb (verse 6). The two names again appear together in Psalm 95:8, a warning to later generations which could refer to this episode.

The name Meribah also occurs (without Massah) in conjunction with *Kadesh, both in a boundary-list (Ezekiel 47:19) and as the location of a similar episode (mainly drawn from P), which results in both Moses and Aaron being denied the privilege of entering the promised land (Numbers 20:1–13 [compare verse 24]; 27:14; Deuteronomy 32:51; Psalm 106:32).

Both narratives are aetiological, *i.e.* imply that the names were given as a result of these events of the Mosaic period. But because of the legal connotations of the verb *rîḇ* it has often been suggested that Meribah was first of all a place where legal disputes were settled (compare En-mishpat, 'well of judgment', another name for Kadesh [Genesis 14:7]). This can only be a hypothesis, but there are other reasons for wondering whether the straightforward explanation of the names is historically correct.

The attempt has frequently been made to separate out a Massah-story and a Meribah-story in Exodus 17:1–7, but, although there is a little unexpected repetition (verses 2–3), it is not sufficient to justify analysis into two separate stories, deriving from different sources. The same must be said for Numbers 20:1–13. What is more likely is that, in both cases, there has been some amplification of the original account by a later author. In Exodus 17:1–7 this amplification may be responsible for the introduction of the allusion to Meribah (and perhaps Massah also) in verses 2 and 7.

Deuteronomy 33:8 and Psalm 81:7, where these names also occur, can scarcely refer to the same episodes, since here there is no hint of criticism and it is God, not the people of Israel, who is doing the 'testing'. The theme of God testing Israel is one that is encountered several times in Exodus (15:25; 16:4; 20:20). It seems likely that other events, perhaps mentioned elsewhere in the Bible (Exodus 32?), perhaps not, were at one time connected with these places. To date, no fully satisfactory correlation of the various passages has been made, and it may be that the literary and historical problems are insoluble. For some ingenious, if speculative, suggestions see H. Seebass, *Mose und Aaron*, 1962, pp. 61ff

G. I. Davies.

*Further reading*

B. S. Childs, *Exodus*, 1974, pp. 305–309

**MECONAH** (Hebrew *m^e^kōnâh*). A town near Ziklag occupied by the Jews after the Exile (Nehemiah 11:28). Grollenberg (*Atlas*, index) suggests that it might be the Machbena of 1 Chronicles 2:49, near *Madmannah; Simons (in *GTT*, p. 155) takes all three as the same and suggests Khirbet umm ed-Deimineh as the location. It is not known whether this site was occupied in the post-exilic period.

J. P. U. Lilley

**MEDEBA** (Hebrew *mêḏ^e^ḇā'*, possibly 'water of quiet'). A plain and city of Reuben (Joshua 13:9, 16) north of the Arnon. An old Moabite town taken from Moab by Sihon (Numbers 21:21–30), it was used by the Syrian allies of Ammon as a camping-site after their defeat at the hand of Joab (1 Chronicles 19:6–15). Thereafter it seems to have changed hands several times. It is mentioned in the Moabite Stone as having been taken by Omri, perhaps from Moab, and as recovered by Mesha and fortified. Recaptured from Moab by Jeroboam II, it is again Moabite in Isaiah 15:2.

Medeba figured also in the history of the intertestamental era (1 Maccabees 9:36ff. as 'Medaba'; Josephus, *Jewish War* 1.63), before

**Continued on p. 210**

# MASADA

Herod, who had gained his throne with the help of Mark Antony after a vicious civil war within Judaea, never felt safe. To guard against insurrection from within and attack from without, he built a string of fortresses and watchtowers on the borders of his kingdom.

Herod was especially afraid that Antony would hand Judaea over to the Egyptian Queen Cleopatra. Against this eventuality, he needed a safe retreat where he could sit out a prolonged siege. Masada became this retreat. His fortifications on top of the 434-metre-high rock and his ingenious storage systems for water made this natural fortress almost impregnable as the Romans later found to their cost.

## Safety first

The Masada rock was originally part of a high plateau looming above the south-western shores of the Dead Sea. Millions of years of erosion had isolated it so that it formed a natural fortress. The Hasmonaean kings had built a castle on Masada, and it was here that Herod had fled when his life was in danger a year before he became king. Leaving his family behind at Masada, he had set off to find Mark Antony and plead for Roman support. During the months he was away, Masada had been besieged, and his family had almost died of thirst. When he was eventually able to free the citadel, Herod had determined that thirst should never be a problem again.

After he became king, Herod built a casemate wall all around the summit of Masada. He strengthened this wall with 30 towers, building them mainly around the western and eastern sides, since it was impossible for any army to scale the northern and southern sides of the rock. He then set about improving the water supply.

Along the north-west face of Masada Herod had two parallel cisterns cut into the rock face, above the Ben Yair ravine. He then dammed both this ravine and the Masada valley and built channels and aqueducts from the water in the valleys to the cisterns. It has been calculated that these cisterns could hold up to 40,000 cubic metres of water. This water was laboriously carried up by manpower and donkey power to large underground water cisterns on the summit.

**Part of the Northern Palace, Masada.**

The site of Masada, showing the grcat ramp built by the Romans to capture the stronghold.

Plan of the fortress of Masada.

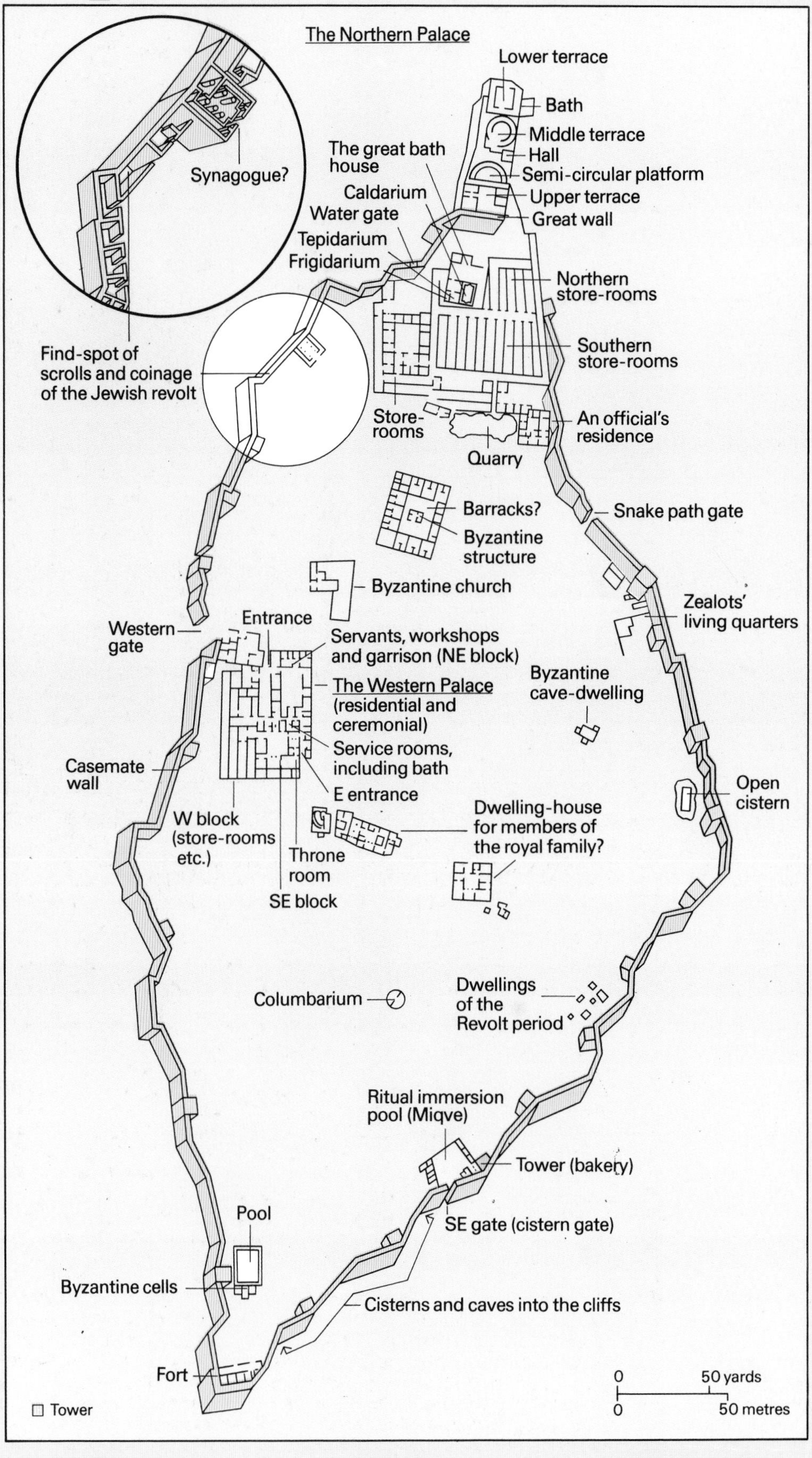
The Northern Palace
Lower terrace
Bath
Middle terrace
Hall
Semi-circular platform
Upper terrace
Great wall
The great bath house
Caldarium
Water gate
Tepidarium
Frigidarium
Synagogue?
Find-spot of scrolls and coinage of the Jewish revolt
Northern store-rooms
Southern store-rooms
Store-rooms
An official's residence
Quarry
Barracks?
Byzantine structure
Snake path gate
Byzantine church
Zealots' living quarters
Western gate
Entrance
Servants, workshops and garrison (NE block)
The Western Palace (residential and ceremonial)
Byzantine cave-dwelling
Service rooms, including bath
Casemate wall
E entrance
Open cistern
W block (store-rooms etc.)
Throne room
SE block
Dwelling-house for members of the royal family?
Columbarium
Dwellings of the Revolt period
Ritual immersion pool (Miqve)
Tower (bakery)
SE gate (cistern gate)
Pool
Byzantine cells
Cisterns and caves into the cliffs
Fort
Tower
0
50 yards
0
50 metres

## ıe palaces

ʻod anticipated that Masada might be home for a very long period of time, ɬ he did not intend to live a spartan life. therefore built storage rooms to hold ɨt quantities of food and constructed ı luxurious palaces. The larger was the stern Palace, just within the fortified ls on the summit. This was Herod's ɬe palace. It included a throne room, ıg rooms, bedrooms, administrative ɪms, and Roman-style bathrooms.

'he more spectacular and magnificent ace was the northern palace, called the ɪnging palace' because it stood on ɜe tiers on the north cliff. The Hanging ace was clearly built to provide ɪxation and pleasure for Herod and his ɪnds. The living rooms were in the upper ace, built on the summit of the north 's. A curved balcony gave superb views ɪe bleak rocky wilderness. Square-cut stairs spiralled down the rock to the two lower levels. Only the foundations remain of the rooms on the middle terrace, some 20 metres below the summit.

The lowest level was 35 metres down the cliff face. This consisted of a square platform on which was built a courtyard surrounded on 4 sides by columns with a small bath-house leading off on the eastern side. Impressive frescoes and eyecatching floor mosaics remain to this day.

### Masada's last stand

In the summer of AD 66 the Zealots, the Jewish revolutionary movement, rose in all-out rebellion against Roman domination. Early in the rebellion an extremist group called the Sicarii ('dagger men') seized Masada, slaughtering its Roman garrison. It was an impossible war. When Jerusalem fell to Rome in AD 70, the Sicarii fled to Masada.

For 3 years about a thousand men, women and children withstood a Roman siege. The Roman commander eventually overcame the fortress by building a giant ramp, topped by a stone platform. This took 7 months to construct. Though the fortress walls collapsed under the impact of the iron battering ram, the Romans were unable to breach the mountains of earth and timber with which the defenders had strengthened the wall. Eventually they set fire to this backing wall.

At last they entered the city – to find that only 2 women and 5 children were alive; 960 people had killed themselves in a suicide pact.

ɜw from the stronghold of Masada, showing the cliff-like slopes surrounding it.

Byzantine church, Masada.

Frescoes in the Northern Palace.

**Continued from p. 205**
being captured by Hyrcanus after a long siege (Josephus, *Antiquities* 13.11, 19).

The site, today called Mādabā, is 10 kilometres south of Heshbon. There in 1896, during excavation of the site of a church, was discovered a 6th-century AD mosaic map showing part of Palestine from Bethshan to the Nile. See M. Avi-Yonah, *The Madaba Mosaic Map*, 1954.

In addition, there are considerable ruins, dating mainly from the Christian era, including a large temple and extensive cisterns. Tombs so far provide the only evidence of occupation during the late Bronze and Iron Ages.

J. D. Douglas

**MEDIA, MEDES** (Hebrew *madai*; Assyrian *(A)mada*; Old Persian *Mada*; Greek *Medai*).

Media was the name for north-western Iran, south-west of the Caspian Sea and north of the Zagros Mountains, covering the modern state of Azerbaijan and part of Persian Kurdistan. The inhabitants were called Medes or Medians and were Japhethites (Genesis 10:2), whose Aryan lineage is confirmed by Herodotus (7.62), Strabo (15.2.8) and by the surviving traces of their language.

*Conquered by Assyria*

The Medes were steppe-dwellers whose name is first mentioned by Shalmaneser III who raided their plains in 836 BC to obtain their famous, finely bred horses. Later Assyrian kings followed him and sought to keep the eastern passes open to the traders. Adad-nirari III (810–781 BC) claims to have conquered 'the land of the Medes and Parsua (Persia)', as did Tiglath-pileser III (743 BC) and Sargon II (716 BC). The latter transported Israelites to Media (2 Kings 17:6; 18:11) after he had overrun the part of the land ruled by Dayaukku (Deioces), whom he exiled for a time to Hamath.

*Independence*

Esarhaddon bound his Median vassals by treaty (*Iraq* 20, 1958, pp. 1–91), but they soon rebelled and joined the Scythians (Ashguza) and Cimmerians against the declining power of Assyria after 631 BC. Under Phraortes there began the open attacks which culminated in the fall of Nineveh (612 BC) and Harran (610 BC) to Kyaxares of Media and his Babylonian allies. The Medes controlled all lands to the north of Assyria and clashed with Lydia until peace was ratified in 585 BC.

*Conquered by Persia*

In 550 BC Cyrus of Anshan (see also *ELAM) defeated Astyages and brought Media under control, capturing the capital Ecbatana and adding 'King of the Medes' to his titles. Many Medes were given positions of responsibility and their customs and laws were combined with those of the Persians (Daniel 6:8, 15).

Media was sometimes used to denote Persia but more usually combined with it as a major part of the new confederation (Daniel 8:20; Esther 1:19). The Medes, according to the prophets Isaiah (13:17) and Jeremiah (51:11, 28), took part in the capture of Babylon (Daniel 5:28). The new ruler of Babylon, Darius, was called 'the Mede' (Daniel 11:1), being the son of Ahasuerus of Median origin (Daniel 9:1).

*Later history*

The Medes later rebelled under Darius I and II (409 BC). The history of the Jews in Media is recounted in Esther (1:3, 14, 18–19) and the Medians under Syrians (Seleucids) and Parthians are referred to in 1 Maccabees 14:1–3 and in Josephus, *Antiquities* 10.232. Media was organized as the 11th and 18th Satrapies. The Medes are mentioned, with the Parthians and Elamites, in Acts 2:9. After the Sassanids Media was used only as a geographical term.

D. J. Wiseman

*Further reading*

G. Widengren, *POTT*, pp. 313ff.

**MEGIDDO.** An important Old Testament city which lay in the Carmel range some 30 kilometres south-south-east of the modern port of Haifa.

**Biblical evidence**

The city of Megiddo (Hebrew *m$^e$ḡiddô*) is first mentioned among the cities which Joshua captured during his conquest of Palestine (Joshua 12:21) and was subsequently allotted to Manasseh in the territory of Issachar (Joshua 17:11; 1 Chronicles 7:29). Manasseh, however, did not destroy the Canaanites in the city, but put them to menial labour (Judges 1:28).

A curiously indirect reference is made to Megiddo in the Song of Deborah, where *Taanach is described as 'by the waters of Megiddo' (*'al-mê m$^e$ḡiddô*, Judges 5:19), but no mention of Megiddo a a city as opposed to the name of a watercourse is made (see also *KISHON).

The next reference to the city comes from the time of Solomon, when it was included in his fifth administrative district under Baan (the son of Ahilud) (1 Kings 4:12) an was selected, with Hazor and Gez to be one of his main fortified cities outside Jerusalem, in which he ha accommodation for chariots and horses (1 Kings 9:15–19).

Megiddo is briefly mentioned as the place where Ahaziah of Judah died after being wounded in his flight from Jehu (2 Kings 9:27), and was later the scene of the death of Josiah when he tried to prevent Neco of Egypt from going to the ai of Assyria (2 Kings 23:29–30; 2 Chronicles 35:22, 24).

The name occurs in the form *m$^e$ḡiddôn* in Zechariah (12:11), and is this form which is used in the Ne Testament *Armageddon (Revelation 16:16), from *har-m$^e$ḡiddôn*, 'hill of Megiddo'.

**Extra-biblical sources**

*Excavations*

The site of ancient Megiddo has been identified with the modern deserted mound of Tell el-Mutesellim, which lies on the nort side of the Carmel ridge and commands the most important pas from the coastal plain to the valley Esdraelon. The tell stands nearly 2 metres high, with an area on the summit of over 4 hectares, and the earlier cities lower down in the mound were still larger than this.

The first excavations were carri out by a German expedition under Schumacher from 1903 to 1905. A trench was cut across the top of th mound, and a number of buildings were found, but owing to the limit knowledge of pottery at the time little was learnt.

The site was not excavated agai until 1925, when the Oriental Institute of the University of Chicag under the direction of J. H. Breaste selected it as its first major project an ambitious scheme of excavatio all over the Near East. The work wa directed successively by C. S. Fish (1925–27), P. L. O. Guy (1927–35), and G. Loud (1935–39). The origin intention was to clear the entire mound, level by level, to the base, and to this end an area at the foot the slope was excavated at an earl stage to release it for the subseque dumping of earth from the tell. Wa brought the work to an end, and

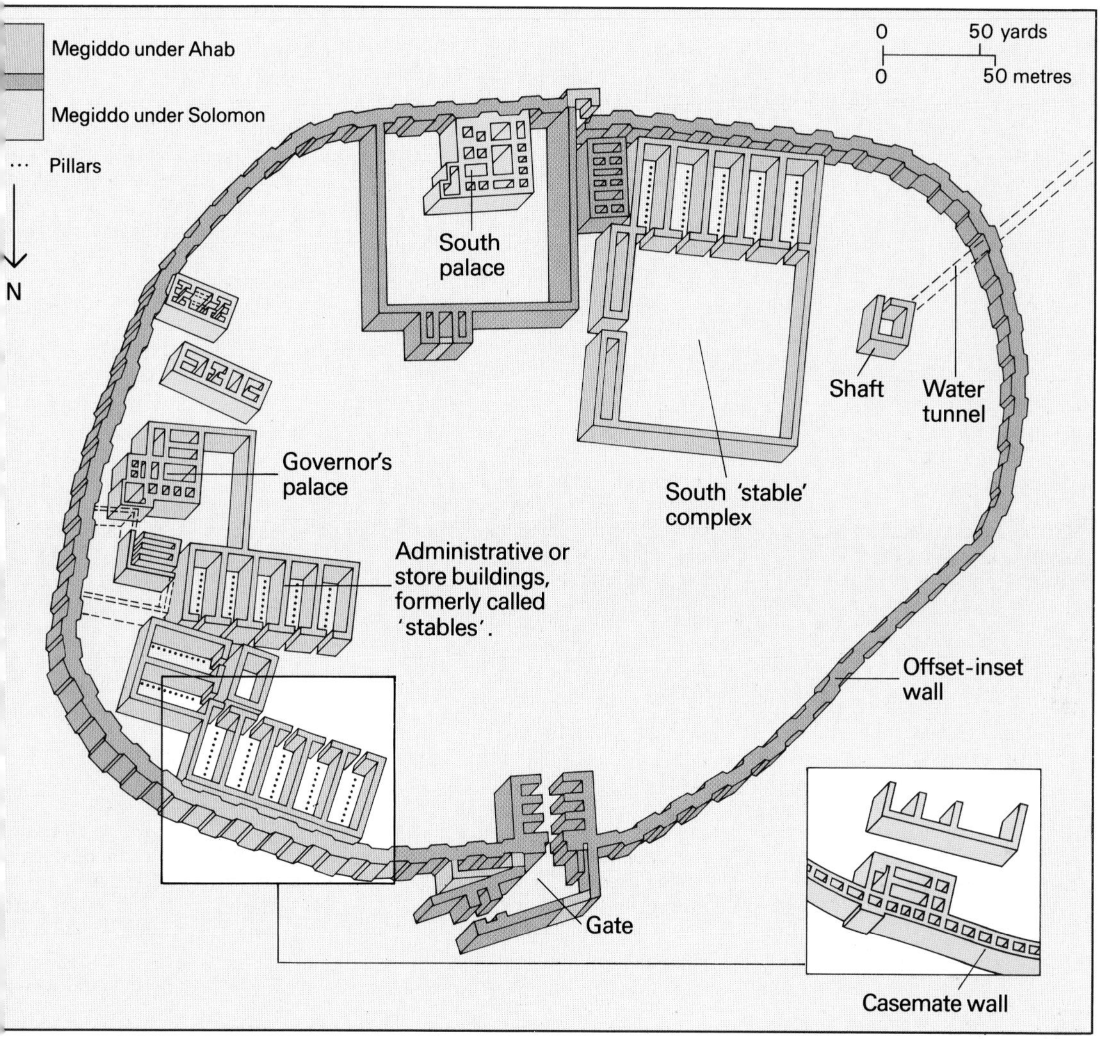


Megiddo, showing the excavated areas of the city in the times of Solomon and Ahab (Levels VA–IVB Solomon, IVA Ahab).

ough the lay-out of the entire city Iron Age times had been revealed, e earlier levels were known only in elatively small area.

Further excavations were carried t in 1960, 1966–67 and 1971 by Y. din to elucidate some problems tstanding from the previous mpaigns.

*rliest levels*

venty main occupation levels were entified, dating back to alcolithic settlements in the early n millennium (levels XX, XIX). An eresting feature of level XIX is a nall shrine with an altar in it. During the Early Bronze Age (3rd llennium) there was a consider-le city at Megiddo (levels 'III–XV), one interesting feature of ich was a circular platform of ulders approached by a flight of ps, which was covered with animal nes and broken pottery. It may be at this was a *bāmâ* or 'high place'. This platform continued in use in e Middle Bronze Age (levels XIV–X; first half of the 2nd millennium), a period of Egyptian influence the start of which was marked by widespread rebuilding, when the circular platform became the nucleus of three megaron-shaped temples with altars. A fine triple-pierced gateway, of a type which originated in Mesopotamia, was also found in these levels, and the necessity of such strong gates was shown by the evidence of a number of major destructions in the latter part of the period, culminating in a great devastation probably to be connected with the Egyptian reconquest of Palestine following the expulsion of the Hyksos from Egypt.

*In the Late Bronze Age*

The evidences of periodical violence are less frequent in the Late Bronze Age (levels VIII, VIIB), and though this was a period of Egyptian domination the culture of Palestine reflected the Canaanite civilization of the north to a considerable extent. It was in this period that perhaps the most fully reported battle of antiquity was fought when Tuthmosis III routed an Asiatic coalition at Megiddo *c.* 1456 BC.

Architectural remains of this period include a temple, a palace and a gate, and the northern cultural influence is clearly seen in a great hoard of over 200 objects of carved ivory which was found in a subterranean treasury under the level VIIA palace. This is one of the earliest collections of a type of art which was well known in Iron Age times from *Samaria and from as far afield as Assyria, and though practically no examples have yet been discovered in Phoenicia it is probable that many of them were made either in Phoenician workshops or by expatriate Phoenician craftsmen. That there were contacts with Mesopotamia at this period is shown by the recent discovery on the edge of the mound of a fragment of the Babylonian Epic of Gilgamesh which can be dated by

Model of the city of Megiddo in the 1st millennium BC, showing storehouses, administrative buildings and gateway.

its cuneiform script to the 14th century BC.

*After the arrival of the Israelites*
A discovery, probably of the period of the Judges (Iron Age I), was the city water-supply systems. An unbuilt zone of the mound was excavated by a pit 37 metres deep, the bottom section of which consisted of a shaft with a staircase round its side, cut into the rock at the base. From the foot of the shaft, the staircase entered a tunnel which, finally levelling off, led some 50 metres farther on, into a cave with a spring of water at the far end. It appeared that this spring had originally (Level VIA) given on to the slope outside the city, but at a later period the tunnel had been cut from inside the city and the cave blocked and masked from the outside for strategic reasons.

Though there are signs of destruction towards the end of the 12th century, some time after the arrival of the Israelites, and evidence of a temporary abandonment following this destruction, the people responsible for resettling the mound (Level V) do not seem to have been Israelites. This would accord with the biblical statement that the inhabitants of Megiddo were not driven out at the time of the Conquest, and were later put to task work (Judges 1:27–28).

*During the Monarchy*
A number of cult objects, limestone horned incense altars, clay incense stands and braziers, from this and the following levels, are probably due to these Canaanites, who, contrary to God's command, were not destroyed. It is probably to the latter part of this and the beginning of the next level (VA–IVB) when the city was in Israelite hands that a six-chambered city gate and associated casemate wall are to be assigned, as Y. Yadin has shown. These are almost identical in plan with examples found at Hazor and Gezer, and are probably to be assigned to the time of Solomon, a fact which illuminates 1 Kings 9:15–19.

The pre-war excavations uncovered an extensive series of buildings which were identified as stables, capable of accommodating up to 450 horses, and the excavators connected these with Solomon, who was known to have instituted a chariot arm in his forces; but Yadin's investigations have shown that these buildings date from the latter part of level IV (IVA), which was probably rebuilt after the destruction of the Solomonic city by the Pharaoh Sheshonq (biblical Shishak). The stables (if that is what they were; some archaeologists now regard them as storehouses) are therefore very probably the work of Ahab, who is known from the Annals of Shalmaneser to have had a chariot force of 2,000 vehicles (probably a mistake for 200).

The final Israelite level (III) was probably destroyed in 733 BC by Tiglath-pileser III, when the city became the capital of an Assyrian province. With the decline in the fortunes of Assyria, this city (level came once more within the territor of Israel, and the defeat and death Josiah there in 609 BC is probably marked by its destruction.

The excavations at Megiddo hav shown what a formidable civilizatic the Israelites under Joshua had to encounter when they invaded the land.

T. C. Mitchell

*Further reading*

G. Schumacher and C. Steuernage *Tell el-Mutesellim* 1, *Fundbericht*, 1908
C. Watzinger, 2, *Die Funde*, 1929
R. S. Lamon and G. S. Shipton, *Megiddo I: Seasons of 1925–1934*, 1939
G. Loud, *Megiddo II: Seasons of 1935–1939*, 1948
H. G. May, *Material Remains of the Megiddo Cult*, 1935
P. L. O. Guy and R. M. Engberg, *Megiddo Tombs*, 1938
G. Loud, *The Megiddo Ivories*, 193
G. I. Davies, *Cities of the Biblical World. Megiddo*, 1986
W. F. Albright, *AJA* 53, 1949, pp. 213–215
G. E. Wright, *JAOS* 70, 1950, pp. 56–60
——, *BA* 13, 1950, pp. 28–46
Y. Yadin, *BA* 33, 1970, pp. 66–96
——, *Hazor* (Schweich Lectures, 1970), 1972, pp. 150–164
Mazar, *AOLOB*, pp. 476–478 (stables)
A. Goetze and S. Levy, 'Fragment the Gilgamesh Epic from Megiddo *'Atiqot* 2, 1959, pp. 121–128
*IDBS*, 1976, pp. 583–585
Y. Aharoni and Y. Shiloh in *NEAEF* III, pp. 1003–1024
Vogel, *HUCA* 42, 1971, pp. 59–60; 52, 1981, pp. 58–59
G. I. Davies, 'King Solomon's Stabl – Still at Megiddo?', *BARev* 20/1, Jan–Feb 1994, pp. 44–49
I. Finkelstein and D. Ussishkin, 'Ba to Megiddo', *ibid.*, pp. 26–43


**MEKONAH.** See *MECONAH.

**MELITA.** See *MALTA.

**MEMPHIS** (Egyptian *Mn-nfr*; Hebrew *Mōp̄* and *Nōp̄*). Situated o the west bank of the Nile, about 2 kilometres south of Cairo, Memph was a foundation of Menes, the pharaoh who united Upper and Lower Egypt, and was originally known as the 'White Fortress'. Th name *Mn-nfr* is short for that of th

**The pyramid of Djeser (Zoser), Memphis (Saqqara). Stages were added over the original mastaba (bench-tomb) to form this first stepped pyramid, 3rd Dynasty (Old Kingdom), c. 2686–2613 BC.**

menos of the pyramid of Pepi (*c.* 400 BC), *i.e. Pepi-mn-nfr*, meaning epi is Firm and Fair'.

Memphis was the capital of Egypt ıring the Old Kingdom. It remained ı important city up to the conquest y Alexander the Great (332 BC). The rincipal gods were Ptah, the emiurge, Sekhmet, Nefertem and okaris. The name *Hwt-k'-Ptḥ*, ıansion of the Ka of Ptah', is the igin of the name Egypt.

Very little remains of the city of the ving (the modern site of Mît-Rahîna); the necropolis is better ıown with the important ruins of ieser at Saqqara, the pyramid of jedefrê at Abu Rawash, the yramids of Kheops, Khephren and ykerinos at Gîza, and those of the h Dynasty at Abusîr.

Ramesses II, Merenptah and sammetichus pursued extensive uilding in the region. The temple is escribed by Herodotus (2.153), and riters of old describe the place here the living Apis bull was kept.

During the New Kingdom, as a onsequence of Asiatic immigration, e find that foreign gods, such as adesh, Astarte and Baal, were orshipped at Memphis.

The city was taken by the thiopians (Piankhy 730 BC), the ssyrians (Esarhaddon 671, shurbanipal 666) and the Persians Cambyses 525).

From the 7th century BC, colonies of foreigners established themselves in the place, and, after the destruction of Jerusalem, also Jews (Jeremiah 44:1). The city is mentioned several times by the prophets (Hosea 9:6; Isaiah 19:13; Jeremiah 2:16; 46:14, 19; Ezekiel 30:13, 16).

C. de Wit

*Further reading*

F. Petrie, *Memphis* 1, 2, 3, 1909–10

Kees, in *RE*, under 'Memphis'

Porter and Moss, *Topographical Bibliography* 3, 1931

**MEONENIM, OAK OF.** This is the RV rendering of the phrase *'ēlôn m^e'ôn^enîm* in Judges 9:37, which is translated 'plain of Meonenim' in the AV and 'Diviners' Oak' in the RSV. The word *m^e'ôn^enîm* is the intensive participle of the verb *'ānan*, 'to practise soothsaying', used, for instance, in 2 Kings 21:6 and 2 Chronicles 33:6 (RV 'observed times') and Leviticus 19:26, where the practice is forbidden. The participial form, meaning 'soothsayer' or 'diviner', occurs also in Deuteronomy 18:10 and 14 and in Micah 5:12 (13, Hebrew) but is treated only as a proper name by the AV and RV in the passage in Judges.

The reference is probably to a tree where Canaanite or apostate Israelite soothsayers carried out their business. The site is unknown.

T. C. Mitchell

**MEREMOTH.** See *ARAD.

**MEROM, WATERS OF** (Hebrew *mērôm*). Rendezvous of the Hazor confederacy against Joshua, who surprised and routed them there (Joshua 11:5, 7). A city called Merom is mentioned in the conquest-records of Tuthmosis III and Ramesses II, and of the Assyrian Tiglath-pileser (*ANET*, p. 283).

The site at Meiron has not yielded any remains from the period. Aharoni (*LOB*, pp. 225f.) proposed Tell el-Khirbeh, 3 kilometres south-south-west of Maroun er-Ras and 12 kilometres north of Meiron. This seems an unlikely place to concentrate an army; the 'Waters' may refer to the lower course of a river, and the battlefield may have been in the Huleh basin or even north-west of Lake Galilee, where a river drains the area beyond modern Meiron (Meirun), 5 kilometres west of Safad (Zefat).

J. P. U. Lilley

**MERONOTH, MERONOTHITE.** Jehdeiah (1 Chronicles 27:30) and Jadon (Nehemiah 3:7) were Meronothites. Nehemiah 3:7 seems to suggest that Meronoth was close to Gibeon and Mizpah, but Mizpah is a doubtful reading (*GTT*, p. 387). Grollenberg, in his *Atlas*, identifies it as Beitûniyeh, north-west of Gibeon, following earlier studies.

A. R. Millard

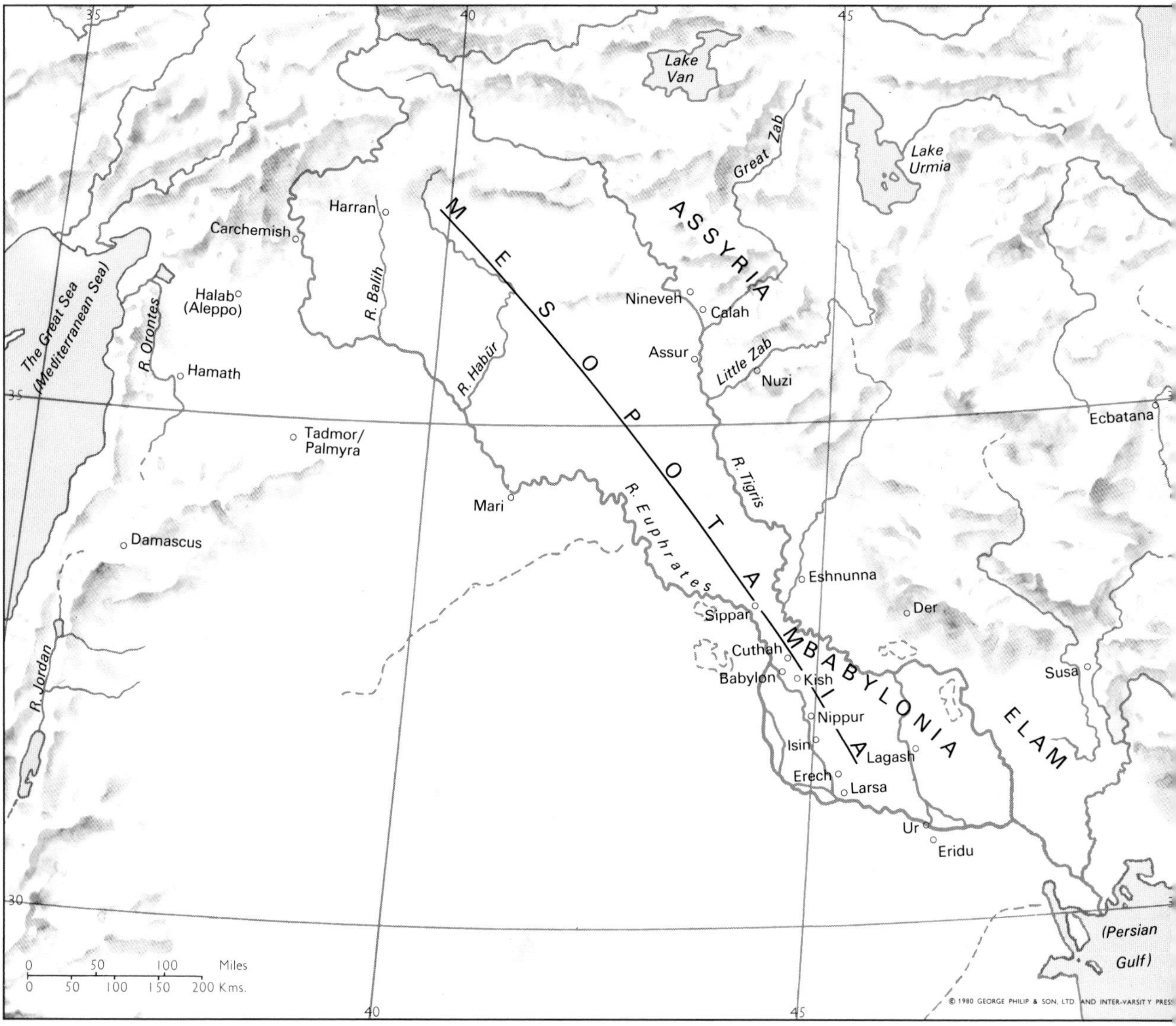

Mesopotamia.

**MEROZ** (Hebrew *mērôz*), in Judges 5:23 a town (doubtfully identified with Khirbet Maruṣ, near *Hazor) on which Deborah pronounces a curse for its failure to take part in the campaign against Sisera. The bitterness of the curse suggests that Meroz was under a sacred obligation to obey Barak's summons.
F. F. Bruce

**MESHA.** A place mentioned as the limit of the territory of the descendants of Joktan (Genesis 10:30), the other limit being *Sephar.

Some scholars would identify Mesha with *maśśā'* in northern Arabia, but the probable location of Sephar in southern Arabia suggests a similar locality for Mesha, though no place of that name has been suggested in that region.
T. C. Mitchell

**MESOPOTAMIA.** The Greek *Mesopotamia*, 'between the two rivers', is AV borrowing from the Septuagint to render the Hebrew *'ᵃram nahᵃrayim* (except in the title of Psalm 60). This was the fertile land east of the river Orontes covering the upper and middle Euphrates and the lands watered by the rivers Habur and Tigris, *i.e.* modern eastern Syria–northern Iraq. It includes Harran (to which Abraham moved after leaving Ur in Babylonia) and its surrounding townships, to which Eliezer was sent to find a wife for Isaac (Genesis 24:10).

Mesopotamia was the original home of Balaam (Deuteronomy 23:4; see also *PEOR) and was the country ruled by Cushan-rishathaim when he oppressed Israel (Judges 3:8–10).

In David's time Mesopotamia provided charioteers and horsemen to support his Ammonite opponents (1 Chronicles 19:6). This accords with the evidence for the occupation of this whole area by horse-rearing Indo-Aryan Mitanni and Hurrians i the 2nd millennium.

Greek and Roman writers after th 4th century BC extended the use of 'Mesopotamia' to describe the whol Tigris-Euphrates valley, that is, the modern state of Iraq. Thus Stephen referred to Abraham's original hom of Ur in Babylonia as in 'Mesopotamia, before he lived in Haran' (Acts 7:2).

The inclusion of Mesopotamians with Parthians, Medes and Elamite may indicate that the Jews of the Diaspora in Babylonia were presen in Jerusalem to hear Peter (Acts 2:9) Thus the New Testament follows th wider use of the geographical nam which is still adopted by some modern scholars.

See also *ARAM, *SYRIA, and for th history of the region *ASSYRIA and *BABYLONIA.
D. J. Wiseman

*ırther reading*
J. Finkelstein, *JNES* 21, 1962, ). 73–92

**ETHEG-AMMAH.** Apparent xtual corruption in 2 Samuel 8:1 akes this name difficult to ıderstand. No certainty seems )ssible, and at least three ternative interpretations present emselves.

That it is a place-name, evidently ear Gath in the Philistine plain (see ill of Ammah', 2 Samuel 2:24).

That the RV translation, 'the bridle the mother city', be preferred – *i.e.* garding it as a figurative name for ath, a chief city of the Philistines ee 1 Chronicles 18:1).

That the Septuagint be followed ıd the verse rendered as 'and David ok the tribute out of the hand of the ıilistines'.

D. Douglas

**ICHMASH, MICHMAS.** A city of enjamin east of Bethel and 12 lometres north of Jerusalem, 600 etres above sea-level, on the pass om Bethel to Jericho. In Geba, just )uth of this pass, Jonathan made a successful foray against the Philistine garrison (1 Samuel 13:3), whereupon the Philistines gathered a large well-equipped army and occupied Michmash, causing the scattered flight of the Hebrews (13:5ff.). Thereafter Saul's army camped at Geba (or Gibeah) with the Philistines on the other side of the pass (13:23).

Unknown to Saul, Jonathan and his armour-bearer descended from Geba and, ascending the southern slope, surprised the Philistines and caused confusion in the enemy camp (for a description of this feat, see S. R. Driver, *Notes on the Hebrew Text of the Books of Samuel*, 2nd edition, 1913, p. 106; see also J. M. Miller, *CBQ* 36, 1974, pp. 157–174). Aided by Hebrew prisoners who had been in Philistine hands, by refugees from the previous defeat and by Saul's army, they put the Philistines to rout (1 Samuel 14:1ff.).

In his prophetic description of the coming attack on Jerusalem Isaiah (10:24, 28) represents the taking of Michmash by the Assyrians. After the Exile members of the Jewish community lived in Michmash (Ezra 2:27; Nehemiah 7:31; 11:31), and it was later the residence of Jonathan Maccabaeus (1 Maccabees 9:73).

It is probably the present Mukhmâs, a ruined village on the northern ridge of the Wadi Suweinit, though the paucity of finds there has led to the alternative suggestion that it lay 1 kilometre farther north, at Khirbet el-Hara el-Fawqa.

J. D. Douglas

**MIDIANITES.** They consisted of five families, linked to Abraham through Midian, son of the concubine Keturah. Abraham sent them away, with all his other sons by concubines, into the east (Genesis 25:1–6). Thus the Midianites are found inhabiting desert borders in Transjordan from Moab down past Edom.

They were desert-dwellers associated with Ishmaelites and Medanites (Genesis 37:28, 36) when Joseph was sold into Egypt; for the partial overlap of these three terms, see Judges 8:24, where the Midianites defeated by Gideon are said to have been Ishmaelites because of their use of gold ear- or

The river Euphrates flowing through Eastern Syria, part of Mesopotamia.

nose-rings. Moses had a Midianite wife, Zipporah, father-in-law, Jethro/Reuel (Exodus 2:21; 3:1, *etc.*), and brother-in-law, Hobab (Numbers 10:29; Judges 4:11). As a man of the desert, Hobab was asked by Moses to guide Israel in travelling through the steppe (or 'wilderness') (Numbers 10:29–32).

Later, in the plains of Moab, the chiefs of Midian and Moab combined in hiring Balaam to curse Israel (Numbers 22ff.) and their people led Israel into idolatry and immorality (Numbers 25), and so had to be vanquished (Numbers 25:16–18; 31). The five princes of Midian were confederates of the Amorite king Sihon (Joshua 13:21).

In the time of the judges, through Gideon and his puny band (Judges 6–8; 9:17), God delivered Israel from the scourge of camel-riding Midianites, Amalekites and other 'children of the east', an event remembered by psalmist and prophet (Psalm 83:9; Isaiah 9:4; 10:26). This is at present the earliest-known reference to full-scale use of camels in warfare (W. F. Albright, *Archaeology and the Religion of Israel*, 1953, pp. 132–133), but by no means the first occurrence of domesticated camels (see W. G. Lambert, *BASOR* 160, 1960, pp. 42–43 for indirect Old Babylonian evidence, and M. Ripinski, *JEA* 71, 1985, pp. 134–141 for Egyptian evidence).

The dromedaries of Midian recur in Isaiah 60:6. In Habakkuk 3:7 Midian is put in parallel with Cushan, an ancient term that probably goes back to *Kushu* mentioned in Egyptian texts of *c.* 1800 BC (see W. F. Albright, *BASOR* 83, 1941, p. 34, note 8; compare G. Posener, *Princes et Pays d'Asie et de Nubie*, 1940, p. 88, and B. Maisler, *Revue d'Histoire Juive en Égypte* 1, 1947, pp. 37–38).

*'Midianite' pottery*

During the 13th to early 11th centuries BC, we have one possible trace of the Midianites in their general area: pottery known as Qurayyah ware, and sometimes called 'Midianite' pottery. It is known from sites in the Arabah valley between Sinai and Edom, up to the Dead Sea, in eastern and western Palestine, and (going back southwards) especially at the type site of Qurayyah in north-western Arabia, where kilns for its manufacture were found (on this site, see P. J. Parr and others, *Bulletin, Institute of Archaeology, University of London* 8/9, 1969/70, pp. 219–241).

At the mining site of Timnah, 'Midianite' pottery is associated with the Egyptian occupation of the 13th/12th centuries BC, followed by Midianite occupation, when a tent-shrine or 'tabernacle' was erected there (on which, see B. Rothenberg, *Timna*, 1972, pp. 152, 184; for a fuller treatment, see B. Rothenberg and others, *The Egyptian Mining Temple at Timna*, 1988, pp. 272–273, 277–278).

K. A. Kitchen

*Further reading*

For discussions of the 'Midianite' pottery:

P. J. Parr in D. T. Potts (ed.), *Araby the Blest*, Copenhagen, 1988, pp. 73–89

——, in P. Bienkowski (ed.), *Early Edom and Moab*, 1992, pp. 41–46, following on from:

P. J. Parr in A. Hadidi (ed.), *Studies in the History and Archaeology of Jordan* 1, 1982, pp. 127–133

B. Rothenberg, J. Glass, in J. F. A. Sawyer, D. J. A. Clines (eds.), *Midian, Moab and Edom*, 1983, pp. 65–124 and map (p. 70)

**MIGDOL.** The name is used of a Canaanite fort. It is mentioned as a place-name in Exodus 14:2, Numbers 33:7, Jeremiah 44:1, 46:14, Ezekiel 29:10 and 30:6.

Several Migdols were built in the neighbourhood of the Egyptian border, but none of them can be accurately located. The Migdol of the Prophets, in the north of Egypt (possibly at Tell el-Her), is different from that farther south, but still in the eastern Delta (P. Anastasi V), which is probably the Migdol of Succoth (Old Egyptian *ṯkw*).

The Migdol in the north may be the Magdolum of *Itinerarium Antonini*, 12 Roman miles from Pelusium.

C. de Wit

**MIGRON. 1.** A place mentioned in 1 Samuel 14:2 situated on the outskirts of Saul's home at Gibeah, where he remained during the first stage of the Philistine invasion after his election as king. It is possibly to be located at Tell Maryam, 1 kilometre south-west of *Michmash.

**2.** A locality mentioned in the march of the Assyrian army in Isaiah 10:28. It may be the same as **1**, or it could be an ancient name for the Wadi Suweinit (see P. M. Arnold, *ABD* 4, pp. 822–823).

J. D. Douglas

**MILETUS.** The most southerly of the great Ionian (Greek) cities on the western coast of Asia Minor. It flourished as a commercial centre, and in the 8th, 7th and 6th centuries BC established many colonies in the Black Sea area and also had contact with Egypt.

Pharaoh Neco dedicated an offering in a Milesian temple after his victory at Megiddo in 608 BC (2 Kings 23:29; 2 Chronicles 35:20ff.). The Milesians resisted the expansion of Lydia, and in 499 BC initiated the Ionian revolt against Persia, but their city was destroyed in 494 BC.

In its period of great prosperity Miletus was the home of the first Greek philosophers Thales, Anaximander and Anaximenes, and of Hecataeus the chronicler. Its woollen goods were world famous.

After its Persian destruction the city had many vicissitudes, and when Paul called there on the way to Jerusalem and summoned the Ephesian elders (Acts 20:15; 2 Timothy 4:20) it was largely living on its past glories. It had long been part of the Roman province of Asia. Due to the silting up of its harbour (nowadays an inland lake) by deposits from the river Maeander it was declining commercially.

An inscription in the ruins shows the place reserved in the stone theatre for Jews and 'god-fearing' people.

K. L. McKay

**MILLO.** A place-name derived from the verb *mālē'*, 'to be full', 'to fill'. It is used in Judges 9:6 and 20 of a place near Shechem, the 'house of Millo', perhaps a fortress; but its principal use is in connection with *Jerusalem where it evidently formed part of the Jebusite city, for it was already in existence in the time of David (2 Samuel 5:9 and 1 Chronicles 11:8).

Millo was rebuilt by Solomon (1 Kings 9:15, 24; 11:27; the 'breach' here referred to was probably a different thing) as part of his programme of strengthening the kingdom, and was again strengthened some 2½ centuries later when Hezekiah was preparing for the Assyrian invasion (2 Chronicles 32:5). This verse is taken by some to indicate that Millo was another name for the whole city of David, but it can very plausibly be connected with a system of terraces consisting of retaining walls with levelled filling, discovered by Kathleen Kenyon on the eastern slope of Ophel Hill at Jerusalem and excavated more thoroughly since 1978 by Yigal Shiloh. These terraces provided space for the construction of buildings on the slope.

The Baths of Faustina, Miletus.

Millo is otherwise mentioned as the ace where Joash was murdered (2 ngs 12:20). The Septuagint usually anslates Millo by the name Akra, ıt this was a Maccabean structure ıd therefore did not exist in the Old estament period.

C. Mitchell

*ırther reading*
Simons, *Jerusalem in the Old estament*, 1952, pp. 131–144
M. Kenyon, *Digging Up rusalem*, 1974, pp. 100–103
Shiloh, *Excavations at the City of avid* I, 1984, pp. 16–17, 25–27

**INAEANS.** The people of the ngdom of Ma'īn which flourished south-western Arabia (in the orth of modern Yemen) in the 1st illennium BC. The name is that of a ibe which became dominant in a ate known from inscriptions to ave been established with arnāwu as its capital by about 400 . It was active in establishing trade nks with the north, having colonies ong the Red Sea coastal route to alestine, the best known being Dedan.

Late in the 1st century BC Ma'īn as absorbed by the expansion of its outhern neighbour Saba (see also SHEBA, **2**) and its northern colonies st their Minaean identity to the abataeans.

The name does not occur with ertainty anywhere in the Bible, ough some scholars would see it in udges 10:12 (Maonites); Chronicles 4:41 (AV 'habitation'); Chronicles 20:1 (altering mmonites); 2 Chronicles 26:7 Mehunims); or Ezra 2:50 and ehemiah 7:52 (Mehunim). (See also MAON; *ARABIA.)

C. Mitchell

*Further reading*
J. A. Montgomery, *Arabia and the Bible*, 1934, pp. 60–61, 133–138, 182–184
S. Moscati, *Ancient Semitic Civilizations*, 1957, pp. 184–194
F. V. Winnett, *BASOR* 73, 1939, pp. 3–9 (old but still useful)
G. Garbini, *Inscrizioni Sudarabiche*, I, *Inscrizioni Minee*, 1974
A. F. L. Beeston, *Sabaic Grammar*, 1984, pp. 58–64

**MINNI.** A people summoned by Jeremiah, with Ararat (Armenia) and Ashkenaz, to make war on Babylonia (Jeremiah 51:27). The Mannai, whose territory lay south-east of Lake Urmia, are frequently named in texts of the 9th–7th centuries BC. The Assyrians dominated them until 673 BC, when they were controlled by the Medes (verse 28).

In the light of Jeremiah, it is interesting to note that the Mannai were allied with the Assyrians, their former enemies, against the Babylonians in 616 BC (Babylonian Chronicle). They were probably present with the Guti and other hill-folk at the capture of Babylon in 539 BC.

D. J. Wiseman

**MINNITH** (Hebrew *minnîṯ*). It is mentioned in Judges 11:33 as the limit of Jepthah's invasion of Ammon. Eusebius (*Onomasticon*) indicates that it lay at the head of a natural route from the Jordan to the uplands between Rabbath-Ammon (Amman) and Heshbon. The exact site is unknown.

Ezekiel 27:17 may refer to the same place, though the text requires some emendation; renderings such as 'olives' are conjectural. Zimmerli, *Ezekiel* (Fortress, 1983), suggests that the name might have become an attribute of quality.

J. P. U. Lilley

**MISREPHOTH-MAIM** (Hebrew *miśrᵉp̄ôṯ mayim*, 'burnings of waters'). A limit of pursuit from the battle at the Waters of *Merom (Joshua 11:8); formerly the southern border of Sidon (Joshua 13:6). It is usually identified with the headland Rosh Haniqra at the northern end of the Acre plain; if so, Khirbet el-Musheirifeh to the south preserved the name. It has no Late Bronze/Iron remains (*LOB*, p. 238; R. Amiran, *IEJ* 2, 1952, p. 142); but the text does not imply a settlement.

There is a Khirbet el-Musheirifeh near the southern end of Lake Huleh, by a wadi of the same name and close to Hazor, but this hardly suits the context of Joshua 13:6.

J. P. U. Lilley

**MITYLENE.** An ancient republic of the Aeolian Greeks and the principal state of the island of Lesbos. Its situation at the cross-roads of Europe and Asia frequently placed its political fortunes in jeopardy, until under the pax Romana it settled down as an honoured subordinate, highly favoured by the Romans as a holiday resort.

A capacious harbour facing the mainland of Asia Minor across the straits made it a natural overnight stop for Paul's vessel on the southern run to Palestine (Acts 20:14).

E. A. Judge

*Further reading*
R. Herbst, *RE*, 16.2.1411

**MIZAR.** A hill mentioned in Psalm 42:6, in connection with Mount Hermon. It may be presumed that Hermon was visible from it; in which case it would have been in the Galilee region – note the reference to the Jordan.

The word in Hebrew (*miṣ'ār*) means 'smallness'. Some scholars emend the text of Psalm 42:6 slightly, making *miṣ'ār* an adjective, 'small', referring to Mount Zion. In this case the psalmist would be stating his preference for Zion rather than Hermon's great bulk.

D. F. Payne

**MIZPAH, MIZPEH.** The basic meaning of the word is 'watch-tower', 'place for watching'. It is vocalized as *miṣpâ* and *miṣpeh*, and is found usually with the article. It is natural to look for places so named on high vantage-points. The following may be distinguished:

**1.** The place where Jacob and Laban made a covenant and set up a cairn of stones as a witness (Galeed, *gal'ēḏ* in Hebrew, or *y$^{e}$ḡar śāh$^{a}$ḏûṯā'* in Aramaic). God was the watcher between them (Genesis 31:44–49).

**2.** Either the same place as **1** or a town in Gilead, east of the Jordan. The article is used both in Genesis 31:49 (*hammiṣpâ*) and in Judges 10:17, 11:11 and 34. The place features in the story of Jephthah. When Ammon encroached on Gilead the Israelites assembled at Mizpah (Judges 10:17), the home of Jephthah, from which he commenced his attack and to which he returned to carry out his rash vow (Judges 11:11, 29, 34).

Its identification with Ramoth-gilead is urged by some writers (J. D. Davis, *Westminster Dictionary of the Bible*, p. 401), but is rejected by F. M. Abel and du Buit, who identify it with Jal'ûd. It is possibly the same as Ramath-mizpeh or height of Mizpeh (Joshua 13:26).

**3.** A place in Moab to which David took his parents for safety (1 Samuel 22:3), possibly the modern Rujm el-Meshrefeh, west-south-west of Madaba.

**4.** A place at the foot of Mount Hermon (Joshua 11:3), referred to as 'the land of Mizpeh' or 'the valley of Mizpeh' (verse 8), the home of the Hivites. Opinions differ as to its identification, but Qal'at eṣ-Ṣubeibeh on a hill 3 kilometres north-east of Banias has much support.

**5.** A town in the Shephelah (lowlands) of Judah named along with Joktheel, Lachish and Eglon (Joshua 15:38–39). The sites of Khirbet Ṣāfiyeh, 4 kilometres north-east of Beit Jibrin, and Ṣufiyeh, 10 kilometres to the north, are possible choices for this Mizpeh.

**6.** A town of Benjamin (Joshua 18:26), in the neighbourhood of Gibeon and Ramah (1 Kings 15:22). In the days of the Judges, when the Benjaminites of Gibeah outraged the Levite's concubine, the men of Israel assembled here (Judges 20:1, 3; 21:1, 5, 8). Here Samuel assembled Israel for prayer after the ark had been restored to Kiriath-jearim (1 Samuel 7:5–6). The Philistines attacked them, but were driven back (verses 7, 11), and Samuel erected a stone of remembrance near by at Ebenezer (verse 12). Here also Saul was presented to the people as their king (1 Samuel 10:17). Mizpeh was one of the places visited by Samuel annually to judge Israel (1 Samuel 7:16).

King Asa fortified Mizpeh against Baasha of Israel, using materials his men took from Baasha's fort at Ramah, after Asa had asked the Syrian Ben-hadad to attack Israel (1 Kings 15:22; 2 Chronicles 16:6).

After the destruction of Jerusalem by Nebuchadrezzar in 587 BC, Gedaliah was appointed governor of the remainder of the people, the governor's residence being fixed at Mizpeh (2 Kings 25:23, 25). The prophet Jeremiah, released by Nebuzaradan, the captain of the guard, joined Gedaliah at Mizpeh (Jeremiah 40:6), and refugee Jews soon returned (Jeremiah 40:8, 10, 12–13, 15).

Soon after, Ishmael of the royal seed slew Gedaliah and the garrison at the instigation of Baalis, king of Ammon. Two days later he murdered a company of pilgrims and threw their bodies into the great cistern Asa had built. He imprisoned others and sought to carry them to Ammon, but was frustrated by Johanan (Jeremiah 41:1, 3, 6, 10, 14, 16).

Two references to a Mizpah in post-exilic times occur in Nehemiah 3:15 and 19. It is possible that one or both of these refer to Mizpah of Benjamin, though they may represent different places.

Mizpah was the scene of an important assembly in the days when Judas Maccabaeus called the men of Judah together for counsel and prayer (1 Maccabees 3:46), 'because Israel formerly had a place of prayer in Mizpah'.

Two identifications are offered today – Nebi Samwil 7 kilometres north-west of Jerusalem, 895 metres above sea-level and 150 metres above the surrounding country, and Tell en-Nasbeh on the top of an isolated hill about 13 kilometres north of Jerusalem. The evidence in favour of Tell en-Nasbeh is stronger than for Nebi Samwil, because it can be seen how the consonants *mzph* could become *nzbh* phonetically and the archaeological evidence supports the identification.

The site itself is ancient and was occupied in the Early Bronze Age, to judge from tombs in the area. It seems to have been deserted in the Middle and Late Bronze periods but was re-occupied in the Iron I period and continued during the years *c.* 110–400 BC, so that it belongs to the period of Israelite settlement. In the days of the kings and during the Persian period the town was prosperous, as the relatively rich tombs suggest.

Prosperity is also suggested by architectural remains, the massive gate, a large number of cisterns and silos, some dye-plants, numerous spinning-whorls, loom-weights, wine and oil presses, pottery, beads of semi-precious stones, pins, bangles and metal jewellery. The city expanded beyond its walls during the Iron II period, but began to decline in the 5th century BC. Fragments of Greek pottery in the later city suggest trade with the Aegean areas. Numerous epigraphic discoveries, scarabs, stamped jar handles bearing the letters *MṢH* and *MṢP* (*i.e.* Miṣpah), a cuneiform inscription bearing the words *šar kiššati*, 'king of the universe', dating to the period *c.* 800–650 BC, and a beautiful seal bearing the inscription *ly'znyhw 'bd hmlk*, 'belonging to Jaazaniah, slave of the king', all attest the importance of the town.

J. A. Thompson

*Further reading*

F. M. Abel, *Géographie de la Palestine* 2, 1933, pp. 388–390

*LOB, passim*

D. Diringer, 'Mizpah', in *AOTS*, pp. 329–342

C. C. McCowan, *Excavations at Tell En-Nasbeh*, 2 vols., 1947

**MIZRAIM. 1.** *miṣrayim* is the regular Hebrew (and common Semitic) term for Egypt. For details on this name, see *EGYPT (Name).

**2.** In 1 Kings 10:28–29, it is possible to argue that the first *miṣrayim* is not Egypt but a land Muṣur in south-eastern Asia Minor and to render (modifying RSV) 'Solomon's import of horses was from Muṣur and from Que' (Cilicia), but this would require the *miṣrayim* of 2 Chronicles 9:28 to be taken also as Muṣur and not Egypt. It is perhaps better to render *miṣrayim* as Egypt in these two passages as in all other Old Testament references.

K. A. Kitchen

*Further reading*

P. Garelli, *Muṣur*, in *DBS* 5, fascicle 29, 1957, columns 1468–1474

H. Tadmor, 'Que and Muṣri', *IEJ* 11, 1961, pp. 143–150

**MOAB, MOABITES.** Moab (Hebrew *mô'āḇ*) was the son of Lot by incestuous union with his eldest daughter (Genesis 19:37). Both the descendants and the land were known as Moab, and the people also as Moabites (*mô'āḇî*).

The core of Moab was the plateau east of the Dead Sea between the wadis Arnon and Zered, though for considerable periods Moab extended well to the north of the rnon. The average height of the lateau is 100 metres, but it is cut by eep gorges. The Arnon itself ivides about 21 kilometres from the ead Sea and several times more arther east into valleys of iminishing depth, the 'valleys of the rnon' (Numbers 21:14). The Bible as preserved the names of many loabite towns (Numbers 21:15, 20; 2:3; Joshua 13:17–20; Isaiah 5–16; Jeremiah 48:20ff.).

*istory*

loab was occupied and had settled illages from the Early Bronze Age nwards. Nelson Glueck's theory hat there was a gap in sedentary ccupation from about 1900 BC until he 13th century BC must now be bandoned in the light of ubsequent surveys and excava-ions. Occupation was continuous hroughout the Bronze Age and into he Iron Age. Lot's descendants ound a population already there, nd must have intermarried with hem to emerge at length as the ominant group who gave their ame to the whole population.

The Moabites overflowed their nain plateau and occupied areas orth of the Arnon, destroying the ormer inhabitants (Deuteronomy :10–11, 19–21; see Genesis 14:5). 'hese lands were shared with the losely related Ammonites.

Just prior to the Exodus, these ands north of the Arnon were vrested from Moab by Sihon, king of he Amorites. When Israel sought ermission to travel along 'the ing's Highway' which crossed the lateau, Moab refused (Judges 1:17). They may have had ommercial contact (Deuteronomy :28–29). Moses was forbidden to ttack Moab despite their nfriendliness (Deuteronomy 2:9), lthough Moabites were henceforth o be excluded from Israel Deuteronomy 23:3–6; Nehemiah 3:1).

Balak, king of Moab, distressed by ne Israelite successes, called for the rophet Balaam to curse Israel now ettled across the Arnon (Numbers 2–24; Joshua 24:9).

As Israel prepared to cross the ordan, they camped in the 'plains of loab' (Numbers 22:1; Joshua 3:1) nd were seduced by Moabite and lidianite women to participate in lolatrous practices (Numbers 25; osea 9:10).

In the days of the Judges, Eglon, ing of Moab, invaded Israelite lands s far as Jericho and oppressed srael for 18 years. Ehud the enjaminite assassinated him (Judges 3:12–30). Elimelech of Bethlehem migrated to Moab and his sons married Moabite women, Orpah and Ruth. Ruth later married Boaz and became the ancestress of David (Ruth 4:18–22; Matthew 1:5–16).

Saul warred with the Moabites (1 Samuel 14:47) and David lodged his parents there while he was a fugitive (1 Samuel 22:3–4). Later David subdued Moab and set apart many Moabites for death (2 Samuel 8:2, 12; 1 Chronicles 18:2, 11). After Solomon's death, Moab broke free, but was subdued by Omri of Israel (as we learn from the Moabite Stone).

Towards the close of Ahab's life Moab began to break free again under the leadership of Mesha. Jehoram of Israel sought the help of Jehoshaphat, king of Judah, and the king of Edom to regain Moab, but the campaign was abortive (2 Kings 1:1; 3:4–27). Later, Jehoshaphat's own land was invaded by a confederacy of Moabites, Ammonites and Edomites, but confusion broke out and the allies attacked one another so that Judah was delivered (2 Chronicles 20:1–30).

In the year of Elisha's death, bands of Moabites raided Israel (2 Kings 13:20). During the latter part of the 8th century BC Moab was subdued by Assyria and compelled to pay tribute (Isaiah 15–16), but after Assyria fell Moab was free again. Moabites entered Judah in the days of Jehoiakim (2 Kings 24:2).

At the fall of Jerusalem in 587 BC some Jews found refuge in Moab, but returned when Gedaliah became governor (Jeremiah 40:11ff.). Moab was finally subdued by Nebuchad-rezzar (Josephus, *Antiquities* 10.181) and fell successively under the control of the Persians and various Arab groups. The Moabites ceased to have independent existence as a nation, though in post-exilic times they were known as a race (Ezra 9:1; Nehemiah 13:1, 23). Alexander Jannaeus subdued them in the 2nd century BC (Josephus, *Antiquities* 13.374).

In the prophets they are often mentioned and divine judgment pronounced on them (see Isaiah 15–16; 25:10; Jeremiah 9:26; 25:21; 27:3; Ezekiel 25:8–11; Amos 2:1–3; Zephaniah 2:8–11).

*Archaeology*

The archaeological story of Moab is slowly being unravelled. Excavation in Jordan has not proceeded as rapidly as it has in areas to the west of the Jordan, although in recent decades the programme has been increased. Important sites which have yielded significant results are Dibon, Aroer, Bab edh-Dhra and several sites in the area of the Lisan.

Our knowledge of Moab in early archaeological periods has been greatly expanded with new information about the transition between the Chalcolithic and the Early Bronze Ages. At Bab edh-Dhra a vast cemetery of the Early Bronze Age has provided material from EB I to EB IV. Aroer and Dibon were typical of important Iron Age walled settlements contemporary with the period of the kings of Israel. At Dibon the important Moabite (or Mesha) Stone was discovered.

A small fragment of a Moabite stele was found on the surface of the mound in 1950, probably antedating the Moabite Stone by a few decades but there was not sufficient writing preserved to permit a reading. But it provided evidence that there were evidently other inscriptions in Moab than the Moabite Stone.

Two other fragmentary texts have been discovered, at Khirbet Bālū' and Kerak. The latter refers to a king of Moab who may be the father and predecessor of Mesha. Excavation has been carried on at several other sites in Moab, including Heshbon. Sedentary life in these sites declined from the end of the 6th century BC down to the end of the 4th century.

J. A. Thompson

*Further reading*


F. M. Abel, *Géographie de la Palestine* 1, 1933, pp. 278–281

M. du Buit, *Géographie de la Terre Sainte*, 1958, pp. 142–143

N. Glueck, *The Other Side of Jordan*, 1940, pp. 150ff.

——, *AASOR* 14–15, 18–19

G. L. Harding, *The Antiquities of Jordan*, 1967

A. D. Tushingham, *The Excavations at Dibon (Dhiban) in Moab, AASOR* 40, 1972

A. H. van Zyl, *The Moabites*, 1960

J. R. Bartlett, 'The Moabites and Edomites', in *POTT*, pp. 229–258

N. Avigad, 'Ammonite and Moabite Seals', in J. A. Sanders (ed.), *Near Eastern Archaeology in the Twentieth Century*, 1970, pp. 284–295

J. M. Miller, 'Recent Archaeological Developments Relevant to Ancient Moab,' in A. Hadidi (ed.), *Studies in the History and Archaeology of Jordan* I, Amman, 1982, pp. 169–173

P. Bienkowski (ed.), *Early Edom and Moab*, 1992


**MOLADAH** (Hebrew *moladah*). A town in southern Judah (Joshua

15:26), Simeonite before David's reign (Joshua 19:2; 1 Chronicles 4:28). It was occupied by returning Judahite exiles (Nehemiah 11:26).

The later Idumaean fortress Malatha and the Roman headquarters Moleatha, known to Eusebius as Malaatha, may have been Tell el-Milh, Tel Malhata (20 kilometres east of Beersheba), but this is now thought to have been *Arad (see also *HORMAH) of the Canaanites rather than Moladah. J. Simons, *GTT*, p. 144, favours Quseife, Hurvat Kasif; but Aharoni, in *LOB*, pp. 261 and 439, tentatively suggests Khirbet el-Waten, Hurvat Yittan, 12 kilometres east of Beersheba.
J. P. U. Lilley

**MOREH** (Hebrew *mōreh*, 'teacher', 'diviner'). **1.** The name of a place near Shechem mentioned in Genesis 12:6, where *'ēlôn mōreh* may be translated 'the teacher's oak' (or 'terebinth'). Deuteronomy 11:30 makes reference to the 'oak of Moreh' in the district of Gilgal (*i.e.* the Shechemite Gilgal). It is recorded that Abraham pitched his camp there on arriving in Canaan from Harran, and it was there that God revealed himself to Abraham, promising to give the land of Canaan to his descendants (see also *MAMRE).

This tree may also be the one mentioned in Genesis 35:4 where Jacob hid foreign gods, and a reference to the place also occurs in the story of Abimelech (Judges 9:37).

**2.** The hill of Moreh at the head of the northern side of the valley of Jezreel, south of Mount Tabor, 2 kilometres south of Nain, and *c.* 13 kilometres north-west of Mount Gilboa, is the modern Jebel Dahi; it features in Judges 7:1, where, in the encounter between Gideon and the Midianites, the Midianites encamped in the valley, by the hill of Moreh, to the north of Gideon's camp by the spring of Harod.
R. A. H. Gunner, F. F. Bruce

**MORESHETH-GATH.** Home-town of the prophet Micah (Micah 1:1; Jeremiah 26:18) near the Philistine territory of Gath (Micah 1:14); probably the modern Tell ej-Judeideh, 32 kilometres south-west of Jerusalem and 10 kilometres north-east of Lachish. Surveys have revealed pottery of the Early Bronze, Iron I, Iron II, Persian and later periods.

Moresheth-gath (Micah 1:14) is one of twelve cities listed by the prophet Micah, whose names are by word-play associated with the form of their imminent judgment through invasion. Lachish, so to speak, will have to give a parting bridal-gift or dowry (compare 1 Kings 9:16) to Moresheth (*môrešeṯ*, which sounds like *m$^{e}$'ôrešeṯ*, betrothed), as that city is lost to the enemy.
N. Hillyer

**MORIAH.** In Genesis 22:2 God commanded Abraham to take Isaac to 'the land of Moriah' (*'ereṣ hammōriyyâ*) and there to offer him as a burnt offering upon one of the mountains (*har*). The mountain chosen was three days' journey (22:4) from the land of the Philistines (21:34; the region of *Gerar), and was visible from a distance (22:4).

The only other mention of the name occurs in 2 Chronicles 3:1, where the site of Solomon's temple is said to be 'on mount Moriah (*b$^{e}$har hammôriyyâ*), on the threshing-floor of Ornan the Jebusite where God appeared to David (3:2). It should be noted that no reference is made here to Abraham in connection with this site.

It has been objected that Jerusalem is not sufficiently distant from southern Philistia to have required a 3 days' journey to get there, and that one of the characteristics of Jerusalem is that the temple hill is not visible until the traveller is quite close, so that the correctness of the biblical identification is called in question. The Samaritan tradition identifies the site with Mount Gerizim (as though Moriah equals Moreh; see Genesis 12:6), and this is claimed to fulfil the conditions of Genesis 22:4 adequately.

However, the distance from southern Philistia to Jerusalem is *c.* 80 kilometres, which might well have required 3 days to traverse, and in Genesis the place in question is not a 'mount Moriah' but one of several mountains in a land of that name, and the hills on which Jerusalem stands are visible at a distance. There is no need to doubt therefore that Abraham's sacrifice took place on the site of later Jerusalem, if not on the temple hill.
T. C. Mitchell

*Further reading*
F. M. Abel, *Géographie de la Palestine* 1, 1933, pp. 374–375

**MOSERAH, MOSEROTH.** A camp-site of the Israelites in the wilderness (Numbers 33:30f.), where Aaron died (Deuteronomy 10:6). The name could mean 'chastisement(s)', with reference to the trespass at Meribah (see Numbers 20:24; Deuteronomy 32:51).

The site is unidentified, but may have been close to Mount *Hor, which also figures as the place of Aaron's death and burial (Numbers 20:22–29).
D. F. Payne

*Further reading*
J. A. Thompson, *Deuteronomy,* TOTC, 1974, p. 145

**MOUNTAIN OF THREE LIGHTS.** See *OLIVES, MOUNT OF.

**MOUNT OF OFFENCE.** See *OLIVES, MOUNT OF.

**MYRA.** With its port, about 4 kilometres away, Myra was one of the chief cities of Lycia, a province on the south-western tip of Asia Minor. There Paul and his centurion escort boarded a ship bound for Italy (Acts 27:5–6). It was a principal port for the Alexandrian corn ships.

Called Demre by the Turks, Myra displays some impressive ruins, including a well-preserved theatre.
J. D. Douglas

**MYSIA.** The homeland of one of the pre-hellenic peoples of Asia Minor, never a political unit in classical times, and therefore never precisely defined. It centred on the heavily forested hill country on either side of the main north road from Pergamum to Cyzicus on the Sea of Marmora, a tract which stretched from the border of Phrygia west to the promontory of the Troad. Troas itself, together with Assos and a number of other Greek coastal states, and even Pergamum may be regarded as part of Mysia.

Mysia was the northern portion of the Roman province of Asia. Paul had reached its eastern limits on his way through Phrygia to Bithynia (Acts 16:7) when he was diverted through Mysia (verse 8) to Troas, probably following a route through the south of the region.
E. A. Judge

# N

**IAAMAH** ('pleasant'). A city in ›wland Judah (Joshua 15:41), robably identical to modern ā'neh, 10 kilometres south of ydda. Zophar, one of Job's omforters', was a Naamathite, but is unlikely that he originated from he same Naamah as the book of Job as an Arabian setting.
. W. Grogan

**IABATAEANS.** See p. 222.

**IAHALAL, NAHALOL** (Hebrew *ah$^{a}$lol, nah$^{a}$lōl*). A town in Zebulun, ut held by Canaanites (Joshua 9:15; 21:35; Judges 1:30), probably n the north-western side of the Vale f Jezreel.

J. Simons (*GTT*, p. 182) suggested 'ell el-Beida, 1 kilometre south of nodern Nahalal. Ma'lul (Mahalul of he Talmud, *Megilla* 1:1) is not old nough. Albright (*AASOR* 2–3, 1923, . 26) suggested Tell en-Nahl near Iaifa. The names are sufficiently imilar but this is outside the tribal rea of Zebulun as presently nderstood; see *LOB*, p. 235. Both 'ell el-Beida and Tell en-Nahl have uitable occupational histories. At resent the location remains nresolved.
P. U. Lilley

**IAHALIEL** (Hebrew *naḥ$^{a}$lî'ēl*, valley of God'). Situated north of the rnon (Numbers 21:19), now the Vadi Zerka Ma'in, it was famous in oman times for its warm springs, vhich flow into the Dead Sea 16 ilometres from the Jordan (Pliny, *Iatural History* 5:16, 72; Josephus, *'ewish War* 1.33.5, 7.6.3).
P. U. Lilley

**IAIN.** Nain is mentioned only in uke 7:11. There is a small village till bearing this name in the Plain of ezreel, a few miles south of azareth, at the edge of Little ermon, and it is generally accepted s the scene of the gospel narrative. It is certainly to be distinguished from the Nain of Josephus, *Jewish War* 4.511, which was east of the Jordan.

The name is perhaps a corruption of the Hebrew word *nā'îm*, 'pleasant', which adjective well describes the area and the views, if not the village itself. It was once thought that the reference to the city gate (Luke 7:12) raised a problem, as the ancient town appeared to have been unwalled. However, a survey in 1982 concluded that ancient Nain had in fact been a walled town.
D. F. Payne, J. Bimson

**NAIOTH.** A place or quarter in Ramah where Samuel supervised a community of prophets and to which David fled from Saul (1 Samuel 19:18–19, 22–23). When Saul sent messengers there to seek David, each in turn 'prophesied'. Later, when Saul came in person he too 'prophesied' (verse 24), giving rise to a proverb: 'Is Saul also among the prophets?'

The Hebrew word *nāyôṯ* is related to *nāweh*, 'pasture ground' or 'abode', and is commonly translated 'habitation'.
J. A. Thompson

**NAPHTALI** (Hebrew *napṯālî*, 'wrestler'). The sixth son of Jacob, and the second son of Bilhah, Rachel's maidservant; the younger brother of Dan, with whom he is usually associated (Genesis 30:5–8).

*Extent*

In most of the administrative lists the tribe of Naphtali comes last (*e.g.* Numbers 1:15, 42f.; 2:29ff.; 7:78; 10:27). The Blessing of Moses commands Naphtali to 'possess the lake and the south' (Deuteronomy 33:23) and following the settlement its tribal portion comprised a broad strip west of the Sea of Galilee and the upper Jordan, including the greater portion of east and central Galilee. This territory is roughly delineated in Joshua 19:32–39, including 19 fortified cities. But the northern boundary is undefined and since two of the cities mentioned, Beth-anath and Beth-shemesh, parts of a chain of Canaanite fortresses extending from the coast across upper Galilee, are noted in Judges 1:33 as not completely subjugated, it is probable that it varied considerably in the earlier period.

*Canaanite influence*

Naphtali included also the largest Canaanite city, *Hazor, covering about 80 hectares and dominating a vital trade route. Hazor, although destroyed by the Israelites under Joshua (Joshua 11:10f.), reasserted itself and, whilst never regaining its former prestige, it was not finally vanquished until well into the Judges' period (Judges 4:2, 23f.). Another important city was *Kedesh, a levitical city and one of the cities of refuge (Joshua 20:7; 21:32).

The strong Canaanite element is reflected in Judges 1:33, 'Naphtali . . . dwelt among the Canaanites'. This would encourage syncretism and partly accounts for the relative insignificance, historically, of this tribe.

*History*

But there were moments of glory. Barak, Deborah's partner in delivering Israel from Canaanite domination, was a Naphtalite (Judges 4:6) and his tribe was conspicuous in the same campaign (Judges 5:18).

A later generation served valiantly under Gideon (Judges 6:35; 7:23), and the Chronicler records their support for David (1 Chronicles 12:34, 40). Thereafter, Naphtali, vulnerable because of its frontier situation, suffered from attacks from the north. During the reign of Baasha its territory was ravaged by Ben-hadad I of Syria (1 Kings 15:20).

Approximately 150 years later (734 BC) the tribe of Naphtali was the first west of the Jordan to be deported (2 Kings 15:29). A probable reconstruction of Tiglath-pileser III's account of this campaign notes his annexation of the region, '. . . the wide land of Naphtali, in its entire extent, I united with Assyria'. Isaiah 9:1 alludes to the same event.

The territory of Naphtali included some of the most fertile areas of the entire land. During David's reign its 'chief officer' was Jeremoth (1 Chronicles 27:19). It was one of the districts from which Solomon provisioned his court; at this time its governor was one of Solomon's sons-in-law, Ahimaaz (1 Kings 4:15). Hiram, the principal architect of Solomon's temple, was the son of 'a widow of the tribe of Naphtali' (1 Kings 7:14).

In Ezekiel's redistribution of the tribal allotments, Dan, Asher and Naphtali are assigned portions in the north, but the other northern tribes, Issachar and Zebulun, are included farther south (Ezekiel 48:1–7, 23–29).

**Continued on p. 224**

# NABATAEANS

**NABATAEANS.** Nebaioth, son of Ishmael and brother-in-law of Edom (Genesis 25:13; 28:9), is possibly to be considered the ancestor of the Nabataeans, who may also be the Nabaiate of inscriptions of Ashurbanipal of Assyria (*c.* 650 BC, *ANET*, pp. 298–299). A difference in spelling between these two names (with *tāw*) and the native *nbṭw* (with *ṭēth*) precludes certain identification.

*3rd–2nd centuries BC*

Diodorus Siculus (*c.* 50 BC) brings the Nabataeans into recorded history in his account of the end of the Persian empire and the career of Alexander. Quoting from an earlier source, he describes them as a nomadic Arab tribe who neither built houses nor tilled the soil. Their territory, the area south and east of the river Jordan, straddled the trade routes from the Orient to the Mediterranean, and their capital, Petra, 80 kilometres south of the Dead Sea, formed a base from which caravans could be attacked.

Antigonus, who gained power in Syria after Alexander's death, sent 2 expeditions to Petra to subdue the Nabataeans and gain control of the trade (312 BC). Both were unsuccessful. It is clear that at this time Petra was at least a stronghold, and Greek potsherds of *c.* 300 BC found there suggest a permanent settlement.

Contact with the settled communities of Palestine during the 2nd and 3rd centuries BC resulted in the development of Nabataean villages and towns and in intensive cultivation of formerly barren areas. This was aided by well-organized lines of frontier posts to guard against Arab marauders and by the skill of Nabataean engineers in constructing irrigation systems to conserve the scanty rainfall. Many of their dams and reservoirs are still usable. Petra is surrounded by high cliffs, pierced by narrow ravines, which form an almost impregnable defence.

*1st century BC–1st century AD*

From the 1st century BC onwards the Nabataeans built towns in the Negeb such as Oboda (Avdat), Nessana and Elusa as caravan centres, and these were joined a little later by Mampsis (Mamshit) and Sobata (Shivta). Explorations at these sites have revealed parts of town plans and water supply systems.

When a Nabataean ruler arose (the earliest known king is Aretas I, *c.* 170 BC, 2 Maccabees 5:8) who was able to safeguard the caravans, Nabataean merchants led trade from southern Arabia and from the Persian Gulf to Petra, whence it was forwarded to the coast, particularly Gaza. Increased demands by the Roman world for spices, silks and other luxuries from India and China swelled enormously the revenues of a power which could levy tolls on all goods passing through its territory. The redirection of the trade routes across the Red Sea to Egypt after Augustus' failure to conquer Arabia

Caravan routes of Nabataean times.

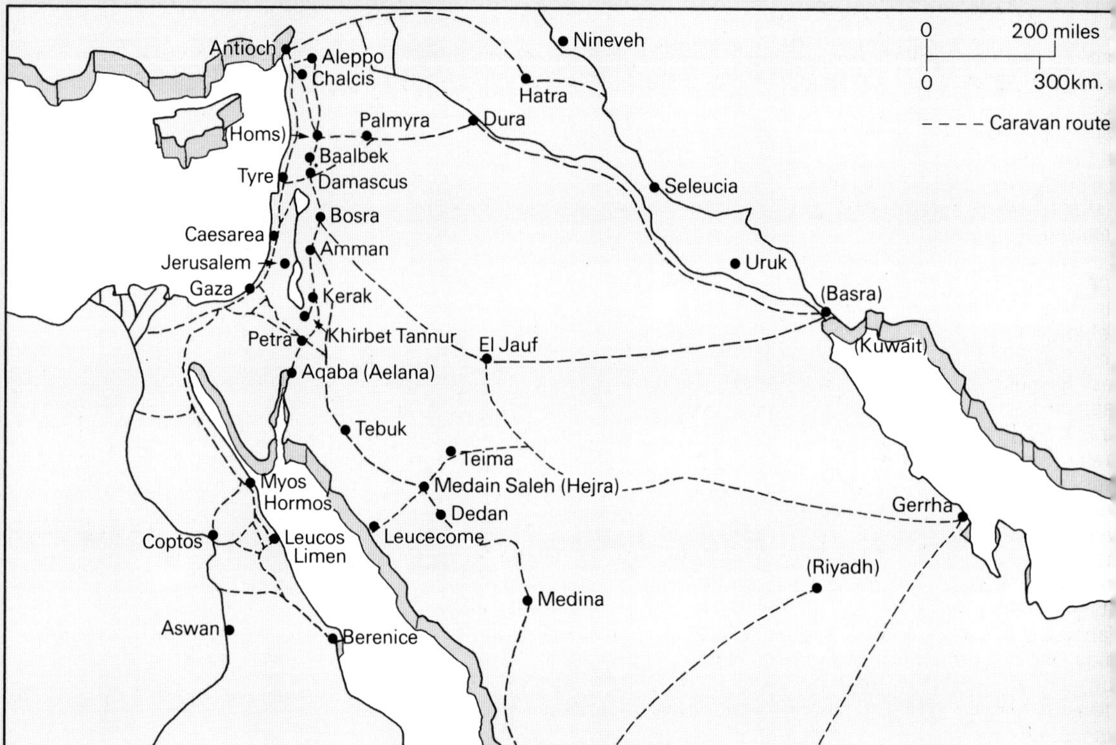

5 BC) was an important factor in the ecline of Nabataean prosperity.

Nabataean history, as reconstructed from incidental references ' Jewish and Greek authors, nsists mainly of struggles to gain ntrol of the Negeb in the south and Damascus in the north. Aretas III 70 BC) and Aretas IV (*c.* 9 BC – AD 40) cceeded in holding both these eas for a few years, so obtaining mplete control of east–west trade. was an officer (Greek *ethnarchēs*) Aretas IV who attempted to detain ul in Damascus (2 Corinthians :32).

*eligion and culture*

ative records (coins and dedicatory scriptions) are written in Aramaic a curiously heightened form of the quare' script. Papyri from the daean desert and ostraca from etra exhibit a cursive form of this riting from which the Arabic ripts are derived.

The use of Aramaic indicates a ide assimilation to the culture of ighbouring settled peoples. This evidenced by Nabataean ulptures which contain features und in Syrian work and traceable early Islamic ornamentation. It ay be seen also in the acceptance Syrian deities, Hadad and targatis (Astarte-Anat) into the abataean pantheon. These two ay have been identified with ushara and his consort Allat, the ational deities. Many open-air rines (*e.g.* the high place at Petra) d temples (*e.g.* Khirbet et-Tannur) ave been discovered on isolated ll-tops. The gods worshipped were specially associated with weather d fertility.

Nabataean potters developed a istinctive ware of their own nsurpassed in Palestine.

*he final years*

alichus III and Rabbel II, the last abataean kings, moved the capital om Petra to Bostra, 112 kilometres ast of Galilee. This became the apital of the Roman province of rabia following Trajan's conquests AD 106. Petra enjoyed considerable osperity during the 2nd century AD hen many of the rock-cut façades ere made. The rise of Palmyra verted the trade which formerly ent to Petra from the east, and that ty gradually declined. The abataean people, subject to Arab ids, became absorbed in the urrounding population, although e script continued in use into the h century.

R. Millard

The Khazneh (treasury) at Petra. Probably the work of Greek masons brought in by the Nabataeans in the 1st century AD. The name comes from a legend that the urn on top of the façade held a treasure.


*Further reading*

N. Glueck, *Deities and Dolphins*, 1966

P. Hammond, *A History of the Nabataeans, Studies in Mediterranean Archaeology*, 1975

Y. Meshorer, *Nabataean Coins*, 1975

S. Moscati, *The Semites in Ancient History*, 1959, pp. 117–119

A. Negev, *Nabatean Archaeology Today*, 1986

**Continued from p. 221**

*In the New Testament*
Jesus spent the greatest part of his public life in this area which, because of its chequered history of deportations and infusion of new settlers, was greatly despised by the Jews of Jerusalem, an attitude which partly explains why Galilee became the headquarters of the reactionary Zealots, bitterly opposed to Roman rule.
A. E. Cundall

*Further reading*
Y. Aharoni, *The Settlement of the Israelite Tribes in Upper Galilee*, 1947
——, *LOB*, pp. 201f., 238f.

The modern town of Nazareth, dominated by the striking Church of the Annunciation.

**NAPTHUHIM.** It is classed with Mizraim (Egypt) in Genesis 10:13 and 1 Chronicles 1:11. Napthuhim's identity is uncertain, but Lower Egypt, specifically the Nile Delta, would be appropriate alongside Pathrusim (see also *Pathros) for Upper Egypt. Hence Brugsch and Erman emended the Hebrew to fit the Egyptian *p' t'-mḥw*, 'Lower Egypt'.

Another Egyptian equivalent, without emendation, might be a *n'(-n-)/n'(yw-) p'idḥw*, 'they of the Delta (literally, marshland)', Lower Egypt(ians). Alternatively, *nap̄tuḥîm* may be an Egyptian *n'(-n-)/n'(yw-) p't' wḥ'(t)*, 'they of the Oasis-land', *i.e.* the oases (and inhabitants) west of the Nile valley.
K. A. Kitchen

**NAZARETH.** A town of Galilee where Joseph and Mary lived, and the home of Jesus for about 30 years until he was rejected (Luke 2:39; 4:16, 28–31). He was therefore called Jesus of Nazareth.

*'Can anything good come from there?'*
Nazareth is not mentioned in the Old Testament, the Apocrypha, by Josephus, or in the Talmud. (The earliest Jewish reference to it is in a Hebrew inscription excavated at Caesarea in 1962, which mentions it as one of the places in Galilee to which members of the 24 priestly courses emigrated after the foundation of Aelia Capitolina in AD 135.)

The reason for this silence was first geographical and later theological. Lower Galilee remained outside the main stream of Israelite life until New Testament times, when Roman rule first brought security. Even then Sepphoris was the chief town of the area, a little to the north of Nazareth. But Nazareth lay close enough to several main trade-routes for easy contact with the outside world, while at the same time her position as a frontier-town on the southern border of Zebulun overlooking the Esdraelon plain produced a certain aloofness. It was this independence of outlook in Lower Galilee which led to the scorn in which Nazareth was held by strict Jews (John 1:46).

*Location*
Nazareth is situated in a high valley among the most southerly limestone hills of the Lebanon range; it runs approximately from south-south-west to north-north-east. To the south there is a sharp drop down to the plain of Esdraelon. The base of the valley is 370 metres above sea-level. Steep hills rise up on the northern and eastern sides, while on the western side they reach up to 500 metres and command an impressive view.

Major roads from Jerusalem and Egypt debouched into the Esdraelon plain in the south; caravans from Gilead crossed the Jordan fords and passed below; the main road from Ptolemais to the Decapolis and the north, along which the Roman legions travelled, passed a few kilometres above Nazareth.

Such a location may have given rise to the name, which is possibly derived from the Aramaic *nāṣ^e^raṯ*, 'watch-tower'. Another suggested derivation is from the Hebrew *nēṣer*, 'shoot', advocated in Eusebius' *Onomasticon* and by Jerome (*Letters* 46, *To Marcellus*).

The mild climate in the valley causes wild flowers and fruit to flourish.

*The New Testament town*
To judge by the rock-tombs, the earl[y] town was higher up the western hi[ll] than the present Nazareth. The Ne[w] Testament town probably began during the 3rd century BC. By the start of the 1st century AD the settlement probably covered an are[a] about 900 × 200 metres and had a population of less than 500.

There are two possible water-supplies. The first, which is the larger, lies in the valley and has been called 'Mary's Well' since AD 1100, but there is no trace of early dwellings nearby. The second is a very small fountain, called 'the New Well', in an angle formed by a projection of the western hill; the Byzantine church and town lay closer to this.

The steep scarp of Jebel Qafsa, overlooking the plain, is traditional[ly] but erroneously called 'the Mount o[f] Precipitation', since this was not th[e] hill 'on which their city was built' (Luke 4:29).
J. W. Charley

*Further reading*
G. H. Dalman, *Sacred Sites and Ways*, 1935, pp. 57ff.
D. Pileggi, 'Life in Ancient Nazareth', *Bible Times* 1/1, 1988, pp. 36–46
Jerome Murphy-O'Connor, *The Hol[y] Land*, 3rd edition, 1992, pp. 379–38[3]
B. Bagatti in *NEAEHL* III, pp 1103–1105

**NEAPOLIS** (the 'new city'). A town, modern Kavalla, in Macedonia whic[h] served as the port of Philippi, 16 kilometres inland. Originally thought to have been called Daton, i[t] occupied a position on a neck of lan[d] between two bays, which gave it a useful harbour on both.

Paul arrived here from Troas on hi[s]

›cond missionary journey (Acts ;:11), after receiving his call to .acedonia. He may have visited it ı his third journey also.
H. Paterson

**€BO. 1.** Mount Nebo, from which ʹoses viewed the Promised Land, a ːominent headland of the ɾansjordan plateau range, *Abarim, ʹith which it is sometimes equated )euteronomy 32:49; 34:1). It is ɜually identified with Jebel en ‹eba, some 16 kilometres east of the ɔrthern end of the Dead Sea. It ɔmmands extensive views from [ount Hermon to the Dead Sea. Jebel Osha, about 45 kilometres .rther north, is preferred by local .uslim tradition and some scholars ‹ee G. T. Manley in *The Book of the ɜw*, 1957, pp. 163f.), but is outside ıe land of Moab. The original border ʹas near Wadi Hesban (Numbers 1:26ff.; the Moabite Stone also ɒplies Jebel en Neba). (See also ⁝BARIM, *PISGAH.)

**2.** A town in Moab (Numbers 32:3, 3; Isaiah 15:2), possibly Khirbet ʹyn Musa or Khirbet el Mukkayet ɜar Jebel en Musa. Excavations at ıe latter site (in the 30s, 60s, 1973 ɿd 1976) revealed ruins of churches f the 4th century AD and later. It was ıken by Mesha of Moab *c.* 830 BC. ɜe M. Piccirillo in *NEAEHL* III, ɒ. 1106–1115; *LA* 16, 1966, ɒ. 165–298; 17, 1967, pp. 5–64; *DAJ* 21, 1976, pp. 55–59.

**3.** A town in Judah (Ezra 2:29; ‹ehemiah 7:33).
. G. Garner

**€EGEB.** Hebrew *negeḇ*, 'the dry', ›fers to the southern lands of ɜlestine. Misconceptions arise from s translation as 'the South' in both ıe AV and RV, where some 40 ɜssages have described it ıaccurately in this way.

*xtent*
n indefinite region, it covers *c.* 2.000 square kilometres or nearly ɜlf the area of modern Israel. The ɔrthern boundary may be drawn ɔnveniently south of the aza–Beersheba road, roughly the )-centimetre mean annual isohyet, ıen due east of Beersheba to the ‹ead Sea through Ras ez-Zuweira. he southern boundary which .erged traditionally into the ıghlands of the Sinai Peninsula is ow drawn politically south of the /adi el-Arish to the head of the Gulf ʹ Aqabah at Eilat. The Wadi rabah, now the political frontier ith Jordan, is overlooked to the ɜst by the Arabah escarpment, the traditional boundary. For the description of the geographical features of the Negeb, see *PALESTINE.

*In the Old Testament*
Mention of the Negeb is almost entirely confined to pre-exilic times, apart from allusions in Zechariah 7:7 and Obadiah 20. Five districts in the northern Negeb are referred to: the Negeb of Judah, of the Jerahmeelites, of the Kenites (1 Samuel 27:10), of the Cherethites and of Caleb (1 Samuel 30:14). These occupied the grazing and agricultural lands between Beersheba and Bir Rikhmeh and the western slopes of the central highlands of Khurashe-Kurnub.

This district was settled by the Amalekites (Numbers 13:29), the ruins of whose fortified sites are still seen between Tell Arad (Numbers 21:1; 33:40), 32 kilometres east of Beersheba and Tell Jemmeh or Gerar (Genesis 20:1; 26:1). At the Exodus the spies had been awed by their defences (Numbers 13:17–20, 27–29), which lasted until the early 6th century BC, when they were probably destroyed finally by the Babylonians (Jeremiah 13:19; 33:13).

The sites of the 29 cities and their villages in the Negeb (Joshua 15:21–32) are unknown, only Beersheba ('well of seven', or 'well of oath', Genesis 21:30), Arad, Khirbet Ar'areh or Aroer (1 Samuel 30:28), Fein or Penon (Numbers 33:42), and Tell el-Kheleifeh or Ezion-geber, having been identified.

*Importance*
The strategic and economic importance of the Negeb has been significant. The 'Way of Shur' crossed it from central Sinai north-east to Judaea (Genesis 16:7; 20:1; 25:18; Exodus 15:22; Numbers 33:8), a route followed by the Patriarchs (Genesis 24:62; 26:22), by Hadad the Edomite (1 Kings 11:14, 17, 21–22), and probably the escape route used by Jeremiah (43:6–12) and later by Joseph and Mary (Matthew 2:13–15). The route was dictated by the zone of settled land where well-water is significant, hence the frequent references to its wells (*e.g.* Genesis 24:15–20; Joshua 15:18–19; Judges 1:14–15).

Uzziah reinforced the defence of Jerusalem by establishing cultivation and defensive settlements in his exposed southern flank of the northern Negeb (2 Chronicles 26:10). It seems clear from the history of the Near East that the Negeb was a convenient vacuum for resettlement whenever population pressure forced out migrants from the Fertile Crescent.

Between the 4th century BC and the beginning of the 2nd century AD, when the Nabataeans finally disappeared, these Semitic people of southern Arabian origin created a brilliant civilization of small hydraulic works in the Negeb. Deployed across the strategic trade routes between Arabia and the Fertile Crescent, they waxed rich on the spice and incense trade of Arabia, and other exotic goods from Somaliland and India.

Later, in the Christian era, the Negeb became a stronghold of Christianity. Glueck has identified some 300 early Christian Byzantine sites in the Negeb, dating from the 5th and 6th centuries AD.
J. M. Houston

*Further reading*
Y. Aharoni, *IEJ* 8, 1958, pp. 26ff.; 10, 1960, pp. 23ff., 97ff.
N. Glueck, *Rivers in the Desert*, 1959
——, *Deities and Dolphins (The story of the Nabataeans)*, 1966
C. L. Woolley and T. E. Lawrence, *The Wilderness of Zin*, 1936
I. Finkelstein and A. Perevolotsky, *BASOR* 279, 1990, pp. 67–88

**NEPHTOAH.** Mentioned only in the expression 'the spring of the Waters of Nephtoah' (Joshua 15:9; 18:15), where the context shows that it was on the borders of Judah and Benjamin. It is usually identified with Lifta, a village 4 kilometres north-west of Jerusalem. The linguistic equation Nephtoah = Lifta is very doubtful, but no other site seems to have strong claims.
L. L. Morris

**NETOPHAH** ('a dropping'). A city, or group of villages (1 Chronicles 9:16; Nehemiah 12:28), near Bethlehem (Nehemiah 7:26). The inhabitants are called Netophathites in the English versions. 'Netophathi' in Nehemiah 12:28, AV, should be 'the Netophathites' as in the RSV.

Netophah was the home of some of David's mighty men (2 Samuel 23:28–29). It is mentioned as a place to which returning exiles came (Ezra 2:22). That it was near Bethlehem is clear, but it cannot be identified conclusively with any modern site.
G. W. Grogan

**NICOPOLIS** ('city of victory'). A town built as the capital of Epirus by Augustus on a peninsula of the Ambraciot Gulf, where he had camped before his victory at Actium in 31 BC. It was a Roman colony, and derived some of its importance from the Actian games, also established by Augustus. These were of equal rank with the Olympian Games.

Although there were other towns named Nicopolis, this was the only one of sufficient standing to warrant Paul's spending a whole winter in it (Titus 3:12), and its geographical position would suit its selection as a rendezvous with Titus. Paul may have planned to use it as a base for evangelizing Epirus. There is no ancient authority for the AV subscription to the Epistle to Titus.
K. L. McKay

## NILE

### Terminology

The origin of the Greek *Neilos* and Latin *Nilus*, our 'Nile', is uncertain. In the Old Testament, with a few rare exceptions, the word *yᵉ'ôr*, 'river, stream, channel', is used whenever the Egyptian Nile is meant. This Hebrew word is itself directly derived from the Egyptian *itrw* in the form *i'r(w)* current from the 18th Dynasty onwards, meaning 'Nile-river, stream, canal', *i.e.* the Nile and its various subsidiary branches and channels. (A. Erman and H. Grapow, *Wörterbuch der Aegyptischen Sprache* 1, 1926, p. 146; T. O. Lambdin, *JAOS* 73, 1953, p. 151).

In the AV the word *yᵉ'ôr* is hidden under various common nouns, 'river, flood', *etc.* Just once the word *nāhār*, 'river', is used of the Nile as the river of Egypt in parallel with the Euphrates, the *nāhār*, 'river' *par excellence*, the promised land lying between these two broad limits (Genesis 15:18).

*naḥal*, 'wadi', is apparently never used of the Nile, but of the Wadi el-'Arish or 'river of Egypt', while the Shihor is the seaward end of the eastern Delta branch of the Nile (see also *EGYPT, RIVER OF).

### Course of the river

*The sources of the Nile*

The ultimate origin of the Nile is the streams such as the Kagera that flow into Lake Victoria in Tanzania; from the latter, a river emerges northwards, *via* Lake Albert Nyanza and the vast Sudd swamps of the southern Sudan, to become the White Nile. At Khartoum this is joined by the Blue Nile flowing down from Lake Tana in the Ethiopian (Abyssinian) highlands, and their united stream is the Nile proper.

*The Nile*

After being joined by the Atbara river some 320 kilometres north-east of Khartoum, the Nile flows for 2,700 kilometres through the Sudan and Egypt north to the Mediterranean without receiving any other tributary; the total length of the river from Lake Victoria to the Mediterranean is roughly 5,600 kilometres.

Between Khartoum and Aswan, six 'sills' of hard granite rocks across the river's course give rise to the six cataracts that impede navigation on that part of its course.

Within Nubia and Upper Egypt, the Nile stream flows in a narrow valley which in Egypt is never much more than 20 kilometres wide and often much less, bounded by hills or cliffs, beyond which stretch rocky deserts to the east and west (see also *EGYPT, Natural features).

*The Delta*

Some 20 kilometres north of Cairo, the river divides into two main branches that reach the sea at Rosetta in the west and Damietta in the east respectively; between and beyond these two great channels extend the flat, swampy lands of the Egyptian Delta.

In Pharaonic Egypt three main branches of the Delta Nile seem to have been recognized ('Western river', Canopic branch?; 'the Great river', very roughly the present Damietta branch; 'the Waters of Rē' or Eastern, Pelusiac branch, Hebrew Shihor), besides various smaller branches, streams and canals. Gree

The Nile, showing the fertile land watered by it.

ʼavellers and geographers reckoned
om five to seven branches and
ouths of the Nile.
See A. H. Gardiner, *Ancient
gyptian Onomastica* 2, 1947,
p. 153*–170*, with map between
p. 131* and 134*, on this tricky
uestion; also J. Ball, *Egypt in the
lassical Geographers*, 1942; M.
ietak, *Tell El-Dab'a* 2, 1975.

**he inundation and agriculture**

he most remarkable feature of the ile is its annual rise and flooding ver its banks, or inundation. In pring and early summer in Ethiopia nd southern Sudan the heavy rains nd melting highland snows turn the pper Nile – specifically the Blue ile – into a vast torrent bringing own in its waters masses of fine, eddish earth in suspension which it sed to deposit on the banks in gypt and Nubia.

Thus, until the perennial rigation-system of dams at Aswan nd elsewhere was instituted last entury, those areas of the Egyptian alley and Delta within reach of the oods received every year a thin, ew deposit of fresh, fertile mud. he muddy flood-waters used to be eld within basins bounded by arthen banks, to be released when ne level of the Nile waters sank gain.

*griculture*

n Egypt the Nile is lowest in May; its se there begins in June, the main oodwaters reach Egypt in uly/August, reach their peak there n September and slowly decline gain thereafter.

But for the Nile and its inundation, gypt would be as desolate as the eserts on either hand; wherever he Nile waters reach, vegetation an grow, life can exist. So sharp is he change from watered land to esert that one can stand with a foot n each.

Egypt's agriculture depended vholly on the inundation, whose evel was checked off against iver-level gauges or Nilometers. A igh flood produced the splendid rops that made Egypt's agricultural vealth proverbial. A low Nile, like rought in other lands, spelt famine; oo high a Nile that swept away rigation-works and brought estruction in its wake was no etter.

*rophetic judgment*

he regular rhythm of Egypt's Nile vas familiar to the Hebrews (see saiah 23:10; Amos 8:8; 9:5), and kewise the dependence of Egypt's

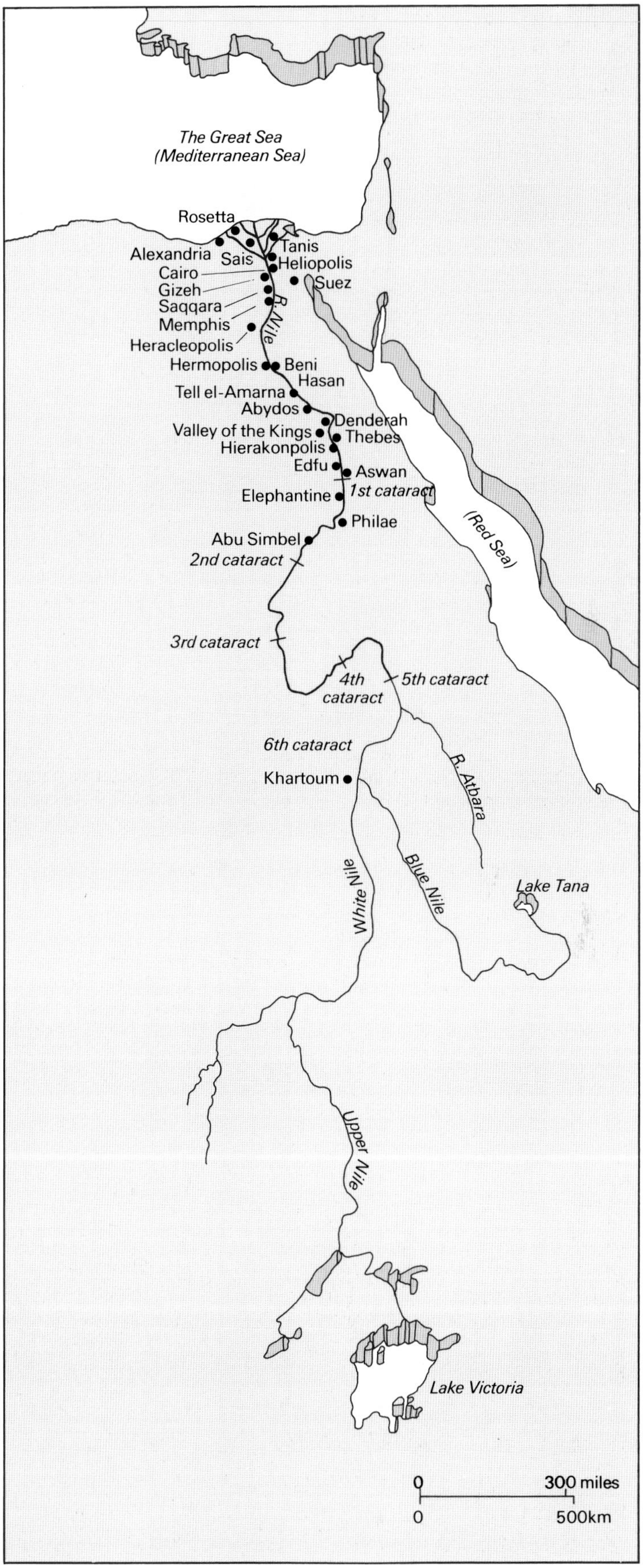


The course of the river Nile.

cultivators, fisherfolk and marshes on those waters (Isaiah 19:5–8; 23:3). More than one prophet proclaimed judgment on Egypt in terms of drying up the Nile (Ezekiel 30:12; compare 29:10; Zechariah 10:11), as other lands might be chastised by lack of rain. Jeremiah (46:7–9) compares the advance of Egypt's army with the surge of the rising Nile.

On the inundation of the Nile, see G. Hort, *ZAW* 69, 1957, pp. 88–95; J. Ball, *Contributions to the Geography of Egypt*, 1939, *passim*; D. Bonneau, *La crue du Nil*, 1964.

**Other aspects**

The Nile in dominating Egypt's agriculture also affected the form of her calendar, divided into three seasons (each of four 30–day months and excluding 5 additional days) called *'Akhet*, 'Inundation'; *Peret*, 'Coming Forth' (*i.e.* of the land from the receding waters); and *Shomu*, 'Dry(?)' or Summer season.

The waters of the Nile not only supported crops but formed also the marshes for pasture (see Genesis 41:1–3, 17–18) and papyrus, and contained a wealth of fish caught by both line and net (Isaiah 19:8), see R. A. Caminos, *Late-Egyptian Miscellanies*, 1954, pp. 74, 200 (many sorts), and G. Posener and others, *Dictionnaire de la Civilisation Égyptienne*, 1959, figures on pp. 214–215.

For Nahum 3:8, see *THEBES. The Assyrians boast of drying up Egypt's streams (2 Kings 19:24 and Isaiah 37:25) may refer to moats and similar river-defence works.

The Nile was also Egypt's main arterial highway; boats could sail north by merely going with the stream, and could as readily sail south with the aid of the cool north wind from the Mediterranean.

In the religious beliefs of the Egyptians the spirit of the Nile-flood was the god Ha'pi, bringer of fertility and abundance.

K. A. Kitchen

**NIMRAH**. See *BETH-NIMRAH.

**NIMRIM, WATERS OF.** The waters of Nimrim are mentioned twice (Isaiah 15:6; Jeremiah 48:34). In substantially identical terms the prophets tell of the overthrow of Moab; cries of anguish go up from the cities of Moab, and 'the waters of Nimrim are a desolation'.

Both in Isaiah and (especially) in Jeremiah the sequence of place-names suggests a site in southern Moab, the now-customary identification with Wadi en-Numeirah, 16 kilometres south of the Dead Sea. This is to be distinguished from Nimrah (Numbers 32:3) or Beth-nimrah (Numbers 32:36) about 16 kilometres north of the Dead Sea.

J. A. Motyer

**NINEVEH.** A principal city, and the last capital, of Assyria. The ruins are marked by the mounds called Kuyunjik and Nabi Yunus ('Prophet Jonah') on the river Tigris opposite Mosul, northern Iraq.

**Name**

The Hebrew *nînᵉwēh* (Greek *Nineuē*; classical *Ninos*) represents the Assyrian *Ninua* (Old Babylonian *Ninuwa*), a rendering of the earlier Sumerian name *Nina*, a name of the goddess Ishtar written with a sign depicting a fish inside an enclosure. Despite the comparison with the history of Jonah, there is probably no connection with the Hebrew *nūn*, 'fish'.

**History**

*Beginnings*

According to Genesis 10:11 Nineveh was one of the northern cities founded by Nimrod or Ashur after leaving Babylonia. Excavation 25 metres down to virgin soil shows that the site was occupied from prehistoric times (*c.* 4500 BC). 'Ubaid (and Samarra) type pottery and pisée-buildings may indicate a southern influence.

Although first mentioned in the inscriptions of Gudea of Lagash who campaigned in the area *c.* 2200 BC, the texts of Tukulti-Ninurta I (*c.* 1230 BC) tell how he restored the temple of the goddess Ishtar of Nineveh founded by Manishtusu, son of Sargon, *c.* 2300 BC.

*Growing importance*

By the early 2nd millennium the city was in contact with the Assyrian colony of Kanish in Cappadocia, and when Assyria became independent under Shamshi-Adad I (*c.* 1800 BC) the same temple of Ishtar (called E-mash-mash) was again restored.

Hammurapi of Babylon (*c.* 1750 BC) adorned the temple, but the expansion of the town followed the revival of Assyrian fortunes under Shalmaneser I (*c.* 1260 BC).

*A royal residence*

By the reign of Tiglath-pileser I (1114–1076 BC) Nineveh was established as an alternative royal residence to Assur and Calah. Both Ashurnasirpal II (883–859 BC) and Sargon II (722–705 BC) had palaces there. It was, therefore, likely that it was to Nineveh itself that the tribute of Menahem in 744 BC (2 Kings 15:20) and of Samaria in 722 BC (Isaiah 8:4) was brought.

Sennacherib, with the aid of his west Semitic queen Naqi'a-Zakutu, extensively rebuilt the city, its defensive walls, gates and water-supply. He built a canal leading 48 kilometres from a dam on the river Gomel to the north, and controlled the flow of the river Khasr which flowed through the city, by the erection of another dam at Ajeila to the east. He also provided new administrative buildings and parks. The walls of his new palace were decorated with reliefs depicting his victories, including the successful siege of *Lachish.

The tribute received from Hezekiah of Judah (2 Kings 18:14) was sent to Nineveh, to which Sennacherib himself had returned after the campaign (2 Kings 19:36; Isaiah 37:37). It is possible that the temple of Nisroch, where he was murdered, was in Nineveh. His account of his attack on Hezekiah in Jerusalem is recorded on clay prisms used as foundation inscriptions in Nineveh.

Ashurbanipal (669–*c.* 627 BC) again made Nineveh his main residence, having lived there as crown prince. The bas-reliefs depicting a lion hunt (British Museum), which were made for his palace, are the best examples of this form of Assyrian art.

*Fall of Nineveh*

The fall of the great city of Nineveh as predicted by the prophets Nahum and Zephaniah, occurred in August 612 BC. The Babylonian Chronicle tells how a combined force of Medes, Babylonians and Scythians laid siege to the city, which fell as a result of the breaches made in the defences by the flooding rivers (Nahum 2:6–8). The city was plundered by the Medes, and the king Sin-shar-ishkun perished in the flames, though his family escaped.

The city was left to fall into the heap of desolate ruin which it is today (Nahum 2:10; 3:7), a pasturing-place for the flocks (Zephaniah 2:13–15), which gives the citadel mound its modern name of Tell Kuyunjik ('mound of many sheep'). When Xenophon and the retreating Greek army passed in 401 BC it was already an unrecognizable mass of debris.

*In the book of Jonah*

At the height of its prosperity

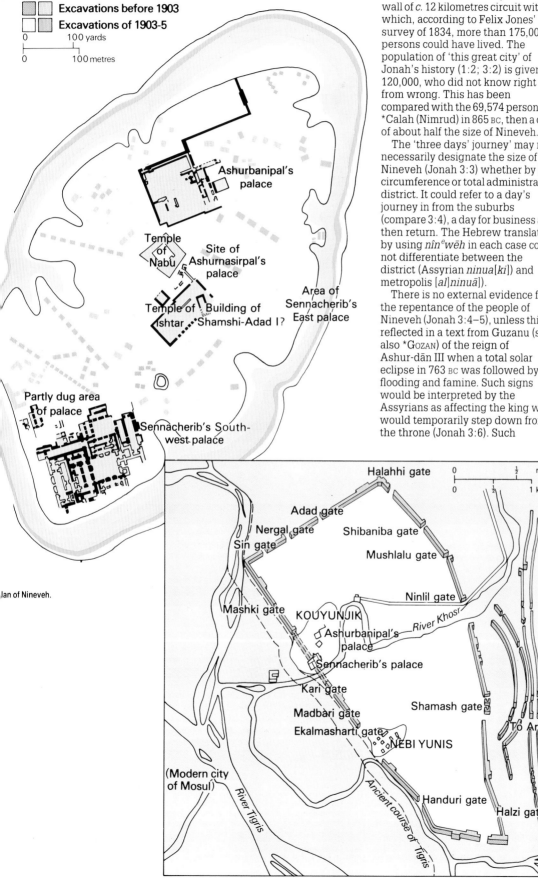

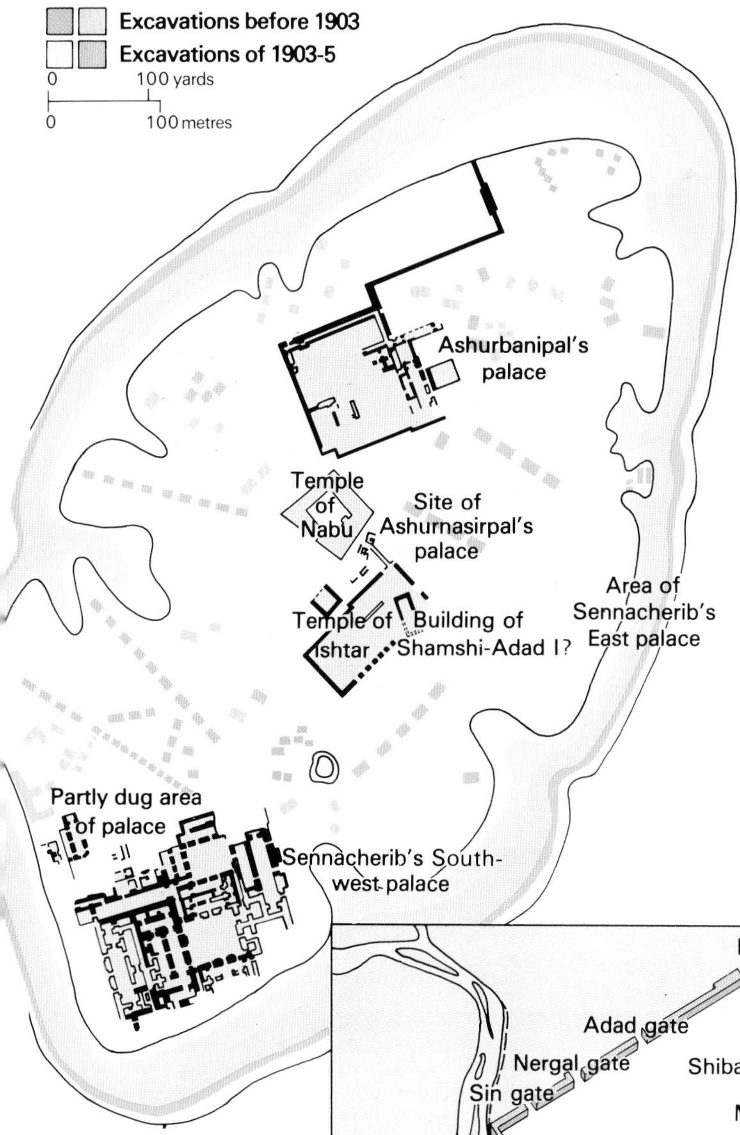


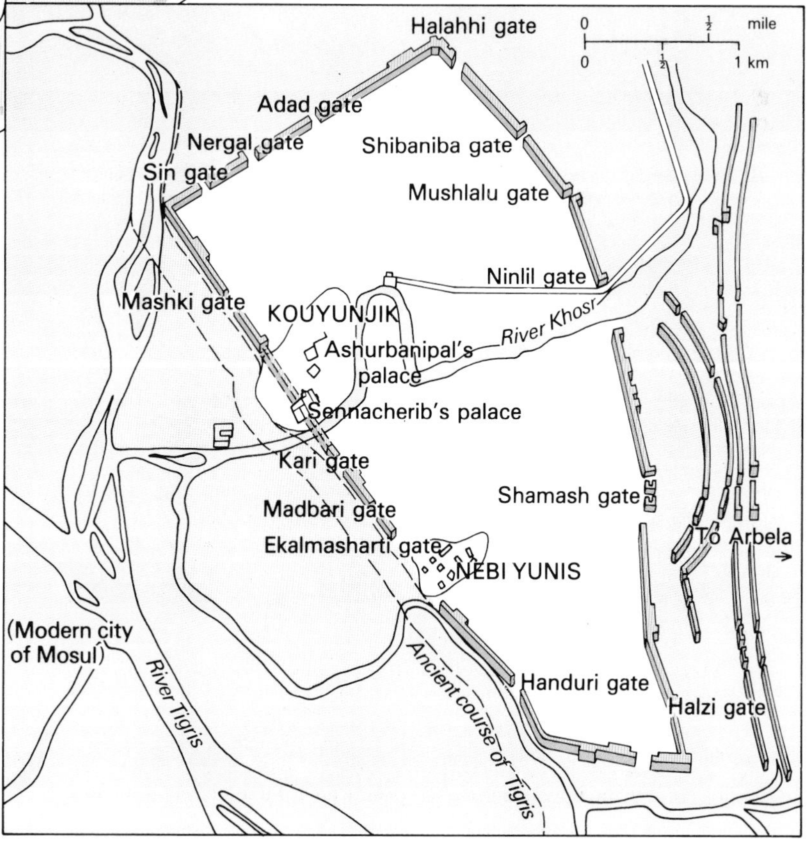


lan of Nineveh.

Nineveh was enclosed by an inner wall of *c.* 12 kilometres circuit within which, according to Felix Jones' survey of 1834, more than 175,000 persons could have lived. The population of 'this great city' of Jonah's history (1:2; 3:2) is given as 120,000, who did not know right from wrong. This has been compared with the 69,574 persons in *Calah (Nimrud) in 865 BC, then a city of about half the size of Nineveh.

The 'three days' journey' may not necessarily designate the size of Nineveh (Jonah 3:3) whether by its circumference or total administrative district. It could refer to a day's journey in from the suburbs (compare 3:4), a day for business and then return. The Hebrew translation by using *nînᵉwēh* in each case could not differentiate between the district (Assyrian *ninua*[*ki*]) and metropolis [*al*]*ninuā*]).

There is no external evidence for the repentance of the people of Nineveh (Jonah 3:4–5), unless this is reflected in a text from Guzanu (see also *GOZAN) of the reign of Ashur-dān III when a total solar eclipse in 763 BC was followed by flooding and famine. Such signs would be interpreted by the Assyrians as affecting the king who would temporarily step down from the throne (Jonah 3:6). Such portents, including an earthquake about the time of Jonah ben Amittai (2 Kings 14:25), could well have made the Ninevites take the step commended by Jesus (Luke 11:30; Matthew 12:41).

### Exploration

Following reports made by such early travellers as John Cartwright (17th century) and plans drawn by C. J. Rich in 1820, interest was reawakened in the discovery of the Old Testament city. Excavation was at first undertaken by P. E. Botta (1842–43), but with little success, and he abandoned the site, believing Khorsabad (16 kilometres to the north) to be the biblical Nineveh.

However, the diggings of Layard and Rassam (1845–54), which resulted in the discovery of the reliefs from the palaces of Sennacherib and Ashurbanipal together with many inscriptions, placed the identification beyond question.

Following the discovery, among the 25,000 inscribed tablets from the libraries of Ashurbanipal and of the temple of Nabu (see also *ASSYRIA), of a Babylonian account of the Flood (Epic of Gilgamesh) in 1872, the British Museum reopened the excavations under G. Smith (1873–76); E. A. W. Budge (1882–91); L. W. King (1903–05) and R. Campbell Thompson (1927–32). The Iraqi Government has continued work at the site (1963, 1966–74). The mound of Nabi Yunus covering a palace of Esarhaddon has been as yet little explored because it is still inhabited.

Nineveh, with its many reliefs and inscriptions, has done more than any other Assyrian site to elucidate the ancient history of *Assyria and *Babylonia, while the epics, histories, grammatical and scientific texts and letters have made Assyrian literature better known than that of any ancient Semitic peoples except the Hebrews.

D. J. Wiseman

*Further reading*

R. Campbell Thompson and R. W. Hutchinson, *A Century of Exploration at Nineveh*, 1929
A. Parrot, *Nineveh and the Old Testament*, 1955
The exploration of Nineveh is described in full in:
A. H. Layard, *Nineveh and its Remains*, 1849
G. Smith, *Assyrian Discoveries*, 1875
R. Campbell Thompson and others, *Liverpool Annals of Archaeology and Anthropology* 18, 1931, pp. 55–116; 19, 1932, pp. 55–116; 20, 1933, pp. 71–186
*Archaeologia* 79, 1929
*Iraq* 1, 1934, pp. 95–105
*Sumer* 23, 1967, pp. 76–80

**NIPPUR.** See *CALNEH.

**NOB.** A locality mentioned in three passages of the Old Testament, all of which may refer to the same place.

In 1 Samuel 22:19 it is referred to as a city of priests; presumably Yahweh's priests had fled there with the ephod after the capture of the ark and the destruction of Shiloh (1 Samuel 4:11).

David visited Nob after he had escaped from Saul when Ahimelech was priest there and ate holy bread (1 Samuel 21:6). When Saul heard that the priest of Nob had assisted the fugitive David he raided the shrine and had Ahimelech, along with 85 other priests, put to death (1 Samuel 22:9, 11, 18–19).

Isaiah prophesied that the Assyrian invaders would reach Nob, between Anathoth, 4 kilometres north-east of Jerusalem, and the capital (Isaiah 10:32), and the city is also mentioned in Nehemiah 11:32 as a village which was reinhabited after the return from exile.

The latter two references indicate a locality near Jerusalem, probably the modern Râs Umm et-Tala on the eastern slopes of Mount Scopus, north-east of Jerusalem (Grollenberg, *Atlas of the Bible*, 1956).

S. R. Driver (*Notes on the Hebrew Text of the Books of Samuel*, 2nd edition, 1913, p. 172) suggests perhaps a spot on the Rās el-Meshārif, under 2 kilometres north of Jerusalem, a ridge from the brow of which (818 metres) the pilgrim along the northern road still catches his first view of the holy city (790 metres).

R. A. H. Gunner

**NOBAH** (Hebrew *nōḇaḥ*). An Amorite locality settled and renamed by the clan of Nobah (Numbers 32:42). The Amorite name Kenath corresponds to Eusebius' *Kanatha*, modern Kanawat, on the slopes of the Jebel Druze.

The mention of a road to the east in Judges 8:11 does not suit this position, however; see *Jogbehah, *Kenath, and D. Baly, *Geography*, pp. 214f., note 5.

J. P. U. Lilley

**NOD.** A land east of, or in front of, Eden (*qiḏmaṯ-'ēḏen*, Genesis 4:16), to which Cain was banished by God after he had murdered Abel. The name (*nôḏ*) is the same in form as the infinitive of the verb *nûḏ* (*nwd*), 'to move to and fro, wander', the participle of which is used in Genesis 4:14 when Cain bemoans the fact that he will become a 'vagabond' (RSV 'wanderer').

The name is unknown outside the Bible, but its form and the context suggest that it was a region where nomadic existence was necessary, such as is today found in several parts of the Middle East.

T. C. Mitchell

**NOHAH.** See *MANAHATH.

**NUZI.** The excavations at Nuzi (Yorghan Tepe) and adjacent mounds near Kirkuk, Iraq, were carried out by E. Chiera and others between 1925 and 1931 through the co-operation of the American Schools of Oriental Research, the Iraq Museum and the Semitic Museum, Harvard.

The earliest level of occupation was dated to the Ubaid period, while the latest traces came from Roman times. The two main periods of occupation were in the 3rd millennium BC when the site was known as Gasur, and in the 15th–14th centuries BC when the town was under Hurrian influence and known as Nuzi.

In the palace and private homes more than 4,000 clay tablets were found, written in a local Hurrian dialect of Akkadian. These included several archives, among which those of Tehiptilla (*c.* 1,000 tablets), prince Shilwateshub and a successful business woman, Tulpunnaya, are the best known. The texts cover approximately five generations, thus providing a detailed picture of life in an ancient Mesopotamian community in a comparatively short period.

The tablets from Nuzi contain mainly private contracts and public records. Apart from lists of various kinds of goods and equipment, a wide range of topics is covered, including land, prices, family law, women, law and order, and slaves. Of particular importance are documents relating to various kinds of adoption, wills, marriage, lawsuits, antichretic security and exchange of persons, goods and land. Until comparatively recently several of the Nuzi text types were scarcely represented elsewhere, but excavation at Tell al-Fikhar (Kurruhanni), *c.* 30 kilometres south-west of Nuzi, has revealed similar material of comparable date, though it remains largely

ıpublished.
By contrast, the political history ıd religious life is poorly ıderstood. Nuzi appears to have een situated within the Hurrian ngdom of Mitanni, though the xtant texts make little reference to ıis or to the rising power of Assyria. ıterature, including myths, epics, isdom texts and scholarly ocuments, is also sparsely epresented.

The Nuzi texts contain a gnificant number of points of ontact with the Old Testament, otably with the patriarchal arratives. These links between the ustoms and social conditions of the eople of Nuzi and the biblical atriarchs have led some scholars to rgue for a similar 15th-century date or Abraham and his descendants, ıough there is evidence that many f these customs had already been bserved for centuries.

More recently attempts have been ıade to reduce considerably any onnection between Nuzi and the atriarchs (Thompson, van Seters). he examples listed below, owever, indicate the existence of everal significant parallels, and ome of the customs concerned are lso found elsewhere in Mesopotamia. Nuzi practice, in fact, ollowed mainly a Mesopotamian ather than a Hurrian pattern.

*ıheritance*

A large group of documents deal vith inheritance. Throughout the ncient Near East an eldest son eceived a larger inheritance share han his brothers, though the exact roportion varied. The double share, vhich is most prominent at Nuzi and vhich also appears in other nd-millennium cuneiform texts, is losely paralleled in Deuteronomy 1:17, though the Patriarchs seem to ave followed a different practice Genesis 25:5–6). The most frequent escription of the eldest son at Nuzi *rabû*, 'eldest'), also found at Ugarit, Alalakh and in Middle Assyrian exts, occurs in Hebrew (*rab*) in Genesis 25:23 instead of the usual *ᵉḵôr*.

It remains uncertain whether or ot one's birthright could be exchanged at Nuzi, as in the case of acob and Esau (Genesis 25:29–34). Although several examples are nown where at least part of an nheritance changed hands between rothers, in no instance can an ldest son be definitely identified in uch transactions. In any case, similar examples of the transfer of an nheritance occur in Assyria and Babylonia and are not confined to Nuzi.

However, any heir could be disinherited. Such drastic action was permitted only for offences against the family and the references to 'disrespect' and 'disobedience' towards parents provides a useful background to Reuben's demotion (Genesis 35:22; 49:3–4), though again similar examples can be found elsewhere.

The suggestion has been made that possession of the household gods in Nuzi formed an effective entitlement to an inheritance and that Rachel's theft of Laban's images, perhaps on Jacob's behalf, could be similarly explained (Genesis 31:19ff.). It is more probable, however, that the family deities could only be bequeathed by the father, normally to the first-born son, and that their theft did not improve an heir's claim.

*Adoption*

Adoption also occupies an important place in the Nuzi texts. A man without an heir could adopt an outsider who would carry out certain responsibilities towards his adoptive parents, though of course similar customs are known from other Mesopotamian texts. The duties included the provision of food and clothing, particularly in old age, and ensuring proper burial and mourning rites, while in return the adoptee received an inheritance. It is quite possible that Abram adopted Eliezer in this manner prior to Isaac's birth (Genesis 15:24), especially since at Nuzi a son born subsequently usually gained a larger inheritance share than any adoptee and that the adoption of slaves is occasionally mentioned.

The process of adoption at Nuzi was also extended to become a fiction whereby property, apparently legally inalienable, could be sold. Tehiptilla, for example, was 'adopted' in this way some 150 times!

*Childless marriage*

Apart from adoption, the Nuzi texts mention three further solutions for a childless marriage. The husband could remarry or take a concubine or the wife could present her own slave-girl to her husband. The latter custom, which afforded the barren wife some protection, parallels that of Sarah, Rachel and Leah (Genesis 16:1–4; 30:1–13), and though only one example occurs at Nuzi (*HSS* 5.67), others are known from Babylonia and Assyria.

A son born to a slave-girl in this way would normally have to be adopted or legitimated by the father according to Mesopotamian custom, though the Nuzi text is not specific on this point. *HSS* 5.67 does indicate, however, that the wife maintained authority over her slave-girl's children and there are indications that Sarah, Rachel and Leah took responsibility for their slave-girls' offspring right from the naming of the children.

Although the Nuzi texts do not refer to a paternal blessing such as in Genesis 27:29, 33 or in 48:1ff., they do occasionally contain oral statements which were clearly regarded as having legal validity. One of these was made by a father to his son while the former lay ill in bed (compare Isaac). In both Nuzi and Genesis such oral statements were supported by legal or customary safeguards, and symbolic actions involving the hands were frequently used.

*Women's rights*

Women are often mentioned in the Nuzi documents. The right of daughters to inherit property is attested, usually in the absence of sons, as in Babylonian contracts (compare Numbers 27:8). Sometimes a marriage contract included a clause prohibiting the husband from marrying a second wife, a safeguard sought for Rachel by Laban (Genesis 31:50). Not every bride was so fortunate, however. A girl could be acquired by a man for optional marriage to himself or to his son (see Exodus 21:7–11), while the complaint of Laban's daughters that their father had held back their dowry (Genesis 31:15) is paralleled by an identical phrase (*kaspa akālu*) in 5 Nuzi texts.

*Business negotiations*

Several Nuzi references to business transactions have some relevance to the Old Testament. Land was sometimes apportioned by lot (Numbers 26:55f.; Joshua 18:2–10) and there was a periodic 'release' from debt (Deuteronomy 15).

Sale of land was sometimes confirmed by the seller lifting his foot and placing the buyer's on the soil, while shoes functioned as legal symbols in some transactions (compare Ruth 4:7–8; 1 Samuel 12:3, Septuagint; Amos 2:6; 8:6). 1 Samuel 1:24 has been reinterpreted in the light of Nuzi evidence to read 'a bullock, three years old'.

Finally, the Nuzi references to *'apiru* (*habiru*), indicating various

persons, many apparently foreigners who had accepted voluntary servitude, recalls the phrase 'Hebrew slave' and the derogatory use of 'Hebrews' by Egyptians and Philistines when referring to Israelites (Genesis 39:14; Exodus 1:15; 21:1–6; 1 Samuel 14:21).
M. J. Selman

*Further reading*

Archaeology:
R. F. S. Starr, *Nuzi, Report on the Excavations at Yorghan Tepe,* 2 vols., 1939
Texts:
E. Chiera and others, *Joint Expedition at Nuzi*, 6 vols., 1927–39
E. R. Lacheman and others, *Excavations at Nuzi*, 8 vols., 1929–62
General:
C. H. Gordon, *BA* 3, 1940, pp. 1–12
H. H. Rowley, *The Servant of the Lord*, 2nd edition, 1965, pp. 312–317
C. J. Mullo Weir, in *AOTS*, pp. 73–86
M. Dietrich and others, *Nuzi-Bibliographie*, 1972
T. L. Thompson, *The Historicity of the Patriarchal Narratives*, 1974, pp. 196–297
J. van Seters, *Abraham in History and Tradition*, 1975, pp. 65–103
M. J. Selman, *TynB* 27, 1976, pp. 114–136

# O

**OLIVES, MOUNT OF.** Olivet, or the Mount of Olives, is a small range of four summits, the highest being 830 metres, which overlooks Jerusalem and the Temple Mount from the east across the Kidron Valley. Thickly wooded in Jesus' day, rich in the olives which occasioned its name, the mount was denuded of trees during the siege of Jerusalem by Titus.

All the ground is holy, for Christ unquestionably walked there, though particularized sites, with their commemorative churches, may be questioned. From the traditional place of Jesus' baptism, on Jordan's bank, far below sea-level, Olivet's distant summit 1,200 metres higher, a traditional site of the Ascension, is clearly visible, for Palestine is a small land of long perspectives.

*In the Old Testament*

The Old Testament references to Olivet at 2 Samuel 15:30, Nehemiah 8:15; and Ezekiel 11:23 are slight. 1 Kings 11:7 and 2 Kings 23:13 refer to Solomon's idolatry, the erection of high places to Chemosh and Molech, which probably caused one summit to be dubbed the Mount of Offence. In the eschatological future the Lord will part the Mount in two as he stands on it (Zechariah 14:4).

Jews resident in Jerusalem used to announce the new moon to their compatriots in Babylonia by a chain of beacons starting on Olivet, each signalling the lighting of the next. But since Samaritans lit false flares, eventually human messengers had to replace the old beacons. G. H. Dalman considers the Mishnaic claim that this beacon service stretched as far afield as Mesopotamia perfectly feasible (*Sacred Sites and Ways*, 1935, p. 263, note 7).

The Mount has close connections with the red heifer and its ashes of purification (Numbers 19; *Parah* 3.6–7, 11), as with other ceremonies of levitical Judaism.

*Legends*

According to one legend, the dove sent forth from the ark by Noah plucked her leaf from Olivet (Genesis 8:11; Midrash *Genesis Rabba* 33.6).

Some believed that the faithful Jewish dead must be resurrected in Israel, and those who died abroad would eventually be rolled back through underground cavities (*Ketuboth* 111a), emerging at the sundered Mount of Olives (H. Loewe and C. G. Montefiore, *A Rabbinic Anthology*, 1938, pp. 660ff.).

When the Shekinah, or radiance of God's presence, departed from the temple through sin, it was said to linger for 3½ years on Olivet, vainly awaiting repentance (*Lamentations Rabba*, Proem 25; compare Ezekiel 10:18).

*'Mountain of Three Lights'*

The name comes from the glow of the flaming temple altar reflected on

The Mount of Olives seen from the Old City of Jerusalem, with the Church of All Nations prominent in the foreground.

e hillside by night, the first beams sunrise gilding the summit, and e oil from the olives which fed the emple lamps.

*ethsemane*
ear the Church of All Nations, at e base of Olivet, are some nerable olive-trees, not emonstrably 2,000 years old. This is e area of Gethsemane, and the ecise spot of the Agony, though ndetermined, is close by. Half-way the hill is the Church of Dominus evit.

But why should our Lord weep ere, half-way down? It has been gently argued (in Hastings' *ctionary of the Bible*) that he really pproached Jerusalem by way of ethany, round the southern oulder of Olivet, weeping when e city suddenly burst into view.

*he Ascension*
succession of churches of the scension have long crowned the puted summit of our Lord's sumption, and his supposed otprints are carefully preserved ere as a tangible fulfilment of echariah 14:4. Yet Luke's Gospel vours the Bethany area as the real ene of the Ascension. The visitor Palestine learns the futility of ondering insolubles.
A. Stewart

*urther reading*
Wilkinson, *Jerusalem as Jesus new It*, 1978, pp. 125–131, 173–175

**LIVET.** See *OLIVES, MOUNT OF.

**N.** A venerable city, Egyptian *wnw* ('city of the pillar'), Greek eliopolis, now represented by cattered or buried remains at Tell isn and Maṭariyeh, 16 kilometres orth-east of Cairo. From antiquity it as the great centre of Egyptian un-worship, where the solar deities ē' and Atum were especially onoured, and the home of one of gypt's several theological ystems'.

The pharaohs embellished the emple of Rē' with many obelisks – ll, tapering, monolithic shafts of quare or rectangular section, each nding at the top in a pyramidally haped point; such a 'pyramidion' presented the *benben* or sacred one of Rē', as first to catch the rays f the rising sun. Each pharaoh from e 5th Dynasty onward (25th entury BC) was styled 'son of Rē'', nd the priestly corporations of n/Heliopolis were equalled in ealth only by that of the god Ptah of Memphis and exceeded only by that of the god Amūn of Thebes, during *c.* 1600–1100 BC.

The prominence of On is reflected in Genesis 41:45, 50 and 46:20, where Joseph as Pharaoh's new chief minister is married to Asenath, daughter of Potiphera, 'priest of On'. This title might mean that Potiphera was high priest there. His name, very fittingly, is compounded with that of the sun-god Rē'. (See also A. Rowe, *PEQ* 94, 1962, pp. 133–142.)

On next recurs in Hebrew history under the appropriate pseudonym Beth-shemesh, 'House of the Sun', when Jeremiah (43:13) threatens that Nebuchadrezzar will smash 'the pillars of Beth-shemesh', *i.e.* the obelisks of On/Heliopolis. Whether Isaiah's 'city of the sun' (19:18) is On is less clear.

Aven (Hebrew *'awen*) of Ezekiel 30:17 is a variant pointing of *'ôn*, 'On', perhaps as a pun on *'awen*, 'trouble, wickedness', in Ezekiel's judgment on Egypt's cities.
K. A. Kitchen

*Further reading*
A. A. Saleh, *Excavations at Heliopolis*, I, II, 1981, 1983

**ONO.** A town first mentioned in the lists of Thothmes III (1479–1425 BC). The Benjaminites rebuilt it after the conquest of Canaan (1 Chronicles 8:12) and reoccupied it after the Exile (Nehemiah 11:31–35). Identified with Kafr 'Anâ, it lay near Lydda. The area was called the Plain of Ono (Nehemiah 6:2).
D. F. Payne

**OPHIR** (Hebrew *'ôp̄ir*, Genesis 10:29; *'ôp̄îr*, 1 Kings 10:11). The country from which fine gold was imported to Judah (2 Chronicles 8:18; Job 22:24; 28:16; Psalm 45:9; Isaiah 13:12), sometimes in large quantities (1 Chronicles 29:4), and with valuable almug(sandal?)-wood (1 Kings 10:11), silver, ivories, apes and peacocks (1 Kings 10:22), and precious stones (2 Chronicles 9:10).

Ophir was reached by Solomon's fleet from Ezion-geber on the Gulf of Aqabah (1 Kings 9:28) employing 'ships of *Tarshish' (1 Kings 22:48). These voyages took 'three years', that is perhaps one entire year and parts of two others. The trade was sufficiently well known for Ophir to be synonymous with the fine gold which was its principal product (Job 22:24). In Isaiah 13:12 Ophir is paralleled with *'ôqir*, 'I will make precious' (*HUCA* 12–13, 1937–38, p. 61). A confirmation of this trade is given in an ostracon, found at Tell Qasileh north-east of Tel Aviv in 1946, inscribed *zhb 'p̄r lbyt ḥrn š*, that is, 'gold from Ophir for Beth Horon 30 shekels' (*JNES* 10, 1951, pp. 265–267).

Various theories have been put forward for the site of Ophir.

*a.* Southern Arabia. A tribe of this name is known from pre-Islamic inscriptions (G. Ryckmans, *Les noms propre sud-sémitiques*, 1934, pp. 298, 339f.). Their area lies between Saba in the Yemen and Ḥawilah (Ḥawlān), as indicated in Genesis 10:29. R. North links (Š)ōpha(i)r(a) (Ophir) with Parvaim (Farwa) in Yemen as the source of Sheba gold (compare Psalm 72:15; Isaiah 60:6). This accords with modern excavation of gold at Madh al Dhabah between Sheba and Havilah (compare Genesis 10:29).

*b.* South-eastern Arabia: Oman. These are not far from Ezion-geber, and it is necessary to assume both that the 3-year voyage included laying up during the hot summer and that some commodities (*e.g.* apes) not commonly found in southern Arabia were brought to Ophir as an entrepôt from more distant places.

*c.* East African coast: Somaliland, *i.e.* the Egyptian *Punt*, a source of the frankincense and myrrh and those items described as from Ophir (W. F. Albright, *Archaeology and the Religion of Israel*, 1953, pp. 133–135, 212; van Beek, *JAOS* 78, 1958, p. 146).

*d.* (S)upāra, 75 kilometres north of Bombay, India. Josephus (*Antiquities* 8.164), the Septuagint and the Vulgate (Job 28:16) interpreted Ophir as India. In favour of this interpretation are the facts that all the commodities named are familiar in ancient India, and it is known that from the 2nd millennium BC there was a lively sea-trade between the Persian Gulf and India.

*e.* Other, more doubtful, suggestions include Apir, Baluchistan (possibly ancient Meluhha, see *BSOAS* 36, 1973, pp. 554–587) and Zimbabwe.
D. J. Wiseman

*Further reading*
V. Christides, *RB* 77, 1970, pp. 240–247
R. North, *Fourth World Congress of Jewish Studies*, Papers 1, 1967, pp. 197–202

**OPHRAH** (Hebrew *'op̄râh*). **1.** A town in Benjamin (Joshua 18:23; 1 Samuel 13:17); called Ephron (*Q$^e$rē' 'ep̄rain*) (2 Chronicles 13:19); modern et-Taiyibeh. It stands on a commanding height 11 kilometres north of the gorge of *Michmash and 7 kilometres north-east of Bethel (Beitin).

Arabs often substituted *taiyibeh* ('fortunate') where the place-name *'oprah* persisted in the Middle Ages, as the latter suggested black magic (Abel in *JPOS* 17, 1937, p. 38; *LOB*, p. 121).

It is not certain that *Ephraim* in John 11:54 refers to the same place; the names are distinct in Hebrew, but Greek sometimes drops *'ayin* (K.-D. Schunck in *VT* 11, 1961, pp. 188–200; J. Heller in *VT* 12, 1962, pp. 339ff.).

**2.** Ophrah of Abiezer in Manasseh, Gideon's home, where his altar of Jahweh-shalom (Judges 6:24, AV) was shown in later times. Possible sites are:

*a.* Fer'ata, west of Mount Gerizim, near Shechem but this is rather remote from the area of conflict, and is more probably *Pirathon of Judges 12:15.

*b.* et-Taiyibeh, half-way between Bethshan and Tabor (Abel), which was, however, in Issachar, and is probably the Hapharaim of Joshua 19:19.

*c.* Afula, in the centre of the valley of Jezreel, in a very exposed position but with Israelite remains (*LOB*, p. 263).

J. P. U. Lilley

**OREB** (Hebrew *'ōrēḇ*, 'raven'). The rock of Oreb, named after the prince defeated by Gideon (Judges 7:25; Isaiah 10:26). The Ephraimites cut off the enemy's retreat at the Jordan fords, presumably opposite Jezreel.

Bethbarah (Judges 7:24) might be a ford (*'āḇar*, 'cross') some 20 kilometres south of Lake Galilee.

J. P. U. Lilley

# P

**PADDAN, PADDAN-ARAM.** The 'field' or 'plain' of Aram (RSV *'Mesopotamia') is the name given in the area around Harran in Upper Mesopotamia, north of the junction of the rivers Ḫabur and Euphrates in Genesis 25:20, 28:2 and 31:18, *etc.*, and is identical with Aram-naharaim, 'Aram of the rivers', of Genesis 24:10, Deuteronomy 23:4 and Judges 3:8.

Abraham dwelt in this area before emigrating to Canaan. He sent his servant there to obtain a bride for Isaac, and thither Jacob fled from Esau.

For a suggested identification of Paddan-aram, near Harran, see A. Malamat in Wiseman (ed.), *POTT*, pp. 134f., 140.

R. A. H. Gunner

**PALESTINE.** See p. 236.

**PALMYRA.** See *TADMOR.

**PAMPHYLIA.** A coastal region of southern Asia Minor on the great bay of *Lycia and *Cilicia. According to tradition, the area was colonized by Amphilochus and Calchas (or Mopsus, his rival and successor) after the Trojan War. Linguistic evidence confirms a mixed settlement. The chief towns were Attaleia, Paul's probable landing-place; Aspendus, a Persian naval base; Side; and *Perga.

The region was under Persian rule until Alexander, after which, apart from brief occupations by Ptolemy I and Ptolemy III, it passed to the possession of the Seleucids of Syria.

After the defeat of Antiochus III, C. Manlius took the region over for Rome and the main cities were associated in alliance. The Attalids at this time (189 BC) received the coastal strip, where they founded Attaleia.

In 36 BC Antony made the territory over to his ally Amyntas, king of Galatia, and Pamphylia was part of the province of Galatia until AD 43. In that year Claudius formed the province of Lycia-Pamphylia. There were later reorganizations under Galba and Vespasian.

The church founded at Perga is the only one mentioned in the 1st century, but there were at least 12 foundations at the time of Diocletian's persecution in AD 304.

Pamphylia is mentioned in Acts 13:13, 14:24 and 15:38 in connection with Paul's first journey, a visit which Ramsay believed was cut short through illness and the enervating climate (*St Paul the Traveller and Roman Citizen*, pp. 89ff.).

E. M. Blaiklock

*Further reading*

A. H. M. Jones, *Cities of the Eastern Roman Provinces*, 2nd edition, 1971, pp. 123ff.

**PAPHOS.** The name of 2 settlements in south-western Cyprus in New Testament times, distinguished by scholars as Old and New Paphos. The former was a Phoenician foundation of great antiquity lying slightly inland from the coast.

New Paphos grew up, after the Romans annexed the island in 58 BC as the centre of Roman rule, and it was here that Paul met the proconsul Sergius (Acts 13:6–7, 12) on his first missionary journey. Here, too, he had his encounter with Elymas the sorcerer (Acts 13:6–11).

Old Paphos was the site of a famous shrine, probably of Phoenician or Syrian origin, but later devoted to the worship of Aphrodite.

J. H. Paterson

*Further reading*

A. Nobbs, 'Sergius Paulus', in A. R. Millard and B. W. Winter (eds.), *Documents of New Testament Times*, 1993

**PARAN.** A wilderness situated in the eastern central region of the Sinai peninsula, north-east from the traditional Sinai and south-south-east of Kadesh, with the Arabah and the Gulf of Aqabah as its eastern border. It was to this wilderness that Hagar and Ishmael went after their expulsion from Abraham's household (Genesis 21:21). It was crossed by the Israelites following their exodus from Egypt (Numbers 10:12; 12:16), and from here Moses despatched men to spy out the land of Canaan (Numbers 13:3, 26). The wilderness was also traversed by Hadad the Edomite on his flight to Egypt (1 Kings 11:18).

1 Samuel 25:1 records that David went to the wilderness of Paran on

e death of the prophet Samuel, but this instance we may read with e Greek 'wilderness of Maon'. El-paran, mentioned in Genesis :6 as on the border of the ilderness, may have been an ıcient name for Elath. Mount Paran the Song of Moses (Deuteronomy :2) and of Habakkuk 3:3 was ossibly a prominent peak in the ountain range on the western shore the Gulf of Aqabah. (See also *ZIN.)
A. H. Gunner

**ARTHIA.** Parthia, a district uth-east of the Caspian Sea, was rt of the Persian empire conquered Alexander the Great. In the iddle of the 3rd century BC Arsaces d the Parthians in revolt against eir Seleucid (Macedonian) rulers, d his successors eventually tended their empire from the ıphrates to the Indus. Their xclusive use of cavalry-bowmen ade them a formidable enemy, as e Romans discovered to their cost.
In 54 BC the Romans under Crassus ıffered a humiliating defeat in ıttle with the Parthians at *Harran. 51 BC the Parthians invaded the oman province of Syria, but were iven back after reaching Antioch. 40 BC, under the leadership of ıcorus, they conquered Syria, ıoenicia and Palestine, but Rome gained the lost territories by 38 BC.
In the 1st century AD the Parthians ıanged their capital from Ecbatana Ctesiphon and sought to revive e Iranian elements of their vilization at the expense of the reek.
The Parthians were governed by a nd-owning aristocracy, and ontrolled the lucrative trade with e Far East. Their own religion was anian Mazdaism, but they were enerally tolerant of other peoples' ligions.
Parthia was one of the districts in hich the deported Israelites had een settled, and according to osephus their descendants ontinued to speak an Aramaic ialect and to worship the true God, ending tribute to the temple at erusalem. Consequently the arthians in Jerusalem on the Day of entecost (Acts 2:9) were probably ews from that district ('language' in erse 8 could equally well be ialect'), but there may have been arthian proselytes with them.
L. McKay

*urther reading*
. C. Debevoise, *Parthia*, 1938
I. A. R. Colledge, *The Parthians*, 967

**PARVAIM.** The place which produced the gold used for ornamenting Solomon's Temple (2 Chronicles 3:6). The location is obscure. Some suggest Farwa in Yemen. Gesenius, identifying it with the Sanskrit *parvam*, understands it to be a general term for the eastern regions. (See also *OPHIR.)
J. D. Douglas

**PATARA.** A seaport of south-western *Lycia, in the Xanthus valley. Besides local trade it was important as being a suitable starting-point for a sea passage direct to Phoenicia.
According to the commonly accepted Alexandrian text of Acts 21:1, Paul trans-shipped at Patara on his way to Jerusalem. The Western Text, possibly influenced by Acts 27:5–6, adds 'and Myra', which would imply that he coasted farther east before trans-shipment (see also *MYRA). There is reason to believe that the prevailing winds made Patara the most suitable starting-point for the crossing, and Myra the regular terminal for the return journey.
Patara was also celebrated for its oracle of Apollo.
K. L. McKay

**PATHROS, PATHRUSIM.** Classed under Mizraim (Egypt) in Genesis 10:14 and 1 Chronicles 1:12, Pathros is Egyptian *p' t'-rs(y)*, 'the Southland', *i.e.* Upper Egypt, the long Nile valley extending north–south between Cairo and Aswan; the name is attested in Assyrian inscriptions as Paturisi. Thus, the terms Mizraim for Egypt, especially Lower Egypt, Pathros for Upper Egypt and *Cush for 'Ethiopia' (northern Sudan) occur in this significantly geographical order both in a prophecy of Isaiah (11:11) and in a subsequent inscription of Esarhaddon, king of Assyria, who also boasts himself 'king of Muṣur, Paturisi and Cush'.
Jeremiah similarly identifies Pathros with Egypt (Jeremiah 44:15) and specifically Upper Egypt as distinct from the cities (and land) of Lower Egypt (Jeremiah 44:1). Pathros also appears as Upper Egypt and as the homeland of the Egyptian people in Ezekiel 29:14 and 30:14.
K. A. Kitchen

**PATMOS.** An island off the Dodecanese, lying some 55 kilometres off the south-west coast of Asia Minor, at 37° 20′ N, 26° 34′ E. To this island the apostle John was banished from Ephesus, evidently for some months about the year AD 95, and here he wrote his Revelation (Revelation 1:9).
The island is about 12 kilometres long, with a breadth of up to 7 kilometres, and it has been suggested that the scenery of its rugged volcanic hills and surrounding seas find their reflection in the imagery of the Apocalypse. See Pliny, *Natural History* 4.69.
J. H. Paterson

*Further reading*
C. J. Hemer, 'The Patmos Background', *The Letters to the Seven Churches of Asia in their Local Setting*, 1986, ch. 2

**PEKOD.** A small *Aramaean tribe and its area east of the lower Tigris. Akkadian sources record the temporary subjugation of *Puqūdu* under Tiglath-pileser III (747–727 BC), Sargon II (722–705 BC) and Sennacherib (705–681 BC).
Mentioned in Jeremiah's oracle against Babylon (50:21), Pekod is also among other Mesopotamian peoples who, though formerly lovers of Israel, will rise against Jerusalem (Ezekiel 23:23). It is eponymous for a city and irrigation system mentioned in the Babylonian Talmud (*Beṣah* 29a, *Kethuboth* 27b, *Ḥullin* 127a).
D. W. Baker

*Further reading*
S. Parpola, *Neo-Assyrian Toponyms*, 1970, pp. 280–281
M. Dietrich, *Die Aramäer Südbabyloniens*, 1970

**PENUEL.** 'The face of God' was the name that Jacob gave to the place where he crossed the Jabbok on his way back to meet Esau (Genesis 32:30–31; the variant spelling Peniel occurs in verse 30). It is possible that it had been called Penuel before, perhaps after a peculiarly shaped rock, and that Jacob endorsed the name as a result of his experience with the angel.
S. Merrill (followed by H. Gunkel) suggested that the place-name originated as the name of the profile of a projecting crag, and cites a reference by the ancient geographer Strabo (*Geography* 16.2.15f.) to a Phoenician foothill called in Greek *Prosōpon Theou* ('face of God'). The name therefore clearly occurred in more than one geographical context.
That Penuel was the site of an important pass is shown by the fact that a fortress was built there, which Gideon destroyed after defeating the Midianites (Judges 8:8ff.), and
**Continued on p. 243**

# PALESTINE

*Name*

The name 'Palestine' is derived ultimately from the Philistines. The 5th-century BC historian Herodotus used the term *Palaistine Syria* (Philistine Syria) to refer to southern Syria, and later Greek writers applied it to the whole region between Phoenicia and the Lebanon mountains in the north and Egypt in the south.

In AD 135, after putting down the second Jewish revolt against Rome, the emperor Hadrian changed the name of the province of Judaea to *Prinvincia Syria Palaestina* (the Lati equivalent of the Greek term). This was later shortened to *Palaestina*, from which the modern 'Palestine' derived.

The name does not occur in the Bible. (In the AV we do find 'Palestin in Joel 3:4 and 'Palestina' in Exodu 15:14 and Isaiah 14:29, but all shoul read 'Philistia', as in the modern versions.) Today it is unfortunately term freighted with political connotations; for many people its use is a sensitive issue because it

Map to illustrate the patriarchal narratives, where locations are known.

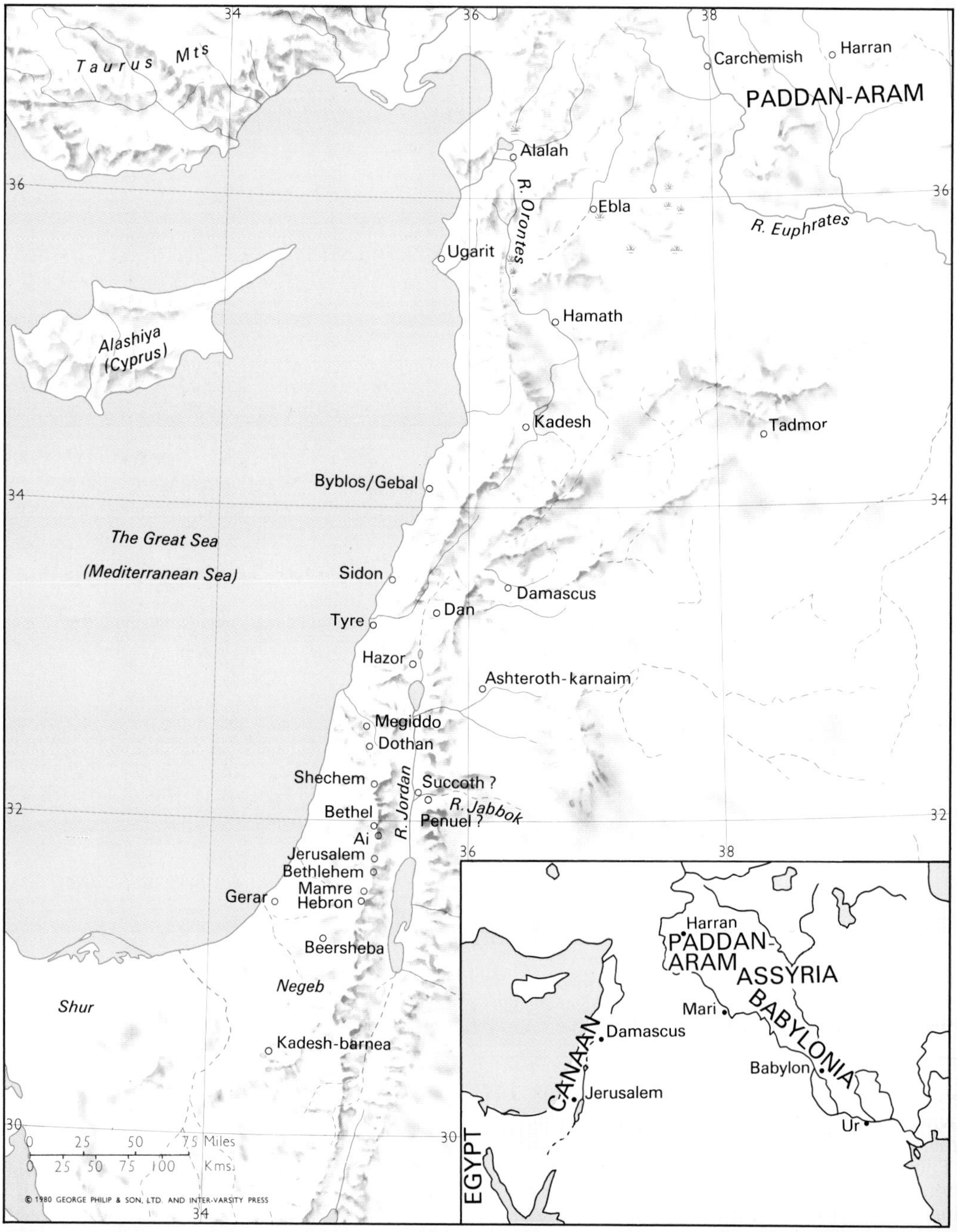

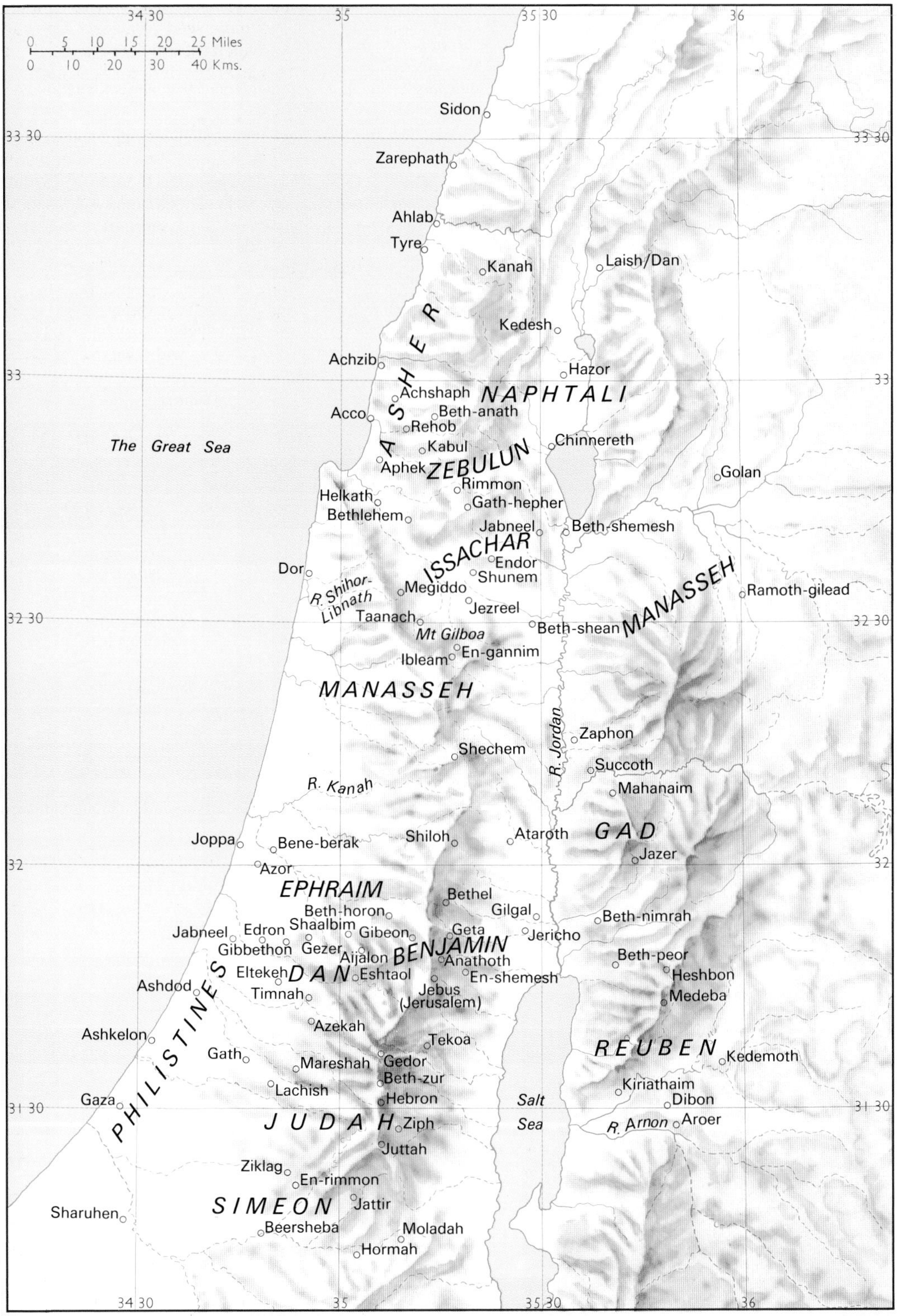


The Tribes of Israel.

ecalls Hadrian's attempt to deny the ewish character of the Roman rovince.

Equally sensitive, however, is the lternative *Eretz-Israel* (Land of srael), an expression which does ccur in the Bible (1 Samuel 13:19 *etc.*; compare Matthew 2:20). In biblical usage this does not mean 'the land called Israel' but rather 'the land belonging to (the people) Israel', since Israel was primarily the name of a people, the descendants of Jacob-Israel. In an attempt to create a neutral term, the expression 'Israel-Palestine' has recently been coined.

The term 'Holy Land' was adopted in the Middle Ages (compare Zechariah 2:12).

The cities allocated to the Levites.

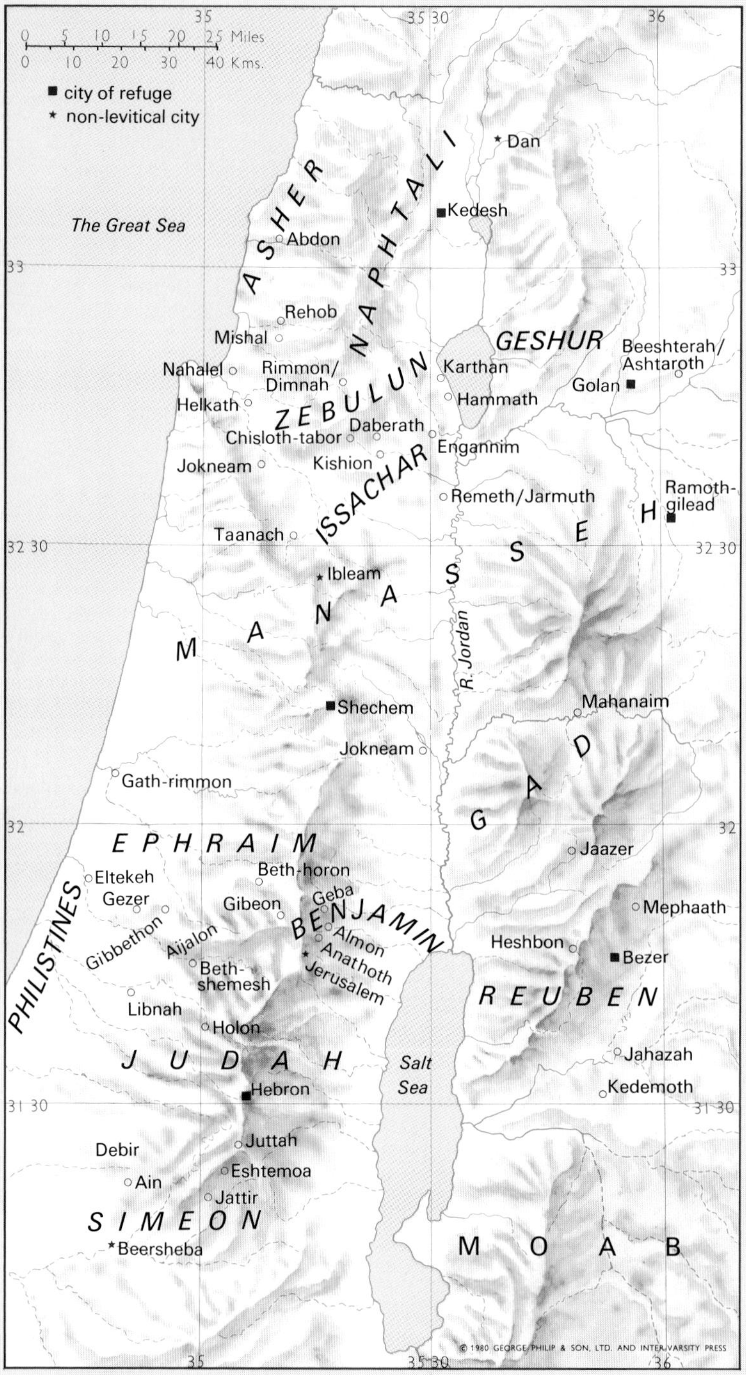


*Central position*
The mediaeval belief that Jerusalem was the centre of the world was not entirely absurd; the thin Syrian corridor bounded by the Mediterranean, Black, Caspian and Red Seas and the Persian Gulf unites Europe, Asia and Africa, and all important international and intercontinental routes must pass through it. The 3 great north–south routes in ancient times were the Trunk Road running along the coast from Egypt to the Vale of Esdraelon then skirting the Lake of Galilee to Damascus; the King's Highway following the edge of the Transjordan Plateau from the Gulf of Aqabah to Damascus; and another through central Palestine linking all the major cities. A number of minor east–west routes cross these.

Perched between the sea and the desert which they feared, the Hebrew highlanders sought to be independent from both environments and their peoples.

*Geographical structure*
The region, which runs 675 kilometres from the Egyptian border to Asia Minor, contains 5 geological zones: the coastal plain, the western mountain chain, the rift valleys, the eastern mountains, and the deserts of Syria and the Negeb. These vary in character from north to south; for example, north of Acre the mountains run almost into the sea, creating natural harbours, whereas south of Mount Carmel the coastal plain is broad and almost harbourless.

The rocks of Palestine are notably chalk and limestone (the central highlands), volcanic rocks (around Galilee), and recent deposits such as marls, gravels and sands.

The Rift Valley (which is traceable southwards to the East African Lakes) has acted like a hinge; areas west of it are formed of rocks laid down under the sea, whereas the eastern (Arabian) block has been

*Right:* Snow-capped Mount Hermon.
*Far right:* The view from the 'Mount of Beatitudes', on the north shore of the Sea of Galilee.

*Far left:* The barren hills of the Judaean Wilderness.
*Left:* Palestine in the time of the Judges.

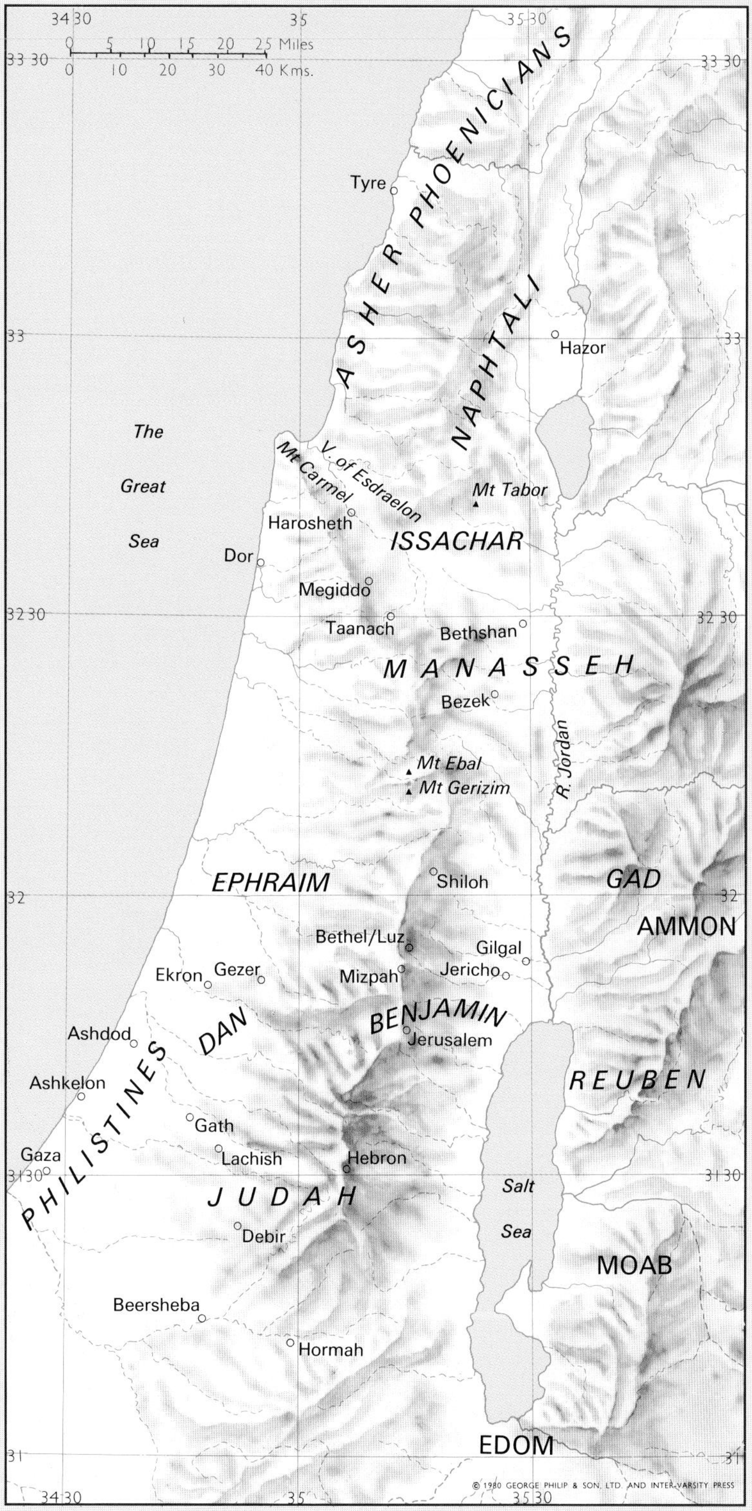


rmed of continental rocks.
The earth's crust is unstable in the ea, and volcanic eruptions curred until the 13th century AD. ne fate of Sodom and Gomorrah as some kind of volcanic action obably associated with the trusion of sulphurous gas and uid asphalt (Genesis 14:10; :24f.). There are also biblical cords of earthquakes (*e.g.*, Samuel 14:15) and geological ulting (Numbers 16:31ff.). Under e semi-arid conditions, badland lief is typical, with hilly areas eeply dissected by wadis.

*ysical features*

ne coastal plains stretch for 200 lometres from Lebanon to Gaza. land from them the Plain of sdraelon or the Jezreel valley was major significance for Israel where rategic cities such as Megiddo, zrel and Bethshan were located.
The Central Hills run 300 lometres from Galilee down to nai. In the south, Judah has gently ndulating folds except in the east, sing to 1,000 metres; in the north e hills of Samaria fall to 300 metres ith Ebal (945 metres) and Gerizim 90 metres) towering above them. orth-west of Galilee, the mountains ach 900 metres.
The Jordan follows the Rift Valley, tering the Sea of Galilee 200 etres below sea-level. To the east e desert tablelands of rock and nd blasted by hot winds.

*imate and vegetation*

nere are 3 climatic zones, each with s own distinct vegetation – editerranean, steppe, and desert. ne coastal plain as far south as aza enjoys mild winters (12°C in nuary at Gaza) and hot summers 6°C in July at Gaza); more centrally Jerusalem the corresponding mperatures are 6° and 23°C.
Less than one-fifteenth of the annual rainfall occurs in the summer (June–October); it varies from 35–40 centimetres on the coast to 75 centimetres on the Judaean and Galilean mountains. Around Beersheba and parts of the Jordan valley the steppe climate produces only 20–30 centimetres of rain.
The deep trough of the Jordan has sub-tropical temperatures; at Jericho in summer the daily average is over 38°C. There is no evidence that the climate has changed since biblical times; for example, Roman gutters excavated near the Gulf of Aqabah still fit the springs for which they were constructed.

*Flora*

The flora of Palestine is very rich (about 3,000 plants) for such a small area because of the great variation in land height. There were few dense forests but much of the woodland in Old Testament times (Joshua 17:18) has disappeared.

Pastoral farming has been partly to blame for deforestation, leading to serious deterioration of once-fertile land into poor scrub in some areas. One estimate suggests that since Roman times 2,000–4,000 million cubic metres of soil have been eroded from the eastern side of the Judaean hills – sufficient for 4,000–8,000 square kilometres of good farmland.

The kingdoms of Israel and Judah.

*'ater supply and agriculture*
ɒart from the Jordan, a few of its ibutaries and some coastal streams d by springs, all the rivers of ılestine are seasonal. There is a ıdden spate after the autumn rains ee Matthew 7:27). Wells were common and irrigation well known; cisterns were built for water storage.

Wheat and barley, figs, grapes and olives were the main crops in biblical times.

*Settlements*
Some 622 place names west of the Jordan are recorded in the Bible, and they are sometimes difficult to identify with certainty. The Jordan valley seems to have been occupied since earliest times. A semblance of

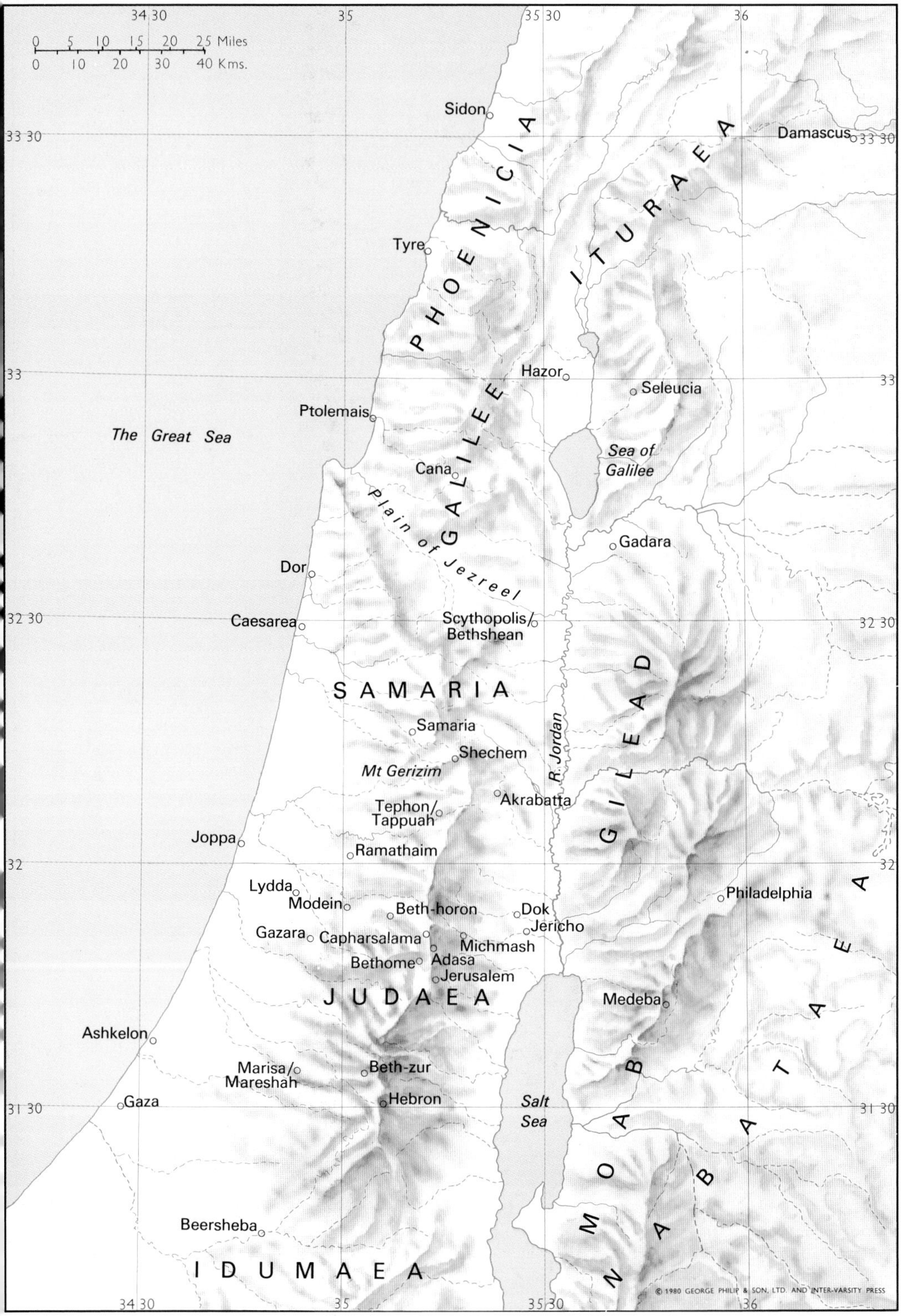


**Israel in the intertestamental period.**

urban life existed at Jericho by *c.*8000–6000 BC. Of 70 settlements in the valley many were established over 5,000 years ago but only 35 were still inhabited in Israelite times. Until about 1200 BC there were relatively few settlements in the Central Hills, perhaps because of forestation, but they included important towns such as Hebron, Jerusalem, Bethel, Shechem and Samaria. The coastal plain south of Carmel favoured fairly dense settlement but farther north, where water was more abundant, the thick woodland made settlement difficult. Location of towns was largely determined by water supply, and the strategic value of occupying important crossroads such as those at Hebron, Jerusalem, Megiddo, Hazor and Samaria.

J. M. Houston, J. Bimson

*Further reading*

D. Baly, *The Geography of the Bible*, 2nd edition, 1974
G. Dalman, *Sacred Sites and Ways*, 1935
N. Glueck, *The River Jordan*, 1946
J. Rogerson, *New Atlas of the Bible*, 1985
G. A. Smith, *The Historical Geography of the Holy Land*, 25th edition, 1931
*National Atlas of Israel* (in Hebrew), in course of publication since 1958

See also *JORDAN, *NEGEB, *SHARON, *ZIN. For archaeology of Palestine, see individual sites.

**The areas administered by the tetrarchs in Palestine.**

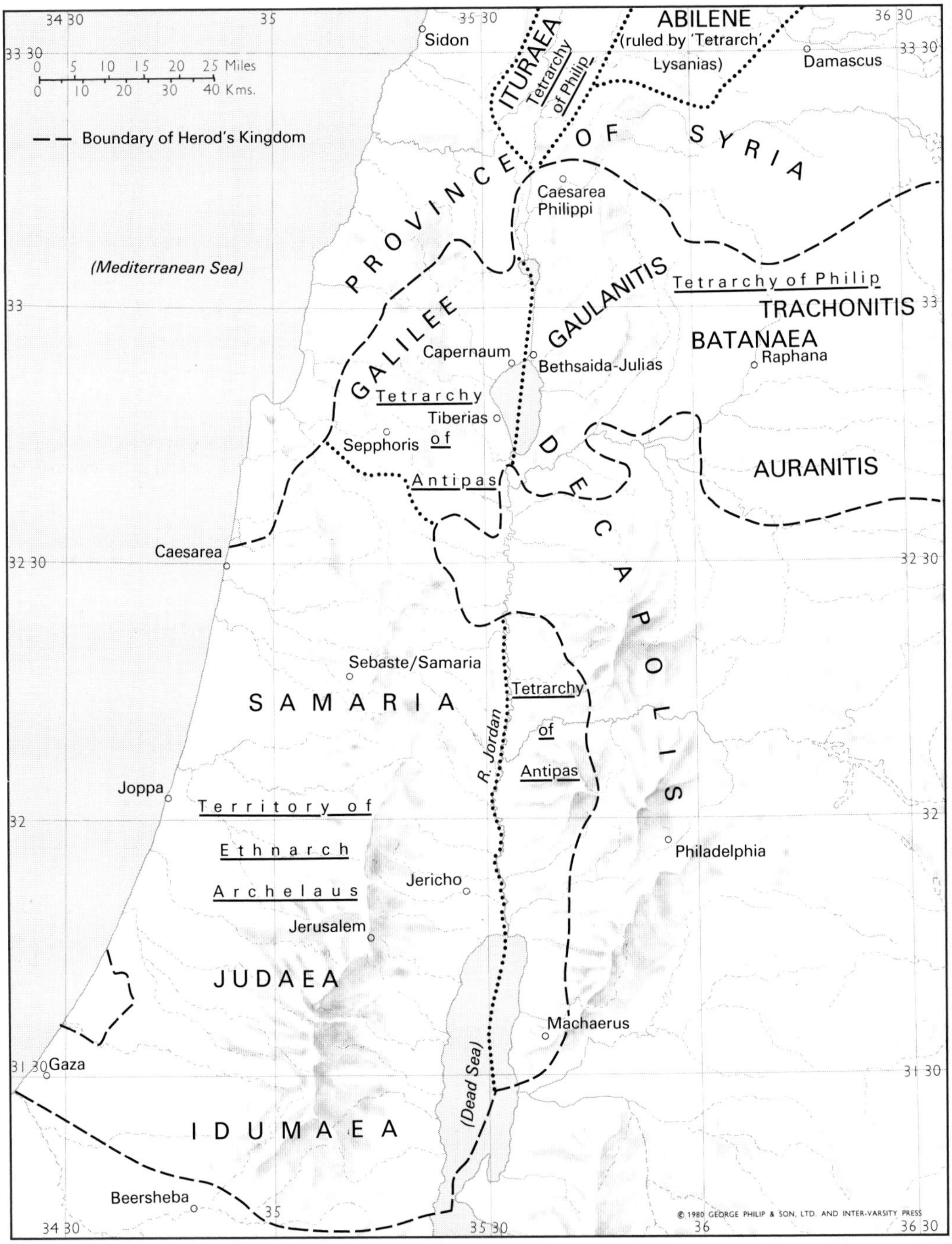

**ontinued from p. 235**
roboam rebuilt the city there, esumably to defend the invader's ute from the east to his new capital Shechem (1 Kings 12:25).

The exact site is unknown, but S. errill in *East of Jordan*, 1881, ). 390–392, makes a good case for e ancient ruins 6 kilometres east of ccoth on 2 hills called Tulul -Dahab.

B. Job, J. Bimson

**EOR.** A mountain somewhere to e north of the Dead Sea and pposite Jericho, described as oking towards the desert, but its cation is not certainly identified. It as the last place from which alaam blessed Israel (Numbers :28).

R. Millard

*ırther reading*

A. Jaussen and R. Savignac, *'ission en Arabie*, 1909, pp. 2, 650f.

**ERAEA.** A district in Transjordan, rresponding roughly to the ilead of the Old Testament. It is ever mentioned by name in the ew Testament (except in variant adings of Luke 6:17) but is the strict referred to several times (*e.g.* atthew 19:1) as the land 'beyond rdan'.

The name Peraea came into use ter the Exile, to denote an area east the Jordan *c.* 16 kilometres wide, retching from the river Arnon in e south to some point between the abbok and the Yarmuk in the north erhaps to the Wadi Jabis). It mprised essentially the edge of e 1,000-metre scarp overlooking e Jordan, with its towns, and was us a highland region, with lequate (75 centimetres per mum) rainfall and tree cover in its gher parts. At intermediate evations there were olives and nes, and cultivation tailed off to the ast through the wheatfields and en the steppe pastures of lower nds.

Peraea was evidently an attractive gion in Old Testament times, for ter seeing it and adjacent areas the ibes of Gad and Reuben (Numbers 2:1–5) lost interest in crossing rdan with their cattle.

In the time of Christ Peraea was cupied by Jews and ruled by erod Antipas, and by Jews it was garded as possessing equality of atus with Judaea and Galilee. As it djoined both of these across the rdan, it was possible by traversing s length to follow an all-Jewish ute from Galilee to Judaea, thus by-passing the territory of the Samaritans.

J. H. Paterson

**PERGA.** An ancient city of unknown foundation in *Pamphylia; well sited in an extensive valley, watered by the Cestrus. It was the religious capital of Pamphylia, like Ephesus, a 'cathedral city' of Artemis, whose temple stood on a nearby hill. Like most cities on that pirate-ridden coast, Perga stands a little inland, and was served by a river-harbour.

Attaleia, founded in the 2nd century BC, later served as Perga's port, but also absorbed her prosperity. Some ruins remain giving a pleasant impression of the ancient Perga, but Attaleia survives as an active port, the modern Adalia, one of the beauty-spots of Anatolia, so completely did Attalus' foundation overwhelm the more ancient towns.

Acts 13:13–14 records Perga as the place where Paul, Barnabas and John Mark landed after Cyprus and where John Mark left for Jerusalem while the others sailed to Pisidian Antioch.

E. M. Blaiklock

**PERGAMUM.** A city of the Roman province of Asia, in the west of what is now Asiatic Turkey. It occupied a commanding position near the seaward end of the broad valley of the Caicus, and was probably the site of a settlement from a very early date.

Pergamum became important only after 282 BC, when Philetaerus revolted against Lysimachus of Thrace and made it the capital of what became the Attalid kingdom, which in 133 BC was bequeathed by Attalus III to the Romans, who formed the province of *Asia from it.

The first temple of the imperial cult was built in Pergamum (*c.* 29 BC) in honour of Rome and Augustus. The city thus boasted a religious primacy in the province, though *Ephesus became its main commercial centre.

*The church in Pergamum*

Pergamum is listed third of the 'seven churches of Asia' (Revelation 1:11): the order suits its position in geographical sequence. This was the place 'where Satan's throne is' (Revelation 2:13). The phrase has been referred to the complex of pagan cults, of Zeus, Athena, Dionysus and Asclepius, established by the Attalid kings, that of Asclepius Soter (the 'saviour', 'healer') being of special importance.

These cults are illustrative of the religious history of Pergamum, but the main allusion is probably to emperor worship. This was where the worship of the divine emperor had been made the touchstone of civic loyalty under Domitian. It marked a crisis for the church in Asia. Antipas (verse 13) is probably cited as a representative (perhaps the first) of those who were brought to judgment and execution here for their faith.

This letter is the primary source for the Nicolaitans, who are emphatically equated with Balaam, and seem to be a party which advocated compromise under pagan pressures.

Here Christ possesses the real and ultimate authority, symbolized by the 'sharp two-edged sword' (verse 12), in the place where the Roman proconsul exercised the 'power of the sword' in judgment. The church is blamed for tolerating a party whose teaching would subvert it

**The Trajanum, ancient Pergamum.**

into idolatry and immorality like that of Balaam. But the 'conqueror' receives a pledge of Christ's inward relationship with him.

The meaning of the 'white stone' (verse 17) is uncertain: it is properly a 'pebble' or *tessera* (tablet; Greek *psēphos*). These had many uses, more than one of which may be apposite here. They represented acquittal, or served as a token or ticket of many kinds. The written name here is of the individual, and marks Christ's individual acceptance of the believer.

A small town (Bergama) still stands on the plain below the acropolis of the ancient city.

M. J. S. Rudwick, C. J. Hemer

*Further reading*

W. M. Ramsay, *The Letters to the Seven Churches of Asia*, 1904, chs. 21–22

C. J. Hemer, 'Pergamum', *The Letters to the Seven Churches of Asia in their Local Setting*, *JSOT*, 1986, ch. 5

**PERSIA, PERSIANS.** The Indo-European Persians, nomadic pastoralists from southern Russia, probably entered the Iranian plateau late in the 2nd millennium BC.

In 836 BC Shalmaneser III of Assyria received tribute from rulers of a Parsua near Lake Urmia. His successor found the land of Parsuash in the south where several tribes finally settled. This area, east of the Persian Gulf, is still called Farsistan. Persepolis and Parsagarda were the chief towns. The Hebrew *pāras*, 'Persia', refers to this land.

## Persian and Jewish history

The early traditions of the Persian people are recorded in the sacred book, the Zend-Avesta. The earliest recorded kings ruled from Anshan, north-west of Susa. The Achaemenes who was claimed as founder of the dynasty by later kings probably reigned *c.* 680 BC. His grandson, Cyrus I, opposed Ashurbanipal of Assyria, but later submitted.

*The Medes and the Persians*

Cyrus II, grandson of Cyrus I, rebelled against his Median suzerain, Astyages, killing him and taking over his capital, *Ecbatana, in 550 BC. Thereafter Median language and customs had strong influence on the Persians. This success was followed by the subjugation of Anatolia and the conquest of Croesus of Lydia (547 BC).

*The conquest of Babylonia*

Cyrus then turned east to extend his realm into north-west India. By 540 BC he was sufficiently strong to attack Babylonia. After several battles he entered Babylon in triumph on 29 October 539 BC, 17 days after the city had fallen to his army (Daniel 5:30f.). The king soon returned to Susa, but his son Cambyses remained in Babylon to represent him in religious ceremonies.

The whole empire was divided into large regions ruled by satraps, chosen from Persian or Median nobles but with native officers unde them (see Daniel 6). Various statue of gods which had been collected into Babylon by the last native king Nabonidus (perhaps reflected in Isaiah 46:1f.), were returned to the own shrines.

*End of the Jewish Exile*

As there was no image of Yahweh return to Jerusalem, Cyrus gave back to the Jews the precious vessels looted from the temple by Nebuchadrezzar (Ezra 1:7ff.; compare *DOTT*, pp. 92–94). More important, he gave royal authoriza- tion for the rebuilding of the templ to any Jew who wished to return to Judah (Ezra 1:1–4). One Sheshbazz was appointed governor (Ezra 5:14

The governor of the province of 'Across the River' (the country wes of the Euphrates) was clearly unaware of Cyrus' edict when in 52 BC he attempted to delay the work. His letter went to his superior, the satrap who had charge of Babylon and the west. No record was found among the archives kept at Babylo but a memorandum was found at Ecbatana, where Cyrus had reside during his first regnal year. Darius (522–486 BC) confirmed the decree and ordered his officials to help the Jews.

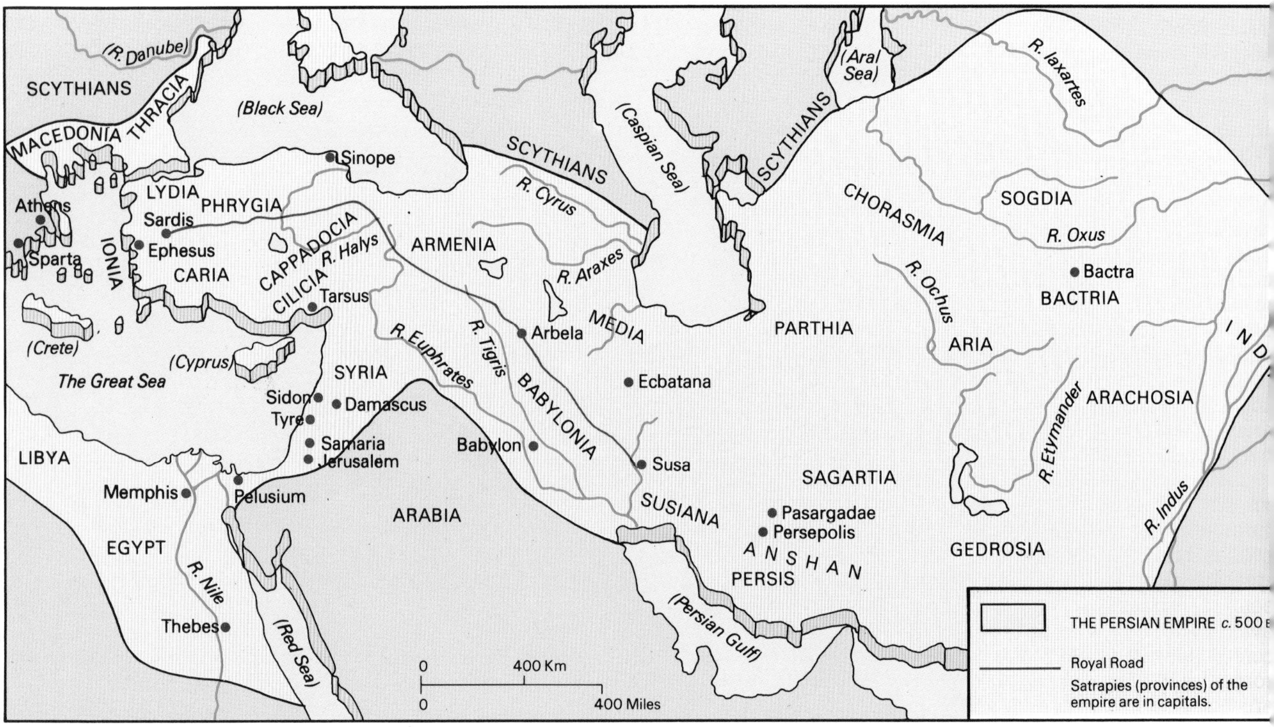


The Persian Empire, 550–330 BC.

Remains of the columned throne-room of the palace of the Persian Kings Xerxes (*c.* 486–465 BC) and Artaxerxes I (465–424 BC) at Persepolis, Iran.

*he Persian empire*
arius and his successor Xerxes I
86–465 BC) expended considerable
nergy in an attempt to conquer the
reeks of the Peloponnese, almost
e only area remaining outside the
ersian empire in the known world,
r Cambyses II (530–522 BC) had
nnexed Egypt in 525 BC. The defeat
Marathon (490 BC) by a small
reek army was the only rebuff
uffered by Darius.
The reorganization of the
atrapies by Darius, his system of
ilitary commanders, and his
troduction of coinage, legal and
ostal systems lasted as long as the
mpire. These facilities coupled with
e considerable degree of
utonomy allowed to subject
eoples contributed greatly to the
ability of the empire and allowed
ich a small community as Judah to
urvive, Jewish officers acting as
overnors (*pḥh*) there.

*zra and Nehemiah*
nder Artaxerxes I (465–424 BC)
ewish affairs had official
presentation at court. Ezra, it
eems, was 'Secretary of State for
ewish Affairs' (Ezra 7:12). He was
ccredited as special envoy to
eorganize the temple services at
erusalem (458 BC).

The eager Jews were led on by the encouragement they received to exceed the terms of Ezra's commission and rebuild the city wall. This was reported to the king by the governor of Samaria. The royal reply (Ezra 4:17–23) ordered the cessation of the work, for search of the records had shown that the city had revolted against earlier kings. Artaxerxes was faced with rebellion in Egypt (*c.* 460–454 BC), so he could not allow the construction of a fortress so near to that country. However, the royal cupbearer was a Jew, Nehemiah, who was able to reverse the effects of this decree by having himself appointed governor of Judah (Hebrew *tiršāṯā'*, a Persian word, Nehemiah 8:9) with permission to rebuild the walls (445 BC).

No record remains of relations between the Persian rulers and the Jews after this period. When the Persian empire was in the power of Alexander (331 BC) the Jews simply transferred their allegiance from one monarch to another.

**Persian culture**
The Indo-European Persian language was written in a cuneiform script composed of 51 simple syllabic signs but this was restricted to imperial monuments almost exclusively. The imperial chancery used the Aramaic language and characters for official communications (*e.g.* the letters in Ezra, compare *DOTT*, pp. 256–269). Translations were made into local tongues (see Esther 3:12; 8:9).

The luxury of the Persian court as described in the book of Esther is attested by objects found at several sites. A number of stone bas-reliefs depict the king and his courtiers and the tribute of the vanquished. Portraits of the different racial groups are especially fine examples of Persian stone carving.

The Oxus treasure (now mostly in the British Museum) and other chance finds show the skill of goldsmiths and jewellers. Solid gold and silver bowls and vases illustrate the wealth of the kings. Greek influences may be seen in some Persian works and Greek craftsmen appear among lists of palace dependants.

**Persian religion**
The early Persians revered gods of nature, fertility and the heavens. The tribe of the Magi were nearly exclusively the priests. Some time after 1000 BC Zoroaster proclaimed a religion of lofty moral ideals based on the principle 'Do good, hate evil'.

For him there was one god, Ahura-mazda, the Good, represented by purifying fire and water. Opposed to the good was a dark power of Evil. This creed was adopted by Darius I, but soon became lost among the more ancient cults.

Zoroaster's doctrines survived and were spread abroad. Their influence has been traced in the writings of early Judaism and, by some scholars, in the New Testament.

A. R. Millard

*Further reading*

A. T. Olmstead, *History of the Persian Empire*, 1948
J. Bright, *A History of Israel*, 3rd edition, 1980, pp. 405–412
R. N. Frye, *The Heritage of Persia*, 2nd edition, 1975
E. Porada, *Ancient Iran*, 1965
M. Boyce, *A History of Zoroastrianism* 1, 1975
E. M. Yamauchi, *Persia and the Bible*, 1990
H. G. M. Williamson, 'The Governors of Judah Under the Persians', *TynB* 39, 1988, pp. 59–82
G. W. Ahlström, *The History of Ancient Palestine,* 1993, pp. 812–906

**PETHOR.** A city of northern Mesopotamia, south of Carchemish, mentioned in Numbers 22:5 as by the river (*i.e.* the Euphrates) and in Deuteronomy 23:4 as in Mesopotamia, it was the home of Balaam. Thither Balak sent messengers to call him to curse Israel.

Pethor in 'Amaw is the Pitru of Assyrian texts (compare *ANET*, p. 278), described as on the river Sāgūr (modern Sājūr), near its junction with the Euphrates. On 'Amaw, see Albright in *BASOR* 118, 1950, pp. 15–16, note 13, and for 'the eastern mountains (or hills)' note that in a 15th-century BC Egyptian text, chariot-wood from 'Amaw is said to come from 'god's land [meaning the East] in the hill-country of Naharen' – *i.e.* hills overlooking 'Amaw on the Sājūr river flowing into the Euphrates on its western bank; this western extension of (Aram-) Naharaim is attested by both Hebrew and Egyptian references.

R. A. H. Gunner

**PHARATHON.** See *PIRATHON.

**PHARPAR** ('swift'). One of the two 'rivers of Damascus' of which Naaman boasted (2 Kings 5:12). It is 64 kilometres long, and is one of the tributaries of the *Abana or Barada, flowing east from Hermon a little south of Damascus. Today it is called the 'Awaj'.

J. D. Douglas

**PHILADELPHIA.** A city in the Roman province of Asia, in the west of what is now Asiatic Turkey. It was perhaps founded by Eumenes, king of Pergamum, in the 2nd century BC, and certainly named after his brother Attalus, whose loyalty had earned him the name Philadelphus.

Philadelphia was situated near the upper end of a broad valley leading down through Sardis to the sea near Smyrna; and it lay at the threshold of a very fertile tract of plateau country, from which much of its commercial prosperity derived.

The area was subject to frequent earthquakes. A severe one in AD 17 destroyed the city; and as the shocks continued intermittently the people took to living outside the city (Strabo, *Geography* 12.8.18 [579]; 13.4.10 [628]). After an imperial bounty had helped it to recover, the city voluntarily assumed the new name of Neocaesarea. Later, under Vespasian, it took another imperial name, Flavia.

The city was remarkable for the number of its temples and religious festivals. The site is now occupied by the town of Alaşehir.

*The church in Philadelphia*

The letter to 'the angel of the church in Philadelphia' (Revelation 3:7–13) probably alludes to some of the circumstances of the city. As Philadelphus was renowned for his loyalty to his brother, so the church, the true Philadelphia, inherits and fulfils his character by its steadfast loyalty to Christ (verses 8, 10).

As the city stands by the 'open door' of a region from which its wealth derives, so the church is given an 'open door' of opportunity to exploit (verse 8; compare 2 Corinthians 2:12). The symbols of the 'crown' and the 'temple' (verses 11–12) point to a contrast with the games and religious festivals of the city. In contrast with the impermanence of life in a city prone to earthquakes, those who 'overcome' are promised the ultimate stability of being built into the temple of God.

As at Smyrna, this church had met rejection from the Jews in the city (verse 9), but the conqueror shall enjoy final acceptance by the Lord whose name he had confessed (verse 8), signified again by the conferring on him of the divine names (verse 12), which recall the new names taken by the city from the divine emperors.

Ignatius later visited the city on his way from Antioch to martyrdom in Rome, and sent a letter to the church there.

M. J. S. Rudwick

*Further reading*

W. M. Ramsay, *The Letters to the Seven Churches of Asia*, 1904, chs. 27–28
C. J. Hemer, 'Philadelphia', *The Letters to the Seven Churches of Asia in their Local Setting*, *JSOT*, 1986, ch. 8

**PHILIPPI.** In the course of his apostolic travels Paul received in a vision an invitation from a man of Macedonia who implored, 'Come over to Macedonia, and help us' (Acts 16:9). Interpreting this plea as a summons from God, Paul and his party sailed for Neapolis, the port of Philippi, 13 kilometres south of the city and the terminus of the Egnatian Way, a military road which joined Rome and the East as a much valued line of communication.

The arrival at Philippi is marked in Acts 16:12 by a description of the city: 'the leading city of Macedonia and a Roman colony'. The stages by which the city attained the rank of this noble description may be traced.

*History*

The town derives its name from Philip of Macedon, who took it from the Thasians about 360 BC. He enlarged the settlement, and fortified it to defend his frontiers against the Thasians.

At this time the gold-mining industry was developed, and gold coins were struck in the name of Philip and became commonly recognized. After the battle of Pydna in 168 BC it was annexed by the Romans; and when Macedonia was divided into four parts for administrative purposes Philippi was included in the first of the four districts. This fact supports a proposal of *prōtēs* in place of the Received Text's *prōtē* in Acts 16:12, suggested by F. Field and accepted by F. Blass, who explained it by this reference to the division of Macedonia into four districts by Aemilius Paullus in 167 BC (Livy, 45.17–18, 29); compare the commentaries on Acts by H. Conzelmann and E. Haenchen. On this emended reading the verse runs: 'a city of the first division of Macedonia'.

If the text is not changed, Philippi's claim to be 'chief city of the district' can be accepted only in a general sense, as A. N. Sherwin-

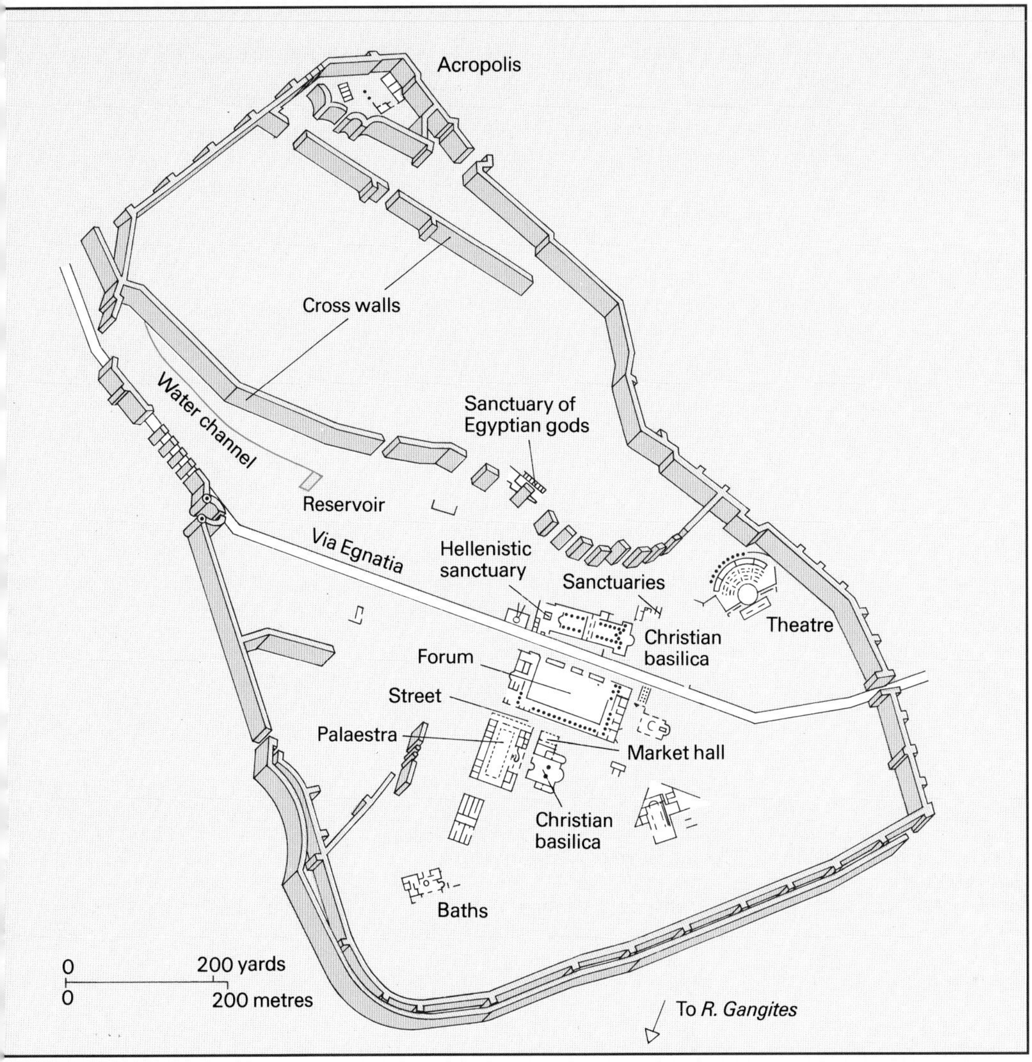


**Plan of the site of Philippi, the 'leading city of the district of Macedonia' in Paul's day (Acts 16:12).**

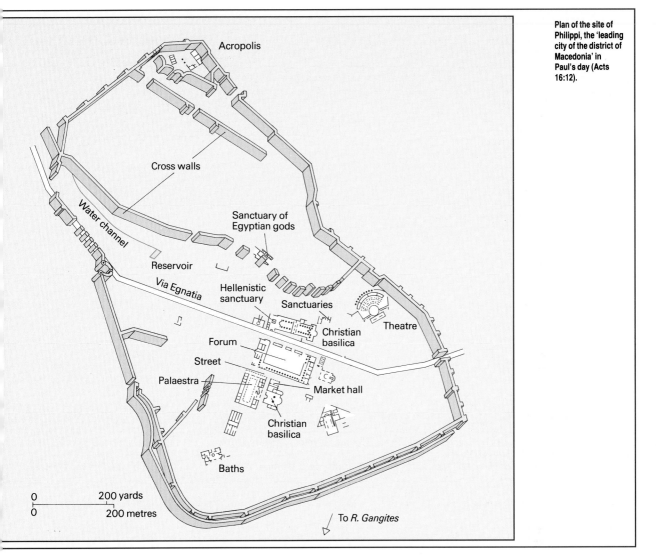

White observes (in *Roman Society and Roman Law in the New Testament*, 1963, pp. 93ff.). The comment possibly reflects Luke's special interest in the city, which may have been his birth-place.

In 42 BC the famous battle of Philippi was fought with Antony and Octavian ranged against Brutus and Cassius. After this date the town was enlarged, probably by the coming of colonists; the title *Colonia Iulia* is attested at this time. This prominence was enhanced further when, after the battle of Actium in 31 BC, in which Octavian defeated the forces of Antony and Cleopatra, the town 'received a settlement of Italian colonists who had favoured Antony and had been obliged to surrender their land to the veterans of Octavian' (Lake and Cadbury, p. 187).

Octavian gave the town its notable title, *Col(onia) Iul(ia) Aug(usta) Philip(pensis)*, which has appeared on coins. Of all the privileges which this title conferred, the possession of the 'Italic right' (*ius Italicum*) was the most valuable. It meant that the colonists enjoyed the same rights and privileges as if their land were part of Italian soil.

*Paul in Philippi*

The civic pride of the Philippians (who are given the equivalent of their Latin name *Philippenses* in Paul's letter, 4:15) is a feature of the Acts narrative, and reappears in allusions the apostle makes in the Epistle (see Acts 16:21 and compare 16:37). Official names are used (*duoviri* in 16:20, 22, and 'lictors' in 16:35). The Greek word translated 'uncondemned' in 16:37 probably reflects the Latin *re incognita* or *indicta causa*, *i.e.* 'without examination'.

In the letter to the Philippian church two passages, 1:27 and 3:20, speak of 'citizenship', a term which would have special appeal to the readers; and the virtues listed in 4:8 are those which the Roman mind would particularly appreciate.

After the apostle's first visit with his preaching, imprisonment and release, his further contact with the city is inferred from references in Acts 20:1, 6 and 1 Timothy 1:3.

R. P. Martin

*Further reading*

Historical details are supplied in:
*BC* 1, 4, 1933, *ad loc.*
R. P. Martin, *Philippians* (NCB), 1976, Introduction, section 1, which describes the religious *milieu* of the city at the time of Paul's arrival there
For archaeological information:
P. Collari, *Philippes, ville de Macédoine*, 2 vols., containing plates and text, 1937
W. A. McDonald, *BA* 3, 1940, pp. 18–24

## PHILISTIA, PHILISTINES.

### Name

In the Old Testament the name Philistine is written *p^e^lištî*, usually with the article, and more commonly in its plural form *p^e^lištîm* (rarely *p^e^lištiyyîm*) generally without the article.

The territory which they inhabited was known as 'the land of the Philistines' (*'ereṣ p^e^lištîm*) or Philistia (*p^e^lešeṯ*). It is from these that the modern name 'Palestine' derives. In the Septuagint the word is variously rendered *Phylistieim* (mainly in the Pentateuch, Joshua and Judges), *Hellēnas* (Isaiah 9:12 [11, Hebrew]), and *allophylos, -oi*, 'stranger, foreigner' (but not in the Pentateuch or Joshua). It is probable that the name is to be identified with *prst* in the Egyptian texts (the hieroglyphic script having no separate symbol for the *l* sound) and *palaštu* in the Assyrian cuneiform inscriptions.

### In the Bible

*Origin of the Philistines*

The Philistines derived from Casluhim, the son of Mizraim (Egypt) the son of Ham (Genesis 10:14; 1 Chronicles 1:12). When they later appeared and confronted the Israelites they came from *Caphtor (Amos 9:7).

*In the time of the Patriarchs*

Abraham and Isaac had dealings with a Philistine, Abimelech, the king of Gerar, and his general Phichol (Genesis 20–21; 26). In the time of the Monarchy the Philistines were almost proverbially aggressive, but Abimelech was a reasonable man. He had adopted many of the customs of the country, for he bore a Semitic name, and engaged with Isaac in a covenant.

*At the time of the Exodus and the Judges*

When the Israelites left Egypt they were obliged to detour inland to avoid 'the way of the land of the Philistines' (Exodus 13:17). The adjacent section of the Mediterranean was in fact referred to as the sea of the Philistines (Exodus 23:31). It is uncertain whether these terms are being used retrospectively or whether Philistines were already extensively settled along the coastal strip between Egypt and Gaza at the time of the Exodus. It is presumably the Philistines in this area who are referred to as Caphtorim in Deuteronomy 2:23.

The Israelites did not encounter the Philistines in Canaan during the Conquest, but by the time Joshua was an old man they were established in the five cities of Gaza, Ashkelon, Ashdod, Ekron and Gath (Joshua 13:23). From this time for many generations these people were used by God to chastise the Israelites (Judges 3:2–3). Shamgar ben Anath repulsed them temporarily (Judges 3:31), but they constantly pressed inland from the coast plain, and the Israelites even adopted their gods (Judges 10:6–7).

The great Israelite hero of the period of the Judges was Samson (Judges 13–16). In his time there were social links between Philistines and Israelites, for he married a Philistine wife, and later had relations with Delilah, who, if not a Philistine herself, was in close contact with them. The hill-country was not under Philistine control, and Samson took refuge there after his raids. When he was finally taken by them he was bound with bronze fetters (16:21) and forced to make sport for them while they watched from inside and on the roof of a pillared building (16:25–27).

*In the reigns of Saul and David*

It was probably largely due to the continuing pressure of the Philistines that the need for a strong military leader was felt in Israel. The ark was captured by the Philistines in a disastrous battle at Aphek and the shrine at Shiloh was destroyed (1 Samuel 4). At this time they probably controlled Esdraelon, the coast plain, the Negeb, and much of the hill-country. They also controlled the distribution of iron, and thus prevented the Israelites from having useful weapons (1 Samuel 13:19–22).

Saul was anointed king by Samuel, and after a victory over the Philistines at Michmash, drove them from the hill-country (1 Samuel 14). His erratic rule, however, allowed the Philistines to continue to assert themselves, as when they challenged Israel at Ephes-dammim, and David killed Goliath (1 Samuel 17–18).

Saul turned against David, who became an outlaw and finally a vassal of Achish king of Gath (1 Samuel 27). He was not called upon to fight against Israel at the battle of Mount Gilboa when Saul and his sons were killed, and when he took over the kingship of Israel he must have remained on peaceful terms with Gath at least, and in fact maintained a personal Philistine bodyguard throughout his reign.

A final conflict had to come, however. David drove the Philistines out of the hill-country and struck a heavy blow in Philistia itself (2 Samuel 5:25), putting an end to the power of the Philistines as a serious menace.

*During the divided Monarchy*

The Philistines continued to cause trouble throughout the Monarchy. With the weakening of the kingdom at the death of David the Philistine cities (except for Gath, 2 Chronicles 11:8) were independent and there was fighting on the frontier (1 Kings 15:27; 16:15). Jehoshaphat received tribute from some of the Philistines (2 Chronicles 17:11), but under Jehoram the border town of Libnah was lost to Israel (2 Kings 8:22).

The Philistines were still aggressive in the time of Ahaz (Isaiah 9:8–12). The last time they are mentioned in the Bible is in the prophecy of Zechariah, after the return from the Exile.

### Philistia

The area which took its name from the Philistines was that of the nucleus of their settlement. This centred on the five main Philistine cities of Gaza, Ashkelon, Ashdod, Ekron and Gath, and comprised the coastal strip south of Carmel, extending inland to the foothills of Judah.

Other cities particularly associated with the Philistines in the Bible are *Bethshean and *Gerar. There is still uncertainty concerning the identification of the sites of some of the five principal Philistine cities (see under separate city names).

### In the inscriptions

The Philistines are first mentioned by name (*prst*) in the annals of Ramesses III for his 5th and 8th years (1180 and 1177 BC), inscribed in his temple to Ammon at Medinet Habu near Thebes. This describes his campaign against an invasion of Libyans (Year 5) and various other peoples generally known as the 'Sea Peoples' (Year 8), of whom the *prst* were one.

Other members of the 'Sea Peoples' had already been mentioned in the inscriptions of Merenptah, Ramesses II and in the 14th-century Amarna Letters (Lukku, Sherden, Danuna).

The carved reliefs in the temple at Medinet Habu show the 'Sea Peoples' arriving with their families and chattels by wagon and ship, and the *prst* and another group closely associated with them, the *ṯkr*

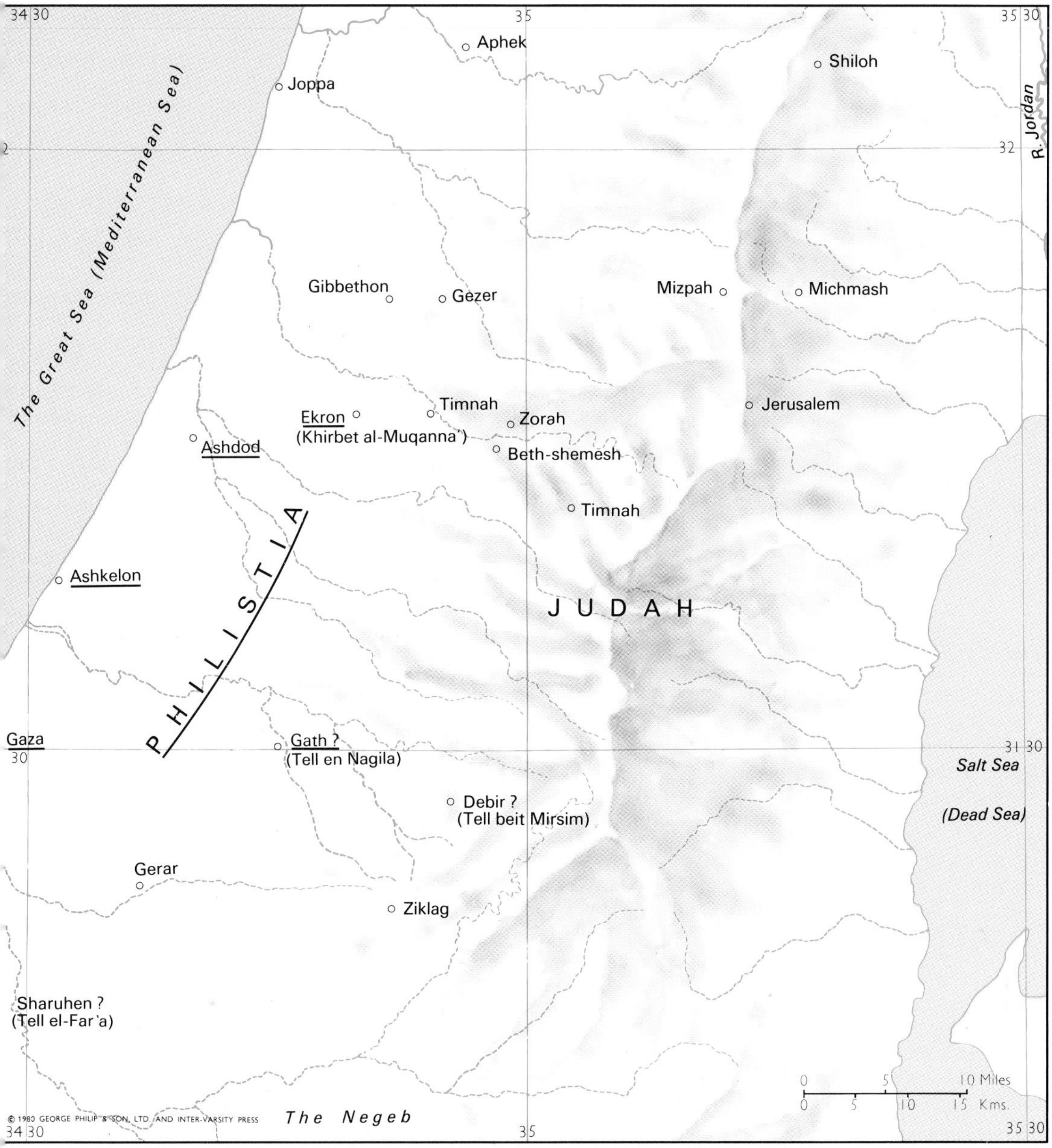


**The cities of the Philistines and their neighbours.**

Tjekker), are depicted clean-shaven and wearing head-dresses of feathers rising vertically from a horizontal band. However, not all prst are depicted this way. Also at Medinet Habu is a *prst* wearing a beard and tight-fitting cap, so generalisations should be avoided.

The Assyrian inscriptions of the first millennium BC mention Philistia as an area often in revolt. The first occurrence is in an inscription of Adad-nirari III (810–782 BC), where Philistia is mentioned among other tribute-paying states, including Israel. The Philistines are subsequently mentioned in the annals of Tiglath-pileser III, Sargon and Sennacherib, usually as defeated rebels.

In a group of cuneiform documents of the time of the Exile found at Babylon, the issue of rations to expatriates is recorded. Among these are mentioned men from Philistia.

## Archaeology

*Pottery*

A distinctive type of painted pottery has been found in a number of sites centring on Philistia and from levels of the late 2nd millennium BC. Since this was the area and period of the Philistines, this pottery is usually attributed to them.

In its decoration it shows marked affinities with that of the Aegean, and excavations at Enkomi and Sinda in Cyprus have brought to light locally-made pottery (*c.* 1225–1175 BC) which is classified as Mycenaean IIIC1b, deriving from Aegean originals, and most probably representing the forerunner of the Philistine pottery. This pottery has been found at those cities of the pentapolis which have been excavated (Ashdod, Ashkelon and Ekron) and also particularly at Tell Qasile and Tell Batash (probably Timna) showing them to have been Philistine centres.

It is clear also that there were Philistine enclaves at a number of other sites, notably Gezer, Beth-shemesh and Deir el-Balah.

*Clay coffins*

Clay coffins, each with a face moulded in relief at the head end, have been discovered at *Beth-shean,

Deir el-Balah, Tell el-Far'a, Lachish and in Transjordan, which are probably to be connected with similar coffins found in Egypt, notably at Tell el-Yehudiyeh in the Delta. The date and distribution of these suggest that they may be attributed to Egyptian officers and officials, and foreign mercenaries, including Philistines (whose coffins have faces surmounted by a row of vertical strokes, perhaps indicating the feathered head-dress), serving under them.

*Weapons*

The Egyptian reliefs show the *prst*, with the Tjekker and Sherden, as armed with lances, round shields, long broadswords and triangular daggers. They arrived in Palestine at the period of transition from the Bronze to Iron Age, so that the biblical statements that they bound Samson with fetters of bronze but, by the time of Saul, controlled the iron industry of the area are quite consistent.

## Culture

The Philistines, while retaining a few cultural features bespeaking their foreign origin, were largely assimilated to the Canaanite culture that surrounded them.

*Government*

The five Philistine cities were each ruled by a *seren* (Joshua 13:3; Judges 3:3; 16:5, 8, 18, 27, 30; 1 Samuel 5:8, 11; 6:4, 12, 16, 18; 7:7; 29:2, 6–7; 1 Chronicles 12:19). The term is probably cognate with the Luwian (Hieroglyphic Hittite) *tarwanas*, 'judge' or the like, and the pre-Hellenic (probably Indo-European) Greek *tyrannos*, 'absolute ruler'. The precise meaning of *seren* is uncertain, but 'ruler' (RSV) is a reasonable rendering.

*Language*

No Philistine inscriptions have been recovered, and the language is unknown, though some scholars have surmised that it may have derived from a possibly Indo-European, pre-Greek speech of the Aegean area. Certain words in the Bible may be Philistine loan-words. In addition to *seren*, the word for helmet, whose foreign origin is betrayed in the variant spellings *kôḇa'* and *qôḇa'*, is usually attributed to the Philistines. Another word which some scholars would label as Philistine is *'argāz*, 'box' (1 Samuel 6:8, 11, 15, AV 'coffer').

From time to time other words have been designated as Philistine, but without general assent. Among the names, Achish (*'āḵîš*) is probably the same as *'kš*, which is listed as a *kftyw* (see also *CAPHTOR) name in an Egyptian inscription of the 16th century BC, and Goliath (*golyat*) is perhaps linked by its *-yat* termination with Luwian (Hieroglyphic Hittite) and Lydian names ending respectively in *-wattaš* and *-uattes*.

Aside from these few words, it is clear that the Philistines adopted the Semitic tongue of the peoples they dispossessed.

*Religion*

Knowledge of the Philistine religion depends mainly upon the Bible. The three gods mentioned, Dagon, Ashtoreth and Baalzebub, were all Near Eastern, and it is perhaps to be assumed that they identified their own gods with those they found in Palestine, and accommodated their own religion to that already there.

The excavator of Bethshean suggested that two temples found there might be those of Dagon and Ashtoreth, where Saul's trophies were hung, and three successive temples at Tell Qasile (strata XII–X), while they show some Canaanite influence, have similarities with temples found in the Aegean and Cyprus.

The Philistines offered sacrifices (Judges 16:23) and wore charms in battle (2 Samuel 5:21). Remains of sacrifices were found in the Tell Qasile temples.

## Origin and role

The cumulative evidence leaves little doubt that the Philistines came immediately, though probably not ultimately, from the Aegean. Some scholars would equate the name with that of the *Pelasgoi*, the pre-Greek inhabitants of the Aegean, a view which is weighted by the occurrence of the name twice in Greek literature, spelt with a *t* rather than a *g*. This view is still debated, and even granting it, the classical references to the *Pelasgoi* are too inconsistent to be helpful.

It seems that the Philistines were one of the 'Sea Peoples' who, in the later 2nd millennium, moved out of the Aegean, probably as a result of the arrival of the Greeks, and migrated by land and sea, some *via* Crete and Cyprus, to the Near East, where they forced a foothold, first as mercenary troops of the pharaohs, the Hittite kings and the Canaanite rulers, and finally as settlers who were absorbed in the basic population.

Though they retained their name for many centuries, the biblical Philistines, the Tjekker who occupied an adjacent coastal region and doubtless others of the 'Sea Peoples', became for all practical purposes Canaanites.

## Philistines in the patriarchal narratives

Since the Philistines are not named in extra-biblical inscriptions until the 12th century BC, and the archaeological remains associated with them do not appear before this time, many commentators reject references to them in the patriarchal period as anachronistic. Two considerations must be entertained, however.

First, there is evidence of a major expansion of Aegean trade in the Middle Minoan II period (*c.* 1900–1700 BC; see also *CRETE) and objects of Aegean manufacture or influence have been found from this period at Ras Shamra in Syria, Hazor and perhaps Megiddo in Palestine, and Tôd, Harageh, Lahun and Abydos in Egypt. It is likely that a large part of this trade consisted in perishable goods such as textiles. A new type of spiral design which appears in Egypt and Asia (Mari) at this time may support this. Further evidence of contacts is afforded by a tablet from Mari (18th century) recording the sending of gifts by the king of Hazor to Kaptara (see also *CAPHTOR).

Secondly, ethnic names in antiquity were not used with particular precision, so the absence of one name from the inscriptions may simply mean that the particular group was not sufficiently prominent to find special mention. The 'Sea Peoples', and their predecessors who traded with the Near East, arrived in waves, and dominant in a 12th-century wave were the Philistines, who consequently figured in the records. There is no reason why small groups of Philistines could not have been among the early Aegean traders, not prominent enough to be noticed by the larger states.

T. C. Mitchell

*Further reading*

R. A. S. Macalister, *The Philistines, Their History and Civilization*, 1914
W. F. Albright, *AASOR* 12, 1932, pp. 53–58
O. Eissfeldt in *RE* 38, 1938, cols. 2390–2401
A. H. Gardiner, *Ancient Egyptian Onomastica*, Text 1, pp. 200*–205*
T. Dothan, *The Philistines and their Material Culture*, 1982

—, *BARev* 16/1, 1990, pp. 26–36
. E. Wright, *BA* 22, 1959, pp. 54–66
. C. Mitchell in *AOTS*, pp. 404–427
A. Kitchen in *POTT*, pp. 53–78
. Mazar, *IEJ* 35, 1985, pp. 95–107
*OLOB*, pp. 300–328, 531–536
. K. Sandars, *The Sea Peoples*, 1978

**HOENICIA, PHOENICIANS.** The rritory on the eastern Mediterra-ean coast covering *c.* 240 lometres between the rivers Litani nd *Arvad (modern Lebanon and outhern Latakia) and its habitants.

Phoenicia (AV Phenice) as such is amed only in the New Testament as ne place of refuge for Christians eeing from persecution following ne death of Stephen (Acts 11:19); rough this land Paul and Silas urneyed on their way from Samaria Antioch (Acts 15:3). Later Paul nded on the Phoenician coast near yre on his way to Jerusalem (Acts 1:2–3).

In the time of Christ Phoenicia was eferred to as 'the sea-coast and istrict of Tyre and Sidon' (Matthew 5:21; Luke 6:17), and the habitants, including Greeks, were onsidered 'Syro-Phoenicians' (Mark :26).

In Old Testament times the rritory occupied by the Phoenicians as called by the Hebrews 'Canaan' saiah 23:11), 'Canaanite' (*i.e.* nerchant') being probably the ame applied by the inhabitants to ne common practice in all periods to efer to Phoenicia by the name of its rincipal cities (see *TYRE, *SIDON), nce there was little political ohesion between them except for eriods such as the reign of Hiram I. ther major settlements were Arvad, Simyra, *Gebal/Byblos, e(i)rut and Zarephath (see ZAREPHATH).

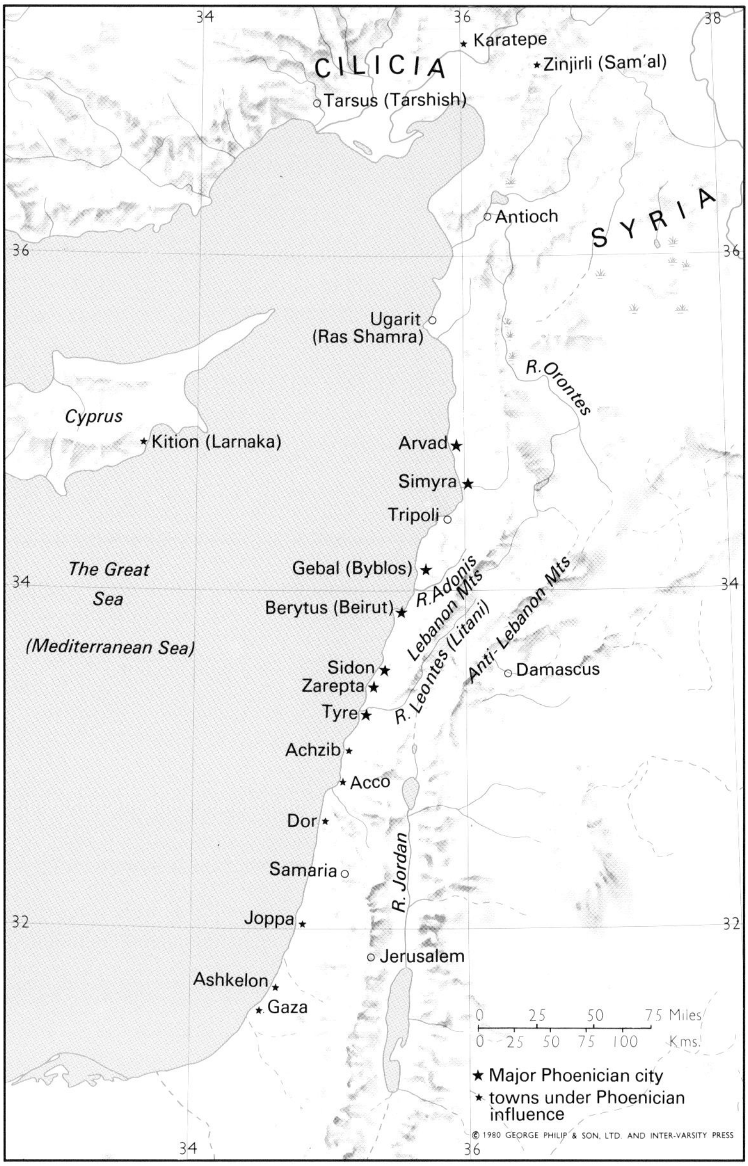


The major cities of Phoenicia.

## istory

### *eginnings*

he origin of the sea-faring hoenicians is obscure, though ccording to Herodotus (1.1; 7.89) ney arrived overland from the ersian Gulf area, via the Red Sea, nd first founded Sidon. The earliest rchaeological evidence of their resence may come from the roto-Phoenician' finds at Byblos ncient Gubla or Gebal, Ezekiel 7:9, modern Gebail) dated *c.* 3000 C.

This important site has been xcavated since 1924 by the French nder Montet and Dunand. Byblian hips are depicted on Egyptian eliefs of the time of Sahure in the 5th Dynasty (*c.* 2500 BC) and there can be no doubt that by the 18th century there was an extensive trade in timber and artistic commodities between Phoenicia and Egypt. The Phoenicians by this time had settled in their first colonies along the coast at Joppa, Dor (Judges 1:27–31), Acre and Ugarit (Ras Shamra). They chose easily defensible natural harbours and gradually dominated the local population as at Ras Shamra (level IV).

### *In the time of the Exodus and Judges*

For some centuries Phoenicia was under the economic and quasi-military control of the Egyptian 18th and 19th Dynasties, and Arvad was among the places claimed to have been captured by Tuthmosis III (*c.* 1457 BC). Nevertheless, the letters written by Rib-Addi of Byblos and Abi-milki of Tyre to Amenophis III at Amarna in Egypt show that, by *c.* 1350 BC, Ṣumur and Berut had disaffected and with Sidon, which appears to have maintained its independence, were blockading Phoenician cities (see also *AMARNA).

When the 'Sea Peoples' invaded the coast soon after 1200 BC, Byblos, Arvad and Ugarit were destroyed and the Sidonians fled to Tyre, which now became the principal port, or, as Isaiah claims, the 'daughter of Sidon' (23:12).

### *In the reigns of David and Solomon*

By the time of David, Tyre was ruled by Hiram I, the son of Abi-Baal, and his reign began a golden age. Phoenicia was allied commercially with David (2 Samuel 5:11; 1 Kings 5:1) and Hiram by treaty supplied Solomon with wood, stone and craftsmen for the construction of the temple and palace (1 Kings 5:1–12; 2 Chronicles 2:3–16), and ships and navigators to assist the Judaean fleet and to develop the port of Ezion-geber as a base for long voyages (1 Kings 9:27). This aid resulted in territorial advantages, for Tyre was given 20 villages on her border in part payment (verses 10–14).

Phoenicia, herself long influenced by Egyptian art, motifs and methods, was now in a position to influence Hebrew thought. Hiram was a conqueror and builder of several temples at Tyre, and a successful administrator who settled colonial revolts (W. F. Albright, in the *Leland Volume*, 1942, pp. 43f.). It was probably due to his initiative that by the 9th century Phoenician colonies were founded in Sardinia (Nova, Tharros), Cyprus (Kition) and Karatepe (northern Taurus). Utica had been settled in the 12th century and Carthage, Sicily (Motya) and Tunisia by the 8th.

*During the divided Monarchy*

Hiram's successor, a high priest named Ethbaal, furthered the alliance with Israel by the marriage of his daughter Jezebel to Ahab (1 Kings 16:31), with the consequence that the worship of the Phoenician Baals was increased (1 Kings 18:19). Elijah fled for a while to Zarephath, which was part of the coast controlled by Sidon, and therefore at this time independent of Tyre (1 Kings 17:9).

The Assyrian advances brought pressure on the Phoenician cities. Ashurnasirpal II (884–859 BC) counted among the tribute he received from Tyre, Sidon, Gebal and Arvad garments and dyed cloth, precious metals and carved ivory and wood. This tribute was renewed when Shalmaneser III besieged Damascus and marched to the Mediterranean coast at the Dog river in 841 BC. The act of submission to him and the gifts sent by Tyre and Sidon are pictured on the bronze gates set up in the Assyrian temple at Balawat (see *ANEP*, pp. 356–357).

Adad-nirari III claimed Tyre and Sidon among his vassals in 803 BC (*DOTT*, p. 51). Hirammu of Tyre, Sibitti-Bi'ili of Gubla (Byblos) sent tribute to Tiglath-pileser III during his siege of Arpad (*c.* 741 BC) about the same time as Menahem of Israel submitted to him.

A few years later the Assyrian sent his *rab šaqe*-official to collect taxes from Metenna of Tyre. Letters addressed to the Assyrian king show that Tyre and Sidon were under the direct supervision of an Assyrian official, who forwarded the taxes, mostly paid in timber and goods, direct to Calah (*Iraq* 17, 1955, pp. 126–154). In 734 BC Tiglath-pileser captured the fortress of Kashpuna, which guarded the approaches to Tyre and Sidon, who were now allied in defence.

Sargon continued to raid the Phoenician coastlands, and Sennacherib (*c.* 701 BC) captured Ušše near Tyre and carried Phoenician prisoners off to Nineveh to build his new palace (as shown on reliefs) and to Opis to build the fleet planned to pursue the rebel Merodach-baladan across the Persian Gulf.

Nevertheless, the larger cities clung to their independence until Esarhaddon sacked Sidon and settled the survivors from it in a new town called 'Walled City of Esarhaddon' and in 15 adjacent villages. Other towns were placed under Ba'ali of Tyre, who was bound by treaty to Esarhaddon. This named Arvad, Acre, Dor, Gebal and Mount Lebanon and regulated trade and shipping. However, Ba'ali, incited by Tirhakah of Egypt, revolted. Tyre was besieged and Phoenicia subordinated to a province. The rulers of the cities, including Milki-asapa of Gebal, and Matan-Ba'al of Arvad, were made to 'bear the corvée basket', that is, to act as labourers at the foundation of Esarhaddon's new palace at Calah, as Manasseh did in Babylon (2 Chronicles 33:11).

Ashurbanipal continued the war against Phoenicia, containing Ba'ali by an attack in 665 BC prior to his advance on Egypt. He took Ba'ali's daughters as concubines and also received a heavy tribute. On the death of Ba'ali Azi-Ba'al was made king and Yakinlu appointed to rule Arvad.

With the decline of Assyria the cities regained their independence and traded with new ports opened in Egypt. Their Punic kinsfolk founded colonies in Algeria, Spain and Morocco in the 7th–5th centuries and by a naval victory over the Etruscans in 535 BC finally closed the western Mediterranean to the Phoenician traders.

*From Nebuchadrezzar to Alexander*

Nebuchadrezzar II of Babylon in his advance towards Egypt besieged Tyre for 13 years *c.* 585–573 BC (Ezekiel 26:1–28:26), but, though Ithobaal was carried off prisoner to Babylon, the city retained a measure of autonomy, which it held throughout the Neo-Babylonian and Persian rule, trading with Egypt (Zephaniah 1:11) and supplying fish and other commodities to Jerusalem (Nehemiah 13:16) and in return probably receiving wood and homespun textiles (Proverbs 31:24).

Alexander the Great captured the island city of Tyre by means of an artificially constructed causeway. The slaughter and destruction was heavy, but the city recovered and, like Sidon, was prosperous in Hellenistic and Roman times (*e.g.* Matthew 15:21).

## Religion

The idolatrous religion of Phoenicia was condemned by Elijah (1 Kings 18–19) and later Hebrew prophets (Isaiah 65:11). The early period, seen in the Ras Shamra texts, reveals a polytheistic and natural mythology centred on Baal, also called Melek, 'king', the sun-god Saps, and Reshep (Mikkal) an underworld deity.

Fertility cults honoured 'Anat (Astarte, Ashtart) and the popular blend of Semitic and Egyptian ideas resulted in the cult of Adonis and Tammuz, in which the former was identified with Osiris. Other deities included Eshmun, the god of healing (Greek Asklepios), and Melqart.

## Art

The syncretistic tendencies of Phoenician religions are to be seen in the art, which combines Semitic, Egyptian and Hurrian elements. This is due to the geographical location and the interchange of materials and influence which followed trade. The Phoenicians were primarily sea-traders and artists. They exported silk, linen and wool, dyed, woven and embroidered locally, hence the name Phoenicia may be derived from the Greek *phoinikoi*, 'red-purple folk' (the Akkadian *kinahhi/kina'ain*, *i.e.* Canaan) (*POTT*, p. 34) and from their unbounded supplies in the hinterland of the Lebanon shipped wood and its products.

The craftsmen worked stone (*e.g.* the Ahiram sarcophagus *c.* 900 BC; *BASOR* 134, 1954, p. 9; *Syria* 11, 1930, pp. 180ff.), ivory and glass, and though the Hebrews did not themselves allow images or the portrayal of the human figure, Phoenician silver and bronze coins are found inland in numbers from the 4th century BC onwards.

The requirements of their trade led to the development of writing (the so-called Phoenician, Byblian and Ugaritic alphabets), the *abacus*

ɔr counting, and papyrus books. It is ɪuch to be regretted that the hoenician literature, including the ɪythology of Sanchuniathon of yblos and the history of Menander f Tyre, has survived only in a few uotations in later authors, for it was robably through their literature ɪat much of the learning of the East eached Greece.
. J. Wiseman

*urther reading*
. B. Harden, *The Phoenicians*, 1962
. Moscati, *The World of the hoenicians*, 1968
. R. Ap-Thomas, 'The Phoenicians', ɪ *POTT*, pp. 259–286
. J. Katzenstein, *The History of yre*, 1973

**HOENIX.** The harbour (AV 'Phenice') the nautical experts, espite Paul's entreaties, made for in winter (Acts 27:12). Data given by trabo, Ptolemy and other writers eem to indicate the Cape Mouros rea, where modern Loutro is the nly safe harbour in southern Crete James Smith, *Voyage and hipwreck of St. Paul*, 4th edition, 880, p. 90 note). But Luke says hoenix 'lies toward the south-west nd north-west [winds]', *i.e.* faces vest, while Loutro faces east. A arrow peninsula separates it from a vest-facing bay, but one offering ttle shelter. Smith, urging the anger of westerly winter gales, uggested that Luke meant the irection *towards which* the winds lew, *i.e.* looking north-east and outh-east (compare RV and RSV); but his is unsubstantiated unless the erms arise from the complexity of he nomenclature of winds in autical idiom.

Ramsay thought that Luke might ave excusably misunderstood 'aul's account of the discussion, but eft open the possibility of a change ɪ coastline (see *HDB*). Ogilvie's ecent examination strongly uggests this occurred. The western ay was once better protected, and arthquake disturbance has pparently covered an inlet facing orth-west in classical times. A outh-west-facing inlet remains, and he disused western bay is still alled Phinika. Ogilvie also found hat locally the winter winds are orth and east: in Acts 27 it was an ast north-east wind which caused he disaster.

There is an inscription at Phoenix edicated to Jupiter and other gods nd the emperor Trajan by the ersonnel of a ship wintering there *CIL* 3.3) and confirms that the decision of the centurion, pilot and captain of Paul's ship was based on the knowledge that Phoenix traditionally provided a known safe shelter.
A. F. Walls, B. Winter

*Further reading*
J. B. Lightfoot on *1 Clement* 25
J. Smith, *Voyage and Shipwreck of St. Paul*, 4th edition, 1880, pp. 87ff., 251ff.
R. M. Ogilvie in *JTS* n.s.9, 1958, pp. 308ff.
C. J. Hemer, *The Book of Acts in the Setting of Hellenistic History*, Tübingen, 1989, pp. 139ff.

**PHRYGIA.** A tract of land centred on the western watershed of the great Anatolian plateau, and reaching northwards into the valley of the upper Sangarius, south-west down the valley of the Maeander, and south-east across the plateau, perhaps as far as Iconium.

The Phrygians formed the (legendary?) kingdom of Midas. They fell under direct Hellenic influence during the era of the Attalid kings of Pergamum, and in 116 BC most of Phrygia was incorporated by the Romans into their province of Asia. The eastern extremity (Phrygia Galatica) was included in the new province of Galatia in 25 BC.

The Romans were deeply impressed by the ecstatic Phrygian cult of Cybele, and the national fanaticism apparently lies behind the defiant tombstones, presumably Montanist, of the 2nd century AD, which represent the earliest extant public manifesto of Christianity.

There is no evidence of any indigenous Christian church in New Testament times, however. Such churches as fall technically within Phrygia (Laodicea, Hierapolis, Colossae, Pisidian Antioch and probably Iconium) were established in Greek communities. It was most probably Jewish members of these Greek states who visited Jerusalem (Acts 2:10).

If Colossians 2:1, as is just possible, is not taken to exclude a visit by Paul, it would be natural to assume that it is the first three of these cities, on the upper Maeander, that are referred to in Acts 16:6 and 18:23. Failing that, we may resort to the view that 'the region of Phrygia and *Galatia' is a composite technical term for Phrygia Galatica and refers in particular to the churches at Iconium and Pisidian Antioch. Otherwise we cannot identify the disciples Paul left in 'Phrygia'.
E. A. Judge

*Further reading*
Strabo, *Geography* 12
J. Friedrich, *RE* 20, 1, pp. 781–891
W. M. Ramsay, *Cities and Bishoprics of Phrygia*, 1895–97
A. H. M. Jones, *Cities of the Eastern Roman Provinces*, 1937
D. Magie, *Roman Rule in Asia Minor*, 2 vols., 1950
W. M. Calder, *AS* 5, 1955, pp. 25–38

**PHUT.** See *PUT.

**PI-BESETH.** Bubastis (Egyptian *Pr-B'stt*, 'mansion of the goddess Ubastet'), today Tell Basta, is situated on the Nile (Tanitic branch) south-east of Zagazig. It is mentioned in Ezekiel 30:17 with the more important city of Heliopolis (On or Aven). Of the main temple described by Herodotus (2.138), little remains. Ubastet was a lioness or cat-goddess.

Bubastis existed already in the time of Kheops and Khephren (4th Dynasty, *c.* 2600 BC) and Pepi I (6th Dynasty, *c.* 2400 BC). There are a few remains of the 18th Dynasty (14th century BC).

The town was important under the Ramesside kings (19th–20th Dynasties, 13th–12th centuries BC) and gave its name to the 22nd (Bubastite) Dynasty – that of Shishak, *c.* 945 BC – for whom it served as a residence like Tanis or Qantir.
C. de Wit

*Further reading*
E. Naville, *Bubastis*, 1891
——, *The Festival Hall of Osorkon II*, 1892
Labib Habachi, *Tell Basta*, 1957

**PIHAHIROTH.** An unidentified place on the border of Egypt (Exodus 14:2, 9; Numbers 33:7–8). Of Egyptian equivalents proposed, the likeliest is either *Pi-Ḥrt*, 'House of the goddess *Ḥrt*' (*BASOR* 109, 1948, p. 16) or *P'-ḥr*, a canal near Ra'amses (see Caminos, *Late-Egyptian Miscellanies*, 1954, p. 74, two mentions).
C. de Wit, K. A. Kitchen

**PIRATHON** (Hebrew *pir'āṯôn*). Home of the Ephraimite judge Abdon ben Hillel (Judges 12:13, 15); and of David's captain Benaiah (2 Samuel 23:30; 1 Chronicles 11:31; 27:14); modern Fer'ata, 9 kilometres west south-west of Shechem.

The district was known as the Amalekite Hills (Judges 12:15, Massoretic Text and Septuagint (B), compare 5:14; Septuagint (A) at 12:15 reads 'Hills of Lanak' and at

5:14 'in the valley' – *ba'emeq*). See J. Soggin, *Judges*, 1981, p. 224.

Although the name Abdon is otherwise Benjaminite, Pharathon in Benjamin (fortified by the Maccabees, 1 Maccabees 9:50) is to be distinguished from Pirathon.

J. P. U. Lilley

**PISGAH, ASHDOTH-PISGAH.** Always accompanied by the definite article, Pisgah is associated with the ascent and either 'top' (head) or 'slope' (Ashdoth). From these facts it may be deduced that Pisgah is a common noun denoting a ridge crowning a mountain or hill. 'The Pisgah' would then be one or more of the ridges common on the Transjordan plateau.

'The slopes of Pisgah' (Ashdoth-pisgah) may refer to the entire edge of the Moabite plateau east of the Dead Sea (Deuteronomy 3:17, AV; 4:49; Joshua 12:3; 13:20). These references relate to the territorial borders of the Amorites and later of the Reubenites.

Apart from the general plateau, Pisgah refers to a specific ridge or peak associated with Mount *Nebo. Numbers 21:20, a location on the route of the Israelites, and Numbers 23:14, one peak from which Balaam tried to curse God's people, are both close to the wilderness north and east of the Dead Sea (see also *JESHIMON), so also probably refer to the same ridge.

It was from 'the top of Pisgah, Mount Nebo' that Moses viewed the promised land before his death (Deuteronomy 3:27; 34:1). This plateau headland is probably to be identified with Ras es Siyaghah, the second and slightly lower northern ridge of Mount Nebo. As this ridge protrudes further west, it provides a wider and less obstructed view over the land, and so is more likely to be the place of Moses' vision.

G. G. Garner

*Further reading*

G. T. Manley, *EQ* 21, 1943, pp. 81–92

**PISIDIA.** A highland area in Asia Minor bounded by Lycaonia to the east and north, Pamphylia to the south, and the province of Asia to the north and west. The district lay at the western end of the Taurus range, and was the home of lawless mountain tribes who defied the efforts of the Persians and their Hellenistic successors to subdue them.

The Seleucids founded Antioch (called 'the Pisidian' to distinguish it rather from the Phrygian Antioch on the Maeander than from the Seleucid capital of Syria) in order to control the Pisidian highlanders, and Amyntas with like aim founded a colony there about 25 BC, and linked the city with similar strongpoints by a system of military roads.

Paul's 'perils of robbers . . . perils in the wilderness' (2 Corinthians 11:26) may have reference to this area, and it is a fair guess that, even in his day, the tradition of predatory independence was not yet dead among the mountaineers.

Pisidia was part of the kingdom of Galatia assigned by Antony to Amyntas in 36 BC, and it was in warfare against the Pisidian hill tribes that Amyntas perished in 25 BC. Sulpicius Quirinius finally imposed some sort of order, and incorporated the region in the province of Galatia. The Roman Peace brought prosperity to the district and in the 2nd century several prosperous towns sprang up together with at least 6 strong churches.

E. M. Blaiklock

**PITHOM** (Old Egyptian *Pr-itm*, 'mansion of the god Atum'). A city of Egypt where the Israelites were afflicted with heavy building burdens (Exodus 1:11). Most accept that it was situated in Wadi Tumilat, at Tell el-Maskhuta or Tell er-Retaba. Not far away from this place was the migdol of Tjeku, which may be the biblical Succoth (Exodus 12:37; 13:20; Numbers 33:5–6).

In Papyrus Anastasi, V, 19.5–20.6 we read that the chief of the archers went to Tjeku to prevent slaves from running away, but he came too late. Somebody had seen them crossing the northern wall of the migdol of Seti-Merenptah. A second report, in Papyrus Anastasi, V, 18.6–19.1, refers to Libyan mercenaries who tried to flee and were taken back to Tjeku. A third mention, in Papyrus Anastasi, VI, 5.1, emanates from a civil servant who had finished passing Shasu-nomads from Edom, south of the Dead Sea, into Egypt, at the fort of Tjeku, towards the marshes of Pithom of Merenptah of Tjeku.

These texts make best sense if Tell el-Maskhuta is the site of Tjeku and biblical Succoth, leaving Tell er-Retaba, 14 kilometres to the west, as the site of Pithom.

C. de Wit

*Further reading*

E. Naville, *The Store-City of Pithom*, 1903

Montet, *Géographie de l'Égypte ancienne* 1, 1957, pp. 214–219

**PLAIN, CITIES OF THE.** The cities of the plain were, chiefly, Sodom, Gomorrah, Admah, Zeboiim and Bela or Zoar (Genesis 14:2).

*Location*

It has been held that these were located north of the Dead Sea, where the Jordan Valley broadens into the 'Circle' or 'Plain' of the Jordan (see Deuteronomy 34:3), the evidence being 'that Abraham and Lot looked upon the cities from near Bethel (Genesis 13:10), that *Circle of Jordan* is not applicable to the south of the Dead Sea, that the presence of five cities there is impossible and that the expedition of the Four Kings (Genesis 14:7), as it swept north from Kadesh-barnea, attacked Hazazon-tamar, probably Engedi, *before* it reached the Vale of Siddim and encountered the king of Sodom and his allies' (G. A. Smith, *Historical Geography of the Holy Land*, 25th edition, 1931, pp. 505f.).

On the other hand, the view that the cities lie buried beneath the shallow waters of the southern tip of the Dead Sea (G. E. Wright, *Westminster Historical Atlas*, 1945, pp. 26, 65–66; and his *Biblical Archaeology*, 1957, p. 50) can be maintained. First, Genesis 13:10 says that Lot saw, not the cities of the plain, but the 'Circle' of Jordan. He was attracted not by urban facilities but by good pasturage.

Secondly, refusal to give the name 'Circle of Jordan' to, and denial of the possibility of five cities at, the southern end of the Dead Sea depends on present-day configuration, and disregards any alterations made by the overthrow and by changed water-levels (there is good reason to believe that the area south of the el-Lisan peninsula was not submerged until after the time of the Crusades).

Thirdly, there is the identification of Hazazon-tamar with En-gedi. This depends on 2 Chronicles 20:2, where the advancing Moabites and Ammonites are said to be 'in Hazazon-tamar (that is, En-gedi)'. The qualifying phrase ought not to be taken in this case as identifying the two places (as, for example, in Genesis 14:3), unless we make the absurd assumption that after the time of Jehoshaphat the name En-gedi replaced Hazazon-tamar, thus necessitating an explanation of the archaism. The qualification 'that is, En-gedi' must, therefore, state more precisely where the enemy was in the general district designated by the first place-name. This suits the usage in Genesis 14:7

,here, in a chapter full of
arenthetic explanations of archaic
lace-names, Hazazon-tamar is left
nexplained.

We may therefore picture the
ities of the plain as sited in the
ow-flooded area which once
ormed the southern extension of the
ircle of the Jordan.

An alternative view would identify
ne five cities with the sites of Bab
dh-Dhra', Numeria, es-Safi, Feifeh
nd Khanazir, all located in wadis on
ne eastern side of the Dead Sea from
ne el-Lisan peninsula southwards.
lowever, it seems probable that
nese cities came to an end no later
nan 2300 BC, which is earlier than
ne biblical date for Abraham.

*estruction*

s Lot saw it, the Circle was
upremely attractive from every
aterial viewpoint (Genesis 13:10),
ut it was to become desolate. The
fficient cause of this destruction of
ne cities was probably an
arthquake, with an accompanying
elease and explosion of gaseous
eposits. Biblically and fundamen-
lly it was God's judgment,
emembered again and again
nroughout the Bible (Deuteronomy
9:23; Isaiah 1:9; Jeremiah 49:18;
amentations 4:6; Amos 4:11; Luke
7:29; 2 Peter 2:6); and Sodom
ecame synonymous with brazen
n (Isaiah 3:9; Lamentations 4:6;
ude 7). Whereas Ezekiel 16:49–51
sts the sins of Sodom as pride,
rosperous complacency and
bominations', Genesis 19:4–5
oncentrates on sexual perversion,
articularly homosexuality. Lot's
icious offer of his daughters (verse
) indicates the life and demoralizing
nfluence of Sodom.

The story of Sodom does not
erely warn, but provides a
neologically documented account of
ivine judgment implemented by
natural' disaster. The history is
ith's guarantee that the Judge of
l the earth does right (Genesis
8:25). Being personally persuaded
f its justice and necessity (Genesis
8:20–21), God acts; but in wrath he
emembers mercy, and in judgment
iscrimination (Genesis 19:16, 29).

A. Motyer

*urther reading*

J. C. van Hattem, *BA* 44/2, 1981,
p. 87–92

Rogerson, *The New Atlas of the
ible*, 1985, pp. 194–196

**LAIN OF MEONENIM.** See
MEONENIM, OAK OF.

**PLAIN OF ONO.** See *ONO.

**PONTUS.** The coastal strip of northern Asia Minor, reaching from Bithynia in the west into the highlands of Armenia to the east. The region was politically a complex of Greek republics, temple estates and Iranian baronies in the interior.

One of these houses established a kingdom whose greatest ruler, Mithridates, temporarily ejected the Romans from Asia Minor early in the 1st century BC. After his defeat the western part of Pontus was administered with Bithynia as a Roman province, the eastern part being left under a Greek dynasty.

The Jews from Pontus (Acts 2:9; 18:2) presumably came from the Greek coastal states. We know nothing of the origin of Christianity there, but it was represented by the time of 1 Peter 1:1.

E. A. Judge

*Further reading*

J. Keil, *CAH* 11, pp. 575ff.

D. Magie, *Roman Rule in Asia Minor*, 2 vols., 1950

**POOL OF SILOAM.** See *SILOAM.

**POTTERS FIELD.** See *AKELDAMA.

**PRAETORIUM.** Originally the tent of the commander, or praetor, and, in consequence, the army headquarters (Livy, 7.12; Caesar, *Civil War* 1.76). By extension the word came to mean the residence of a provincial governor. In the gospels the word Praetorium refers to the Jerusalem residence of Pontius Pilate (Matthew 27:27; Mark 15:16; John 18:28, 33; 19:9; the NIV has 'palace' in all three instances in John).

There is some debate over the identification of the building in which Pilate questioned Jesus. Tradition identifies it with the Antonia Fortress, which stood at the north-western corner of the temple area; hence the Via Dolorosa begins where this fortress (destroyed in AD 70) once stood. However, Josephus (*Jewish War*, 2.301) and Philo (*Embassy to Gaius*, 38.229 and 39.306) both refer to Roman governors residing in the palace of Herod the Great when staying in Jerusalem. This occupied a large rectangular area on the western hill (the Upper City) and was lavishly adorned with towers, gardens and apartments. Mark 15:16 supports this location for Pilate's examination of Jesus, referring to it as 'the palace (that is, the praetorium)'.

Another praetorium is mentioned in Philippians 1:13. If Paul was writing from Rome, this may refer to the emperor's residence on the Palatine. The word seems not to have been used for the permanent camp of the praetorian guards by the Porta Viminalis. It does, however, sometimes mean the forces of the praetorian guards (*CIL*, 5.2837; 8.9391), and, whether the letter was written at Ephesus or Rome, this gives good sense to Paul's phrase. Detachments of *praetoriani* were sent to the provinces, and in Rome they would have charge of prisoners in imperial custody.

E. M. Blaiklock, J. Bimson

**PTOLEMAIS**

**In the Old Testament**

The name given in the late 3rd or early 2nd century BC by Ptolemy I or II of Egypt to the seaport of Acco, on

Pisidian Antioch, visited by Paul on his early missionary journeys.

the northern point of the Bay of Acre (named from Acco), about 13 kilometres north of the Carmel headland which faces it across the bay. Acco was the only natural harbour on the coast south of Phoenicia in Old Testament times, and various routes connected it with Galilee and its lake, the Jordan valley and beyond.

The only reference to Acco in the Old Testament is in Judges 1:31, where it is assigned to Asher, but the tribe failed to capture it, and it probably remained Phoenician throughout the Old Testament period.

Some would emend Ummah in Joshua 19:30 to read Acco (*e.g. GTT*, p. 139), though this is but a conjecture.

*In non-biblical texts*

Acco is more frequently mentioned in non-biblical texts. A prince of Acco (Egyptian *'ky*) is apparently already mentioned in the Egyptian Execration Texts of the 18th century BC (G. Posener, *Princes et Pays d'Asie et de Nubie*, 1940, p. 87, E49; *ANET*, p. 329, note 9).

Acco later appears in topographical lists of the 15th and 13th centuries BC, in the Amarna tablets of the 14th century BC (*e.g. ANET*, pp. 484–485, 487), and in an Egyptian satirical letter of *c.* 1240 BC (*ANET*, p. 477b).

In later days Sennacherib of Assyria mentions Acco as part of the realm of Tyre and Sidon on his Palestinian campaign of 701 BC (*ANET*, p. 287b), and Ashurbanipal attacked it in the 7th century BC (*ANET*, p. 300b). On the relation of Acco to Asher and Galilee inland, see D. Baly, *Geography of the Bible*, 2nd edition, 1974, pp. 121–124. On excavations, see Z. Goldmann and others, 'Acco', *NEAEHL*, I, pp. 16–31.

K. A. Kitchen

**In the New Testament**

During the intertestamental period the name Acco was changed to Ptolemais, presumably in honour of Ptolemy Philadelphus (285–246 BC). Under this name it played an important role in the Jews' struggle for freedom under the Maccabees (see 1 Maccabees 5:15; 12:45–48), but is only once noticed in the New Testament (Acts 21:7). Paul, sailing from Tyre to Caesarea towards the end of his missionary journey, put in at Ptolemais, and while his ship lay at anchor in the harbour he spent a day with the Christians of the place. This was probably not the only time he passed through the city, since he came along the Phoenician coast several times. In Paul's day Ptolemais was a *colonia*, the emperor Claudius having settled a group of veterans there.

*After the Roman period*

When Roman power ended, the city assumed its original name 'Akka and has maintained it to the present day.

During the Crusades Ptolemais rose to importance under the Gallicized name Acre or St Jean d'Acre. Today it is overshadowed by the prominence of the city of Haifa, which lies directly across the bay.

W. W. Wessel

**PUT, PHUT.** Warriors of Put, alongside those of Lubim, Egypt and Ethiopia, were unable to save No-Amon (Thebes) from Assyria (Nahum 3:9). Elsewhere the word i found only in Jeremiah 46:9 and Ezekiel 30:5 (as Egyptian allies), in Ezekiel 38:5 (in Gog's armies; AV 'Libya[ns]') and in Ezekiel 27:10 (warriors of Tyre).

Put is certainly African, but its location is disputed. Claiming that Lubim (Libyans) and Put are distinc in Nahum 3:9, some wish to equate Put with the *Pw(n)t* (eastern Sudan? of Egyptian texts. But the Old Persian *putiya* and Babylonian *puṭa* (Hebrew *pûṯ*) become *T' Ṯmḥw*, 'Libya', in Egyptian thus making Pu Libya (G. Posener, *La Première Domination Perse en Égypte*, 1936, pp. 186–187).

Lubim and Put in Nahum 3:9 are lik Lubim and *Sukkiim in 2 Chronicles 12:3. Also, Tyre would employ Libya rather than Somali auxiliaries.

*pûṯ* may derive from the Egyptia *pḏty*, 'foreign bowman', or similar; especially as the Libyans were archers (W. Hölscher, *Libyer und Ägypter*, 1937, pp. 38–39).

K. A. Kitchen

**PUTEOLI.** Modern Pozzuoli, near Naples, a Samian colony from Cuma founded in the 6th century BC. Puteo probably fell into Roman hands wit Capua in 338 BC, and rapidly becam an important arsenal and trading por Livy mentions a garrison of 6,000 during the Hannibalian invasion (24.13), and the embarkation of larg reinforcements for Spain (26.17).

Rome's eastern traffic, notably th Egyptian grain, passed through Puteoli. Seneca describes the arriva of the Alexandrian corn-fleet (*Letters* 77), and Paul arrived on an Alexandrian freighter (Acts 28:13).

The recently discovered chapel i Herculaneum probably marks the home of some who met Paul at nearby Puteoli. The Via Domitiana linked Puteoli with the Via Appia.

E. M. Blaiklock

Remains of the Flavian amphitheatre at Puteoli (modern Pozzuoli).

# Q

**QUICKSANDS.** See *SYRTIS.

# QUMRAN

**UMRAN,** the name of a wadi and of
n ancient ruin in its vicinity,
orth-west of the Dead Sea. The
erivation of the name is uncertain;
ttempts (*e.g.* by F. de Saulcy) to
onnect it with Gomorrah are
nacceptable.
The name was recorded by a
umber of travellers who passed that
ay, but was practically unknown
ntil the manuscript discoveries in
eighbouring caves, in 1947 and the
llowing years, put it on the map.

*he people of the Dead Sea Scrolls*
he excavations carried out at
hirbet Qumran ('ruin of Qumran')
etween 1951 and 1955 are
enerally regarded as demonstrating
hat this complex of buildings
ormed the headquarters of the
ommunity which produced the
ead Sea Scrolls. A cemetery lying
etween Khirbet Qumran and the
ead Sea (investigated by C. S.
lermont-Ganneau in 1873) was
robably the burying-ground of the
ommunity; over 1,000 burials have been identified here, but only a small proportion have been excavated, the bodies lying north and south, with the head to the south.

The site was evidently first occupied in the period of the Judaean Monarchy, to which period a circular cistern is assigned (compare 2 Chronicles 26:10; see also *SALT, CITY OF). The most interesting phases of occupation, however, are those generally associated with the 'people of the scrolls'.

*Phase I*
Phase Ia (often dated *c.* 130–110 BC, though it could have been slightly later) was marked by the clearing of the old circular cistern and the construction of two new rectangular cisterns, together with a few rooms and a potter's kiln.

This was followed by Phase Ib, marked by a thoroughgoing reconstruction of the headquarters on an elaborate scale, evidently to meet the requirements of a greatly enlarged community. This phase came to an end *c.* 40 BC, perhaps because of the *Parthian invasion.

Sandstone cliffs beside the Dead Sea. Qumran cave 4 is in the foreground.

*Far left top:* Remains of the pottery, Qumran. *Far left bottom:* One of the cisterns, Qumran.

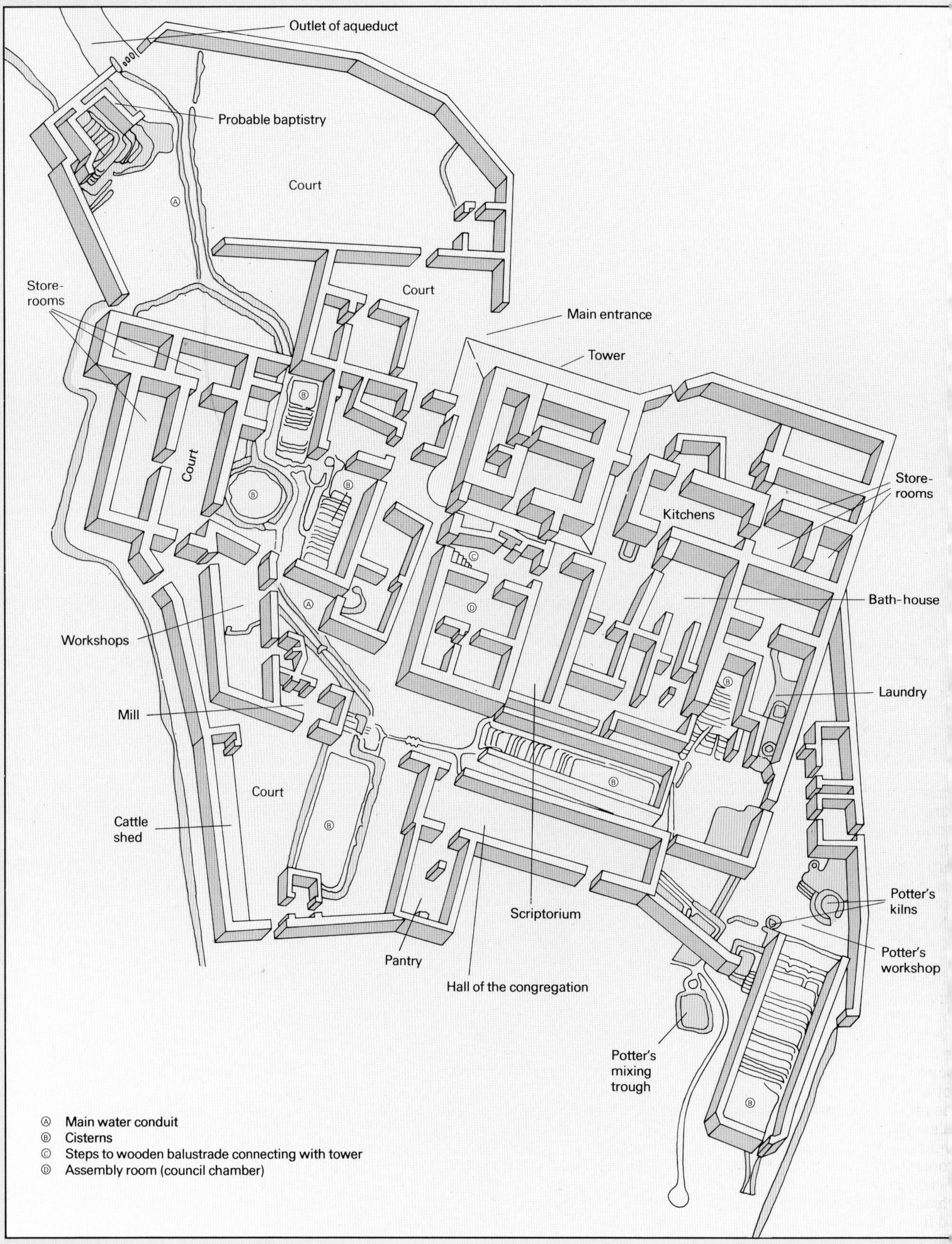


**Plan of the settlement excavated at Qumran. 1st century BC–1st century AD.**

Overview of the settlement remains at Khirbet Qumran, believed to have been occupied by an Essene community. The Dead Sea can be seen in the distance.

*hase II*
uring the temporary absence of the ommunity the buildings were eriously damaged by the arthquake of 31 BC (mentioned in osephus, *Antiquities* 15.121f.). The te probably lay derelict until *c.* 4 BC, hen the damaged buildings were epaired and strengthened. This arks the beginning of Phase II, uring which the place evidently erved the same purpose as it had one during Phase Ib.

Among the installations which can e clearly identified are assembly ooms, scriptorium, kitchen, laundry, ottery factory (the best-preserved ne thus far known from ancient alestine), flour mills, storage bins, vens, smelting furnaces, metal orkshops and an elaborate system f cisterns and ritual baths, into hich water was led by an aqueduct ed from rock-hewn cisterns in the ills to the north-west.

The phases of occupation are fairly early indicated by the coin record, everal hundreds of contemporary coins having been found in the course of the excavations. This record suggests that Phase II came to an end *c.* AD 68.

*Destruction*
Evidence of another kind shows that the end of Phase II was violent; the walls were demolished, a layer of black ash covered the site and a quantity of arrow-heads added their silent testimony to the general picture. It is tempting to connect these events with mopping-up operations in that region at the time of the Roman occupation of Jericho in the summer of AD 68. Whether the Qumran community had remained in possession up to that time, or an insurgent garrison had taken over such well-built headquarters, remains uncertain.

A few rooms were built over the ruins and manned for some years by a Roman garrison (Phase III).

Since the excavation of Khirbet Qumran it has been widely identified with the Essene settlement referred to by Pliny the Elder (*Natural History* 5.17) as lying above En-gedi.

F. F. Bruce

*Further reading*
H. Bardtke, *Die Handschriften am Toten Meer,* 2 vols., 1953, 1958
J. van der Ploeg, *The Excavations at Qumran*, 1958
R. de Vaux, *Archaeology and the Dead Sea Scrolls*, 1973
E. M. Laperrousaz, *Qoumrân: l'établissement essénien des bords de la Mer Morte*, 1976
P. R. Davies, *Qumran*, 1982
H. Shanks, 'The Qumran Settlement – Monastery, Villa or Fortress?', *BARev* 19/3, May-June 1993, pp. 62–65
M. Broshi in *NEAEHL* IV, pp. 1235–1241

# R

**RAAMAH** (Hebrew *ra'mâ, ra'mā*, 'trembling'). A 'son' of Cush (Genesis 10:7; 1 Chronicles 1:9). The tribe of Raamah has not been identified, but inscriptions found in Sheba suggest a location north of Marib in Yemen. With Sheba, Raamah sold spices, precious stones and gold to Tyre (Ezekiel 27:22).
A. R. Millard

**RA'AMSES, RAMESES** (Egyptian *Pr-R'mssw*, Pi-Ramessē, 'Domain of Ramesses'). A city of Egypt mentioned with Pithom, where the Hebrews were afflicted with heavy burdens (Exodus 1:11; 12:37; Numbers 33:3). This was the famous East-Delta residence of Ramesses II (*c.* 1290–1224 BC).

Scholars once located Pi-Ramessē at Pelusium, then at Tanis (see also *ZOAN), following Montet's excavations there. But all the Ramesside stonework at Tanis is re-used material from elsewhere. Remains of a palace, a glaze-factory and of houses of princes and high officials (with trace of a temple) at and near Qantir, 30 kilometres south of Tanis, almost certainly mark the real site of Ra'amses/Pi-Ramessē.

Excavations conducted here since 1966 have revealed almost continuous occupation from the 19th–11th centuries BC. The work in which the Hebrews were involved was therefore part of a rebuilding or expansion programme. The long-held view that the area was not occupied during the 18th Dynasty (*c.* 1550–1300 BC) has been disproved by recent finds.

The Exodus began from Ra'amses (Exodus 12:37) (see also *ENCAMPMENT BY THE SEA). Centuries before, Jacob had settled in the district (Genesis 47:11).
C. de Wit, K. A. Kitchen

*Further reading*
A. H. Gardiner, *JEA* 5, 1918, pp. 127–138, 179–200, 242–271
P. Montet, *RB* 39, 1930, pp. 5–28
L. Habachi, *ASAE* 52, 1954, pp. 443–562
J. van Seters, *The Hyksos*, 1966, pp. 127–151
M. Bietak, *Tell el-Dab'a* 2, 1975, especially pp. 179–221, plates 44f.
M. Bietak, *Avaris and Piramesse*, 2nd edition, 1986

**RABBAH. 1.** A town with associated villages in the hill country of Judah (Joshua 15:60), possibly Rubute of the Amarna Letters and Tuthmosis III, which lay in the region of Gezer.

**2.** The capital of Ammon, now Amman, capital of Jordan, 35 kilometres east of the river Jordan. Its full name occurs in Deuteronomy 3:11, 2 Samuel 12:26, 17:27, Jeremiah 49:2 and Ezekiel 21:20 as 'Rabbah of the Ammonites' (*rabbat $b^e$nê ammôn*), and is shortened to Rabbah (*rabbâ*) in 2 Samuel 11:11, 12:27 and Jeremiah 49:3, *etc.* The name evidently means 'Main-town' (the Septuagint has *akra*, 'citadel', at Deuteronomy 3:11). The iron coffin of Og, king of Bashan, rested there (Deuteronomy 3:11; AV 'iron bedstead').

Ammonite power grew simultaneously with Israelite, so that David faced a rival in Hanun, son of Nahash. After defeating Hanun's Aramaean allies and the Ammonite army, David and Joab were able to overrun Ammon, Joab besieging Rabbah, but leaving David the honour of taking the citadel. The inhabitants were put to forced labour (2 Samuel 10; 12:26–31; 1 Chronicles 19:20). After Solomon death, Ammon reasserted her independence and troubled Israel. The prophets spoke against Rabbah as representing the people of Ammon (Jeremiah 49:2–3; Ezekiel 21:20; 25:5; Amos 1:14).

Rabbah, rebuilt and renamed *Philadelphia by Ptolemy Philadelphus (285–246 BC), became one of the cities of the Decapolis an an important trading centre.

*Excavations*
Considerable archaeological remains exist in the vicinity of Amman today. At the airport a building of the 13th century BC (Late Bronze IIB) has been unearthed. It was used as a depository for cremated human remains, many of them of young children, perhaps sacrificed to Molech.

On the citadel itself are extensive ruins of the mediaeval, Byzantine, Roman and Hellenistic cities. Traces of a Middle Bronze Age fortification

The Roman theatre, Amman, viewed from the citadel.

ave also been noticed and pottery uggests continuing occupation in ie Late Bronze Age. Evidence of ccupation in the early Iron Age is parse, but finds from the 8th–6th enturies BC (Iron Age IIB–C) are bundant and include sculptures nd inscriptions.

A. Thompson, A. R. Millard

*'urther reading*
. M. Abel, *Géographie de la 'alestine* 2, 1933, pp. 423–425
. L. Harding, *Antiquities of Jordan*, 967, pp. 61–70
. B. Hennessy, *PEQ* 98, 1966, p. 155–162
. M. Bennett, *Levant* 10, 1978, p. 1–9
. T. Geraty and L. Herr (eds.), *The rchaeology of Jordan and Other tudies*, 1986, pp. 11–17

**AMAH.** The Hebrew name *rāmâ*, om the root *rûm*, 'to be high', was sed of several places, all of them on levated sites.

**1.** Ramah of Benjamin, near Bethel, n the area of Gibeon and Beeroth Joshua 18:25), was a resting-place n the road north. Here the Levite nd his concubine planned to stay Judges 19:13). Deborah the rophetess lived close by (Judges :5). When Asa of Judah and Baasha f Israel were at war, Baasha built a ort here, but when the Aramaeans ttacked Israel Asa destroyed it and uilt Geba and Mizpah with the naterials (1 Kings 15:17, 21–22; Chronicles 16:1, 5–6).

Here Nebuzaradan gathered the xiles after the fall of Jerusalem and eleased Jeremiah (Jeremiah 40:1). The town was reoccupied after the eturn from Babylon (Ezra 2:26; Nehemiah 11:33).

Ramah features in the messages of ome of the prophets (Hosea 5:8; saiah 10:29; Jeremiah 31:15). It is robably to be identified with Er-Ram, 8 kilometres north of Jerusalem, or Ramat Rahel, near the raditional tomb of Rachel (Jeremiah 31:15; 1 Samuel 10:2; Matthew 2:18; Josephus, *Antiquities* 8.303).

**2.** The birthplace and subsequent ome of Samuel (1 Samuel 1:19; 2:11), also called Ramathaim-zophim n the hill country of Ephraim (1 Samuel 1:1), from which he went n circuit annually (1 Samuel 7:17). Here Saul first met him (1 Samuel 9:6, 10), and here the elders of Israel came to demand a king (1 Samuel 8:4ff.). After his dispute with Saul Samuel came here (1 Samuel 15:34ff.). David found refuge in Ramah and later fled to Nob (1 Samuel 19:18; 20:1).

There are three sites proposed for Ramah today: Ramallah, 13 kilometres north of Jerusalem; Beit Rama, 19 kilometres north-west of Bethel; and Er-Ram, the Ramah of Benjamin. The latter identification depends on the view that Samuel's home was in fact the same as **1**. This involves emending 1 Samuel 1:1 to read that Elkanah was 'from Ramah, a Zuphite from the hill country of Ephraim'.

The word is also used as the name for **3**, a town on the boundary of Asher (Joshua 19:29), possibly Ramieh, 17 kilometres east of Rosh Ha-Niqra.

**4.** A walled town of Naphtali (Joshua 19:36), probably modern er-Rameh, 12 kilometres south-west of Safed.

**5.** A town of Simeon (Joshua 19:8; 1 Samuel 30:27) which Aharoni suggests identifying with the Negeb site of Horvat 'Uzza.

**6.** An abbreviation for Ramoth-gilead (see 2 Kings 8:28–29 and 2 Chronicles 22:5–6).

J. A. Thompson, J. Bimson

*Further reading*
F. M. Abel, *Géographie de la Palestine* 2, 1933, p. 427
D. Baly, *Geography of the Bible*, 2nd edition, 1974
*LOB*, pp. 261, 441
P. M. Arnold, *ABD*, vol. V, pp. 613–614

**RAMATH-LEHI.** See *LEHI.

**RAMESES.** See *RA'AMSES.

**RAMOTH.** See *JARMUTH.

**RAMOTH-GILEAD.** A walled city in the territory of Gad, east of the Jordan, which featured frequently in Israel's wars with Aram. It was one of the *cities of refuge (Deuteronomy 4:43; Joshua 20:8) and was assigned to the Merarite Levites (Joshua 21:38; 1 Chronicles 6:80).

Ramoth-gilead has been identified with Mizpeh, Mizpeh of Gilead (Judges 11:29) and Ramath-mizpeh ('height of Mizpeh', Joshua 13:26). Modern identifications suggested are Huṣn-'Ajlûn and Remtheh, but the suggestion of Nelson Glueck (*BASOR* 92, 1943) that it is Tell-Rāmîth, near the modern border with Syria, has strong claims in view of the site's Iron Age pottery and commanding location.

It was probably the home of Jephthah (Judges 11:34). Ben-geber, one of Solomon's 12 administrators, governed Gilead and Bashan from here (1 Kings 4:13). According to Josephus (*Antiquities* 8.399), the city was taken by Omri from Ben-hadad I.

The town changed hands between Israel and the Aramaeans several times. Even after Ahab had defeated the Aramaeans (1 Kings 20), it remained in their hands and Ahab enlisted the help of Jehoshaphat of Judah to retake it (1 Kings 22:3–4). He was wounded and died (1 Kings 22:1–40; 2 Chronicles 18). His son Joram took up the attack but was likewise wounded (2 Kings 8:28ff.).

During his absence from the camp at Ramoth-gilead, Jehu the army captain was anointed at Elisha's instigation (2 Kings 9:1f.; 2 Chronicles 22:7). Jehu later murdered all the seed royal, but Josephus says that the city was taken before Jehu departed (*Antiquities* 9.105).

J. A. Thompson

*Further reading*
N. Glueck, 'Ramoth Gilead', *BASOR* 92, 1943, pp. 10ff.
F. M. Abel, *Géographie de la Palestine* 2, 1933, pp. 430–431
H. Tadmor, 'The Southern Border of Aram', *IEJ* 12, 1962, pp. 114–122
D. Baly, *Geography of the Bible*, 2nd edition, 1974
L. T. Geraty and L. G. Herr (eds.), *The Archaeology of Jordan and Other Studies*, 1986, pp. 64–65

**RAS SHAMRA.** See *UGARIT.

**RED SEA.** In modern geography, the sea that divides north-east Africa from Arabia and extends some 1,900 kilometres from the straits of Bab el-Mandeb near Aden northwards to the southern tip of the Sinai peninsula. For nearly another 300 kilometres, the Gulfs of Suez and Aqabah continue the sea northwards on the western and eastern sides of the Sinai peninsula respectively.

In classical antiquity the name Red Sea (*erythra thalassa*) included also the Arabian and Indian Seas to the north-western coast of India. In the Old Testament the term *yam sûp̄*, 'sea of reeds' (and/or 'weed'), is used to cover: *a* the Bitter Lakes region in the Egyptian Delta north of Suez along the line of the present Suez Canal; and *b* the Gulfs of Suez and Aqabah and possibly the Red Sea proper beyond these.

### The Bitter Lakes region

In general terms, the Israelites were led from Egypt on the way of the wilderness and the *yam sûp̄* (Exodus 13:18). Exodus 14 and 15 are more specific: on leaving Succoth (Tell el-Maskhuta) and Etham, Israel were to turn back and camp before Pihahiroth, between Migdol and the 'sea', before Baal-zephon (Exodus 14:1–2, 9; see *Encampment by the Sea).

It was this 'sea', near all these places, that God drove back and divided by a 'strong east wind' for Israel to cross dryshod, and then brought back upon the pursuing Egyptians (Exodus 14:16, 21–31; 15:1, 4, 19, 21).

From the 'sea of reeds', *yam sûp̄*, Israel went into the wilderness of Shur (Exodus 15:22; Numbers 33:8) and then on towards Sinai.

*Location of the Exodus*

Various points suggest that this famous crossing, the Exodus in the narrow sense, took place in the Bitter Lakes region, roughly between Qantara (48 kilometres south of Port Said) and just north of Suez. First, geographically, the wilderness of Shur, which Israel entered directly from crossing the *yam sûp̄* (Exodus 15:22), is opposite this very area (see also *Shur).

Secondly, geophysically, the reedy waters of the Bitter Lakes and Lake Menzaleh can be affected by strong easterly winds precisely in the way described in Exodus 14:21 and experienced on a small scale by Aly Shafei Bey in 1945–46 (*Bulletin de la Société Royale de Géographie d'Égypte* 21, 1946, pp. 231ff.; compare also *JTVI* 28, 1894–95, pp. 267–280).

Thirdly, philologically, the Hebrew word *sûp̄* is generally admitted to be a loan-word from the Egyptian *ṯwf(y)*, 'papyrus', and *p'-ṯwf*, a location, 'the papyrus-marshes' *par excellence* in the north-eastern part of the Delta between Tanis (Zoan), Qantir and the present line of the Suez Canal north of Ismailia, on the former Pelusiac arm of the Nile.

For details and references, see A. H. Gardiner, *Ancient Egyptian Onomastica* 2, 1947, pp. 201*–202*; R. A. Caminos, *Late-Egyptian Miscellanies*, 1954, p. 79; Erman and Grapow, *Wörterbuch d. Aegypt. Sprache* 5, 1931, p. 359: 6–10.

Psalm 78:12, 43, puts the great events preceding the Exodus in the 'field of Zoan', *i.e.* in the north-eastern Delta.

**The Gulfs of Suez and Aqabah**

Turning south from Shur *via* Etham, Marah and Elim, the Israelites pitched by the *yam sûp̄* and then went on to Sin and Dophkah (Numbers 33:10–11). This would appear to refer to the Gulf of Suez. Whether Exodus 10:19 during the plagues refers to the Lakes region, the Gulf of Suez or the Red Sea proper is not certain; see G. Hort in *ZAW* 70, 1958, pp. 51–52. The *yam sûp̄* of Exodus 23:31 is ambiguous, but perhaps it is the Gulf of Aqabah.

Various references clearly show that the term *yam sûp̄* applied to the Gulf of Aqabah. After their first halt at Kadesh-barnea (see also *Kadesh), the Israelites were ordered into the wilderness by the way to the *yam sûp̄* (Numbers 14:25; Deuteronomy 1:40; 2:1), *i.e.* by the Arabah towards the Gulf of Aqabah as suggested by the physical circumstances in which the earth swallowed Korah and his company (see also *Wilderness of Wandering; G. Hort, *Australian Biblical Review* 7, 1959, pp. 19–26).

After a second sojourn at Kadesh, Israel went by the way of the *yam sûp̄* to go round Edom (Numbers 21:4; Judges 11:16), again with reference to the Gulf of Aqabah. Solomon's seaport of Ezion-geber or *Elath on this gulf is placed on the *yam sûp̄* by 1 Kings 9:26; Teman in Edom is associated with it (Jeremiah 49:21).

That the term *yam sûp̄* should have a wider use for the two northern arms of the Red Sea as well as the more restricted application to the line of reedy lakes from Suez north to Lake Menzaleh and the Mediterranean is not specially remarkable or unparalleled. About 1470 BC, for example, Egyptian texts of a single epoch can use the name *Wadj-wer*, 'Great Green (Sea)', of both the Mediterranean and Red Seas (Erman-Grapow, *op. cit.*, 1, p. 269: 13–14, references), and *Ta-neter*, 'God's Land', of both Punt (eastern Sudan?) in particular and eastern lands generally (*ibid.*, 5, p. 225: 1–4, references).

K. A. Kitchen

**REFUGE, CITIES OF.** See *Cities of Refuge.

**REHOB** (Hebrew $r^{e}$ḥōḇ, 'open place, market-place [of town or village]', a name occurring in the Bible as a personal and as a place-name).

**1.** The most northerly city observed by Joshua's spies in Canaan (Numbers 13:21). It was an Aramaean centre which supplied the Ammonites with troops in the time of David (2 Samuel 10:6–8).

The name is written 'Beth-rehob' in 2 Samuel 10:6 and in Judges 18:28, which latter passage suggests that it was situated near the source of the Jordan, though the precise location is unknown. Two suggestions are Tell el-Balat, 16 kilometres east of Rosh Ha-Niqra, and Tell er-Raḥb, 7 kilometres to the south-east. Both are too far west to be the (Beth-)Rehob of Numbers 13:21 and 2 Samuel 10:6–8, which some scholars therefore consider to have been a separate place.

**2.** A city in Canaan which fell to the lot of Asher (Joshua 19:28, 30) and was declared a levitical city (Joshua 21:31; 1 Chronicles 6:75), though it was among the cities not taken at the time of the Conquest (Judges 1:31). The suggested identification with Tell eṣ-Ṣârem south of Bethshean is unsubstantiated and many scholars prefer Tell el-Bir el-Gharbi, 8 kilometres east south-east of Acco.

(See also *Rehoboth; *Rehoboth-Ir.)

T. C. Mitchell, J. Bimson

*Further reading*

W. F. Albright, *BASOR* 83, 1941, p. 3[illegible]

J. Garstang, *Joshua–Judges*, 1931, pp. 73–74, 241

H. Tadmor, *Scripta Hierosolymitana* 8, 1961, p. 245

**REHOBOTH** (Hebrew $r^{e}$ḥōḇôṯ, 'broad places, room'; Septuagint *eurychōria*). **1.** A well dug by Isaac near Gerar (Genesis 26:22), so named because no quarrel ensued with the herdsmen of Gerar. It was probably located in the Wadi Ruḥaybeh, south-west of Beersheba.

**2.** A city 'by the river' (Genesis 36:37), probably beside the Wadi el-Hesā, which divides Moab from Edom. 'The River' is normally the Euphrates (see RSV), but the context here forbids it.

J. W. Charley

**REHOBOTH-IR** (Hebrew $r^{e}$ḥōḇōṯ 'îr). One of four cities built by As(s)hur (RSV Nimrod) in Assyria (Genesis 10:11–12). Of these Nineveh and Calah are well known, but no Assyrian equivalent is known for this place. Since the large and ancient city of Aššur (80 kilometres south of Nineveh) would be expected in the context, some consider this name an interpretation from the Sumerian *AŠ.UR* (*AŠ* is the Assyrian *rebātu*; *UR* is the Assyrian *ālu*; Hebrew *'îr*).

A suburb of Nineveh (*rebit Ninua*) is mentioned in Assyrian texts (Esarhaddon), and this may have been founded at the same time. The phrase 'open-places of the city' may here be a description of Nineveh itself. The Septuagint read as a

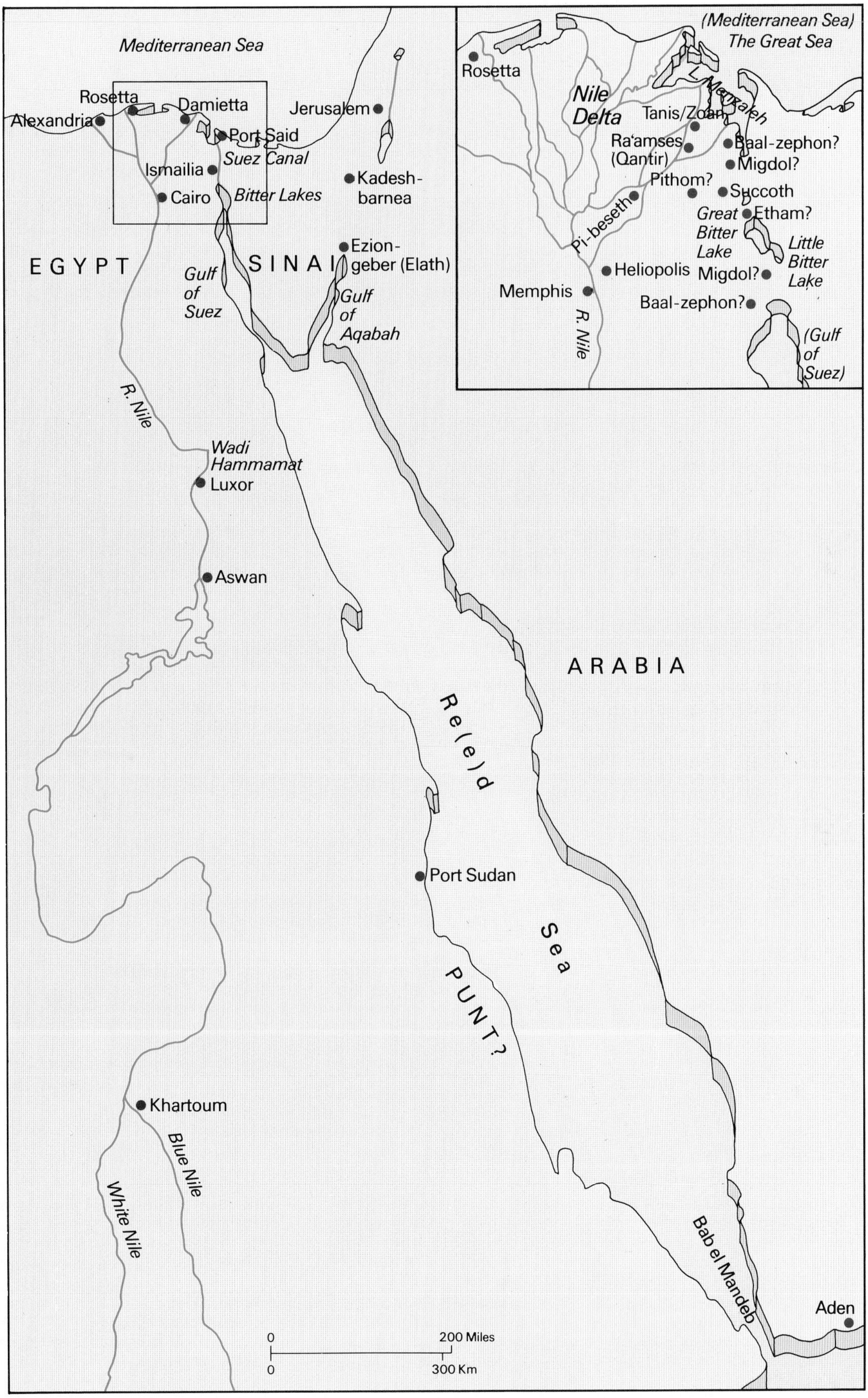


The modern Red Sea and its northern reaches at the time of the Exodus (inset).

proper name (*Rhoōbōth*).
D. J. Wiseman

*Further reading*
G. Dossin, *Le Muséon* 47, 1934, pp. 108ff.
W. F. Albright, *Recent Discoveries in Bible Lands*, 1955, p. 71
J. M. Sasson, *RB* 90, 1983, pp. 94–96

**REMETH.** See *JARMUTH.

**REPHIDIM.** The last stopping-place of the Israelites on the Exodus from Egypt, before they reached Mount Sinai (Exodus 17:1; 19:2; Numbers 33:14–15). Here the Israelites under Joshua fought against Amalek, and the successful outcome of the battle depended on Moses' holding up his hands, which he did with the support of Aaron and Hur (Exodus 17:8–16). After the battle, Jethro, Moses' father-in-law, persuaded Moses to give up judging the people entirely by himself, and to appoint deputies for this purpose (Exodus 18).

The site of Rephidim is uncertain, the usual suggestion being the Wadi Refayid in south-western Sinai, while the Wadi Feiran has been favoured by tradition since the Byzantine period.
T. C. Mitchell

*Further reading*
B. Rothenberg, *God's Wilderness*, 1961, pp. 143, 168

**RESEN** (Greek *Dasen*). The city located between Nineveh and Calah founded by Nimrod or Ashur (so AV) and with them part of a great populated area (Genesis 10:12).

*rēš-êni* ('fountain-head') designated a number of places in Assyria. The sites of this name on the Ḫabur and Khosr Rivers (north-east of Nineveh) do not, however, easily fit the geographical situation given in Genesis 10. The proposed equation with Selamiyeh (3 kilometres north of Calah) is based on the false identification of this place with Larissa (Xenophon, *Anabasis* 3.4), now known to be the Greek name for Calah itself.

A possible site for Resen is the early ruins of Hamam Ali with its adjacent sulphur springs on the right bank of the river Tigris about 13 kilometres south of Nineveh.
D. J. Wiseman

**REUBEN** (Massoretic Text *r^e'ûḇēn*; Septuagint *Roubēn*; Peshitta *Roubîl*; Josephus *Roubēlos*; Arabic *Ra'ûbîn*; Latin *Rubin*). The first-born of Jacob by Leah (Genesis 29:32), whose choice of name is connected with the phrase, 'the Lord *has looked upon my affliction*' (Hebrew *rā'â . . . b^e'onyî*).

The tribe of Reuben was involved in the rebellion in the wilderness (Numbers 16:1). The tribe was linked with Gad and occupied territory east of Jordan. In the north it was contiguous with Gad, in the south it was bounded by the Arnon.

The tribe's pursuits would be mainly pastoral, but those to the west of Jordan were mainly agricultural. This may have led to a separation of interests, for Reuben took no part in repelling the attack of Sisera (Judges 5:15f.). In the time of Saul they united with Gad and Manasseh in an attack on the Hagarites, apparently a nomad people (1 Chronicles 5:10, 19f.).

Though there is mention of Gad on the Moabite Stone, there is none of Reuben, and thus it appears that at that time, *c.* 830 BC, they had lost their importance as warriors. However, they were never forgotten by their brethren; a place is reserved for the tribe of Reuben in Ezekiel's reconstructed Israel (Ezekiel 48:7, 31), and they are numbered among the 144,000 sealed out of every tribe of the children of Israel, in the Apocalypse of John (Revelation 7:5).
R. J. A. Sheriffs

**REZEPH.** A town destroyed by the Assyrians and named in a letter to Hezekiah sent by Sennacherib as a warning to Jerusalem of the fate of those cities who resisted their demands for surrender (2 Kings 19:12 and Isaiah 37:12). The details of any revolt or sack of Assyrian Raṣappa are not known, though Assyrian texts mention the town and name several governors in the years 839–673 BC.

This important caravan-centre on the route from the Euphrates to Hamath was identified by Ptolemy (5.16; Greek *Rhēsapha*) and is the modern *Resāfa*, about 200 kilometres east north-east of Hama, Syria.
D. J. Wiseman

**RHEGIUM.** The modern Reggio di Calabria, a port-city on the Italian shore of the Strait of Messina, in southern Italy. An old Greek colony, Rhegium owed its importance under the Roman empire to its position in relation to the navigation of the Strait and the Italian western coast.

With the whirlpool of Charybdis and the rock of Scylla endangering navigation through the Strait, it was important to attempt the passage only with the most favourable sailing wind, and shipping moving north would wait at Rhegium for a south wind. This was done by the master of the ship which was taking Paul to Rome (Acts 28:13).
J. H. Paterson

**RHODES.** The large island extending towards Crete from the south-western extremity of Asia Minor, and thus lying across the main sea route between the Aegean and the Phoenician ports. It was partitioned among three Greek states, of Dorian stock, early federated and sharing a common capital at the north-eastern point of the island. It was this city, also called Rhodes, that Paul touched at on his last journey to Palestine (Acts 21:1).

After Alexander's conquests, and the establishment of the Macedonian kingdoms and many Hellenized states throughout the eastern periphery of the Mediterranean, Rhodes grew to be the leading Greek republic, outstripping those of the old homeland. This was not only because she was now the natural clearing-house for the greatly increased east–west traffic, but because her position gave her an effective diplomatic leverage against the pressures of the rival kingdoms who disputed the hegemony of the strategic Aegean islands.

As the champion of the old autonomy principle, Rhodes took the lead in calling for Roman intervention to protect it. She fell from favour with the Romans, however, who deliberately advanced Delos to destroy her ascendancy. By Paul's time her importance was gone, except as a resort of mellow distinction in learning and leisure.
E. A. Judge

*Further reading*
M. Rostovtzeff, *CAH* 8, pp. 619–642

**RIBLAH, RIBLATH. 1.** A place in the district of Hamath, on the river Orontes in Syria, on the right bank of which are ruins near a modern village, Ribleh, 56 kilometres north-east of Baalbek and south of Hama. The site is easily defended and commands the main route from Egypt to the Euphrates as well as the neighbouring forests and valleys, from which ample supplies of food or fuel are obtained.

For such reasons Riblah was chosen by Neco II as the Egyptian headquarters, following his defeat of Josiah at Megiddo and the sack of adesh in 609 BC. Here he deposed ehoahaz, imposed tribute on Judah nd appointed Jehoiakim its king 2 Kings 23:31–35).

When Nebuchadrezzar II defeated ne Egyptians at Carchemish and Hamath in 605 BC he likewise chose iblah as his military base for the ubjugation of Palestine. From it he irected operations against erusalem in 589–587 BC, and here vas brought the rebel Zedekiah to e blinded after watching the death f his sons (2 Kings 25:6, 20–21; eremiah 39:5–7; 52:9–27).

The AV Diblath (RV 'Diblah') of zekiel 6:14 may be the same place see RSV), since an otherwise nknown situation is unlikely in the ontext.

**2.** Riblath at the north-eastern orner of the ideal boundary of Israel Numbers 34:11) might be the same lace as **1**, though the border is enerally considered to lie farther outh (compare Ezekiel 47:15–18). 'he suggestion commonly adopted, hat this is to be read 'to Harbel' Septuagint), modern Harmel in the Beqa', helps little in evaluating the order, since this place lies only 13 ilometres south-west of Riblah **1** self.

. J. Wiseman

**IMMON** (Hebrew *rimmôn*, pomegranate'). **1.** En(Ain)-Rimmon vas a place in the Negeb near Edom ssigned to Simeon (Joshua 19:7; Chronicles 4:32) but incorporated nto the Beersheba district (Joshua 5:32). Zechariah envisaged it as the outhern part of the high plateau een from Jerusalem (14:10). It was ettled by returning exiles Nehemiah 11:29).

Although Rimmon has been dentified with Khirbet er-Ramamim . 16 kilometres north-north-east of Beersheba, recent excavations have evealed no trace of occupation in he Old Testament period. A more romising site is Tel Halif, 1 ilometre farther north. This is erved by two springs (hence n-Rimmon, 'Pomegranate Spring') nd has remains from the Iron Age nd the Persian period. See O. Borowski, *BA* 51/1, 1988, pp. 21–27.

**2.** A village in Zebulun (Joshua 9:13), possibly modern Rummaneh 0 kilometres north-north-east of Nazareth (the Crusader Romaneh). 'he AV 'Remmon-methoar' is to be ranslated 'Rimmon as it bends owards . . .', as in the RSV. A Levitical ity (1 Chronicles 6:77), Dimnah Joshua 21:35), read by some ersions as Remmon, may be the ite; it was captured by the Assyrians *en route* to Jerusalem (so Isaiah 10:27, RSV).

**3.** A rocky cliff with caves near Gibeah, to which the Benjaminites escaped (Judges 20:45–47); perhaps modern Rammon, 8 kilometres east of Bethel.

**4.** Rimmon-perez, an Israelite encampment of the wilderness journeys (Numbers 33:19–20), location unknown.

D. J. Wiseman, J. Bimson

**ROMAN EMPIRE.** The term in its modern usage is neither biblical nor even classical, and does not do justice to the delicacy and complexity of Roman methods of controlling the peoples of the Mediterranean.

The word *imperium* signified primarily the sovereign authority entrusted by the Roman people to its elected magistrates by special act (the *lex curiata*). The *imperium* was always complete, embracing every form of executive power, religious, military, judicial, legislative and electoral. Its exercise was confined by the collegiality of the magistracies, and also by the customary or legal restriction of its operation to a particular *provincia*, or sphere of duty.

With the extension of Roman interests abroad, the province became more and more often a geographical one, until the systematic use of the magisterial *imperium* for controlling an 'empire' made possible the use of the term to describe a geographical and administrative entity. In New Testament times, however, the system was still far from being as complete or rigid as this implies.

## The nature of Roman imperialism

The creation of a Roman province, generally speaking, neither suspended existing governments nor added to the Roman state.

### *The 'governor'*

The 'governor' (there was no such generic term, the appropriate magisterial title being used) worked in association with friendly powers in the area to preserve Rome's military security, and if there was no actual warfare his work was mainly diplomatic. He was more like the regional commander of one of the modern treaty organizations which serve the interests of a major power than the colonial governor with his monarchical authority.

### *The 'governed'*

The solidarity of the 'empire' was a product of the sheer preponderance of Roman might rather than of direct centralized administration. It embraced many hundreds of satellite states, each linked bilaterally with Rome, and each enjoying its individually negotiated rights and privileges. While the Romans obviously had it in their power to cut their way clean through the web of pacts and traditions, this suited neither their inclination nor their interest, and we find them even struggling to persuade dispirited allies to enjoy their subordinate liberties.

At the same time there was going on a process of piecemeal assimilation through individual and community grants of Roman citizenship which bought out the loyalty of local notabilities in favour of the patronal power.

## Growth of the provincial system

### *In Italy*

The art of diplomatic imperialism as explained above was developed during Rome's early dealings with her neighbours in Italy. Its genius has been variously located in the principles of the fetial priesthood, which enforced a strict respect for boundaries and allowed no other grounds for war, in the generous reciprocity of early Roman treaties, and in the Roman ideals of patronage, which required strict loyalty from friends and clients in return for protection.

For whatever reason, Rome soon acquired the leadership of the league of Latin cities, and then over several centuries, under the impact of the sporadic Gallic and German invasions, and the struggles with overseas powers such as the Carthaginians and certain of the Hellenistic monarchs, built up treaty relations with all of the Italian states south of the Po valley. Yet it was not until 89 BC that these peoples were offered Roman citizenship and thus became municipalities of the republic.

### *The Mediterranean world and beyond*

Meanwhile a similar process was taking place throughout the Mediterranean. At the end of the first Punic War Sicily was made a province (241 BC), and the Carthaginian threat led to further such steps in Sardinia and Corsica (231 BC), Hither and Further Spain (197 BC), and finally to the creation of a province of Africa itself after the destruction of Carthage in 146 BC.

By contrast the Romans at first hesitated to impose themselves on the Hellenistic states of the East, until after the repeated failure of free negotiation provinces were created for Macedonia (148 BC) and Achaia (146 BC).

In spite of a certain amount of violence, such as the destruction of both Carthage and Corinth in 146 BC, the advantages of the Roman provincial system soon became recognized abroad, as is made clear by the passing of 3 states to Rome by their rulers' bequest, leading to the provinces of Asia (133 BC), Bithynia and Cyrene (74 BC). The Romans had been busy tidying up on their own account, and the threat to communications caused by piracy had by this time led to the creation of provinces for Narbonese Gaul, Illyricum and Cilicia.

The careerism of Roman generals now began to play a prominent part. Pompey added Pontius to Bithynia and created the major new province of Syria as a result of his Mithridatic command of 66 BC, and in the next decade Caesar opened up the whole of Gaul, leaving the Romans established on the Rhine from the Alps to the North Sea.

The last of the great Hellenistic states, Egypt, became a province after Augustus' defeat of Antony and Cleopatra in 31 BC. From this time onwards the policy was one of consolidation rather than expansion. Augustus pushed the frontier up to the Danube, creating the provinces of Raetia, Noricum, Pannonia and Moesia.

In the next generation local dynasties were succeeded by Roman governors in a number of areas. Galatia (25 BC) was followed by Cappadocia, Judaea, Britain, Mauretania and Thrace (AD 46).

*By the time of the New Testament*

The New Testament thus stands at the point where the series of provinces has been completed and the whole Mediterranean has for the first time been provided with a uniform supervisory authority. At the same time the pre-existing governments still flourished in many cases, though with little prospect of future progress.

The process of direct incorporation into the Roman republic went ahead until Caracalla in AD 212 extended citizenship to all free residents of the Mediterranean. From this time onwards the provinces are imperial territories in the modern sense.

### The administration of the provinces

Until the 1st century BC the provinces had fallen to the Roman magistrates either for their year of office itself or for the immediately subsequent year, when they continued to exercise the *imperium* as pro-magistrate. For all the high sense of responsibility of the Roman aristocrat, and his life-long training in politics and law, it was inevitable that his province was governed with a single eye to his next step in the capital. The first standing court at Rome was established for the trial of provincial governors for extortion.

So long as the competition for office remained unrestrained, the creation of 3-, 5- and 10-year commands only worsened the position. They became the basis for outright attempts at military usurpation. The satellite states were left in a hopeless plight. They had been accustomed to protect their interests against capricious governors by seeking the patronage of powerful houses in the senate, and justice was done in the long run.

Now during the 20 years of civil war that followed the crossing of the Rubicon (49 BC) they were compelled to take sides and risk their wealth and liberty in an unpredictable conflict. Three times the great resources of the East were mustered for an invasion of Italy itself, but in each case the invasion was abortive.

*Professional administration*

It then fell to the victor, Augustus, during 45 years of unchallenged power to restore the damage. He first accepted a province for himself embracing most of the regions where a major garrison was still needed, notably Gaul, Spain, Syria and Egypt. This grant was renewed periodically until the end of his life, and the custom was maintained in favour of his successors. Regional commanders were appointed by his delegation, and thus a professional class of administrators was established, and consistent long-term planning was possible for the first time.

The remaining provinces were still allotted to those engaged in the regular magisterial career, but the possibilities of using the position improperly were ruled out by the overwhelming strength of the Caesars, and inexperience tended to defer to them in any case, so that the Caesarian standard of administration was widely maintained.

If it came to the worst a maladministered province could be transferred to the Caesarian allotment, as happened in the case of Bithynia in Pliny's day.

*Duties of a governor*

Three of the main responsibilities of the governors are well illustrated in the New Testament. The first was military security and public order. Fear of Roman intervention on this ground led to the betrayal of Jesus (John 11:48–50), and Paul was arrested by the Romans on the assumption that he was an agitator (Acts 21:31–38). The governments at Thessalonica (Acts 17:6–9) and at Ephesus (Acts 19:40) demonstrate the paralysis that had crept in through fear of intervention. On the other hand, among the Phoenician states (Acts 12:20) and at Lystra (Acts 14:19) there are violent proceedings with no sign of Roman control.

The second major concern was with the revenues. The Caesars straightened out the taxation system and placed it on an equitable census basis (Luke 2:1). Jesus (Luke 20:22–25) and Paul (Romans 13:6–7) both defended Roman rights in this matter.

The third and most onerous of their duties was jurisdiction. Both by reference from the local authorities (Acts 19:38) and by appeal against them (Acts 25:9–10) litigation was concentrated around the Roman tribunals. Long delays ensued as the cost and complexity of procedure mounted up. Hard-pressed governors struggled to force the onus back on to local shoulders (Luke 23:7; Acts 18:15). Christians, however, freely joined in the chorus of praise for Roman justice (Acts 24:10; Romans 13:4).

### The Roman empire in New Testament thought

While the intricate relations of governors, dynasts and republics are everywhere apparent in the New Testament and familiar to its writers, the truly imperial atmosphere of the Caesarian ascendancy pervades it all. Caesar's decree summons Joseph to Bethlehem (Luke 2:4). He is the antithesis of God in Jesus' dictum (Luke 20:25). His distant envoy seals Jesus' death warrant (John 19:12). Caesar commands the perjured loyalty of the Jews (John 19:15), the spurious allegiance of the Greeks (Acts 17:7), the fond confidence of the apostle (Acts 25:11). He is the 'emperor' to whom Christian obedience is due (1 Peter 2:13).

Yet his very exaltation was fatal t

:hristian loyalty. There was more han a grain of truth in the repeated nsinuation (John 19:12; Acts 17:7; 5:8). In the last resort the Christians vill defy him. It was the hands of awless' men that crucified Jesus Acts 2:23). The vaunted justice is to e spurned by the saints 1 Corinthians 6:1). When Caesar etaliated (Revelation 17:6) the lasphemy of his claims revealed his oom at the hand of the Lord of lords nd King of kings (Revelation 17:14).
Thus, while Roman imperial peace pened the way for the gospel, oman imperial arrogance flung own a mortal challenge.
. A. Judge

*urther reading*
*:AH*, 9–11
. H. Stevenson, *Roman Provincial dministration*, 1949
. N. Sherwin-White, *Roman Society nd Roman Law in the New estament*, 1963
. E. Adcock, *Roman Political Ideas nd Practice*, 1959
. Millar, *The Roman Empire and its Neighbours*, 1967
I. Mattingly, *Roman Imperial Civilization*, 1957
. P. V. D. Balsdon, *Rome: the Story of n Empire*, 1970
. A. Judge, *The Social Pattern of the Christian Groups in the First Century*, 1960

**ROME.** See p. 268.

**ROSH.** In the RV and NEB this word ccurs in the title of Gog who is escribed as 'prince of Rosh' (Ezekiel 8:2–3; 39:1). The AV, RV margin, RSV nd NIV interpret the word as a title tself, 'chief', 'prince'. However, the ame of a northern people or country uch as Meshech and Tubal is more robable. Gesenius suggested ussia, but this name is not attested n the area, and a very distant people amed thus early is unlikely in the ontext. Most follow Delitzsch in dentifying Rosh with Assyrian *Rašu* n the north-western border of Elam *.e.* in Media).
). J. Wiseman

**RUMAH.** Mentioned in 2 Kings 23:36 nly as the home of Zebidah, mother f King Jehoiakim. Josephus, in a arallel account (*Antiquities* 10.5.2), alls it 'Abouma', and probably neans 'Arumah'.
A place of this name is mentioned n Judges 9:41, often assumed to be ear Shechem, but an Arumah is also ttested in the annals of Tiglath-ileser III and has been identified vith Khirbet al-Rumah, some 35 kilometres inland from Mount Carmel. This could be the Galilean town of Rumah mentioned by Josephus (*Jewish War* 3.7.21). In view of the links which Josiah, Jehoiakim's father, forged with the north (2 Chronicles 34:6–7), it could also be the Rumah of 2 Kings 23:36.
Some would also locate the Arumah of Judges 9:41 here, but it is possible that this should be sought somewhere nearer to Shechem.
D. F. Payne, J. Bimson

*Further reading*
*LOB*, pp. 372, 403

# S

**SALAMIS.** A town on the east coast of the central plain of *Cyprus, not to be confused with the famous island off the coast of Attica. It rivalled in importance Paphos, the Roman capital of the whole island, and eventually superseded it. The harbour which made Salamis a great commercial centre is now completely silted up.
In the 1st century AD the Jewish community in Salamis was large enough to have more than one synagogue (Acts 13:5). Destroyed by earthquakes, the town was rebuilt in the 4th century AD as Constantia. Its ruins are 5 kilometres from Famagusta.
K. L. McKay

**SALECAH, SALCAH.** A place in the extreme east of *Bashan (Deuteronomy 3:10; Joshua 12:5; 13:11). Though Bashan was allotted to Manasseh, the area occupied by Gad included Salecah (1 Chronicles 5:11). It probably was within the area conquered by David, but after Solomon's time it lay outside Israelite territory.
The site is possibly the modern Ṣalḫad (Nabataean *ṣlḫd*) on a southern spur of the Ḥauran, though this identification is not universally accepted. See *LOB*, p. 441.
T. C. Mitchell

**SALEM.** The place where Melchizedek ruled (Genesis 14:18; Hebrews 7:1, 8) near the valley of Shaveh (Genesis 14:17; explained as 'the King's Valley'). It is mentioned in parallel with Zion (Psalm 76:2).
Following Josephus (*Antiquities* 1.180), Salem is usually identified with the ancient site of *Jerusalem, the city of Salem, *Uru-salem, uru-salimmu* of the cuneiform and Egyptian inscriptions. This would suit the route probably taken by Abraham on his return from Damascus to Hebron when he encountered Melchizedek. Those
**Continued on p. 271**

# ROME

**ROME.** Founded traditionally in 753 BC on its seven hills (the bluffs formed where the Latin plain falls away into the Tiber bed at the first easy crossing up from the mouth), Rome, as the excavations have shown, was in origin a meeting-place and a melting-pot, rather than the home of a pre-existing people.

The process of accretion, stimulated at an early stage by the strategic requirements of the Etruscan states to the north and south, acquired its own momentum, and by a liberal policy of enfranchisement unique in antiquity Rome attracted to herself men and ideas from all over the Mediterranean, until nearly 1,000 years from her beginning she had incorporated every other civilized community from Britain to Arabia.

Rome was cosmopolitan and all the world was Roman. Yet this very comprehensiveness destroyed the uniqueness of the city, and the strategic centrality that had dictated her growth was lost with the opening up of the Danube and the Rhine, leaving Rome in the Middle Ages little more than a provincial city of Italy.

*The New Testament city*

In New Testament times Rome was in the full flush of her growth. Multi-storey tenement blocks housed a proletariat of over a million, drawn from every quarter. The aristocracy, becoming just as international through the domestic favours of the Caesars, lavished the profits of three continents on suburban villas and country estates. The Caesars themselves had furnished the heart of the city with an array of public buildings perhaps never equalled in any capital.

The same concentration of wealth provided the over-crowded masses with generous economic subsidies and entertainment. It also attracted literary and artistic talent from foreign parts. As the seat of the senate and of the Caesarian administration Rome maintained diplomatic contact with every other state in the Mediterranean, and the traffic in foodstuffs and luxury goods fortified the links.

## Rome in New Testament thought

*The book of Acts*

The Acts of the Apostles has often been supposed to be an apostolic odyssey set between Jerusalem and Rome as the symbols of Jew and Gentile. The opposite pole to Jerusalem is, however, given as the 'end of the earth' (Acts 1:8), and, while the narrative certainly concludes at Rome, no great emphasis is laid on that.

Attention is concentrated on the legal struggle between Paul and his Jewish opponents, and the journey to Rome serves as the resolution of this, culminating in Paul's denunciation of the Jews there and the unhindered preaching to the Gentiles. The theme of the book seems to be the release of the gospel from its Jewish matrix, and Rome provides a clear-cut terminal point in this process.

*The book of Revelation*

In Revelation, however, Rome acquires a positively sinister significance. 'The great city, which has dominion over the kings of the earth' (Revelation 17:18), seated upon seven mountains (verse 9), and upon 'the waters' which are 'peoples and multitudes and nations and tongues' (verse 15), is unmistakably the imperial capital.

The seer, writing in Asia Minor, the greatest centre of luxury trade in antiquity, discloses the feelings of those who suffered through the consortium with Rome. He scorns the famous compromise with 'the kings of the earth' who 'were wanton with her' (Revelation 18:9), and catalogues the sumptuous traffic (verses 12–13) of the 'merchants of the earth' who have 'grown rich with the wealth of her wantonness' (verse 3). He stigmatizes the artistic brilliance of the city (verse 22).

How widespread such hatred was we do not know. In this case the reason is plain. Rome has already drunk the 'blood of the martyrs of Jesus' (Revelation 17:6).

## The origin of Christianity at Rome

So far as the New Testament goes, it is not clear how the circle of Christians was established in Rome nor even whether they constituted a church in the regular way. There is no unequivocal reference to any meeting or activity of the church as such, let alone to bishops or sacraments. The church of Rome simply fails to appear in our documents. Let it be said at once that this need not mean that it was not yet formed. It may merely be the case that it was not intimately connected with Paul, with whom most of our information is concerned.

*Paul, Aquila and Priscilla*

Paul's first known link with Rome

Part of the ancient forum, Rome.

**Part of the Colosseum, Rome, built by Vespasian and completed by Titus. It was used as a place of persecution of some Christians.**

vas when he met Aquila and riscilla at Corinth (Acts 18:2). They ad left the city as a result of laudius' expulsion of the Jews. ince it is not stated that they were lready Christians, the question nust be left open.

Suetonius says (*Claudius*, 25) that he trouble in Rome was caused by a ertain Chrestus. Since this could be variant of Christus, it has often een argued that Christianity had already reached Rome. Suetonius, however, knew about Christianity, and, even if he did make a mistake, agitation over Christus could be caused by any Jewish Messianic movement, and not necessarily by Christianity alone.

There is no hint in the Epistle to the Romans that there had been any conflict between Jews and Christians at Rome, and when Paul himself reached Rome the Jewish leaders professed personal ignorance of the sect (Acts 28:22). This not only makes it unlikely that there had been a clash, but sharpens the question of the nature of the Christian organization at Rome, since we know that by this stage there was a considerable community there.

*Paul and the Christians in Rome*

Some few years after meeting Aquila and Priscilla, Paul decided that he 'must also see Rome' (Acts 19:21). When he wrote the Epistle shortly afterwards his plan was to visit his friends in the city on the way to Spain (Romans 15:24). A considerable circle of these is named (chapter 16), they had been there 'many years' (Romans 15:23), and were well known in Christian circles abroad (Romans 1:8).

Paul's reference to his not building 'on another man's foundation' (Romans 15:20) does not necessarily refer to the situation in Rome; it need only mean that this was the reason why his work abroad had been so lengthy (Romans 15:22–23); indeed, the authority he assumes in the Epistle leaves little room for an alternative leader. The most natural

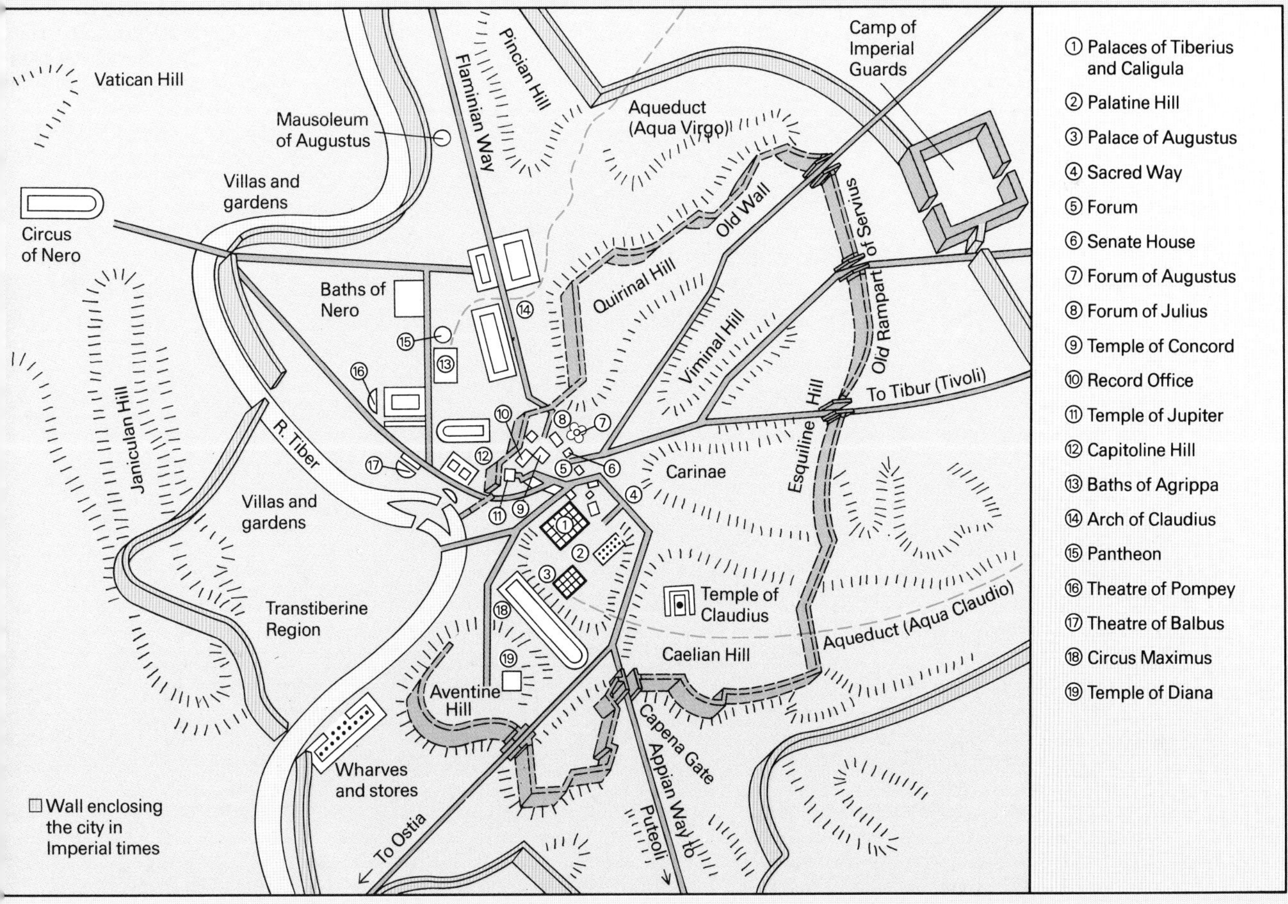


**Plan of the city of Rome in AD 64, the year of Nero's massacre of the Christians.**

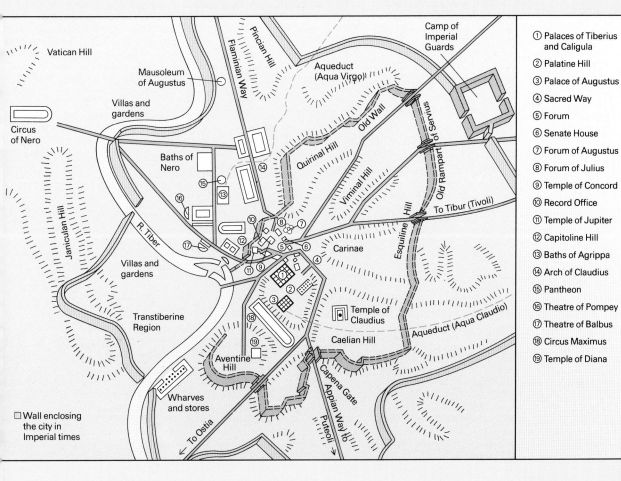

**Vespasian's Arch, built to commemorate the victories in the east.**

assumption, on the internal evidence, is that Paul is writing to a group of persons who have collected in Rome over the years after having had some contact with him in the various churches of his foundation. A number of them are described as his 'kinsmen', others have worked with him in the past. He introduces a new arrival to them (Romans 16:1).

Although some bear Roman names, we must assume that they are recently enfranchised foreigners, or at least that the majority of them are not Romans, since Paul's references to the government allude to its capital and taxation powers over non-Romans in particular (Romans 13:4, 7). Although some are Jews, the group seems to have a life of its own apart from the Jewish community (chapter 12). The reference in at least five cases to household units (Romans 16:5, 10–11, 14–15) suggests that this may have been the basis of their association.

*Paul in Rome*

When Paul finally reached Rome several years later, he had been met on the way by 'the brethren' (Acts 28:15). They do not appear again, however, either in connection with Paul's dealings with the Jewish authorities or, so far as the brief notice goes, during his 2 years' imprisonment. The seven letters that are supposed to belong to this period do sometimes contain greetings from 'the brethren', though they are mainly concerned with personal messages.

The reference to rival preachers (Philippians 1:15) is the nearest we come to any positive New Testament evidence for a non-Pauline contribution to Roman Christianity. On the other hand, the assumption of a church organized independently of Paul might explain the amorphous character of Roman Christianity in his writings.

**Was Peter ever in Rome?**

In the late 2nd century AD the tradition appears that Peter had worked in Rome and died there as a martyr, and in the 4th century the claim that he was the first bishop of the Roman church appears. These traditions were never disputed in antiquity and are not inconsistent with New Testament evidence. On the other hand, nothing in the New Testament positively supports them.

Most students assume that 'Babylon' (1 Peter 5:13) is a cryptic designation for Rome, but, although there are parallels for this in apocalyptic literature, it is difficult to see what the need for secrecy was in a letter, nor who was likely to be deceived in this case when the meaning was supposed to be plain to so wide a circle of readers.

The so-called *First Epistle of Clement*, written when the memory of the apostles was still preserved by living members of the church at Rome, refers to both Peter and Paul in terms which imply that they both died martyrs' deaths there. The tantalizing fact that this is not positively asserted may, of course, simply mean that it was taken for granted.

From about a century later comes the information that there were 'trophies' of Peter on the Vatican hill and of Paul on the road to Ostia. On the assumption that these were tombs, the two churches bearing the apostolic names were erected over them at later times. The Vatican excavations have revealed a monument which could well be the 2nd-century 'trophy' of Peter. It is associated with a burial-ground that was used in the late 1st century.

We still lack any positive trace of Peter in Rome, however. The excavations strengthen the literary tradition, of course, and in default of further evidence we must allow the distinct possibility that Peter died in Rome. That he founded the church there and ruled it for any length of time has much feebler support in tradition, and faces the almost insuperable obstacle of the silence of Paul's Epistles.

*Nero's massacre of Christians*

The tradition of the martyrdom of the apostles is supplied with a lurid occasion by the massacre of AD 64. The account by Tacitus (*Annals* 15.44) and the shorter notice by Suetonius (*Nero* 16) supply us with several surprising points about the Christian community at Rome. Its numbers are described as very large. Its connection with Jesus is clearly understood, and yet it is distinguished from Judaism. It is an object of popular fear and disgust for reasons which are not explained, apart from a reference to 'hatred of the human race'. Thus Nero's mad atrocities merely highlight the revulsion with which the Christians were received in the metropolis of the world.

E. A. Judge

*Further reading*

See under *ROMAN EMPIRE
J. P. V. D. Balsdon, *Life and Leisure in Ancient Rome*, 1974
O. Cullmann, *Peter: Disciple, Apostle, Martyr*, 1962
C. P. Thiede, *Simon Peter: From Galilee to Rome*, pp. 153–193

**ontinued from p. 267**
ᵊho assume his return down the ɔrdan valley look for a more easterly ᵊcation such as *Salim.

The Samaritans link Salem with Shalem, a city of Shechem (Genesis 3:18, AV, but compare the RSV and ɪv), east of Nablus, but this may be ue to their ancient rivalry with udah, where a 'Valley of Salem' is nown as late as Maccabean times udith 4:4). In Jeremiah 41:5 the eptuagint (B) reads Salem for hiloh.

The name *šālēm* (Greek *Salem*) eans 'safe, at peace', though erusalem has been interpreted as salem founded' implying a divine ame Salem. For the early ccurrence of this name form, ɔmpare *šillēm* (Genesis 46:24; umbers 26:49).

. J. Wiseman

**ALIM.** An apparently well-known lace (Greek *Saleim*) near Aenon on ɪe river Jordan where John aptized (John 3:23). It seems to ave been located west of the river John 3:26).

Of the many identifications roposed, the Salim (Salumias) or ell Abu Sus about 12 kilometres ɔuth of Beisan (*Bethshan-cythopolis) is the most likely. The uins of Tell Ridgha or Tell Sheikh elim, as it is also called after the ɔcal shrine, lie near several springs which might have been called Aenon Arabic *'ain*, 'spring'). This site would be under the control of cythopolis. Salim is mentioned by usebius, and marked on the 6th entury AD Medaba map.

The Salim east of Nablus with which the Samaritans identify the Salem of Genesis 14:18 lies in the eart of Samaria and is therefore uch less likely, as many Jews would have avoided the area.

The land of Salim (RSV 'Shaalim') is region in hilly Ephraim, possibly etween Aijalon and Ramah Samuel 9:4).

. J. Wiseman

*urther reading*

V. F. Albright, *The Archaeology of Palestine*, 1960, p. 247

—, in *The Background of the New Testament and its Eschatology* (ed. V. D. Davies and D. Daube), 1956, . 159

ee also *SHAALBIM

**ALMONE.** A promontory at the xtreme eastern end of Crete, now nown as Cape Sidero. On his way to ome Paul's ship was prevented by a orth-westerly wind from proceeding from off Cnidus along the northern coast of Crete, and, tacking past Salmone, sheltered in the lee of the island (Acts 27:7).

K. L. McKay

**SALT, CITY OF** (Hebrew *'îr hammelaḥ*). In Joshua 15:62 one of the frontier posts of the tribal territory of Judah 'in the wilderness', south of Middin, *Secacah and Nibshan (now identifiable, on the basis of excavations, with the Buqei'a Iron Age II settlements at Khirbet Abū Ṭabaq, Khirbet es-Samrah and Khirbet el-Maqāri), and north of En-gedi.

An identification with Khirbet Qumran, first suggested by M. Noth (*Josua*, 1938, p. 72; *ZDPV* 71, 1955, pp. 111ff.), has been confirmed by the discovery of an Iron Age II fortress beneath the *Qumran community settlement (compare F. M. Cross Jr., J. T. Milik, in *BASOR* 142, 1956, pp. 5ff.; R. de Vaux, *Archaeology and the Dead Sea Scrolls*, 1973, pp. 91ff.).

F. F. Bruce

**SALT, VALLEY OF.** Saline encrustations in steppe and desert lands are common. Some are of climatic origin; in other cases the climate has preserved geological salinity in the rocks. It is not possible to identify one topographic location from the biblical references.

David and his lieutenant Abishai had memorable victories over the Edomites in the Valley of Salt (2 Samuel 8:13; 1 Chronicles 18:12). Later Amaziah had a similar victory (2 Kings 14:7; 2 Chronicles 25:11).

Traditionally the site has been accepted as the plain south-south-west of the Dead Sea, opposite the oasis of the Zered delta, where a plain 10–13 kilometres long is overlooked by the salt range of Jebel Usdum, 8 kilometres long and 200 metres high. This plain passes imperceptibly into the glistening lowland of the Sebkha to the south-east, a soft, impassable waste of salt marsh, where an army could well be routed in confusion.

But, equally well, the site could be Wadi el-Milh (salt), east of Beersheba, also overlooked by a rocky hill, Tel el-Milh. All that the more precise reference of 2 Chronicles 25:11 suggests is that the plain was overlooked by a rocky hill, somewhere between Judah and Edom, presumably in the Arabah.

J. M. Houston

**SAMARIA.** The name of the northern Israelite capital and of the territory surrounding it.

## History

*Omri's capital*

After reigning 6 years at Tirzah, Omri built a new capital for the northern kingdom on a hill 11 kilometres north-west of Shechem commanding the main trade routes through the Esdraelon plain. He purchased the site for 2 talents of silver and named it after its owner Shemer (1 Kings 16:24). The place is otherwise unknown unless it is to be identified with Shamir, the home of Tola (Judges 10:1; F. M. Abel, *Géographie de la Palestine* 2, p. 444).

The hill, which is *c.* 100 metres high and commands a view over the plain, was impregnable except by siege (2 Kings 6:24), and the name (*šōmᵉrôn*) may be connected with the Hebrew 'watch-post'.

Omri allowed the Syrians of Damascus to set up bazaars (AV

**The view from the site of ancient Samaria.**

'streets') in his new city (1 Kings 20:34). For 6 years he worked on the construction of Samaria, and this was continued by Ahab, who built a house decorated or panelled with ivory (1 Kings 22:39).

*Idolatrous worship*
In a temple for Baal of Sidon (Melqart), the deity whose worship Jezebel encouraged (1 Kings 18:22), Ahab set up a pillar (*'ăšērâ*) near the altar; Jehoram later removed this pillar (2 Kings 3:2).

Other shrines and buildings used by the idolatrous priests must have been in Samaria from this time until the reform undertaken by Jehu (2 Kings 10:19). Samaria itself was long considered by the prophets a centre of idolatry (Isaiah 8:4; 9:9; Jeremiah 23:13; Ezekiel 23:4; Hosea 7:1; Micah 1:6).

*God's intervention*
Ben-hadad II of Syria besieged Samaria, at first unsuccessfully (1 Kings 20:1–21), but later the Syrians reduced it to dire famine (2 Kings 6:25). It was relieved only by the panic and sudden withdrawal of the besiegers, which was discovered and reported by the lepers (2 Kings 7).

Ahab was buried in the city, as were a number of Israelite kings who made it their residence (1 Kings 22:37; 2 Kings 13:9, 13; 14:16). His descendants were slain there (2 Kings 10:1), including Ahaziah, who hid in vain in the crowded city (2 Chronicles 22:9).

Samaria was again besieged in the time of Elisha and miraculously delivered (2 Kings 6:8ff.).

*Taken by Assyria*
Menahem preserved the city from attack by paying tribute to Tiglath-pileser III (2 Kings 15:17–20). His son Pekah, however, drew the Assyrian army back again by his attack on Judah, then a vassal-ally of Assyria.

The city, called *Samerina* or *Bit-Ḫumri* ('House of Omri') in the Assyrian Annals, was besieged by Shalmaneser V of Assyria in 725–722 BC. 2 Kings records that he captured the city, agreeing with the Babylonian Chronicle, but evidently his death intervened before it was finally secured for Assyria.

The citizens, incited by Iau-bi'di of Hamath, refused to pay the tax imposed on them, and in the following year (721 BC) Sargon II, the new king of Assyria, initiated a scheme of mass deportation for the whole area. According to his annals, Sargon carried off 27,270 or 27,290 captives, and the effect was to terminate the existence of the northern kingdom of Israel as a homogeneous and independent state.

*Recolonisation*
The exiles were despatched to places in Syria, Assyria and Babylonia and replaced by colonists from other parts of the Assyrian empire (2 Kings 17:24). The 'Samaritans' (RSV) of verse 29 should not be confused with the later sect of that name, with which they have no connection. Here it means simply 'people of Samaria' (as in NIV). The resultant failure to cultivate the outlying districts led to an increase in the incursions of lions (verse 25).

Some Israelites still inhabited part of the city and continued to worship at Jerusalem (Jeremiah 41:5). The town, according to a cuneiform inscription (*HES*, 247) and other records, was under an Assyrian governor and both Esarhaddon (Ezra 4:2) and Ashurbanipal (Ezra 4:9–10) brought in additional peoples from Babylonia and Elam. The contention between Samaria and Judah, of earlier origin, gradually increased in intensity, though Samaria itself declined in importance.

*A Greek city*
The discovery of papyri from Samaria in a cave of the Wadi ed-Dâliyeh 14 kilometres north of Jericho seems to confirm the reports of ancient historians that Samaria was initially favourable to Alexander who captured the city in 331 BC. However, while Alexander was in Egypt they murdered his prefect over Syria.

On his return, Alexander destroyed Samaria, massacred the city's leaders in the cave to which they had fled and resettled the area with Macedonians. Information contained in the papyri enables a list of Samaritan governors to be constructed, beginning with Sanballat I *c.* 445 BC.

*Sebaste*
Samaria was besieged by John Hyrcanus, and the surrounding countryside was devastated *c.* 111–107 BC. Pompey and Gabinius began to rebuild (Josephus, *Antiquities* 14.75), but it was left to Herod to embellish the city, which he renamed Sebaste (Augusta) in honour of his emperor. In it he housed 6,000 veterans, including Greeks.

On Herod's death, Samaria became part of the territory of Archelaus and later a Roman colony under Septimus Severus.

*In the New Testament*
Despite the mutual antagonism between Judah and Samaria, Jesus Christ took the shorter route through Samaria to Galilee (Luke 17:11), resting at Sychar near Shechem, a Samaritan city (John 4:4).

Philip preached in Samaria, but perhaps the district rather than the city is intended, since the definite article is absent in Acts 8:5.

**Archaeology**
The site was occupied in the Early Bronze Age, then deserted until the Iron Age. Sixteen levels of occupation were recognized by the Harvard (1908–10) and, later, joint Harvard-Hebrew University-British School of Archaeology in Jerusalem expeditions (1931–35). Further excavations were made by the Department of Antiquities of Jordan in 1965 and the British School of Archaeology in Jerusalem in 1968.

*Levels I–II, Omri to Ahab*
The site is difficult to work because of the dense and continuous habitation, with constant rebuilding. Of the periods of occupation unearthed, the following were assigned by K. M. Kenyon to the Israelites: Levels I–II, Omri–Ahab (28 years).

The inner (1·5 metres thick) and outer (6 metres thick) fortification wall, completed by the latter king, enclosed the summit. A main gateway seems to have had a columned entrance court. The palace, which was later adapted by Jeroboam II, had a wide court in which lay a reservoir or pool (10 × 5 metres), probably the one in which Ahab's bloodstained chariot was washed down (1 Kings 22:38).

In an adjacent storeroom more than 200 plaques or fragments of ivories were discovered. These show Phoenician and pseudo-Egyptian styles and influences and some may well have been inlays for furniture in Ahab's 'ivory house' (1 Kings 22:39). Others probably date from the reign of Jeroboam II in the following century (see Amos 3:15; 6:4).

Sixty-five ostraca, inscribed in Old Hebrew, noted the capacity and original owners of the wine-jars, with the date of their contents (*DOTT*, pp. 204–208). These are probably to be assigned to the reign of Jeroboam II and attest the taxation system then in operation.

**Part of the remains of a colonnaded street from Herod's Roman city of Sebaste (Samaria).**

*evels III–VI, Jehu to fall of Samaria*
evel III marks the period of Jehu vith adaptations of earlier uildings. Then, after an interval, ome levels IV–VI, the Israelite eriod covering Jeroboam and the th century BC. The city was repaired n the last decades before its fall to he Assyrians in 722 BC, which is narked by the destruction level of VI.

*evels VII–IX, Foreign occupation*
ost-Israelite eras are represented y levels VII (Assyrian administra-ion), VIII (Babylonian period) and IX Persian rule). Occupation continued uring the Hellenistic and Roman eriods.

The remains of the Hellenistic uildings are well preserved, with a ound tower standing 19 courses of tone high, a fortress, the city wall near the West Gate), coins, stamped ar-handles and Greek pottery emaining.

*Ierod's city*
he Roman city of Herod is notable or the great temple dedicated to ugustus, built over the Israelite alaces. Other remains include the nclosure wall, and West Gate, with round towers, a 820-metre-long olonnaded street bordered by orticos and shops, the temple of Isis ededicated to Kore, a basilica (68 × 2 metres), divided into 3 naves by orinthian columns, a forum, a tadium and an aqueduct.

Many of the visible ruins are robably to be dated to later estorers, especially Septimus everus (AD 193–211).

. J. Wiseman, J. Bimson

*Further reading*
A. Parrot, *Samaria*, 1958
J. W. Crowfoot, K. M. Kenyon and others, *Samaria* 1, *The Buildings at Samaria*, 1943; 2, *Early Ivories at Samaria*, 1938; 3, *The Objects from Samaria*, 1957
*BA* 26, 1963, pp. 110–121
J. B. Hennessy, 'Excavations at Samaria-Sebaste 1968', *Levant* 2, 1970, pp. 1–21
P. W. and N. L. Lapp, *Discoveries in the Wâdī ed-Dâliyeh*, *AASOR* 41, 1974
N. Avigad in *NEAEHL* IV, pp. 1300–1310

**SAMOS.** One of the larger islands in the Aegean Sea, off the coast of Asia Minor south-west of Ephesus. An Ionian settlement, it had been an important maritime state. Under the Romans it was part of the province of Asia until Augustus made it a free state in 17 BC.

On his way back to Judaea from his third missionary journey Paul sailed between Samos and the mainland (Acts 20:15).

K. L. McKay

**SAMOTHRACE** (modern Samothraki). A small mountainous island in the north of the Aegean off the coast of Thrace, with a town of the same name on the north side. One of its peaks rises above 1,700 metres, forming a conspicuous landmark.

Sailing north-west from Troas on his way to Neapolis, Paul must have had a favourable wind to reach Samothrace in one day and Neapolis in one more (Acts 16:11; compare 20:6).

Samothrace was renowned as a centre of the mystery cult of the Kabeiroi, ancient fertility deities who were supposed to protect those in danger, especially at sea.

K. L. McKay

**SARDIS.** A city in the Roman province of Asia, in the west of what is now Asiatic Turkey. It was the capital of the ancient kingdom of Lydia, the greatest of the foreign powers encountered by the Greeks during their early colonization of Asia Minor. Its early prosperity, especially under Croesus, became a byword for wealth; its riches are said to have derived in part from the gold won from the Pactolus, a stream which flowed through the city.

The original city was an almost impregnable fortress-citadel, towering above the broad valley of the Hermus, and nearly surrounded by precipitous cliffs of treacherously loose rock. Its position as the centre of Lydian supremacy under Croesus was ended abruptly when the Persian king Cyrus besieged the city and took the citadel (546 BC), apparently by scaling the cliffs and entering by a weakly defended point under cover of darkness.

The same tactics again led to the fall of the city in 214 BC, when it was captured by Antiochus the Great. Though it lay on an important trade route down the Hermus valley, it never regained under Roman rule the spectacular prominence it had had in earlier centuries. In AD 26 its claim for the honour of building an imperial temple was rejected in favour of its rival Smyrna.

There is now only a small village (Sart) near the site of the ancient city.

*The church in Sardis*

The letter to 'the angel of the church in Sardis' (Revelation 3:1–6) suggests that the early Christian community there was imbued with the same spirit as the city, resting on its past reputation and without any present achievement, and failing, as the city had twice failed, to learn from its past and be vigilant.

The symbol of 'white garments' was rich in meaning in a city noted for its luxury clothing trade: the faithful few who are vigilant shall be arrayed to share in the triumphal coming of their Lord.

*Excavations*

Important current excavations have brought much to light, including a superb late synagogue. Sardis had evidently been for centuries a principal centre of the Jewish Diaspora, and was probably the Sepharad of Obadiah 20.

E. M. B. Green

*Further reading*

W. M. Ramsay, *The Letters to the Seven Churches of Asia*, 1904, chs. 25, 26

D. G. Mitten, *BA* 29, 1966, pp. 38–68

G. M. A. Hanfmann, regular reports in *BASOR*

C. J. Hemer, *NTS* 19, 1972–73, pp. 94–97

——, 'Sardis', *The Letters to the Seven Churches in their Local Setting*, 1986, ch. 7

**SAREPTA.** See *ZAREPHATH.

**SARID.** A town on the southern boundary of Zebulun (Joshua 19:10, 12). Some ancient manuscripts of the Septuagint read *Sedoud*, and this has given rise to the common identification with Tell Shadud, 8 kilometres south-east of Nazareth (*LOB*, p. 117). The weight of textual evidence, however, favours the Massoretic Text's Sarid of unknown location.

W. Osborne

**SCYTHOPOLIS.** See *SALIM.

**SEA OF ARABAH.** See *DEAD SEA.

**SEA OF GALILEE.** See *CHINNERETH.

**SEA OF REEDS.** See *RED SEA.

**SEA OF TIBERIAS.** See *CHINNERETH.

**SEBA.** A land and people in southern Arabia, apparently closely related to the land and people of *Sheba; in fact *s$^{e}$ḇā'* (Seba) and *š$^{e}$ba'* (Sheba) are commonly held to be simply the Old Arabic and Hebrew forms of the one name of a people, *i.e.* the well-known kingdom of Sheba.

In a psalm (72:10) dedicated to Solomon, he is promised gifts from 'the kings of Sheba and (or: "yea") Seba'. In Isaiah's prophecies, Israel's ransom would take the wealth of Egypt, Ethiopia (Cush) and Seba (Isaiah 43:3), and the tall Sabaeans were to acknowledge Israel's God (Isaiah 45:14), first fulfilled in the wide spread of Judaism and first impact of Christianity there during the first 5 centuries AD.

The close association of Seba/ Sheba with Africa (Egypt and Cush) may just possibly reflect connections across the Red Sea between southern Arabia and Africa from the 10th century BC onwards; for slender indications of this, see W. F. Albright in *BASOR* 128, 1952, p. 45 with notes 26–27 and Abdel-Aziz Saleh in *JEA* 58, 1972, pp. 140–158.

Strabo (*Geography* 16.4.8–10) names a town Sabai and harbour Saba on the western or Red Sea coast of Arabia.

K. A. Kitchen

*Further reading*

H. von Wissmann, *Über die frühe Geschichte Arabiens und das Entstehen des Sabäerreiches – Die Geschichte von Saba I*, 1975, pp. 87–88, compare 89ff.

**SEBAM.** See *SIBMAH.

**SECACAH** (Hebrew *s$^{e}$ḵāḵâh*). A settlement in north-eastern Judah (Joshua 15:61); tentatively identified with Khirbet es-Samrah, the largest (68 metres × 40 metres) of 3 fortified sites in el-Buqei'a, an upland vale to the west of Qumran controlling irrigation works which made it possible to settle in this area; first occupied in the 9th century BC.

Other possible sites for the 'desert' settlements have been found along the shore of the Dead Sea, including Khirbet *Qumran which has some Iron Age remains. (See also *SALT, CITY OF.)

J. P. U. Lilley

*Further reading*

F. M. Cross, J. T. Milik, *BASOR* 142, 1956, pp. 5–17

P. Bar-Adon, *RB* 77, 1970, pp. 398–400

L. E. Stager, *BASOR* 221, 1976, pp. 145–158

*LOB*, p. 356

**SECU** (RSV), **SECHU** (AV). The Hebrew name, perhaps meaning 'outlook', of a place near Ramah, which Saul visited when seeking David and Samuel (1 Samuel 19:22). A possible but uncertain identification is Khirbet Shuweikeh, 5 kilometres north of el-Râm (probably biblical *Ramah).

Some manuscripts of the Septuagint read the unknown town Sephi, which represents, according to some scholars, the Hebrew *š$^{e}$p̄î*, 'bare hill'; and the Peshitta similarly renders *sûp̄â*, 'the end'; but other Greek manuscripts and the Vulgate support the Massoretic Hebrew.

J. A. Thompson

*Further reading*

F. M. Abel, *Géographie de la Palestine* 2, 1938, p. 453

C. R. Conder and H. H. Kitchener, *The Survey of Western Palestine* 3, 1883, p. 52

**SEIR. 1.** The word *śē'îr* defines a mountain (Genesis 14:6; Ezekiel 35:15), a land (Genesis 32:3; 36:21; Numbers 24:18) and a people (Ezekiel 25:8) in the general area of old Edom with which it is sometimes (*e.g.* Deuteronomy 1:44) synonymous.

Esau went to live in Seir (Genesis 32:3), and his descendants overcame the original inhabitants, the Horites (Genesis 14:6; 36:20; Deuteronomy 2:12; Joshua 24:4). The Simeonites later destroyed some Amalekites who took refuge there (1 Chronicles 4:42–43).

**2.** A landmark on the boundary of Judah (Joshua 15:10).

J. A. Thompson

**SELA.** Etymologically the Hebrew word *(has-)sela'* means '(the) rock' or 'cliff' and may be used of any rocky place. The name occurs several times in the Bible.

**1.** A fortress city of Moab, conquered by Amaziah king of Judah and renamed Joktheel (2 Kings 14:7; 2 Chronicles 25:12). Obadiah, in condemning Edom, refers to those who dwelt in the clefts of the rock (Sela, Obadiah 3). Isaiah 42:11 may refer to the same place.

For centuries the site has been identified with a rocky outcrop behind Petra, an identification which goes back to the Septuagint, Josephus and Eusebius. The massive rocky plateau Umm el-Biyara towers 300 metres above the level of Petra (the Greek translation of Sela), and 1,130 metres above sea level.

It was investigated by Nelson Glueck in 1933 and W. H. Morton in 1955. Part of an Iron Age Edomite settlement there was excavated by Mrs C. M. Bennett in 1960–65, and the houses found belong to the 7th century BC, but may have replaced older ones. The site was taken by the Nabataeans *c.* 300 BC and they converted the great valley to the north, some 1,370 metres long and 225–450 metres across, quite enclosed by mountain walls, into the amazing rock-cut city of Petra – the 'rose-red city half as old as time'.

More recently it has been claimed that another Iron Age site, *es-Sela'*, 4 kilometres north-west of Bozra (Buseira), suits the biblical and post-biblical evidence better. This site was a fortified city during the 9th–7th centuries BC. It was previously overlooked because of the impressive and continuous support for Petra. (See A. F. Rainey in *IDBS*, p. 100.)

**2.** An unidentified site, on the border of the Amorites in the time of the Judges (Judges 1:36), apparently within Judah.

**3.** Isaiah, referring to the coming judgment of Moab, spoke of fugitive Moabites sending tribute to Judah from distant Sela (Isaiah 16:1). The site is unidentified.

J. A. Thompson

*Further reading*
On Umm el-Biyara:
N. Glueck, *AASOR* 14, 1933–34, pp. 77f.
W. H. Morton, *BA* 19, 1956, pp. 26f.
*RB* 71, 1964, pp. 250–253
C. M. Bennett, *RB* 73, 1966, pp. 372–403
On the identity of Sela:
J. Starcky, *DBS*, 1966, cols. 886–900
S. Hart, *PEQ* 118, 1986, pp. 91–95

**SELEUCIA.** The former port of Antioch in Syria (1 Maccabees 11:8) which lay 8 kilometres north of the mouth of the Orontes river and 25 kilometres away from Antioch.

Seleucia (*Seleukeia*) was founded by Seleucus Nicator in 301 BC, 11 years after he had established the Seleucid kingdom. The city lay at the foot of Mount Rhosus, to the north, and was itself in the north-eastern corner of a fertile plain still noted for its beauty.

Seleucia was fortified on the south and west and surrounded by walls, but, although regarded as impregnable, it was taken by the Ptolemy Euergetes (1 Maccabees 11:8) in the Ptolemaic-Seleucid wars and remained in the hands of the Ptolemies till 219 BC, when Antiochus the Great recaptured it. He greatly beautified it, and, although it was lost again for a short time to Ptolemy Philometor in 146 BC, Seleucia was soon retaken.

The Romans under Pompey made it a free city in 64 BC, and from then on it flourished until it began to decay fairly early in the Christian era.

It is known in the Bible only in Acts 13:4, as the port of embarkation of Paul and Barnabas after they had been commissioned by the church in Antioch. From Seleucia they set sail for Cyprus on their first missionary journey. It is probably the port inferred in Acts 14:26 and 15:30, 39, though it is not named.

Seleucia today is an extensive ruin, subject to archaeological investigation by a number of expeditions since 1937. The city area can be traced, and evidence of buildings, gates, walls, the amphitheatre, the inner harbour and the great water conduit built by Constantius in AD 338 in solid rock to carry off the mountain torrent from the city are all to be seen. The channel which connected the inner harbour to the sea has, however, long since been silted up.

J. A. Thompson

**SENAAH.** In the list of exiles who returned with Zerubbabel there are 3,630 (Ezra 2:35) or 3,930 (Nehemiah 7:38) belonging to the town of Senaah. In Nehemiah 3:3 the name of the town occurs again with the definite article. Since in both passages Jericho is mentioned in close proximity, Senaah may have been near Jericho. However, some scholars prefer to regard it as the name of a Benjaminite clan.

J. S. Wright

**SENEH** ('pointed rock') and **BOZEZ** ('slippery') were two rocks between which Jonathan and his armour-bearer entered the garrison of the Philistines (1 Samuel 14:4ff.). (See also *MICHMASH.)

No precise identification of the location of these two rocky crags has been made, but see *GTT*, p. 317.

J. D. Douglas

**SENIR.** According to Deuteronomy 3:9, Senir is the Amorite name for Mount Hermon (*śᵉnîr*; AV Shenir); but in Song of Songs 4:8 and 1 Chronicles 5:23, it is apparently one of the peaks in the ridge, the name being loosely applied to the whole.

Manasseh expanded northwards to Senir (1 Chronicles 5:23), and the slopes supplied fir for Tyrian ships, Lebanon yielding cedars (Ezekiel 27:5). Shalmaneser III names Senir (*sa-ni-ru*) as a stronghold of Hazael, king of Aram (2 Kings 8:7–15, *etc.*) (*ANET*, p. 280).

A. R. Millard

**SEPHAR.** The name of a 'mountain of the east' (*har haq-qeḏem*), mentioned in the Table of Nations in defining the boundary of the territory of the sons of Joktan (Genesis 10:30). Judging from the names of other sons of Joktan, a mountain or promontory in southern Arabia seems likely, and the coastal town of Ẓafār in the eastern Hadramaut has been suggested. In view, however, of the lack of precision in the Bible statement, and the discrepancy in the sibilants, there can be no certainty.

T. C. Mitchell

*Further reading*
J. A. Montgomery, *Arabia and the Bible*, 1934, p. 41

**SEPHARAD.** The place in which captives from Jerusalem were exiled (Obadiah 20). The location is as yet unidentified.

Of many conjectures, the most plausible identifies the place as Sardis, capital of Lydia in Asia Minor. Known in Persian times as Sfard, it is written in Aramaic with the same consonants as in Obadiah. It may be the Saparda named in the Assyrian Annals of Sargon and Esarhaddon as a country allied to the Medes. The Targum of Jonathan interpreted it as Spain, hence the term Sephardim for Spanish Jews. A location in Anatolia is favoured by the Vulgate (*in Bosphoro*).

D. J. Wiseman

*Further reading*
*JNES* 22, 1963, pp. 128–132

**SEPHARVAIM.** A city captured by the Assyrians (2 Kings 17:24, 31; 18:34; 19:13; Isaiah 36:19; 37:13). The context implies that it lies in Syria or adjacent territory and this is supported by the name of its deities (Adrammelech; Anammelech).

The place is unidentified, though Halévy's suggestion that it is the same as the later Sibraim near Damascus (Ezekiel 47:16) is possible. It cannot be the same as the Šab/mara'in of the Babylonian Chronicle, as this is Samaria.

The usual interpretation of Sepharvaim as the twin cities of Sippar (of Šamaš and Anunitum) in Babylonia is unsupportable (though Sippar-amnanim is mentioned in texts), as Sippar had no independent

king (compare 2 Kings 19:13).
D. J. Wiseman

**SEPULCHRE OF THE KINGS, SEPULCHRE OF DAVID.** The Bible indicates that the kings of Israel were buried in a special area near Jerusalem. Expressions like 'tombs of the kings of Israel' (2 Chronicles 28:27), 'sepulchres of David' (Nehemiah 3:16), 'tombs of the sons of David' (2 Chronicles 32:33), refer specifically to the royal tombs of the Judaean kings of David's line in the city of David. These tombs were close to the King's Garden and the pool of Shelah (1 Kings 2:10; 2 Chronicles 21:20; Nehemiah 3:15–16). Thus when Nehemiah was building the wall of Jerusalem one of his parties worked 'over against the sepulchres of David', not far from the 'pool of Shelah (Shiloah)' (Nehemiah 3:15–16).

Most of the kings from David to Hezekiah were buried in the city of David, though some kings had their own private sepulchres, *e.g.* Asa (2 Chronicles 16:14), and possibly Hezekiah (2 Chronicles 32:33), Manasseh (2 Kings 21:18), Amon (2 Kings 21:26) and Josiah (2 Kings 23:30; 2 Chronicles 35:24).

Several kings died outside the bounds of Palestine: Jehoahaz in Egypt, Jehoiachin and Zedekiah in Babylon. Possibly Jehoiakim was not buried at all (Jeremiah 22:19), and Jehoram, Joash, Uzziah and Ahaz were not admitted to the royal sepulchre (2 Chronicles 21:20; 24:25; 26:23; 28:27).

The location of the tombs in the city of David was still referred to after the Exile. Josephus reported that they were plundered by the Hasmonean king John Hyrcanus and also by Herod (*Antiquities* 13.249; 16.179).

In the New Testament the sepulchre of David was still remembered (Acts 2:29) and Josephus (*Jewish War*, 5.147) spoke of the third wall passing by the sepulchred caverns of the kings. An inscribed tablet found by E. Sukenik states that the bones of King Uzziah had been removed to the top of the Mount of Olives.

*The site of the tombs*

The exact site of the tombs of the kings is not known today. Monuments in the Kedron Valley are late, both architecture and epigraphy pointing to the time of Herod the Great.

The term 'City of David' in the vicinity of which these tombs lay does not denote the entire city of Jerusalem but merely the citadel of the stronghold of Zion. Evidence points to the spur which juts to the south between the Tyropoean and Kedron valleys, later known as Ophel, as the location of the City of David. It overlooks the gardens and pools of Siloam. In this general area long horizontal tunnels have been found in the rock and these may have been the burial-place of the kings of David's line. But the site was desecrated and destroyed, possibly at the time of the Bar Kokhba revolt (AD 135), and thereafter the exact location forgotten.

Various other sites have been proposed over the centuries. A popular tradition reaching back for 1,000 years places the tomb of David on the western hill at the place now called Mount Zion. This site was accepted by Jewish, Muslim and Christian traditions, and Benjamin of Tudela (*c.* AD 1173) reported the miraculous discovery of David's Tomb on Mount Zion during the repair of a church on the site. Pilgrimages are still made to the site, but there is little to commend its authenticity.

The so-called Tombs of the Kings of Judah some distance to the north of the modern wall mark the tomb of Helen, queen of Adiabene, a district in Upper Mesopotamia, whose burial in Jerusalem is referred to by Josephus (*Antiquities* 20.17, 35). This burial complex dates from the 1st century AD.

However, when Josephus (*Jewish War*, 5.147) speaks of 'the caves of the kings' he is not referring to these late tombs but probably to another area of rock-hewn sepulchres closer to the present Damascus Gate. These tombs, in the grounds of the Church of St. Étienne, are of late Iron Age date, and their style suggests they belonged to wealthy and important people. It has therefore been suggested that this was the burial-place of Judah's later kings, perhaps from the time of Manasseh (A. Kloner in *Levant* 18, 1986, pp. 121–129).
J. A. Thompson, J. Bimson

*Further reading*
S. Krauss, 'The Sepulchres of the Davidic Dynasty', *PEQ* 1947, pp. 102–112
S. Yeivin, 'The Sepulchres of the Kings of the House of David', *JNES* 7, 1948, pp. 30–45

**SERPENT'S STONE** (RSV; 'Stone of Zoheleth', AV, NIV) (*'eḇen hazzōḥeleṯ*). A stone near En-rogel, to the south-east of Jerusalem, the scene of the slaughtering of animals by Adonijah (1 Kings 1:9).

The meaning of *zōḥeleṯ* is uncertain, but it is usually connected with *zāḥal*, 'to withdraw, crawl away'. From this, some would interpret the phrase as 'the stone of slipping' and connect it with a steep and slippery rock slope, called by the Arabs *zaḥweileh*, or some neighbouring surface, near Siloam.
T. C. Mitchell

*Further reading*
J. Simons, *Jerusalem in the Old Testament*, 1952, pp. 160–162

**SEVENEH.** The RV, ASV rendering of the Massoretic Text *sᵉwēnēh* (Egyptian *Swn*, 'place of barter', 'market', Coptic *Suan*, Arabic *'Aswân*) in Ezekiel 29:10 and 30:6, where the AV, RSV and NEB retain the classical form, *Syene.

Located on the first cataract of the Nile, Syene (modern 'Aswân) marked the boundary between Egypt and Ethiopia. 'From Migdol ('tower' in the AV and RV) to Syene' means 'the length of Egypt from north to south'. The Massoretic Text *sᵉwēnēh* should be read *sᵉwēnâ* or *sᵉwānâ*, the *â* signifying direction: 'to Syene'. A border fortress and a base for expeditions up the Nile, a terminus for river traffic and a source of red granite for Egyptian monuments (syenite), Syene was of special importance to the Jews because of its proximity to the island of Elephantine, which housed a colony of Jews who sought refuge in Egypt after Jerusalem fell (587 BC).

The Qumran manuscript of Isaiah suggests that 'Syenites' should replace *sînîm* (Isaiah 49:12); the Septuagint reads *Syene* for *Sin* in Ezekiel 30:16.
D. A. Hubbard

*Further reading*
E. G. Kraeling, 'New Light on the Elephantine Colony', *BA* 15, 1952, pp. 50–68

**SHAALBIM.** A village inhabited by Amorites near Mount Heres and Aijalon when they withstood the Danites. Later the Amorites were subjugated by the house of Joseph (Judges 1:35). With Makaz, Beth-shemesh and Elon-beth-Hanan Shaalbim formed part of Solomon's second administrative district (1 Kings 4:9).

Shaalbim is almost certainly the same as Shaalabbin, included with Aijalon in the list of Dan's territory (Joshua 19:42), and Shaalbon, the house of Eliahba, one of David's

The so-called Tombs of the Kings of Judah, Jerusalem, mark the tomb of Helen, queen of Adiabene.

warriors (2 Samuel 23:32; 1 Chronicles 11:33). Because of the similar area covered it has been suggested that Shaalbim of Judges 1:35 and 1 Kings 4:9 may also be the same place.

The position of modern Selbit, 5 kilometres north-west of Aijalon and 13 kilometres north of Beth-shemesh, suits all these contexts well, though the name is philologically different. Shaalbim, *etc.*, may mean 'haunt of foxes'.

D. J. Wiseman

**SHAARAIM** (Hebrew *ša'$^{a}$raim*, 'two gates'). **1.** On the line of the Philistine flight from Azekah, before the ways to Gath and Ekron parted (1 Samuel 17:52); it lay in the *Socoh district of Judah (Joshua 15:36) but cannot be more precisely located. See J. Simons, *GTT*, p. 318.

**2.** In 1 Chronicles 4:31, it refers to *Sharuhen.

J. P. U. Lilley

**SHALEM.** A word treated by the AV as the name of a place near Shechem, which was visited by Jacob (Genesis 33:18). The RV ('in peace') and RSV, NEB, NIV ('safely'), however, prefer to take it in an adverbial sense, from the verb *šālēm*, 'to be complete, sound', and this appears to make better sense.

The word *šālēm*, identical in form, does occur as a place-name in connection with Melchizedek, but is given as *Salem in the English versions.

T. C. Mitchell

**SHALISHAH.** The district reached by Saul after passing through the hills of Ephraim and before reaching the land of Shaalim, or *Salim, in pursuit of his father's lost asses (1 Samuel 9:4). The place seems to have had its own deity or shrine, Baal-shalishah (2 Kings 4:42).

Since the places in conjunction with which Shalishah is cited are of uncertain location, its own situation is not known. Conder proposed the ruins of Khirbet Kefr Thilth, 30 kilometres north-east of Jaffa.

D. J. Wiseman

**SHAMIR.** See *SHAPHIR.

**SHAPHIR** (SAPHIR, AV). A town in the Shephelah against which Micah prophesied (Micah 1:11). The exact site is uncertain, but may be es-Sūāfir near Ashdod, or, more probably, Khirbet el-Kôm, west of Hebron. The identification of Shaphir with Shamir (Joshua 15:48; Judges 10:1–2) is tenuous.

R. J. Way

**SHARON** (Hebrew *šārôn*; 'Saron', Acts 9:35, AV) means a level place or plain. It comprises the largest of the coastal plains in northern Palestine.

*Physical features*

Lying between the extensive marshes of the lower Crocodile river (Nahr ez-Zerka) and the valley of Aijalon and Joppa in the south, it runs some 80 kilometres north to south and is 15 kilometres wide. Its features have been largely determined by the Pleistocene shorelines and deposits.

Inland from the belt of recent sand-dunes which divert and choke some of the coastal rivers, rises a zone of Mousterian red sands to *c.* 60 metres, forming in the north a continuous belt of some 30 kilometres. Formerly, this zone was thickly forested with oaks, probably *Quercus infectoria*, and today this is one of the richest agricultural districts of Israel, planted with citrus groves.

Inland from the belt of Mousterian sands, the streams have partially excavated a longitudinal trough along the foothills of an earlier Pleistocene shoreline.

The river valleys, especially in the north of this trough, tended to be marshy until modern drainage developments. In the past, only in the southern border of Sharon was the land more favourable for settlement, and it is clear that most of Sharon was never colonized by the Israelites (but Tell Qasile, north of Joppa, was founded *c.* 1200 BC).

*In the Bible*

In the north, Socoh, a district centre under Solomon (1 Kings 4:10), and Gilgal, seat of the petty kings defeated by Joshua (Joshua 12:23), lay in the Samaritan foothills east of the plain.

References to Lod and Ono in the south, which were both fortified outposts (1 Chronicles 8:12; Ezra 2:33; Nehemiah 7:37), and 'the valley of the craftsmen' separating them (Nehemiah 11:35; compare 1 Samuel 13:19–20) appear to indicate they were settled by the returning exiles.

The 'majesty' of Sharon (Isaiah 35:2), like the 'jungle' of Jordan (Jeremiah 12:5; 49:19), would suggest the dense vegetation cover rather than the fertility which Sharon has subsequently proved to possess in its Pleistocene sands, now under orange groves.

For settlement it has long remained a 'desert' (Isaiah 33:9), and was used only for pasturage (1 Chronicles 5:16; Isaiah 65:10). It was here that Shitrai supervised King David's flocks (1 Chronicles 27:29).

The 'rose of Sharon' (Song of Songs 2:1–3) suggests the flowers of the dense undergrowth. Four red flowers still follow each other in quick succession, an anemone (*Anemone coronaria*), a buttercup (*Ranunculus asiaticus*), a tulip (*Tulipa montana*) and a poppy (*Papaver species*).

J. M. Houston

*Further reading*

D. Baly, *The Geography of the Bible*, 1957, pp. 133–137

**SHARUHEN** (Hebrew *šārûḥēn*). Only mentioned in Joshua 19:6, as a Simeonite settlement (but it may be the Shilhim of Joshua 15:32). Egyptian sources refer to *Srhn* as a Hyksos city which resisted Ahmose I for 3 years, *c.* 1550 BC, barring his way to the north (*ANET*, pp. 233f.); it must have been a large and strong

The land of Sheba.

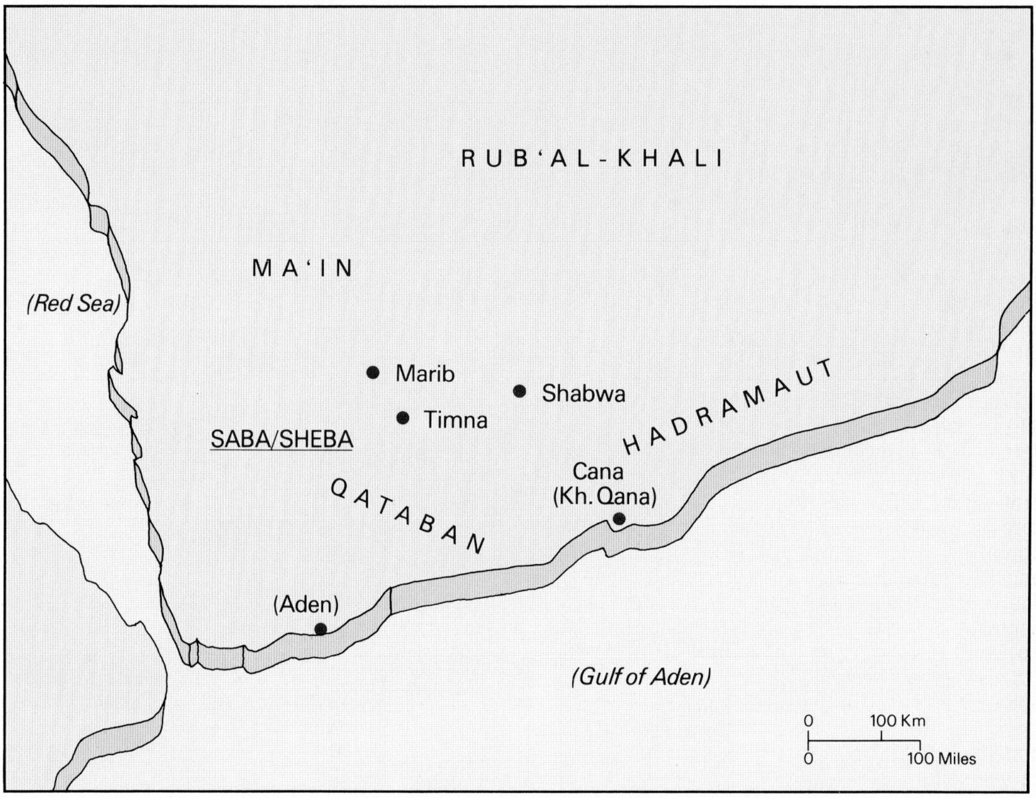


position controlling the coast road.

Tell el-Ajjul (6 kilometres south-west of Gaza) and Tell el-Far'a (24 kilometres south of Gaza) have been proposed; neither is free from difficulty, and the whole area looks so unlikely for Simeonite settlement that the biblical site has been sought either at Tel Halif, Tell el-Huweilifeh (Albright, *JPOS* 4, 1924, p. 158; but this is hardly possible if the site is only 0·5 kilometres from, or identified with, *Rimmon); or at Tel Sera', Tell esh-Shariah (20 kilometres north-west of Beersheba) (Garstang, *Joshua*, p. 87; but E. D. Oren considers this to be *Ziklag [*BA* 45, 1982, pp. 155–166]).

J. P. U. Lilley

*Further reading*

Albright, *BASOR* 33, 1929, p. 7
Abel, *Géographie* 2, 1937, pp. 451, 462
A. Kempinski, *IEJ* 24, 1974, pp. 145–152
W. Shea, *IEJ* 29, 1979, pp. 1–5
J. Weinstein, *BASOR* 241, 1981, pp. 1–28
J. K. Hoffmeier, *Levant* 21, 1989, pp. 182–184

**SHAVEH, VALLEY OF.** A valley near *Salem (Genesis 14:17f.), also known as 'the King's Valley', where Absalom raised his memorial pillar (2 Samuel 18:18).

If Salem is Jerusalem, the site may be at the top of the Valley of Hinnom. But an ancient Jewish tradition reads *ś-r-h*, another word meaning 'king', for *š-w-h* ('Shaveh'). (This involves only one slight consonantal change.)

D. F. Payne

**SHAVEH-KIRIATHAIM.** See *KIRIATHAIM.

**SHEBA. 1**. A city (Hebrew *šeḇa'*) in the territory allotted to Simeon in southern Palestine near Beersheba and Moladah (Joshua 19:2; the Massoretic Text at 1 Chronicles 4:28 omits it in the parallel list, but the Septuagint has 'Sama'). The Septuagint reads 'Samaa' in manuscript B (compare Joshua 15:26) and 'Sabee' in manuscript A.

S. Cohen (in *IDB*, 4, p. 311) suggests that Sheba ('seven') was named for the seven lambs with which Abraham made covenant with Abimelech (Genesis 21:28–29) and may have been the older part of Beersheba.

**2.** The land (*š*$^{e}$*ḇā'*) whose queen visited Solomon (1 Kings 10:1ff.; 2 Chronicles 9:1ff.) was in all probability the home of the Sabaeans in south-western Arabia. J. A. Montgomery (*Kings* [ICC], 1951, pp. 215f.) contends that the Sabaeans were still in northern Arabia in the 10th century BC although they controlled the trade routes from southern Arabia.

On the other hand, J. Bright (*History of Israel*, 3rd edition, 1980, p. 215), while recognizing that the Sabaeans were originally camel nomads, affirms, with greater probability, that by Solomon's time they had settled in the eastern area of what is modern Yemen. So also G. W. Van Beek (*IDB* 4, p. 145).

*Sabaea and Sheba*

The relationship between the Sabaeans and the three Shebas mentioned in Genesis (10:7; 10:28; 25:3) is by no means clear. They may be distinct tribes, but the similarities among the groupings are striking: Raamah's sons (Genesis 10:7), Hamites, bear the same names as Abraham's grandsons – Sheba and Dedan (25:3); both Cush, the Hamite (10:7), and Joktan, the Semite, have descendants named Sheba and Havilah (10:28–29).

The Table of Nations in Genesis 10 may reflect both the Semitic origin of the Sabaeans and also the fact that they settled in close proximity to Hamitic groups, *i.e.* Egyptians and Ethiopians. Indeed, classical Abyssinian culture testifies to a blending of Hamitic and Semitic elements, and the role that southern Arabians who crossed the Bab al-Mandab as traders and colonists played in shaping this culture is impressive.

*Gold, spices and jewels*
It is as traders or raiders (Job 1:15, although E. Dhorme, *Job*, English translation, 1967, p. xxv, identifies Sheba here with an area near Tema and Dedan, oases substantially north of the Sabaean homeland) that the Old Testament most frequently speaks of the people of Sheba. Gold (1 Kings 10:2; Psalm 72:15; Isaiah 60:6), frankincense (Isaiah 60:6; Jeremiah 6:20), spices and jewels (1 Kings 10:2; Ezekiel 27:22) were brought to northern markets in their caravans (Job 6:19). Commercial opportunists, they were not above engaging in slave trade according to Joel 3:8 (where less preferably the Septuagint reads 'into captivity' for 'to the Sabaeans').

This extensive trading activity apparently led the Sabaeans to found colonies at various oases in northern Arabia. These served as caravan bases and probably gave the colonists a degree of control over the northern area. Testimony to intercourse between Sheba and Canaan is found in a southern Arabian clay stamp (*c.* 9th century BC) unearthed at Bethel (*BASOR* 151, 1958, pp. 9–16).

*Rulers and religion*
The most prominent of the Arab states (which included Hadramaut, Ma'īn and Qatabān) during the first half of the 1st millennium BC, Sheba was ruled by *mukarribs*, priest-kings, who supervised both the political affairs and the polytheistic worship of the sun, moon and star gods.

Explorations by the University of Louvain with H. St J. Philby (1951–52) and the American Foundation for the Study of Man (1950–53) found some outstanding examples of Sabaean art and architecture, especially the temple of the moon-god at Mārib, the capital, which dates from the 7th century BC, and the sluices, hewn through solid rock at the dam in Mārib (*c.* 6th century BC).

D. A. Hubbard

*Further reading*
R. L. Bowen, Jr., and F. P. Albright, *Archaeological Discoveries in South Arabia*, 1958
*GTT*
S. Moscati, *Ancient Semitic Civilizations*, 1957, pp. 181–194
G. Ryckmans, *Les religions arabes préislamiques,* 2nd edition, 1951
J. Ryckmans, *L'Institution monarchique en Arabie méridionale avant l'Islam*, 1951
G. W. Van Beek in *BA* 15, 1952, pp. 2–18
——, 'South Arabian History and Archaeology', in G. E. Wright (ed.), *The Bible and the Near East*, 1961
——, 'The Land of Sheba', in J. B. Pritchard (ed.), *Solomon and Sheba*, 1974, pp. 40–63
A. K. Irvine in *POTT*, pp. 299ff.
D. T. Potts (ed.), *Araby the Blest*, 1988

**SHEBAH.** See *SHIBAH.

**SHEBAM.** See *SIBMAH.

**SHECHEM.** An important town in central Palestine with a long history and many historical associations. Normally it appears in the Bible as

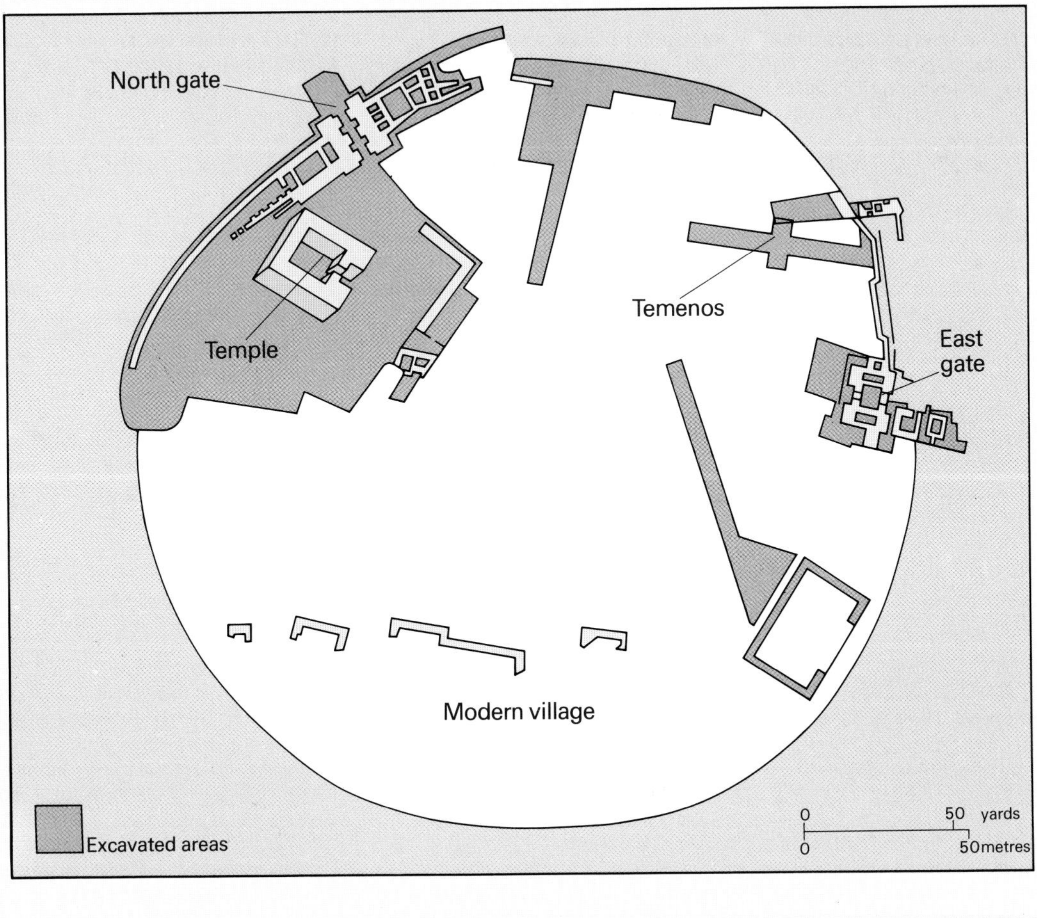


Plan of the site of Shechem, showing the areas of excavations.

Shechem ($š^{e}\underline{k}em$), but also once as Sichem (Genesis 12:6, AV) and twice as Sychem (Acts 7:16, AV). It was situated in the hill country of Ephraim (Joshua 20:7), in the neighbourhood of Mount Gerizim (Judges 9:7). The original site is today represented by Tell Balaṭa, which lies at the eastern end of the valley running between Mount Ebal on the north and Mount Gerizim on the south, about 50 kilometres north of Jerusalem and 9 kilometres south-east of Samaria.

*In the time of the Patriarchs*

Shechem (Sichem) is the first Palestinian site mentioned in Genesis. Abram encamped there at the 'oak of Moreh' (Genesis 12:6). The 'Canaanite was then in the land', but the Lord revealed himself to Abram and renewed his covenant promise. Abram thereupon built an altar to the Lord (Genesis 12:7).

Abram's grandson, Jacob, on his return from Harran, came to Shechem, and pitched his tent (Genesis 33:18–19) on a parcel of ground which he bought from Hamor, the Hivite prince of the region (Genesis 33:18–19; 34:2). When Shechem, the son of Hamor, defiled Dinah, Simeon and Levi killed the men of the region (Genesis 34:25–26), and the other sons of Jacob pillaged the town (verses 27–29), though Jacob condemned the action (Genesis 34:30; 49:5–7).

Here Jacob buried the 'strange gods' under the oak (Genesis 35:1–4) and raised an altar to El-elohe-Israel ('God, the God of Israel', Genesis 33:20). Joseph later sought his brothers near the rich pasture-lands round Shechem (Genesis 37:12ff.).

We learn from the Amarna letters that in the mid-14th century BC the town was ruled by Labayu, a shrewd rebel against the Egyptian administration and ambitious to extend his territory (*ANET*, pp. 477, 485–487, 489–490). The name Shechem probably occurs earlier in Egyptian records dating back to the 19th–18th centuries BC (*ANET*, pp. 230, 329).

*In Joshua and Judges*

After the Israelite conquest of Palestine Joshua called for a renewal of the covenant at Shechem. Various features of the typical covenant pattern well known in the East, 1500–700 BC, may be identified in Joshua 8:30–35. Before his death, Joshua gathered the elders again to Shechem, reiterated the covenant, and received the oath of allegiance to God, the King (Joshua 24). Many modern scholars see in these assemblies a strong suggestion of an amphictyonic league centred at Shechem (see M. Noth, *The History of Israel*, 1958).

The boundary between Ephraim and Manasseh passed near the town (Joshua 17:7), which was one of the cities of refuge, and a levitical city assigned to the Kohathite Levites (Joshua 20:7; 21:21; 1 Chronicles 6:67). The town lay in Ephraim (1 Chronicles 7:28). Here the Israelites buried the bones of Joseph which they had brought from Egypt (Genesis 50:25; Joshua 24:32).

In the time of the Judges, Shechem was still a centre of Canaanite worship and the temple of Baal-berith ('the lord of the covenant') features in the story of Gideon's son Abimelech (Judges 9:4), whose mother was a Shechemite woman.

Abimelech persuaded the men of the city to make him king (Judges 9:6; compare 8:22–23). He proceeded to slay the royal seed, but Jotham, one son who escaped the bloody purge, spoke a parable about the trees as he stood on Mount Gerizim (Judges 9:8–15), appealing to the citizens of Shechem to forsake Abimelech. This they did after 3 years (verses 22–23), but Abimelech destroyed Shechem (verse 45) and then attacked the stronghold of the temple of Baal-berith and burnt it over the heads of those who sought refuge there (verses 46–49).

*During the divided kingdom*

After Solomon's death the assembly of Israel rejected Rehoboam at Shechem and made Jeroboam king (1 Kings 12:1–19; 2 Chronicles 10:1–11). Jeroboam restored the town and made it his capital for a time (1 Kings 12:25), but later moved the capital to Penuel, and then to Tirzah. The town declined in importance thereafter, but continued in existence long after the fall of Samaria in 722 BC, for men from Shechem came with offerings to Jerusalem as late as 586 BC (Jeremiah 41:5).

*After the Exile*

In post-exilic times Shechem became the chief city of the Samaritans (Ecclesiasticus 50:26; Josephus, *Antiquities* 11.340), who built a temple on Mount Gerizim. In 128 BC John Hyrcanus destroyed the Samaritan temple, and in 108 BC the city also fell (Josephus, *Antiquities* 13.255).

In the time of the first Jewish revolt Vespasian camped near Shechem, and after the war the town was rebuilt and named Flavia Neapolis (Flavia Newtown) in honour of the emperor Flavius Vespasianus (hence the modern Nablus).

*Excavations*

Important excavations conducted at Tell Balaṭa by C. Watzinger (1907–09), E. Sellin and his colleagues (between 1913 and 1934), by G. E. Wright (1956–68) and subsequent investigations in 1969 and 1972 have revealed the story of this site from the mid-4th millennium BC down to *c.* 100 BC when the Hellenistic city came to an end.

Although there was a sizeable Chalcolithic village during the 4th millennium BC, the city of the historical period arose *c.* 1800 BC in the Middle Bronze Age and reached the height of its prosperity during the Hyksos period (*c.* 1700–1550 BC).

During these years several courtyard temples and city walls were built. About 1650 BC a massive stone wall was erected, earlier walls covered over and a fortress temple built on the filling.

The entire city was destroyed at the end of the Middle Bronze Age (in the period 1550–1500 BC) but was rebuilt around 1450 BC. The temple was also rebuilt; it survived with some changes until *c.* 1100 BC and may well represent in its later stages the temple of Baal-berith (Judges 9:4) known to the early Israelites.

The town remained important until the 9th–8th centuries BC when it began to deteriorate. Masses of fallen brick and burnt debris attest the destruction of the city by the Assyrians in 724–721 BC.

For 4 centuries the town reverted to a village until it gained new life, probably as a Samaritan centre, between *c.* 325 and *c.* 108 BC. There is a continuous coin record for this period. The town ceased to exist after its destruction by John Hyrcanus *c.* 108 BC.

It is unlikely that Shechem is the same as the *Sychar of John 4:5. There are only a few traces of Roman occupation at Tell Balaṭa, and probably none later than the 1st century BC. Sychar may have lain in the same general vicinity, perhaps at modern Askar.

J. A. Thompson, J. Bimson

*Further reading*

E. F. Campbell, Jr., and J. F. Ross, 'The Excavation of Shechem and the Biblical Tradition', *BA* 26, 1963, pp. 2–26

E. Nielsen, *Shechem, A Traditio-Historical Investigation*, 1955
E. Sellin, in *ZDPV*, 1926, 1927, 1928
—— and H. Steckeweh in *ZDPV*, 1941
G. E. Wright, *Shechem, The Biography of a Biblical City*, 1965
'Shechem', in *AOTS*, pp. 355–370
E. F. Campbell and I. Magen, 'Shechem', *NEAEHL*, IV, pp. 1345–1359
W. G. Dever, *BASOR* 216, 1974, pp. 341–352
L. E. Toombs, in F. M. Cross (ed.), *Symposia*, 1979, pp. 69–83
D. P. Cole, *Shechem I*, 1984

**SHEEP-POOL.** See *Bethesda.

**SHELAH.** See *Siloam.

**SHENIR.** See *Senir.

**SHEPHELAH** (Hebrew *šᵉp̄ēlâ*), a geographical term for the low hill tract between the coastal plain of *Palestine and the high central ranges. The term is used only in the AV of 1 Maccabees 12:38, which elsewhere translates it as 'vale', 'valley' or (low) 'plain(s)', although the district is frequently referred to in the Old Testament. The RV rendering 'lowland' (sometimes also in the RSV) would give a truer picture if used in the plural form, to indicate its rolling relief of both hills and valleys. But its root-meaning ('to humble' or 'make low') suggests more accurately a district of relatively low relief at the foot of the central mountains.

In the RSV 'Shephelah' occurs in 1 Kings 10:27, 1 Chronicles 27:28, 2 Chronicles 1:15, 9:27, 26:10, 28:18, Jeremiah 17:26, 32:44, 33:13 and Obadiah 1:19. Passages such as 2 Chronicles 26:10 and 29:18 clearly distinguish it from the coastal plain.

The location of the 'Shephelah' of Joshua 11:2 and 16 is distinct. There it refers to the hills around the town of Carmel (verse 2). 'Israelite Shephelah' in verse 16, according to G. A. Smith, may mean the land between Carmel and Samaria, a structural continuation of the true Shephelah farther south.

J. M. Houston

*Further reading*
D. Baly, *The Geography of the Bible*, 1957, pp. 142–147
*LOB*

**SHIBAH.** The name of a well dug by Isaac's servants and named Shibah (Hebrew *šiḇ'â*), Shebah (Genesis 26:33, AV), because of a covenant with Abimelech. The word itself means 'seven' or 'oath'.

Already, before Isaac's time, Abraham had encountered trouble with Abimelech king of Gerar and had finally entered into a covenant (Genesis 21:22–34). Seven ewe lambs were presented to Abimelech as a witness to the fact, and Abraham preserved the memory of this covenant by calling the place *Beersheba ('well of seven', 'well of an oath').

Isaac revived the old name, using the feminine form *šiḇ'ậ* of the word *šeḇā'*.

J. A. Thompson

**SHIHOR.** See *Egypt, River of.

**SHIHOR-LIBNATH.** A small river forming part of the southern boundary of the tribe of Asher (Joshua 19:26). Probably it is the modern Nahr ez-Zerqa, which runs south of Mount Carmel (see also *Egypt, River of).

T. C. Mitchell

*Further reading*
*GTT*, p. 190, note 78
L. H. Grollenberg, *Atlas of the Bible*, 1957, pp. 58–59
*LOB*, pp. 257–258 (arguing for the *Kishon)

**SHILOH.** According to Judges 21:19, Shiloh is situated 'north of Bethel, on the east of the highway that goes up from Bethel to Shechem, and south of Lebonah'. This identifies it as the modern Seilūn, a ruined site on a hill about 14 kilometres north of Bethel (Beitīn) and 5 kilometres south-east of el-Lubbān.

*Excavations*
The site was excavated by Danish expeditions in 1926–29 and 1932, and by an Israeli team under I. Finkelstein, 1981–84. There was a Middle Bronze Age city (*c.* 2100–1550 BC), massively fortified in its later stages (Stratum VII). There was no settlement during the Late Bronze Age but for a time (perhaps from *c.* 1500 BC until *c.* 1400 BC or slightly later) the site was a cultic centre to which offerings and sacrifices were brought (Stratum VI).

The site was resettled in the Iron Age (Stratum V, 12th–11th centuries BC) and destroyed by fire *c.* 1050 BC. This may have been the work of the Philistines following the battle of Ebenezer. There was a small village on the site during the later Iron Age, followed by Hellenistic and Roman occupation.

*A religious centre*
According to the biblical record, it was at Shiloh that the tent of meeting was set up in the early days of the Conquest (Joshua 18:1), and it was the principal sanctuary of the Israelites during the time of the Judges (Judges 18:31). It was the site of a local annual festival of dancing in the vineyards, perhaps at the Feast of Ingathering (Exodus 23:16), which once provided the men of Benjamin with an opportunity to seize the maidens for wives (Judges 21:19ff.), and this festival probably developed into the annual pilgrimage in which Samuel's parents were later to take part (1 Samuel 1:3).

By the time of Eli and his sons, the sanctuary had become a well-established structure for centralized worship, and the tent of Joshua had been replaced by a temple (*hêḵāl*) with door and door-posts (1 Samuel 1:9). No trace of such a temple has been found from the early Iron Age stratum. Although Scripture does not refer directly to its destruction, it seems from the archaeological evidence that this did take place and this would fit in well with the references to Shiloh as an example of God's judgment upon his people's wickedness (Psalm 78:60; Jeremiah 7:12, 14; 26:6, 9).

Ahijah the Shilonite is mentioned in 1 Kings 11:29 and 14:2, and other inhabitants of Shiloh in Jeremiah 41:5 in keeping with the evidence that limited occupation continued after 1050 BC, but the priesthood transferred to Nob (1 Samuel 22:11; compare 14:3) and Shiloh ceased to be a religious centre.

*The meaning of Genesis 49:10*
A reference of peculiar difficulty comes in Genesis 49:10, 'the sceptre shall not depart from Judah, nor the ruler's staff from between his feet, until Shiloh come' (RV). The Hebrew *'aḏ kî-yāḇō' šîlōh* can be rendered in several ways.

*a.* As RV, taking Shiloh as a Messianic title.
*b.* As RV margin 'till he come to Shiloh', with the subject as Judah and the fulfilment in the assembling of Israel to Shiloh in Joshua 18:1, when the tribe of Judah nobly relinquished the pre-eminence it had formerly enjoyed.
*c.* By emending *šîlōh* to *šellōh* and translating with the Septuagint 'until that which is his shall come', *i.e.* 'the things reserved for him', a vaguely Messianic hope.
*d.* By emending *šîlôh* to *šay lô*, as in the NEB, 'so long as tribute is paid to him'.
*e.* Following a variant reading in the

Septuagint, 'until he comes to whom it belongs' (RSV), whatever 'it' may be (Onkelos says it is the kingdom).

The last of these was generally favoured by the Fathers, while the first does not seem to have been put forward seriously until the 16th century except in one doubtful passage in the Talmud.

Against *a* is its uniqueness: nowhere else is Shiloh used as a title for the Messiah and the New Testament does not recognize it as a prophecy. If it were taken as a title it would have to mean something like 'the peace-giver', but this is not very natural linguistically.

*b* is plausible, but it scarcely fits in with what we know of the subsequent history of Judah; nor is it usual for a patriarchal blessing to have such a time-limit. A variant to get round that objection is the translation 'as long as people come to Shiloh', *i.e.* 'for ever', but it strains the Hebrew.

*c, d* and *e* involve a minor emendation, and the renderings leave much to the imagination, but Ezekiel 21:27 (verse 32 in the Hebrew) shows that a similar construction can stand; indeed, Ezekiel 21:27 is probably a deliberate echo and interpretation of Genesis 49:10. The use of *še-* for the relative particle is, however, normally regarded as late (but compare Judges 5:7).

J. B. Taylor, J. Bimson

*Further reading*

For reviews of the possible interpretations, see especially the commentaries of J. Skinner and E. A. Speiser; an interesting theory by J. Lindblom is found in *VT Supp.* 1 (= Congress Volume, 1953), pp. 78–87.

For archaeological information:

W. F. Albright in *BASOR* 9, 1923, pp. 10f.

H. Kjaer in *PEQ* 63, 1931, pp. 71–88

M.-L. Buhl and S. Holm-Nielsen, *Shiloh . . . : The Pre-Hellenistic Remains*, 1969

I. Finkelstein (ed.), 'Excavations at Shiloh 1981–84', *TA* 12, 1985, pp. 123–180

A. Kempinski and I. Finkelstein in *NEAEHL* IV, pp. 1364–1370

**SHIMRON-MERON.** A Canaanite city whose king was allied with Hazor (Joshua 11:1, simply 'Shimron') and so defeated by Joshua in his Galilean war (Joshua 12:20). Probably it was identical with Shimron in the territory assigned to Zebulun, in the Bethlehem district (Joshua 19:15), *i.e.* the northern (Zebulonite) Bethlehem. If so, it is most probably to be identified with a mound variously called Tell es-Semuniyeh, Khirbet Sammuniya, and now Tel Shimon; this very large site is approximately 5 kilometres south-south-east of Zebulonite Bethlehem and about 5 kilometres west of Nazareth.

The ancient name also varied, being *Šmw'nw* in the Egyptian 'Execration Texts' of *c.* 1800 BC, and *Šm'n* in Egyptian records of *c.* 1450 BC (*Šamḫuna* in cuneiform, in the Amarna letters, *c.* 1350 BC), giving a form *Šam'ona* (becoming *Symoōn* in the Septuagint), and assimilated to Simonia(s) in Hellenistic times. The origin of the Hebrew form with *r* in place of the *'ayin*-sound is obscure. See A. F. Rainey, *Tel Aviv* 3, 1976, pp. 57–69 and plate 1.

K. A. Kitchen

**SHINAR.** The land in which were situated the great cities of Babylon, Erech and Akkad (Genesis 10:10). It lay in a plain to which early migrants came to found the city and tower of Babel (Genesis 11:2) and was a place of exile for the Jews (Isaiah 11:11; Daniel 1:2).

The Septuagint interprets Shinar as 'Babylonia' (Isaiah 11:11) or the 'land of Babylon' (Zechariah 5:11), and this accords with the location implied in Genesis 10:10. (See also *ACCAD or Agade, which gave its name to northern Babylonia.)

The Hebrew *šin'ār* represents *šanhar* of cuneiform texts from the Hittite and Syrian scribal schools of the 2nd millennium BC, and was certainly a name for Babylonia, perhaps a Hurrian form of Sumer. This equation is proved by several texts (see H. G. Güterbock in *JCS* 18, 1964, p. 3), ruling out older ideas.

D. J. Wiseman

**SHITTIM. 1.** One of the names given to the final Israelite encampment before they crossed the Jordan, opposite Jericho (Numbers 25:1; Joshua 2:1; 3:1; compare Micah 6:5). Numbers 33:49 uses a longer form of the name, Abel-shittim ('the brook (?) of the acacias', since *šiṭṭîm* means 'acacias'), for one extremity of the camp.

Josephus mentions a city of his time called Abila, which was 60 stades from the Jordan in this general area (*Antiquities* 5.4), which appears to represent the element 'Abel' of this name. Glueck and Aharoni argue that Abila was probably located at Tell el-Hammam, though other scholars have preferred Tell el-Kefrein, which lies a little to the north-west. (See *IDB* 4, p. 339.)

**2.** The 'valley of Shittim/acacias' in Joel 3:18, which is to be watered by a stream flowing from the temple (compare Ezekiel 47:1–12), cannot be the same place, because a location for it west of the Jordan is required. It is most likely to be either a general term for the wadis of the Judaean wilderness or a name for the lower part of the Kidron valley, which leads into the Dead Sea from the west (rather than referring to the Wadi es-Sanṭ).

G. I. Davies

*Further reading*

H. W. Wolff, *Joel and Amos* (Hermeneia), 1977, pp. 83–84, on Joel 4:18 (3:18)

**SHUAL, LAND OF.** A district in Benjamin mentioned as lying in the path of a company of plundering Philistines, as they moved from Michmash to Ophrah (1 Samuel 13:17). Unknown outside the Bible, but probably near Michmash, Shual ('fox') is identified by some with Shaalim where Saul searched for lost donkeys (1 Samuel 9:4). (See also *SHALISHAH.)

T. C. Mitchell

**SHULAMMITE.** A feminine noun (*šûlammîṯ*) applied to the heroine in Song of Songs 6:13, 'Shulammite' has been a formidable problem to scholars. Some (*e.g.* Koehler's *Lexicon*) have connected it with an unknown town, Shulam; some (*e.g. ISBE*) classify it as a variant of Shunammite (below); others (*e.g.* L. Waterman and H. Torczyner) identify the Shulammite with Abishag, the Shunammite.

E. J. Goodspeed (*AJSL* 50, 1934, pp. 102ff.) and H. H. Rowley (*AJSL* 56, 1939, pp. 83–91) deny any connection with *Shunem but view the word as a feminine counterpart of Solomon, 'the Solomoness'. Attempts have been made to derive the names Solomon and Shulammite from the god Shelem.

D. A. Hubbard

*Further reading*

H. H. Rowley, *The Servant of the Lord,*, 1952, p. 223

**SHUNEM, SHUNAMMITE.** A town in the territory of Issachar near Jezreel (Joshua 19:18), Shunem (*šûnēm*) was the site of the Philistine camp before the battle of Gilboa (1 Samuel 28:4). It is probably modern Solem, where surface pottery suggests occupation

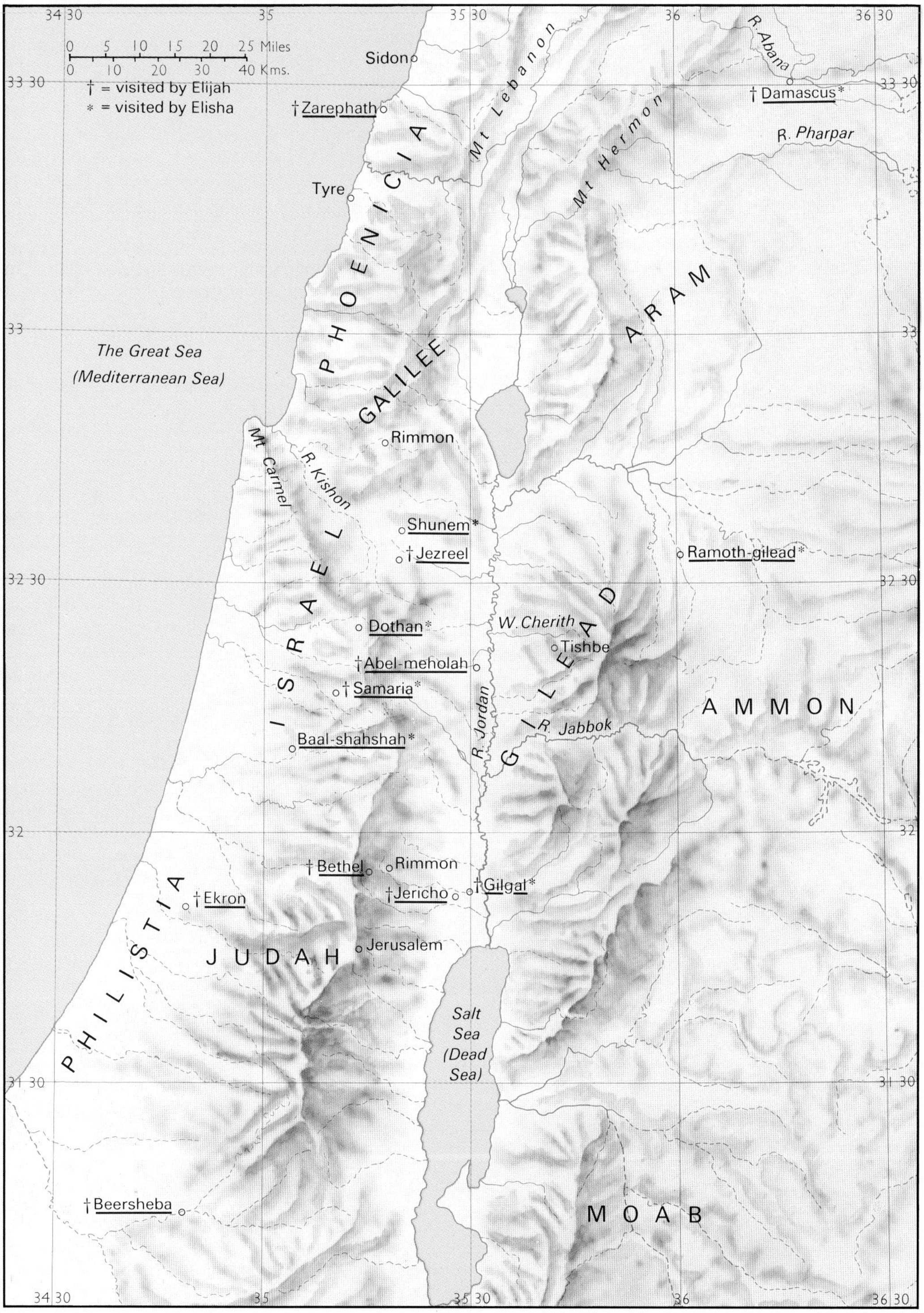


**Places associated with Elijah and Elisha.**

throughout the biblical period.

Elisha frequently stayed in Shunem in the home of a generous woman (called the Shunammite, a feminine adjective derived from Shunem) whose son, born according to Elisha's prediction, was miraculously raised up by the prophet after being smitten with sun-stroke (2 Kings 4:8ff.). It is this woman whose property was restored at Gehazi's request after she had temporarily abandoned it to seek relief from famine in Philistia (2 Kings 8:1–6).

From Shunem also David's men brought the beautiful Abishag to comfort their aged king (1 Kings 1:3, 15). Adonijah's request for her hand in marriage cost him his life (1 Kings 2:17, 21–22). (See also *SHULAMMITE.)

D. A. Hubbard

**SHUR.** A wilderness-region in the north-western part of the Sinai isthmus, south of the Mediterranean coastline and the 'way of the land of the Philistines', between the present line of the Suez Canal on its west and the 'River of *Egypt' (Wadi el-'Arish) on its east. Abraham and Sarah's handmaid Hagar fled to a well past Kadesh on the way to Shur (Genesis 16:7).

For a time Abraham 'dwelt between Kadesh and Shur' and then sojourned at Gerar (Genesis 20:1); Ishmael's descendants ranged over an area that reached as far as 'Shur, which is opposite [*i.e.* east of] Egypt' (Genesis 25:18).

After passing through the sea (see also *RED SEA), Israel entered the wilderness of Shur before going south into Sinai (Exodus 15:22). Shur lay on the direct route to Egypt from southern Palestine (1 Samuel 15:7 and, most explicitly, 27:8).

K. A. Kitchen

**SHUSHAN.** See *SUSA.

**SIBMAH.** A town wrested from Sihon king of the Amorites and allotted by Moses to the tribe of Reuben (*śibmâ*, Joshua 13:19, 21). It is identical with Sebam ('Shebam', AV); possibly its name was changed when it was rebuilt (Numbers 32:3, 38). By the time of Isaiah and Jeremiah, who bewailed its devastation, it had reverted to the Moabites (Isaiah 16:8–9; Jeremiah 48:32).

Originally a land for cattle (Numbers 32:4), it became famous for its vines and summer fruit. Jerome (*Commentary on Isaiah* 5) placed it about 500 paces from Heshbon: Khirbet Qurn el-Qibsh, 5 kilometres west-south-west, is a feasible site, though some would prefer to locate it farther to the south on the plain of Medeba.

J. W. Charley

**SICHEM.** See *SHECHEM.

**SIDDIM, VALLEY OF** (Hebrew *siddîm*, perhaps derived from the Hittite *siyantas*, 'salt'). In Genesis 14:3 and 10 it is the name of a valley identified with the 'Salt Sea' and described as 'full of bitumen pits'. Here the kings of the Jordan pentapolis were defeated by Chedorlaomer and his allies from the east.

It may have been the plain which now lies beneath the shallow extension of the Dead Sea south of the Lisan peninsula. There is evidence that this area was still above water in Roman times and perhaps as late as the Crusades. From the bituminous products of the Dead Sea (still in evidence) the Greeks called it *Asphaltitis*. (See also *PLAIN, CITIES OF THE.)

F. F. Bruce

*Further reading*

J. P. Harland, 'Sodom and Gomorrah', *BA* 5, 1942, pp. 17ff.; 6, 1943, pp. 41ff.

**SIDON** (Hebrew *ṣîḏôn, ṣîḏōn*). A major walled city and port in ancient *Phoenicia (now located on the coast of Lebanon). Sidon (AV also 'Zidon'; modern Saida) had twin harbours and was divided into Greater Sidon (Joshua 11:8) and Lesser Sidon.

*History*

According to tradition, Sidon was the first Phoenician city to be founded and became a principal Canaanite stronghold (Genesis 10:19; 1 Chronicles 1:13). For some centuries the harbour was subordinate to the Egyptian 18th–19th Dynasties. With declining Egyptian military control the city ruler Zimri-ada committed defection *c.* 1350 BC (so *Amarna tablets).

It is possible that the attempt to include Dor in Sidonian territory led to war with the Philistines, who *c.* 1150 BC plundered Sidon, whose inhabitants fled to Tyre. The city was, however, strong enough to oppose Israel (Judges 10:12), and during a period of active colonization apparently made an unsuccessful attempt to settle at Laish in the Upper Jordan (Judges 18:7, 27).

Opposition to Phoenician expansion came also from the Assyrians, who under Tiglath-pileser I, *c.* 1110 BC, began to exact tribute from the ports, including Sidon. Ashurnasirpal II (*c.* 880 BC) claimed the city as a vassal, and in 841 BC Shalmaneser III marched to the Dog river to receive the tribute of Tyre, Sidon and Israel, and depicted this on the temple gates at Balawat (now in the British Museum).

The Assyrian demands increased and the Sidonians rebelled. Tiglath-pileser III captured Tyre and perhaps Sidon in 739–738 (H. Tadmor, in *Scripta Hierosolymitana* 8, 1961, p. 269, makes Zechariah 9:2 refer to this time). When Sennacherib marched, in an attack foretold by Isaiah (23:2–12), Luli fled and died in exile and was replaced by Ethba'al (Tuba'lu) when Great and Little Sidon had been captured.

On Sennacherib's death Sidon once more revolted and Esarhaddon invaded Sidon, killed the ruler Abdi-milkutti, sacked the port and moved its inhabitants to Kar-Esarhaddon, and brought prisoners from Elam and Babylonia to replace the depleted population.

Sidon recovered its independence with the decline of the Assyrians, only to be besieged again and captured by Nebuchadrezzar *c.* 587 BC as foretold by Jeremiah (25:22; 27:3; 47:4). Under the Persians it provided the majority of the Persian fleet (see Zechariah 9:2).

About 350 BC, under Tabnit II (Tannes), Sidon led the rebellion of Phoenicia and Cyprus against Artaxerxes III (Ochus). The city was betrayed and 40,000 perished, the survivors burning the city and fleet. The fortifications were never rebuilt. The city under Strato II yielded to Alexander the Great without opposition and helped his siege of Tyre.

Under Antiochus III Sidon was a prosperous part of the kingdom of Ptolemy and later passed to the Seleucids and then to the Romans, who granted it local autonomy.

*In New Testament times*

Through all its history the principal temple was that of Eshmun, the god of healing. It is thus significant that it was in the region of Sidon that Christ healed the Syro-Phoenician woman's daughter (Mark 7:24–31; compare Matthew 11:21). Many Sidonians listened to his teaching (Mark 3:8; Luke 6:17; 10:13–14).

Herod Agrippa I received a delegation from Sidon at Caesarea (Acts 12:20) and Paul visited friends in the city on his way to Rome (Acts 27:3). The inhabitants of Sidon, which was renowned as a centre of philosophical learning, were mainly Greek (compare Mark 7:26).

*Archaeological findings*

Many coins bear inscriptions of Sidonian rulers, and among the discoveries in the area are remains from the Middle Bronze Age onwards, the inscribed sarcophagus of Eshmunazar (*c.* 300 BC) and buildings in the port area of New Testament times (A. Poidebard and J. Lauffray, *Sidon,* 1951).

For Phoenician inscriptions from Sidon, see G. A. Cooke, *North Semitic Inscriptions*, 1903, pp. 26–43, 401–403.

D. J. Wiseman

**SILOAH.** See *SILOAM.

**SILOAM.** One of the principal sources of water supply to Jerusalem was the intermittent pool of Gihon ('Virgin's Fountain') below the Fountain Gate (Nehemiah 3:15) and east south-east of the city. This fed water along an open canal, which flowed slowly along the south-eastern slopes, called *šilôaḥ* ('Sender'; Septuagint *Silōam*, Isaiah 8:6). It

**The 'pool of Siloam' and the mouth of Hezekiah's tunnel.**

followed the line of the later 'second aqueduct' (Wilson) which fell only 5 centimetres in 300 metres, discharging into the Lower or Old Pool (modern *Birket el-Ḥamra*) at the end of the central valley between the walls of the south-eastern and south-western hills. It thus ran below 'the wall of the Pool of Shelah' (Nehemiah 3:15) and watered the 'king's garden' on the adjacent slopes.

*The Pool of Siloam*

This Old Pool was probably the 'Pool of Siloam' in use in New Testament times for sick persons and others to wash (John 9:7–11). The 'Tower of Siloam' which fell and killed 18 persons – a disaster well known in our Lord's day (Luke 13:4) – was probably sited on the Ophel ridge above the pool which, according to Josephus (*Jewish War* 5.145), was near the bend of the old wall below Ophlas (Ophel).

According to the Talmud (*Sukkoth* 4.9), water was drawn from Siloam's pool in a golden vessel to be carried in procession to the temple on the Feast of Tabernacles.

Though there are traces of a Herodian bath and open reservoir (about 18 metres × 5 metres, originally 22 metres square with steps on the western side), there can be no certainty that this was the actual pool in question.

It has been suggested that the part of the city round the Upper Pool (*'Ain Silwān*) 100 metres above was called 'Siloam', the Lower being the King's Pool (Nehemiah 2:14) or Lower Gihon.

*Hezekiah's tunnel*

When Hezekiah was faced with the threat of invasion by the Assyrian army under Sennacherib he 'stopped all the springs', that is, all the rivulets and subsidiary canals leading down into the Kedron 'brook that flowed through the land' (2 Chronicles 32:4). Traces of canals blocked at about this time were found by the Parker Mission. The king then diverted the upper Gihon waters through a 'conduit' or tunnel into an upper cistern or pool (the normal method of storing water) on the western side of the city of David (2 Kings 20:20).

Ben Sira tells how 'Hezekiah fortified his city and brought water into the midst of it; he tunnelled the sheer rock with iron and built pools for water' (Ecclesiasticus 48:17–19). Hezekiah clearly defended the new source of supply with a rampart (2 Chronicles 32:30). The digging of the reservoir may be referred to by Isaiah (22:11).

In 1880 bathers in the upper pool (also called *birket silwān*) found about 5 metres inside the tunnel a cursive Hebrew inscription, now in Istanbul, which reads: '. . . was being dug out. It was cut in the following manner . . . axes, each man towards his fellow, and while there were still 3 cubits to be cut through, the voice of one man calling to the other was heard, showing that he was deviating to the right. When the tunnel was driven through, the excavators met man to man, axe to axe, and the water flowed for 1,200 cubits from the spring to the reservoir. The height of the rock above the heads of the excavators was 100 cubits' (D. J. Wiseman, in *IBA*, pp. 61–64).

When this remarkable Judaean engineering feat was excavated the marks of the picks and deviations to effect a junction midway were traced. The tunnel traverses 540 metres (or 643 metres, Ussishkin), twisting to avoid constructions or rock faults or to follow a fissure, to cover a direct line of 332 metres. It is about 2 metres high and in parts only 50 centimetres wide.

Modern buildings prevent any archaeological check that the upper pool is the 'reservoir' (*b*$^{e}$*rēḵâ*) of Hezekiah or that from this the waters overflowed direct to the lower pool. The pool was probably underground at first, the rock roof collapsing or being quarried away later.

*The Jebusite water-shaft*

Hezekiah's tunnel begins from an earlier tunnel which channelled water from the spring of Gihon to the bottom of a shaft which rises to join an inclined tunnel which led to a point inside the city. Some scholars have argued that this shaft and tunnel system was built by the Jebusites to provide a secure water-supply and is possibly the 'gutter' or 'water shaft' (*ṣinnôr*) that David's men climbed to capture the city (2 Samuel 5:8). But others doubt whether the system can be early enough to be the work of the Jebusites.

*Rock-cut tombs*

Below the modern village of Siloam (Silwān, first mentioned in 1697) on the eastern escarpment opposite the hill of Ophel are a number of rock-cut tombs. These were prepared for the burial of ministers and nobles of the kingdom of Judah. One of these bore a Hebrew inscription, the epitaph of a royal steward, probably the Shebna who was rebuked by Isaiah (22:15–16). See *IBA*, p. 59; *IEJ* 3, 1953, pp. 137–152; K. M. Kenyon, *Digging Up Jerusalem*, 1974, pp. 153–159.

D. J. Wiseman

*Further reading*

J. Simons, *Jerusalem in the Old*

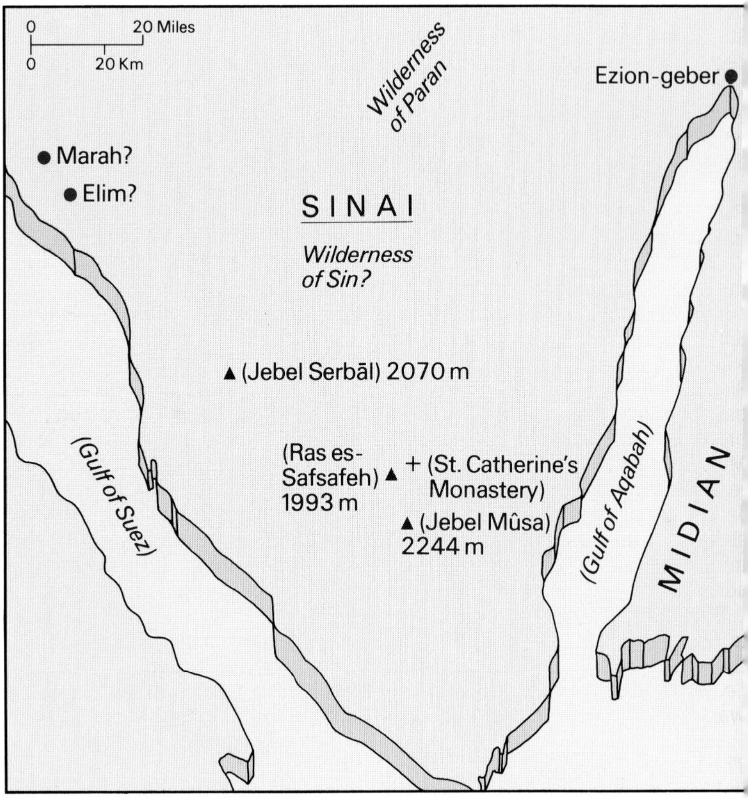

The Sinai peninsula.

*Testament*, 1952
D. Ussishkin, 'The Original Length of the Siloam Tunnel', *Levant* 8, 1976, pp. 82–95
J. Wilkinson, 'The Pool of Siloam', *Levant* 10, 1978, pp. 116–125

**SIN, WILDERNESS OF.** A wilderness through which the Israelites passed between Elim and Mount Sinai (Exodus 16:1; 17:1; Numbers 33:11–12). It is usually identified with Debbet er-Ramleh, a sandy tract below Jebel et-Tih in the south-west of the Sinai peninsula; but another suggested location is on the coastal plain of el-Markhah. As its position depends on the fixing of Mount *Sinai, which is uncertain, it is impossible to determine the exact site.
J. M. Houston

## SINAI, MOUNT

### Situation

The location of this mountain is uncertain. The following mountains are regarded by various scholars as Mount Sinai: Jebel Mûsa, Ras eṣ-ṣafṣafeh, Jebel Serbal and a mountain near al-Hrob.

The tradition in favour of Jebel Serbāl can be traced back as far as Eusebius; the tradition in favour of Jebel Mûsa only as far as Justinian. The situation of Jebel Serbāl, *e.g.* the fact that there is no wilderness at its foot, makes it improbable as the mountain of the covenant.

The once widely accepted view of A. Musil that the volcanic mountain near al-Hrob is to be identified with Mount Sinai is no longer popular with scholars, because it makes the reconstruction of the route of the Exodus impossible and it reads too much into Exodus 19. Modern attempts to identify Sinai with volcanic mountains east of the Gulf of Aqaba are so uncertain that not much can be derived from them.

This leaves two possibilities: Jebel Mûsa and Ras eṣ-ṣafṣafeh. These two mountains are situated on a short ridge of granite of about 4 kilometres stretching from north-west to south-east. Ras eṣ-ṣafṣafeh (1,993 metres) is situated at the northern edge and Jebel Mûsa (2,244 metres) at the southern one. Tradition and most of the modern scholars accept Jebel Mûsa as Mount Sinai.

There is, none the less, a strong preference among certain scholars for Ras eṣ-ṣafṣafeh as the mountain of the covenant because of the considerable plain at its foot which would have been spacious enough for the large body of Israelites (see Exodus 20:18: 'they stood afar off'). However, tradition in favour of Jebel Mûsa is so ancient (about 1,500 years) and the granite formations so imposing that it is quite probably Mount Sinai. Furthermore, a few stations *en route* to the mountain point to the same conclusion.

### In the Old Testament

Mount Sinai is also called Horeb in the Old Testament. Travelling past Marah and Elim, the Israelites reached Sinai in the 3rd month after their departure from Egypt (Exodus 19:1), and camped at its foot on a plain from which the top was visible (Exodus 19:16, 18, 20). The Lord revealed himself to Moses on this mountain and gave the Ten Commandments and other laws. The covenant made here between God and the people played a major role in binding the tribes together and moulding them into one nation serving one God.

Although the authenticity of this account is rejected by certain modern schools, it is clear from Judges 5:5 that the Sinai tradition is an ancient part of Israelite belief. The prominent role of Mount Sinai in the Old Testament and the strong tradition attached to it provide ample evidence in support of the historicity of the account.

At the foot of Jebel Mûsa is the monastery of St Catherine. It was here that Tischendorf discovered the famous 4th-century uncial manuscript of the Greek Bible called Codex Sinaiticus. The library of St Catherine has ancient manuscripts in Greek, Arabic, Ethiopic and Syriac (many of which have recently been made generally available on microfilm).
F. C. Fensham

*Further reading*

B. Rothenberg, *God's Wilderness*, 1961
W. Beyerlin, *Origins and History of the Oldest Sinaitic Traditions*, 1965
M. Harel, *The Route of the Exodus of the Israelites from Egypt and their Wanderings in the Sinai Desert: A Geographic Study*, 1965, pp. 115ff.
G. I. Davies, *The Way of the Wilderness*, 1979, pp. 63–69
A. Perevolotsky and I. Finkelstein, *BARev* XI/4, 1985, pp. 26–41
I. Beit-Arieh, *BARev* XIV/3, 1988, pp. 28–37
I. Finkelstein, *BARev* XIV/4, 1988, pp. 46–50

### In the New Testament

*Stephen's speech*

During his last speech before martyrdom, Stephen twice mentions Mount Sinai in a reference to the theophany to Moses at the burning bush (Acts 7:30, 38; in Exodus 3:1ff.

the synonym Horeb is used). Stephen reminds his accusers that even a Gentile place like Sinai in north-western Arabia became holy ground because God was pleased to reveal himself there; he was not limited by Jewish geography.

*Paul's letter to the Galatians*
In Galatians 4:21–31 Paul uses an allegory to identify Israel first with the slave-wife Hagar (Genesis 16:15; 21:2, 9) and then with Mount Sinai 'in Arabia' (*i.e.* appropriately in a barren wilderness area). Hagar and Sinai are symbolic respectively of being outside the covenant of promise and of bondage to the law of Moses. Together they are taken as representing 'the present Jerusalem', *i.e.* Judaism, which is slavery (to the Law and its intolerable burden of Pharisaic additions as well as to the Romans).

By contrast 'the Jerusalem above' is 'free' (freeborn) and 'our mother', the mother of all who are Christians, *i.e.* 'children of promise, as Isaac was'.

*The letter to the Hebrews*
In Hebrews 12:19–29, although not named directly, Mount Sinai, symbolizing the old covenant, is contrasted with Mount Zion, symbolizing the offer of the gospel under the new covenant. The awesome terrors of Sinai at the giving of the Law are described in terms of Exodus 19:16–19; 20:18–21; Deuteronomy 4:11f.; and the reader is warned that rejecting the gospel and its privileges incurs a far more dreadful judgment even than that which followed disobedience to the Law.
N. Hillyer

*Further reading*
C. Brown, *NIDNTT* 3, pp. 1013–1015
E. Löhse, *TDNT* 7, pp. 282–287

**SINITES.** See *Syene.

**SION.** A synonym for, or part of, Mount Hermon (Deuteronomy 4:48, AV; compare RSV margin). It is probably another form of 'Sirion' (Deuteronomy 3:9); indeed, the Peshitta reads 'Sirion' here, as also do the RSV and NEB. A different word from 'Zion'.
J. D. Douglas

**SIRAH, CISTERN OF** (AV 'well of Sirah'). The place from which Joab secretly recalled Abner, former captain of Saul's armies, following his visit to David to discuss the surrender of Israel. Unknown to David, Joab slew Abner (2 Samuel 3:26).

Probably it is modern Ain Sarah, 2·5 kilometres north-west of Hebron.
J. A. Thompson

**SIRION** (Hebrew *śiryōn*). The Canaanite name for Mount *Hermon as used in the Bible by the Sidonians (Deuteronomy 3:9; compare Psalm 29:6) and found in the form *šryn* in the Ugaritic texts. See C. H. Gordon, *Ugaritic Textbook*, 1965, p. 495. (See also *Sion.)
T. C. Mitchell

**SITNAH** (Hebrew *śiṭnâ*, 'hatred', 'contention'). A name given to a well which Isaac's servants dug in Gerar (Genesis 26:21) and which was seized by the servants of Abimelech. For its general location, see *Gerar.
J. D. Douglas

**SMYRNA.** A city in the Roman province of Asia, on the Aegean shore of what is now Asiatic Turkey. There was a Greek colony nearby from very early times, but it was captured and destroyed by the Lydians about the end of the 7th century BC and virtually ceased to exist until it was refounded on its present site by Lysimachus in the early 3rd century BC.

Smyrna grew to be one of the most prosperous cities in Asia Minor. It was the natural port for the ancient trade route through the Hermus valley, and its immediate hinterland was very fertile. The city was a faithful ally of Rome long before the Roman power became supreme in the eastern Mediterranean. Under the empire it was famous for its beauty and for the magnificence of its public buildings.

It is now Izmir, the second largest city in Asiatic Turkey.

*The church in Smyrna*
The gospel probably reached Smyrna at an early date, presumably from Ephesus (Acts 19:10). The 'angel of the church in Smyrna' is the recipient of the second (Revelation 2:8–11) of the letters to the 'seven churches . . . in Asia'. As in other commercial cities, the church encountered opposition from the Jews (Revelation 2:9; compare 3:9).

The description of the Christ as the one who was dead and lived again (verse 8) may allude to the resurgence of the city to new prosperity after a long period in obscurity. The 'crown' (verse 10) was rich in associations at Smyrna. It may suggest the victor's wreath at the games, or current forms of eulogy which used the image of the beauty and glory of the city and its buildings. Compare also James 1:12.

The call to faithfulness (verse 10) is a call to the church to fulfil in the deepest way the historic reputation of the city. It was exemplified in the courage with which the aged bishop Polycarp refused to recant; he was martyred there *c.* AD 155 or later.
E. M. B. Green, C. J. Hemer

*Further reading*
W. M. Ramsay, *The Letters to the Seven Churches of Asia*, 1904, chs. 19–20
C. J. Cadoux, *Ancient Smyrna*, 1938
C. J. Hemer, 'Smyrna' in *The Letters to the Seven Churches of Asia in their Local Setting*, 1986, ch. 4

**SOCOH** (Hebrew *śôḵōh*, 'hedge').
**1.** A town south-east of Azekah in the Shephelah (Joshua 15:35); scene of the Philistine defeat in 1 Samuel 17 (see G. A. Smith, *Historical Geography*, 1966, pp. 161f. for a tactical description). Khirbet Abbad (Hurvat Sokho), 20 kilometres north-west of Hebron, overlooks the Wadi Sunt (Vale of Elah) from the south, where the wadi running north from *Keilah is joined by two which drain the hills west of Bethlehem. (The name is preserved at Khirbet Suweike 0·5 kilometre east, occupied in Roman–Byzantine times.)

Either this Socoh or **2** below was fortified by Rehoboam (2 Chronicles 11:7). Socoh is one of the cities named on royal jar-handle stamps found at *Lachish and other sites, which probably points to its importance as a major administrative centre in the reign of Hezekiah (Joshua 15:35); see *LOB*, pp. 394–399. The Philistines captured it from Ahaz (2 Chronicles 28:18).

**2.** A place in the highlands near *Debir (Joshua 15:48 and probably 1 Chronicles 4:18); Khirbet Shuweikeh, 3 kilometres east of Dhahiriya.

**3.** A town in Solomon's Hepher district (1 Kings 4:10); probably the Bronze Age–Byzantine site Khirbet Shuweiket er-Ras, 3 kilometres north of Tulkarm in the Plain of Sharon; see *ANET* pp. 246f.; *LOB*, pp. 49, 60, 310 *etc.*
J. P. U. Lilley

**SODOM.** See *Plain, Cities of the.

**SOREK, VALLEY OF.** The home of Delilah (Judges 16:4). There is little doubt that this may be equated with the Wadi al-Sarar, a large valley lying between Jerusalem – starting some

20 kilometres from it – and the Mediterranean.

The Valley of Sorek must always have offered a convenient route inland (it is today followed by the railway line). There is a ruin near the valley called Khirbet Surik, preserving the biblical name. Eusebius and Jerome made the same identification.

D. F. Payne

**SPAIN.** For the discussion of possible Old Testament references to Spain, see *TARSHISH. A series of Greek commercial colonies founded from Massilia (Marseilles) introduced Spain into world history, and in the 3rd century BC it became a theatre for the long struggle between Carthage and Rome.

By 197 BC, the Carthaginians being dispossessed, two Roman provinces, Hispania Citerior and Hispania Ulterior, were set up; but the forcible reconciliation of the Spanish tribes to Roman rule took almost 2 centuries more. Later, however, Spain developed, economically and culturally, perhaps faster than any other part of the empire.

Augustus reorganized the peninsula into 3 provinces, Hispania Tarraconensis, Baetica and Lusitania: Vespasian extended Latin status to all the Spanish municipalities. The Senecas, Lucan, Quintilian, Martial and other prominent Latin writers of that age, as well as the emperors Trajan and Hadrian, were of Spanish birth.

*Paul in Spain?*

These things show how forward-looking was Paul's plan to travel beyond Rome to Spain (Romans 15:24, 28), a project in which he clearly expects the co-operation of the Roman Christians. Even if his first object was the Hellenized towns, 'it marks the beginning of an entirely new enterprise; behind it lies Gaul and perhaps Germany and Britain. He is about to pass over from the Greek into the distinctly Roman half of the civilized world' (J. Weiss, *History of Primitive Christianity* 1, 1937, p. 359).

Whether Paul achieved his ambition remains uncertain. The silence of the Pastorals may indicate a change of plan. Clement of Rome, *c.* AD 95, says that Paul reached 'the boundary of the West' (*1 Clement* 5) – most naturally interpreted, not of Rome, but of the Pillars of Hercules. The 2nd-century *Acts of Peter* and the Muratorian Fragment are more explicit, but may reflect assumptions based on Romans 15. The earliest surviving Spanish traditions are too late to help, and later Roman theory was interested in proving that all western churches were founded by Peter's lieutenants (Innocent, *Letters* 25.2, AD 416).

A. F. Walls

*Further reading*

Strabo, *Geography* 3
C. H. V. Sutherland, *The Romans in Spain 217 BC–AD 117*, 1939
Th. Zahn, *INT*, 1909, 2, pp. 61ff., 73ff.
P. N. Harrison, *The Problem of the Pastoral Epistles*, 1921, pp. 102ff.
F. F. Bruce, *Paul: Apostle of the Free Spirit*, 1977, pp. 445ff.

**STRAIGHT STREET.** See *DAMASCUS.

**SUCCOTH. 1.** First site on the journey of the Israelites during the Exodus, possibly equivalent to the Old Egyptian *ṯkw*, which was in the eastern part of Wadi Tumilat (Exodus 12:37; 13:20; Numbers 33:5–6). It is probably to be identified with the site of Tell el-Maskhuta. This was the normal way in or out of Egypt for displaced persons. We find it mentioned in the Story of Sinuhe, in Papyrus Anastasi V and VI. (See also *PITHOM.)

**2.** City of the tribe of Gad (Joshua 13:27) in the Jordan Valley not far from a water passage (Judges 8:5, 16) and from Zarethan (1 Kings 7:46).

Two sites have been proposed: Tell el-Ekhsas and Tell Deir 'Allah, about 2·5 kilometres apart on the eastern side of the River Jordan near the Jabbok (Nahr Zerqa). Tell Deir 'Allah has remains from the appropriate periods, but the excavator (H. Franken) does not consider the Iron Age finds to be Israelite and therefore prefers Tell el-Ekhsas (H. Franken, 'The Identity of Tell Deir 'Allah', *Akkadica* 14, 1979, pp. 11–15). Others continue to prefer Tell Deir 'Allah.

The name Succoth is explained in Genesis 33:17, where it is connected with 'booths', since Jacob established himself there.

C. de Wit, J. Bimson

*Further reading*

On **1**:
E. L. Bleiberg, 'The Location of Pithom and Succoth', *The Ancient World* 6, 1983, pp. 21–27

**SUMER, SUMERIANS.** The lower part of ancient Mesopotamia or southern Iraq between the area of modern Baghdad and the Persian Gulf and south of the region was known as *Akkad. This flat area of *c.* 26,000 square kilometres is traversed by the rivers *Tigris and *Euphrates. Although not directly referred to in the Old Testament it may be *Shinar (*šin'ar*; Sumerian *keñir* and *šumer*). The Sumerian civilization may lie behind the narratives of Genesis 1–11 (see History, below).

The region was settled from *c.* 4500 BC by Sumerians until *c.* 1750 BC when they were finally absorbed by the Semites who inhabited the same area. The origin of the Sumerians is not known, though theories on this include migration from the east.

### History

The history of the Sumerians falls into three periods: Early Sumerian, 3000–2700 BC; Classic Sumerian, 2700–2250 BC; and Neo-Sumerian, 2100–1960 BC. It is reconstructed in each of these respective periods chiefly from epic poems, scattered historical records and hundreds of thousands of business documents.

*Early Sumerian*

The first period was dominated by three major cities: Uruk, Aratta and Kish. The three leading figures, all rulers of Uruk, were Enmerkar, Lugalbanda and especially Gilgamesh, who is the most famous hero of all Sumerian history.

Since the historical figures and events were recovered not from contemporaneous records but from later literary compositions, it is difficult to assign the events to a given archaeological level of any of the cities mentioned. Furthermore, very little of this period has been uncovered in either Kish or Uruk. The epoch is a shadowy one, from which come faint echoes of lusty deeds performed by a young and vigorous people.

*Classic Sumerian*

The classic period centres chiefly on four cities: Ur, Kish, Umma and Lagash. The best-known rulers are Eannatum, Urukagina and Gudea of Lagash and Lugalzaggisi of Umma. By this time contemporaneous documents are extant bearing the names and recording some of the exploits of these rulers. We can therefore frequently identify many of the cities and even buildings to which reference is made in the documents.

Rather more is known archaeologically than historically of Ur at this time. The names of the kings are known without reference to significant events. But the greatest treasure of all time from Mesopotamia belongs to this period

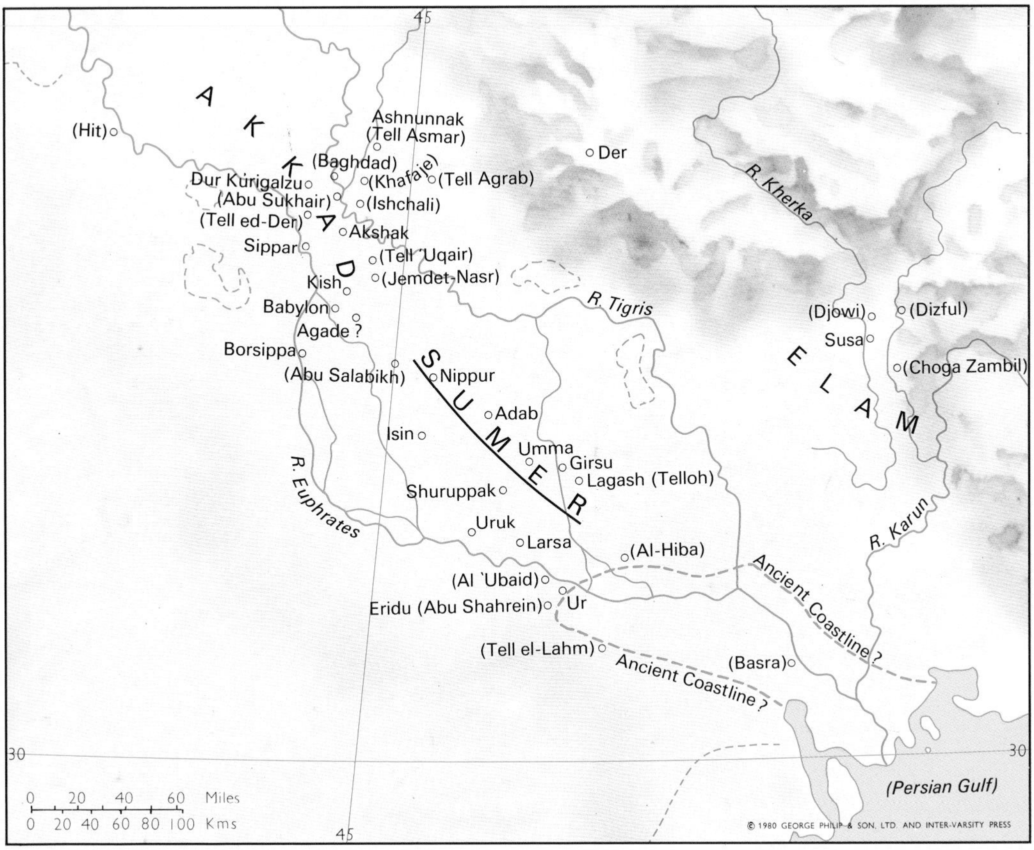


**Sumer, the southern part of Babylonia.**

– the fabulously rich 'royal tombs'.

The first true historical document of any length also comes from this period and deals with strife between Umma and Lagash. Inscribed about 2400 BC at the time of Entemena of Lagash, it contains much economic and social data as well as history. But a later governor of Lagash, Gudea, is more widely known today, since scores of inscribed statues of him are extant, witnessing to the skill of sculpture in hard stone at this time. His inscriptions yield abundant data on economic and religious life.

Lugalzaggisi, the last Sumerian king of the period, fell prey to the famous Semitic dynast Sargon of Agade.

*Neo-Sumerian*

Nearly 2 centuries later the Neo-Sumerian epoch with its capital at Ur rose on the ruins of the Akkadian dynasty. But Sumerian blood had thinned drastically as a result of the widespread immigration of other peoples, chiefly Amorites. Only the first two of Ur's five kings actually bore Sumerian names. Nevertheless, even after all Sumerians disappeared and the language was no longer spoken it was still the language of religion, science, business and law for many more centuries.

## Literature

*Language and writing*

The invention of writing *c.* 3200 BC, as known from texts at *Erech, is attributed to the Sumerians. The language, in several dialects including 'fine speech' (*eme.-sal*), is agglutinative in form and non-Semitic. It cannot be related reliably with any known language group, though it shares elements which feature in several.

Originally developed for the purposes of recording legal transactions and economic and administrative texts which comprise 75% of all extant documents in Sumerian using the cuneiform script, it soon was employed for all types of literature as later known throughout the ancient Near East. The script and literary genres were adapted and developed by subsequent *Babylonians, *Assyrians, Hittites, Hurrians, *Canaanites and *Elamites.

*Historiography*

This includes building and votive inscriptions, military accounts of inter-state relations (Lagash–Umma; Stela of Vultures), king-lists, year formulae for dating, royal correspondence and significant detailed documents (Tummal) and poetic explanations of major events ('The Curse of Agade'). Epico-historic accounts of the exploits of Sargon of Agade and Ur-Nammu and nine *Epic*-tales attest other forms of historiography. The latter reflect the relations of the city-states with their neighbours, *e.g.*, Enmerkar and Aratta, Lugalbanda with Enmerkar and Gilgamesh with Agga of Kish.

*Myths*

In Sumerian myths the heroes are deities and cover the themes of creation ('Enlil and Ninlil: the birth of the Moon-god', 'The Creation of the Pick-axe', 'Enlil and Ninmah: the Creation of Man'); of civilization ('Enki and the World Order: the Organization of the earth and its Cultural Processes', 'Inanna and Enki: the transfer of the arts of Civilization from Eridu to Erech') and of a 'heroic age' ('Enlil and Ninhursag: the Sumerian Paradise Myth') as well as of man's failure ('Inanna and Shukalletuda: the Gardener's Mortal Sin'). The goddess Inanna (later Ishtar) and

Dummuzi (Tammuz) play a leading role in myths about the descent of gods into the nether world.

The Flood, though known in Sumerian translation, may well be of Semitic literary origin (compare Epic of Atrahasis). Similar themes occur in Old Testament early historiography (Genesis 1–11).

*Hymns, lamentations and wisdom literature*
The Sumerians also composed highly sophisticated hymns extolling gods, kings and temples, and lamentations bewailing the destruction of city-states and cities (Ur, Nippur) or the death of the god Tammuz.

Other Sumerian genres comprise the beginning of the so-called 'wisdom' literature with collections of instructions, essays, fables, proverbs and riddles. All these gained a currency through their use in the educational system of schools where instruction covered writing, rhetoric, music and other forms, including examinations. The school 'contest' literature gives us the contrasts between the 'Summer and Winter', 'Pickaxe and Plough', *etc.* Other contests were used to describe the school system (*é.dub.ba*).

**Culture**
Originally Sumerian society appears to have grouped villages and towns around the larger cities into city-states controlled by a council of senators and young men of military status under the leadership of a 'lord' (*en*), later the *lugal*, 'chief man, king'.

Alongside such institutions arose a bureaucracy of the temple and priests which also owned property and occasionally dominated this 'democratic' and highly organized society. Human government was thought to reflect on earth what happened in heaven. The king was but the vicegerent of the chief god of the city who both called him to office and required him to account for his stewardship in office as dispenser of law and justice.

The king later ruled through provincial governors and through certain cities designated to control the economy in its relations with the surrounding nomads.

**Legacy**
In addition to its literary heritage Sumer gave to later civilizations its concepts of law and government backed by a 'scientific technology'. The latter was based on empirical methods (data in lists) and practice.

Astronomy and mathematics used both the decimal and sexagesimal systems, including the subdivision of time and area into degrees from which we derive our hours, minutes and linear measurements.

The wheel was developed both for transport and for the potter in his work.

Architectural practices included the arch, vault, dome, niches, columns as well as the decorative techniques of stucco and inlay used on temple façades, the temple platform and the stepped pyramid (*ziggurat*). In art, the engraved stamp and cylinder seal was closely associated with its long tradition of writing.

F. R. Steele, D. J. Wiseman

*Further reading*
S. N. Kramer, *The Sumerians: their history, culture and character*, 1963
T. Jacobsen, *Treasures of Darkness*, 1976
H. Ringgren, *Religions of the Ancient Near East*, 1975
For history:
*CAH*, 3rd edition, I.2, pp. 71–92
For texts:
*ANET*, 3rd edition, 1969, pp. 37–39 (myths, epics), 159ff. (laws), 265ff. (historical texts), 455ff. (lamentations), 589ff. (proverbs), 575ff. (hymns)

**SUPH.** In Deuteronomy 1:1 this may be a place-name (so in the RV and RSV, 'over against Suph') whose location is quite uncertain (see *GTT*, section 431, p. 255, note 223). In rendering 'over against the Red Sea', the AV understands Suph as standing for *yam-sûp̄*, referring to the Gulf of Aqabah, which is also possible (see also *Red Sea).

In Numbers 21:14, Suph(ah), 'storm' (?), is perhaps an area in which Waheb is located, in the brief quotation from the *Book of the Wars of the Lord*. Its relation to Suph in Deuteronomy 1:1 is uncertain. Musil suggested it might be Khirbet Sufah, some 6 kilometres south-south-east of Madaba (*GTT*, section 441, pp. 261–262, note 229 end).

On Suph and Suphah, see also E. G. Kraeling in *JNES* 7, 1948, p. 201.

K. A. Kitchen

**SUSA** (AV **SHUSHAN**), the ruins of which lie near the river Karun (see also *Ulai), south-western Persia, was occupied almost continuously from prehistoric times until it was abandoned by the Seleucids. Here was the capital of *Elam, whose royal inscriptions of the 2nd millennium have been recovered.

Susa maintained its importance under the Kassites and its independence until sacked in 645 BC by Ashurbanipal, who sent men of Susa (Susanchites) to exile in Samaria (Ezra 4:9). Under the Achaemenids Susa flourished as one of the three royal cities (Daniel 8:2; Nehemiah 1:1). Darius I built his palace here, the ruins of which, restored by Artaxerxes I (Longimanus) and II (Mnemon), remain, with the Apadana, one of the outstanding Persian architectural features of the 5th century BC. This palace figures prominently in the book of Esther (1:2, 5; 2:3; 3:15, *etc.*).

The site was first excavated by Loftus in 1851, and subsequently extensive operations have been undertaken there by the French.

D. J. Wiseman

*Further reading*
R. Ghirshman, *Iran*, 1963
E. M. Yamauchi, *Near East Archaeological Society Bulletin* 8, 1976, pp. 5–14

**SYCHAR.** The Samaritan town whence the woman came to fetch water from Jacob's well, where she met Jesus who taught her the nature of spiritual worship (John 4).

Sychar is commonly identified with Askar, a village 1 kilometre north of Jacob's well, on the eastern slope of Mount Ebal. An alternative theory identifies it with Shechem, but archaeological evidence suggests that Shechem had ceased to be occupied by the 1st century BC.

A. R. Millard

**SYCHEM.** See *Shechem.

**SYENE** (AV **SINIM, SINITES**). **1.** Hebrew *sînîm*. A distant land from which the people will return (Isaiah 49:12), named with the north and west, so it is either in the far south or east (so the Septuagint 'land of the Persians'). Scholars have looked for a connection with classical Sinae (China), but it is unlikely that Jews had settled in so distant a place by this period. Therefore Sin (Pelusium, Ezekiel 30:15) or Sin in Sinai (Exodus 16:1) has been proposed.

Most likely is the identification with Syene of Ezekiel 29:10 and 30:6, on the far southern border of Egypt. This is the Egyptian *swn* 'market', Coptic *Suan*, modern *'Aswān*. A Jewish community living there in the 5th century BC has left us many Aramaic papyri in which the place name is written *swn*, hence the RV and RSV *Seveneh in Ezekiel 29 and 30, better taken as 'to Seven'.

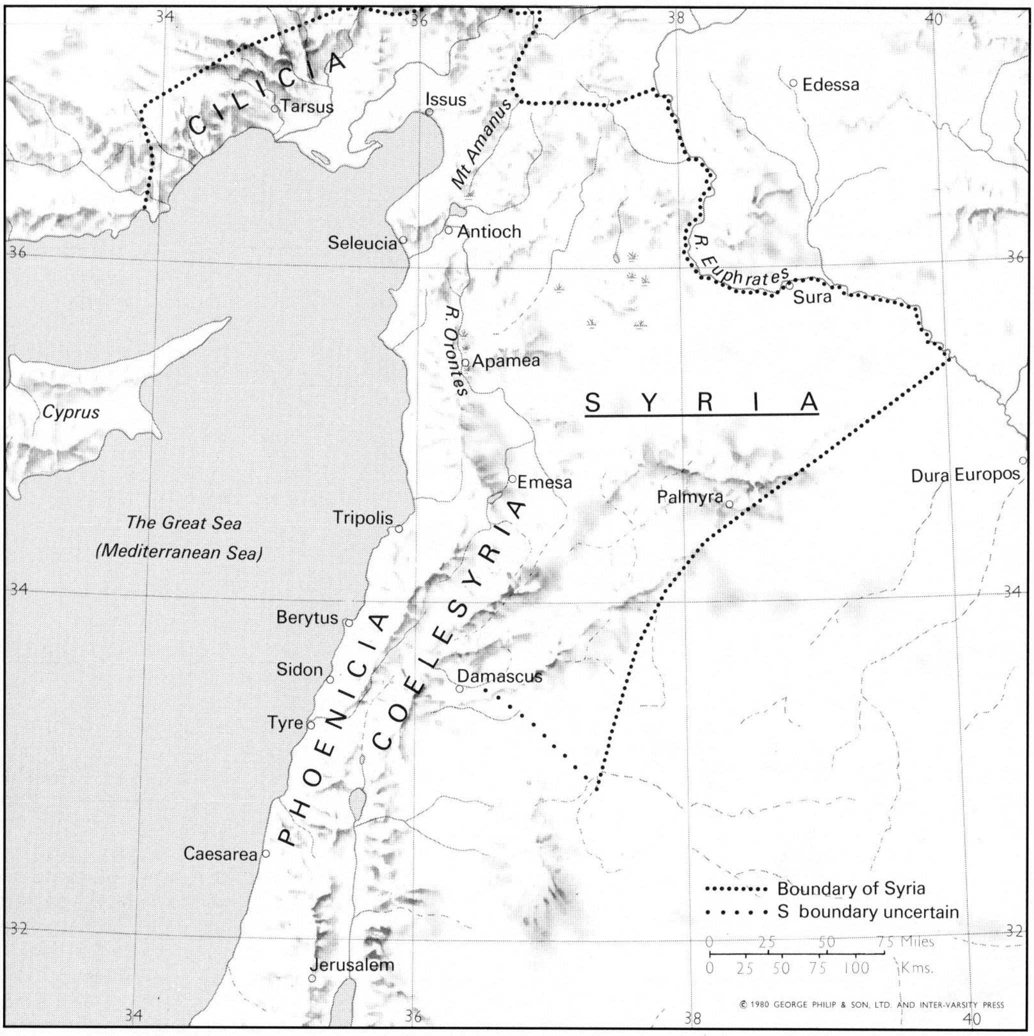


Syria in New Testament times.

'From Migdol (AV and RV 'tower') to Syene' means from one end of Egypt to the other. Syene, on the first cataract of the Nile, was a fortress and base for expeditions into Nubia (Cush), a terminus for river traffic and a source of red granite for monumental buildings (syenite).

The Qumran manuscript of Isaiah (1QIs[a]) suggests that 'Syenites' should replace *sînîm* (Isaiah 49:12); the Septuagint has *Syene* for *Sin* in Ezekiel 30:16.

**2.** Sinites (Hebrew *sînî*) were a Canaanite people (Genesis 10:17; 1 Chronicles 1:15), probably to be identified with a region, near Arqā, on the Lebanon coast, named in texts from *Mari and possibly *Ebla. The name survives in Nahr as-Sinn and is the Ugaritic *syn*, Akkadian *siyanu*.
D. J. Wiseman

*Further reading*
E. G. Kraeling, *BA* 15, 1952, pp. 50–68
*The Brooklyn Museum Aramaic Papyri*, 1953, p. 21

**SYRACUSE.** A city with a large harbour on the eastern coast of Sicily. Founded in 734 BC by Corinthian colonists, it had by the end of the 5th century BC become the most important city, politically and commercially, in Sicily, especially under the tyrants Gelon and Dionysius I. With its allies it was strong enough to defeat the great Athenian expedition to Sicily in 415–413 BC.

The Romans captured Syracuse in 212 BC, in spite of a defence strengthened by the inventions of the great mathematician Archimedes, and made it the seat of government of the province of Sicily, which became one of the sources of grain for Rome. Syracuse continued to flourish down to the 3rd century AD.

On the last stage of his journey to Rome Paul's ship stayed there for 3 days (Acts 28:12), presumably waiting for a suitable wind.
K. L. McKay

**SYRIA, SYRIANS.** In the English Old Testament this merely denotes *Aram, Aramaeans.

The geographical entity Syria is bounded by the Taurus Mountains in the north, the western bend of the Euphrates river and the Arabian desert-edge from there to the Dead Sea in the east, the Mediterranean Sea on the west, and the Sinai isthmus at the extreme south (see R. Dussaud, *Topographie Historique de la Syrie Antique et Médiévale*, 1927, pp. 1–2, *etc.*; see this work generally).

'Syria' is a Greek term; Nöldeke derived it from *Assyrios*, 'Assyria(n)', and this suggestion is open to the least objection. Compare F. Rosenthal, *Die Aramäistische Forschung*, 1939, p. 3, note 1.

Historically, ancient Syria existed as a political *unit* only during the period of the Hellenistic Seleucid monarchy, founded by Seleucus I (312–281 BC), who ruled over a realm that stretched from eastern Asia

Minor and northern Syria across Babylonia into Persia to the border of India. In 198 BC all 'Syria' belonged to this kingdom when Antiochus III finally gained Palestine from Ptolemy V of Egypt. But from 129 BC, with the death of Antiochus VII, everything east of the Euphrates was lost, and the Seleucids held Syria only. After this, internal dynastic strife disrupted the shrinking state until Pompey annexed the region for Rome in 64 BC.

Syria as defined in the second paragraph above constituted the Roman province of Syria, with which Cilicia was closely associated (Judaea being separate from AD 70). See also *ANTIOCH (Syrian), *UGARIT, *ALALAKH, *etc.*, and also *CAH*.

K. A. Kitchen

**SYROPHOENICIA.** In New Testament times Phoenicia was part of the Roman province of Cilicia and Syria. It was a Syrophoenician woman (*syrophoinikissa*), a Greek from the region of Tyre and Sidon, who pleaded with Jesus to heal her daughter (Mark 7:26; compare Matthew 15:21–28). The parallel verse in Matthew 15:22 calls the woman a Canaanite, using the ancient name by which these people were known.

The name Syrophoenician combines the area of Phoenicia which included Tyre and Sidon, and the larger Roman province of Syria. Phoenicians who lived in Carthage were called Libyphoenicians.

J. A. Thompson

**SYRTIS.** (Greek for 'sandbank'; see Acts 27:17 [AV 'the quicksands'].) The ship in which Paul was travelling found it necessary to take precautions against being driven on to the Greater Syrtis, quicksands west of Cyrene on the North African coast. Now called the Gulf of Sidra, its treacherous sands and waters were greatly feared by sailors.

J. D. Douglas

# T

**TAANACH.** Modern Tell Ta'annek on the southern edge of the valley of Jezreel, guarding a pass across Mount Carmel following the Wadi Abdullah.

Tuthmosis III mentions Taanach in the account of his conquest of western Palestine (*c.* 1450 BC; *ANET*, pp. 234ff.), as does Shishak. Amarna letter 248 complains of a raid by men of Taanach on Megiddo, which was loyal to Egypt. The Israelites defeated the king of this city, but the tribe to which it was allotted, Manasseh, was unable to take possession of it (Joshua 12:21; 17:11; Judges 1:27). It was one of the levitical cities (Joshua 21:25) and was also occupied by Issachar (1 Chronicles 7:29).

Taanach and Megiddo are closely associated in Solomon's administrative division of Israel (1 Kings 4:12) and in the Song of Deborah, where 'Taanach, by the waters of Megiddo' (Judges 5:19) is the site of the Canaanite defeat.

Excavations in 1901–04, 1963, 1966 and 1968 revealed an Early Bronze Age city, a Middle Bronze II occupation with typical glacis fortification, destroyed violently, a town of Late Bronze I burnt, perhaps by Tuthmosis III, and a prosperous town of the 14th century BC (14 Akkadian cuneiform tablets were found), but no town of the 13th century.

Iron Age occupation began in the first half of the 12th century and was interrupted by violent destruction, perhaps the work of Deborah's men. In the debris a clay tablet inscribed in a Canaanite cuneiform alphabet was found. The Early Iron Age city, containing a supposed cultic building with stone stelae, numerous pig bones and an elaborate pottery incense-stand, appears to have been destroyed by Shishak. Thereafter the city declined.

A. R. Millard

*Further reading*

E. Sellin, *Tell Ta'annek*, 1904
P. W. Lapp, *BA* 30, 1967, pp. 1–27
*BASOR* 173, 1964, pp. 4–44; 185, 1967, pp. 2–39; 195, 1969, pp. 2–49
D. R. Hillers, *BASOR* 173, 1964, pp. 45–50
A. Glock, *BASOR* 204, 1971, pp. 17–30
W. E. Rast, *Taanach* 1, *Studies in the Iron Age Pottery*, 1978
A. Glock in *NEAEHL* IV, pp. 1428–1433

**TABOR.** If Joshua 19:22, Judges 8:18 and 1 Chronicles 6:77 refer to the same place, Tabor was on the Zebulun–Issachar border; and it was presumably on or near Mount Tabor.

The 'oak', or 'terebinth' (NEB), of 1 Samuel 10:3 must have been at a different Tabor, in Benjaminite territory.

D. F. Payne

**TABOR, MOUNT.** A notable mountain rising from the Plain of Jezreel to 588 metres above sea-level. Its slopes are steep, and the views from the summit magnificent; hence it was considered worthy of comparison with Mount Hermon, in spite of the latter's much greater bulk and height (see Psalm 89:12).

Mount Tabor was the scene of Barak's mustering (Judges 4:6) and of an idolatrous shrine in Hosea's day (see Hosea 5:1). In later times there was a town on the summit, which was taken and then fortified by Antiochus III in 218 BC. In 53 BC it was the scene of a battle between the Romans and Alexander the son of Aristobulus. Josephus, in his role as Jewish general, gave the town on the summit a defensive rampart in AD 66; remains of this wall can still be seen. The mountain also figured in the events of Crusader times.

Since the 4th century AD, and perhaps earlier, tradition has held that Mount Tabor was the scene of the Transfiguration. This is not very likely in view of the fact that a town stood on the summit in the 1st century; the Transfiguration probably took place in the Hermon region (see J. Rogerson, *The New Atlas of the Bible*, 1985, pp. 140–141).

It is possible that Mount Tabor is intended in Deuteronomy 33:19. The Arabs called the mountain Jabal al-Tur; the Israelis have given it its old Hebrew name, *Har Tāḇôr*.

D. F. Payne

**TADMOR.** This place-name occurs twice in the AV and NIV (1 Kings 9:18; 2 Chronicles 8:4), and is usually

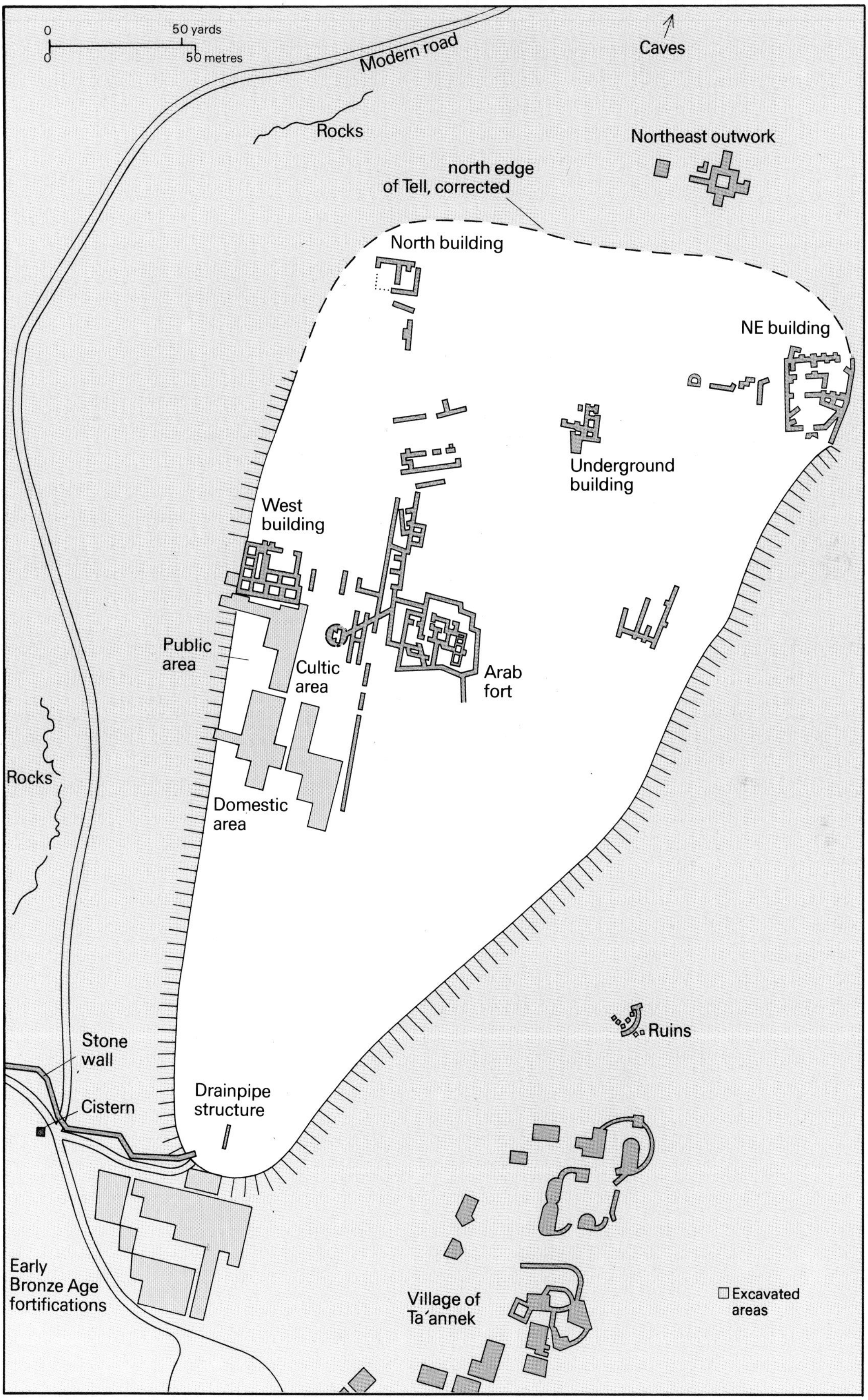


**The mound of Taanach (Tell Ta'annek), showing excavated areas.**

identified with modern Tudmur, 'Palmyra', 200 kilometres north-east of Damascus; mentioned as *Tadmar* in Assyrian texts *c.* 1110 BC. Tadmor in the AV and NIV in 1 Kings 9:18 is based on *q$^e$rē'* and the ancient versions. The *k$^e$tîḇ* is *tāmār*. The ancient versions have 'Palmyra' (Greek for 'palm tree', which is the Hebrew *tāmār*). The problem is whether the Tamar of 1 Kings 9:18 (RV, RSV) is identical with the Tadmor of 2 Chronicles 8:4. The following solutions are proposed:

*a.* Later in the time of the Chronicler, when the government of Solomon was idealized, the unimportant Tamar of the Judaean desert was changed to the then well-known, illustrious Tadmor in the Syrian desert.

*b.* *Q$^e$rē'* and the ancient versions are to be followed in identifying the place in 1 Kings 9:18 with Tadmor, the later Palmyra in the Syrian desert.

*c.* Tamar of 1 Kings 9:18 and Tadmor of 2 Chronicles 8:4 are different places. Tamar, the modern *Kurnub*, called *Thamara* in the *Onomasticon* of Eusebius, was situated on the route between Elath and Hebron. This city was fortified to protect the trade with southern Arabia and the seaport Elath. Tadmor was the famous trading-centre north-east of Damascus and could have been brought under Solomon's rule with the operations against the Syrian Hamath and Zobah.

The third solution is acceptable, because Tamar in 1 Kings 9:18 is expressly called 'in the land' and thus in Israelite territory (compare also Ezekiel 47:19; 48:28).

F. C. Fensham

*Further reading*

J. Starcky, *Palmyra*, 1952

**TAHPANHES.** An important Egyptian settlement in the eastern Delta, named with Migdol, Noph (Memphis), *etc.* (Jeremiah 2:16; 44:1; 46:14; Ezekiel 30:18 as Tehaphnehes), to which certain Jews fled *c.* 586 BC, taking thither the prophet Jeremiah (Jeremiah 43).

The same consonantal spelling *Tḥpnḥs* recurs in a Phoenician papyrus letter of the 6th century BC found in Egypt (see A. Dupont-Sommer in *PEQ* 81, 1949, pp. 52–57). The Septuagint form Taphnas, Taphnais, probably equates Tahpanhes with the Pelusian Daphnai of Herodotus (2.30, 107) where the 26th Dynasty pharaoh Psammetichus I (664–610 BC) established a garrison of Greek mercenaries.

On grounds of geographical location, the equivalence of Arabic Defneh with Daphnai, and the excavation at Defneh of Greek pottery and other objects, Tahpanhes-Daphnai is located at modern Tell Defneh ('Defenneh'), about 43 kilometres south-south-west of Port Said.

The Egyptian for Tahpanhes is not inscriptionally attested, but may be *T'-ḥ(wt)-p'-nḥsy*, 'mansion of the Nubian', names compounded with *nḥsy*, 'Nubian', being known elsewhere in Egypt (so Spiegelberg).

'Pharaoh's house in Tahpanhes' and the 'brickwork' (RV) at its entry in which Jeremiah hid stones to presage Nebuchadrezzar's visitation there (Jeremiah 43:9) may just possibly be the fortress of Psammetichus I, with traces of a brick platform on its north-western side, excavated by Petrie (*Nebesheh (Am) and Defenneh (Tahpanhes)* bound with *Tanis II*, 1888).

K. A. Kitchen

**TAHTIM-HODSHI.** In 2 Samuel 24:6 a place in the north of David's realm, near the frontier with the kingdom of Hamath, mentioned in his census record. On the basis of the Septuagint and Massoretic Text *'ereṣ taḥtîm ḥodšî* (AV, NIV 'the land of Tahtim-hodshi') has been very plausibly emended to *qādēš 'ereṣ ha-ḥittîm ḥodšî* (RSV 'Kadesh in the land of the Hittites'). (See also *KADESH.)

F. F. Bruce

**TAPPUAH** ('quince'?). **1.** A village in the *Shephelah, east of Azekah (Joshua 15:34, 53, Beth-tappuah), sometimes identified with Beit Netif, *c.* 18 kilometres west of Bethlehem. The place-name may derive from a Calebite from Hebron (1 Chronicles 2:43).

**2.** A town in Ephraim territory (Joshua 16:8) on the southern border of Manasseh (Joshua 17:7–8), possibly modern Sheikh Abu Zarad, *c.* 12 kilometres south of Shechem. Its Canaanite king was defeated by Joshua (Joshua 12:17; *Testament of Judah* 3:2; 5:6). If 2 Kings 15:16 refers to this same place (so RSV, after the Septuagint; compare AV Tiphsah), it was later attacked by Menahem of Israel.

D. J. Wiseman

**TARSHISH. 1.** The son of Javan, grandson of Noah (Genesis 10:4; 1 Chronicles 1:7). The name Tarshish (*taršîš*), which occurs 4 times in the AV as Tharshish (1 Kings 10:22 (twice); 22:48; 1 Chronicles 7:10), refers both to the descendants and to the land.

*Identification*

Several of the references in the Old Testament are concerned with ships and suggest that Tarshish bordered on the sea. Thus Jonah embarked on a ship sailing to Tarshish (Jonah 1:3; 4:2) from Joppa in order to flee to a distant land (Isaiah 66:19). The land was rich in such metals as silver (Jeremiah 10:9), iron, tin, lead (Ezekiel 27:12), which were exported to places like Joppa and Tyre (Ezekiel 27).

A land in the western Mediterranean where there are good deposits of mineral seems a likely identification, and many have thought of Tartessus in Spain. According to Herodotus (4.152), Tartessus lay 'beyond the Pillars of Hercules', and Plinius and Strabo placed it in the Guadalquivir Valley. Certainly the mineral wealth of Spain attracted the Phoenicians, who founded colonies there. Interesting evidence comes from Sardinia, where monumental inscriptions erected by the Phoenicians in the 9th century BC bear the name Tarshish.

W. F. Albright has suggested that the very word Tarshish suggests the idea of mining or smelting, and that in a sense any mineral-bearing land may be called Tarshish, although it would seem most likely that Spain is the land intended. An old Semitic root found in the Akkadian *rašāšu* means 'to melt', 'to be smelted'. A derived noun *taršīšu* may be used to define a smelting-plant or refinery (Arabic *ršš*, 'to trickle', *etc.*, of liquid). Hence any place where mining and smelting were carried on could be called Tarshish.

*'Ships of Tarshish'*

The Old Testament itself suggests that the name referred to more than one place. According to 1 Kings 10:22 Solomon had a fleet of ships of Tarshish that brought gold, silver, ivory, monkeys and peacocks to Ezion-geber on the Red Sea, and 1 Kings 22:48 mentions that Jehoshaphat's 'ships of Tarshish' sailed from Ezion-geber for Ophir. Further, 2 Chronicles 20:36 says that these ships were made in Ezion-geber for sailing to Tarshish. These latter references appear to rule out any Mediterranean destination but point to a place along the Red Sea or in Africa.

Another possibility is that the expression *'$^o$nî ṯaršîš*, navy of

Tarshish or Tarshish fleet, may refer more generally to ships which carried smelted metal either to distant lands from Ezion-geber or to Phoenicia from the western Mediterranean.

Another view is that Tarshish vessels were deep seagoing vessels named after the port of Tarsus, or the Greek *tarsos*, 'oar'.

These ships symbolized wealth and power. A vivid picture of the day of divine judgment was to portray the destruction of these large ships in that day (Psalm 48:7; Isaiah 2:16; 23:1, 14). The fact that Isaiah 2:16 compares the ships of Tarshish with 'the pleasant place' (RSV 'beautiful craft') suggests that whatever the original identification of Tarshish may have been, it became in literature and in the popular imagination a distant paradise from which all kinds of luxuries might be brought to such areas as Phoenicia and Israel.

J. A. Thompson

*Further reading*

W. F. Albright, 'New Light on the Early History of Phoenician Colonization', *BASOR* 83, 1941, pp. 14ff.

'The Role of the Canaanites in the History of Civilization', *Studies in the History of Culture*, 1942, pp. 11–50, especially p. 42

C. H. Gordon, 'Tarshish', *IDB* 4, pp. 517f.

**TARSUS.** A city on the Cilician plain, watered by the Cydnus, and some 16 kilometres inland after the fashion of most cities on the Asia Minor coast. To judge from the extent of its remains, Tarsus must have housed a population of no less than half a million in Roman times. The lower Cydnus was navigable, and a port had been skilfully engineered. A major highway led north to the Cilician Gates, the famous pass through the Taurus range some 50 kilometres distant.

*Origin*

Nothing is known of the foundation of Tarsus. It was probably a native Cilician town, penetrated at a very early date by Greek colonists. The name of Mopsus is traditionally associated with Greek settlement in Cilicia, and may indicate, as Ramsay believed (*The Cities of St. Paul*, 1907, pp. 116f.), early Ionian settlement. Genesis 10:4, 'The sons of Javan, Elishah, Tarshish . . .' may support this theory. Josephus' identification of Tarshish with Tarsus in this passage does not preclude a different interpretation in other contexts. The antiquity of Genesis 10 is a graver objection, but the words may be evidence of Ionian intrusion of very remote date.

*In Old Testament times*

Tarsus appears sporadically in history. It is mentioned in the Black Obelisk of Shalmaneser as one of the cities overrun by the Assyrians in the middle of the 9th century BC.

Median and Persian rule followed, with that typically loose organization which permitted the rule of a Cilician subject-king. Xenophon, passing through in 401 BC, found Tarsus the royal seat of one Syennesis, ruling in such capacity. This petty king may have been deposed for his association with Cyrus' revolt which brought Xenophon and the Ten Thousand to Cilicia, for Alexander, in 334 BC, found the area in the hands of a Persian satrap.

The coinage of the period suggests a mingling of Greek and Oriental influence, and gives no indication of autonomy. Ramsay professes to trace a decline of Greek influence under the Persian rule.

'Cleopatra's Gate', Tarsus.

*Under Seleucid and Roman rule*
Nor did the Seleucid kings, who ruled after Alexander, promote the influence of the Greeks in Tarsus. Their general policy, here as elsewhere, was to discourage the Greek urge to city autonomy and its attendant liberalism. It is possible that the shock of the Roman defeat of Antiochus the Great and the peace of 189 BC reversed the process. The settlement limited the Syrian domain to the Taurus, and Cilicia became a frontier region. This fact seems to have prompted Syria to some reorganization, and the granting of a form of autonomy to Tarsus. The Tarsus of Paul's birth (Acts 22:3), with its synthesis of East and West, Greek and Oriental, dates from this time.

A story in 2 Maccabees 4:30–36 reveals the rapid growth of independence, and the reorganization of the city which a Tarsian protest won from Antiochus Epiphanes in 171 BC. The formation of a 'tribe' of Jewish citizens after the Alexandrian fashion may date from this time. (Antiochus' anti-semitism was against metropolitan recalcitrance.)

Tarsian history in the rest of the 2nd century BC is obscure. The 1st century BC is better known. Roman penetration of Cilicia began in 104 BC, but Roman and Greek influence were both overwhelmed in Asia by the Oriental reaction under Mithridates (83 BC). Pompey's settlement in 65–64 BC reconstituted Cilicia as a 'sphere of duty', which is the basic meaning of 'province', rather than a geographical entity, and the governors, Cicero among them (51 BC), had a roving commission to pacify the pirate coast and hinterlands and to protect Roman interests.

In spite of Roman experimentation with the land at large, Tarsus flourished, played some part in the civil wars, was visited by Antony, and favoured by Augustus as the home town of Athenodorus, his teacher at Apollonia and life-long friend. The Roman citizenship of some Tarsian Jews dates probably from Pompey's settlement.
E. M. Blaiklock

**TAVERNS, THREE.** See *THREE TAVERNS.

**TEHAPHNEHES.** See *TAHPANHES.

**TEKOA.** A town in Judah, the home of Amos (Amos 1:1). When Joab 'perceived that the king's heart went out to Absalom' he sent to Tekoa for a wise woman who might reconcile David and Absalom (2 Samuel 14:1f.). Rehoboam fortified the town (2 Chronicles 11:6). Later, when Jehoshaphat was faced by Ammonites and Moabites, he consulted with the people in 'the wilderness of Tekoa' (2 Chronicles 20:20). Jeremiah called for the blowing of a trumpet in Tekoa in the face of the advancing enemy (Jeremiah 6:1).

After the Exile the town was re-inhabited (Nehemiah 3:5, 27). In Maccabean and Roman times the place was known, and the name lingers today as Khirbet Taqû'a, a ruined village of some 2 hectares, which lies 17 kilometres south of Jerusalem. Finds from the Iron Age I and II periods make its identification with Old Testament Tekoa probable.

(Some scholars have suggested that Amos came from a Tekoa in Galilee, unknown from the Old Testament but mentioned in the Talmud; however, Amos 7:12 provides strong confirmation of the prophet's Judaean origins.)
J. A. Thompson, J. Bimson

*Further reading*
F. M. Abel, *Géographie de la Palestine* 2, 1933, p. 478
D. Baly, *Geography of the Bible*, 2nd edition, 1974, pp. 89, 182
H. W. Wolff, *Joel and Amos*, 1977, p. 123

**TELAIM.** The place where Saul gathered his army before his attack on the Amalekites (1 Samuel 15:4). The incident described in 1 Samuel 15, in which Saul disobeyed God's word given by the prophet Samuel, provoked the severe rebuke of 1 Samuel 15:22–23, 'to obey is better than sacrifice'.

Telaim (Hebrew *ṭᵉlā'îm*) is identified by some with Telem (Joshua 15:24), in the Negeb. The exact location is unknown. Some manuscripts allow of an occurrence of the word in 1 Samuel 27:8, and read 'they of Telaim' for 'of old'.
J. A. Thompson

**TELASSAR.** A place inhabited by the 'children (sons) of Eden' and cited by Sennacherib's messengers to Hezekiah as an example of a town destroyed in previous Assyrian attacks (as also *GOZAN, *HARAN, *REZEPH).

The name *tᵉla'śśār* (2 Kings 19:12) or *tᵉlaśśār* (Isaiah 37:12) represents Tell Assur ('mound of Assur'), Akkadian Til-Aššur. The *bᵉnê 'eḏen* probably lived in the area between the Euphrates and Baliḫ rivers, called in Assyrian Bît-Adini (Beth-Eden), but no Til-Aššur has been found in this region, although the area does suit the context. A Til-Aššur named in the annals of Tiglath-pileser III and Esarhaddon appears to lie near the Assyrian border with Elam.

The common form of the place-name means that it may not yet be identified. There is no need to emend to Tell Bassar (Basher), south-east of Raqqa on the Euphrates (as L. Grollenberg, *Atlas of the Bible*, 1956, p. 164).
D. J. Wiseman

**TELEM.** See *ELAIM.

**TELL EL-AMARNA.** See *AMARNA.

**TEMA.** The name (Hebrew *tēmā'*) of the son and descendants of Ishmael (Genesis 25:15; 1 Chronicles 1:30) and of the district they inhabited (Job 6:19). It is mentioned, with Dedan and Buz, as a remote place (Jeremiah 25:23) and as an oasis in the desert on a main trade route through Arabia (Isaiah 21:14).

The modern site is Taima', about 400 kilometres north-north-west of Medina in north-western Arabia. It became an urban centre around 600 BC and excavations show that it reached its peak of prosperity in the 5th century BC. Several Aramaic inscriptions date from this period.

The city (Babylonian *Tema'*) is also named in documents recording its occupation by Nabonidus during his exile in northern Arabia, 553–543 BC (*AS* 8, 1958, p. 80; *ANET*, 3rd edition, p. 562).
D. J. Wiseman

**TEMAN.** The grandson of Esau (Genesis 36:11; 1 Chronicles 1:36), who may have given his name to the district, town or tribe of that name in northern Edom (Jeremiah 49:20; Ezkeiel 25:13; Amos 1:12).

The inhabitants were renowned for wisdom (Jeremiah 49:7; Obadiah 8–9). Eliphaz the Temanite was one of Job's comforters (Job 2:11, *etc.*).

A chief (*'allûp̄*) of Teman (*têmān*) is named among the chiefs of Edom (Genesis 36:15, 42; 1 Chronicles 1:53), and Husham was one of the early rulers (Gensis 36:34).

The prophets include Teman among Edomite towns to be destroyed (Jeremiah 49:20; Ezekiel 25:13; Amos 1:12; Obadiah 9).

Habakkuk in his great vision saw God the Holy One coming from Teman (Habakkuk 3:3).

N. Glueck (*The Other Side of Jordan,* 1940, pp. 25–26) identified it

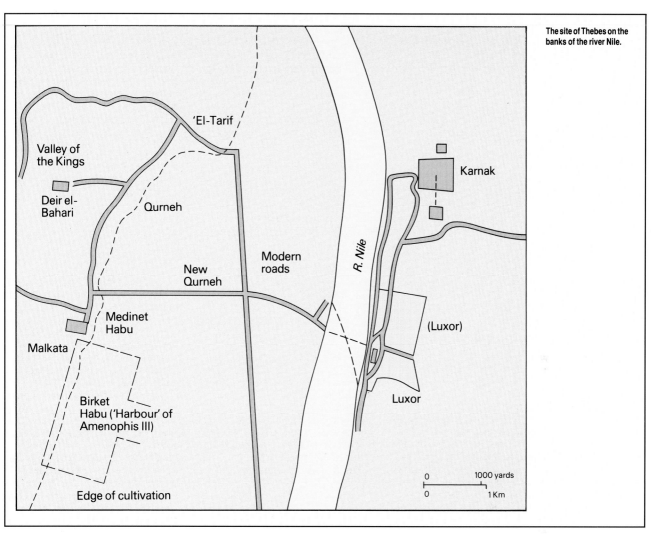

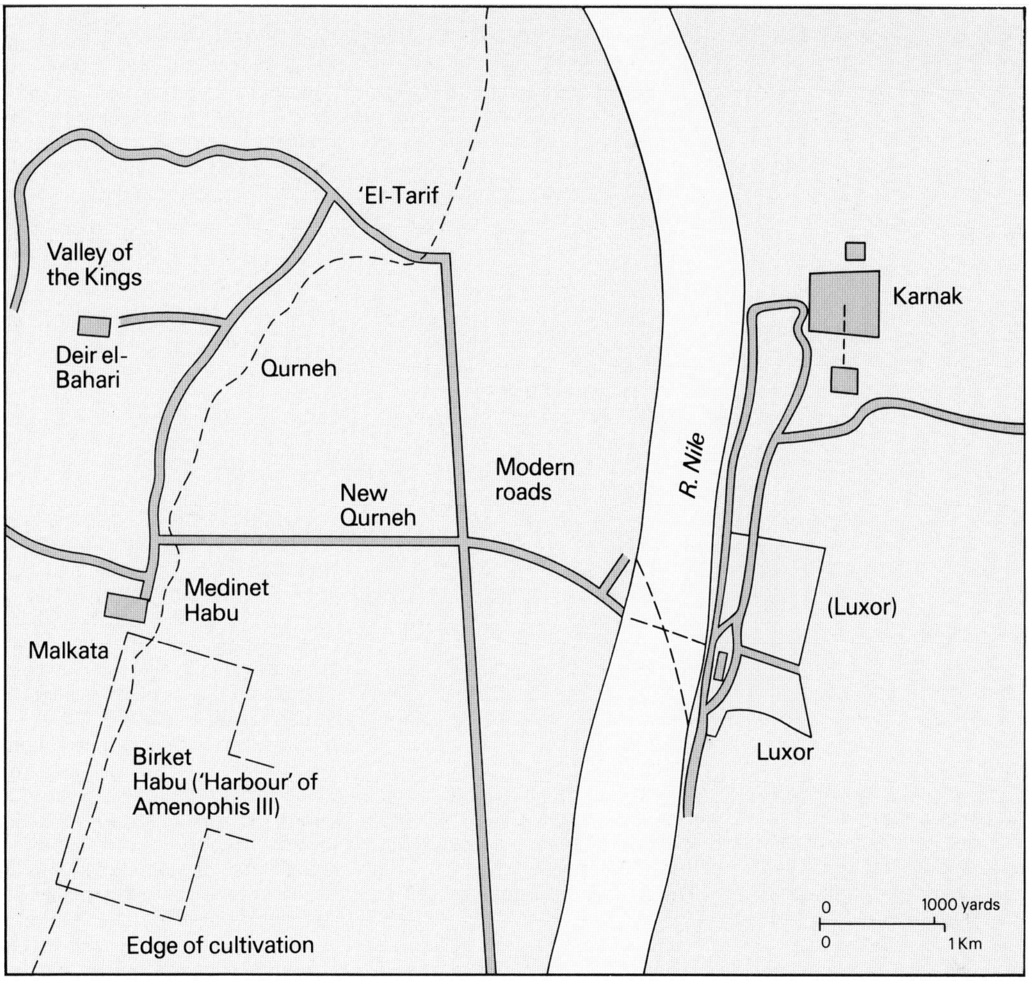


The site of Thebes on the banks of the river Nile.

with Tawilân, since excavated to show a large Edomite town of the 8th to 6th centuries BC (*RB* 76, 1969, pp. 386ff.). R. de Vaux argued that it denoted southern Edom (*RB* 77, 1969, pp. 379–385).

J. A. Thompson

**THARSHISH.** See *TARSHISH.

**THEBES** (Hebrew *No*, as the AV). Once Egypt's most magnificent capital. The Hebrew *No* corresponds to the Egyptian *niw*(*t*), 'the City' *par excellence*, and No-Amon to the Egyptian phrase *niw*(*t*), 'the City of (the god) Amūn'. In Greek it is called both Thebes, the usual term in modern writings, and Diospolis Magna.

Some 530 kilometres upstream from Cairo as the crow flies, its site on the two banks of the Nile is marked on the eastern side by the two vast temple-precincts of the god Amūn (Amon), now known by the Arabic names Karnak and Luxor, and on the western side by a row of royal funerary temples from modern Qurneh to Medinet Habu, behind which extends a vast necropolis of rock-cut tombs.

Thebes first rose to national importance in the Middle Kingdom (early 2nd millennium BC), as the home town of the powerful pharaohs of the 12th Dynasty (see also *EGYPT, History); however, the land was then administered not from Thebes in the far south, but from the better placed Itjet-Tawy just south of ancient *Memphis and modern Cairo.

During the Second Intermediate Period Thebes became the centre of Egyptian opposition to the foreign Hyksos kings, and from Thebes came the famous 18th Dynasty kings, who finally expelled them and established the Egyptian empire (New Kingdom).

During the imperial 18–20th Dynasties, *c.* 1550–1070 BC, the treasures of Asia and Africa poured into the coffers of Amūn of Thebes, now state god of the empire. All this wealth plus the continuing gifts of Late Period pharaohs such as Shishak fell as spoil to the conquering Assyrians under Ashurbanipal in 663 BC amid fire and slaughter. In predicting mighty Nineveh's fall, no more lurid comparison could Nahum (3:8–10) draw upon than the fate of Thebes. The force of this comparison rules out attempts occasionally made to identify Nahum's No-Amon with a Lower Egyptian city of the same name.

The Nile, Nahum's 'rivers', was truly Thebes' defence. The Late Period pharaohs made full use of its eastern Delta branches and irrigation and drainage canals as Egypt's first line of defence, with sea-coast forts at the Nile mouths and across the road from Palestine – perhaps alluded to in the phrase 'wall(s) from the sea' (coast inwards?). To this protection was added Thebes' great distance upstream, which invaders had to traverse to reach her.

In the early 6th century BC Jeremiah (46:25) and Ezekiel (30:14–16) both spoke against Thebes.

K. A. Kitchen

*Further reading*

C. F. Nims, *Thebes*, 1965

For the monuments at Thebes, full references are given in:

B. Porter, R. L. B. Moss, E. M. Burney, *Topographical Bibliography of Ancient Egyptian Hieroglyphic Texts, Reliefs & Paintings*, 2nd edition, I:1, 1960, I:2, 1964, and II, 1972

**THEBEZ** (Hebrew *tēḇēṣ*, 'brightness'). A fortified city in Mount Ephraim, in the course of capturing which Abimelech was mortally wounded by a millstone hurled down on him by a woman (Judges 9:50ff.; 2 Samuel 11:21).

Thebez is the modern Tūbās, about 16 kilometres north of Nablus, and north-east of Shechem on the road to Bethshan.

J. D. Douglas

**THESSALONICA.** Founded after the triumph of Macedonia to grace her new position in world affairs, the city rapidly outstripped its older neighbours and became the principal metropolis of Macedonia. Situated at the junction of the main land route from Italy to the east with the main route from the Aegean to the Danube, her position under the Romans was assured, and she has remained a major city to this day.

*Paul in Thessalonica*

Thessalonica was the first place where Paul's preaching achieved a numerous and socially prominent following (Acts 17:4). His opponents, lacking their hitherto customary influence in high places, resorted to mob agitation to force the government's hand. The magistrates, known as politarchs, neatly trapped by the imputation of disloyalty towards the imperial power, took the minimum action to move Paul on without hardship to him.

In spite of his success, Paul made a point of not placing himself in debt to his followers (Philippians 4:16f.; 1 Thessalonians 2:9). Not that they were themselves without generosity (1 Thessalonians 4:10); Paul was apparently afraid that the flourishing condition of the church would encourage clients to continue to be supported by patrons unless he himself set the strictest example of self-support (2 Thessalonians 3:8–12).

The two Epistles to the Thessalonians, written soon after his departure, reflect also his anxiety to preserve his ethical integrity as a teacher compared with secular orators (1 Thessalonians 2:1–12) and from disillusionment in the face of further civic agitation (1 Thessalonians 3:3). He need not have feared. Thessalonica remained a triumphant crown to his efforts (1 Thessalonians 1:8).

E. A. Judge, B. W. Winter

*Further reading*

E. Oberhummer, *RE*, under 'Thessalonika'

B. W. Winter, '"If a man does not wish to work . . ." A Cultural and Historical Setting for 2 Thessalonians 3:6–16', *TynB* 40.2, 1989, pp. 303–315

——, 'The Entries and Ethics of Orators and Paul (1 Thessalonians 2:1–12)', *TynB* 44:1, 1993, pp. 55–74

G. H. R. Horsley, 'Politarchs' in A. R. Millard and B. W. Winter (eds.), *Documents of New Testament Times*, 1993

**THREE TAVERNS** (Latin *Tres Tabernae*). This was a station about 50 kilometres from Rome on the Via Appia, which led south-east from the city. It is situated at the crossing of the road from Norba to Autium and is mentioned by Cicero in his correspondence with Atticus (2.10). When the apostle Paul and his company were on their way from Puteoli to Rome, Christians came out of the city and met him here (Acts 28:15).

B. F. C. Atkinson

**THYATIRA.** A city in the Roman province of Asia, in the west of what is now Asiatic Turkey. It occupied an important position in a low-lying 'corridor' connecting the Hermus and Caicus valleys. It was a frontier garrison, first on the western frontier of the territory of Seleucus I of Syria, and later, after changing hands, on the eastern frontier of the kingdom of Pergamum. With that kingdom, it passed under Roman rule in 133 BC.

But Thyatira remained an important point in the Roman road-system, for it lay on the road from Pergamum to Laodicea, and thence to the eastern provinces. It was also an important centre of manufacture; dyeing, garment-making, pottery and brass-working are among the trades known to have existed there. A large town (Akhisar) still stands on the same site.

The Thyatiran woman Lydia, the 'seller of purple' whom Paul met at Philippi (Acts 16:14), was probably the overseas agent of a Thyatiran manufacturer; she may have been arranging the sale of dyed woollen goods which were known simply by the name of the dye. This 'purple' was obtained from the madder root, and was still produced in the district, under the name 'Turkey red', into the present century.

*The church in Thyatira*

The Thyatiran church was the fourth (Revelation 1:11) of the 'seven churches of Asia'. Some of the symbols in the letter to the church (Revelation 2:18–29) seem to allude to the circumstances of the city. The description of the Christ (verse 18) is appropriate for a city renowned for its brass-working (*chalkolibanos*, translated 'fine brass', may be a technical term for some local type of brassware).

The terms of the promise (verses 26–27) may reflect the long military history of the city. 'Jezebel' (the name is probably symbolic) was evidently a woman who was accepted within the fellowship of the church (verse 20). Her teaching probably advocated a measure of compromise with some activity which was implicitly pagan. This is likely to have been membership of the social clubs or 'guilds' into which the trades were organized. These bodies fulfilled many admirable functions, and pursuance of a trade was almost impossible without belonging to the guild; yet their meetings were inextricably bound up with acts of pagan worship and immorality.

M. J. S. Rudwick, C. J. Hemer

*Further reading*

W. M. Ramsay, *The Letters to the Seven Churches of Asia,* 1904, chs. 23–24

C. J. Hemer, 'Thyatira' in *The Letters to the Seven Churches of Asia in their Local Setting*, 1986, ch. 6

**TIBERIAS.** A city on the western shore of the Sea of *Galilee which subsequently gave its name to the lake. It was founded by Herod Antipas about AD 20 as a new capital in place of Sepphoris, and named after the emperor Tiberius.

The principal factors influencing Herod's choice of site seem to have been, first, a defensive position represented by a rocky projection above the lake, and, second, proximity to some already-famous warm springs which lay just to the south. Otherwise, the site offered little, and the beautiful buildings of the city (which became Herod's capital) rose on ground that included a former graveyard, and so rendered the city unclean in Jewish eyes.

Tiberias is mentioned only once in the gospels (John 6:23; 'sea of Tiberias' appears in John 6:1; 21:1), and there is no record of Christ ever visiting it. It was a largely Gentile city, and he seems to have avoided it in favour of the numerous Jewish towns of the lake shore.

By a curious reversal, however, after the destruction of Jerusalem it became the chief seat of Jewish learning, and both the Mishnah and the Palestinian Talmud were compiled there, in the 3rd and 5th centuries respectively.

Of the towns which surrounded the Sea of Galilee in New Testament times, Tiberias is the only one which remains of any size at the present day.

J. H. Paterson

**TIBHATH.** A town in the Aramaean kingdom of Zobah (*ṣôḇâ*). After David defeated a composite force of Aramaeans, including men from Zobah and Damascus, he pressed on to the towns of Tibhath (*ṭiḇhaṯ*) and Chun, from which he took booty (1 Chronicles 18:8).

The precise location of Tibhath is unknown but it may have been situated in the region between Tunip and Baalbeck.

J. A. Thompson

**TIGRIS.** The Greek name for one of the 4 rivers marking the location of Eden (*Hiddekel*; Genesis 2:14; Akkadian *Diglat*; Arabic *Dijlah*). It rises in the Armenian Mountains and runs south-east for 1,900 kilometres via Diarbekr through the Mesopotamian plain to join the river *Euphrates 64 kilometres north of the Persian Gulf, into which it flows.

The Tigris is a wide river as it meanders through Babylonia (Daniel 10:4) and is fed by tributaries from the Persian hills, the Greater and Lesser Zab, Adhem and Diyala rivers. When the snows melt, the river floods in March–May and October–November.

Nineveh, Calah and Assur are among the ancient cities which lay on its banks.

D. J. Wiseman

**TIMNAH** (Hebrew *timnâh*). **1.** A town on the northern boundary of Judah, formerly counted as Danite (Joshua 15:10; 19:43). It changed hands more than once between Israelites and Philistines (Judges 14:1; 2 Chronicles 28:18). Samson's first wife lived there. Tel Batash, in the northern lower Shephelah, 30 kilometres west of Jerusalem, is probably the site, though the name is preserved at Khirbet Tibneh, 5 kilometres to the south-east.

The town lay at the mouth of the Vale of Sorek, below Beth Shemesh. Genesis 38:12 probably refers to this Timnah (note the connection with *Adullam).

**2.** A town in the south of Judah (Joshua 15:57). Identifications suggested for its neighbours point to a location south-west of Hebron, but no precise identification can be offered.

J. P. U. Lilley, J. Bimson

*Further reading*

On **1**:

B. Mazar, *IEJ* 10, 1960, pp. 65–73

*LOB*, pp. 220, 274 *etc.*

G. Kelm and A. Mazar, *BASOR* 248, 1982, pp. 1–36

*RB* 91, 1984, pp. 410–420

Continuing excavation reports in *IEJ*

The famous warm springs at Tiberias.

**TIMNATH-HERES, TIMNATH-SERAH** (Hebrew *timnaṯ ḥeres, timnaṯ seraḥ*). The personal inheritance of Joshua, where he was buried (Joshua 19:50; 24:30; Judges 2:9). The Samaritans claimed Kafr Haris, 16 kilometres south-west of Shechem, as the site; but Herzberg (*PJB* 22, 1926, pp. 89ff.) proposed Khirbet Tibneh, 24 kilometres south-west of Shechem, a Late Bronze–Early Iron site on the southern side of a deep ravine (compare Joshua 24:30); the traditional tomb of Joshua, mentioned by Eusebius, is in the side of the valley towards the east.

The Hebrew *ḥeres* is a rare word for 'sun' (Judges 1:35; 8:13; Job 9:7; possibly Isaiah 19:18, but the reading is uncertain). If it had idolatrous implications, the variant *seraḥ* ('extra') was perhaps intended to avoid them; but this leaves unexplained the retention of *ḥereṣ* in Judges 2:9 and of *šemeš*, which also means 'sun', in other place-names. *Seraḥ* may therefore have been a deliberate adaptation for Joshua's

inheritance.
J. P. U. Lilley

*Further reading*
J. A. Soggin, *Judges*, 1981, p. 39
R. G. Boling, *Joshua* (Anchor), 1982, p. 469

**TIPHSAH** (Hebrew *tip̄saḥ*, 'a ford', 'a passage'). Probably Thapsacus, an important crossing on the western bank of the Middle Euphrates. At the north-eastern boundary of Solomon's territory (1 Kings 4:24), it was placed strategically on a great east–west trade route. See *LOB*, pp. 276–277.
J. D. Douglas

**TIRZAH.** A Canaanite town noted for its beauty (Song of Songs 6:4) which lay in the northern part of Mount Ephraim at the head of the Wadi Far'ah along which passed the road from Transjordan to the central hill country where Shechem, Samaria, Dothan and other towns lay.

Tirzah was captured by Joshua (Judges 12:24) and was assigned to Manasseh (Joshua 17:2–3). Jeroboam I lived there (1 Kings 14:17) and the town became the capital of the northern kingdom in the time of Baasha (1 Kings 15:21, 23; 16:6), Elah and Zimri (1 Kings 16:8–9, 15). Zimri burnt the palace over his own head when trapped there by Omri (1 Kings 16:17–18). After 6 years Omri transferred the capital to Samaria which was more central and easier to defend. In *c.* 752 BC Menahem, a resident of Tirzah, was able to overthrow Shallum and usurp the throne (2 Kings 15:14, 16).

De Vaux identified the large mound of Tell el-Far'ah, about 11 kilometres north-east of Nablus, as the site of Tirzah and over the course of several years excavation revealed the archaeological story of the site. There was continuous settlement here from Chalcolithic times, before 3000 BC, down to Assyrian times. The Israelite occupation during the days of the northern kingdom is represented by Levels I–III. The 9th-century level showed a standard type of house over a wide area with one larger administrative building near the gate (Level III).

By the 8th century there were several large houses, a great administrative building and a considerable number of very poor houses, confirming the picture drawn by the 8th-century prophets (Amos 5:11; Isaiah 9:8–10). (However, note the argument of T. L. McClellan, that these poor houses actually belong to Level III, which is characterized by poorer standards than Level II.) This latter phase of the city ended with the Assyrian invasion of 723–721 BC (Level II).

The last period of the city's life (Level I) represents the years of Assyrian domination culminating in the destruction of the city at the end of the 7th century, possibly by Nebuchadrezzar.
J. A. Thompson

*Further reading*
W. F. Albright, 'The site of Tirzah and the Topography of Western Manasseh', *JPOS* 11, 1931, pp. 241–251
R. de Vaux and A. M. Steve, several articles in *RB* from 1947 (Vol. 54) to 1962 (Vol. 69), especially Vol. 62, 1955, pp. 587–589
'Tirzah' in *AOTS*, pp. 371–383
'The Excavation at Tell el-Far'h and the site of ancient Tirzah', *PEQ*, 1956, pp. 125–140
G. E. Wright, *BA* 12, 1949, pp. 66–68
T. L. McClellan, *BASOR* 267, 1987, pp. 84–86

**TISHBITE, THE** (Hebrew *hattišbî*). An epithet of Elijah (1 Kings 17:1; 21:17, 28; 2 Kings 1:3, 8; 9:36). Generally seen as denoting one from a town Tishbeh in Gilead. N. Glueck read 1 Kings 17:1 as 'Jabeshite, from Jabesh-Gilead'. A town Tishbeh in Gilead is not otherwise known (Tobit 1:2 places one in Naphtali), but tradition locates it at al-Istib, 12 kilometres north of the Jabbok.

The word has been read as *hattōšᵉb̲î*, 'the sojourner', related to the following word 'settlers' (RSV margin).
D. W. Baker

*Further reading*
N. Glueck, *AASOR* 25–28, 1951, part 1, pp. 218, 225–227
F. M. Abel, *Géographie de la Palestine* 2, 1937, p. 486

**TOB.** The name of an Aramaean city and principality lying north of Gilead, mentioned in connection with Jephthah and David (Judges 11:3; 2 Samuel 10:6); the district named in 1 Maccabees 5:13 is probably identical.

The likely location of the city is al-Taiyiba (preserving the ancient name), some 20 kilometres east-north-east of Ramoth-gilead. For its history, see B. Mazar, *BA* 25, 1962, pp. 98–120.
D. F. Payne

**TOMBS, ROYAL.** See *SEPULCHRE OF THE KINGS.

**TOPHEL.** Mentioned only in Deuteronomy 1:1 as the locality where Moses addressed the Israelites. The identification with el-Tafileh, 25 kilometres south-east of the Dead Sea, is philologically unlikely (N. Glueck, *AASOR* 18–19, 1939, pp. 42–43). Tophel may well have been a stopping-place in the Israelites' wilderness itinerary.

Aharoni (*LOB*, p. 203) suggested a location between Punon and the Wadi Zered, but this would lie south of Moabite territory and would therefore conflict with Deuteronomy 1:5.
D. J. Wiseman, J. Bimson

**TOPHETH** (AV **TOPHET**). This was a 'high place' in the valley of *Hinnom just outside Jerusalem, where child sacrifices were offered by fire to a deity Molech (Jeremiah 7:31). Isaiah spoke of it metaphorically as a place prepared for the destruction of Israel's enemies (Isaiah 30:33, NIV, RSV margin). Josiah defiled this idolatrous shrine (2 Kings 23:10), and Jeremiah prophesied that the place would be used as a cemetery (Jeremiah 7:32f.).

The root of the noun seems to be the *tpt* of Aramaic and Arabic denoting 'fireplace'. The vowels are artificial, taken from the Hebrew noun *bōšet̲*, 'shame'.
D. F. Payne

**TOWER OF BABEL.** See *BABEL, TOWER OF.

**TOWER OF SILOAM.** See *SILOAM.

**TRACHONITIS.** The only biblical reference is Luke 3:1, where, linked with *Ituraea, it is called the tetrarchy of Philip (the brother of Herod, tetrarch of Galilee).

Trachonitis must have been the district around Trachon (Josephus uses both names); Trachon corresponds with the modern al-Laja', a pear-shaped area of petrified volcanic rock some 900 square kilometres in area, to the east of Galilee and south of Damascus. It is on the whole extremely unproductive, but here and there are patches of fertile ground, with a spring or two.

The cracked and broken nature of the terrain made Trachonitis ideal for outlaws and brigands. Among others Varro (governor of Syria under Augustus), Herod the Great and Herod Agrippa I endeavoured to civilize the area, with varying success. Later on a Roman road was built through it.

Targum Jonathan identifies the Old Testament *Argob with Trachonitis.
D. F. Payne

**TRANSJORDAN.** See *GILEAD.

**TROAS.** The principal seaport of north-western Asia Minor, established some 20 kilometres south-south-west of the site of Troy (Ilium) by the successors of Alexander the Great, and named Alexandria after him. 'Troas' was originally a distinguishing epithet, but it became the usual designation of the city after Augustus made it a Roman colony.

The place grew rapidly around its artificial harbour-basins, which provided necessary shelter from the prevailing northerlies at a focal meeting-point of sea-routes, close to the mouth of the Hellespont (Dardanelles). Troas was the port for the crossing to *Neapolis in Macedonia for the land-route to Rome.

*In the New Testament*
Though rarely mentioned in secular literature, Troas had a strategic function in the Roman system of communication, and its importance emerges clearly from unobtrusive references both in Acts and the Epistles. It was the scene of the vision of the 'man of Macedonia' (Acts 16:8–11) and of the raising of Eutychus (Acts 20:5–12). The former incident was the occasion of the coming of the gospel from Asia to Europe, though this aspect is not stressed in Acts. Perhaps this also marks the meeting of Paul with Luke, for the 'we-passages' begin at Acts 16:10.

Later Paul found an 'open door' at Troas (2 Corinthians 2:12), and again stayed there as long as possible when in haste to reach Jerusalem (Acts 20:6, 13). Paul's urgent request in 2 Timothy 4:13 may reflect a hurried departure from Troas under arrest. Ignatius, too, after sending three of his epistles from Troas, had to sail in haste for Neapolis as a prisoner bound for Rome (*Letter to Polycarp* 8), when the weather permitted.

The site of Troas at Dalyan is now deserted, but there are remains of the harbour, baths, stadium and other buildings, and several kilometres of the walls may be traced.

C. J. Hemer

*Further reading*
C. J. Hemer, 'Alexandria Troas', *TynB* 26, 1975, pp. 79–112

**TROGYLLIUM** (or Trogyllia). A promontory of the west coast of Asia Minor between Ephesus and Miletus, and reaching to within 2 kilometres of Samos. Paul's delay there (Acts 20:15) was no doubt due to the difficulty of navigating a strait in darkness. The mention of this landmark in the Western text, though not preferred by the United Bible Societies text, is geographically apposite.

K. L. McKay

**TROY.** See *TROAS.

**TYRE, TYRUS.** The principal seaport on the Phoenician coast, about 40 kilometres south of Sidon and 45 north of Acco, Tyre (modern Ṣûr; Hebrew *ṣôr*; Assyrian *Ṣur(r)u*; Egyptian *Ḏaru*; Greek *Tyros*) comprised two harbours. One lay on an island, the other 'Old' port on the mainland may be the Uššu of Assyrian inscriptions. The city, which was watered by the river Litani, dominated the surrounding plain, in the north of which lay Sarepta (see also *ZAREPHATH).

## History

*Beginnings*
According to Herodotus (2.44), Tyre was founded *c.* 2700 BC; it is mentioned in Execration Texts from *Egypt (*c.* 1850 BC) and in a Canaanite poem (Keret, *ANET*, pp. 142f.) from Ras Shamra (see also *UGARIT). It took an early and active part in the sea-trade in trade and luxuries with Egypt which led to the Egyptian campaigns to control the Phoenician coast.

During the Amarna period the local ruler of Tyre, Abimilki, remained loyal, writing to Amenophis III of the defection of surrounding towns and requesting aid against the Amorite Aziru and king of Sidon.

When the Philistines plundered Sidon (*c.* 1200 BC) many of its inhabitants fled to Tyre, which now became the 'daughter of Sidon' (Isaiah 23:12), the principal Phoenician port.

By the late 2nd millennium BC Tyre was counted as a strongly defended city on the border of the land allocated to Asher (Joshua 19:29), and this reputation continued (2 Samuel 24:7; RSV 'fortress').

*In the time of David and Solomon*
With the decline of Egypt Tyre was independent, its rulers dominating most of the Phoenician coastal cities, including the Lebanon hinterland. Hiram I was a friend of David and supplied materials for building the royal palace at Jerusalem (2 Samuel 5:11; 1 Kings 5:1; 1 Chronicles 14:1), a policy he continued during the reign of Solomon, when he sent wood and stone for the construction of the temple (1 Kings 5:1–12; 2 Chronicles 2:3–16) in return for food supplies and territorial advantages (1 Kings 9:10–14). Tyrians, including a bronze-caster also named Hiram, assisted in Solomon's projects (1 Kings 7:13–14).

During Solomon's reign Hiram I linked the mainland port with the island by an artificial causeway and built a temple dedicated to the deities Melqart and Astarte. As part of his policy of colonial expansion and trade he assisted Solomon's development of the Red Sea port of Ezion-geber for southern voyages (1 Kings 9:27), his ships reaching distant places (1 Kings 9:28; see also *OPHIR).

From this time, often called 'the golden age of Tyre', the people became the merchant princes of the eastern Mediterranean (Isaiah 23:8), and were henceforth noted for their seafaring prowess (Ezekiel 26:17; 27:32). The primary trade was in their own manufactured glass and the special scarlet-purple dyes, called 'Tyrian', made from the local *murex* (see also *PHOENICIA).

The Canon of Ptolemy is still a primary source for the king list, though, despite correlations with Assyrian and Hebrew history, there remains a divergence of about 10 years in the chronology of the earlier rulers. Thus Hiram I is dated *c.* 979–945 BC (Albright and Katzenstein prefer *c.* 969–936 BC).

*During the divided Monarchy*
Hiram's successor Baal-eser I (Balbazeros) was followed by Abd-Ashtart, who was murdered by his brothers, the eldest of whom, Methus-Astartus, usurped the throne. Phelles, who succeeded Astarymus *c.* 897 BC, was overthrown by the high priest Ethbaal (Ithobal), whose daughter Jezebel was married to Ahab of Israel to confirm the alliance made between their countries (1 Kings 16:31). Ethbaal was also a contemporary of Ben-hadad I. His success against Phelles may have been connected with the invasion of Ashurnasirpal II of Assyria, who took a heavy tribute from Tyre.

*Assyrian dominance*
The port suffered another blow in 841 BC, when, in his 18th regnal year, Shalmaneser III of Assyria received tribute from Ba'alimanzar at the

same time as Jehu paid him homage at the Nahr-el-Kelb (see *Sumer* 7, 1951, 3–21). Baalezer II was followed by Mattan I (*c.* 829–821) and by Pygmalion (Pu'myaton), in whose 7th year (825 BC; others 815 BC) Carthage was founded from Tyre.

Assyrian pressure on Phoenicia continued, and Tyre paid tribute to Adad-nirari III of Assyria in 803 BC and its king Hiram II sent gifts to Tiglath-pileser III, who claims that his Rab-shakeh took 150 talents of gold from Mattan II, the next king of Tyre (*c.* 730 BC; *ANET*, p. 282). By peaceful submission the city retained a large measure of autonomy.

According to Josephus (*Antiquities* 9.283), Shalmaneser V of Assyria (whose own records are wanting) laid siege to Tyre in 724, and the city fell with Samaria into the hands of Sargon II in 722 BC. Local Assyrian officials supervised the return of taxes in kind to Nineveh, but considerable unrest was fomented from Egypt, to whom the Tyrians turned for help. This led to the denunciation of Tyre by the Hebrew prophets who followed Isaiah and by Joel (3:5–6) for their selling them as slaves to the Greeks. Tyre came under the domination of Sidon, and when Sennacherib approached its ruler Luli (Elulaeus) fled and died in exile. This saved the city from assault, for the Assyrians installed their nominee Tuba'alu (Ethbaal III) in 701 BC.

Esarhaddon, who was keeping the route open to attack Egypt, executed Abdi-milkitti of Sidon (*c.* 677 BC) and set Ba'ali (I) on the throne, binding him by treaty to Assyria. However, Tyre, instigated by Tirhakah of Egypt, rebelled and Esarhaddon besieged the port, which did not, however, fall since Ba'ali submitted. His influence and independence must have been great in Phoenicia, since he retained the throne throughout his life. When he rebelled again in 664 BC the city fell to Ashurbanipal, who made Azi-Baal king, taking his sisters and many officials as hostages to Nineveh.

*Babylonian rule*

With the decline of Assyria at the end of the reign of Ashurbanipal (*c.* 636–627 BC), Tyre regained her autonomy and much of her former sea-trade. Nevertheless, Jeremiah prophesied Tyre's subjection to the Babylonians (25:22; 27:1–11), as did Ezekiel later (26:1–28:19; 29:18–20) and Zechariah (9:2ff.). Nebuchadrezzar II besieged Tyre for 13 years, *c.* 587–574 BC (Josephus, *Antiquities* 10.228; *JBL* 51, 1932, pp. 94ff.), but no contemporary record of this remains (compare Ezekiel 29:18–20). The city (under Ba'ali II) eventually recognized Babylonian suzerainty, and a number of Babylonian contracts confirm this and give the names of the local Babylonian officials. For a decade the city was ruled by 'judges' (*špṭ*).

*Into the New Testament*

In 332 BC Alexander the Great laid siege to the island port for 7 months and captured it only by building a mole to the island fortress. Despite heavy losses, the port soon recovered under Seleucid patronage. Herod I rebuilt the main temple, which would have been standing when our Lord visited the district bordering Tyre and Sidon (Matthew 15:21–28; Mark 7:24–31). People of Tyre heard him speak (Mark 3:8; Luke 6:17), and he cited Tyre as a heathen city which would bear less responsibility than those Galilean towns which constantly witnessed his ministry (Matthew 11:21–22; Luke 10:13–14).

Christians were active in Tyre in the 1st century (Acts 21:3–6), and there the scholar Origen was buried (AD 254).

### Archaeology

The main extant ruins date from the fall of the Crusader city in AD 1291, but excavations from 1921 (*Syria* 6, 1922), and from 1937 in the harbour, have traced some of the earlier foundations. The many coins minted in Tyre from the 5th century BC onwards, found at sites throughout the ancient Near East and Mediterranean, attest its greatness.

The 'ladder of Tyre' (Josephus, *Jewish War* 2.188), which marked the division between Phoenicia and Palestine proper (1 Maccabees 11:59), is identified with the rocky promontory at Ras en-Naqara or Ras el-'Abyad.

D. J. Wiseman

*Further reading*

N. Jidejian, *Tyre through the Ages*, 1969
H. J. Katzenstein, *The History of Tyre*, 1973

# U

**UGARIT, RAS SHAMRA.** This important trade centre flourished as the capital of a city-state in northern Syria throughout the second millennium BC. It is mentioned in the *Mari and *Amarna letters, though not in the Old Testament. The site, known as Ras Shamra ('Fennel Hill'), lies *c.* 1 kilometre from the Mediterranean coast, and *c.* 15 kilometres north of Latakia.

*Excavations*

Excavations were begun in 1929 after a peasant had uncovered a tomb on the sea coast in what proved to be the port of Ugarit, ancient Ma'hadu (now Minet el-Beida). C. F. A. Schaeffer directed a team of French archaeologists for many years (1929–39, 1948–73), and the work continues.

Occupation from pre-pottery Neolithic (*c.* 6500 BC) to Roman times has been traced in 15 levels. Among major buildings cleared are two temples, one dedicated to El (at first thought to be Dagan's) founded in Level II, *c.* 2100 BC and associated by the excavator with the Amorites.

An enormous palace, over 900 metres square, was the major building of the Late Bronze Age (*c.* 1550–1180 BC). Houses of officials, scribes, and a high priest living in the same time were also uncovered. The city had been sacked, perhaps by the 'Sea People' (see also *PHILISTINES) soon after 1200 BC, so many objects lay buried in the ruins.

A vivid picture of Ugarit's wealth and trading connections can be built up on the evidence of pottery and ivory carvings imported from Crete and Greece, of Egyptian and Babylonian products and things from Asia Minor and Cyprus, as well as the first local 'Canaanite' work in gold and silver, bronze and stone so far unearthed.

*Written documents*

Most important of all is the large number of written documents recovered from the palace and various houses. Egyptian, Cypriot and Hittite writing systems were all

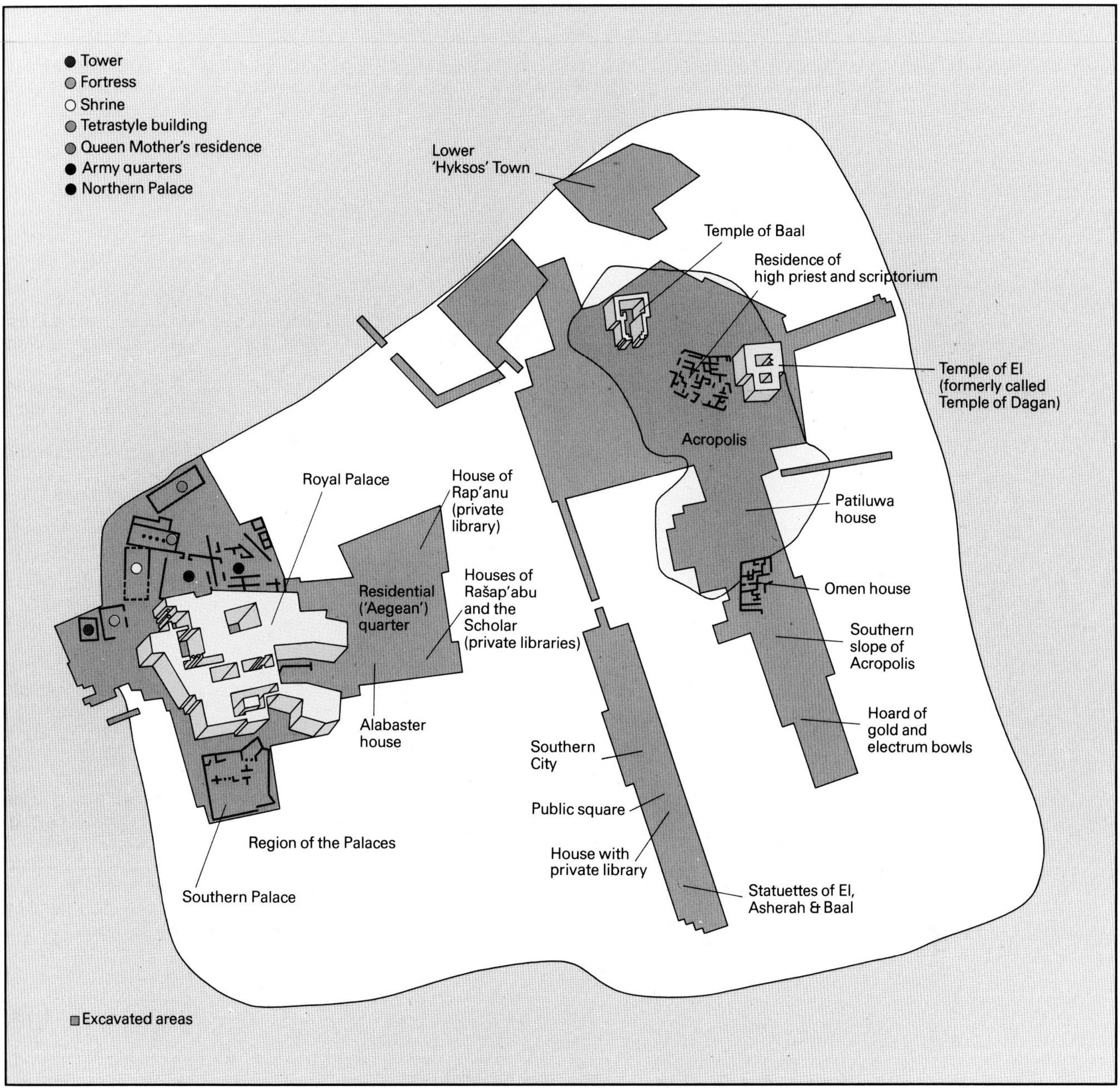


**Plan of the mound of Ugarit (Ras Shamra) showing where excavation has been undertaken and some of the main buildings uncovered.**

known in the city, but Babylonian cuneiform was the most commonly used. The scribes learnt this writing in Ugarit, and some of their exercises and reference books survive. They copied Babylonian literature, or composed variations of it. Examples include an account of the Flood (Atrahasis), a story about Gilgamesh and a unique version of the 'Babylonian Job'. There are also proverbs, riddles and love-lyrics. A hymn in Hurrian has notes which provide clues to its musical accompaniment (*RA* 68, 1974, pp. 69–82).

Babylonian was not the scribes' native language, so beside the standard lists of Sumerian and Akkadian words, they compiled others giving equivalents in their own western Semitic language ('Ugaritic') and in Hurrian, another current tongue. These lists are of great value for our understanding of the lesser-known languages. Babylonian was used in daily life for business and administration in the temples, the palace and the big houses. It was the international diplomatic language, so was used for writing treaties.

The kings of Ugarit in the 14th and 13th centuries BC traced their dynasty back to an ancestor who ruled the city *c.* 1850 BC. The later kings were subject to the Hittites, and several treaties made with them, or at their suggestion, are available for study. In those texts elements of the pattern displayed by *Hittite treaties and the Old Testament covenant texts appear.

*The alphabetic script*

In order to write their own language, the scribes of Ugarit imitated the idea of the alphabet which had been invented by the Canaanites to the south. Instead of using signs based on pictures, they combined wedges to make 29 cuneiform letters, each representing one consonant. The letters were learnt in an order which is the same as the Hebrew, with additions. Over 1,300 inscriptions in this alphabet, dating from 1400 BC onwards, have been found at Ugarit, a few dozen at a site called Ras Ibn

**Continued on p. 306**

# UR

**UR OF THE CHALDEES.** The city which Terah and Abram left to go to Harran (Genesis 11:28, 31; 15:7; Nehemiah 9:7). It was considered by Stephen to be in Mesopotamia (Acts 7:2, 4). An old identification of the Hebrew *'ûr* with Urfa (Edessa), 32 kilometres north-west of Harran, is unlikely on philological grounds, and *Ura'* is the name of several places known in Asia Minor. Moreover, such an identification would require Abraham to retrace his steps eastwards before setting out westwards towards Canaan. This identification requires that the 'Chaldea' which identifies the location must be equated with Ḫaldai (part of ancient Armenia). The *Chaldeans were a Semitic people known in Babylonia from at least the end of the 2nd millennium BC, but there are no references to their presence in northern Mesopotamia.

The Septuagint wrote 'the land (*chōra*) of the Chaldees', perhaps being unfamiliar with the site. However, Eupolemus (*c.* 150 BC) refers to Ur as a city in Babylonia called Camarina ('the moon') or Ouria. The Talmudic interpretation of Ur as Erech is unlikely since the latter is distinguished in Genesis 10:10.

The most generally accepted identification is with the ancient site of Ur (*Uri*), modern Tell el-Muqayyar, 14 kilometres west of Nasiriyeh on the river Euphrates in southern Iraq. Excavations at this site in 1922–34 by the joint British Museum and University Museum, Philadelphia, expedition under Sir C. L. Woolley traced the history of the site from the 'Al 'Ubaid period (5th millennium BC) until it was abandoned about 300 BC. Many spectacular discoveries were made, especially in the royal cemeteries of the early Dynastic 3 period (*c.* 2500 BC).

Beneath these a layer of silt was at first equated with the flood of the Epic of Gilgamesh and Genesis (see now *Iraq* 26, 1964, pp. 65ff.). The ruins of the temple tower (*ziggurat*) built by Ur-Nammu, the founder of the prosperous 3rd Dynasty (*c.* 2150–2050 BC) still dominate the site (see also *BABEL).

The history and economy of the city is well known from thousands of inscribed tablets and the many buildings found at the site. The principal deity was Nannar (Semitic Sin or Su'en), who was also worshipped at Harran. The city was later ruled by the Neo-Babylonian (Chaldean) kings of Babylonia.

D. J. Wiseman

*Further reading*

C. L. Woolley, *Excavations at Ur*, 1954

H. W. F. Saggs, 'Ur of the Chaldees', *Iraq* 22, 1960

C. J. Gadd, 'Ur', *AOTS*, 1967, pp. 87–101

*CAH* 1/2, 1971, pp. 595–617

*Orientalia* 38, 1969, pp. 310–348

**Marshlands in southern Iraq, near biblical Ur.**

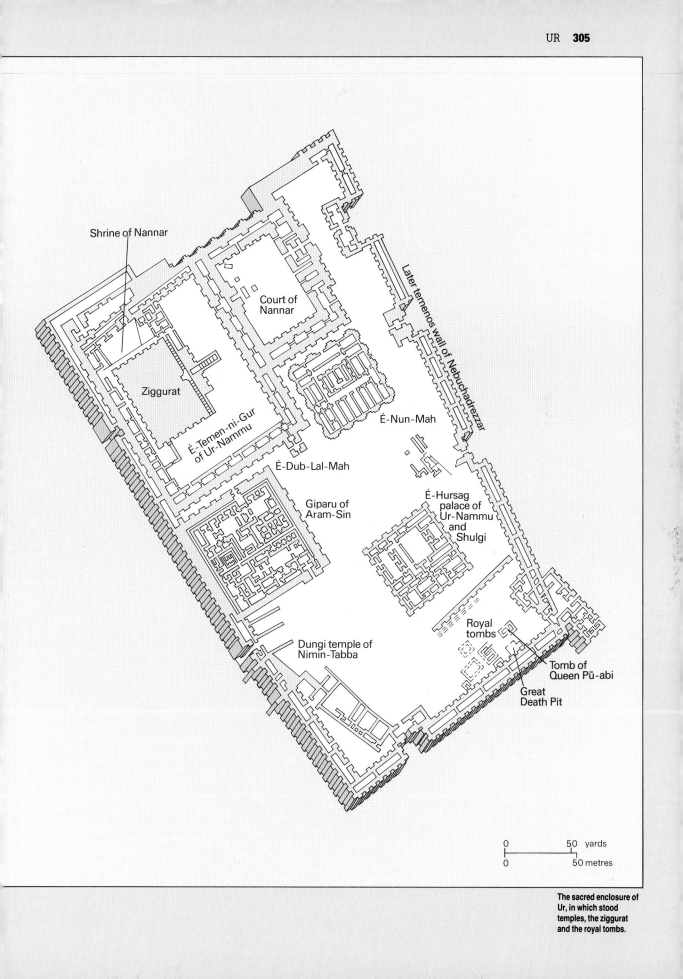

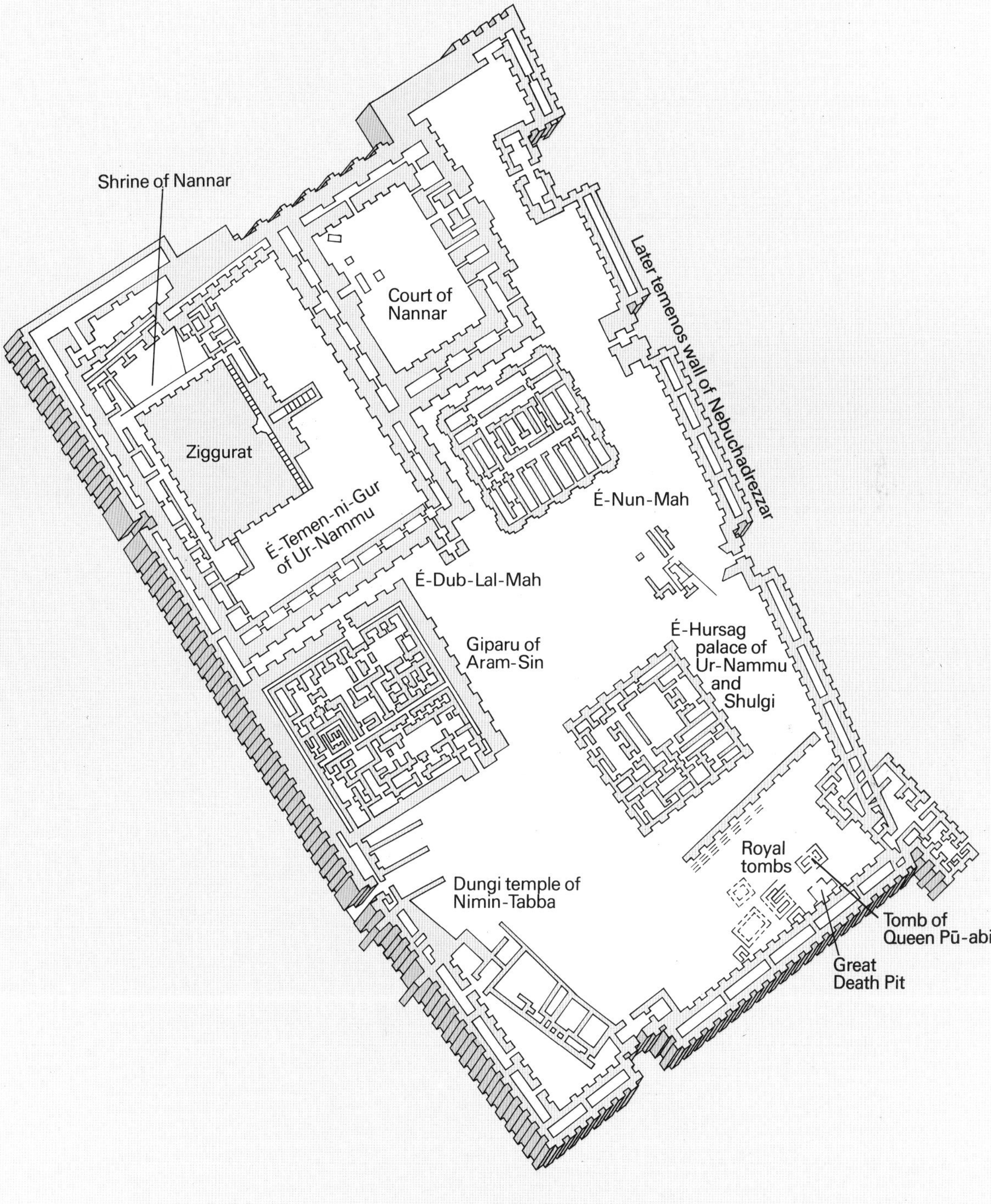


**The sacred enclosure of Ur, in which stood temples, the ziggurat and the royal tombs.**

**Continued from p. 303**
Hani to the south and one at Tell Sukas farther down the coast.

A shorter form of this alphabet, having only 22 letters, was more widely known. Beside three examples from Ugarit, single inscriptions have been unearthed at *Kadesh in Syria, Kamid el-Loz and *Zarephath in Lebanon, and *Beth-shemesh, *Taanach and near Mount Tabor in Palestine.

*Ugaritic and Hebrew*
Ugaritic is closely related to Hebrew and has broadened appreciation of the language of the Old Testament in many ways. It is necessary to realize, however, that the languages are not identical, so what is true of one may not be applied automatically to the other.

There is similarity between the terminology of the elaborate Ugaritic ritual system and that in Leviticus. Thus the whole burnt-offering (Ugaritic *kll*; Deuteronomy 33:10), burnt- (*šrp*), communion- (*šlmn*), trespass- (*'asm*), and tribute- or gift- (*mtn*) offerings, and offerings made by fire (*'est*) are named, though their use differs from Old Testament spirit and practice.

The epics, myths and hymns from Ugarit (see below) have a distinct poetic style, with irregular metre, repetitions and parallelisms, which have led Albright and his students to argue for a date of the 13th–10th century BC or earlier for some Hebrew poetic passages, *e.g.* for the Songs of Miriam (Exodus 15; *JNES* 14, 1955, pp. 237–250), and Deborah (Judges 5); the blessing of Moses (Deuteronomy 33; *JBL* 67, 1948, pp. 191–210) and Psalms 29 and 58 (*HUCA* 23, 1950–51, pp. 1–13).

Many phrases which occur in Hebrew poetry are found in these texts; a few examples may be cited: 'flashing (*ysr*) his lightning to the earth' is similar to the probable reading of Job 37:3; 'the dew of heaven and the fat (*smn*) of the earth' can be compared with Genesis 27:28, 39; and 'LTN the swift . . . the crooked serpent' is the Leviathan of Isaiah 27:1 and Job 26:13.

In this way the meaning and exegesis of a number of difficult Hebrew passages can be elucidated. The 'fields of offerings' of 2 Samuel 1:21 (AV) is rather the Ugaritic 'swelling of the deep', and the Ugaritic root *spsg*, 'glaze', helps to translate Proverbs 26:23 correctly as 'like glaze upon a potsherd'.

The study of Ugaritic grammar and syntax, especially of such prepositions and particles as *b, l, 'el, k*(*i*), has shown that many of the old emendations proposed for the Massoretic Text are unnecessary.

*Epics, myths and hymns*
Texts in the alphabetic script include a number of epics or myths, several hundred lines in length. Ever since their discovery, their significance has been disputed, some arguing they are dramas acted in the cult, some claiming a basis in the annual cycle of seasons for the *Baal Epics*, others seeing a seven-year cycle.

The *Baal Epics* tell how that god met his rivals Yam ('Sea') and Mot ('Death') and overcame them with the weapons fashioned by the craftsman god Ktr(whss). These were probably thunder (a mace or drumstick) and lightning (a lance or thunderbolt), as shown on bronze statuettes of the god Baal found there. Following a successful war in which Baal's sister Anat, probably to be identified with the Phoenician Ashtart, a goddess of war, love and fertility, played a major part, the craftsman-god built Baal a temple at the command of El. Mot later rebelled and Baal appears to have journeyed to the underworld to stay for half a year while the earth wilted until he was rescued by the Sun-goddess.

The *Keret* legend tells of a godly king who had no heir until El appeared to him in a dream and told him to march to besiege Udm to win Huriya, the daughter of King Pabil. In time he had sons and daughters by her but, failing to repay a vow to the goddess Atherat, he fell sick and died. During this time his eldest son Yassib was disinherited in favour of the younger (compare Genesis 25:29–34).

The *Aqhat* texts record the doings of the pious hero King Danel (compare Ezekiel 14:20) who died following a misunderstanding about the bow of the goddess Anat he had acquired and refused to give up in answer to a promise of wealth and immortality.

The texts show the degrading results of the worship of these deities; with their emphasis on war, sacred prostitution, sensuous love and the consequent social degradation. They reveal aspects of Canaanite religious thought and practice, but care should be taken in estimating any influence they may have had on the Hebrews.

The same applies to the use of Ugaritic in the clarification of the Old Testament text. Other deities met here include the 'Lady of the Sea' (Asherah, *Aššuratum*). She was the chief goddess of Tyre, where she was known also as *Qudšu*, 'Holy'. Her name was sometimes used for 'goddess' in general and linked with Baal (compare Judges 3:7).

Among the prayers to Baal is one in which the worshipper pleads for deliverance for his city: '. . . "the bulls for Baal we will consecrate, we will fulfil the vows made to Baal; we will dedicate the first-born to Baal; we will pay tithes to Baal; we will go up to the sanctuary of Baal; we will go up the path to the temple of Baal." Then Baal will hear your prayer; he will drive away the strong one from your gate, the warrior from your walls.'

Lists of gods, Babylonian, Hurrian and Ugaritic, in both cuneiform scripts, give more than 250 names, but of these only some 15–28 were classified in the primary pantheon. This was headed by *'l ib* ('god of the fathers or spirits'), followed by El, Dagan (Dagon), Ba'al of the heights and seven Baals. In the second rank were the sun, moon (Yerih), Reshef (Habakkuk 3:5) and several goddesses, including Baalat, Anat, Pidriya, and 'Athirat of the grove. Since several of the gods listed have foreign associations, there were probably frequent cases of syncretism.

*Significance of the Ugarit documents*
The alphabetic script was used as freely as the Babylonian for writing letters, business documents, magical spells and every sort of document, even medical prescriptions for horses. It fell into oblivion with the city of Ugarit; its recovery is one of the major landmarks of 20th-century archaeology.

D. J. Wiseman

*Further reading*
General:
C. F. A. Schaeffer, *Mission de Ras Shamra* 1–18, 1929–78 (includes *Ugaritica*, 1–7)
Alphabetic texts:
A. Herdner, *Corpus des tablettes en cunéiformes alphabétiques découvertes à Ras Shamra de 1929–1939*, 1963
*Ugaritica* 2, 6–7
Cuneiform (Akkadian) texts:
J. Nougayrol, *Palais royal d'Ugarit* 3, 1955; 4, 1956; 6, 1970
*Ugaritica* 5, 1968, pp. 1–446
See also:
*Syria*
*UF* 1, 1969
*ANET*, pp. 129–155
M. Dietrich and others, *Ugarit-Bibliographie 1928–1966*, 1973
J. Gray, *The Legacy of Canaan*, 196[illegible]

**ULAI.** The canal or river flowing east of Susa in Elam (south-western Persia) where Daniel heard a man's voice (Daniel 8:16). The river (Hebrew *'ûlāi*; Assyrian *Ulai*; classical *Eulaeus*) has changed its course in modern times, and the present Upper Kherkhah and Lower Karun (Pasitigris) rivers may then have been a single stream flowing into the delta at the north of the Persian Gulf.

The river is illustrated in the Assyrian reliefs showing Ashurbanipal's attack on Susa in 646 BC (R. D. Barnett, *Assyrian Palace Reliefs*, 1960, plates 118–127).
D. J. Wiseman

**UMMAH.** See *PTOLEMAIS.

**UPHAZ.** An unidentified location from which came fine gold (Jeremiah 10:9; Daniel 10:5). It may, however, be a technical term for 'refined gold' itself (so 1 Kings 10:18, *mûpāz*; compare *mippāz*, Isaiah 13:12) similar to the definition 'pure gold' (*zāhāḇ ṭāhôr*; 2 Chronicles 9:17).

Others, with some support from the versions, read *'ûpîr* (see also *OPHIR; compare Jeremiah 10:9) for *'ûpāz* owing to the similarity of Hebrew *z* and *r*.
D. J. Wiseman

**UPPER EGYPT.** See *PATHROS.

**UR OF THE CHALDEES.** See p. 304.

**UZ.** The land of Uz was Job's homeland (Job 1:1; compare Jeremiah 25:20 and Lamentations 4:21), the location of which is uncertain. Of the numerous suggestions (*e.g.* near Palmyra, near Antioch, or in northern Mesopotamia) the two most likely are Hauran, south of Damascus, and the area between Edom and northern Arabia. The former is supported by Josephus (*Antiquities* 1.145) and both Christian and Muslim traditions. On this view (favoured by F. I. Andersen, *Job*, 1976) Uz is the land settled by the son of Aram.

Many modern scholars (*e.g.* E. Dhorme, *Job*, English translation 1967) incline towards the more southerly location. Job's friends seem to have come from the vicinity of Edom, *e.g.* Eliphaz the Temanite (Job 2:11). Uz appears to have been accessible both to Sabaean bedouin from Arabia and Chaldean marauders from Mesopotamia (Job 1:15, 17).

The postscript to the Septuagint locates Uz 'in the regions of Idumaea and Arabia', but partly on the basis of a spurious identification of Job with Jobab (Genesis 36:33). Uz in Jeremiah 25:20 is coupled with Philistia, Edom, Moab and Ammon, while Lamentations 4:21 indicates that the Edomites were occupying the land of Uz. However, the Septuagint omits Uz in both of these passages, and the identity of this land of Uz with Job's is not certain.

The fact that Job is numbered with the people of the East (1:3; compare Judges 6:3, 33; Isaiah 11:14; Ezekiel 25:4, 10) seems to substantiate a location east of the great rift (Arabah) in the area where Edom and western Arabia meet.
D. A. Hubbard

**UZAL.** In Ezekiel 27:19, the AV translates 'Dan also and Javan going to and fro occupied in thy fairs' from the Hebrew *w^eḏān w^eyāwān m^e'ûzzāl b^e'izbônayiḵ nāṯānû*, which the RV margin renders 'Vedan and Javan traded from Uzal for thy wares', while the RSV reads 'and wine from Uzal they exchanged for your wares' (following the Septuagint).

Uzal may be identified with Izalla in north-eastern Syria, whence Nebuchadrezzar obtained wine (S. Langdon, *Neubabylonische Königsinschriften*, no. 9, I, line 22; compare line 23 'wine from *Ḫilbunim*' with Helbon of Ezekiel 27:18). The alteration of *w^eyāwān* to *w^eyayin*, 'and wine', is very slight.

Although *w^eḏān* may be omitted as a scribal error due to the proximity of Dedan (verse 20), it might be a cognate of the Akkadian *dannu* (and Ugaritic *dn*), 'a large jar or vat used for storing wine or beer'. This would lead to a translation, 'and vat(s) of wine from Uzal they exchanged for your wares'; compare NEB.
A. R. Millard

*Further reading*
A. R. Millard, *JSS* 7, 1962, pp. 201–203

# V

**VALLEY OF DECISION.** See *DECISION, VALLEY OF.

**VALLEY OF JEHOSHAPHAT.** See *JEHOSHAPHAT, VALLEY OF.

**VALLEY OF SALT.** See *SALT, VALLEY OF.

**VALLEY OF SHAVEH.** See *SHAVEH, VALLEY OF.

**VALLEY OF SOREK.** See *SOREK, VALLEY OF.

**VEDAN.** See *UZAL.

# W

**WELL OF SIRAH.** See *SIRAH, CISTERN OF.

**WILDERNESS.** In Scripture the words rendered 'wilderness' or 'desert' include not only the barren deserts of sand dunes or rock that colour the popular imagination of a desert, but also steppe-lands and pasture lands suitable for grazing livestock.

The commonest Hebrew word rendered thus is *miḏbār*, a word already well-attested in Canaanite epics from Ugarit (14th century BC, going back to earlier origin) as *mdbr* (Gordon, *Ugaritic Manual* 3, 1955,

p. 254, No. 458). This word can indicate grassy pastures (Psalm 65:12; Joel 2:22), supporting sheep (compare Exodus 3:1), sometimes burnt up by the summer droughts (Jeremiah 23:10; Joel 1:19–20), as well as denoting desolate wastes of rock and sand (Deuteronomy 32:10; Job 38:26). The same applies to the Greek *erēmos* in the New Testament; note that the 'desert' (AV; RSV 'lonely place') of Matthew 14:15 does not lack 'much grass' (John 6:10).

The Hebrew *y^ešîmôn*, sometimes rendered as a proper name 'Jeshimon', is used of relatively bare wildernesses in Judaea in 1 Samuel 23:19, 24 and 26:1, 3. The wilderness viewed from Pisgah (Numbers 21:20; 23:28; compare Deuteronomy 34:1ff.) would doubtless include the marly waste-lands on either side of the Jordan's channel before it entered the Dead Sea, the slopes of Pisgah and its range into the Jordan valley, and perhaps the edges of the Judaean wilderness opposite, behind Jericho and north and south of Qumran. For general references, see Deuteronomy 32:10, Psalm 107:4 and Isaiah 43:19.

Besides its use as a proper name for the long rift valley from the Dead Sea to the Gulf of Aqabah, the term *'^arāḇâ* can be used as a common noun for steppe or scrubland where wild creatures must seek out their food (Job 24:5; Jeremiah 17:6) or else of barren desert (Job 39:6 in parallel with saltflats).

The words *ṣiyyâ*, 'dry lands' (Job 30:3; Psalm 78:17) and *tōhû*, 'empty waste' (Job 6:18; 12:24; Psalm 107:40) likewise refer to barren, uninhabitable deserts.

K. A. Kitchen

## WILDERNESS OF WANDERING

### Limits

After leaving Egypt by crossing the Sea of Reeds (Exodus 14:10–15:27), and until they finally by-passed Edom and Moab to reach the Jordan (Numbers 20ff.), Israel spent long years in the intervening territory, comprising, *a*, the peninsula of Sinai flanked by the Gulfs of Suez and Aqabah and separated from the Mediterranean on the north by the dusty 'way of the land of the Philistines' that linked Egypt to Palestine, *b*, the long Arabah rift-valley extending south from the Dead Sea to the Gulf of Aqabah, and, *c*, the wilderness of Zin south of Beersheba.

### Physical features

The road from Egypt by 'the way of the land of the Philistines' to Raphia (Rafa) and Gaza, runs roughly parallel with the Mediterranean coast, passing through and along the northern fringes of a barren sandy desert – the wilderness of *Shur – which lies between the line of the modern Suez Canal and the Wadi el-'Arish (River of *Egypt), and then through cultivable land which becomes more evident between El-'Arish and Gaza (see also *NEGEB; compare A. H. Gardiner, *JEA* 6, 1920, pp. 114–115; C. S. Jarvis, *Yesterday and Today in Sinai*, 1931, p. 107).

About 30–60 kilometres south of the coast road runs the 'way of the wilderness of Shur', from Egypt to the region of Kadesh and north-east to Beersheba.

South of this road there gradually rise the hills and wadis of the limestone plateau of Et-Tih which, from a 'baseline' north of a line drawn between the heads of the Suez and Aqabah Gulfs, occupies a great semicircle projecting into the peninsula of Sinai. Across the plateau to Aqabah ran an ancient trade-route.

South of the plateau is a triangular-shaped area of granite, gneiss and other hard, crystalline rocks forming mountain ranges, which include the traditional Mount Sinai, several peaks rising to 2,000 metres. This region is separated at its north-western and north-eastern corners from the limestone plateau by sandstone hills containing deposits of copper ores and turquoise. In the east the limestone plateau of Et-Tih gives way to the jumbled rocks and wadis of the southern Negeb, bounded by the Rift Valley of the Arabah between the Dead Sea and the Gulf of Aqabah.

There are wells and springs at intervals of a day's journey all down the west coast from the Suez region to Merkhah; the water-table is generally close to the gravelly ground-surface. The wadis usually have some kind of scanty vegetation; where more permanent streams exist, notably in the broad Wadi Feiran (the finest oasis in Sinai), the vegetation flourishes accordingly. There is a 'rainy season' (up to 20 days) during winter, with mists, fogs and dews.

In the past, there has been much and persistent wholesale destruction of tamarisk and acacia groves for firewood and charcoal, there being a steady export of the latter to Egypt in the 19th century (Stanley, *Sinai and Palestine*, 1905 edition, p. 25). Thus, in ancient times the Sinai peninsula may have had more vegetation in its wadis and consequently better rains; but there has apparently been no fundamental climatic change since antiquity.

### The route of the journeyings

The precise route taken by Israel from the Sea of Reeds (between Qantara and Suez; see also *RED SEA) to the edges of Moab is still conjectural, as almost none of the names of Israelite stopping-places has survived in the late, fluid and descriptive Arabic nomenclature of the peninsula of Sinai.

Various stopping-places were named by the Israelites in relation to events that occurred on their travels, *e.g.* Kibroth-hattaavah, 'graves of craving' (Numbers 11:34), but they left no sedentary population behind to perpetuate such names. Furthermore, the traditions attaching to the present Mount *Sinai (Jebel Mûsa and environs) have not been traced back beyond the early Christian centuries; this does not of itself prove those traditions wrong, but permits of no certainty.

*Traditional route*

The traditional route ascribed to the Israelites is certainly a possible one. From the wilderness of *Shur they are usually considered to have passed southwards along the western coast-strip of the Sinai peninsula, Marah and Elim often being placed at 'Ain Hawarah and Wadi Gharandel respectively.

That the camp after Elim (Exodus 16:1) is 'by the *yam sûp̄*' (Hebrew of Numbers 33:10), *i.e.* the Sea of Reeds, or here by extension the Gulf of Suez (see also *RED SEA), indicates clearly that Israel had kept to the western side of the Sinai peninsula and not gone northwards (the way of the Philistines). The Gulf of Aqabah is too far away to be the *yam sûp̄* in this passage.

Somewhat later, Israel encamped at Dophkah. This name is sometimes considered to mean 'smeltery' (G. E. Wright, *Biblical Archaeology*, 1957, p. 64; Wright and Filson, *Westminster Historical Atlas of the Bible*, 1957 edition, p. 39) and so to be located at the Egyptian mining centre of Serabit el-Khadim. For copper and especially turquoise mining in that area, see Lucas, *Ancient Egyptian Materials and Industries*, 1962, pp. 202–205, 404–405; J. Černý, A. H. Gardiner and T. E. Peet, *Inscriptions of Sinai* 2, 1955, pp. 5–8.

As Egyptian expeditions visited this region only during January to March (rarely later), and did not live

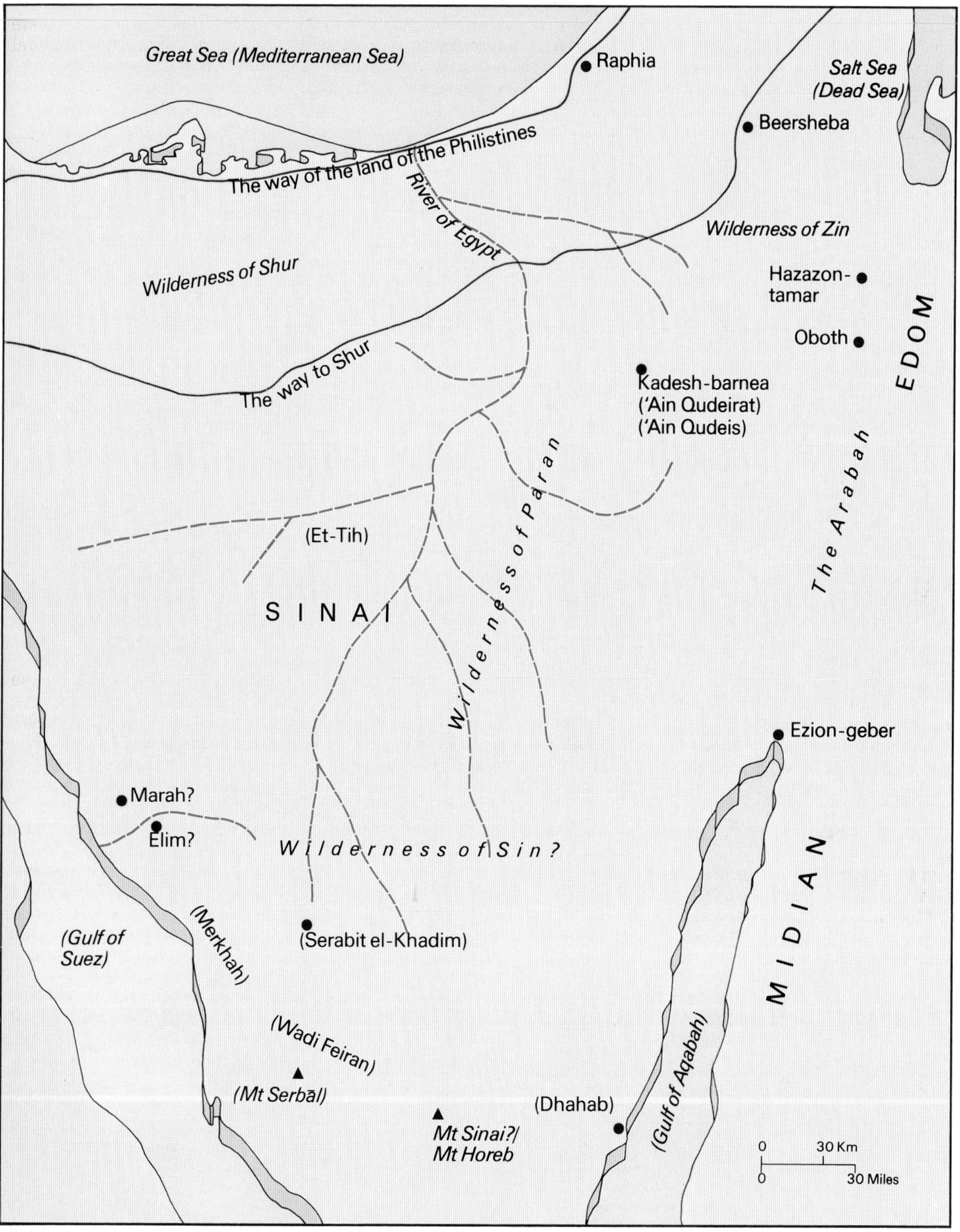


The 'wilderness' or desert through which Israel wandered during the Exodus.

permanently at the mines (see Petrie, *Researches in Sinai*, 1906, p. 169), the Israelites would not meet them there, as they left Egypt in the month Abib (Exodus 13:4), *i.e.* about March, and left Elim a month later (Exodus 16:1), *i.e.* about April. However, Dophkah could be any copper-mining spot in the metalliferous sandstone belt across southern central Sinai (which favours a southern route for Israel in any case).

Rephidim is sometimes identified with Wadi Feiran, sometimes with Wadi Refayid, and Mount Sinai with the summits of Jebel Mûsa (or, less likely, Mount Serbal near Feiran). See the works of Robinson, Lepsius, Stanley and Palmer (*Further reading*, below).

Beyond Mount Sinai, Dhahab on the east coast might be Di-zahab (Deuteronomy 1:1; so Y. Aharoni, *Antiquity and Survival* 2. 2/3, 1957, pp. 289–290, figure 7); if so, Huderah on a different road is less likely to be the Hazeroth of Numbers 11:35 and 33:17–18.

The next fixed points are Kadesh-barnea (see also *KADESH) on the borders of the wilderness(es) of Zin and Paran (Numbers 12:16; 13:26) at 'Ain Qudeirat or 'Ain Qudeis and the surrounding region, including 'Ain Qudeirat, and Ezion-geber at the head of the Gulf of Aqabah (Numbers 33:35f.).

*Korah, Dathan and Abiram*
For the phenomenon of the earth swallowing up Korah, Dathan and Abiram (Numbers 16), a most interesting explanation was offered by G. Hort in *Australian Biblical Review* 7, 1959, pp. 2–26, especially 19–26. She would locate this incident in the Arabah Rift Valley between the Dead Sea and the Gulf of Aqabah. Here are to be found mudflats known as *kewirs*. A hard crust of clayey mud overlying layers of hard salt and half-dry mud, about 30 centimetres thick, eventually forms over the deep mass of liquid mud and ooze. When this crust is hard it may be walked on with impunity, but increased humidity (especially rainstorms) will break up the crust and turn the whole into gluey mud.

Dathan, Abiram and Korah's adherents withdrew from the main camp probably to one of these deceptively level, hard mudflats. From his long years of experience in Sinai and Midian (Exodus 2–4), Moses had probably learnt of this phenomenon, but not so the Israelites. When a storm approached he saw the danger and called the Israelites away from the tents of the rebels. The crust broke up and the rebels, their families and their possessions were all swallowed up in the mud. Then the storm broke, and the 250 men with censers were struck by lightning – smitten down by the fire of the Lord.

Miss Hort thought that this incident occurred at Kadesh-barnea, and therefore that Kadesh should be located in the Arabah. But there are possible reasons for locating *Kadesh in the region of 'Ain Qudeis and 'Ain Qudeirat, and in fact Numbers 16 does *not* state that the revolt(s) of Korah, Dathan and Abiram occurred at Kadesh.

It should be noted that it is the whole, unitary account of the twin rebellions in Numbers 16 and their awesome end that alone makes sense and fits the physical phenomena in question; the supposed sources obtained by conventional documentary literary analyses severally yield fragmentary pictures that correspond to no known realities.

*The route past Edom*
The long list of names in Numbers 33:19–35 falls into the 38 years of wandering, and cannot be located at present. The precise route past Edom (Numbers 20:22ff.; 21; 33:38–44) is also obscure. Some of the incidents in these long journeys reflect the natural phenomena of the area. The repeated phenomenon of water coming from the smitten rock (Exodus 17:1–7; Numbers 20:2–13) reflects the water-holding properties of Sinai limestone: an army NCO once produced quite a good flow of water when he accidentally hit such a rock face with a spade! (See Jarvis, *Yesterday and Today in Sinai,* 1931, pp. 174–175.)

The digging of wells as recorded in Numbers 21:16–18 (compare Genesis 26:19) reflects the known occurrence of sub-surface water in various regions of Sinai, the Negeb and southern Transjordan (see references above, and N. Glueck, *Rivers in the Desert*, 1959, p. 22).

*Quail*
The references to the catching of quail (Exodus 16:13; Numbers 11:31–35) have been interpreted by some as requiring a northern route for the Exodus along the Mediterranean (*e.g.* Jarvis, *op. cit.*, pp. 169–170; compare J. Bright, *A History of Israel*, 1960, p. 114, after J. Gray in *VT* 4, 1954, pp. 148–154; G. E. Wright, *Biblical Archaeology*, 1957, p. 65). But that route was explicitly forbidden to Israel (Exodus 13:17f.), and in any case the quails land on the Mediterranean coast of Sinai (from Europe) only in the *autumn* and at dawn, whereas Israel found them in the *spring* in the evening, in or following Abib, *i.e.* March (Exodus 16:13), and a year and a month later (Numbers 10:11; 11:31).

These two points exclude the Mediterranean coast from Israel's route on these two occasions, and directly favour the southern route by the Gulfs of Suez and Aqabah *via* 'Mount Sinai'. The quails return to Europe in the spring – the season when Israel twice had them – across the upper ends of the Gulfs of Suez and Aqabah, and in the evening (Lucas, *The Route of the Exodus*, 1938, pp. 58–63 and references, and p. 81, overstressing Aqabah at the expense of Suez).

*An alternative route*
A minority view would make Israel cross the Sinai peninsula more directly to the head of the Gulf of Aqabah and locate Mount Sinai in Midian. Among the best advocates of such a view is Lucas (*The Route of the Exodus*, 1938) who does not invoke non-existent active volcanoes as some have done. However, this view is no freer of topographical difficulties than any other, and fails entirely to account for the origin of the traditions of the Christian period that attached themselves to the peninsula now called Sinai and not to Midian or north-western Arabia.

For a good comparative table of the data on the route and stopping-places on Israel's wanderings in Exodus–Numbers, Numbers 33 and Deuteronomy, see J. D. Davies and H. S. Gehman, *Westminster Dictionary of the Bible*, pp. 638–639; for the literary background, see G. I. Davies in *TynB* 25, 1974, pp. 46–81; for Bronze Age sites in Sinai, see T. L. Thompson, *The Settlement of Sinai and the Negev in the Bronze Age*, 1975.

**The numbers of the Israelites**
When Israel left Egypt there went '600,000 men on foot' besides their families and the mixed multitude, while from a census of the men from the tribes other than Levi held at Sinai comes the total of 603,550 men over 20 who could bear arms (Numbers 2:32). These figures are commonly held to imply a total number of Israelites – men, women and children – of somewhat more than two million.

That the slender resources of Sinai were of themselves insufficient to support such a multitude is indicated by the Bible itself (as well as suggested by exploration) in that Israel's chief sustenance came from God-given manna (Exodus 16; compare verses 3–4, 35).

Israel never went wholly without (Deuteronomy 2:7), although the water-supply sometimes nearly failed them (*e.g.* at Rephidim, Exodus 17:1, and Kadesh, Numbers 20:2). In any case, they would soon learn to subsist on very little water per head indeed, as illustrated by Robinson's guide in Sinai, who was able to go without water for a fortnight by living on camel's milk, while sheep and goats as well as camels can sometimes go without water for 3–4 months if they have had fresh pasture (E. Robinson, *Biblical Researches* 1, 1841 edition, p. 221).

Furthermore, it is wholly misleading to imagine the Israelites marching in long 'columns of four' up and down Sinai, or trying to encamp all together *en masse* in some little wadi at each stop. They would be spread out in their tribal and family groups, occupying a variety of neighbouring wadis for all their scattered encampments; after they left Sinai with the ark and tabernacle (as baggage when on the move), the sites where these were successively lodged would be the focus of the various tribal camps, as in Numbers 2.

In various parts of Sinai the water-table is near the ground-surface; the scattered Israelite encampments would thus often get the little they needed by digging small pits over an area. See Robinson, *Biblical Researches* 1, 1841, pp. 100 (general observations), 129; Lepsius, *Letters, etc.*, 1853, p. 306; Currelly in Petrie, *Researches in Sinai*, 1906, p. 249; Lucas, *The Route of the Exodus*, 1938, p. 68.

*Census-lists*

There have been many attempts down the years to interpret the census-lists in Numbers 1 and 26 and related figures in Exodus 12:37 and 38:24–29, besides the levitical reckoning (Numbers 4:21–49) and other figures (*e.g.* Numbers 16:49), in order to gain from the Hebrew text a more modest total for the number of the people of Israel involved in the Exodus from Egypt through Sinai to Palestine.

For recent attempts, see R. E. D. Clark in *JTVI* 87, 1955, pp. 82–92 (taking *'lp* as 'officer' instead of '1,000' in many cases); G. E. Mendenhall in *JBL* 77, 1958, pp. 52–66 (taking *'lp* as a tribal sub-unit instead of '1,000'), who refers to earlier treatments; and J. W. Wenham, *TynB* 18, 1967, pp. 19–53, especially 27ff., 35ff.

While none of these attempts accounts for all the figures involved, they indicate several possible clues to a better understanding of various apparently high figures in the Old Testament. The fact is that these records must rest on some basis of ancient reality; the apparently high figures are beyond absolute disproof, while no alternative interpretation has yet adequately accounted for all the data involved.

**Later significance**

Theologically, the wilderness period became the dual symbol of God's leading and providing and of man's rebellious nature typified by the Israelites (see, *e.g.*, Deuteronomy 8:15–16 and 9:7; Amos 2:10 and 5:25 [compare Acts 7:40–44]; Hosea 13:5–6; Jeremiah 2:6; Ezekiel 20:10–26, 36; Psalms 78:14–41, 95:8–11 [compare Hebrews 3:7–19] and 136:16; Nehemiah 9:18–22; Acts 13:18; 1 Corinthians 10:3–5).

K. A. Kitchen

*Further reading*

E. Robinson, *Biblical Researches in Palestine, Mount Sinai and Arabia Petraea* 1, 1841 edition, pp. 98–100, 129, 131, 179
C. R. Lepsius, *Letters from Egypt, Ethiopia and the Peninsula of Sinai*, 1853, pp. 306–307
A. P. Stanley, *Sinai and Palestine*, 1905 edition, pp. 16–19, 22, 24–27
E. H. Palmer, *The Desert of the Exodus* 1, 1871, pp. 22–26
W. M. F. Petrie and C. T. Currelly, *Researches in Sinai*, 1906, pp. 12, 30, 247–250, 254–256 (Feiran), 269
C. L. Woolley and T. E. Lawrence, *Palestine Exploration Fund Annual* 3, 1915, p. 33
C. S. Jarvis, *Yesterday and Today in Sinai*, 1931, p. 99
A. E. Lucas, *The Route of the Exodus*, 1938, pp. 19, 44–45, 68
W. F. Albright, *BASOR* 109, 1948, p. 11 (El-'Arish rains; scrub vegetation in the north)
G. I. Davies, *The Way of the Wilderness: A Geographical Study of the Wilderness Itineraries in the Old Testament*, 1979
——, 'The Wilderness Itineraries and Recent Archaeological Research', in J. A. Emerton (ed.), *Studies in the Pentateuch* (*VT Supp.* XLI), 1990, pp. 161–175
For Sinai scenery, see:
G. E. Wright, *Biblical Archaeology*, 1957, pp. 62–64, figures 33–35
L. H. Grollenberg, *Shorter Atlas of the Bible*, 1959, pp. 76–77
Petrie, *Researches in Sinai*, 1906, *passim*
B. Rothenberg, *God's Wilderness*, 1961, *passim*
On the southern route, and conspectus of identification of Mount Sinai, see:
I. Beit-Arieh, *BARev* 14/3, 1988, pp. 28–37

# Z

**ZAANAN.** A place mentioned in Micah 1:11, in a passage which vividly foretells the consequences of an enemy invasion. It is probably identical with Zenan in the Shephelah of Judah listed in Joshua 15:37. Its identification with 'Arâq el-Kharba, west of Lachish, has been suggested but there is no agreement on the matter.

As with other towns in the list of Micah 1:10–15, the name is used as the basis for a word-play. As the name Zaanan sounds like the Hebrew for 'get out', the line could be roughly rendered: 'There will be no way out for Exit-town [*i.e.* Zaanan]'.

J. D. Douglas, J. Bimson

**ZAANANNIM** (Hebrew *ṣa'ᵃnannîm*). On the southern border of Naphtali, near *Kedesh and west of *Adami-nekeb (Joshua 19:33); Heber the Kenite camped there (Judges 4:11; the AV, following the the Massoretic Text *kᵉṯîḇ*, translates as 'Zaanaim'). The complete place-name may have been Elon-in-Zaanannim but most English versions translate this as 'the oak [or large tree] in Zaanannim' (compare RSV, NIV).

Khan et-Tuggar, 4 kilometres north-north-east of Mount Tabor, is the most likely site, and preserves the Arabic equivalent of the name ('traveller').

At Judges 4:11 Abel and Simons prefer Khan Leggun, between Tell abu Qudeis and Megiddo; but this involves distinguishing it from the place named in Joshua 19. It is more probable that Sisera escaped away from the flooded Kishon; and if he was deliberately seeking sanctuary with friends (Judges 4:17), there is no point in looking for Zaanannim nearer to his home-city. (See also *KEDESH.)

J. P. U. Lilley

*Further reading*

J. A. Soggin, *Judges*, 1981, p. 75
R. G. Boling, *Joshua* (Anchor), 1982, p. 458

**ZAIR.** 2 Kings 8:21 records that King Joram passed over to Zair to crush a revolt of the Edomites, hence its probable location was on the border of Edom. Some manuscripts of the Septuagint read here Z(e)ior, and Zair may possibly be identical with *Zior, listed in Joshua 15:54, in the Judaean hill-country. On the other hand, a location for Zair somewhere south-east of the Dead Sea seems more probable.

R. A. H. Gunner, J. Bimson

**ZALMON. 1.** The name of a mountain in the vicinity of the tower of Shechem (Judges 9:48). Its identification is far from certain; both Gerizim and Ebal have been suggested.

**2.** Another mountain, mentioned in Psalm 68:14 (spelt Salmon in the AV). Some have equated it with **1**, but

this mountain would appear to have been to the east of the Jordan and is usually identified with Jebel Ḥaurân.
D. F. Payne

**ZANOAH** (Hebrew *zānôaḥ*). **1.** A town in the Shephelah (Joshua 15:34; Nehemiah 3:13; 11:30); it is Khirbet Zanu' (Hurvat Zanoah), 4 kilometres south-east of Beth-shemesh.

**2.** A town in the hills near *Juttah (Joshua 15:56; 1 Chronicles 4:18); it may be Khirbet Beit Amra, 11 kilometres south-south-east of Hebron, overlooking the Nahal Hevron, part of which is called Wadi abu Zenah (J. Simons, *GTT*, p. 150; Abel, *Géographie* 2, p. 489).

Rudolph, in his *Chronicles* (commenting on 1 Chronicles 4:18), suggested Khirbet Zanuta, but no pre-Roman settlement has been found. Noth, in *Josua* (commenting on 15:56), emended to 'Zanoah of Kain' (Khirbet Yaqin), as the Septuagint runs the names together; but the readings are doubtful.
J. P. U. Lilley

**ZAPHON. 1.** A town referred to in Joshua 13:27 and Judges 12:1, lying in Gadite territory in the Jordan valley. The Jerusalem Talmud identifies it with the Amathus of Josephus, which is to be located at Tell 'Ammatah; but this is improbable. Other proposed locations for Zaphon are Tell al-Sa'idiya and Tell al-Qos.

**2.** A mountain (modern Jebel el-Aqra') near the mouth of the River Orontes in northern Syria. As the word *ṣāpôn* is generally used to mean 'north' in the Old Testament, it is not always easy to decide when the mountain is being referred to. There is very probably a reference in Psalm 48:2 (NIV, NEB margin) and possibly another in Psalm 89:12 (NEB); some scholars also think the mountain is intended in Job 26:7 and Isaiah 14:13.

In Canaanite mythology Mount Zaphon was the sacred mountain of the god Baal and believed to be the site of his palace. Psalm 48:2 may therefore be scoring a theological point by comparing Mount Zion favourably with Mount Zaphon (thus the NIV: 'Like the utmost heights of Zaphon is Mount Zion, the city of the Great King'). (R. Clifford, *The Cosmic Mountain in Canaan and the Old Testament*, 1972.)
D. F. Payne

**ZAREPHATH** ('smelting place'); Akkadian *ṣariptu*; compare *ṣarāpu*, 'to refine (metals), to fire (bricks)'. A small Phoenician town (modern Sarafand), originally belonging to *Sidon, it appears in the late-13th-century Papyrus Anastasi I (*ANET*, 3rd edition, p. 477). It was captured by Sennacherib in 701 BC (Zarebtu, *ANET*, 3rd edition, p. 287) and by Esarhaddon, *c.* 680–669 BC, who gave it to Ba'ali, king of Tyre (see J. B. Pritchard, 'Sarepta in History and Tradition', in J. Reumann (ed.), *Understanding the Sacred Text*, 1971, pp. 101–114).

Situated about 13 kilometres south of Sidon on the Lebanese coast on the road to *Tyre, it is mentioned in 1 Kings 17:9ff. as the place to which Elijah went during the drought in Ahab's reign and where he restored life to the son of the widow with whom he lodged. Luke 4:26 refers to this incident, the town there being called by the Greek and Latin name, Sarepta.

Obadiah prophesied that in the Day of the Lord those of the children of Israel who were deported by Sargon after the fall of Samaria should possess Phoenicia as far as Zarephath.
R. A. H. Gunner

*Further reading*
For excavations begun in 1969, see: *AJA* 74, 1970, p. 202; 76, 1972, p. 216
*Archaeology* 24, 1971, pp. 61–63
J. Pritchard, *Sarepta*, 1975

**ZARETAN, ZARETHAN.** This town is spelt variously Zaretan, Zartanah and Zarthan in the AV; and the name appears as Zeredah (AV Zeredathah) in 2 Chronicles 4:17.

Zarethan is mentioned in connection with Bethshean, Adam and Succoth, and lay in the Jordan valley, near a ford over the river (Joshua 3:16; 1 Kings 4:12). Its exact site has been debated, but it almost certainly lay west of the Jordan.

One suggested location, Qarn Sartaba, perhaps recalls the name Zarethan; but most authorities prefer Tell al-Sa'idiya. (Excavated by J. B. Pritchard, 1964–67; see *Expedition* 6–11, 1964–1968.) However, this is too far (17 kilometres) north of Tell ed-Damiya (Adam) to explain the phrase 'Adam . . . that is beside Zarethan' (Joshua 3:16). Tell Umm Ḥamâd is another possibility.
D. F. Payne, J. Bimson

**ZARTANA.** See *ZARETAN.

**ZARTHAN.** See *ZARETAN.

**ZEBOIIM** (NEB **ZEBOYIM**). One of the cities of the *plain (Genesis 14:2) eventually destroyed with *Sodom and Gomorrah (Deuteronomy 29:23). Its location seems to have been in the vicinity of *Admah.
D. F. Payne

**ZEBOIM. 1.** A valley near Michmash in Benjaminite territory (1 Samuel 13:18), modern Wadi Abu Daba'. The Hebrew phrase means 'ravine of hyenas' (*gê ṣ$^{e}$ḇō'îm*).

**2.** A Benjaminite town of post-exilic times, near Lydda (Nehemiah 11:34). Khirbet Sabiyah has been suggested as the site.
D. F. Payne

**ZEBOYIM.** See *ZEBOIIM.

**ZEBULUN.** The tenth son of Jacob and the sixth son of Leah (Genesis 30:19f.). The original form of the name may have been Zebulon or Zebul, the name of Abimelech's lieutenant (Judges 9:26–41).

*Extent*
Zebulun was able to possess more of its allotted territory than most of the tribes, possibly because it comprised largely virgin country, with no great cities (Joshua 19:10–16). Kitron (perhaps the Kattath of Joshua 19:15) and Nahalol are mentioned as incompletely conquered (Judges 1:30).

Generally speaking, Zebulun occupied a broad wedge in southern Galilee between Asher and Naphtali with Manasseh to the south-west and Issachar to the south-east. The southern boundary was probably the river Kishon in the Valley of Esdraelon, which gave Zebulun, like Issachar, control over the trade routes.

The Blessing of Jacob (Genesis 49:13) promises Zebulun access to the sea, although it is not clear whether Galilee or the Mediterranean is meant. In either case this was never realized, but the reference may be to the strategic commercial position shared with Issachar (see Deuteronomy 33:18f.). These tribes also shared the same holy mountain (Deuteronomy 33:19), probably Tabor (see Judges 4:6), on the fringe of Zebulun's territory.

Although one of the smaller tribal areas, Zebulun was fertile, being exposed to the rain-bearing westerly winds. With 57,400 and 60,500 warriors respectively in the two census lists (Numbers 1:31; 26:27), it was the fourth largest tribe.

*History*
In the great covenant-renewal ceremony at Shechem, Zebulun was assigned an inferior place with Reuben and the 'handmaiden' tribes

The Wilderness of Zin, near Sde Boker.

(Deuteronomy 27:13). But in the Judges period it distinguished itself in the conflicts against the Canaanites and Midianites (Judges 4:6, 10; 5:14, 18; 6:35). One of the minor judges, Elon, came from Zebulun (Judges 12:11). When David became king over a united Israel, considerable initial military and economic support was supplied (1 Chronicles 12:33, 40). The prophet Jonah was a Zebulunite from Gath-hepher (2 Kings 14:25; compare Joshua 19:18).

Zebulun suffered severely in the Assyrian invasion of 733/32 BC under Tiglath-pileser (2 Kings 15:29; compare Isaiah 9:1), many of its inhabitants were deported and its territory was assimilated into the Assyrian empire. However, its tribal identity survived, and its inhabitants are included among the participants in Hezekiah's Passover (2 Chronicles 30:10–22).

In the New Testament, apart from the quotation in Matthew 4:13–16, Zebulun is mentioned only in Revelation 7:8, but Nazareth, where Jesus spent his early years, was within its traditional borders.

A. E. Cundall

*Further reading*

*LOB*, pp. 248, 257, 304, 315

**ZEDAD.** One of the sites on the northern border of the promised land (Numbers 34:8), mentioned also in Ezekiel's vision of the limits of restored Israel (Ezekiel 47:15). There are two main candidates for identification with it, corresponding to the two views that are taken about the line of the northern border described in these texts as a whole.

The dominant view (*e.g.* Aharoni) sees the name as preserved at Ṣadad, *c.* 110 kilometres east-north-east of Byblos; this accords well with the preferred location for the 'entrance of *Hamath', the adjacent point on the boundary.

A minority of scholars advocate a more southerly position, at Khirbet Ṣerādā, a few miles north of Dan, reading the name as Zerad, with the Septuagint and the Samaritan text.

R. A. H. Gunner, G. I. Davies

*Further reading*

G. B. Gray, *Numbers*, 1903, p. 459

G. A. Cooke, *Ezekiel* (ICC), 1936, p. 527

*LOB,* pp. 65–67

**ZELZAH.** After Samuel had anointed Saul 'prince over his people Israel' (1 Samuel 10:1), one of the signs given to Saul was that he would meet 'two men by Rachel's tomb . . . at Zelzah' (1 Samuel 10:2). The Septuagint translates Zelzah by 'leaping furiously' (from *ṣōl$^{e}$ḥîm*), and the Vulgate 'in the south'. The village Beit Jala between Bethel and Bethlehem, to the west, may be the location.

R. A. H. Gunner

**ZEMARAIM. 1.** A Benjaminite town, listed with Beth-arabah and Bethel (Joshua 18:22). Proposed locations are Khirbet al-Samra, Ras al-Zaimara and Ras al-Tâḥûna (*LOB*, p. 385).

**2.** A mountain in the hill country of Ephraim (2 Chronicles 13:4). Bethel was presumably in the same general locality (compare verse 19), so probably the mountain was near to, and named after, the town Zemaraim.

D. F. Payne

**ZENAN.** See *Zaanan.

**ZEPHATHAH** (Hebrew *ṣ$^{e}$p̄aṯâh*). 'In the valley of Zephathah at (*l$^{e}$*) Mareshah' (2 Chronicles 14:10; verse 9, Massoretic Text). The Septuagint apparently read *baggai missapon* ('in the valley to the north') for *b$^{e}$gê' ṣ$^{e}$p̄aṯâh*. Complex re-entrants in gently-sloping country lie north and south of *Mareshah.

However, if Zephathah is to be understood as the name of a specific locality, it should probably be identified with the Wadi es-Safiyeh.

J. P. U. Lilley, J. Bimson

**ZER.** A fortified city in the territory of Naphtali (Joshua 19:35). No satisfactory location has been suggested but it is not necessary to adopt the Septuagint reading *Tyros, i.e.* Tyre, which presupposes a Hebrew reading *ṣōr* instead of the Massoretic Text *ṣēr.*

J. D. Douglas

**ZERAD.** See *Zedad.

**ZERED,** a mountain-torrent (Hebrew *nahal*) or wadi crossed by the Israelites on their journey round the frontiers of Edom and Moab (Numbers 21:12; Deuteronomy 2:13f.). In Numbers it is mentioned as a camping-ground, which accords with the order to 'rise up' in Deuteronomy 2:13.

Its identification is disputed; probably it is modern Wadi el-Hesâ, which runs into the Dead Sea from the south-east. The comments which follow in Deuteronomy 2:14ff. show that its crossing was regarded as an important stage in the journey.

G. T. Manley

**ZEREDAH.** See *Zarethan.

**ZEREDATHAH.** See *Zarethan.

**ZIDON.** See *Sidon.

**ZIKLAG.** Ziklag appears in Joshua 15:31 as being in the Negeb, near the southern border of Judah. It was apportioned to the Simeonites, but later fell into Philistine hands. David, when a Philistine vassal, ruled it and was later able to retain and incorporate it in his own realm (1 Samuel 27:6; 30:1–26; 2 Samuel 1:1–9). It remained in the hands of Judah in both pre-exilic and post-exilic times (Nehemiah 11:28).

At least four locations have been proposed, of which Tell al-Shari'a (Tel Sera'), *c.* 25 kilometres south-east of Gaza, seems the most probable. Excavations directed by E. D. Oren have revealed evidence of occupation from the Chalcolithic to the Islamic periods, including strata from the appropriate times to equate the site with biblical Ziklag. (E. D. Oren. 'Tel Sera', *NEAEHL* IV, pp. 1329–1335.)

D. F. Payne, J. Bimson

**ZIN** (Hebrew *ṣin*). A name loosely applied to the Wilderness of Zin traversed by the Israelites in the Exodus, close to the borders of Canaan (Numbers 13:21). It refers to the extensive area between the camping-place of the Israelites at the oasis of *Kadesh-barnea in north-eastern Sinai, to the Ascent of Aqrabbim or Scorpion Pass constituting the limit between Edom and Judah (Joshua 15:1–4; compare Numbers 34:1–5). The wilderness of Paran lay to the south of it, though Kadesh appears to have been included in both territories, and the two wildernesses occur within the broader term *'Negeb'.

J. M. Houston

*Further reading*

C. L. Woolley and T. E. Lawrence, *The Wilderness of Zin*, 1936

**ZIOR.** A city listed in Joshua 15:54 in the Judaean hill-country north-east of Hebron and allocated to the tribe of Judah; modern Si'ir (see also *Zair). A suitable location has yet to be proposed; modern Sair lies too far to the north.

J. D. Douglas

**ZIPH. 1.** A town in southern Judah, near the Edomite boundary (Joshua 15:24), perhaps to be located at Khirbet ez-Zeifeh, south-west of Kurnub.

**2.** A town in the hill-country of Judah (Joshua 15:55), associated with David and with Rehoboam, who fortified it. It is commonly identified with Tell Zif, 7 kilometres south-east of Hebron, but this view is yet to be tested by excavations.

Ziph is named on royal jar-handle stamps found at *Lachish and other sites, which probably points to its importance as a major Judaean administrative centre in the reign of Hezekiah. The adjoining area was known as the Wilderness of Ziph.

D. F. Payne

**ZIZ.** The name of an ascent used by the Moabites and Ammonites in a campaign against Jehoshaphat of Judah (2 Chronicles 20:16). Their army lay previously at Engedi, on the western shore of the Dead Sea; and they reached the wilderness of Tekoa. These details make the Wadi Hasasa, just north of Engedi, a virtually certain identification.

D. F. Payne

**ZOAN.** Ancient city, Egyptian *ḏ'n*(*t*) to which the Hebrew *ṣō'an* exactly corresponds. The Greek Tanis and the modern site of Ṣan el-Ḥagar near the southern shore of Lake Menzaleh in the north-eastern Delta. The curious note in Numbers 13:22 that Hebron was built 7 years before Zoan in Egypt may indicate a refounding of Zoan in the Middle Kingdom (*c.* 2000–1800 BC) or at some later date which cannot be established at present (see *Hebron).

Psalm 78:12 and 43 places the Exodus miracles in 'the field of Zoan', precisely the Egyptian *sḫt ḏ'*(*nt*), 'field of Dja'(ne)', a term apparently applied to the region near Zoan; Zoan and Ra'amses are not to be identified.

From 1100 BC until about 660 BC, Zoan was the effective capital of Egypt in the 21st–23rd Dynasties, and the northern base of the Ethiopian 25th Dynasty. Hence the prominence of Zoan as the seat of pharaoh's counsellors and princes (Isaiah 19:11, 13; 30:4) and among Egypt's great cities in Ezekiel's (30:14) word of judgment.

K. A. Kitchen

*Further reading*

On Zoan/Tanis, see:

A. H. Gardiner, *Ancient Egyptian Onomastica* 2, 1947, pp. 199*–201*

P. Montet, *Les Énigmes de Tanis*, 1952

H. Kees, *Tanis,* 1964

H. Coutts (ed.), *Gold of the Pharaohs*, 1988, pp. 10–27

**ZOAR.** See *Plain, Cities of the.

**ZOBAH.** An Aramaean kingdom which flourished during the early Hebrew Monarchy, and which took the field against Saul and David. One of its kings was Hadadezer (2 Samuel 8:3). It lay between Hamath, to its north, and Damascus to its south, and at its height its influence reached these cities.

It is unnecessary to postulate two Zobahs, one of them south of Damascus, merely because it is listed with Beth-rehob and Maacah in 2 Samuel 10:6 (both south of Damascus).

D. F. Payne

*Further reading*

B. Mazar, 'The Aramaean Empire and Its Relations with Israel', *BA* 25, 1962, pp. 98–120

J. Bright, *A History of Israel*, 3rd edition, 1980, pp. 200–205

**ZOHELETH, STONE OF.** See *Serpent's Stone.

**ZOPHIM.** This place-name comes from the Hebrew *ṣōp̄îm*, 'watchers'. The location of 'the field of the watchers' (Numbers 23:14, AV) is difficult to determine. It must have been on a high part of the Pisgah Mountains, from which Balaam could see the encampment of the Israelites at Shittim.

Some propose to take the Hebrew *śāḏeh* here in the meaning of the Akkadian *šādû*, 'mountain' ('the mountain of the watchers'). The word 'watcher' is sometimes used in the sense of prophet (see Isaiah 52:8; 56:10) and is thus especially applicable to Balaam (compare Ramathaim-zophim; Ramah, 1 Samuel 1:1).

F. C. Fensham

**ZORAH.** A town in the lowlands of Judah (Joshua 15:33), closely connected with the Samson stories (Judges 13:2, 25; 16:31). Its site is Ṣar'a, on the northern side of the Wadi al-Ṣarar, the biblical valley of Sorek. The Amarna letters refer to it as Zarkha.

Zorah was fortified by Rehoboam (2 Chronicles 11:10) and reoccupied after the Babylonian Exile (Nehemiah 11:29). The references to Hebron and Beersheba in these two passages, however, may suggest that there was another similarly named city a considerable distance south of Samson's territory. (See *LOB*, pp. 272, 443.)

D. F. Payne

# INDEX

Figures in *italics* indicate that an illustration appears on that page.

If a placename does not appear in this index, it may nevertheless be included in the list on pages 7–13.

# PHOTOGRAPHIC ACKNOWLEDGEMENTS

Barnabys: p. 245
Bible Scene (Maurice S. Thompson): pp. 21, 113, 123, 260, 313
British Museum: p. 193
R. Harding: p. 223
F. N. Hepper: pp. 29, 41
J. P. Kane: pp. 76, 89, 164
K. A. Kitchen: p. 111
A. R. Millard: pp. 37, 93
A. M. Morris: p. 57 (bottom)
A. Parrot: p. 46
R. Pitt: p. 100
R. Sheridan: p. 256
J. Simson: pp. 17, 39, 304
Three's Company/Tiger Colour Library: pp. 2–3, 7, 8, 9, 11, 12, 15, 43, 49, 50, 51, 61, 65, 67, 68, 69, 72, 74, 75, 78, 79, 83, 84, 98, 108–109, 110, 117, 128, 131, 135, 139, 151, 153, 159, 166, 169, 171, 175, 176, 177, 179, 189, 195, 199, 201, 206, 207, 209, 213, 217, 224, 226, 232, 238, 239, 243, 255, 257, 259, 268, 269, 270, 271, 273, 277, 295, 299
D. J. Wiseman: pp. 53, 57 (top), 96

**Relief maps** © Copyright George Philip and Son Ltd and Inter-Varsity Press
These maps appear on pp. 16, 17, 29, 40, 45, 47, 77, 80, 81, 88, 90, 94, 99, 100, 106, 125, 137, 140, 157, 165, 178, 180, 181, 183, 194, 196, 214, 236, 237, 238, 239, 240, 241, 242, 249, 251, 283, 289, 290

**Diagrams, charts and town plans**
The publishers are glad to acknowledge their indebtedness to a variety of sources as indicated below. 'After' indicates that the material remains essentially as it appears in the source acknowledged but has been redrawn. 'Based on' means that the substance of the source material has been retained but reinterpreted.

**Alexandria,** p. 23
After H. T. Davis, *Alexandria the Golden City* (Principia Press, 1957), vol. 1, p. 5.
**Amarna,** p. 24
After H. Frankfort and J. D. S. Pendlebury, *The City of Akhenaton* (OUP, 1933), pl. 1.
**Antioch,** p. 27
After *ACA*, p. 222.
**Arad,** p. 32
After *EAEHL*, vol. 1, pp. 75, 77 and 83.
**Babel,** p. 53
After Sir Leonard Woolley, *Ur Excavations,* vol. 5, *The Ziggurat and its surroundings* (Philadelphia, 1939), p. 86.
**Beersheba,** p. 64
After Y. Aharoni, 'Tel-Aviv 2 (1975), The Beersheba Excavations' in *Journal of Tel-Aviv University Institute of Archaeology*, p., 148.
**Bethshean,** p. 71
After *EAEHL*, vol. 1, pp. 209, 212.
**Caesarea,** p. 76
After *EAEHL*, vol. 1, p. 270.
**Calvary,** p. 78
After K. M. Kenyon, *Digging up Jerusalem* (Ernest Benn, 1974), p. 233.
**Capernaum,** p. 85
Based on V. Corbo, *Studia Hiersolymitana* (Franciscan Press, Jerusalem, 1976), vol. 1, p. 161, fig. 1.
**Carchemish,** p. 87
After C. L. Woolley, *Carchemish 1921–52* (British Museum), vol. 2, pl. 3 and vol. 3, pl. 41a.
**Corinth,** p. 92
After *ACA*, p. 155.
**Karnak,** p. 112
After A. A. M. van der Heyden, in A. R. David, *The Egyptian Kingdoms* (Elsevier, 1975), p. 22.
**Ephesus,** p. 129
After *ACA*, p. 212.
**Gezer,** p. 143
After K. M. Kenyon, *The Bible and Recent Archaeology* (Colonnade, 1978), p. 6.
**Gibeon,** p. 145
After *EAEHL*, vol. 2, p. 449.
**Jericho,** p. 167
Based on E. Netzer, *IEJ* 25, 1975, p. 98.
**Jerusalem,** pp. 168, 169, 170
Based on Walter de Gruyter (ed.), *Atlas of Jerusalem*, Maps 3:1, 3:2 and 3:6 (Jewish History Publications, 1973).
**Water system,** p. 170
Based on W. G. Dever and S. M. Paul, *Biblical Archaeology* (Keter Publishing House, Jerusalem, 1973), p. 132, fig. b.
**Jerusalem,** p. 172
After *EAEHL*, vol. 2, p. 598.
**Jerusalem,** p. 173
Based on Y. Yadin (ed.), *Jerusalem Revealed* (The Israel Exploration Society and Yale University Press, 1976), p. 27.
**Temple,** p. 174
Based on information from J. Wilkinson, *Jerusalem as Jesus knew it* (Thames and Hudson, 1978), pp. 77 and 84.
**Mari,** p. 204
Based on A. Parrot, *Sumer* (Thames and Hudson, 1960), pp. 257f.
**Masada,** p. 208
Based on Y. Yadin, *The Excavation of Masada, 1963–4*, Preliminary Report (Israel Exploration Society, 1965).
**Megiddo,** p. 211
Based on K. M. Kenyon, *The Bible and Recent Archaeology* (Colonnade Books), pp. 63 and 71.
**Nineveh,** p. 229
After B. Mazar and M. Avi-Yonah and others (eds.), *Views of the Biblical World* (International Publishing Co. Ltd, Jerusalem, 1960), vol. 3, p. 253 and R. Campbell Thompson, *Iraq I* (British School of Archaeology in Iraq, 1934), p. 97, fig. 1.
**Philippi,** p. 247
Based on *ACA*, p. 176.
**Qumran,** p. 258
Based on R. de Vaux, *Archaeology and the Dead Sea Scrolls* (Oxford University Press, 1973), pl. 39.
**Rome,** p. 269
Based on T. G. Tucker, *Life in the Roman World* (Macmillan), fig. 17.
**Shechem,** p. 279
Based on *EAEHL*, vol. 4, p. 1083.
**Taanach,** p. 293
Based on *EAEHL*, vol. 4, p. 1140.
**Thebes,** p. 297
Based on J. Hawkes, *Atlas of Ancient Archaeology* (William Heinemann, 1974), p. 155.
**Ugarit,** p. 303
Based on *IDBS*, p. 929.
**Ur,** p. 305
Based on J. Hawkes, *Atlas of Ancient Archaeology* (William Heinemann, 1974), p. 173.